Take a look

at a powerful new teaching tool. Send today for a 30-day preview of

The American Nation Videodisc Program

and see how this new *curriculum-based videodisc* product can help you motivate your students — whatever their learning styles, interests, or abilities. Use

the two-disc package you'll receive to guide students through an exciting, engaging exploration of major events in our nation's history. Complete lesson plans and student activity sheets in the accompanying *Teacher's Guide* provide solid instructional support. This **easy-to-use** program is integrated directly into *The American Nation in the Twentieth Century.* See for yourself how *The American Nation Videodisc Program* complements your curriculum and expands your teaching options. To order your preview copy today — just **complete and return the attached reply card** or **fax** a copy of the completed card to **1-512-314-6787.**

HOLT
RINEHART
WINSTON

Preview *The American Nation Videodisc Program* for 30 days.

Preview *The American Nation Videodisc Program* for 30 days.

If you decide to keep the product, simply pay the invoice by the date indicated. Or return the product to us in saleable condition within 30 days from the invoice date and receive full credit. You can even arrange for pre-paid return by calling 1-800-544-6678.

Order by Fax:
Fax a copy of this completed form to 1-512-314-6787.

HOLT RINEHART WINSTON

TEAR OFF

YES, I want to learn more about using technology-based teaching tools to help motivate my students. Please send me a 30-day preview of *The American Nation Videodisc Program.*

Date _____

Purchase Order Number _____

Is Purchase Order Enclosed? ☐ Yes ☐ No

Tax Exempt Notice:
If you are ordering for the first time and are exempt from state sales and use taxes, be sure to attach an exemption certificate.

Preferred Shipping Method _____

Send Product and Invoice Here:
Prices are subject to change without notice.
H96982-4............................$597.00

Name _____

Telephone Number _____

Title _____

School _____

Address _____

City, State, Zip _____

Authorized Signature _____

Title _____

TEAR OFF

YES, I want to learn more about using technology-based teaching tools to help motivate my students. Please send me a 30-day preview of *The American Nation Videodisc Program.*

Date _____

Purchase Order Number _____

Is Purchase Order Enclosed? ☐ Yes ☐ No

Tax Exempt Notice:
If you are ordering for the first time and are exempt from state sales and use taxes, be sure to attach an exemption certificate.

Preferred Shipping Method _____

Send Product and Invoice Here:
Prices are subject to change without notice.
H96982-4............................$597.00

Name _____

Telephone Number _____

Title _____

School _____

Address _____

City, State, Zip _____

Authorized Signature _____

Title _____

WHAT DO *YOU* WANT FROM TECHNOLOGY?

When HRW decided to develop technology products, we started by asking teachers what they needed in the classroom. We polled thousands of educators, and their ideas and advice became our starting point.

The first thing we learned is that most technology products available today share a common flaw — they aren't integrated with the curriculum. Most of them were created by people who know a great deal about RAM and ROM, but not very much about the other three Rs. The result for teachers: frustration and hours of planning time wasted trying to mix and match.

Because HRW has been creating educational curriculum since 1866, we know that the focus of the classroom is the student, not the technology. That's why we've organized our new technology materials around your curriculum, and that's why — before we tell you how fast it runs or how many images you can access in 30 seconds — we want to show you the instructional content and value that characterize every product in the new **HRW Multimedia Curriculum Systems.** Look for this special logo to identify these curriculum-based products, and to remind you that at HRW technology is not an extra; it's part of an integrated approach to classroom management and instruction.

The American Nation Videodisc Program is one of these new products and this is your opportunity to preview it for 30 days. Order today and see for yourself the difference it makes when a technology product is developed to expand a student's capacity, not showcase a machine's.

Like all **HRW Multimedia Curriculum Systems** materials, **The American Nation Videodisc Program** —

- **Requires less planning time because we've already matched its content to fit your curriculum goals and sequence**

- **Addresses the diversity of learning styles found in today's classroom**

- **Offers greater flexibility with both English and Spanish soundtracks**

- **Is teacher friendly so you don't have to be a technical whiz to use it successfully**

- **Provides a Teacher's Guide containing all the information you need to use the program — ready-made teaching plans, ideas for customizing instruction, and barcodes — all correlated directly to The American Nation in the Twentieth Century**

- **Organizes barcodes chronologically, thematically, or topically for unsurpassed instructional flexibility**

That's our story. For a glimpse of the future that's ready for the classroom today, please let us send you **The American Nation Videodisc Program** to preview for 30 days. Just complete the attached order form and either fax or mail it to us today.

William A. Talkington
President
Holt, Rinehart and Winston

HOLT RINEHART WINSTON

201H95AO7
9-99-711626-7

THE
AMERICAN
NATION

IN THE
20th
Century

THE AMERICAN NATION

IN THE 20th Century

PAUL BOYER
STERLING STUCKEY

HOLT, RINEHART AND WINSTON
Harcourt Brace & Company
Austin • New York • Orlando • Atlanta
San Francisco • Boston • Dallas • Toronto • London

About the Authors
PAUL BOYER

*P*aul Boyer is Merle Curti Professor of History at the University of Wisconsin, Madison, and a senior member of the university's Institute for Research in the Humanities. Dr. Boyer is the author of numerous works, including *By the Bomb's Early Light: American Thought and Culture at the Dawn of the Atomic Age.*

STERLING STUCKEY

*S*terling Stuckey is Professor of History and Religious Studies and holds the President's Chair at the University of California, Riverside. Dr. Stuckey is the author of *Slave Culture: Nationalist Theory and the Foundations of Black America* and *Going Through the Storm: The Influence of African American Art in History.*

Cover Photo: Ralph Brunke Photography

Cover: (front to back) Photo of Statue of Liberty, Historical Pictures/Stock Montage; Stock certificate, Manhattan-Dearborn Corporation; Jose Lopez, courtesy Jose Lopez; Five Presidents, AP/Wide World Photos; Angel Island Entry Card, Angel Island Immigration Station Foundation; U.S. Olympic pin, U.S. Olympic Committee; Sandra Day O'Connor, Bettmann; United Farm Workers, M. Richards/PhotoEdit; Native American, The Lilly Library, Indiana University, Bloomington, IN; 3-D glasses, The Waite Group, Mill Valley, CA; Amelia Earhart, Culver Pictures; Hand held TV, Casio; Vietnam Military currency, courtesy Bob Hoyt; AFL-CIO pin, American Federation of Labor and Congress of Industrial Organizations; Martin Luther King from *Time* Magazine, Robert Vickrey, Time, Inc.; Patch, courtesy Kathy Condo; Kennedy and Khrushchev, AP/Wide World Photos; Mount Suribachi, AP/Wide World Photos.

Front and Back End Page: Ralph Brunke Photography; Stock Montage for Statue of Liberty

Half Title Page and Title Page: Ralph Brunke Photography; Stock Montage for Statue of Liberty

Some material in this work was previously published in Todd & Curti's The American Nation, Annotated Teacher's Edition, copyright © 1995 by Holt, Rinehart and Winston, Inc. All rights reserved.

For acknowledgments, see page 836, which is an extension of the copyright page.

Printed in the United States of America

ISBN 0-03-094973-4

2 3 4 5 6 7 8 9 032 98 97 96 95

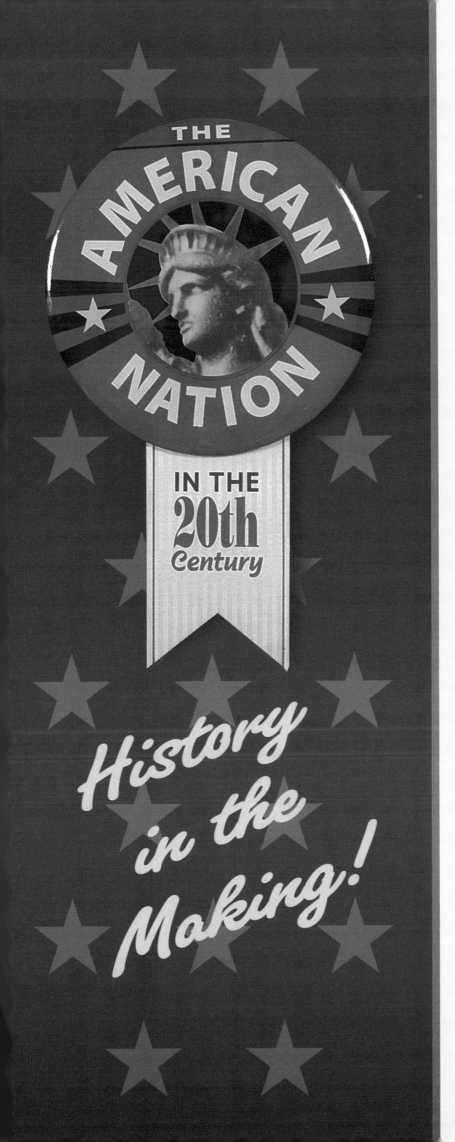

THE

AMERICAN
NATION

IN THE
20th
Century

History in the Making!

IN CLASSROOMS AROUND the country, *The American Nation in the Twentieth Century* is making history—and we want you to be a part of it. Our fully integrated instructional package helps your students see, hear and *experience* history like never before! Best of all, this unique program gives you the ability to choose the combination of materials that meets the instructional objectives of *your* classroom. ❖

The American Nation in the Twentieth Century

❖ Focuses on the twentieth century, making history relevant to students' lives

❖ Includes extensive pre-twentieth century coverage, giving students the background they need to put recent history in context

❖ Looks at global issues in a unique, thematic unit—The American Experience in Global Context

❖ Interweaves social history and multicultural perspectives throughout the text

❖ Captures the emotion of history with stunning artwork, compelling quotes, and moving literature

❖ Encourages students to become active historians by developing critical-thinking skills

❖ Makes history accessible and appealing to *all* students with its student-friendly design

❖ Integrates videodisc support directly into the text with on-page barcodes

TRUMAN BARKLEY

"The only thing new in the world is the history you don't know."

— Harry S. Truman

N O MATTER HOW WELL YOU KNOW America's story, *The American Nation in the Twentieth Century* will intrigue you. An exciting narrative filled with firsthand accounts, memorable quotes, and stirring primary source readings gives students a view of history that's so revealing, they'll feel like they're experiencing it themselves. ❖

Social History Perspectives

The text's social history perspective looks at events from more than one point of view, helping students realize that history is more than the legacy of the famous—it's a record of the past that belongs to all of us. ❖

Through Others' Eyes bring a global perspective to American history.
▶

EURO DISNEY

THROUGH OTHERS' EYES

"This is the '90s" declared Disney's head, Michael Eisner, "the decade we reinvent the Disney experience not just in California, but worldwide." However, not everyone welcomed Eisner's vision. When Euro Disney opened outside Paris in April 1992, critics called it a "cultural Chernobyl." "It took a money-hungry little mouse to trigger a debate on issues that we have been evading," noted Jean-Marie Rouart in the Paris newspaper Le Figaro. "Should we allow culture to be ruled by profitability?"

Such concerns on the part of some of the French were not new. In 1982, a decade before Euro Disney opened, France's minister of culture, Jack Lang, warned the world about what he called American cultural imperialism: "Certain great nations who taught us about freedom and called on people to rise up against oppression, yet who today . . . have no other morality than that of profit, . . . seek to impose a uniform culture on the whole world."

UNIT 6

American Letters

The Pains of War

Numerous wars have marked the 20th century. Some, such as World Wars I and II, have affected Americans as well as many peoples around the world. But all wars are significant to those who experience them personally. Nigerian poet and playwright Wole Soyinka, Romanian-born concentration-camp survivor Elie Wiesel, Vietnamese writer Nguyen Thi Vinh, and Chilean novelist Isabel Allende are among those who have experienced and written about war.

▲ Elie Wiesel

Civilian and Soldier
by Wole Soyinka

My apparition rose from the fall of lead,
Declared, "I'm a civilian." It only served
To aggravate your fright. For how could I
Have risen, a being of this world, in that hour
Of impartial death! And I thought also: nor is
Your quarrel of this world.

You stood still
For both eternities, and oh I heard the lesson
Of your training sessions, cautioning—
Scorch earth behind you, do not leave
A dubious neutral to the rear. Reiteration
Of my civilian quandary,[1] burrowing earth
From the lead festival of your more eager friends
Worked the worse on your confusion, and when
You brought the gun to bear on me, and death
Twitched me gently in the eye, your plight
And all of you came clear to me.

I hope some day
Intent upon my trade of living, to be checked
In stride by your apparition in a trench,
Signaling, I am a soldier. No hesitation then
But I shall shoot you clean and fair
With meat and bread, a gourd of wine
A bunch of breasts from either arm, and that
Lone question—do you friend, even now, know
What it is all about? ❖

1 ghost-like appearance
2 dilemma

From Night
by Elie Wiesel

In front of us flames. In the air that smell of burning flesh. It must have been about midnight. We had arrived—at Birkenau, reception center for Auschwitz.
The cherished objects we had brought with us thus far were left behind in the train, and with them, at last, our illusions.
Every two yards or so an SS man held his Tommy gun[1] trained on us. Hand in hand we followed the crowd.
An SS noncommissioned officer came to meet us, a truncheon in his hand. He gave the order:
"Men to the left! Women to the right!"
Eight words spoken quietly, indifferently, without emotion. Eight short, simple words. Yet that was the moment when I parted from my mother. I had not had time to think, but already I felt the pressure of my father's hand: we were alone. For a part of a second I glimpsed my mother and my sisters moving away to the right. Tzipora held Mother's hand. I saw them disappear into the distance; my mother was stroking my sister's fair hair, as though to protect her, while I walked on with my father and the other men. And I did not know that in that place, at that moment, I was parting from my mother and Tzipora forever. I went on walking. My father held onto my hand.
Behind me, an old man fell to the ground. Near him was an SS man, putting his revolver back in its holster.

From Thoughts of Hanoi
by Nguyen Thi Vinh

The night is deep and chill
as in early autumn. Pitchblack,
it thickens after each lightning
flash.
I dream of Hanoi:
Co-ngu Road
ten years of separation
the way back sliced by a frontier
of hatred. . . .

Brother,
how is Hang Dao now?
How is Ngoc Son temple?
Do the trains still run
each day from Hanoi
to the neighboring towns?
To Bac-ninh, Cam-giang, Yen-bai,
the small villages, islands
of brown thatch in a lush green
sea! . . .

Stainless blue sky,
jubilant voices of children
stumbling through the alphabet,
village graybeards strolling to
the temple,
grandmothers basking in twilight
sun,
chewing betel leaves
while the children run—

Brother,
how is all that now?
Or is it obsolete?
Are you like me,
reliving the past,
imagining the future?
Do you count me as a friend
or am I the enemy in your eyes?
Brother, I am afraid
that one day I'll be with the
March-North Army
meeting you on your way to
the South.
I might be the one to shoot
you then

or you me
but please
not with hatred.

For don't you remember how
it was,
you and I in school together,
plotting our lives together?
Those roots go deep!

Brother, we are men,
conscious of more
than material needs.
How can this happen to us
my friend
my foe? ❖

From The House of the Spirits
by Isabel Allende

Then came the roar of the airplanes, and the bombing began. Jaime threw himself to the floor with everyone else, unable to believe what he was seeing; until the day before, he had been convinced that nothing like this would ever happen in his country and that even the military respected the law. Only the President was on his feet. He walked to the window carrying a bazooka and fired it at the tanks below. Jaime inched his way to him and grabbed him by the calves to make him get down, but the President replied with a curse and rem... utes late... in flame... breathe... and the... among... bits of p... around... attempt... but he could only offer words of comfort and close the eyes of the dead. In a sudden pause in the shooting, the President gathered the survivors and told them to leave because he did not want any martyrs or needless sacrifice; everyone had a family, and important tasks lay ahead. "I'm going to call a truce so you can leave," he added. But no one moved. Though a few of them were trembling, all were in apparent possession of their dignity. The bombing was brief, but it left the palace in ruins. By two o'clock in the afternoon the fire had consumed the old drawing rooms that had been used since colonial times, and only a handful of men were left around the President. Soldiers entered the building and took what was left of the first floor. Above the din was heard the hysterical voice of an officer ordering them to surrender and come down single file with their hands on their heads. The President shook each of them by the hand. "I'll go last," he said. They never ❖

THINKING AND WRITING ABOUT LITERATURE

1. What views regarding the shooting of civilians during warfare does Wole Soyinka present in his poem?
2. Why does Elie Wiesel attribute so much importance to the eight words spoken by the SS officer?
3. How does the speaker in Nguyen Thi Vinh's poem recall Hanoi? How has war changed the speaker's relationship with childhood companions?
4. Why do you think the bombing described by Isabel Allende occurred? Where do the author's sympathies lie?

742 ❖ UNIT 6

AMERICAN LETTERS ❖ 743

◀ *American Letters features use primary sources—including literature, poetry, and song lyrics—to give students a cultural overview of each unit.*

A Global Context

The final unit—The American Experience in Global Context—looks at how the United States has shaped and been shaped by significant global issues such as international relations, human rights, and the environment. The flexibility of this unit allows you to teach it at the end of the course or incorporate it into the chapters throughout the year. ❖

Unsurpassed Curriculum Design

THE AMERICAN NATION
VIDEODISC PROGRAM
Vietnam and the Media

2B   13498   5:43

Chapter 23

IMPERIALISM TO NEW WORLD ORDER

▉ LINK TO THE PAST

The American colonies were established as outposts of the British Empire during the first age of European imperialism. But the success of the American Revolution made the nation a "child" of anti-imperialism. Both imperialism and anti-imperialism continued to shape the history of the United States and the world.

FOCUS

UNDERSTANDING THE MAIN IDEA

The 20th century began as the great age of European empires. Even the United States briefly engaged in imperialism. But two world wars weakened the empires, which dissolved after World War II. Only the Soviet Union's empire survived into the 1980s, and it too had collapsed by the early 1990s. Yet many legacies of imperialism remain.

THEMES

▉ DEMOCRATIC VALUES
Can a democratic nation hold an empire and still be upholding the principles of democracy?

▉ CULTURAL DIVERSITY
How do empires promote cultural diversity? How do they discourage it?

▉ GLOBAL RELATIONS
How might small nations avoid becoming entangled in major world rivalries?

During a meeting with a delegation of Methodist missionaries in 1898, President McKinley explained his position regarding annexation of the Philippines. The president said he had prayed long and hard for guidance.

❝ And one night late it came to me this way—I don't know how it was, but it came: (1) That we could not give them back to Spain—that would be cowardly and dishonorable; (2) that we could not turn them over to France or Germany—our commercial rivals in the Orient—that would be bad business and discreditable; (3) that we could not leave them to themselves—they were unfit for self-government—and they would soon have anarchy and misrule over there worse than Spain's was; and (4) that there was nothing left for us to do but to take them all, and to educate the Filipinos, and uplift and civilize and Christianize them. ❞

McKinley's attitude was typical of the time. At the height of imperialism, it combined arrogance, ignorance (nearly all the Filipinos were already Christians), and benevolence. But times would change.

Sir Hiram S. Maxim, inventor of the first fully-automatic machine gun (1883)

U.S. soldiers in Shanghai, China, during the Boxer Rebellion, 1900

1898	1934	1947	1955	1967
Battle of Omdurman leaves thousands of Africans dead.	U.S. Congress passes Tydings-McDuffie Act.	Britain grants India and Pakistan independence.	Bandung Conference held in Indonesia.	Civil war breaks out in Nigeria.

IMPERIALISM TO NEW WORLD ORDER ▉ 621

Give your students a framework for learning about history that will stand the test of time. The student-friendly *Pupil's Edition* provides in-depth coverage of topics, complemented by recurring themes and reading strategies to help students understand main ideas and retain what they've read. ❖

❖ **Theme questions** help students trace the development of seven basic themes over the course of U.S. history.

❖ **Link to the Past** shows students how historical periods are influenced by earlier events.

❖ **Chapter timelines** present events visually, summarizing significant events and issues from each chapter.

❖ **First-person accounts** reveal the opinions, emotions, and conflicts of the time.

❖ Point-of-use barcodes make it easy to incorporate **videodisc lessons, support segments,** and **still images** into the lessons.

Videodisc lessons from The American Nation Videodisc Program *enable students to view, discuss, and analyze topics such as* A Nation of Immigrants, Malcom X, *and more.*

Revolutionary Teaching Support

Multimedia components—including videodiscs, transparencies, and maps—help you address all your students' learning styles. Completely integrated into the lessons, these resources expand history from something your students read about to something they experience. ❖

I HAVE SEEN THE FUTURE

"We must define the common good, and begin again to shape a common future."

—Barbara Jordan

Excerpted from the Keynote Address to the Democratic National Convention, 1976.

IF STUDENTS KNOW HOW TO INTERPRET the past, it can teach them valuable lessons—lessons that will enable them to make better and more informed decisions in the future. *The American Nation in the Twentieth Century* teaches students those lessons with a comprehensive program designed to develop critical-thinking, decision-making, and map skills. ❖

Thinking Critically About History

Strategies for Success develops students' critical-thinking skills and provides activities to apply them to social studies topics. In addition, a Skills Handbook teaches students vital skills such as identifying main ideas, building vocabulary, and writing papers. ▶

Linking Geography to History

America's Geography features explore a wide range of social studies themes using maps and charts to show the influence of geographical factors on U.S. history. ◀

Introduction to the Program

The study of American history, like history itself, is an ever-evolving process. Over the course of the 20th century, historians have expanded their inquiry beyond the analysis of great events and great leaders to include an examination of the contributions of all members of society to America's story. Central to this enriched historical inquiry is an appreciation of the importance of cultural diversity, geography, democratic values, economics, global relations, and technology in shaping America's past, present, and future. American history today is both multicultural and multidisciplinary. **The American Nation in the Twentieth Century** is a reflection of this broadened perspective. **The American Nation in the Twentieth Century** draws on political history, social history, multicultural perspectives, geography, literature, and economics to paint a more complete and accurate picture of America's history.

The American Nation in the Twentieth Century has three major goals. The first goal is to inform and excite students about our nation's past. The second is to promote respect for the nation's rich cultural diversity and for the contributions of diverse peoples to its history. The third goal is to strengthen students' critical thinking skills, study skills, and map and chart skills—skills that are vital to subjects across the curriculum and to effective participation in a democratic society. The components of **The American Nation in the Twentieth Century** program—the Pupil's Edition, the Annotated Teacher's Edition, the Core Resources Binder, the Visual Resources Binder, and a variety of other program resources—work together to achieve these goals.

Program Components

THE PUPIL'S EDITION

The Pupil's Edition provides coverage of American history from prehistory to the present, while concentrating on the 20th century. The text consists of 27 chapters divided into 5 chronological units and a sixth thematic unit. The last unit examines the American experience in the context of world events. Because this unit is organized thematically, it can be taught as a whole or integrated as appropriate into earlier chapters. All units in the book present a blend of social and political history to provide students with a broad view of America's past and present.

The book's commitment to telling the history of all Americans is reinforced through in-text **Biographies** and **Commentaries** and through such features as **American Almanac, American Letters, Through Others' Eyes, Then and Now, Changing Ways, History in the Making,** and **Presidential Lives.** Geographic coverage is woven into the running text and is reinforced in the map skills program, in the **America's Geography** feature, and in chapter review exercises. Seven broad themes in American history—Global Relations, Constitutional Heritage, Democratic Values, Technology and Society, Cultural Diversity, Geographic Diversity, and Economic Development—are examined in the running text and in chapter opener and review questions to help students see connections between events over time. Critical thinking and study skills are taught and reinforced in the **Strategies for Success** unit feature, **Skills Handbook,** and all section and chapter reviews. And a wide range of review and assessment questions and activities, including portfolio assessment, are presented in the section, chapter, and unit reviews.

THE ANNOTATED TEACHER'S EDITION

The Annotated Teacher's Edition (ATE) of *The American Nation in the Twentieth Century* is designed to reduce teacher preparation time and to provide full instructional support for the Pupil's Edition. *The American Nation in the Twentieth Century* ATE contains all Pupil's Edition pages, slightly reduced to create side and top margins. An **interleaf** at the beginning of each chapter helps to plan chapter instruction. Within each chapter, page margins contain a variety of point-of-use instructional strategies and resources. ATE top text provides **teaching strategies** correlated to each section's learning objectives. The side-margin **annotations** include a wealth of supplementary information to engage students and to enhance their understanding.

Planning and Resources

The two-page **chapter interleaf** facilitates effective planning and teaching. The chapter's main points are overviewed, and the Pupil's Edition themes are explored. Alternative strategies for meeting individual students' needs are suggested.

A **Chapter Planning Guide** lists ancillaries that support chapter instruction and identifies which of the program's resources might be used to introduce or review the chapter. The guide also indicates where material from Unit 6 may be integrated into the chapter. These print and multimedia materials are also correlated for chapter or section use in **resource organizers** on the opening pages of each chapter and section in the ATE. In addition, transparencies and videodisc segments are cited in ATE side margins at their suggested points of use.

Teaching from the Annotated Teacher's Edition

Each chapter in *The American Nation in the Twentieth Century* ATE begins in the same way. Specialized strategies tie chapter content to previous learning and introduce students to the chapter's main ideas, events, and themes.

Section lessons also follow an identical format. A **Preview Workshop** lists the important people, places, and terms that will be encountered in the reading. The Pupil's Edition Focus questions are restated as **learning objectives.** Following these introductory elements is the lesson itself.

Answers to all chart, graph, and map questions, section reviews, and chapter reviews are provided in the ATE at point of appearance in the Pupil's Edition.

THE TEACHING LESSON

The teaching lesson for each section is based on a six-step instructional model—**Motivating, Teaching, Practice, Review** and **Assessment, Closure,** and **Extension:**

1 MOTIVATING activities engage students by tying their own experiences, previous learning, or current knowledge to the content of the upcoming section.

2 TEACHING THE SECTION strategies address each section learning objective. They may be teacher-directed; require students to work independently, in pairs, or as a class; or involve cooperative learning or other group efforts. They also encourage students to be imaginative and self-expressive, both orally and in writing.

3 PRACTICE strategies for each section begin with a **Guided Practice,** which allows the teacher to model, monitor, and remediate students' learning or skills. An accompanying **Independent Practice** asks students, in class or as homework, to individually utilize the Guided Practice model without teacher direction.

4 REVIEW AND ASSESSMENT exercises check students' achievement of section objectives and then evaluate the learning that has taken place. Reteaching strategies are provided for students who need remediation.

5 CLOSURE strategies tie section objectives together and apply or evaluate learning .

6 EXTENSION offers activities to enrich or extend learning.

Side-Margin Annotations

The side margins of *The American Nation in the Twentieth Century* ATE include a variety of enrichment and extension materials at points appropriate to the content of textbook pages. Among the annotations that appear frequently are **Global Connections,** which place events and trends in American history in a global context and **Multicultural Perspectives,** which offer observations of ethnic Americans and insights from other cultures about the American experience. Point-of-use references to *The American Nation Videodisc Program* provide barcodes and information about disc number, side, location, and length of video segments that support instruction.

THE TEACHER'S RESOURCES

The teacher's resources for *The American Nation in the Twentieth Century* provide a variety of effective materials for extending and enriching learning, reinforcing and reteaching content, and evaluating student performance.

Core Resources Binder

To facilitate access to materials, all instructional support in the **Core Resources Binder** is organized by unit and chapter. The binder offers the following reproducible blackline masters for each unit and chapter:

AMERICAN ALMANAC WORKSHEETS require students to analyze and apply information in the unit's American Almanac.

BUILDING YOUR PORTFOLIO WORKSHEETS assist students in completing a unit portfolio project.

AMERICA'S GEOGRAPHY WORKSHEETS and teaching strategies synthesize and apply information from the textbook feature.

GRAPHIC ORGANIZERS visually organize and reinforce each chapter's content and themes.

SOCIAL STUDIES SKILLS WORKSHEETS reinforce skills that are emphasized throughout the program.

GEOGRAPHY WORKSHEETS explore the links between geography and important chapter themes and ideas.

LITERATURE WORKSHEETS reinforce chapter themes and main ideas through historical prose and poetry.

DAILY QUIZZES provide a short objective assessment for each section of the chapter.

CHAPTER TESTS provide two comprehensive tests, combining objective and essay questions, for each chapter.

RETEACHING WORKSHEETS reorganize and review each chapter's content, providing students with another chance to master its main ideas.

UNIT ANSWER KEY contains answers to all worksheets.

The **Core Resources Binder** also includes the following program-wide booklets:

WRITING ABOUT AMERICAN HISTORY develops students' skills in historical research, writing, and test-taking.

ALTERNATIVE ASSESSMENT FORMS include student and teacher guidelines for various types of self-assessment, peer assessment, portfolio assessment, and teacher assessment.

OUTLINE MAPS contain outline maps of the continents, major subcontinents, and the world.

VIDEODISC RESOURCES provide correlations and barcodes for *The American Nation* Videodisc Program.

Visual Resources Binder

The **Visual Resources Binder** provides 36 four-color **LINKING HISTORY AND GEOGRAPHY** transparencies, including overlays and worksheets. It also contains 33 **EVERYDAY LIFE IN AMERICA** social history transparencies and worksheets, and an Answer Key and Teacher's Notes for both transparency packages.

Program Resources

Other resources available for use with *The American Nation in the Twentieth Century* include the following:

THE AMERICAN NATION IN THE TWENTIETH CENTURY **TEST GENERATOR** permits custom-designed tests on Macintosh or IBM-compatible hardware.

THE AMERICAN NATION **VIDEODISC PROGRAM** offers video lessons in English or Spanish, support segments, and still images on two discs with Teacher's Guide.

ART IN AMERICAN HISTORY is a package of 49 four-color transparencies with teacher notes and student worksheets.

EYEWITNESSES AND OTHERS provides two volumes of primary source readings in American history.

CONTENTS

A 12th-century map
of the world

George Washington

Slaves escaping from Maryland.

Poster commemorating the Emancipation Proclamation

Sitting Bull

An immigrant mother and her children arriving at Ellis Island

UNIT 3 · *Prosperity and Crisis* 1920–1945

World War II
victory medal

UNIT 4 *Postwar America* 1945–1975

Campaign doll, 1964

U.S. soldiers in Korea, 1952

MUST YOU TAKE EVERY THING THE INDIANS OWN ??

Tuscarora boy protesting in 1958

Hippies in the Haight-Ashbury district of San Francisco

UNIT 6 CONTINUED

The NSFnet

Antinuclear protester Susan Ginzberg with her son, 1961

Reference Section

Features

CONTENTS

Sara Matthews/ Swarthmore College Peace Collection

Charts and Maps

Charts

Maps

Themes in American History

The American Nation in the Twentieth Century begins every chapter with a set of theme questions. These questions are drawn from seven broad themes central to American history: global relations, our Constitutional heritage, democratic values, technology and society, cultural diversity, geographic diversity, and economic development. They provide a context for the historical events in each chapter. This context will help you understand the connections between historical events and see how past events are relevant to today's social, political, and economic concerns.

As you begin each chapter, examine the theme questions and answer them based on your own experiences or prior knowledge. At the end of each chapter, you will be asked to answer another set of theme questions, this time using specific facts learned from studying the chapter. This process will help you develop critical thinking skills and encourage you to synthesize the information you have learned. In addition, by tracing the themes through the book, you will be able to see how each theme has developed over time.

■ GLOBAL RELATIONS

This theme asks you to explore the global context in which the United States exists. From its settlement by Asian immigrants tens of thousands of years ago to the first arrival of European, African, and later Asian immigrants to today, America has influenced and been influenced by other parts of the world. Your exploration of the Global Relations theme will help you understand how the relations the United States has maintained with other countries over time have affected our nation's political, social, and economic development. It also will help you appreciate the problems and possibilities of living in an interdependent world community.

■ CONSTITUTIONAL HERITAGE

The study of American history would not be complete without an exploration of the Constitution, the legal framework that structures our democratic government. The Constitutional Heritage theme questions ask you to think about the origin of the Constitution and the ways in which the Constitution has been interpreted and amended over time. You will explore how the laws and government institutions established in the 18th century have evolved through amendments, Supreme Court rulings, and congressional actions. Your examination of this theme will encourage you to understand the part individuals play in promoting the goals—such as justice and democratic rights—enshrined in the Constitution's preamble.

■ DEMOCRATIC VALUES

This theme concerns the continuing struggle to define and protect such democratic values as individual liberty, political representation, freedom of religion, and freedom of speech. The Democratic Values theme questions ask you to consider the impact of changing social, economic, and political conditions on these values. For example, in the years before the Civil War, enslavement of African Americans—a violation of the democratic value of individual liberty—was practiced in the South. Some slaveholders justified this practice by arguing that the democratic value of right to property should be the overriding concern. It took a bloody civil war to settle the issue. Conflicts over democratic values recur throughout American history, and this theme explores the attempts at resolution.

■ TECHNOLOGY AND SOCIETY

From computers in your homes and classrooms to communications satellites orbiting the earth, technology influences many aspects of society. The Technology and Society theme questions ask you to trace technological developments and explore their influence on the economy and our lives.

■ CULTURAL DIVERSITY

Different ethnic, racial, and religious groups have all contributed to the creation of America's rich and unique culture. The Cultural Diversity theme questions ask you to explore how the United States has dealt with diversity from the days of the first encounters between Native Americans and Spanish and English settlers to its status today as a haven for immigrants from all over the world.

■ GEOGRAPHIC DIVERSITY

The majestic old-growth forests of the Pacific Northwest, the rich coal deposits of the Appalachian and Rocky mountains, the oil fields of Texas and Alaska, and the tropical plantations on the volcanic islands of Hawaii have enriched the U.S. economy. The Geographic Diversity theme questions ask you to consider how the development of the nation's diverse natural resources has shaped U.S. society, politics, and the economy. The questions also explore how government and public awareness of the effects of natural resource development on the environment has changed over time.

■ ECONOMIC DEVELOPMENT

The United States has developed one of the world's strongest economies. The Economic Development theme questions explore the influence of the nation's economy on domestic politics and social life and on international relations. The theme questions ask you to explore the implications of such economic issues as trade, depression and expansion, poverty, taxation, government regulation, and the status of workers.

Chapter Opener

The **Chapter Opener** theme questions raise broad issues relevant to the chapter.

The **Chapter Review** theme questions recast the introductory theme questions in terms of chapter content.

REVIEWING THEMES

1. **Democratic Values** How did reformers seek to curb political corruption and to make government more democratic in the early 20th century?
2. **Economic Development** How did President Roosevelt attempt to regulate business without discouraging free enterprise?
3. **Constitutional Heritage** How might reformers have used the Nineteenth Amendment as a means of accomplishing reform in politics and business?

from the Chapter Review

Critical Thinking and the Study of History

*T*hroughout *The American Nation in the Twentieth Century,* you are asked to think critically about the events and issues that have shaped U.S. history. Critical thinking is the reasoned judgment of information and ideas. People who think critically study information to determine its accuracy. They evaluate arguments and analyze conclusions before accepting them. Critical thinkers are able to recognize and define problems and develop strategies for resolving them.

The development of critical thinking skills is essential to effective citizenship. Such skills empower you to exercise your civic rights and responsibilities. For example, critical thinking skills equip you to judge the messages of candidates for office and to evaluate news reports.

Helping you develop critical thinking skills is an important goal of *The American Nation in the Twentieth Century.* The following 14 critical thinking skills appear in the section reviews and chapter reviews. Additional skills strategies can be found in each unit's Strategies for Success and in the Skills Handbook, which begins on page 748.

Union mortar battery

understand that the Europeans did not "discover" the Americas. They encountered a land already settled by people with rich cultures.

3 **Recognizing Point of View** means identifying the factors that color the outlook of an individual or group. Editorial cartoons, for example, present points of view about issues, events, and people. A person's point of view includes beliefs and attitudes that are shaped by factors such as age, gender, religion, race, and economic status. This thinking skill helps us

1 **Using Historical Imagination** is mentally stepping into the past to consider an event or situation as people at the time would have considered it. In putting yourself in their place, you might note whether they lived *before* or *after* historical turning points. Ask yourself: Did these people live before or after major medical advances such as penicillin? before or after technological advances such as the automobile? before or after World War II? Keep in mind what the people of the time knew and did not know. For example, to grasp the experience of a soldier wounded in the Civil War, you need to understand that little was known then about the causes of disease and infection.

2 **Gaining a Multicultural Perspective** means viewing historical events and situations in ways that are fair and sensitive to all cultural groups affected. A multicultural perspective broadens your understanding of American history while deepening your appreciation of the nation's diversity. For example, studying Native American cultures before the arrival of Columbus helps you

Toltec pillar

SLAVERY AS IT EXISTS IN AMERICA.

SLAVERY AS IT   EXISTS IN ENGLAND.

This proslavery editorial cartoon from the 1850s distorts the reality of slavery by falsely suggesting that southern slaves led easier lives than English factory workers.

The Granger Collection, New York

Struggle at Concord Bridge

examine why people see things as they do and reinforces the realization that people's views may change over time, or with a change in circumstances. When the point of view of an individual or a group is highly personal or based on unreasoned judgment, it is considered *bias*.

4 **Comparing and Contrasting** is examining events, situations, or points of view for their similarities and differences. *Comparing* focuses on both the similarities and the differences. *Contrasting* focuses on only the differences. For example, a comparison of early Irish and Chinese immigrants to the United States would point out that both groups were recruited to help build the nation's transcontinental railroad and that both groups faced discrimination and experienced difficulties in finding well-paying jobs. In

contrast, language and racial barriers generally proved more of a problem for Chinese immigrants. Other factors to compare and contrast could include reasons for immigrating to the United States.

5 **Identifying Cause and Effect** is part of interpreting the relationships between historical events. A *cause* is any action that leads to an event; the outcome of that action is an *effect*. To explain historical developments, historians may point out multiple causes and effects. For instance, the actions of the colonists as well as those of the British government brought about the American Revolution, which in turn had many far-reaching effects. (For a more detailed discussion of Identifying Cause and Effect, see page 749 in the Skills Handbook.)

6 **Analyzing** is the process of breaking something down into its parts and examining the relationships between them. Analysis enables you to better understand the whole. To analyze the outcome of the 1912 presidential election, for example, you might study a map such as the one on the next page. Analyzing the results state by state shows how Woodrow Wilson won a majority in the electoral college without winning a majority of the popular vote.

Railroad laborers

Election of 1912

WILSON'S STRENGTH Wilson's strength was in the South. Although he won the electoral vote by a landslide, the only states outside the old Confederacy where he won at least half the popular vote were Kentucky, Maryland and Oklahoma.

? LOCATION Which state split its electoral vote?

	Electoral Vote	Popular Vote	% of Pop. Vote
Wilson	435*	6,296,547	41.9%
T. Roosevelt	88	4,118,571	27.4
Taft	8	3,486,720	23.2
Debs		900,672	6.0
Other parties		235,025	1.6

*Two electors in California voted for Wilson.

- Wilson (Democratic)
- T. Roosevelt (Progressive)
- Taft (Republican)

7 Assessing Consequences means studying an action, an event, or a trend to predict its long-term effects—and to judge the desirability of those effects. *Consequences* often are effects that are indirect and unintended. They may appear long after the event that led to them. An example of assessing consequences is the federal government's weighing of the positive and negative elements of a new drug or medical procedure before permitting its use. Consequences include side effects and other possible risks, as well as benefits.

8 Distinguishing Fact from Opinion means separating the facts about something from what people say about it. A fact can be proved or observed; an opinion, on the other hand, is a personal belief or conclusion. We often hear facts and opinions mixed in everyday conversation on such issues as the environment—as well as

American Museum of Natural History

American buffalo

L. J. Cranstone's painting depicting a slave auction

the North and the South over control of the United States' western frontier. The historian would then organize the available evidence to support this hypothesis and to challenge other explanations of the war's causes.

11 **Synthesizing** is combining information and ideas from several sources or points in time to gain a new understanding of a topic or event. Much of the narrative writing in *The American Nation in the Twentieth Century* is a synthesis. It pulls together historical data from many sources into a chronological story of our nation. Synthesizing the history of the Great Depression, for example, might involve studying

in advertising, in political debate, and in historical sources. Although some opinions can be supported by facts, in an argument opinions do not carry as much weight as facts. (For a more detailed discussion of Distinguishing Fact from Opinion, see page 750.)

9 **Identifying Values** involves recognizing the core beliefs that a person or group holds. Values are more deeply held than opinions and are less likely to change. Values commonly concern matters of right and wrong and may be viewed as desirable in and of themselves. The values of freedom and justice, for example, motivated the struggle to abolish slavery, just as the value of equality has been a foundation of the civil rights and women's movements.

10 **Hypothesizing** is forming a possible explanation for an event, a situation, or a problem. A hypothesis is not a proven fact. Rather it is an "educated guess" based on available evidence and tested against new evidence. A historian, for instance, might hypothesize that the Civil War was primarily the result of a power struggle between the ruling classes of

Migrant Mother, photographed by Dorothea Lange during the Great Depression

economic statistics from the 1930s and photographs taken by Walker Evans, Ben Shahn, Arthur Rothstein, and Dorothea Lange for the Farm Security Administration, together with interviews of Americans who lived through the period.

12 **Problem Solving** is a process of reviewing a situation and making decisions and recommendations for improving or correcting it. Before beginning, however, the problem must be clearly identified and stated. For instance, in considering a solution to the nation's drug-abuse crisis, you might state the problem in one of the following ways:

1. in terms of the relationship of drug addiction to violent crime,

2. in terms of the economics of the drug trade,

3. in terms of the effects of drug abuse on families,

4. in terms of the economic impact on society of treatment, enforcement, and correctional institutions.

You would then propose and evaluate possible solutions or courses of action, selecting the one you think is best and giving the reasons for your choice.

Progressive reformer Robert M. La Follette

Woman suffragist

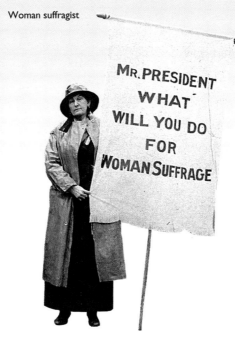

MR. PRESIDENT WHAT WILL YOU DO FOR WOMAN SUFFRAGE

13 **Evaluating** is assessing the significance or overall importance of something, such as the success of a reform movement or the legacy of a president. You should base your judgment on standards that others will understand and are likely to share. An evaluation of the early women's movement, for example, might assess the short- and long-term effects of the focus on women's suffrage.

14 **Taking a Stand** is identifying an issue, deciding what you think about it, and persuasively expressing your position. Your stand should be based on specific information gathered from reliable sources. In taking a stand, even on controversial or emotional issues, state your position clearly and give carefully thought-out reasons to support it.

UNIT 1

American Roots ❖ Beginnings–1900

Introducing the Unit

- **Chapter 1**
  BEGINNINGS TO 1763
  Prehistory–1763
- **Chapter 2**
  CREATING A NATION
  1763–1830
- **Chapter 3**
  GROWTH AND CHANGE
  1815–1860
- **Chapter 4**
  WAR AND REUNIFICATION
  1861–1900
- **Chapter 5**
  THE WESTERN CROSSROADS
  1860–1910
- **Chapter 6**
  THE NATION TRANSFORMED
  1865–1910

UNIT OVERVIEW

The first Americans migrated from Asia to North America thousands of years ago, followed in the 16th, 17th, and 18th centuries by Europeans who established colonies throughout the Americas. During the late 1700s, the United States won its independence from Britain. International conflicts were accompanied by domestic turmoil, as 19th-century expansion called attention to the institution of slavery and led to the Civil War. During the second half of the century, settlers continued westward. By the end of the 19th century, the United States was prepared to enter the international arena.

CORE RESOURCES

- **American Almanac Worksheet 1**
- **Building Your Portfolio Worksheet 1**
  You may wish to preview the Unit 1 Review and Building Your Portfolio performance assessment activities on p. 163.

Using the Almanac

Review the almanac entries with students. Ask students to note inventions and products that are still used today. Have students also note any activities that are still practiced today.

American ALMANAC

❖ The American People

Life expectancy in 1989 is more than twice that of 1789!

LIFE EXPECTANCY

Women
Men

Years

80 70 60 50 40 30 20 10 0

1789   1989

Source: Bureau of the Census

POPULATION DENSITY

People per Square Mile

80 60 40 20 0

1860   1990

Source: Bureau of the Census

◀ Between 1861 and 1900 more than 14 million immigrants arrive on American shores!

▲ Mission San José today in San Antonio

❖ Peoples of the West

1758 Mission San José de Aguayo in present-day Texas includes 84 houses; fields of corn, beans, and sugarcane; sugar mill; carpentry shop; chickens; 30 yoke of oxen; 1,500 cattle; 3,376 sheep; 80 mares; and several "swimming pools"; 281 Native Americans live there.

1867 Between 1867 and 1881 more than four million cattle are driven north from Texas; roughly a third of the cowboys are African American, Mexican American, or Mexican.

1890 Non-Indian population triples from about one million in 1870 to more than three million; in some western states men still outnumber women by nearly two to one.

1900 Native American population hits its lowest level—about 150,000.

❖ Inventing America

1760s Ben Franklin invents bifocal lenses.

1769 Mansion in Maryland is built with only known indoor toilet.

1800 William Young of Philadelphia makes "left" and "right" shoes; before, shoes were interchangeable.

1834 African American Henry Blair receives patent for corn harvester.

◀ Ben Franklin's own eyeglasses

▶ Ben Franklin

1853 In New York, Native American chef George Crum makes first potato chips.

1876 Alexander Graham Bell receives patent for the telephone.

1886 Dr. John Pemberton brews a new drink—Coca Cola.

1894 First Hershey bar is made (and eaten!).

The American People

Note that the graph shows life expectancy *at birth* and reflects the impact of child mortality. People who reached age 21 in the late 1700s could expect to live about 40 more years.

■■ Have students check a current almanac to determine life expectancy in the United States today.

Inventing America

In 1754 African American astronomer Benjamin Banneker constructed the first clock made entirely in America—even though he had never seen a working clock before. It ran accurately for 20 years.

■■ Have students suggest why Banneker's invention was of importance to everyday life in 18th-century America.

Peoples of the West

By the beginning of the 20th century, Native Americans were confined to about 170 reservations scattered about the country. Beset by loss of land and culture, and afflicted by malnutrition and disease, they struggled merely to survive.

■■ Have students research Native Americans' status today.

Daily Life

Cycling was the greatest exercise craze of the 1890s, with serious riders numbering more than 100,000. According to some, cycling satisfied the spiritual as well as the physical needs of persons attempting to adjust to city life.

■■ Ask students to identify today's exercise crazes.

Hot off the Presses

Freedom's Journal, the first African American newspaper, focused on the antislavery movement. The most widely read African American abolitionist newspaper may have been Frederick Douglass's *North Star,* first published in 1847.

■■ Have students identify present-day publications that are associated with a particular social cause.

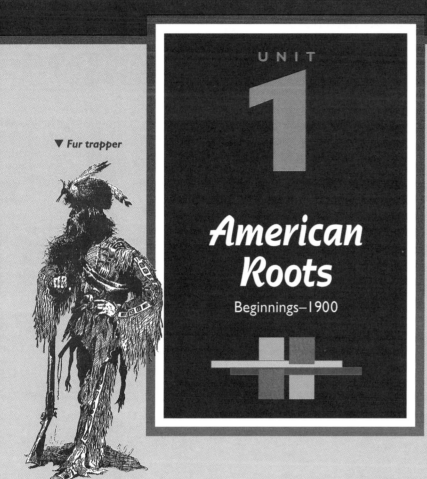

▼ Fur trapper

UNIT

1

American Roots

Beginnings—1900

▲ Phillis Wheatley

❖ Hot off the Presses

1773 British readers rave over book of poetry by young Boston slave Phillis Wheatley, who couldn't find an American printer.

1823 James Fenimore Cooper writes *The Pioneers*—considered by some to be the first truly American novel.

1828 *Cherokee Phoenix* is first newspaper published in a Native American language—Cherokee.

1852 *Uncle Tom's Cabin* by Harriet Beecher Stowe causes a sensation.

❖ Daily Life

1620 First public library in the English colonies opens in Virginia.

1656 Eavesdropping, scolding, bad grinding at a mill, and pulling hair are crimes in Massachusetts.

1700s English colonial recreation includes rabbit hunting, cockfighting, horseracing, and card playing.

1830s Fandango, a lively Spanish dance that can last several days, is popular in the California territory.

1874 Tennis arrives from England. It's popular with women, who can play while wearing their fashionable long skirts.

1880s Bicycling becomes popular for getting around—and for fun!

◀ Advertisement for theater production of Uncle Tom's Cabin

◀ Dime novels

1853 *Clotel,* William Wells Brown's story of a slave born in Thomas Jefferson's household, is the first published novel by an African American.

1860s "Dime novels" about the West, like Buffalo Bill, the King of the Border Men, and Frontier Angel, are popular.

BEGINNINGS TO 1763

Prehistory–1763

THE AMERICAN NATION VIDEODISC PROGRAM
A variety of still images, short videos, and activities are available for you to use as you teach this chapter. See Videodisc Resources in the Core Resources Binder for barcode correlations and suggestions for using the program.

Chapter Overview

The first Americans migrated from Asia to North America between 12,000 and 60,000 years ago. Over the centuries, they spread throughout the Americas and developed distinct cultures. During the 1400s Europeans began to look beyond their own borders. Voyages of exploration eventually brought them to the Americas, where the Spanish and the English built huge colonial empires. In the process, they drove the Native Americans from their lands and established the practice of enslaving Africans.

In the 1700s struggles between European powers drew the American colonies into a number of wars. Britain emerged victorious, gaining control of all of North America east of the Appalachians.

Chapter Planning Guide

CHAPTER 1	CORE RESOURCES	AUDIOVISUAL RESOURCES	PROGRAM RESOURCES
INTRODUCTION pp. 2–3	■ Building Your Portfolio Worksheet 1		
TEACHING THE CHAPTER pp. 4–19	■ Graphic Organizer 1 ■ Social Studies Skills Worksheet 1 ■ Geography Worksheet 1 ■ Literature Worksheet 1 ■ Outline Maps 1, 2, 3, 7, 8, 11, 12, 13, 14, 17	■ *The American Nation Videodisc: Inquiry and Exploration; The Spanish Mission System* ■ Linking Geography and History Transparencies and Worksheets 1, 2, 3, 4, 5, 6, 7 ■ Everyday Life in America Transparencies and Worksheets 1, 2, 3	■ Art in American History Transparencies and Worksheets 1, 2 ■ *Eyewitnesses and Others*, Volume 1: Readings 1, 2, 3, 4, 5, 6, 7, 8, 9, 10, 11, 12, 14, 15, 16, 18, 19
REVIEW AND ASSESSMENT pp. 20–21	■ Chapter 1 Daily Quizzes ■ Reteaching Worksheet 1 ■ Chapter 1 Tests ■ Alternative Assessment Forms		■ Test Generator

Additional Resources

BOOKS FOR TEACHERS

Hawke, David Freeman. *Everyday Life in Early America*. HarperCollins, 1989. Shows how early European settlers adjusted to life in North America.

Josephy, Alvin M., Jr., ed. *America in 1492*. Newberry, 1991. Examines Native American civilizations before the arrival of Columbus.

Wright, Ronald. *Stolen Continents: The Americas Through Indian Eyes Since 1492*. Houghton Mifflin, 1992. Examines European colonization from the Native American perspective.

BOOKS FOR STUDENTS

*Adams, Simon. *The Middle Ages: A.D. 456–1450*. Warwick Press, 1990. Reviews medieval times in Africa, the Americas, China, Europe, and the Islamic world.

Dor-Ner, Zvi, and William Scheller. *Columbus and the Age of Discovery*. William Morrow, 1991. Companion volume to PBS documentary.

Scott, John. *Settlers on the Eastern Shore, 1607–1750*. Facts on File, 1990. Primary source materials describe colonial life.

* for students reading below grade level

MULTIMEDIA MATERIALS

As It Was in Colonial America. Video, 59 min. January Productions. Shows lifestyles of colonial Americans.

The Incas Remembered. Video, 60 min. SSSS. Documentary explores the achievements of the Inca people.

Native Americans: The History of a People, Volume 1. Video, 25 min. Knowledge Unlimited/SSSS. Historical overview of Native Americans before the arrival of the Europeans.

USE WITH PAGES 2–3

Listed on the right are the themes emphasized in Chapter 1. The questions in boldface type stimulate critical thinking and provide students with an opportunity to discuss the themes within a broadened context. The questions also appear in the pupil's edition on p. 2.

■ GEOGRAPHIC DIVERSITY

How might differences in environment and land use result in diverse ways of life? Students should note that environmental factors—types and abundance of resources, terrain—help determine the types of economic activities a people can pursue. This, in turn, affects the distribution of the population, the growth of cities, and the development of cultural practices.

■ GLOBAL RELATIONS

What positive and negative effects might result from interactions between countries? Students' examples of positive effects could include increased trade and the exchange of technological developments and new crops. Negative effects might include conflicts over control of resources and the domination of one country over the other.

■ CULTURAL DIVERSITY

How might the cultural backgrounds of settlers influence the development of a region? Students might note that settlers bring their cultural beliefs and practices with them. If an area is settled by people with similar beliefs and practices, the region may develop a society that is opposed to change or diversity. Areas settled by people from diverse cultures, on the other hand, might be more tolerant of differing views and practices and, thus, more varied and dynamic.

CHAPTER STRATEGIES FOR MEETING INDIVIDUAL NEEDS

LIMITED ENGLISH PROFICIENT LEARNERS

Organize students into small groups and assign each group a section from the chapter. Have groups develop definitions for the Preview Workshop for their section. Then ask groups to write sentences and draw sketches using each term. Have groups share their work with the class.

TACTILE/KINESTHETIC LEARNERS

Have students work in groups to create a large annotated map of voyages of exploration. Assign each group a specific voyage to chart and annotate.

LEARNERS HAVING DIFFICULTY

Have students work in pairs to create biography cards of the chapter's key people and groups. One side should list the name of the person or group; the other should list pertinent actions, events, and issues. Have students use the cards to quiz each other.

AUDITORY LEARNERS

Suggest that students work individually or in groups to prepare (and tape-record, if possible) a dramatic reading on one of the major events discussed in the chapter. Have students present their readings to the class.

VISUAL LEARNERS

Have students use materials in the school and public libraries to locate visual materials that depict aspects of life in the English colonies (crafts, housing, customs). Have volunteers share their visuals.

GIFTED LEARNERS

Have students research and write a report on an American Indian tribe mentioned in the chapter. Reports should discuss the tribe's way of life and, if applicable, its interaction with Europeans.

USING THE CHAPTER FOCUS

■ UNDERSTANDING THE MAIN IDEA

Call on a volunteer to read the Understanding the Main Idea paragraph aloud. Then ask students to suggest, using a world map, why some early civilizations had little or no contact. *(separated by great distances and physical barriers, such as mountain ranges and oceans)* Have students speculate what developments broke the isolation. *(desire to trade, technological innovations, desire to explore, etc.)* List student responses on a flip chart. Have students evaluate their responses after they have completed the chapter.

THEMES

Have students work individually or in small groups to answer the questions under Themes. Save students' responses so that they can compare them with their responses after studying the chapter. (See p. 1B for suggested answers.)

■ THE TIME LINE

Ask students to list the time line entries in their notebooks. Have students note each entry's significance as they read the chapter. Upon completing the chapter, have students compare notes.

CORE RESOURCES

- **Graphic Organizer 1**
- **Social Studies Skills Worksheet 1**
- **Outline Maps 1, 2, 3, 7, 8, 11, 12, 13, 14, 17**
- **Building Your Portfolio Worksheet 1**

ABOUT THE ILLUSTRATION

Machu Picchu stands as a testament to the engineering and construction skills of the Incas. The walls of the city's nearly 200 rooms were made of huge granite blocks. No mortar was used to hold these blocks together. Rather, carved ridges and grooves locked the stones to one another. Built in the Andes at an elevation of about 10,000 feet, Machu Picchu may have served as the Incas' last stronghold against the Spanish conquistadors. Ask students how this city might demonstrate the complexity of Incan society.

Chapter 1

Prehistory–1763

BEGINNINGS TO 1763

FOCUS

UNDERSTANDING THE MAIN IDEA

For thousands of years great civilizations rose and fell throughout the world. Some of these civilizations had little or no contact with one another. During the Middle Ages, however, trade increasingly linked most of these cultures. By the 1400s the desire for an all-sea route to Asia propelled Europeans beyond the frontiers of their known world. As a result, in 1492 the Americas became linked with the rest of the world.

THEMES

■ **GEOGRAPHIC DIVERSITY**
How might differences in environment and land use result in diverse ways of life?

■ **GLOBAL RELATIONS**
What positive and negative effects might result from interactions between countries?

■ **CULTURAL DIVERSITY**
How might the cultural backgrounds of settlers influence the development of a region?

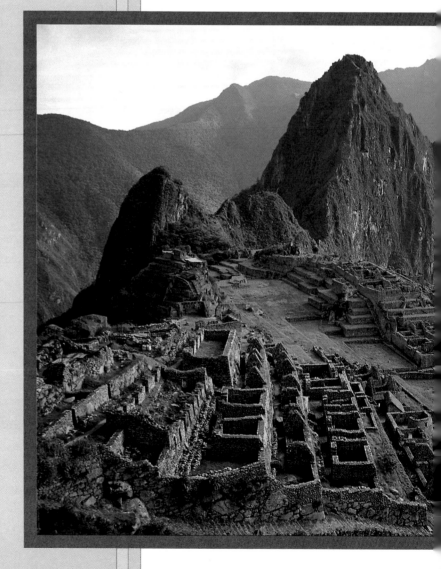

c.8000 B.C.	A.D. 610	c.700	1096	1492	1607	1763
Rise of farming in Mexico.	Muhammad founds Islam.	Rise of Mississippian culture.	Crusades begin.	Columbus lands in the Americas.	Jamestown founded.	Treaty of Paris signed.

■■ ▶ LINK TO THE FUTURE

On a large wall map of the world, indicate the distance overland between Spain and China. Ask students to speculate why the major trading nations of Europe sought new sea routes to Asia. Call on volunteers to suggest ways in which European exploration and settlement of the Western Hemisphere that resulted from this quest would set dramatic changes in motion for European, Native American, and African peoples after 1492.

:: LINK TO THE FUTURE

In the 1400s, Europeans were eager to trade with Asia and Africa. Seeking a westward sea route to Asia to replace the dangerous overland routes, explorers encountered the rich and varied cultures of the Americas. The Americas soon drew thousands of European colonists who staked claims and established settlements, often in harsh environments. In the process they created new American cultures.

*T*ens of thousands of years ago, a momentous migration began. Ice Age peoples, perhaps clothed in mammoth furs and carrying their few possessions, stalked herds of animals across a bridge of land linking present-day Siberia to what is now Alaska. In a series of waves, these first Americans fanned out across two continents and wove a tapestry of distinct cultures.

But many centuries would pass before the Americas were permanently linked to the rest of the world. The desire for luxury goods—from the precious silks and porcelains of China and the spices of India, to the plentiful gold of Africa—launched Europeans on remarkable journeys of exploration that eventually brought them to the shores of the Americas.

In 1492, with Christopher Columbus's daring voyage, worlds apart became worlds in contact—and conflict. Columbus and the explorers and colonists who followed him carved out new lives for themselves in the Americas. Other new arrivals came unwillingly, brought from Africa to work on American plantations and mines after the devastating decline of the Native American population. The colonies produced riches for European nations, who went to war for control of the Americas.

National Maritime Museum Picture Library

World map published in 1486

Incan ruins at Machu Picchu, Peru

Following is a list of the significant people, places, and terms in this section. You may wish to use this list as a section preview.

People
- Kublai Khan
- Johannes Gutenberg

Places
- Beringia
- Mexico
- Cahokia

Terms
- hunter-gatherers
- Paleo-Indians
- glyph
- Qur'an

- Crusades
- Renaissance
- monopoly
- African diaspora

FOCUS OBJECTIVES

- Describe how the environment influenced the cultures of the first Americans.

- Assess the role trade played in linking most of the world in the Middle Ages.

- Determine how the Crusades and the expansion of trade helped change European society.

- Examine how Portugal gained control of East-West trade.

BUILDING VOCABULARY

The prefix *paleo*, often used in terms that refer to things prehistoric, is derived from *palaiós*, a Greek word meaning "old" or "ancient."

Section 1

THE WORLD BY 1500

FOCUS

- **How did the environment influence the cultures of the first Americans?**
- **What role did trade play in linking most of the world in the Middle Ages?**
- **How did the Crusades and the expansion of trade help change European society?**
- **How did Portugal gain control of East-West trade?**

Bronze figurine of a flute player from Benin, West Africa

Trade played a dynamic role in linking most of the world during the Middle Ages (roughly A.D. 500–1500). Merchants traded silks, spices, and other goods between Asia, Africa, and Europe. In Europe, trade helped transform a warring group of isolated kingdoms into a continent of powerful nations. Trade eventually propelled Europeans to the Americas, where men and women originally from Asia had created diverse cultures.

NATIVE AMERICAN CULTURES

Most archaeologists—the scientists who study the remains of past cultures—agree that the first people to reach the vast American wilderness came from Asia during the last Ice Age. Groups of **hunter-gatherers**, peoples who stalked game and gathered edible plants, probably followed animal herds across **Beringia**, a wide land bridge between Siberia and Alaska. Scholars estimate that these first Americans, known as **Paleo-Indians**, arrived between 12,000 and 60,000 years ago.

Empires of the Americas. Groups of Paleo-Indians spread throughout the Americas, and eventually some of them shifted from hunting and gathering to agriculture. Archaeologists have found evidence that by 8000 B.C. people in Mexico were growing maize (corn), and by 2000 B.C. people in the Andes Mountains were growing potatoes. As people settled down to grow their own food, small villages formed. Over time, some villages gave way to cities and complex societies.

The earliest complex societies arose in the areas where agriculture first took hold: Mesoamerica (Central America and the southern and central regions of Mexico) and the Andes region of South America. In Mesoamerica, the Olmec civilization flourished from about 1200 to 400 B.C. The Olmecs practiced slash-and-burn agriculture, in which farmers cut down and burned sections of the forest and then planted crops in the ash-enriched soil.

▼ **Olmec sculptors carved thousands of jade figures—often of infants and dwarfs—and buried them underneath their ceremonial courts.**

Ask students what they know about the world in the 1500s from books, television, and films. Offer guidance by asking: *What was happening in Europe at this time? What was happening in Africa in the 1500s?* and so on. Record student responses on a flip chart so they can see whether their preconceptions are supported by information in the section.

Teaching the Section

ENVIRONMENTAL INFLUENCES

Using a physical wall map of the Americas, point to various regions mentioned in the Native American Cultures subsection. Call on volunteers to describe the environment of each of these regions. Then call on other volunteers to suggest how these environments might have influenced the ways Native Americans lived. Have students use these suggestions to write a generalization on the relationship between environment and culture.

Native American Culture Areas

CULTURAL DIVERSITY By 1500 Native Americans occupied every corner of the Americas. They thrived in vastly different geographic settings: frozen tundra, mountains, dry grasslands, deserts, lush woodlands, and tropical forests.

? HUMAN–ENVIRONMENT INTERACTION Scholars often group Native Americans into broad culture areas based on geographic location. They do this because they believe that environment influences a people's culture. Why might environment influence culture?

Legend:
- Arctic
- Subarctic
- Northwest Coast
- Plateau
- Great Plains
- Northeast
- Great Basin
- California
- Southwest
- Southeast
- Mesoamerica
- Circum-Caribbean

Aztec, Maya, and Inca Empires

- Aztec
- Maya
- Inca

Map Caption Answer
People must adapt to their environment: the resources, physical characteristics, and climate of their region. These adaptations become part of a group's culture.

MULTICULTURAL PERSPECTIVES

Most American Indian tribes originally gave themselves names that meant "people," or "human beings." The names by which Native American peoples call themselves usually differ from the names given to them by others. The name *Navajo,* for example, is the Spanish name for one tribe whose members prefer to call themselves *Dinneh.* Likewise the name *Hopi* is an English mispronunciation of the tribe name *Hopiti.*

COOPERATIVE LEARNING

Organize the class into small groups and assign each group one of the culture areas shown on the map on this page. Have them use reference materials to create a two-page illustrated essay on their culture area. Students should divide tasks—research, design and art, and caption writing. Have groups display their work.

Teaching the Section

TRADE ROUTES IN THE MIDDLE AGES

Provide students with outline maps of the world. Have students use atlases, world history texts, and information from the Trade Networks subsection to create a map titled *Trade Routes in the Middle Ages*. Suggest that they show the principal trade routes that connected the various regions of the world and key goods traded along those routes. Then ask students to write a paragraph on the role trade played in linking most of the world in the Middle Ages. Students may wish to include their maps and paragraphs in their portfolios.

MULTICULTURAL PERSPECTIVES

The people of the Mississippian culture were highly artistic and spiritual. In addition to their elaborate mounds, they crafted a variety of tools, jewelry, and ceremonial objects from clay, shell, marble, copper, and other minerals. Many of their artifacts reflect the Mississippians' obsession with death. The Mississippians were so conscious of death that many scholars refer to their religious practices as the Death Cult. Scholars also believe, however, that a mutual fear of death may have helped prevent warfare among the Mississippian groups.

The Olmecs developed an accurate calendar to help farmers chart the seasons. They also invented a writing system—a form of **glyph**, or picture, writing—that helped merchants keep track of the food and other goods they traded. Olmec merchants may have helped spread Olmec culture to other peoples, including the Mayas. Mayan scholars improved the Olmecs' calendar and writing system and devised a number system that included zero.

Both Olmec and Mayan societies had distinct social classes, and the people believed their kings were divine beings. Later societies, including the Aztecs, had divine kings, but a warrior class was dominant. The Aztecs conquered their neighbors, demanded tribute, and took captives to sacrifice to their gods. Like the Aztecs, the Incas of the Andes region created a militaristic empire. By the 1400s, it included some six to nine million subjects.

Cultures of North America. By the 1400s hundreds of distinct cultural groups lived in the Americas. In North America, where the population was smaller and less dense, very few of these cultural groups created societies as large as those in Mesoamerica or the Andes.

American Indians in the Southwest developed irrigation to overcome dry conditions. Agriculture allowed the Anasazi (ahn-uh-SAHZ-ee) to settle in large villages. Between A.D. 800 and 1100 the Anasazi began to construct multistory rock and adobe dwellings. Many of these buildings nestled against cliffs and contained as many as 800 rooms.

In the woodlands of the East, the Adenas and Hopewells flourished from about 1000 B.C. to A.D. 700. Called the Mound Builders because of the distinctive earthworks they created, they based their

▲ The Adenas and Hopewells built elaborate earthen mounds in the shape of animals as burial places for their dead. This aerial photograph shows the **Great Serpent Mound**, near present-day **Hillsboro, Ohio**.

societies on hunting, gathering, and farming. After about A.D. 700, the Mississippian culture dominated much of the Southeast and Midwest. The largest Mississippian settlement was Cahokia (kuh-HOH-kee-uh) near present-day St. Louis. Cahokia's rulers controlled trade routes that stretched from the Great Lakes into Mesoamerica.

■■ **As Native Americans adapted to the different environments in which they lived, they developed varied cultures.**

*T*RADE NETWORKS

Just as many cultures of the Americas were linked through trade, trade linked the cultures of Asia, Africa, and Europe. Trade between these regions dated from at least the first century A.D., when a route, known as the Silk Road, was established between present-day Iran and China. Wars and raiding often disrupted trade, but in the seventh century, the Tang dynasty in China and the Muslim empire in Southwest Asia revitalized the trade.

China. The Tang dynasty, which began in 618, expanded the western boundaries of China and kept the Silk Road to Central Asia clear of raiders. China's flourishing economy, which produced silk, paper, bronze artifacts, and porcelain, attracted foreign merchants. In the 1200s invaders from Mongolia overran the country. The Mongol leader Kublai Khan (KOO-bluh KAHN) made China the world's largest empire and protected the Silk Road. After Kublai Khan's death in 1294, however, the Silk Road trade declined. Later Chinese leaders emphasized sea routes, and in 1405 China launched a series of maritime expeditions. The expeditions—the most far-reaching the world had ever seen—sailed to Southeast Asia, India, the Arabian Peninsula, and East Africa. But in 1433 China officially ended foreign trade, though Asian merchants continued to trade Chinese goods.

The Islamic world. In the seventh century the Muslim empire helped link China with the West. The empire originated with Muhammad, a merchant and prophet who began to preach the religion of Islam in about 610. Muhammad united the Arabian Peninsula, and his successors conquered surrounding empires. At its height, the

THE IMPACT OF THE CRUSADES AND TRADE

On the chalkboard draw a chart with the following headings: *Political, Economic, Social,* and *Intellectual.* Have students suggest changes in these areas brought about by the Crusades and the expansion of trade. Enter responses in the appropriate columns. Have students copy the chart and include it in their portfolios.

PORTUGAL, SLAVERY, AND EAST-WEST TRADE

Have students record on an annotated map or illustrated time line the various stages in Portugal's search for an all-water route to the East. Captions and entries should indicate areas affected, goods exchanged, and the development of the slave trade. Have students display their maps and time lines on the bulletin board. Students may wish to include their work in their portfolios.

Muslim empire covered northern Africa, the Iberian Peninsula, and Southwest Asia.

Although Muslim armies helped spread the Islamic faith, many people were converted by merchants. Muslim merchants launched expeditions from Baghdad, which became the Muslim empire's capital in 762. Located on the Tigris River, Baghdad had access to the Persian Gulf and thus to India and China. Baghdad was also linked to the western end of the Silk Road, where Muslim and Jewish merchants controlled much of the trade. These merchants carried Persian rugs and textiles and African gold to eastern Asia and returned with porcelain and jewels. The Muslim merchants also carried the **Qur'an** (kuh-RAN)—the holy book of Islam—and tirelessly preached their religion.

Trade fostered other cultural exchanges. Muslims introduced Chinese technologies, such as silk and paper production, to the West. Mathematical ideas from India influenced al-Khwārizmī, a Muslim mathematician who developed algebra. Ibn Sina (IB-uhn SEE-nah), a Baghdad physician, compiled a medical encyclopedia that became a standard textbook beyond Muslim lands. Islamic maps also found their way to other lands.

Africa. Islamic culture spread to Africa through conquest and trade. In the seventh century Arab armies captured Egypt and North Africa. In East Africa, African traders brought gold and ivory to the coast, where other traders—most of them Arabs—shipped the goods to the Arabian Peninsula and then to India and China. The most sought-after item was gold, which the Muslim empire needed to mint coins used in international trade. Over time Arabs and East Africans created a unique African culture, whose language, Swahili (swah-HEE-lee), blended Bantu and Arabic languages.

In West Africa, African merchants had early on established a trade in gold and salt across the Sahara Desert. The kingdom of Ghana flourished from this trade until the region was overrun by Muslims in the 11th century. The kingdom of Mali then rose to power, eventually controlling a huge empire that stretched from the upper Niger (NY-juhr) River westward to the Atlantic coast.

Muslim traders converted many West African rulers. Mansa Mūsā, who ruled Mali from 1307 to 1332, was a devout Muslim. After his death, Mali declined and the state of Songhai (SAWNG-hy) became the dominant power in West Africa. Songhai grew rich from the trade in gold, ivory, and

◀ Mansa Mūsā made a pilgrimage to Mecca in 1324.

slaves and became a center of Islamic learning. Its city of Tombouctou (tohn-book-TOO) was home to three universities and some 180 Islamic schools.

Europe. From North Africa Muslim armies moved into Europe. By 714 they had conquered most of present-day Spain and Portugal. Muslims introduced irrigation systems and Asian crops, such as rice. Jewish traders sold these crops, together with fine steel products and textiles, all around the Mediterranean.

■■ Through trade, the world's regions shared new technologies and religious and scientific ideas.

THE TRANSFORMATION OF EUROPE

In the 10th century, trading cities in Italy arose that traded goods from Spain and the rest of the Muslim empire throughout Europe. By the early 1100s Venice, the most powerful of these cities, dominated the eastern Mediterranean trade. Venice, like most of Europe, was Christian under the leadership of the Roman Catholic Church. Christianity had spread to Europe after its founding in the first century A.D. in present-day Israel. Because Jesus Christ had been born there, Christians considered it to be the Holy Land. Muslims also considered the area holy. When they restricted Christians' access to the city of Jerusalem, the Europeans waged a series of wars against the Muslims. These wars, known as the **Crusades**, took place between 1096 and the late 1200s.

In the First Crusade, European soldiers captured Jerusalem and established several kingdoms in the area. (The Muslims retook the city in the late

Practice

GUIDED PRACTICE

Have groups of students role-play merchants from China, Africa, the Islamic world, and Europe. Ask groups to explain how they exchange ideas, cultural practices, and goods with other parts of the world.

INDEPENDENT PRACTICE

Have students use information gained from the Guided Practice to write a Middle Ages travel brochure expounding the cultural diversity of China, Africa, or Europe.

Review and Assessment

REVIEW Have students write a paragraph on the world in the Middle Ages using the terms listed in the Preview Workshop. Ask for volunteers to read their paragraphs to the class. Then assign the Section 1 Review on p. 9.

ASSESS Assign the **Section 1 Daily Quiz** in *Core Resources*.

GLOBAL CONNECTIONS

The goods imported from the East by Italian traders traveled to the outskirts of Europe by way of markets and fairs. The center of exchange was the French province of Champagne, which held fairs approximately six times a year. There, exotic goods from Byzantium and Africa, Flemish cloth, French wine, English wool, and a profusion of other products changed hands in a frenzy of trade.

MAKING CONNECTIONS
Government

A historical move toward representative government in Europe began in 1215 with the signing of the Magna Carta, the document that limited the power of the English king. Although the charter primarily benefited the nobility, one provision served the interests of the newly created middle class by protecting trade.

"All merchants shall have safe and secure conduct to go out of, and to come into, England. . . . by land as by water, for buying and selling by the ancient and allowed customs, without any unjust tolls, except in time of war."

1100s.) Though later Crusades were never as successful, the wars had important consequences for trade. Venetian merchants and bankers helped fund the Crusades in return for trading privileges.

This trade helped change Europe's political and social order. Increased trade created opportunities for merchants and bankers who formed a new social class—the middle class. This new class supported strong rulers who could protect trade; in return for their support, the middle class demanded greater political and economic freedom. Kings and lords reluctantly granted towns self-government. Some monarchs even organized assemblies, which were the forerunners of modern parliaments.

By the 1400s strong national monarchies existed in Portugal, France, England, and Spain. Henry VII unified England in 1485 after 30 years of fighting. Spain created a unified nation in 1492, after the kingdoms of Castile and Aragon united by marriage and Muslims and Jews were forced to leave.

◀ The 12th-century Arab geographer Abū al-Idrīsī developed a map of the world that consisted of many different sections. One section displaying the "Seven Climatic Zones" is shown.

The Crusades and trade also promoted a rebirth of European learning and creativity known as the **Renaissance**. Crusaders and traders brought to Europe classical Greek and Roman works and new ideas from the Byzantine Empire (the eastern half of the former Roman Empire) and from the Islamic world. These ideas spread throughout Europe after the 1450s, when Johannes Gutenberg invented a printing press that produced books quickly and cheaply. The wealth won from trade supported the work of Renaissance artists and architects.

■■ The Crusades and trade helped broaden a new social class's political freedoms, spurred the creation of strong national monarchies, and fostered the Renaissance.

Then and Now — THE FIVE THEMES OF GEOGRAPHY

Historical events cannot be fully understood without an understanding of the geographical settings in which they take place. History and geography, therefore, are closely linked. To organize information, geographers study the following five themes: location, place, human-environment interaction, movement, and region.

Location can be expressed in two ways. *Absolute location* is a site's exact spot on the earth. The absolute location of Chicago, for example, is 41°52' north latitude and 87°37' west longitude. *Relative location*, on the other hand, describes the position of a place in relation to other places. For instance, Chicago lies along the southwest shore of Lake Michigan.

Place refers to the physical and human characteristics of an area. Climate is an example of a physical characteristic, while population size is an example of a human characteristic.

Human-environment interaction deals with the ways in which people both adapt to and change their natural surroundings. The shelters people build to protect themselves against cold or heat are a form of adaptation. Actions that people take to change the environment include clearing forests and setting up irrigation systems.

Movement describes the way people interact as they travel, communicate, and trade goods and services. Movement includes human migration as well as the exchange of goods.

A *region* is an area defined by common physical or cultural characteristics, such as climate or religion. Geographers have divided the earth into many regions and subregions.

RETEACH Organize students into four groups and assign each group one of the Focus questions on p. 4. Have group members discuss and write an answer to their question. Ask group representatives to share their answers with the class.

Closure

Have students work individually or in small groups to write a generalization explaining how and why Europeans set out to explore the world at the end of the 1400s and some of the consequences. Have students or groups present and explain their generalizations to the class.

Extension

RESEARCH Have students work in pairs to research and report on a pre-1500 Native American culture in their state. Encourage students to contact local historical societies and visit museums for information.

CREATE Encourage students to research and draw diagrams of a navigational or sailing development made at Prince Henry's center at Sagres.

THE LURE OF TRADE AND EXPLORATION

By the early 1400s, goods from Africa and Asia were available in Europe, but very costly. The emerging nations of Europe wanted to share in the huge profits to be earned from this trade. But to do so, they needed to break Genoa and Venice's **monopoly**, or exclusive control, of East-West trade, by finding a new route to the East.

Portuguese exploration. Portugal, a small country with a long seafaring tradition, led the way in exploration. Prince Henry of Portugal oversaw Portuguese exploration in the 15th century. He sought to find the African "gold kingdoms" he had heard of while fighting the Muslims in Morocco.

In 1419 Prince Henry established a center for the study of navigation at Sagres (SAH-greesh), which produced accurate maps and new ships and navigation methods. Henry put the results to use by sponsoring voyages of exploration down the African coast. By the 1460s, the Portuguese had ventured nearly around the great bulge of West Africa.

The slave trade. The first Portuguese traders to land in West Africa sought gold and spices. In time, however, they turned to the sale of enslaved Africans. The Portuguese did not introduce the slave trade—slavery had long existed in Europe, Asia, and Africa. But prior to the Portuguese, Africans pressed into slavery were often criminals or captives of war. Most could marry, and their children were not slaves.

By the end of the 1500s, the slave trade had become a major economic activity. It eventually resulted in the **African diaspora** (dy-AS-pruh)—the forcible resettlement of millions of Africans to the Americas. Estimates suggest that in the four centuries the slave trade operated, more than 10 million Africans crossed the Atlantic as slaves.

The slave trade devastated African society. Warfare among West African nations increased as each sought to capture slaves. Many other slaves were captured in raids. In 1444 a Portuguese observer described the painful experience of captured Africans:

> 66 Mothers would clasp their infants in their arms and throw themselves on the ground to cover them with their bodies, disregarding any injury to their own persons, so that they could prevent their children from being separated from them. 99

But such observations did not stop the slave trade. The Portuguese continued to trade and to search for a new route to Asia. In 1488 Bartolomeu Dias rounded Africa's southern tip, and 10 years later Vasco da Gama's expedition reached India. Over the next half century, the Portuguese established trading forts in West and East Africa, India, Southeast Asia, and southern China, thereby gaining control of East-West trade. Soon other European nations sponsored voyages of exploration, this time venturing west to the Americas.

■■ Portuguese explorers sailed around Africa and established a new East-West trade route.

SECTION 1 REVIEW

IDENTIFY and explain the significance of the following: hunter-gatherers, Beringia, Paleo-Indians, glyph, Kublai Khan, Qur'an, Crusades, Renaissance, Johannes Gutenberg, monopoly, African diaspora.

LOCATE and explain the importance of the following: Mexico, Cahokia.

1. **MAIN IDEA** Why was there great variety in Native American cultures?
2. **MAIN IDEA** How were the world's regions linked during the Middle Ages?
3. **MAIN IDEA** In what ways did the Crusades change economic, political, and social life in Europe?
4. **WRITING TO PERSUADE** Imagine you are Vasco da Gama. Write a letter to the Portuguese monarchs explaining why it would be in their interests to fund your attempts to find a new route to Asia.
5. **SYNTHESIZING** What led to the spread of Islam and Islamic culture?

SECTION

2

*Introducing
the Section*

PREVIEW WORKSHOP

Following is a list of the significant people and terms in this section. You may wish to use this list as a section preview.

People
- Christopher Columbus
- Bartolomé de Las Casas
- Ferdinand Magellan
- Hernán Cortés

- Francisco Pizarro
- Juan Ponce de León
- Friar Junípero Serra

Terms
- *Reconquista*
- *encomienda*
- Columbian exchange
- Treaty of Tordesillas
- circumnavigate

- conquistadors
- Pueblo Revolt
- peons

FOCUS OBJECTIVES

- Describe some results of the Columbian exchange.

- Explain how conquistadors helped build a Spanish empire in the Americas; describe how Native Americans responded to the conquistadors.

- List elements of their culture the Spanish colonists introduced to the Americas.

HISTORICAL SIDELIGHTS

Maritime Skills

Columbus was an expert in a navigational skill called "dead reckoning," which calculates a ship's position by estimating course and speed. Columbus measured the ship's speed by watching the flow of water along the hull while assessing the effects of winds and currents.

CORE RESOURCES

- **Section 2 Daily Quiz**
- **Literature Worksheet 1**

AV RESOURCES

- ***The American Nation Videodisc: The Spanish Mission System***
- **Linking Geography and History Transparency** and **Worksheet 6**
- **Everyday Life in America Transparency** and **Worksheet 2**

Section 2

SPANISH AMERICA

- **What were some of the results of the Columbian exchange?**
- **How did the conquistadors help build a Spanish empire in the Americas? How did Native Americans respond to the conquistadors?**
- **What elements of their culture did Spanish colonists introduce to the Americas?**

Few dates in American history are as instantly recognizable as 1492. With Christopher Columbus's daring voyage, worlds apart became worlds in contact—and conflict. The explorers and colonists who came to the Americas after Columbus carved out new lives for themselves and began a new era of trade. Tragically, however, Europeans introduced diseases to the Americas that decimated Indian populations.

Flora and fauna of the Americas

FIRST CONTACT

Christopher Columbus, a mariner from Genoa, doubted that the Portuguese route around Africa was the most direct route to Asia. He went to Lisbon, Portugal, the center of European knowledge about sea travel, and studied charts and books. Columbus concluded that the western sea could not be very large and that the great trading cities of Asia lay only about 2,400 miles west of Portugal.

In the 1480s Columbus tried to persuade various European monarchs to sponsor a westward voyage. King John II of Portugal rejected the plan because he doubted Columbus's calculation of the distance to Asia. (In fact, Columbus had underestimated the distance by about five times.) Initially, Columbus had no better luck with the Spanish monarchs, Ferdinand and Isabella. His luck changed in 1492, however, when the monarchs completed the *Reconquista*—the reconquest of Spain from the Muslims. With that massive task accomplished, the Spanish rulers were able to back Columbus, who had persuaded them with promises of great riches and new Catholic converts.

At dawn on August 3, 1492, Columbus and his experienced crew of 90 men departed from Palos, Spain. More than two months later, Columbus's fleet—the *Santa María,* the *Niña,* and the *Pinta*—reached a tiny coral island in the central Bahamas and claimed the land for Spain.

◀ **This detail from the *Fall of Granada* by Pradilla shows Ferdinand and Isabella receiving the surrender of the Kingdom of Granada from the Moors in 1492.**

Teaching the *Section*

RESULTS OF THE COLUMBIAN EXCHANGE

Draw students' attention to the Commentary on pp. 11–12. Then organize the class into three groups. Ask one group to develop a list of the pros or cons of the Columbian exchange from the Native American perspective. The other groups should develop similar lists from the European and African perspectives. Have groups present and explain their lists.

■■ Ask students to give examples of ways in which the Columbian exchange affects their lives today.

▶

The residents of the island, the Tainos (TY-nohs), greeted the strange visitors. Columbus described their hospitality:

> ❝ They . . . brought us parrots and balls of cotton and spears and many other things, which they exchanged for the glass beads and hawks' bells. They willingly traded everything they owned. ❞

Though these were not the luxury items of the Indies Columbus sought, he saw potential profit in the situation. Noting that the Tainos—who he called "Indios," or inhabitants of the Indies, because he still believed he had reached Asia—did not have metal weapons, he concluded: "They would make fine servants. . . . With 50 men we could subjugate [conquer] them all."

Columbus expected the Tainos to lead him to gold. He sailed from island to island—naming and claiming each for Spain—in his search. Though the search yielded some gold, it produced conflict. The Spaniards' excessive demands for gold and food wore down the Tainos' generosity and led to battles between the two groups. Another source of conflict was the *encomienda* (en-koh-mee-EN-duh) system, which Columbus informally introduced. Under this system the colonists, or *encomenderos* (en-koh-muhn-DE-rohs), received the right to have a certain number of Indians work for them. The *encomenderos* used the Indians to mine gold, provide food, and build houses.

Most *encomenderos* overworked the American Indian laborers and prevented them from growing food for themselves. One prominent critic, Bartolomé de Las Casas, demanded an end to the *encomienda*. In his *Apologetic History of the Indies* (1566), Las Casas argued that Native Americans should not be enslaved because their humanity and wisdom equaled that of Europeans:

> ❝ Not only have [the Indians] shown themselves to be very wise peoples and possessed of lively and marked understanding, . . . governing and providing for their nations, . . . but they have equaled many diverse nations of the . . . past and present. ❞

The end of the *encomienda* would not come through official action but through the catastrophic decline of the American Indian population. The

▲ This illustration from an Aztec manuscript shows the devastating effects of smallpox. Smallpox, measles, and malaria were just a few of the diseases brought by Europeans that caused epidemics among Native American peoples.

devastating effects of European disease, overwork, and malnutrition reduced the Indian population in some areas by over 90 percent by the mid-16th century. To replace the Indian laborers, the Spanish imported African slaves.

COMMENTARY

The Columbian Legacy

Historians offer different interpretations of the significance of Columbus's voyages to the Americas. Some applaud him for his courage and vision; others blame him for introducing the encomienda *system and for the drastic decline of the Native American population. But certainly a useful way to understand the legacy of Columbus's voyages is to see the enormous effect they had on the world. The transfer of people, ideas, plants, animals, and diseases between the Americas, Europe, Asia, and Africa that Columbus's journeys initiated has come to be called the* **Columbian exchange**.

The Columbian exchange transformed the world. Gold, silver, and other resources from the Americas made many European nations wealthy and powerful. Crops from the Americas, such as corn, potatoes, and tomatoes, became staples for people everywhere. Through settlement and

MULTICULTURAL PERSPECTIVES

To illustrate the cultural differences between the Spanish and the Native Americans, Las Casas told the story of Hathvey, an Indian chief who fled to Cuba from Hispaniola. Hathvey explained to the Indians that the Spaniards believed gold to have supernatural powers. He suggested that if the Indians prayed to these same powers, the Spanish might possibly be placated. Following Hathvey's advice, the Indians prayed to a gold-filled chest.

In 1511 the Spaniards traveled to Cuba, where they captured Hathvey and burned him alive for worshipping false gods. As the chief neared death, a monk extolled the glories of the Spaniards' heaven to him. Hathvey replied, "Let me go to hell that I may not come where they [the Spanish] are."

PRIMARY SOURCES

Description of Change: excerpted and bracketed
Rationale: excerpted to focus on main idea; bracketed to clarify meaning

Teaching the Section

CONQUISTADORS' ROLES

Have students work in small groups to do research to write reports from either Cortés or Pizarro to the Spanish Crown, describing and explaining the actions taken by the conquistadors. Suggest that groups illustrate their reports with maps and other visuals. Have volunteer groups present their reports to the class.

NATIVE AMERICANS' RESPONSE

Have students take the identity of 16th-century American Indians and write journal entries on the effects of Spanish conquests on their way of life and the actions they took to survive. Ask volunteers to share their entries. Students may wish to include their journal entries in their portfolios.

SPANISH CULTURE

Create a four-column chart on the chalkboard with the following headings: *government, architecture, labor systems,* and *social structure.* Ask students for examples of the Spanish contribution to the Americas in each category. Suggest to the class that some contributions may fit more than one category. When the chart is complete, have students survey the contributions and identify which remain part of the Americas' Spanish heritage today.

 GLOBAL CONNECTIONS

Not surprisingly, the rest of Europe did not recognize the Treaty of Tordesillas. Elizabeth I of England declared that the sea was common to all nations. Foreshadowing the coming struggle between England and Spain, she added, "Since the sea belongs to everyone, it belongs to me."

PRIMARY SOURCE

Description of Change: excerpted and bracketed
Rationale: excerpted to focus on main idea; bracketed to clarify meaning

the slave trade, the lands formerly inhabited only by American Indians were gradually peopled with Europeans, Africans, and Asians. The introduction of European animals transformed the American landscape.

The exchange also introduced deadly diseases, such as smallpox, measles, and malaria, to North America. Because Native Americans lacked resistance to these diseases, the Indian population experienced a catastrophic decline. Scholars estimate that the population of the Americas before the Europeans arrived was between 8.4 million and 112.5 million. Several centuries later, the Native American population had declined to perhaps 4 to 4.5 million.

The tragic effects of disease and military conquest on American Indians and of the introduction of African slavery understandably overshadow many of the positive aspects of the Columbian exchange. But when determining the significance of Columbus's voyages, we must take into account the global transformations he set in motion.

■■ The Columbian exchange resulted in the transfer of people, precious metals, crops, and animals between the Americas and Europe, Asia, and Africa.

THE CONQUEST OF THE MAINLAND

Columbus's voyages also fueled the rivalry between Spain and Portugal. To avoid open conflict, the two nations signed the **Treaty of Tordesillas** (tawrd-uh-SEE-uhs) in 1494. The treaty drew an imaginary line of demarcation, or separation, around the world: Territory west of the line would belong to Spain; east of the line, to Portugal.

The Spanish Crown soon sponsored new voyages. Ferdinand Magellan set out in 1519 to find a westward route to Asia. After sailing around the southern tip of South America and into the Pacific Ocean, the expedition accomplished its goal. Surviving crew members returned to Spain in 1522—the first people to **circumnavigate**, or sail completely around, the world.

Other explorers claimed lands in Central America and South America. In 1512 Vasco Nuñez de Balboa (NOON-yays day bahl-BOH-uh) explored

THE SLAVE TRADE

Nzinga Mbemba (en-ZING uhm-BEM-buh), "Lord of the Congo," was a central-African ruler who hoped to increase contact and trade between the Congo states and the leading European powers. To aid this effort, he even adopted the Christian faith and assumed a new name: Dom Afonso. His dreams turned sour, however, as he watched Portuguese slave ships take more and more of his people by force to the Americas. In 1526 he urged King John III of Portugal to curb this practice:

THROUGH OTHERS' EYES

❝**W**e cannot reckon how great the damage is, since the . . . [slave] merchants daily seize our subjects, sons of the land and sons of our noblemen and vassals and our relatives. . . . Thieves and men of evil conscience take them . . . and cause them to be sold: and so great, Sir, is their corruption . . . that our country is being utterly depopulated.❞

Afonso's pleas went unheeded, however. Spain and other European nations followed Portugal's lead. By 1600 several hundred thousand Africans were in bondage in the Americas.

Practice

GUIDED PRACTICE

Work with students to create a chart on the board titled *Organization of Spanish America* with the column headings *Social, Economic,* and *Political*. Have volunteers suggest entries for each heading, giving a brief explanation of each.

INDEPENDENT PRACTICE

Have students imagine that they are Spanish colonists in the late 1700s. Have them use information in the Guided Practice chart to write a letter to a friend in Europe. The letter should describe the extent of Spanish settlement in the Americas and the organization of daily life in their colony.

Review and Assessment

REVIEW Organize students into small groups and provide each group with a piece of butcher paper. Then ask groups to create a mural that illustrates life in Spanish America. Have groups display their murals on the bulletin board. Then assign the Section 2 Review on p. 14.

ASSESS Assign the **Section 2 Daily Quiz** in *Core Resources.*

▶

▲ Magellan–Elcano Expedition

Panama and was probably the first European to glimpse the Pacific Ocean from the Americas. Lured by stories of gold, Spanish **conquistadors** (kawng-KEES-tuh-dawrs), or conquerors, soon followed the explorers. In 1521 Hernán Cortés conquered the Aztec Empire in Mexico, and Francisco Pizarro conquered the vast Inca Empire in the 1530s.

The Spanish conquistadors were aided by divisions within the Indian empires and by the devastating spread of diseases. To maintain control over the conquered Indians, the Spanish tried to wipe out Native American cultures. They tore down temples, destroyed art, and reorganized settlements. In Mexico, the Spanish leveled the Aztec capital of Tenochtitlán (tay-nawch-tee-TLAHN) and built their capital of Mexico City over its ruins.

American Indian cultures were not completely destroyed. Survival, however, usually meant the mixing of Spanish and Native American peoples and cultures. For example, many Indians developed a new religion by combining their rituals with Catholic rituals. Over time American Indian and Spanish ways blended, creating new cultures.

■■ **The conquistadors added vast territory and wealth to the Spanish American empire. Many Native Americans fought the conquistadors, while others blended their culture with Spanish ways.**

SPANISH SETTLEMENT

Since North America boasted no empires as wealthy as the Aztecs or Incas, Spanish exploration and colonization there proceeded slowly. The main goals of settlement were providing ports for ships sailing up the Atlantic coast on their way back to Spain, establishing missions to convert American Indians, and preventing other countries from colonizing Spanish territory. Beginning in the mid-1500s, Spain founded settlements from coast to coast in what is now the continental United States.

Spain's northern lands. Spanish explorers first turned their attention to La Florida, the entire eastern seaboard from present-day Florida to Newfoundland. Florida's first European explorer, Juan Ponce de León (PAWN-say day lay-AWN), sought the mythical "Fountain of Youth" in 1513, but established no settlements. A much more practical goal—establishing a port—motivated later explorers. In 1565, after two earlier colonizers had failed, an expedition led by Pedro Menéndez de Avilés (may-NAYN-days day ah-bee-LAYS) succeeded in planting a permanent settlement. This was St. Augustine, the oldest city founded by Europeans in what is now the United States.

In 1609, some 1,500 miles west of St. Augustine, the Spanish established Santa Fe as the capital of New Mexico. The Pueblo Indians bitterly opposed Spanish rule. In 1680 the Pueblos, resentful of Spanish taxes and demands that they give up their religion, drove out the Spanish. After the **Pueblo Revolt,** the Pueblos attempted to return to their former way of life. However, a new governor, Diego de Vargas, reestablished Spanish rule in the 1690s.

▲ The Pueblo Indians skillfully decorated pottery with beautiful symbols and designs.

At the same time, the Spanish began moving into Arizona. Father Eusebio Kino (ay-oo-SAYB-yoh KEE-noh) built missions near present-day Nogales (noh-GAL-uhs) in 1687 and Tucson in 1700. During the 1700s, fear of French and British expansion prompted the Spanish to speed up their colonization of Arizona and New Mexico. France's colonizing activity also spurred Spain to strengthen its hold on Texas. The San Francisco de los Tejas mission was established in 1690, and the San Antonio de Valero mission was built in 1718. Other settlements emerged along the Rio Grande, but the absence of gold and silver and the Apaches' and Comanches' constant raiding discouraged further settlement.

California was the last of Spain's northern territories to be colonized. Juan Rodríguez Cabrillo (kah-BREE-yoh) explored much of the California

RETEACH For each subsection in the section, have students write a sentence that summarizes the main idea. Select students to read their sentences aloud. Have the class choose the best summary sentence for each subsection.

Closure

Have students each determine and record the one word that they think best describes life in Spanish America. Call on students to reveal and explain their choices.

Extension

INVESTIGATE Encourage students to investigate the impact of the Columbian exchange on European diet.

CREATE Have students research Spanish missions and create models or detailed diagrams showing their layout and organization.

SECTION REVIEW ANSWERS

IDENTIFY

For significance, see the following pages:
Christopher Columbus (p. 10)
Reconquista (p. 10)
encomienda (p. 11)
Bartolomé de Las Casas (p. 11)
Treaty of Tordesillas (p. 12)
Ferdinand Magellan (p. 12)
circumnavigate (p. 12)
Hernán Cortés (p. 13)
Francisco Pizarro (p. 13)
Juan Ponce de León (p. 13)
Pueblo Revolt (p. 13)
Friar Junípero Serra (p. 14)
peons (p. 14)

1. *Exchanges mentioned might include: transfer of crops and people among regions, diseases brought to the Americas, slave trade in Africa, influence of American gold and silver on European economies.*
2. *conquered Aztec and Incan land; transferred great wealth to Spain*
3. *Spanish language, Catholicism, architecture, ranching, different foods and crops, social structure*
4. *Essays might mention that some fought Spanish or escaped; others allied themselves with Spanish and adapted Spanish customs to their own.*
5. *Murals should show Tainos helping Spanish and later being enslaved by them.*

---

coastline as early as 1542. But not until the late 1700s did Spain, alarmed by Russian explorations in northern California, attempt to set up permanent settlements. San Diego was founded in 1769, and San Francisco in 1776. Friar Junípero Serra (hoo-NEE-pay-roh SER-rah), a scholarly missionary, also founded a string of missions along California's coast.

Colonial life. From California to Florida, colonists transplanted Spanish political and social institutions. The Spanish influence found today throughout the southwestern United States dates from this period. Spain's northern colonies were part of the viceroyalty, or province, of New Spain and were administered by a viceroy in Mexico City. But because transportation between the capital at Mexico City and northern New Spain was long and difficult, colonists usually exercised some independence in local government.

The Spanish founded more than 150 missions in the present-day United States to convert Native Americans to the Catholic faith. At the center of the missions were the churches, whose architecture ranged from rustic to ornate. In their zeal to teach the Native Americans Spanish ways, missionaries suppressed Indian cultures and sometimes enforced a harsh labor system. Many Indians fled from the missions or died from European diseases.

Outside the missions, colonists established estates and settlements, which were usually guarded by presidios (forts). **Peons**, or workers who owned no land of their own, worked on haciendas—the biggest estates. Many peons remained tied to a hacienda by debts or by lack of other opportunities. Owners of *ranchos,* or smaller estates, usually worked alongside their laborers.

The Granger Collection, New York

▲ A Mexican hacienda owner, his wife, an overseer, and a *vaquero* are shown in this watercolor from the early 1830s.

The Spanish *vaqueros* (vah-KER-ohs), the horsemen who worked on cattle ranches, established many of the ranch practices that became the models for later North American cowboys.

People living on haciendas, in missions, and in the bustling cities of Spanish America developed a unique social structure. *Peninsulares* (pay-nin-SOO-LAHR-uhs), Spaniards born in Spain, and *criollos* (kree-OH-yohs), Spaniards born in the colonies, held the most privileged positions in the Americas. Below the Spaniards were *mestizos* (me-STEE-zohs), men and women born of European-Indian unions. Roughly equal in status to the *mestizos* were mulattoes, people of African-European ancestry. At the bottom of the social structure were Native Americans, Africans, and *zambos*, people of Indian-African ancestry.

■■ **Colonists brought Spanish government, architecture, and customs to the Americas.**

SECTION 2 REVIEW

IDENTIFY and explain the significance of the following: Christopher Columbus, *Reconquista, encomienda,* Bartolomé de Las Casas, Treaty of Tordesillas, Ferdinand Magellan, circumnavigate, Hernán Cortés, Francisco Pizarro, Juan Ponce de León, Pueblo Revolt, Friar Junípero Serra, peons.

1. **MAIN IDEA** What exchanges between the Americas, Europe, Asia, and Africa took place as a result of Columbus's journeys?
2. **MAIN IDEA** What roles did the conquistadors play in helping Spain build an American empire?
3. **MAIN IDEA** What elements of Spanish culture were transplanted to Spanish America?
4. **WRITING TO EXPLAIN** Write an essay explaining how Native Americans kept their cultures alive in spite of the conquistadors' efforts to destroy their cultures.
5. **USING HISTORICAL IMAGINATION** Imagine you are a Taino living in the Bahamas. Draw a plan for a mural that portrays your interactions with the Spanish explorers.

PREVIEW WORKSHOP

Following is a list of the significant people and terms in this section. You may wish to use this list as a section preview.

People
- Olaudah Equiano
- William Penn

Terms
- Protestant Reformation
- Spanish Armada
- joint-stock companies
- Puritans
- Separatists
- Mayflower Compact
- Great Migration
- commonwealth
- freemen
- indentured servants
- Middle Passage
- abolition
- Iroquois League

Section 3

THE ENGLISH COLONIES

- **How did English colonization methods differ from Spanish methods?**
- **Why did settlers come to England's North American colonies? What kinds of societies did they establish?**
- **What were the main causes and results of the French and Indian War?**

In the 1500s, as the Spanish began settling North America, other European nations—especially England and France—claimed large areas of the continent. By the end of the 17th century, English colonies flourished in North America, and the colonists, with the help of Native Americans, created distinctive societies. The 18th century, however, brought increasing conflicts with American Indians and the French over control of the land.

NOVA BRITANNIA.
OFFERING MOST
Excellent fruites by Planting in
VIRGINIA.
Exciting all such as be well affected
to further the same.

LONDON
Printed for SAMVEL MACHAM, and are to be sold at
his Shop in Pauls Church-yard, at the
Signe of the Bul-head.
1609.

English pamphlet promoting colonization in 1609

FOCUS OBJECTIVES

- Compare the English method of colonization with that of the Spanish.

- Explain why settlers came to England's North American colonies; describe the kinds of societies they established.

- Identify the main causes and results of the French and Indian War.

HISTORICAL SIDELIGHTS

Sea Dogs
Chief among English sea dogs was John Hawkins. In the 1560s he transported African slaves to the West Indies and the Spanish Main. But he soon discovered a quicker—though riskier—way to make a fortune: preying on Spanish treasure ships.

EARLY ENGLISH SETTLEMENT

Shortly after Columbus's first voyage, mariner John Cabot searched for a northwestern route to Asia. In 1497 and 1498 Cabot claimed Newfoundland, Nova Scotia, and New England for England. But England delayed colonizing its new territory. England was embroiled in the **Protestant Reformation**—the religious upheaval that established new churches as alternatives to Catholicism. The struggle between Protestants and Catholics became not only religious but also territorial and political. England, which became a Protestant nation in 1534, began to challenge Catholic Spain for religious and political dominance in Europe and in the Americas.

▶ The faster English ships outmaneuvered the ships of the Spanish Armada.

English pirates, known as "sea dogs," attacked Spanish galleons and seized their cargoes. To retaliate, the Spanish king, Philip, launched an attack on England in 1588. The English navy defeated Philip's force of some 130 ships, known as the **Spanish Armada**. Spain's defeat revealed Spanish military and economic weaknesses. The way was thus open for England to begin colonization.

Attempts at colonization had been made in the 1580s, but they had failed. In 1606, however, King James I issued a charter licensing two merchant groups to organize settlements in Virginia and "to dig, mine, and search for all manner of mines of gold, silver, and copper." The two groups, the Plymouth Company and the London Company, were **joint-stock companies**, which operate somewhat like corporations do today. Investors shared the cost of starting and maintaining the company; they also shared any profits or

CORE RESOURCES

- **Section 3 Daily Quiz**
- **Geography Worksheet 1**

AV RESOURCES

- **Linking Geography and History Transparency** and **Worksheet 7**
- **Everyday Life in America Transparency** and **Worksheet 3**

MOTIVATING: LINK TO TODAY

Have students identify English influences in their lives. Suggest such subjects as language, system of government, and customs and traditions. List responses on the chalkboard. Then ask students to speculate on why English influences remain strong in the United States today.

Teaching the Section

COMPARING ENGLISH AND SPANISH COLONIZATION

Organize students into pairs and have them create a chart in which they compare the Spanish and English methods of colonization. Ask a volunteer pair to present their chart and discuss the similarities and differences with the class.

ENGLISH SETTLERS TO NORTH AMERICA

Draw a web on the chalkboard, with *English Settlers Come to America* as the center. Ask for volunteers to complete the web by offering reasons why people left England for America. Have students copy the web into their notebooks, and suggest that they include the web in their portfolios.

HISTORICAL SIDELIGHTS

Orders to Settlers

Among the other orders given to the Jamestown settlers were: find a safe port at the entrance of a river that runs far inland; set your houses in a straight line; make wide streets with a marketplace in the town square. They were also warned not to write any letters that would discourage others from joining them.

Map Caption Answer
New Hampshire

MULTICULTURAL PERSPECTIVES

At the time the Pilgrims signed the Mayflower Compact, a form of democratic government already existed in North America. The Great Law of Peace, the constitution of the Iroquois League, was more democratic than were European governmental systems of the time. Iroquois leaders were regarded as servants of the people, rather than as their masters. In addition, the Great Law of Peace endorsed freedom of speech and worship and allowed women a role in government.

losses. Unlike the Spanish government, which itself organized settlements in the Americas, the English Crown left early colonization to these private companies.

■■ Great Britain, unlike Spain, played an indirect role in settling its American colonies.

Quickly following up on its charter, the London Company in 1607 sent some 100 men to Virginia, where they founded Jamestown on the Chesapeake Bay. The company insisted that the settlers search for gold. With little time to build good shelters or to plant crops, many colonists died. In 1608, to avert disaster, John Smith called off the fruitless search for gold and ordered wells dug, new shelters built, land cleared, and crops planted. The Powhatans, a confederation of some 30 small tribes, aided the settlers by giving them food and teaching them how to cultivate corn.

The colony became prosperous after the introduction of tobacco in 1612. However, tobacco required large amounts of land. Tobacco farmers soon expanded onto the Powhatans' hunting grounds. The Native Americans viewed the taking of their lands as an act of war and attacked, killing some 350 settlers. The English struck back fiercely. Thus ended peaceful relations between settlers and Indians.

*T*HE THIRTEEN COLONIES

After Jamestown's success, English settlers flocked to the Americas. They came for varied reasons. The prospect of religious freedom drew many colonists to New England. By contrast, most settlers in the Chesapeake colonies of Virginia and Maryland came as laborers seeking a better life. Later colonies, including New York, Pennsylvania, and the Carolinas, also drew settlers from Europe. These settlers created distinctive regional societies.

New England. Not all English colonists came to the Americas to find gold or to grow tobacco. Some fled religious upheaval, which had raged since England had become a Protestant nation. Some Protestants, including the **Puritans**, wished to "purify" the Church of England of all Catholic traditions. The most radical of the Puritans—the **Separatists**, who had broken entirely with the

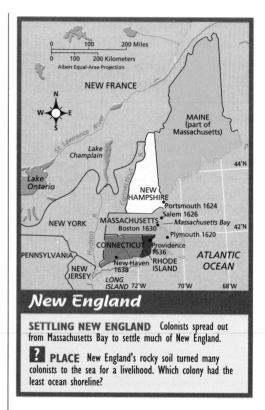

New England

SETTLING NEW ENGLAND Colonists spread out from Massachusetts Bay to settle much of New England.

❓ PLACE New England's rocky soil turned many colonists to the sea for a livelihood. Which colony had the least ocean shoreline?

church—were persecuted. They fled to the Netherlands after King James I threatened to "harry [force] them out of the land or else do worse."

In 1620 the Separatists, known as Pilgrims, left the Netherlands and established the Plymouth colony at Massachusetts' Cape Cod Bay. They adopted the **Mayflower Compact**, a document that established a self-governing colony based on the majority rule of male church members. The Mayflower Compact set a precedent for local government based on written agreements and the consent of the governed.

Growing religious persecution and economic difficulties drove other Puritans from England. Many Puritan tenant farmers were driven off their lands when landowners fenced their holdings and began to raise sheep. Then in the 1620s crop failures and an economic depression hit Puritan farmers and weavers. Beginning in 1630, in what is known as the **Great Migration**, some 60,000 Puritans left England for the Americas. Some 10,000 to 20,000 settled in Massachusetts.

In the first year of the Great Migration, some 1,000 Puritans established a colony by royal charter

ENGLISH COLONIES IN AMERICA

Ask students to imagine they are visitors from Europe touring the English colonies in America. Have them write a letter to a friend in Europe detailing the differences and similarities of life in New England, the Chesapeake region, South Carolina, and Pennsylvania. Ask for volunteers to read their letters to the class. Students may wish to include their letters in their portfolios.

THE FRENCH AND INDIAN WAR

Work with students to develop a chalkboard chart on the French and Indian War. Suggest that chart entries address causes, strategies and tactics, turning points, and outcomes. Then have students work in small groups to write summary paragraphs based on the chart. Ask group representatives to read their paragraphs to the class.

▶

in Massachusetts Bay. These Puritans built a Bible **commonwealth**, in which everyone, guided by English law and the Bible, was expected to work together for the common good. All **freemen**—that is, adult male church members who owned property—could vote and participate in government. The success of the community depended on educated people who could understand the Bible. Laws thus required parents to teach their children to read and, after 1647, required towns to establish schools.

Olaudah Equiano

New England's plentiful food and healthful climate encouraged the growth of large families. New Englanders with large families had little need for servants or slaves. Fathers and sons farmed, and mothers and daughters made many of the goods their families needed.

To pay for supplies and luxury items from England, some New Englanders turned to fishing, shipping, and business. They distilled rum and built ships. They sold fish, grain, meat, naval stores (turpentine, pitch, and rosin), and lumber to England, Spain, Portugal, the West Indies, and England's other American colonies.

Chesapeake colonies. Colonists created a completely different culture in the Chesapeake—the land surrounding Chesapeake Bay. Most white colonists who came to the Chesapeake came as **indentured servants**, who were bound for a period of years to serve the person who paid for the voyage to America. Some 75 percent of indentured servants were male. Because there were so few white women in the early years, many men never married.

The vast majority of Chesapeake colonists lived on widely scattered farms and plantations. They produced tobacco for export and grew or made many of the things they needed. Since there was little need for a central market, few towns arose.

Slavery. Slavery also set the Chesapeake apart from New England. As the supply of indentured servants dwindled, the demand for slaves increased. Slave raiders began moving far into the interior of West Africa in search of Africans to enslave. Their constant attacks destroyed the African countryside and emptied villages.

Once captured, the slaves endured many horrors. In the mid-1700s, 11- or 12-year-old Olaudah Equiano (oh-LOW-duh ek-wee-AHN-oh) was kidnapped and sold into slavery. He described his ordeal during the dread **Middle Passage**—the voyage across the Atlantic—in his autobiography. Once aboard the slave ship, he was taken below deck:

66 There I received such a salutation in my nostrils as I had never experienced in my life; so that with the loathesomeness of the stench, and crying together, I became so sick and low that I was not able to eat. . . . I now wished for the last friend, death, to relieve me. 99

Equiano survived the voyage, but countless others did not. In the crowded and unhealthy conditions many died from suffocation, disease, or violence. Some captives killed themselves, leaping overboard, rather than face further horrors.

After Equiano arrived in the Americas, he was sold to a series of masters. By 1766 Equiano had earned enough money to buy his freedom. After working as a seaman, Equiano settled in England and began lecturing for the antislavery, or **abolition**, movement. His popular autobiography, published in 1789, convinced many people of the need to end the slave trade.

Equiano's experience was uncommon, for he did not suffer the hardships of plantation life. Laws called "slave codes" forbade slaves to leave the

▲ When this 1786 slave ship diagram was drawn, Africans had long been in British North American. Africans first arrived in Jamestown in 1619, probably as indentured servants.

HISTORICAL SIDELIGHTS

Indentured Servitude
In the Chesapeake, colonial laws forbade masters to abuse their servants "with intolerable oppression and hard usage." However, these laws were rarely enforced, and masters were free to use servants as they wished. They kept discipline among servants largely through brute force and had the right to fine, flog, or brand those whom they believed guilty of disobedience. Masters also could rent out, bequeath, and even sell their servants.

BIO GRAPHY PERSONALITIES IN HISTORY

Equiano was born inland of the Guinea Coast in the Kingdom of Benin—an area that today is in southern Nigeria. Before his capture he had never seen the ocean nor had he heard of the existence of white people.

PRIMARY SOURCE

Description of Change: excerpted
Rationale: excerpted to focus on main idea

*P*ractice

GUIDED PRACTICE

On the chalkboard draw a chart with the following headings: *Colony, Purpose, Economic Activities*. Ask for volunteers to fill in information on the English colonies in North America. Students may wish to copy the chart to include in their portfolios.

MAKING CONNECTIONS

Language Arts

Yankee—the nickname that identifies Americans in other nations—is probably of Dutch origin. The English often referred disparagingly to Dutch seamen as *Jan Kee*—Dutch for "Little John." Later this term also referred to New England sailors. Over time *Jan Kees* became *Yankee* and, by the Revolution, the British were applying it to all American colonists.

MAKING CONNECTIONS

Sociology

German immigrants arrived at a rate of about 2,000 per year between 1727 and 1750. Almost all of them settled in Pennsylvania. Indeed, by the time of the American Revolution they probably made up one third of the colony's population. They brought with them many interesting customs— the communal barn raising, for example. Friends and neighbors would help a farmer erect a barn and then celebrate by holding a dance in the new building.

INDEPENDENT PRACTICE

Ask students to write a paragraph explaining in which of the English colonies they would rather have settled and why. Students who select the same colony may compare reasons for their choice before writing the final drafts of their paragraphs.

plantation, to meet together, to learn to read or write, or to own weapons. Such harsh rules did not prevent rebellion, however. Slaves often ran away. There were also a few uprisings. Most slaves, however, resisted in other, less direct ways, such as by destroying property or working slowly.

Proprietary colonies. Slavery was also important in another colony—South Carolina. In 1663 Charles II granted some of his supporters a large tract of land between Virginia and Spanish Florida. The proprietors, or owners, later split the colony into North and South Carolina. Slaves from rice-growing regions in Africa transformed the swampy coastal areas of South Carolina into profitable rice plantations. By 1720 African slaves made up about 70 percent of the population of the colony. The thriving port of Charles Town attracted a diverse group of settlers, including Scots, Scotch-Irish, Germans, European Jews, West Indians, and French Huguenots (Protestants).

The king established other proprietary colonies in the 1660s. To cripple Dutch trading interests, Charles sent out a fleet to capture the Dutch colony of New Netherland. Without a shot being fired, the colony fell into English hands. Charles made his brother, James, the Duke of York, the proprietor. James renamed part of the colony New York and gave the rest—New Jersey—to two friends.

Another proprietary colony was founded in these years as a religious experiment. In 1681 William Penn, a Quaker, founded Pennsylvania as a place where people of different nationalities and religious beliefs could live peacefully together.

▼ This extract from *Colonial Office Papers* shows the earliest land grants, beginning in 1674, given to settlers in South Carolina. By 1765 more than 11,000 names appeared on this list.

*R*eview and *A*ssessment

REVIEW Have students work in small groups to develop an annotated time line of the most important events surveyed in the section. Display time lines on the bulletin board. Then assign the Section 3 Review on p. 19.

ASSESS Assign the **Section 3 Daily Quiz** in *Core Resources*.

▲ *The Peaceable Kingdom* was one of several paintings Edward Hicks made of animals living in harmony with nature. In this version, William Penn is shown in the background, meeting with other colonists.

Pennsylvania attracted thousands of poor immigrants from England, Denmark, and Germany. The settlers found fertile land that they could purchase cheaply and a mild climate. Farmers soon exported flour and salted meat to the West Indies.

While Pennsylvania began as a "Holy Experiment," Georgia was a social experiment. The last colony was founded in 1732 to give the English poor a fresh start. However, proprietor James Oglethorpe and his partners wanted to aid only the most "virtuous and industrious" poor. Very few debtors qualified, and the colony attracted few other settlers. By 1760 Georgia's European population numbered only some 6,000. The colony mainly served as a buffer between South Carolina's prosperous plantations and Spanish Florida.

■■ Colonists came to the English colonies for religious and economic reasons. They built religious communities in New England, tobacco and rice plantations in the Chesapeake and in South Carolina, and small farms in Pennsylvania.

*T*HE FRENCH AND INDIAN WAR

Unlike Georgia, the populations of Great Britain's other colonies grew rapidly during the 18th century. Many colonists expanded into the frontier regions of New York, Massachusetts, Pennsylvania, Virginia, and North Carolina.

RETEACH Organize students into three groups and assign each group one of the section's subsections. Have groups write 5 to 10 true/false statements based on the content of their subsections. Ask group representatives to read statements to the class and have class members identify them as true or false. Call on volunteers to recast false statements to make them correct.

Closure

Ask students to discuss why England became the dominant European power in North America. Have them write sentences that summarize the main points of their discussion.

Extension

RESEARCH Have students research Native American tribes of New England or the Chesapeake region during the 1600s and 1700s and present their findings on a map.

FORMULATE Have students write scenarios of how the southern colonies might have developed without slave labor. Ask for volunteers to explain their scenarios.

Conflicts arose, however, as colonists established farms on lands claimed by Native Americans and by the French.

Both the English and the French often violated American Indian land rights. Both frequently battled American Indians to capture their lands. However, one group, the powerful **Iroquois League**—a confederation of tribes in New York and Pennsylvania formed in the 15th or 16th century—had maintained their land and independence. The league skillfully played the English and French against each other.

The French and English competition in North America stemmed from a worldwide struggle for empire. Overseas colonies were vitally important to France and England as sources of raw materials and as markets for European goods. France's North American territory, which stretched from northeastern Canada across the interior of the continent to the Gulf of Mexico, was sparsely settled but supplied precious furs. In 1749, when Virginia land speculators started to build a fort in disputed territory in the Ohio Valley, the French drove the Virginians off. The French completed the fort and named it Fort Duquesne (doo-KAYN).

The territorial conflict touched off the **French and Indian War** (1754–1763). The French won the early battles of the war. Britain's fortunes improved, however, when cabinet minister William Pitt assumed control of the war effort. His efforts paid off in July 1758 when the British captured Fort Louisbourg, effectively cutting off French supplies. Further British victories convinced the Iroquois to abandon their neutral stance and side with the

◀ **George Washington** experienced his first taste of military service during the French and Indian War.

Washington/Curtis/Lee Collection, Washington and Lee University, Lexington, Virginia.

British. Abandoned by their Indian allies in the Ohio Valley, French troops withdrew to Canada.

British forces followed, capturing Quebec in 1759 and Montreal the following year. With these defeats France lost the last of its Canadian holdings. Fighting dragged on for two more years in other parts of the world. In 1763 the Treaty of Paris officially ended all hostilities. The treaty granted Great Britain Canada and all French holdings east of the Mississippi except New Orleans. Spain, which had sided with the French, had earlier received France's vast Louisiana territory west of the Mississippi. By the terms of the treaty, Spain surrendered Florida to Britain.

■■ **Competition for the North American interior touched off the French and Indian War. The war cost France most of its North American holdings.**

SECTION REVIEW ANSWERS

IDENTIFY

For significance, see the following pages:
Protestant Reformation (p. 15)
Spanish Armada (p. 15)
joint-stock companies (p. 15)
Puritans (p. 16)
Separatists (p. 16)
Mayflower Compact (p. 16)
Great Migration (p. 16)
commonwealth (p. 17)
freemen (p. 17)
indentured servants (p. 17)
Olaudah Equiano (p. 17)
Middle Passage (p. 17)
abolition (p. 17)
William Penn (p. 18)
Iroquois League (p. 19)

1. *Spanish Crown was directly involved in colonization; English government played an indirect role in settling its American colonies.*
2. *religious freedom, economic opportunity*
3. *New England: religious communities based on farming and trade; Chesapeake and South Carolina: large plantations growing tobacco and rice*
4. *Letters should discuss early struggles, leadership of John Smith, introduction of tobacco, conflict with Native Americans.*
5. *Conflicts over Ohio Valley sparked French and Indian War; France lost most of its holdings at end of war.*

■■ ■■
S E C T I O N 3 R E V I E W

IDENTIFY and explain the significance of the following: Protestant Reformation, Spanish Armada, joint-stock companies, Puritans, Separatists, Mayflower Compact, Great Migration, commonwealth, freemen, indentured servants, Olaudah Equiano, Middle Passage, abolition, William Penn, Iroquois League.

1. **MAIN IDEA** How did the English colonization process differ from the Spanish process?
2. **MAIN IDEA** For what reasons did settlers come to the English colonies in North America?
3. **CONTRASTING** How did the societies established by colonists in New England differ from the societies established in the Chesapeake and in South Carolina?
4. **WRITING TO DESCRIBE** Imagine you are one of the original colonists at Jamestown. Write a letter home to England, describing some of the challenges you have faced.
5. **LINKING HISTORY AND GEOGRAPHY** How did competition for land in North America cause conflicts between Britain and France? How did these conflicts end?

Chapter Review Answers

WRITING A SUMMARY
See Essential Points in each section for main ideas.

REVIEWING CHRONOLOGY

4, 2, 5, 1, 3
Linking History and Geography
Both events selected should illustrate one of the five themes of geography.

IDENTIFYING PEOPLE AND IDEAS

1. *wide land bridge between Siberia and Alaska*
2. *Holy Book of Islam, carried by followers of the prophet Muhammad as they spread the faith throughout Asia, Africa, and Europe*
3. *rebirth of European learning and creativity*
4. *forcible resettlement of Africans to the Americas from 1500s to 1800s*
5. *labor system under which Spanish colonists received right to have certain number of Indians work for them*
6. *explorer who sought a westward route to Asia; his crew members were the first to circumnavigate the world*
7. *founded a string of missions along California's coast*

8. *movement, beginning in 1630, of some 60,000 Puritans from England to North America*
9. *ex-slave whose autobiography described the Middle Passage*
10. *confederation of Native American tribes of New York and Pennsylvania*

UNDERSTANDING MAIN IDEAS

1. *They wanted to break the monopoly on East-West trade held by Genoa and Venice.*
2. *Mexico, Central America, much of South America, and modern-day southern U.S.; missions, haciendas, ranchos, ports, and cities*
3. *Spanish government itself organized settlements; English government awarded charters to private companies that organized settlements.*
4. *Some fled to escape contact with Europeans, others revolted against Europeans or blended cultural elements.*

🎗 REVIEWING THEMES

1. *Types and abundance of resources, differing terrain helped to determine types of economic activities American Indians could pursue; influencing the development of Native Americans' cultural practices.*

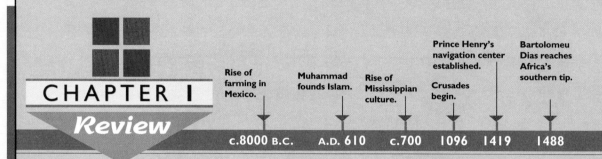

				Prince Henry's navigation center established.	Bartolomeu Dias reaches Africa's southern tip.
Rise of farming in Mexico.	Muhammad founds Islam.	Rise of Mississippian culture.	Crusades begin.		
c.8000 B.C.	A.D. 610	c.700	1096	1419	1488

CHAPTER 1
Review

WRITING A SUMMARY
Using the essential points of the chapter as a guide, write a summary of the chapter.

REVIEWING CHRONOLOGY
Number your paper 1 to 5. Study the time line above, and list the following events in the order in which they happened by writing the first next to 1, the second next to 2, and so on. Then complete the activity below.

1. Pueblo Revolt drives the Spanish from Santa Fe.
2. Bartolomeu Dias reaches Africa's southern tip.
3. Treaty of Paris signed.
4. Rise of Mississippian culture.
5. Jamestown established.

Linking History and Geography Pick two of the events above and explain how each illustrates one of the five themes of geography.

IDENTIFYING PEOPLE AND IDEAS
Explain the historical significance of each of the following people or terms.

1. Beringia
2. Qur'an
3. Renaissance
4. African diaspora
5. *encomienda*
6. Ferdinand Magellan
7. Friar Junípero Serra
8. Great Migration
9. Olaudah Equiano
10. Iroquois League

UNDERSTANDING MAIN IDEAS
1. Why did the Portuguese want to find a new route to Asia in the 15th century?
2. What territories in the Americas did Spain acquire following Columbus's voyages? What kinds of settlements were established in these territories?
3. How was the British government's role in colonization in the Americas less direct than the role played by the Spanish government?
4. How did American Indians respond to both Spanish and English colonization?

🎗 REVIEWING THEMES
1. **Geographic Diversity** What effects did geographical and environmental factors have on Native American cultures?
2. **Global Relations** What were the positive and negative results of the Columbian exchange?
3. **Cultural Diversity** How did the cultural backgrounds of the colonists affect the development of the English colonies in which they settled?

THINKING CRITICALLY
1. **Analyzing** How did Muslims influence cultural diffusion between Africa, Asia, and Europe?
2. **Synthesizing** Describe the various labor systems that were used by Spanish and English colonists in the Americas.
3. **Hypothesizing** How might North American territories have been divided differently in 1763 if France had won the French and Indian War?

STRATEGY FOR SUCCESS
Review the Skills Handbook entry on Identifying the Main Idea on page 748. Read the following excerpt from a 1705 study of American Indian culture. Then identify the main idea of the selection.

> 66 They [Native Americans] have on several accounts reason to lament [regret] the arrival of the Europeans, by whose means they seem to have lost their felicity [happiness] as well as their innocence. The English have taken away [a] great part of their country and consequently made everything less plenty amongst them. They have introduced drunkenness and luxury amongst them, which have multiplied their wants and put them up to desiring a thousand things they never dreamt of before. 99

2. positive—transfer of foods, animals, technologies, and ideas; negative—conquest, enslavement, transfer of disease
3. Primarily Puritan New England developed a fairly uniform culture; other regions attracted a wider range of immigrants and had more diverse cultures.

THINKING CRITICALLY

1. Africa—Muslim influence on development of Swahili language; Asia—Muslim traders carried Chinese technologies to the West and adapted mathematical knowledge from India to Arabic numeral system; Europe—fostered advances in medicine and cartography

2. The Spanish encomienda system essentially enslaved Native Americans, but a drastic decline of the American Indian population caused the Spanish to adopt African slavery. Similarly a decline in the supply of indentured servants caused some English colonies to rely on African slavery.
3. France probably would have won all the territory in the Ohio Valley and would have increased their possessions in Canada.

STRATEGY FOR SUCCESS

Europeans devastated Native American cultures by taking away their land and introducing new vices.

WRITING ABOUT HISTORY

Essays should point out that as the supply of indentured servants dwindled, the demand for slaves increased. They should also point out that the slave trade caused the forcible removal of some 10 million people from Africa over a period of 400 years and that slaves endured unending hardship on American plantations.

USING PRIMARY SOURCES

Essays should note that the judge's basic argument was that the demise of American Indians was their own fault. Students might counter this argument by pointing out that many of the problems the judge mentioned did not exist until the arrival of the Spanish.

LINKING HISTORY AND GEOGRAPHY

Lists will vary but should identify the culture area, the American Indian tribes present, the features of each group, and the traces of each group still evident.

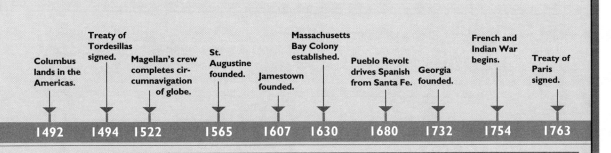

| 1492 | 1494 | 1522 | 1565 | 1607 | 1630 | 1680 | 1732 | 1754 | 1763 |

Columbus lands in the Americas. — Treaty of Tordesillas signed. — Magellan's crew completes circumnavigation of globe. — St. Augustine founded. — Jamestown founded. — Massachusetts Bay Colony established. — Pueblo Revolt drives Spanish from Santa Fe. — Georgia founded. — French and Indian War begins. — Treaty of Paris signed.

WRITING ABOUT HISTORY

Writing to Evaluate Write an essay about the introduction of slavery to the Americas. Be sure to include the effects of the slave trade on Africa as well as the effects of slavery on enslaved Africans.

Slaves loading tobacco barrels at a Virginia wharf

USING PRIMARY SOURCES

Read the following excerpt from a 17th-century Spanish judge's defense of Spanish treatment of Native Americans. Then write an essay summarizing the judge's arguments and evaluating how these arguments might be countered.

66 *At each step they [critics] throw in our faces the fact that the Indians have been badly treated and that in many places they have completely disappeared. . . .*

In many places the Indians gave cause for their mistreatment or for war to be made against them, either because of their bestial [brutal] and savage customs or because of the excesses and treason that they attempted or committed against our people. . . .

Moreover, it is not the Spaniards who have exterminated them, but their own vices and drunkenness or the earthquakes and repeated epidemics of smallpox and other diseases with which God in His mysterious wisdom has seen fit to reduce their numbers. 99

LINKING HISTORY AND GEOGRAPHY

Study the map on page 5. Locate the culture area in which your community is found, and list the American Indian tribes who lived in your area in 1500. Then write down the influences of any of these tribes that still exist locally—either through place-names, artifacts, or customs.

BUILDING YOUR PORTFOLIO

Complete the following projects independently or cooperatively.

1. **THE ECONOMY** Imagine you are a geographer who specializes in patterns of world trade throughout history. Prepare a map that shows trade routes between Europe, Africa, Asia, and the Americas during the 1400s, 1500s, and 1600s. Draw symbols on the map to indicate major items of trade.

A trade card advertisement

2. **CULTURAL DIVERSITY** Imagine you are a museum researcher preparing an exhibit on cultural exchanges in the Americas. With drawings and captions, dramatic readings of first-person accounts, charts, or other suitable materials, illustrate some of the cultural exchanges that took place between American Indians, Africans, and Europeans.

BUILDING YOUR PORTFOLIO

Have students refer to **Building Your Portfolio Worksheet 1**, assigned at the beginning of Unit 1. Use the worksheet to help students monitor their progress on the portfolio projects.

Assessment

Core Resources
• Reteaching Worksheet 1
• Chapter 1 Tests
• Alternative Assessment Forms
Test Generator

EUROPEAN EXPLORATION AND SETTLEMENT

HISTORICAL SIDELIGHTS

False Diamonds

By establishing a settlement on the St. Lawrence, Jacques Cartier hoped to gain control of Saguenay, a territory somewhere to the north that was believed to be rich in precious metals. Indeed, Cartier did find quantities of what appeared to be gold and diamonds close to the settlement. On his return to France, however, his precious discoveries turned out to be nothing more than iron pyrites and quartz. This probably gave rise to the French saying "false as Canadian diamonds."

America's GEOGRAPHY

EUROPEAN EXPLORATION AND SETTLEMENT

COLUMBUS'S landing introduced the Americas to the rest of the world, thus beginning a new era of exploration, trade, colonization, and cultural exchange. European explorers rushed west to search for new trade routes, seek riches, and stake out territories for the nations sponsoring them. In the 1500s the Spanish began settling North America. At the same time, other European nations—especially England and France—began claiming large areas of the continent. Nearly a century would pass, however, before the French and English successfully colonized North America. The communities the colonists founded developed in different ways, giving rise to distinctive societies.

Spain, England, and France sponsored most of the explorations of North America in the 16th and early 17th centuries. In general, the areas explored by each country were the areas that that country claimed and settled, as indicated by the maps below and at right. Spain explored and settled the southern and western parts of the continent; Britain explored and settled the eastern and northern regions; and France explored and settled the central and northeastern areas.

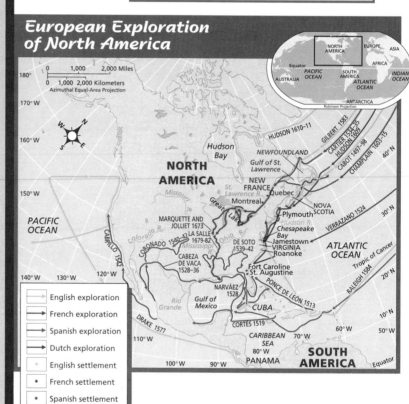

European Exploration of North America

- → English exploration
- → French exploration
- → Spanish exploration
- → Dutch exploration
- · English settlement
- · French settlement
- · Spanish settlement

Most of the 16th-century explorers were inspired by Christopher Columbus's four round-trip voyages to the Americas between 1492 and 1504. On the final two voyages Columbus visited not only the Caribbean islands but also parts of Central and South America. Most of the lands Columbus and his crew saw became part of Spanish America.

Lands seen by Columbus and his crew

Columbus's Voyages

North America in 1754

British **French**
Spanish **Russian**
– – – Boundary of Iroquois League

The rivalry in Europe between Great Britain and France carried over to North America. Both nations' desire for the lands of the Ohio Valley sparked the French and Indian War.

PACIFIC OCEAN

Hudson Bay

NEW FRANCE

Disputed

NEWFOUNDLAND

NOVA SCOTIA

LOUISIANA

THIRTEEN COLONIES

Tropic of Cancer

Disputed

ATLANTIC OCEAN

NEW SPAIN

FLORIDA

Gulf of Mexico

West Indies

CARIBBEAN SEA

0   600   1,200 Miles
0   600   1,200 Kilometers
Azimuthal Equal-Area Projection

Equator

120° W   110° W   100° W   90° W

The Thirteen Colonies

British Colonies
New England colonies
Middle colonies
Southern colonies
Dominion of New England boundary, 1688
• Cities

NEW FRANCE

NOVA SCOTIA

ME (MA)

Lake Huron   Lake Ontario   Albany   NH   Portsmouth
NY   Cape Cod
Lake Erie   MA   Boston
                              CT   Providence
                                       RI
                              New York City
                        PA   NJ
                        Philadelphia
                   MD   Baltimore   DE
                        Annapolis
              VA
              Richmond   Chesapeake Bay
                        James R.   Williamsburg

APPALACHIAN MTS.

NC   New Bern

SC   Wilmington

GA   Charles Town   ATLANTIC OCEAN

Savannah

SPANISH FLORIDA

0   100   200 Miles
0   100   200 Kilometers
Albers Equal-Area Projection

85° W   80° W   75° W

Spanish Missions

Miller Projection

NORTH AMERICA

ROCKY MTS.

San Francisco 1776
Monterey 1770
NEW SPAIN

Mississippi R.

APPALACHIAN MTS.

San Diego 1769
Santa Fe   Albuquerque
San Xavier del Bac 1700
Ysleta
La Bahia   San Antonio   St. Augustine
Nogales
Monterrey

GEORGIA

Present-day boundaries   FLORIDA

PACIFIC OCEAN 1687
Mexico City ★

Havana
CUBA   HISPANIOLA
Tropic of Cancer

CARIBBEAN SEA
ATLANTIC OCEAN   15° N

0   750   1,500 Miles
0   750   1,500 Kilometers

Equator 0°

★ Capital of viceroyalty
■ Mission
• City or Spanish settlement

Spanish Missions

CALIFORNIA
ARIZONA
NEW MEXICO
TEXAS

Colorado R.
Rio Grande
Nueces R.

Present-day boundaries

120° W   105° W   90° W   75° W   60° W   45° W   15° S
                                              Tropic of Capricorn

Spanish North America in 1785

Even within an area settled by a single European country, regional differences existed. For example, the diverse ethnic, economic, social, and religious backgrounds of the people in the 13 British colonies—as well as diverse geographical features—helped to create societies distinct from one another and from Great Britain.

By the 1780s Spanish America was one of the largest colonial empires the world had ever known. Because of the vast size of the territory, colonists often organized their own settlements. The mission was one form of settlement established by the Spanish in the Americas.

Geography

Settlers on their way to the Pennsylvania and Virginia frontiers took the Great Wagon Road, a route that stretched about 700 miles along the eastern edge of the Appalachians from Philadelphia to Georgia. Although little more than a rutted track, it was the most traveled highway in colonial America.

CREATING A NATION

1763–1815

Chapter Overview

When Britain sought to gain greater control over the colonies after the French and Indian War, the colonists objected. Tensions grew until they exploded into revolt and war. Years of struggle ended in 1781, and the colonies won independence. Prominent Americans soon devised a Constitution that established a strong central government while reserving important powers for the states.

The nation grew and prospered as it acquired new territory. But the political scene proved turbulent as new political parties disagreed over domestic and foreign policy. Although the nation tried to stay clear of foreign entanglements, in 1812 it was once again drawn into war with Britain.

THE AMERICAN NATION VIDEODISC PROGRAM A variety of still images, short videos, and activities are available for you to use as you teach this chapter. See Videodisc Resources in the Core Resources Binder for barcode correlations and suggestions for using the program.

Chapter Planning Guide

CHAPTER 2	CORE RESOURCES	AV AUDIOVISUAL RESOURCES	PROGRAM RESOURCES
INTRODUCTION pp. 24–25	■ Building Your Portfolio Worksheet 1		
TEACHING THE CHAPTER pp. 26–67	■ Graphic Organizer 2 ■ Social Studies Skills Worksheet 2 ■ Literature Worksheet 2 ■ Geography Worksheet 2 ■ Outline Maps 1, 2, 8, 9, 14, 19	■ *The American Nation Videodisc: Patriotism & Propaganda: The Boston Massacre; Designing a Nation; A Native American Confederacy* ■ Everyday Life in America Transparencies and Worksheets 4, 5, 6 ■ Linking Geography and History Transparencies and Worksheets 8, 9	■ *Eyewitnesses and Others,* Volume 1: Readings 13, 20, 21, 22, 23, 24, 25, 26, 27, 28, 29, 30, 32, 33, 36, 38, 39, 40 ■ Art in American History Transparencies and Worksheets 3, 5, 6
REVIEW AND ASSESSMENT pp. 68–69	■ Chapter 2 Daily Quizzes ■ Reteaching Worksheet 2 ■ Chapter 2 Tests ■ Alternative Assessment Forms		■ Test Generator

Additional Resources

BOOKS FOR TEACHERS

Bernstein, Richard B., and Kym S. Rice. *Are We to Be a Nation? The Making of the Constitution.* Harvard University Press, 1987. Perspectives on the Constitutional Convention.

Middlekauff, Robert. *The Glorious Cause.* Oxford University Press, 1985. Dramatic account of crucial Revolution events.

Smith, Page. *The Shaping of America: A People's History of the Young Republic,* Vol 3. Viking Penguin, 1989. In-depth analysis of the nation's formative years.

BOOKS FOR STUDENTS

Holder, Angela R. *The Meaning of the Constitution,* 2nd ed. Barron's, 1987. Clause-by-clause explanation of the Constitution.

*Marrin, Albert. *The War for Independence.* Atheneum, 1988. Retells Revolution events through eyes of historical characters.

Wheeler, Richard. *Voices of 1776: The Story of the American Revolution in the Words of Those Who Were There.* Meridian, 1991. Eyewitness accounts of the Revolution.

* for students reading below grade level

MULTIMEDIA MATERIALS

The American Revolution: Two Views. Video, 60 min. Educational Audio Visual, Inc. Examines the Revolution from colonial and British viewpoints.

The Constitution: The Compromise that Made a Nation. Video, 27 min. Learning Corporation of America/SSSS. Award-winning film dramatizes debate over equal representation.

Women in the Revolution: Legend and Reality. Video, 20 min. Multi-Media Productions/SSSS. Examines the roles of women in the Revolution.

THEMES IN AMERICAN HISTORY

USE WITH PAGES 24–25

Listed on the right are the themes emphasized in Chapter 2. The questions in boldface type stimulate critical thinking and provide students with an opportunity to discuss the themes within a broadened context. The questions also appear in the pupil's edition on p. 24.

■ ECONOMIC DEVELOPMENT

How might the economic interests of one country conflict with those of another? Students should note that countries try to establish economic policies—tariffs, duties, and other taxes; strategies for resource use; import and export limits; etc.—that benefit their own economic development. These policies often run counter to the economic needs and desires of their trading partners. Students might draw specific examples from U.S. trade relations with Japan, Mexico, or Canada.

■ CONSTITUTIONAL HERITAGE

How does the organization of government affect the way power is distributed and exercised? Students should note that government organization determines how power is distributed and exercised. In an absolute monarchy or a dictatorship, power is concentrated at the top of the government in the hands of a few. In a democracy, power ultimately rests with the people. How that power is translated into government responsibilities depends on the government's structure. In the United States these responsibilities are shared between a strong federal government and the states.

■ DEMOCRATIC VALUES

How might a democracy encourage the formation of political parties? Students will note that democracy encourages people to express their views. In order to get their voices heard, people with similar views on economic, political, and social issues may join together to form political parties.

CHAPTER STRATEGIES FOR MEETING INDIVIDUAL NEEDS

LIMITED ENGLISH PROFICIENT LEARNERS

After they have read the chapter, have pairs of students create illustrated time lines of the chapter's major events. Students should write brief captions for each entry and present their work to the class.

TACTILE/KINESTHETIC LEARNERS

Organize the class into small groups of three or four and provide each group with newspapers or news magazines. Instruct each group to locate articles that reflect constitutional issues or matters related to the relationship between the federal and state governments. Have each group select a spokesperson to present its findings to the class.

LEARNERS HAVING DIFFICULTY

As the class studies each section, ask students to write questions about events and concepts of which they are not certain. Have them work in pairs to find answers and quiz each other.

AUDITORY LEARNERS

Read aloud to the class the first ten amendments to the U.S. Constitution and then call on volunteers to paraphrase each amendment. Elicit a class discussion about the relevance of the Bill of Rights to students' lives today.

VISUAL LEARNERS

Have students skim the chapter and locate the visual they think best illustrates the chapter title: Creating a Nation. Call on students to explain their choices to the class.

GIFTED LEARNERS

Suggest that students research the ideas of Enlightenment thinkers as well as documents and institutions providing the foundations for self-government. Ask students to explain how these ideas influenced the framers of the Constitution.

USING THE CHAPTER FOCUS

■ **UNDERSTANDING THE MAIN IDEA**

Call on a volunteer to read aloud the Understanding the Main Idea paragraph. Then ask students to jot down in their notebooks information on political upheavals that have recently appeared in the media. As students read the chapter, have them look for comparisons between these events and the conflict between the colonies and Britain.

 THEMES
Have students work individually or in groups to answer the questions under Themes. Save students' responses so that they can compare them with their responses after studying the chapter. (See p. 23B for suggested answers.)

■ **THE TIME LINE**

Ask students to jot down important points about each time-line event as they study the chapter. When the chapter is completed, ask volunteers to discuss the points they noted.

ABOUT THE ILLUSTRATION

This detail from the painting *Battle of Princeton* by William Mercer illustrates the Americans' ambush of British troops on January 3, 1777. The successful attack by the Patriot army at Princeton was made possible when George Washington outsmarted the British command at nearby Trenton. After the American victory over Hessian troops there, General Cornwallis prepared to launch a counterattack. Washington left campfires burning to mislead the British into thinking they were still in the area. Then the Patriots slipped past Cornwallis on the flank side and made their way to Princeton, where they surprised the enemy again.

Chapter 2

1763–1815

CREATING A NATION

FOCUS

UNDERSTANDING THE MAIN IDEA

Colonial conflicts with the British erupted into a war that established American independence. A need for a strong central government to guide the new nation led to the framing of the Constitution of the United States of America. Domestic and foreign problems, however, plagued the country in its early years.

 THEMES

■ **ECONOMIC DEVELOPMENT** How might the economic interests of one country conflict with those of another?

■ **CONSTITUTIONAL HERITAGE** How does the organization of government affect the way power is distributed and exercised?

■ **DEMOCRATIC VALUES** How might a democracy encourage the formation of political parties?

1775	1783	1788	1803	1812
Revolutionary War begins.	Treaty of Paris signed.	U.S. Constitution ratified.	U.S. completes Louisiana Purchase.	War declared against Great Britain.

Ask students to recall the results of the French and Indian War. Have students suggest the problems that might develop between Britain and the colonies as a consequence of the war. Have students check the accuracy of their predictions as they work through the chapter.

■■ LINK TO THE PAST

Through their victory in the French and Indian War, the British gained control of most of North America east of the Mississippi River. They now faced the tasks of governing, protecting, and financing their expanded empire.

HISTORICAL SIDELIGHTS

Vergennes's Prediction
Vergennes played a significant role in making his prophecy about the American colonies come true. He was instrumental in persuading France's King Louis XVI to support the Americans in their revolution.

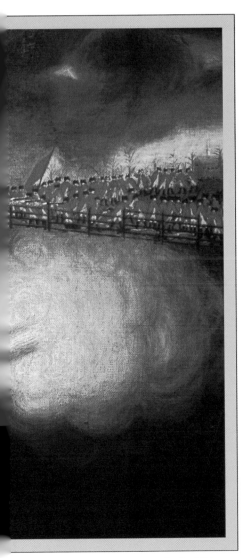

With the signing of the Treaty of Paris in 1763, Great Britain's future looked bright. Many people in Great Britain and elsewhere realized, however, that the British Empire faced new challenges. One of these observers, a French government official named Charles Gravier (**grawv-yay**) Comte de Vergennes (**ver-ZHEN**), believed that Great Britain's North American colonies would prove especially troublesome.

Mindful that France had lost its colonial claim in North America, Vergennes predicted a similar fate for Great Britain. "The American colonies stand no longer in need of England's protection," he said. "England," he continued, "will call on them to help contribute toward supporting the burden they have helped to bring on her, and they will answer by striking off all dependence."

Vergennes's prophecy would prove accurate. Thirteen years after his prediction, the British colonies along the Atlantic seaboard declared independence—and fought to win it. Although the fight was successful, the new nation faced a number of challenges. Establishing a workable form of government, easing domestic tensions, and resolving conflicts with foreign powers were among these challenges.

Battle of Princeton

Continental soldier

FOCUS OBJECTIVES

- Determine why the Crown imposed taxes on the colonists. Examine how the colonists reacted to these taxes.

- Identify the actions taken by the First Continental Congress and the Second Continental Congress.

- Explain how the Declaration of Independence justified America's break with Great Britain.

- Determine how the Americans were able to defeat the British.

CORE RESOURCES

- Section 1 Daily Quiz
- Social Studies Skills Worksheet 2

AV RESOURCES

- *The American Nation* Videodisc: Patriotism & Propaganda: The Boston Massacre
- Linking Geography and History Transparency and Worksheet 9
- Everyday Life in America Transparency and Worksheet 4

Section 1

INDEPENDENCE!

FOCUS

- **Why did the Crown impose taxes on the colonists? How did the colonists react to these taxes?**
- **What actions did the First Continental Congress and the Second Continental Congress take?**
- **How did the Declaration of Independence justify America's break with Great Britain?**
- **How were the Americans able to defeat the British?**

Victory in the French and Indian War left Great Britain with a huge debt and more territory to govern and defend. When the British tried to make the American colonists help pay the costs of administering this expanded empire, the colonists protested. But colonial protests were unsuccessful, pushing the colonies to declare their independence, to fight for it, and, ultimately, to win it.

Protests took many forms.

A RICH NEW TERRITORY

The Treaty of Paris of 1763 forced the French to give up their North American empire. With the stroke of a pen, the British gained control of Spanish Florida, Canada, and the land between the Appalachian Mountains and the Mississippi River. It was a rich land. Indian agent and trader George Croghan, who traveled through the western territory in 1765, noted in his diary that "a good hunter, without much fatigue to himself, could here daily supply one hundred men with meat."

▲ Settlers and traders to the Ohio Valley saw many colorful and unusual species of flora, such as this wild honeysuckle painted by naturalist artist Edwin Whitefield.

Such glowing reports drew pioneer farmers and speculators to the region. Ignoring Native American claims to the land, they demanded that the territory be opened for settlement. But Native Americans, whose ways of life had already been disrupted by European trade, resented the flow of settlers into their lands.

When a series of Indian uprisings convinced British authorities that they could not effectively protect British settlers on the frontier, Great Britain issued the **Proclamation of 1763**, barring settlement west of the Appalachian Mountains. But the proclamation was difficult to enforce. Land-hungry colonists resented the measure and continued to stream into the territory.

TAXATION AND PROTEST

The royal proclamation was not the only British policy the colonists resented. They were also angered by Parliament's efforts to make them pay part of the costs of "protecting and securing" the

Ask students what actions they might take to protest a school rule that they regard as unfair, and write their suggestions on the chalkboard. As students study this section, have them compare these suggested actions with those used by the colonists to protest British policies.

Teaching the Section

BRITISH TAXES AND COLONIAL PROTESTS

Divide the class into two groups. Have students in one group imagine that they are members of the British Parliament. Ask them to write a brief speech explaining why they intend to pass the Sugar Act, the Stamp Act, and the Townshend Acts. Have students in the other group imagine that they are American colonists. Have them write protest statements to Parliament expressing their opposition to these acts. Statements should include the actions the colonists will take if Parliament does not change its taxation policies. Call on volunteers to read their speeches or statements.

▲ This 1766 British cartoon celebrates the repeal of the Stamp Act. As members of the British government carry the dead act in a coffin, background ships show that trade with America is already resuming.

frontier. One of the first taxes Parliament passed to raise revenue in the colonies was the **Sugar Act** of 1764, which set an import tax on foreign sugar, molasses, and several other items. Then in 1765 Parliament passed the **Stamp Act**. Far more sweeping than the Sugar Act, the Stamp Act levied a tax on all printed matter such as newspapers, playing cards, and legal documents.

Because the colonists had no direct representation in Parliament, they felt that they were being taxed unjustly. A series of resolutions passed by the Virginia House of Burgesses in 1765 asserted that "the taxation of the people by themselves" or by their representatives was "the distinguishing characteristick of British freedom."

To protest the Stamp Act, colonial merchants resolved not to buy or import British goods. Besides this boycott, colonists also used demonstrations, petitions, public meetings, and pamphlets to rally support against the taxes. Though most protests were peaceful, some did turn violent. One of the most violent demonstrations occurred in Boston on a hot August night in 1765, when a mob wrecked a building belonging to a stamp agent and then beheaded an effigy—a crude likeness—of the agent.

The colonial protests and the boycott of British goods persuaded Parliament to repeal the Stamp Act in March 1766, but Parliament's efforts to raise revenue in the colonies continued. In 1767 Parliament passed the **Townshend Acts**, which imposed an import tax on such common items as tea, lead, glass, and dyes. The law, as well as British attempts to enforce it, aroused powerful opposition. In February 1768 the Massachusetts

legislature drafted a letter attacking taxation without representation. The British government responded by dissolving the Massachusetts assembly. This only served to fuel more protests.

In 1768 British troops were sent to Boston to quiet the protests. But tensions exploded into one violent confrontation after another. On March 5, 1770, an angry crowd gathered and began to harass a small group of British soldiers. When one soldier's gun accidentally discharged, the others opened fire on the crowd. Five colonists, including Crispus Attucks—a sailor and an escaped slave—ultimately died as a result of what colonists soon dubbed the **Boston Massacre**.

Although a partial repeal of the Townshend Acts quieted the general unrest, the calm was short-lived. Another key protest erupted in Boston in 1773, after Parliament passed an act that American merchants feared would place them at a disadvantage selling tea. On December 16, a well-organized group of colonists dressed as Mohawk Indians boarded British tea ships in Boston Harbor and dumped 90,000 pounds of tea into the water.

Many colonists cheered the **Boston Tea Party**, but British officials were furious. In 1774 Parliament passed the Coercive Acts, four laws designed to punish Massachusetts and reinforce

▶ Crispus Attucks

▼ Crispus Attucks, a sailor and runaway slave, was one of the men British troops killed during the Boston Massacre.

THE AMERICAN NATION VIDEODISC PROGRAM

Patriotism & Propaganda: The Boston Massacre

1A   38399   3:24

Teaching the Section

CONTINENTAL CONGRESSES

Organize students into two groups. Have both groups design and construct the first page of a colonial newspaper. One group's articles and headlines should focus on the actions of the First Continental Congress; the other's should show those of the Second Continental Congress. Ask students to identify the intervening events that made these two front pages so different.

THE DECLARATION OF INDEPENDENCE

Organize students into small groups. Have each group read the Declaration of Independence (pp. 30–33) and then make a list paraphrasing the colonial grievances outlined in the document. Call on group representatives to read their lists to the class. Use these readings as the starting point for a class discussion on the following question: *Was the colonial break with Britain justified?*

MAKING CONNECTIONS

Literature

"The shot heard round the world" comes from Ralph Waldo Emerson's poem "Concord Hymn": "By the rude bridge that arched the flood,/Their flag to April's breeze unfurled./Here once the embattled farmers stood/And fired the shot heard round the world." Written in 1836, the poem commemorates the completion of the Concord Monument honoring the minutemen.

BIOGRAPHY PERSONALITIES IN HISTORY

When George Washington received his commission to lead the Continental Army, he declined the monthly salary Congress had voted to provide to him, and instead asked only reimbursement for expenses at the end of the war. In 1783 Washington submitted an expense report for less than 2000 pounds, which included costs of his wife's trips to camp headquarters, travel, supplies, and payments for intelligence. Auditors reported that Washington's figures were within one American dollar of their own calculations.

British control over the colonies. The colonists referred to these laws as the **Intolerable Acts** and regarded them as part of a growing pattern of oppression by the British.

■■ **The British government taxed the colonies to finance their empire. But colonists protested "taxation without representation" through petitions, boycotts, and demonstrations.**

*M*OVE TOWARD INDEPENDENCE

In 1774, delegates from 12 colonies gathered at the **First Continental Congress** in Philadelphia to discuss their grievances. While expressing loyalty to the British crown, the Congress's final resolution outlined the colonists' rights as British subjects and asserted the people's right to the "exclusive power of legislation in their several provincial legislatures." To put teeth in their demands, the colonists also called for a ban on all trade with Great Britain.

For King George III the Continental Congress was the last straw. He declared the New England governments to be "in a State of Rebellion," and Parliament ordered General Thomas Gage to reassert royal authority. On April 18, 1775, Gage began a march to Concord, Massachusetts, to seize rebel supplies. But Paul Revere and William Dawes galloped ahead of Gage to warn the Patriots that "the British are coming!" As a result, the colonial forces met the British on the way to Concord, in Lexington. Suddenly someone—each side accused the other— fired the "shot heard round the world." A barrage of British gunfire followed, leaving 8 colonists dead and 10 wounded.

The British marched on to Concord, destroyed the Patriot supplies, and started back to Boston. But from behind stone walls, Patriots fired

◀ Carpenter's Hall in Philadelphia was the site of the Second Continental Congress.

steadily at the British troops, whose traditional marching formations made them easy targets. While the Patriots suffered fewer than 100 casualties, British casualties numbered 273. A humbled British officer wrote: "Whoever looks upon them [the Patriots] as an irregular mob will find himself much mistaken."

With the news of the battles at Lexington and Concord on everyone's lips, the **Second Continental Congress** opened in Philadelphia in May. By June, the delegates had agreed to establish the Continental Army and chose George Washington of Virginia to command it.

BIOGRAPHY Born February 22, 1732, George Washington first worked as a surveyor, later assuming control of the family's large Virginia plantation, Mount Vernon. Washington acquired military experience and a reputation for bravery while fighting for the British in the French and Indian War. He also served twice as a delegate to the Continental Congress. With the colonies preparing for war, Washington devoted himself and his fortune to the "glorious cause" of American independence.

▶ George Washington

■■ **The First Continental Congress demanded the restoration of colonists' rights; the Second established the Continental Army.**

One of the first battles the Patriots fought was the **Battle of Bunker Hill**. On June 17, 1775, New England militiamen dug in atop two hills overlooking Boston Harbor—Bunker Hill and Breed's Hill—awaiting an onslaught of British troops. To save ammunition, an American commander ordered his men: "Don't one of you fire until you see the whites of their eyes." Although the British took both hills after mounting three assaults, they suffered 1,054 casualties. Fewer than 450 Americans were killed or injured.

INDEPENDENCE FOR WHOM?

Have students write newspaper editorials praising the Declaration of Independence for its support of the ideals of liberty and freedom. Call on volunteers to read their editorials to the class. Then have students write letters to the editor from the viewpoint of women and African Americans, questioning whether the Declaration truly supported those ideals. Students may wish to include their editorials and letters in their portfolios.

■■ Ask students who have written letters to the editor to discuss the experience.

VICTORY OVER THE BRITISH

Have students take the role of George Washington. Have them write a report to Congress explaining how the Continental Army was able to defeat the British in the Revolutionary War. Suggest that they cover three areas in their reports: special knowledge held by Continental soldiers; tactics used by the Continental Army; support provided by outside powers. Call on volunteers to present their reports to the class. ▶

Even after the battle, conservatives worked to avoid a permanent break with Great Britain. They persuaded the Continental Congress to send a final plea to George III. This plea—the Olive Branch Petition—professed the colonists' loyalty to the king and asked for his help in ending the conflict. The king refused to accept the petition. Instead he ordered the Royal Navy to blockade all shipping to the colonies and sent more soldiers there as well.

𝕴NDEPENDENCE DECLARED

Although fighting had begun, most colonists insisted that they were merely resisting unjust acts of Parliament, not waging war. But to others, the time was ripe for independence. Thomas Paine's pamphlet *Common Sense,* published in January 1776, urged revolution. "The period of debate is closed," declared the pamphlet. "Every thing that is right or reasonable pleads for separation. . . . 'TIS TIME TO PART."

In June 1776 the Second Continental Congress appointed Thomas Jefferson, a Virginia lawyer and planter, and four others to draft a **Declaration of Independence**. On July 4 the Congress formally adopted the Declaration. The Declaration's immediate purpose was to win support for independence, both at home and abroad. To undermine loyalty to George III, the document listed his misdeeds. It also asserted that governments exist to secure their citizens' rights:

❝ We hold these truths to be self-evident, that all men are created equal, that they are

endowed by their Creator with certain unalienable Rights, that among these are Life, Liberty, and the pursuit of Happiness. ❞

Furthermore, the Declaration claimed, "whenever any Form of Government becomes destructive of these ends, it is the Right of the People to alter or to abolish it." Those who signed the document knew they were now traitors in the eyes of the Crown. The price for failing to win independence might well be imprisonment or even death.

■■ **The Declaration of Independence asserted the right of people to overthrow an unjust government.**

COMMENTARY

Independence for Whom?

Thomas Jefferson's words "all men are created equal" have, almost from the beginning, been a source of controversy. What exactly did he mean? Remember that 18th-century colonial America, like Europe, was full of social, political, and economic inequalities. Besides, the delegates to the Continental Congress were seeking to justify a political, not a social, revolution.

Nevertheless, the Declaration and the revolution it symbolized had social consequences. Many women participated in protests. During the war women took over the work of the absent men or cared for troops. As a result, some women argued for a greater voice in politics.

Whether the delegates intended the words men *and* mankind *to include women is debatable. It is more certain that they did not intend the words to apply to slaves. While some delegates opposed slavery, others supported it. In drafting the Declaration of Independence America's leaders, for the first but not the last time, sidestepped the explosive issue of slavery.*

▶ **Mum Bett, a Massachusetts slave, believed that the words "all men are created equal" should apply to her. In 1781 she successfully sued for her freedom. Her lawyer's daughter, Susan Sedgwick, painted this portrait of her.**

The Declaration of Independence

HISTORICAL SIDELIGHTS

Selecting an Author
Jefferson thought that John Adams ought to write the first draft of the Declaration. Adams responded that Jefferson should write the document: "Reason 1st. You are a Virginian and a Virginian ought to be at the head of this business. Reason 2nd. I am obnoxious, suspected and unpopular; you are very much otherwise. Reason 3rd. You can write ten times better than I can."

BUILDING VOCABULARY

The word *despotism* derives from the Greek word *despotēs*, which means "master" or "chief." Over the years, many of the leaders upon whom the title *despotēs* was bestowed ruled in a repressive fashion. By the late-18th century, *despot* had come to mean an absolute, tyrannical ruler.

HISTORICAL Document

The Declaration of Independence

Thomas Jefferson wrote the first draft of the Declaration in a little more than two weeks.

In the first paragraph, the signers are justifying why they are separating from Great Britain.

impel: force

endowed: provided

Natural or "unalienable" rights (the rights to life, liberty, and the pursuit of happiness) cannot be taken away. The signers supported John Locke's view that people created governments to protect their natural rights. A government, therefore, must have the consent of the governed. If a government abuses its powers, it is the right as well as the duty of the people to do away with that government.

usurpations: wrongful seizures of power
despotism: unlimited power

tyranny: oppressive power exerted by a government
candid: fair

In Congress, July 4, 1776 The unanimous Declaration of the thirteen united States of America,

When in the Course of human events, it becomes necessary for one people to dissolve the political bands which have connected them with another, and to assume among the powers of the earth, the separate and equal station to which the Laws of Nature and of Nature's God entitle them, a decent respect to the opinions of mankind requires that they should declare the causes which impel them to the separation.

We hold these truths to be self-evident, that all men are created equal, that they are endowed by their Creator with certain unalienable Rights, that among these are Life, Liberty, and the pursuit of Happiness.

That to secure these rights, Governments are instituted among Men, deriving their just powers from the consent of the governed,

That whenever any Form of Government becomes destructive of these ends, it is the Right of the People to alter or to abolish it, and to institute new Government, laying its foundation on such principles and organizing its powers in such form, as to them shall seem most likely to effect their Safety and Happiness. Prudence, indeed, will dictate that Governments long established should not be changed for light and transient causes; and accordingly all experience hath shown, that mankind are more disposed to suffer, while evils are sufferable, than to right themselves by abolishing the forms to which they are accustomed. But when a long train of abuses and usurpations, pursuing invariably the same Object evinces a design to reduce them under absolute Despotism, it is their right, it is their duty, to throw off such Government, and to provide new Guards for their future security.

Such has been the patient sufferance of these Colonies; and such is now the necessity which constrains them to alter their former Systems of Government. The history of the present King of Great Britain is a history of repeated injuries and usurpations, all having in direct object the establishment of an absolute Tyranny over these States. To prove this, let Facts be submitted to a candid world.

He has refused his Assent to Laws, the most wholesome and necessary for the public good.

He has forbidden his Governors to pass Laws of immediate and pressing importance, unless suspended in their operation till his Assent should be obtained; and when so suspended, he has utterly neglected to attend to them.

He has refused to pass other Laws for the accommodation of large districts of people, unless those people would relinquish the right of Representation in the Legislature, a right inestimable to them and formidable to tyrants only.

He has called together legislative bodies at places unusual, uncomfortable, and distant from the depository of their public Records, for the sole purpose of fatiguing them into compliance with his measures.

He has dissolved Representative Houses repeatedly, for opposing with manly firmness his invasions on the rights of the people.

He has refused for a long time, after such dissolutions, to cause others to be elected; whereby the Legislative powers, incapable of Annihilation, have returned to the People at large for their exercise; the State remaining in the meantime exposed to all the dangers of invasion from without, and convulsions within.

He has endeavored to prevent the population of these States; for that purpose obstructing the Laws for Naturalization of Foreigners; refusing to pass others to encourage their migrations hither, and raising the conditions of new Appropriations of Lands.

He has obstructed the Administration of Justice, by refusing his Assent to Laws for establishing Judiciary powers.

He has made Judges dependent on his Will alone, for the tenure of their offices, and the amount and payment of their salaries.

He has erected a multitude of New Offices, and sent hither swarms of Officers to harass our people, and eat out their substance.

Here the Declaration lists the charges that the colonists had against King George III. How does the language of the list appeal to people's emotions?

relinquish: release, yield

inestimable: priceless

formidable: causing dread

Why do you think the king had his legislatures in the colonies meet in places that were hard to reach?

annihilation: destruction

convulsions: violent disturbances

naturalization of foreigners: the process by which foreign-born persons become citizens

appropriations of land: setting aside land for settlement

tenure: term

a multitude of: many

HISTORICAL SIDELIGHTS

Accusing the King

Today the list of grievances presented in the Declaration generally elicits little interest. The list, however, is the part of the document that was most debated and changed by the Continental Congress. In England attention also focused on the list of grievances. John Lind, a pamphleteer for Lord North, wrote an answer to the Declaration in which he devoted 110 out of a total of 129 pages to a consideration of the grievances.

BUILDING VOCABULARY

Tenure derives from the Latin verb *tenēre*, which means "to hold." In the Declaration *tenure* refers to the length of time judges may hold office.

◄ **The Continental Congress is shown voting for independence in this painting by Robert Pine and Edward Savage.**

HISTORICAL
Document

HISTORICAL
Document

HISTORICAL SIDELIGHTS

Rebellion to Tyrants

The sentiments expressed in the Declaration appeared in the proposals for the design of the seal of the United States. Franklin suggested that the motto "Rebellion to tyrants is obedience to God" should be used on the seal. This recommendation was eventually rejected. Jefferson, however, liked the saying so much that he adopted it as his personal motto, stamping it in the wax with which he sealed his letters.

What wrongful acts does the Declaration state have been committed by the king and the British Parliament?

The "neighboring Province" that is referred to here is Quebec.
arbitrary: not based on law
render: make

abdicated: given up

foreign mercenaries: soldiers hired to fight for a country not their own

perfidy: violation of trust

insurrections: rebellions

petitioned for redress: asked formally for a correction of wrongs

---

He has kept among us, in times of peace, Standing Armies without the Consent of our legislatures.

He has affected to render the Military independent of and superior to the Civil power.

He has combined with others to subject us to a jurisdiction foreign to our constitution, and unacknowledged by our laws; giving his Assent to their Acts of pretended Legislation:

For quartering large bodies of armed troops among us:

For protecting them, by a mock Trial, from punishment for any Murders which they should commit on the Inhabitants of these States:

For cutting off our Trade with all parts of the world:

For imposing Taxes on us without our Consent:

For depriving us in many cases, of the benefits of Trial by Jury:

For transporting us beyond Seas to be tried for pretended offences:

For abolishing the free System of English Laws in a neighboring Province, establishing therein an Arbitrary government, and enlarging its Boundaries so as to render it at once an example and fit instrument for introducing the same absolute rule into these Colonies:

For taking away our Charters, abolishing our most valuable Laws, and altering fundamentally the Forms of our Governments:

For suspending our own Legislatures, and declaring themselves invested with power to legislate for us in all cases whatsoever.

He has abdicated Government here, by declaring us out of his Protection and waging War against us.

He has plundered our seas, ravaged our Coasts, burnt our towns, and destroyed the Lives of our people.

He is at this time transporting large Armies of foreign Mercenaries to complete the works of death, desolation and tyranny, already begun with circumstances of Cruelty & perfidy scarcely paralleled in the most barbarous ages, and totally unworthy the Head of a civilized nation.

He has constrained our fellow Citizens taken Captive on the high Seas to bear Arms against their Country, to become the executioners of their friends and Brethren, or to fall themselves by their Hands.

He has excited domestic insurrections among us, and has endeavored to bring on the inhabitants of our frontiers, the merciless Indian Savages, whose known rule of warfare, is an undistinguished destruction of all ages, sexes and conditions.

In every stage of these Oppressions We have Petitioned for Redress in the most humble terms: Our repeated Petitions have been answered only by repeated injury. A Prince, whose character is thus marked by every act which may define a Tyrant, is unfit to be the ruler of a free people.

32

32 ■■ CHAPTER 2

Nor have We been wanting in attentions to our British brethren. We have warned them from time to time of attempts by their legislature to extend an unwarrantable jurisdiction over us. We have reminded them of the circumstances of our emigration and settlement here. We have appealed to their native justice and magnanimity, and we have conjured them by the ties of our common kindred to disavow these usurpations, which would inevitably interrupt our connections and correspondence. They too have been deaf to the voice of justice and of consanguinity. We must, therefore, acquiesce in the necessity, which denounces our Separation, and hold them, as we hold the rest of mankind, Enemies in War, in Peace Friends.

We, therefore, the Representatives of the united States of America, in General Congress, Assembled, appealing to the Supreme Judge of the world for the rectitude of our intentions, do, in the Name, and by Authority of the good People of these Colonies, solemnly publish and declare, That these United Colonies are, and of Right ought to be Free and Independent States; that they are Absolved from all Allegiance to the British Crown, and that all political connection between them and the State of Great Britain, is and ought to be totally dissolved; and that as Free and Independent States, they have full Power to levy War, conclude Peace, contract Alliances, establish Commerce, and to do all other Acts and Things which Independent States may of right do.

And for the support of this Declaration, with a firm reliance on the protection of divine Providence, we mutually pledge to each other our Lives, our Fortunes and our sacred Honor.

unwarrantable jurisdiction: unjustified authority

magnanimity: generous spirit

conjured: called upon

consanguinity: common ancestry

acquiesce: consent to

rectitude: rightness

In this paragraph, the signers state their actual declaration of independence. What rights would the new United States of America now have as an independent nation?

Congress adopted the final draft of the Declaration of Independence on July 4, 1776. A formal copy, written on parchment paper, was signed on August 2, 1776.

John Hancock	Benjamin Harrison	Lewis Morris
Button Gwinnett	Thomas Nelson, Jr.	Richard Stockton
Lyman Hall	Francis Lightfoot Lee	John Witherspoon
George Walton	Carter Braxton	Francis Hopkinson
William Hooper	Robert Morris	John Hart
Joseph Hewes	Benjamin Rush	Abraham Clark
John Penn	Benjamin Franklin	Josiah Bartlett
Edward Rutledge	John Morton	William Whipple
Thomas Heyward, Jr.	George Clymer	Samuel Adams
Thomas Lynch, Jr.	James Smith	John Adams
Arthur Middleton	George Taylor	Robert Treat Paine
Samuel Chase	James Wilson	Elbridge Gerry
William Paca	George Ross	Stephen Hopkins
Thomas Stone	Caesar Rodney	William Ellery
Charles Carroll	George Read	Roger Sherman
of Carrollton	Thomas McKean	Samuel Huntington
George Wythe	William Floyd	William Williams
Richard Henry Lee	Philip Livingston	Oliver Wolcott
Thomas Jefferson	Francis Lewis	Matthew Thornton

HISTORICAL SIDELIGHTS

Signing the Declaration

Some of the signers of the Declaration were not in Philadelphia on August 2, 1776, so not all 56 signatures were affixed on that date. Evidence suggests that a few of the signers did not put their names on the document until October or November.

BUILDING VOCABULARY

John Hancock, the president of the Congress, was the first to sign the Declaration. Boldly signing his name in large letters, he declared that the king would be able to read it without his glasses. Today, *John Hancock* is a synonym for a signature or autograph.

Practice

GUIDED PRACTICE

Have students suggest entries for a time line on the American Revolution. Record suggestions on the chalkboard as they are offered. Have volunteers explain why each entry should be included on the time line.

INDEPENDENT PRACTICE

Have students design a handbill (containing a slogan and/or a sketch) that illustrates the American or British view of one of the entries from the Guided Practice time line. Display handbills in the classroom. Students may wish to include their handbills in their portfolios.

Review and Assessment

REVIEW Have students work in pairs to prepare newspaper headlines summarizing the main events discussed in Section 1. Then assign the Section 1 Review on p. 35.

ASSESS Assign the **Section 1 Daily Quiz** in *Core Resources*.

HISTORICAL SIDELIGHTS

Building an Army
Washington bitterly complained that Congress's insistence on short-term enlistments of one year (and even as little as three months in some cases) undermined the war effort. By the time his recruits gained the experience to be good soldiers, their enlistment was up.

MULTICULTURAL PERSPECTIVES

Many enslaved African Americans fought in the Continental Army hoping to secure their freedom. As an indication of their hopes, they often assumed surnames such as "Freedom," "Freeman," and "Liberty" upon enlistment.

Map Caption Answer
approximately 315 miles

THE WAR FOR INDEPENDENCE

To declare independence was one thing: to fight for it was another. The lack of a central government hindered the American war effort. The Second Continental Congress, with little real authority, could ask the states for supplies, troops, and funds, but it could not force them to comply.

Fighting the war. Without a strong government behind it, the Continental Army faced constant supply shortages. As a result, Washington's troops suffered, enduring hunger and bitter winters. In addition, unsanitary conditions led to dysentery, which caused thousands of deaths.

Washington also faced a shortage of troops. Recruiting went well only after victories, and the soldier-farmers often deserted at planting or harvesting time. And because enlistments were short-term, the training of troops was especially difficult. But despite these problems, the Patriot forces enjoyed two key advantages: they fought on familiar ground, and they were inspired by a revolutionary cause.

Among the troops were about 5,000 African Americans. Numerous black soldiers, such as Salem Poor and Peter Salem, two of many African Americans who fought at Bunker Hill, received official recognition for their courage. Hundreds more served bravely but anonymously. African Americans served the war effort in another important way as well: they provided the slave labor used in the production of tobacco. Tobacco, in turn, provided the colonies with a key source of funding for the revolution.

A few Patriot women also fought in the war, while others undertook dangerous missions as spies or messengers. Many other women accompanied the troops and worked as laundresses, nurses, and cooks. But most stayed behind and supported the war effort by distributing medical supplies, making uniforms, manufacturing bullets, and managing businesses and farms.

Both the British and the Patriots tried to recruit members of the Iroquois League. After holding a council to discuss the war in 1777, the League split over the issue. Some tribes chose to join the British; others sided with the Patriots.

The war in the North. In the summer of 1776, British general William Howe sailed into New York Harbor and easily routed Washington's

troops in New York City. Thinking the war was almost won, Howe prepared to celebrate Christmas, taking few precautions against a possible Patriot attack.

But Washington and his troops ignored the customary winter halt in fighting. On Christmas night they set out to attack the foe at Trenton, New Jersey. Surprising the enemy, the Patriots quickly won a stunning victory. British plans to end the war quickly were, as one London official wrote, "blasted by the unhappy affair at Trenton."

Still in control of Canada to the north and New York City to the south, the British planned to cut off New England from the other rebel colonies. What the British did not realize—or ignored—

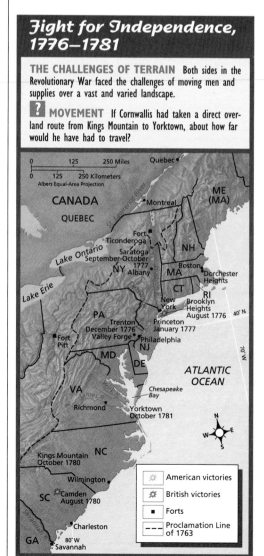

Fight for Independence, 1776–1781

THE CHALLENGES OF TERRAIN Both sides in the Revolutionary War faced the challenges of moving men and supplies over a vast and varied landscape.

❓ **MOVEMENT** If Cornwallis had taken a direct overland route from Kings Mountain to Yorktown, about how far would he have had to travel?

RETEACH Direct students to write who, what, when, where, and why questions and answers for each of the section's subsections. Collect question sheets and use them to quiz students on section content.

*C*losure

Ask students to design a time capsule for the American Revolution. Have them make suggestions for artifacts to place in the time capsule. Ask them to explain why these artifacts should be included.

*E*xtension

CREATE Encourage students to create a biographical dictionary of the American Revolution. Students may wish to include their dictionaries in their portfolios.

EVALUATE Have students evaluate the outcome of the American Revolution by writing a paragraph answering the following question: *Did the Revolution attain all its goals?*

was that their lines of attack crossed lakes, swamps, hills, and forests teeming with Patriots. British strategy failed, and in the fall of 1777 the outfoxed and outmanned British suffered defeat at the **Battle of Saratoga**.

Saratoga was a turning point for the Americans. Encouraged by the victory, the French signed a formal alliance with the Patriots in February 1778. French aid provided Americans with money, supplies, a fleet, and troops. By 1780 Spain and the Netherlands were also aiding the Patriots.

The war in the South. Late in 1778 the British focused their attacks on the southern colonies, where they anticipated strong support from **Loyalists** (also known as Tories)—colonists who remained loyal to Great Britain. After crushing the Americans in the Battle of Camden in South Carolina in 1780, British and Loyalist forces under General Charles Cornwallis marched toward North Carolina.

Patriot commander Nathanael Greene stopped the British advances. Greene was a master of the tactics of **guerrilla warfare**—wearing down the enemy in surprise hit-and-run skirmishes while avoiding direct battles. The use of guerrilla tactics allowed the Patriots to make the most of their limited numbers and frustrated British hopes of winning in the South.

During the summer of 1781, Cornwallis moved his army into Yorktown, Virginia, where he had access to the British fleet and supplies. When the

◀ **Bernardo de Gálvez, the Spanish governor of Louisiana, defeated the British at Baton Rouge, Natchez, Mobile, and Pensacola.**

The Historic New Orleans Collection, Museum/Research Center

French fleet moved to cut off this access, Washington's army, along with a French force, rushed south to Yorktown, completing the trap. In October, after attempts to break out failed, Cornwallis admitted defeat at the **Battle of Yorktown**. The British surrendered as their band played "The World Turned Upside Down."

▪▪ Familiarity with the terrain, unconventional tactics, and European support helped the Patriots defeat the British.

In the peace talks that followed the surrender, American negotiators won generous terms. The **Treaty of Paris**, signed on September 3, 1783, granted the United States independence. It also gave the new nation the land from the Atlantic coast westward to the Mississippi River and from the Great Lakes south to Florida.

SECTION REVIEW ANSWERS

IDENTIFY

For significance, see the following pages:
Proclamation of 1763 (p. 26)
Townshend Acts (p. 27)
Crispus Attucks (p. 27)
Boston Massacre (p. 27)
Boston Tea Party (p. 27)
Intolerable Acts (p. 28)
George Washington (p. 28)
Battle of Bunker Hill (p. 28)
Thomas Paine (p. 29)
Declaration of Independence (p. 29)
Loyalists (p. 35)
guerrilla warfare (p. 35)
Treaty of Paris (p. 35)

LOCATE

For locations, see the map on page 34.

1. *to raise revenue for Great Britain; protests through boycotts and demonstrations*
2. *discussed grievances, asserted colonists' rights, called for ban on trade with Britain; established Continental Army, issued Olive Branch Petition, adopted Declaration of Independence*
3. *listed George III's misdeeds, asserted citizens' rights, declared people's right to overthrow unjust government*
4. *Letters might point out advantages France would gain—defeat of enemy, possible new claims to lands in Americas.*
5. *unprepared for guerrilla warfare tactics and Patriots' use of terrain*

S E C T I O N 1 R E V I E W

IDENTIFY and explain the significance of the following: Proclamation of 1763, Townshend Acts, Crispus Attucks, Boston Massacre, Boston Tea Party, Intolerable Acts, George Washington, Battle of Bunker Hill, Thomas Paine, Declaration of Independence, Loyalists, guerrilla warfare, Treaty of Paris.

LOCATE and explain the importance of the following: Trenton, New Jersey; Battle of Saratoga; Battle of Yorktown.

1. **MAIN IDEA** What was the purpose of the Sugar Act and the Stamp Act? What reaction did these measures provoke?
2. **MAIN IDEA** How did the First and Second Continental Congresses respond to British actions?
3. **MAIN IDEA** What arguments did the Declaration of Independence offer in support of revolution?
4. **WRITING TO PERSUADE** Imagine you are a delegate to the Second Continental Congress. Write a letter to the government of France encouraging the French to aid the Patriots.
5. **ASSESSING CONSEQUENCES** British soldiers were well trained in traditional military procedures and tactics. How might this have been a disadvantage in the Revolutionary War?

PREVIEW WORKSHOP

Following is a list of the significant people and terms in this section. You may wish to use this list as a section preview.

People
- James Madison

Terms
- republic

- Articles of Confederation
- Land Ordinance of 1785
- Northwest Ordinance
- inflation
- depression
- Shays's Rebellion
- Constitutional Convention
- Virginia Plan
- federalism

- tariffs
- delegated powers
- reserved powers
- concurrent powers
- supremacy clause
- separation of powers
- checks and balances
- impeachment
- elastic clause

Section 2

FROM CONFEDERATION TO FEDERAL UNION

FOCUS

- **What were the weaknesses of the Articles of Confederation? What problems did these weaknesses cause?**
- **What issues threatened the framing and ratification of the Constitution?**
- **What are the major provisions of the Constitution?**

During the war the colonies replaced their royal charters with republican constitutions. The Continental Congress then drafted the Articles of Confederation to guide the new nation. Soon after the Revolution, however, economic problems and political unrest led the Congress to call for revision of the Articles. In response, the Constitutional Convention drafted the Constitution of the United States of America, a blueprint for a flexible and enduring system of government.

Great Seal of the Supreme Court

THE ARTICLES OF CONFEDERATION

The American Revolution brought an end to monarchical rule in America, leaving a void in place of the government. To fill this void, the Second Continental Congress advised the colonies "under the authority of the people" to form new governments. Between 1776 and 1780 all of the states ratified new constitutions or revised their royal charters.

To form the new governments, the state legislatures relied on republican theory. A **republic** is a form of government in which political leaders receive from the citizens the authority to make and enforce laws. Despite differences in economy, geography, and population, all of the states adopted similar constitutions, defining executive power and voting rights.

Many states also took steps to separate church and state. Before the Revolution, some colonies had collected taxes to support official churches. But many people opposed this close relationship between the government and one particular religion. In 1779 Thomas Jefferson drafted the Virginia Statute for Religious Freedom, declaring that "No man shall be compelled to . . . support any religious worship. . . . All men shall be free to profess their . . . opinion in matters of religion." By 1833 all of the states had forbidden the establishment of official state churches supported by tax dollars.

A plan for confederation.

The state constitutions established frameworks of government for each of the former colonies, but no

◀ **Many American statesmen used the political theories of John Locke when framing state constitutions.**

MOTIVATING: PRIOR KNOWLEDGE

Direct students to identify the aims of the American Revolution. Then point out that Benjamin Rush, a signer of the Declaration of Independence, suggested that the Revolutionary War was simply "the first act of the great drama" of revolution. Ask students what they think Rush meant by this statement. Have them speculate what acts would complete the drama.

Teaching the Section

WEAKNESSES OF THE ARTICLES

Call on volunteers to identify weaknesses of the Articles of Confederation and the problems they caused. List responses on the chalkboard as they are offered. Then have other students suggest how these weaknesses might be corrected. Note the suggestions in the appropriate place on the chalkboard. Then, direct students to write a letter to their representative in the Confederation government. The letter should indicate the government's weaknesses and the problems caused by these weaknesses and should suggest how these weaknesses could be corrected. Students may wish to include their letters in their portfolios.   ▶

such framework existed on the national level. To secure national unity, the Continental Congress knew it had to create a plan for a central government. On July 12, 1776, a committee of the Congress presented the **Articles of Confederation** to the other congressional delegates. The Articles created a confederation, or an alliance, of states while guaranteeing each state its "sovereignty, freedom, and independence."

▲ *Articles of Confederation cover*

The Articles authorized Congress—in which each state had one vote—to borrow and coin money, conduct foreign affairs, and settle disputes between the states. In addition, Congress could ask the states to contribute money to the central government and to provide recruits for the military. Most powers, however, were retained by the states, who were willing to join in a loose union but were reluctant to give up much authority to a national government. By 1781 all of the states had agreed to enter the Confederation.

The problem of land.

The 13 states were now officially "The United States of America." But a problem remained: who would control the land between the Appalachian Mountains and the Mississippi River? To regulate disposal of the land, Congress passed the **Land Ordinance of 1785**, which marked off the land into townships. Each township was 6 miles square and divided into 36 sections of 640 acres. The ordinance permitted the cash sale of 35 of the sections but reserved one for the establishment of a school.

Two years later, with the **Northwest Ordinance**, Congress established a system for governing the Northwest Territory. This area extended north of the Ohio River to the Great Lakes and west of Pennsylvania to the Mississippi River. The ordinance also outlined the steps to statehood, reflecting Congress's intent that states would be carved out of the Northwest Territory. Besides ensuring eventual self-rule in the territory, the ordinance guaranteed settlers their basic civil rights and banned slavery in the territory.

Weaknesses in the Confederation.

The land ordinances established a pattern of land settlement for the next 75 years and marked an important achievement for the Confederation. But Congress could point to few other noteworthy accomplishments. On paper the Confederation government enjoyed broad powers, but in reality it was weak. Proposed changes to the Articles needed the consent of all 13 states, and major legislation needed the approval of at least 9 states. Agreements were hard to reach because northern and southern delegates often had conflicting interests.

The government also had financial problems. Congress desperately needed cash to pay the war debt. But it could not tax the people directly; it could only ask the states for funds that some were reluctant to provide. During the war Congress had responded to the revenue shortage by printing paper money, which led to **inflation**, or an increase in prices. By 1781 people needed 100 paper dollars to purchase a product worth a dollar in gold. The

▼ The Continental Congress had authorized states to print paper money to finance the Revolution. By 1779 more than $241 million in paper dollars, called "Continentals," had been issued. The dollars shown here were printed in Philadelphia in 1779.

MULTICULTURAL PERSPECTIVES

The Northwest Ordinance pledged that Native Americans would always be treated with the "utmost of good faith," and that "their land and property [would] never be taken away from them without their consent." Many settlers ignored these promises, however, moving onto Indian lands or violating treaties and agreements in other ways. In 1794 Mohawk leader Thayendanegea warned that Native Americans' patience with the settlers was wearing thin. Emphasizing Indian rights to use the land, he said, "We, as the original inhabitants of this country, and sovereigns of the soil, look upon ourselves as . . . independent, and free as any other nation. . . . This country was given to us by the Great Spirit above; we wish to enjoy it."

Teaching the Section

ISSUES THREATENING THE CONSTITUTION

Organize the class into an even number of groups and provide each group with a piece of butcher paper. Direct half the groups to design and construct on their butcher paper a broadside titled *The Issues that Threatened the Framing of the Constitution.* Have the other groups do the same for a broadside titled *The Issues that*

Threatened the Ratification of the Constitution. Explain that broadsides, common during the American Revolution, were posted in public areas. Remind students that broadsides can include news stories, poems, songs, cartoons, and sketches. Display completed broadsides on the bulletin board.

Confederation's economic worries multiplied in 1786, when the nation experienced a **depression**, a sharp drop in business activity accompanied by rising unemployment.

■■ The limitations on congressional power under the Articles of Confederation caused serious economic problems.

Shays's Rebellion. The weak Confederation also proved unable to help farmers, who had been particularly hard hit by the war and its aftermath. The depression left farmers with fewer markets in which to sell their goods and no access to credit. They also had little money to pay their debts to merchants for equipment and other goods.

In Massachusetts the merchant-controlled legislature imposed a heavy tax on land and began seizing property if the tax was not paid. Outraged farmers protested to the legislature; when the legislature did not address the issue, the farmers rebelled. Under the leadership of such men as Daniel Shays, a former Revolutionary War captain, angry farmers took up arms to defend their property rights and political representation in what became known as **Shays's Rebellion**.

▲ This 1884 painting by Howard Pyle shows Daniel Shays and his men taking possession of a courthouse.

In January 1787, Shays and some 1,200 farmers attempted to seize the federal arsenal in Springfield, Massachusetts. But when the militia killed four of the farmers, Shays's men fled. By the end of February, the militia had crushed the rebellion. Yet despite Shays's defeat, the rebellion raised doubts about the national government's ability to deal with civil unrest. As a result many people who had previously objected to a strong central government began calling for new powers for the Confederation.

DRAFTING AND RATIFYING THE CONSTITUTION

With the weaknesses of the Confederation becoming more and more apparent, congressional leaders issued a call for a **Constitutional Convention** to strengthen the government. The proceedings began in Philadelphia in May 1787.

Although charged by Congress to revise the Articles of Confederation, some delegates believed that the Articles should be replaced with a new plan of government. One such plan was James Madison's **Virginia Plan**. This plan shifted political power away from the states and toward the central government, reflecting Madison's belief that the nation's survival depended on **federalism**—the division of powers between a strong central government and the state governments. The plan gave the federal legislature vast powers, such as the rights to overturn state laws and to tax the states.

Compromise at the convention. A dispute quickly arose over the number of representatives each state could send to the legislature. States with large populations naturally favored representation based on population. But states with small populations insisted on an equal number of representatives for each state.

To balance the interests of the large and small states, a compromise was fashioned. This **Great Compromise** proposed a two-house, or bicameral, legislature. Each state, regardless of size, would have an equal voice in the upper house. In the lower house, representation would be according to population. The delegates narrowly approved this proposal, ending what Madison later described as "the most serious and threatening excitement" of the convention.

Write the following terms on the chalk-board, leaving space between each term: *federalism, separation of powers, checks and balances, amendment process, elastic clause.* Call on volunteers to come to the board and write definitions of the listed terms. Then have students use the terms to write a paragraph explaining why the framers thought it necessary to include these provisions in the Constitution. Select students to read their paragraphs to the class.

■■ Ask students if the principles of separation of powers and of checks and balances are present in their student council or other clubs to which they belong. Call on volunteers to give examples.

The delegates resolved one dispute only to see several others arise. Conflict between small states and large states gave way to conflict between northern and southern states as delegates debated whether slaves should be counted as part of a state's population to determine representation. In the end, delegates accepted the **Three-Fifths Compromise**, which counted three fifths of the slave population in determining state population.

Northern and southern delegates also clashed over control of commerce. Northern delegates favored giving the national government the power to regulate all of the nation's trade. But the southern economy depended on exports, and southerners feared that if the national government imposed **tariffs**, or taxes, on exports, sales would be hurt. Another compromise resolved the issue—Congress would be able to levy tariffs on imports but not on exports.

Once again, however, problems arose. Planters now worried that Congress might use its powers to tax imports to restrict or abolish the slave trade. Bowing to southern pressure, convention delegates voted to permit the slave trade until the end of 1807. They also gave slaveholders the right to pursue runaway slaves across state lines.

With these conflicts resolved, delegates began drafting the Constitution on July 26, 1787. After weeks of hammering out the details, the final document was ready for the delegates' signatures on September 17, 1787. The Constitution then went to the states for ratification.

The Federalists and the Antifederalists.

To win ratification, the Constitution required the approval of 9 of the 13 states. Most convention delegates hoped for unanimous approval as a show of national unity. But when local newspapers printed copies of the Constitution, many Americans were shocked by what they read. They

▲ This 1788 woodcut commemorates the ratification of the Constitution.

expected a revision of the Articles; what they saw was a new framework of government. Citizens soon divided over the issue of ratification.

One group, the **Federalists**, favored ratification. Wealthy merchants, planters, and lawyers generally were Federalists. They advocated a strong national government that would assure a sound currency and protect property rights. Many Americans who were not wealthy also supported the Constitution, believing that a strong national government would provide stability and security against political unrest like Shays's Rebellion. As one Massachusetts farmer explained:

❝ I have lived in a part of the country where I have learned the worth of good government by the lack of it. There was a black cloud of rebellion that rose in the east last winter and spread over the west. . . . Now when I saw this Constitution, I found it was a cure for these disorders. ❞

The other group, called **Antifederalists** by their opponents, opposed ratification. They believed that a powerful national government would destroy states' rights and that the concentration of power in a central government violated the principle of liberty that had guided the Revolution.

HISTORICAL SIDELIGHTS
Two Philadelphia Meetings
The Pennsylvania Society for Promoting the Abolition of Slavery was meeting in Philadelphia at the same time as the Constitutional Convention. Society members drew up a petition calling on the Convention to "make the Suppression of the African [slave] trade in the United States" a part of its deliberations. These members hoped that Benjamin Franklin would present the petition to the Convention, but Franklin remained silent on their petition.

PRIMARY SOURCE
Description of Change: excerpted
Rationale: excerpted to focus on main idea

▶ *The Pennsylvania Packet, and Daily Advertiser* was one of several newspapers that carried the full text of the Constitution on September 19, 1787. The preamble to the Constitution is shown here.

The Pennſylvania Packet, *and Daily Advertiſer.*

[Price Four-Pence.]   WEDNESDAY, SEPTEMBER 19, 1787.   [No. 2690.]

WE, the People of the United States, in order to form a more perfect Union, eſtabliſh Juſtice, inſure domeſtic Tranquility, provide for the common Defence, promote the General Welfare, and ſecure the Bleſſings of Liberty to Ourſelves and our Poſterity, do ordain and eſtabliſh this Conſtitution for the United States of America.

Practice

GUIDED PRACTICE

Call on volunteers to compose headlines detailing the main ideas of the three subsections of this section. Write headlines on the chalkboard. Then, have students suggest elements for a newspaper story that might accompany each headline. Note responses under the appropriate headline.

INDEPENDENT PRACTICE

Direct students to choose one of the headlines and, using the notes developed in the Guided Practice, write a news story that might appear under that headline. Students may wish to include their stories in their portfolios.

Review and Assessment

REVIEW Organize the class into groups and assign each group one of the section's main heads. Tell groups to create a graphic that reflects the content of their assigned heading. Have groups present their graphic in the order in which the topics appear in the section. Then assign the Section 2 Review on p. 41.

ASSESS Assign the **Section 2 Daily Quiz** in *Core Resources*.

HISTORICAL SIDELIGHTS

A Bitter Debate

In Virginia a bitter personal exchange between Edmund Randolph and Patrick Henry enlivened the debate over ratification. Randolph refused to sign the Constitution but later championed its ratification. Henry openly ridiculed Randolph for changing his mind. Randolph, visibly angry, responded with a sarcastic rejection of Henry's arguments. At the end of the exchange, both men seemed ready to settle their differences in a duel. Tempers cooled, however, and the duel did not take place.

MAKING CONNECTIONS

Political Science

The distinction between state and federal powers enabled state governments to discriminate against groups that, under a unitary form of government, would have been protected under the Constitution's Bill of Rights. For example, New Jersey, which in 1776 had granted women the right to vote, revoked women's suffrage in 1807, largely because women were voting against incumbent candidates.

PRIMARY SOURCE

Description of Change: excerpted and bracketed
Rationale: excerpted to focus on main idea; bracketed to clarify meaning

The question of federalism versus states' rights was at the heart of the ratification struggle. Another crucial issue was individual rights. Unlike most state constitutions, the U.S. Constitution did not have a bill of rights. Some citizens, such as Amos Singletary of Massachusetts, feared that the Constitution would take away individual rights:

> 66 We contended [fought] with Great Britain . . . because they claimed a right to tax us and bind us in all cases whatever. And does not this Constitution do the same? . . . These lawyers, and men of learning, and moneyed men . . . expect to be the managers of this Constitution, and get all the power and all the money into their own hands, and then they will swallow up all us little folks. 99

■■ **Issues of representation, commerce, states' rights, and individual rights caused divisions that threatened the framing and ratification of the Constitution.**

Bitter debates took place in many of the states' ratifying conventions. By May 29, 1790, all 13 states had ratified the Constitution, some by the narrowest of margins. Americans could now hope to launch constitutional government in the United States with solid prospects for success.

THE CONSTITUTION: A LIVING DOCUMENT

Drawing on their experiences with British rule and with the Confederation, the delegates to the Constitutional Convention had worked to frame a constitution that would provide for a strong central government while protecting states' rights. Once the delegates settled on a federal system of government, they had to decide which powers would fall to the federal government and which powers the states would retain.

▶ The state seal of New York is shown here. State legislatures use seals such as this on official public documents.

They decided to give the federal government authority in matters of concern to all the people. These **delegated powers** include the rights to coin money, to regulate trade with foreign nations and among the states, and to raise and support an army and a navy. All powers not specifically granted to the federal government or denied to the states are kept, or reserved, by the states. Examples of the states' **reserved powers** include establishing local governments, overseeing schools, conducting elections, regulating businesses, and making marriage laws.

The powers that are held jointly by the federal government and the state governments are called **concurrent powers**. Examples of concurrent powers include levying and collecting taxes, borrowing money, providing for the public welfare, and establishing courts.

Recognizing that disputes might arise if the national government and the state governments passed laws that conflicted with one another, the delegates added the **supremacy clause** to Article VI of the Constitution. This clause states that the federal constitution and all federal laws override state constitutions and state laws.

To prevent the federal government from abusing its powers, the framers separated it into three branches: legislative, executive, and judicial. Each branch has specific powers the other branches cannot claim. The legislative branch makes laws, the executive branch sees that they are carried out, and the judicial branch interprets them and punishes lawbreakers. This **separation of powers** keeps any part of the federal government from becoming too powerful.

The separation of powers is upheld by a system of **checks and balances** that gives each branch of government the means to restrain the other two. Congress, for example, has the responsibility to check presidential power. The most extreme restraint on presidential authority is the legal process of **impeachment**. The House of Representatives may impeach, or charge, a president who is thought to be guilty of "treason, bribery, or other high crimes and misdemeanors." The president would then be tried by the Senate and, if found guilty, removed from office.

There are other checks and balances among the three branches. The president can make treaties and appoint important officials, but only with the approval of the Senate. Congress can also check the president by refusing to spend the monies necessary to fund a presidential action. The president,

Closure

Point out that Thomas Jefferson once wrote that constitutions must "keep pace with the times." Have students comment on whether the work of the framers satisfies Jefferson's requirements.

Extension

CREATE Suggest that small groups of students create maps of the original states and dates of ratification. Have groups conduct research to find areas of Federalist and Antifederalist support.

COMPARE Encourage students to research the constitution of another country. Ask students to construct a chart comparing it with the U.S. Constitution.

---

in turn, can curb the powers of Congress by vetoing, or rejecting, laws passed by Congress. Although Congress possesses the power to override, or overrule, a presidential veto, the two-thirds majority necessary to do so is often difficult to obtain. The president can also check Congress's power through influence and pressure. Both the executive and legislative branches balance the judicial branch: the Senate must approve the president's appointment of federal judges, and Congress has the power to impeach judges.

The Constitution has remained effective for more than 200 years because it is a living document that can adapt to changes in our society. To allow for needed changes, the framers specified a procedure by which the Constitution may be amended. But the amendment process is difficult. Only 27 amendments have been added to the Constitution since 1789.

The Constitution's **elastic clause** has also increased the document's flexibility. To the specific powers granted to Congress, this clause adds the power "to make all Laws which shall be necessary and proper for carrying into Execution the foregoing Powers." The elastic clause allows Congress to stretch its powers in ways not specifically outlined in the Constitution.

■■ Federalism, separation of powers, checks and balances, and the amendment process are among the Constitution's most significant provisions.

COMMENTARY

Evaluating the Constitution

The goal of the men who wrote the Constitution was not to remake the United States but to set the new nation on more stable political, economic, and social foundations. In this sense many of these men were conservatives. They did not, for example, wish to grant political power to all members of society, such as women and African Americans. Nor did they squarely face the issue of slavery. Some were willing to sidestep the issue because they mistakenly believed that slavery was a dying institution. But whatever the reason, the failure to end slavery at this time—when it could have been most easily accomplished—set the stage for more than 70 years of bitter debate and a civil war.

Yet the Constitution also had revolutionary implications. As the antislavery and women's movements would show, the promise of the Constitution was not lost on those excluded from power. In pressing for the same rights and liberties granted to free white men, all groups stood to benefit from the Constitution.

IDENTIFY

For significance, see the following pages:
republic (p. 36)
Land Ordinance of 1785 (p. 37)
Northwest Ordinance (p. 37)
inflation (p. 37)
depression (p. 38)
Shays's Rebellion (p. 38)
Constitutional Convention (p. 38)
James Madison (p. 38)
Virginia Plan (p. 38)
federalism (p. 38)
tariffs (p. 39)
delegated powers (p. 40)
reserved powers (p. 40)
concurrent powers (p. 40)
supremacy clause (p. 40)
separation of powers (p. 40)
impeachment (p. 40)
elastic clause (p. 41)

1. *needed 13 states to change Articles and 9 to add new laws, could not tax; led to economic and diplomatic problems*
2. *Delegates compromised over political representation, commerce, and slavery.*
3. *because amendment process and elastic clause allow it to adapt to changing conditions*
4. *Speeches will vary but should show understanding of the Federalist or Antifederalist view of government power.*
5. *by causing stalemate between government branches*

SECTION 2 REVIEW

IDENTIFY and explain the significance of the following: republic, Land Ordinance of 1785, Northwest Ordinance, inflation, depression, Shays's Rebellion, Constitutional Convention, James Madison, Virginia Plan, federalism, tariffs, delegated powers, reserved powers, concurrent powers, supremacy clause, separation of powers, impeachment, elastic clause.

1. **MAIN IDEA** What limits did the Articles of Confederation place on federal power? What were some of the consequences of these limits?
2. **MAIN IDEA** What were the major compromises that came out of the Constitutional Convention?
3. **MAIN IDEA** Why can the Constitution be considered a flexible, living document?
4. **WRITING TO PERSUADE** Imagine you are a Federalist or an Antifederalist delegate to a state ratifying convention. Write a speech explaining why you support or oppose ratification of the Constitution.
5. **EVALUATING** How might a system of checks and balances prevent government from being effective at times?

The Constitution of the United States of America

HISTORICAL
Document

The Constitution of the United States of America

HISTORICAL SIDELIGHTS

Gouverneur Morris

The Preamble to the Constitution was written by only one man: Gouverneur Morris of Pennsylvania. Serving on the Committee on Style, Morris alone was charged with writing the Preamble. He began it with the simple words *We the People of the United States. . . .* By using the name "United States" rather than listing the 13 states individually, the Preamble emphasized that the Constitution was not the product of states or state governments but of the citizens of a nation truly unified.

MAKING CONNECTIONS

Government

The "most numerous branch" of a state legislature is the one with the most members. If a person is eligible to vote for members of the "most numerous branch," he or she is eligible to vote for members of Congress. All states except Nebraska have a two-house legislature. With certain constitutional restrictions or restrictions of federal law, the states decide who can vote for state legislators. The Fifteenth, Nineteenth, Twenty-fourth, and Twenty-sixth amendments forbid the states to deny or restrict a citizen's right to vote because of race, sex, failure to pay a tax, or age (if the person is at least 18 years old).

Preamble
The short and dignified Preamble explains the goals of the new government under the Constitution.

Legislative Branch
Article I explains how the legislative branch, called Congress, is organized. The chief purpose of the legislative branch is to make the laws. Congress is made up of the Senate and the House of Representatives. The decision to have two bodies of government solved a difficult problem during the Constitutional Convention. The large states wanted the membership of Congress to be based entirely on population. The small states wanted every state to have an equal vote. The solution to the problem of how the states were to be represented in Congress was known as the Great Compromise.

The number of members of the House is based on the population of the individual states. Each state has at least one representative. The current size of the House is 435 members, set by Congress in 1929. If each member of the House represented only 30,000 people, the House would have more than 8,000 members.

PREAMBLE

We the People of the United States, in Order to form a more perfect Union, establish Justice, insure domestic Tranquility, provide for the common defense, promote the general Welfare, and secure the Blessings of Liberty to ourselves and our Posterity, do ordain and establish this Constitution for the United States of America. *

ARTICLE I

Section 1. All legislative Powers herein granted shall be vested in a Congress of the United States, which shall consist of a Senate and House of Representatives.

Section 2. The House of Representatives shall be composed of Members chosen every second Year by the People of the several States, and the Electors in each State shall have the Qualifications requisite for Electors of the most numerous Branch of the State Legislature.

No Person shall be a Representative who shall not have attained to the Age of twenty-five Years, and been seven Years a Citizen of the United States, and who shall not, when elected, be an inhabitant of that State in which he shall be chosen.

Representatives and direct Taxes shall be apportioned among the several States which may be included within this Union, according to their respective Numbers, which shall be determined by adding to the whole Number of free Persons, including those bound to Service for a Term of Years, and excluding Indians not taxed, three fifths of all other Persons. The actual Enumeration shall be made within three Years after the first Meeting of the Congress of the United States, and within every subsequent Term of ten Years, in such Manner as they shall by Law direct. The Number of Representatives shall not exceed one for every thirty Thousand, but each State shall have at Least one Representative; and until such enumeration shall be made, the State of New Hampshire shall be entitled to choose three; Massachusetts eight; Rhode Island and Providence Plantations one; Connecticut five; New York six; New Jersey four;

* Parts of the Constitution that have been ruled through are no longer in force or no longer apply.

Qualifications to Serve
In 1806 Henry Clay of Kentucky was appointed to fill an unexpired term in the Senate. He was only 29, a few months younger than the minimum age, but no one challenged his appointment. In 1793 Albert Gallatin was elected to the Senate from Pennsylvania. He was barred from taking office because he had not been a citizen for the required nine years.

Pennsylvania eight; Delaware one; Maryland six; Virginia ten; North Carolina five; South Carolina five; and Georgia three.

When vacancies happen in the Representation from any State, the Executive Authority thereof shall issue Writs of Election to fill such Vacancies.

The House of Representatives shall choose their Speaker and other Officers; and shall have the sole Power of Impeachment.

Section 3. The Senate of the United States shall be composed of two Senators from each State, chosen by the Legislature thereof, for six Years; and each Senator shall have one Vote.

Immediately after they shall be assembled in Consequence of the first Election, they shall be divided as equally as may be into three Classes. The Seats of the Senators of the first Class shall be vacated at the Expiration of the second Year, of the second Class at the Expiration of the fourth Year, and of the third Class at the Expiration of the sixth Year, so that one third may be chosen every second Year; and if Vacancies happen by Resignation, or otherwise, during the Recess of the Legislature of any State, the Executive thereof may make temporary Appointments until the next Meeting of the Legislature, which shall then fill such Vacancies.

No Person shall be a Senator who shall not have attained to the Age of thirty Years, and been nine Years a Citizen of the United States, and who shall not, when elected, be an Inhabitant of that State for which he shall be chosen.

The Vice President of the United States shall be President of the Senate, but shall have no Vote, unless they be equally divided.

The Senate shall choose their other Officers, and also a President pro tempore, in the Absence of the Vice President, or when he shall exercise the Office of President of the United States.

The Senate shall have the sole Power to try all Impeachments. When sitting for that Purpose, they shall be on Oath or Affirmation. When the President of the United States is tried, the Chief Justice shall preside: And no Person shall be convicted without the Concurrence of two thirds of the Members present.

Judgment in Cases of Impeachment shall not extend further than to removal from Office, and disqualification to hold and enjoy any Office of honor, Trust or Profit under the United States: but the Party convicted shall nevertheless be liable and subject to Indictment, Trial, Judgment and Punishment, according to Law.

Section 4. The Times, Places and Manner of holding Elections for Senators and Representatives, shall be prescribed in each State by the Legislature thereof; but the Congress may at any time by Law make or alter such Regulations, except as to the Places of choosing Senators.

The Congress shall assemble at least once in every Year, and such Meeting shall be on the first Monday in December, unless they shall by Law appoint a different Day.

Every state has two senators. Senators serve a six-year term, but only one third of the senators reach the end of their terms every two years. In any election, at least two thirds of the senators stay in office. This system ensures that there are experienced senators in office at all times.

The only duty that the Constitution assigns to the vice president is to preside over meetings of the Senate. Modern presidents have given their vice presidents more and varied responsibility.

The House charges a government official of wrongdoing, and the Senate acts as a court to decide if the official is guilty.

Congress has decided that elections will be held on the Tuesday following the first Monday in November of even-numbered years. The Twentieth Amendment states that Congress shall meet in regular session on January 3 of each year. The president may call a special session of Congress whenever necessary.

HISTORICAL SIDELIGHTS

Compensation

Section 6 prohibits members of Congress from creating jobs to which they can be appointed, from raising the salaries of jobs they hope to hold in the future, and from holding office in other branches of government. In 1909 Senator Philander C. Knox resigned from the Senate to become secretary of state, but the salary of the secretary of state had been increased during Knox's term as senator. So that Knox might accept the post, Congress withdrew the salary increase for the period of Knox's unfinished term.

Congress makes most of its own rules of conduct. The Senate and the House each have a code of ethics that members must follow. It is the task of each house of Congress to discipline its own members. Each house keeps a journal, and a publication called the **Congressional Record** records what happens in congressional sessions. The general public can learn how their representatives voted on bills by reading the *Congressional Record*.

The framers of the Constitution wanted to protect members of Congress from being arrested on false charges by political enemies who did not want them to attend important meetings. The framers also wanted to protect members of Congress from being taken to court for something they said in a speech or in a debate.

The power of taxing is the responsibility of the House of Representatives. Because members of the House are elected every two years, the framers felt that representatives would listen to the public and seek its approval before passing taxes.

Section 5. Each House shall be the Judge of the Elections, Returns and Qualifications of its own Members, and a Majority of each shall constitute a Quorum to do Business; but a smaller Number may adjourn from day to day, and may be authorized to compel the Attendance of absent Members, in such Manner, and under such Penalties as each House may provide.

Each House may determine the Rules of its Proceedings, punish its Members for disorderly Behavior, and, with the Concurrence of two thirds, expel a Member.

Each House shall keep a Journal of its Proceedings, and from time to time publish the same, excepting such Parts as may in their Judgment require Secrecy; and the Yeas and Nays of the Members of either House on any question shall, at the Desire of one fifth of those Present, be entered on the Journal.

Neither House, during the Session of Congress, shall, without the Consent of the other, adjourn for more than three days, nor to any other Place than that in which the two Houses shall be sitting.

Section 6. The Senators and Representatives shall receive a Compensation for their Services, to be ascertained by Law, and paid out of the Treasury of the United States. They shall in all Cases, except Treason, Felony and Breach of the Peace, be privileged from Arrest during their Attendance at the Session of their respective Houses, and in going to and returning from the same; and for any Speech or Debate in either House, they shall not be questioned in any other Place.

No Senator or Representative shall, during the Time for which he was elected, be appointed to any civil Office under the Authority of the United States, which shall have been created, or the Emoluments whereof shall have been increased during such time; and no Person holding any Office under the United States, shall be a Member of either House during his Continuance in Office.

Section 7. All Bills for raising Revenue shall originate in the House of Representatives; but the Senate may propose or concur with Amendments as on other Bills.

Every Bill which shall have passed the House of Representatives and the Senate, shall, before it become a Law, be presented to the President of the United States; If he approve he shall sign it, but if not he shall return it, with his Objections to that House in which it shall have originated, who shall enter the Objections at large on their Journal, and proceed to reconsider it. If after such Reconsideration two thirds of that House shall agree to pass the Bill, it shall be sent, together with the Objections, to the other House, by which it shall likewise be reconsidered, and if approved by two thirds of that House, it shall become a Law. But in all such Cases the Votes of both Houses shall be determined by Yeas and Nays, and the Names of the Persons voting for and against the Bill shall be entered on the

Journal of each House respectively. If any Bill shall not be returned by the President within ten Days (Sundays excepted) after it shall have been presented to him, the Same shall be a Law, in like Manner as if he had signed it, unless the Congress by their Adjournment prevent its Return, in which Case it shall not be a Law.

Every Order, Resolution, or Vote to which the Concurrence of the Senate and House of Representatives may be necessary (except on a question of Adjournment) shall be presented to the President of the United States; and before the Same shall take Effect, shall be approved by him, or being disapproved by him, shall be repassed by two thirds of the Senate and House of Representatives, according to the Rules and Limitations prescribed in the Case of a Bill.

Section 8. The Congress shall have Power To lay and collect Taxes, Duties, Imposts and Excises, to pay the Debts and provide for the common Defense and general Welfare of the United States; but all Duties, Imposts and Excises shall be uniform throughout the United States;

To borrow Money on the credit of the United States;

To regulate Commerce with foreign Nations, and among the several States, and with the Indian Tribes;

To establish an uniform Rule of Naturalization, and uniform Laws on the subject of Bankruptcies throughout the United States;

To coin Money, regulate the Value thereof, and of foreign Coin, and fix the Standard of Weights and Measures;

To provide for the Punishment of counterfeiting the Securities and current Coin of the United States;

To establish Post Offices and post Roads;

To promote the Progress of Science and useful Arts, by securing for limited Times to Authors and Inventors the exclusive Right to their respective Writings and Discoveries;

To constitute Tribunals inferior to the supreme Court;

To define and punish Piracies and Felonies committed on the high Seas, and Offenses against the Law of Nations;

To declare War, grant Letters of Marque and Reprisal, and make Rules concerning Captures on Land and Water;

To raise and support Armies, but no Appropriation of Money to that Use shall be for a longer Term than two Years;

To provide and maintain a Navy;

To make Rules for the Government and Regulation of the land and naval Forces;

To provide for calling forth the Militia to execute the Laws of the Union, suppress Insurrections and repel Invasions;

To provide for organizing, arming, and disciplining, the Militia, and for governing such Part of them as may be employed in the Service of the United States, reserving to the States respectively, the

The veto power of the president and the ability of Congress to override a presidential veto are two of the important checks and balances in the Constitution.

The framers of the Constitution wanted a national government that was strong enough to be effective. This section lists the powers given to Congress. The last sentence in Section 8 (see page 170) contains the famous "elastic clause," which can be stretched (like elastic) to fit many different circumstances. The clause was first disputed when Alexander Hamilton proposed a national bank. Thomas Jefferson said that the Constitution did not give Congress the power to establish a bank. Hamilton argued that the bank was "necessary and proper" in order to carry out other powers of Congress, such as borrowing money and regulating currency. This argument was tested in the court system in 1819 in the case of *McCulloch* v. *Maryland*, when Chief Justice Marshall ruled in favor of the federal government. Powers given to the government by the "elastic clause" are called implied powers.

Undeclared Wars
Only Congress can officially declare war. More than one president, as commander in chief of the armed forces, has engaged the United States in war without a declaration by Congress. The major undeclared war in American history was the Vietnam War. The Korean War and the Persian Gulf War were also undeclared but were fought under United Nations auspices.

HISTORICAL
Document

HISTORICAL SIDELIGHTS

Slave Trading

As a compromise, Congress was not allowed to ban the importation of slaves for 20 years. In 1807 President Thomas Jefferson signed a law prohibiting the importation of slaves. The law went into effect in 1808, but illegal slave trading continued for several decades. In 1860 Captain Nathaniel Gordon was arrested and tried after attempting to bring 900 West African slaves to the United States. Found guilty of breaking the law, Gordon was executed. Captain Gordon was the only American slave trader ever executed by the United States.

If Congress has implied powers, then there also must be limits to its powers. Section 9 lists powers that are denied to the federal government. Several of the clauses protect the people of the United States from unjust treatment. For instance, Section 9 guarantees the writ of *habeas corpus* and prohibits bills of attainder and *ex post facto* laws.

Section 10 lists the powers that are denied to the states. In our system of federalism, the state and federal governments have separate powers, share some powers, and are denied other powers. The states may not exercise any of the powers that belong to Congress.

Appointment of the Officers, and the Authority of training the Militia according to the discipline prescribed by Congress.

To exercise exclusive Legislation in all Cases whatsoever, over such District (not exceeding ten Miles square) as may, by Cession of particular States, and the Acceptance of Congress, become the Seat of the Government of the United States, and to exercise like Authority over all Places purchased by the Consent of the Legislature of the State in which the Same shall be, for the Erection of Forts, Magazines, Arsenals, dock-Yards, and other needful Buildings;—And

To make all Laws which shall be necessary and proper for carrying into Execution the foregoing Powers, and all other Powers vested by this Constitution in the Government of the United States, or in any Department or Officer thereof.

Section 9. ~~The Migration or Importation of such Persons as any of the States now existing shall think proper to admit, shall not be prohibited by the Congress prior to the Year one thousand eight hundred and eight, but a Tax or duty may be imposed on such Importation, not exceeding ten dollars for each Person.~~

The Privilege of the Writ of Habeas Corpus shall not be suspended, unless when in Cases of Rebellion or Invasion the public Safety may require it.

No Bill of Attainder or ex post facto Law shall be passed.

No Capitation, or other direct, Tax shall be laid, unless in Proportion to the Census or Enumeration herein before directed to be taken.

No Tax or Duty shall be laid on Articles exported from any State.

No Preference shall be given by any Regulation of Commerce or Revenue to the Ports of one State over those of another: nor shall Vessels bound to, or from, one State, be obliged to enter, clear, or pay Duties in another.

No Money shall be drawn from the Treasury, but in Consequence of Appropriations made by Law; and a regular Statement and Account of the Receipts and Expenditures of all public Money shall be published from time to time.

No Title of Nobility shall be granted by the United States: And no Person holding any Office of Profit or Trust under them, shall, without the Consent of the Congress, accept of any present, Emolument, Office, or Title, of any kind whatever, from any King, Prince, or foreign State.

Section 10. No State shall enter into any Treaty, Alliance, or Confederation; grant Letters of Marque and Reprisal; coin Money; emit Bills of Credit; make any Thing but gold and silver Coin a Tender in Payment of Debts; pass any Bill of Attainder, ex post facto Law, or law impairing the Obligation of Contracts, or grant any Title of Nobility.

No State shall, without the Consent of the Congress, lay any Imposts or Duties on Imports or Exports, except what may be absolutely necessary for executing its inspection Laws: and the net Produce of all Duties and Imposts, laid by any State on Imports or Exports, shall be for the Use of the Treasury of the United States; and all such Laws shall be subject to the Revision and Control of the Congress.

No State shall, without the Consent of Congress, lay any Duty of Tonnage, keep Troops, or Ships of War in time of Peace, enter into any Agreement or Compact with another State, or with a foreign Power, or engage in War, unless actually invaded, or in such imminent Danger as will not admit of delay.

ARTICLE II

Section 1. The executive Power shall be vested in a President of the United States of America. He shall hold his Office during the Term of four Years, and, together with the Vice President, chosen for the same Term, be elected, as follows.

Each State shall appoint, in such Manner as the Legislature thereof may direct, a Number of Electors, equal to the whole Number of Senators and Representatives to which the State may be entitled in the Congress: but no Senator or Representative, or Person holding an Office of Trust or Profit under the United States, shall be appointed an Elector.

~~The Electors shall meet in their respective States, and vote by Ballot for two Persons, of whom one at least shall not be an Inhabitant of the same State with themselves. And they shall make a List of all the Persons voted for, and of the Number of Votes for each; which List they shall sign and certify, and transmit sealed to the Seat of the Government of the United States, directed to the President of the Senate. The President of the Senate shall, in the Presence of the Senate and House of Representatives, open all the Certificates, and the Votes shall then be counted. The Person having the greatest Number of Votes shall be the President, if such Number be a Majority of the whole Number of Electors appointed; and if there be more than one who have such majority, and have an equal Number of Votes, then the House of Representatives shall immediately choose by Ballot one of them for President; and if no Person have a Majority, then from the five highest on the List the said House shall in like Manner choose the President. But in choosing the President, the Votes shall be taken by States, the Representation from each State having one Vote; A quorum for this Purpose shall consist of a Member or Members from two thirds of the States, and a Majority of all the States shall be necessary to a Choice. In every Case, after the Choice of the President, the Person having the greatest Number of Votes of the Electors shall be the Vice President. But if there should~~

Executive Branch
The president is the chief of the executive branch. It is the job of the president to enforce the laws. The framers wanted the president and vice president's term of office and manner of selection to be different from those of members of Congress. They decided on four-year terms, but they had a difficult time agreeing on how to select the president and vice president. The framers finally set up an electoral system, which varies greatly from our electoral process today. The Twelfth Amendment changed the process by requiring that separate ballots be cast for president and vice president. The rise of political parties has since changed the process even more.

GLOBAL CONNECTIONS

The framers of the Mexican Constitution of 1824 were greatly influenced by the success of the U.S. system of government, and they modeled their constitution after that of the United States. The Mexican constitution established a federal government with powers divided among the executive, legislative, and judicial branches. The legislature was bicameral, with an upper house consisting of two senators per state, and a lower house consisting of one representative per 80,000 residents. Important differences included the election of the president and vice president by state legislatures and the establishment of the Catholic Church as the official state church.

HISTORICAL
Document

In 1845 Congress set the first Tuesday after the first Monday in November of every fourth year as the general election date for selecting presidential electors.

The youngest elected president was John F. Kennedy; he was 43 years old when he was inaugurated. (Theodore Roosevelt was 42 when he assumed office after the assassination of McKinley.) The oldest elected president was Ronald Reagan; he was 69 years old when he was inaugurated.

Emolument means "salary, or payment." In 1969 Congress set the president's salary at $200,000 per year. The president also receives an expense account of $50,000 per year. The president must pay taxes on both.

The oath of office is administered to the president by the chief justice of the United States. Washington added "So help me, God." All succeeding presidents have followed this practice.

The framers wanted to make sure that an elected representative of the people controlled the nation's military. Today the president is in charge of the army, navy, air force, marines, and coast guard. Only Congress can decide, however, if the United States will declare war. This section also contains the basis for the formation of the president's cabinet. Every president, starting with George Washington, has appointed a cabinet.

Most of the president's appointments to office must be approved by the Senate.

~~remain two or more who have equal Votes, the Senate shall choose from them by Ballot the Vice President.~~

The Congress may determine the Time of choosing the Electors, and the Day on which they shall give their Votes; which Day shall be the same throughout the United States.

No Person except a natural born Citizen, ~~or a Citizen of the United States, at the time of the Adoption of this Constitution,~~ shall be eligible to the Office of President; neither shall any Person be eligible to that Office who shall not have attained to the Age of thirty-five Years, and been fourteen Years a Resident within the United States.

In Case of the Removal of the President from Office, or of his Death, Resignation, or Inability to discharge the Powers and Duties of the said Office, the Same shall devolve on the Vice President, and the Congress may by Law provide for the Case of Removal, Death, Resignation or Inability, both of the President and Vice President, declaring what Officer shall then act as President, and such Officer shall act accordingly, until the Disability be removed, or a President shall be elected.

The President shall, at stated Times, receive for his Services, a Compensation, which shall neither be increased nor diminished during the Period for which he shall have been elected, and he shall not receive within that Period any other Emolument from the United States, or any of them.

Before he enter on the Execution of his Office, he shall take the following Oath or Affirmation:—"I do solemnly swear (or affirm) that I will faithfully execute the Office of President of the United States, and will to the best of my Ability, preserve, protect and defend the Constitution of the United States."

Section 2. The President shall be Commander in Chief of the Army and Navy of the United States, and of the Militia of the several States, when called into the actual Service of the United States; he may require the Opinion, in writing, of the principal Officer in each of the executive Departments, upon any Subject relating to the Duties of their respective Offices, and he shall have Power to grant Reprieves and Pardons for Offenses against the United States, except in Cases of Impeachment.

He shall have Power, by and with the Advice and Consent of the Senate, to make Treaties, provided two thirds of the Senators present concur; and he shall nominate, and by and with the Advice and Consent of the Senate, shall appoint Ambassadors, other public Ministers and Consuls, Judges of the supreme Court, and all other Officers of the United States, whose Appointments are not herein otherwise provided for, and which shall be established by Law: but the Congress may by Law vest the Appointment of such inferior Officers, as they think proper, in the President alone, in the Courts of Law, or in the Heads of Departments.

The President shall have Power to fill up all Vacancies that may happen during the Recess of the Senate, by granting Commissions which shall expire at the End of their next Session.

Section 3. He shall from time to time give to the Congress Information of the State of the Union, and recommend to their Consideration such Measures as he shall judge necessary and expedient; he may, on extraordinary Occasions, convene both Houses, or either of them, and in Case of Disagreement between them, with Respect to the Time of Adjournment, he may adjourn them to such Time as he shall think proper; he shall receive Ambassadors and other public Ministers; he shall take Care that the Laws be faithfully executed, and shall Commission all the Officers of the United States.

Section 4. The President, Vice President and all civil Officers of the United States, shall be removed from Office on Impeachment for, and Conviction of, Treason, Bribery, or other high Crimes and Misdemeanors.

ARTICLE III

Section 1. The judicial Power of the United States, shall be vested in one supreme Court, and in such inferior Courts as the Congress may from time to time ordain and establish. The Judges, both of the supreme and inferior Courts, shall hold their Offices during good Behavior, and shall, at stated Times, receive for their Services, a Compensation, which shall not be diminished during their Continuance in Office.

Section 2. The judicial Power shall extend to all Cases, in Law and Equity, arising under this Constitution, the Laws of the United States, and Treaties made, or which shall be made, under their Authority;—to all Cases affecting Ambassadors, other public Ministers and Consuls;—to all Cases of admiralty and maritime Jurisdiction;—to Controversies to which the United States shall be a Party;—to Controversies between two or more States;— between a State and Citizens of another State; —between Citizens of different States;—between Citizens of the same State claiming Lands under Grants of different States, and between a State, or the Citizens thereof, and foreign States, Citizens or Subjects.

In all Cases affecting Ambassadors, other public Ministers and Consuls, and those in which a State shall be Party, the supreme Court shall have original Jurisdiction. In all the other Cases before mentioned, the supreme Court shall have appellate Jurisdiction, both as to Law and fact, with such Exceptions, and under such Regulations as the Congress shall make.

The Trial of all Crimes, except in Cases of Impeachment, shall be by Jury; and such Trial shall be held in the State where the said Crimes shall have been committed; but when not committed within

Every year the president presents to Congress a State of the Union message. In this message, the president explains the legislative plans for the coming year. This clause states that one of the president's duties is to enforce the laws.

Judicial Branch
The Articles of Confederation did not make any provisions for a federal court system. One of the first things that the framers of the Constitution agreed upon was to set up a national judiciary. With all the laws that Congress would be enacting, there would be a great need for a branch of government to interpret the laws. In the Judiciary Act of 1789, Congress provided for the establishment of lower courts, such as district courts, circuit courts of appeals, and various other federal courts. The judicial system provides a check on the legislative branch; it can declare a law unconstitutional.

HISTORICAL SIDELIGHTS

State of the Union Addresses
Presidents George Washington and John Adams delivered their State of the Union messages to Congress in person. For more than 100 years after that, most presidents sent a written message that was read in Congress. President Woodrow Wilson delivered his messages in person, as did President Franklin D. Roosevelt. The presidents' messages often have great influence on public opinion and thus on Congress.

BUILDING VOCABULARY

Cases in which the Supreme Court has *original jurisdiction* are those that go directly to the Supreme Court. Such cases include those affecting the representatives of foreign countries and those in which a state is a party. In those cases in which the Supreme Court has *appellate jurisdiction*, the cases are tried first in a lower court and may come up to the Supreme Court for review. Congress cannot take away or modify the original jurisdiction of the Supreme Court, but it can create exceptions to the right to appeal to that court and set the conditions one must meet to present an appeal.

HISTORICAL
Document

HISTORICAL
Document

BUILDING VOCABULARY

A *republican government* is one in which the people elect representatives to govern. The Supreme Court ruled that Congress, not the courts, must decide whether a government is republican. According to the Supreme Court, if Congress admits a state's senators and representatives, that action indicates that Congress considers the government to be republican.

Congress has the power to decide the punishment for treason, but it can punish only the guilty person. *Corruption of blood* means punishing the family of a person who has committed treason. It is expressly forbidden by the Constitution.

The States
States must honor the laws, records, and court decisions of other states. A person cannot escape a legal obligation by moving from one state to another.

Section 3 permits Congress to admit new states to the Union. When a group of people living in an area that is not part of an existing state wishes to form a new state, it asks Congress for permission to do so. The people then write a state constitution and offer it to Congress for approval. The state constitution must set up a representative form of government and must not in any way contradict the federal Constitution. If a majority of Congress approves of the state constitution, the state is admitted as a member of the United States of America.

any State, the Trial shall be at such Place or Places as the Congress may by Law have directed.

Section 3. Treason against the United States, shall consist only in levying War against them, or in adhering to their Enemies, giving them Aid and Comfort. No Person shall be convicted of Treason unless on the Testimony of two Witnesses to the same overt Act, or on Confession in open Court.

The Congress shall have Power to declare the Punishment of Treason, but no Attainder of Treason shall work Corruption of Blood, or Forfeiture except during the Life of the Person attainted.

ARTICLE IV

Section 1. Full Faith and Credit shall be given in each State to the public Acts, Records, and judicial Proceedings of every other State. And the Congress may by general Laws prescribe the Manner in which such Acts, Records and Proceedings shall be proved, and the Effect thereof.

Section 2. The Citizens of each State shall be entitled to all Privileges and Immunities of Citizens in the several States.

A Person charged in any State with Treason, Felony, or other Crime, who shall flee from Justice, and be found in another State, shall on Demand of the executive Authority of the State from which he fled, be delivered up, to be removed to the State having Jurisdiction of the Crime.

~~No Person held to Service of Labor in one State, under the Laws thereof, escaping into another, shall, in Consequence of any Law or Regulation therein, be discharged from such Service or Labor, but shall be delivered up on Claim of the Party to whom such Service or Labor may be due.~~

Section 3. New States may be admitted by the Congress into this Union; but no new State shall be formed or erected within the Jurisdiction of any other State; nor any State be formed by the Junction of two or more States, or Parts of States, without the Consent of the Legislatures of the States concerned as well as of the Congress.

The Congress shall have Power to dispose of and make all needful Rules and Regulations respecting the Territory or other Property belonging to the United States; and nothing in this Constitution shall be so construed as to Prejudice any Claims of the United States, or of any particular State.

Section 4. The United States shall guarantee to every State in this Union a Republican Form of Government, and shall protect each of them against Invasion; and on Application of the Legislature, or of the Executive (when the Legislature cannot be convened) against domestic Violence.

ARTICLE V

The Congress, whenever two thirds of both Houses shall deem it necessary, shall propose Amendments to this Constitution, or, on the Application of the Legislatures of two thirds of the several States, shall call a Convention for proposing Amendments, which, in either Case, shall be valid to all Intents and Purposes, as Part of this Constitution, when ratified by the Legislatures of three fourths of the several States, or by Conventions in three fourths thereof, as the one or the other Mode of Ratification may be proposed by the Congress; Provided that no Amendment which may be made prior to the Year One thousand eight hundred and eight shall in any Manner affect the first and fourth Clauses in the Ninth Section of the first Article; and that no State, without its Consent, shall be deprived of its equal Suffrage in the Senate.

ARTICLE VI

All Debts contracted and Engagements entered into, before the Adoption of this Constitution, shall be as valid against the United States under this Constitution, as under the Confederation.

This Constitution, and the Laws of the United States which shall be made in Pursuance thereof; and all Treaties made, or which shall be made, under the Authority of the United States, shall be the supreme Law of the Land; and the Judges in every State shall be bound thereby, any Thing in the Constitution or Laws of any State to the Contrary notwithstanding.

The Senators and Representatives before mentioned, and the Members of the several State Legislatures, and all executive and judicial Officers, both of the United States and of the several States, shall be bound by Oath or Affirmation, to support this Constitution; but no religious Test shall ever be required as a Qualification to any Office or public Trust under the United States.

ARTICLE VII

The Ratification of the Conventions of nine States, shall be sufficient for the Establishment of this Constitution between the States so ratifying the Same.

DONE in Convention by the Unanimous Consent of the States present the Seventeenth Day of September in the Year of our Lord one thousand seven hundred and Eighty seven and of the Independence of the United States of America the Twelfth. IN WITNESS whereof We have hereunto subscribed our Names.

George Washington—
President and deputy from Virginia

The Amendment Process

America's founders may not have realized just how enduring the Constitution would be, but they did make provisions for changing or adding to the Constitution. They did not want to make it easy to change the Constitution. There are two different ways in which changes can be proposed to the states and two different ways in which states can approve the changes and make them part of the Constitution.

National Supremacy

One of the biggest problems facing the delegates to the Constitutional Convention was the question of what would happen if a state law and a national law conflicted. Which law would be followed? Who decided? The second clause of Article VI answers those questions. When a national and state law disagree, the national law overrides the state law. The Constitution is the supreme law of the land. This clause is often called the "supremacy clause."

Ratification

The Articles of Confederation called for all 13 states to approve any revision to the Articles. The Constitution required that the vote of 9 out of the 13 states would be needed to ratify the Constitution. The first state to ratify was Delaware, on December 7, 1787. The last state to ratify the Constitution was Rhode Island, which finally did so on May 29, 1790, almost two and a half years later.

Religious Tests

At the time that the Constitution was written, all but two states—New York and Virginia—had religious qualifications for stateholders. Delaware, for example, would let only "Protestants who accepted the Holy Trinity" serve in the state legislature. Pennsylvania required its state officers to have a "belief in God and the inspiration of the Scriptures." When Charles Pinckney III of South Carolina proposed that the Constitution specifically prohibit these religious tests, a heated debate followed. Some delegates believed that electing officials who espoused Christian beliefs would help ensure that their leaders would rule fairly. The majority of delegates, however, favored the ban on religious tests. Pinckney's motion passed.

HISTORICAL
Document

New Hampshire	Delaware
John Langdon	*George Read*
Nicholas Gilman	*Gunning Bedford, Jr.*
	John Dickinson
Massachusetts	*Richard Bassett*
Nathaniel Gorham	*Jacob Broom*
Rufus King	
	Maryland
Connecticut	*James McHenry*
William Samuel Johnson	*Daniel of St. Thomas Jenifer*
Roger Sherman	*Daniel Carroll*
New York	Virginia
Alexander Hamilton	*John Blair*
	James Madison, Jr.
New Jersey	
William Livingston	North Carolina
David Brearley	*William Blount*
William Paterson	*Richard Dobbs Spaight*
Jonathan Dayton	*Hugh Williamson*
Pennsylvania	South Carolina
Benjamin Franklin	*John Rutledge*
Thomas Mifflin	*Charles Cotesworth Pinckney*
Robert Morris	*Charles Pinckney*
George Clymer	*Pierce Buttler*
Thomas FitzSimons	
Jared Ingersoll	Georgia
James Wilson	*William Few*
Gouverneur Morris	*Abraham Baldwin*

Attest: *William Jackson*, Secretary

Bill of Rights

One of the conditions set by several states for ratifying the Constitution was the inclusion of a Bill of Rights. Many people feared that a stronger central government might take away basic rights of the people that had been guaranteed in state constitutions. If the three words that begin the preamble—We the people—were truly meant, then the rights of the people needed to be protected.

THE AMENDMENTS

ARTICLES in addition to, and Amendment of the Constitution of the United States of America, proposed by Congress, and ratified by the Legislatures of the several states, pursuant to the fifth Article of the original Constitution.

[The First through Tenth amendments, now known as the Bill of Rights, were proposed on September 25, 1789, and declared in force on December 15, 1791.]

First Amendment

Congress shall make no law respecting an establishment of religion, or prohibiting the free exercise thereof; or abridging the freedom of speech, or of the press; or the right of the people peaceably to assemble, and to petition the Government for a redress of grievances.

Second Amendment

A well regulated Militia, being necessary to the security of a free State, the right of the people to keep and bear Arms, shall not be infringed.

Third Amendment

No Soldier shall, in time of peace, be quartered in any house, without the consent of the Owner, nor in time of war, but in a manner to be prescribed by law.

Fourth Amendment

The right of the people to be secure in their persons, houses, papers, and effects, against unreasonable searches and seizures, shall not be violated, and no Warrants shall issue, but upon probable cause, supported by Oath or affirmation, and particularly describing the place to be searched, and the persons or things to be seized.

Fifth Amendment

No person shall be held to answer for a capital, or otherwise infamous crime, unless on a presentment or indictment of a Grand Jury, except in cases arising in the land or naval forces, or in the Militia, when in actual service in time of War or public danger; nor shall any person be subject for the same offense to be twice put in jeopardy of life or limb; nor shall be compelled in any criminal case to be a witness against himself, nor be deprived of life, liberty, or property, without due process of law; nor shall private property be taken for public use, without just compensation.

Sixth Amendment

In all criminal prosecutions, the accused shall enjoy the right to a speedy and public trial, by an impartial jury of the State and district wherein the crime shall have been committed, which district shall have been previously ascertained by law, and to be informed of the nature and cause of the accusation; to be confronted with the witnesses against him; to have compulsory process for obtaining witnesses in his favor, and to have the Assistance of Counsel for his defense.

Seventh Amendment

In Suits at common law, where the value in controversy shall exceed twenty dollars, the right of trial by jury shall be preserved,

---

The First Amendment protects freedom of speech and thought, and forbids Congress to make any law "respecting an establishment of religion" or restraining the freedom to practice religion as one chooses.

A police officer or sheriff may enter a person's home with a search warrant, which allows the law officer to look for evidence that could convict someone of committing a crime.

The Fifth, Sixth, and Seventh amendments describe the procedures that courts must follow when trying people accused of crimes. The Fifth Amendment guarantees that no one can be put on trial for a serious crime unless a grand jury agrees that the evidence justifies doing so. It also says that a person cannot be tried twice for the same crime.

The Sixth Amendment makes several promises, including a prompt trial and a trial by a jury chosen from the state and district in which the crime was committed. The Sixth Amendment also states that an accused person must be told why he or she is being tried and promises that an accused person has the right to be defended by a lawyer.

The Seventh Amendment guarantees a trial by jury in cases that involve more than $20, but in modern times, usually much more money is at stake before a case is heard in federal court.

MAKING CONNECTIONS

Government

The First Amendment prohibits Congress from setting up or supporting an *established* or official church. The amendment also forbids Congress from passing laws limiting religious worship, and it has been interpreted to forbid government endorsement of religious doctrines. The guarantee of freedom of religion does not mean, however, that all religious practices must be allowed. In the 1800s some Mormons believed that it was a man's religious duty to have more than one wife. The Supreme Court ruled that Mormons had to obey the laws forbidding that practice.

HISTORICAL SIDELIGHTS

Due Process of Law

The due process clause is one of the most important in the Constitution. The statement expresses the idea that life, liberty, and property are not subject to the uncontrolled power of the government. Until the mid-1900s, the Court used the due process clause to strike down laws that prevented people from using their property as they wished. Today the courts use the due process clause primarily to strike down laws that interfere with personal liberty.

HISTORICAL SIDELIGHTS

Capital Punishment

In the 1972 case *Furman* v. *Georgia,* the Supreme Court ruled that capital punishment (death penalty), as it was then imposed, violated the Eighth Amendment. The Court held that capital punishment was cruel and unusual punishment because it was not applied fairly and uniformly. After that decision, many states adopted new capital-punishment laws designed to meet the objections of the Supreme Court. The Court has ruled that the death penalty may be imposed if certain standards are applied to guard against arbitrary results in capital cases.

HISTORICAL Document

The Ninth and Tenth amendments were added because not every right of the people or of the states could be listed in the Constitution.

The Twelfth Amendment changed the election procedure for president and vice president. This amendment became necessary because of the growth of political parties. Before this amendment, electors voted without distinguishing between president and vice president. Whoever received the most votes became president, and whoever received the next highest number of votes became vice president. A confusing election in 1800, which resulted in Thomas Jefferson's becoming president, caused this amendment to be proposed.

and no fact tried by a jury shall be otherwise reexamined in any Court of the United States, than according to the rules of the common law.

Eighth Amendment

Excessive bail shall not be required, nor excessive fines imposed, nor cruel and unusual punishments inflicted.

Ninth Amendment

The enumeration in the Constitution, of certain rights, shall not be construed to deny or disparage others retained by the people.

Tenth Amendment

The powers not delegated to the United States by the Constitution, nor prohibited by it to the States, are reserved to the States respectively, or to the people.

Eleventh Amendment

[Proposed March 4, 1794; declared ratified January 8, 1798]

The Judicial power of the United States shall not be construed to extend to any suit in law or equity, commenced or prosecuted against one of the United States by Citizens of another State, or by Citizens or Subjects of any Foreign State.

Twelfth Amendment

[Proposed December 9, 1803; declared ratified September 25, 1804]

The Electors shall meet in their respective states and vote by ballot for President and Vice President, one of whom, at least, shall not be an inhabitant of the same state with themselves; they shall name in their ballots the person voted for as President, and in distinct ballots the person voted for as Vice President, and they shall make distinct lists of all persons voted for as President, and of all persons voted for as Vice President, and of the number of votes for each, which lists they shall sign and certify, and transmit sealed to the seat of the government of the United States, directed to the President of the Senate;—The President of the Senate shall, in the presence of the Senate and House of Representatives, open all the certificates and the votes shall then be counted;—The person having the greatest number of votes for President, shall be the President, if such number be a majority of the whole number of Electors appointed; and if no person have such majority, then from the persons having the highest numbers not exceeding three on the list of those voted for as President, the House of Representatives shall choose immediately, by ballot, the President. But in choosing the President, the votes shall be taken by states, the representation from each state having one vote; a quorum for this purpose shall consist of a member or members from two thirds of the states, and a majority of all the states shall be necessary to a choice. ~~And if the House of Representatives shall not choose a President whenever the right of choice shall devolve upon them, before the fourth day of March next following, then the Vice President shall act as President, as in the case of the death or other constitutional disability of the President;~~ The person having the greatest number of votes as Vice President, shall be the Vice President, if such number be a majority of the whole number of Electors appointed, and if no person have a majority, then from the two highest numbers on the list, the Senate shall choose the Vice President; a quorum for the purpose shall consist of two thirds of the whole number of Senators, and a majority of the whole number shall be necessary to a choice. But no person constitutionally ineligible to the office of President shall be eligible to that of Vice President of the United States.

Thirteenth Amendment

[Proposed January 31, 1865; declared ratified December 18, 1865]

Section 1. Neither slavery nor involuntary servitude, except as a punishment for crime whereof the party shall have been duly convicted, shall exist within the United States, or any place subject to their jurisdiction.

Section 2. Congress shall have power to enforce this article by appropriate legislation.

Although some slaves had been freed during the Civil War, slavery was not abolished until the Thirteenth Amendment took effect.

Fourteenth Amendment

[Proposed June 13, 1866; declared ratified July 28, 1868]

Section 1. All persons born or naturalized in the United States and subject to the jurisdiction thereof, are citizens of the United States and of the State wherein they reside. No State shall make or enforce any law which shall abridge the privileges or immunities of citizens of the United States; nor shall any State deprive any person of life, liberty, or property, without due process of law; nor deny to any person within its jurisdiction the equal protection of the laws.

Section 2. Representatives shall be apportioned among the several States according to their respective numbers, counting the whole number of persons in each State, ~~excluding Indians not taxed.~~ But when the right to vote at any election for the choice of electors for President and Vice President of the United States, Representatives in Congress, the Executive and Judicial officers of a State, or the members of the Legislature thereof, is denied to any of the ~~male~~ inhabitants of such State, being ~~twenty-one years of age, and~~ citizens of the United States, or in any way abridged, except for participation in rebellion, or other crime, the basis of representation therein shall be reduced in the proportion which the number of such ~~male~~ citizens shall bear to the whole number of ~~male~~ citizens ~~twenty-one years of age~~ in such State.

Section 3. No person shall be a Senator or Representative in

In 1833 Chief Justice John Marshall ruled that the Bill of Rights limited the national government but not the state governments. This ruling meant that states were able to keep African Americans from becoming state citizens. If African Americans were not citizens, they were not protected by the Bill of Rights. The Fourteenth Amendment defines citizenship and prevents states from interfering in the rights of citizens of the United States.

MAKING CONNECTIONS

Government

The phrase "due process of law" has been construed to prohibit states from violating most rights protected by the Bill of Rights. It also has been interpreted as protecting other rights by its own force. The statement that a state cannot deny anyone "equal protection of the laws" has provided the basis for many Supreme Court rulings on civil rights. For example, the Court has outlawed segregation in public schools, declaring that "equal protection" means that all children, regardless of race, must have an equal opportunity to be educated.

MAKING CONNECTIONS

Government

African Americans who had been enslaved became citizens under the terms of the Fourteenth Amendment, but the Fifteenth Amendment does not specifically say that they must be allowed to vote. The amendment states that a voter cannot be denied the ballot because of race. However, the states are free to set qualifications for voters, and some states attempted to deny the ballot to African Americans through indirect means, such as the poll tax. Such measures have been overturned by Supreme Court decisions, by federal laws, and by the Twenty-fourth Amendment.

HISTORICAL
Document

The Fifteenth Amendment extended the right to vote to African American males.

The Sixteenth Amendment made legal the income tax described in Article I.

The Seventeenth Amendment required that senators be elected directly by the people instead of by the state legislature.

Congress, or elector of President and Vice President, or hold any office, civil or military, under the United States, or under any State, who, having previously taken an oath, as a member of Congress, or as an officer of the United States, or as a member of any State legislature, or as an executive or judicial officer of any State, to support the Constitution of the United States, shall have engaged in insurrection or rebellion against the same, or given aid or comfort to the enemies thereof. But Congress may by a vote of two thirds of each House, remove such disability.

Section 4. The validity of the public debt of the United States, authorized by law, including debts incurred for payment of pensions and bounties for services in suppressing insurrection or rebellion, shall not be questioned. But neither the United States nor any State shall assume or pay any debt or obligation incurred in aid of insurrection or rebellion against the United States, ~~or any claim for the loss or emancipation of any slave;~~ but all such debts, obligations and claims shall be held illegal and void.

Section 5. The Congress shall have power to enforce, by appropriate legislation, the provisions of this article.

Fifteenth Amendment

[Proposed February 26, 1869; declared ratified March 30, 1870]

Section 1. The right of citizens of the United States to vote shall not be denied or abridged by the United States or by any State on account of race, color, or previous condition of servitude.

Section 2. The Congress shall have power to enforce this article by appropriate legislation.

Sixteenth Amendment

[Proposed July 12, 1909; declared ratified February 25, 1913]

The Congress shall have power to lay and collect taxes on incomes, from whatever source derived, without apportionment among the several States, and without regard to any census or enumeration.

Seventeenth Amendment

[Proposed May 13, 1912; declared ratified May 31, 1913]

The Senate of the United States shall be composed of two Senators from each State, elected by the people thereof, for six years; and each Senator shall have one vote. The electors in each State shall have the qualifications requisite for electors of the most numerous branch of the State legislatures.

When vacancies happen in the representation of any State in the Senate, the executive authority of such State shall issue writs of election to fill such vacancies: *Provided,* That the legislature of any

State may empower the executive thereof to make temporary appointments until the people fill the vacancies by election as the legislature may direct.

This amendment shall not be so construed as to affect the election or term of any Senator chosen before it becomes valid as part of the Constitution.

Eighteenth Amendment

[Proposed December 18, 1917; declared ratified January 29, 1919; repealed by the Twenty-first Amendment December 5, 1933]

Section 1. After one year from the ratification of this article the manufacture, sale, or transportation of intoxicating liquors within, the importation thereof into, or the exportation thereof from the United States and all territory subject to the jurisdiction thereof for beverage purposes is hereby prohibited.

Section 2. The Congress and the several States shall have concurrent power to enforce this article by appropriate legislation.

Section 3. This article shall be inoperative unless it shall have been ratified as an amendment to the Constitution by the legislatures of the several States, as provided in the Constitution, within seven years from the date of the submission hereof to the States by the Congress.

Although many people felt that Prohibition was good for the health and welfare of the American people, the amendment was repealed 14 years later.

Nineteenth Amendment

[Proposed June 4, 1919; declared ratified August 26, 1920]

The right of citizens of the United States to vote shall not be denied or abridged by the United States or by any State on account of sex.

Congress shall have power to enforce this article by appropriate legislation.

Abigail Adams was disappointed that the Declaration of Independence and the Constitution did not specifically include women. It took almost 150 years and much campaigning by women's suffrage groups for women finally to achieve voting privileges.

Twentieth Amendment

[Proposed March 2, 1932; declared ratified February 6, 1933]

Section 1. The terms of the President and Vice President shall end at noon on the 20th day of January, and the terms of Senators and Representatives at noon on the 3rd day of January, of the years in which such terms would have ended if this article had not been ratified; and the terms of their successors shall then begin.

Section 2. The Congress shall assemble at least once in every year, and such meeting shall begin at noon on the 3rd day of January, unless they shall by law appoint a different day.

Section 3. If, at the time fixed for the beginning of the term of the President, the President elect shall have died, the Vice President elect shall become President. If a President shall not have been chosen before the time fixed for the beginning of his term, or if the President elect shall have failed to qualify, then the Vice President

In the original Constitution, a newly elected president and Congress did not take office until March 4, which was four months after the November election. The officials who were leaving office were called "lame ducks" because they had little influence during those four months. The Twentieth Amendment changed the date that the new president and Congress take office. Members of Congress now take office on January 3, and the president takes office on January 20.

The debate over the Fourteenth and Fifteenth amendments gave suffragists the hope that women would be given the vote along with African Americans. The Fourteenth Amendment, however, defined an eligible voter as a male over 21 years of age, and for the first time, women thus were specifically excluded from the vote. Until then, voting rights had been considered a state matter, and it had been possible to interpret some state laws to include women as citizens and voters. Some women property owners previously had voted, often in local elections. The direct exclusion of women by the Fourteenth Amendment angered and disappointed suffragists, who ultimately would have to work 50 more years to gain the vote.

HISTORICAL
Document

elect shall act as President until a President shall have qualified; and the Congress may by law provide for the case wherein neither a President elect nor a Vice President elect shall have qualified, declaring who shall then act as President, or the manner in which one who is to act shall be selected, and such persons shall act accordingly until a President or Vice President shall have qualified.

Section 4. The Congress may by law provide for the case of the death of any of the persons from whom the House of Representatives may choose a President whenever the right of choice shall have devolved upon them, and for the case of the death of any of the persons from whom the Senate may choose a Vice President whenever the right of choice shall have devolved upon them.

~~*Section 5.* Sections 1 and 2 shall take effect on the 15th day of October following the ratification of this article.~~

~~*Section 6.* This article shall be inoperative unless it shall have been ratified as an amendment to the Constitution by the legislatures of three fourths of the several States within seven years from the date of its submission.~~

Twenty-first Amendment
[Proposed February 20, 1933; declared ratified December 5, 1933]

Section 1. The eighteenth article of amendment to the Constitution of the United States is hereby repealed.

Section 2. The transportation or importation into any State, Territory, or possession of the United States for delivery or use therein of intoxicating liquors, in violation of the laws thereof, is hereby prohibited.

~~*Section 3.* This article shall be inoperative unless it shall have been ratified as an amendment to the Constitution by conventions in the several States, as provided in the Constitution, within seven years from the date of the submission hereof to the States by the Congress.~~

Twenty-second Amendment
[Proposed March 24, 1947; declared ratified March 1, 1951]

Section 1. No person shall be elected to the office of the President more than twice, and no person who has held the office of President, or acted as President, for more than two years of a term to which some other person was elected President shall be elected to the office of the President more than once. ~~But this Article shall not apply to any person holding the office of President when this Article was proposed by the Congress, and shall not prevent any person who may be holding the office of President, or acting as President, during the term within which this Article becomes operative from holding the office of President or acting as President during the remainder of such term.~~

The Twenty-first Amendment is the only amendment that has been ratified by state conventions rather than by state legislatures.

From the time of President Washington's administration, it was a custom for presidents to serve no more than two terms of office. Franklin D. Roosevelt, however, was elected to four terms. The Twenty-second Amendment made into law the old custom of a two-term limit for each president, if reelected.

Section 2. This Article shall be inoperative unless it shall have been ratified as an amendment to the Constitution by the legislatures of three fourths of the several States within seven years from the date of its submission to the States by the Congress.

Twenty-third Amendment

[Proposed June 16, 1960; declared ratified April 3, 1961]

Section 1. The District constituting the seat of Government of the United States shall appoint in such manner as the Congress may direct:

A number of electors of President and Vice President equal to the whole number of Senators and Representatives in Congress to which the District would be entitled if it were a State, but in no event more than the least populous State; they shall be in addition to those appointed by the States, but they shall be considered, for the purposes of the election of President and Vice President, to be electors appointed by a State; and they shall meet in the District and perform such duties as provided by the twelfth article of amendment.

Section 2. The Congress shall have power to enforce this article by appropriate legislation.

Twenty-fourth Amendment

[Proposed August 27, 1962; declared ratified February 4, 1964]

Section 1. The right of citizens of the United States to vote in any primary or other election for President or Vice President, for electors for President or Vice President, or for Senator or Representative in Congress, shall not be denied or abridged by the United States or any State by reason of failure to pay any poll tax or other tax.

Section 2. The Congress shall have power to enforce this article by appropriate legislation.

Twenty-fifth Amendment

[Proposed July 6, 1965; declared ratified February 23, 1967]

Section 1. In case of removal of the President from office or of his death or resignation, the Vice President shall become President.

Section 2. Whenever there is a vacancy in the office of the Vice President, the President shall nominate a Vice President who shall take office upon confirmation by a majority vote of both Houses of Congress.

Section 3. Whenever the President transmits to the President pro tempore of the Senate and the Speaker of the House of Representatives his written declaration that he is unable to discharge the powers and duties of his office, and until he transmits to them a written declaration to the contrary, such powers and duties shall be discharged by the Vice President as Acting President.

Until the Twenty-third Amendment, the people of Washington, D.C., could not vote in presidential elections.

The illness of President Eisenhower in the 1950s and the assassination of President Kennedy in 1963 were the events behind the Twenty-fifth Amendment. The Constitution did not provide a clear-cut method for a vice president to take over for a disabled president or for the death of a president. This amendment provides for filling the office of the vice president if a vacancy occurs, and it provides a way for the vice president to take over if the president is unable to perform the duties of that office.

BUILDING VOCABULARY

A *poll tax* is a tax collected equally from everyone. Some states once used such taxes to keep poor people and African Americans from voting. The term *poll tax* does not mean a tax on voting. It comes from the word *poll* meaning "head."

HISTORICAL SIDELIGHTS

Appointing a Vice President

In 1973 Gerald R. Ford became the first person ever chosen vice president under the terms of the Twenty-fifth Amendment. He was nominated by President Richard M. Nixon after Vice President Spiro Agnew resigned. In 1974 Nixon resigned and Ford became president. Nelson Rockefeller then became the new vice president under the new procedure. For the first time, the United States had both a president and a vice president who had not been elected to their offices. Before this amendment, tradition and practice dictated that vacancies in the vice presidency remain unfilled until the next presidential election.

Section 4. Whenever the Vice President and a majority of either the principal officers of the executive departments or of such other body as Congress may by law provide, transmit to the President pro tempore of the Senate and the Speaker of the House of Representatives their written declaration that the President is unable to discharge the powers and duties of his office, the Vice President shall immediately assume the powers and duties of the office as Acting President.

Thereafter, when the President transmits to the President pro tempore of the Senate and the Speaker of the House of Representatives his written declaration that no inability exists, he shall resume the powers and duties of his office unless the Vice President and a majority of either the principal officers of the executive department or of such other body as Congress may by law provide, transmit within four days to the President pro tempore of the Senate and the Speaker of the House of Representatives their written declaration that the President is unable to discharge the powers and duties of his office. Thereupon Congress shall decide the issue, assembling within forty-eight hours for that purpose if not in session. If the Congress, within twenty-one days after receipt of the latter written declaration, or, if Congress is not in session, within twenty-one days after Congress is required to assemble, determines by two-thirds vote of both Houses that the President is unable to discharge the powers and duties of his office, the Vice President shall continue to discharge the same as Acting President; otherwise, the President shall resume the powers and duties of his office.

Twenty-sixth Amendment
[Proposed March 23, 1971; declared ratified July 5, 1971]

Section 1. The right of citizens of the United States, who are eighteen years of age or older, to vote shall not be denied or abridged by the United States or by any State on account of age.

Section 2. The Congress shall have power to enforce this article by appropriate legislation.

Twenty-seventh Amendment
[Proposed September 25, 1789; declared ratified May 7, 1992]

No law, varying the compensation for the services of the Senators and Representatives, shall take effect, until an election of Representatives shall have intervened.

The Voting Act of 1970 tried to set the voting age at 18 years old. But the Supreme Court ruled that the act set the voting age for national elections only, not state or local elections. This ruling would make necessary several different ballots at elections. The Twenty-sixth Amendment gave 18-year-old citizens the right to vote in all elections.

PREVIEW WORKSHOP

Following is a list of the significant people and terms in this section. You may wish to use this list as a section preview.

People
- Sacagawea
- Tecumseh

Terms
- Bill of Rights

- Judiciary Act
- Whiskey Rebellion
- national bank
- strict construction
- loose construction
- Jay's Treaty
- Pinckney's Treaty
- sectionalism
- Alien and Sedition Acts
- Kentucky and Virginia

Resolutions
- *Marbury* v. *Madison*
- judicial review
- Twelfth Amendment
- Trans-Appalachian West
- Louisiana Purchase
- Embargo Act
- Battle of Tippecanoe
- Battle of New Orleans
- Treaty of Ghent

Section 3

A STRONG START FOR THE NATION

F O C U S

- **What steps did Congress take to strengthen the federal government?**
- **What international and domestic issues were important to the United States between 1790 and 1800?**
- **Why was the Louisiana Purchase important?**
- **What were the major causes of the War of 1812?**

*D*omestic and foreign problems plagued America in its early years. The new federal government successfully addressed some of the problems at home. But relations with Europe threatened to draw the nation into war and divided Americans along political party lines. These intrigues would eventually erupt into the War of 1812.

U.S. cannon, 1815

FOCUS OBJECTIVES

- Identify the steps Congress took to strengthen the federal government.

- Determine the international and domestic issues that were important to the United States between 1790 and 1800.

- Explain the importance of the Louisiana Purchase.

- List the major causes of the War of 1812.

THE AMERICAN NATION
VIDEODISC PROGRAM

Designing a Nation

1A   06322   4:24

CORE RESOURCES
- **Section 3 Daily Quiz**
- **Geography Worksheet 2**

AV RESOURCES
- *The American Nation Videodisc: Designing a Nation; A Native American Confederacy*
- **Linking Geography and History Transparency** and **Worksheet 8**
- **Everyday Life in America Transparency** and **Worksheet 6**

*F*ORGING A NATION

When Congress opened the ballots from the states on April 6, 1789, the unanimous choice for the nation's first president was George Washington. But while crowds cheered and towns celebrated Washington's inauguration, the task of shaping the new government belonged to the First Congress.

Molding the government. Congress's first order of business was to add a protection of individual liberties to the Constitution. Congress recommended twelve amendments for adoption; of these, 10 were ratified by the states in 1791 and became known as the **Bill of Rights**.

Another task of Congress was the creation of a federal court system, achieved by the **Judiciary**

▶ This sampler celebrates Washington's inauguration.

Act of 1789. Congress also created three departments to assist the president: the State Department to handle foreign affairs, the War Department to manage military affairs, and the Treasury Department to oversee the nation's finances. The president appointed the heads, or secretaries, of these departments to serve as his advisers. Over time these advisers became known as the president's cabinet.

Restoring the nation's credit. Next, Congress tackled the nation's finances, for the government had inherited serious financial problems. Not only did the Treasury lack funds to pay off war debts, it did not have enough money to run the country. Lawmakers turned to Secretary of the Treasury Alexander Hamilton for help.

Hamilton believed that America's future depended on a strong national government controlled by the rich and well born. He also believed that one of the best ways to strengthen the government, both financially and

MOTIVATING:
LINK TO TODAY
Have students identify as many present-day government agencies as they can. List responses on the chalkboard. Ask students how and why they think these agencies came into being.

MAKING CONNECTIONS

Geography

The District of Columbia was originally a 100-square-mile territory set aside for the federal government and made up of the towns of Alexandria, Georgetown, and Washington (the site chosen for the new capital). After Alexandria was given back to Virginia in 1846, and Georgetown annexed by Washington in 1878, the city of Washington had the same boundaries as the District of Columbia. Refer students to the maps on p. 98 and p. 102 to show the district's boundaries.

COOPERATIVE LEARNING

Organize the class into groups and encourage them to research and report on a current issue, such as gun control or music censorship, from the standpoints of strict construction and loose construction of the Constitution. Each group should divide the tasks of research, report preparation, and report presentation among its members.

politically, was to establish economic policies that helped business and industry. If business people believed the federal government had their best interests at heart, they would support it.

As a first step toward winning over the merchant class, Hamilton advised Congress to strengthen the nation's credit by paying off the national debt and by taking over the debts of the states. Hamilton knew that a nation that did not pay its debts would have trouble borrowing additional money. Despite strong resistance, particularly from the southern states, Congress eventually passed these measures. But in return for southern votes, Hamilton's supporters pledged that the nation's capital would be moved south to a site across the Potomac River from Virginia. The site was later named Washington, D.C.

In order to pay the national debt, of course, Hamilton had to raise money. Unlike today, the government did not have the power to collect an income tax. So Hamilton asked Congress to impose a tax on a few domestically produced items, most notably whiskey. The tax, to be paid by producers, hit western farmers the hardest. News of the tax infuriated them, and in the summer of 1794, farmers in western Pennsylvania rose in what became known as the **Whiskey Rebellion**. A federal force, however, quickly subdued the "Whiskey Boys."

Hamilton's bank proposal. Establishing good credit was not the only solution to the nation's financial woes. The government also lacked the means to manage the nation's money supply. Hamilton believed that the creation of a **national bank** would solve this problem, and

▲ An excise officer is tarred and feathered by a mob in 1794.

asked Congress to create such a bank. This proposal met with stiff opposition from many Americans who feared that the bank would be controlled by wealthy northeastern merchants.

Thomas Jefferson raised a more serious charge: nowhere in the Constitution was the federal government given the power to set up a bank. Jefferson believed that the government could only do what the Constitution specifically allows. This philosophy of constitutional interpretation is called **strict construction**. Hamilton, on the other hand, believed that the government could do anything the Constitution does not specifically forbid—the philosophy called **loose construction**.

The members of Congress debated the issue for months. In the end, President Washington sided with Hamilton, and Congress chartered the Bank of the United States in 1791. The charter granted the Bank the right to operate for 20 years, when it would again be subject to congressional approval.

■■ To strengthen the government, Congress set up a court system, established executive departments, enhanced the nation's credit, and created a national bank.

𝓐 DANGEROUS WORLD

Hamilton intended his financial program to enrich the American economy. In the 1790s, however, economic independence was not yet a reality. Americans still needed British money and technology to strengthen commerce and to develop manufacturing. France provided an important market for American agricultural products.

Thus, when France declared war on Great Britain, Spain, and the Netherlands in 1793, the resulting conflict disrupted American trade and threatened to draw the United States into war. Both France and Great Britain ignored the American declaration of neutrality and seized American vessels bound for enemy ports. In addition, Britain's **impressment**—or kidnapping—of U.S. sailors aroused American hostility.

The French, meanwhile, tried to stir up pro-French passions among Americans by reminding them of their 1778 military alliance treaty with France. But Washington, knowing that the United States was unprepared for war, refused to give in

Teaching the Section

STRENGTHENING THE FEDERAL GOVERNMENT

Have students work with partners to list the steps taken by Congress to strengthen the federal government. *(passed Bill of Rights, set up a federal court system, established three executive departments, enhanced the nation's credit, created a national bank)*

Have volunteers present their lists to the class. Ask students to explain how each action was important to the success of the new government.

▶

PRESIDENTIAL LIVES

GEORGE WASHINGTON
1732–1799

in office 1789–1797

JOHN ADAMS
1735–1826

in office 1797–1801

THOMAS JEFFERSON
1743–1826

in office 1801–1809

JAMES MADISON
1751–1836

in office 1809–1817

---

to pressure. On April 22, 1793, he issued a proclamation forbidding Americans to offer support to any nation at war.

Washington managed to avoid foreign entanglements, but trouble brewed in the Northwest Territory. By the terms of the Treaty of Paris of 1783, the British granted this land to the United States. Native Americans, however, considered the territory theirs. To defend their homes, some 1,500 American Indians of various tribes joined together in a loose confederation. The confederation won several battles against American troops in 1790 and 1791, but fresh federal forces defeated the confederation in the summer of 1794. This defeat severely weakened Native American resistance and led to the surrender of additional Indian lands.

The American Indians had received weapons from British forts in the Northwest Territory. The existence of these forts violated the 1783 Treaty of Paris. This situation further strained America's shaky relations with Great Britain. Hoping to avert a war that he believed the United States could not win, President Washington sent Chief Justice John Jay to Great Britain in 1794 to negotiate a settlement. Under the terms of **Jay's Treaty** the British agreed to abandon their forts,

▶ **Miami chief Little Turtle led American Indians in successful battles against American troops in the Northwest Territory during 1790–1791.**

and the U.S. government agreed to pay debts owed to the British.

Fearing that an American alliance with Britain would threaten Spanish territory in North America, Spain moved to settle its disputes with the United States. The result was **Pinckney's Treaty**, negotiated in 1795 by Thomas Pinckney of South Carolina. This treaty set the southern U.S. boundary near Florida at the 31st parallel. It also guaranteed American navigation rights on the Mississippi River and use of the port at New Orleans for three years.

DOMESTIC BATTLES

By the mid-1790s heated debates over whether to side with Great Britain or France had already deepened political differences in the United States. **Sectionalism**, or loyalty to a particular part of the country, helped to create two political parties: the Federalists and the Democratic-Republicans (who soon became known as the Republicans—though the party has no historical connection to today's Republican party).

Merchants, manufacturers, and lawyers from New England and the Atlantic seaboard tended to support the Federalist party. Federalists favored a strong

---

HISTORICAL SIDELIGHTS

Jay's Treaty
Great Britain did not stop arming Native Americans, impressing American sailors, or seizing British ships. These acts angered many Americans who thought Jay had sold out to the British. Mobs burned Jay in effigy, and the nation's political divisions deepened. When Alexander Hamilton spoke in favor of Jay's Treaty in New York, he was stoned from the platform. Later, in response to Republican goading, he offered to duel the Republicans, one at a time. Although the Republicans accepted, the duels never took place. In spite of the turmoil, Congress ratified the treaty. Washington had realized his major goal—preventing war with Great Britain.

Teaching the Section

INTERNATIONAL AND DOMESTIC CHALLENGES

Divide the chalkboard into two columns, labeled *International* and *Domestic*. Fill in the columns by calling on volunteers to give examples of international and domestic issues the United States faced between 1790 and 1800. Then, ask students to write two paragraphs, one stating the most impor-

tant international issue confronting the United States, the other stating the most important domestic issue. Both paragraphs should include students' reasons for their choices. Have students compare their paragraphs.

■■ Ask students to identify the major international and domestic challenges facing the United States today.

RECOGNIZING PREJUDICE

The Alien and Sedition Acts reflected a strong antiforeign sentiment in the U.S. during this period. Discuss with students why countries often feel threatened by immigrants and other "foreign" groups.

■■ Ask students to identify any antiforeign movements currently active in the world.

HISTORICAL SIDELIGHTS

Elections

At the time of the 1800 election, voting was a rowdy public event. Each man declared his vote in the presence of a crowd and both candidates. A voter could be heard to shout at a political opponent, "You, sir, ought to have your mouth smashed." Candidates could thank their supporters personally; one told a supporter that he would "treasure that vote in my memory." Some people, wishing to maintain good relations with both candidates, would try to avoid voting, but party leaders did their best to seek them out and bring them, physically, to the polls.

▲ The Republican party believed in an agricultural America full of orderly farms, such as the one shown here.

national government and wanted to promote the development of commerce, especially with Great Britain. In contrast, the Republican party included planters, small farmers, and wage earners. The party was particularly strong on the frontier and in the South, but also found considerable support in the middle states. Republicans' main aim was to protect states' rights and individual liberties by limiting the federal government. Because they distrusted the aristocratic British, they tended to be pro-French.

The Federalists come to power. In the election of 1796 Federalists John Adams and Thomas Pinckney faced off against Republicans Thomas Jefferson and Aaron Burr. According to the Constitution, the candidate who received the most votes became president; the runner-up became vice president. When the votes were counted, however, Adams was elected president, and Jefferson—his Republican opponent—was vice president!

President Adams faced many challenges during his term. One of his goals was to improve relations with the French, who viewed Jay's Treaty as further evidence of pro-British leanings and continued to seize American ships bound for British ports. Adams's attempts to negotiate with France, however, turned into a crisis when the French made demands that seemed unreasonable to the Americans. Fortunately for Adams, a change of government in France led to an agreement.

The crisis with France increased the bad blood between the Federalists and the Republicans. In 1798 the Federalist majority in Congress added

fuel to the fire by passing the **Alien and Sedition Acts**. The Alien Act and the Alien Enemies Act authorized the president to imprison or expel "all such aliens [foreigners] as he shall judge dangerous to the peace and safety of the United States." The Sedition Act targeted American citizens, and Republicans in particular. It stated that anyone who wrote, said, or printed anything "false, scandalous, and malicious" about the government "with intent to defame" could be fined or jailed. Throughout the country, Republican newspaper editors and politicians were arrested for sedition; 25 were indicted and 10 convicted.

Many Americans saw the Sedition Act as an attempt to curb individuals' rights—rights that were guaranteed by the First Amendment. Furious Republicans voiced their protests through the **Kentucky and Virginia Resolutions**, written by Thomas Jefferson and James Madison. These resolutions declared the Alien and Sedition Acts unconstitutional. The states, they argued, had created the federal government as their agent; therefore the states had the right—and duty—to void any unconstitutional laws.

Because the Federalists controlled most state governments, the resolutions failed to win wide support. They had, however, raised an important question: Who should decide when a federal law or a government action violates the U.S. Constitution?—the states?—the Supreme Court? The resolutions came down on the side of the states. But Supreme Court chief justice John Marshall, Adams's most significant judicial appointment, took a different view a few years later in the case of *Marbury* v. *Madison* (1803). In this case, Marshall established the principle of **judicial review**—the right of the Supreme Court to declare an act of Congress unconstitutional. The Supreme Court thus acquired its most important role—that of final interpreter of the Constitution.

■■ **Conflicts among European countries, disputes with Native Americans, a growing sectionalism, and rivalry between political parties caused tension in the United States.**

Jefferson takes office. In the election of 1800 the Republicans swept to power, gaining control of Congress. But another electoral crisis arose concerning the presidency: Jefferson and Burr, the

CONSEQUENCES OF THE LOUISIANA PURCHASE

Organize students into small groups and provide each group with a piece of butcher paper. Direct groups to construct on their butcher paper a two-column chart titled *Consequences of the Louisiana Purchase.* One column should be headed *Positive,* the other *Negative.* Display a number of finished charts. Use these as a starting point for a discussion on the following questions:

What if the U.S. had not made the Louisiana Purchase? How would the country's development have been different?

CAUSES OF WAR OF 1812

Have groups create a cause-effect flowchart showing the events leading to the War of 1812. The chart should show how the actions of the British, Native Americans, and westerners influenced the decision to go to war. Ask a volunteer from each group to present the group's chart and discuss it with the class.

▶

---

two Republican candidates, had received the same number of votes! As dictated by the Constitution, the election was thrown to the House of Representatives. After a lengthy stalemate, the House selected Jefferson. To prevent future electoral crises, Congress proposed the **Twelfth Amendment** to the Constitution. Ratified in 1804, this amendment requires electors to vote for presidential and vice-presidential candidates on separate ballots.

To fulfill his promise of moderation, Jefferson left untouched some Federalist programs, including the national bank and the debt payment plan. But Jefferson had not abandoned his view that a federal government with too much power threatened individual freedoms and states' rights. Thus he led the Republican-controlled Congress in repealing taxes, cutting military funding, and reducing the size of the army and the navy.

THE NATION EXPANDS

In the election of 1800, the Republicans won every state that had a frontier on the **Trans-Appalachian West**, the area between the Appalachian Mountains and the Mississippi River. Republicans favored expansion, and Jefferson imagined "distant times, when our rapid multiplication will expand [the nation] . . . & cover the whole northern if not southern continent." This view appealed to settlers who were always seeking new land because their farming practices were hard on the soil.

Fertile land was not enough, however. Western farmers also needed access to the Mississippi River and to the port of New Orleans to get their produce to market. When Jefferson learned that Spain had secretly transferred the territory surrounding the river to France, he was alarmed. French control of the river might severely limit American trade and block westward expansion. To remedy the situation, Jefferson was prepared to offer Napoléon, France's ruler, as much as $10 million for New Orleans and West Florida. But to the surprise of the American negotiators, Napoléon's representative asked how much the United States would pay for *all* of Louisiana—the enormous territory consisting roughly of the northern and western reaches of the Mississippi River basin. The astonished Americans quickly agreed to pay about $15 million for the entire area in the

Louisiana Purchase.

President Jefferson assigned the task of mapping the huge new territory to two skilled frontiersmen, Meriwether Lewis and William Clark. The Lewis and Clark expedition, numbering about 45 men, left St. Louis in May 1804. Many Native Americans aided the expedition but none more than Sacagawea, a Shoshone woman, who proved to be invaluable as a guide and interpreter. The expedition traveled up the Missouri River, crossed the Rocky Mountains, and canoed down the Snake

THE LOUISIANA PURCHASE

*S*pain was unpleasantly surprised to discover in 1803 that France planned to sell Louisiana to the United States. Earlier, Spain had transferred the land to France on the condition that the French never part with it. Spain feared that if the United States acquired this vast territory, the young nation would threaten Spain's other colonies in North America, such as California and Mexico.

The Marques de Casa Irujo (eer-oo-hoh), Spain's minister to the United States, wrote a harsh letter to Secretary of State James Madison denying the United States' right to buy Louisiana: "The sale of that province to the United States is founded on the violation of a promise so absolute that it ought to be respected—a promise without which the king, my master, would not under any circumstances have let Louisiana go."

In a letter to his own government, Casa Irujo called the Louisiana Purchase "truly an evil" for the United States. He predicted the U.S. government would be unable to hold such a vast territory of diverse peoples together: "One does not need extraordinary wisdom to anticipate that the acquisition of Louisiana, far from consolidating the strength and vigor of this nation, will rather contribute to weaken it."

THROUGH OTHERS' EYES

HISTORICAL SIDELIGHTS

Tons of Money

Federalists criticized the Louisiana Purchase for a number of reasons, not the least of which was its cost. Federalist newspapers noted that if the $15 million were stacked up in silver dollars, the stack would be three miles high. They also marveled that it would take 25 ships to carry that much money.

THROUGH OTHERS' EYES

Discuss with students whether Casa Irujo's prediction about the impact of the Louisiana Purchase on the United States came true.

*P*ractice

GUIDED PRACTICE

Organize the class into small groups and provide each group with a copy of the list of terms included in the Preview Workshop on p. 61. Have groups discuss and then write a paragraph explaining how these various terms relate to the development of the United States in its first 25 years. Call on group representatives to read their paragraphs to the class.

INDEPENDENT PRACTICE

Ask students to create illustrated time lines of this section, using information developed in the Guided Practice paragraphs. Students may wish to include their time lines in their portfolios.

*R*eview and *A*ssessment

REVIEW Have students work in small groups to create cause-event-effect graphic organizers showing the main events discussed in the section. Then assign the Section 3 Review on p. 67.

ASSESS Assign the **Section 3 Daily Quiz** in *Core Resources*.

BIO GRAPHY PERSONALITIES IN HISTORY

Tecumseh planned to recruit young men for his confederation because he believed that older chiefs and tribal leaders had been corrupted by whites. Tecumseh's father had been killed in Lord Dunmore's War, an elder brother had died during the American Revolution, and another brother was killed at the Battle of Fallen Timbers. Although he had no love for whites, Tecumseh, who was made a brigadier general, fought for the British in the War of 1812. He saw the war as an opportunity to win a homeland for all Native American groups. Tecumseh died in the Battle of the Thames in 1813.

THE AMERICAN NATION VIDEODISC PROGRAM

A Native American Confederacy

1A	00598 3:11

▲ Americans pushed westward as new territories opened. This engraving shows a family crossing the Appalachians on their way to Pittsburgh.

and Columbia rivers to the Pacific Ocean. After nearly two and a half years, the expedition returned—bringing with it detailed journals and various specimens from the explored areas.

The Louisiana Purchase added all or part of 13 future states to the nation. This increased size gave the United States greater international stature. And as Americans devoted more energy to developing the frontier, they increasingly looked west, rather than east across the Atlantic. This shift promoted a stronger sense of national identity. The purchase, however, had a negative effect on Native Americans, whose claims to the land were not considered, and on many African Americans, who became slaves in the new territory.

▪▪ **Although the Louisiana Purchase had negative consequences for some peoples, it added to U.S. prestige and helped build national identity.**

---

*T*HE WAR OF 1812

Events across the Atlantic, however, by no means went unnoticed. When Napoléon's war in Europe spilled over into the Atlantic, America was again caught in the cross fire between France and Britain. Great Britain had forbade all neutral vessels from trading with France; France reacted by threatening to seize all foreign ships that cooperated with the British navy.

In the summer of 1807, events took an ugly turn when Britain stepped up the impressment of American sailors. In response, Jefferson urged Congress to pass the **Embargo Act** of 1807, which stopped shipments of food and other American products to all foreign ports. But public pressure from American merchants, farmers, and workers led Congress to repeal the embargo in 1809.

Problems abroad were compounded by events at home. Rapid westward expansion fueled tensions between settlers and Indians, who continued to look to Britain for assistance. Westerners were particularly alarmed by the activities of the Shawnee leader Tecumseh.

BIO GRAPHY Settlers had a tireless and resourceful opponent in Tecumseh (1768–1813). When whites killed his father, Tecumseh was adopted by the Shawnee chief Blackfish. As he grew older, Tecumseh became convinced that Native Americans' best hope for survival rested in a military alliance among the Indian nations.

In the early 1800s Tecumseh set out to rally the Indian nations east of the Mississippi River. From the Great Lakes to the Gulf of Mexico, Tecumseh urged Native

Tecumseh

Americans not to sell land to the settlers. As Tecumseh gained support, settlers pressured the government to take action. In the fall of 1811, General William Henry Harrison decided to move against Tecumseh's stronghold on the Tippecanoe River in Indiana Territory. The **Battle of Tippecanoe** ended in defeat for Native Americans, shattering Tecumseh's dream of a united confederation. Two years later, he was killed in battle.

The British had supplied Tecumseh's forces with weapons. Thus, the clamor for war against Britain again arose in Congress. James Madison, who had succeeded Jefferson as president in 1809, asked for a declaration of war. In his message to Congress on June 1, 1812, Madison cited Britain's repeated violations of neutral rights, continued impressment of American sailors, and support of American Indian uprisings on the frontier as reasons for the declaration. After some debate, Congress voted to declare war.

▪▪ **Frustration over violations of neutral rights, impressment of U.S. sailors, and British support of Native Americans led to war.**

RETEACH Write each Focus question from p. 61 on a separate sheet of butcher paper. Organize students into four groups and give each group one of the sheets. Have groups create a chart that answers its assigned question. Have each group present its chart and ask other groups if they wish to make additions. Post completed charts on the bulletin board.

Closure

Have students outline what events in the section support the section's heading *A Strong Start for the Nation.*

Extension

EVALUATE Have students find and read Washington's Farewell Address and write an essay explaining what his reaction might be to U.S. foreign policies today.

RESEARCH Have students research and report on a major event in the War of 1812 (a naval battle, the burning of Washington, the Battle of New Orleans). Encourage use of graphics, such as maps.

American war strategy focused on the conquest of Canada. With the British preoccupied by their struggle to stop Napoléon, Americans were confident of a quick victory. But repeated attempts to invade Canada failed. The United States did, however, enjoy early successes at sea. In the first eight months of the war, U.S. frigates won many victories against British warships, and American privateers disrupted British commerce. Encouraged by the naval victories, General Harrison crossed into Canada with some 4,500 troops and defeated the British and their American Indian allies. The British hold on the Northwest Territory was finally broken.

The second phase of the war took a different turn. Soon after ending its war against France early in 1814, Great Britain sent some 14,000 reinforcements to Canada. British strategists planned to invade the United States from the north through Canada and from the south through New Orleans. They would also continue to raid the Atlantic coast to disrupt American commerce.

On the night of August 24, 1814, British forces struck Washington, D.C. Within a day they had captured the city, burning the executive mansion and other public buildings before moving on. The next target for a coastal assault was the city of Baltimore, where British vessels bombarded Fort McHenry. The fort's brave stand—immortalized in Francis Scott Key's poem "The Star-Spangled Banner"—was a setback for the British.

Great Britain then assembled about 7,500 troops to strike at New Orleans. General Andrew

▲ British troops were defeated as they attacked the line of earthworks built for the defense of New Orleans. Painted by H. Charles McBarron, Andrew Jackson is shown here mounted on a horse.

Jackson, a ruthless Indian-fighter and commander of a frontier militia, led the American forces in defense. When the invasion finally came on January 8, 1815, well-protected U.S. troops easily won the **Battle of New Orleans**. Few Americans were killed, but British casualties topped 2,000.

Tragically, the fighting at New Orleans came after peace negotiations had produced the **Treaty of Ghent**, signed on Christmas Eve, 1814. The treaty consolidated American control over the Northwest Territory through the defeat of American Indians and the removal of their British allies. In addition, it resulted in a peace between the United States and Great Britain that marked the beginning of a long partnership.

SECTION 3 REVIEW

IDENTIFY and explain the significance of the following: Bill of Rights, Judiciary Act, Whiskey Rebellion, national bank, strict construction, loose construction, Jay's Treaty, Pinckney's Treaty, sectionalism, Alien and Sedition Acts, Kentucky and Virginia Resolutions, *Marbury v. Madison*, judicial review, Twelfth Amendment, Trans-Appalachian West, Sacagawea, Embargo Act, Battle of Tippecanoe, Battle of New Orleans, Treaty of Ghent.

1. **MAIN IDEA** What actions did Congress take to establish the federal government and to strengthen the nation's finances?
2. **MAIN IDEA** How did conflicts in Europe cause political tension among Americans in the 1790s?
3. **ASSESSING CONSEQUENCES** What consequences did the Louisiana Purchase have for the United States?
4. **WRITING TO EXPLAIN** Write a paragraph explaining the causes of the War of 1812.
5. **ANALYZING** Imagine you are Tecumseh. Why do you believe Native Americans should form a confederation?

SECTION REVIEW ANSWERS

IDENTIFY

For significance, see the following pages:
Bill of Rights (p. 61)
Judiciary Act (p. 61)
Whiskey Rebellion (p. 62)
national bank (p. 62)
strict construction (p. 62)
loose construction (p. 62)
Jay's Treaty (p. 63)
Pinckney's Treaty (p. 63)
sectionalism (p. 63)
Alien and Sedition Acts (p. 64)
Kentucky and Virginia Resolutions (p. 64)
Marbury v. Madison (p. 64)
judicial review (p. 64)
Twelfth Amendment (p. 65)
Trans-Appalachian West (p. 65)
Sacagawea (p. 65)
Embargo Act (p. 66)
Battle of Tippecanoe (p. 66)
Battle of New Orleans (p. 67)
Treaty of Ghent (p. 67)

1. *passed Bill of Rights, set up federal courts, formed executive departments, created national bank*
2. *U.S. trade disrupted, events threatened to draw U.S. into war, impressment caused resentment*
3. *doubled size of U.S., increased U.S. stature, enhanced national identity, threatened Native American lands, allowed slavery to expand*
4. *Paragraphs should mention frustration over violations of neutrality, impressment of U.S. sailors, and British support of Native Americans.*
5. *because Native American alliance is best hope*

Chapter Review Answers

WRITING A SUMMARY

See Essential Points in each section for main ideas.

REVIEWING CHRONOLOGY

2, 5, 1, 4, 3
Evaluating
Paragraphs will vary but should stress the significance of the event.

IDENTIFYING PEOPLE AND IDEAS

1. *colonist whose pamphlet, Common Sense, urged revolution*
2. *an American battlefield victory that was a turning point because it prompted a French military alliance with the Patriots*
3. *hit-and-run battle technique used by colonists*
4. *leader of farmers' revolt against high taxes and heavy debts*
5. *compromise in which a slave was counted as three-fifths of a person to determine state population*
6. *division of powers among three branches of federal government to prevent any one branch from becoming too powerful*
7. *constitutional interpretation that states government can do anything Constitution does not specifically forbid*
8. *required electors to vote*

for presidential and vice-presidential candidates on separate ballots
9. Shoshone woman who acted as guide and interpreter on Lewis and Clark expedition
10. treaty that ended War of 1812

UNDERSTANDING MAIN IDEAS

1. restrictions on westward expansion, taxation without representation
2. to proclaim freedom, to gain support for independence at home and abroad, to undermine loyalty to the British Crown, to list reasons for rebellious

actions, and to assert the right of citizens to overthrow unjust government
3. representation in Congress; slaves counted as three-fifths people; tariffs set only on imports; slave trade permitted until end of 1807
4. added Bill of Rights; created federal judiciary; established treasury, war, and state departments
5. wars in Europe; capture of U.S. ships; impressment of U.S. sailors; arming of Native Americans

CHAPTER 2
Review

Proclamation of 1763 issued.

Stamp Act enacted.

Boston Massacre occurs.

Intolerable Acts passed. First Continental Congress meets.

Articles of Confederation adopted.

Declaration of Independence issued.

1763 1765 1770 1775

WRITING A SUMMARY

Using the essential points of the chapter as a guide, write a summary of the chapter.

REVIEWING CHRONOLOGY

Number your paper 1 to 5. Study the time line above, and list the following events in the order in which they happened by writing the first next to 1, the second next to 2, and so on. Then complete the activity below.

1. U.S. Constitution ratified.
2. Intolerable Acts passed.
3. U.S. completes Louisiana Purchase.
4. Bill of Rights ratified.
5. Declaration of Independence issued.

Evaluating Select an event on the time line, and in a paragraph, state its significance in U.S. history.

IDENTIFYING PEOPLE AND IDEAS

Explain the historical significance of each of the following people or terms.

1. Thomas Paine
2. Battle of Saratoga
3. guerrilla warfare
4. Daniel Shays
5. Three-Fifths Compromise
6. separation of powers
7. loose construction
8. Twelfth Amendment
9. Sacagawea
10. Treaty of Ghent

UNDERSTANDING MAIN IDEAS

1. What were the main reasons the colonists protested British actions?
2. Why did the Second Continental Congress issue the Declaration of Independence?
3. What were the main compromises reached during the Constitutional Convention?
4. What steps were taken by the First Congress to organize the federal government?
5. What events pushed the United States toward war with Great Britain in the early 1800s?

⭐ REVIEWING THEMES

1. **Economic Development** How did British attempts to raise revenues in the colonies conflict with colonial interests?

2. **Constitutional Heritage** How does the way the government was organized reflect concern about a powerful national government?
3. **Democratic Values** Why did two political parties form in the 1790s? How did the two parties differ?

THINKING CRITICALLY

1. **Evaluating** Some historians claim that wise leaders could have resolved the differences between Great Britain and the colonies before 1775. Do you agree? Explain.
2. **Identifying Cause and Effect** How did the experience of governing the nation under the Articles of Confederation influence the actions of the framers of the Constitution?
3. **Gaining a Multicultural Perspective** Why did Native Americans resist settlers moving west?

STRATEGY FOR SUCCESS

Review the Skills Handbook entry on Reviewing Map Basics beginning on page 752. Then number your paper 1 to 13. Study the map below, noting the numbers on it. It illustrates the states, either in full or in part, that were formed from the Louisiana Purchase. Write the name of the state next to the corresponding number.

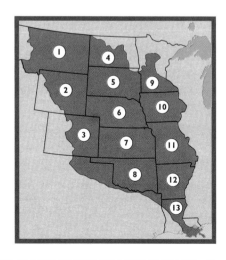

REVIEWING THEMES

1. British revenue measures cut into colonial profits from trade and smuggling; colonists objected to being taxed by Parliament, where they had no representation.
2. Responsibilities were shared between the federal government and states, each with defined powers.
3. Sectionalism helped to create the two political parties—the Federalists and the Democratic-Republicans. Federalists favored a strong central government. Democratic-Republicans wanted to protect states' rights and individual liberties by limiting federal government.

THINKING CRITICALLY

1. Students should consider how leaders could have balanced the Crown's need for revenue against the colonists' desire for self-government.
2. Because of the weaknesses of the Articles, the framers of the Constitution wanted to create a strong central government while still protecting states' rights.
3. fought disruption of Indian way of life and destruction of natural resources

British surrender at Yorktown. States officially become "The United States of America."

Treaty of Paris signed.

Constitutional Convention meets.

U.S. Constitution ratified.

Washington inaugurated.

Bill of Rights ratified.

Alien and Sedition Acts passed.

U.S. completes Louisiana Purchase.

War declared against Great Britain.

Treaty of Ghent signed.

1781   1785   1790   1800   1814

WRITING ABOUT HISTORY

Writing to Persuade Imagine you are a business owner in New England who supports the Constitution. Write a letter to the editor of your local newspaper, explaining why you support the new plan of government over the Articles of Confederation.

USING PRIMARY SOURCES

At first some Patriot leaders opposed enlisting African Americans in the fight for freedom. However, when soldiers were needed for the southern campaign, Washington's aide, Alexander Hamilton, suggested recruiting African Americans. Read the following excerpt from a letter by Hamilton, in which he outlines his plan. Then write a summary of the points outlined in the letter.

> *Head Quarters March 14th 79*
> *Dear Sir:*
>
> *Colonel Laurens, who will have the honor of delivering you this letter, is on his way to South Carolina, on a project . . . to raise two, three, or four battalions of Negroes . . . by contributions from owners in proportion to the number they possess. . . .*
>
> *I have not the least doubt that the Negroes will make very excellent soldiers, with proper management. . . .*
>
> *I foresee that this project will have to combat much opposition from prejudice and self-interest. The contempt we have been taught to entertain for the blacks makes us fancy many things that are founded neither in reason nor experience. . . . An essential part of the plan is to give them their freedom with their muskets. This will secure their fidelity, animate their courage, and I believe will have a good influence upon those who remain, by opening a door to their emancipation [freedom]. . . .*
>
> *—Alexander Hamilton*

LINKING HISTORY AND GEOGRAPHY

British forces fought the Revolutionary War in physical settings that were often unfamiliar to them. Study the map on page 34. Select one of the battles or campaigns included on the map and indicate how geography might have helped or hurt British efforts.

Struggle at Concord Bridge

BUILDING YOUR PORTFOLIO

Complete the following projects independently or cooperatively.

1. **CONFLICT** Imagine you are a public official assigned to oversee the American war effort either in the Revolutionary War or in the War of 1812. Create a chart showing how you will recruit and train troops, coordinate and transport supplies, communicate with field commanders, and achieve whatever else might be necessary to maintain an effective military force and strategy.

2. **INDIVIDUAL RIGHTS** Imagine you are the editor of a colonial newspaper. Write an editorial arguing for the expansion of colonists' rights under British rule. Your editorial should list specific grievances and should explain how an expansion of rights would address these grievances.

GROWTH AND CHANGE

1815–1860

Chapter Overview

In the years after the War of 1812, the United States experienced tremendous change as the economy grew and Americans sought greater opportunities and an increase of democracy. But growth did not affect all sections in the same way. In the North and the Middle West, commerce and industry brought major social change. The South, however, remained largely agrarian, and the economy depended heavily on slavery. The expansion of slavery quickly became a major political issue as settlers pushed westward and brought new territories into the Union. During the 1840s and 1850s, slavery and other sectional issues drove the North and the South farther apart. Only a series of political compromises kept the Union intact.

Chapter Planning Guide

CHAPTER 3	CORE RESOURCES	AUDIOVISUAL AV RESOURCES	PROGRAM RESOURCES
INTRODUCTION pp. 70–71	■ Building Your Portfolio Worksheet 1		
TEACHING THE CHAPTER pp. 72–91 ■ For expanded coverage of p. 82, see Chapter 26.	■ Graphic Organizer 3 ■ Social Studies Skills Worksheet 3 ■ Literature Worksheet 3 ■ Geography Worksheet 3 ■ Outline Maps 1, 2, 9, 10, 11, 12, 13, 14, 19	■ *The American Nation* Videodisc: Free at Last; The Reform Movement; Community Ties: San Francisco's Chinatown ■ Linking Geography and History Transparencies and Worksheets 10, 11, 12, 13 ■ Everyday Life in America Transparencies and Worksheets 7, 8, 9	■ *Eyewitnesses and Others,* Volume 1: Readings 41–77 ■ Art in American History Transparencies and Worksheets 7, 8, 9, 10, 11, 12
REVIEW AND ASSESSMENT pp. 92–93	■ Chapter 3 Daily Quizzes ■ Reteaching Worksheet 3 ■ Chapter 3 Tests ■ Alternative Assessment Forms		■ Test Generator

Additional Resources

BOOKS FOR TEACHERS

Brown, Dee. *Wondrous Times on the Frontier.* HarperCollins, 1992. Describes life on the frontier.

Oakes, James. *Slavery and Freedom.* Knopf, 1990. Analysis of slavery, capitalism, and the American ideal of freedom.

Remini, Robert V. *Andrew Jackson and the Course of American Democracy.* Harper & Row, 1984. Three-volume study by Jackson's foremost contemporary biographer.

BOOKS FOR STUDENTS

Hindle, Brooke, and Steven Lubar. *Engines of Change: The American Industrial Revolution, 1790–1860.* Smithsonian, 1986. Pictorial history of U.S. Industrial Revolution.

*Van Steenwyk, Elizabeth. *California Gold Rush: West with the Forty-Niners.* Watts, 1991. Account of the gold rush in California.

White, Deborah Gray. *Ar'n't I a Woman?* Norton, 1987. In-depth study of slave women by a historian who specializes in African studies.

* for students reading below grade level

MULTIMEDIA MATERIALS

As the Wind Rocks the Wagon: An American Odyssey. Video, 52 min. APL Educational Video/SSSS. Diaries and memoirs of pioneer women traveling the Oregon Trail.

Erie Canal. Video, 21 min. Phoenix/SSSS. Period music and historical illustrations tell history of Erie Canal.

Slavery: America's Peculiar Institution. Video, 32 min. Zenger. Two-part program traces origins of slavery and describes slavery in the U.S.

USE WITH PAGES 70–71

Listed on the right are the themes emphasized in Chapter 3. The questions in boldface type stimulate critical thinking and provide students with an opportunity to discuss the themes within a broadened context. The questions also appear in the pupil's edition on p. 70.

■ ECONOMIC DEVELOPMENT

What are some of the factors that might influence a region's economic development? Students might mention natural resources, climate, geography, population size, ease of transportation, and the balance between urban and rural areas as factors that could affect a region's economic development.

Why might regions within a large country develop different economies? Students might suggest that variations in factors that influence economic development could explain development of distinct regional economies in a large country.

■ DEMOCRATIC VALUES

How might people who feel left out of the democratic process bring about change in a society? Students might suggest that people could take their grievances to the courts, call on government to make changes, or take violent action to win changes.

■ GLOBAL RELATIONS

How might territorial expansion lead to international as well as domestic conflicts? Students might mention that not all people may support expansion. Some people might object to expanding at another country's expense. Others might disagree over how new territory should be governed. Students should also consider that international disputes may arise when one country seizes territory from another.

CHAPTER STRATEGIES FOR MEETING INDIVIDUAL NEEDS

LIMITED ENGLISH PROFICIENT LEARNERS

As the class studies the chapter, have students work in small groups to create a collage showing the major changes in the U.S. from 1815 to 1860. Groups should present their collages, explaining each image.

TACTILE/KINESTHETIC LEARNERS

Have students work in groups and write on index cards each of the terms in Identify in the Section Review. Have students take turns "acting out" the cards by using drawings or gestures. Other members of the group should identify what is on each card.

LEARNERS HAVING DIFFICULTY

Have students create three concept webs: one with "Nationalism and Economic Power" in the center, one with "Separate Societies: North and South" in the center, and one with "Expansion and Conflict" in the center. Ask students to identify the main ideas of each section by placing them in strands at the end of the correct web.

AUDITORY LEARNERS

Organize students into small groups and assign each group a prominent person discussed in the chapter. Have each group prepare and present a speech by its subject, stating his or her view of the chapter's events.

VISUAL LEARNERS

After they have read the chapter, have students work in groups to prepare illustrated time lines showing major events in the chapter. Ask students to prepare a caption for each event.

GIFTED LEARNERS

Have students hold a panel discussion on how the major developments that took place between 1815 and 1860 contributed to conflict between the North and the South. Panel members should field questions from the class.

USING THE CHAPTER FOCUS

■ UNDERSTANDING THE MAIN IDEA

Tell students that the expansion of slavery fueled political debate between free states and slave states in the halls of government and throughout the nation. In 1858 Abraham Lincoln said, "[This nation] will become all one thing, or all the other." Ask students to discuss what Lincoln meant.

THEMES

Have students work individually or in groups to answer the questions under Themes. Save students' responses so that they can compare them with their responses after studying the chapter. (See p. 69B for suggested answers.)

■ THE TIME LINE

Ask students to recall how earlier expansion of the U.S. affected Native Americans. *(It led to battles between white settlers and Native Americans, and many Native Americans were pushed from their lands.)* Ask students to look at the time line and speculate about the U.S. policy toward Native Americans in the mid-1800s. *(The Indian Removal Act of 1830 indicates that the policy was to continue to push the Native Americans from their lands.)*

CORE RESOURCES

• Graphic Organizer 3
• Building Your Portfolio Worksheet 1

70

ABOUT THE ILLUSTRATION

By the 1820s many states had removed restrictions on suffrage and allowed all white males to vote. Ask students how this fact is reflected in the painting on these two pages. Tell students that George Caleb Bingham is known for his paintings that depict scenes from everyday life on the frontier. His paintings of election scenes are keen studies of town life in the mid-1800s. Ask volunteers to characterize the general mood of the people in this painting. Then ask if they note anything missing from the scene *(women)* and if so, why. *(Women were not part of the election process at this time.)*

Chapter 3

1815–1860

GROWTH AND CHANGE

FOCUS

UNDERSTANDING THE MAIN IDEA

After the War of 1812, the United States entered a period of growth. As its territory expanded and new transportation systems linked different regions of the country, the economy grew and national markets were established for the first time. Politics became more democratic in the 19th century. But growth also led to new tensions, especially over slavery.

THEMES

■ **ECONOMIC DEVELOPMENT** What are some of the factors that might influence a region's economic development? Why might regions within a large country develop different economies?

■ **DEMOCRATIC VALUES** How might people who feel left out of the democratic process bring about change in a society?

■ **GLOBAL RELATIONS** How might territorial expansion lead to international as well as domestic conflicts?

1820	1830	1836	1848	1857
Missouri Compromise passed.	Indian Removal Act passed.	Texas declares independence from Mexico.	Seneca Falls Convention held.	*Dred Scott* case decided.

:: LINK TO THE PAST

The War of 1812, although producing no clear-cut victory for the United States, proved that the country could stand up to a major European power. Americans began to believe that the United States could become a power in its own right, free from Europe's influence and control.

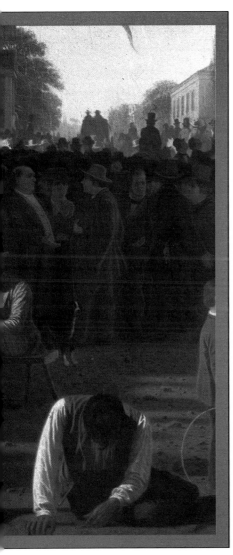

Verdict of the People (1855) by George Caleb Bingham

𝒢n 1828 Fanny Wright, a world traveler, social reformer, and sometime U.S. resident, delivered a Fourth of July speech at New Harmony, Indiana. She praised the United States as the protector of "human liberty [and] the favored scene of human improvement." Soon, she predicted, "all mankind" would celebrate "the Jubilee of Independence."

The United States was far from granting liberty to all in 1828, as Native Americans and enslaved African Americans well knew. Yet the national pride and optimism expressed in Wright's speech were widespread. One British visitor noted that American national pride "blazes out everywhere and on all occasions."

The new confidence that burst forth in this era took many forms. The United States built new roads and canals, developed new industries, launched a period of economic growth, secured its borders, and warned Europe to stay out of Latin America. American optimism also fostered a renewal of religious faith and led to a variety of reform movements. The expansionist ambitions of some Americans were boundless as they envisioned a continental empire.

But growth, expansion, and reform also produced new tensions, especially between the increasingly separate societies of the North and the South. By midcentury slavery cast an ever-lengthening shadow over the future of the nation.

Fanny Wright

MULTICULTURAL PERSPECTIVES

Frederick Douglass, an escaped slave and prominent abolitionist, articulated the feelings of many African Americans in the mid-1800s about Independence Day and the spirit of democracy: "What, to the American slave, is your 4th of July? I answer; a day that reveals to him, more than all other days in the year, the gross injustice and cruelty to which he is the constant victim. To him, your celebration is a sham; . . . your sounds of rejoicing are empty and heartless; . . . your shouts of liberty and equality, hollow mockery."

SECTION 1

Introducing the Section

FOCUS OBJECTIVES

■ Describe the steps taken by the U.S. after the War of 1812 to secure its place in the world and to develop its economy.

■ Explain how sectional tensions between the North and the South were eased in the 1820s and 1830s.

■ Identify some of the effects of Andrew Jackson's policies.

MAKING CONNECTIONS

Economics
By mid-1814 the war with Britain had drained the U.S. Treasury. Since Congress had refused to recharter the national bank in 1811, the Treasury had to rely on scores of state banks for loans. Many of these banks were unstable. One such bank in Ohio was known as the Saddlebag because its backer reputedly had carried all its capital resources in his saddlebags.

CORE RESOURCES

• **Social Studies Skills Worksheet 3**
• **Section 1 Daily Quiz**

AV RESOURCES

• **Linking Geography and History Transparencies and Worksheets 10, 11**
• **Everyday Life in America Transparency and Worksheet 7**

Section 1

NATIONALISM AND ECONOMIC POWER

F O C U S

■ **After the War of 1812 what steps did the United States take to secure its place in the world and to develop its economy?**

■ **How were sectional tensions between the North and the South eased in the 1820s and 1830s?**

■ **What were some of the effects of Andrew Jackson's policies?**

The War of 1812 filled Americans with national pride and sparked the growth of the domestic economy. Soon, a new spirit of democracy swept the nation, as symbolized by "the man of the people," Andrew Jackson. But sectional tension and economic downturns eroded his party's strength.

Flag of the United States, 1818

The Granger Collection, New York

THE RISE OF NATIONALISM

The United States emerged from the War of 1812 with a new sense of **nationalism**, or national pride and loyalty. In addition, the war's end ushered in a period of political harmony known as the Era of Good Feelings. The newfound harmony was largely due to the collapse of the Federalist party, which had angered many Americans by opposing the war.

The young nation had successfully stood up to Great Britain, and now the new president, James Monroe, moved to secure the nation's borders. An agreement with Great Britain set much of the U.S.–Canadian border. The United States and Great Britain also agreed to occupy **Oregon Country**— the disputed area of the Pacific Northwest—jointly for 10 years, with a boundary to be set later. An agreement with Spain set the southern and western boundaries of the Louisiana Purchase and transferred Florida to the United States.

American foreign policy interests did not stop at the nation's borders. American officials were worried about reports that France was prepared to help Spain retake the newly independent countries of Latin America. In 1823, in what came to be called the **Monroe Doctrine**, the president declared that the United States would consider any European attempt to revive old colonies or establish new ones in the Western Hemisphere "as dangerous to our peace and safety."

■■ **The United States secured its borders and declared the Americas off-limits to European colonization.**

PROMOTING ECONOMIC GROWTH

Americans were looking inward as well as outward after the War of 1812. While the war had given U.S. manufacturing a boost, it had also revealed weaknesses in the nation's financial system. Furthermore, the difficulty and expense of moving goods and troops during the war had underscored the nation's transportation problems. By 1815 many people were calling for national measures to improve these systems.

Henry Clay, a congressman from Kentucky, came up with a program of federal support for

Teaching the Section

FOREIGN POLICY, ECONOMIC GROWTH

Divide the class into small groups. Have some groups write newspaper headlines on how the Monroe Doctrine affected America's standing in the world. Have other groups write newspaper headlines about how the American System, technological developments, the market revolu-

tion, and the Industrial Revolution contributed to the country's economic growth. Have groups present their headlines while the class fills in details of stories that might appear under each headline.

▶

economic development. Clay's program, known as the **American System**, had three main features. The first was the re-creation of a national bank to provide for a sound currency and greater federal control over the nation's financial system. (The previous national bank's charter had been allowed to expire in 1811.) Congress agreed and chartered the Second Bank of the United States in 1816.

The second feature of Clay's program—a protective tariff to encourage manufacturing—also met with Congress's approval. The **Tariff Act of 1816** put a 25 percent duty on most imported factory goods, making them more expensive than their U.S.-produced counterparts.

The third feature of the American System was a national transportation system to unite northern manufacturers, western farmers, and southern planters. This feature failed to be enacted into law, and states and private companies built most roads and canals. New York, for example, began building the Erie Canal in 1817. This 363-mile-long canal linked the Hudson River with Lake Erie, reducing the cost of moving goods between Buffalo and

New York City by more than 90 percent. The success of the Erie Canal spurred massive canal projects in other states. By 1840 rivers and canals combined to provide a waterway that stretched from Illinois to the Atlantic.

Technological advances also furthered the transportation revolution. The steam-powered locomotive came into commercial use in the 1830s. Between 1840 and 1850, railroads reached many isolated parts of the country as companies spent more than $200 million laying nearly 9,000 miles of track. By making it easier and cheaper to move goods long distances, new transportation systems created national markets for the first time. Regions no longer had to be relatively self-sufficient; they could import some goods and produce what was most profitable.

This creation of national markets has come to be known as the **market revolution**. The market revolution both increased profits and changed the way farmers and manufacturers did business. Before the market revolution, for example, entire families worked most northern farms. They grew

U.S. Boundaries, 1820

SECURING U.S. BORDERS The Convention of 1818 and the Adams-Onís Treaty settled major U.S. boundary disputes with Great Britain and Spain.

? **ABSOLUTE LOCATION** About how many miles was the permanent boundary agreed upon by the Convention of 1818? What was its absolute location?

Albers Equal-Area Projection

Claimed by U.S., ceded to Great Britain in 1818

British Territory

Lake of the Woods

49° N

Disputed

PACIFIC OCEAN

ROCKY MOUNTAINS

49th Parallel

Oregon Country

Great Lakes

Michigan Territory

Mississippi R.

0 225 450 Miles
0 225 450 Kilometers

ME

VT NH
NY MA
CT RI

42° N

40° N

42nd Parallel

Unorganized Territory

PA

NJ

OH

IL IN

MD DE

The United States and Great Britain jointly occupied Oregon Country until 1846, long past the 10 years called for by the Convention of 1818.

Spanish Territory

Arkansas R.

Missouri Territory

KY

APPALACHIAN MOUNTAINS

VA

NC

ATLANTIC OCEAN

70° W

120° W

Red River

Arkansas Territory

TN

SC

Sabine R.

MS AL GA

LA

By the terms of the Adams-Onís Treaty, Spain ceded East Florida to the United States and gave up all claims to West Florida.

Unorganized Territory

Gulf of Mexico

90° W 80° W

Convention of 1818
Adams-Onís Treaty of 1819
Louisiana Purchase
Florida Cession
British Cession of 1818

Teaching the Section

THE RISE OF SECTIONAL TENSIONS

Organize students into pairs. Have members of half the pairs take the role of either a free-state representative or a slave-state representative to debate whether Missouri should be admitted to the union as a free state or a slave state. Have members of the other pairs take the role of either a northern business leader or a southern planter to debate the protective tariff of 1828. Call on pairs to hold their debates for the class. Then lead the class in a discussion of how these issues contributed to sectional tensions and how well the Missouri Compromise and the Tariff of 1833 eased these tensions.

JACKSON'S POLICIES

Draw a three-column chart on the chalkboard with these headings: *Policies, Effectiveness, Effects on the Nation.* Write students' responses in the appropriate columns. Then have students use information in the chart to write a pamphlet that either attacks or defends one of Jackson's policies. Suggest that they cite the policy's effectiveness and its long-term impact on the nation to support their arguments. Students may wish to include their pamphlets in their portfolios.

HISTORICAL SIDELIGHTS

The Missouri Compromise

Although the Missouri Compromise called for the admission of both Missouri and Maine, only Maine immediately became a state. Missouri's admission was delayed 17 months, until it had an acceptable state constitution. At first, a provision prohibited free blacks from entering Missouri. Not until the Missouri legislature agreed to respect the rights of all citizens did Missouri become the 24th state, in August 1821.

MAKING CONNECTIONS

Geography

Passage of the Missouri Compromise restricted the options of slaveholders who wanted to live on the frontier. Only the Arkansas Territory remained open to slavery. Consequently, southerners became increasingly interested in moving beyond the borders of the Louisiana Purchase to settle in the Mexican territory called Texas.

their own food and sold their crops locally. After the market revolution northern farmers hired laborers to help produce large cash crops to sell in national and international markets.

The market revolution was tied to a change in manufacturing. The increasing demand for goods led manufacturers to divide tasks to speed up production and to invest in new machinery that increased output. This shift from hand to machine production was part of the **Industrial Revolution**, which began in Great Britain in the mid-1700s with the invention of new spinning machines. The machines revolutionized the textile industry by allowing for mass production—the manufacture of large quantities of goods.

In the United States, inventors made their own contributions to industrialization. Eli Whitney pioneered the use of interchangeable, machine-produced parts in the manufacture of firearms. Another innovation was Francis Cabot Lowell's factory system. Lowell cut costs and increased output by using machines—housed under one roof—to accomplish every step of the manufacturing process.

■■ **After the War of 1812, the transportation, market, and industrial revolutions promoted the nation's economic development.**

By 1818, largely due to the growth of national markets, all sections of the country prospered. Many people borrowed money to buy land or build factories. The state banks lent more money than they could back with **specie**, or gold and silver coin. The result was the **Panic of 1819**, a chain reaction of bank failures and foreclosures.

THE RISE OF SECTIONAL TENSIONS

The United States faced more than economic problems in 1819. The nation was also plagued by political conflict caused by westward expansion. In that year the Missouri Territory, which contained some 10,000 enslaved African Americans, was applying for statehood. Because the nation was equally divided between slave and free states, Missouri's entrance as a slave state would tip the congressional balance in favor of the South. An angry debate erupted.

To resolve the issue, Henry Clay led Congress in working out the **Missouri Compromise** in 1820. The agreement admitted Missouri as a slave state and Maine as a free state, thus maintaining the congressional balance. Moreover, slavery was banned in the rest of the Louisiana Purchase north of latitude 36°30'. The compromise calmed the sectional crisis, but many Americans worried that the slavery issue would reemerge.

The protective tariff was another issue dividing the nation. To protect U.S. manufacturers Congress passed a tariff in 1828 that doubled the 1816 rates for some items. Outraged southern planters, who feared that the British would retaliate by buying less southern cotton, accused Congress of favoring the industrial North. Outlining the South's position, then–Vice President John C. Calhoun argued that the states, as creators of the federal union, had the right to nullify, or refuse to obey, any act of Congress they considered unconstitutional. This view became known as the **doctrine of nullification**.

South Carolina, finding this doctrine useful, declared Congress's recent tariffs null and void and threatened to secede if the federal government tried to collect the tariffs within the state. Again Clay arranged a compromise, convincing Congress to pass a tariff in 1833 that lowered rates over a 10-year period. The crisis subsided, but sectional tensions continued to grow.

■■ **The Missouri Compromise and the 1833 tariff settled immediate conflicts between the North and the South but left fundamental differences unresolved.**

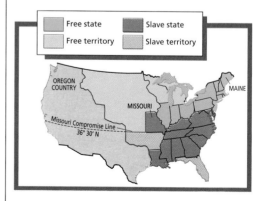

| | Free state | | Slave state |
| Free territory | | Slave territory |

▲ **The Missouri Compromise**

Practice

GUIDED PRACTICE

Draw a line down the center of the chalk-board. On one side of the line write *Panic of 1819;* on the other write *Panic of 1837.* Discuss with students the events surrounding these two economic crises. Then call on pairs of volunteers to come to the board and draw flowcharts of the causes and effects of the two panics.

INDEPENDENT PRACTICE

Have students use the Guided Practice flowcharts to create political cartoons illustrating the causes and effects of the Panic of 1819 or the Panic of 1837. Call on students to display and explain their completed cartoons. Students may wish to include their cartoons in their portfolios.

Review and Assessment

REVIEW Have students imagine that they are living in the mid-1800s. Ask them to work in pairs and interview each other about why they feel optimistic or pessimistic about the nation's future. Then assign the Section 1 Review on p. 76.

ASSESS Assign the **Section 1 Daily Quiz** in *Core Resources.* ▶

THE JACKSONIAN ERA

Presiding over the nullification crisis was Tennessean Andrew Jackson. Known as "Old Hickory" because of his toughness, Jackson portrayed himself as a "man of the people." Defeated by John Quincy Adams in the controversial election of 1824, Jackson had won the presidency in 1828 by a wide margin.

Jackson owed his victory in part to more democratic voting laws, particularly in the frontier states. His image as a "common man" won the support of farmers, laborers, and frontier settlers. "The virtuous portion of the people have well sustained me," Jackson rejoiced. "I am filled with gratitude."

Jackson's supporters eventually became known as the Democratic party (the origin of today's party of the same name). Once in office, Jackson rewarded some of his supporters by giving them government jobs. This practice became known as the **spoils system.**

Jackson's Indian policy. Andrew Jackson put his stamp on a decade, and his policies shaped the nation for years. Some of his most important policies involved the Native Americans occupying millions of acres of fertile land in the Southeast that white farmers and land speculators wanted. Jackson, who viewed the continued presence of American Indians in the East as a barrier to "the waves of population and civilization . . . rolling westward," agreed that the Indian lands should be opened for white settlement.

Jackson cloaked his calls for removal in humanitarian terms, claiming that Indians would be moved west for their own protection. In 1830 Congress passed the **Indian Removal Act**, providing for the relocation—by force, if need be—of tribes living east of the Mississippi to Indian Territory in present-day Oklahoma (see map on page 86). Jackson promised eastern Indians the land for "as long as the grass grows, or the water runs."

By 1840, most Native Americans—among them Creeks, Chickasaws, Choctaws, Cherokees, and Seminoles—had been driven from the Southeast. Few, however, went willingly. Some appealed to Congress in the name of "liberty and justice." Others hoped the judicial system would support their cause. When Georgia seized Cherokee land to sell to white settlers, the Cherokees went to the Supreme Court. Although

▲ *The Intruders* (1966) by Native American artist Jerome Tiger portrays the Florida home of the Seminoles.

National Museum of the American Indian

the Court ruled in their favor, Jackson would not enforce the ruling, and Georgia kept on taking Cherokee land. Unable to hold out, the Cherokees were forced to move to Indian Territory in 1838. Some 4,000 Cherokees died on the 800-mile trek that came to be known as the **Trail of Tears**.

Other Indians, like the Seminole leader Osceola, urged outright resistance to removal:

f My Brothers! . . . the white man says I shall go, and he will send people to make me go; but I have a rifle, and I have some powder and some lead. I say, we must not leave our homes and lands. 99

In Florida, resistance to removal led to the **Second Seminole War** (1835–1842), which was one of the most costly Indian wars in U.S. history. Although the Seminoles fought bravely, most were eventually killed or removed to Indian Territory.

■■ **In order to open land to white settlement, Jackson and the U.S. government forced most eastern Indians to move west.**

The Panic of 1837. Indian removal remains one of the Jacksonian era's most controversial legacies. Yet for many Americans at the time, other economic issues—particularly regarding the Second Bank of the United States—seemed more important. Making the banking issue a personal crusade, Jackson attacked the Bank as a dangerous monopoly that benefited rich investors at the public's expense. To shut down the Bank, Jackson stopped depositing federal funds in it. New deposits went to state banks

MULTICULTURAL PERSPECTIVES

Seminole resistance to the Indian Removal Act was encouraged by the African Americans who lived among them. Believing the Seminoles to be a branch of the Creek nation, the U.S. government long had forced the Creeks to compensate planters for escaped slaves who sought refuge with the Seminoles. (For decades runaway slaves had crossed the Georgia-Florida border and settled near or in Seminole communities.) Because the government planned for the Seminoles and Creeks to live together in Indian territory, the African Americans in the area feared that the Creeks would seize them. Many former slaves, who had influence with Seminole leaders, were understandably reluctant to leave Florida.

PRIMARY SOURCE

Description of Change: excerpted
Rationale: excerpted to focus on main idea

RETEACH Have students work in groups, assigning pairs in each group the task of turning Section Review questions into statements by supplying answers. Ask pairs to share their work with the group.

Closure
Ask for examples from this section that support or contradict the following view expressed by Daniel Webster: "Our age is wholey [sic] of a different character from the past. Society is full of excitement."

Extension
RESEARCH Have students research and prepare a report on the Erie Canal, focusing on its location, dimensions, and purpose. Students might include a diagram or model with their report.

ANALYZE Have students research and report on the current situation of a Native American group affected by Indian removal in the 1830s. Encourage use of statistics, graphs, maps, and primary sources.

SECTION REVIEW ANSWERS

IDENTIFY
For significance, see the following pages:
nationalism (p. 72)
Tariff Act of 1816 (p. 73)
American System (p. 73)
market revolution (p. 73)
Industrial Revolution (p. 74)
specie (p. 74)
Missouri Compromise (p. 74)
doctrine of nullification (p. 74)
spoils system (p. 75)
Indian Removal Act (p. 75)
Osceola (p. 75)
Second Seminole War (p. 75)
pet banks (p. 76)

LOCATE
For locations, see the maps on pp. 73 and 74.

1. *transportation—made shipment of goods cheaper and easier; market— national markets allowed regions to specialize*
2. *1819—banks made loans they could not back with specie; 1837—Jackson's crusade against national bank, pet banks, bank failures*
3. *Missouri, as slave state, threatened balance in Congress; 1828 tariff hurt southern economy, leading to doctrine of nullification and secession threats. Through the Missouri Compromise and the compromise tariff of 1833.*
4. *Editorials might suggest that the U.S. had become a major world power.*
5. *Selections might express fear, anger, or sadness.*

PRESIDENTIAL LIVES

JAMES MONROE
1758–1831

in office 1817–1825

JOHN QUINCY ADAMS
1767–1848

in office 1825–1829

ANDREW JACKSON
1767–1845

in office 1829–1837

MARTIN VAN BUREN
1782–1862

in office 1837–1841

WILLIAM HENRY HARRISON
1773–1841

in office 1841

JOHN TYLER
1790–1862

in office 1841–1845

---

chosen for their officers' loyalty to the Democratic party—**pet banks**, as Jackson's enemies called them.

Jackson won his bank war, but by weakening federal control over banking, he invited a financial crisis. His pet banks fueled inflation by issuing their own bank notes and making loans without enough specie to back them. To curb inflation, Jackson in 1836 ordered the Treasury to accept only gold and silver as payment for public land. Many people began demanding that their banks exchange bank notes for gold or silver. Unable to do this, hundreds of banks failed. Jackson left office before the inflationary bubble burst, leaving his successors—among them members of the new Whig party—to suffer the consequences of the country's mounting economic and sectional crises.

■■ **Jackson's monetary policies helped cause the economic crisis of the late 1830s.**

SECTION 1 REVIEW

IDENTIFY and explain the significance of the following: nationalism, Tariff Act of 1816, American System, market revolution, Industrial Revolution, specie, Missouri Compromise, doctrine of nullification, spoils system, Indian Removal Act, Osceola, Second Seminole War, pet banks.

LOCATE and explain the significance of the following: Oregon Country, Indian Territory.

1. **MAIN IDEA** How was the U.S. economy helped by the transportation and market revolutions?
2. **MAIN IDEA** What conditions led to the Panics of 1819 and 1837?
3. **MAIN IDEA** Why did Missouri's petition for statehood and Congress's 1828 tariff cause sectional tension? How were these conflicts resolved?
4. **WRITING TO EXPLAIN** Imagine you are the editor of a European newspaper in 1823. Write an editorial explaining the significance of the Monroe Doctrine.
5. **GAINING A MULTICULTURAL PERSPECTIVE** Imagine you are a Cherokee on the Trail of Tears. Write a poem or diary entry explaining your feelings at being forced to leave your home.

Chapter 3

SECTION 2

Introducing the Section

PREVIEW WORKSHOP

Following is a list of the significant people and terms in this section. You may wish to use this list as a section preview.

People
- Harriet Tubman
- Horace Mann
- Frederick Douglass

Terms
- middle class
- strike
- nativism
- yeoman farmers
- cotton gin
- overseers
- drivers
- Underground Railroad
- spirituals
- Second Great Awakening
- utopias
- rehabilitation
- temperance movement
- prohibition
- American Anti-Slavery Society
- Seneca Falls Convention
- suffrage

Section 2

SEPARATE SOCIETIES: NORTH AND SOUTH

FOCUS
- **How did the market and industrial revolutions affect life in the North?**
- **Why did the demand for slaves increase in the South? How did slave laborers attempt to shape their lives?**
- **What ideas and movements did reformers support in the first half of the 19th century?**

The market and industrial revolutions changed northern and southern societies. In the North, new social divisions and new ways of working emerged. In the South, the dominance of cotton strengthened the slave-based social order. Throughout the nation, some changes in society alarmed Americans and inspired them to launch a variety of reform movements.

Carrying cotton from southern fields

FOCUS OBJECTIVES
- Explain how the market and industrial revolutions affected life in the North.
- Analyze why the demand for slaves increased in the South. Explain how slave laborers attempted to shape their lives.
- Identify ideas and movements reformers supported in the first half of the 19th century.

HISTORICAL SIDELIGHTS
Lowell Mill Workers
Female textile workers in Lowell, Massachusetts, lived in closely supervised, company-owned boarding-houses. Mill owners organized cultural activities and required them to attend church. Housekeepers enforced curfews, banned alcohol, and reported on the workers' behavior.

CORE RESOURCES
- **Literature Worksheet 3**
- **Section 2 Daily Quiz**

AV RESOURCES
- **The American Nation Videodisc: Free at Last; The Reform Movement**
- **Linking Geography and History Transparency** and **Worksheet 12**
- **Everyday Life in America Transparencies** and **Worksheets 8, 9**

NORTHERN SOCIETY

The market and industrial revolutions profoundly affected the North. New social divisions arose as a wide gap opened between the rich—merchants, bankers, and manufacturers who lived in huge, lavish homes—and the poor, who crowded into small apartments with few conveniences. And between the wealthy and the poor arose a new social class— the **middle class**. Prosperous farmers, artisans, shopkeepers, ministers, lawyers, and their families made up the new middle class. Middle-class families lived in modest but comfortable homes and had the income to buy food, clothing, and other products made available by the market revolution.

Changing working conditions. The ways people worked also changed during the early 19th century. Previously, whole families had worked together at home or in mills. But as factories needing hundreds of employees sprang up, owners found it more practical to hire individuals instead of families.

In some places, such as the textile mills of Lowell, Massachusetts, young, single women became factory workers. These women were cheaper to hire than men, since they were not seen as having to support their families. Children, too, often worked in the mills. By 1832, two out of five New England factory workers were children. Supervisors often forced children to run machines late into the night and kept the children awake by splashing water in their faces.

Children were not the only ones who faced difficult working conditions, particularly as industrialization expanded. Owners—searching for larger profits—cut wages, sped up production, and increased working hours. As conditions worsened, workers organized more than 60 unions to fight for reforms, such as the 10-hour workday.

Labor unions used many methods to press for reforms. A common tactic was the **strike**—the refusal to work until employers meet union demands. During the 1830s, workers led more than 100 strikes, mostly to protest low wages or to avoid wage reductions. Workers' protests,

MOTIVATING: PRIOR KNOWLEDGE

Have students recall the developments that led to the market revolution. Then ask students to speculate on how the market revolution might change life in the northern and middle-western states. Have students review and adjust their speculations as they study this section.

Teaching the Section

DIFFERENCES AMONG SOCIAL CLASSES

Create a three-column chart on the chalkboard with the headings *The Rich, The Middle Class,* and *The Poor.* Call on volunteers to suggest which occupations members of each class might have filled during the mid-1800s. Then have students describe the lifestyles of each class. Record responses on the chart.

■■ Using the chart, ask students if they think the information given still applies to life in the United States today.

 GLOBAL CONNECTIONS

During the "famine years" of 1845 to 1855 that resulted from the potato blight, more people left Ireland than in its previous recorded history. Although 75 percent of these emigrants came to the United States, hundreds of thousands settled in Britain, Australia, and Canada. The ocean journeys aboard steamships were difficult. Most emigrants could only afford the cheapest accommodations and were crammed below deck in makeshift berths that invited sickness because of the cramped quarters. In 1847, for example, more than one in three Irish emigrants bound for Canada died at sea or shortly after landing.

MULTICULTURAL PERSPECTIVES

Realizing illiteracy's costly effects, many Irish immigrants were determined that their descendants would receive an education. They not only supported parochial schools but also founded Notre Dame, Holy Cross, Villanova, Georgetown, and other colleges and universities. Have students research the founding of these colleges and universities and share their information with the class.

---

however, had little success, as more job seekers competed for factory positions.

■■ **The market and industrial revolutions created a new middle class and changed the ways people worked.**

Immigration. Many of the job seekers were new immigrants. In the 1830s, more than 500,000 newcomers—eager for work, land, and equality—poured into the country. By 1860, immigrants made up about 14 percent of the U.S. population.

The largest group of immigrants—more than 1.9 million—came from Ireland. Poverty, hunger, and mistreatment by the British had driven them from their homeland. Most settled in cities, where they lived in crowded slums and often took the most dangerous and undesirable jobs. The second largest group of immigrants came from the states that make up present-day Germany. Some German immigrants sought religious freedom or refuge from political conditions. But most were displaced artisans or farmers seeking economic opportunity.

Though the Irish and Germans faced hardships in making a new life in America, they were able to forge their own communities. The Irish established hundreds of Roman Catholic churches and played an active role in local politics. Germans formed tightly knit neighborhoods, complete with European-style beer gardens where families met to socialize. Many communities also published newspapers in German.

Some native-born Americans were troubled by the immigrants' customs. They disapproved of the "clannishness" of the Germans and feared the Roman Catholicism and growing political power of the Irish. Such feelings gave rise to **nativism**—the favoring of native-born Americans over the foreign-born. Some nativists urged limiting immigrants' rights to vote and hold public office. At times nativists' fears led to violence. Anti-Catholic riots hit cities such as Boston, New York, and Philadelphia from the 1830s through the 1850s.

■■ **Irish and German immigrants left economic and social hardships in Europe to seek opportunities in the United States.**

*T*HE MIDDLE WEST

Not all immigrants settled in northern cities. Many, especially Germans, Swiss, Scandinavians, and Dutch, sought opportunity in the Middle West. This region was newly prosperous because growing northeastern factories and cities needed more farm products, which middle western farmers began to supply.

As the market revolution made many manufactured products less expensive, farm families began to purchase items, such as cloth, they had previously made at home. Farmers also bought machines that increased crop yields. Soon they were able to focus on growing a single crop, such as wheat or corn, for the market.

Women also began to make items to sell. For example, women earned so much money making butter and cheese that some farms began to specialize in dairy production. This work was handled by women who also performed other home and farm chores.

*S*OUTHERN SOCIETY

Like the Middle West, the South was primarily agricultural. In 1860, the South had 35 percent of the nation's population but only 15 percent of the manufacturing centers. Accordingly, most southern whites were farmers.

A slave-owning planter minority dominated southern society and politics. Below the planters on the social ladder were the hundreds of thousands of **yeoman farmers** who made up the majority of southern whites. Most of these small farmers grew their own food and raised some crop (often grain)

The Granger Collection, New York

▲ This 1844 picture shows an anti-Catholic mob battling the state militia in Philadelphia.

REASONS FOR IMMIGRATION

Have students work in pairs to prepare dialogues in which an Irish immigrant and a German immigrant discuss their reasons for coming to the United States and their hopes for improving their lives. Have volunteers present their dialogues to the class. Have the class take notes, and then ask the class as a whole to categorize the reasons into political, economic, or social, as you write them on the chalkboard.

COTTON AND SLAVERY

Work with students to create on the chalkboard a cause-effect diagram showing how agriculture in the Lower South became increasingly dependent on slave labor. Then have students write a brief paragraph that explains the relationships shown in the diagram. Call on volunteers to read their paragraphs to the class.

▶

for cash. Below the yeoman farmers were the poorest whites who farmed the least-fertile soils and often had to depend on hunting and fishing for survival.

King Cotton and slave labor.
Despite its agricultural emphasis, the South, too, felt the impact of market and industrial changes. In particular, the invention of new weaving machines that cut the cost and time of making cloth sent the demand for cotton skyrocketing.

POPULATION IN THE SOUTH, 1860

Total Population: 47%, 1%, 2%, 16%, 34%

Slaveholding Households: 72%, 1%, 2%, 25%

Nonslaveholding whites — Slaveholding whites — Slaves — Free blacks — Others

Less than 10 slaves — 10–49 slaves — 50–99 slaves — 100 or more slaves

Sources: *Historical Statistics of the United States; Slavery and the Southern Economy; The Black American Reference Book*

SLAVERY IN THE SOUTH Although slavery played an important part in the southern economy, only a small minority of southerners owned slaves.

❓ BUILDING GRAPH SKILLS Which group made up the largest section of the population in the South? What percent of all slaveholders owned 50 or more slaves?

Southern planters were able to open new lands to production and increase output thanks to another mechanical invention—the **cotton gin.** Invented by Eli Whitney in 1793, the cotton gin made it possible for a person to clean 50 times as much cotton in a day as a person working by hand.

As cotton production expanded, the demand for slaves rose. The number of slaves grew from about 1.5 million in 1820 to some 4 million by 1860. The Upper South, with more slaves than the region needed, sold slaves to the cotton-producing states of the Lower South.

While some slaves lived in the cities and worked at skilled trades, more than 75 percent labored on southern plantations and farms. Field hands worked long hours, especially during harvest. Ex-slave Peter Clifton wrote, "The rule on the place was: Wake up the slaves at daylight, begin work when they can see, and quit work when they can't see." Some slaves—especially women—served the plantation household as maids, cooks, or nannies.

■■ **The rising demand for cotton led to an increased demand for slaves as planters sought to boost cotton production.**

On small farms slaveholders usually supervised their slaves directly. On the larger plantations **overseers**—who were usually planters' sons, other relatives, small farmers, or skilled workers—managed slaves. To help supervise the slaves,

overseers used **drivers**—assistants picked from among the slaves. Drivers had the difficult task of directing the work of their fellow slaves.

The living conditions and treatment of slaves varied from place to place. To make a profit using slave labor, planters had to make sure slaves were fed, clothed, and free from illness. However, housing was cramped and sparsely furnished. Furthermore, slaves usually had to supplement their meager rations of meat, rice, grits, and meal with food they caught or grew themselves.

While some planters used rewards to get slaves to work, others relied on the use or threat of violence. Whipping was the most common form of punishment. William Wells Brown, a former slave and the author of the first published novel by an African American, wrote that the whip was used "very frequently and freely, and a small offence on the part of a slave furnished an occasion for its use." Perhaps the worst threat held over slaves was that of being sold "down river"—away from relatives and community ties.

Resistance.
African Americans resisted slavery in various ways—from running away to open rebellion. In the first half of the 19th century there were several small uprisings involving slaves in the South. Open rebellion, however, was rare. Slaves generally protested their bondage through individual actions. They might fake illness, slow their work pace, or damage tools in an effort to disrupt the plantation routine.

Graph Caption Answer
nonslaveholding whites; 3%

MAKING CONNECTIONS
Science
The vitamin-deficient slave diet, which consisted primarily of corn products, led to many nutritional diseases. The most severe of these diseases was pellagra, a condition caused by lack of protein and niacin (an essential acid of the vitamin B complex). Pellagra usually leads to severe skin disorders and deterioration of the digestive and nervous systems.

THE AMERICAN NATION VIDEODISC PROGRAM

Free at Last

1B   15914   2:57

Teaching the Section

LIFE AS A SLAVE

Lead the class in a brainstorming session to develop a list of terms that describe slave life in the mid-1800s. Prompt students with such clue words as *Living Conditions, Treatment, Resistance,* and *Culture.* List the results of the brainstorming session on the chalkboard. Then organize students into pairs. Direct each pair to choose 10 terms from the list and to use each in a sentence that describes slave life. Select pairs to read their sentences to the class.

REFORMING SOCIETY

Organize students into groups to construct charts listing the social problems discussed in the paragraphs under the heading *Reforming institutions,* the solutions that reformers offered to address each problem, and the reformers' reasons for wanting reform. Call on groups to present and discuss their charts. Then have students use information from the charts to develop statements about how the efforts at reform showed the reformers' spirit of optimism about American society.

■■ Have students identify the social issues that are the focus of reform movements today.

SHOUTS ACROSS THE OCEAN

SETTING THE SCENE

Many of the characteristics of break dancing also have roots in traditional dances of Africa. The circle formation of break dancing and the way break-dancers take turns giving solo performances in the middle of the circle are characteristic of the African *juba* dance. African Americans combined the shuffle steps of the *juba* with the steps and movements of the Irish Jig to form the tap dance. Tap dance led to flash dancing, a tap-dance style that incorporates acrobatic movements such as splits and flips. Black tap dancers also experimented with dance steps borrowed from the Russians, such as drops, squats, and sweeps. Many of these tap-dance and flash-dance movements are evident in the movements and body control of break-dancers.

The most tempting form of resistance was to run away, whether for only a few days or permanently. Chances of success were slim, and punishment if caught was brutal. Some aid came from the **Underground Railroad,** a loose network of white and black abolitionists who helped slaves escape to freedom in the North or in Canada. Escaping slaves were hidden in attics and haylofts by day and taken by "conductors" to the next safe house at night. Harriet Tubman, the most famous and successful conductor and an escaped slave herself, led more than 300 slaves to safety.

Although slaves' lives were controlled during the workday, their time was mostly their own after dark and on Sundays and rare holidays. Then slaves devoted time to relatives and community, creating a unique culture. At its center were family, religion, music, folktales, and humor. Laughter helped slaves deal with painful situations and kept them from being crushed by slavery. Slaves' songs and tales often represented an indirect means of protest, one that could be made without inviting retribution. "We would sing and dance and make others laugh," former slave John Little explained. "We did it to keep down trouble, and to keep our hearts from being completely broken." Religion, too, played a vital role, and services often blended Christian and African elements. For example, the

---

HISTORY
in the Making

BY DR. STERLING STUCKEY

Shouts Across the Ocean

When Africans were forcibly brought to North America as slaves, their traditions crossed the ocean with them. Today, African influences are visible throughout American society. American dance and music, for example, have roots in African dances and musical forms.

In much of Africa, religious and ceremonial dances are performed in a ring, with dancers slowly moving counterclockwise in a circle. The ring often symbolizes the life cycle—the cycle of birth and death. Thus, it is an important part of many burial ceremonies, used to show respect for one's ancestors.

The African ring dances were the source of the ring shout in American slave culture. Slaves sang, shouted, and clapped their hands as they moved counterclockwise in a circle. As in Africa, the dancing and singing were forms of spiritual expression directed to ancestors.

Over time the ring shout and other African dances inspired new forms of dance in America. The influence of African dance was probably most widespread in the 1920s. Few people realize that the wildly popular Charleston was based on an African religious dance.

With new forms of dance came new forms of music. Some slaves adapted songs with Christian lyrics to the ring shout. The result was the Negro spiritual, which remains an important part of many African American religious ceremonies. Several leading concert artists, such as Paul Robeson, Marian Anderson, and Roland Hayes, helped popularize spirituals.

The rhythms and emotional tones of the ring shout greatly influenced blues music

▲ Shown here are members of the **Bradford Singers, a noted gospel group.**

as well. And the blues, in turn, shape today's popular music. Rock musicians, such as the Rolling Stones and Eric Clapton, have drawn on the blues.

Well-known performers, such as James Brown and Aretha Franklin, trained in the musical traditions of the black church, have also influenced a new generation of artists, among them Janet Jackson. In all these ways, African dance and music, like other features of African culture, have left strong and lasting imprints on American life.

CRUSADING FOR RIGHTS

Write the following headings on the chalkboard: *Arguments Against Slavery, Arguments Supporting Women's Rights.* Call on volunteers to note appropriate arguments under these headings. Have students assume the role of a volunteer participating in a petition drive calling for legislation abolishing slavery or calling for women's suffrage. Ask them to use information on the chalkboard to write a script they would use when presenting the petition to a prospective signer. Students may wish to include their scripts in their portfolios.

---

haunting religious songs called **spirituals**, or "Sorrow Songs," were modeled in part on Christian hymns and in part on African rituals and musical forms.

■■ **In spite of harsh conditions, African Americans resisted slavery and developed a unique culture.**

*R*ELIGIOUS ZEAL AND SOCIAL REFORM

Religion was an important part of life for many Americans. Beginning in the 1790s, waves of religious revivals swept the country. From the urban Northeast to the frontier areas of Kentucky, Ohio, Tennessee, and South Carolina, preachers promised that all sinners—not just a chosen few—could find salvation. Known as the **Second Great Awakening** because of an earlier wave of revivals, this renewal of faith reflected a widespread belief in the power of religion to reform people's lives.

Reforming institutions. Some Americans translated their faith in human perfection into attempts to reform society. Some men and women created **utopias**—communities that experimented with new ways of organizing family life, work, and property ownership in an attempt to create the ideal society. However, more Americans—notably those in the Northeast who were troubled by the effects of rapid industrialization—began to direct their religious zeal toward solving social problems. Middle-class women took the lead in many of these reform efforts.

In 1843 Dorothea Dix shocked the public with a report on the treatment of the mentally ill. During 18 months of visiting jails and poorhouses, Dix had found that the mentally ill were kept "in *cages, closets, cellars, stalls, pens! Chained, naked, beaten with rods, and lashed* into obedience." Dix convinced people of the need to offer the mentally ill **rehabilitation**, or treatment to restore them to a useful place in society.

▲ **Dorothea Dix helped found or enlarge more than 30 mental hospitals.**

Other reformers worked to rehabilitate prisoners and the poor. New systems of prison organization placed prisoners in individual cells so that they would think about their crimes and repent. Prisons also set up strict routines to teach inmates how to live disciplined lives. New poorhouses taught work skills and discipline to help the poor become self-supporting.

Some concerned people organized the **temperance movement** to persuade others to limit alcohol consumption, which was blamed for nearly all social problems including mental illness, poverty, and crime. In 1846 Maine became the first state to enact **prohibition**, or a ban on alcohol. A few other states followed, as did some communities. Many other states strictly licensed taverns and imposed heavy liquor taxes. By the middle of the 19th century, alcohol consumption had declined substantially.

In the 1840s and 1850s, reformers turned their attention to education. Arguing that existing schools—most of them private—were inadequate to educate citizens for participation in an expanding democracy, reformers sought to establish free public schools. In Massachusetts, Horace Mann's reforms as the state's first secretary of education established a model for free public education. Mann united local school districts into a state system, raised teachers' salaries, extended school terms, and updated the curriculum.

Not everyone supported public education. Some farming and working-class families opposed it because they depended on their children's labor. Also opposed were many Catholics who viewed public schools as a means of spreading Protestant beliefs. The public schools also failed to benefit many African American children born to free blacks; they were rarely allowed to attend public schools. And educational reform had little effect in the South. The antislavery movement made the South defensive about its "peculiar institution," and many southerners increasingly viewed all reform with suspicion.

■■ **Inspired to improve society, reformers supported rehabilitation, temperance, and public education.**

HISTORICAL SIDELIGHTS
Temperance's Impact
The work of temperance societies drastically reduced the consumption of alcohol by Americans. By 1840 consumption had dropped from close to four gallons per person a year to less than one and a half gallons. Temperance societies were most effective in New England and western New York. Over three quarters of the recorded temperance pledges came from New York, New Jersey, and Pennsylvania.

HISTORICAL SIDELIGHTS
Separation of Church and State
Horace Mann refused to let the public schools teach religion. The Bible could be read but not discussed in the classroom. Although this position was severely criticized, Mann went on to become one of the most influential American educators of the century.

THE AMERICAN NATION VIDEODISC PROGRAM
The Reform Movement

| 1A | 14239 | 4:02 |

*P*ractice

GUIDED PRACTICE
On the chalkboard create a chart on the reformers mentioned in this section, using the following headings: *Name, Issue, Actions/Ideas.* Ask students to supply information to fill in the blanks in the chart.

INDEPENDENT PRACTICE
Have students use the Guided Practice chart to create short biographies for a reformers' "Who's Who." Biographies should include such information as the subject's ideas, important actions, and connections to various reform movements. Call on volunteers to read their "Who's Who" to the class.

*R*eview and *A*ssessment

REVIEW Have students chart on a time line the major events discussed in this section and briefly describe the significance of each. Then assign the Section 2 Review on p. 83.

ASSESS Assign the **Section 2 Daily Quiz** in *Core Resources.*

The crusade for abolition. With the transportation, market, and industrial revolutions of the early 19th century, regional economic differences heightened the existing social and political tensions between the North and the South. As the division between the systems of slave and free labor became more pronounced, support for abolition increased among northerners.

In the 1830s black and white abolitionists began to join forces to call for an immediate end to slavery. The appearance of two important publications, David Walker's *Appeal to the Colored Citizens of the World* (1829) and William Lloyd Garrison's *Liberator* (1831), marked the start of a bold, energetic, and more organized attack on the institution of slavery. Then in 1833, abolitionists formed the first national antislavery organization devoted to immediate abolition—the **American Anti-Slavery Society**.

The society, which soon claimed more than 200 branches across the North and the Middle West, papered the country with antislavery publications and organized petition drives to protest legislation supporting slavery. Most important, the society sponsored national lecture tours of abolitionists

Sojourner Truth

who hoped to convince audiences that slavery was morally wrong. One of the most effective speakers was Frederick Douglass, a fugitive slave from Maryland. Douglass was also a powerful writer. His autobiography, *Narrative of the Life of Frederick Douglass* (1845), became a classic indictment of the slave system.

BIO GRAPHY Another former slave who worked tirelessly for the American Anti-Slavery Society was Sojourner Truth (c. 1797–1883). She was born Isabella Baumfree on the estate of a wealthy Dutch landowner. After escaping from her last master in 1827, she joined religious reformers who preached on the streets of New York City. In 1843 Baumfree said she had a religious vision in which God instructed her to find a new mission and a new identity. Adopting the name Sojourner (visitor) Truth, she traveled through New England preaching the "truth"—abolition and women's rights.

By 1840, abolitionists had recruited some 200,000 northerners to their cause. Southern slaveholders, of course, felt threatened by the growing movement. But some northerners also opposed abolition, sometimes violently. Elijah Lovejoy, an abolitionist editor in Alton, Illinois, was killed in 1837 as he tried to prevent a mob from destroying his printing press. Much of the opposition to the antislavery cause was based on prejudice against blacks. In addition, many northern wage earners feared competing with free blacks for jobs, and northern merchants feared abolition would disrupt cotton production.

Women's rights. Women's support for African Americans' rights eventually led many women to view abolition and women's rights as parts of the same struggle. As Angelina Grimké explained, "the discussion of the rights of the slave has opened the way for the discussion of other rights."

The link between abolition and women's rights endured as the call for equal rights for women grew stronger in the 1840s. When two American abolitionists, Elizabeth Cady Stanton and Lucretia Mott, were refused the opportunity to speak at the World's Anti-Slavery Convention in London in

▲ Abolitionists used antislavery songs to protest the evils of slavery. One notable example was "The Fugitive's Song," composed in honor of Frederick Douglass's escape from slavery.

RETEACH Organize students into small groups and assign each group a subsection of Section 2. Tell each group to create a poster, drawing, or cartoon that illustrates the main idea of its subsection. Have each group explain its creation.

Closure

Have students debate the following statement: *Abolition was the most important issue of the reform movement of the mid-1800s.*

Extension

RESEARCH Students might wish to research the Underground Railroad and create an illustration of one route that indicates how escapees traveled, where they stayed, and where they settled.

COMPARE Have students conduct research in order to compare the goals of the abolitionists with the goals of the African American civil rights movement of the 1950s and 1960s.

1840, they decided to launch a movement to end the daily discrimination women faced.

Their efforts led to the first U.S. women's rights convention, held in Seneca Falls, New York, in 1848. More than 300 women and men attended the **Seneca Falls Convention**, which marked the birth of the organized women's rights movement in the United States. The convention adopted a Declaration of Sentiments modeled on the Declaration of Independence:

66 We hold these truths to be self-evident: that all men and women are created equal; that they are endowed by their Creator with certain inalienable rights. . . .
  Now, . . . because women do feel themselves . . . fraudulently deprived of their most sacred rights, we insist that they have immediate admission to all the rights and privileges which belong to them as citizens of the United States. 99

The Declaration of Sentiments also called for reforms to strengthen women's legal position. Most importantly—and controversially—it called for **suffrage**, or the right to vote. Stanton said attaining the right to vote was crucial to winning full equality because "the power to choose rulers and make laws, was the right by which all others could be secured."

The grievances expressed at the Seneca Falls Convention were primarily white, middle-class, married women's concerns. Most African American

▲ A commemorative printing of the Declaration of Sentiments is shown above. The declaration called for legal reforms such as granting women the right to vote and married women the right to be awarded custody of their children in the event of a divorce.

and white working-class women, however, had concerns different from those of middle-class women and therefore did not participate in the mainstream movement. Instead, they either joined groups that shared their concerns or formed their own organizations and found a separate path to equality.

▪▪ Movements supporting abolition and women's rights gained strength in the 1830s and 1840s.

PRIMARY SOURCE

Description of Change: excerpted
Rationale: excerpted to focus on main idea

SECTION REVIEW ANSWERS

IDENTIFY

For significance, see the following pages:
middle class (p. 77)
strike (p. 77)
nativism (p. 78)
yeoman farmers (p. 78)
cotton gin (p. 79)
overseers (p. 79)
drivers (p. 79)
Underground Railroad (p. 80)
Harriet Tubman (p. 80)
spirituals (p. 81)
Second Great Awakening (p. 81)
utopias (p. 81)
rehabilitation (p. 81)
temperance movement (p. 81)
prohibition (p. 81)
Horace Mann (p. 81)
American Anti-Slavery Society (p. 82)
Frederick Douglass (p. 82)
Seneca Falls Convention (p. 83)
suffrage (p. 83)

1. *North—middle class, factories, immigration grew; Middle West—crop specialization, more products available*
2. *technology increased production, raised prices and labor needs*
3. *prison reform, treatment, education*
4. *should mention goals, disputes within movement*
5. *workers went on strike, slaves rebelled*

■■
■■

S E C T I O N   2   R E V I E W

IDENTIFY and explain the significance of the following: middle class, strikes, nativism, yeoman farmers, cotton gin, overseers, drivers, Underground Railroad, Harriet Tubman, spirituals, Second Great Awakening, utopias, rehabilitation, temperance movement, prohibition, Horace Mann, American Anti-Slavery Society, Frederick Douglass, Seneca Falls Convention, suffrage.

1. **MAIN IDEA** What changes did the market and industrial revolutions cause in the North and Middle West?

2. **MAIN IDEA** What factors led to an increased demand for slaves in the South?

3. **MAIN IDEA** What were some of the reforms people advocated to reduce social problems such as crime and poverty?

4. **WRITING TO DESCRIBE** You are a woman abolitionist in 1840. Write a letter to a friend describing the obstacles you face and your experiences in the movement.

5. **COMPARING AND CONTRASTING** Write an essay comparing and contrasting the lives of northern workers with the lives of southern slaves. How did each group protest or resist difficult conditions?

PREVIEW WORKSHOP

Following is a list of the significant people, places, and terms in this section. You may wish to use this list as a section preview.

People
- James K. Polk
- Dred Scott

Places
- Rio Grande
- Mexican Cession

Terms
- manifest destiny
- Texas Revolution
- Mexican War
- Treaty of Guadalupe Hidalgo
- Gadsden Purchase

- Oregon Trail
- forty-niners
- Mariposa War
- popular sovereignty
- Free-Soil party
- Fugitive Slave Act
- Kansas-Nebraska Act
- Dred Scott decision

FOCUS OBJECTIVES

- Describe how the U.S. gained territory in the Southwest.

- Explain why settlers were attracted to the Far West.

- Analyze why U.S. expansion caused conflict between the North and the South. Determine how successfully this conflict was resolved.

- Identify the factors that led to a rise in northern antislavery sentiments.

- Explain why the results of the 1860 presidential election caused a crisis.

CORE RESOURCES

- **Geography Worksheet 3**
- **Section 3 Daily Quiz**

AV RESOURCES

The American Nation Videodisc:
Community Ties: San Francisco's Chinatown
- **Linking Geography and History Transparency** and **Worksheet 13**
- **Everyday Life in America Transparency** and **Worksheet 10**

Section 3

EXPANSION AND CONFLICT

FOCUS

- **How did the United States gain territory in the Southwest?**
- **Why were settlers attracted to the Far West?**
- **Why did U.S. expansion cause conflict between the North and the South? How successfully was this conflict resolved?**
- **What factors led to a rise in northern antislavery sentiments?**
- **Why did the results of the 1860 presidential election cause a crisis?**

Poster advertising a voyage to California

After 1820, U.S. settlers moved west in increasing numbers, and by 1850 U.S. territory extended to the Pacific. The addition of new lands, and the accompanying argument over the extension of slavery into the West, caused the rift between the North and the South to widen. When the North elected a Republican president in 1860, the Deep South made good its threat to secede.

AMERICAN EXPANSION

As the United States gained territory, population, and economic might during the first half of the 19th century, the idea that the United States was destined to extend its territory to the Pacific Ocean became popular. This view, known as **manifest destiny**, inspired a generation of American expansionists to claim vast new territories for the country.

Texas independence. After winning its independence from Spain in 1821, Mexico encouraged U.S. immigration to its northern territory in an effort to boost Texas's non-Indian population. By 1830 non-Mexicans outnumbered Tejanos (native Mexicans living in Texas) by about two to one. Fearing that the increase in the American population might lead to a rebellion in Texas or to a U.S. invasion, the Mexican government closed the Texas border to further U.S. immigration. But immigration continued illegally, and by 1835 about 25,000 Americans, including some 3,000 slaves, lived in Texas.

When General Antonio López de Santa Anna seized control of the Mexican government in 1834 and tightened control over Texas, outraged American settlers and Tejanos rose up in revolt the next year. Isolated clashes quickly grew into a full-scale rebellion known as the **Texas Revolution**.

To put down the revolt, Santa Anna led several thousand Mexican troops in an assault on rebel-controlled San Antonio in February 1836. From the Alamo, a former Spanish mission, 187 Texas rebels fought off repeated attacks by Santa Anna's troops. On March 6, Mexican troops finally overran the fort; few of the defenders survived. The Mexicans, who suffered some 1,500 casualties, paid a heavy price for their victory.

Santa Anna won the siege of the Alamo, but six weeks later a Texas army under the command of Sam Houston surprised Santa Anna near the San Jacinto River. Shouting "Remember the Alamo!" the Texans killed about 630 Mexicans in 20 minutes and took Santa Anna prisoner. With his forces

Teaching the Section

THE MEXICAN WAR

Organize students into small groups and tell them that their task is to create a "TV documentary" on the Mexican War. Ask groups to outline a script that discusses the causes, fighting, and outcome of the war. Suggest that groups also include a commentary titled *Was the War Inevitable?* Select groups to present their scripts to the class.

▶

diminished and supplies low, Santa Anna agreed to grant Texas its independence.

Many Texans wanted to become part of the United States; and from 1836, when Texas won its independence, to 1845, the question of annexing the Republic of Texas never died. Supporters of annexation argued that if the United States did not admit Texas to the Union, Great Britain—which was interested in Texas as a source of cotton and a market for British goods—might increase its influence there. Opponents feared Texas's admission would upset the balance between slave and free states. These fears, coupled with Mexico's warning that it would consider U.S. annexation of Texas "equivalent to a declaration of war against the Mexican Republic," kept the U.S. Congress from acting. For nine years Texas remained an independent republic.

The Mexican War. The issue of western expansion dominated the 1844 presidential election, which was narrowly won by Democrat James K. Polk, an ardent expansionist. Once elected, Polk immediately called for Texas annexation. On March 28, 1845, in the wake of the congressional resolution annexing Texas, Mexico broke diplomatic relations with the United States.

Polk fueled the Mexican government's anger by demanding that Mexico recognize the Rio Grande as Mexico's northern border. Mexico, however, claimed all the land south of the Nueces (nooh-AY-suhs) River, about 100 miles north of the Rio Grande. To back up his demand, Polk ordered troops under General Zachary Taylor into the disputed area. Although Polk insisted that the troops were only defending U.S. territory, he hoped Mexico would commit an act that would justify war.

On May 9, 1846, Polk received the news that Mexican troops had crossed the Rio Grande and had attacked a U.S. patrol. Polk sent his war message to Congress. "Mexico," he said, has "shed American blood upon the American soil." On May 13 Congress declared war. Although some Americans, particularly Whigs and northerners, viewed the **Mexican War** as unjustified, most—eager to gain new lands—supported it.

While Taylor led American forces in fierce—and costly—fighting in northern Mexico, U.S. forces seized New Mexico and California. Then in March 1847 General Winfield Scott led some 10,000 U.S. troops on a march along the long mountainous road from Veracruz on the Gulf of Mexico to Mexico City. In spite of fierce resistance, Scott's troops captured the capital on September 14.

In February 1848 the United States dictated the terms of the **Treaty of Guadalupe Hidalgo** (GWAHD-uh-loop-ay ee-DAL-goh). Mexico gave up all claims to Texas and surrendered the territory known as the **Mexican Cession**. With this treaty, some 80,000 Spanish-speaking people became U.S. citizens. The United States acquired more Mexican territory in 1853 when U.S. diplomat James Gadsden negotiated the **Gadsden Purchase**.

■■ **American expansionism led to war with Mexico and the addition of a vast new southwestern territory.**

West to the Pacific. At the same time that Polk was fighting Mexico for the territories of the Mexican Cession, he was negotiating with Great Britain over Oregon Country. Since 1818, when Great Britain and the United States had agreed to occupy Oregon Country jointly, Great Britain had several times refused American requests for division of Oregon at the 49th parallel. Now Polk astounded the British by claiming all of Oregon up to the southern border of present-day Alaska.

Polk was bluffing. He hoped the threat of war would persuade the British to accept the old U.S. offer of division at the 49th parallel. In June 1846 the two sides finally agreed on the border that exists today.

Even before the boundary dispute was settled, U.S. settlers had flocked to Oregon Country. Between 1840 and 1848, thousands of settlers made the difficult journey along the **Oregon Trail** from Independence, Missouri, to Portland, Oregon. Most settlers headed for the fertile Willamette Valley, where they established farms.

White settlement of Oregon came at the expense of the region's Native Americans. Increasing contact

▲ **Missionary Narcissa Whitman was one of the first white women to travel along the Oregon Trail and across the Rocky Mountains.**

HISTORICAL SIDELIGHTS

Life on the Oregon Trail

The nearly 2,000 mile journey on the Oregon Trail averaged about four and a half to six months, depending on weather conditions, equipment failure, and various mishaps. The rugged passage west required that travelers pool their resources. The migrants helped one another repair broken equipment, shared information about the trail, and traded goods. Some of the larger traveling groups even wrote codes of law and elected officers for the journey. Traveling in large groups also helped the pioneers deal with such obstacles as ravines, deep mud, heavy snow, and swollen rivers. Rivers, in particular, posed a serious problem because there were no bridges or ferries, and it sometimes took days to cross—often exacting a toll in human and animal lives.

Teaching the Section

NEW TERRITORIES

Have students identify on a map of the modern United States the territories acquired as a result of the Mexican War and the Gadsden Purchase. Ask students to point out Spanish place-names that indicate the extent of Hispanic settlement in the present-day United States.

WEST TO THE PACIFIC

Organize students into groups of six. Assign group members the following roles: two settlers in the Oregon Country, two forty-niners, two Native Americans. Have these pairs within the groups prepare short speeches that describe their lives in the West. Oregon settlers and forty-niners should explain why they came west, how they came, and how their lives changed by moving west. Native Americans should describe how their lives were changed by the arrival of the newcomers. Have groups present their speeches to the class.

■■ Have students discuss why people move from one place to another today. Call on volunteers to explain why they or their friends have moved in the past and why they might do so in the future.

---

between settlers and northwestern Indian tribes such as the Chinooks, Makahs, and Klickitats spread diseases to which the Indians had no immunity. In addition, non-Indians destroyed much of the wildlife the Indians depended on for survival.

The rush to California. Settlers also flocked to California after gold was discovered there in 1848. News of this discovery spread over the following year and drew thousands of hopeful gold seekers. Many of the U.S. **forty-niners**—so called because of the year, 1849—trekked overland to California along the California Trail, which forked off southward from the Oregon Trail. By the end of May 1849, more than 40,000 people had made this dangerous journey.

The gold rush added to the diversity of California's population, which up to this point had consisted mainly of Native Americans and Californios (the descendants of early Spanish settlers). Though nearly 80 percent of the forty-niners were Anglos or African Americans from the United States and about 8 percent were from Mexico, others came from South America, Europe, Australia, and China. This international mix of gold seekers helped swell California's non-Native American population from some 14,000 in 1848 to more than 200,000 in 1852. Anglos soon took control of the gold fields and pushed Californios, as well as Chinese and African American gold seekers, from the mines.

The gold rush also increased pressure on the Native Americans of California. Miners forced

---

U.S. Boundaries, 1853

TERRITORIAL EXPANSION Many Americans supported westward expansion, believing that more territory would help ease social and economic problems.

? **PLACE** How many states were admitted to the Union between 1820 and 1853?

OREGON TREATY 1846
The treaty extended the 49th parallel boundary from the Rockies to Puget Sound, then through the channel around Vancouver Island to the Pacific.

WEBSTER-ASHBURTON TREATY OF 1842
The treaty with Britain settled the boundary between Maine and Canada. The treaty also adjusted the U.S.–Canadian border from Maine westward to the Lake of the Woods.

MEXICAN CESSION 1848
In the Treaty of Guadalupe Hidalgo, Mexico gave up much of its land in return for $15 million.

GADSDEN PURCHASE 1853
Pushed by southern transcontinental railroad builders, the United States paid Mexico $10 million for this land, which rounded out the boundaries of the continental United States.

Map labels: VANCOUVER I., Puget Sound, 49th Parallel, Lake of the Woods, CANADA, Washington Territory, Columbia R., Oregon Territory, ROCKY MOUNTAINS, Great Salt Lake, Utah Territory, San Francisco, CA 1850, PACIFIC OCEAN, Colorado River, Gila River, Santa Fe, New Mexico Territory, Claimed by Texas, Great Plains, Missouri River, Minnesota Territory, Unorganized Territory, Indian Territory, Mississippi River, Lake Superior, Lake Huron, Lake Michigan, Lake Erie, L. Ontario, WI 1848, MI 1836, Detroit, Chicago, Cleveland, IA 1846, IL, IN, OH, Cincinnati, St. Louis, MO 1821, KY, TN, AR 1836, MS, AL, GA, LA, Mobile, New Orleans, Galveston, Brownsville, San Antonio, TX 1845, Gulf of Mexico, FL 1845, Charleston, SC, NC, VA, MD, Washington, Baltimore, Philadelphia, DE, PA, NJ, New York City, NY, Buffalo, Boston, MA, CT, RI, VT, NH, ME 1820, APPALACHIAN MOUNTAINS, ATLANTIC OCEAN, MEXICO, 120°W, 90°W, 80°W, 70°W, 40°N, 30°N

0   200 Miles
0   200 Kilometers
Albers Equal-Area Projection

Legend:
- Acquired by Oregon Treaty
- Mexican Cession
- Gadsden Purchase
- Texas Annexation
- 1845 Date admitted to the Union
- Acquired by Webster-Ashburton Treaty

CONTROVERSY OVER NEW TERRITORY

Call on a volunteer to explain why the admission of Texas to the Union and the acquisition of new territory from Mexico created conflict in Congress. Then organize students into groups and have groups role-play a debate among supporters of each of the four proposed solutions to the problem. After the role-play session, have the class comment on the solutions and explain which one they would have supported and why.

THE COMPROMISE OF 1850

Ask students to cite the terms of Clay's compromise proposal and write their responses on the chalkboard. Then create a two-column chart titled *Opposition to the Compromise of 1850*. Label one column *Northern Opposition* and the other *Southern Opposition*. Have the class list each group's reasons for opposing the compromise.

▶

Native Americans off their gold-rich lands. Many were pressed into service in the mines; others had their villages raided by the army and volunteer militia. In what became known as the **Mariposa War** some Indians fought back. The Miwoks and the Yokuts in the Sierra Nevada and the San Joaquin Valley, whose lands had been taken over by miners, led raids on Anglo property in 1850 and in 1851. But by 1860 disease, starvation, and violence had reduced California's Indian population to about 35,000.

■■ **The fertile farmland of Oregon and the discovery of gold in California prompted migration to the Far West at mid-century.**

EXPANSION LEADS TO CONFLICT

The addition of new territories rekindled old arguments between the North and the South over slavery. When Texas was admitted to the Union as a slave state in 1845, the balance of power in Congress tipped toward the South. After the U.S. victory over Mexico, proslavery and antislavery forces in Congress quickly took sides on the issue of whether to allow slavery in territories acquired in the war.

To quiet the debate, several solutions were suggested. President Polk proposed extending the Missouri Compromise line to the Pacific Ocean.

Senators Lewis Cass of Michigan and Stephen A. Douglas of Illinois offered **popular sovereignty** as a solution: let the citizens of each new territory decide whether to permit slavery.

Neither proposal satisfied the hard-liners. Congressman David Wilmot of Pennsylvania proposed the Wilmot Proviso, an amendment banning slavery in all lands acquired from Mexico. Senator John C. Calhoun of South Carolina introduced resolutions in the Senate arguing, in part, that any ban on slavery was unconstitutional.

As the 1848 national election approached, Congress still had not settled the issue. The Democrats chose Lewis Cass, who favored popular sovereignty, as their presidential candidate. The Whigs nominated Mexican War hero General Zachary Taylor, a southerner whose political views were virtually unknown.

Angered by the reluctance of the major parties to address the slavery issue, antislavery advocates formed the **Free-Soil party** in August 1848. The Free-Soilers, who nominated former president Martin Van Buren as their candidate, demanded that Congress prohibit the expansion of slavery into the territories. Though the Free-Soil party won only about 10 percent of the vote, it tipped the election in favor of Taylor. It also demonstrated that the slavery question could no longer be ignored.

When Congress assembled in 1849, it was deeply divided over problems involving the

HISTORICAL SIDELIGHTS

Wilmot Proviso

After President Polk witnessed the strong emotions evoked in Congress by the Wilmot Proviso, he made a dire prediction. Writing in his diary, he noted that slavery "cannot fail to destroy the Democratic party, if it does not ultimately threaten the Union itself."

𝒯eaching the 𝒮ection

VIEWS ON SLAVERY

Have students imagine they are northerners in the 1850s. Call on volunteers to explain how the Fugitive Slave Act, the Kansas-Nebraska Act, and the *Dred Scott* decision have affected their views of slavery. Note their responses on the chalkboard. Have students use the information on the chalkboard to create a poster or political cartoon that illustrates changing attitudes toward slavery in the North during the 1850s. Select students to display and explain their posters or cartoons for the class.

MULTICULTURAL PERSPECTIVES

Frederick Douglass's co-editor of the *North Star*, African American physician Martin R. Delany, was particularly incensed by Henry Clay's proposal for a tougher fugitive slave law. He defiantly declared against anyone who came to his house searching for a slave, "I care not who he may be, whether constable or sheriff, magistrate or even judge of the Supreme Court . . . if he crosses the threshold of my door, and I do not lay him a lifeless corpse at my feet, I hope the grave may refuse my body a resting place."

MAKING CONNECTIONS

Literature

In writing *Uncle Tom's Cabin*, Harriet Beecher Stowe drew upon her experiences in Cincinnati with runaway slaves and on her observances of slavery in Kentucky. No previous antislavery publication approached the national impact of her novel, which quickly sold more than one million copies.

PRIMARY SOURCE

Description of Change: excerpted

Rationale: excerpted to focus on main idea

---

territories newly acquired from Mexico. California wanted to join the Union as a free state, which southern members of Congress hotly opposed. In addition, Texas was claiming that its boundary extended westward into an area the federal government considered part of the New Mexico Territory. Despite opposition from southern lawmakers, the antislavery members of Congress were intent on limiting the size of Texas and on barring slavery from New Mexico.

In early 1850, a weary Henry Clay again urged northern and southern senators to compromise. Clay proposed admitting California as a free state and paying Texas $10 million to abandon its claim to the eastern part of the New Mexico Territory. To persuade southerners to accept these terms, Clay further proposed organizing the New Mexico Territory into two territories on the basis of popular sovereignty. He also advocated the passage of a tougher fugitive slave law to aid the capture of runaway slaves.

Congress angrily debated Clay's proposals for months. The most bitter attack came from the South's elder statesman, John C. Calhoun. In a speech that Calhoun was too ill to deliver himself, Calhoun argued against compromise, insisting that the nation could avoid civil war only if the North allowed slavery to exist in the territories:

❝ If something decisive is not now done . . . , the South will be forced to choose between abolition and secession. . . . The responsibility of saving the Union rests on the North, and not the South. ❞

Many northern members of Congress also opposed Clay's compromise. They wanted to ban slavery from the territories and were against stricter fugitive slave legislation. Many agreed with Senator William H. Seward of New York when he declared that compromise on an issue like slavery was "radically wrong and essentially vicious."

When the 73-year-old Clay became too exhausted to continue the fight for compromise, Senator Douglas assumed leadership of the cause. By September 20, 1850, Douglas had pushed all of the compromise measures through Congress. Many people considered the **Compromise of 1850** a triumph of national unity, but deep sectional divisions remained. More importantly, the basic issue—whether slavery would be allowed to expand—remained unresolved.

■■ **The acquisition of new territories reopened the fierce debate over slavery in the West. The Compromise of 1850 kept the Union together but did not resolve the issue of slavery.**

𝒞OMPROMISE COMES TO AN END

Although many people were dissatisfied with the Compromise of 1850, most Americans hoped that it had settled the slavery question. To tap into this optimistic mood, both major political parties adopted platforms supporting the compromise, vowing to avoid further debate over slavery.

The Fugitive Slave Act. The Compromise of 1850, however, soon began to crumble, largely because of the **Fugitive Slave Act**. This law made it a crime to assist runaway slaves and authorized the arrest of escaped slaves, even in states where slavery was illegal.

Harriet Beecher Stowe's 1852 novel *Uncle Tom's Cabin,* which dramatized the plight of runaway slaves, helped stir northern opposition to the law. Many northerners also reacted in horror as they came face to face with slave catchers in action. One observer wrote, "We went to bed one night old fashioned conservative Compromise Union Whigs and waked up stark mad Abolitionists." Several northern states defiantly passed "personal liberty" laws, which prevented state officials from aiding the capture and return of slaves to their owners. Some northerners took direct action. In New York and Massachusetts angry mobs freed runaway slaves who had been taken into custody and helped them on their way to freedom in Canada.

▲ **Slaves escaping from Maryland are shown here.**

SECESSION

Have students write newspaper headlines that describe the reaction in the South to the presidential election of 1860. Select a few headlines and write them on the chalkboard. Then ask students to write an article to accompany one of the headlines. Suggest that students include in their articles details of the South's reaction to the election and reasons why the South felt justified in seceding from the Union. Call on volunteers to present their articles to the class. Students may wish to include their articles in their portfolios.

The Kansas-Nebraska Act. Early in 1854, Senator Douglas inflamed passions further by reigniting the debate over slavery in the West. To clear the way for construction of a railroad from his home state of Illinois to the Pacific Ocean, Douglas introduced the **Kansas-Nebraska Act**. The act organized Kansas and Nebraska into territories—a step necessary for the railroads—on the basis of popular sovereignty. It would allow new states formed from the territories to "be received into the Union with or without slavery, as their constitution may prescribe at the time of their admission."

Passage of the act in May 1854 renewed southern hopes of expanding slavery. Antislavery northerners were outraged; many viewed the South as intent on dominating the nation. Other critics of the act feared that slavery in the territories would force out white workers and replace them with slave labor.

Within months a fierce battle erupted between proslavery and antislavery forces as they vied for control of the new territories. Groups in the North helped antislavery families move to Kansas; proslavery forces countered by urging southerners to migrate there as well. "We are playing for a mighty stake," warned Senator David Atchinson of Missouri. "If we win, we carry slavery to the Pacific Ocean."

Incidents of destruction and savagery soon plagued the new territories. In May 1856 a proslavery mob of some 700 burned the town of Lawrence, Kansas. In revenge, a group led by abolitionist John Brown attacked a proslavery settlement and brutally murdered five men. This sparked yet more violence in what newspapers began calling "Bleeding Kansas."

The *Dred Scott* decision. On July 6, 1854, at a convention in Jackson, Michigan, a group of antislavery Whigs and Democrats, together with some Free-Soilers, founded the Republican party, which firmly opposed the expansion of slavery. In 1856 the Republicans nominated the popular western explorer John C. Frémont for president. Frémont finished second to the Democratic candidate, James Buchanan, but the race established the importance of the new party.

A few days after Buchanan took office, the Supreme Court issued a decision that would further

The Granger Collection, New York

▲ A posse of proslavery men from Missouri are shown here on their way to plunder and burn Lawrence, Kansas, in 1856. Months of intense and bloody fighting followed the raid, giving rise to the phrase "Bleeding Kansas."

divide the North and the South. The controversial case involved a Missouri slave named Dred Scott, who had accompanied his owner John Emerson to the free state of Illinois. In 1846, after Emerson's death, Scott sued for his freedom, arguing that his residence in a free state entitled him to it.

In 1857 the case reached the U.S. Supreme Court. The Court ruled against Scott, saying that he was not a citizen of the United States and thus could not bring suit. Chief Justice Roger B. Taney, one of five southerners on the Court, wrote in the majority opinion that the nation's founders had viewed blacks as "beings of an inferior order," having "no rights which the white man was bound to respect."

The Court also ruled that Scott's claim had no merit because Congress had acted unconstitutionally in passing the Missouri Compromise. The Court held that the Fifth Amendment to the Constitution, which forbids Congress to deny the right to property without "due process of law," had been violated since slaves were legally classified as property.

The ***Dred Scott*** decision outraged abolitionists and all who opposed the extension of slavery. There seemed to be no way to keep slavery from spreading into the territories.

▓ **The Fugitive Slave Act, violence in Kansas, and the *Dred Scott* decision all strengthened antislavery feelings in the North.**

COOPERATIVE LEARNING

Organize students into small groups and have them assume the roles of members of Congress in 1854. Ask each group to create a proposal for organizing the Kansas-Nebraska territories that preserves the Union. Direct each student in the group to contribute one idea for the group's proposal. Have volunteers from each group present its proposal to the class. Encourage comments from other students.

HISTORICAL SIDELIGHTS

Opinions on *Dred Scott* Supreme Court justices John McLean of Ohio and Benjamin Curtis of Massachusetts, neither a Democrat, wrote dissents in the *Dred Scott* decision. These became the basis for the Republican position— that Scott remained a free man because of his residency in a free territory and that he was also a citizen under the Constitution.

*P*ractice

GUIDED PRACTICE

Call on students to identify and describe events from the 1830s to 1860 that helped to create the conflict that eventually led to secession. List their responses on the chalkboard.

INDEPENDENT PRACTICE

Instruct students to use the Guided Practice list to create a cause-event-effect flowchart. Ask them to add annotations at each step in the flowchart that suggest what, if anything, might have eased tensions and averted secession. Students may wish to include their flowcharts in their portfolios.

*R*eview and *A*ssessment

REVIEW Have students imagine it is the 1850s. Ask them to write an editorial for their local newspaper, reflecting on how slavery has come to dominate national politics. Then assign the Section 3 Review on p. 91.

ASSESS Assign the **Section 3 Daily Quiz** in *Core Resources.*

BIO GRAPHY PERSONALITIES IN HISTORY

Today people are accustomed to seeing pictures of a bearded Lincoln. However, it wasn't until shortly before the 1860 presidential election that Lincoln grew his beard. It seems a clean-shaven Lincoln received a letter from an 11-year-old girl in Westfield, New York. She suggested that he grow a beard, saying that "you would look a great deal better for your face is so thin." Lincoln took her advice.

HISTORICAL SIDELIGHTS

Brown's Warning
John Brown wrote the following note of warning to the nation before he was hanged: "I, John Brown, am now quite certain that the crimes of this guilty land will never be purged away but with blood. I had, as I now think, vainly flattered myself that without much bloodshed it might be done."

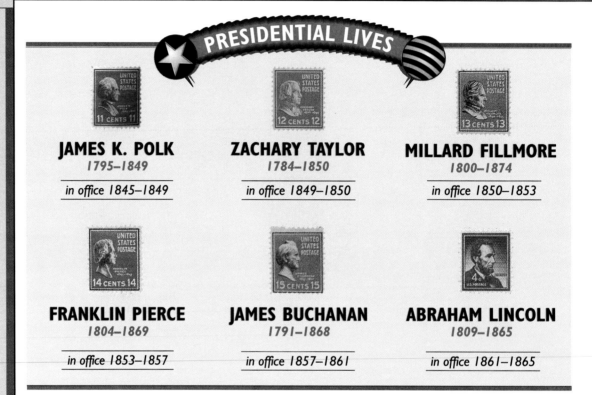

PRESIDENTIAL LIVES

JAMES K. POLK
1795–1849
in office 1845–1849

ZACHARY TAYLOR
1784–1850
in office 1849–1850

MILLARD FILLMORE
1800–1874
in office 1850–1853

FRANKLIN PIERCE
1804–1869
in office 1853–1857

JAMES BUCHANAN
1791–1868
in office 1857–1861

ABRAHAM LINCOLN
1809–1865
in office 1861–1865

---

*O*N THE BRINK OF WAR

The 1858 U.S. Senate race in Illinois became the forum for debate over the *Dred Scott* decision and the slavery issue. Running against incumbent Stephen Douglas was Republican Abraham Lincoln.

BIO GRAPHY Born in a log cabin in 1809, Abraham Lincoln had grown up in the backwoods of Kentucky, Indiana, and Illinois. He was intelligent and ambitious. During childhood he often walked miles to borrow books.

Lincoln left home when he was 22 and settled in New Salem, Illinois, where he worked at various jobs before deciding to study law. Shortly after being admitted to the bar, Lincoln moved to Springfield, where he courted and married Mary Todd, who was from a well-to-do Kentucky family.

An able politician as well as a successful lawyer, Lincoln served in the Illinois state legislature and then in the U.S. House of Representatives. Then in 1858, largely due to his opposition to slavery, he was selected as the Republican party's candidate for the U.S. Senate seat that Douglas held. Lincoln used a quotation from the Bible as the foundation for his acceptance speech at the party's convention: "A house divided against itself cannot

stand." The nation, he argued, could not remain divided into slave and free states for long.

Lincoln challenged Douglas to a series of debates between August and October 1858. In the debates, Lincoln attacked the *Dred Scott* decision and condemned slavery as "a moral, social, and political wrong." He was willing to tolerate slavery in the South, but he firmly opposed its expansion. Although Douglas narrowly defeated him in the Senate race, Lincoln had won a national reputation.

The year after the Lincoln-Douglas debates, John Brown again grabbed national attention. On October 16, 1859, John Brown and a band of some 20 men, including 5 blacks, seized the federal arsenal at Harpers Ferry, Virginia. Apparently, Brown planned to arm slaves for a rebellion. Two days later, federal troops assaulted Brown's position, killing half his men and capturing the rest. Brown was convicted of murder and other charges and was hanged. Many believed Brown got what he deserved. However, some abolitionists, among them Henry David Thoreau, saw Brown as a hero. In Congress, tension ran high.

Thus divided, the nation approached the presidential election of 1860. The election results mirrored the nation's sectional strife: votes were

RETEACH Have students work in groups, assigning individuals or pairs the task of outlining subsections. Direct individuals or pairs to exchange outlines and use them to ask questions of other members of the group.

Closure

Ask students if they think secession was inevitable. Have them provide reasons for their answers.

Extension

IDENTIFY Direct students to research, identify, and map the Native American groups who lived in the Oregon Country and California in the 1840s. Ask students to include on their maps annotations describing each group's way of life.

INTERPRET Have students research the Lincoln-Douglas debates and prepare dramatic readings and interpretations of key passages.

divided among four major candidates more or less along sectional lines. Republican candidate Abraham Lincoln won almost every northern state, as well as Oregon and California. Although Lincoln had received only about 40 percent of the popular vote and had failed to carry any of the southern states, his electoral victory was a landslide.

That a president had been elected without winning a single southern state confirmed the South's deepening sense of political powerlessness and mobilized southern leaders to action. Within days, the South Carolina legislature voted unanimously to leave the Union. Though some southern leaders urged restraint, Mississippi, Florida, Alabama, Georgia, Louisiana, and Texas soon passed similar acts of secession.

Early in 1861, delegates from six of the seven seceding states met at Montgomery, Alabama, and drafted a constitution for the Confederate States of America. The Confederate Constitution resembled the U.S. Constitution except that it guaranteed the right to own slaves and stressed that each state was "sovereign and independent." The convention chose former U.S. senator Jefferson Davis as president of the Confederacy.

Abraham Lincoln

The southern secessionists used the doctrine of states' rights to justify their actions, asserting that since individual states had come together to form the Union, a state had the right to withdraw from the Union. The issue went beyond states' rights, however. Also at stake was southern determination to protect slavery. Southerners feared that restricting slavery in the territories would ensure that the slave states remained a minority voting bloc. Then the northern majority in Congress could not only prohibit slavery in the territories but also abolish it in the South.

Northern Republicans maintained that states did not have the right to secede and that majority rule was a fundamental principle of republican government. Abraham Lincoln, in a message to Congress, declared that the South had to accept the election results. "When ballots have fairly and constitutionally decided," he said, "there can be no successful appeal back to bullets." Many in the South thought otherwise.

■■ **Seven southern states decided to secede when Abraham Lincoln won the presidency.**

SECTION REVIEW ANSWERS

IDENTIFY

For significance, see the following pages:
manifest destiny (p. 84)
Texas Revolution (p. 84)
James K. Polk (p. 85)
Mexican War (p. 85)
Treaty of Guadalupe Hidalgo (p. 85)
Oregon Trail (p. 85)
forty-niners (p. 86)
Mariposa War (p. 87)
popular sovereignty (p. 87)
Free-Soil party (p. 87)
Dred Scott (p. 89)

LOCATE

For locations, see the map on p. 86.

1. *Texas—annexation; Mexican Cession—after Mexican War; Gadsden Purchase—negotiations*
2. *whether to allow slavery in territories; admitting California as free state, organizing New Mexico Territory on basis of popular sovereignty*
3. *Northerners became more committed to abolition.*
4. *Articles should mention states' rights doctrine, which held that because states had freely joined Union they had right to withdraw from it.*
5. *Answers will note that while Oregon settlers found fertile lands and forty-niners found gold, Native Americans were driven off their land, killed, and ravaged by European diseases.*

■■
■■ ## S E C T I O N **3** R E V I E W

IDENTIFY and explain the significance of the following: manifest destiny, Texas Revolution, James K. Polk, Mexican War, Treaty of Guadalupe Hidalgo, Oregon Trail, forty-niners, Mariposa War, popular sovereignty, Free-Soil party, Dred Scott.

LOCATE and explain the importance of the following: Rio Grande, Mexican Cession, Gadsden Purchase.

1. **MAIN IDEA** What new territories did the United States acquire in the 1840s and 1850s, and what were the methods of acquisition?

2. **MAIN IDEA** What major issue regarding the new territories divided northerners and southerners? How did the Compromise of 1850 attempt to resolve this issue?

3. **ASSESSING CONSEQUENCES** How did northerners respond to the Fugitive Slave Act, the Kansas-Nebraska Act, and the *Dred Scott* decision?

4. **WRITING TO INFORM** Imagine you are a political commentator writing for a southern magazine. Write an article that explains to your readers the arguments the South has used to justify its actions after the election of 1860.

5. **SYNTHESIZING** Using the settlement of Oregon Country or the California gold rush as an example, explain how one group's good fortune can cause problems for other groups.

CHAPTER 3
Review

DEVELOPING THEMES

Return to the "Themes" section on p. 70. Have students discuss these again and compare their original responses to those given now. (See p. 69B for suggested answers.)

Chapter Review Answers

WRITING A SUMMARY
See Essential Points in each section for main ideas.

REVIEWING CHRONOLOGY
4, 5, 3, 1, 2
Synthesizing
Paragraphs might mention battles in Kansas, Dred Scott decision, Lincoln-Douglas debates, John Brown's raid, and secession of southern states.

IDENTIFYING PEOPLE AND IDEAS
1. *called for national bank, protective tariffs, transportation system*
2. *declaration that states could nullify federal laws*
3. *Seminole leader who urged outright resistance to Indian removal*
4. *prejudices favoring native-born Americans over immigrants*
5. *escaped slave, most famous "conductor" on Underground Railroad*
6. *Massachusetts's first secretary of education and reformer of the public school system*
7. *the right to vote*
8. *idea that U.S. was destined to extend its territory to Pacific Ocean*
9. *raids by Miwoks and Yokuts against Anglos in California during 1850 and 1851*

92

10. *compromise plan giving settlers power to decide for or against slavery in their territory*

UNDERSTANDING MAIN IDEAS
1. *Southeastern Native Americans were forced off their land and ordered to move west to Indian Territory. It created a financial crisis in the late 1830s that affected the whole nation.*
2. *production rates, working hours increased, wages fell; women, children, immigrants*
3. *poor—advocated teaching work skills and discipline in the poorhouses, supported temperance as a solution to poverty, favored free public education;*

slaves—formed organizations devoted to immediate abolition, lectured on abolition, helped slaves escape on Underground Railroad; women—founded women's rights movement, called for women's suffrage
4. *reopened debate over expansion of slavery; extension of Missouri Compromise line, popular sovereignty, Wilmot Proviso, and extension of slavery*
5. *Lincoln's victory without winning one southern state made the South feel powerless.*

CHAPTER 3
Review

Missouri Compromise passed. | Monroe Doctrine issued. | Andrew Jackson elected president. | Indian Removal Act passed. | American Anti-Slavery Society established. | Texas declares independence from Mexico.

1820 1825 1830 1835

WRITING A SUMMARY
Using the essential points of the chapter as a guide, write a summary of the chapter.

REVIEWING CHRONOLOGY
Number your paper 1 to 5. Study the time line above, and list the following events in the order in which they happened by writing the first next to 1, the second next to 2, and so on. Then complete the activity below.

1. Seneca Falls Convention held.
2. Kansas-Nebraska Act passed.
3. Cherokees begin Trail of Tears.
4. Missouri Compromise passed.
5. Texas declares independence from Mexico.

Synthesizing In a paragraph, provide evidence that neither the Missouri Compromise nor the Kansas-Nebraska Act settled the issue of slavery in the new territories.

IDENTIFYING PEOPLE AND IDEAS
Explain the historical significance of each of the following people or terms.

1. American System
2. doctrine of nullification
3. Osceola
4. nativism
5. Harriet Tubman
6. Horace Mann
7. suffrage
8. manifest destiny
9. Mariposa War
10. popular sovereignty

UNDERSTANDING MAIN IDEAS
1. What effects did Andrew Jackson's wish to open more land for white settlement have on Native Americans? How did his bank war affect the nation as a whole?
2. How did working conditions in factories change as a result of the Industrial Revolution? What groups of people did factory owners tend to hire?
3. How did reformers work to improve the lives of poor Americans, slaves, and women?
4. Why did western expansion cause conflict? How did various members of Congress propose to deal with the issue from the 1820s through the 1850s?

5. Why did the presidential election of 1860 lead to southern secession?

REVIEWING THEMES
1. **Economic Development** How did the transportation and market revolutions lead to regional differences in economic development? How did the economies of the North, the Middle West, and the South differ?
2. **Democratic Values** How did Native Americans, slaves, and women protest discriminatory treatment in the first half of the 19th century?
3. **Global Relations** What international issues did Americans consider when debating the U.S. annexation of Texas?

THINKING CRITICALLY
1. **Synthesizing** What did the Monroe Doctrine reveal about the way the United States viewed its role in the Western Hemisphere?
2. **Hypothesizing** How might slavery have been affected if industrialization in the South had advanced as it did in the North?
3. **Contrasting** How did the reasons most people moved to California differ from the reasons most people moved to Oregon Country?
4. **Evaluating** Do you think antislavery northerners were justified in disobeying the Fugitive Slave Act or in supporting John Brown? Explain your answer.

STRATEGY FOR SUCCESS
Review the Skills Handbook entry on Studying Primary and Secondary Sources beginning on page 758. Then study the following verses from a slave spiritual. How do the words of the song relate to the life of a slave in southern society? What 19th-century people and places might be represented by Moses, Israel, Egypt, and the Pharaoh?

❝ Go down Moses,
'Way down in Egypt land,
Tell ole Pharaoh,
To let my people go.

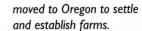

★ REVIEWING THEMES

1. *New transportation created national markets, allowing regions to specialize. North—heavily industrial; Middle West—primarily agricultural, focusing on a single crop, such as wheat or corn; South—economy dominated by cotton and slave labor.*

2. *Native Americans took their concerns to the courts; when this course of action failed, they resisted violently. Slaves, too, resisted violently. They also created an African American culture that helped them to bear ill-treatment by slaveowners. Escaped slaves traveled to the North, calling for abolition. Women formed organizations to protest discrimination and*

issued a Declaration of Rights that called for equality.

3. *fears that Great Britain would extend its commercial interests in Texas; threats of war with Mexico*

THINKING CRITICALLY

1. *that the U.S. viewed itself as responsible for events in its own hemisphere*

2. *Answers might mention that slavery may have ended as manufacturing increased the profitability of wage labor over slavery.*

3. *People moved to California in search of gold, people*

moved to Oregon to settle and establish farms.

4. *Answers should weigh a group's goals and the methods used to achieve those goals.*

STRATEGY FOR SUCCESS

Students should note that the song is a plea to end slavery. Moses might represent Harriet Tubman; Israel = the 19th-century American slaves; Egypt = the South; Pharaoh = the president or slaveowner

WRITING ABOUT HISTORY

Speeches will vary but should offer specific political solutions to one of the social problems.

USING PRIMARY SOURCES

new land would not be as suitable; their people if moved would not thrive; whites would soon move onto western land

LINKING HISTORY AND GEOGRAPHY

U.S. boundaries moved westward to Pacific Ocean. MO, IA, AR, LA, CA, TX granted statehood; NM, UT, WA, MN Territories added.

Cherokees begin Trail of Tears.	Dorothea Dix begins crusade for mentally ill.	Seneca Falls Convention held. Gold discovered in California. Treaty of Guadalupe Hidalgo signed.	Compromise of 1850 enacted.	Kansas-Nebraska Act passed. Republican party formed.	Dred Scott case decided.	Abraham Lincoln elected president. South Carolina secedes.	

1840   1845   1850   1855   1860

When Israel was in Egypt land,
Let my people go,
Oppressed so hard they could not stand,
Let my people go.
Thus spoke the Lord, bold Moses said,
Let my people go,
If not I'll smite [strike] your first-born dead,
Let my people go. 🞂🞂

WRITING ABOUT HISTORY

Writing to Express a Viewpoint Imagine you are a politician running for office in the 1850s. Write a short speech that explains your position on one of the following issues: rehabilitation, prohibition, public education, abolition, or women's rights.

USING PRIMARY SOURCES

When the U.S. government first began pressuring the Chickasaws to exchange their lands in the Southeast for lands in Indian Territory, the Chickasaw leaders offered the following reply. What reasons did the Chickasaws give for not wanting to move westward?

🞄🞄 *We never had a thought of exchanging our land for any other, as we think that we would not find a country that would suit us as well as this we now occupy, it being the land of our forefathers, if we should exchange our lands for any other, fearing the consequences may be similar to transplanting an old tree, which would wither and die away, and we are fearful we would come to the same. . . .*

We have no lands to exchange for any other. We wish our father [the President] to extend his protection to us here, as he proposes to do on the west of the Mississippi, as we apprehend [fear] we would, in a few years, experience the same difficulties in any other section of the country that might be suitable to us west of the Mississippi. 🞂🞂

LINKING HISTORY AND GEOGRAPHY

Study the maps on pages 73 and 86. How did U.S. boundaries change between 1820 and 1853? How did internal state and territorial boundaries change?

"Tom Thumb" locomotive racing a horse-drawn car, 1830

The Granger Collection, New York

BUILDING YOUR PORTFOLIO

Complete the following projects independently or cooperatively.

1. **THE ECONOMY** In Chapter 1 you created a map of international trade routes. Building on that material, imagine you are a textile manufacturer in the northern United States in the 1840s. Create an illustrated chart for a new factory that shows how you will obtain cotton, what techniques you will use to produce cloth from the cotton, and how you will transport your products to markets.

2. **INDIVIDUAL RIGHTS** In Chapter 2 you wrote an editorial arguing for the expansion of American colonists' rights under British rule. Building on that material, imagine you are a women's rights activist in the mid-1800s. Prepare a political poster calling for women's rights.

3. **CULTURAL DIVERSITY** In Chapter 1 you created a museum exhibit showing cultural exchanges between Native Americans, Africans, and Europeans. Building on that material, imagine you are an African American slave in the South. Write a story about slave life that shows how enslaved African Americans have combined elements from different cultures to create a new, unique culture.

BUILDING YOUR PORTFOLIO

Have students refer to **Building Your Portfolio Worksheet 1,** assigned at the beginning of Unit 1. Use the worksheet to help students monitor their progress on the portfolio projects.

Assessment

Core Resources
• Reteaching Worksheet 3
• Chapter 3 Tests
• Alternative Assessment Forms
Test Generator

WAR AND REUNIFICATION

1861–1900

Chapter Overview

Between 1861 and 1865, the country was torn apart by a bloody civil war. The Confederacy's defensive strategy and outstanding military leadership led to several early successes. Ultimately, however, the North's superior resources brought about a Union victory. A struggle over how best to reconstruct the South soon developed between the president and Congress. Radical Republicans in Congress eventually gained control of Reconstruction. As a result, blacks—many of whom had been slaves freed by the war—were granted suffrage and took part in Reconstruction governments. By 1877, however, Reconstruction had ended, and many blacks found themselves in situations that closely resembled prewar conditions.

THE AMERICAN NATION VIDEODISC PROGRAM
A variety of still images, short videos, and activities are available for you to use as you teach this chapter. See Videodisc Resources in the Core Resources Binder for barcode correlations and suggestions for using the program.

Chapter Planning Guide

CHAPTER 4	CORE RESOURCES	AUDIOVISUAL (AV) RESOURCES	PROGRAM RESOURCES
INTRODUCTION pp. 94–95	■ Building Your Portfolio Worksheet 1		■ *Eyewitnesses and Others,* Volume 1: Reading 80
TEACHING THE CHAPTER pp. 96–115	■ Graphic Organizer 4 ■ Social Studies Skills Worksheet 4 ■ Literature Worksheet 4 ■ Geography Worksheet 4 ■ Outline Map 9	■ *The American Nation* Videodisc: The American Red Cross; Building an Army; The Tuskegee Institute ■ Everyday Life in America Transparency and Worksheet 13 ■ Linking Geography and History Transparency and Worksheet 14	■ Art in American History Transparencies and Worksheets 13, 14 ■ *Eyewitnesses and Others,* Volume 1: Readings 78, 79, 81, 82, 83, 84, 85; Volume 2: Readings 3, 4, 19, 21
REVIEW AND ASSESSMENT pp. 116–117	■ Chapter 4 Daily Quizzes ■ Reteaching Worksheet 4 ■ Chapter 4 Tests ■ Alternative Assessment Forms		■ Test Generator

Additional Resources

BOOKS FOR TEACHERS

Foner, Eric, and Olivia Mahoney. *A House Divided: America in the Age of Lincoln.* Norton, 1990. Illustrated history of the war years.

McPherson, James M. *Ordeal by Fire: the Civil War and Reconstruction.* McGraw-Hill, 1985. Account of Civil War and its aftermath.

Sutherland, Daniel E. *The Expansion of Everyday Life, 1860–1876.* HarperCollins, 1990. Social history from 1860 to 1876.

BOOKS FOR STUDENTS

Franklin, John Hope. *Reconstruction: After the Civil War.* University of Chicago Press, 1962. Classic account of American life during Reconstruction.

McPherson, James M. *Marching Toward Freedom: Blacks in the Civil War, 1861–1865.* Facts on File, 1990. African Americans in the Civil War.

* Ray, Delia. *Behind the Blue and Gray.* Dutton, 1991. The daily life of soldiers in the Civil War.

* for students reading below grade level

MULTIMEDIA MATERIALS

The Background of the Reconstruction Period. Video, 20 min. BFA/SSSS. Focuses on historical and political issues of Reconstruction.

The Civil War. 9 videos, 11 hrs. PBS. Award-winning series on Civil War.

"*Separate But Equal.*" Video, 8 min. Britannica. Describes how Jim Crow laws, KKK, *Plessy v. Ferguson* maintained inequality.

THEMES IN AMERICAN HISTORY

USE WITH PAGES 94–95

Listed on the right are the themes emphasized in Chapter 4. The questions in boldface type stimulate critical thinking and provide students with an opportunity to discuss the themes within a broadened context. The questions also appear in the pupil's edition on p. 94.

■ GEOGRAPHIC DIVERSITY

How might geography help or hinder a war effort? Students might note that military tactics in a war, campaign, or battle are often linked to geographic features such as terrain or vegetation. They might consider the importance of rivers as a barrier to attack or in transporting troops. Also, the capture of a river could divide enemy territory or block the enemy's access to important ports. Rough terrain could make the fighting of a battle more difficult. Proximity of strategic enemy sites might make it easier to fight the war, since armies would not have to travel long distances or bring large areas under control.

■ CONSTITUTIONAL HERITAGE

Why is it necessary that a plan of government be adaptable? Students might suggest that a plan of government must be able to adapt to changing social, economic, environmental, and other conditions because the future is unknowable.

What might happen if a plan of government cannot adapt to changes in society? If a government cannot adapt, citizens might attempt to force change on government.

■ DEMOCRATIC VALUES

Why might a nation's definition of a democratic society change over time? Students might suggest that a society's view of who should be allowed to participate in a democratic government could be altered by social changes. For example, property qualifications for voting might be lowered or eliminated if society no longer believed that only the rich were qualified to govern.

CHAPTER STRATEGIES FOR MEETING INDIVIDUAL NEEDS

LIMITED ENGLISH PROFICIENT LEARNERS

Have pairs of students pick visuals from each section and explain to the class how each visual relates to the main ideas of the lesson.

TACTILE/KINESTHETIC LEARNERS

Ask students to work in small groups to create scripts for skits about one of the main ideas in the chapter. Have them perform the skits for classmates.

LEARNERS HAVING DIFFICULTY

Direct students to work in pairs to pick three events in each section that they consider important and write two or three sentences explaining the importance of each event. As a class, create a time line showing all events.

AUDITORY LEARNERS

Direct students to select a quotation from each section and write an introduction to the quote, explaining its subject, its source, and how it is related to the section. Have students read their selections and introductions to the class.

VISUAL LEARNERS

Organize students into three groups to create a photo documentary of the Civil War and Reconstruction. Assign each group one of the chapter's sections and have them research books containing photographs that relate to their assigned section. Have groups bring their selections to class and present them.

GIFTED LEARNERS

Have students prepare and present oral reports on the legacy, positive *and* negative, of the Civil War and Reconstruction.

ABOUT THE ILLUSTRATION

Chattanooga, Tennessee's location and value to the South as an industrial center made it a target of Union strategy. In September 1863 Union general William Rosecrans took the city with little resistance. However, Confederate general Braxton Bragg positioned his forces on hills around Chattanooga and trapped Rosecrans's army. In November, Union general Ulysses S.

Grant arrived to lift the siege of the city. In a fierce three-day battle, Grant's forces and troops from within Chattanooga defeated Bragg and opened the way for the Union to divide the South through Georgia. Have students study the illustration and assess the role that geography played in this battle. Ask how the illustration conveys a sense of the battle's intensity.

USING THE CHAPTER FOCUS

■ **UNDERSTANDING THE MAIN IDEA**

Call on a volunteer to read aloud the Understanding the Main Idea paragraph. Drawing on what they have learned in previous chapters, ask students to describe the advantages of the North and the South at the onset of the Civil War. Write responses on the board. Then have students suggest reasons for the advantages each side held and make predictions about the strategies each might use. Keep a copy of the predictions for review and further discussion after completing the chapter answers.

 THEMES
Have students work individually or in groups to answer the questions under Themes. Save students' responses so that they can compare them with their responses after studying the chapter. (See p. 93B for suggested answers.)

■ **THE TIME LINE**

Point out that Lincoln began to plan for Reconstruction two years before the Civil War ended. Then have students note how long Reconstruction lasted.

CORE RESOURCES

- Graphic Organizer 4
- Outline Map 9
- Building Your Portfolio Worksheet 1

AV **RESOURCES**

- Everyday Life in America Transparency and Worksheet 13

94

Chapter 4

1861–1900

WAR AND REUNIFICATION

▼ **FOCUS**

UNDERSTANDING THE MAIN IDEA

The Civil War dragged on far longer than anyone anticipated in 1861. Despite the South's defensive strategy and superior military leadership, the staying power of the northern forces ultimately led the Union to victory. When the war ended, the nation struggled to restore the southern states to the Union and to determine the status of the freed slaves.

THEMES

■ **GEOGRAPHIC DIVERSITY**
How might geography help or hinder a war effort?

■ **CONSTITUTIONAL HERITAGE** Why is it necessary that a plan of government be adaptable? What might happen if a government cannot adapt to changes in society?

■ **DEMOCRATIC VALUES**
Why might a nation's definition of a democratic society change over time?

1861	1863	1865	1867	1877
Fort Sumter falls.	Emancipation Proclamation goes into effect.	Lee surrenders at Appomattox.	Reconstruction Acts passed.	Reconstruction ends.

Call on volunteers to list on the chalkboard the key points of the Missouri Compromise. Have a volunteer explain why the North and the South had been willing to compromise at that time but by 1861 were once again approaching a crisis.

The Missouri Compromise and the Compromise of 1850 had each proved only temporary solutions to the slavery issue. The Fugitive Slave and Kansas-Nebraska acts and the Supreme Court's Dred Scott decision soon reignited tensions between the North and the South. Republican Abraham Lincoln's victory in the 1860 presidential election brought the crisis to a head.

HISTORICAL SIDELIGHTS

Raising an Army

Lincoln's call for recruits was met with an avalanche of volunteers. For example, Ohio was asked for 13 regiments but had enough for 20. The town of Flint, Michigan, had enough troops for its own regiment. The nation's immigrants formed units of Irish, Italian, and German volunteers. In New York City, some men showed support for the Union by wearing postage stamps on their hats. Some women sewed red, white, and blue ribbons on their bonnets.

PRIMARY SOURCE

Description of Change: excerpted and bracketed
Rationale: excerpted to focus on main idea; bracketed to clarify meaning

The Granger Collection, New York

The Battle of Chattanooga, 1863

On April 15, 1861, President Abraham Lincoln declared that the nation faced an armed revolt. Mary Ashton Livermore, who would soon join the war effort as a volunteer for the United States Sanitary Commission, recorded the reaction in Boston to the president's call to arms:

66 Monday dawned, April 15. Who that saw that day will ever forget it! For now . . . there rang out the voice of Abraham Lincoln calling for seventy-five thousand volunteers for three months. . . . This proclamation was like the first peal of a surcharged thunder-cloud, clearing the murky air. The . . . whole North arose as one man. . . .

Hastily formed companies marched to camps of rendezvous, the sunlight flashing from gun-barrel and bayonet. . . . Merchants and clerks rushed out from stores, bareheaded, saluting them as they passed. Windows were flung up; and women leaned out into the rain, waving flags and handkerchiefs. Horse-cars and omnibuses halted for the passage of the soldiers, and cheer upon cheer leaped forth from [their] thronged doors and windows. . . .

I had never seen anything like this before. I had never dreamed that New England . . . could be fired with so warlike a spirit. 99

This "warlike spirit" pervaded the nation in early 1861. Amid the excitement, few Americans imagined the death and destruction that lay ahead. And perhaps even fewer imagined the difficulties they would face once the war was over—both in restoring the Union and in deciding the fate of the nearly four million newly freed slaves.

Union drum with federal eagle insignia

PREVIEW WORKSHOP

Following is a list of the significant people, places, and terms in this section. You may wish to use this list as a section preview.

People
- Elizabeth Blackwell
- Clara Barton
- Martin Delany

Places
- Richmond
- Gettysburg
- Vicksburg
- Atlanta
- Appomattox Courthouse

Terms
- First Battle of Bull Run
- Gettysburg Address

- conscription
- Copperheads
- Emancipation Proclamation
- war of attrition
- total war

FOCUS OBJECTIVES

- Analyze the military advantages each side possessed at the beginning of the war.

- Contrast the military strategies of the North and the South.

- Explain why some northerners opposed the war.

- Analyze how and why the Union's war aims shifted.

- Describe the strategies Grant and Sherman employed to win the war.

Section 1

THE CIVIL WAR

FOCUS

- **What military advantages did each side possess at the beginning of the war?**
- **How did the military strategies of the North and the South differ?**
- **Why did some northerners oppose the war?**
- **How and why did the Union's war aims shift?**
- **What strategies did Grant and Sherman employ to win the war?**

As war became inevitable, both sides prepared for what they believed would be a short conflict. The war, however, would become a bloody struggle that lasted for years instead of months.

The Spirit of '61 recruiting poster

THE UNION DISSOLVES!

When Abraham Lincoln took office on March 4, 1861, the nation was on the brink of collapse. South Carolina, Mississippi, Florida, Alabama, Georgia, Louisiana, and Texas had already seceded, and other southern states seemed likely to follow.

▲ The firing on Fort Sumter on April 12, 1861, marked the beginning of four long, bloody years of war.

The fall of Fort Sumter. The Confederacy had immediately taken over the federal forts, mints, and arsenals within its borders. However, one fort important to the South—Fort Sumter, in Charleston, South Carolina—remained in federal hands.

The North knew that losing this fort would be an admission that South Carolina had truly left the Union. But Lincoln hesitated to use force. He feared that the leaders of the eight slave states remaining in the Union would make good their threat to secede if force were used against the South.

Realizing, however, that inaction would signify weakness, Lincoln moved to send Fort Sumter desperately needed supplies. When the local Confederate commander, General P.G.T. Beauregard, learned that the supply ships were on the way, he ordered Fort Sumter evacuated. The fort's commander, Major Robert Anderson, refused.

On April 12 the Confederates opened fire. On April 14, with much of the fort ablaze, Anderson and his men formally surrendered. The next day Lincoln proclaimed the existence of a rebellion "too powerful to be suppressed by the

Ask students to relate some planning strategies they have used to compete in sporting events. Discuss what they needed to know about their team's and the opposing team's strengths and weaknesses. Then tell them that in this section they will learn about the military strategies used by the North and the South.

Teaching the *Section*

MILITARY ADVANTAGES

Have students work in small groups as northern or southern military strategists. Have each group draw up a list of its own strengths and weaknesses and its opponent's strengths and weaknesses. When lists are complete, have each group speculate on how it can best utilize its strengths and compensate for its weaknesses and how it can defend against its opponent's strengths and take advantage of any weaknesses. Have groups put their recommendations in a strategy paper and choose a spokesperson to read it to the class.

▶

---

ordinary course of judicial proceedings." He asked the governors of the loyal states to provide 75,000 militiamen to put down the rebellion.

In response to Lincoln's request, four states—Virginia, Arkansas, Tennessee, and North Carolina—decided to secede. Four other slave states—Delaware, Missouri, Kentucky, and Maryland—remained in the Union. The mountainous counties of northwestern Virginia stayed loyal to the Union as well. They set up their own government and joined the Union in 1863 as West Virginia.

The Upper South remained divided over secession, and sections of several southern states raised Union regiments. Some families split apart as members fought for different sides. Kentucky's Senator John Crittenden saw one son become a Union general; another, a Confederate general.

Comparing North and South. On the face of it, the war that loomed after the fall of Fort Sumter seemed a mismatch. The North—with more than 22 million people—could recruit more soldiers than could the South—with a population of some 9 million, nearly 4 million of whom were slaves.

The North also enjoyed an economic advantage. It had over 85 percent of the nation's industries and almost all known supplies of iron, copper, gold, and other metals. With such resources the North could easily produce war materials; the agrarian South could not. In addition, the North had most of the nation's railroad lines and could move troops at will. The South had few connecting routes and lacked the resources to replace worn-out railroad equipment. And the North held superiority at sea—most of the U. S. Navy supported the Union.

The South, however, had two advantages. Fighting a defensive war, the South had only to protect its territory until the Union quit the fight. The South—where most of the nation's military academies were located—also had brilliant military leadership.

■■ **The North had numerical and economic advantages in the war, but the South had the advantage of fighting on its own soil under brilliant military leaders.**

RESOURCES OF THE NORTH AND SOUTH, 1861

	North	South
Total Population	22,000,000	9,000,000*
Bank Deposits	$189,000,000	$47,000,000
Railroad Mileage	20,000 miles	9,000 miles
Number of Factories	100,500	20,600

* Southern population includes slaves.

Source: American Heritage Picture History of the Civil War, Encyclopedia of American History

NORTH vs. SOUTH At the beginning of the Civil War, the North's abundant resources gave it a military advantage over the South.

? EVALUATING Which resource do you think had the greatest influence on the outcome of the Civil War? Why?

---

*F*IGHTING THE WAR

After the fall of Fort Sumter, Lincoln hoped to end the war quickly. In mid-July 1861 he sent General Irvin McDowell and 35,000 barely trained troops to capture Richmond, Virginia, the Confederate capital. Laughing and joking along the way, the troops were joined by sightseers and reporters who expected a quick Union victory.

But on July 21, 1861, Confederate forces, also numbering around 35,000, met the Union troops near Manassas (muh-NAS-uhs) Junction, 25 miles outside Washington. Under General Joseph E. Johnston, the Confederates dug in behind a creek called Bull Run.

At first the battle (called the **First Battle of Bull Run** in the North; the Battle of Manassas in the South) went in the Union's favor. But then southern general Thomas "Stonewall" Jackson and his men charged, filling the air with an eerie scream. Eventually known as the rebel yell, the sound struck fear in the hearts of the enemy. Union colonel Andrew Porter wrote: "Soon the slopes . . . were swarming with our retreating and disorganized forces, while riderless horses and artillery teams ran furiously through the flying crowd" of soldiers and sightseers headed for Washington.

After Bull Run, everyone realized that the war would last longer than a few months. Each side began training its forces and planning strategy. Lincoln and his advisers chose a three-part strategy: (1) capture Richmond, (2) control the Mississippi River, and (3) institute a naval blockade of the South. The naval blockade would keep the South from importing supplies and exporting cotton.

Chart Caption Answer
Students might mention that population influenced army size; bank deposits affected wartime investments; railroad mileage determined the mobility of supplies and troops; and the number of factories decided wartime production.

HISTORICAL SIDELIGHTS
Families and War
Divisions among family members affected people at the heart of Civil War politics. Mary Todd, Lincoln's wife and a Southerner by birth, had four brothers and three brothers-in-law fighting in the Confederate army.

HISTORICAL SIDELIGHTS
Northern Firepower
The North not only outnumbered the South but also outgunned it. In 1860 New England manufactured more than $2 million worth of firearms, 60 times as much as the entire South.

Teaching the Section

PLANNING FOR WAR

Organize the class into four groups—two of northerners and two of southerners—to prepare military briefings, complete with charts and maps, on their side's strategies after the First Battle of Bull Run. Have each group appoint two students to conduct its briefing. Ask the rest of the class to be reporters who attend the briefing and ask questions.

MAKING CONNECTIONS

Technology

The introduction of the Colt and Spencer repeating rifles changed warfare dramatically. Such rifles could be loaded more rapidly and aimed more accurately than any previous weapons. They enabled soldiers to fire many more shots without reloading, greatly increasing casualties and making warfare more deadly.

■■ Have students name some technological advances in warfare since the Civil War.

Map Caption Answer
Gettysburg in Pennsylvania; Antietam in Maryland

AV **TRANSPARENCY**

Linking Geography and History Transparency and **Worksheet 14**

Much of the North's plan depended on geography. The Appalachian Mountains divided most of the action in the Civil War into two arenas: the eastern theater, east of the Appalachian Mountains, and the western theater, between the mountains and the Mississippi River. Control of the Mississippi would give the North access to the Deep South and keep the Confederacy from resupplying western forces.

The South hoped to win by taking Washington, D.C., and moving north into Maryland and Pennsylvania. This offensive move, they believed, would shatter the North's morale, disrupt Union communications, and speed the war's end. The South also hoped to win European support. Because France and Great Britain depended heavily on cotton, the Confederacy expected one of those nations would respond to the North's naval blockade by aiding the South. This, however, did not happen.

The War in the East, 1861–1863

MISSED OPPORTUNITIES General George B. McClellan's caution and delays meant that the Union failed to capture Richmond.

? **LOCATION** What two battles were fought on Union soil?

■■ **The North's strategy centered on dividing the South geographically, while the South planned to capture Washington, D.C., invade the North, and win European aid.**

The war in the East. The South won most of the early battles of the war, as the Union army struggled to take Richmond and the Confederacy attempted to make inroads into Union territory (see chart on page 100). The skillful military leadership provided by Joseph E. Johnston, Robert E. Lee, and Stonewall Jackson played a decisive role in the South's early victories.

Lincoln, however, had no luck finding a general during the first years of the war, and the Union's forces in the East had five different commanders in just one year. The first of them, General George B. McClellan, trained his men well, but he hesitated to commit them to battle. (Lincoln once grew so frustrated with McClellan's delays that he threatened to send a letter asking if he could borrow the army if the general had no use for it.) After McClellan allowed the defeated Confederates to escape after the Battle of Antietam in September 1862, Lincoln lost patience with McClellan and fired the overcautious general.

The revolving door for Union generals whirled on. By the time of the **Battle of Gettysburg** in July 1863, General George Gordon Meade was in command. Meade led the Union to victory, but at a staggering cost: Union casualties from the three days of fighting numbered more than 23,000. Furthermore, the Union army failed to end the war while it had the opportunity. A disappointed President Lincoln lamented, "Our Army held the war in the hollow of their hand and they would not close it." Nevertheless, the battle marked a turning point in the war. The Union army had proved that the Confederacy could be beaten.

In November 1863 Lincoln helped dedicate a cemetery at the Gettysburg battlefield. Lincoln's brief **Gettysburg Address** remains a classic statement of democratic ideals (see page 768).

The war in the West. From the start the war went far better for the Union army in the West. In February 1862 General Ulysses S. Grant moved into Tennessee and led his army swiftly through the state. In April he paused at Shiloh Church near the Mississippi state line. Nearby Confederates under

MILITARY LIFE

Have students draw a sketch or diagram of a Civil War military encampment. Drawings should include drilling areas, living quarters, and provision storage areas. Ask volunteers to share their drawings with the class.

WOMEN AND THE WAR

Have students work in pairs to create patriotic posters that celebrate women's roles in the Civil War. Tell students that the text and illustrations for their posters should inspire other women to contribute to the war effort. Have pairs present and explain their posters to the class.

generals Albert Sidney Johnston and P.G.T. Beauregard launched a surprise attack, but Grant forced the Confederates to retreat.

To achieve a decisive victory in the West, however, the Union had to gain control of the Mississippi River. Toward this end, David Farragut, commander of a Union naval squadron, captured New Orleans in April 1862. Despite this victory, Grant knew that gaining full control of the river meant taking Vicksburg, Mississippi. More than a year passed, however, before Grant and his men were in position to lay siege to the city and force its surrender. By July 8, 1863, the Union controlled the entire Mississippi, cutting off Arkansas, Louisiana, and Texas from the rest of the Confederacy.

The military experience. While high-level leaders were executing battle strategies, the officers under them had to train young, inexperienced recruits to fight the war. Training and field officers also had to contend with shortages of food, clothing, and even rifles—especially in the Confederate army. Eventually soldiers received their Union blue or Confederate gray uniforms, but many troops never had adequate shoes or coats. Under these difficult conditions, soldiers felt homesick, lonely, and bored. Some deserted, but most found ways to cope through activities such as card-playing and singing.

The lack of provisions, coupled with unsanitary conditions in most field camps, led to disease. Thousands died from illnesses such as typhoid, pneumonia, and influenza. And minor injuries often led to infection. In fact, disease, infection, and malnutrition were responsible for over 65 percent of troop deaths. Conditions were especially horrible in filthy, overcrowded prisoner-of-war camps.

Women and the war. Many women in both the North and the South responded to the armies' overwhelming need for medical care. The first group of women to volunteer for medical duty were Catholic nuns, who transformed convents into emergency hospitals throughout the North and South. These "nuns of the battlefield" treated all victims of the war, becoming the only group recognized by both Union and Confederate forces.

In the North, Elizabeth Blackwell, America's first licensed female doctor, helped run the U.S. Sanitary Commission, which worked to battle wartime diseases and infections. About 3,000 women served in the Union army as nurses. Some, like Clara Barton, ministered to the wounded on the battlefield. After the war, Barton founded the American Red Cross. In the South, Sally Louisa Tompkins founded small hospitals and clinics. Eventually

MAP

Union state / **Confederate state** / **Union occupied** / **Union forces** / **Confederate forces** / ☆ **Union victory** / ☆ **Confederate victory**

0   75   150 Miles
0   75   150 Kilometers
Albers Equal-Area Projection

UNION STRATEGY
Control of the Mississippi would split the Confederacy and enable northern forces to reach the Deep South.

IL   IN   Louisville
Ohio River   KY
Paducah   Ft. Donelson Feb. 1862   Cumberland River
MO
Ft. Henry Feb. 1862   Nashville   Murfreesboro Dec. 1862–Jan. 1863
AR   Shiloh April 1862   TN   Chattanooga Nov. 1863
Memphis   Corinth   JOHNSTON   Chickamauga Sept. 1863
Birmingham   Atlanta
AL   GA
MS
Vicksburg May–July 1863   Jackson
LA   GRANT
TX
Port Hudson May–July 1863   Mobile   FL
Baton Rouge   New Orleans April 1862
FARRAGUT
UNION BLOCKADE   **Gulf of Mexico**

After the Union victories at Murfreesboro and Chattanooga, the Union's western armies were in position to divide the Upper and Lower South.

The War in the West, 1862–1863

JOINT OPERATIONS The Union army and navy cooperated in gaining control of the Mississippi.

❓ LOCATION Union victories at Fort Henry and Fort Donelson prevented the Confederates from moving into which Union state?

▶ **Sally Tompkins**

◀ **Elizabeth Blackwell**

MULTICULTURAL PERSPECTIVES

Native Americans from the Indian Territory also played a role in the War in the West. The Creeks fought for the North in Grant's campaign, while Cherokees, Chocktaws, and Chickasaws fought for the Confederacy in such battles as Wilson's Creek, Missouri (1861), and Pea Ridge, Arkansas (1862). Cherokee leader Stand Watie became the only Native American promoted to the rank of brigadier general in the Confederate army and was one of the last Confederate officers to surrender when the war ended.

THE AMERICAN NATION VIDEODISC PROGRAM
The American Red Cross

1B   49210   45

Ꭲeaching the Section

OPPOSING THE WAR

Have students assume the roles of northerners who oppose the war. Ask them to write letters to the editor of a northern newspaper explaining their position. Point out that northern opposition was driven by a number of reasons. Have volunteers read their letters to the class. Make sure that every reason for opposition is presented. Students may wish to include their letter in their portfolios.

■■ Ask students if they believe that the government should be empowered to limit civil liberties during a time of emergency, such as a natural disaster or war.

Chart Caption Answer
Battle of Antietam

THE AMERICAN NATION VIDEODISC PROGRAM

Building an Army

1B   00600   4:27

THE EARLY DAYS OF THE STRUGGLE: SIGNIFICANT BATTLES 1861–1863	
EASTERN CAMPAIGN	
First Battle of Bull Run July 21, 1861	The Union suffered some 3,000 casualties, the South some 2,000. The battle was a tactical victory for the Confederacy and boosted southern confidence.
Battle of Seven Pines May 31–June 1, 1862	This battle was a tactical victory for the North. Confederate casualties numbered some 6,000; Union losses totaled some 5,000. Confederate general Joseph E. Johnston was severely wounded, and Robert E. Lee took command.
Seven Days' Campaign June 25–July 1, 1862	Despite some 20,000 casualties, the campaign was considered a victory for the South because McClellan retreated. (Union casualties numbered nearly 16,000.) Lincoln gave the field command to John Pope.
Second Battle of Bull Run August 29–30, 1862	A Confederate victory, this battle prepared the way for the South to invade the North. Pope's losses totaled some 16,000, and Lincoln placed McClellan back in command.
Battle of Antietam September 17, 1862	In one of the bloodiest days of the war, the South suffered more than 13,000 casualties; the North more than 12,000. While not a clear-cut Union victory, this failure of a major Confederate offensive cost the South any hope of European support. Lincoln replaced McClellan with Ambrose E. Burnside.
Battle of Fredericksburg December 13, 1862	Burnside sent his men out onto an open plain. Lee's army controlled the surrounding hillsides and easily picked off Union soldiers. The North suffered more than 12,000 casualties, the South some 5000. Lincoln put Joseph Hooker in command.
Battle of Chancellorsville May 1–4, 1863	Hooker withdrew in defeat, and morale in the North plummeted. Lee lost his most valued general, Stonewall Jackson, who was wounded by his own men. The North suffered some 17,000 casualties, the South some 13,000.
Battle of Gettysburg July 1–3, 1863	The Union's decisive victory at Gettysburg is considered the turning point of the war in the East. The battle cost the North some 23,000 casualties, the South more than 20,000.
WESTERN CAMPAIGN	
Battle of Shiloh April 6–7, 1862	Although taken by surprise, the Union forces won a costly victory. The Union suffered some 13,000 casualties, the Confederacy more than 10,000.
Vicksburg May 18–July 4, 1863	Vicksburg's surrender (which coincided with the Union victory at Gettysburg) and Port Hudson, Louisiana's fall four days later put the Union in control of the Mississippi.

MILITARY STRATEGY The South won most of the early battles but failed to make inroads into the North.

? **BUILDING CHART SKILLS** In which battle did the South fail to achieve one of its strategic goals?

commissioned as a captain, Tompkins became the Confederate army's only female officer.

Women on both sides helped in other ways. Some women, such as Loreta Jeneta Velázquez (vuh-LAHS-kuhs), dressed liked men so they could fight. Others served as spies. Elizabeth Bowser, who was a maid in Confederate president Jefferson Davis's home, and Harriet Tubman both supplied information to the Union from behind enemy lines.

Women also replaced men in offices and factories. Nearly 450 women worked in the Treasury Department as clerks—the government's first female office workers. In addition, some 100,000 women worked in factories, sewing rooms, and military arsenals.

ᴏPPOSITION TO THE WAR

While women helped meet the demand for workers at home, neither the North nor the South could fill their armies with volunteers. To raise troops the Confederate government passed a **conscription**, or draft, act in April 1862—the first draft law in American history. In March 1863 the Union also passed a draft law. Although all social classes fought, the draft laws put the burden of fighting on poor farmers and workers. In the North, wealthy men could hire substitutes to serve for them or pay the government to be exempted from service. The South exempted anyone owning 20 or more slaves.

Exemptions caused resentment in both the North and South. In the North, poor whites, especially immigrants, rioted in protest. In New York City some newspapers whipped readers into a frenzy, claiming that the draft forced white workers to fight for the freedom of African Americans who would then come north and steal their jobs. Men and women—many of them poor Irish immigrants—raged through African American neighborhoods, leaving more than 100 people dead. Draft riots did not occur in the South, but, as in the

FREEING THE SLAVES

Divide the class into pairs. Ask one member of each pair to be an interviewer, and the other member to be a former slave who fought for the Union after the Emancipation Proclamation. Have the interviewer ask about wartime experiences. Invite volunteers to reprise their interviews before the class.

WAR AIMS SHIFT

Draw a line dividing the chalkboard into two columns. Label columns *War Aims Before September 1862* and *War Aims After September 1862*. Call on volunteers to describe the Union's war aims in each period and list them on the chalkboard. Have students identify reasons for the North's shift in priorities and explain why Lincoln's timing was important in announcing the Emancipation Proclamation.

North, many whites criticized the draft, claiming it proved the conflict was a "rich man's war and a poor man's fight."

There were others, particularly in the North, who also voiced displeasure with the war itself. Some believed that the war was too costly in terms of money and human life. Some northern Democrats, labeled **Copperheads**, opposed the war because they sympathized with the South. Most Copperheads limited antiwar activities to speeches and newspaper articles. But to quiet them Lincoln suspended some civil liberties. At one time or another, thousands of Copperheads and other opponents of the war were arrested and held without trial.

■■ **The draft, fear of unemployment, concern over costs, and sympathy for the South led some northerners to protest the war.**

THE FINAL PHASE

Even northerners who fully supported the war began to rethink the war's aim. As more and more lives were lost, many northerners wondered whether saving the Union without ending slavery was worth such a high price. Slavery, they decided, must end. Yet Lincoln insisted: "My paramount object in the struggle *is* to save the Union, and is *not* either to save or to destroy slavery."

The Emancipation Proclamation. Privately, however, the president had concluded that slavery was too important to the southern war effort to ignore. The Confederacy depended on slaves to raise food, haul supplies, and work in factories. Lincoln hoped that if slaves heard the North was fighting to free them, they would desert their masters, thereby weakening the South's economy.

Lincoln lacked the constitutional authority to abolish slavery, but he had the power to issue military measures. In September 1862 Lincoln issued the **Emancipation Proclamation**, which declared that all slaves in areas rebelling against the United States would become free on January 1, 1863. Because the proclamation applied only to areas held by the Confederacy, it did not change the status of slaves in the border states. Another three years would pass before slavery was abolished everywhere in the United States.

The Emancipation Proclamation brought a decisive change in the war. By inspiring some 500,000 slaves to leave their masters whenever Union troops were nearby, it struck a serious blow to the South's economy. The proclamation also encouraged African Americans to enlist as soldiers. The first official black regiments were organized in August 1862 in South Carolina. Frederick Douglass, who had been pressing for black troops, saw military service as an important step toward citizenship for African Americans:

❝ Let the black man get upon his person the brass letters, U.S.; let him get . . . a musket on his shoulder and bullets in his pocket, and there is no power on earth which can deny that he has earned the right to citizenship. ❞

By war's end nearly 180,000 African Americans had served in the Union army. The 166 all-black regiments fought 449 engagements. More than 20 African Americans won the Congressional Medal of Honor, and over 32,000 died for the Union cause.

Although the Union army accepted African Americans, it did not offer full equality. For much of the war, black soldiers earned less than half the pay of whites. In addition, white officers commanded every black regiment. Only about 100 African Americans were commissioned as junior officers, and it was not until 1865 that Martin Delany became the first black promoted to major.

▼ Poster commemorating the Emancipation Proclamation

■■ **The North enlarged its war aims to include freeing the slaves in the hopes of weakening the South.**

A war of attrition. Emancipation provided Lincoln with one key to Union success. Another key was General Grant, who became commander of all Union forces. Grant's strategy was to use the North's advantages in terms of soldiers and

PRIMARY SOURCE

Description of Change: excerpted
Rationale: excerpted to focus on main idea

🌐 GLOBAL CONNECTIONS

One immediate effect of the Emancipation Proclamation was to end all hope of support for the Confederacy. One London newspaper called the decree "a gigantic stride in the paths of Christian and civilized progress." No leaders of European governments were willing to risk the outrage of public opinion by fighting against a country waging a war against slavery.

Teaching the Section

WINNING THE WAR

Pair students to role-play Grant and Sherman. Have them write and exchange letters explaining and justifying their military tactics. Select pairs to read their letters to the class. Then discuss with students how Grant's and Sherman's strategies differed from the strategies of previous Union commanders, how they built upon Union strengths and Confederate weaknesses, and what were the potential costs and risks for the Union army.

■■ Ask students if they believe "war of attrition" and "total war" to be appropriate military strategies today. Ask students to cite some recent examples of these strategies in use.

Map Caption Answer
The distance between Savannah and Columbia is about 135 miles; this averages about 8 miles a day.

HISTORICAL SIDELIGHTS

March to the Sea

As Sherman's army marched through Georgia, they made sure they destroyed railroads. Soldiers pried up tracks, heated them over bonfires, and then twisted them around trees so they could not be reused. Union soldiers called the twisted metal they left behind "Sherman hairpins" or "Jeff Davis neckties."

The Final Campaigns, 1864–1865

GRANT'S CAMPAIGN Although he suffered defeat after defeat, Grant kept on the attack. When he failed to take Petersburg, Grant laid siege to the city for 9 months. Defeated at Five Forks, Lee abandoned Petersburg and Richmond on April 2. A week later Lee surrendered to Grant.

❓ **MOVEMENT** Sherman's army took 17 days to march from Savannah to Columbia. On average how many miles did his army need to cover each day?

supplies against an enemy reeling from shortages. Grant planned a **war of attrition**—to fight until the South ran out of men, supplies, and will. He would march on Richmond, take his losses, and press on.

In May 1864 Grant began his campaign against Lee's troops in Virginia. Although the Union suffered high casualties, Grant pushed his troops on, mile after bloody mile. His actions forced Lee to keep weary men in the field. At Spotsylvania Court House, Virginia, Union and Confederate forces clashed several times between May 10 and May 19. As before, Union losses were heavy. Shocked by the number of casualties, a southern soldier remarked of Grant: "We have met a man this time, who either does not know when he is whipped, or who cares not if he loses his whole army."

By mid-June Grant's army had suffered some 60,000 casualties. He called off the direct assault of Petersburg, Virginia, and settled down to besiege the city. Grant was achieving his goal, however. Lee's army was dwindling, with no reserves available.

Matching Grant in determination was the Union commander of the Tennessee army, General William Tecumseh Sherman. While Grant was heading to Richmond in early May, Sherman moved about 100,000 troops out of Tennessee toward Atlanta, Georgia. His troops entered the city on September 2, 1864, and cut the only Confederate railroad link across the Appalachians.

After burning much of Atlanta, Sherman marched toward Savannah, Georgia. Sherman's men, cut off from their supply line, took what they needed and destroyed what remained. They uprooted crops, burned houses, slaughtered livestock, and tore up railroad tracks, leaving nearly stripped a swath 60 miles wide and almost 300 miles long.

Such destruction was part of Sherman's tactic of fighting a **total war**. He believed that it was not enough to fight enemy troops. To win the war, the Union had to strike at the enemy's economic resources. Sherman succeeded, but his actions left bitter scars across the South. After capturing Savannah, Sherman and his troops turned north to link up with Grant.

GUIDED PRACTICE

Make a time line on the chalkboard for the years 1861 through 1865. Have students take turns offering significant events in headline form and add them to the time line. When the time line is complete, have students identify turning points in the war and suggest the places where a southern victory was still possible and why.

INDEPENDENT PRACTICE

Direct students to choose a headline from the time line developed in Guided Practice and write an article to accompany it. Call on volunteers to read their articles to the class. Students may wish to include their articles in their portfolios.

REVIEW Have students write 10 questions based on Section 1 on individual notecards with the answers on the reverse side. Then divide students into groups of four. Ask them to use their notecards to question the other members of their group. Then assign the Section 1 Review on p. 104.

ASSESS Assign the **Section 1 Daily Quiz** in *Core Resources*.

▶

■■ In 1864 Grant began wearing down the Confederates through a war of attrition, and Sherman waged total war to defeat the South economically as well as militarily.

As Sherman's army moved northward through the Carolinas, Grant's troops hammered at Richmond. On April 2, 1865, with Grant close behind, Lee withdrew. Within hours, Union troops poured into the Confederate capital. Lee tried to make a run to the west, hoping to join up with more troops. But Grant cut off Lee's escape. With his once-proud army reduced to 30,000 men, many without shoes, Lee asked for terms of surrender.

▲ Sherman's troops left a wake of destruction behind them, including torn-up railroad tracks and burned-out factories.

Grant and Lee met in the tiny village of Appomattox Courthouse on April 9, 1865. The terms of surrender were simple. Confederate

Changing Ways

THE COURAGEOUS 54TH

LINK TO TODAY

Have students contrast the roles African Americans play in the military today with their roles at the time of the Civil War. (*No longer in segregated units, African American officers may hold all ranks in the military including chairman of the joint chiefs of staff for the armed services.*)

Changing Ways THE COURAGEOUS 54TH

On July 18, 1863, the men of the 54th Massachusetts Infantry sat in camp on Morris Island in South Carolina's Charleston Harbor. Three quarters of a mile away, guarding the harbor entrance, Fort Wagner rose above the sands. More than 1,700 Confederates stood ready to defend the fort.

The Confederates held not only Fort Wagner but all the forts and batteries around Charleston, South Carolina. The Union campaign to seize control of Charleston's defenses had begun on July 10. Eight days later, despite Union bombardment, Fort Wagner was still in Confederate hands. So General Truman Seymour decided to send some 6,000 Union troops in a frontal attack against the fort—with the 54th regiment in the lead.

The 54th was no ordinary regiment. It was composed of

some of the first African American soldiers recruited for the Union army. And this battle was the first time black troops had been assigned a key role. It was up to them to break through the Confederate line, and they would surely suffer great losses. These troops also faced a danger that white Union soldiers did not. Captured blacks were shot, hanged, or sold into slavery.

As night fell, the 54th's commanding officer, Colonel Robert Gould Shaw, gave the order "Forward!" and the troops advanced. The evening exploded in a storm of gunfire. Confederate cannons all around opened fire, but somehow Colonel Shaw and his men clawed their way to the top of

▲ Charles and Lewis Douglass, sons of Frederick Douglass, both served with the 54th Massachusetts, shown here charging Fort Wagner.

Fort Wagner's walls. There, they fought hand to hand against the Confederate defenders inside. The casualties were extremely heavy.

Union troops continued the siege until September 6, when the Confederates, no longer able to hold out, evacuated the fort. Four survivors of the regiment received the Gillmore Medal for gallantry, and their courage won the 54th Regiment an honored place in U.S. military history.

RETEACH Organize students into small groups and assign each a subsection of the section. Tell each group to compose a poem, song, or rap that expresses the main idea of its subsection. Have each group perform its composition.

Closure

Have students explain these statements from p. 101: "Emancipation provided Lincoln with one key to Union success. Another key was General Grant, who became commander of all Union forces." Have students suggest other keys to the Union victory.

Extension

INTERPRET Have students research and read Civil War soldiers' letters to their families and friends. Students should choose one of these letters and write a response to it from a loved one back home.

RESEARCH Have students research and report on the roles played by African Americans or women in the Civil War.

Graph Caption Answer
about 250,000; about 150,000

SECTION REVIEW ANSWERS

IDENTIFY

For significance, see the following pages:
First Battle of Bull Run (p. 97)
Gettysburg Address (p. 98)
Elizabeth Blackwell (p. 99)
Clara Barton (p. 99)
conscription (p. 100)
Copperheads (p. 101)
Emancipation Proclamation (p. 101)
Martin Delany (p. 101)
war of attrition (p. 102)
total war (p. 102)

LOCATE

For locations, see the maps on pp. 98, 99, and 102.

1. *North—large population, majority of resources, naval superiority; South—on own soil, talented military leaders*
2. *North—capture Richmond, control Mississippi River, institute blockade, divide South; South—capture Washington, D.C., enlist European aid*
3. *changed from ending rebellion to freeing slaves; to weaken South by removing labor force*
4. *Democrats opposed war for political reasons; some whites feared that freed African Americans might take their jobs.*
5. *strategies wore down the South militarily, economically, and psychologically*

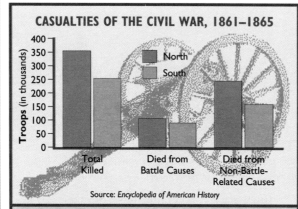

CASUALTIES OF THE CIVIL WAR, 1861–1865

Troops (in thousands) — North, South

Total Killed | Died from Battle Causes | Died from Non-Battle-Related Causes

Source: Encyclopedia of American History

COST OF CONFLICT The Civil War was one of the bloodiest wars in U.S. history. Of the more than 2.6 million Union and Confederate soldiers, more than 600,000 died during the four-year struggle.

? BUILDING GRAPH SKILLS About how many Union deaths resulted from non-battle-related causes? About how many Confederate deaths resulted from non-battle-related causes?

officers could keep their sidearms, and all soldiers could keep their horses. Lee acknowledged that "this will do much toward conciliating [uniting] our people."

As Lee rode off, Union troops started to cheer, but Grant silenced them. "The war is over," he said; "the rebels are our countrymen again." After the surrender, Lee quietly told his men to resume their lives and "become as good citizens as you were soldiers." On April 26, 1865, General Joseph Johnston surrendered to General Sherman.

The consequences of war. No other war on American soil has been as tragic as the Civil War in terms of human costs. Some 360,000 Union and 285,000 Confederate soldiers died. More Americans were killed in the Civil War than in all other American wars combined.

In the South the war devastated the economy and left southerners facing an uncertain future. Almost four million former slaves were without homes and ways to earn a living. Tens of thousands of Confederate veterans were also homeless and jobless.

In the North the war benefited the economy. Agriculture and industry had expanded to meet military needs, and many northern industries—steel, petroleum, food processing, manufacturing, and finance—continued to expand after the war.

The North's victory also made the Republican party the dominant political force. Moreover, it resolved the long-debated issue of slavery. Never again would the U.S. government sanction the legalized enslavement of a group of people.

◄ Defeated Confederates rolling up their flag

The West Point Museum, United States Military Academy

SECTION 1 REVIEW

IDENTIFY and explain the significance of the following: First Battle of Bull Run, Gettysburg Address, Elizabeth Blackwell, Clara Barton, conscription, Copperheads, Emancipation Proclamation, Martin Delany, war of attrition, total war.

LOCATE and explain the importance of the following: Richmond, Gettysburg, Vicksburg, Atlanta, Appomattox Courthouse.

1. **MAIN IDEA** What were the North's military strengths at the beginning of the Civil War? What were the South's strengths?
2. **MAIN IDEA** How did the North's strategy differ from the South's at the beginning of the Civil War?
3. **MAIN IDEA** How and why did the North change its war aims during the Civil War?
4. **RECOGNIZING POINTS OF VIEW** What reasons did some northern Democrats and working-class whites have for opposing the war?
5. **ASSESSING CONSEQUENCES** How did Grant's and Sherman's military strategies bring an end to the war?

*Introducing
the Section*

Following is a list of the significant people and terms in this section. You may wish to use this list as a section preview.

People
- Thaddeus Stevens
- Elizabeth Cady Stanton

Terms
- Reconstruction
- freedpeople
- Thirteenth Amendment
- black codes
- Civil Rights Act of 1866
- Fourteenth Amendment
- Reconstruction Acts
- Fifteenth Amendment

- Enforcement Acts
- Civil Rights Bill of 1875
- Compromise of 1877

Section 2

RECONSTRUCTION

FOCUS

- **How did the Civil War affect southern life?**
- **How did Lincoln, Johnson, the Moderate Republicans, and the Radicals differ in their approaches to Reconstruction?**
- **How did African Americans participate in rebuilding the South?**
- **What factors led to the end of Reconstruction?**

*A*fter the Civil War, Americans faced complex problems. Politicians disagreed about how to restore the Union, and whites and blacks struggled to define the rights of former slaves.

An African American addressing Congress

FOCUS OBJECTIVES

- Explain how the Civil War affected southern life.
- Explain how Lincoln, Johnson, the Moderate Republicans, and the Radical Republicans differed on Reconstruction.
- Determine how African Americans participated in rebuilding the South.
- List the factors that led to the end of Reconstruction.

HISTORICAL SIDELIGHTS

Searching for Families
Many African Americans spent years trying to find relatives from whom they had been separated during slavery. Well into the 1880s, African American newspapers in the North and in the South carried advertisements by former slaves requesting any information about their relatives.

PRIMARY SOURCES

Description of Change: excerpted
Rationale: excerpted to focus on main idea

THE OLD SOUTH DESTROYED

As the war ended, most of the nearly four million former slaves, or freedmen, found themselves without money or homes. "It came so sudden on 'em," recalled freedman Parke Johnston:

66 Just think of whole droves of people, that had always been kept so close, and hardly ever left the plantation before, turned loose all at once, with nothing in the world, but what they had on their backs. **99**

Despite the obstacles, however, most former slaves eagerly looked to the future. They hoped to get an education, to establish churches, to legalize their marriages, and especially to find family members who had been sold away.

Above all, they wanted land to support themselves and to protect their independence. In fact, many believed that it was their due. "Our wives, our children, our husbands, has been sold over and over again to purchase the

lands we now locates upon," argued freedman Bayley Wyat; "we have a divine right to the land."

The planters still had land, but even they found their world "literally kicked to pieces." Mary Boykin Chesnut wrote about the despair many white southerners felt: "We are shut in here—turned with our faces to a dead wall. No mails. . . . We are cut off from the world—to eat out our own hearts."

The Union army had laid waste to parts of the South—destroying railroad lines and stripping homes, barns, and gardens. Many cities, too, lay in ruins. Disease, the grim companion of hunger and bad sanitation, swept the South—especially cities, and thousands died in the year after the war.

After the Civil War parts of the South lay in ruins and many southerners faced poverty. The former slaves, however, looked forward to shaping their own destinies.

◄ This family record, showing a prosperous African American family, was marketed to former slaves after the war.

CORE RESOURCES
- **Literature Worksheet 4**
- **Section 2 Daily Quiz**

AV **RESOURCES**
- **Everyday Life in America Transparency and Worksheet 13**

MOTIVATING: LINK TO TODAY

Have students describe recent situations in which the president and Congress have come into conflict. Ask them to describe the conflicts and explain how they were resolved. Tell students that in this section they will read about clashes between Congress and the president during Reconstruction.

Teaching the Section

CIVIL WAR'S EFFECTS ON SOUTHERN LIFE

Call on two volunteers to role-play southerners after the Civil War. Ask one to testify about what life was like for African Americans and the other to relate what life was like for planters. The volunteers also should state what their character thinks the future might bring. Then have the remaining class members compare changes in the ways of life for African Americans and Southern planters after the Civil War. Encourage students to write a paragraph summarizing the class comparison. Have volunteers read their paragraphs aloud.

HISTORICAL SIDELIGHTS

Lincoln on Suffrage
In Lincoln's last speech, given on April 11, 1865, he said that he favored African American suffrage, but with limits. "I would myself prefer that [the vote] were now conferred on the very intelligent, and on those who serve our cause as soldiers."

PRIMARY SOURCES

Description of Change: excerpted
Rationale: excerpted to focus on main idea

THROUGH OTHERS' EYES

Although emancipation of serfs is considered by many historians to be Alexander II's greatest achievement, he also carried out numerous reforms in the courts, in education, and in government to improve the quality of life in Russia and to strengthen its economy.

PRESIDENTIAL RECONSTRUCTION

President Lincoln had gone to war not to destroy the South but to preserve the Union. Even before war's end, he had begun to plan for **Reconstruction**—rebuilding the rebelling states and reuniting the nation. In December 1863 he had issued the Proclamation of Amnesty and Reconstruction, which offered a full pardon to almost all southerners who would swear allegiance to the U.S. Constitution and accept federal laws on slavery. The proclamation also permitted a state to rejoin the Union when 10 percent of the state's residents who had voted in 1860 swore their loyalty to the United States.

Many members of Congress objected to Lincoln's plan. They did not trust the rebels to be loyal or to protect the rights of former slaves. In 1864 Congress laid out its own Reconstruction plan in the Wade-Davis Bill. It called for former Confederate states to abolish slavery and for a *majority* of each state's white males to take a loyalty oath. Lincoln vetoed the bill because he was not ready to "be inflexibly committed to any single plan." In his Second Inaugural Address, Lincoln clarified his goal for Reconstruction:

66 With malice toward none, with charity for all, with firmness in the right as God gives us to see the right, let us strive on . . . to bind up the nation's wounds . . . to do all which may achieve and cherish a just and lasting peace. 99

■■ **Unlike Congress, Lincoln favored a flexible, lenient policy toward the former Confederates.**

What course Reconstruction might have taken under Lincoln's direction will never be known. On April 14, 1865, just days after Lee's surrender, John Wilkes Booth, a half-crazed Confederate sympathizer, shot the president.

Upon Lincoln's death the following day, Vice President Andrew Johnson—a Democrat from Tennessee and a former slaveholder—became president. Johnson was ill-suited to the challenges of Reconstruction and of defining African Americans' new rights. He suffered, one contemporary observed, from "almost unconquerable prejudices against the African race." Moreover, he lacked tact and political skill.

At first Johnson denounced southern treason, even suggesting that Jefferson Davis and other high-ranking Confederates be hanged as traitors. In May 1865, however, in a startling about-face, Johnson issued a blanket pardon to all rebels except ex-Confederate officeholders and the richest planters. These he pardoned individually. Johnson was equally lenient with the rebel states.

THE EMANCIPATION PROCLAMATION

In 1861, two years before President Lincoln issued the Emancipation Proclamation, Czar Alexander II of Russia promised more than 20 million Russian serfs freedom and land. Though the czar's own land policies eventually failed, in 1879 he criticized the proclamation for having sidestepped the issue of land. The czar charged that the decree had freed the American slaves but had left them with no means to support themselves. Alexander boasted:

66 I did more for the Russian serf in giving him land as well as personal liberty, than America did for the Negro slave set free by the Proclamation of President Lincoln. I am at a loss to understand how you Americans could have been so blind as to leave the Negro slave without tools to work out his salvation. . . . Without property of any kind he cannot educate himself and his children. I believe the time must come when many will question the manner of American emancipation of the Negro slaves in 1863. 99

THROUGH OTHERS' EYES

DIFFERING VIEWS ON RECONSTRUCTION

Have students work in pairs to make a chart that compares and contrasts Lincoln's Proclamation of Amnesty and Reconstruction and the provisions of the Wade-Davis Bill. Call on volunteer pairs to draw their charts on the chalkboard. Discuss which plan was more flexible and lenient toward former Confederates.

JOHNSON'S PLAN FOR RECONSTRUCTION

Call on volunteers to list the provisions of Johnson's plan for Reconstruction as you write them on the chalkboard. Then have students imagine they are members of Congress during Reconstruction and present arguments for or against each provision.

CONGRESSIONAL RECONSTRUCTION

Ask students to develop a flowchart showing the major events of Congressional Reconstruction. Suggest that they begin their flowcharts with the disagreement between Moderate and Radical Republicans over the goals of Reconstruction. Ask for volunteers to present their flowcharts to the class. Students may wish to include their flowcharts in their portfolios.

▶

▲ After Lincoln's assassination, the War Department offered a reward for the capture of John Wilkes Booth.

For readmission to the Union, Johnson asked only that they nullify secession, abolish slavery, and refuse to pay Confederate debts.

Johnson's plan allowed former Confederate leaders—some still proudly wearing Confederate uniforms—to take charge of Reconstruction. When they complained of the "painful humiliation" caused by the presence of black soldiers, Johnson withdrew the soldiers. When Mississippi refused to ratify the **Thirteenth Amendment**—which Congress had passed in January 1865 to abolish slavery—Johnson recognized the state's new government anyway.

Johnson's actions encouraged former Confederates to adopt laws limiting the former slaves' freedom. These **black codes**, which African Americans denounced as "a disgrace to civilization," resembled prewar slave codes. Mississippi simply used its old code, substituting the word *freedman* for *slave.*

Under these laws African Americans could not hold meetings unless whites were present. They could not travel without permits or own guns. Blacks in New Orleans could not be on the streets after 10 o'clock at night, just one hour later than the previous slave curfew. The editor of the city's African American newspaper noted: "Four years of a bloody war have been fought to gain that one hour."

Above all, the codes reestablished white control over black labor. Because whites were desperate to make former slaves return to field work, some codes required freedpeople to sign labor contracts. The laws were so restrictive that one black

veteran demanded: "If you call this Freedom, what do you call Slavery?"

■■ Johnson's leniency toward ex-Confederates allowed them to dominate Reconstruction and to limit the rights of African Americans.

CONGRESSIONAL RECONSTRUCTION

President Johnson's support of the former Confederates and his failure to protect African Americans' rights angered many members of Congress. Even Republicans, however, were divided over the course Reconstruction should take. The Moderates, who made up the party majority, viewed Reconstruction as a practical matter of restoring southern states to the Union. Their main concern was keeping ex-Confederates out of government. And though they favored giving African Americans civil equality, they did not think the former slaves should have voting rights.

Radical Republicans, on the other hand, insisted that African Americans be given the right to vote. They wanted Reconstruction to create a new South where all men would have equal rights. In addition, Thaddeus Stevens, the outspoken Radical from Pennsylvania, believed that land reform could change southern society. He agreed with Senator Charles Sumner of Massachusetts, who insisted that "the great plantations . . . must be broken up, and the freedmen must have the pieces." According to Stevens, economic independence for the former slaves would ensure their freedom and destroy the rebel leaders' power. But land reform never won wide support. Even many Radicals believed that the ballot, civil equality, and free labor were enough to give African Americans a chance to succeed.

Congress versus Johnson. The split between Moderates and Radicals did not last. In 1866 Congress held hearings on conditions in the South. Witness after witness recounted stories of murder and of homes, schools, and churches reduced to "ashes and cinders." These reports and others like them convinced the Moderates to join forces with the Radicals. They began work on

COOPERATIVE LEARNING

Organize students into groups of six, subdivided into pairs. Direct each pair to write down a different provision of the black codes and to explain how that provision was like a continuation of slavery. Then have each pair read the provision and explanation to their group.

HISTORICAL SIDELIGHTS

Land Distribution
Thaddeus Stevens advocated federal seizure of the 400 million acres belonging to the wealthiest 10 percent of southerners. Each freedman would receive 40 acres, and the remaining 90 percent of the land would be sold, in small lots, to the highest bidders. Proceeds from land sales would provide pensions for Civil War veterans and pay off most of the national debt.

Teaching the Section

THE FREEDMEN'S BUREAU

Divide the class into groups of four. Have each group represent Freedmen's Bureau administrators in the South. Groups should discuss the needs of African Americans after the Civil War, developing a plan that will provide former slaves with homes, jobs, and other needs. Each group should select one member to present the plan to the remainder of the class.

▲ This cartoon is a reaction to Johnson's veto of the Freedmen's Bureau Bill.

legislation to protect the rights and safety of the ex-slaves. This effort included extending the life of the Freedmen's Bureau, which Congress had established in 1865.

Originally authorized to operate for one year, the Freedmen's Bureau had been designed to aid the millions of southerners, particularly ex-slaves, left homeless by the war. The bureau distributed food, served as an employment agency, and ran hospitals and schools. While African Americans thought the Freedmen's Bureau too often encouraged blacks to remain on plantations and sign labor contracts, they acknowledged that the bureau's very presence forced white southerners to recognize emancipation.

In February 1866 Congress passed the Freedmen's Bureau Bill to keep the agency in operation. Johnson promptly vetoed the bill.

A furious Congress quickly passed the **Civil Rights Act of 1866**, which declared that everyone born in the United States was a citizen with full civil rights. Again, Johnson issued a veto, partly because he believed the bill would "operate . . . against the white race." Congress overrode the veto. Then Congress returned to the matter of the Freedmen's Bureau, passed a new bill, and over-rode yet another veto.

Fearing that a future Democrat-controlled Congress might repeal the Civil Rights Act, Republicans wrote its provisions into the **Fourteenth Amendment**, passed in June 1866. The amendment required states to extend equal citizenship to all people "born or naturalized in the United States," including African Americans. The amendment's ratification in July 1868 created a national citizenship with rights—enjoyed equally by all—that were to be enforced by the federal government. The amendment did not guarantee blacks voting rights.

However, it encouraged states to grant those rights by reducing the number of representatives a state could send to Congress in proportion to the number of the state's male citizens denied the right to vote.

The Radicals come to power. In the 1866 congressional elections, Johnson appealed to voters to support candidates who opposed the Fourteenth Amendment. Few voters were receptive. Many were troubled by the ongoing violence against blacks in the South. In Memphis in May 1866, for example, white rioters killed 46 blacks and burned 12 schools and 4 churches. Fearing they might lose the fruits of their Civil War victory, northerners overwhelmingly elected Republicans in 1866.

Now firmly in command of Congress, the Republicans seized control of Reconstruction. Over Johnson's angry vetoes, Republicans passed the **Reconstruction Acts** of 1867. These acts divided the former Confederacy (except already-reconstructed Tennessee) into five military districts to be overseen by Union troops. To gain readmission to the Union, states were required to ratify the Fourteenth Amendment and to submit to Congress new constitutions giving all men the vote.

Tensions between Johnson and Congress continued to mount. In February 1868 Johnson ousted Secretary of War Edwin Stanton—an ally of the Radicals—without congressional approval. This was a violation of the Tenure of Office Act, and the House responded by voting to impeach the president. The vote in the Senate in May fell one short of the number needed to remove him from office.

▲ This 1866 poster mocks the effectiveness of the Civil Rights Act of 1866. As punishment for crimes, one freedman is being sold at auction while another is being whipped.

AFRICAN AMERICANS GAIN CIVIL RIGHTS

Have students work in pairs to create graphic organizers summarizing the expansion of civil rights brought by the Fourteenth and Fifteenth amendments and the criticisms of the amendments. Ask volunteers to share their graphic organizers with the class. After several organizers have been presented, encourage the class to discuss how citizenship and voting rights affected African Americans. Students may wish to include their organizers in their portfolios.

▼ A ticket of admission to the U.S. Senate galleries was required for people wishing to attend the impeachment trial of President Johnson.

The Granger Collection, New York

The attempt to force Johnson from office cost the Radical Republicans some popular support. To retain voters in the 1868 election, they chose popular war hero General Ulysses S. Grant as their presidential candidate. Grant won the election by a slim margin.

As worried Republicans studied the election returns, they realized that new African American voters had given them their narrow win. Eager to protect their power in both the North and the South, the Republicans drew up the **Fifteenth Amendment**, which Congress passed in 1869. Short and to the point, it stated that the right "to vote shall not be denied or abridged . . . on account of race, color, or previous condition of servitude."

■■ At first Moderate and Radical Republicans were divided over African American suffrage.

But postwar events led them to join forces to protect African Americans' rights.

The ratification of the Fifteenth Amendment in 1870 was a triumph for African Americans. The amendment did not, however, guarantee them the right to hold office. Nor did it prevent states from limiting voting rights through discriminatory requirements, such as literacy tests.

The amendment also failed to extend the vote to women. Some women's rights leaders, believing that "this hour belongs to the negro," had urged women to wait for the more controversial women's suffrage. Elizabeth Cady Stanton replied: "My question is this: Do you believe the African race is composed entirely of males?" Stanton and others had opposed ratification until all women gained the vote. The bitter debate divided the women's suffrage movement for over 20 years and alienated many African American women from the movement.

RECONSTRUCTION IN THE SOUTH

During the debate over African American suffrage, Congress imposed its Reconstruction plan. The advent of Radical Reconstruction rekindled the former slaves' hopes for equal citizenship. Some southern blacks took dramatic actions, such as chasing overseers from plantations. But many more registered to vote and turned to political activity to press for the equality promised by the Civil Rights Act and the Fourteenth Amendment. Even the churches found that "politics got in our midst" and overtook "our revival or religious work," one freedman minister recalled.

ANDREW JOHNSON

1808–1875

in office 1865–1869

ULYSSES S. GRANT

1822–1885

in office 1869–1877

ᵀeaching the Section

THE END OF RECONSTRUCTION

Ask students to identify the factors that contributed to the end of Reconstruction. List responses on the chalkboard. Then ask students to choose a factor from the list and create a political cartoon illustrating that factor. Encourage students to present and explain their cartoons to the class. Students may wish to include their work in their portfolios.

HISTORICAL SIDELIGHTS

New State Constitutions

When the new southern state constitutions were submitted to the voters for approval, many whites stayed away from the polls in an attempt to deprive the Radicals of the majority of registered voters that was needed for adoption. But Congress reacted to this tactic by passing a law that allowed new state constitutions to be approved by a simple majority of those voting.

BUILDING VOCABULARY

Ku Klux is most likely taken from a misspelling of the Greek word *kuklos*, meaning "ring" or "circle." *Klan* is the English word *clan* spelled with a *k*.

PRIMARY SOURCE

Description of Change: excerpted
Rationale: excerpted to focus on main idea

AV TRANSPARENCY

Everyday Life in America Transparency and **Worksheet 13**

African Americans also joined political clubs, such as the Union League. Begun in the North as a patriotic club, the league brought the views of the Republican party to the freed slaves and to poor whites. It provided blacks in particular with a place to develop their political skills.

Most importantly, African Americans served as delegates to the 1867 conventions held to draft new state constitutions. In Louisiana and South Carolina, black delegates outnumbered whites. In other states they made up 10 to 40 percent of the delegates. Many of these delegates were ex-slaves or free-born southern blacks, but northern blacks participated, too. Many northern African American communities watched their most talented professionals go south to help with Reconstruction.

Reconstruction governments. Most convention delegates were northern Republicans or white southern Unionists. Ex-Confederates resented the northern Republicans—white or black—whom they called carpetbaggers. The newcomers, they jeered, were "needy adventurers" of "the lowest class" who could carry all their belongings in a carpetbag (cheap suitcase). Ex-Confederates heaped even more scorn on southern whites who had backed the Union and supported Reconstruction. These whites, dubbed scalawags, were considered traitors.

The alliance of groups favoring Reconstruction allowed for political change in the South. New state constitutions abolished property qualifications for jurors and for candidates for public office and guaranteed white and black men the vote. Nine states also expanded married women's property

▲ **W.L. Sheppard sketched** *Electioneering in the South* **for** *Harper's Weekly* **in 1868 to illustrate African American interest in voting.**

rights. Once Congress approved the new constitutions, state legislators raised taxes to pay for new road, bridge, and railroad construction and for increased services, such as free public education.

■■ **Reconstruction legislatures, which included African Americans, made their state governments more democratic and increased services.**

Many ex-Confederates ridiculed the new state constitutions and pointed out corruption. During Reconstruction, some southern legislators did use their offices to enrich themselves just as they had done under slavery. But the scandals involving Reconstruction governments paled in comparison with government scandals in the North (see Chapter 6).

The Ku Klux Klan. The Reconstruction governments' reforms and African Americans' growing political participation stirred a vicious backlash. Angry white southerners formed secret terrorist groups to keep blacks from voting. The best known group was the Ku Klux Klan. Founded in the mid-1860s, the Klan grew quickly, attracting members from all social classes.

▲ **These two members of the Ku Klux Klan, shown in their uniforms, were captured at Huntsville, Alabama, during an 1868 riot.**

The Klan did not limit its attacks to politically active white and black Republicans. Klansmen beat and killed thousands of blacks whom they regarded as "uppity" or too successful. Sarah Song, an ex-slave from Louisiana, recalled how some 20 or 30 Klansmen killed her husband:

❝ He was shot in the head while he was in bed sick. . . . They came into the room. . . . Then one . . . put the pistol to his head and shot him three times. . . . Then one of them kicked him, and another shot him again when he was down. ❞

Practice

GUIDED PRACTICE

Organize students into small groups to create a class time line. Give each group a different main event of Reconstruction to illustrate and annotate on butcher paper. Have a member from each group work with the others to assemble the time-line panels for the class to study.

INDEPENDENT PRACTICE

Instruct students to select two events from the Guided Practice time line and to write a paragraph that explains how one event helped cause, or was an effect of, the other event.

Review and Assessment

REVIEW Invite students to imagine that as southern African Americans they are writing a letter to the editor of a northern newspaper. Ask them to explain to northerners what Reconstruction has accomplished and why it should not be abandoned. Then assign the Section 2 Review on p. 112.

ASSESS Assign the **Section 2 Daily Quiz** in *Core Resources*. ▶

Klansmen also burned homes and schools and stole livestock and land in an often effective effort to chase blacks and pro-Reconstruction whites from the South.

As violence mounted, African Americans demanded that Congress act to "enable us to exercise the rights of citizens." Between 1870 and 1871, Congress responded by passing three **Enforcement Acts**. The acts empowered the federal government to combat terrorism with military force and to prosecute suspects. In Mississippi alone, the federal government charged some 700 Klansmen. But most local whites resented federal intervention and seldom made convictions.

THE DEFEAT OF RECONSTRUCTION

For a time government intervention decreased Klan violence. But Republicans, and northern voters in general, began to turn their attention to economic issues and political corruption in the North. What remained of the Republicans' commitment to Reconstruction died with a severe economic downturn in 1873.

Faced with threats of strikes and hard-hit workers' and farmers' demands for relief, an Ohio Republican noted that "the overwhelming labor question has dwarfed all other questions." The partnership between northern businesspeople—the heart of the Republican party—and the former slaves had never been a stable one, and under economic pressure it dissolved altogether. "I suppose," said a former slave, "it is a fight between the poor people and the rich man now." Concerned with their own problems, many northerners began to accept southern whites' racist propaganda that portrayed blacks as unfit for self-government.

Economic discontent turned voters against the Republican-controlled Congress. In the 1874 congressional elections, Democrats gained a majority in the House. In the South they had won white Republicans' votes with promises of lower taxes and with racist appeals to white supremacy.

When Congress reconvened, Republicans made one final effort to enforce Reconstruction. They pushed through the **Civil Rights Bill of 1875**, which prohibited discrimination by hotels and other businesses serving the public. Yet even white Republicans who supported the bill had begun to see Reconstruction as a political liability.

▲ This Thomas Nast engraving, entitled *To Thine Own Self Be True*, commemorates the passage of the Civil Rights Bill of 1875.

The Granger Collection, New York

Convinced that the federal government would not stop them, Democrats in the South moved to "redeem," or win back, their states from the Republicans. Beginning in 1875 the "Redeemers" openly used terrorism to win state elections. Senator Ben Tillman of South Carolina later admitted: "We took the government away. We stuffed ballot boxes. We shot them [blacks]." Whites armed with rifles—even cannons—kept blacks away from the polls. A black official called the period "the most violent time that ever we have seen."

In 1876 the Redeemers focused on the presidential election, which pitted Democrat Samuel J. Tilden of New York against Republican Rutherford B. Hayes of Ohio. Opponents of Reconstruction vowed to win the election even "if we have to wade in blood knee-deep." In the popular vote they were successful. But challenges to the election results in four states meant that the electoral vote was another story.

An electoral commission set up to rule on the validity of the returns gave Hayes the presidency by one electoral vote. The Democrats in the House protested, and a deal was struck to end the crisis. The exact terms of the **Compromise of 1877** remain a matter of dispute. It is clear, however, that in return for Democrats' acceptance of Hayes as president, Republicans agreed not to use the military to enforce Reconstruction legislation.

Denied federal protection, the last of the Reconstruction governments fell. Once in power the Redeemers rewrote state constitutions and overturned many of the Reconstruction governments' reforms, trimmed spending, and cut services. Some states even did away with public education systems.

■■ By the early 1870s conditions in the North undermined Republicans' commitment to Reconstruction.

HISTORICAL SIDELIGHTS

Southern Redeemers
In addition to keeping African Americans out of Southern governments, the Redeemers reduced state aid to public works and social programs. Across the South, railroads lost state funding, and public schools in Texas began to charge fees for attendance.

HISTORICAL SIDELIGHTS

Politics
Grant realized that national support for Reconstruction was eroding. Asked why he had refused to send federal troops to Mississippi to protect black voters in the 1875 state elections, he replied that a delegation of prominent Republicans had told him the Republicans would lose Ohio to the Democrats if he did so.

RETEACH Have students work in pairs using the Essential Points in the section as major topics for an outline titled "Reconstruction in the South." Ask students to fill in the outline by listing appropriate subtopics for each major topic and by briefly summarizing each entry in the outline.

*C*losure

Ask students to judge whether Radical Reconstruction was a success or a failure. Encourage students to consider the Radicals' goals, the South's response, and the long-term legacy of Reconstruction in making their evaluation.

*E*xtension

INTERPRET Have students work in groups to find primary sources illustrating conditions for freedpeople after the Civil War. Ask groups to prepare dramatic readings from the sources.

CREATE Have students work in groups to research, assign roles, and prepare scripts to re-create the impeachment trial of Andrew Johnson.

SECTION REVIEW ANSWERS

IDENTIFY

For significance, see the following pages:
Thirteenth Amendment
   (p. 107)
black codes (p. 107)
Thaddeus Stevens (p. 107)
Civil Rights Act of 1866
   (p. 108)
Fourteenth Amendment
   (p. 108)
Reconstruction Acts (p. 108)
Fifteenth Amendment (p. 109)
Elizabeth Cady Stanton (p. 109)
Enforcement Acts (p. 111)
Civil Rights Bill of 1875
   (p. 111)
Compromise of 1877 (p. 111)

1. *much of South in ruins; many southerners poor; African Americans hopeful about future*
2. *Johnson—allowed ex-Confederates to dominate Reconstruction, limit African American rights; Radical Republicans—sought to punish ex-Confederates, protect and broaden rights of African Americans.*
3. *Intimidation and violence discouraged white Republicans and blacks from voting; Congress responded with Enforcement Acts.*
4. *Speeches might mention the need to participate in politics through churches and political clubs.*
5. *Students may note that a stronger economy might have allowed Republicans to keep their majority in the House and to continue Reconstruction.*

C O M M E N T A R Y

Reconstruction Perspectives

In the late 19th century, many white southerners remembered Reconstruction as a time when they were bullied by Union soldiers, lorded over by former slaves, and exploited by carpetbaggers and scalawags. Similarly, many northerners came to believe that Radical Reconstruction was a mistake.

Such views were for many years reflected in American history textbooks and in popular culture. For example, both Thomas Dixon's 1905 novel The Clansman and D. W. Griffith's 1915 film Birth of a Nation, based on Dixon's book, glorified the Klan and ridiculed Congress. Unfortunately, most white Americans accepted these views as fact, and such ideas only reinforced white southerners' opposition to African Americans' rights.

Blacks had a different perspective. They knew that their active participation had helped shape Radical Reconstruction. Francis L. Cardozo ably served as South Carolina's treasurer from 1872 to 1876. Hiram R. Revels, who had

recruited African Americans for the Union army and had taught school, represented Mississippi in the U.S. Senate. Blanche K. Bruce, a wealthy black planter from Mississippi, served as sheriff, tax collector, superintendent of education, and U.S. senator. The Reconstruction governments, asserted John R. Lynch, a black who served as speaker of Mississippi's House and as a representative to Congress, "were the best governments those States ever had."

These men and others left behind a positive social legacy that benefited both blacks and whites. They built roads, hospitals, and established free public schools. Blacks also built up their own communities, creating churches and strong family networks that helped sustain them through the post-Reconstruction years. Later generations drew on these institutions to build the civil rights movement.

Reconstruction also left a legal legacy. Although practically ignored for almost a century, the Civil Rights Act of 1866 and the Fourteenth and Fifteenth amendments provided an important legal framework. They enabled later civil rights leaders to win back voting rights for African Americans and to end legal segregation.

S E C T I O N   **2**   R E V I E W

IDENTIFY and explain the significance of each of the following: Thirteenth Amendment, black codes, Thaddeus Stevens, Civil Rights Act of 1866, Fourteenth Amendment, Reconstruction Acts, Fifteenth Amendment, Elizabeth Cady Stanton, Enforcement Acts, Civil Rights Bill of 1875, Compromise of 1877.

1. **MAIN IDEA** How did southern life change after the Civil War?
2. **MAIN IDEA** How did Reconstruction under the Radical Republicans differ from Reconstruction under Andrew Johnson?
3. **ASSESSING CONSEQUENCES** How did the Ku Klux Klan affect Reconstruction?
4. **WRITING TO PERSUADE** Imagine you are an African American living in the South during Reconstruction. Write a speech to deliver to community members recommending a course of action to help shape Reconstruction.
5. **HYPOTHESIZING** How might the course of Reconstruction have been different if the United States had not experienced an economic downturn in 1873? Explain your answer.

Chapter 4

SECTION 3

Introducing the Section

PREVIEW WORKSHOP

Following is a list of the significant people and terms in this section. You may wish to use this list as a section preview.

People
- Booker T. Washington
- Ida Wells-Barnett

Terms
- sharecropping
- crop-lien system
- poll taxes
- literacy tests
- Jim Crow laws
- *Plessy* v. *Ferguson*

MOTIVATING: PRIOR KNOWLEDGE

Ask students to recall the social structure of southern plantations before the Civil War. Ask students to suggest why this structure would no longer be workable during and after Reconstruction. Point out that this section explains the new structure and discusses people's reactions to it.

Section 3

THE NEW SOUTH

FOCUS
- **What new labor arrangements appeared in the South after the emancipation of the slaves?**
- **How did Reconstruction's end affect African Americans?**
- **How did African Americans respond to segregation and to the loss of civil and political rights?**

During the 1880s white business leaders began to speak of the "New" South, urging that the region move away from its dependence on cotton toward a more varied economy. Although southerners worked to build up the region's manufacturing enterprises, many remained in rural poverty. And for blacks in the South, racial discrimination made life harsher still.

Grant Hamilton's *From Darkness to Light* (1895) shows a New South rising from the ashes of the Civil War.

FOCUS OBJECTIVES
- Describe the new labor arrangements that appeared in the South after the emancipation of the slaves.
- Explain how Reconstruction's end affected African Americans.
- Recognize how African Americans responded to segregation and to the loss of civil and political rights.

MAKING CONNECTIONS

Economics

Interest rates on goods purchased on credit often exceeded 50 percent, a result of the South's shortage of capital and of fraud by rural merchants.

■■ Ask students what current interest rates are on car loans, mortgages, and credit cards. Discuss the difficulty of repaying loans with interest rates of 50 percent or more.

TENANT FARMING AND SHARECROPPING

After the Civil War, planters in the South faced a common problem: a shortage of labor. Few ex-slaves or whites wanted to work for the low wages planters were willing—or, in many cases, able—to pay. Many planters turned to **sharecropping** as a solution.

Under this system a sharecropper, or cropper, agreed to work a parcel of the planter's land in return for a share of the crop, a cabin, seed, tools, and a mule. Sharecropping appealed both to planters, because they got their lands worked without having to pay cash, and to the croppers—most of whom were ex-slaves—who received places to live and lands to work.

The system had a serious drawback, however. Croppers had no income until harvesttime. To obtain needed supplies, they promised their crops to local merchants who sold them goods on credit. Any debts they could not pay to the mer-

chants in a given year were added to the next year's bills.

This arrangement, known as the **crop-lien system**, made it nearly impossible for croppers—white or black—to work their way out of poverty. "Until he [the cropper] has paid the last dollar of his indebtedness, he is subject to . . . constant oversight and direction," economist Matthew Hammond noted at the time. In the judgment of former slave Thomas Hall, the system was "little better than slavery."

■■ **Many southern landowners turned to sharecropping and the crop-lien system to keep cotton production up and wages down.**

The crop-lien system also kept the southern economy tied to one-crop agriculture. Merchants would only give credit to farmers who grew certain crops, most often cotton. As a result, cotton displaced other crops to such an extent that southerners had to import food and animal feed from the North.

CORE RESOURCES
- **Section 3 Daily Quiz**

AV RESOURCES
- *The American Nation Videodisc: The Tuskegee Institute*

Teaching the Section

LIFE IN THE NEW SOUTH

Have pairs of students develop charts with three sections: New Labor Arrangements, African American Life After Reconstruction, and African American Responses. Have students use details from the text to complete their charts.

Practice

GUIDED PRACTICE

Ask students how each boldfaced term affected African Americans in the New South. List responses on the board.

INDEPENDENT PRACTICE

Tell students to imagine they are lawyers for African Americans who are suing for economic damages in the New South. Have students write opening trial arguments.

Review and Assessment

REVIEW
Have students work in pairs to write a conversation between a former slave who fled the South before the Civil War and a relative who never left the South. Encourage pairs to read their conversations to the class. Then assign the Section 3 Review on p. 115.

ASSESS
Assign the **Section 3 Daily Quiz** in *Core Resources*.

MULTICULTURAL PERSPECTIVES

After Reconstruction, as one freedman observed, "The whole South . . . got into the hands of the very men that held us slaves." As a result, some African Americans headed west. By 1880 about 15,000 freedpeople were in Kansas, farming, working in new towns, or founding new communities. Frederick Douglass and other African American leaders deplored this exodus. But some, like Sojourner Truth, encouraged it. Truth helped organize an association to assist migrants until they found employment.

THE AMERICAN NATION VIDEODISC PROGRAM

The Tuskegee Institute

1B   33609   3:53

▲ After the Civil War, the South began a slow course of industrialization. This photograph shows a worker at White Oaks Mills, a factory near Greensboro, North Carolina.

Some southerners argued that one-crop agriculture kept the South in poverty and too economically dependent on the North. They envisioned a New South that would manufacture its own goods. Supporters of the New South joined with northern and British investors to finance factories, steel mills, textile mills, improvements in railroads, and other enterprises.

Not everyone benefited equally from industrialization in the South, however. Factory owners and investors profited at the expense of workers who earned wages that were some 40 percent below what their northern counterparts earned. Most African Americans, meanwhile, could not find factory work at any wage. Many industrial workers were forced to buy goods on credit from the company store and to live in ramshackle company houses. Like sharecroppers, they soon found themselves locked in a cycle of debt.

TURNING BACK THE CLOCK

For African Americans the New South was starting to look very much like the Old South. Tied to the land through sharecropping and excluded from most factory jobs, African Americans had few economic opportunities. Moreover, Democrats, now firmly in control of the southern state legislatures, stepped up their attempts to strip blacks of their rights.

In an effort to deprive African Americans of the right to vote, southern state legislatures instituted **poll taxes**—fixed taxes imposed on every voter—and **literacy tests**—tests supposedly intended to limit the vote to those who could read. Technically, these measures did not violate the Fifteenth Amendment. However, since most black southerners were poor and had been denied an education, these laws accomplished their purpose.

To further deprive African Americans of their rights, states passed laws designed to enforce segregation, or separation, of the races. The first of these so-called **Jim Crow laws**, passed by Tennessee in 1881, required separate railway cars for blacks and whites. By the 1890s all southern states had legally segregated public transportation and schools. Segregation soon extended to parks, cemeteries, and other public places.

African Americans sued for equal treatment under the Civil Rights Act of 1875, but the Supreme Court refused to overturn the Jim Crow laws. The final blow came in 1896, when the Supreme Court's *Plessy v. Ferguson* decision ruled that "separate but equal" facilities did not violate the Fourteenth Amendment.

■■ After Reconstruction, African Americans were deprived of their rights and had few economic opportunities.

BLACK SOUTHERNERS ORGANIZE

Confronted by segregation and denied basic political and civil rights, some African Americans left the South for the Midwest or moved to northern cities. Most, however, stayed in the South, where their ancestors had lived for generations. To improve their lives, African Americans formed mutual aid societies, started businesses, strengthened churches, and built schools.

The key question facing African American leaders after 1877 was how to fight discrimination. Two influential leaders, Booker T. Washington, a former slave who founded Alabama's Tuskegee Institute in 1881, and Ida Wells-Barnett, a teacher and journalist, offered different answers to the discrimination question.

Washington believed that African Americans should concentrate on economic advancement. To further blacks' economic independence—which he

Closure

Read these words of African American leader W.E.B. Du Bois: *"The slave went free; stood a brief moment in the sun; then moved back again toward slavery."* Ask students to explain what Du Bois meant.

Extension

FORMULATE Have students research Justice John Marshall Harlan's dissenting opinion in *Plessy* v. *Ferguson.* Ask students to formulate an opinion dissenting from that of the majority on the Court.

RESEARCH Invite students to read biographies and write annotations about African American leaders during the 1870s and 1880s. Compile annotations into a *Who's Who* book.

◄ Tuskegee Institute was founded in 1881 to teach African Americans trades and professions. A printing class is shown here.

believed was the key to political and social equality—Washington urged blacks to seek practical training in trades and professions. He also discouraged them from protesting against discrimination, arguing that such protesting merely increased whites' hostility. If economic and social progress was to be made, he claimed, blacks would need "the cooperation of the Southern whites" because "they control government and own the property."

Ida Wells-Barnett

The Granger Collection, New York

BIO GRAPHY Many African American leaders did not agree with Washington's position. They argued instead that blacks should protest unfair treatment. One such leader was Ida Wells-Barnett (born Ida Bell Wells). Born to a slave family in 1862, Ida Wells was educated in a Mississippi freedmen's school and became a teacher herself at age 14. In 1884 Wells moved to Tennessee, where she lost her teaching job when she began protesting discrimination and segregated schools.

Ida Wells then turned to journalism, becoming part owner of the *Memphis Free Speech.* In 1892, after whites lynched three of her friends, she vowed to put a stop to lynching and wrote a fiery editorial on the subject. Angry whites responded by destroying her newspaper office.

Wells then left Memphis for New York, where she continued her crusade against lynching. After moving to Chicago and marrying lawyer Ferdinand Barnett in 1895, she published *A Red Record,* the first statistical study of lynching. Though lynchings decreased only slightly in the early 1900s, Wells's tireless efforts kept the public's attention focused on the issue.

■■ African Americans built their own institutions, and they adopted several approaches to fighting discrimination.

SECTION REVIEW ANSWERS

IDENTIFY

For significance, see the following pages:
sharecropping (p. 113)
crop-lien system (p. 113)
poll taxes (p. 114)
literacy tests (p. 114)
Jim Crow laws (p. 114)
Plessy v. Ferguson (p. 114)
Booker T. Washington (p. 114)
Ida Wells-Barnett (p. 115)

1. *turned to sharecropping and the crop-lien system to provide cheap labor*
2. *still denied rights and still had few economic opportunities*
3. *built their own institutions, adopted strategies such as economic advancement and protest to fight discrimination*
4. *Essays may mention that the sharecropper might be no better off because of low wages and being tied to a company's housing and store.*
5. *harmed African Americans, southern Unionists, and northern carpetbaggers; benefited former Confederates, white Democrats, and factory owners and investors*

SECTION 3 REVIEW

IDENTIFY and explain the significance of the following: sharecropping, crop-lien system, poll taxes, literacy tests, Jim Crow laws, *Plessy v. Ferguson,* Booker T. Washington, Ida Wells-Barnett.

1. **MAIN IDEA** After slavery had been abolished, how did plantation owners deal with the shortage of labor?
2. **MAIN IDEA** In what ways did the New South resemble the Old South (before Reconstruction) for African Americans?
3. **MAIN IDEA** What actions did blacks take in response to their loss of rights?
4. **WRITING TO EVALUATE** Write an essay evaluating the consequences for a white sharecropper of leaving the land to seek work in a southern factory.
5. **SYNTHESIZING** How did changes in the post-Reconstruction New South harm some groups of people and benefit others?

Return to the "Themes" section on p. 94. Have students discuss these again and compare their original responses to those given now. (See p. 93B for suggested answers.)

Chapter Review Answers

WRITING A SUMMARY
See Essential Points in each section for main ideas.

REVIEWING CHRONOLOGY
2, 5, 1, 4, 3
Assessing Consequences
Answers will vary but should make clear the reasons for assessments.

IDENTIFYING PEOPLE AND IDEAS
1. *commander of Confederate forces after 1862*
2. *first professionally licensed female doctor in America*
3. *Northern Democrats who sympathized with South*
4. *first African American to rise to rank of major in Union army*
5. *Ulysses S. Grant's strategy of fighting until South ran out of men, supplies, and will*
6. *laws limiting the freedom of ex-slaves*
7. *declared that everyone born in the U.S. was a citizen with full civil rights; passed over President Johnson's veto*
8. *deal in which Democrats accepted Hayes as president and Republicans agreed not to use the military to enforce Reconstruction legislation*

9. *system under which a person agrees to work a parcel of land in return for a share of the crop, a cabin, seed, tools, and a mule*
10. *women's rights leader who wanted to tie women's suffrage to African American suffrage*

UNDERSTANDING MAIN IDEAS
1. *political—changed from repressing rebellion to freeing slaves; military—shifted from dividing South to waging a war of attrition*
2. *North—growth of agriculture and industry; South—ruin of economy, end of slavery; both—loss of lives*

3. *Lincoln's and Johnson's plans were more lenient than the Radicals' plan.*
4. *African Americans participated in government and voted.*
5. *Sharecropping and crop-lien systems kept farmers poor; some industrial and other new opportunities increased, but many remained in poverty.*
6. *As white Democrats gained control of state governments, they passed laws to legalize segregation and to strip blacks of their newly won rights.*

CHAPTER 4
Review

Lincoln inaugurated. Fort Sumter falls. Union and Confederate forces collide at First Battle of Bull Run.	Emancipation Proclamation goes into effect. Draft riots in North. South defeated at Gettysburg. Vicksburg falls.	Lee surrenders at Appomattox. War ends. Thirteenth Amendment passed. Freedmen's Bureau established.	Civil Rights Act passed. Fourteenth Amendment passed.
1861	1863	1865	1866

WRITING A SUMMARY
Using the essential points of the chapter as a guide, write a summary of the chapter.

REVIEWING CHRONOLOGY
Number your paper 1 to 5. Study the time line above, and list the following events in the order in which they happened by writing the first next to 1, the second next to 2, and so on. Then complete the activity below.

1. Lee surrenders at Appomattox.
2. First Jim Crow law passed in Tennessee.
3. Emancipation Proclamation goes into effect.
4. Reconstruction ends.
5. Reconstruction Acts passed.

Assessing Consequences Choose the two events that you think had the greatest effects on the lives of African Americans, and explain the reasons for your assessment.

IDENTIFYING PEOPLE AND IDEAS
Explain the historical significance of each of the following people or terms.

1. Robert E. Lee
2. Elizabeth Blackwell
3. Copperheads
4. Martin Delany
5. war of attrition
6. black codes
7. Civil Rights Act of 1866
8. Compromise of 1877
9. sharecropping
10. Elizabeth Cady Stanton

UNDERSTANDING MAIN IDEAS
1. How did the goals of the North change as the Civil War progressed?
2. What were the consequences of the war for the North and the South?
3. How did the Reconstruction plans of Lincoln, Johnson, and the Radical Republicans differ?
4. What political roles did African Americans play during Reconstruction?
5. How did conditions for southern farmers and laborers change from 1865 to 1900?

6. How did changes in the New South reverse the policies of the Reconstruction period?

REVIEWING THEMES
1. **Geographic Diversity** What role did geography play in helping the North win the war?
2. **Constitutional Heritage** How did the Thirteenth, Fourteenth, and Fifteenth amendments attempt to adapt the U.S. Constitution to changing conditions after the Civil War?
3. **Democratic Values** How was democratic society in the U.S. expanded during Reconstruction? How did the expansion prepare for further changes in America's definition of democracy?

THINKING CRITICALLY
1. **Hypothesizing** How might the outcome of the Civil War have been different if European powers had aided the South?
2. **Evaluating** Why did many southern whites react so strongly to gains made by African Americans during Reconstruction?
3. **Synthesizing** Compare and contrast the views of Booker T. Washington and Ida Wells-Barnett on how African Americans should deal with discrimination.

STRATEGY FOR SUCCESS
Review the Skills Handbook entry on Reading Charts and Graphs beginning on page 756. Then study the chart below. How did the value of cotton goods produced in the South change during this period? How did southern production compare with that of the New England and Middle Atlantic regions?

VALUE OF COTTON GOODS PRODUCED 1880–1900 (in millions of dollars)			
Region	**1880**	**1890**	**1900**
New England	143	181	191
Middle Atlantic	29	40	48
Southern	16	41	95
Source: The American South			

REVIEWING THEMES

1. The North was able to divide the South along the Mississippi River, weaken its economy with a naval blockade, and capture its capital, which was close to northern territory.
2. provided framework to define some African American rights but failed to foresee how those rights would be undermined in New South
3. by extending political rights to black males; encouraged women to fight for their voting rights

THINKING CRITICALLY

1. Students might consider the impact of European money, manpower, and supplies in affecting the outcome.
2. Because the changes overturned the old class structure based on race, they evoked resentment and prejudice.
3. Washington focused on economic progress and social separation; Wells-Barnett said blacks should protest unfair treatment.

STRATEGY FOR SUCCESS

value grew by nearly 600 percent; the South was the fastest growing region, passing the Middle Atlantic region about 1890, though still far behind New England

WRITING ABOUT HISTORY

Essays should balance the goal of victory against the destructive implications of total war.

USING PRIMARY SOURCES

The demands include calls for equal treatment and protection before the law; the vote; and secure access to schools, churches, and the press. The demands are based on the principles of U.S. government.

LINKING HISTORY AND GEOGRAPHY

Paragraphs should mention how unreliable information about terrain may have led to difficulty in moving men and supplies and created delays in organizing military campaigns.

Reconstruction Acts passed.	Fifteenth Amendment passed.	Reconstruction ends.	First Jim Crow law passed in Tennessee.	Ida Wells-Barnett publishes first statistical study of lynching.	Supreme Court issues ruling in *Plessy* v. *Ferguson*.
1867	1869	1877	1881	1895	1896

WRITING ABOUT HISTORY

Writing to Evaluate The wisdom of Sherman's total-war tactics has been debated by historians. Write an essay evaluating whether such tactics would be practical in every war.

USING PRIMARY SOURCES

Read the following excerpt from a November 1865 letter that a group of African Americans from South Carolina wrote to the U.S. Congress. Then summarize the letter's main demands and explain the suggested basis for these demands.

66 *We would ask for no rights or privileges but such as rest upon the strong basis of justice. . . . We ask first, that the strong arm of law and order be placed alike over the entire people of this State; that life and property be secured, and the laborer free to sell his labor as the merchant his goods. . . .*

We ask that the three great agents of civilized society—the school, the pulpit, the press—be as secure in South Carolina as in Massachusetts or Vermont.

We ask that equal suffrage be conferred upon us, in common with the white men of this State.

This we ask, because "all free governments derive their just powers from the consent of the governed"; and we are largely in the majority in this State, bearing for a long period the burden of onerous taxation, without a just representation. 99

LINKING HISTORY AND GEOGRAPHY

The Civil War was commanded by generals whose knowledge of the terrain was often hampered by inaccurate maps. Read the following excerpt from T. Harry Williams's *Lincoln and His Generals* (1952). Then, in a paragraph, explain how unreliable information may have affected military campaigns in both the North and the South.

66 General Henry W. Halleck was running a campaign in the western theater in 1862 with maps he got from a book store. . . . Not until 1863 did the Army of the Potomac [the Union army] have an accurate map of northern Virginia, its theater of operations. . . . As late as 1864 there was not an office in Washington that could tell a general organizing a campaign what railroads were under military control . . . or how many men and supplies they could transport. 99

 BUILDING YOUR PORTFOLIO

Complete the following projects independently or cooperatively.

1. **CONFLICT** In Chapter 2 you examined the logistics of organizing a war effort from a government official's point of view. Building on that experience, imagine you are a soldier drafted into a Civil War army regiment—either for the Union or for the Confederacy—in 1864. Write a journal entry expressing your reactions to the war in general and to the draft, and describing the details of your military experience.

2. **INDIVIDUAL RIGHTS** In chapters 2 and 3 you argued for the expansion of rights for various groups in American society prior to the Civil War. Building on that experience, imagine you are a lawyer representing a group of African Americans in Mississippi in the second half of the 19th century. Prepare a closing statement arguing that your clients' rights have been violated by the black codes, Jim Crow laws, or the actions of groups such as the Ku Klux Klan.

 BUILDING YOUR PORTFOLIO

Have students refer to **Building Your Portfolio Worksheet 1**, assigned at the beginning of Unit 1. Use the worksheet to help students monitor their progress on the portfolio projects.

Assessment

Core Resources
• Reteaching Worksheet 4
• Chapter 4 Tests
• Alternative Assessment Forms
Test Generator

CONQUERING DISTANCE

Ordering Workers

Many Asian laborers who made their way to America in the 19th century were initially "imported" to work on American-owned plantations in Hawaii. Hawaiian plantation owners often spoke of their Asian workers as if they were property to be bought and sold. In 1890, for example, the owners of a plantation company sent a memo to a local manager requesting supplies. The order read in part as follows:

> bonemeal
> canvas
> Japanese laborers
> macaroni
> a Chinaman

America's GEOGRAPHY

CONQUERING DISTANCE

𝒯HE late 19th century was a period of massive population shifts for the United States. Between 1860 and 1910 some 23 million immigrants crossed the Atlantic and Pacific oceans to get here. Many of these immigrants joined the migration across the country as millions of people settled the American West. This westward migration was aided by dozens of railroad lines, trails, and improved systems of communication. These means of transportation and communication linked numerous western cities together, forming the basis of a modern transcontinental economy that eventually lured some western immigrants to the East Coast.

Conquering Distance Overseas

JAPAN 158,000
CHINA 290,000
NORTH AMERICA
UNITED STATES
ASIA
SCANDINAVIA 1.9 MILLION
RUSSIA & THE BALTICS 2.36 MILLION
IRELAND 2.3 MILLION
GREAT BRITAIN 2.79 MILLION
GERMANY 3.86 MILLION
ITALY 3.07 MILLION
EUROPE

IMMIGRATION TO THE U.S., 1860–1910

Other 28%
Japan <1%
China 1%
Germany 17%
Scandinavia 8%
Russia & Baltics 10%
Italy 13%
Ireland 10%
Great Britain 12%

Compared to European immigrants, immigrants from Asia had to travel twice as far to reach the United States. The vast majority of Chinese immigrants in the late 19th century came from the province of Guangdong. Although most initially settled along the Pacific coast, particularly in the San Francisco area, some eventually journeyed across the United States. In 1870 a Massachusetts factory owner began to recruit Chinese laborers from California to take the place of striking workers. As this practice caught on, more Chinese Californians made the trek to the east coast. Today the thriving Chinatowns of Boston, New York, and San Francisco are all the results of the 19th century journeys from Guangdong.

From Across the Pacific to the Atlantic Coast

CHINA
GUANGDONG
Canton
Hong Kong
HONG KONG TO SAN FRANCISCO, 6,951 MILES
San Francisco
SAN FRANCISCO TO BOSTON, 3,179 MILES
SAN FRANCISCO TO NEW YORK CITY, 3,036 MILES
New York City
ME
VT
NH
NY
MA
CT
RI
Boston
CA

PERCENTAGE OF CALIFORNIA CHINESE LIVING IN SAN FRANCISCO

San Francisco 24%
Rest of CA 66%
1870

San Francisco 45%
Rest of CA 55%
1900

CHINESE AMERICAN AREAS OF RESIDENCE

California 77%
All other areas 23%
1870

California 51%
North Atlantic 16%
All other areas 33%
1900

Conquering Distance Across the West

Railroad
Cattle trail
Other trail
Area settled by 1890
DUTCH Ethnic settlement area
SIOUX Indian reservation

0   200   400 Miles
0   200   400 Kilometers
Albers Equal-Area Projection

As the railroads and western population increased, many small towns grew into thriving cities within a few short years. Many followed the pattern of Omaha, Nebraska. The small settlement of Omaha, which was a popular stopping point for settlers headed to Colorado, officially became a town in 1857. After the first tracks of the Union Pacific Railroad were laid there in 1865, Omaha's population soared. Located in the heart of cattle country, the city developed a thriving meat-processing industry in the 1880s. This new industry attracted many settlers, particularly poor immigrants from southern and central Europe.

POPULATION OF OMAHA

1860	1,833
1900	102,555

Omaha

WESTERN POPULATION GROWTH, 1860–1910

1860	29%	71%	619,000 total
1870	32%	68%	991,000 total
1880	28%	72%	1,801,000 total
1890	25%	75%	3,134,000 total
1900	20%	80%	4,309,000 total
1910	20%	80%	7,082,000 total

25% % Foreign born
75% % Native born

Literature

One of the best-known series of books on the personal lives of the settlers who conquered distance was written by Laura Ingalls Wilder. Wilder's stories of growing up on the Plains during the late 19th century became best-sellers during the 20th century. Among her most popular works is the classic *Little House on the Prairie*, which was the basis for a hit television series. In recent years more historians have begun to value the Wilder books as examples of the daily lives of settlers.

■■ Ask students if they have read any of the works of Laura Ingalls Wilder. Ask what they learned about prairie life from their reading.

THE WESTERN CROSSROADS

1860–1910

Chapter Overview

Beginning in the years after the Civil War, the Native Americans of the Great Plains and the Far West fought a desperate battle to maintain their homelands and ways of life. Spearheaded by the U.S. Army and supported by land-hungry settlers, the Indian wars pushed the Native Americans from the Plains. Land acts and the spread of railroads across the Plains greatly increased the number of non-Indian settlers in the area, who then established farms and cattle ranches. The free grazing land in the West created a cattle boom that lasted about 20 years. Gold and silver drew thousands more westward, and eventually mining became the province of big business.

Chapter Planning Guide

CHAPTER 5	CORE RESOURCES	AUDIOVISUAL RESOURCES	PROGRAM RESOURCES
INTRODUCTION pp. 120–121	■ Building Your Portfolio Worksheet 1	■ Everyday Life in America Transparency and Worksheet 14	■ *Eyewitnesses and Others,* Volume 2: Reading 9
TEACHING THE CHAPTER pp. 122–137	■ Graphic Organizer 5 ■ Social Studies Skills Worksheet 5 ■ Geography Worksheet 5 ■ Literature Worksheet 5 ■ Outline Maps 8, 9	■ *The American Nation Videodisc: Crossroads of Cultures; Linking the Nation* ■ Linking Geography and History Transparencies and Worksheets 10A, 12A	■ Art in American History Transparencies and Worksheets 15, 17 ■ *Eyewitnesses and Others,* Volume 1: Reading 77; Volume 2: Readings 1, 2, 5, 7, 8, 10
REVIEW AND ASSESSMENT pp. 138–139	■ Chapter 5 Daily Quizzes ■ Reteaching Worksheet 5 ■ Chapter 5 Tests ■ Alternative Assessment Forms		■ Test Generator

Additional Resources

BOOKS FOR TEACHERS

Nabokov, Peter, ed. *Native American Testimony.* Viking Penguin, 1992. History of relations between Native Americans and whites, using Native American first-person accounts.

Painter, Nell. *Exodusters.* University Press of Kansas, 1986. Study of the African American migration to Kansas after Reconstruction.

White, Richard. *"It's Your Misfortune and None of My Own": A History of the American West.* University of Oklahoma Press, 1991. Scholarly history of the creation of the West.

BOOKS FOR STUDENTS

*Editors of Time-Life Books. *The Wild West.* Warner, 1993. Illustrated general history of the settlement of the West.

Hook, Jason. *American Indian Warrior Chiefs.* Sterling, 1990. Biographies of Crazy Horse, Chief Joseph, Geronimo, and Tecumseh.

Schlissel, Lillian, et al. *Far from Home: Families of the Westward Journey.* Schocken, 1989. Social history of western pioneers.

*for students reading below grade level

MULTIMEDIA MATERIALS

The American West: Myth and Reality. Video, 52 min. EAV/SSSS. Debunks television and movie myths about the West.

Ghost Town Hunters. Video, 50 min. SSSS. Tour of mining camps and other boom and bust towns.

Nez Percé: Portrait of a People. Video, 23 min. National Park Service/SSSS. History of the Nez Percé.

THEMES IN AMERICAN HISTORY

**USE WITH PAGES
120–121**

Listed on the right are the themes emphasized in Chapter 5. The questions in boldface type stimulate critical thinking and provide students with an opportunity to discuss the themes within a broadened context. The questions also appear in the pupil's edition on p. 120.

■ GEOGRAPHIC DIVERSITY

What strategies might people use to survive and prosper in arid or semi-arid environments? Students might consider ways people could adapt to these environments, including conserving water, raising crops and animals best suited to these regions, or devising farming methods that use the available water efficiently.

■ CULTURAL DIVERSITY

What problems might arise when one group attempts to force another group to give up its way of life? Students should discuss a group's rights to retain its own values, beliefs, and practices. They should consider that forcing a group to give up its culture might result in disruption of the group's economic and social organization, perhaps accompanied by resistance to these events.

■ ECONOMIC DEVELOPMENT

How might a government promote economic development in a new territory? Students might weigh the ability of settlers to develop the economy of a new territory against the difficulty settlers might encounter with such problems as establishing transportation and communication networks, legal rights to land, or relations with people already in the territory. They might also consider the impact that a government's land policies, and its ability to protect people in the new territory, could have on the territory's economic development.

CHAPTER STRATEGIES FOR MEETING INDIVIDUAL NEEDS

LIMITED ENGLISH PROFICIENT LEARNERS

Have students work in pairs to create scenes depicting life in the West in the late 19th century. Ask volunteers to compile the finished scenes into a slide presentation for the class. You may also wish to have LEP students work with visual learners in executing that activity.

TACTILE/KINESTHETIC LEARNERS

Organize students into groups to make models, dioramas, or diagrams of a Sioux Indian encampment, a sod farmhouse, a cattle ranch, or a mining camp.

LEARNERS HAVING DIFFICULTY

Organize students into four groups. Assign each group the Focus questions for a section. Have the groups identify the pages on which information to answer the questions can be found, take notes, and put their answers in sentence form. Have groups share their answers.

AUDITORY LEARNERS

Have students pick cowboy songs for a presentation, explaining how the songs depict cowboy life. A resource for this is *Cowboy Songs and Other Frontier Ballads* by J. A. and Allan Lomax.

VISUAL LEARNERS

Have students create a series of "Western Crossroads" postage stamps showing life on the Plains for Native Americans, farmers, cowboys, and miners. They can use the people cited in each section's Preview Workshop for possible choices.

GIFTED LEARNERS

Have students research and write an essay on myths about the West. The essay should identify how these misconceptions started, any inaccuracies they contain, reasons why they gained acceptance, and any effects they caused.

USING THE CHAPTER FOCUS

■ **UNDERSTANDING THE MAIN IDEA**

Call on a volunteer to read aloud the Understanding the Main Idea paragraph. Ask students to identify types of people who would be most likely to have moved West in the 1860s and later. Then ask them to write sentences describing how they think each of these groups might have viewed the West. Discuss similarities and differences among the groups' views and speculate on potential areas of conflict among them and with groups that occupied the land.

 THEMES

Have students work individually or in groups to answer the questions under Themes. Save students' responses so that they can compare them with their responses after studying the chapter. (See p. 119B for suggested answers.)

■ **THE TIME LINE**

Ask students to copy the events on the time line in their notebooks. After they read about each event in the chapter, ask them to write a paragraph that explains the causes and effects of that event.

CORE RESOURCES

• **Graphic Organizer 5**
• **Building Your Port-folio Worksheet 1**

AV RESOURCES

• *The American Nation* Videodisc: **Crossroads of Cultures**

120

ABOUT THE ILLUSTRATION

Although some women mined alongside their husbands, others, like the woman in this rare 1852 photograph, only visited the mine sites. Ask students to study the photograph on these pages and read the caption. Call on volunteers to suggest, based on the photograph, the kinds of tools and supplies a prospective miner would need to buy. Then ask them to speculate about the living and working conditions of the miners shown in the photograph.

Chapter 5

1860–1910

THE WESTERN CROSSROADS

 FOCUS

UNDERSTANDING THE MAIN IDEA

After the Civil War the regions of the West—the Great Plains, the Southwest, and the Far West—played important roles in U.S. economic growth. People moved to the West, encouraged by the U.S. government's offers of free land and the promise of profits from ranching, farming, lumbering, and mining. In many years of conflict and treaty negotiations, the U.S. government forced Native Americans to give up much of their lands.

THEMES

■ **GEOGRAPHIC DIVERSITY**
What strategies might people use to survive and prosper in arid or semiarid environments?

■ **CULTURAL DIVERSITY**
What problems might arise when one group attempts to force another group to give up its way of life?

■ **ECONOMIC DEVELOP-MENT** How might a government promote economic development in a new territory?

1862	1869	1876	1879	1896
The Homestead Act passed.	First transcontinental railroad completed.	Battle of Little Bighorn occurs.	Exodusters trek west.	Gold discovered in the Klondike.

LINK TO THE PAST

Have students recall previous conflicts between Native Americans and non-Indian settlers. Discuss what caused these conflicts and how they were resolved. Ask students to predict, based on previous conflicts, how Native Americans might respond to increasing pressures on their lands and resources from non-Indian settlers. Write students' responses on the chalkboard and have them check their accuracy as they read the chapter.

▶ **LINK TO THE PAST**

The resolution of the Oregon boundary dispute in 1846 and the Treaty of Guadalupe Hidalgo in 1848 opened up millions of acres of western land for U.S. settlement. Native Americans faced increasing pressure on their lands and resources as non-Indian settlers moved to the Far West.

Miners at Auburn Ravine, California, 1852

Ever since the Spanish planted settlements in the present-day southwestern United States, the West has been a crossroads where Native American and Asian, African, and European cultures met and influenced each other. European horses and guns, for example, changed the culture of the Plains Indians, allowing them to hunt buffalo more successfully and to move permanently from the mountains to the Plains. The Comanches—possibly the most-skilled horse raisers of the Plains—used the guns and horses to raid settlements and to dominate other Indian tribes on the southern Plains.

The Comanche way of life, however, required abundant land and buffalo. The Comanche freedom to roam the Plains was threatened after 1859, when the U.S. government stepped up its efforts to settle the Comanches on reservations in present-day Oklahoma. Ten Bears, a Comanche leader, argued against the government's plan:

❝ When I was in Washington the Great Father told me that all the Comanche land was ours, and that no one should hinder us in living on it. So, why do you ask us to leave the rivers, and the sun, and the wind, and live in houses? ❞

The federal government's reasons were overwhelmingly economic. As the U.S. government limited Native Americans to reservations, non-Indians rushed to the West to establish farms and ranches and to stake out mining claims. Soon the West began supplying the United States and the rest of the world with wheat, lumber, minerals, and cattle and sheep.

American buffalo

American Museum of Natural History

MULTICULTURAL PERSPECTIVES

Ten Bears argued against the government's plan to settle the Comanches on reservations at a meeting between government officials and Indian leaders. The officials asked why Native Americans were still raiding in Texas and Kansas. Ten Bears explained: "If the Texans had kept out of my country, there might have been peace. But that which you now say we must live in, is too small. The Texans have taken away the places where the grass grew the thickest and the timber was best. Had we kept that, we might have done the things you ask. But it is too late."

PRIMARY SOURCE

Description of Change: excerpted
Rationale: excerpted to focus on main idea

THE AMERICAN NATION VIDEODISC PROGRAM
Crossroads of Cultures

1A   21501   6:22

THE WESTERN CROSSROADS ▪▪ 121

Introducing the Section

FOCUS OBJECTIVES

- Analyze why the U.S. government adopted the reservation policy.

- Explain why so much conflict erupted between Native Americans and the federal government in the late 1800s.

- Describe how the federal government tried to "Americanize" Native Americans.

PREVIEW WORKSHOP

Following is a list of the significant people, places, and terms in this section. You may wish to use this list as a section preview.

People
- Sitting Bull
- George Armstrong Custer
- Wovoka
- Chief Joseph

- Geronimo
- Helen Hunt Jackson
- Sarah Winnemucca

Places
- San Carlos Reservation

Terms
- Treaty of Fort Laramie
- Bureau of Indian Affairs

- Sand Creek Massacre
- Treaty of Medicine Lodge
- Battle of the Little Bighorn
- Wounded Knee Massacre
- Long Walk
- assimilation
- Dawes General Allotment Act

Section 1

NATIVE AMERICAN RESISTANCE

FOCUS

- **Why did the U.S. government adopt the reservation policy?**
- **Why did so much conflict erupt between Native Americans and the federal government in the late 1800s?**
- **How did the federal government try to "Americanize" Native Americans?**

Until the 1850s most non-Indians who ventured to the West settled in California, Oregon, or Texas. By mid-century, however, non-Indians began settling on the Great Plains and in other parts of the West. To make room for the settlers, the government forced Native Americans onto reservations, provoking nearly a half century of conflict.

Sioux doll

INDIAN COUNTRY

By 1850 nearly all Native Americans—some 360,000—lived west of the Mississippi River. Indians from the old Northwest and the Southeast were confined to Indian Territory, in present-day Oklahoma. On the southern Plains, the Kiowas shared the land with the powerful Comanches. The Sioux, Blackfeet, and Crows dominated the northern Plains. In the Southwest the Apaches ranged throughout New Mexico, Arizona, and northern Mexico, while the Navajos and Hopis lived in farming or ranching communities.

In the Far West, disease and conflict associated with nearly a century of contact with Hispanic and other non-Indian settlers had reduced the Indian population, including the Paiutes (PY-oots), Pimas, Miwoks, and Maidus. In California alone their numbers had dropped from an estimated 300,000 in 1769 to some 35,000 by 1860.

In the 1851 **Treaty of Fort Laramie**, the U.S. government had promised the Sioux, Cheyenne, and other tribes control of the Plains—the bulk of Indian Country. In return, each tribe had accepted a defined territory, pledged not to attack settlers moving west, and allowed the government to build roads and forts in its territories. The government, however, soon broke the promises made in the treaty.

Hearing tales (both exaggerated and accurate) about the mineral wealth and fertile land in the West, thousands of non-Indians streamed into the territory. In a series of new treaties, the government forced Native Americans to move to reservations. The treaties promised reservation land,

Museum of the Great Plains

◄ **Driven out of Montana by the Cheyennes and Sioux, the Kiowas settled on the southern Plains, in an area stretching from Kansas to Mexico.**

MOTIVATING: PRIOR KNOWLEDGE

Ask students to recall how the attitudes of earlier settlers toward the land were different from those of Native Americans. (Areas for comparison should include attitudes toward natural resources, occupancy, land use, and land ownership.) Tell students that in this section they will learn how these differences once again became apparent in the late 1800s.

Teaching the Section

RESERVATION POLICY

Select several students to role-play a team of federal officials who are to convince a group of Native Americans to move to a reservation. Ask the rest of the class to play the Indians. The officials should attempt to convince the Indians why the move will benefit them. The Native Americans should challenge the officials about the proposed move, about the benefits of reservation life, and about any government promises made to them. When the presentation is complete, have the Indians discuss whether or not to move and vote on the issue. If the Indians vote not to move, ask them to predict possible consequences of their action.

money, and yearly supplies. The task of administering the reservations went to the **Bureau of Indian Affairs**, established in 1824 within the War Department. The close ties between the army and the bureau sent a clear message: Indians who resisted confinement on reservations would be dealt with by force.

Even when Native Americans went quietly to reservations, the government rarely kept its side of the bargain. Corrupt bureau agents often lined their pockets by selling the supplies intended for Native Americans to non-Indians. Furthermore, the government regularly reduced the size of reservations as settlers demanded more land. As a newspaper editor noted in 1869, the government's actions showed that "when the march of our empire demands this reservation of yours, we will assign you another; . . . so long as we choose, this is your home, your prison, your playground."

■■ **The U.S. government attempted to restrict Native Americans to reservations to make room for non-Indian settlers.**

YEARS OF STRUGGLE

Angered by the government's double-dealings, several Plains tribes, including the Cheyennes, Comanches, and Sioux, fought back. To them a life without buffalo hunting was no life at all.

The Plains peoples faced strong opposition. Some 20,000 U.S. Army troops, many of them Civil War veterans, enforced Indian removal. Some 4,000 were African Americans, nicknamed "buffalo soldiers," who served in four segregated units. The army enlisted Indians as scouts or as soldiers by playing on rivalries among tribes. For example, many Pawnees, Crows, and Shoshones helped U.S. forces battle the Sioux.

Sand Creek. One of the earliest confrontations in the West between the military and American Indians occurred in Colorado Territory. The territory's non-Indian population had been growing rapidly since the Colorado gold rush of 1858. Eager to open more land to U.S. settlers, John Evans, the territorial governor, pressured the Cheyennes and Arapahos to move to reservations. When some Cheyenne and Arapaho leaders refused to leave, Evans feared an uprising.

▲ Some time between 1875 and 1880, Cheyenne-Arapaho artist No Horse drew this scene, entitled *Women Honoring Warriors.*

No Horse, Women Honoring Warriors (1875–1880), Collection of Heard Museum, Phoenix, Arizona

Throughout the summer of 1864, Indian forces clashed with the local militia. By fall Black Kettle, a Cheyenne chief, was tired of fighting. He and his group made their way to Fort Lyon to surrender. When they stopped to camp along Sand Creek, most of the men left to hunt. In their absence, some 700 troops under Colonel John Chivington attacked the camp, killing some 200 Cheyennes, most of them women and children.

The **Sand Creek Massacre** horrified U.S. authorities. But Chivington was unrepentant. "Damn any man who sympathizes with Indians!" he exclaimed. "I have come to kill Indians, and believe it is right . . . to use any means under God's heaven to kill Indians."

News of the slaughter swept across the Plains, sparking raids by the Arapahos and Cheyennes. The Sioux, engaged in a long-standing war against the U.S. Army, also stepped up their efforts. But neither side emerged victorious. To end the fighting, U.S. authorities and American Indian leaders signed the **Treaty of Medicine Lodge** in 1867 and the second Treaty of Fort Laramie in 1868. In these treaties, the southern Plains Indians and the Sioux agreed to move to reservations.

The treaties did not end the fighting, however. As an editor of the *Army and Navy Journal* observed: "One of our hands holds the rifle and the other the peace-pipe, and we blaze away with both instruments at the same time. The chief consequence is a great *smoke*—and there it ends."

Sioux resistance. In 1875 the U.S. Army was again campaigning against the Sioux. Impatient to open up the Sioux's sacred Black Hills to gold prospectors, U.S. authorities ordered the Sioux to

HISTORICAL SIDELIGHTS

Buffalo Soldiers

When the Union Army was reorganized after the Civil War, officers created four African American units: the 24th and 25th infantries and the 9th and 10th cavalries. All four served in the West. These regiments had the highest reenlistment rates and the lowest desertion rates of any on the frontier. The soldiers responded proudly to the nickname given them by the Plains Indians. A Montana newspaper wrote admiringly of them, "There are no better troops in the service."

BUILDING VOCABULARY

Many Native American groups are known today by the pejorative names given to them by their enemies. The name *Sioux,* for example, is the French version of the Chippewa word for "snake." The Sioux called themselves *Oceti Shakowin,* the "Seven Council Fires," referring to the seven tribal groups that once made up their nation.

Teaching the Section

NATIVE AMERICANS AND FEDERAL GOVERNMENT CLASH

Create a six-column chart on the chalkboard titled *The U.S.-Native American Struggle*. Label each column as follows: *Event, Year, Participants, Causes, Outcome,* and *Consequences*. Starting with the Treaty of Fort Laramie and concluding with the Wounded Knee Massacre, have the class provide in chronological order information about battles, treaties, and other confrontations that occurred between Native Americans and the government, the army, or settlers during the period. When the chart is complete, ask volunteers to generalize about why the period was characterized by so much conflict between Native Americans and the government.

BIO GRAPHY PERSONALITIES IN HISTORY

In 1883 the Department of the Interior arranged a 15-city tour for Sitting Bull in order to separate him from the other Sioux at Standing Rock. He proved so popular that he became a member of Buffalo Bill's Wild West Show in 1885, but declined to go to Europe with the show in 1887. Sitting Bull continued to live at Standing Rock until 1890, when he was killed by Indian police sent to arrest him.

AV TRANSPARENCY

Linking Geography and History Transparency and **Worksheet 12A**

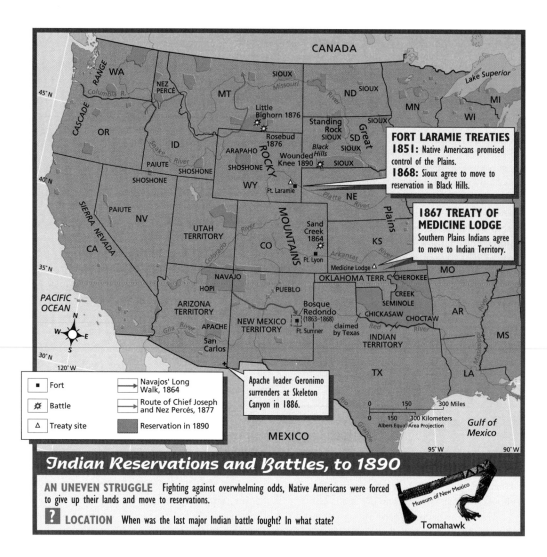

FORT LARAMIE TREATIES
1851: Native Americans promised control of the Plains.
1868: Sioux agree to move to reservation in Black Hills.

1867 TREATY OF MEDICINE LODGE
Southern Plains Indians agree to move to Indian Territory.

Apache leader Geronimo surrenders at Skeleton Canyon in 1886.

■ Fort
☼ Battle
△ Treaty site
→ Navajos' Long Walk, 1864
→ Route of Chief Joseph and Nez Percés, 1877
▨ Reservation in 1890

0   150   300 Miles
0   150   300 Kilometers
Albers Equal-Area Projection

Indian Reservations and Battles, to 1890

AN UNEVEN STRUGGLE Fighting against overwhelming odds, Native Americans were forced to give up their lands and move to reservations.

? LOCATION When was the last major Indian battle fought? In what state?

Tomahawk
Museum of New Mexico

settle near the agencies, the local offices of the Bureau of Indian Affairs.

Among those urging resistance to the government's efforts was Tatanka Iyotake, a medicine man whom non-Indians called Sitting Bull. One of the principal leaders of the Sioux nation, Sitting Bull was born around 1831. He joined his first war party at 14 and soon gained a reputation for courage and military skill.

Sitting Bull mocked those who gave in to reservation life. "You are fools," he argued, "to make yourselves slaves to a piece of fat bacon, some hard-tack [biscuits], and a little sugar and coffee."

◄ **Sitting Bull signed his name to this 1880s photograph shortly after it was taken.**

Many Sioux and Cheyennes agreed. They joined forces under Sitting Bull and Ta-sunko-witko (Crazy Horse). By late June 1876 Sitting Bull and Crazy Horse's camp on the Little Bighorn River contained almost 2,000 men prepared to fight.

The army, misjudging the size of the Indian fighting force, decided to strike first. The Native Americans, outnumbering the army troops and led by Crazy Horse, fought off two army attacks. On June 25, General George Armstrong Custer divided his force to strike the camp from three sides. Custer led a battalion of over 200 men. After the final attack, which lasted less than an hour, Custer and all his battalion lay dead.

The **Battle of the Little Bighorn** gave the Indians only a brief triumph. Their forces broke into

ASSIMILATION

Ask volunteers to identify ways by which the federal government attempted to "Americanize" Native Americans. List students' responses on the chalkboard. Then direct students to assume the role of an army officer assigned to direct the assimilation of the Navajos at Bosque Redondo in New Mexico. Have each student write a memorandum from the officer to a government official explaining why the plan for "Americanization" of the Navajos is not working. Ask volunteers to read their memorandums to the class. Then discuss how the government responded to the plan's failure and the resulting effects on the Navajos.

▶

smaller groups to evade army troops, but group by group, they were forced to surrender and settle near the agencies. Sitting Bull fled to Canada but later returned and settled on Standing Rock Reservation, where he continued to oppose non-Indian settlement of Sioux lands.

The Ghost Dance. A tragic final chapter of the Plains Indian–U.S. Army wars unfolded on the plains of South Dakota. The seeds of this conflict were planted in 1889 when Wovoka (woh-VOH-kuh), a Paiute holy man, began the Ghost Dance religion. Wovoka proclaimed that traditional Indian ways of life would revive if Indians performed the Ghost Dance. A Sioux explained the appeal of Wovoka's message:

▲ Some Ghost Dance performers wore Ghost Shirts similar to this one. They believed that the symbols of stars, birds, and animals on the garment protected them from harm.

Field Museum of Natural History

66 The rumor got about: "The dead are to return. The buffalo are to return. The Dakota [Sioux] people will get back their own way of life. The white people will soon go away, and that will mean happier times for us once more!"

That part about the dead returning . . . appealed to me. To think I should see my dear mother, grandmother, brothers and sisters again! 99

Wovoka preached peace. The Sioux living on reservations in the Dakotas, however, added a militant tone to the religion by donning "Ghost Shirts," whose special symbols, they believed, could stop bullets. Government agents, fearing the Ghost Dance would inspire Indian resistance, moved to suppress the religious movement.

In late December 1890, about 500 soldiers of the 7th Cavalry were sent to bring in some Sioux followers of the Ghost Dance who had left their reservation. The army encountered the Sioux at Wounded Knee Creek. As the army set about disarming them, someone fired a rifle—possibly during a scuffle, possibly as a signal. Gunfire immediately erupted between U.S. soldiers and Indians. Some 300 Sioux were killed, including women and children. About 30 U.S. soldiers also died. The **Wounded Knee Massacre** marked the end of the Indian wars on the Great Plains.

CONFLICT IN THE FAR WEST

Native Americans west of the Great Plains also faced resettlement. The government tried to force the Navajos in northwestern New Mexico and northeastern Arizona to give up sheep herding and become settled farmers. To enforce the government's plan, the army waged a campaign against the Navajo in 1863, destroying homes and sheep herds. Soldiers then forced the Navajos to walk to the Bosque Redondo reservation. This came to be known as the **Long Walk.**

The government gave the Navajos seeds and farming tools, but the land proved unsuitable for farming. Living conditions were harsh, and many Navajos died from malnutrition or disease. In 1868 the government, recognizing that its plan was unworkable, granted the Navajos a reservation in New Mexico and Arizona. There the Navajos rebuilt their communities, concentrating on raising sheep, weaving, and silver-smithing.

Farther north in the Wallowa (wah-LOW-uh) River Valley of northeastern Oregon, the Nez Percés also tried to avoid relocation. Although the Nez Percés had long maintained good relations with the U.S. government and white settlers, the government ordered the Nez Percés to move to an Idaho reservation in 1877. Their leader, Chief Joseph, reluctantly agreed. Before his people could leave, however, a few Nez Percés killed some white settlers, whom they viewed as intruders. Joseph's group, fearing attack, fled.

Pursued by army troops for three months, the Nez Percés journeyed east and north through Idaho, Wyoming, and Montana, picking up additional followers along the way. They planned to escape to Canada, but as winter approached, travel became harder. The Nez Percés surrendered only 30 miles from the Canadian border. An interpreter wept as he relayed Chief Joseph's surrender statement:

66 I am tired of fighting. Our chiefs are killed. . . . It is cold and we have no blankets. The little children are freezing to death. . . . My heart is sick and sad. From where the sun now stands, I will fight no more forever. 99

MAKING CONNECTIONS
Anthropology
Much of the information on the Ghost Dance religion from the Sioux perspective was gathered by anthropologist Ella Deloria from 1927 to the 1940s and published in *Speaking of Indians* (1944). Deloria was born on the Yankton Indian Reservation in South Dakota in 1888. She did fieldwork under the supervision of Frank Boas and Ruth Benedict, both pioneering anthropologists.

PRIMARY SOURCE
Description of Change: excerpted and bracketed
Rationale: excerpted to focus on main idea; bracketed to clarify meaning

PRIMARY SOURCE
Description of Change: excerpted
Rationale: excerpted to focus on main idea

Practice

GUIDED PRACTICE

Write the quotation from the *Army and Navy Journal* on p. 123 on the chalkboard and lead a class discussion on its meaning. Have students give examples of "rifles" and "peace-pipes" and interpret the use of the term *smoke*.

INDEPENDENT PRACTICE

Direct students to read the quote by the newspaper editor on p. 123 (first column, first full paragraph). Have students write an explanation of the passage, including an interpretation of the terms *prison* and *playground*.

Review and Assessment

REVIEW Pair students and have them create illustrated time lines for the period 1850 to 1890. For each event on the time line, have students include a brief annotation describing its effect on Native Americans. Then assign the Section 1 Review on p. 127.

ASSESS Assign the **Section 1 Daily Quiz** in *Core Resources.*

 GLOBAL CONNECTIONS

Canada also adopted some assimilation policies in the late 19th century, and in 1884 passed an anti-pot-latch law. Potlatch is an Indian ceremony that includes masked dancing and a lavish distribution of gifts. Some white men believed the ceremony to be barbaric and anti-Christian. A Kwakiutl Indian reacted to the law: "Do we ask the white man, 'Do as the Indian does'? No, we do not. Why then do you ask us, 'Do as the white man does'?"

■■ Ask students to suggest examples of ways non-Indians showed they considered Native American cultures inferior to their own. Ask students how they think such views allowed non-Indians to justify taking Indian lands.

MULTICULTURAL PERSPECTIVES

When choosing their 160-acre allotments, few Native Americans were concerned with their acreage's potential as farmland. Some selected acreage within traditional hunting grounds or at the site of an old encampment. Others chose land that had religious or personal significance.

▲ Before reaching the Canadian border, Chief Joseph surrendered to Colonel Nelson A. Miles on October 5, 1877. Shown here is *Chief Joseph Rides to Surrender* by Howard Terpning.

The Nez Percés, however, were not the last American Indians to surrender to the U.S. Army. The Apaches of the desert and canyon lands of New Mexico and Arizona mounted a long campaign against government control. The conflict began when settlers moved into Apache territory in the 1850s. Raids and attacks by both sides produced a climate of fear and hatred. In 1877 the U.S. government forced the seminomadic Apaches to settle on San Carlos Reservation in Arizona.

Most Apaches complied, but life on the reservation proved harsh. In 1881, amid rumors of an Indian uprising, army troops moved into the territory. Fearing an attack, Geronimo, an Apache chief, fled the reservation with about 75 followers. For the next five years, Geronimo's group raided settlements and evaded capture. But on September 4, 1886, with his followers outnumbered, Geronimo gave up. "Once I moved about like the wind," he told his captors. "Now I surrender to you and that is all." His surrender marked the end of armed resistance to the reservation system.

■■ **The U.S. Army and Native Americans clashed as the U.S. government took away Indian lands.**

*R*ETHINKING INDIAN POLICY

By the 1880s Native Americans had been forced to surrender more than 450 million acres to the U.S. government. The Indians had been driven off their land and onto reservations by a number of pres-

sures. While the army forced Indians onto reservations, U.S. settlers, whose presence increased as railroads snaked across the West, moved onto Indian lands and killed off most of the buffalo herds. "Kill every buffalo you can," advised Colonel R. I. Dodge. "Every buffalo dead is an Indian gone." With the loss of the buffalo, Native Americans had little hope of maintaining an independent existence on the Plains.

At the same time, a small but active group of reformers was voicing alarm at the mistreatment of Native Americans. Helen Hunt Jackson's influential book, *A Century of Dishonor,* attacked the government for its years of broken promises and corrupt dealings with Indians. Another important reformer was Thoc-me-tony (Shell-Flower), a Paiute woman known as Sarah Winnemucca. Outraged by the Paiutes' forced removal to Yakima Reservation in Washington Territory in 1878, she began lecturing to non-Indians about the Paiutes' plight. Later she reached a wider audience with her book *Life Among the Piutes.*

▲ Sarah Winnemucca brought the plight of Native Americans to the nation's attention in the 1880s.

Many government officials, as well as reformers interested in Indian welfare, viewed **assimilation**, or cultural absorption, of Native Americans into "white America" as the only way to ensure Native American survival. The federal government urged Native Americans to become farmers and to move out of their dwellings and live in wooden houses. To encourage assimilation, the government passed laws to force Native Americans to abandon their traditional appearance and to dress like "Americans." One law ordered Indian men to cut their long hair. Another outlawed Indian religious practices.

To speed assimilation, the government set up a system of Indian schools. Some Indian children attended reservation schools, while others were forced to leave home to attend boarding schools. The Carlisle Indian School in Pennsylvania

Closure

Write on the chalkboard the following statement from *Extraordinary American Indians* by Susan Avery and Linda Skinner: *"Removal and allotment were both attempts to control Indian destiny that sprang from alliances of greed and misguided humanitarian impulses."* Have volunteers explain why they agree or disagree with this statement.

Extension

INTERVIEW Direct students to research the life of one of the Native American leaders discussed in the section. Have students present their information in the form of a question-and-answer interview.

ANALYZE Have students investigate the life of Native Americans on reservations today and write editorials comparing reservation conditions in the late 1800s with conditions today.

◀ A group of Navajos from New Mexico arrived at the Carlisle Indian School in the 1880s. Six months after arrival they posed for this photograph, outfitted in school uniforms.

typified the boarding school system. Students were forced to speak only English, wear "proper" clothes, and change their names to "American" ones. The school's founder summed up his aim: to "kill the Indian and save the man."

The government's most important assimilation strategy, however, was forcing Indians to give up tribal ownership of land in favor of private ownership. Private ownership, the government argued, lay at the heart of Americanization. Western settlers and developers wanted Native Americans to give up tribal ownership of land for another reason: if Native Americans could be forced onto small plots, settlers and developers could then buy up surplus reservation land.

The passage of the **Dawes General Allotment Act** in 1887 established private ownership of Indian land. The act required that Indian lands be surveyed and Indian families claim an allotment of 160 acres of reservation land for farming. The remaining land would be sold.

The Dawes Act proved to be a disaster for Native Americans. In less than 50 years, they lost two thirds of their land. In addition to the surplus land sold to settlers and developers, American Indians sold or were cheated out of their allotments. By 1890 forced assimilation and warfare had reduced the U.S. Indian population to fewer than 250,000.

By outlawing Indian customs, establishing boarding schools, and enforcing private land ownership, the U.S. government attempted to assimilate Native Americans.

SECTION REVIEW ANSWERS

IDENTIFY

For significance, see the following pages:
Bureau of Indian Affairs (p. 123)
Sand Creek Massacre (p. 123)
Treaty of Medicine Lodge (p. 123)
Sitting Bull (p. 124)
George Armstrong Custer (p. 124)
Battle of the Little Bighorn (p. 124)
Wovoka (p. 125)
Wounded Knee Massacre (p. 125)
Chief Joseph (p. 125)
Geronimo (p. 126)
Helen Hunt Jackson (p. 126)
Sarah Winnemucca (p. 126)
Dawes General Allotment Act (p. 127)

LOCATE

For location, see the map on p. 124.

1. *to make room for non-Indian settlers; clashed with troops in many battles*
2. *Treaty of Fort Laramie promised Native Americans control of Great Plains. Later, U.S. government forced Native Americans onto reservations.*
3. *forbade Indian customs, set up schools, enforced private land ownership*
4. *Essays might mention hope offered by "Ghost Dance" and protection promised by "Ghost Shirt."*
5. *harsh living conditions at Bosque Redondo land not unsuitable for farming*

SECTION 1 REVIEW

IDENTIFY and explain the significance of the following: Bureau of Indian Affairs, Sand Creek Massacre, Treaty of Medicine Lodge, Sitting Bull, George Armstrong Custer, Battle of the Little Bighorn, Wovoka, Wounded Knee Massacre, Chief Joseph, Geronimo, Helen Hunt Jackson, Sarah Winnemucca, Dawes General Allotment Act.

LOCATE and explain the importance of the following: San Carlos Reservation.

1. **MAIN IDEA** Why did the U.S. government attempt to resettle Native Americans on reservations? How did Native Americans respond to this attempt?
2. **MAIN IDEA** How did the government's policy toward Native Americans as outlined in the Treaty of Fort Laramie differ from the government's policy in the late 1800s?
3. **MAIN IDEA** What did the U.S. government do to try to assimilate Native Americans?
4. **WRITING TO EXPLAIN** Imagine you are a Sioux who took part in the Ghost Dance religion. Write an essay explaining the meaning of the Ghost Dance and Ghost Shirt.
5. **ANALYZING** Why was the government's attempt to relocate Navajos unsuccessful?

FOCUS OBJECTIVES

- Analyze why many farmers moved to the West in the late 1800s.

- Describe the innovations that helped farmers cope with the western environments.

- List the factors that led to the rise and fall of the cattle boom in the 1870s and 1880s.

PREVIEW WORKSHOP

Following is a list of the significant people, places, and terms in this section. You may wish to use this list as a section preview.

People
- Joseph Glidden

Places
- Central Pacific Railroad

- Union Pacific Railroad
- Red River Valley

Terms
- Homestead Act
- Pacific Railway Act
- Morrill Act
- Exodusters
- U.S. Department of Agriculture

- dry farming
- bonanza farm
- Texas longhorn
- long drives
- railhead
- open range

Section 2

WESTERN FARMERS AND CATTLE RANCHERS

FOCUS

- **Why did many farmers move to the West in the late 1800s?**
- **What innovations helped farmers cope with the western environments?**
- **What factors led to the rise and fall of the cattle boom in the 1870s and 1880s?**

Windmill on the western Great Plains

Attracted by the promise of free or cheap land, thousands moved to the West after the Civil War. Farmers were able to take advantage of this opportunity because new technologies enabled them to deal with the West's harsh environment. The new railroads that crossed the West provided farmers and ranchers access to eastern markets and made possible the cattle ranching boom.

ECONOMIC DEVELOPMENT OF THE WEST

After the southern states seceded from the Union, northern Republicans saw a chance to develop the West along northern lines. The Republicans wanted the new western states and territories to be free of slavery and populated by independent farmers who would develop the land. To attain these goals, Republicans passed a series of acts in 1862 to put public lands to productive use.

Land acts. Three government land acts increased non-Indian settlement of the Great Plains. The **Homestead Act** granted a 160-acre homestead, or farm, to any citizen or prospective citizen willing to live in the Great Plains and cultivate the land for five years. Some 400,000 families took advantage of this offer. The **Pacific Railway Act** gave land to railroad companies to build a transcontinental railroad linking both coasts. The **Morrill Act** granted land to the states to set up agricultural colleges, which would help farmers develop the West.

◀ Daniel Freeman filed this claim in Brownsville, Nebraska, for 160 acres of land in January 1863. He received this homestead certificate after certifying that he had built a "part log & part frame" house on his claim.

MOTIVATING: STUDENT EXPERIENCES

Have students suggest phrases and images they associate with farming in the West and with cowboys and cattle ranching. Discuss where these impressions of western life came from and to what extent they have been influenced by movies and other media. Then tell students that in this section they can check the accuracy of their impressions against the historical reality.

*T*eaching the *S*ection

WHY FARMERS MOVED WEST

Have students work in small groups and act as writers and artists hired by railroad companies to create full-page newspaper ads to attract settlers to Oklahoma or Kansas. Tell the groups that their ads should combine appealing images with lists of incentives that convinced farmers to settle on the Great Plains. Have groups present their completed advertisements. Then ask the class to summarize, based on the advertisements, why farmers moved to the West in the late 1800s.

■■ Have students discuss what factors might cause them to move to another part of the country. ▶

Competition for land was fierce. In Oklahoma in 1889, for example, a flood of would-be settlers responded to a government offer of free homesteads. In March, President Benjamin Harrison announced that former Seminole and Creek lands would become available on April 22 to the first takers. By the appointed day, some 50,000 prospective homesteaders gathered to race for the land. At exactly noon the stampede began. Settler Hamilton S. Wicks noted the result:

66 On the morning of April 23, a city of 10,000 people, 500 houses, and innumer-able tents existed where twelve hours before was nothing but a broad expanse of prairie. 99

Subsequent "runs" took place in other parts of Oklahoma. As a result, Native Americans lost more than 11 million acres to non-Indian settlers.

The railroads. Railroad companies also helped lure settlers to the West. Between 1869 and 1883 the companies built four transcontinental lines (see map, page 132). To pay the huge costs of laying the tracks, the companies sold settlers land

PRIMARY SOURCE

Description of Change: excerpted
Rationale: excerpted to focus on main idea

THE AMERICAN NATION VIDEODISC PROGRAM
Linking the Nation

| 1B | 29399 | 2:20 |

AV **TRANSPARENCY**
Linking Geography and History Transparency and **Worksheet 10A**

Changing Ways

A TRANSCONTINENTAL RAILROAD

In the mid-1800s there was no easy way to get from the East Coast to the West Coast. Both the overland journey and the boat trip around the tip of South America could take months. To help open the West to settlers, Congress passed the Pacific Railway Act in 1862. The act awarded contracts to build a transcontinental railroad to the Central Pacific and the Union Pacific railroad companies.

The track had to cross some 1,500 miles of wilderness. The Central Pacific Railroad would lay track eastward from Sacramento, California, over the Sierra Nevada. The Union Pacific would work westward from Omaha, Nebraska, and cross the rugged Rockies.

To encourage the companies to take on the job, the federal government gave them land. The project soon became a

▲ Laborers from different ethnic backgrounds helped build the transcontinental railroad. This 1886 photograph shows a Northern Pacific Railroad crew.

contest to see which company would lay more track.

The railroad companies recruited thousands of workers for the often perilous work. Work crews competed against nature as well as each other as they blasted, shoveled, and pick-axed their way across the continent. During the winters snowdrifts and avalanches blocked mountain passes. Some laborers died doing the dangerous blasting work. The crews also faced attacks by Indians,

who tried to prevent "the wagons which make a noise" from invading their land.

Most of the Union Pacific's 10,000 workers were Irish immigrants. After the Civil War, veterans from both sides also signed on. The Central Pacific's work force consisted mostly of Chinese laborers. One observer called the sound of the crews' progress "a grand Anvil Chorus" that played "in triple time: three strokes to the spike; ten spikes to the rail; 400 rails to the mile." After seven years the crews met at Promontory, Utah, on May 10, 1869.

Railroad officials, politicians, and workers looked on as the last railroad tie—made of laurel wood, a symbol of victory in a contest of strength—was put into place. Leland Stanford, president of the Central Pacific and former governor of California, then drove a golden spike to complete the railroad. The telegraph built alongside the tracks flashed the news from coast to coast.

Changing Ways

A TRANSCONTINENTAL RAILROAD

SETTING THE SCENE

The work crews of the Central Pacific Railroad faced blizzards and other natural hazards in the winter of 1866–67 as they laid tracks over the Sierra Nevada. Since few whites wanted the dangerous job of blasting through the mountains, the Chinese took these jobs. They were suspended from cliff tops in wire baskets to drill holes and plant explosives in the cliff sides. Once they lit the explosives, they faced certain death if not pulled back up in time.

Teaching the Section

ADAPTING TO WESTERN ENVIRONMENTS

Make a three-column chart on the chalkboard labeled *Problem, Effect, Solutions.* In the first column list challenges western farmers faced, such as lack of water, lack of trees, harsh winters, strong winds, and heavy topsoil. Have students complete the chart, indicating the effects of each problem, and how each problem was solved.

MULTICULTURAL PERSPECTIVES

The African American migrants to Kansas were known as "Exodusters" because they believed that, like the Israelites depicted in Exodus (the second book of the Bible), God would help them flee the land of slavery and find their freedom.

GLOBAL CONNECTIONS

From 1870 to 1910, close to 1.5 million Scandinavians (Nowegians, Danes, and Swedes) immigrated to the U.S. During this period the homelands of these immigrants had experienced population explosions, land shortages, and the shift of their economies from agriculture to industry. Most Scandinavian immigrants moved to Plains states where the farming conditions and climate reminded them of home.

donated by federal, state, and local governments. The federal government, for example, gave the railroads more than 100 million acres of land. To attract buyers, the railroads offered free transportation and credit.

Railroads also stimulated the midwestern and western lumbering industry. Vast pine forests in Michigan, Wisconsin, Minnesota, and eventually the Pacific Northwest supplied wood for railroad ties, railroad cars, and buildings that sprang up along the railroad routes. But uncontrolled lumbering destroyed wildlife habitats, caused erosion, and had other important ecological consequences little recognized at the time.

Who moved to the West? Economic motives, the search for racial tolerance, and the promise of a better life drew three main groups to the West after the Civil War. They were (1) white Americans from the East; (2) African Americans from the South; and (3) immigrants from Europe and Asia.

Most white newcomers came from more settled areas of the United States. As a Nebraska settler explained, "I am well satisfied that I can do better here than I can in Illinois." The high cost of transporting supplies to the West also meant that most settlers were middle-class farmers and businesspeople who could afford the move.

While African Americans moved west to obtain land, they also sought to escape violence and persecution. Kansas, where John Brown had first fought against slavery, especially appealed to African American settlers. The biggest rush of black settlers occurred during the Kansas Fever Exodus of 1879. From 20,000 to 40,000 African Americans fled the South after violence erupted during the 1878 elections. Poor and ill-equipped, these black settlers, known as **Exodusters**, were helped by established black settlers. The Exodusters eventually settled some 20,000 acres.

European immigrants also flocked to the western United States. "America Fever" infected thousands of Norwegians, Swedes, and Danes. In 1882 alone more than 100,000 came to the American West. In addition, many Irish who had helped build the railroads and a great number of Germans who had settled in the Mississippi Valley decided to move to the Plains. They were joined by Mennonites, Protestant pacifists who fled persecution in Russia. Their experience growing wheat on the Russian steppes, or grasslands, proved particularly useful on the Great Plains.

Many Chinese immigrants who had come to California during the gold rush of 1849 also turned to farming. In California in 1880 some 3,200 Chinese raised crops. Throughout the West, they worked on their own farms or as farm laborers, sharecroppers, or produce vendors.

■■ **Farmers moved onto the Great Plains for a variety of motives, but the main incentive was readily available land.**

▲ Between 1830 and 1910 some 90 percent of all pioneers west of the Missouri River lived in sod houses. Shown here is the Scott family, photographed outside their Nebraska home in 1889.

WESTERN FARMS

Environmental conditions in the West posed special problems for farmers. The cold winters and arid conditions of the Great Plains required new crops and farming techniques. The scarcity of trees meant that farmers had to find new building materials. Turning to sod, they built houses and barns out of sod chunks cut from the heavy topsoil and stacked like bricks. Sod houses were well insulated, windproof, and fireproof but also dank, dirty, full of insects, and far from rainproof.

The **U.S. Department of Agriculture**, created in 1862, helped farmers adapt to the Plains environment. Department experts sought out and publicized new varieties of wheat that would grow in the cold winters of the northern Plains.

BONANZA FARMS

Ask students to write magazine articles titled "Bonanza Farms" that analyze why bonanza farms developed, where they were located, and why they eventually failed. Students may wish to include maps with their articles. Have volunteers read their articles to the class. Students may wish to include their magazine articles in their portfolios.

CATTLE INDUSTRY: BOOM AND BUST

Have students work in several small groups to create two graphic organizers. Half the groups should create organizers showing the factors that led to the growth of cattle ranching. (*cheap land, railroads, growing eastern markets, hardy cattle*) The other groups should create organizers showing factors that led to its decline. (*overgrazing,* *oversupply, price declines, barbed wire, bad weather*) Have groups present and explain their graphic organizers.

◀ Bonanza farms applied the techniques of the factory system to agriculture. By 1890 there were some 300 farms in the Red River Valley that covered about 1,000 acres each. This photograph shows one such operation in the San Fernando Valley of California.

▶

Department of Agriculture agents also taught **dry farming** techniques, planting and harvesting methods that conserve moisture. For example, agents advised farmers to plow deep furrows to bring moisture to the surface and to break up the soil after a rainfall to prevent evaporation.

To tap water deep underground, Plains farmers adapted drilling machinery developed by petroleum companies. They also used new models of windmills—wind-powered water pumps designed to withstand the Plains' strong winds.

Lack of water was a problem for farmers further west, too. In parts of the Southwest, Hispanic and Native American farmers had developed irrigation systems that used canals, sloping fields, and dams to control water flow. They had also established farms that fanned out in thin strips from water sources so that all community residents had access to water. The new settlers had to adopt these methods to survive.

On the Plains new farm equipment also helped farmers. James Oliver's factory in South Bend, Indiana, produced thousands of plows with sharp, durable blades to slice through the tough prairie sod. "Self-binding" harvesters not only cut wheat but also tied it into bundles. The combine—a sort of factory on wheels—cut, threshed, and cleaned the grain all in one operation.

■■ **Government support, innovative farming practices, and new technologies helped make farming on the Plains possible.**

Efficient new farm machinery and cheap, abundant land made possible the creation of a new kind of large-scale operation, the **bonanza farm**. Most bonanza farms were owned by companies and run like factories, with professional managers.

At planting and harvesting times foremen often supervised some 500 to 1,000 extra workers.

The first bonanza farms were established in the Red River Valley in Dakota Territory and Minnesota in the mid-1870s. They were located close to the Northern Pacific Railroad which transported their wheat to market.

Investors also organized bonanza farms farther west. In California's Central Valley one of the largest wheat farms covered more than 66,000 acres. Although California led the country in wheat production in the 1880s, by the 1890s most California farmers had turned to more-profitable fruit and vegetable crops. Farmers shipped these crops east in refrigerated railcars.

When weather and market conditions were good, bonanza farms made large profits; buying seeds and equipment in bulk meant lower production costs. But in times of drought or low wheat prices, their profits fell. Family farmers, with fewer workers to pay and less money invested in equipment, could better handle boom-and-bust cycles. Thus by the 1890s most bonanza farms had been broken up into smaller farms.

Plains farming demanded hard work from everyone in the family. Men did most of the heavy labor of building houses, fencing the land, and farming. Women, in addition to household and child-rearing tasks, also worked in the fields. One woman was her husband's "sole help in getting up and stacking at least 25 tons of hay and oats."

Children had to do their share, too. They fetched water, tended gardens, and did such routine chores as churning butter.

■■ **Large-scale bonanza farms were profitable during boom times, but family farms were better able to keep costs down.**

Practice

GUIDED PRACTICE

On the chalkboard draw a two-column chart with the headings *Benefits* and *Costs*. Have students list all the possible benefits for a homesteader moving to the Great Plains. Then have them suggest the possible costs of such a change, including the social costs of isolation and initial lack of schools as well as the personal and economic risks.

INDEPENDENT PRACTICE

Have students review the chart from the Guided Practice and use it to write an essay about why they would, or would not, have moved west in the late 1800s.

Review and Assessment

REVIEW Have students make a list of topics for an encyclopedia article titled "Life in the West During the Late 1800s." Have volunteers share their lists with the class, explaining why each topic should be included in the article. Then assign the Section 2 Review on p. 133.

ASSESS Assign the **Section 2 Daily Quiz** in *Core Resources*.

HISTORICAL SIDELIGHTS

Woman Trailblazer

In 1871 Amanda Burks was one of the first women to join one of the long drives herding longhorns. In the months that she traveled with her husband on the drive, she endured many difficulties, including severe storms, homesickness, rustlers, and extreme heat. But the freedom of outdoor life outweighed the dangers, as she reflected on her return home: "For what woman, youthful and full of spirit and the love of living, need sympathy because of availing herself of the opportunity of being . . . in the great out-of-door world!"

COOPERATIVE LEARNING

Have students work in small groups and imagine they are employed by a cattletown newspaper. Students can take roles as editors, reporters, cartoonists, and headline writers. Ask each group to prepare a four-page newspaper covering activities that might have taken place during the course of a week.

Map Caption Answer
Central Pacific, Union Pacific; Southern Pacific, Atlantic & Pacific; Southern Pacific, Texas & Pacific; Northern Pacific

𝒯HE CATTLE BOOM

The factors that made bonanza farms possible—the growth of eastern markets, completion of the railroad, and access to land—also led to a boom in cattle ranching after the Civil War.

The first ranches were in Texas. There English cattle had bred with cattle first introduced by the Spanish in the 1500s. By the 1850s they had produced a new breed—the **Texas longhorn**. Although their meat was tough, the hardy longhorns could survive **long drives**, treks of hundreds of miles, to a **railhead**, a town along the railroad. There they were sold and shipped east for slaughter. In 1866 a steer that would bring about $4 in Texas could be sold for $40 to $50 in eastern markets.

On a typical long drive, a trail boss managed a crew of about 10 cowboys. Out of approximately 35,000 cowboys, about a third were African American, Mexican, or Mexican American. Some of the African American cowboys had been brought west as slaves before the Civil War; others left the South after the war. In an era when most African Americans faced segregation, black cowboys worked, bunked, and ate alongside other cowboys and received the same wages they did.

In the 1880s most Mexican and Mexican American cowboys worked on South and West Texas ranches. Although Mexican *vaqueros* had developed many ranching practices, many Anglo ranchers considered the *vaqueros* inferior to Anglo cowboys. Mexican cowboys were not allowed to supervise non-Mexicans, and they worked and lived separately from Anglo cowboys.

Cattle ranching spread west into New Mexico and Colorado and north into Kansas, Nebraska, the Dakotas, Wyoming, and Montana as the government converted Indian territory into public land. The government allowed ranchers to use it as common grazing land or **open range**. Although many families established ranches, it was mainly large companies financed by eastern

Railroads and Cattle Trails, 1870–1890

ROUTES TO THE WEST The railroads sped passengers and goods across the United States. Linked to western ranches by the cattle trails, the railroads made it possible for ranchers to ship cattle to eastern markets.

[?] **LOCATION** Which rail lines formed the first transcontinental route?

Rope and branding iron

On May 10, 1869, Leland Stanford drove the golden spike marking the completion of the first transcontinental railroad.

- - - - Cattle trail
━━━ Transcontinental railroad
━━━ Railroad

RETEACH For each subsection in the section, have students write a sentence that summarizes the main idea. Select students to read their statements aloud. Have the class choose the best summary sentence for each subsection.

Closure

Have students provide evidence from the section to support the following assessment: *On the Great Plains nature was sometimes the farmer's friend but more often the farmer's foe.*

Extension

INTERPRET

Encourage students to read diaries and letters of homesteaders like those in Lillian Schlissel's *Women's Diaries of the Westward Journey.* Have them choose three excerpts and discuss the contributions women made to the settlement of the West.

CREATE Have students compose a song or write a poem about life on the long drive.

and European investors that took advantage of government land. Access to this free pasture land made cattle ranching profitable. The introduction of higher-grade cattle breeds from Europe led to even bigger profits.

Sheep ranching, also introduced by the Spanish, was another important economic activity. Native Americans, including the Pueblos and Navajos, raised sheep in New Mexico and Arizona. Thousands of sheep were herded west to California to feed the miners during the gold rush.

Both cattle and sheep ranches demanded hard work from everyone. As one Texan explained, the ranch owners "got right out with the boys on the trail" and "did just as much work."

This description also applied to women, who played an integral role in ranch life. On most ranches, women did housework, cooked for all the cowboys, and helped with fence-mending, herding, or other chores. Many women organized their own ranch-related businesses. For example, Ella Bird accumulated her first herd of cattle by trading hand-sewn leather gloves and vests for yearlings.

Ranch children often took on adult responsibilities at a young age. In addition to doing chores around the house, some boys and girls broke horses and herded cattle. The cowboy life offered children some interesting experiences, but the work was hard. John Norton, a young cowboy, said that he and his brother "leaped with joy" when the cattle they were herding were finally shipped for slaughter.

The cattle boom lasted only about 20 years. Several factors led to its end. First, ranchers filled the free range land with too many cattle, which led to overgrazing. The vast herds also increased the supply of beef. Prices and profits crashed in 1885, as supply far exceeded demand.

Furthermore, open-range ranching declined after the invention of barbed wire, which Joseph Glidden patented in 1874. Farmers and ranchers used this cheap fencing to control access to land and water, limiting the amount of open range land.

Bad weather dealt the final blow. On the southern Plains a severe winter in 1885–86 and a drought in 1886 diminished many herds. The following year, blizzards struck the northern Plains, killing up to 90 percent of some herds.

▲ **Ex-slave Nat Love, also known as Deadwood Dick, claimed to have carried the marks of 14 bullet wounds on his body and boasted that any one of his wounds would have killed an ordinary man.**

Furthermore, the end of the open range meant that ranchers had to buy their own range land. They also had to invest more in their operations. Learning from the blizzards of the mid-1880s, they began to raise hay to feed their cattle during the winters. By the 1890s the cattle boom was over.

■■ **The cattle boom began when new railroads provided access to eastern markets. The boom ended because of overgrazing, fencing of the open range, and bad weather.**

SECTION 2 REVIEW

IDENTIFY and explain the significance of the following: Homestead Act, Pacific Railway Act, Morrill Act, Exodusters, U.S. Department of Agriculture, dry farming, bonanza farm, Texas longhorn, long drives, railhead, open range, Joseph Glidden.

LOCATE and explain the importance of the following: Central Pacific Railroad, Union Pacific Railroad, Red River Valley.

1. **MAIN IDEA** What groups of people moved west in the late 1800s? Why did they move?
2. **MAIN IDEA** How were farmers able to adapt to western environments?
3. **MAIN IDEA** Why was cattle ranching so profitable in the late 1800s? Why did the cattle boom come to an end?
4. **WRITING TO DESCRIBE** Imagine you are a member of an Exoduster family in the late 1800s. Write a journal entry explaining why you left the South for Kansas.
5. **EVALUATING** How might the development of the Great Plains have been different if the government and the railroads had not been involved?

PREVIEW WORKSHOP

Following is a list of the significant people and terms in this section. You may wish to use this list as a section preview.

People
- William H. Seward

Terms
- Comstock Lode
- *patio* process
- Klondike Gold Rush
- hydraulic mining
- hard-rock mining

MOTIVATING: PRIOR KNOWLEDGE

Ask students to recall facts about the California Gold Rush of 1849. Ask volunteers to describe the forty-niners and to characterize that mining boom. Remind students to be alert for comparisons and contrasts with that boom as they study this section.

FOCUS OBJECTIVES

- Locate where important mining discoveries took place in the late 1800s.

- Explain how early mining camps differed from more-developed mining towns.

- Analyze why mining became big business.

HISTORICAL SIDELIGHTS

The Comstock Lode
The Comstock Lode made Virginia City one of the most famous boomtowns in the West. About one year after the vein's discovery, Virginia City had 202 businesses. By the 1870s it had 30,000 people and more than 100 saloons. However, by the 1880s the Comstock Lode was out of silver, and Virginia City became a ghost town.

CORE RESOURCES

- Section 3 Daily Quiz

Section 3

A MINING BOOM

FOCUS

- **Where did important mining discoveries take place in the late 1800s?**
- **How did early mining camps differ from more-developed mining towns?**
- **Why did mining become big business?**

Ever since the forty-niners had flocked to California after the discovery of gold in the Sierra Nevada, miners from all over the world had been drawn to the American West. After the richest California diggings were claimed, hundreds of forty-niners moved eastward and northward into the Rockies and beyond. A few individuals prospered from new mineral discoveries. But large mining companies reaped the greatest profits.

Chinese miner in Alaska

WESTERN MINING

The first promising mining discoveries after the California gold rush were made in Colorado. Prospectors found gold near Pikes Peak late in 1858. In 1859 another center of frantic prospecting was the Carson River Valley in present-day Nevada. In addition to gold, the area contained the famous **Comstock Lode**, one of the world's richest silver veins. Over 20 years its mines yielded more than $500 million worth of precious metals.

Some miners turned south into Arizona. Since the mid-1700s Hispanics had been mining silver there using techniques developed in Mexico and South America. These included a mill for separating gold from quartz and the *patio* **process**—which used mercury to extract silver from the ore. The newer arrivals used these methods to mine the Comstock Lode and in the region around Tucson. Others, trekking northward, made strikes in Idaho and Montana.

By the late 1850s others had pushed into the Fraser River Valley of British Columbia. This push into Canada had important consequences. Russia, which owned Alaska, feared a territorial dispute with the United States. To avoid this, the Russians offered to sell Alaska to the Americans. U.S. Secretary of State William H. Seward agreed to purchase Alaska in 1867 for $7,200,000—about two cents an acre. Many Americans considered Alaska worthless, calling the purchase "Seward's Folly."

But Seward's belief that Alaska "possesses treasures . . . equal to those of any other region" would prove correct. In 1896, prospectors found gold in Canada's Klondike district, which bordered Alaska. This discovery launched the **Klondike Gold Rush**. By the summer of 1897, Klondike miners had extracted gold deposits worth more than a million dollars. Gold discoveries in Alaska in 1898 and 1902 attracted settlers, who later established fish canneries, lumber companies, and coal and copper mining enterprises.

Mining booms attracted prospectors to present-day Colorado, Nevada, Arizona, Idaho, Montana, and Alaska.

Teaching the Section

SITES OF MINING DISCOVERIES

Organize students into groups to create maps showing the location of the major mining discoveries of the late 1800s. Have groups present their maps. Use these presentations as a starting point for a class discussion on the difficulties prospectors from New York or San Francisco might encounter traveling to the various mining sites.

MINING CAMPS AND MINING TOWNS

Draw a two-column chart on the chalkboard labeled *Mining Camps* and *Mining Towns* and have students complete the chart, listing living conditions and activities they associate with each. Have volunteers use the completed chart to generalize about similarities and contrasts between the two types of communities.

FROM LONE MINER TO BIG BUSINESS

Organize students into pairs to role-play a conversation between a mining engineer and a prospector. Conversations should cover the following topics: their differences in discovering and mining ore, why mining is becoming big business, and what this trend will mean for the lives of lone miners. Select pairs to reenact their conversations for the class.

▶

LIFE IN MINING COMMUNITIES

Mining camps grew up almost overnight wherever news of possible wealth brought prospectors together. At first most mining communities were inhabited almost entirely by men. Unlike ranching or farming, prospecting generally was not a family enterprise.

Mining camps drew a wide range of settlers. In the mining zones of southern California in the 1860s, Mexicans, Californios, Peruvians, and Chileans formed separate settlements. In other regions, the prospectors included a mixture of U.S. citizens, Irish and Chinese men who had worked on the railroads, and miners from Cornwall, England. Some were seeking wealth; others were fleeing difficult circumstances.

At first, life in the mining camps was crude and comforts were few. J. Ross Browne described the first shelters of Virginia City, Nevada:

66 Frame shanties . . . ; tents of canvas, . . . of potato sacks . . . , with empty whisky-barrels for chimneys; smoky hovels of mud and stone; coyote holes in the mountain side forcibly seized and held by men. 99

The atmosphere in most camps was one of intense competition. Prospector William Parsons remembered a "furious race for wealth, in which men lost their identity almost, . . . and lived a . . . fearfully excited life; forgetting home and kindred; abandoning old, steady habits."

▲ The lure of gold and silver drew many people to the mining camps of the West. This photograph of an African American mining family in Colorado was taken in the late 19th century.

Competition and ethnic conflicts sometimes led to violence. Miners in Colorado's Cripple Creek camp forcibly excluded Hispanics and eastern and southern Europeans. In other camps, Cornish miners fought with Irish, German, and Chinese miners. Gamblers and con men swarmed in, and conflicts over claims set off brawls.

But stability came to the mining camps as they grew into towns. Mining towns attracted a host of businesses eager to feed and clothe the miners. In fact, owners of saloons and stores were more apt to strike it rich than miners. Cooking and providing lodging were especially lucrative. One woman managed to earn nine hundred dollars in nine weeks by washing miners' clothes. Elizabeth Collins, later known as the "cattle queen of

HISTORICAL SIDELIGHTS

Lawlessness

In the period that preceded the transformation of many mining towns into stable communities, mining towns often lacked law officers, and violence was a part of everyday life. "Every morning from one to three or four dead men were picked up back of the dance halls and saloons," complained one citizen. Sometimes the leading citizens of a town organized a vigilance committee to track down lawbreakers and sometimes acted as judge and jury as well.

PRIMARY SOURCES

Description of Change: excerpted
Rationale: excerpted to focus on main idea

THE WILD WEST

Fantastic stories about the untamed western lands of the United States could be heard far from America's shores in the late 1800s. Fascination with outlaw gangs, shoot-outs, and man-eating wild animals lured many European travelers to America to see for themselves. But the "Wild West" rarely lived up to its reputation. Windham T. Dunraven, a British earl, wrote about what he did *not* find in the American West:

66 *I never have an adventure worth a cent; nobody ever scalps me; I don't get 'jumped' by highwaymen. It never occurs to a bear to hug me, and my very appearance inspires feelings of dismay or* disgust in the breast of the puma or mountain lion. It is true that I have often been horribly frightened, but generally without any adequate cause. 99

Practice

GUIDED PRACTICE

Draw a two-column chart on the chalkboard with the headings *Positive* and *Negative*. Call on volunteers to give the positive and negative effects of big business on mining. List students' responses on the chart as they are offered.

INDEPENDENT PRACTICE

Direct students to use the information from the chart developed in Guided Practice to write an editorial for a mining-town newspaper assessing the positive and negative impacts of the takeover of mining by big businesses. Students may wish to include their editorials in their portfolios.

Review and Assessment

REVIEW Have students write paragraphs or draw scenes about mining life "before" and "after" big business came in, and "before" camp and "after" town. Then assign the Section 3 Review on p. 137.

ASSESS Assign the **Section 3 Daily Quiz** in *Core Resources.*

▲ As settlement grew in the West, so did the need for schools. Blanche Lamont posed with members of her school at Hecla, Montana, in October 1893.

Montana," was offered a job as cook for 18 men at a mining camp. "Prompted by kindness," she later wrote, and "also craving for the $75 per month—I promptly accepted the offer."

The few children in the camps hunted for gold dust and stray nuggets under sidewalks or panned and scavenged for gold dust after the miners were done for the day. Much more profitable, however, was selling fresh food to the miners. One brother and sister made $800 one summer selling butter and bacon to the miners.

As more families arrived, many camps turned into permanent communities. With prosperity came law and order as well as schools, hospitals, churches, newspapers, and singing clubs. Denver, Colorado, for example, started out as a mining camp.

■■ **At first, mining camps were crude. With prosperity, however, came families, community life, and law and order.**

MINING AS BIG BUSINESS

Individual prospectors roaming the West made the earliest mining discoveries, or strikes. But the day of the lone miner did not last. Within a few years of a strike, most of the easily accessible mineral deposits were "worked out." To get at the ore, miners had to use one of two methods: (1) **hydraulic mining**, which used water pressure to wash away mountains of gravel and expose the minerals

underneath; or (2) **hard-rock mining**, which involved sinking deep shafts to get at ore locked in veins of quartz.

Both of these methods required large sums of money—far beyond a lone prospector's resources. Thus mining became the province of large, well-financed companies. These companies relied on science rather than luck. Corps of college-educated engineers helped locate the ore and instructed the companies on how best to extract the zinc, lead, copper, and iron eastern factories demanded.

The federal government also helped develop mineral resources. It sent out several western expeditions in the 1860s. In 1879 the government organized the U.S. Geological Survey, which gathered and coordinated data about new mines.

■■ **As mineral deposits became more expensive to extract, big business dominated mining.**

Big mining companies also changed working conditions in the mines. The big companies used new machinery and hired armies of laborers who sank the shafts, built the tunnels, drilled, and processed the ore. Miners, no longer spurred on by the hope of sudden riches, grew dissatisfied with wages and working conditions.

In some communities miners formed unions. Dues paid to the unions often helped workers injured in the dangerous mines or the families of miners killed on the job. Unions also negotiated with owners who tried to cut wages. Many also fought against the hiring of Chinese miners, who received lower wages. Union resistance to wage cuts proved most effective during boom times. In the early 1880s, union miners at the Comstock

▼ New mining techniques removed ore quickly from the ground, but also eroded entire hillsides.

RETEACH Organize the class into small groups and assign each group a subsection. Direct each group to develop questions about the main ideas in its subsection. Then have each group exchange its questions with another group and work to answer the questions it receives.

*C*losure

Write the last sentence from the Commentary on p. 137 on the chalkboard. Call on students to cite evidence from the section to explain how the statement applies to the experiences of miners.

*E*xtension

RESEARCH Have students research and report on the vigilante movements that sprang up in mining and cattletowns during the late 1800s.

CREATE Have students create a model of a mine, mining camp, or mining town.

Lode successfully maintained their four-dollar-a-day salaries and eight-hour workdays.

When mining became big business, the land suffered. In their haste to extract ore, mining companies often ignored the environmental effects of their practices. Hydraulic mining leveled mountains and often left eroded hills in its wake. Hydraulic mining also dumped tons of earth and rocks into rivers, thus raising riverbeds and causing flooding. Flooding in some areas swept away towns and destroyed farmland. Forests disappeared as hard-rock mining companies felled acres of trees to get wood for mine shafts.

COMMENTARY

Western Myths

The solitary miner, prospecting for gold on a remote mountain stream, is a well-known character in books, movies, and television programs. So is the cowboy who rides off alone into the sunset. Almost equally familiar is the farm or ranch family in its isolated home on the vast, empty plains. All these legendary western figures represent the American ideal of rugged individuals conquering barren and uninhabited land. But these images, while powerful, are inaccurate.

Most westerners, including cowboys on ranches and prospectors in mining camps, *worked for or with others. The lands where ranchers or farmers grazed their cattle or sheep had been settled for centuries by American Indians or Hispanics. Most of the crowded, noisy mining camps were established on or near lands inhabited by Hispanics or Native Americans. And the large companies, not the independent ranchers, farmers, or miners, generally made the biggest profits.*

Furthermore, Americans who settled the West could not have survived without the help of the federal government. The U.S. Army used force to open Native American land for non-Indian settlement. The army also maintained forts to guard trails and protect settlements. The Department of the Interior, through its Bureau of Indian Affairs, resettled Native Americans and ran the reservations on which it placed them. The General Land Office disposed of public land at low rates, while Congress subsidized railroad development. The Department of Agriculture helped Plains farmers, and the Geological Survey aided mining interests.

Novels, songs, and traveling shows spread the myth of the "Wild West" as a region of outlaws, lone cowboys, and isolated pioneers. In reality, men and women lived and worked together in a West shaped as much by technology, big business, and the federal government.

SECTION REVIEW ANSWERS

IDENTIFY

For significance, see the following pages:
Comstock Lode (p. 134)
patio process (p. 134)
William H. Seward (p. 134)
hydraulic mining (p. 136)
hard-rock mining (p. 136)

1. *Later camps enjoyed some stability, permanence, and law and order as they grew into towns; earlier camps were crude, lawless, and violent and witnessed ethnic conflict.*
2. *Only large companies could afford the technology needed to extract mineral deposits after the easily accessible ore was gone.*
3. *Colorado, Nevada, Arizona, Idaho, Montana, and Alaska*
4. *Essays should contrast myths—the outlaw, isolated cowboy, and solitary pioneer—with westerners who worked for or with other people and depended on the federal government for assistance.*
5. *Answers should mention eroded hills and mountains, flooding, and destruction of forests and farmland.*

SECTION 3 REVIEW

IDENTIFY and explain the significance of the following: Comstock Lode, *patio* process, William H. Seward, hydraulic mining, hard-rock mining.

1. **MAIN IDEA** How did later mining camps differ from earlier mining camps?
2. **MAIN IDEA** Why did mining become the domain of large companies?
3. **GEOGRAPHY: LOCATION** Where did the most important mining discoveries take place in the late 19th century?
4. **WRITING TO EXPLAIN** Write an essay contrasting the myth of the rugged individual of the West with westerners' lives in the late 1800s.
5. **EVALUATING** How did western mining affect the environment?

9. secretary of state who negotiated purchase of Alaska in 1867
10. mining method using water pressure to expose minerals

UNDERSTANDING MAIN IDEAS

1. availability of land, railroad links to eastern markets, and business opportunities
2. Farming was a family enterprise. Mining camps were crude and violent and, initially, mainly male.

3. mining sites—present-day states of CO, NV, AZ, ID, MT, and AK; bonanza farms—Dakota Territory, MN, and CA
4. Boom times ended for cattle ranching; big business dominated mining.

Chapter Review Answers

WRITING A SUMMARY
See Essential Points in each section for main ideas.

REVIEWING CHRONOLOGY

5, 3, 4, 2, 1
Identifying Cause and Effect
Answers will vary but should make the cause and effect of events clear.

IDENTIFYING PEOPLE AND IDEAS

1. *forced relocation of Navajos to Bosque Redondo in 1864*
2. *Sioux medicine man who prophesied victory over U.S. Army*
3. *Paiute leader who publicized the plight of Native Americans*
4. *1862 law granting railroads land to develop transcontinental line*
5. *black settlers who went to Kansas in 1879 to escape violence in the South*
6. *overland cattle drive from Texas to railheads in Kansas, Missouri, Nebraska, and Wyoming*
7. *public lands used for grazing*
8. *one of the world's richest silver veins; discovered in 1859 in present-day Nevada*

CHAPTER 5
Review

Timeline:
- The Homestead Act passed.
- Sand Creek Massacre occurs.
- Treaty of Medicine Lodge signed. Seward negotiates purchase of Alaska.
- Second Treaty of Fort Laramie signed.
- First transcontinental railroad completed.

1860   1865   1870

WRITING A SUMMARY
Using the essential points of the chapter as a guide, write a summary of the chapter.

REVIEWING CHRONOLOGY
Number your paper 1 to 5. Study the time line above, and list the following events in the order in which they happened by writing the first next to 1, the second next to 2, and so on. Then complete the activity.

1. Beef prices crash.
2. Exodusters trek west.
3. First transcontinental railroad completed.
4. Battle of Little Bighorn occurs.
5. The Homestead Act passed.

Identifying Cause and Effect Select two events on the time line, and in a paragraph, explain the cause-and-effect relationship between them.

IDENTIFYING PEOPLE AND IDEAS
Explain the historical significance of each of the following people or terms.

1. Long Walk	6. long drives
2. Sitting Bull	7. open range
3. Sarah Winnemucca	8. Comstock Lode
4. Pacific Railway Act	9. William H. Seward
5. Exodusters	10. hydraulic mining

UNDERSTANDING MAIN IDEAS
1. What caused settlers to travel to the West in the late 19th century?
2. How did farm life differ from life in the early mining camps?
3. In what areas were key mining sites and bonanza farms developed?
4. How had the businesses of cattle ranching and mining changed by the late 1890s?

★★ REVIEWING THEMES
1. **Geographic Diversity** How did western farmers adapt to the weather and environment?
2. **Cultural Diversity** What problems arose from the federal government's attempt to assimilate Native Americans?

3. **Economic Development** How did the U.S. government promote western land development and settlement?

THINKING CRITICALLY
1. **Hypothesizing** How might Helen Hunt Jackson's *A Century of Dishonor* and Sarah Winnemucca's lectures have shaped public opinion in the late 1800s?
2. **Evaluating** What positive and negative consequences resulted from development of the West?
3. **Synthesizing** How did different cultures influence one another in the West?

STRATEGY FOR SUCCESS
Review the Skills Handbook entry on Studying Primary and Secondary Sources beginning on page 758. Then read the selections below. In the first selection, Priscilla Merriam Evans describes some of her responsibilities on a farm in Utah. In the second, author Hamlin Garland describes his mother's life. Compare and contrast their points of view.

66 We made our own cloth, which was mostly gray in color, for dresses. . . . With . . . Indigo . . . and other roots, I have colored beautiful fast colors. We were kept busy in those days carding, spinning, knitting, and doing all of our own sewing by hand. 99

66 All her toilsome, monotonous days rushed through my mind with a roar like a file of gray birds in the night . . . how tragically small her joys, and how black her sorrows, her toil, her tedium. 99

WRITING ABOUT HISTORY
Writing to Express a Viewpoint Imagine you are a prospector in a small mining camp. Write a speech expressing your views about the growth of big mining companies.

REVIEWING THEMES

1. used irrigation and dry-farming methods, adopted mechanized farm equipment, grew new varieties of wheat
2. Resentment over assaults on customs and tribal lands led to conflict. Harsh life on reservations caused conflict and starvation when land proved unsuitable for farming and federal agents proved corrupt.
3. provided free land to railroads and settlers, removed Indians to reservations to make more land available, supported railroad construction, aided farmers and miners by creating new government agencies

THINKING CRITICALLY

1. A Century of Dishonor and Sarah Winnemucca's lectures might have caused people to see the need for reform of U.S. policies in dealing with Native Americans.
2. positive—economic growth through farming, ranching, and mining; negative—conflict with Native Americans and damage to the environment
3. People from many culture groups provided the farmers, cowboys, miners and other workers that brought about development and change, which Native Americans resisted.

STRATEGY FOR SUCCESS

Both views reflect the self-reliance of farm life, but Garland's selection shows more harshness.

WRITING ABOUT HISTORY

Speeches might mention that big companies were able to spend large sums of money on scientific mining techniques to reach ore deposits not available to prospectors, but that they often had a negative impact on the lifestyles of individual miners.

USING PRIMARY SOURCES

Chief Joseph expected equality and freedom for Native Americans. The government limited Native Americans to reservations and attempted to make them give up their customs.

LINKING HISTORY AND GEOGRAPHY

Railroads opened the U.S. Southwest and Great Plains and connected the Pacific coast with the Mississippi Valley and the East. The railroads brought non-Indian farmers, ranchers, and miners and linked the West to eastern markets.

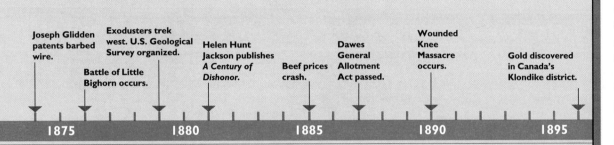

Joseph Glidden patents barbed wire.

Battle of Little Bighorn occurs.

Exodusters trek west. U.S. Geological Survey organized.

Helen Hunt Jackson publishes *A Century of Dishonor.*

Beef prices crash.

Dawes General Allotment Act passed.

Wounded Knee Massacre occurs.

Gold discovered in Canada's Klondike district.

1875   1880   1885   1890   1895

USING PRIMARY SOURCES

The following excerpt is from "Chief Joseph's Own Story," an 1879 account by the Nez Percé leader who had long been committed to peaceful relations with non-Indians. Based on the selection below, how did Chief Joseph's expectations differ from the reality of U.S. policies toward Native Americans?

❝ We only ask an even chance to live as other men live. We asked to be recognized as men. We ask that the same law shall work alike on all men. . . .

Let me be a free man—free to travel, free to stop, free to work, free to trade where I choose, free to choose my own teachers, free to follow the religion of my fathers, free to think and talk and act for myself—and I will obey every law, or submit to the penalty.

Whenever the white man treats the Indian as they treat each other, then we shall have no more wars. We shall be all alike—brothers of one father and one mother, with one sky above us and one country around us, and one government for all. Then the Great Spirit Chief who rules above will smile upon this land, and send rain to wash out the bloody spots made by brothers' hands upon the face of the earth. ❞

Chief Joseph

LINKING HISTORY AND GEOGRAPHY

Review the map on page 132. What areas did railroad lines open to non-Indian settlers in this period, and how did the railroads foster development of these areas?

Railroad station, c.1870s

 BUILDING YOUR PORTFOLIO

Complete the following projects independently or cooperatively.

1. **CONFLICT** In chapters 2 and 4 you looked at conflict from the points of view of a government official and a drafted soldier. Building on that experience, imagine you are a Sioux living on a reservation in South Dakota in 1895. Compose an oral account that describes how conflict between the Sioux and farmers, ranchers, and miners has affected you and other Sioux. Be sure to work in details of the conflict.

2. **THE ECONOMY** In chapters 1 and 3 you explored such economic issues as trade and manufacturing. Building on that experience, imagine you are a land speculator who hopes to establish a small railhead in Nebraska. Prepare a plan for the town that shows the businesses and other public buildings—stockyard, rail station, church, school, and so on—you will include to attract residents.

BUILDING YOUR PORTFOLIO

Have students refer to **Building Your Portfolio Worksheet 1**, assigned at the beginning of Unit 1. Use the worksheet to help students monitor their progress on the portfolio projects.

*A*ssessment

Core Resources
• Reteaching Worksheet 5
• Chapter 5 Tests
• Alternative Assessment Forms
Test Generator

THE NATION TRANSFORMED

1865–1910

THE AMERICAN NATION VIDEODISC PROGRAM
A variety of still images, short videos, and activities are available for you to use as you teach this chapter. See Videodisc Resources in the Core Resources Binder for barcode correlations and suggestions for using the program.

Chapter Overview

In the late 1800s the U.S. experienced a surge of industrial growth, fostering a "new industrial order." During the same period, millions of immigrants, fleeing poverty or persecution at home, sought a better life in America.

As industry expanded, the gap between the lavish lifestyles of the rich and the working and living conditions of laborers widened. Many workers joined labor movements to fight for reform. Likewise, farmers who felt disenfranchised in the new industrial order organized politically to protect their interests. At the same time, other Americans pushed for reforms to end corruption in politics.

Chapter Planning Guide

CHAPTER 6	CORE RESOURCES	AUDIOVISUAL RESOURCES	PROGRAM RESOURCES
INTRODUCTION pp. 140–141	■ Building Your Portfolio Worksheet 1	■ Linking Geography and History Transparency and Worksheet 11A	■ *Eyewitnesses and Others*, Volume 2: Reading 27
TEACHING THE CHAPTER pp. 142–157 ■ For expanded coverage of pp. 141–145, see Chapter 24, pp. 648–652; for coverage of pp. 147–149, see Chapter 25, pp. 674–678.	■ Graphic Organizer 6 ■ Social Studies Worksheet 6 ■ Literature Worksheet 6 ■ Geography Worksheet 6 ■ Outline Maps 1, 2, 9, 14, 15, 20	■ *The American Nation Videodisc: The Standard Oil Company; Community Ties: San Francisco's Chinatown* ■ Linking Geography and History Transparency and Worksheet 13A ■ Everyday Life in America Transparencies and Worksheets 15, 16	■ Art in American History Transparencies and Worksheets 16, 19 ■ *Eyewitnesses and Others*, Volume 2: Readings 6, 11, 12, 16, 17, 20, 22, 24, 25, 29, 31
REVIEW AND ASSESSMENT pp. 158–159	■ Chapter 6 Daily Quizzes ■ Reteaching Worksheet 6 ■ Chapter 6 Tests ■ Alternative Assessment Forms		■ Test Generator

Additional Resources

BOOKS FOR TEACHERS

Daniels, Roger. *Coming to America*. HarperCollins, 1990. Study of immigration to the U.S.

McMath, Robert C. *American Populism: A Social History, 1877–1898*. Hill & Wang, 1993. Social history of the 19th-century agrarian revolt.

Schlereth, Thomas J. *Victorian America: Transformations of Everyday Life, 1876–1915*. HarperCollins, 1991. Surveys late-19th-century U.S. social history.

BOOKS FOR STUDENTS

Clark, Judith Freeman. *America's Gilded Age: An Eyewitness History*. Facts on File, 1992. Firsthand accounts of major events in the late 1880s.

*James, Portia P. *The Real McCoy*. Smithsonian Institution Press, 1989. Examines African American inventions and innovations.

Meltzer, Milton. *Bread & Roses: The Struggle of American Labor, 1865–1915*. Facts on File, 1990. Discusses the formative years of the American labor movement.

* for students reading below grade level

MULTIMEDIA MATERIALS

The Golden Door: Our Nation of Immigrants. Video, 20 min. Knowledge Unlimited/SSSS. Shows the immigrant experience.

Women in American Life—1880–1920. Video, 17 min. National Women's History Project. Explores changes in women's lives.

Populism: Where Historians Disagree. 2 filmstrips. Random House Media. Presents opposing viewpoints on Populist party.

USE WITH PAGES 140–141

Listed on the right are the themes emphasized in Chapter 6. The questions in boldface type stimulate critical thinking and provide students with an opportunity to discuss the themes within a broadened context. The questions also appear in the pupil's edition on p. 140.

■ ECONOMIC DEVELOPMENT

How might technological change affect a nation's economy? Students may mention that a new technology might improve a nation's economy by creating new products, making existing manufacturing processes less expensive, streamlining the way businesses operate, and changing the ways that products are marketed and sold.

■ CULTURAL DIVERSITY

What challenges might an influx of people with different ways of life present to a community? Students might suggest the adjustments that some newcomers must make—finding new employment, adjusting to unfamiliar customs and behaviors, perhaps mastering a new language—and consider how these factors might affect life in a community. They may debate what responsibilities a community might have in making these adjustments easier.

■ DEMOCRATIC VALUES

What actions might citizens take to bring about change in society? Students might mention supporting reform candidates for political office; supporting organized groups that are working for change, such as labor unions and political parties; and protests, riots, or other radical violent actions.

CHAPTER STRATEGIES FOR MEETING INDIVIDUAL NEEDS

LIMITED ENGLISH PROFICIENT LEARNERS

This chapter introduces a number of terms that might be unfamiliar to LEP students. Ask pairs of students to write sentences and draw sketches that illustrate the meaning of the terms in the Preview Workshops. Have students compare their sentences and sketches.

TACTILE/KINESTHETIC LEARNERS

Have students create and perform skits about the experiences of immigrants who came to the U.S. in the late 1800s.

LEARNERS HAVING DIFFICULTY

Organize students into pairs to construct an annotated outline, section by section, as they read through the chapter. Encourage pairs to compare their outlines.

AUDITORY LEARNERS

Direct small groups of students to select short readings from the titles listed in Books for Students on page 139A. One group member should read the selection to the class. Other members should explain the selection's significance.

VISUAL LEARNERS

Have students review the chapter to locate the visual they think best illustrates the chapter title—"The Nation Transformed." Call on students to explain their choices.

GIFTED LEARNERS

Have students write and deliver a speech on poverty in the U.S. in the late 1800s that either a Social Gospel minister or Social Darwinist might have given.

ABOUT THE ILLUSTRATION

In the late 1800s it was not uncommon for young children to work in factories. Tell students that the children in this photograph are working at a mill in Macon, Georgia. Because they were small, children often were made to climb onto the spinning machines to mend broken threads or replace empty bobbins. Ask students to assume the role of union leaders and write letters to the editor in which they protest the dangerous conditions under which children work and demand a change in child labor laws.

Chapter 6

1865–1910

THE NATION TRANSFORMED

FOCUS

UNDERSTANDING THE MAIN IDEA

New technologies and new forms of business organization helped usher in a second industrial age in late-19th-century America. Millions of immigrants arrived during this period, lured by the prospect of work. By 1900 these developments had transformed the United States into an urban nation and an industrial power. The transformation, however, did not benefit everyone equally, and people formed numerous organizations to reform society or to improve their lot.

THEMES

■ **ECONOMIC DEVELOPMENT** How might technological change affect a nation's economy?

■ **CULTURAL DIVERSITY** What challenges might an influx of people with different ways of life present to a community?

■ **DEMOCRATIC VALUES** What actions might citizens take to bring about change in society?

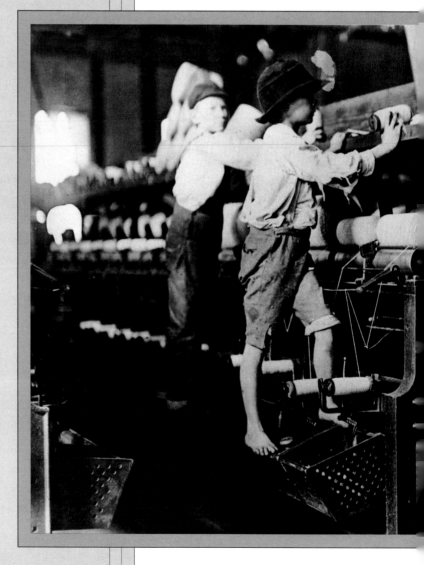

1869	1876	1882	1889	1892
Knights of Labor founded.	Alexander Graham Bell patents telephone.	Congress passes Chinese Exclusion Act.	Jane Addams establishes Hull House.	Populist party founded.

Have volunteers recall the major industrial advances and waves of immigration during the first half of the 1800s. Direct students to list the major points of the discussion in their notebooks. Then as students read the chapter, have them compare items on their lists to events and developments in the second industrial age and the new immigration.

AV TRANSPARENCY
Linking Geography and History Transparency and **Worksheet 11A**

⊞ LINK TO THE PAST ▶

Industrialization and immigration helped fuel the growth of the United States in the first half of the 1800s. However, the United States remained primarily a rural nation whose people continued to depend on agriculture for a living.

Child factory laborers

In the second half of the 1800s, the United States underwent another wave of industrialization. To many this process seemed almost a natural outcome of American life. "The American mechanizes as an old Greek sculptured, as the Venetian painted," the London *Times* noted in 1878. A debate quickly developed, however, over whether the negative side effects of industrialization—such as grinding poverty existing side-by-side with great wealth—were natural outcomes as well.

Critical of the new industrial order, economist Henry George condemned the growing contrast "between the House of Have and the House of Want." He argued that the poor should not have to suffer so that a few could be rich. Yale professor William Graham Sumner took the opposite view, claiming that the rich and the poor were just where nature intended and that any change would slow progress and harm society. Not all industrialists agreed with Sumner. Some proposed that they use part of their wealth to benefit all of society. But social reformer Frederic Howe argued that if industrialists really had the well-being of society at heart, they "would stop the twelve-hour day . . . increase wages and put an end to the cruel killing and maiming" of workers. Although this debate produced no solid answers about how to reconcile the existence of poverty in the midst of great wealth, it did lead to efforts to reform the worst abuses of the industrial order.

The Edison phonograph

SECTION

1

Introducing the Section

FOCUS OBJECTIVES

- Identify the technological innovations that contributed to the rise of the new industrial order.

- Explain how businesses increased their profits in the late 1800s.

- Describe how the government attempted to regulate businesses.

PREVIEW WORKSHOP

Following is a list of the significant people and terms in this section. You may wish to use this list as a section preview.

People
- Lewis Latimer
- John D. Rockefeller

Terms
- trunk lines
- proprietorships
- partnerships
- corporation
- stock
- stockholders
- dividends
- trust
- monopoly
- economies of scale
- vertical integration
- horizontal integration
- laissez-faire capitalism
- Sherman Antitrust Act

Section 1

INDUSTRY'S GOLDEN AGE

FOCUS

- **What technological innovations contributed to the rise of the new industrial order?**
- **How did businesses increase their profits in the late 1800s?**
- **How did the government attempt to regulate businesses?**

From 1865 to 1910 the United States experienced a surge of industrial growth. These decades witnessed the beginnings of a "second industrial revolution." A "new industrial order" was created with the development of cheap steel, the completion of a nationwide rail network, the invention of the telephone, the introduction of new sources of energy, and the rise of big business.

First telephone, 1876

TECHNOLOGICAL INNOVATIONS

America's first industrial revolution had been driven by coal and steam. But it was steel—not steam—that spurred industrialization in the late 1800s. The heavy machinery used to mass-produce goods, the rails that enabled trains to move people and products, the bridges that spanned the rivers, and the tall buildings that dotted the cities all required steel.

In the 1850s Henry Bessemer in England and William Kelly in the United States independently developed a new method of producing steel. The Bessemer process, as the method came to be called, could produce more steel in a day than older techniques could turn out in a week. Using and improving on this technique, America's annual steel production grew from about 15 thousand tons in 1865 to over 28 million tons by 1910. As production increased, prices dropped. Steel that had sold for $100 a ton in 1873 sold for $12 by the late 1890s.

The availability of cheaper steel encouraged railroads to lay thousands of miles of new track. By the end of the century, almost a half-dozen

trunk lines, or major railroads, crossed the Great Plains to the Pacific coast. Feeder, or branch, lines connected the trunk lines to surrounding areas. This huge railroad grid joined every state and linked remote towns to urban centers.

The economic impact of the railroads was immeasurable. Not only were the railroad companies the country's major employers for much of the late 1800s, they also spurred the growth of other industries. The railroads' demands for rails, locomotives, and railcars poured money into the steel industry. Innovations like refrigerated freight cars helped develop the meat-packing industry. In addition, the network of railroad lines helped strengthen a national market. Now a Pennsylvania steel foundry could obtain iron ore from the Great Lakes region, or a Philadelphia furniture company could sell its products in small midwestern towns.

With the growth of this national market came an increased need to communicate across long distances. Samuel F. B. Morse's telegraph had attracted little attention when patented in 1837, but people now saw its business potential. Using Morse's dot-and-dash code, a telegraph operator could send a business order to a distant location in

MOTIVATING: PRIOR KNOWLEDGE

Have students draw upon information learned in previous chapters to identify inventions and technological innovations that were important to the industrial revolution of the early 1800s. As students read the section, have them compare these inventions and innovations with those that drove the second industrial revolution.

Teaching the Section

A NEW INDUSTRIAL ORDER

Organize the class into small groups. Ask groups to create graphic organizers titled "Making A New Industrial Order." Suggest that they divide their organizers into four parts: contributions of steel, contributions of railroads, contributions of communications, and contributions of energy. Have groups display and explain their completed graphic organizers.

NEW BUSINESS PRACTICES

Encourage students to write letters to the editor commenting on late-19th-century business practices from the viewpoint of a successful industrialist or of a small-business owner. Select representatives of both viewpoints to read their letters to the class. Have the class discuss ways the government tried to regulate these business practices.

minutes. By 1866 Western Union, the leading telegraph company, had over 2,000 offices.

The "talking telegraph," or telephone, which Alexander Graham Bell patented in 1876, had an even greater impact. Big businesses quickly found the telephone indispensable. By the end of the 1800s, more than a million telephones had been installed in U.S. offices and homes.

Innovations in transportation and communications depended on abundant sources of energy. In the late 1800s inventors began to tap into two new sources of power—oil and electricity. While the existence of both had been known about for years, neither had been seen as having practical uses. Oil was seen by some as having, at best, medicinal value, while electricity was considered little more than a puzzling natural phenomenon.

Then in the late 1850s, American chemist Benjamin Silliman, Jr., released a report noting that oil could be refined to make kerosene, which, when burned, produces light. Prospectors hurried to sink oil wells as the demand for this inexpensive fuel rose. By the 1880s, oil wells dotted Pennsylvania, Ohio, and West Virginia, producing more than 25 million barrels of oil in 1880 alone.

Electricity's potential became clear in the mid-1800s, when European and American scientists and engineers developed the dynamo, or electric generator. Driven by steam, water, or other energy source, the dynamo produced enough electrical power to run a factory. At his workshop in Menlo Park, New Jersey, inventor Thomas Alva Edison and a team of researchers worked to find practical uses for electricity. Edison's lab produced many innovations, ranging from the incandescent

light bulb to the phonograph to a central electric power plant. Edison and his associates were not the only ones trying to perfect electric lighting. Lewis Latimer—who later worked for Edison—also contributed to light bulb design.

■■ **Innovations in steel production, railroads, communications, and energy spurred industry's golden age.**

THE RISE OF BIG BUSINESS

Along with these technological developments emerged new forms of business organization that added to industries' productivity—and profits. At the close of the Civil War, most businesses were **proprietorships**—small enterprises owned by individuals or families—or **partnerships**—enterprises owned by two or more people. These forms of business organization were inadequate to manage giant new industries like railroads, steel, or oil. Nor could they raise the capital needed to finance such ventures. As a result, business leaders turned to another form of business organization—the **corporation**.

In a corporation organizers raise capital by selling shares of **stock**, or certificates of ownership, in the company. Selling stock to many people allows a corporation to raise enormous sums of money. Furthermore, because a corporation is distinct from its owners, it continues to exist no matter who owns the stock. **Stockholders**—those who buy the shares—receive a percentage of the corporation's profits in the form of **dividends**, but they are not responsible for the corporation's debt or its daily operations.

Bigger is better. Some corporations responded to the fierce economic climate of the late 1800s by joining together to form an even more powerful organization—a **trust**. In a trust, a group of companies turn control of their stock over to a board of directors. The directors then run the companies as a single enterprise. A trust that gains exclusive control of an industry becomes a **monopoly**.

Andrew Carnegie, a Scot who immigrated to the United States in 1848, established some of the first monopolies. Entering the steel business in the early 1870s, Carnegie beat out his competitors by buying supplies in bulk and producing goods in large quantities. By following this principle,

▼ African American Lewis Latimer, pictured at age 70, was one engineer who worked to improve light bulb design.

The Granger Collection, New York

▲ Thomas Edison

Practice

GUIDED PRACTICE

On the chalkboard write the first and last entries for a cause-effect chain on American industrialization—*Technological Innovations* and *America Becomes an Industrial Power*. Ask for volunteers to come to the board and add links to the chain.

INDEPENDENT PRACTICE

Encourage students to imagine they are correspondents for a foreign business magazine. Ask them to use information from the cause-effect chain developed in Guided Practice to write an article for their country's readers on the conditions that made possible America's industrial growth in the late 1800s.

Review and Assessment

REVIEW Ask students to work in pairs to write sentences that explain how each entry in the Preview Workshop is related to the main idea of the subsection in which it is located. Have pairs share their sentences with the class. Then assign the Section 1 Review on p. 145.

ASSESS Assign the **Section 1 Daily Quiz** in *Core Resources*.

THE PRICE OF INDUSTRIALIZATION

In 1871 Austrian diplomat Joseph Alexander, Graf von Hübner, visited the United States. Von Hübner was impressed by the opportunities Americans enjoyed in an industrializing society. But he also saw that fierce competition in business took its toll on working people. Von Hübner said:

> 66 *In the New World man is born to conquer. Life is a perpetual struggle, . . . a race in the open field across terrible obstacles, with the prospect of enormous rewards for reaching the goal. The American cannot keep his arms folded. He must embark on something, and once embarked he must go on and on forever; for if he stops, those who follow him would crush him under their feet. His life is one long campaign, a succession of never-ending fights, marches, and countermarches.*
>
> *In such a militant existence, what place is left for the sweetness, the repose [rest], the intimacy of home or its joys? Is he happy? Judging by his tired, sad, exhausted, anxious, and often delicate and unhealthy appearance, one would be inclined to doubt it. Such an excess of uninterrupted labor cannot be good for any man.* 99

---

known as **economies of scale**, Carnegie was able to lower production costs and increase profits. Carnegie also used **vertical integration** to control costs—that is, he acquired companies that provided materials and services upon which his enterprises depended. For example, Carnegie purchased iron and coal mines, which provided the raw materials for his steel mills, steamship lines, and railroads. Marveled one admirer:

> 66 From the moment these crude stuffs were dug out of the earth until they flowed in a stream of liquid steel in the ladles, there was never a price, profit, or royalty paid to an outsider. 99

◄ Eastman Johnson completed this formal portrait of John D. Rockefeller in 1895.

Because Carnegie controlled businesses at each stage of production, he could sell steel at a much lower price than his competitors.

Like Carnegie, oil tycoon John D. Rockefeller used vertical integration to make his company—Standard Oil—more competitive, eventually acquiring oil fields, barrel factories, pipelines, railroad tanker cars, and oil-storage facilities. But Rockefeller's main method of expansion was **horizontal integration**—one company's ownership of other companies involved in the same business, in this case, oil refining. What companies Standard Oil could not buy, it tried to control through the establishment of a trust.

Rockefeller also drove his competitors out of business by making deals with suppliers and transporters to receive cheaper supplies and freight rates. By 1899 the Standard Oil Company controlled some 90 percent of the country's petroleum refining capacity and had annual profits of some $45 million.

Mass marketing. Industrialists knew that cutting production costs and reducing competition were not the only ways to increase profits. They also developed new methods of marketing to sell their products. Some companies used brightly colored packages and distinctive logos to entice consumers. Advertising, too, became an important promotional tool. Newspapers, magazines, and roadside billboards carried advertisements urging people to buy "The Purest" soap and telephones "warranted to work *one mile*, unaffected by changes in the weather."

In cities, an unprecedented variety of goods became available at a new kind of store. Pioneered by John Wanamaker in Philadelphia, Marshall

RETEACH Organize students into groups and assign each group a subsection of the section. Have each group develop several questions and answers about the main ideas in its assigned material. Then have each group quiz the other groups with its questions.

Closure

Have students work in small groups to draw up a list of the items they might include in a museum exhibit titled "American Industry's Golden Age." Suggest that they divide their exhibits into four sections: Technological Innovations, New Sources of Energy, The Rise of Big Business, Mass Marketing. Have groups compare their lists.

Extension

CREATE Have students research 19th-century advertising techniques and use them to create an advertisement for a modern-day product. Ask for volunteers to display their advertisements on the bulletin board.

RESEARCH Ask students to research and diagram one of the inventions discussed in this section. Have them present their diagrams to the class.

Field in Chicago, and R. H. Macy in New York City, the department store offered shoppers shoes, clothing, hardware, and appliances—all under one roof. The department store bought products in bulk and, as a result, could offer low prices to consumers.

While department stores catered to the urban market, mail-order companies like Montgomery Ward or Sears, Roebuck, and Co. appealed to rural consumers. Customers selected goods from a catalog, then ordered, paid for, and received the merchandise by mail.

▲ Colorful advertisements such as these for processed baby food and flour flooded newspapers and magazines by the end of the 19th century.

■■ **Businesses used corporations, trusts, vertical and horizontal integration, and mass marketing to increase profits.**

*B*USINESS AND GOVERNMENT

Historians refer to the late 1800s as the age of **laissez-faire capitalism**. (*Laissez faire* is French for "let it be.") The theory of laissez-faire capitalism calls for no government regulation of economic matters. Most business leaders argued that if businesses were freed from government regulation, the economy would prosper.

In reality, companies benefited from certain government policies, such as those limiting foreign competition. By placing high tariffs on imports, the federal government allowed U.S. businesses to

dominate the home market. In 1875, for example, Congress increased tariff rates to make imported steel 40 percent more expensive than domestic steel.

At the same time, however, public pressure pushed the government to take modest steps to regulate businesses. As Carnegie Steel and Standard Oil grew in power, many Americans—including some who had been driven out of their own small businesses—demanded that trusts be outlawed. Congress responded in 1890 by passing the **Sherman Antitrust Act**, which declared all monopolies and trusts in restraint of trade illegal. While its intentions appeared clear, the law failed to define what constituted a monopoly or trust. Thus the law proved difficult to enforce.

■■ **The federal government adopted the Sherman Antitrust Act in an effort to eliminate monopolies.**

SECTION REVIEW ANSWERS

IDENTIFY

For significance, see the following pages:
trunk lines (p. 142)
Lewis Latimer (p. 143)
proprietorships (p. 143)
partnerships (p. 143)
corporation (p. 143)
stock (p. 143)
stockholders (p. 143)
dividends (p. 143)
trust (p. 143)
monopoly (p. 143)
economies of scale (p. 144)
vertical integration (p. 144)
horizontal integration (p. 144)
laissez-faire capitalism (p. 145)
Sherman Antitrust Act (p. 145)

1. *Steel provided needed building materials; railroads consumed industrial products, built markets, spurred other industries; innovations improved business communication.*
2. *corporations, trusts, and vertical and horizontal integration; brand names, packaging, advertising, department stores, and mail-order companies*
3. *public pressure; outlawed all monopolies and trusts in restraint of trade*
4. *Letters might mention that without antitrust legislation, the small company will not be able to compete with Rockefeller and will go out of business.*
5. *Growth of large industries led to development of corporations and trusts to increase efficiency or reduce competition.*

■■ SECTION **1** REVIEW

IDENTIFY and explain the significance of the following: trunk lines, Lewis Latimer, proprietorships, partnerships, corporation, stock, stockholders, dividends, trust, monopoly, economies of scale, vertical integration, horizontal integration, laissez-faire capitalism, Sherman Antitrust Act.

1. **MAIN IDEA** How did steel, railroads, and innovations in communications contribute to American industry?
2. **MAIN IDEA** What organizational and selling methods did businesspeople use to increase their profits in the late 1800s?
3. **MAIN IDEA** Why did Congress pass the Sherman Antitrust Act in 1890? How did the act attempt to accomplish its purpose?
4. **WRITING TO EXPLAIN** Imagine you are the owner of a small oil company that John D. Rockefeller is trying to drive out of business. Write a letter to your congressperson explaining the need for antitrust legislation.
5. **EVALUATING** What was the effect of the new industrial order on business organization?

PREVIEW WORKSHOP

Following is a list of the significant people and terms in this section. You may wish to use this list as a section preview.

People
- Jacob Riis

Terms
- conspicuous consumption
- new immigrants
- benevolent societies
- Chinese Exclusion Act
- Immigration Restriction League
- mass transit
- settlement houses
- Social Gospel
- Social Darwinism
- philanthropy

FOCUS OBJECTIVES

- Analyze the effect of the new industrial order on society.

- Describe how immigration changed in the late 1800s. Explain how some native-born Americans responded to the new immigrants.

- Describe how American cities changed in the late 1800s.

- Identify the ways people tried to improve urban conditions.

Section 2

IMMIGRATION AND URBAN LIFE

F O C U S

- **How did the new industrial order affect society?**
- **How did immigration change in the late 1800s? How did some native-born Americans respond to the new immigrants?**
- **How did American cities change in the late 1800s?**
- **In what ways did people try to improve urban conditions?**

Chicago's Masonic Temple

Spurred by industrialization, American cities grew dramatically during the second half of the century. In 1865 only 14 American cities had populations of more than 100,000 and only 20 percent of Americans lived in urban areas. By 1900 the nation was 40 percent urban and had 29 cities with populations in excess of 100,000. With growth came other changes, and a distinct urban culture developed.

CORE RESOURCES

- **Social Studies Worksheet 6**
- **Geography Worksheet 6**
- **Section 2 Daily Quiz**

AV RESOURCES

- ***The American Nation* Videodisc: Community Ties: San Francisco's Chinatown**
- **Linking Geography and History Transparencies and Worksheets 11A, 13A**

A NEW SOCIAL ORDER

In the cities the new industrial order gave rise to a new social order. The urban upper class that emerged in the late 1800s was a new breed whose wealth dwarfed that of the old upper-class merchants and bankers. These new rich had made their money in the new industries, such as railroads, iron and steel, mining, or publishing.

For the new rich, author William Dean Howells noted sarcastically, "the dollar is the measure of every value, the stamp of every success." This new class built lavish houses in the cities—some decorated like Gothic castles or Renaissance palaces. The new rich thought nothing of spending thousands of dollars to stage one night's amusement. They were often criticized for such **conspicuous consumption**, that is, spending money for the sake of showing off their wealth.

The new industrial age also created a new middle class. By the late 1800s modern corporations had swelled the ranks of the middle class with managers, engineers, accountants, clerks, and salespeople. In addition, technological innovations and the rise of big business created a new range of jobs, such as telephone operator, stenographer, salesclerk, and secretary. Business owners increasingly hired young, single middle-class women to fill these positions, paying them lower wages than men. As a result, by 1910 nearly 35 percent of the more than 1.9 million clerical workers were women.

However, most married middle-class women worked at home. Smaller families, greater reliance on purchased goods, and new household technology

▲ **During the late 19th century, many native-born middle-class women began filling clerical positions.**

Teaching the Section

A NEW SOCIAL ORDER

Draw a two-column chart on the chalkboard with *Social Class* and *Characteristics* as headings. Call on volunteers to name the three social classes discussed in the section and to list the identifying characteristics of each class. Note their suggestions on the chart. Then ask students to use the chart to generalize about differences in the lifestyles of urban upper, middle, and industrial working classes.

▶

such as running water, water closets, and home canning changed middle-class women's domestic work. The advent of hot and cold running water meant that doing laundry no longer required pumping, hauling, and heating the water. With more leisure time, many women joined social clubs or participated in reform movements (see Chapter 7).

Industry created a demand not only for managers and clerical workers, but also for laborers. Millions of workers were needed to staff factories, furnish raw materials, and transport finished goods. Hundreds of thousands of rural Americans moved to the cities in search of jobs. Among this group were thousands of African Americans from the South who came to the North in hope of securing industrial work, from which they were often barred in the South. But industrial employment was denied to most. The best jobs still went to native-born whites or to immigrants.

By 1890 nearly 50 percent of industrial workers lived below the poverty line. As a result the ranks of women workers more than doubled between 1870 and 1890 as wives, daughters, and sisters labored to put food on the table. The number of children in the work force doubled during this period for the same reason. By 1890 close to 20 percent of American children between ages 10 and 15 worked for wages.

In the end, the great demand for labor was met, in large part, by floods of immigrants who came to the United States during the late 1800s. By 1900 one third of the country's industrial workers were foreign-born.

■■ **The new industrial order created a new wealthy class, expanded the ranks of the middle class, and increased the demand for industrial workers.**

*T*HE NEW IMMIGRANTS

Prior to 1880, most of the immigrants who had come to the United States were Protestants from northwestern Europe. In the late 1800s, however, a new wave of immigrants swept over the United States. In contrast to the previous immigrants, about 70 percent of these **new immigrants** were from southern or eastern Europe, and most were Catholic, Jewish, or Greek Orthodox. French Canadians, Armenians, Arabs, Chinese, and Japanese also arrived by the thousands.

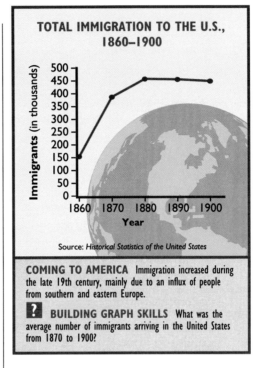

TOTAL IMMIGRATION TO THE U.S., 1860–1900

Immigrants (in thousands)

500
450
400
350
300
250
200
150
100
50
0

1860 1870 1880 1890 1900
Year

Source: *Historical Statistics of the United States*

COMING TO AMERICA Immigration increased during the late 19th century, mainly due to an influx of people from southern and eastern Europe.

? **BUILDING GRAPH SKILLS** What was the average number of immigrants arriving in the United States from 1870 to 1900?

Many of these new immigrants came to the United States to escape poverty or persecution. Most of the southern European immigrants were Italian or Slavic males who sought economic opportunities in the United States that were scarce in their home countries. The eastern European immigrants, meanwhile, included Hungarian and Polish farmers and Jews from many countries. Most of the Jewish and Armenian families fled their homelands to escape religious or political persecution.

■■ **Most new immigrants were southern or eastern Europeans who came to America to find jobs or to escape persecution.**

▶ **This immigrant mother and her children arrived at Ellis Island, New York, around 1910.**

HISTORICAL SIDELIGHTS
Coming to America
Many immigrants learned of the opportunities available in the United States from railroad and steamship companies. In fact, convincing foreigners that the United States was the land of opportunity became a major business activity in the late 1800s. The agents of steamship companies and railroads swarmed over Europe, one observer noted, "as the locusts covered Egypt!" They painted a tempting—and often false—picture of America. Some railroad companies exaggerated the employment opportunities available in the United States, and steamship lines charged rock-bottom fares to attract customers.

Teaching the Section

NEW IMMIGRATION AND THE NATIVIST RESPONSE

Call on some students to portray new immigrants to the U.S. in the late 1800s. Have them address the class, explaining where they came from and why they came to the U.S. Ask other students to act as nativists and present their view of the new immigration. Have students use information provided in the presentations to write a newspaper editorial supporting or challenging the nativist view of immigration. Students may wish to include their editorials in their portfolios.

CHANGES IN AMERICAN CITIES

Write these terms on the chalkboard: *elevator, skyscraper, mass transit, suburb, tenement.* Ask students to explain how each brought about changes in American cities in the late 1800s. Write responses under the appropriate term. Then have students use the information on the chalkboard to write a descriptive paragraph titled "The Changing American City." Call on volunteers to read their paragraphs to the class.

HISTORICAL SIDELIGHTS

Becoming Americans
Newspapers helped people adapt to life in America. In the early 1900s more than 1,000 foreign-language papers were printed in the U.S. The largest was New York's *Jewish Daily Forward,* which had a daily circulation of 175,000.

MULTICULTURAL PERSPECTIVES

Chinese Americans felt that nativists' attitudes toward them reflected cultural ignorance. In 1852, a Chinese American pointed out that "when your [a California governor's] nation was a wilderness, . . . we exercised most of the arts and virtues of civilized life; ... we are possessed of a language and literature, and . . . men skilled in sciences and the arts are numerous among us. . . . We are not the degraded race you would make us."

THE AMERICAN NATION
VIDEODISC PROGRAM
Community Ties: San Francisco's Chinatown

1B   15914   4:23

By the early 1900s, about 60 percent of the people living in the nation's 12 largest cities either were foreign-born or had foreign-born parents. Many big cities of the Northeast and Midwest became patchworks of ethnic neighborhoods as new immigrants settled among others from their homelands. Social reformer Jacob Riis (himself an immigrant from Denmark) suggested that an 1890s map of New York City, colored according to nationality, "would show more stripes than . . . a zebra, and more colors than any rainbow."

In these close-knit neighborhoods, residents spoke the same languages and followed the customs of the old country. Neighborhood churches and synagogues helped immigrants maintain a sense of identity and belonging. Most cities also had **benevolent societies**, or support organizations, to aid newcomers.

As with earlier immigrants, however, the vast majority of newcomers did not find paradise at the end of the difficult voyage to America. Confined to dingy slums, they worked at menial jobs for low wages. Many did the country's "dirty work"—or, as one observer put it, "the shoveling."

Furthermore, many native-born Americans viewed immigration as a threat. They agreed with Thomas Bailey Aldrich, who, in his poem "The Unguarded Gates," warned against a "wild motley throng" bringing "unknown gods and rites." Many felt that the newcomers were just too different ever to fit in. Others went further, blaming immigrants for all of society's ills.

Nativists also charged that the willingness of immigrants to work cheaply robbed native-born Americans of jobs and lowered wages for all. On

▼ Chinese immigrants formed their own communities and businesses after arriving in the United States. This photograph is of San Francisco's Chinatown district.

the West Coast, where Chinese laborers had worked for years, the new nativist Workingmen's Party of California angrily cried "The Chinese must go" in response to mounting unemployment in the 1870s. White mobs attacked the Chinese, killing some and burning the property of others.

In some cases, nativists successfully pushed for restrictions on immigration. For example, in 1882 the U.S. Congress passed the **Chinese Exclusion Act**, which denied citizenship to people born in China and prohibited the immigration of Chinese laborers. Other attempts at limiting immigration, however, were less successful. The **Immigration Restriction League**, founded in 1894 by a group of well-to-do Bostonians, sought to make literacy a requirement for admission into the country. Congress passed such a measure, but President Grover Cleveland vetoed it in 1897, calling it "illiberal, narrow, and un-American."

Despite the efforts to impose restrictions, immigration continued. And contrary to nativists' arguments, the immigrants' varied cultures added new dimensions to American life, especially in the cities, where most immigrants settled.

▪▪ Prejudice and fear prompted nativists to try to restrict immigration.

URBAN LIFE

As more and more immigrants and migrants from rural areas poured into American cities, these urban areas did not just expand. Growth was accompanied by changes in the very structure and layout of cities.

The changing city. The urban areas of the mid-1800s were compact. Few buildings were taller than two or three stories. And even in the largest cities, most people lived less than a 45-minute walk from the city center, where most businesses and industries were located. But by the late 1800s, technological innovations and the great flood of people began to transform the urban landscape.

Contributing to the transformation were steel, new building techniques, and Elisha Otis's mechanized elevator, all of which allowed cities to grow upward as well as outward. No longer restricted by the number of stairs people could comfortably climb, architects designed multistory buildings, or skyscrapers.

Ask students to imagine they are young men or women about to start work in a settlement house or a church-sponsored reform group. Have them write letters to a family member or friend explaining the purpose of the organization, why it is needed, and what they hope to contribute by working there. Ask for volunteers to read their letters to the class.

■■ Ask students to identify and describe institutions in their community today that are similar to the settlement houses of the 1880s.

▶

▲ Trolley cars were an important part of many urban mass-transit systems. This photograph was taken in New York City around 1895.

Moreover, the development of **mass transit**—commuter trains, subways, and trolley cars—made it possible for cities to spread outward because workers no longer had to live within walking distance of their jobs. Soon, suburbs arose as some wealthier residents moved away from crowded city centers to live in "light and air."

The tenements. While some could afford to enjoy the healthy life of the suburbs, many urban Americans remained trapped by poverty in crowded, and often unhealthy, tenement houses. These dark, airless buildings sometimes housed as many as 12 families per floor. Jacob Riis described one of the apartments:

66 A room perhaps a dozen feet square, with walls and ceiling that . . . were now covered with a brown crust that, touched with the end of a club, came off in shuddering showers of crawling bugs. 99

Outside the tenements, raw sewage and piles of garbage fouled unpaved streets and alleys. Worse still, the slums usually adjoined industrial areas where factories belched pollution. "The stink is enough to knock you down," one New York resident complained. In such an environment, sickness and death were common. Diseases like tuberculosis spread rapidly through tightly packed slums.

While the conditions faced by residents of poor neighborhoods were hard, those who experienced the greatest difficulties were African

▶ Crowded tenements, such as these lining Hester Street in New York City, sprang up as urban populations swelled.

Americans. Widespread discrimination meant that most of them could get only poorly paid jobs. Moreover, African Americans had to pay outrageous rents for the most appalling apartments, and they faced almost constant police harassment. Yet many preferred the North to the South. As one African American journalist explained:

66 They sleep in peace at night; what they earn is paid them, if not they can appeal to the courts. They vote without fear of the shotgun, and their children go to school. 99

■■ New technologies allowed cities to expand upward and outward. Wealthier people moved to the suburbs, but many of the poor had no choice but to live in crowded tenements.

THE DRIVE FOR REFORM

As urban poverty grew and received more publicity, people debated how best to help the poor. Some saw education as the solution to the problems plaguing the cities. After 1860 more and more states passed compulsory school attendance laws and lengthened the school year from 78 to 144 days. From 1870 to 1900 the number of students in school grew from

*P*ractice

GUIDED PRACTICE

On the chalkboard write the term *urban life.* Ask volunteers to explain what this term means to them. List their responses on the chalkboard. Direct the class to use the information on the list to develop a one-sentence definition of the term *urban life.*

INDEPENDENT PRACTICE

Organize students into small groups. Have groups use the list and definition developed in Guided Practice to prepare a script outline for a "TV documentary" on urban life in the late 1800s. Suggest that groups cover such topics as different classes and different lifestyles, the changing city, urban reform movements, and leisure time. Call on volunteers to present their groups' script outlines to the class.

*R*eview and *A*ssessment

REVIEW Ask students to write newspaper headlines that summarize the content of each heading and subheading in the section. Have students compare and discuss their headlines. Then assign the Section 2 Review on p. 151.

ASSESS Assign the **Section 2 Daily Quiz** in *Core Resources.*

GLOBAL CONNECTIONS

The settlement-house movement began in Great Britain. Toynbee Hall, the first settlement house, was established in the East End of London by Canon Samuel Barnett in 1884. It was named for Arnold Toynbee, a prominent British social reformer.

BIO **PERSONALITIES** **GRAPHY** **IN HISTORY**

Jane Addams strongly believed that every opinion, no matter how odious or unpopular, had a right to be heard. In 1920 she took action to advance this belief by helping to found the American Civil Liberties Union (ACLU).

HISTORICAL SIDELIGHTS

Inventor and Volunteer
At the Henry Street Settlement in New York, African American Lewis Latimer taught courses that helped immigrants adjust to living in the U.S.

---

some 7 million to more than 15 million. Many of these new students were young women.

The settlement houses. To confront the problem of poverty more directly, some young Americans established and lived in **settlement houses**—community service centers—in poor neighborhoods. At the forefront of this effort was Jane Addams.

BIO GRAPHY Born in 1860 to a well-to-do family in Cedarville, Illinois, Jane Addams grew up in an atmosphere of politics and charitable activity. Her Quaker father was a passionate abolitionist, and as a state senator he had worked to pass social reform legislation. The young Addams decided to dedicate her life to helping the urban poor.

In time, Addams's work included other causes. She tirelessly worked for women's suffrage and served as president of the Women's International League for Peace and Freedom from 1919 to 1935. Worldwide recognition for her work came in 1931, when she and Nicholas Murray Butler won the Nobel Peace Prize.

Addams began her settlement-house work in 1889, when she and Ellen Gates Starr established Hull House in one of Chicago's immigrant neighborhoods. The mission of Hull House, as stated in its charter, was "to provide a center for a higher civic and social life" and "to investigate and improve the conditions in the industrial districts of Chicago."

The Hull House volunteers were mostly young, college-educated women. They set up a day nursery and kindergarten for the children of working mothers and gave adult education classes. They offered recreational facilities and staffed an employment agency. And when the city failed to pick up garbage in poor neighborhoods, Addams secured an appointment as a garbage inspector to make sure the much-needed service was provided.

Hull House served as a model for others hoping to aid the poor. For example, in 1890 African American teacher Janie Porter Barrett founded one of the first African American settlement houses—

Jane Addams

▲ In this early 1900s photograph, nurses from New York's Henry Street Settlement House are on their way to help the poor and needy.

the Locust Street Social Settlement—in Hampton, Virginia. By 1900 almost 100 settlement houses had opened across the country.

Other reform movements. At the same time that the settlement houses began their work, a number of Protestant religious leaders developed the idea of the **Social Gospel**, which called for people to apply Christian principles to address social problems. Many churches attempted to implement the Social Gospel by providing libraries, job training, counseling, and other social services.

Many religious groups joined the battle against urban poverty. In the 1880s the Salvation Army, an evangelical group founded in Great Britain, began offering food, clothing, and shelter to the poor to help put them on the path to physical and spiritual salvation.

Some people—particularly wealthy ones such as steel baron Andrew Carnegie—opposed direct aid, or handouts, to the poor. Such handouts, Carnegie argued, rewarded equally both the unworthy beggar and the worthy worker fallen on hard times. Carnegie was a firm believer in **Social Darwinism**, a theory that sought to apply the biological principles of natural selection and evolution to society. Social Darwinists thought that the "fittest" people should and would rise to positions of wealth and power, while the "unfit" would fail.

RETEACH Have students work in small groups to create charts showing the major ideas and events presented in the section. Direct each group to indicate on its chart how each item addresses one of the section's Focus questions.

Closure

Have students use information they have learned from the section to suggest comparisons between immigration and urban life in the late 1800s and immigration and urban life today.

Extension

INTERPRET Have students read "The New Colossus" by Emma Lazarus. Ask them to write a paragraph that summarizes the poem's main ideas. Ask for volunteers to read their summaries to the class.

CREATE Have students select a city and create a model or map that shows its growth pattern from the mid-1800s to the turn of the century. Have students display their models or maps.

Instead of direct aid, Carnegie advocated **philanthropy**, charitable efforts to promote public welfare. The best way to benefit the lower class, he argued, was "to place within its reach the ladders upon which the aspiring can rise." Carnegie's "ladders" included universities and libraries, and he gave some $350 million to such causes.

■■ **Some people attempted to solve urban problems through settlement houses, the Social Gospel, and philanthropy.**

*L*EISURE TIME

Philanthropic efforts often served to enrich urban cultural life for all. In addition to supporting universities and libraries, some wealthy people financed museums and art galleries and established new theater groups and symphony orchestras.

Such institutions were not the only forms of recreation urban dwellers enjoyed. Expanded education meant that by 1900 some 90 percent of Americans could read, and many did. The dramatic increase in the number of daily newspapers—from less than 600 in 1870 to some 2,600 by 1910—reflected the growth in literacy. Many people also read popular fiction—romances, mysteries, and westerns. Young boys favored Horatio Alger's success stories about hardworking street urchins who rose to middle-class respectability by courage—and luck.

Older readers enjoyed realistic books about urban life. For example, Edith Wharton's *House of Mirth* (1905) described the conflicts between the

▲ Shown here is the 1866 championship game at Elysian Field, in Hoboken, New Jersey.

new rich and the old elite. William Dean Howells's *Rise of Silas Lapham* (1885) wove a tale of greed and social ambition. Stephen Crane and Frank Norris depicted the grimmer aspects of urban life.

Sports became another popular form of recreation. In 1876, with the founding of the first professional league, baseball became a popular spectator sport—in one contemporary sportswriter's words, "the national game of the United States." But even sports could be discriminatory; widespread racism led to the exclusion of African Americans from major league baseball teams until 1947.

For children, Barnum & Bailey's Circus provided "The Greatest Show on Earth." Vaudeville shows, with roots in working-class variety acts, attracted middle-class as well as working-class audiences. Also popular, especially among working-class families, were amusement parks with their roller coasters and Ferris wheels.

■■ **An urban culture with diverse educational and leisure activities developed in the late 1800s.**

IDENTIFY

For significance, see the following pages:
conspicuous consumption (p. 146)
new immigrants (p. 147)
Jacob Riis (p. 148)
benevolent societies (p. 148)
Chinese Exclusion Act (p. 148)
Immigration Restriction League (p. 148)
mass transit (p. 149)
settlement houses (p. 150)
Social Gospel (p. 150)
Social Darwinism (p. 150)
philanthropy (p. 151)

1. *Immigration soared, with most new immigrants from southern and eastern Europe; nativists thought immigrants would take jobs, drive down wages.*
2. *skyscrapers and mass transit systems built, cities spread out, rise of suburbs*
3. *Settlement-house movement offered social services for the poor, Social Gospel movement used Christian principles to address social problems.*
4. *Letters should focus on poverty and conditions in the tenements.*
5. *drew many young, single middle-class women into the work force as salesclerks and secretaries; gave more leisure time to married middle-class women who did not work; drew thousands of working-class women into work force because they needed money for food*

■■
S E C T I O N 2 R E V I E W

IDENTIFY and explain the significance of the following: conspicuous consumption, new immigrants, Jacob Riis, benevolent societies, Chinese Exclusion Act, Immigration Restriction League, mass transit, settlement houses, Social Gospel, Social Darwinism, philanthropy.

1. **MAIN IDEA** What change occurred in immigration in the late 1800s? Why did nativists oppose the new immigrants?
2. **MAIN IDEA** In what ways did American cities change in the late 1800s?
3. **CONTRASTING** How did efforts to reform urban conditions differ from each other?
4. **WRITING TO DESCRIBE** Imagine you are visiting a New York tenement house in 1895. Write a letter to a friend describing your visit and observations about tenement life.
5. **SYNTHESIZING** How did technology and the new industrial order affect the lives of middle- and working-class women?

FOCUS OBJECTIVES

- Explain why many Americans called for civil service reform.

- Identify the problems that led Americans to organize labor unions.

- Determine what prompted farmers to organize after the Civil War.

BUILDING VOCABULARY

The term *graft* has similar meanings in horticulture and politics. In work with plants, a part from one plant is grafted onto another so that it eventually becomes a permanent part of that plant. In politics the term is used to designate money obtained fraudulently, because it usually results from illegal practices "grafted" to the official duties of an officeholder.

PRIMARY SOURCE

Description of Change: excerpted
Rationale: excerpted to focus on main idea

Following is a list of the significant people, places, and terms in this section. You may wish to use this list as a section preview.

People
- Mary Harris Jones

Places
- Haymarket Square
- Homestead steel plant
- Pullman sleeping car factory

Terms
- Gilded Age
- political machines
- Pendleton Civil Service Act
- Knights of Labor
- Great Upheaval
- Haymarket Riot
- anarchists
- blacklists
- yellow-dog contracts
- lockouts

- strikebreakers
- American Federation of Labor
- National Grange
- cooperatives
- Interstate Commerce Act
- Farmers' Alliance
- graduated income tax
- Populist party

Section 3

POLITICS AND PROTEST

FOCUS

- **Why did many Americans call for civil service reform?**
- **What problems led Americans to organize labor unions?**
- **What prompted farmers to organize after the Civil War?**

𝓣*he abuses of power that seemed to characterize the late–19th-century political scene left many Americans deeply troubled. Some people called for political reform. Others—such as industrial workers and farmers—took matters into their own hands, organizing to protect their interests and to win their share of prosperity.*

THE
GILDED AGE
A TALE OF TO-DAY

BY
MARK TWAIN
(SAMUEL L. CLEMENS)
AUTHOR OF "INNOCENTS ABROAD," "ROUGHING IT," ETC.
AND
CHARLES DUDLEY WARNER
AUTHOR OF "MY SUMMER IN A GARDEN," "BACK LOG STUDIES," ETC.

FULLY ILLUSTRATED FROM NEW DESIGNS
BY HOPPIN, STEPHENS, WILLIAMS, WHITE, ETC., ETC.

SOLD BY SUBSCRIPTION ONLY.

HARTFORD:
AMERICAN PUBLISHING COMPANY.
W. E. BLISS & CO., TOLEDO, OHIO.
1874.

The Gilded Age

RESTORING HONEST GOVERNMENT

In their 1873 novel *The Gilded Age*, authors Mark Twain and Charles Dudley Warner suggested that, like the base material that hides beneath the glittering gold surface of a gilded picture frame, corruption and greed lurked below the polite and prosperous luster of late-19th-century American society. The image struck a chord, and the era became known as the **Gilded Age**. Corruption and greed seemed particularly evident in the politics of the time.

Graft and corruption. The rapid growth of cities in the late 19th century led to the creation of powerful **political machines**—party organizations whose primary goal was to obtain and then keep local political power. The political bosses who ran the big-city machines got their candidates elected by dispensing favors to people in return for votes. One observer described a boss's methods:

❝ To this one he lends a dollar; for another he obtains a railroad ticket without payment; he has coal distributed in the depth of winter; . . . he sometimes sends poultry at Christmas time; he buys medicine for a sick person; he helps bury the dead. ❞

Once in power, bosses used any means necessary—the rigging of elections, bribery, even violence—to stay in power. And many took advantage of their positions to plunder public treasuries.

The most notorious political machine was Tammany Hall, the Democratic party machine that controlled New York City's government. Tammany Hall's reputation for graft and corruption was launched by William Marcy Tweed, who along with his cronies—the Tweed Ring—robbed the city treasury of some $200 million between 1865 and 1871.

Politicians in Washington, D.C., played the same games, often for higher stakes. President Ulysses S. Grant's first term was marred by several financial scandals. The greatest of these surfaced in 1872 and involved Grant's vice-president, Schuyler Colfax. In 1867, the directors of the Union Pacific Railroad had formed the Crédit Mobilier Company and awarded it contracts to build part of the transcontinental railroad. Crédit Mobilier overcharged Union Pacific by more than $20 million. These "excess profits" were paid to Crédit

MOTIVATING: STUDENT EXPERIENCES

Have students identify any examples of local, state, or federal political corruption or scandal. Have volunteers describe the public reaction to these events. Ask students about any reforms that the corruption and scandals prompted. Tell students that this section, in part, deals with government corruption and attempts at political reform in the late 1800s.

Teaching the Section

CIVIL SERVICE REFORM

Have students write letters, as Americans living in the Gilded Age, to their senator or representative. Letters should express their views of conditions in government and why civil service reform is needed. Tell students to use examples from the text to support their arguments. Have each student exchange his or her letter with a classmate, who will offer a spoken response in the role of a senator or representative. Students may wish to include their letters in their portfolios.

▶

Mobilier's stockholders, many of whom were members of Congress, including then–Speaker of the House Colfax.

The struggle for reform. Critics charged that corruption in national political life was in large part the result of the spoils system, in which successful political candidates rewarded their supporters with civil service jobs. Reformers proposed that appointments to government jobs be based on ability, as determined on competitive exams, rather than on party affiliation.

Political corruption and civil service reform became important issues in every presidential election between 1872 and 1888. The Republican party even split into two factions over the issue of patronage.

Because of the controversy over the issue, reform was slow to come. A spark to change, however, came on July 2, 1881, when Charles Guiteau (guh-TOH), a disappointed and mentally unstable government job seeker, shot and killed President James A. Garfield. Chester A. Arthur, who became president on Garfield's death, responded to the shooting by helping gain passage of the **Pendleton Civil Service Act** in 1883. This act established a Civil Service Commission to administer competitive examinations to those seeking government jobs.

Yet critics charged that the Pendleton act was of limited value because it covered only about 10 percent of federal jobs. And although President Grover Cleveland, a Democrat, doubled the number of jobs requiring a civil service exam after his election in 1884, many elected officials continued to make appointments based on patronage rather than on merit.

■■ **Convinced that the spoils system led to political corruption, many Americans called for civil service reform.**

The LABOR MOVEMENT

Preoccupied with political reform, the government overlooked one of the major trends of the late 1800s—the growing gulf between the haves and the have-nots. By 1890 close to 75 percent of the nation's wealth was controlled by just 10 percent of the population, and many American industrial workers lived in poverty.

Working life. All industrial workers labored long hours for little pay. Most white unskilled male laborers worked at least 10 hours a day, 6 days a week, for less than $10 a week. Many African American, Mexican American, and Asian American men worked the same number of hours for even lower wages. And wages for women were lower than those for men. In 1883, the average earnings of women in Boston were estimated to be less than $5 a week. Children, too, faced terrible conditions in the labor force. In some textile mills, children worked 12-hour shifts—often at night—for pennies a day.

▲ In the 1870s the Knights of Labor campaigned for legislation to protect child workers. But children continued to experience wretched working conditions throughout the next few decades.

Long hours left workers exhausted. Fatigue increased the danger in already unsafe working surroundings. In 1881 alone, some 30,000 railway workers were killed or injured on the job. Most employers felt no responsibility for work-related deaths and injuries and made little effort to improve workplace safety.

The Knights of Labor. As conditions worsened, workers clamored for change and banded together to make people listen. One of the earliest national unions was the **Knights of Labor**, founded in 1869. Under Terence V. Powderly, who became the leader of the Knights of Labor in 1879, the union fought for the eight-hour workday, equal pay for equal work, and an end to child labor.

Powderly—in contrast to the leaders of most other unions—opened the Knights' membership to both skilled and unskilled laborers and to women. A number of women played prominent roles in the union. Mary Harris Jones, for example, organized strikes, marches, and demonstrations. Her activities earned her the title "the most dangerous woman in America." But because she looked more motherly than radical, most people called her Mother Jones.

Teaching the Section

LIFE FOR THE WORKING CLASS

Call on volunteers to role-play the following figures in the late 1800s: African American coal miner, child textile-mill worker, Russian laundress, Mexican American cannery worker, Chinese American cook, male and female Italian garment workers, German railroad worker. Ask them to explain their jobs, working conditions, family economic situations, and prospects for the future. Have the class respond, as late-1800s American citizens, by writing letters to the editor regarding what they have learned about the plight of these workers. Ask volunteers to share their letters with the class.

THE GREAT UPHEAVAL

Organize students into groups of three to role-play a "broadcast journalist" conducting a short interview with a labor union official and a factory manager in the 1880s. The interview should concern the cause of the Great Upheaval, its effect on the general public, and its potential consequences for the workers, unions, and factory owners. Call on groups to present their interviews to the class.

Map Caption Answer
the Midwest

MULTICULTURAL PERSPECTIVES

Not all African Americans felt that they were treated fairly by the Knights. One North Carolina mason said, "The white Knights of Labor prevent me from getting employment because I am a colored man, although I belong to the same organization."

PRIMARY SOURCE

Description of Change: excerpted and bracketed
Rationale: excerpted to focus on main idea; bracketed to clarify meaning

Labor Strikes, 1870–1900

STRIKES INCREASE The strike became the chief means for workers to improve wages and working conditions.

? **LOCATION** Where did the majority of railroad-related strikes occur?

1886 HAYMARKET RIOT
Bomb kills police breaking up labor rally; public turns against workers.

1875–1876 MOLLY MAGUIRES
Irish miners accused of murdering foreman; 24 convicted, 10 hanged.

1892 HOMESTEAD STRIKE
Skilled iron and steel workers' strike at Carnegie Steel Company fails.

Great railroad strike of 1877 | Miners' strike
Other railroad strike | Other strike or riot
Counties with strike activity, 1881–1900

Powderly also opened the union to African Americans. By the mid-1880s the Knights claimed some 60,000 black members. The Knights were not equality-minded when it came to everyone, however. Powderly, like many working-class Americans, actively opposed Chinese workers, claiming they took jobs from white Americans. At his urging, for instance, West Coast branches of the Knights of Labor vigorously campaigned for passage of the Chinese Exclusion Act.

Industrial unrest. In 1886, the nation entered a year of intense strikes and violent labor confrontations that would become known as the **Great Upheaval.** An economic depression in the early 1880s had led to massive wage cuts. Workers needed—and demanded—relief. When negotiations with management failed, many workers took direct action. By the end of 1886, some 1,500 strikes, involving more than 400,000 workers, had swept the nation. Many of these strikes turned violent, as angry strikers clashed head-on with their employers and the police. Perhaps the best-known of these confrontations was the **Haymarket Riot.**

The seeds for the Haymarket Riot were sown when some 40,000 Chicago workers struck on May 1, 1886. On May 3 a confrontation between the police and the strikers left two strikers dead. In protest, the strikers called a meeting for the next day in Chicago's Haymarket Square. Peaceful and sparsely attended, the rally was about to break up when nearly 200 police officers appeared. Suddenly a bomb exploded in the midst of the police. The police responded with gunfire. When the smoke cleared, more than 70 people lay wounded, and seven police officers and one civilian were dead.

The police arrested eight well-known **anarchists** (people who oppose all forms of government), even though only one of them had actually attended the meeting. All eight were found guilty of incitement to murder; four went to the gallows. On the final day of the trial, one of the defendants warned:

❝ I have told [Chicago Police] Captain Schaack, . . . "if you cannonade us, we shall dynamite you." . . . Let me assure you I die happy on the gallows, so confident am I that the hundreds and thousands to whom I have spoken will remember my words; . . . they will do the bomb throwing! ❞

FARMERS' PLIGHT

Tell students to imagine that they have been selected to speak before a Senate committee on the plight of debt-ridden farmers in the Midwest. Have students prepare a compelling description of the problems farmers face. Have volunteers read their statements to the class. Encourage students to respond to the statements in the role of members of the Senate committee.

FARMERS ORGANIZE

Have students imagine they are reporters: some are attending an Alliance rally, some a Grange rally and others a Populist party rally. Have them write newspaper articles detailing the goals of the movement, the methods proposed to achieve these goals, and the special activities taking place at the rally. Have volunteers from each group present their articles to the class. Then, on the basis of the articles, have students compare and contrast the Grange, Alliance, and Populist movements. Students may wish to include their articles in their portfolios.

But worker activism actually decreased by the close of the year. Emboldened by the Haymarket convictions, employers struck back. They drew up **blacklists**—lists of union supporters—that they shared with one another. Blacklisted workers found it almost impossible to get jobs. Many employers also made job applicants sign agreements—called **yellow-dog contracts** by the workers—promising not to join unions. When these measures failed and workers struck anyway, many companies instituted **lockouts**, barring workers from the plant, and brought in nonunion **strikebreakers**, often African Americans or others who felt abandoned by the unions.

As labor suffered repeated defeats and the tide of public sentiment turned against workers, union membership—including the Knights'—shrank. Many of the workers who remained in unions were skilled workers who joined the newly formed **American Federation of Labor** (AFL), founded by Samuel Gompers in 1886. The AFL was a collection of independent skilled craft unions committed to advancing the interests of skilled workers.

After a few years of relative peace, industrial unrest broke out again in the 1890s. At Andrew Carnegie's Homestead steel plant in Pennsylvania, workers went on strike in 1892 after a wage cut was announced. Violence between the strikers and hired plant guards resulted in 16 deaths. The violence soon spread to other plants, and order was restored only after the state militia was called in. Then in 1894, workers at the Pullman sleeping-car factory in Chicago went on strike, again largely in response to a wage cut. The American Railway Union (ARU) supported the workers, and the strike escalated, drawing in the railroad owners and the federal government. Federal troops were ordered into Chicago, sparking violence that left scores of casualties. Within days the strike had been broken and the ARU destroyed.

▪▪ Industrial workers formed unions and staged strikes and protests to try to win better wages and working conditions.

THE RISE AND FALL OF POPULISM

The development of the new industrial order affected not only workers, but farmers as well. The rapidly growing population in the nation's cities needed to be supplied with food. The farmers responded, each year producing larger crops and more livestock. Unfortunately for the Americans, farmers in other nations did the same. Soon prices tumbled as supply exceeded demand. But railroad freight prices continued to spiral upward, as did the cost of new machinery. As farm profits plunged, farmers tried to produce more just to break even. But greater production only pushed prices even lower.

To make matters worse, almost all farm families had borrowed money to pay for their land or to buy new equipment, generally putting their farms up as security. Those who could not repay the loans lost their farms. Many ended up as tenant farmers, paying rent to the new owners. Others were forced to become farm laborers.

Early movements. In an effort to better their lot, farmers organized. The first major farmers' organization, the Patrons of Husbandry, or the **National Grange**, was founded by Oliver Hudson Kelley in 1867. The Grange began primarily as a social organization. But as membership increased and farmers' financial problems grew, the Grange began tackling economic and political issues.

To lower costs, some Grange farmers formed **cooperatives**. Cooperative members sold their products directly to big-city markets and bought farm equipment and other goods in large quantities at wholesale prices—thereby cutting costs.

The Grange's main focus, however, was on trying to get the railroads, which shipped farm products to markets, to lower freight rates. A leading granger complained that "the cost of transportation to the East eats up about one-half the value of the wheat." In response to pressure from farmers, Illinois, Iowa, Minnesota, and Wisconsin

▲ African American farmers joined the Colored Farmers' Alliance to protect their interests against monopolies and unfair freight prices. Shown here are Virginia homesteaders during the 1890s.

BUILDING VOCABULARY

The use of *blacklists* dates to medieval times. Black books were used by early British universities to record cases of student misconduct. Merchants later used similar books to list the names of people who were poor credit risks.

GLOBAL CONNECTIONS

Cooperative retailing was established by the Rochdale Society of Equitable Pioneers, which opened a store in Rochdale, England, in 1844. The store provided quality goods at reasonable prices for members, and profits were shared among members in proportion to the value of purchases they made. Membership in the society was open to all, regardless of race, sex, religion, or political affiliation. And each member had one vote in decision making. In the mid-1870s the National Grange attempted to organize its cooperatives according to the Rochdale system.

 TRANSPARENCY

Everyday Life in America Transparency and **Worksheet 16**

Practice

GUIDED PRACTICE

Create a chart on the chalkboard with *Workers* and *Farmers* as vertical headings and *Problems They Faced, Goals of Organizations,* and *Methods Used by Organizations* as horizontal headings. Call on volunteers to fill in the information on the chart.

INDEPENDENT PRACTICE

Have students use information developed in Guided Practice to write a letter from a farmer to an industrial worker, or from an industrial worker to a farmer. Letters should explain the hardships they faced, why they organized, the goals of their organization, and how their counterparts could benefit by supporting these goals. Students may wish to include their letters in their portfolios.

Review and Assessment

REVIEW Have students create fliers or handbills for the civil-service reform, workers', or farmers' movements that took place in the late 1800s. Fliers or handbills should clearly spell out the goals and methods of the movement. Select students to explain their fliers or handbills to the class. Then assign the Section 3 Review on p. 157.

ASSESS Assign the **Section 3 Daily Quiz** in *Core Resources.*

COOPERATIVE LEARNING

Organize students into six groups and assign to each group one of the following topics: Government Corruption, Political Reform, Labor Organizes, The Great Upheaval, Farmers Organize, The Election of 1896. Have groups work as editorial boards to develop the front page of a special-edition newspaper on their assigned subject. Display completed front pages on the bulletin board.

HISTORICAL SIDELIGHTS

Regional Alliances

Several Farmers' Alliances developed in different regions of the country to meet needs of local farmers. The Southern Farmers' Alliance was founded in Texas in 1875 as a form of protection against horse thieves and land sharks. Although the regional alliances did not officially unite, leaders realized that state governments were not able to solve farmers' problems.

RUTHERFORD B. HAYES
1822–1893

in office 1877–1881

JAMES A. GARFIELD
1831–1881

in office 1881

CHESTER A. ARTHUR
1829–1886

in office 1881–1885

GROVER CLEVELAND
1837–1908

in office 1885–1889
and 1893–1897

BENJAMIN HARRISON
1833–1901

in office 1889–1893

WILLIAM McKINLEY
1843–1901

in office 1897–1901

---

passed laws in the early 1870s to fix maximum railroad rates. Then in 1887, Congress passed the **Interstate Commerce Act**, which stated that railroad rates had to be "reasonable and just." However, the act proved hard to enforce. The railroads almost always won when the government took them to court for violating the law.

While the Grange was fighting for railroad legislation, a more powerful farm organization—the **Farmers' Alliance**—arose. Offering a strong message of solidarity and hope, the movement had attracted some 400,000 members by 1890. Like the Grange, the Alliance organized cooperatives to buy equipment. It also offered farmers low-cost insurance and lobbied for tougher bank regulations, government ownership of the railroads, and a **graduated income tax** that taxed higher incomes at a higher rate.

The Alliance also echoed the demand that farmers had been making since the end of the Civil War: expand the money supply by printing more greenbacks, the paper money used during the war. The resulting inflation would benefit farmers by allowing them to

▲ Farm family, 1881

charge more for their products and by making it easier to repay their bank loans.

Such prospects alarmed eastern bankers who opposed increasing the amount of money in circulation. Since the money supply was backed by gold, they argued, it was limited by the amount of gold held in the U.S. Treasury. The farmers responded by demanding that the government back the money with silver (which was plentiful in the West) as well as with gold.

In the elections of 1890, Alliance members supported any candidate who accepted their pro-farmer programs. The results were remarkable. Alliance-backed candidates won 38 U.S. congressional seats, 4 southern governorships, and numerous other political offices.

▪▪ **Falling prices and rising costs led many farmers to join the Grange and Farmers' Alliance movements— organizations that sought economic and political change.**

Closure

Ask volunteers to offer words and phrases describing the challenges facing civil-service reformers, workers, and farmers in the late 1880s. List responses on the chalkboard. Then have students evaluate if and how well the civil-service reform movement, the labor movement, and farmers' organizations addressed these challenges.

Extension

CREATE Have students research and create a visual display including sketches and political cartoons of the labor strikes during this period.

RESEARCH Have students research the life of Mary Elizabeth Lease and prepare an oral report on their findings.

The Populist party. Elated, Alliance leaders sought to build on these successes by forming a new political party. At a national convention in St. Louis in February 1892, a gathering of farmers, labor leaders, and reformers founded the People's party, which became more commonly known as the **Populist party.** Politician and author Ignatius Donnelly of Minnesota opened the convention with a thunderous address:

> 66 We meet in the midst of a nation brought to the verge of moral, political, and material ruin. Corruption dominates the ballot-box, the Legislatures, the Congress. . . . We seek to restore the government of the Republic to the hands of the "plain people." 99

The Populists nominated James B. Weaver to run in the 1892 presidential election. Although Democrat Grover Cleveland won the presidency, the Populist party elected 3 senators, 11 congressmen, 3 governors, and numerous state legislators. And Weaver polled a very respectable one million popular votes, carrying 4 western states and 22 electoral votes.

In the presidential election of 1896, the debate on the money supply became a central issue. The Populists threw their support to the Democratic candidate, William Jennings Bryan. Bryan, a two-term congressman from Nebraska, supported the Populists' demand for a silver-

► While Bryan traveled 13,000 miles and gave 600 speeches during the 1896 campaign, McKinley stayed home and received visitors on the front porch of his Ohio home. Ribbons from McKinley's campaign are shown here.

backed currency. Bryan swept the South and much of the West, but he made no headway at all in the urban industrial East or in the mixed industrial and farm states of the Midwest. When the popular votes were counted, Republican William McKinley had beaten Bryan by some 500,000 votes.

Although the power of the Populist party declined after the election, the movement stands as the first example of a large-scale effort by a disadvantaged group in the modern industrial era to use the political process to advance its interests. Furthermore, the Populist platform laid the groundwork for future reform (see Chapter 7). As Populist leader Mary Elizabeth Lease noted in 1914, "the seeds we sowed out in Kansas did not fall on barren ground."

■■ The Populist party drew attention to problems faced by farmers and laid the groundwork for later reforms.

SECTION REVIEW ANSWERS

IDENTIFY

See the following pages:
Gilded Age (p. 152)
political machines (p. 152)
Pendleton Civil Service Act (p. 153)
Knights of Labor (p. 153)
Mary Harris Jones (p. 153)
Great Upheaval (p. 154)
anarchists (p. 154)
blacklists (p. 155)
yellow-dog contracts (p. 155)
lockouts (p. 155)
strikebreakers (p. 155)
American Federation of Labor (p. 155)
National Grange (p. 155)
cooperatives (p. 155)
Interstate Commerce Act (p. 156)
Farmers' Alliance (p. 156)
graduated income tax (p. 156)

LOCATE
See the map on p. 154.

1. *Controversy over spoils system slowed reform.*
2. *8-hour workday, equal pay, end to child labor*
3. *falling prices, rising costs, heavy debts*
4. *changes—eight-hour workday, better pay and treatment; reasons—higher morale, more productivity*
5. *farmers wanted easier debt payment; bankers feared devaluation, profit loss*

SECTION 3 REVIEW

IDENTIFY and explain the significance of the following: Gilded Age, political machines, Pendleton Civil Service Act, Knights of Labor, Mary Harris Jones, Great Upheaval, anarchists, blacklists, yellow-dog contracts, lockouts, strikebreakers, American Federation of Labor, National Grange, cooperatives, Interstate Commerce Act, Farmers' Alliance, graduated income tax.

LOCATE and explain the importance of the following: Haymarket Square, Homestead steel plant, Pullman sleeping car factory.

1. **MAIN IDEA** What obstacles did reformers face in the fight against political corruption?
2. **MAIN IDEA** What changes did the Knights of Labor want for working people?
3. **MAIN IDEA** What conditions led to the rise of the Populist party?
4. **WRITING TO EXPRESS A VIEWPOINT** Imagine you are a member of an industrial workers' union in the late 1800s. Write a proposal for changes in work rules and conditions to present to management. State why you think these changes should be made.
5. **ANALYZING** Why did expansion of the money supply appeal to farmers but not to eastern bankers?

Chapter Review Answers

WRITING A SUMMARY
See Essential Points in each section for main ideas.

REVIEWING CHRONOLOGY
2, 5, 3, 1, 4
Evaluating
improved conditions for urban poor by providing employment, day care, education, recreation, and sanitation services

IDENTIFYING PEOPLE AND IDEAS
1. *major railroad lines*
2. *invented incandescent light bulb*
3. *situation where a business has exclusive control of an industry*
4. *southern and eastern European immigrants to U.S.*
5. *theory that sought to apply the biological principles of natural selection and evolution to society*
6. *social reformer, immigrant from Denmark*
7. *party organizations whose primary goal was to obtain and then keep local political power*
8. *"Mother Jones," strong labor activist from 1870s to 1930*
9. *company practice barring workers from plant where they were employed*

10. *farm organization that organized cooperatives to buy farm equipment, offered farmers low-cost insurance, and lobbied for pro-farm legislation*

UNDERSTANDING MAIN IDEAS
1. *Sherman Antitrust Act declared all monopolies and trusts illegal.*
2. *Bessemer process enabled steel to be produced cheaply, thereby providing materials for mass transit and skyscrapers.*
3. *to improve immigrants' well-being through community services*

4. *They believed that the spoils system led to political corruption.*
5. *Workers faced dangerous working conditions, low pay, and long hours. Farmers had huge debts from falling farm prices and rising costs.*

REVIEWING THEMES
1. *Technological developments made improved production, transportation and communication possible—all changes that strengthened the economy by lowering costs, expanding markets, and increasing profits.*

CHAPTER 6
Review

National Grange founded.
Knights of Labor founded.
Crédit Mobilier scandal surfaces.
Mark Twain and Charles Dudley Warner publish *The Gilded Age.*
Alexander Graham Bell patents telephone.
Lewis Latimer invents the incandescent light bulb.

1865   1870   1875   1880

WRITING A SUMMARY
Using the essential points of the chapter as a guide, write a summary of the chapter.

REVIEWING CHRONOLOGY
Number your paper 1 to 5. Study the time line above, and list the following events in the order in which they happened by writing the first next to 1, the second next to 2, and so on. Then complete the activity below.

1. Jane Addams establishes Hull House.
2. National Grange founded.
3. Congress passes Chinese Exclusion Act.
4. Standard Oil's profits reach some $45 million.
5. Crédit Mobilier scandal surfaces.

Evaluating How did the establishment of Hull House contribute to social reform?

IDENTIFYING PEOPLE AND IDEAS
Explain the historical significance of each of the following people or terms.

1. trunk lines
2. Lewis Latimer
3. monopoly
4. new immigrants
5. Social Darwinism
6. Jacob Riis
7. political machines
8. Mary Harris Jones
9. lockouts
10. Farmers' Alliance

UNDERSTANDING MAIN IDEAS
1. How did the government attempt to restrict big businesses in 1890?
2. How did technological advances promote changes in American cities in the late 1800s?
3. What goals were shared by benevolent societies and by reformers involved in the settlement-house and Social Gospel movements?
4. Why did some Americans support civil service reform?
5. What problems did American industrial workers and farmers face in the late 1800s?

REVIEWING THEMES
1. **Economic Development** How did changes in technology affect the nation's economy in the late 1800s?

2. **Cultural Diversity** Why did some native-born Americans oppose immigration, and what actions did they take to prevent it?
3. **Democratic Values** What steps did reformers take to bring about social, political, and economic change in American society in the late 1800s?

THINKING CRITICALLY
1. **Evaluating** What advantages did large companies have over smaller ones in the new industrial order?
2. **Analyzing** How did the new industrial order lead to changes in the composition of the upper, middle, and working classes?
3. **Synthesizing** Was government intervention in the workers' strikes of the 1880s and 1890s in keeping with the theory of laissez-faire capitalism? Explain.

STRATEGY FOR SUCCESS
Review the Skills Handbook entry on Identifying Cause and Effect on page 749. Write a paragraph tracing the rise of big business from the development of the Bessemer process to the eventual government legislation limiting monopolies and trusts. Be sure to show the connections between causes and effects.

WRITING ABOUT HISTORY
Writing to Create
Among the best-selling books of the late 19th century were dime novels, books with paper covers that sold for 10 cents. Dime novels offered plots with lots of action and suspense. Using a 19th-century tycoon, immigrant, urban resident, reformer, or industrial worker as a main character, write an outline for a dime novel.

2. They felt that immigrants threatened jobs and social stability; they pressed for legal restrictions and sometimes used violence against immigrants.
3. established settlement houses and other welfare institutions, pushed for reform legislation, organized political groups, supported reform candidates

THINKING CRITICALLY

1. Large companies could buy materials in bulk, produce goods in large quantities and sell at lower prices. Large companies could also cut deals with suppliers and transporters to lower costs.

2. New industrial order created urban upper class, who often made a show of wealth through conspicuous consumption. It also created a new middle class of managers, engineers, accountants, clerks, and salespeople. Finally, it expanded the urban working class, drawing people to work in factories.
3. Answers may vary. Some students will answer no, since with laissez-faire capitalism the workers and owners should be left to solve the problems themselves. Others may answer yes, pointing out that the strikes threatened to shut down the whole economy. By stepping in, the government was enabling the economy to continue to function.

STRATEGY FOR SUCCESS

Paragraphs might mention the role of technology in fostering industrial growth, which led to the development of new business practices, which, in turn, led to concerns over monopoly and eventual government intervention.

WRITING ABOUT HISTORY

Outlines might develop the opportunities for, and obstacles to, success in the late 19th century, and the struggle of the main character against those obstacles.

USING PRIMARY SOURCES

Students should note the agricultural problems described in the passage, but even when these problems were not present, the overwhelming problem of mortgage debt was always there.

LINKING HISTORY AND GEOGRAPHY

Most strikes occurred in the Midwest, because it was the hub of heavy industry and railroad activity.

Timeline:

Congress passes Chinese Exclusion Act.

Pendleton Civil Service Act passed.

Jane Addams establishes Hull House.

Haymarket Riot occurs.

Sherman Antitrust Act passed. Janie Porter Barrett founds Locust Street Social Settlement.

Homestead strike occurs. Populist party founded.

Pullman strike occurs.

William McKinley elected president.

Standard Oil's profits reach some $45 million.

Edith Wharton publishes *House of Mirth.*

1885 — 1890 — 1895 — 1900 — 1905 — 1910

USING PRIMARY SOURCES

In the late 19th century, farmers faced a variety of problems, from unpredictable weather and pests to railroad price-fixing. Read the poem below, written by a Georgia farmer in 1890. Then explain how it reflects the problems that led to the formation of farmers' groups. What was the most severe problem?

> 66 We worked through spring and summer,
> through winter and through fall;
> But the mortgage worked the hardest
> and the steadiest of them all;
> It worked on night and Sunday, it
> worked each holiday;
> It settled down among us and it never
> went away.
>
> Whatever we kept from it seemed
> almost as bad as theft;
> It watched us every minute and ruled
> us right and left
> The rust and blight was with us
> sometimes, and sometimes not;
> The dark brown scowling mortgage was
> forever on the spot.
>
> The weevil and the cut worm, they
> went as well they came;
> The mortgage stayed forever, eating
> hearty all the same
> It nailed up every window, stood
> guard at every door;
> And happiness and sunshine made their
> place with us no more. 99

LINKING HISTORY AND GEOGRAPHY

Review the map on page 154. In which region did most labor strikes take place? Why do you think this was so?

BUILDING YOUR PORTFOLIO

Complete the following projects independently or cooperatively.

1. THE ECONOMY In chapters 1, 3, and 5 you explored such economic issues as trade, manufacturing, and regional development. Building on that experience, imagine you are an industrial worker and a union president in the late 1800s. Write a speech to the members of your union recommending the ways by which workers might best adapt or respond to the new industrial order.

UMW emblem, 1890

2. CULTURAL DIVERSITY In chapters 1 and 3 you examined the effects of cultural contact and exchange between various groups. Building on that experience, imagine you are an immigrant who has just arrived from southern or eastern Europe. Create a series of poems and graphics that illustrate the problems you face in your new home and your hopes for the future.

BUILDING YOUR PORTFOLIO

Have students refer to **Building Your Portfolio Worksheet 1**, assigned at the beginning of Unit 1. Use the worksheet to help students monitor their progress on the portfolio projects.

Assessment

Core Resources
• Reteaching Worksheet 6
• Chapter 6 Tests
• Alternative Assessment Forms
Test Generator

MARK TWAIN'S AMERICA

UNIT I

American Letters

SETTING THE SCENE

First published in serial form in *The Atlantic Monthly* during 1875, *Life on the Mississippi* (1883) recounts Twain's apprenticeship as a riverboat pilot. Twain tells how in many journeys up and down the Mississippi he gains the intimate knowledge of the river that a pilot needs. The story concludes with a triumph, but also with a tragedy. Twain achieves his boyhood dream of becoming a pilot, but the Civil War ends the pilot's way of life on the river.

In *The Gilded Age* (1873), Twain and Warner skillfully skewer political corruption and introduce one of the great characters in American humor: Colonel Beriah Sellers. Part confidence artist and part dreamer, Sellers constantly schemes to make a fortune. His schemes are as questionable as the actions of a crooked politician, but they are so vast, wild, and imaginative that everyone is taken in. By portraying Sellers in such a loving fashion, Twain recognizes the role that such speculators played in building the United States.

Mark Twain's America

Samuel Langhorne Clemens—Mark Twain to generations of readers—remains one of America's greatest humorists and chroniclers of the American character. In the following two selections, Twain explores life in two very different settings—the Mississippi River and Washington, D.C.

▲ **Mark Twain**

From *Life on the Mississippi*

by Mark Twain

The river's earliest commerce was in great barges—keelboats, broadhorns. They floated and sailed from the upper rivers to New Orleans, changed cargoes there, and were tediously warped and poled back by hand. A voyage down and back sometimes occupied nine months. In time this commerce increased until it gave employment to hordes of rough and hardy men; rude, uneducated, brave, suffering terrific hardships with sailor-like stoicism; heavy drinkers, coarse frolickers in moral sties like the Natchez-under-the-hill of that day, heavy fighters, reckless fellows, every one, elephantinely jolly, foul-witted, profane, prodigal of their money, bankrupt at the end of the trip, fond of barbaric finery, prodigious braggarts; yet, in the main, honest, trustworthy, faithful to promises and duty, and often picturesquely magnanimous.

By and by the steamboat intruded. Then, for fifteen or twenty years, these men continued to run their keelboats downstream, and the steamers did all of the upstream business, the keelboatmen selling their boats in New Orleans, and returning home as deck-passengers in the steamers.

But after a while the steamboats so increased in number and in speed that they were able to absorb the entire commerce; and then keelboating died a permanent death. The keelboatman became a deckhand, or a mate, or a pilot on the steamer; and when steamer-berths were not open to him, he took a berth on a Pittsburgh coal-flat, or on a pine raft constructed in the forests up toward the sources of the Mississippi.

In the heyday of the steamboating prosperity, the river from end to end was flanked with coal-fleets and timber-rafts, all managed by hand, and employing hosts of the rough characters whom I have been trying to describe. . . .

By way of illustrating the keelboat talk and manners, and that now departed and hardly remembered raft life, I will throw in, in this place, a chapter from a book which I have been working at. . . . The book is a story which details some passages in the life of an ignorant village boy, Huck Finn, son of the town drunkard. . . . He has run away from his persecuting father, and from a persecuting good widow who wishes to make

▼ *Mississippi riverboat*

a nice, truth telling respectable boy of him; and with him a slave of the widow's has also escaped. They have found a fragment of a lumber-raft (it is high water and dead summer-time), and are floating down river by night, and hiding in the willows by day— bound for Cairo, [Illinois,] whence the Negro will seek freedom in the heart of the free states. But, in the fog, they have passed Cairo without knowing it. By and by they begin to suspect the truth, and Huck Finn is persuaded to end the dismal suspense by swimming down to a huge raft which they have seen in the distance ahead of them, creeping aboard under cover of the darkness, and gathering the needed information by eavesdropping: . . .

I swum down along the raft till I was most abreast the campfire in the middle, then I crawled aboard and inched along and got in among some shingles on the weather side of the fire. There was thirteen men there—they was the watch on deck of course. And a mighty rough-looking lot, too. . . .

The man they called Ed said the muddy Mississippi water was wholesomer to drink than the clear water of the Ohio; he said that if you let a pint of this yaller Mississippi water settle, you would have about a half to three-quarters of an inch of mud in the bottom, according to the stage of the river, and then it warn't no better than Ohio water—what you wanted to do was to keep it stirred up—and when the water was low, keep mud on hand to put in and thicken the water up the way it ought to be.

The Child of Calamity said that was so; he said there was nutritiousness in the mud, and a man that drunk Mississippi water could

grow corn in his stomach if he wanted to. He says:

"You look at the graveyards; that tells the tale. Trees won't grow worth shucks in a Cincinnati graveyard, but in a Sent Louis graveyard they grow upwards of eight hundred foot high. It's all on account of the water the people drunk before they laid up. A Cincinnati corpse don't richen a soil any." ❖

From *The Gilded Age*

by Mark Twain and Charles Dudley Warner

Every individual you encounter in the City of Washington almost—and certainly every separate and distinct individual in the public employment, from the highest bureau chief, clear down to the maid who scrubs the Department halls . . . —represents Political Influence. Unless you can get the ear of a Senator, or a Congressman, or a Chief of a Bureau or Department, and persuade him to use his "influence" in your behalf, you cannot get an employment of the most trivial nature in Washington. Mere merit, fitness and capability, are useless baggage to you without "influence." The population of Washington consists pretty much entirely of government employés and the people who board them.

There are thousands of these employés, and they have gathered there from every corner of the Union and got their berths through the intercession (command is nearer the word) of the Senators and Representatives of their respective States. It would be an odd circumstance to see a girl get employment at three or four dollars a week . . . without any political grandee to back her, but merely because she was worthy, and competent, and a good citizen of a free country that "treats all persons alike." Washington would be mildly thunderstruck at such a thing as that. If you are a member of Congress, (no offence,) and one of your constituents who doesn't know anything, and does not want to go into the bother of learning something, and has no money, and no employment, and can't earn a living, comes besieging you for help, do you say, "Come, my friend, if your services were valuable you could get employment elsewhere—don't want you here?" Oh, no. You take him to a Department and say, "Here, give this person something to pass away the time at—and a salary"— and the thing is done. You throw him on his country. He is his country's child, let his country support him. There is something good and motherly about Washington, the grand old benevolent National Asylum for the Helpless. ❖

(see pp. 152–153)

THINKING AND WRITING ABOUT LITERATURE

1. Toward which group does Mark Twain seem most sympathetic—the Mississippi boatmen or the public servants in Washington? Provide evidence to support your answer.
2. Twain and Charles Dudley Warner published *The Gilded Age* in 1873. What events in Washington might have influenced the tone of the book?

THINKING AND WRITING ABOUT LITERATURE

1. *the Mississippi boatmen; Twain describes the boatmen as rude and uneducated but honest, trustworthy, and hardworking; the public servants in Washington, according to Twain, get paid for doing nothing*
2. *scandals in President Ulysses S. Grant's first administration (see pp. 152–153), including the Crédit Mobilier scandal, which surfaced in 1872*

INTERPRETING EDITORIAL CARTOONS

Guide students through the explanation of how to interpret editorial cartoons, and have them complete the Practicing the Strategy exercise. Then divide students into groups of three, and have groups assign each person the task of identifying either the main symbol and its meaning, the meaning of the title and label, or the point of view of an editorial cartoon clipped from a newspaper or magazine. Assign the class a different topic, such as a news event or a recent event in school, and ask the groups to draw an editorial cartoon about it. Have the groups present their cartoons, explaining the symbols, labels, and point of view of their drawing.

PRACTICING THE STRATEGY

1. *Northern visitors to the South, southern slaveholders, enslaved African Americans, English textile workers and poor people, an English gentleman; the activities of the black slaves are caricatured*
2. *Dancing and banjo playing symbolize the supposedly happy, carefree life of slaves.*
3. *The label "Cloth Factory" is not particularly important, since the speech of the characters makes the subject of factory work clear. The title suggests a contrast is being drawn between slavery in the American South and the sad conditions of textile workers and coal miners in England.*
4. *(a) that of a defender of slavery who is critical of industrialization*
   (b) that enslaved African Americans in the South have a shorter workday and better working conditions, and therefore an easier life, than do the working class of England

Strategies for Success

INTERPRETING EDITORIAL CARTOONS

Editorial cartoons are drawings that present points of view on the issues, ideas, people, and events of the day. They usually appear in the editorial sections of newspapers and newsmagazines. Although some express a positive outlook, many are critical of a person or policy.

To communicate their message, editorial cartoonists frequently use caricature and symbolism. A *caricature* is a drawing that exaggerates or distorts physical features. *Symbolism* is the use of one thing to stand for something else. For instance, cartoonists often use Uncle Sam to represent the United States, an elephant to symbolize the Republican party, and a donkey to stand for the Democrats.

Many editorial cartoons rely on labels to help identify symbols or other aspects of the picture. Most also include captions or "speech balloons," which may serve as a sort of punchline.

How to Interpret Editorial Cartoons

1. **Identify the caricatures.** Identify each figure and object. Note any distortions or exaggerations, and decide whether they cast the figure in a positive or negative light.
2. **Identify the symbols used.** Determine what each symbol stands for.
3. **Read the title and labels.** Read and determine the meaning of any title and labels.

4. **Consider the cartoonist's purpose.** Identify the points of view being expressed in the speech balloons or caption. Try to determine the cartoonist's message.

Applying the Strategy

Andrew Jackson was a popular subject for editorial cartoonists of his day. In the cartoon on this page, Jackson is shown wearing a crown and kingly robe, holding a scepter like a club and a "veto" as if it were a royal decree. Tattered papers labeled "Constitution of the United States," "Internal Improvements," and "U.S. Bank" and a book titled *Judiciary of the U. States* are strewn underfoot.

According to his critics, Jackson had abused his constitutional authority by his vetoes of bills that would have rechartered the national bank and provided for internal improvements. The cartoonist uses symbols of monarchy to accuse Jackson of acting more like a king than the president of a republic. This point is reinforced by the condition and position of the papers and by the title: "King Andrew the First."

Practicing the Strategy

Study the editorial cartoon on page xix of your textbook. Then, on a separate sheet of paper, answer the following questions.

1. Who are the central figures in the cartoon? Are they portrayed realistically, or are they caricatures?
2. What symbols does the cartoon contain?
3. How do the labels and the title help make the cartoonist's point of view and message clear?
4. What is **(a)** the cartoonist's point of view and **(b)** the cartoon's message?

▼ **Cartoon satirizing Andrew Jackson**

BUILDING YOUR PORTFOLIO

Each portfolio project described below is the culmination of the Building Your Portfolio activities in the chapter reviews of Unit 1. First, decide whether you wish students to work individually or in groups on these unit projects. Then permit each student to choose the project on which he or she desires to work. Provide students with copies of **Building Your Portfolio Worksheet 1** from *Core Resources*. This worksheet will guide students step by step to complete their projects.

UNIT

1

Review

BUILDING YOUR PORTFOLIO

Outlined below are four projects. Independently or cooperatively, complete one and use the products to demonstrate your mastery of the historical concepts involved.

1 THE ECONOMY
The search for better trade routes first brought Europeans to the Americas, and economic factors continued to influence the United States during its early history. Using the portfolio materials you designed in chapters 1, 3, 5, and 6, create a board game tracing the nation's economic development from the time of the first European arrivals to 1900. Games should consider transportation, technology, markets, and labor.

2 CULTURAL DIVERSITY
The history of the United States is a history of the rich intermingling of a variety of cultures. Using the portfolio materials you designed in chapters 1, 3, and 6, prepare a series of one-scene plays showing experiences of and exchanges between American Indians, Africans, and Europeans in America up to 1900. Plays might describe daily life in different time periods or might focus on specific historical events and people.

3 CONFLICT
Wars and other social conflicts in early American history often affected different people or groups in different ways. Using the portfolio materials you designed in chapters 2, 4, and 5, conduct a panel discussion about the nature of conflict that showcases the views of soldiers, government planners or others responsible for organizing a war effort, and others involved in conflicts. Use specific examples.

4 INDIVIDUAL RIGHTS
American colonists protested British rule in an effort to secure individual rights, and as time passed, others also struggled to win their rights. Using the portfolio materials you designed in chapters 2, 3, and 4, prepare a presentation discussing the different ways in which individual rights can be violated and the methods by which rights can be secured.

PORTFOLIO ASSESSMENT

1. *Games should illustrate how the development of roads, canals, and railroads provided better access to markets; how technological developments encouraged the shift from hand production to mechanized production; how the market revolution changed the economy; and how growth of the industrial class led to unionization.*
2. *Plays should illustrate sources of conflict between groups as well as attempts to improve the status of groups.*
3. *Panels should address the issues that contributed to a particular conflict and the developments that led to war.*
4. *Presentations should discuss violations of individual rights and ways people have tried to secure rights.*

Videodisc Review
In assigned groups, develop an outline for a video collage of America from prehistory through 1900. Choose images that best illustrate the major topics of the period. Write a script to accompany the images. Assign narrators to different parts of the script, and present your video collage to the class.

Further Reading
Foner, Eric. *A Short History of Reconstruction, 1863–1877.* HarperCollins (1990). Overview of the Reconstruction years.
Luchetti, Cathy, and Carol Olwell. *Women of the West.* Orion (1982). Firsthand accounts of women's lives in the West.
Meltzer, Milton, ed. *Voices from the Civil War.* HarperCollins (1989). Northern and southern views of the war and its effects.

Nash, Gary B. *Red, White, and Black: The Peoples of Early North America.* Prentice Hall (1992). Account of interaction between Native Americans, Africans, and whites during colonial times.
Schlereth, Thomas J. *Victorian America: Transformations in Everyday Life 1876–1915.* HarperCollins (1991). Overview of the impact of immigration, expansion, and industrialization on U.S. society.

Introducing the Unit

- **Chapter 7**
  THE AGE OF REFORM
  1897–1920
- **Chapter 8**
  THE PROGRESSIVE
  PRESIDENTS
  1900–1920
- **Chapter 9**
  AMERICA AND THE WORLD
  1898–1917
- **Chapter 10**
  WORLD WAR I
  1914–1920

UNIT OVERVIEW

By the turn of the century, many Americans had begun to focus on economic and social problems, which had accompanied industrialization and the growth of cities. Some reformers fought for social change. Others sought to reform government at all levels. As the world's major powers pursued policies of economic and political imperialism, the U.S. also sought to extend its influence in the Pacific, the Caribbean, Latin America, and Asia. However, the U.S. attempted to avoid the conflict that imperialism and nationalism caused in Europe itself. Eventually the U.S. became embroiled in World War I. At war's end, President Wilson tried to negotiate a just peace, but the treaty was rejected by the Senate.

CORE RESOURCES

- **American Almanac Worksheet 2**
- **Building Your Portfolio Worksheet 2**
  You may wish to preview the Unit 2 Review and Building Your Portfolio performance assessment activities on p. 273.

Using the Almanac

Review the almanac entries with students. Then ask students to use information in the almanac to write a one-paragraph portrait of the period. Call on volunteers to read their portraits to the class.

American ALMANAC

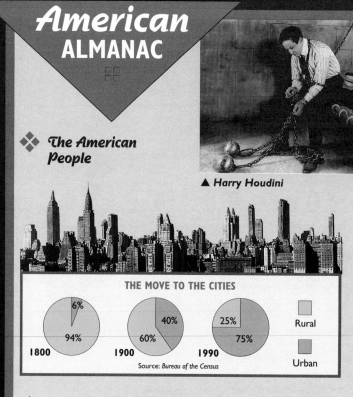

▲ *Harry Houdini*

❖ The American People

THE MOVE TO THE CITIES

- 1800: 6% Urban / 94% Rural
- 1900: 40% Urban / 60% Rural
- 1990: 75% Urban / 25% Rural

Rural
Urban

Source: *Bureau of the Census*

❖ Off to Work

1900 Industry workers make about 29¢ per hour; farm workers earn $1 per day.

1900 Booker T. Washington organizes National Negro Business League.

1900 A 1,000-man logging camp consumes 1,200 lbs. of meat, 1 ton of fruit and vegetables, 900 lbs. of flour, 600 lbs. of sugar, 190 lbs. of butter, and 240 dozen eggs daily.

1900 Nearly 126,000 Americans serve in the U.S. armed forces at home and abroad.

1909 W.E.B. Du Bois helps found the new National Association for the Advancement of Colored People (NAACP).

▶ *Naval Aviation Camp at Guantánamo Bay, Cuba, 1913*

1916 Montana representative Jeannette Rankin is first woman elected to Congress.

1916 Ezequiel de Baca elected governor of New Mexico—attaining highest elected office held by a Hispanic American to date.

▶ *Ezequiel de Baca*

❖ At Your Leisure

1899 Scott Joplin's "Maple Leaf Rag" makes him "King of Ragtime."

1900 Eastman Kodak's $1.00 Brownie Box Camera boosts amateur photography.

1903 Baseball's Boston Americans win first World Series.

1904 Cy Young is first major league player to pitch a perfect game.

1908 Escape artist Harry Houdini attracts huge crowds.

1910 Boy Scouts and Camp Fire Girls founded.

1912 Fox-trot, crab step, kangaroo dip, chicken scratch, and bunny hug dances are big hits!

1912 Stores are bursting with consumer products: Crayola crayons, Campbell's soup, Pepsi-Cola, Jell-O, ice cream cones, Corn Flakes, Life Savers, and Oreos.

1915 Charlie Chaplin is sensation of the year; in his career he produces, directs, or acts in more than 80 films!

1920 National Negro Baseball League is formed—enabling African Americans to play professional baseball.

The American People

Mention that the rate of urbanization was rapid in the first 20 years of the 1900s. A report published by the Census Bureau in 1921 showed that 51 percent of the population lived in urban areas.

■■ Ask students to research the population count that made up an urban area in the early 1900s and in the 1890s.

Off to Work

Point out that in 1900 unskilled male laborers earned 10¢ per hour on average, and young girls working a loom at a textile factory often took home as little as $2 for a 50- to 55-hour week.

■■ Have students who work compare their pay rates with the pay rates of 1900.

At Your Leisure

Cy Young was elected to the National Baseball Hall of Fame in 1937. Today, at the end of each baseball season, the Cy Young Award is given to the outstanding pitcher in each major league.

■■ Have students identify and discuss other awards named for famous people.

Firsts in Science and Technology

Henson had accompanied Peary on a number of expeditions prior to the one that took them to the North Pole. "I cannot get along without him," Peary commented.

■■ Ask students what might motivate them to take part in a voyage of exploration.

The Automobile

Point out that the automobile was very much a part of American life by the beginning of the 1920s. One of every four American families bought or sold a car each year.

■■ Ask students what impact the automobile has had on life today.

The Latest Looks

By 1920 factory-made, ready-to-wear clothes in standardized sizes were available in most clothing stores.

■■ Ask students to describe today's "latest looks."

UNIT

2

A World Power

1897–1920

▲ Model T Ford

❖ The Automobile

1900 People spend $1,250 for a new Oldsmobile; a horse and buggy costs $400.

1904 Official speed limits are set in New York: 10 mph in cities, 15 in villages, 20 on country roads.

1909 Ford produces the Model T, priced at $950; price drops to $290 by 1924.

1920 Auto sales climb to 1,905,500—up from 4,100 in 1900!

▼ Blanche Stuart

◀ Wright brothers' airplane

❖ Firsts in Science and Technology

1900 Only about 2% of U.S. households have a telephone; today about 95% have one.

1909 Robert E. Peary and African American Matthew Henson reach North Pole.

1909 U.S. Army buys its first airplane—from the Wright brothers.

1910 Blanche Stuart is first American woman to fly an airplane.

❖ The Latest Looks

1890s First factory-made clothes appear.

1907 Annette Kellerman is arrested for wearing "shocking" attire on a Boston beach: a bathing suit.

THE AGE OF REFORM

1897–1920

Chapter Overview

By the beginning of the 20th century, the U.S. was witnessing the benefits—as well as the ills—of industrialization and rapid urbanization. Americans from all walks of life focused on the basic economic and social inequities that existed in the nation. Muckraking journalists exposed corrupt political and corporate practices as well as racial and economic injustices, while novelists and intellectuals publicized social problems and theorized about solutions. Social reformers fought for changes in the workplace and tackled problems in housing and public health, and issues of personal morality. Nonwhite reformers organized to address problems of discrimination and prejudice, but with mixed results.

THE AMERICAN NATION VIDEODISC PROGRAM
A variety of still images, short videos, and activities are available for you to use as you teach this chapter. See Videodisc Resources in the Core Resources Binder for barcode correlations and suggestions for using the program.

Chapter Planning Guide

CHAPTER 7	CORE RESOURCES	AUDIOVISUAL AV RESOURCES	PROGRAM RESOURCES
INTRODUCTION pp. 166–167	■ Building Your Portfolio Worksheet 2	■ Everyday Life in America Transparency and Worksheet 17	
TEACHING THE CHAPTER pp. 168–185 ■ For expanded coverage of pp. 183–184, see Chapter 26.	■ Graphic Organizer 7 ■ Social Studies Skills Worksheet 7 ■ Literature Worksheet 7 ■ Geography Worksheet 7 ■ Outline Map 9	■ Linking Geography and History Transparencies and Worksheets 11A, 13A	■ Art in American History Transparency and Worksheet 20 ■ *Eyewitnesses and Others*, Volume 2: Readings 18, 26, 30
REVIEW AND ASSESSMENT pp. 186–187	■ Chapter 7 Daily Quizzes ■ Reteaching Worksheet 7 ■ Chapter 7 Tests ■ Alternative Assessment Forms		■ Test Generator

Additional Resources

BOOKS FOR TEACHERS

Brasch, Walter M. *Forerunners of Revolution: Muckrakers & the American Social Conscience.* University Press of America, 1990. Examines role of muckrakers.

Davis, Allen F. *Spearheads for Reform: The Social Settlements & the Progressive Movement, 1890 to 1914.* Rutgers University Press, 1985. Scholarly history of the Progressive movement.

Rosenberg, Rosalind. *Divided Lives: American Women in the Twentieth Century.* Hill and Wang, 1992. History of the 20th-century women's movement.

BOOKS FOR STUDENTS

Brady, Kathleen. *Ida Tarbell: Portrait of a Muckraker.* University of Pittsburgh Press, 1989. Biography of Tarbell.

Schneider, Carl, and Dorothy Schneider. *American Women in the Progressive Era, 1900–1920.* Facts on File, 1992. History of women in the Progressive Era.

*Tames, Richard. *Nineteen Hundred to Nineteen Nineteen.* Watts, 1991. Photographic history of the first two decades of the 20th century.

*for students reading below grade level

MULTIMEDIA MATERIALS

Muckrakers and Reformers. Sound filmstrip, 10 min. Multi-Media Productions/SSSS. Examines goals of reformers.

The Progressive Era: Reform Works in America. Video, 23 min. Britannica. Examines the Progressive Era.

Progressives, Populists and Reform in America (1890–1917). Video, 32 min. Guidance Associates/SSSS. Primary sources show reformers' work.

THEMES IN AMERICAN HISTORY

USE WITH PAGES 166–167

*L*isted on the right are the themes emphasized in Chapter 7. The questions in boldface type stimulate critical thinking and provide students with an opportunity to discuss the themes within a broadened context. The questions also appear in the pupil's edition on p. 166.

■ ECONOMIC DEVELOPMENT

How might state governments justify regulating how businesses treat workers? Students might suggest that a state is obligated to protect the rights of all its citizens, even within the workplace.

■ DEMOCRATIC VALUES

How might reform groups help extend opportunities to all citizens? Students might note that by calling attention to social and economic injustices, reform groups can heighten public awareness of important issues, which may result in increased pressure on local, state, or national business or political leaders for widespread change.

■ CONSTITUTIONAL HERITAGE

How might reform movements lay the groundwork for constitutional change? Students might suggest that reform efforts could bring to light concerns about issues so basic to American society that some people might believe constitutional change to be the appropriate remedy. Once the general public is made aware of such issues, a ground swell of support may build for constitutional amendments that will institute needed changes.

CHAPTER STRATEGIES FOR MEETING INDIVIDUAL NEEDS

LIMITED ENGLISH PROFICIENT LEARNERS

As students read through the chapter, have them work in pairs to select an illustration from each section. Ask pairs to write an extended caption for each illustration, explaining its relation to the section content. You may also wish to involve these students in the simulated 1905 strike activity.

TACTILE/KINESTHETIC LEARNERS

Encourage students to act out a 1905 union strike against a factory. Students may want to create banners, signs, and other visuals to use in their presentation.

LEARNERS HAVING DIFFICULTY

Organize students in pairs to create biography cards of the chapter's key people and groups. Have one side list the name of the person or group and the other list pertinent actions, events, and issues. Encourage students to use the cards to quiz each other.

AUDITORY LEARNERS

Have students assume roles of the persons quoted in the chapter's primary sources. Allow time for them to dramatize the quotes before the class.

VISUAL LEARNERS

Invite students to view a sound filmstrip such as *Muckrakers and Reformers* (see Multimedia Materials, p. 165A). Then have students write a muckraking story based on information in the chapter.

GIFTED LEARNERS

Have students create a pictorial exhibit titled "Progressive Reformers," showing the actions of each reformer and his or her impact on society.

165B

■ **UNDERSTANDING THE MAIN IDEA**

Call on a volunteer to read aloud the Understanding the Main Idea paragraph. Ask students to suggest measures that reformers might take to overcome the negative effects of industrialization and rapid urbanization. List their responses on a flip chart. At the end of the chapter, compare student solutions with those of the progressive reformers.

 THEMES
Have students work individually or in small groups to answer the questions under Themes. Save students' responses so that they can compare them with their responses after studying the chapter. (See p. 165B for suggested answers.)

■ **THE TIME LINE**
Have students study the time line at the bottom of the page. Ask them to explain how the entries in the time line reflect the title of the chapter.

CORE RESOURCES

- **Graphic Organizer 7**
- **Social Studies Skills Worksheet 7**
- **Outline Map 9**
- **Building Your Portfolio Worksheet 2**

AV RESOURCES

- **Everyday Life in America Transparency and Worksheet 17**

166

ABOUT THE ILLUSTRATION

Tell students that the 1913 painting by C. C. Cooper of New York City's Fifth Avenue illustrates typical conditions in large cities in the U.S. in the early 1900s. Ask students to study the illustration and to write a short paragraph describing the conditions they see in this painting and suggesting reasons why people in the early 1900s might have sought to change these conditions.

Chapter 7

1897–1920

THE AGE OF REFORM

FOCUS

UNDERSTANDING THE MAIN IDEA

A new reform mood swept the United States during the early 1900s. With great optimism and faith in scientific efficiency, reformers set out to conquer the negative effects of industrialization and rapid urbanization: unsafe working conditions, long hours, poor wages, and slum housing.

THEMES

■ **ECONOMIC DEVELOPMENT** How might state governments justify regulating how businesses treat workers?

■ **DEMOCRATIC VALUES** How might reform groups help extend opportunities to all citizens?

■ **CONSTITUTIONAL HERITAGE** How might reform movements lay the groundwork for constitutional change?

1900	1904	1909	1912	1919
ILGWU established.	National Child Labor Committee formed.	NAACP founded.	Massachusetts passes minimum-wage law.	Eighteenth Amendment ratified.

■■ ▶ LINK TO THE PAST

Call on volunteers to review the social and economic
changes brought on by the growth of American business and industry in the Gilded Age. Ask other volunteers to describe how the reform work of Jane
Addams and of supporters of the Social Gospel movement addressed some of these problems.

■■ LINK TO THE PAST ▶ *While the Gilded Age had promoted industrial development and generated great profits for some, it had also created many problems. The
Populist movement had brought to the nation's attention the plight of
farmers and urban workers. Gilded Age reformers like Jane Addams
and the men and women involved in the Social Gospel movement had
worked to improve conditions for the urban poor.*

Fifth Avenue in New York, 1913

*I*n 1906 Upton Sinclair published *The Jungle,* a novel about the
meat-packing industry in Chicago. In an effort to alert the public to
what he saw as the consequences of capitalist greed, Sinclair
described industry practices in graphic detail:

> ❝ There was never the least attention paid to what was cut up for
> sausage. . . . There would be meat that had tumbled out on the floor,
> in the dirt and sawdust. . . . There would be meat stored in great
> piles in rooms; and the water from leaky roofs would drip over it,
> and thousands of rats would race about on it. . . . These rats were
> nuisances, and the packers would put poisoned bread out for them,
> they would die, and then rats, bread, and meat would go into the
> hoppers together. ❞

Sinclair's images were so vivid that they made some readers
physically sick. "I aimed at the public's heart," Sinclair remarked,
"and by accident I hit it in the
stomach." In response to *The
Jungle*, Americans demanded
federal laws prohibiting
unhealthful conditions in
food-processing industries.

The Jungle was part of a
reform movement that swept
the country in the early 20th
century. Most reformers recognized the benefits of indus-
trialism, but they were intent
on correcting its abuses.

Urban child collecting firewood

MAKING CONNECTIONS

Literature
In 1905 President Theodore
Roosevelt and Congress
were locked in battle over
legislation about impurities
in food. Alarmed by reading
page proofs of *The Jungle*
sent to him by a senior partner of the company that was
about to publish the book,
Roosevelt launched an
investigation of the stockyards, then publicly re-
leased part of its findings.
When the public responded
with outrage, Roosevelt
threatened congressional
opponents that he would
release even more lurid
parts of the book unless
they acted. As a result,
Congress passed the Pure
Food and Drug Act and the
Meat Inspection Act.

PRIMARY SOURCE

Description of Change:
excerpted
Rationale: excerpted to
focus on main idea

PREVIEW WORKSHOP

Following is a list of the significant people and terms in this section. You may wish to use this list as a section preview.

People
- John Dewey
- Lincoln Steffens
- Ida Tarbell
- S. S. McClure
- Ray Stannard Baker
- Theodore Dreiser
- Herbert Croly
- Jane Addams

Terms
- progressivism
- muckrakers

FOCUS OBJECTIVES

- List some of the goals of progressivism.

- Explain why some women were attracted to the Progressive movement.

- Identify the roles that muckrakers, writers, and intellectuals played in the Progressive movement.

Section 1

THE PROGRESSIVE MOVEMENT

F O C U S
- **What were some of the goals of progressivism?**
- **Why were many women attracted to the Progressive movement?**
- **What roles did muckrakers, writers, and intellectuals play in the Progressive movement?**

In spite of its name, the Progressive movement—the reform effort that swept the nation between 1900 and 1920—was not a single movement united behind a single goal. Rather it was a collection of reform-minded individuals and groups dedicated to bettering life in the United States. Building on Populist efforts and the work of 19th-century reformers, the progressives publicized the ills of industrial society and sought to remedy them.

"Omnia Vincit Labor"

SAMUEL GOMPERS

President American Federation of Labor

COURT HOUSE

Thursday, June 3

7:45 P. M.

SUBJECT:

Shorter Work Day

Announcement of an AFL meeting, 1897

THE PROGRESSIVE SPIRIT

By the early 1900s industrialization had transformed the United States. Much of the transformation was positive: economic growth, new goods and services, and an expanding middle class. However, economic growth also widened the gap between the rich and the poor and contributed to unsafe working conditions and crowded cities. These ills led to a spirit of reform known as **progressivism**.

This concern over the effects of industrialization was by no means new. In the late 1800s Populists had protested unfair or corrupt corporate practices and had pressed for government legislation to stop them. Populism, however, was mainly a rural movement. Progressivism, on the other hand, focused on urban problems, such as unsafe working conditions, bad sanitation, and corrupt political machines.

Progressives carried on the Populists' struggle to "restore government to the people" by proposing election reforms that would enable people to participate more fully in running their government (see

◀ **In the early 1900s most major labor unions excluded women, even though they made up nearly one fourth of the work force. Seamstresses, such as these shown here, often formed their own unions to fight for better working conditions.**

MOTIVATING: PRIOR KNOWLEDGE

Ask volunteers to recall the goals of the Populists in the late 1800s; write student responses on the chalkboard. Explain that this section identifies the goals of other reformers who were determined to halt the negative effects of industrialization in urban America.

Teaching the Section

PROGRESSIVES' GOALS

Pair students to role-play Populist and progressive reformers. Tell each pair to discuss similarities and differences in their goals for reform. Choose pairs to re-create their conversations for the class. Then ask each student to write a summary sentence about the goals of progressivism. Have students read their sentences aloud.

The Granger Collection, New York

◄ The progressive spirit also influenced a new school of artists during the early 1900s. Known as the Ash Can School for the gritty and realistic subjects of their paintings, the movement included such artists as George Bellows, Robert Henri, John Sloan, George Luks, William Glackens, and Everett Shinn. Many of their paintings, such as George Bellows's *Lone Tenement* (1909), shown at left, depicted the ugly tenements and tough living conditions of poor urban neighborhoods.

MAKING CONNECTIONS
Sociology
Middle-class women reformers believed that the problems brought about by industrial growth had a direct impact on family life. They insisted that government should assume a greater responsibility for the economic well-being of citizens, particularly women and children.

Chapter 8). Progressives believed that the cure for democracy's ills was more democracy.

Progressives also carried on the Populists' demand for a curb on corporate power. Toward this end, they promoted legislation that prohibited monopolies and enabled smaller businesses to compete successfully in the economy.

Like Populists, progressives were inspired by the spirit of social justice. To cap the skyrocketing incomes of the rich, they took up the Populists' demand for a federal graduated income tax. They also supported the Populists' cry for an eight-hour workday. In addition, they sought to institute minimum wages, assure safe working conditions, and end child labor.

The progressive spirit was deeply infused with idealism. Theodore Roosevelt, who would become a leading progressive, aptly reflected this idealism when he wrote:

❝ If we wish to do good work for our country, we must be unselfish, disinterested, sincerely desirous of the well-being of the commonwealth, and capable of devoted adherence to a lofty ideal. ❞

This idealism extended to a firm belief in the power of science and technology to solve social problems. The progressive philosopher John Dewey urged reformers to gather data about society's ills through observation and experimentation and then test solutions. Progressives, assisted by universities, initiated many social research projects.

■■ **Progressives sought a more democratic government, a check on corporate power, and solutions to social problems.**

Although people from all walks of life participated in reform efforts during the Progressive Era, many progressives were native born, middle or upper class, and college educated. Men and women of the urban middle class—social workers, engineers, writers, teachers, doctors, ministers, lawyers, and small-business owners were particularly attracted to progressivism. This class had grown from some 750,000 in 1870 to around 10 million by 1910. In the words of Kansas editor William Allen White, by the 1900s Populism had "shaved its whiskers, washed its shirt, put on a derby, and moved up into the middle class."

Many middle-class women were attracted to the Progressive movement for the same reason earlier generations of women had assisted reform efforts: reform work provided them with one of the

▲ Shown here is a group of Vassar women from the 1920s.

PRIMARY SOURCE
Description of Change: excerpted
Rationale: excerpted to focus on main idea

■■ Ask students if they think it is possible for a president to adhere to such high ideals without politics getting in the way.

Teaching the Section

PROGRESSIVE WOMEN

Ask three volunteers to role-play middle-class women of the early 1900s. Have other students work in small groups to write questions they would ask the women in order to gain a better understanding of their reasons for becoming involved in the Progressive movement. Invite representatives of each group to ask the role-players their questions.

THE MUCKRAKERS

Organize the class into four groups, each group representing the editorial board of a new "muckraking" magazine for the early 1900s. Have each group choose a name for its magazine, draft a statement of purpose to appear in the magazine, and choose titles for five articles to appear in the first issue. Ask a student from each group to present its ideas to the class. Then ask the groups how other writers and intellectuals reinforced the work of the muckrakers.

Graph Caption Answer
about 40 percent

MAKING CONNECTIONS

Literature
Roosevelt used the term *muckraker* in a 1906 speech. His reference was to a character in John Bunyan's 17th-century English classic *Pilgrim's Progress* who was too busy raking the filth on the floor to look up and accept a celestial crown.

BIO GRAPHY PERSONALITIES IN HISTORY

Tarbell's extensively researched articles were compiled into two volumes. Her work aroused public interest and resulted in federal investigations of the Standard Oil Company. That company was dissolved in 1911 under the Sherman Antitrust Act. Although Tarbell gained her fame in her 40s as a writer for *McClure's* magazine, she was the author of numerous articles and books, including several books about Abraham Lincoln. She was planning a new book when she died at age 86.

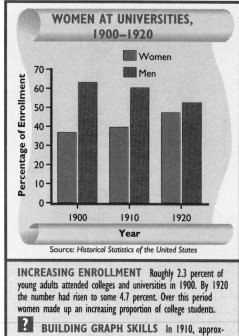

WOMEN AT UNIVERSITIES, 1900–1920

Percentage of Enrollment

■ Women
■ Men

Year

Source: *Historical Statistics of the United States*

INCREASING ENROLLMENT Roughly 2.3 percent of young adults attended colleges and universities in 1900. By 1920 the number had risen to some 4.7 percent. Over this period women made up an increasing proportion of college students.

? **BUILDING GRAPH SKILLS** In 1910, approximately what percentage of university students were women?

few acceptable avenues for influencing politics and society. Although the number of women enrolled in colleges increased during the early 1900s, women's career options were limited. Reform work provided college-educated women with a way to apply their knowledge of medicine, psychology, sociology, and other disciplines. Some women made careers of reform work; others volunteered their time through associations such as the General Federation of Women's Clubs, the Women's Trade Union League, and the National Association of Colored Women.

▪▪ **Not only did reform work provide women with a way to influence social change, it was one of the few career opportunities open to college-educated women.**

INSPIRATION FOR REFORM

Progressive journalists helped spread the reform message. Newly founded mass-circulation magazines like *McClure's, Munsey's,* and *Cosmopolitan* filled their pages with stories that explored

corruption in politics and business as well as such social problems as slums and child labor.

The progressive journalists were relentless in their assaults on social evils, leading Theodore Roosevelt to complain: "Men with a muck-rake are often indispensable to the well-being of society, but only if they know when to stop raking the muck." The vivid image stuck, and the journalists became known as **muckrakers**—a name they accepted with obvious pride.

McClure's publication of "Tweed Days in St. Louis" by journalists Lincoln Steffens and Claude Wetmore in October 1902 marked the beginning of the muckraking school of journalism. The article exposed the political machine in St. Louis, comparing corrupt city government there with New York City's government under Boss Tweed. *McClure's* went on to publish hundreds of articles on political and corporate corruption, poor working conditions, and slum life.

BIO GRAPHY In November 1902, *McClure's* ran the first installment of Ida Tarbell's "History of the Standard Oil Company." Tarbell, the daughter of an independent oil producer, was born in western Pennsylvania in 1857. She grew up admiring the independent oil man "whose ear was attuned to Fortune's call, and who had the daring and the energy to risk everything." Tarbell was deeply angered when John D. Rockefeller's Standard Oil Company began swallowing up independent oil companies. When her father went bankrupt and his partner committed suicide, 15-year-old Tarbell blamed Rockefeller.

In 1876 Tarbell entered Allegheny College, the only female in a freshman class of 40 "hostile or indifferent" males. Soon after graduation she moved to Paris and began her career

▲ **McClure's featured the work of many prominent authors and journalists, including Rudyard Kipling and Ray Stannard Baker.**

Ida Tarbell

Practice

GUIDED PRACTICE

Call on students to identify the types of people who were attracted to progressivism. List their responses on the chalkboard and then review the list, asking why each type of person might be interested in reform.

INDEPENDENT PRACTICE

Have students choose one of the types from the Guided Practice chalkboard list and in the role of such a person write a short essay titled "Why I Am a Progressive." Students may wish to include their essays in their portfolios.

Review and Assessment

REVIEW Have students copy the names of persons listed in the Preview Workshop on p. 168 and write a brief statement about each individual's contribution to progressive reform. Then assign the Section 1 Review on p. 172.

ASSESS Assign the **Section 1 Daily Quiz** in *Core Resources*.

▲ Standard Oil's practice of swallowing up independent oil companies is sharply criticized in this editorial cartoon.

as a writer. By the 1890s she was writing a popular biographical series for *McClure's*.

In 1900 the magazine's reform-minded founder, Scotch-Irish immigrant S. S. McClure, assigned her to investigate Standard Oil. "Out with you. Look, see, report," he urged. "Don't do it," warned her father, knowing too well the power of Standard Oil to punish its enemies. But she went ahead, publishing her findings in a series of 18 articles. Month after month she attacked Standard Oil's business practices:

❝ One of the most depressing features . . . is that instead of such methods arousing contempt, they are more or less openly admired. . . . There is no gaming table in the world where loaded dice are tolerated, no athletic field where men must not start fair. Yet Mr. Rockefeller has systematically played with loaded dice. . . . Business played in this way loses all its sportsmanlike qualities. It is fit only for tricksters. ❞

McClure's readers shared Tarbell's outrage, hailing her as "a modern Joan of Arc" and "the Terror of the Trusts." One reader even called her series "the *Uncle Tom's Cabin* of today." Later, Rockefeller biographer Allan Nevins would call it "the most spectacular success of the muckraking school of journalism, and its most enduring achievement."

Meanwhile, muckraking books poured off the presses. In *The Octopus* (1901) Frank Norris exposed the ways in which railroads misused their vast power. Lincoln Steffens continued to document political corruption in urban America in *The Shame of the Cities* (1904). Jack London wrote *The Iron Heel* (1907) to warn that bloody revolution might result if something was not done to curb capitalism's abuses.

Only a few progressives, however, concerned themselves with racial justice. One who did was Ray Stannard Baker. Baker traveled around the nation in 1904, examining the plight of African Americans. He found that African Americans were segregated, routinely robbed of their right to vote, and otherwise discriminated against. Worst of all, lynchings still took place. In *Following the Color Line* (1908), Baker described a lynching in Springfield, Ohio:

❝ The worst feature of all in this Springfield lynching was the apathy of the public. No one really seemed to care. A "nigger" had been hanged: what of it? But the law itself had been lynched. What of that? . . . If ever there was an example of good citizenship lying flat on its back . . . , Springfield furnished an example of that condition. ❞

■■ Muckrakers exposed political and corporate corruption, difficult working conditions, crowded slums, and racial injustice.

EXPLORING SOCIAL PROBLEMS

Like the muckraking journalists, novelists and intellectuals explored the darker side of the new industrial order's effect on people's behavior and values. Theodore Dreiser, in novels such as *Sister Carrie* (1900) and *The Financier* (1912),

▲ Slum life was a frequent target of muckrakers. This 1910 photograph shows a Jewish immigrant in the home he has made in a coal cellar.

BUILDING VOCABULARY

The term *lynching* derives from a Virginia colonel, Charles Lynch, who presided over an extralegal court that punished—primarily by whipping—Loyalists and other criminals during the American Revolution.

PRIMARY SOURCES

Description of Change: excerpted
Rationale: excerpted to focus on main idea

MULTICULTURAL PERSPECTIVES

Mary Church Terrell, Oberlin College graduate and first president of the National Association of Colored Women (NACW), fought for equal rights and suffrage for all women. But she believed that she and other professional African American women had a special obligation to help those "to whom they are bound by ties of race and sex." Under her leadership, the NACW established kindergartens and day nurseries for the children of black working mothers, fought for employment opportunities for black women, and sought equality in the criminal justice system.

RETEACH Organize students into groups and assign each group a subsection of Section 1. Have each group develop several questions and answers about the main ideas in its assigned material. Then have each group quiz the other groups with its list of questions.

*C*losure

Call on one volunteer to read aloud Theodore Roosevelt's words on p. 169 and another to read Jane Addams's statement on p. 172. Ask students to identify similarities between the two statements. Then discuss ways in which they reflected the ideals of progressive reform.

*E*xtension

ANALYZE Have students read one of the fiction or nonfiction works noted in the section and report on it to the class.

EVALUATE Suggest that students find examples of muckraking in current newspapers and magazines. Display the stories in the classroom. Then have students debate the pros and cons of this type of journalism.

PRIMARY SOURCE

Description of Change: excerpted and bracketed
Rationale: excerpted to focus on main idea; bracketed to clarify meaning

SECTION REVIEW ANSWERS

IDENTIFY

For significance, see the following pages:
progressivism (p. 168)
John Dewey (p. 169)
muckrakers (p. 170)
Lincoln Steffens (p. 170)
Ida Tarbell (p. 170)
S. S. McClure (p. 171)
Ray Stannard Baker (p. 171)
Theodore Dreiser (p. 171)
Herbert Croly (p. 172)
Jane Addams (p. 172)

1. *through more democratic government, checks on corporate power, a federal graduated income tax, labor reforms, and research projects to solve social problems*
2. *political and corporate corruption; difficult working conditions, crowded slums, racial injustice*
3. *offered avenues for influencing politics and society, ways to apply college education; few other career options*
4. *Articles will vary but should offer a solution to the social problem selected.*
5. *Both supported legislation prohibiting corrupt business practices, proposed election reforms, supported graduated income tax and eight-hour workday.*

◀ **Jane Addams started the settlement-house movement in order to provide college-educated women like herself an opportunity to "learn of life from life itself." Her settlement house grew and became a model for social reforms in child labor, health care, urban renewal, and public education.**

depicted workers brutalized by low wages and business owners driven by greed.

Progressive intellectuals proposed solutions. In *The Promise of American Life* (1909), political theorist Herbert Croly praised Alexander Hamilton's call, over a century earlier, for a strong, activist central government. But instead of promoting the interests of only the business class, as Hamilton had favored, Croly held that the government should promote the welfare of all its citizens by expanding opportunities.

Social thinkers urged citizens to take responsibility as well. Jane Addams, by now well known for her settlement-house work among Chicago's immigrants, argued in *Democracy and Social Ethics* (1902) that democracy meant more than the right to vote. It demanded a society in which all citizens showed concern for the poor:

❝ This is the penalty of a democracy—that we are bound to move forward or [slip backward] together. None of us can stand aside; our feet are mired in the same soil, and our lungs breathe the same air. ❞

■■ **Progressive writers and intellectuals publicized social problems and offered theories on how to solve them.**

Although progressives like Addams and Croly wanted to change American society, they remained committed to democracy. Most progressives sought reforms of local government, businesses, and city life to ensure that democratic freedoms were available to all citizens.

SECTION 1 REVIEW

IDENTIFY and explain the significance of the following: progressivism, John Dewey, muckrakers, Lincoln Steffens, Ida Tarbell, S. S. McClure, Ray Stannard Baker, Theodore Dreiser, Herbert Croly, Jane Addams.

1. **MAIN IDEA** In what ways did progressives hope to reform society?
2. **MAIN IDEA** What types of political and social evils did muckrakers expose through their writings?
3. **RECOGNIZING POINTS OF VIEW** Why were middle-class women attracted to the Progressive movement and reform activities?
4. **WRITING TO INFORM** Imagine you are a progressive writer or intellectual in the early 20th century. Write an article for *McClure's* proposing a solution to a social problem of the new industrial order.
5. **COMPARING** In what ways were the goals of Populists and progressives similar?

Chapter 7

SECTION

2

Introducing the Section

PREVIEW WORKSHOP

Following is a list of the significant people and terms in this section. You may wish to use this list as a section preview.

People
- Florence Kelley
- Rose Schneiderman
- Josephine Goldmark
- Louis D. Brandeis

- Samuel Gompers
- "Big Bill" Haywood

Terms
- freedom of contract
- closed shop
- socialism
- open shops

Section 2

REFORMING THE NEW INDUSTRIAL ORDER

FOCUS
- **How did progressives try to reform the workplace?**
- **How did the Supreme Court respond to social legislation?**
- **Which labor organizations represented workers in the Progressive Era? How did these organizations differ?**

The new industrial order changed American society in deep and disturbing ways. Many workers felt victimized by unhealthful working conditions, poor wages, and long workdays. At times progressive reformers and labor organizations joined forces, but more often they organized their own campaigns to improve conditions for workers.

IWW songbook

The Granger Collection, New York

REFORMING THE WORKPLACE

As progressives explored working conditions first-hand, they saw men and women laboring long hours, often in dangerous jobs. In 1900 the average laborer worked nearly 10 hours a day, 6 days a

▼ Child laborers, such as these shown in a textile mill, often worked in unsafe conditions.

week for about $1.50 a day. Women and children workers were paid even less.

Social reformers had long argued that the conditions women and children faced in the workplace undermined home and family life. Progressives and labor-union activists campaigned for laws prohibiting or limiting child labor and improving conditions for women workers. Florence Kelley was one of the women who worked tirelessly for this cause, helping to persuade the Illinois legislature in 1893 to prohibit child labor and to limit the number of hours women could work. In 1904 she helped organize the National Child Labor Committee, which worked to persuade state legislatures to pass laws against employing young children. By 1912 the committee had helped 39 states pass child labor laws. Some states even limited older children's employment to 8 or 10 hours a day and barred them from working at night or in dangerous occupations. But enforcement of such laws was lax. Many employers, claiming that their business success depended on cheap child labor, simply refused to obey the laws and continued to hire child workers.

Progressives also campaigned for laws that would force factories to limit the long hours employers demanded of their adult workers, men

FOCUS OBJECTIVES
- Explain how progressives tried to reform the workplace.
- Analyze the Supreme Court's response to social legislation.
- Cite labor organizations that represented workers in the Progressive Era and identify how they differed.

GLOBAL CONNECTIONS

Like many other progressive goals, the impetus for child labor reform reached America from Europe. Great Britain passed the first child labor law in 1802, but because it did not provide for enforcement it had little effect. A more effective attack on the use of child labor was Charles Dickens's novel *Oliver Twist,* which was published in the 1830s and widely read in Britain and America. Not until 1900, however, was the International Association for Labour Legislation established in Switzerland to promote child labor reform throughout the world.

CORE RESOURCES
- **Geography Worksheet 7**
- **Section 2 Daily Quiz**

AV RESOURCES
- **Everyday Life in America Transparency and Worksheet 17**

MOTIVATING: STUDENT EXPERIENCES

Ask students to name tasks they have performed or jobs they have held for which they have been paid money. Ask them what job conditions they had hoped to have. Then discuss working conditions they would find unacceptable. Tell students that in this section they will learn about progressive reformers' campaigns to improve workers' conditions in the early 1900s.

Teaching the Section

REFORMING THE WORKPLACE

Encourage students to write letters to a 1904 state legislator from the viewpoint of a progressive reformer demanding laws to improve the workplace. Instruct students to suggest specific changes they would make and to cite examples of injustices to back up their demands. Ask volunteers to read their letters aloud. Students may wish to include their letters in their portfolios.

AV TRANSPARENCY

Everyday Life in America Transparency and **Worksheet 17**

Graph Caption Answer
about twice as much

MULTICULTURAL PERSPECTIVES

Long before the Triangle Company fire, women had been trying to improve conditions in the shirtwaist industry. A strike by some 20,000 to 30,000 workers, mostly young female immigrants, brought the industry to a halt in the winter of 1909–10. Theresa Malkiel, a Russian immigrant, stated her feelings about the strike: "There is nothing dishonest in standing up for one's bread. We must warn the newcomers that us girls are out on strike because our boss is paying starvation wages. . . . This land is one big union, and us children were taught very early that united we stand and divided we fall."

PRIMARY SOURCE

Description of Change: excerpted
Rationale: excerpted to focus on main idea

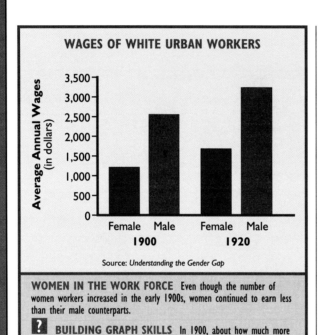

WAGES OF WHITE URBAN WORKERS

Average Annual Wages (in dollars)

3,500 / 3,000 / 2,500 / 2,000 / 1,500 / 1,000 / 500 / 0

Female Male Female Male
1900   **1920**

Source: Understanding the Gender Gap

WOMEN IN THE WORK FORCE Even though the number of women workers increased in the early 1900s, women continued to earn less than their male counterparts.

? BUILDING GRAPH SKILLS In 1900, about how much more were white male workers earning than white female workers?

---

and women alike. In 1903, Florence Kelley helped lobby the Oregon legislature to pass a law limiting women laundry workers to 10 hours a day. Earlier, Utah had enacted a law that limited working days in dangerous occupations like mining and smelting to 8 hours. Other states passed similar laws.

Wages were another target for progressives. Of the some 30 million men and 8 million women employed in 1910, about one third lived in poverty. In 1912, in response to progressive agitation, Massachusetts passed the nation's first minimum-wage law—setting base wages for women and children. Gradually, other states followed suit.

But it would not be until 1938 that the nation passed a minimum-wage law for all workers.

Progressives also worked to improve workplace safety. Tragic events in March 1911 catapulted the need for such reforms onto the front pages of the nation's newspapers.

Late in the afternoon on Saturday, March 25, some 500 employees—most of them young Jewish or Italian immigrant women—were completing their six-day workweek at New York City's Triangle Shirtwaist Company. Shortly before quitting time, as they rose from their crowded worktables and started to leave, a fire erupted in a rag bin. Within moments the entire eighth floor of the 10-story building was ablaze. Escape quickly became impossible—there were only two stairways, and most of the exit doors were locked. Leaping from high windows became the last, desperate way out. Some 60 workers took it—to their death.

Through the night, weeping family members wandered among the crushed bodies on the sidewalk, looking for their loved ones. In all, more than 140 people perished in the Triangle fire, victims of a thoroughly unsafe workplace. Rose Schneiderman, a Women's Trade Union League organizer, argued that only a strong working-class movement could bring real change to the workplace. She noted:

❝ This is not the first time girls have been burned alive in the city. Each week I must learn of the untimely death of one of my sister workers. Every year thousands of us are maimed. The life of men and women is so cheap and property is so sacred. There are so many of us for one job it matters little if 143 of us are burned to death. ❞

▼ Rose Schneiderman's impassioned speech (below) after the Triangle Shirtwaist Company's fire (left) marked the beginning of sweeping reforms that improved factory safety regulations.

Choose nine students to represent Supreme Court justices. Organize the rest of the class into four groups. Two groups should prepare briefs for and against New York's law regulating the workday of bakers. The other two groups should do the same for the Oregon law regulating the workday of female employees. In each case, after each side presents its brief, the justices should discuss the legal and social issues and make their ruling. Conclude the activity by asking the class to hypothesize about why the Court struck down reform in New York but upheld it in Oregon. *(In upholding the Oregon law, the Court was protecting women. The New York law was not linked to gender.)*

THE LABOR UNIONS

Organize the class into small groups. Ask half the groups to write brochures outlining the benefits of becoming a member of the AFL. Have the other groups do the same for the IWW. Ask one volunteer from each group to present the argument in that group's brochure to the class. Ask students what might make a worker choose one union over the other.

▶

But it did matter. The public outcry was so great that it pressured lawmakers to pass protective legislation. The New York legislature responded by enacting the nation's strictest fire safety code.

■■ Progressives sought laws to end child labor, limit working hours, raise wages, and improve safety.

𝒯HE COURT'S RESPONSE

As more states passed laws regulating the workplace, employers fought back through the courts—even to the Supreme Court. Employers appealed to the Fifth and Fourteenth amendments to the Constitution, which prohibit states from depriving any person of "life, liberty, or property, without due process of law." Owners claimed that laws that limited their businesses unfairly deprived them of their "property."

The Supreme Court sided with business owners and declared much of the early social legislation unconstitutional. The Court also ruled that some social legislation violated the constitutional "liberty" of workers by denying them **freedom of contract**. In 1905, for example, in *Lochner* v. *New York,* the Court overturned the New York law limiting bakers' workdays to 10 hours, declaring that the law robbed workers of their "liberty of contract." Workers, the Court argued, should be free to accept any conditions of employment that business owners required—including 14- or 16-hour workdays.

The Court did uphold some social legislation, however. In 1908, in *Muller* v. *Oregon,* an employer challenged the 10-hour workday law Florence Kelley had helped push through the Oregon legislature. Kelley and her co-worker, Josephine Goldmark, swung into action to convince the Court to uphold this hard-won law. Goldmark gathered data for the brief, or legal argument, to defend the law. Kelley recruited Goldmark's brother-in-law, the brilliant Boston lawyer Louis D. Brandeis, to argue the case. The "Brandeis Brief" broke new legal ground. In addition to making sound legal points, the brief included extensive evidence of the bad effects that working long hours had on women's health and well-being. This social research not only convinced the Court to uphold the Oregon law but became a model for the defense of other social legislation.

◀ Josephine Goldmark

▶ Louis Brandeis

■■ On the grounds of property rights and freedom of contract, the Supreme Court struck down much—but not all—progressive legislation.

𝓛ABOR UNIONS

Progressive reformers were not the only ones fighting for workers' rights. Labor unions continued to battle for better conditions and for the

LABOR UNION MEMBERSHIP, 1900–1920

Membership (in millions) — vertical axis: 0, 1, 2, 3, 4, 5, 6

Year — horizontal axis: 1900, 1905, 1910, 1915, 1920

Source: *The Growth of American Trade Unions, 1880–1923*

GROWTH OF UNIONS The spread of industrialization and the efforts of progressive reformers contributed to the growth of labor union membership in the early 1900s.

? BUILDING GRAPH SKILLS During which five-year period was the increase in union membership the smallest? During which period was it the largest?

MAKING CONNECTIONS
Sociology
Brandeis argued in *Muller* v. *Oregon* that women's work hours should be limited because "women are fundamentally weaker than men." In making its decision, the Court noted that women would always depend on men for "protection." Despite the sexism of the argument and the decision, both of which mirrored male attitudes of the time, the outcome benefited working women by limiting their work hours and by breaking with the legal principle that employers had sole control over the terms of employment. Yet the decision had the undermining effect of reinforcing social stereotypes of women.

■■ Ask students if they think this argument could be successfully used today in a court of law.

HISTORICAL SIDELIGHTS
"The People's Attorney"
Brandeis was known as "the people's attorney" because of his support of public causes such as offering life insurance at affordable rates for workers. His support of progressive reforms was a factor in his becoming in 1916 the first Jew to be appointed to the Supreme Court.

Graph Caption Answer
1905–1910; 1915–1920

Practice

GUIDED PRACTICE

Work with students to develop on the chalkboard a web diagram, using *Progressive Reforms* as the hub of the diagram. Then have students complete the diagram by listing conditions that led to progressive reforms in the workplace. Review the completed web with the class, asking students to elaborate on each condition it contains.

INDEPENDENT PRACTICE

Instruct students to choose one of the conditions listed in the Guided Practice web diagram and, in the role of a progressive reformer, to write a letter to the editor protesting the situation and suggesting what should be done about it. Students may wish to include their letters in their portfolios.

Review and Assessment

REVIEW Have students work in small groups to locate in the text the persons and terms listed in the Preview Workshop. Guide students to discuss and write explanations of how each person and term is related to industrial reform. Then ask groups to exchange papers and compare answers. Then assign the Section 2 Review on p. 177.

ASSESS Assign the **Section 2 Daily Quiz** in *Core Resources*.

---

closed shop—a workplace where the employer hires only union members. Some union members favored "working within the system." They wanted to change how workers were treated, but they did not want to threaten capitalism's very existence. Others wanted to replace capitalism with an economic system that workers controlled. Many favored **socialism**, the system under which the government or worker cooperatives, not private interests, own factories, utilities, and transportation and communications systems.

The AFL. The major labor organization in these years remained the American Federation of Labor (AFL). The AFL stood firmly for working within the system. Under Samuel Gompers' leadership, AFL membership grew from some 500,000 in 1900 to about 2 million in 1914. But the AFL

◄ AFL seal, about 1890

excluded most unskilled workers—the majority of whom were immigrant, Asian American, Hispanic American, or African American men and women. This left most urban workers without organized support.

One AFL union that did try to assist unskilled workers was the International Ladies' Garment Workers Union (ILGWU). Established in 1900 in New York City, it sought to unionize workers—mainly Jewish and Italian immigrant women—employed in sewing shops like the Triangle Shirtwaist Company.

In order to organize workers, union leaders generally planned a strike to establish the union's power to negotiate for workers. The International Ladies' Garment Workers Union used this tactic in November 1909 when it staged the "Uprising of the Thirty Thousand." Thousands of women garment workers walked off their jobs to demand that their companies recognize the ILGWU as their union.

The strike lasted through the bitter winter. Hard-pressed strikers received generous aid from progressive groups such as the Women's Trade Union League, an organization of well-to-do women who supported the efforts of working women to form unions.

The strike's results were mixed. Most employers agreed to many of the ILGWU's demands. The employers, however, were determined to run **open shops**—or nonunion workplaces. Thus, they refused to recognize the union.

The IWW. While Gompers and his AFL trade unions negotiated with business owners for worker gains, a new union emerged with a different agenda. The Industrial Workers of the World (IWW), founded in Chicago in 1905, opposed capitalism. Its leader, "Big Bill" Haywood, proclaimed IWW's aim:

66 Fellow workers, this is the continental congress of the working class. We are here to confederate the workers of this country into a working-class movement that shall have for its purpose the emancipation of the working class from the slave bondage of capitalism. 99

THROUGH OTHERS' EYES

The economic development of the Southwest was due in large part to Mexican immigrant labor. One historian estimates that during the first several decades of the 1900s, agricultural labor in the Southwest was 65 to 85 percent Mexican. And from 1900 to 1940 Mexican workers were 60 percent of common labor in mines and 60 to 90 percent of the extra gangs employed by 18 western railroads. Mexico, in turn, benefited; between 1917 and 1927 Mexican laborers in the U.S. sent an average of $10 million a year to relatives back home.

PRIMARY SOURCE

Description of Change: excerpted
Rationale: excerpted to focus on main idea

IMMIGRANT WORKERS

THROUGH OTHERS' EYES

*P*rogressive *reformers won shorter workdays, better working conditions, and other improvements for many U.S. workers. But such changes were unknown to the immigrants who crossed the border from Mexico to work the railroads, mines, and fields of the southwestern United States. These immigrant workers experienced both poor working conditions and prejudice. In 1910 the Mexican newspaper Diario del Hogar wondered what drove "our workingmen, so attached to the land, to abandon the country [Mexico], even at the risk of the Yankee contempt with which they are treated on the other side of the Bravo [Rio Grande]." Indeed, some Mexican laborers were brutally assaulted or lynched. Venustiano Carranza, Mexico's president from 1917 to 1920, claimed that 114 Mexicans had been murdered across the border. And in 1922 the Mexican newspaper Heraldo charged that "Mexicans are still being killed without any effort by the American authorities to punish the murderers."*

RETEACH Organize students into groups and assign individuals or pairs the task of outlining subsections. Have students exchange outlines and use them to ask questions of other members of their group.

Closure

Ask volunteers to state which industrial reform accomplished by the progressives they consider to be most important and why. Discuss students' responses with the class.

Extension

RESEARCH Invite students to research the growth of the AFL (now AFL–CIO) from the time covered in this section to the present. Then ask students to create a time line showing their findings.

COMPARE Challenge students to investigate their state's child labor laws and, using Labor Department information, to compare the laws with those in the early 1900s.

▶ Employers often used armed guards to remove picketing workers. This photograph shows local militiamen aiming their guns at strikers in Lawrence, Kansas.

Haywood denounced the AFL's cooperation with business owners and its failure to include unskilled workers. He vowed to organize migrant farm workers, miners, lumber workers, and textile workers to overthrow the capitalist system. In addition to enlisting African American, Hispanic American, and Asian American workers, the IWW actively recruited women workers and the wives of male workers. An IWW newspaper expressed optimism about the role of union women:

66 The advent of women side by side with men in strikes, will soon develop a fighting force that will end capitalism and its horrors in short order. . . . The industrial union movement seeks to develop the fighting quality of both sexes. 99

The Wobblies, as the members of the IWW came to be called, pursued their goals through general strikes, boycotts, and industrial sabotage. Their greatest hour came in 1912 when they led 20,000 workers in a strike against the textile mills of Lawrence, Massachusetts, to protest a 30-cent wage cut. After a bitter and much publicized two-month strike, the mill owners gave in.

Success was short-lived, however. Several later IWW-led strikes failed miserably. Most Americans grew fearful of IWW's aims, and the government cracked down on the union with increasing force. Disagreements among Wobbly leaders also weakened IWW's power. Within a few years the IWW collapsed and eventually faded from power. The AFL trade unions continued to flourish, but the majority of American industrial workers remained outside the union movement.

■■ **The AFL worked within the system and focused on skilled workers, while the IWW opposed capitalism and focused on unskilled workers.**

PRIMARY SOURCE

Description of Change: excerpted
Rationale: excerpted to focus on main idea

SECTION REVIEW ANSWERS

IDENTIFY

For significance, see the following pages:
Florence Kelley (p. 173)
Rose Schneiderman (p. 174)
freedom of contract (p. 175)
Josephine Goldmark (p. 175)
Louis D. Brandeis (p. 175)
closed shop (p. 176)
socialism (p. 176)
Samuel Gompers (p. 176)
open shops (p. 176)
"Big Bill" Haywood (p. 176)

1. *to end young child labor, to limit working hours and improve workplace safety, and to set minimum wages for women and children*
2. *unconstitutional because they interfered with property rights of owners and denied workers freedom of contract*
3. *AFL worked within the system; IWW opposed cooperation with business owners; sought to overthrow the capitalist system.*
4. *Letters should describe working conditions that contributed to the disaster and how they would be different after legislation was passed to protect workers.*
5. *Students might suggest government regulation of the workplace and strong unions that protect workers while allowing employers to still make a profit.*

SECTION 2 REVIEW

IDENTIFY and explain the significance of the following: Florence Kelley, Rose Schneiderman, freedom of contract, Josephine Goldmark, Louis D. Brandeis, closed shop, socialism, Samuel Gompers, open shops, "Big Bill" Haywood.

1. **MAIN IDEA** What kinds of laws to improve the workplace did progressives seek?
2. **MAIN IDEA** What reasons did the Supreme Court use to justify striking down some progressive legislation?
3. **CONTRASTING** How did the goals of the AFL differ from those of the IWW?
4. **WRITING TO DESCRIBE** Imagine you are a worker in New York City's Triangle Shirtwaist Company in March 1911. Write a letter to a friend that describes work conditions before and after the fire.
5. **USING HISTORICAL IMAGINATION** If you were a progressive in the early 1900s, how would you balance the needs of employers with the needs of employees?

PREVIEW WORKSHOP

*Following is a list of the significant
people and terms in this section.
You may wish to use this list as a
section preview.*

People
- Lawrence Veiller
- Frances Willard
- W.E.B. Du Bois

Terms
- Women's Christian Temperance Union
- Eighteenth Amendment
- National Association for the Advancement of Colored People
- Society of American Indians

FOCUS OBJECTIVES

- Describe steps reformers took to try to solve urban problems.

- Identify the actions taken by African American and Native American progressives to address discrimination.

- Explain why the Progressive movement had mixed results for immigrants.

HISTORICAL SIDELIGHTS

Man with a Mission
Lawrence Veiller was only 28 years old when he hit upon a plan to bring the tenement housing problem to the public's attention. He set up a Tenement Housing Exhibition in New York. His cardboard model of the Canal Street slum demonstrated the conditions in which 2,781 residents shared 264 toilets and not one bathtub. Among the thousands of viewers was Theodore Roosevelt, then governor of New York. He told Veiller, "Tell me what you want and I will help you get it."

178

Section 3

REFORMING SOCIETY

FOCUS
- **What steps did reformers take to try to solve urban problems?**
- **What actions did African American and Native American progressives take to address discrimination?**
- **Why can it be said that the Progressive movement had mixed results for immigrants?**

*P*rogressive reformers were convinced that as citizens they were responsible for the well-being of their communities. While most white progressives concentrated on improving housing, public health, and personal morality, African American and Native American progressives organized to fight discrimination. Other progressives, motivated by nativist sentiments, set out to change immigrants' cultures.

Woman doing laundry, about 1910

REFORMING CITY LIFE

By 1920, for the first time in U.S. history, more than 50 percent of Americans lived in cities. As urban populations soared, the ability of cities to provide garbage collection, safe and affordable housing, health care, police and fire protection, and adequate public education was stretched to the breaking point.

Cleaning up the city. What cities needed, some reformers announced, was "municipal housekeeping," a campaign to make the cities a more healthful and livable home for all residents. "The community is one great family," explained Louise DeKoven Bowen, the president of Chicago's Woman's City Club, and "each member of it is bound to help the other." The Woman's City Club, other women's clubs, various men's clubs, and reform organizations enlisted the aid of local governments to clean up the cities. Some organizations took the cleanup campaign literally, working to rid the cities of garbage. Other reform organizations worked for better housing or to improve public education.

Progressive reformers published articles and books documenting urban problems, even assigning blame for them in some cases. For example, Lawrence Veiller (VYL-uhr), a settlement-house worker, lashed out at irresponsible tenement owners "who for the sake of a large profit on their investments sacrifice the health and welfare of countless thousands."

Veiller campaigned tirelessly for improved housing. In 1901 he succeeded in getting the New York State Tenement House bill passed. The law banned construction of dark and airless tenements. New buildings had to be constructed around an open courtyard that would let in light and air. The law also required that new buildings contain one bathroom for each apartment or for every three rooms, rather than one or two for an entire floor, as was the common practice. Housing reformers in other states used the New York law as a model for their own legislative proposals.

Teaching the Section

URBAN REFORM

Organize students into small groups. Have each group use drawing paper and markers to design a plan for a dream city of the early 1900s. Direct students to label and annotate proposed buildings and land uses. Then call on volunteers from each group to present their plan, citing the urban problems they have addressed and their proposed solutions for those problems.

In another campaign to make the cities more-healthful places to live, a group of physicians and reform-minded citizens formed the National Tuberculosis Association. The association focused on education and on lobbying the government to fund special hospitals to treat victims of tuberculosis. Thanks in part to this effort, by 1915 the death rate from TB had dropped significantly.

Other reformers campaigned for more city parks and playgrounds to provide safe places for children to play. The playground developed earlier at Jane Addams's Hull House in Chicago served as the model, and by 1920, millions of dollars had been spent establishing playgrounds.

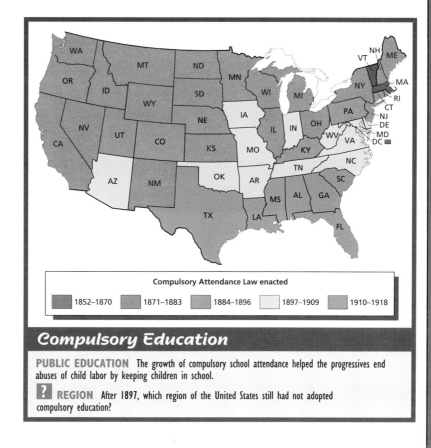

Compulsory Attendance Law enacted

1852–1870	1871–1883	1884–1896	1897–1909	1910–1918

Compulsory Education

PUBLIC EDUCATION The growth of compulsory school attendance helped the progressives end abuses of child labor by keeping children in school.

? REGION After 1897, which region of the United States still had not adopted compulsory education?

City planning. Progressives firmly believed that cleaned-up cities would produce better citizens. Out of this belief grew the city-planning movement. The first National Conference on City Planning was held in 1909. Through wise and careful planning, its members hoped,

◄ **Daniel Burnham**

the spread of slums could be halted and cities could be beautified with lush green parks, sparkling fountains, and tree-shaded streets.

In 1909 Daniel Burnham, a leading architect and city planner, produced a magnificent plan for redesigning Chicago, the first comprehensive plan to redesign an American city. It portrayed a future Chicago of almost dreamlike harmony and beauty. The centerpiece of Burnham's vision for Chicago was a soaring city hall that would inspire all residents to be good citizens. "Make no little plans," said Burnham. "They have no magic to stir men's blood."

City-planning commissions in Washington, D.C., Cleveland, and San Francisco

◄ **Daniel Burnham's plan for Chicago included wide intersecting streets similar to the ones he saw in Paris.**

COOPERATIVE LEARNING

Have students work in groups of three to portray members of a city commission that is formulating a plan for urban reform. One member should be in charge of urban services, another of health and education, and another of moral reform. Encourage groups to present their plans to the class.

■■ Ask students if they have participated in any projects to beautify their community.

AV TRANSPARENCY

Linking Geography and History Transparency and **Worksheet 11A**

Changing Ways

THE ORPHAN TRAINS

LINK TO TODAY

An organization called the Orphan Train Heritage Society of America was formed in 1986. Since then, dozens of former "train orphans" have gathered together to share their stories and to make sure that lessons of the orphan train movement are not forgotten.

CRITICAL THINKING

Have students read the quote from the Children's Aid Society on p. 180. Then read to them the following quote from a 72-year-old former train orphan. "New York missed a good thing when they shipped out so many talented people." Ask students which statement they agree with more and the reasons for their choice.

PRIMARY SOURCE

Description of Change: excerpted
Rationale: excerpted to focus on main idea

Changing Ways   THE ORPHAN TRAINS

▲ **Children whose parents could no longer care for them often were sent to orphanages. Some remained there until they were old enough to take care of themselves; others were placed in homes or ran away.**

In the late 1800s and early 1900s, periodic economic downswings left many people unable to provide for their families. Urban immigrants faced desperate poverty. Many children of broken families, or whose parents could not provide for them, roamed the streets of New York and other eastern cities.

Many of these children died; others ended up in orphanages. But most found a way to survive on the streets. They shined shoes, sold newspapers, or picked pockets by day and curled up to sleep in doorways, garbage heaps, or outhouses at night.

Progressives and other reformers pitied the abandoned children. But they also feared that without parents to teach them right from wrong, the children posed a danger to society. As the Children's Aid Society warned:

❝ They will vote—they will have the same rights as we ourselves though they have grown up ignorant of moral principle. . . . Let society beware, when the vicious, reckless multitude of New York boys, swarming now in every foul alley and low street, come to know their power and use it! ❞

The founding director of the Children's Aid Society, the minister Charles Loring Brace, devised a plan to provide homes for these abandoned children. Brace reasoned that since farmers needed laborers and street urchins needed homes, why not bring these adults and children together? By 1914 the Society would help some 116,000 children leave eastern cities on "orphan trains" for a better life on farms in New England, the South, and the Midwest.

Photojournalist Jacob Riis, a supporter of the Society, described how "big-hearted farmers" came from miles away to meet the trains and choose from the "little troop[s]" of children. "Night falls," he wrote, "upon a joyous band returning home over the quiet country road, the little stranger snugly stowed among his new friends, one of them already, with home and life before him."

Despite the many success stories, there were problems. Some critics justifiably charged that the Society failed to turn away farmers who were looking for no more than cheap labor. Others condemned the lack of adequate follow-up supervision. They argued that such safeguards were necessary to protect children from being taken advantage of economically or abused physically. Still others accused the Society of "dumping" New York's juvenile delinquents. As a result, some states passed laws restricting the placement of children in foster homes across state borders.

Whatever the shortcomings of the program, it provoked a long and fruitful debate on how the nation could provide for abandoned or orphaned children. Before the first orphan train departed in 1854, child-welfare workers saw institutionalization as the only option. By 1900 "placing out"—finding homes for children—had become the preferred solution.

MORAL REFORM

Have students work in pairs to write a newspaper editorial either supporting or opposing prohibition or motion pictures. Then ask each student in each pair to write a letter to the editor, taking the opposite view. Select pairs to read their editorials and letters to the class. Students may wish to include their letters in their portfolios.

▶

---

also engaged Burnham to develop grand schemes for their cities. His plans were never fully realized, but some, such as those for Washington, were a success. Above all, his efforts helped people realize that city planning—building codes, sanitation standards, and zoning—was a necessary function of municipal government.

■■ **Progressives sought to clean up the cities by enlarging the function of government to include housing standards, public health, and city planning.**

URBAN MORAL REFORM

Progressives also wanted to "clean up" what they considered to be immoral behavior. Toward this end, they pushed for prohibition—a ban on the manufacture and sale of alcoholic beverages—and for the closing of the nation's saloons. Reformers believed that prohibition and the elimination of saloons would have several benefits. These reforms would lessen social problems by removing what reformers viewed as two of the chief causes of unemployment: crime and the breakup of families. Such actions would also limit the powers of brewery and liquor interests, groups that exercised considerable influence over the government.

▲ While serving as president of the WCTU, Frances Willard also helped organize the Prohibition party in 1882.

The Anti-Saloon League (ASL) and the **Women's Christian Temperance Union** (WCTU), an offshoot of the mid-19th-century temperance movement, led the crusade against alcohol. By 1902 the ASL had branches in 39 states with 200 paid staff members. It sent out thousands of volunteer speakers, many of them Protestant ministers, to spread the anti-saloon message in the nation's churches.

Billy Sunday, an ex-ballplayer and a Presbyterian minister, preached that the saloon was "the sum of all villainies," and "the parent of crimes and the mother of sins." Frances Willard, who presided over the WCTU from 1879 to 1898, described the zeal she felt as she led a prayer meeting in a saloon early in her career:

> 66 Kneeling on that sawdust floor, with a group of earnest hearts around me, and behind them, filling every corner and extending out into the street, a crowd of unwashed, unkempt, hard-looking drinking men, I was conscious that perhaps never in my life, save beside my sister Mary's dying bed, had I prayed as truly as I did then. 99

A brilliant organizer and magnetic public speaker, Willard eventually made the WCTU a powerful national force for temperance, moral purity, and the rights of women.

Drawing on Americans' spirit of patriotic sacrifice, prohibitionists achieved their goal during World War I. The **Eighteenth Amendment**, which Congress passed in 1917 and the states ratified in 1919, barred the manufacture, sale, or importation of alcoholic beverages. The amendment proved unpopular and difficult to enforce, however, and was repealed in 1933 (see Chapter 12).

The growing popularity of the newly invented motion picture gave urban reformers another source of danger to worry about. The first movie to tell a story, *The Great Train Robbery,* was

▼ Movie theaters attracted large crowds by showing action films such as *The Great Train Robbery.* Early cowboy stars gained worldwide fame from these movie westerns.

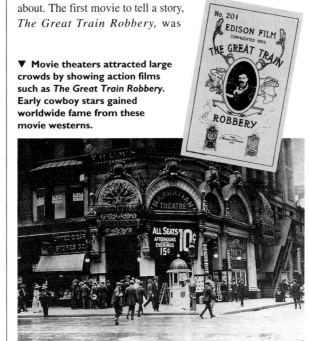

HISTORICAL SIDELIGHTS
A Flamboyant Preacher

Billy Sunday was born in Ames, Iowa, in 1862. After completing high school and holding a variety of odd jobs, he joined the Chicago White Sox baseball team in 1883. For the next eight years he played professional baseball in Chicago, Philadelphia, and Pittsburgh. During this time he experienced a religious conversion. He became a revivalist preacher and was ordained in the Presbyterian church in 1903. Sunday, a flamboyant preacher, gained a huge following and purportedly accumulated a fortune from the offerings of his followers.

Teaching the Section

DISCRIMINATION AND PREJUDICES

Organize students into small groups. Ask half the groups to outline a speech to be given by an African American progressive. Ask the other half to outline a speech to be given by a Native American progressive. Tell students that the speeches should express their feelings as African Americans or Native Americans about progressive reform and reformers and should advocate methods to be used to draw attention to their needs. Then stage a rally for reform with volunteers from each group giving the speeches.

PRIMARY SOURCES

Description of Change: excerpted

Rationale: excerpted to focus on main idea

■■ Ask students how the concerns about movies voiced in the primary source (column 1) compare to concerns about movies today.

BIO GRAPHY PERSONALITIES IN HISTORY

While at Atlanta University in 1897, Du Bois began what he called his "real life work." He began a scientific study of the problems of city blacks, collecting facts to support his theories. His intent was to study and publish the findings of one aspect of African American life each year for 10 years. After the 10-year cycle had been repeated 10 times, 100 years of research material about African American life would be available as a source for scholars and government leaders. After 10 years, however, lack of funds brought the work to an end.

produced in 1903, and by 1910, millions of Americans were attending the movies each week. In 1916 the *New York Times* could declare that films were the fifth-largest U.S. industry.

To the urban poor a 5- to 10-cent movie ticket provided cheap, readily available entertainment. But many middle-class Americans believed that movies—especially the steamy romances—and movie houses were immoral and sources of temptation, particularly for the young. As one writer of the time reported:

> 66 The pictures thrown upon the luminous curtain of the stage have been declared extremely corrupting to the idle young people lurking in the darkness before it. The darkness itself has been held a condition of inexpressible depravity and a means of allurement to evil. 99

Declaring that moviegoing "softens the mental fibre and saps the character," reformers demanded that motion pictures be censored. Several states and cities set up censorship boards to ban movies they considered immoral. In 1909 the movie industry began to censor itself.

■■ **Reformers sought to improve American morals by working for prohibition and censorship of movies.**

*T*HE LIMITS OF PROGRESSIVISM

For nonwhites the Progressive movement had mixed results. While most progressives were concerned about the plight of the poor, few white progressives devoted very much energy to addressing the problems of discrimination and prejudice against African Americans and Native Americans. Some progressives even expressed openly racist or nativist sentiments against these groups. Many African Americans and Native Americans, however, drew on progressive ideas to craft solutions appropriate to their own communities.

BIO GRAPHY One of the most influential black leaders to emerge during this period was W.E.B. Du Bois (doo BOYS). Born in 1868 in Great Barrington, Massachusetts, Du Bois graduated from Fisk University, a black school in Nashville, Tennessee. He then studied history in Germany and at Harvard University. In 1895 he became the first African American to earn a doctorate from Harvard. Two years later he was hired as a professor of history and economics at Atlanta University, a leading African American college, where he taught until 1910.

By the early 1900s Du Bois was recognized as a brilliant thinker and strong advocate of African American civil rights and culture. He believed that a college education, rather than vocational training, would ensure greater progress for African Americans. He also believed that African Americans should be politically active in the struggle for racial equality.

Throughout his life Du Bois maintained a passionate interest in Africa, which he regarded as the spiritual homeland of all blacks. Du Bois eloquently expressed his dual identity as both African and American:

> 66 One feels his two-ness—an American, a Negro, two souls, two thoughts, two unreconciled strivings, two warring ideals. . . .
> The history of the American Negro is the history of this strife. . . . He would not Africanize America. . . . He would not bleach the Negro soul in a flood of white Americanism. . . . He simply wishes to make it possible for a man to be both a Negro and an American, without being cursed and spit upon. 99

W.E.B. Du Bois

In the 1920s, in an effort to forge greater unity among blacks and to promote pride in their African heritage, Du Bois organized a series of Pan-African congresses, which attracted black leaders from around the world.

During the 1930s and 1940s, Du Bois continued his career as a scholar and political activist. By the 1950s he had embraced socialism—which attracted many prominent American intellectuals, both black and white—for its promise

IMMIGRANTS AND PROGRESSIVES

Set up two student "face-off" panels: Ask one panel to assume roles of progressives in the early 1900s and the other panel to represent immigrants. Have the members of each panel discuss how to help the immigrant poor from that panel's point of view. Encourage the rest of the class to question and challenge panel members on their positions. Close the discussion by asking the progressive panel to list proposals on the chalkboard and the immigrant panel to support or reject each proposal and explain why.

of social justice. In 1961, at age 93, Du Bois joined the Communist party and moved to Ghana, where he died two years later.

The fight for racial justice. In 1909, in an effort to end racial discrimination, Du Bois, along with leading white progressives such as Jane Addams, helped found the **National Association for the Advancement of Colored People** (NAACP). Through its magazine, *The Crisis,* which Du Bois edited, the NAACP publicized cases of racial inequality and called for social reforms that would ensure equal rights for African Americans.

The NAACP also worked through the courts to end restrictions on voting and on other civil rights. In 1915 it won its first major victory in *Guinn* v. *United States.* In this case the Supreme Court outlawed the "grandfather clause" that southern states used to ensure that suffrage requirements designed to keep blacks from voting would not apply to whites. Two years later, in *Buchanan* v. *Warley,* NAACP lawyers successfully overturned a

▶ Du Bois served as editor of *The Crisis* from 1910 to 1932. This monthly magazine focused on issues important to African Americans.

Louisville, Kentucky, law requiring segregated housing. As a result, similar laws were struck down across the country. Since then the NAACP has continued to fight for African Americans' legal rights.

Another important organization in the struggle for racial justice during this period was the National Urban League. Founded in 1910 by concerned blacks and whites, the League worked to improve job opportunities and housing for urban

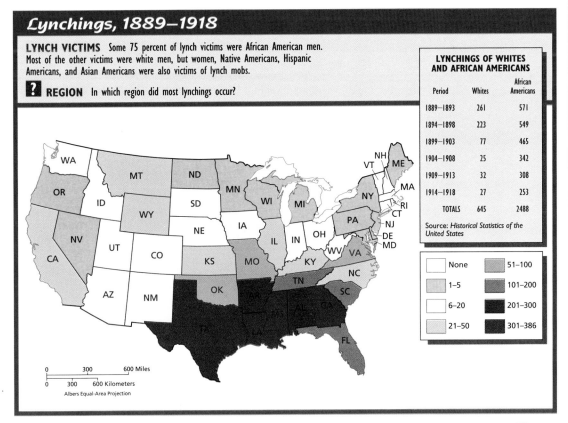

Lynchings, 1889–1918

LYNCH VICTIMS Some 75 percent of lynch victims were African American men. Most of the other victims were white men, but women, Native Americans, Hispanic Americans, and Asian Americans were also victims of lynch mobs.

❓ **REGION** In which region did most lynchings occur?

Period	Whites	African Americans
1889–1893	261	571
1894–1898	223	549
1899–1903	77	465
1904–1908	25	342
1909–1913	32	308
1914–1918	27	253
TOTALS	645	2488

LYNCHINGS OF WHITES AND AFRICAN AMERICANS

Source: *Historical Statistics of the United States*

None	51–100
1–5	101–200
6–20	201–300
21–50	301–386

Practice

GUIDED PRACTICE

Create an outline on the chalkboard, using *Reforming Society* as the title and the section's subheads as the main topics. Leave space under each subhead. Call on students to list details that might appear under each main topic and add them to the outline.

INDEPENDENT PRACTICE

Ask students to choose a main topic and accompanying details from the outline developed in the Guided Practice and use them to write a subsection of an encyclopedia article that might appear under an entry titled "Social Reform."

Review and Assessment

REVIEW Have students use the Essential Points of the section to write an essay that explains how the progressives reformed society. Then assign the Section 3 Review on p. 185.

ASSESS Assign the **Section 3 Daily Quiz** in *Core Resources*.

---

blacks. One of its chief goals was to help African American migrants from the South adjust to life in northern cities. Today the National Urban League carries on its efforts to end racial discrimination and to aid the disadvantaged.

The NAACP and the National Urban League made possible some important gains for black citizens. Nevertheless, most African Americans still faced discrimination, segregation, and denial of equal rights. The long struggle to eliminate racism continued.

■■ **Black leaders and organizations such as the NAACP and the National Urban League fought for racial justice. But racism continued to haunt American life.**

Native American progressives. Most progressives supported the Dawes Act of 1887 (see Chapter 5), which encouraged Native Americans to abandon reservation life and become private landowners. However, progressives realized that this policy had led many Native Americans to lose their property to land speculators and fall deeper into poverty. Thus, many progressives argued for a more gradual approach: slowing down land allotment and maintaining the reservation system for a time.

In 1911 a group of 50 Native Americans, most of them middle-class professional men and women, formed the **Society of American Indians** to address the problems facing Native Americans. One of its members, Seneca historian Arthur C. Parker, urged Native Americans "to strike out into the duties of modern life and . . . find every right that had escaped them before."

While some members supported strengthening tribal values, most favored complete assimilation. The Society publicized the accomplishments of famous Native Americans such as Olympic gold medalist Jim Thorpe and lobbied against the use of such derogatory terms as "buck" and "squaw." They also discussed ways to improve Indian health, education, civil rights, and local government. But the Society's moderate positions on most issues led to disputes among members, thus weakening the organization.

One member, Dr. Carlos Montezuma, a Yavapai-Apache, urged the Society to criticize the Bureau of Indian Affairs for mismanaging

▲ As a founder of the Society of American Indians, Gertrude S. Bonnin fought to protect Native Americans in Oklahoma from exploitation. There, land speculators used every possible tactic to secure oil leases to valuable Indian property.

reservations. Most Society members refused to take such a strong antigovernment stand, and the group's influence dwindled after 1923. While the Society did not last long, it provided a forum for Indian leaders and a basis for later attempts to improve conditions for Native Americans.

■■ **The Society of American Indians worked to improve the image of Native Americans and to solve the problems they faced.**

IMMIGRANTS AND ASSIMILATION

For immigrants the Progressive movement also had mixed results. On the one hand, many reformers sympathized with the plight of the newcomers crowded into urban factories and tenements. These reformers lobbied for laws to improve immigrants' lives and to better conditions in the workplace and in city slums.

At the same time, progressives criticized immigrants, accusing them of immoral behavior—of drinking, gambling, and other vices. They also denounced immigrant support for big-city political machines. As a result, some native-born Americans with progressive ideals also favored restricting immigration. Madison Grant was a case in point. In 1916 Grant, a prominent New Yorker, published

Closure

Discuss how actions of early 1900s reformers still affect life in the 1990s. Ask students to name and comment on programs and organizations begun in the Progressive Era that continue to affect society today. Have students comment on which of the many reforms they think had the greatest impact on future generations.

Extension

INVESTIGATE Have students research reformers who are questioning the impact of TV and movies on society today. Have them compare the present-day crusade with reformers' efforts in the Progressive Era.

COMPARE Have students find newspaper and magazine articles about recent immigrants. Have them write a paper comparing the experiences of today's immigrants with those of the immigrants of the early 1900s.

The Passing of the Great Race. In this book he expressed vicious racist opinions about African Americans, Jews, and immigrants from southern and eastern Europe. Only immigrants from England and northern Europe met Grant's standard of human worth. Yet Grant was also a progressive who supported urban planning and other reforms.

Many progressives, fearing the cultural diversity immigrants brought to American life, believed immigrants should be "Americanized" as quickly as possible. Americanizing, though, often meant denying the value of the immigrants' own culture and trying to reshape them in the mold of the native-born Protestant majority. Russian immigrant Eugene Lyons described the unsettling effects of this process in *Assignment in Utopia*:

▲ In 1890 Arnold Genthe photographed this Chinese immigrant family on an outing in San Francisco.

66 We were "Americanized" about as gently as horses are broken in. . . . We sensed a disrespect for the alien traditions in our homes and came unconsciously to resent and despise those traditions . . . because they seemed [impossible] barriers between ourselves and the adopted land. 99

The immigrant poor and the political bosses who represented them did, however, support middle-class progressives when they fought for practical reforms such as worker protection,

public-health programs, or regulation of slum housing. On such issues the big-city political machines sometimes played a key role. For example, a New York State legislative committee set up to investigate factory conditions after the 1911 Triangle fire won strong backing from New York City's immigrant-based democratic political machine.

■■ Immigrants supported progressive reformers on practical health and welfare issues.

PRIMARY SOURCE
Description of Change: excerpted and bracketed
Rationale: excerpted to focus on main idea; bracketed to clarify meaning

SECTION REVIEW ANSWERS

IDENTIFY

For significance, see the following pages:
Lawrence Veiller (p. 178)
Women's Christian Temperance Union (p. 181)
Frances Willard (p. 181)
Eighteenth Amendment (p. 181)
W.E.B. Du Bois (p. 182)
National Association for the Advancement of Colored People (p. 183)
Society of American Indians (p. 184)

1. *enlarging the function of government to include housing standards, public health, and city planning*
2. *through prohibition, censorship of movies*
3. *African Americans founded organizations such as NAACP to fight for racial justice. Native Americans founded Society of American Indians to solve common problems.*
4. *Pamphlets might mention efforts to protect workers, public-health programs, and housing regulations; or judgmental morality, racism, and disrespect for other cultures.*
5. *to lessen social problems by removing chief causes of unemployment, crime, and the breakup of families*

■
■ ■ **SECTION 3 REVIEW**

IDENTIFY and explain the significance of the following: Lawrence Veiller, Women's Christian Temperance Union, Frances Willard, Eighteenth Amendment, W.E.B. Du Bois, National Association for the Advancement of Colored People, Society of American Indians.

1. **MAIN IDEA** What approach did progressives use to clean up American cities?
2. **MAIN IDEA** How did reformers attempt to improve American morality?
3. **MAIN IDEA** How did African Americans and Native Americans attempt to fight racism and discrimination?
4. **WRITING TO EXPLAIN** Imagine you are an immigrant. Write a brief pamphlet for other immigrants that attempts to explain why you do or do not support the Progressive movement.
5. **ANALYZING** Why did progressives support prohibition and the elimination of saloons?

Review

DEVELOPING THEMES

Return to the Themes section on p. 166. Have students discuss these again and compare their original responses with those given now. (See p. 165B for suggested answers.)

Chapter Review Answers

WRITING A SUMMARY
See Essential Points in each section for main ideas.

REVIEWING CHRONOLOGY

5, 2, 4, 3, 1
Evaluating
created public outcry for new legislation to protect workers

IDENTIFYING PEOPLE AND IDEAS

1. *urban reform movement inspired by spirit of social justice*
2. *reformer and co-worker of Florence Kelley who helped research the "Brandeis Brief"*
3. *progressive journalists who exposed racial injustice and corruption in government and business*
4. *organizer of National Child Labor Committee who worked to prohibit child labor and to limit working hours for women*
5. *principle that workers had right to accept any conditions of employment that business owners required*
6. *architect who developed first comprehensive plan to redesign an American city*
7. *system under which government or worker cooperatives own businesses*
8. *reformer who worked for a law that set standards for urban housing*

9. *president of WCTU (1879–98)*
10. *organization formed by Native Americans, most of whom favored assimilation; worked to improve image, solve problems*
11. *muckraker who documented urban political corruption in The Shame of the Cities*

UNDERSTANDING MAIN IDEAS

1. *Women worked through reform organizations, wrote books and articles, and urged laws to correct social evils; it was one of the few ways in which they could influence social change and use their education, and one of the few careers open to them.*
2. *Muckrakers exposed corruption, urban social problems, and racial injustice. Writers and intellectuals attacked social problems and offered ideas for their solution.*
3. *child labor, long hours, low wages, unsafe working conditions*
4. *worked to clean up and beautify cities; passed housing laws, building codes, public-health measures; campaigned for parks and playgrounds*
5. *founded organizations to help fight racial injustice, improve image, and solve their unique problems*

CHAPTER 7
Review

Ida Tarbell's "History of the Standard Oil Company" begins publication in *McClure's*.

National Child Labor Committee formed.

Ray Stannard Baker's *Following the Color Line* and Upton Sinclair's *The Jungle* published.

ILGWU established.

IWW founded.

1897 1900 1905

WRITING A SUMMARY
Using the essential points of the chapter as a guide, write a summary of the chapter.

REVIEWING CHRONOLOGY
Number your paper 1 to 5. Study the time line above, and list the following events in the order in which they happened by writing the first next to 1, the second next to 2, and so on. Then complete the activity below.

1. Eighteenth Amendment ratified.
2. IWW founded.
3. Massachusetts passes minimum-wage law.
4. NAACP founded.
5. National Child Labor Committee formed.

Evaluating What effect did the Triangle Shirtwaist Company fire have on improving workplace safety?

IDENTIFYING PEOPLE AND IDEAS
Explain the historical significance of each of the following people or terms.

1. progressivism
2. Josephine Goldmark
3. muckrakers
4. Florence Kelley
5. freedom of contract
6. Daniel Burnham
7. socialism
8. Lawrence Veiller
9. Frances Willard
10. Society of American Indians
11. Lincoln Steffens

UNDERSTANDING MAIN IDEAS

1. In what ways did women work for progressive goals? Why were they so active in the Progressive movement?
2. What roles did muckrakers, writers, and intellectuals play in the reform movement?
3. Which labor issues did reformers hope to remedy through legislation?
4. What actions did progressive reformers take to improve conditions in cities?
5. What steps did African American and Native American progressives take to address the problems facing their communities?

REVIEWING THEMES

1. **Economic Development** Why did states pass laws to protect workers' rights?
2. **Democratic Values** How did progressives propose to extend opportunities to all citizens? Were they successful in these efforts? Why or why not?
3. **Constitutional Heritage** How did progressives help win passage of the Eighteenth Amendment?

THINKING CRITICALLY

1. **Analyzing** How did industrialization influence progressive reform efforts?
2. **Hypothesizing** How might the course of reform have been different if the Supreme Court had supported more early social legislation?
3. **Contrasting** How did the AFL and the IWW differ in their views on the scope and nature of labor reform?

STRATEGY FOR SUCCESS
Review the Skills Handbook entry on Reading Charts and Graphs beginning on page 756. Study the two graphs below. This information was compiled as an average for all industries in the period from 1900 to 1910. What conclusions can you draw from the graph data about the impact of progressivism?

AVERAGE DAILY HOURS

AVERAGE HOURLY WAGE

Hours: 10.0, 9.5, 9.0, 8.5, 8.0
1902 1906 1910
Year

Wage (cents): 20, 19, 18, 17, 16, 15
1902 1906 1910
Year

Source: *Historical Statistics of the United States*

REVIEWING THEMES

1. because of pressure on legislatures from reformers to pass such laws
2. by proposing election reforms that would enable people to participate more fully in running their government, by promoting legislation to curb corporate power, by seeking social justice; generally successful because many of their reforms were enacted; however, racist attitudes and lack of respect for ethnic cultures marred the record of progressive reformers
3. by campaigning vigorously for prohibition and elimination of saloons

THINKING CRITICALLY

1. Industrialization contributed to labor abuses and overcrowding, which increased urban problems but also fostered respect for progress; reformers focused on correcting urban problems and believed science and technology could help solve these problems.
2. might have reduced conflicts between employers and workers, led to faster and greater improvement of working conditions
3. AFL worked within system, negotiating with business owners and focusing on skilled workers; IWW opposed capitalism and focused on the needs of unskilled workers.

STRATEGY FOR SUCCESS

Reforms show up in the gradual decrease in average hours worked and in the increase in wages.

WRITING ABOUT HISTORY

Closing arguments should refer to evidence of social research that details the negative effects of long working hours and other specific working conditions on workers' health and well-being.

USING PRIMARY SOURCES

Summaries might mention Du Bois's belief that many career options were available, that training creates opportunities, and that any advances made by African Americans improve opportunities for African American children in the future.

LINKING HISTORY AND GEOGRAPHY

Most of the states were located in the South; historically, white southerners had opposed public education and education of blacks.

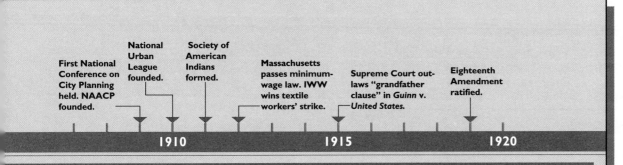

First National Conference on City Planning held. NAACP founded.

National Urban League founded.

Society of American Indians formed.

Massachusetts passes minimum-wage law. IWW wins textile workers' strike.

Supreme Court outlaws "grandfather clause" in *Guinn* v. *United States.*

Eighteenth Amendment ratified.

1910   1915   1920

WRITING ABOUT HISTORY

Writing to Persuade Imagine you are the young Boston lawyer Louis D. Brandeis. Write a closing argument attempting to convince the Supreme Court to uphold laws that guarantee workers' rights. Include specific examples of working conditions to support your arguments.

USING PRIMARY SOURCES

In 1905 W.E.B. Du Bois wrote to an African American student who was discouraged about the career opportunities that would be available to her. Read the following excerpt from his letter and write a summary of his advice to her.

I have heard that you are a young woman of some ability but that you are neglecting your school work because you have become hopeless of trying to do anything in the world. I am very sorry for this. . . .

There are in the U.S. today tens of thousands of colored girls who would be happy beyond measure to have the chance of educating themselves that you are neglecting. If you train yourself as you easily can, there are wonderful chances of usefulness before you: you can join the ranks of 15,000 Negro women teachers, of hundreds of nurses and physicians, of the growing number of clerks and stenographers. . . . Ignorance is a cure for nothing. Get the very best training possible & the doors of opportunity will fly open before you as they are flying before thousands of your fellows. On the other hand every time a colored person neglects an opportunity, it makes it more difficult for others of the race to get such an opportunity. Do you want to cut off the chances of the boys and girls of tomorrow?

LINKING HISTORY AND GEOGRAPHY

Review the map on compulsory education on page 179. Note that most states adopted compulsory attendance laws for school-aged children during the 19th century, but 15 states did not do so until after 1900. Where are most of these 15 states located? Drawing on what you have learned in previous chapters, what factors might help explain the link between geographic region and the timing of passage of compulsory attendance laws for school-aged children?

BUILDING YOUR PORTFOLIO

Complete the following projects independently or cooperatively.

1. **REFORM** Imagine you are a progressive reformer in the early 1900s. Write an editorial for *McClure's, Cosmopolitan,* or another progressive magazine that addresses an urban problem in government, business, the workplace, or the community. Be sure that your editorial suggests a possible solution to the problem. Editorials might examine political machines, corporate abuses, poor working conditions, or public-health concerns.

2. **DEMOCRATIC RIGHTS** Imagine you are a progressive reformer working to promote women's rights. Prepare a speech on women's rights to deliver at an Independence Day celebration. Be sure that the speech outlines the various problems and concerns faced by women in the early 1900s and indicates how progressive reformers intend to address these problems and concerns.

BUILDING YOUR PORTFOLIO

Have students refer to **Building Your Portfolio Worksheet 2,** assigned at the beginning of Unit 2. Use the worksheet to help students monitor their progress on the portfolio projects.

*A*ssessment

Core Resources
- Reteaching Worksheet 7
- Chapter 7 Tests
- Alternative Assessment Forms

Test Generator

THE PROGRESSIVE PRESIDENTS

1900–1920

Chapter Overview

In an effort to improve life for all Americans, the progressives sought to curb corrupt politicians and to mobilize the power of government to improve society. Initial efforts were at the local level, but the spirit of reform soon spread to all levels of government.

Theodore Roosevelt, William Howard Taft, and Woodrow Wilson all used the office of the president to further the aims of progressivism. Some gains were made in cleaning up government and regulating big business, but by 1916 much still remained to be done.

THE AMERICAN NATION VIDEODISC PROGRAM A variety of still images, short videos, and activities are available for you to use as you teach this chapter. See Videodisc Resources in the Core Resources Binder for barcode correlations and suggestions for using the program.

Chapter Planning Guide

CHAPTER 8	CORE RESOURCES	AUDIOVISUAL AV RESOURCES	PROGRAM RESOURCES
INTRODUCTION pp. 188–189	■ Literature Worksheet 8 ■ Building Your Portfolio Worksheet 2	■ Everyday Life in America Transparency and Worksheet 18	
TEACHING THE CHAPTER pp. 190–209 ■ For expanded coverage of pp. 196–198, see Chapter 27, pp. 722–727; for coverage of pp. 207–208, see Chapter 26.	■ Graphic Organizer 8 ■ Social Studies Skills Worksheet 8 ■ Geography Worksheet 8 ■ Outline Map 9	■ *The American Nation* Videodisc: Yosemite National Park	■ *Eyewitnesses and Others,* Volume 2: Reading 28
REVIEW AND ASSESSMENT pp. 210–211	■ Chapter 8 Daily Quizzes ■ Reteaching Worksheet 8 ■ Chapter 8 Tests ■ Alternative Assessment Forms		■ Test Generator

Additional Resources

BOOKS FOR TEACHERS

Broderick, Francis L. *Progressivism at Risk: Electing a President in 1912.* Greenwood Press, 1989. Issues surrounding the 1912 presidential election.

Cashman, Sean D. *America in the Age of the Titans.* New York University Press, 1988. A thorough account of the Progressive Era.

Giese, James R. *The Progressive Era: The Limits of Reform.* 2nd ed. Social Science Education Consortium, 1989. A review of progressive reforms.

BOOKS FOR STUDENTS

Cooper, John Milton, Jr. *Pivotal Decades.* Norton, 1990. Reviews historical developments from 1900 to 1920.

*Fritz, Jean. *Bully for You, Teddy Roosevelt!* Putnam, 1991. Award-winning author explores the life of TR.

*Whitelaw, Nancy. *Theodore Roosevelt Takes Charge.* Albert Whitman, 1992. Chronicles the life of Theodore Roosevelt.

* for students reading below grade level

MULTIMEDIA MATERIALS

TR & His Times. Video, 58 min. PBS. A study of the life and times of Theodore Roosevelt.

The United States in the 20th Century: 1900–1912. Video, 12 min. Coronet Instructional Films. Focuses on the administrations of Roosevelt and Taft.

The United States in the 20th Century: 1912–1920. Video, 12 min. Coronet Instructional Films. Examines the presidency of Woodrow Wilson.

THEMES IN AMERICAN HISTORY

USE WITH PAGES 188–189

Listed on the right are the themes emphasized in Chapter 8. The questions in boldface type stimulate critical thinking and provide students with an opportunity to discuss the themes within a broadened context. The questions also appear in the pupil's edition on p. 188.

■ DEMOCRATIC VALUES

What are some ways in which government can restore political power to the people? Students might suggest that government could restore power to the people by allowing more people to vote, by filling more offices by election instead of by appointment, and by allowing voters a more direct voice in shaping the laws that affect them. Limiting the power of government officials by making them more accountable to the voters who elected them also increases the people's political power.

■ ECONOMIC DEVELOPMENT

How can government regulate business practices without discouraging free enterprise? Students might suggest that a democratically elected government has an obligation to the public that empowers it. This obligation may include some oversight of business practices in the public interest, such as protecting consumers from harmful products or protecting businesses from dishonest competitors. Such business regulation provides for the general welfare without disrupting the free enterprise system.

■ CONSTITUTIONAL HERITAGE

How might people use constitutional change to reform politics and society? Students might suggest that government officials may not always meet the wants or needs of the majority—or even a large minority—of society, and that they may sometimes be more responsive to other powerful interests. In such cases people may call for a constitutional amendment to accomplish a reform. Students may note that reform achieved through amendment is more permanent than change accomplished by laws, which might be changed later or voided by the Supreme Court.

CHAPTER STRATEGIES FOR MEETING INDIVIDUAL NEEDS

LIMITED ENGLISH PROFICIENT LEARNERS

Have students work in small groups to create flyers, banners, and signs that represent various points of view on the issues discussed in the chapter.

TACTILE/KINESTHETIC LEARNERS

Have students work in small groups to create an annotated, illustrated map of the National Parks system. Display the map on the bulletin board.

LEARNERS HAVING DIFFICULTY

Encourage students to write answers to the questions in each section's Focus. Then have them use these answers to write a brief summary of the chapter.

AUDITORY LEARNERS

Guide students to use the books listed on p. 187A to prepare dramatic readings on issues discussed in the chapter—tariff reform, business regulation, conservation, and women's suffrage, for example.

VISUAL LEARNERS

Ask students to review the chapter and other texts on the progressives to locate illustrations that represent the presidencies of Roosevelt, Taft, and Wilson. Call on volunteers to present and explain their selections.

GIFTED LEARNERS

Encourage students to write and present speeches that might have been given by Roosevelt, Taft, or Wilson on one of the issues discussed in the chapter.

USING THE CHAPTER FOCUS

■ **UNDERSTANDING THE MAIN IDEA**

Have students read the Understanding the Main Idea paragraph. Then ask them to suggest what kinds of reform legislation a progressive president like Roosevelt, Taft, or Wilson might propose or support in order to carry the reform agenda to the national level. List student responses on a flip chart. As students read the chapter, have them review and revise the list.

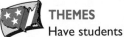 **THEMES** Have students work individually or in small groups to answer the questions under Themes. Save students' responses so that they can compare them with their responses after studying the chapter. (See p. 187B for suggested answers.)

■ **THE TIME LINE**

Have students list the time-line entries in their notebooks. Then, as they read the chapter, have them note what impact each event or incident on the time line had on the advance of progressivism.

CORE RESOURCES

• **Graphic Organizer 8**
• **Literature Worksheet 8**
• **Building Your Portfolio Worksheet 2**

AV RESOURCES

• **Everyday Life in America Transparency and Worksheet 18**

ABOUT THE ILLUSTRATION

Rallies similar to this one were held frequently by supporters of women's suffrage. On March 3, 1913, the day of Wilson's inauguration, the new president was almost upstaged by some 5,000 suffragists who marched down Pennsylvania Avenue. Ask students how they would react if they were members of a group that was denied the same rights as other Americans.

Chapter 8

1900–1920

THE PROGRESSIVE PRESIDENTS

FOCUS

UNDERSTANDING THE MAIN IDEA

Many progressives sought to extend their reform efforts to government itself. They wanted to take power away from corrupt political machines and mobilize the power of the government to improve American life. On the national level, presidents Theodore Roosevelt, William Howard Taft, and Woodrow Wilson tried in varying degrees to implement the progressive reform agenda.

THEMES

■ **DEMOCRATIC VALUES** What are some ways in which government can restore political power to the people?

■ **ECONOMIC DEVELOPMENT** How can government regulate business practices without discouraging free enterprise?

■ **CONSTITUTIONAL HERITAGE** How might people use constitutional change to reform politics and society?

1901	1906	1910	1912	1914	1920
William McKinley assassinated.	Pure Food and Drug Act passed.	Mann-Elkins Act passed.	Progressive party formed.	Federal Trade Commission created.	Nineteenth Amendment ratified.

:: LINK TO THE PAST ▶

Various efforts to reform society had occupied American women and men throughout the 19th century. Reformers had campaigned to end slavery, to secure women's rights, and to correct the problems caused by industrialization and urbanization. Similar new efforts at reform engaged many middle-class Americans early in the 20th century.

HISTORICAL SIDELIGHTS

A Stepping-Stone?

Lincoln Steffens described Roosevelt's work as police commissioner as "pitiless reorganization and absolute publicity." Indeed, it seemed to many people that publicity was all-important to Roosevelt and that the commission was simply a stepping-stone to higher office. That office, Steffens and Riis suspected, was the presidency.

Suffrage rally, 1912

O n the morning of May 6, 1895, two progressive reporters, Jacob Riis and Lincoln Steffens, waited eagerly outside New York City police headquarters. The new head of the city's four-member police commission, Theodore Roosevelt, was due to arrive any minute. The reporters eagerly wished to find out Roosevelt's plans for reforming New York's notoriously corrupt police department.

Riis and Roosevelt were already friends and political allies. Five years before, Riis had gained national attention for his book *How the Other Half Lives,* in which he documented the grim reality of slum life in New York City. Roosevelt wrote to Riis, requesting a meeting, saying, "I have read your book, and I have come to help."

Now Roosevelt would have the chance to reform the nation's largest police force. Arriving at police headquarters, he called the two reporters into his office, leaving his fellow commissioners outside. Motioning Riis and Steffens to sit down, he said, "Now then, what'll we do?" As Steffens later recalled, "It was just as if we three were the Police Board." Within days Roosevelt had fired the police chief and had begun to clean up the department. By the end of the summer, fellow commissioner Avery Andrews noted, "The whole country . . . was talking about Theodore Roosevelt."

Six years later, Roosevelt was president of the United States. He brought to the White House the same boundless energy and progressive spirit he had demonstrated as police commissioner. Under Roosevelt's leadership progressivism moved from state and local politics into the national arena.

First edition cover of Riis's book

FOCUS OBJECTIVES

- Describe the forms that government corruption took.

- Identify election reforms supported by progressives to make government more democratic.

- List reforms enacted in city and state governments during the Progressive Era.

190

PREVIEW WORKSHOP

Following is a list of the significant people, places, and terms in this section. You may wish to use this list as a section preview.

People
- Samuel M. Jones
- Tom Johnson
- Robert M. La Follette

Places
- Wisconsin

Terms
- direct primary
- Seventeenth Amendment
- initiative
- referendum
- recall
- Wisconsin Idea

MOTIVATING: STUDENT EXPERIENCES

Ask the class how candidates are selected for offices in school groups. As volunteers explain each group's process, have students evaluate how democratic each process is. Tell students that in this section they will discover how the process for selecting government officials became more democratic in the early 20th century.

Section 1

REFORMING GOVERNMENT

FOCUS

- **What forms did government corruption take?**
- **What election reforms did progressives support to make government more democratic?**
- **What reforms were enacted in city and state governments during the Progressive Era?**

*P*rogressives did not limit their reform efforts to social ills. They also tackled the task of curbing the political power of the privileged few and removing the corrupt political machines that served them. Toward this end, progressives sought changes in the electoral process that would restore political power to the people.

New York political boss Charles Murphy voting, 1916

GOVERNMENT CORRUPTION

Theodore Roosevelt and other progressive reformers found corruption at all levels of government, from city hall to Washington, D.C. As Lincoln Steffens so graphically reported in *The Shame of the Cities,* urban political machines demanded bribes from anyone wanting to do business with city government.

In Philadelphia, for instance, in order to secure jobs teachers had to pay the political machine $120 of the first $141 they earned. In Pittsburgh, public jobs went to contractors who paid bribes. Of course, they were allowed to pad their bills to make up the losses. One Pittsburgh political boss even opened his own paving firm so that he could take the lion's share of contracts himself—at inflated prices.

Government corruption did not stop at the city level. City machines were often linked to Democratic or Republican state machines. The state machines catered to "special interests," making deals with the railroads, the lumber industry, or anyone else who wanted tax breaks or other favors

from state legislatures. In return, the machines expected generous gifts, often in the form of "campaign contributions."

At the federal level some U.S. senators, who were often put in power by state machines, accepted bribes to vote the way corporations wished. In 1906 the progressive writer David Graham Phillips began

▲ This 1926 cartoon, entitled *The National Gesture,* satirizes the widespread practice of receiving bribes among government officials.

CORRUPT GOVERNMENT

Divide the class into fourths to write letters to the editor. Two groups' letters should explain why as taxpayers or business owners they object to political machines in their city government. Students in the other groups should explain why they believe state or national government to be corrupt and undemocratic. Select students from each group to read their letters aloud.

STRENGTHENING DEMOCRACY

Ask students to list the election reforms that progressive reformers accomplished. Record responses on the chalkboard. Then ask volunteers to explain how each reform made government more democratic and responsive to the people rather than to special interests. Students may wish to consult the letters they wrote in the previous activity to speculate how each reform might address the issues they raised in their letters.

CITY AND STATE REFORM

Organize students into small groups to discuss progressive reform in city and state government. Direct half the groups to analyze the relationship between business and reform of city government. Have the other groups analyze how the Wisconsin Idea reflected progressive ideas about making government serve the people rather than the special interests. Call on a spokesperson from each group to report its findings to the class. ▶

publishing articles that described how special interests influenced American politics. In "The Treason of the Senate," he wrote:

> ❝ The greatest single hold of "the interests" is the fact that they are the "campaign contributors." . . . Who pays the big election expenses of your congressman, of the men you send to the legislature to elect senators? Do you imagine those who foot those huge bills are fools? Don't you know that they make sure of getting their money back, with interest? ❞

▪▪ **Corrupt political bosses and machines accepted bribes from special interests in return for government favors.**

ELECTION REFORMS

Government corruption outraged reformers. To restore honest government, they demanded, "Give the government back to the people!" Only when government heeded the public's voice, they believed, could the problems of American life be remedied.

One way progressives sought to break the powers of the bosses and the special interests was to reform the election process. First, they wanted to take the job of choosing candidates for office away from the machines. Therefore, progressives pushed for the **direct primary**—a nominating election in which voters choose the candidates who will later run in a general election. Wisconsin adopted the direct primary in 1903, and by 1916 most other states had followed suit.

Next, progressives proposed to change the method of electing U.S. senators. At the time, the U.S. Constitution mandated that state legislatures elect senators. To progressives, this law made it easy for the bosses to control government. By 1912 the progressive tide had grown strong enough to pass the **Seventeenth Amendment**, which was ratified the next year. The amendment authorized voters to elect their senators directly.

As another step toward more democratic government, the progressives sought to reform the voting process. At the time, each political party

▲ **Progressives reformed the voting process by eliminating colored ballots. With the secret ballot, people could cast their vote without revealing their party preference.**

printed its own ballot in a distinctive color. On Election Day the colored ballots made it easy to see how people voted. Without secrecy, voters could be pressured to support certain candidates. To lessen this threat, progressives proposed using the secret ballot. Developed in Australia, the ballot lists all candidates on a single sheet of paper and is printed at public expense. By 1910 most states had switched to the secret ballot.

Finally, progressives urged states to adopt three other election reforms: initiative, referendum, and recall. The **initiative** gives voters the power to initiate, or introduce, legislation. If a certain percentage of voters in a state (usually 5 to 15 percent) petition their legislature to enact a measure, the legislature has to consider it. The **referendum** is a companion to the initiative. By securing a specified number of signatures on a petition, voters can compel the legislature to place a measure on the ballot. The **recall** enables voters to remove an elected official from office by calling for a new election.

▪▪ **Progressives supported the direct primary, the direct election of U.S. senators, the secret ballot, and the initiative, referendum, and recall.**

PRIMARY SOURCE

Description of Change: excerpted

Rationale: excerpted to focus on main idea

🌐 **GLOBAL CONNECTIONS**

Because Australia led the way in instituting the secret ballot, it sometimes is referred to as the *Australian* ballot. Adopted first by the colonial government of Victoria in 1856, it spread over western Australia by 1879. During the 1870s it was also adopted in New Zealand, Britain, Canada, and Belgium. The first American states to introduce the secret ballot were Massachusetts and Kentucky in 1888.

HISTORICAL SIDELIGHTS

Election Reform
Referendums and initiatives were not new devices. Massachusetts in 1780 allowed referendums for constitutional ratification. In 1831 the Swiss were first to use referendums to approve laws. They also instituted the initiative in 1845. The recall has more modern origins. It first appeared in the Los Angeles city charter in 1903.

Practice

GUIDED PRACTICE

On the chalkboard draw a two-column chart with *Mayor/Council* and *Commission* as headings. Ask students to provide information about these two forms of city government as you add their responses in the appropriate column.

INDEPENDENT PRACTICE

Have students use the information from the chart developed in the Guided Practice to write a paragraph explaining which form of government they think is the more efficient. Suggest that students read and compare their paragraphs. Students may wish to include their paragraphs in their portfolios.

Review and Assessment

REVIEW Ask students to create an outline of Section 1, using the essential points as their main topic headings. Then assign the Section 1 Review on p. 193.

ASSESS Assign the **Section 1 Daily Quiz** in *Core Resources.*

HISTORICAL SIDELIGHTS

Golden Rule at Work

As a manufacturer of oil-well machinery, Jones treated his employees according to the Golden Rule. The workday was eight hours, and workers kept track of their own time. Workers received a week's paid vacation, Christmas bonuses, and free lunches. Jones also provided a park and a company band for recreation and entertainment.

MULTICULTURAL PERSPECTIVES

Not all urbanites welcomed progressive efforts at reform. In ethnic neighborhoods political bosses were often the only people who seemed willing to stand up for immigrants. One popular but corrupt party boss was Long Island mayor Patrick Jerome Gleason, an Irish immigrant who amassed a large following by fighting big businesses that took advantage of the working class. His most lasting legacy was construction of a school in an Irish American community. Amid the protests of his supporters, he was removed from office after it was revealed that he profited financially from the venture.

Reforming City Government

Efforts to reform government were not motivated solely by a desire for more democracy. Businesspeople supported reform because the costs of political corruption had become too great. John Patterson of the National Cash Register Company argued that individuals "skilled in business management and social service" should run "municipal affairs on a strict business basis." Many agreed. As a result, good-government campaigns put a large number of reform mayors into office. Two of the most successful were elected in Ohio: Samuel M. Jones and Tom Johnson. Both were self-made men who had amassed their fortunes early and then in mid-life had traded business for politics.

Samuel M. "Golden Rule" Jones got his nickname from his belief in the biblical Golden Rule—"Do unto others as you would have them do unto you." Seeking to apply this principle to government, Jones successfully ran for mayor of Toledo in 1897. Over the next seven years he overhauled the police force, improved municipal services, set a minimum wage for city workers, and opened kindergartens for children.

During this same period, Tom Johnson served as Cleveland's mayor. A former streetcar magnate, he knew personally how closely business interests were tied to political bosses, and he worked to sever those ties. His success led writer Lincoln Steffens to call Johnson "the best mayor of the best governed city in the United States."

▶ Samuel M. Jones pushed through so many reforms that his party refused to renominate him for mayor in 1899. He ran as an independent, however, and defeated both of his opponents. The photograph above shows a kindergarten in Toledo, Ohio, in the early 1900s.

A few charismatic mayors alone, however, could not conquer entrenched corruption. Many reformers came to believe that only a change in the structure of city government could break the political machines. The typical city government of the time consisted of a mayor and a city council made up of aldermen. Each alderman was the elected leader of one of the wards into which a city was divided. Under this system a political machine could easily elect its own people and thus run city affairs its own way.

Oddly enough, it was a natural disaster that produced an alternative to this system. In 1900 a hurricane struck Galveston, Texas, killing some 6,000 people and destroying the city. The city's government could not cope with the emergency, so

▶ The disastrous hurricane that struck Galveston, Texas, in 1900 led to a new structure of government.

RETEACH Direct students to summarize the section by writing a sentence for each of the major headings. Call on volunteers to read their summaries to the group.

Closure

Read the following statement to the class: *In America's cities business was often the friend of government reform, but at the state level, business was often its foe.* Ask students whether they agree or disagree with this assessment and to cite evidence from the section to support their opinions.

Extension

RESEARCH Suggest that students research and write a biographical sketch of one of the reform politicians or progressive writers discussed in Section 1.

INVESTIGATE Encourage students to interview a local official about the structure of local government. Suggest that they also ask about operating procedures that safeguard against graft and corruption. Ask them to present their findings to the class.

the state legislature named a five-person city commission to rebuild the area. The commissioners were experts in their fields, not party loyalists. Thus they based their decisions on what would work best rather than on what would benefit the political machine. Citizens praised the commission as more honest and efficient than the previous city government. By 1913, city commissions ran more than 350 U.S. cities.

The desire for increased government efficiency also gave rise to city managers. These were expert administrators hired to run cities as they might run a business—with maximum efficiency.

■■ **Many American cities elected reform mayors, formed city commissions, and hired city managers to increase government efficiency.**

REFORMING STATE GOVERNMENT

The spirit of reform also affected many state governments. In Wisconsin, Governor Robert M. "Fighting Bob" La Follette instituted reforms that turned Wisconsin into what Theodore Roosevelt would call "the laboratory of democracy."

BIO GRAPHY Born in June 1855 in Primrose, Wisconsin, La Follette worked his way through college and law school. Although a loyal Republican, he found himself at odds with Wisconsin's Republican machine, which railroad and lumber interests dominated. After serving as a county district attorney and as a U.S. congressman during the late 1800s, he signaled his break with the party machine by refusing an alleged bribe by a party boss.

La Follette emerged early in the progressive movement as one of its most energetic leaders. A spellbinding orator, he won farmers, the working class, and the middle class to progressivism.

Elected governor in 1900, he vigorously backed a reform program—soon known as the **Wisconsin Idea**—that became a model for other states. First, La Follette brought the direct primary to Wisconsin. He then prodded the state legislature to increase taxes on the railroads and the public utilities—gas, electric, and streetcar companies—and to create commissions to regulate these companies in the public

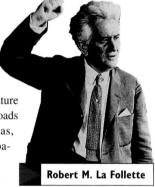
Robert M. La Follette

interest. La Follette also got laws passed to curb excessive lobbying and backed labor legislation, the conservation of Wisconsin's natural resources, and other social legislation. In 1905 the Wisconsin legislature elected La Follette to the U.S. Senate, where he continued to battle for reform until his death in 1925.

■■ **La Follette's Wisconsin Idea provided a model for reforming local and state government and regulating big business.**

SECTION 1 REVIEW

IDENTIFY and explain the significance of the following: direct primary, Seventeenth Amendment, initiative, referendum, recall, Samuel M. Jones, Tom Johnson, Robert M. La Follette.

LOCATE and explain the importance of the following: Wisconsin.

1. **MAIN IDEA** What measures did progressives suggest to make government more democratic?
2. **MAIN IDEA** How did many U.S. cities try to increase government efficiency and lessen corruption?
3. **GEOGRAPHY: HUMAN-ENVIRONMENT INTERACTION** How did the Galveston hurricane help produce a new political structure for cities?
4. **WRITING TO INFORM** Imagine you are David Graham Phillips. Write an article describing political corruption at the local, state, and federal levels.
5. **ANALYZING** What reforms made up the Wisconsin Idea? Why can it be said that these reforms are examples of the progressive spirit?

PREVIEW WORKSHOP

*Following is a list of the significant
people and terms in this section.
You may wish to use this list as a
section preview.*

People
■ Theodore Roosevelt
■ Leon Czolgosz
■ Judge Alton Parker

Terms
■ arbitration
■ Square Deal
■ Elkins Act
■ Hepburn Act
■ Meat Inspection Act
■ Pure Food and Drug Act
■ Newlands Reclamation Act
■ reclamation

FOCUS OBJECTIVES

■ Describe the Square Deal.

■ Explain how Theodore Roosevelt fought corruption in business.

■ List the steps that Roosevelt took to protect the environment.

Section 2

ROOSEVELT AND THE SQUARE DEAL

F O C U S

■ **What was the Square Deal?**

■ **How did Theodore Roosevelt fight corruption in business?**

■ **What steps did Roosevelt take to protect the environment?**

Theodore Roosevelt was the first progressive president of the United States. Taking office after the assassination of President William McKinley, Roosevelt was elected in his own right in 1904. During his two terms as president, he promoted the regulation of big business and helped preserve natural resources for future generations.

Assassination of
President McKinley, 1901

*R*OOSEVELT BECOMES PRESIDENT

In 1900 President McKinley ran for reelection with Theodore Roosevelt as his running mate. The Democrats again nominated William Jennings Bryan and made free silver their campaign issue. But in 1900 most Americans felt prosperous, and McKinley and Roosevelt sailed to victory. Then on September 6, 1901, anarchist Leon Czolgosz shot McKinley. A week later the president died, and Roosevelt became the nation's chief executive.

BIO
GRAPHY Theodore Roosevelt was born in 1858 into a wealthy New York family. A sickly child, he built up his strength through rigorous exercise. From his father, he acquired a love of the outdoors, a strong sense of fair play, and concern for the less fortunate. As a student at Harvard University, he developed a taste for history and politics. After graduating, Roosevelt won election to the New York state legislature, where he served from 1882 to 1884. As a legislator he earned a reputation as a moderate but energetic reformer.

Toward the end of his third term, Roosevelt's wife, Alice Lee,

died following childbirth. Deeply saddened, he did not seek reelection. Instead he headed for his ranch in the Dakota Territory. Roosevelt spent much of the next two years ranching and writing history books, including what would become the four-volume *Winning of the West*. The harsh winter of 1885–86, however, forced him out of the cattle business and back to New York. In December 1886 he married childhood friend Edith Kermit Carow.

In the 1890s Roosevelt served in a variety of federal and state positions. Then, during the Spanish-American War in 1898 (see Chapter 9), he helped organize a volunteer cavalry unit—the Rough Riders—and went off to fight in Cuba. He returned a war hero that same year and was elected governor of New York.

As governor, Roosevelt worked to reform government and to regulate big business. Angered by the governor's progressive efforts, conservative Republican party leaders tried to ease Roosevelt out of state office by having him run as vice president on the McKinley ticket in 1900. Alarmed, the conservative senator Mark Hanna warned that there would be "only one life between

Theodore Roosevelt

MOTIVATING: STUDENT EXPERIENCES

Ask students to recall and list in their notebooks the political reforms promoted by the Populists in the late 1800s. Then, as they read this section, direct students to note if and how the progressives enacted these Populist goals.

Teaching the Section

A SQUARE DEAL

Suggest that students imagine they are speech writers for Teddy Roosevelt. Ask them to write a campaign speech explaining the aims of, and outlining the proposed programs of, the Square Deal. Call on volunteers to deliver their speeches to the class. Students may wish to include their speeches in their portfolios.

PRESIDENTIAL LIVES

THEODORE ROOSEVELT
1858–1919

in office 1901–1909

Theodore Roosevelt relished the limelight. As one of his children remarked, Roosevelt always wanted to be "the bride at every wedding."

This hero of the Rough Riders became a legend in his own time. Roosevelt always lived life to the hilt. "No President has ever enjoyed himself as much as I have enjoyed myself," he claimed. An old friend explained Roosevelt's great love of life: "You must

always remember that the President is about six [years old]."

His energy was legendary. For example, when the French ambassador once visited the White House, he and the president played tennis, jogged, and then worked out. Roosevelt turned to his guest and asked, "What would you like to do now?" "If it's just the same with you, Mr. President," said the ambassador, "I'd like to lie down and die."

Theodore Roosevelt

---

this madman and the Presidency." When Roosevelt moved into the White House a year later, Hanna exclaimed to a colleague, "My God, that . . . cowboy in the White House!"

Teddy, or TR, as he was now commonly called, loved hunting and sports. Only 42 years old, he brought a new style to the presidency. Journalist William Allen White described him as a "rumbling, roaring . . . tornado of a man." His nononsense style and toothy grin made him a favorite target of political cartoonists.

THE SQUARE DEAL

Unlike the presidents of the Gilded Age, who generally took a hands-off approach to government, Roosevelt believed that the president should use his office as a "bully pulpit" to speak out on vital issues. Roosevelt brought dynamic leadership to the progressive movement.

Soon after Roosevelt became president, a labor dispute helped define his approach to the office. In 1902 some 150,000 Pennsylvania coal miners struck for higher wages and recognition of the United Mine Workers union. But the mine owners—mostly railroad companies—would not negotiate.

Roosevelt urged the two sides to accept **arbitration**—to let a third party settle the dispute. When the mine owners refused, the president threatened to take over the mines. The mine

owners backed down. The arbitrators gave both the miners and the mine owners part of what they wanted. The compromise was a landmark: For the first time, the federal government had intervened in a strike to protect the interests of the workers and the public. Satisfied, Roosevelt pronounced the compromise a square deal.

The **Square Deal** became Roosevelt's 1904 campaign slogan. He promised to "see to it that every man has a square deal, no less and no more." This pledge summed up Roosevelt's belief in balancing the interests of labor, business, and consumers. Roosevelt's Square Deal called for limiting the power of trusts, promoting public health and safety, and improving working conditions.

The president was so popular with voters that no Republican dared challenge him for the 1904 nomination. In the election, Roosevelt easily defeated his Democratic opponent, Judge Alton Parker of New York.

■■ **Roosevelt's Square Deal pledged fair treatment for business, workers, and the public.**

REGULATING BUSINESS

One of Roosevelt's goals during both terms in office was to regulate large corporations. While he considered big business essential to the nation's growth, he also believed companies should behave responsibly.

Teaching the Section

ROOSEVELT THE TRUSTBUSTER

Organize the class to debate the following question: *Roosevelt—Does He Deserve the Title "Trustbuster"?* Ask students from both sides of the question to state their views. Suggest that students consider whether a president who left trusts intact unless they were "bad" was a genuine trustbuster.

ENVIRONMENTAL PROTECTION

Have students work in small groups to create a four-page pictorial essay on environmental-protection activity during Roosevelt's presidency. Ask volunteers from each group to present and explain their group's essay to the class.

"We don't wish to destroy corporations," he said, "but we do wish to make them subserve the public good."

Trustbusting. In 1902 the president put this philosophy into practice. He directed the attorney general to sue the Northern Securities Company, which monopolized railroad shipping in the Northwest. In 1904 the Supreme Court ruled that the monopoly violated the Sherman Antitrust Act and therefore ordered the corporation dissolved. Encouraged by this victory, Roosevelt's administration went on a "trustbusting" campaign, filing 44 suits against business combinations deemed "bad." It was not size that mattered, Roosevelt declared, but whether a trust was good or bad for the public as a whole. As he put it, "We draw the line against misconduct, not against wealth."

The Roosevelt administration also promoted railroad regulation. At the president's urging, Congress passed two laws that turned the Interstate Commerce Commission (ICC) into a significant regulatory agency. The first, the 1903 **Elkins Act**, forbade shippers from accepting rebates (money secretly given back to shippers in return for their business). The second, the 1906 **Hepburn Act**, authorized the ICC to set railroad rates and to regulate other companies engaged in interstate commerce, such as pipelines and ferries.

Protecting the consumer. Roosevelt was also concerned about the food and drug industries. By the early 1900s clear evidence existed that some drug companies, meat packers, and food processors were selling dangerous products. Some drug companies sold ineffective over-the-counter medicines that contained dangerous drugs such as cocaine or morphine. Exposing drug industry abuses, journalist Samuel Hopkins Adams wrote:

66 Gullible America will spend this year some seventy-five millions of dollars in the purchase of patent [over-the-counter]

▲ The Pure Food and Drug Act tried to prevent drug manufacturers from making false or exaggerated claims about their products. This advertisement, for example, promises the user will be spared from headaches after taking Carter's liver pills.

medicines. . . . It will swallow huge quantities of alcohol, an appalling amount of opiates and narcotics. 99

The drug companies' claims that their "health tonics" could cure everything from baldness to cancer, Adams charged, amounted to fraud.

In response to these abuses and those of the food industry, Roosevelt and Congress enacted two consumer-protection laws in 1906. The **Meat Inspection Act** required government inspection of meat shipped from one state to another. The **Pure Food and Drug Act** forbade the manufacture, sale, or transportation of food and patent medicine containing harmful ingredients. The law also required that containers of food and medicines carry ingredient labels.

■■ Roosevelt fought corruption in business by breaking up illegal trusts and regulating railroads and the food and drug industries.

Protecting the environment. The president may have achieved his most enduring legacy in the field of conservation. He recognized that America's natural resources were limited and that the needs of business had always taken precedent over the environment. "In the past, we have admitted the right of the individual to injure the future of the Republic for his own present profit," he charged. "The time has come for a change."

Practice

GUIDED PRACTICE

On the chalkboard write *Roosevelt's Square Deal*. Underneath, draw a three-column chart with these headings: *Problem, Promise,* and *Action*. Help students to complete the chart with entries that relate Roosevelt's Square Deal promises and philosophy to the actions he took to address the problems of the early 1900s.

INDEPENDENT PRACTICE

Have students use the information in the Guided Practice chart to "grade" ("A" to "F") Theodore Roosevelt as a reform president and to write paragraphs explaining their evaluations. Students may wish to include their evaluations in their portfolios.

Review and Assessment

REVIEW Direct students to create an annotated time line of domestic affairs during the Roosevelt presidency. Students may wish to include their time lines in their portfolios. Then assign the Section 2 Review on p. 198.

ASSESS Assign the **Section 2 Daily Quiz** in *Core Resources*.

▶

Never content with mere talk, Roosevelt withdrew from sale millions of acres of public land and set aside some 150 million acres as forest reserves. At his urging, Congress created national parks and wildlife sanctuaries and in 1902 passed the **Newlands Reclamation Act**. The act allowed money from the sales of public land to be used for irrigation and **reclamation**—the process of making damaged land productive again. Moreover, a 1908 White House conference on conservation led to the creation of a National Conservation Commission to study natural resource issues and to the establishment of conservation agencies in 41 states.

■■ **Roosevelt saved public lands from destructive development and created wildlife sanctuaries and national parks.**

Then and Now — NATIONAL PARKS

In the late 1800s government, industry, and most Americans still believed there was no end to the nation's natural resources. Between the 1850s and the 1870s alone, millions of acres of public land were sold cheaply or even given away to mining, logging, and railroad companies for development.

However, an increasing number of Americans, including Theodore Roosevelt, believed the country's lands and wildlife were being recklessly destroyed. During his two terms in office, President Roosevelt fought for programs to protect public land and historic sites.

Many opposed Roosevelt's efforts, believing the economic value of the reserved land outweighed the need to conserve it. But in 1916, largely as a result of Roosevelt's efforts, Congress created the National Park Service to maintain and oversee the country's 10 national parks and 21 national monuments. Today, the National Park Service manages some 355 sites on 80 million acres of land.

Although the number and size of parks have increased tremendously since Roosevelt's day, one problem facing the Park Service remains unchanged. The agency is still caught between those who wish to preserve and expand park land and those who want to use the parks' resources.

▲ **Yellowstone National Park was established in 1872. Shown here is a detail from Thomas Moran's painting of the park, *Grand Canyon of the Yellowstone*.**

Conservationists charge that clear-cutting, strip mining, and overdevelopment are destroying wildlife habitats and old-growth forests. Logging and

mining interests counter that the demand for wood and mineral products—not to mention the protection of thousands of industry jobs—requires the use of park resources. Lawmakers are caught in the middle, hoping to please voters on both sides of the issue.

Lawmakers—and Park Service officials—also face the problem of trying to maintain the parks while containing costs. More than 250 million people visit the national parks annually, and some officials argue that the visitors are literally "loving the parks to death." To counteract the strain on park resources, officials have proposed that visitation be limited in certain popular parks.

The future of the national parks is far from settled. But all sides in the debate might well consider Teddy Roosevelt's words: "A nation is obligated to manage its resources for the greatest good of the greatest number over the long run."

Then and Now

Point out that the first director of the National Park Service was Stephen T. Mather, a Chicago businessman. After seeing the impact of overgrazing on Yosemite National Park, Mather wrote a letter noting his concerns to Secretary of the Interior Frank Lane. Lane later invited Mather to run the parks.

THE AMERICAN NATION VIDEODISC PROGRAM

Yosemite National Park

1B   08593   4:04

Map Caption Answer
(for map on p. 198)
Alaska

RETEACH Ask students to draw a chart with the following column headings: *Trustbusting, Protecting the Consumer, Protecting the Environment*. Have students complete the chart by listing the actions taken by Roosevelt in these three areas.

Closure

Have students write a paragraph that answers the following questions: *What do you think was the single most important action taken by President Roosevelt? Why?* Ask volunteers to present and defend their paragraphs.

Extension

COMPARE Encourage students to research the federal government's involvement in conservation today and compare it with the government's role in environmental issues during the early 1900s.

RESEARCH Ask students to research editorial cartoons about Teddy Roosevelt and present their findings to the class.

SECTION REVIEW ANSWERS

IDENTIFY

For significance, see the following pages:
Theodore Roosevelt (p. 194)
Leon Czolgosz (p. 194)
arbitration (p. 195)
Square Deal (p. 195)
Judge Alton Parker (p. 195)
Elkins Act (p. 196)
Hepburn Act (p. 196)
Meat Inspection Act (p. 196)
Pure Food and Drug Act (p. 196)
Newlands Reclamation Act (p. 197)
reclamation (p. 197)

1. *to limit the power of trusts, promote public health and safety, and improve working conditions*
2. *broke up illegal trusts, regulated railroads and other companies engaged in interstate commerce, regulated food and drug industries*
3. *required government inspection of meat shipped between states; forbade the manufacture, sale, or transportation of food and patent medicine with harmful ingredients*
4. *Reports might state that land was destroyed by industry. Action plan might advise creating forest reserves, wildlife sanctuaries, and national parks.*
5. *Possible positions: miners might favor it because government protected the workers; owners might oppose it because it forced them to negotiate.*

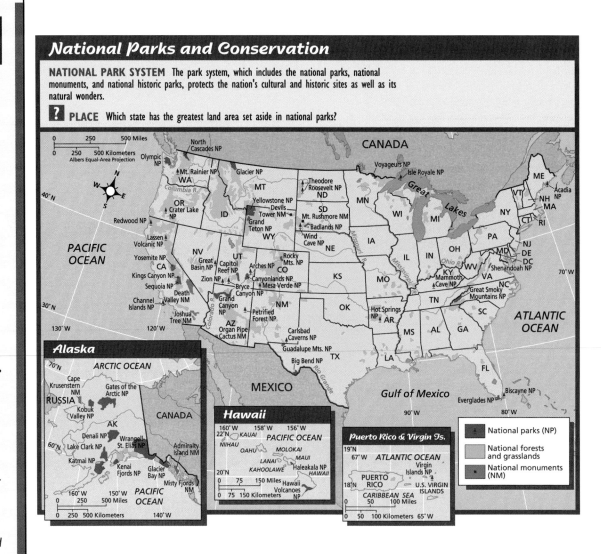

National Parks and Conservation

NATIONAL PARK SYSTEM The park system, which includes the national parks, national monuments, and national historic parks, protects the nation's cultural and historic sites as well as its natural wonders.

? PLACE Which state has the greatest land area set aside in national parks?

Legend:
- ▲ National parks (NP)
- National forests and grasslands
- ■ National monuments (NM)

■■ SECTION 2 REVIEW

IDENTIFY and explain the significance of the following: Theodore Roosevelt, Leon Czolgosz, arbitration, Square Deal, Judge Alton Parker, Elkins Act, Hepburn Act, Meat Inspection Act, Pure Food and Drug Act, Newlands Reclamation Act, reclamation.

1. **MAIN IDEA** What did Roosevelt pledge to accomplish through the Square Deal?
2. **MAIN IDEA** What actions did Roosevelt take against trusts and railroads?
3. **MAIN IDEA** How did the Meat Inspection Act and Pure Food and Drug Act try to protect consumers?
4. **WRITING TO EXPLAIN** Imagine you are a member of the National Conservation Commission. Write a report to the president, evaluating the impact that business has had on natural resources and offering a plan of action for protecting those resources.
5. **TAKING A STAND** Roosevelt's handling of the Pennsylvania coal miners' strike represented a new approach to labor relations. Take a stand either on the side of the miners or the mine owners and explain how that group might feel about Roosevelt's solution.

PREVIEW WORKSHOP

*Following is a list of the significant
people and terms in this section.
You may wish to use this list as a
section preview.*

People
- William Howard Taft
- Nelson Aldrich
- Richard Ballinger
- Gifford Pinchot

- Joseph Cannon
- George Norris
- Woodrow Wilson
- Eugene Debs

Terms
- Mann-Elkins Act
- Sixteenth Amendment
- New Nationalism
- New Freedom

FOCUS OBJECTIVES

- Describe the reforms carried out by President Taft.

- Explain why Taft lost the progressives' support.

- Examine the result of the 1912 election.

Section 3

REFORM UNDER TAFT

F O C U S
- **What reforms did President Taft carry out?**
- **Why did Taft lose the progressives' support?**
- **What was the result of the 1912 election?**

*A*lthough a financial panic and sharp depression hit the nation in 1907, President Roosevelt remained popular. The Republican nomination was his for the asking, but having served almost two full terms, he chose not to run again. The Republicans then turned to William Howard Taft, who easily won the 1908 election. In some ways, Taft carried on Roosevelt's reform program. But as his term wore on, progressives became more and more unhappy with his actions.

Taft and Sherman
campaign banner, 1908

TAFT TAKES OFFICE

At the 1908 Republican convention, Roosevelt supported his secretary of war, William Howard Taft, who won the nomination on the first ballot. The Democrats again nominated William Jennings Bryan, whose prolabor platform won the backing of the American Federation of Labor. Despite labor's support, the Democrats lost the election by a wide margin.

From the start it was clear that Taft would be a different sort of president than Roosevelt. Roosevelt enjoyed being in the public eye. Taft was just the opposite. "I don't like politics," he once wrote. "I don't like the limelight."

A smart but cautious man, Taft stressed the limits on his power as president, rather than his potential for leadership. Nevertheless, he chalked up an impressive list of accomplishments. His administration filed 90 antitrust suits, more than twice the number begun under Roosevelt. At Taft's urging, Congress passed the **Mann-Elkins Act** in 1910, extending the regulatory powers of the Interstate Commerce Commission to telephone and telegraph companies.

Taft also advanced the cause of conservation. He added vast areas to the nation's forest reserves. Taft also supported reforms to aid working people. With his approval, Congress created the Department of Labor to enforce labor laws. It also passed mine-safety laws and established an eight-hour workday for employees of companies holding contracts with the federal government.

The Taft administration was partly responsible, too, for the adoption of the **Sixteenth Amendment**. Proposed in 1909 and ratified in 1913, the amendment authorizes a national tax

CORE RESOURCES

• **Section 3 Daily Quiz**

MOTIVATING: PRIOR KNOWLEDGE

Ask for volunteers to state Roosevelt's reform achievements. Have students write the responses in their notebooks. Then, as students read this section, direct them to compare the reform record of William Howard Taft with that of Roosevelt.

Teaching the Section

TAFT THE REFORMER

On the chalkboard draw a four-column chart with the following headings: *Business Regulation, Conservation, Labor Issues, Economic Policy*. Call on volunteers to enumerate Taft's actions in these areas as you note their responses in the appropriate column. Then have students use the information in the chart to write a paragraph

summarizing Taft's achievements as a reformer. Students may wish to include their summaries in their portfolios.

HISTORICAL SIDELIGHTS

A Tariff for the Rich?

Some people saw the Payne-Aldrich Tariff as an example of how wealthy business leaders controlled conservatives in the Senate. As evidence they pointed to the fact that imported fine art was one of the few items exempted from the tariff. This exemption allowed rich Americans to bring works of art from Europe duty-free. For example, J. Pierpont Morgan, the banker and financier, saved a fortune in tariffs on the importation of his European art collection, which was valued at some $20 million.

HISTORICAL SIDELIGHTS

An Expected Firing

Pinchot was not surprised at being fired, and he held no animosity toward Taft for taking such action. Taft, Pinchot said, "was perfectly justified in firing me. I had asked for it and I could not complain."

■■ Ask students to discuss whether they would risk losing a job over a matter of principle.

PRESIDENTIAL LIVES

WILLIAM H. TAFT
1857–1930

in office
1909–1913

Bill Taft was an unhappy president—at heart a judge, not a politician. He seemed ill suited for public office, dozing off at official dinners or Cabinet meetings, forgetting names, procrastinating, and being tactless at the worst moments. When leaving the White House, he welcomed incoming President Woodrow Wilson by saying, "I'm glad to be going. This is the lonesomest place in the world."

What Taft really wanted was a seat on the U.S. Supreme Court. Taft had had a distinguished legal career, serving as U.S. solicitor general, as a federal judge, as a president of the American Bar Association, and as a law professor at Yale University. In 1921 Taft got his wish—he was appointed chief justice of the Supreme Court. "Presidents come and go," a happy Taft said, "but the Court goes on forever."

based on individual income. Progressives had long supported such a tax as a way to fund needed governmental programs in a fair manner.

■■ **Taft's administration supported the Mann-Elkins Act, conservation programs, labor reforms, and the Sixteenth Amendment.**

*T*AFT ANGERS THE PROGRESSIVES

Despite these reforms, Taft lost the support of progressive Republicans. The split between the

president and the progressives began in April 1909 with the passage of a tariff bill.

Both Taft and the progressives favored tariff reductions to lower the prices of consumer goods. Some members of Congress, however, wanted high tariffs to protect American industry. They won out when the House sent a low-tariff bill to the Senate, and Nelson Aldrich of Rhode Island turned it into a high-tariff measure.

Taft could have vetoed the bill, now called the Payne-Aldrich Tariff, or he could have pressured Aldrich to change the rates. But Taft lacked the political skill to oppose conservative Republicans in Congress. Despite his misgivings, he signed the bill. To make matters worse, he proceeded to call it the best tariff ever passed. Outraged progressives accused Taft of betraying the reform cause.

Progressives also attacked Taft for sabotaging Roosevelt's conservation program. The dispute revolved around Taft's secretary of the interior, Richard Ballinger, who believed that the Roosevelt administration had exceeded its authority when it stopped the sale of public land. Ballinger approved the sale of a vast tract of coal-rich Alaska timberland. The head of the U.S. Forest Service, Gifford Pinchot (PIN-shoh), an ardent conservationist and Roosevelt's friend, attacked Ballinger for favoring private interests over conservation. Taft warned Pinchot to stop criticizing Ballinger. When Pinchot did not stop, Taft fired him.

For progressives the Ballinger-Pinchot affair signaled Taft's weakness on conservation.

▼ This cartoon appeared in the *Tacoma News Tribune* in 1919 and satirizes Taft's awkward position in the Ballinger-Pinchot affair.

PROGRESSIVES CRITICIZE TAFT

Organize students into groups and ask them to imagine they are progressive Republicans during Taft's presidency. Direct each group to prepare a press release explaining why it is dissatisfied with Taft's performance as president and what it intends to do if he seeks reelection. Invite volunteers to present their groups' press releases at a "news conference" and to respond to questions about their positions from class members in the role of reporters.

THE 1912 ELECTION

Organize students into groups of four and assign each group member one of the following roles: a reporter, William Howard Taft, Teddy Roosevelt, Woodrow Wilson. Direct reporters to interview the candidates in the aftermath of the election of 1912. Have reporters ask the candidates to discuss their strengths and weaknesses, the major issues of the election, and the impact a third-party candidate had on the outcome of the election. Ask for volunteer groups to conduct their interviews for the rest of the class. Have the reporters from the remaining groups summarize for the class the results of their interviews.

Although his administration later restored the Alaska land to the federal forest reserve, the episode hurt the Republicans in the 1910 congressional elections. For the first time in 16 years, the Republicans lost control of the House of Representatives.

◀ The Progressive, or Bull Moose, party held its convention in Chicago on August 5, 1912. Delegates paraded through the aisles, singing "Onward Christian Soldiers," and unanimously nominated Theodore Roosevelt for president. Souvenirs from the Bull Moose campaign are shown here.

■■ **Taft lost progressive support when he signed the Payne-Aldrich Tariff and fired conservationist Gifford Pinchot.**

Taft made one particularly dangerous enemy—Theodore Roosevelt, who broke with Taft over the Pinchot controversy. In the congressional elections of 1910, Roosevelt campaigned for progressive Republicans who opposed Taft and the party's conservative wing. In a speech at Osawatomie (oh-suh-WAHT-uh-mee), Kansas, Roosevelt offered his **New Nationalism**—a bold program of social legislation calling for tough laws to protect workers, ensure public health, and regulate business. He declared:

❝ The true friend of property, the true conservative, is he who insists that property shall be the servant and not the master of the commonwealth. . . . The citizens of the United States must effectively control the mighty commercial forces which they have themselves called into being. **❞**

Government, Roosevelt said, must become the "steward of the public welfare." His call for a more activist federal government represented a far more liberal position than he had taken as president. Delighted, reformers hailed the New Nationalism as a revival of the progressive spirit.

𝒯HE REPUBLICAN PARTY DIVIDES

Not long before Roosevelt's speech, a bitter dispute in Congress had further deepened the gulf between Taft and the progressives. In the spring of 1910, progressive Republicans in Congress launched a major attack on Speaker of the House Joseph ("Uncle Joe") Cannon of Illinois, a conservative Republican.

Cannon, a 73-year-old tobacco-chewing poker player, was one of Washington's most powerful politicians. As Speaker he ruled the House with an iron hand, appointing all House committees and naming their chairmen. As head of the powerful Rules Committee, which determined the order of business in the House, Cannon prevented bills he opposed from even reaching the House floor for debate.

Progressives charged that Cannon used his great power to block reform legislation. ("Not one cent for scenery," he had growled in dismissing a call for environmental protection.) In March 1910 Congressman George Norris of Nebraska, a progressive, began an effort to break Cannon's power. Norris proposed that in the future, House members elect the Rules Committee and that the Speaker be excluded from membership.

After a heated debate, Norris's motion passed. A year later, the House also stripped the Speaker of the power to appoint members of the other committees—a major progressive victory. Throughout this bitter dispute, Taft refused to take sides, further alienating progressives.

By 1912 the conservative and the progressive wings of the Republican party were deeply divided. Theodore Roosevelt, by now completely at odds with Taft, decided to run again for the presidency. Borrowing a prizefighting term, he proclaimed: "My hat is in the ring." Roosevelt won almost every Republican state primary, including the one in Taft's own state, Ohio.

At the convention the Taft forces, firmly in control of the party machinery, refused to seat many of Roosevelt's delegates. When Taft won the nomination, Roosevelt's supporters angrily walked out, and held their own convention, adopting a platform based on the New Nationalism and nominating Roosevelt as their presidential candidate. Thus was born the Progressive party, also known as the Bull Moose party after Roosevelt declared that he felt "fit as a bull moose" to run.

HISTORICAL SIDELIGHTS

Low Opinion of Reform "Uncle Joe" Cannon looked upon reform and reformers with complete disdain, reserving special scorn for "the chief muckraker," his name for Roosevelt. Cannon once contemptuously referred to Republican progressives in Congress as being "tainted with Teddyism."

PRIMARY SOURCE

Description of Change: excerpted
Rationale: excerpted to focus on main idea

MAKING CONNECTIONS

Language Arts
"Throw your hat in the ring" is an American term, first recorded in the early 1800s. At country fairs, boxing champions often took on all comers. Throwing a hat in the ring of spectators was a signal that you were willing to fight the champion. The phrase took on the political meaning of declaring candidacy for public office after Roosevelt used it in the 1912 campaign.

Practice

GUIDED PRACTICE

Ask for volunteers to identify the major legislation and issues of Taft's administration. Write their responses on the chalkboard. Guide students to arrange the information on the chalkboard into two columns in their notebooks, one headed *Positive Impact on Reform* and the other headed *Negative Impact on Reform*. Then invite students to share and compare their lists.

INDEPENDENT PRACTICE

Have students use the information from the Guided Practice to create election posters or editorial cartoons that express their views of Taft as a progressive reformer. Students may wish to include their work in their portfolios.

Review and Assessment

REVIEW Suggest that students write the main ideas of the section in the form of newspaper headlines. Ask for volunteers to present their headlines, and have the class discuss what might be included in articles that accompany the headlines. Then assign the Section 3 Review on p. 203.

ASSESS Assign the **Section 3 Daily Quiz** in *Core Resources*.

MULTICULTURAL PERSPECTIVES

French political writer Charles Oster, who came to America to observe the 1912 election, commented on the difficulties Taft had faced during his presidency in following someone with the personality of Roosevelt: "Mr. Taft was not the kind of President the people needed in 1908. The rank and file felt this even when they elected him. Since his election that feeling has increased. . . . The people wanted a fighter . . . a Jefferson or a Jackson, and Mr. Taft is not of that type. . . . With all the good he has done in awakening the country from a long sleep and . . . with all the popularity he won by such a course, Mr. Roosevelt was an overpowering adversary for Mr. Taft."

PRIMARY SOURCE

Description of Change: excerpted
Rationale: excerpted to focus on main idea

Chart Caption Answer
1912

Map Caption Answer
(for map on p. 203)
California, with 11 for Roosevelt, 2 for Wilson

▲ **Part of the speech**
Theodore Roosevelt delivered on October 14, 1912, and the eyeglass case he carried are shown here. Notice the bullet holes made during the attempted assassination.

Roosevelt's candidacy, however, almost ended on October 14, 1912, when a deranged man shot him in the chest during a campaign stop. Roosevelt went ahead with his planned speech, despite the bullet lodged in his body. This reckless display of courage reinforced his image as a larger-than-life hero.

■■ **When Roosevelt failed to win the Republican presidential nomination from Taft, he formed the Progressive party.**

A DEMOCRATIC VICTORY IN 1912

Although Roosevelt's campaign continued to pick up steam, the division in the Republican party practically assured a Democratic victory. Roosevelt and Taft were likely to split the Republican vote, while Democrats united behind one candidate. Their choice was Governor Woodrow Wilson of New Jersey, who ran on a platform calling for tariff reduction, banking reform, laws benefiting wage earners and farmers, and stronger antitrust legislation.

Wilson, a native of Virginia and a political newcomer, had long nurtured dreams of high office. In college he had made calling cards proclaiming "Thomas Woodrow Wilson, Senator from Virginia." He eventually became a professor at Princeton University in New Jersey and later served as its president. He was elected governor in 1910. In his short time as governor, he fought the state's Democratic party bosses and pushed through laws regulating business. As an outspoken reformer and eloquent speaker, Wilson was the presidential choice of progressives in the Democratic party.

In the 1912 campaign, Wilson brilliantly captured the nation's reform mood. His program, the **New Freedom**, called for a revival of small business and a return to an America where the "little guy" was free from the control of big business and government. Wilson asserted:

❝ The only way that government is kept pure is by keeping . . . channels open, so that . . . there will constantly be coming new blood into the veins of the body politic. ❞

RISE OF THE SOCIALIST PARTY
Number of Socialist Votes, 1900–1920

Election Year	1900	1904	1908	1912	1916	1920
Presidential	87,814	402,283	420,793	900,672	585,113	919,799
Gubernatorial	0	73,914	13,694	386,828	125,907	230,907
Congressional	8,021	138,201	113,450	1,599,420	770,230	1,128,200

Sources: *Congressional Quarterly's Guide to U.S. Elections* (for gubernatorial and congressional),
Historical Statistics of the United States (for presidential)

THE SOCIALIST CHALLENGE Dramatic social changes at the turn of the century spurred the popularity of the prolabor, reform-minded Socialist party.

? **BUILDING CHART SKILLS** In which year did Socialist candidates obtain the largest number of overall votes?

RETEACH Have students work in groups and assign individuals or pairs the task of outlining subsections. Have students exchange outlines and use them to ask questions of other members of their group.

Close

Write the following statement on the chalkboard: *Taft was a conservative, not a progressive.* Ask students to present arguments that support or challenge the statement.

Extension

INVESTIGATE Encourage students to investigate other significant third-party or independent presidential candidates, such as George Wallace and H. Ross Perot, and to report on the role they played in presidential elections.

ANALYZE Have students research the New Nationalism program and analyze how it represented the ideals and principles of progressivism.

Although Wilson shared the progressive belief in government as an agent of reform, he believed that making government too strong could stifle individual freedom. He believed that the goal of reform should be to rid the system of corruption so that free competition could flourish, without significantly altering the system itself. In this regard he differed from Roosevelt and especially from another candidate for president, Eugene Debs of the Socialist party. The Socialist party supported worker control of the government and public ownership of all major industries. The party had done very well in the 1910 elections.

Among Debs, Wilson, and Roosevelt, American voters had a choice of three strong reform-minded candidates. Even Taft supported reform programs, although he appeared to represent a more conservative viewpoint.

As expected, Wilson won the election, receiving 435 electoral votes to 88 for Roosevelt and 8 for Taft. Debs won over 900,000 popular votes but no electoral votes. Out of more than 15 million votes cast, the three reform candidates received some 11 million. Some 1,200 Socialist candidates, including 79 mayors, were elected to offices across the country, reflecting the desire for new approaches to government. Although Wilson won just six million popular votes, he took office with a strong mandate for reform.

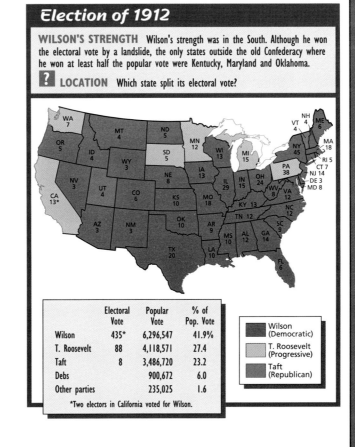

Election of 1912

WILSON'S STRENGTH Wilson's strength was in the South. Although he won the electoral vote by a landslide, the only states outside the old Confederacy where he won at least half the popular vote were Kentucky, Maryland and Oklahoma.

? LOCATION Which state split its electoral vote?

	Electoral Vote	Popular Vote	% of Pop. Vote
Wilson	435*	6,296,547	41.9%
T. Roosevelt	88	4,118,571	27.4
Taft	8	3,486,720	23.2
Debs		900,672	6.0
Other parties		235,025	1.6

*Two electors in California voted for Wilson.

- Wilson (Democratic)
- T. Roosevelt (Progressive)
- Taft (Republican)

■■ The split in the Republican vote and the public support for reform enabled Woodrow Wilson to win the 1912 presidential election.

SECTION REVIEW ANSWERS

IDENTIFY

For significance, see the following pages:
William Howard Taft (p. 199)
Mann-Elkins Act (p. 199)
Sixteenth Amendment (p. 199)
Nelson Aldrich (p. 200)
Richard Ballinger (p. 200)
Gifford Pinchot (p. 200)
New Nationalism (p. 201)
Joseph Cannon (p. 201)
George Norris (p. 201)
Woodrow Wilson (p. 202)
New Freedom (p. 202)
Eugene Debs (p. 203)

1. *supported Mann-Elkins Act, conservation programs, labor reforms, Sixteenth Amendment (income tax)*
2. *signed Payne-Aldrich Tariff, was accused of sabotaging Roosevelt's conservation program*
3. *It split the Republican vote, practically assuring a Democratic victory.*
4. *Speeches should explain New Nationalism (tough laws to protect workers, ensure public health, and regulate business) and should criticize Taft's control of the Republican party.*
5. *no, because Taft's administration extended reforms begun under TR, filed more than twice the number of antitrust suits, preserved much land, did more for labor than TR*

◧ S E C T I O N 3 R E V I E W

IDENTIFY and explain the significance of the following: William Howard Taft, Mann-Elkins Act, Sixteenth Amendment, Nelson Aldrich, Richard Ballinger, Gifford Pinchot, New Nationalism, Joseph Cannon, George Norris, Woodrow Wilson, New Freedom, Eugene Debs.

1. **MAIN IDEA** What contributions did the Taft administration make to reform?

2. **MAIN IDEA** What actions caused Taft to lose the support of progressives?

3. **MAIN IDEA** How did the Progressive party help determine the outcome of the 1912 presidential election?

4. **WRITING TO EXPRESS A VIEWPOINT** Imagine you are Teddy Roosevelt. Write a speech explaining your plan of action and why you formed the Progressive party.

5. **DISTINGUISHING FACT FROM OPINION** Supporters of the Progressive party believed that Taft had not lived up to the progressive ideals of the Roosevelt administration. Comparing Taft's reform record to Roosevelt's, was this a fair assessment? Why or why not?

Following is a list of the significant people and terms in this section. You may wish to use this list as a section preview.

People
- Alice Paul
- Carrie Chapman Catt

Terms
- Underwood Tariff Act
- Federal Reserve Act
- Clayton Antitrust Act
- Federal Trade Commission
- Federal Farm Loan Act
- Adamson Act
- Federal Workmen's Compensation Act
- Keating-Owen Child Labor Act
- Nineteenth Amendment

FOCUS OBJECTIVES

- Outline the achievements of the Wilson administration in the areas of tariff and banking reforms and business regulation.

- Explain how women won the right to vote.

- Determine the major success of progressivism.

PRIMARY SOURCE

Description of Change: excerpted
Rationale: excerpted to focus on main idea

204

Section 4

WILSON'S "NEW FREEDOM"

FOCUS

- **What did the Wilson administration achieve in the areas of tariff and banking reforms and business regulation?**
- **How did women win the right to vote?**
- **What was the major success of progressivism?**

$\mathcal{D}$uring the 1912 campaign, Woodrow Wilson pledged to restore opportunity in American life. Once in office, Wilson moved to lower tariffs, reform banking, regulate corporations, and aid farmers and wage earners. As Wilson began his second term in office, progressives could claim some success in their efforts to improve American life. Yet much remained to be done. Progressives had barely begun to clean up government and regulate business, women still did not have the right to vote, and the pledge of equal opportunity for all Americans remained unfulfilled.

Suffragist demonstrating in front of the White House, about 1916

REFORM ON MANY FRONTS

On March 4, 1913, President Wilson gave his first inaugural address in which he eloquently summed up the spirit of the progressive reform movement:

❝ We have been proud of our industrial achievements, but we have not . . . stopped . . . to count the . . . fearful physical and spiritual cost to the men and women and children upon whom the . . . weight and burden of it all has fallen. . . . This is not a day of triumph; it is a day of dedication. Here muster, not the forces of party, but the forces of humanity. ❞

A month later, Wilson presented his legislative agenda. It included tariff and banking reforms and stronger antitrust laws. Opposed by business groups and lobbyists, Wilson used all his skill to rally support for his program, both in Congress and among the American people.

Wilson's first priority was to lower tariffs. Well aware that big business had blocked tariff reduction during Taft's presidency, Wilson mounted a public campaign to undermine the business lobby and overcome Senate opposition. His

◀ Woodrow Wilson is shown delivering his first inaugural address on March 4, 1913.

MOTIVATING:
LINK TO TODAY

Ask students what they know from newspaper, magazine, and television reports about women's roles in politics today. List responses on a flip chart. As students read the section have them compare the present-day political role of women with their role in 1919.

Teaching the Section

TARIFF AND BANKING REFORM

Organize students into small groups and suggest that they imagine they are public-relations advisers to President Wilson. Inform groups that their task is to develop a media campaign to "sell" to the American public Wilson's reforms for tariff and banking. Invite groups to present and explain their campaigns to the class.

▶

PRESIDENTIAL LIVES
WOODROW WILSON
1856–1924

in office
1913–1921

Woodrow Wilson had a reputation for being very serious and often inflexible. He hated political compromise and at times would oppose legislation he originally proposed if it was amended by someone else. He once told a political associate, "I am sorry for those who disagree with me. . . . Because I know they are wrong."

Yet, despite his public image, Wilson often surprised his close associates with

sudden displays of humorous behavior. Once when Wilson was riding in the country with a Secret Service agent, they passed a small boy on the road. "Did you see what that boy did?" Wilson said to the agent, very seriously "He made a face at me." Then the president asked, "Did you see what I did?" "No, Sir," said the agent. With a boyish grin, Wilson replied, "I made a face right back!"

---

strategy worked. In 1913 Congress passed the **Underwood Tariff Act**, which reduced tariffs to their lowest levels in 50 years. To make up for the lost revenue, the bill imposed a graduated income tax, taxing people with high incomes at a higher rate than those with low incomes.

Next on Wilson's agenda was banking. At the time, there was no central fund that banks could borrow from to prevent collapse during financial panics. Thus, when many people withdrew their deposits at the same time, banks commonly failed. Reform was clearly necessary, but Americans disagreed on how to change the banking system. Conservative business groups wanted to give the nation's large private banks more control. In contrast, many Democrats and progressive Republicans wanted the government to run the system.

The **Federal Reserve Act** of 1913, which Wilson helped pass, combined these two views. It created a three-level banking system. At the top was the Federal Reserve Board, a group appointed by the president and charged with running the system. At the second level were 12 Federal Reserve banks, under mixed public and private control. These "bankers' banks" served other banks rather than individuals. At the third level were private banks, which could borrow from the Federal Reserve banks at interest rates set by the Board.

■■ **Wilson worked to secure passage of the Underwood Tariff Act and the Federal Reserve Act.**

WILSON AND BIG BUSINESS

Having achieved important tariff and banking reforms, Wilson turned to business regulation. He wanted to limit the power of monopolies, which he viewed as a threat to small business. Toward this end, he backed passage of the **Clayton Antitrust Act** of 1914. This act clarified and extended the 1890 Sherman Antitrust Act by clearly stating what corporations could not do. For example, companies could not sell goods below cost to drive competitors out of business. They also could not buy competing companies' stock to create a monopoly.

The Wilson administration also backed the creation of the **Federal Trade Commission** (FTC). The FTC, which Congress established in 1914, was

◀ **This 1913 cartoon portrays Wilson's use of antitrust legislation to protect small businesses from the unfair competition of monopolies and other large corporations.**

HISTORICAL SIDELIGHTS

Income Tax
The first nation to impose a general income tax was Great Britain, which it did in 1799 to finance its war in Europe against Napoleon. In the United States, Congress created an income tax in 1862 to finance the war against the Confederacy, but this tax ended 10 years later. Another income tax was enacted in 1894. However, the Supreme Court ruled that law unconstitutional, a ruling that launched the campaign to amend the Constitution.

HISTORICAL SIDELIGHTS

Clayton's Intentions
Wilson's antitrust legislation was named for its chief author, Democratic Representative Henry D. Clayton of Alabama. Clayton's main intention in writing the bill was to delineate clearly which business practices were illegal—a task that the Sherman Antitrust Act had failed to do.

Teaching the Section

REGULATING BUSINESS, AIDING WORKERS

Randomly assign students the following characters: owner of big business, farmer, union member, railroad worker, federal worker. Have students write 25-word telegrams to President Wilson, urging him to support legislation that affects their characters. Then ask a representative of each character to read his or her telegram to the class.

Changing Ways

THE ARMORY SHOW

SETTING THE SCENE

A number of the American artists involved in the Armory Show were no strangers to controversy or negative criticism. In 1908 they had taken part in an exhibition called "Eight American Painters." The works on display, many of which had been rejected the previous year by the National Academy of Design, featured realistic portrayals of the seedier side of city life—barrooms, back alleys, and so on. As a result, critics contemptuously referred to these eight artists as the "Ash Can School."

CRITICAL THINKING

Point out that new developments in the arts commonly cause controversy. Have students write a paragraph on why such new developments always seem to shock some people.

■ Ask students if they can identify recent examples of art or pop culture that caused controversy.

Changing Ways — THE 1913 ARMORY SHOW

The progressive reform spirit influenced art as well as economic policies in the early 1900s. Just as industry reformers attacked business trusts, progressive artists tackled the leading American museums' monopoly in determining which paintings and sculptures the public saw.

Resistant to change, the mainstream art community in America was hostile to the "radical" ideas and techniques of the growing modern art movement in Europe. Modernists such as Picasso, Van Gogh, Matisse, and Cézanne offered a new art style, which blurred the lines between reality and fantasy.

Resolved to introduce the American public to modern art, a small group of independent artists formed the Association of American Painters and Sculptors (AAPS) in 1912. The group planned an international exhibition, combing galleries and studios in Munich, Berlin, Paris, and the Hague for works to display. On February 17, 1913, the International Exhibition of Modern Art opened in the 69th Regiment Armory in New York City. The Armory Show presented some 1,300 works by both European and American artists.

Newspaper reporters raved about the show, calling it "an event not to be missed."

▲ The Armory Show introduced contemporary European artists and works of art, such as Marcel Duchamp's *Nude Descending a Staircase,* to a curious, but often puzzled, American public.

Art critics were not so kind. They blasted Van Gogh as "unskilled" and Cézanne as "absolutely without talent." As for Duchamp's *Nude Descending a Staircase,* they described it as "a lot of disused golf clubs and bags" and "an explosion in a shingle factory."

Ironically, the critics' remarks boosted attendance, which exceeded the organizers' wildest dreams. People came primarily to gape. "I remember one woman becoming so hysterical with laughter," an artist recalled, "that she actually rolled over on the floor—I also remember [AAPS president] Arthur B. Davies taking Teddy Roosevelt through the show— Roosevelt waved his arms and stomped through the Galleries pointing at pictures and saying 'That's not art!' 'That's not art!'"

Even if it failed to enchant Americans with modern art, the Armory Show was a huge success in terms of attendance and publicity. Before the show moved to Chicago, AAPS honored its "friends and enemies" in the press with a beefsteak dinner. Glasses were raised; speeches were made; diners sang and danced. One critic summed up the general mood: "It was a good show, but don't do it again."

WOMEN AND THE VOTE

Ask students to write newspaper editorials supporting or opposing ratification of the Nineteenth Amendment. Suggest that their editorials might also include commentary on the tactics of the women's movement, the impact that women's suffrage would have on American democracy, or changes the vote might bring for women. Ask volunteers to read their editorials to the class. Students may wish to include their editorials in their portfolios.

THE PROGRESSIVE LEGACY

Organize students into groups of four or five and ask them to list the political, social, and economic accomplishments of the progressives. Instruct each group to use its list to review progressive reform and to draft a statement indicating what it believes to be the progressives' major success. Tell the groups that they must achieve consensus among their members on the statement. Have representatives of each group read its statement to the class and briefly summarize how it was developed. Then use the groups' statements to reach a class determination about the progressives' most important legacy. Also ask the class what it believes to be the most significant shortcoming of progressive reform. *(Students may suggest its implicit racism or its imposition of white middle-class values on ethnic groups.)*

▶

authorized to investigate corporations and issue "cease and desist orders" to those engaged in unfair or fraudulent practices and to use the courts to enforce its rulings. Among the abuses the FTC targeted were mislabeled products and false claims.

■■ **Wilson backed passage of the Clayton Antitrust Act and creation of the Federal Trade Commission.**

WILSON AND WORKERS

The Wilson administration also supported legislation to aid working people. The **Federal Farm Loan Act** provided low-interest loans to farmers. The Clayton Antitrust Act included a provision that affirmed labor's right to strike so long as property was not irreparably damaged. The **Adamson Act** reduced the workday for railroad workers from 10 to 8 hours, with no cut in pay. This law not only won applause from reformers but avoided a threatened railroad strike. With Wilson's support, Congress also passed the **Federal Workmen's Compensation Act**, which provided benefits to federal workers injured on the job.

The Wilson administration was less successful in the campaign against child labor. For years progressives had wanted to get young children out of the mills, factories, and mines (see Chapter 7). As labor organizer Mother Jones later recalled:

❝ Every day little children came into Union Headquarters, some with their hands off, . . . some with their fingers off at the knuckle. They were stooped little things, round shouldered and skinny. Many were not over ten years of age. ❞

Faced with rising protests against child labor from the National Consumers' League and other groups, Congress passed the **Keating-Owen Child Labor Act** in 1916. This act, which had Wilson's backing, outlawed the interstate sale of products produced by child labor. In 1918, however, the Supreme Court declared the law unconstitutional because it restricted commerce instead of directly outlawing child labor. Another law, passed in 1919, met the same fate. Not until the 1930s would the United States outlaw child labor.

𝒯HE STRUGGLE FOR WOMEN'S SUFFRAGE

Another part of the progressive agenda—the campaign for women's suffrage—faced strong opposition. Liquor interests feared that women would vote for prohibition. Businesses feared that the vote would empower women to demand better wages and working conditions. When one state senator expressed the widely held belief that the vote would rob women of their beauty and charm, a suffragist retorted:

❝ We have women working in the foundries. . . . Women in the laundries . . . stand for 13 or 14 hours in the terrible steam and heat with their hands in hot starch. Surely these women won't lose any

WOMEN'S SUFFRAGE

THROUGH OTHERS' EYES

In 1902 the first International Woman Suffrage Conference was held in Washington, D.C. The United States was among the nations represented that had not yet granted women national suffrage. Swedish delegate Emmy Evald remarked that in her homeland women had voted on some level since 1736. She then went on to point out the contradictions in the American situation:

❝*𝒴ou can not trust the ballot into the hands of women teachers in the public schools but you give it to men who can not read or write. You can not trust the ballot to women who are controlling millions of [dollars] and helping support the country but you give it to loafers and vagabonds who know nothing, have nothing and represent nothing. You can not trust the ballot in the hands of women who are the wives and daughters of your heroes but you give it to those who are willing to sell it for a glass of beer and you trust it in the hands of anarchists.* ❞

PRIMARY SOURCES

Description of Change: excerpted
Rationale: excerpted to focus on main idea

THROUGH OTHERS' EYES

The universal nature of the suffrage movement was underscored when conference delegates agreed to establish a permanent organization, the International Woman Suffrage Alliance. Its first meeting, held in Berlin in 1904, was attended by delegates from Australia, Britain, Denmark, Germany, the Netherlands, Norway, Sweden, and the United States.

PRIMARY SOURCE

Description of Change: excerpted and bracketed
Rationale: excerpted to focus on main idea; bracketed to clarify meaning

*P*ractice

GUIDED PRACTICE

Work with students to summarize Wilson's progressive reform accomplishments by creating on the chalkboard a three-column chart with the headings *Issue, Action,* and *Impact.* Ask students to provide and explain entries for the chart.

INDEPENDENT PRACTICE

Have students write letters to Washington during the Wilson administration urging their senator or representative to support one of the actions listed in the Guided Practice. Letters should explain why the writer believes the action is needed and what he or she expects its impact to be. Students may wish to include their letters in their portfolios.

*R*eview and *A*ssessment

REVIEW Have students work together to develop a list of five words that characterize progressivism. Ask students to use these words to write a paragraph that discusses Wilson's accomplishments as a progressive president. Then assign the Section 4 Review on p. 209.

ASSESS Assign the **Section 4 Daily Quiz** in *Core Resources.*

COOPERATIVE LEARNING

Organize students into three groups to create an illustrated time line of important events during the administrations of the three progressive presidents. Assign each group one of the administrations, and suggest that group members share tasks—research, artwork, writing, and so on. Have each group present its time line.

MULTICULTURAL PERSPECTIVES

Wilson's racial policies caused the NAACP in August 1913 to send him an open letter: "Should ten millions of our citizens say that their civic liberties and rights are not safe in your hands? To ask the question is to answer it. They desire a 'New Freedom' too, Mr. President." African American leader Booker T. Washington agreed. Writing to the publisher of the New York *Evening Post,* he observed, "I have never seen the colored people so discouraged and bitter as they are at the present time."

Map Caption Answer
the West

---

more of their beauty and charm by putting a ballot in a ballot box once a year than they are likely to lose standing in foundries or laundries all year. **99**

One leading force in the suffrage movement was the National American Woman Suffrage Association, or NAWSA, founded in 1890. Its first two presidents, Elizabeth Cady Stanton and Susan B. Anthony, took a local approach, trying to get state legislatures to grant women the vote. They achieved few successes in their first few years of lobbying, however.

In 1913 Alice Paul, a militant young Quaker suffragist, broke away from NAWSA and formed another organization, which in 1916 became the National Woman's party. It focused on passing an amendment to the Constitution guaranteeing

▲ Alice Paul

women the right to vote. When Wilson and the Democratic party failed to support woman suffrage in the 1916 election, the Woman's party campaigned against them. Wilson won, but narrowly. (See Chapter 10 for more on the election.)

Paul, who had studied in England, favored using the attention-getting protest tactics employed by British suffragists. For example, in January 1917, with Wilson reelected, the Woman's party began round-the-clock picketing of the White House in an effort to pressure Wilson to support a suffrage amendment. They held banners asking, "Mr. President, What Will You Do for Woman Suffrage?" and "How Long Must Women Wait for Liberty?" Many were arrested. Some went on hunger strikes in prison.

Meanwhile, the NAWSA, energized by the leadership of the highly skilled organizer Carrie Chapman Catt, continued to follow traditional political means to attain voting rights. Launching what came to be called her "Winning Plan" in 1916, the NAWSA won a string of successes for suffrage at the state level. After the United States entered World War I in 1917, leaders of the movement—along with millions of American women—lent strong support to the war effort. Their patriotism helped weaken opposition to women's suffrage. By 1919 thirty states had granted women full or partial voting rights. Finally, in 1919, the U.S. Congress passed the **Nineteenth Amendment**, granting women full voting rights. It was ratified in 1920.

Carrie Chapman Catt cautioned, however, that the vote was only an "entering wedge." Women still had to force their way through the "locked door" of political decision making.

:: In 1920, with ratification of the Nineteenth Amendment, American women won their long battle for the right to vote.

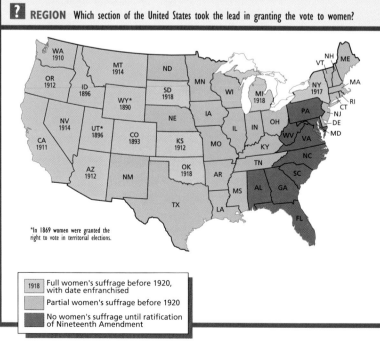

Women's Suffrage, 1920

FIGHTING FOR THE VOTE The National American Woman Suffrage Association worked to convince state legislatures to grant women the vote, while the National Woman's party campaigned for a constitutional amendment.

? **REGION** Which section of the United States took the lead in granting the vote to women?

In 1869 women were granted the right to vote in territorial elections.

| 1918 | Full women's suffrage before 1920, with date enfranchised |
| Partial women's suffrage before 1920 |
| No women's suffrage until ratification of Nineteenth Amendment |

RETEACH Suggest that students work together to divide and assign the section material according to headings and subheadings. Ask each student to write a question on the content of his or her assigned heading or subheading. Then use the questions to quiz the group on the section.

Closure

Ask students to write several sentences explaining which of the three presidents discussed in the chapter has the best claim to the title "progressive." Invite volunteers to reveal and defend their choices.

Extension

INVESTIGATE Have students investigate and report on Carrie Chapman Catt's "Winning Plan."

EVALUATE Suggest that students evaluate the success of progressive reform by responding to the following statement: *The progressives identified the problems but offered few working solutions.*

COMMENTARY

The Progressive Legacy

Although scholars agree that the progressive movement left a lasting legacy, they often disagree over how to define that legacy. Many scholars have noted that progressivism was primarily supported by fairly conservative, middle-class, white Americans trying to maintain some level of political and economic power. Many of the successes and shortcomings of the movement can be tied to its origins in the white middle class.

Progressivism made great strides in many areas; however, some of the economic and political reforms of the movement failed to bring about the radical changes anticipated. Such policies as the creation of the Federal Reserve System and implementation of a federal income tax did improve the government's ability to regulate the economy and pay for new programs. Yet, many regulations on businesses fell short of changing the capitalist system; corporations were eventually able to use the regulations to their own advantage. On the political front, reforms such as the initiative, referendum, and recall were primarily used on the local level and thus had little impact on broad questions of public policy.

One of progressivism's most successful elements, the settlement-house movement, increased emphasis on education, improved opportunities for women, brought great urban reform, and eased the plight of European immigrants. However, the settlement-house workers neglected to address the problems of African Americans, many of whom were new migrants from the rural South. This was one of progressivism's greatest shortcomings.

The progressive presidents certainly showed little interest in racial issues. President Wilson was the least sympathetic to African American concerns. During his administration numerous bills designed to institute segregation were submitted to Congress. Although none passed, Wilson issued an executive order segregating eating and restroom facilities for federal employees. Wilson argued that this policy prevented friction between white and black workers, but African Americans strongly protested it as racist.

Despite these shortcomings, however, progressives took real strides toward making the new industrial society more just and orderly. Their greatest legacy was in demonstrating that America's democratic system could respond and adapt to changes in American life.

■ **Although progressivism fell short of some of its goals and failed to address racism, it made industrial society more just and humane.**

SECTION 4 REVIEW

IDENTIFY and explain the significance of the following: Underwood Tariff Act, Federal Reserve Act, Clayton Antitrust Act, Federal Trade Commission, Federal Farm Loan Act, Adamson Act, Federal Workmen's Compensation Act, Keating-Owen Child Labor Act, Alice Paul, Carrie Chapman Catt, Nineteenth Amendment.

1. **MAIN IDEA** How did Wilson hope to reduce tariffs and reform the banking system?
2. **MAIN IDEA** How did the Wilson administration attempt to regulate business?
3. **MAIN IDEA** What did the passage of the Nineteenth Amendment accomplish?
4. **WRITING TO EVALUATE** Write a paragraph evaluating the legacy of progressivism.
5. **ANALYZING** How successful was Wilson in enlisting the "forces of humanity" to help farmers, railroad and federal workers, and child laborers?

SECTION REVIEW ANSWERS

IDENTIFY

For significance, see the following pages:
Underwood Tariff Act (p. 205)
Federal Reserve Act (p. 205)
Clayton Antitrust Act (p. 205)
Federal Trade Commission (p. 205)
Federal Farm Loan Act (p. 207)
Adamson Act (p. 207)
Federal Workmen's Compensation Act (p. 207)
Keating-Owen Child Labor Act (p. 207)
Alice Paul (p. 208)
Carrie Chapman Catt (p. 208)
Nineteenth Amendment (p. 208)

1. *by passage of the Underwood Tariff Act and the Federal Reserve Act*
2. *supported Clayton Antitrust Act and creation of FTC*
3. *granted women full voting rights*
4. *Paragraphs might mention: improvements in business regulation, education, women's opportunities, urban reform, immigrant aid, more just and humane industry, failure to address racism, and falling short of some goals.*
5. *Despite business opposition, Wilson passed his legislative agenda including support for labor's right to strike and help for farmers, railroad workers, federal employees, and child laborers.*

CHAPTER 8
Review

DEVELOPING THEMES

Return to the Themes section on p. 188. Have students discuss these again and compare their original responses with those given now. (See p. 187B for suggested answers.)

Chapter Review Answers

WRITING A SUMMARY
See Essential Points in each section for main ideas.

REVIEWING CHRONOLOGY
3, 5, 1, 4, 2
Analyzing
obtained funds based on ability to pay by authorizing a graduated income tax; sought to eliminate corruption by providing for direct election of senators

IDENTIFYING PEOPLE AND IDEAS
1. *reform giving voters power to introduce legislation*
2. *reform mayor of Toledo, nicknamed "Golden Rule"*
3. *law authorizing ICC to establish railroad rates and to regulate other companies engaged in interstate commerce*
4. *process of making damaged land productive*
5. *Taft's secretary of interior, opposed restrictions on sale of public land*
6. *Roosevelt's program of social legislation calling for tough laws to protect workers, ensure public health, and regulate business*
7. *Speaker of the House who used his power to block reform legislation*

---

8. *reform legislation passed under Wilson, creating Federal Reserve Board and Federal Reserve banks*
9. *reduced the workday for railroad workers from 10 to 8 hours for same pay*
10. *militant Quaker suffragist who formed National Woman's party*

UNDERSTANDING MAIN IDEAS
1. *because composed of experts, not party loyalists, who made honest, efficient decisions for cities*

---

2. *provided a model for reform in government and for regulating big business*
3. *Both promoted reform in business, for the environment, and on behalf of labor.*
4. *The Payne-Aldrich Tariff and the Ballinger-Pinchot affair convinced TR that Taft was too conservative. TR wanted to push for further reform.*
5. *Clayton Antitrust Act helped define what business could not do; FTC investigated offending corporations and used courts to enforce its rulings.*
6. *that America's democratic system could respond and adapt to changes in American life*

CHAPTER 8
Review

William McKinley assassinated. Theodore Roosevelt becomes president.

Pennsylvania coal miners strike. Newlands Reclamation Act passed.

Elkins Act passed.

Theodore Roosevelt elected president.

Hepburn Act, Meat Inspection Act, and Pure Food and Drug Act passed.

1900   1905

WRITING A SUMMARY
Using the essential points of the chapter as a guide, write a summary of the chapter.

REVIEWING CHRONOLOGY
Number your paper 1 to 5. Study the time line above, and list the following events in the order in which they happened by writing the first next to 1, the second next to 2, and so on. Then complete the activity below.
1. Progressive party formed.
2. Nineteenth Amendment ratified.
3. Pennsylvania coal miners strike.
4. Federal Trade Commission created.
5. William Howard Taft elected president.

Analyzing How did the Sixteenth and Seventeenth amendments promote reform?

IDENTIFYING PEOPLE AND IDEAS
Explain the historical significance of each of the following people or terms.

1. initiative	6. New Nationalism
2. Samuel M. Jones	7. Joseph Cannon
3. Hepburn Act	8. Federal Reserve Act
4. reclamation	9. Adamson Act
5. Richard Ballinger	10. Alice Paul

UNDERSTANDING MAIN IDEAS
1. Why were city commissions effective at achieving efficiency in city government?
2. How did the Wisconsin Idea lay the foundation for further reforms?
3. In what ways were Theodore Roosevelt and William Howard Taft similar in their approaches to reform?
4. Why did Roosevelt challenge Taft in 1912?
5. What were the effects of the Clayton Antitrust Act and the creation of the Federal Trade Commission on the regulation of business?
6. What was the progressive movement's greatest legacy?

REVIEWING THEMES
1. **Democratic Values** How did reformers seek to curb political corruption and to make government more democratic in the early 20th century?
2. **Economic Development** How did President Roosevelt attempt to regulate business without discouraging free enterprise?
3. **Constitutional Heritage** How might reformers have used the Nineteenth Amendment as a means of accomplishing reform in politics and business?

THINKING CRITICALLY
1. **Synthesizing** How did Roosevelt bring dynamic leadership to the progressive movement at the city, state, and national levels?
2. **Evaluating** How did the controversy over tariffs contribute to Taft's defeat in the 1912 election?
3. **Analyzing** What interests worked against the campaign for women's suffrage in the early 20th century?
4. **Hypothesizing** How might life have been different for African Americans if Wilson had pursued a different racial policy?

STRATEGY FOR SUCCESS
Review the Skills Handbook entry on Reading a Time Line on page 751. Then study the time-line entries below, which focus on the years from 1908 to 1912. What cause-and-effect relationship is suggested by the sequence of events listed? How did the events of 1910 relate to those of 1912?

1908	William Howard Taft elected president.
1909	Payne-Aldrich Tariff passed. Taft fires Gifford Pinchot.
1910	Republicans lose control of House of Representatives.
1912	Roosevelt forms Progressive party. Woodrow Wilson elected president.

WRITING ABOUT HISTORY
Writing to Evaluate Write an essay evaluating the progressives' record on racial issues.

210

REVIEWING THEMES

1. through election reforms to make government more directly responsible to the people, such as direct primary; direct election of U.S. senators; secret ballot; and initiative, referendum, and recall

2. Roosevelt limited trustbusting and regulation only to those companies behaving irresponsibly.

3. by encouraging women to vote for female reform candidates and for legislation giving women equality in the labor force

THINKING CRITICALLY

1. fought for political, economic, and social reform as head of New York City's police commission, New York state legislator, governor of New York, and president

2. Taft's signing of high-tariff bill outraged progressives, who threw support to Roosevelt. Resulting party division led to Taft's election defeat.

3. liquor interests and businesses that feared women would demand better wages and working conditions

4. might have made advances sooner and more easily if Wilson had not instituted segregation for federal employees

STRATEGY FOR SUCCESS

Because the public was upset with Taft over the tariff and Pinchot's firing, the Republicans lost votes in the 1910 election; Republican losses in 1910 increased dissatisfaction within the party, resulting in the 1912 Republican split and in the election of a Democrat.

WRITING ABOUT HISTORY

Essays might mention the movement's white, conservative middle-class base and note Wilson's support of segregation.

USING PRIMARY SOURCES

Paragraphs might mention how graphic scenes portrayed in the book may have aroused public indignation and forced government investigation leading to passage of act.

LINKING HISTORY AND GEOGRAPHY

Answers might offer that in the less populated western states women already had a greater role in decision making; therefore, suffrage was not a radical change from established practices.

Timeline:

- Mann-Elkins Act passed.
- William Howard Taft elected president.
- Progressive party formed. Woodrow Wilson elected president.
- Sixteenth and Seventeenth amendments ratified. Underwood Tariff Act and Federal Reserve Act passed.
- Clayton Antitrust Act passed. Federal Trade Commission created.
- Woodrow Wilson reelected president.
- Nineteenth Amendment ratified.

1910   1915   1920

USING PRIMARY SOURCES

In 1906 Upton Sinclair published *The Jungle*, a biting attack on the industrial practices and unsanitary conditions in the Chicago stockyards. Read the following excerpt, which describes the manufacture and processing of canned goods in "Packingtown" (Chicago). Then, in a paragraph, explain how publication of this book might have influenced the passage of the Meat Inspection Act.

> 66 *"Deviled ham" . . . was made out of the waste ends of smoked beef that were too small to be sliced by the machines; and also tripe, dyed with chemicals so that it would not show white, and trimmings of hams and corned beef, and potatoes, skins and all. . . . All this ingenious mixture was ground up and flavored with spices to make it taste like something. Anybody who could invent a new imitation had been sure of a fortune, . . . but it was hard to think of anything new in a place where . . . men welcomed tuberculosis in the cattle they were feeding, because it made them fatten more quickly; and where they bought up all the old rancid [stale] butter . . . rechurned it with skim milk, and sold it in bricks in the cities!* 99

Chicago stockyards, 1919

LINKING HISTORY AND GEOGRAPHY

Study the map on page 208. What might explain the link between geographic region and the granting of women's suffrage?

Sample ballot, 1892

BUILDING YOUR PORTFOLIO

Complete the following projects independently or cooperatively.

1. **REFORM** In Chapter 7 you portrayed a progressive reformer addressing a problem in your city. Building on that experience, write a platform for the Progressive party that translates the problems of political machines, women's suffrage, business regulation, and worker protection into specific reforms your party hopes to institute.

2. **DEMOCRATIC RIGHTS** In Chapter 7 you portrayed a progressive reformer preparing a speech on women's rights to deliver at an Independence Day celebration. Building on that experience, imagine you are the editor of a labor union newspaper. Write an editorial indicating why you believe that progressives are not adequately addressing the needs of working-class women.

BUILDING YOUR PORTFOLIO

Have students refer to **Building Your Portfolio Worksheet 2**, assigned at the beginning of Unit 2. Use the worksheet to help students monitor their progress on the portfolio projects.

AMERICA AND THE WORLD

1898–1917

Chapter Overview

In the late 1800s and early 1900s, the U.S. sought to extend its influence in the Pacific, Latin America, the Caribbean, and Asia. In its drive to become a world power, the U.S. adopted a program of economic and political imperialism. It fought a war with Spain and gained control of Cuba and added the Philippines, Hawaii, and Puerto Rico to its territorial possessions. To link its growing empire, the U.S. built the Panama Canal. To successfully compete with the European powers for trade in Asia, the U.S. formulated the Open Door policy in China. In the Western Hemisphere, U.S. military power protected American business investments in other nations.

Chapter Planning Guide

CHAPTER 9	CORE RESOURCES	AUDIOVISUAL RESOURCES	PROGRAM RESOURCES
INTRODUCTION pp. 212–213	■ Building Your Portfolio Worksheet 2		
TEACHING THE CHAPTER pp. 214–235 ■ For expanded coverage of pp. 214–215, see Chapter 24, pp. 648–655; for coverage of pp. 219–224, see Chapter 23, pp. 622–627.	■ Graphic Organizer 9 ■ Social Studies Skills Worksheet 9 ■ Literature Worksheet 9 ■ Geography Worksheet 9 ■ Outline Maps 1, 2, 8, 11, 12, 13, 20, 21, 24	■ *The American Nation Videodisc: The Panama Canal* ■ Linking Geography and History Transparency and Worksheet 15 ■ Everyday Life in America Transparency and Worksheet 19	■ *Eyewitnesses and Others*, Volume 2: Readings 13, 23
REVIEW AND ASSESSMENT pp. 236–237	■ Chapter 9 Daily Quizzes ■ Reteaching Worksheet 9 ■ Chapter 9 Tests ■ Alternative Assessment Forms		■ Test Generator

Additional Resources

BOOKS FOR TEACHERS

Hall, Linda B. and Don M. Coerver. *Revolution on the Border: The United States and Mexico, 1910–1920.* University of New Mexico Press, 1988. Account of the Mexican Revolution in the U.S.–Mexico borderlands.

LaFeber, Walter. *Panama Canal: The Crisis in Historical Perspective.* Oxford University Press, 1990. Historical perspective of the Panama Canal.

O'Toole, G. J. *The Spanish War: An American Epic, 1898.* Norton, 1986. History of the war and its impact on U.S. foreign policy.

BOOKS FOR STUDENTS

Dolan, Edward F. *Panama & the United States: Their Canal, Their Stormy Years.* Watts, 1990. History of Panama and Panama–U.S. relations from years as a Spanish colony through 1990.

*Marrin, Albert. *The Spanish-American War.* Atheneum, 1991. Explores causes and consequences of war, yellow journalism, and Teddy Roosevelt's role.

Paterson, Thomas G. and Stephen G. Rabe, eds. *Imperial Surge: The United States Abroad, the 1890s–Early 1900s.* Heath, 1992. Explores U.S. imperialism in the 1890s and early 1900s.

* for students reading below grade level

MULTIMEDIA MATERIALS

Becoming a Modern Nation. Video, 28 min. Video Knowledge. Traces U.S. history from Spanish-American War to World War I.

The Lure of Empire: America Debates Imperialism. Video, 27 min. Learning Corporation of America. Dramatizes the debate over the Spanish-American War and U.S. foreign policy in the Pacific.

The Splendid Little War. Video, 55 min. Belle Grove. Uses newsreels, reenactments, and period music to tell the story of the Spanish-American War.

USE WITH PAGES 212–213

*L*isted on the right are the themes emphasized in Chapter 9. The questions in boldface type stimulate critical thinking and provide students with an opportunity to discuss the themes within a broadened context. The questions also appear in the pupil's edition on p. 212.

■ GLOBAL RELATIONS

Why might a country acquire overseas colonies? Students may explain that overseas colonies could provide resources or markets for a country's economic activities. A country might want to colonize another nation in order to achieve the political control it thinks necessary to serve its economic interests there. It also might want colonies in order to resettle some of its population, or for international prestige.

Why might a country resist becoming a colony? Students may suggest that a country might resist colonization because it wants to maintain its political independence or control its own resources.

■ ECONOMIC DEVELOPMENT

How might foreign investors influence a country's economy? Students might suggest that by purchasing land and businesses in foreign countries, foreign investors can come to dominate certain industries. They also might influence another economy by making loans to private businesses in a country, by financing infrastructure improvements, and otherwise creating jobs.

What problems might arise from these investments? Students may suggest that problems could develop if foreign investors try to exert political or economic influence over another nation or deprive its citizens of opportunities to develop their own economy.

■ DEMOCRATIC VALUES

Does the acquisition of colonies conflict with democratic principles? Why or why not? Students might suggest that a colonizing country can establish democratic governments in its colonies. On the other hand, students might indicate that the very act of imposing a system of government on another limits its citizens' freedom to choose their own institutions and form of government.

CHAPTER STRATEGIES FOR MEETING INDIVIDUAL NEEDS

LIMITED ENGLISH PROFICIENT LEARNERS

Organize the class into three groups. Have one group write questions about the People in the Preview Workshop for each section, while other groups write questions about the Places and Terms. Have groups pose their questions to the class.

TACTILE/KINESTHETIC LEARNERS

Direct students to work in groups to make color-coded world maps. Maps should show the locations of U.S. colonies and of countries in which the U.S. intervened militarily or practiced dollar diplomacy.

LEARNERS HAVING DIFFICULTY

Direct students to create a three-column chart for each section labeled *What I Already Know, What I Expect to Learn, What I Learned.* Have them complete columns one and two for each Focus question. After they complete the section, have students fill in column three.

AUDITORY LEARNERS

Have students make an audiotape script—titled "Imperialism Yes! Imperialism No!"—of quotes from the chapter defending, expressing concern about, or opposing U.S. expansion. Suggest that students write brief introductions to the quotes.

VISUAL LEARNERS

Have students create a booklet in the style of a newsmagazine's "People" section, highlighting the various people who took part in the events of this period.

GIFTED LEARNERS

Encourage students to conduct research and write an essay comparing Americans' belief in manifest destiny to U.S. imperialism. Essays should note how these ideas influenced U.S. domestic and foreign policy.

USING THE CHAPTER FOCUS

■ **UNDERSTANDING THE MAIN IDEA**

Call on a volunteer to read aloud the Understanding the Main Idea paragraph and to define the term *foreign policy*. Then ask students why Americans might have believed that the U.S. had a greater right to exercise its power and influence in the Western Hemisphere than did Spain or other major European powers. Encourage students to speculate about possible reasons for growing U.S. interest in the Pacific, the Caribbean, and Latin America.

■ **THEMES**

Have students work individually or in groups to answer the questions under Themes. Save students' responses so that they can compare them with their responses after studying the chapter. (See p. 211B for suggested answers.)

■ **THE TIME LINE**

Invite students to convert time-line entries into newspaper headlines. As they read the part of the chapter that pertains to each headline, have students write brief newspaper articles that explain the who, what, when, where, and why of each event.

CORE RESOURCES

• **Graphic Organizer 9**
• **Outline Maps 1, 2, 8, 11, 12, 13, 20, 21, 24**
• **Building Your Portfolio Worksheet 2**

ABOUT THE ILLUSTRATION

Pictures of battle scenes, such as the one below, received front-page coverage during the Spanish-American War. Newspapers sent journalists overseas to wire dispatches of the most exciting events. News of the Battle of Manila Bay was hard to obtain because the telegraph cable that could have immediately relayed news of the American victory was cut. It was not until May 9, more than a week after the battle, that Dewey officially cabled news of his victory to the U.S. Ask students to compare the coverage of this battle with news coverage of a recent world event, and to speculate about the impact of accurate and immediate news accounts on public opinion.

Chapter 9

AMERICA AND THE WORLD

1898–1917

FOCUS

UNDERSTANDING THE MAIN IDEA

In the waning years of the 19th century, the United States established itself as a world power by defeating Spain and acquiring Spain's last colonies in the Western Hemisphere. The progressive presidents asserted a strong foreign policy, acting to promote U.S. economic and security interests in the Pacific, the Caribbean, Asia, and Latin America.

THEMES

■ **GLOBAL RELATIONS** Why might a country acquire overseas colonies? Why might a country resist becoming a colony?

■ **ECONOMIC DEVELOPMENT** How might foreign investors influence a country's economy? What problems might arise from these investments?

■ **DEMOCRATIC VALUES** Does the acquisition of colonies conflict with democratic principles? Why or why not?

1898	1899	1904	1910	1915
Spanish-American War begins.	U.S. annexes Philippines.	Russo-Japanese War begins.	The Mexican Revolution starts.	Wilson sends marines into Haiti.

Ask students to recall key points of the Monroe Doctrine and the reasons that President Monroe issued it in 1823. Write their responses on the chalkboard. Ask them for examples of domestic concerns in the early and mid-1800s that might have distracted American attention from foreign affairs. Ask students to speculate about the role industrialization might have played in reawakening Americans' interest in foreign affairs. Point out that in this chapter, students will see how America's view of its role in the world changed in the late 1800s and early 1900s, and how these changes influenced the way its leaders made and carried out foreign policy.

▦ **LINK TO THE PAST** ▶

President James Monroe issued the Monroe Doctrine in 1823 as a warning to European powers to keep out of the Americas. But for much of the 19th century, the United States was too involved in domestic affairs to enforce the doctrine.

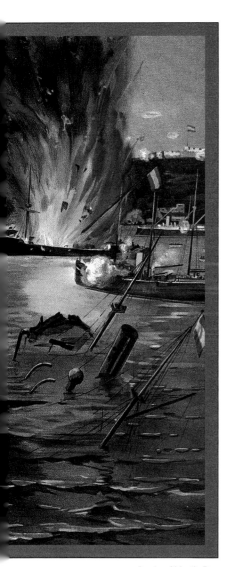

Battle of Manila Bay

D awn was just breaking as the American fleet, its flags flying, steamed across lovely Manila Bay, in the Philippines. It was early morning, May 1, 1898—just 11 days after the United States had declared war on Spain. Commodore George Dewey stood on the bridge of his flagship, *Olympia,* his eyes trained on the Spanish guns aimed at his ships from the shore and from the small Spanish fleet anchored in the harbor.

Sighting the Americans, the Spanish opened fire. Shortly after 5:30 A.M., Commodore Dewey gave an order to his flagship captain: "You may fire when you are ready, Gridley." The boom and flash of naval guns exploded through the bay. Shells crashed into several Spanish vessels, and they erupted into flames.

The Battle of Manila Bay had begun, the first battle of the Spanish-American War. It marked America's emergence on the world stage at the end of the 19th century. Throughout most of the century, Americans had followed George Washington's advice and remained aloof from foreign entanglements. Indeed, as late as 1889, Congressman Henry Cabot Lodge of Massachusetts wrote: "Our relations with foreign nations today fill but a slight place in American politics." But this would soon change as the United States became deeply involved in events abroad, from nearby Cuba and Mexico to distant China.

U.S. soldiers question Filipino women, 1899.

MAKING CONNECTIONS

Music

Dewey's victory at Manila Bay made him an instant hero and the subject of a wildly popular song that included these lines:

O Dewey was the morning
   Upon the first of May,
And Dewey was the
   Admiral
   Down in Manila Bay. . . .
And Dewey feel
   discouraged?
   I Dew not think we Dew.

AMERICA AND THE WORLD ▦ 213

Following is a list of the significant people, places, and terms in this section. You may wish to use this list as a section preview.

People
- Te'o Tuvale
- José Martí
- Valeriano Weyler

- William Randolph Hearst
- William McKinley
- Enrique Dupuy de Lôme
- George Dewey
- Emilio Aguinaldo

Places
- American Samoa
- Santiago, Cuba

- Manila, Philippines
- Puerto Rico
- Guam

Terms
- imperialism
- Teller Amendment
- Spanish-American War

FOCUS OBJECTIVES

- Explain what fueled the quest for overseas territory.

- Analyze why the U.S. declared war on Spain.

- Determine the outcome of the Spanish-American War for the U.S. and for Spain.

HISTORICAL SIDELIGHTS

Influence of Sea Power
Alfred Thayer Mahan's *Influence of Sea Power Upon History, 1660–1783,* was one of the most influential books of the era. Mahan's ideas received strong support from Massachusetts congressman Henry Cabot Lodge, who was fond of telling people that sea power was essential to "the greatness of every splendid people."

Section 1

WAR WITH SPAIN

FOCUS

- **What fueled the quest for overseas territory?**
- **Why did the United States declare war on Spain?**
- **What was the outcome of the Spanish-American War for the United States and Spain?**

In the late 1800s the United States emerged as the world's leading industrial producer and agricultural exporter. This economic success encouraged the nation to establish overseas colonies, just as the European powers were doing. The United States hoped colonization would provide new markets for its goods and new sources of raw materials. U.S. involvement in Samoa and a short war with Spain in 1898 increased the American role in the Pacific and the Caribbean.

Recruiter, 1898

THE IMPULSE FOR IMPERIALISM

In March 1889 seven warships—one British, three German, and three American—faced off in the South Pacific harbor of Apia, in present-day

Western Samoa. But before a shot could be fired, a typhoon struck, destroying all but the British ship. What brought these three powerful nations to the brink of war? **Imperialism**: the quest for colonial empires.

Between 1876 and 1915, vast areas of Africa, Asia, and Latin America fell under the control of a handful of industrialized nations locked in a race to acquire overseas colonies. Great Britain, the leading imperialist power, had colonies flung so far across the globe that the British could boast, "The sun never sets on the British Empire."

What lay behind this wave of imperialism? The desire for power and prestige played a role, but it was also a matter of economics. Industrial workers, aided by efficient machines and abundant capital, produced far more goods than could be consumed at home. In response, industrialists turned to Africa, Asia, and Latin America for new

◄ **Samoan families lived in grass-thatched huts, such as this one in Pago Pago.**

Teaching the Section

IMPERIALISM

Have students work in groups to create a list of the reasons for U.S. interest in becoming an imperial power at the turn of the century. (*industrialization and increased dependence on world trade, desire for overseas military bases and fueling stations, interest in spreading U.S. political system and Christianity*) Direct groups to label each reason as an economic, strategic, cultural, or political motive for imperialism and to identify in the section an example of each reason in practice. Then ask groups to share their lists and examples with the class and discuss them.

▶

customers and new sources of raw materials. The telegraph, steamship, and railroad made even the remotest areas potential markets. To protect these new markets from competition, industrialized nations launched a campaign of colonization.

Although American enthusiasm for overseas expansion never matched that of the Europeans, support grew during the late 1800s. Some supporters, like Alfred Thayer Mahan of the U.S. Naval College, argued that overseas territories would make the United States more powerful and provide sites for naval bases and steamship fueling stations from which to conduct trade. Others claimed that the United States had a duty to spread its political system and the Christian religion to other parts of the world. This belief often went hand-in-hand with feelings of racial superiority. In his widely read book *Our Country* (1885), Josiah Strong, a Protestant minister and social reformer, proclaimed that Anglo-Saxons (people of English ancestry) had a special mission:

66 God, with infinite wisdom and skill, is training the Anglo-Saxon race for an hour sure to come in the world's future. . . .
Then this race . . . the representative, let us hope, of the largest liberty, the purest Christianity, the highest civilization . . . will spread itself over the earth. 99

■■ The quest for empire was fueled by strategic, economic, and cultural motives.

It was the desire for naval bases and fueling stations, rather than cultural concerns, that led the United States, Great Britain, and Germany to square off in Samoa in 1889. The Samoans realized that this competition put them in grave danger. In 1898 Te'o Tuvale, a government official, warned his fellow Samoans:

66 Be kind and don't start a war in Samoa, because if you do the Three Powers [Britain, Germany, and the United States] will take over the conduct of the country and your orators and Chiefs and things that you have been accustomed to will be of no further use. 99

Te'o Tuvale's prophecy was fulfilled the next year when, in the face of overwhelming European and U.S. military might, Samoans surrendered their government. The United States won control over Eastern Samoa, and Germany was granted control over Western Samoa. Today Western Samoa is independent, while Eastern (or American) Samoa remains a U.S. territory (see map on page 220).

CONFLICT IN CUBA

The Caribbean island of Cuba, just 90 miles from the Florida Keys, provided a testing ground for U.S. imperialism. In the late 1800s Cuba simmered with unrest. Along with its Caribbean neighbor Puerto Rico, it was the last of the Spanish colonies in the Americas. Since 1868, Cubans had launched a series of unsuccessful revolts against Spanish rule. To put down the rebellion, the Spanish government exiled many leaders of the independence movement. Foremost among these exiles was the brilliant Cuban poet José Martí, who was forced out of Cuba in 1871 and again in 1879.

From his exile in New York, Martí wrote poems and newspaper articles promoting Cuban independence. He also urged Cuban exiles to mount an invasion of Cuba:

▲ José Martí

66 Let us rise up at once with a final burst of heartfelt energy. . . . Let us rise up for the true republic, those of us who, with our passion for right and our habit of hard work, will know how to preserve it. 99

When Cubans launched another revolt in February 1895, Martí and other exiles joined them. Martí became a martyr for Cuban independence when he was killed a month later in a battle with Spanish soldiers.

In 1896 Spain sent General Valeriano Weyler to put down the uprising. Within days Weyler had imprisoned thousands of farmers in concentration camps to prevent them from supplying the rebels. Over the next two years, starvation and disease claimed the lives of perhaps 200,000 Cubans.

The American press branded Weyler "the Butcher." William Randolph Hearst's *Journal* and Joseph Pulitzer's *World,* two New York City newspapers, outdid each other in publicizing Spanish atrocities. (This type of sensationalized reporting

HISTORICAL SIDELIGHTS

The Two Samoas
Western Samoa experienced further turmoil before finally gaining its independence in 1962. Soldiers from New Zealand occupied the islands from 1914 to 1920. In 1919, Germany relinquished control of Western Samoa. It was later governed by New Zealand under UN auspices until independence. American Samoa, under U.S. jurisdiction, elects a representative to Congress who can vote in committee but has no vote on the House floor.

PRIMARY SOURCES

Description of Change: excerpted
Rationale: excerpted to focus on main idea

PRIMARY SOURCE

Description of Change: excerpted and bracketed
Rationale: excerpted to focus on main idea; bracketed to clarify meaning

RECOGNIZING PREJUDICE

In 1885 American historian John Fiske wrote that Anglo-Saxon culture would soon spread all over the world and that English would be the universal language. Have students compare expansionists' views of non–English-speaking people with attitudes toward Native Americans.

Teaching the **Section**

WAR WITH SPAIN

Work with the class to develop a chalkboard list of reasons that the U.S. went to war with Spain. Discuss each reason as it is recorded on the chalkboard. Then have students imagine they are newspaper editors in 1898 and have them write editorials calling for war with Spain. Ask students to read their editorials aloud. Students may wish to include their editorials in their portfolios.

THE WAR'S OUTCOME

Have students work in groups to discuss the outcomes of the Spanish-American War for the U.S. and Spain and then report to the class about whether they think those outcomes justified U.S. participation in this war.

■■ Direct students to list circumstances or reasons they believe would justify U.S. military intervention in another country today.

was named yellow journalism after "The Yellow Kid," a comic strip published for a time in both papers.) In 1897 Hearst sent artist Frederic Remington to Cuba to send back drawings that documented Spanish cruelty. Hearst hoped to horrify Americans into agitating for war against Spain. Finding nothing to draw, Remington reportedly cabled Hearst: "EVERYTHING IS QUIET. THERE IS NO TROUBLE HERE. THERE WILL BE NO WAR. WISH TO RETURN." Hearst was said to have replied: "PLEASE REMAIN. YOU FURNISH THE PICTURES AND I'LL FURNISH THE WAR."

In addition to U.S. horror at Spanish atrocities, threats to U.S. investments in Cuba convinced many that the United States should aid the Cuban rebels. In the face of mounting war fever, President William McKinley, himself a veteran of the Civil War, struggled to remain neutral and to resist committing American troops. "I have been through one war. I have seen the dead piled up, and I do not want to see another," he explained.

But early in 1898, two shattering events forced his hand. First, on February 9 Hearst's *Journal* printed a letter written by Spain's minister to the United States, Enrique Dupuy de Lôme. Intercepted by a Cuban spy and sold to Hearst, the letter ridiculed President McKinley as "weak, and a bidder for the admiration of the crowd."

Americans were outraged at the Spaniard's remarks, which the *Journal* called "the worst insult to the United States in its history." Then on February 15 the American battleship *Maine*—sent to Havana, Cuba, to protect U.S. lives and property—blew up, killing 260 sailors. "DESTRUCTION OF THE WAR SHIP MAINE WAS THE WORK OF AN ENEMY!" screamed the *Journal*'s headline. Though it was later determined that a fire in a coal bin had probably caused

the explosion, many Americans blamed Spain. "Remember the *Maine*! And to hell with Spain!" became a familiar chant.

Spain tried to calm tensions by agreeing to a U.S.–proposed peace plan. But it was too late. On April 11 President McKinley bowed to public pressure and asked Congress to intervene in Cuba "in the name of humanity, in the name of civilization, and in behalf of endangered American interests."

On April 20 Congress recognized Cuban independence and voted to use U.S. military force to help Cuba attain it. Congress also adopted the **Teller Amendment**, which stated that the United States claimed no "sovereignty, jurisdiction, or control" over Cuba. Once Cuba won its independence from Spain, the amendment promised, the United States would "leave the government and control of the Island to its people."

■■ **To protect U.S. investments and to help Cuba overthrow Spanish rule, the United States declared war on Spain in April 1898.**

WAR WITH SPAIN

The first battles of the **Spanish-American War** were not fought in nearby Cuba, but halfway around the world, in the Spanish-held Philippine Islands. Weeks before war was declared, Assistant Secretary of the Navy Theodore Roosevelt had, without authorization, cabled Commodore George Dewey, commander of the U.S. Navy's Asiatic fleet anchored at Hong Kong. Roosevelt ordered Dewey to keep his ships ready to take offensive action in the Philippines.

On May 1, 1898, less than two weeks after war was declared, Dewey's fleet easily defeated the small Spanish fleet guarding the Philippine city of Manila. In order to capture the city itself, Dewey obtained the support of a rebel army of Filipino patriots led by Emilio Aguinaldo (ahg-ee-NAHL-doh). Filipinos had been fighting for independence from Spain for two years. Now, along with U.S. soldiers, they attacked and captured Manila. Cut off by Commodore Dewey's warships and surrounded by Aguinaldo's forces, Spanish forces in the Philippines surrendered on August 14, 1898.

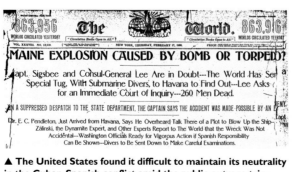

▲ The United States found it difficult to maintain its neutrality in the Cuban-Spanish conflict amid the public outrage triggered by sensationalized news reports. This headline appeared in Joseph Pulitzer's *World*.

GUIDED PRACTICE

List the following on the chalkboard: *Spanish rule in Cuba, Hearst and Pulitzer newspaper stories, U.S. investments in Cuba, De Lôme letter,* and *sinking of the* Maine. Call on students to describe the role that each factor played in encouraging the U.S. to declare war on Spain.

INDEPENDENT PRACTICE

Ask students to choose an item from the Guided Practice and to write a paragraph that supports or disputes it as a good reason for declaring war on Spain. Students may wish to include their paragraphs in their portfolios.

Review and Assessment

REVIEW Have students work in pairs to create time lines of the events in this section, making sure to leave out at least four key events. Instruct pairs to exchange time lines, to identify the missing events, and to enter them in the appropriate places on the time lines. Then assign the Section 1 Review on p. 218.

ASSESS Assign the **Section 1 Daily Quiz** in *Core Resources.* ▶

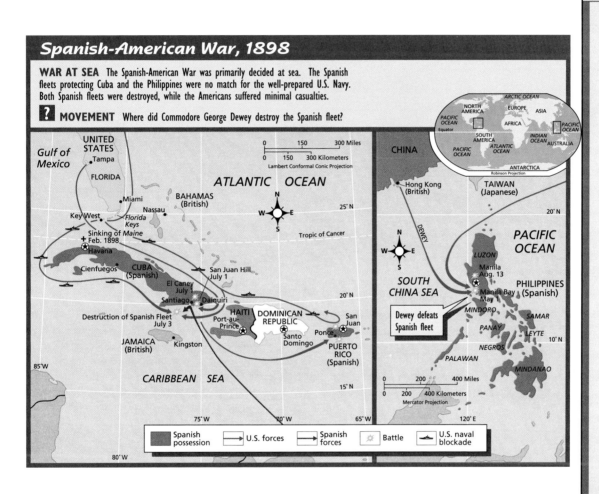

Spanish-American War, 1898

WAR AT SEA The Spanish-American War was primarily decided at sea. The Spanish fleets protecting Cuba and the Philippines were no match for the well-prepared U.S. Navy. Both Spanish fleets were destroyed, while the Americans suffered minimal casualties.

? **MOVEMENT** Where did Commodore George Dewey destroy the Spanish fleet?

Spanish possession | U.S. forces | Spanish forces | ☼ Battle | U.S. naval blockade

Victory in Cuba would not come quite as easily as it had in the Philippines. With a regular army of only some 28,000 soldiers, the U.S. War Department was unprepared for land battles. Thousands of volunteers raced to enlist, but how could they be trained and equipped overnight? With little training and outfitted in heavy wool uniforms (the only ones that army storehouses could supply), U.S. troops sailed for tropical Cuba in mid-June. For rations, the men were issued canned corned beef that was supposed to keep in any weather. "Well," reported one soldier, "it commenced to explode. We had to throw it all overboard." Another soldier described life once the troops arrived in Cuba:

    66 Heavy rains pouring down, no tents for cover, . . . standing in trenches in a foot of water and mud, day and night. . . . Ration issue consisting of a slice of sow belly, hardtack, and some grains of coffee. . . . Then came the issue of fleece-lined underwear in a 132 [degree] climate. . . . Then came on malaria. 99

▲ **Emilio Aguinaldo, shown wearing a vest, sat for this photograph with his advisers in 1896.**

HISTORICAL SIDELIGHTS

Civilian Relief

Cuban civilians faced extreme hardships during the war. Forced into concentration camps and cut off from food imports by a U.S. blockade, thousands died. American Red Cross founder Clara Barton worked throughout the war with the Central Cuban Relief Committee to bring needed supplies to Cuban civilians. Thwarted both by Spanish and by U.S. officials, Barton and the committee were eventually able to distribute hundreds of tons of food and medicine and establish medical facilities on the island.

BUILDING VOCABULARY

The word *tack* was used by sailors to refer insultingly to the ship's food supplies. Sailors called the hard biscuits that lasted months and months at sea *hardtack.*

PRIMARY SOURCE

Description of Change: excerpted and bracketed
Rationale: excerpted to focus on main idea; bracketed to clarify meaning

RETEACH Organize students into groups and assign each group a subsection of the section. Have each group develop several questions and answers about the main ideas in its assigned material. Then have each group quiz the other groups with its questions.

Closure

Ask students to assess whether or not America's involvement in war with Spain was part of the mission outlined by Josiah Strong in the quote on p. 215. Require students to explain and defend their opinions.

Extension

INTERPRET

Have students research Cuban poet José Martí's poems or essays about the U.S. and interpret them for the class.

INVESTIGATE

Students might investigate the lives and activities of the "founders" of yellow journalism: Joseph Pulitzer and William Randolph Hearst.

SECTION REVIEW ANSWERS

IDENTIFY

For significance, see the following pages:
imperialism (p. 214)
Te'o Tuvale (p. 215)
José Martí (p. 215)
Valeriano Weyler (p. 215)
William Randolph Hearst
(p. 215)
William McKinley (p. 216)
Enrique Dupuy de Lôme
(p. 216)
Teller Amendment (p. 216)
Spanish-American War
(p. 216)
George Dewey (p. 216)
Emilio Aguinaldo (p. 216)

LOCATE

For locations, see the maps on pp. 217 and 220.

1. *new markets for growing industries, bases and fueling stations to reach and protect those markets*
2. *sensational reports of Spanish atrocities, threats to U.S. investments in Cuba, Dupuy de Lôme's letter, destruction of the Maine, public pressure*
3. *U.S. gained Puerto Rico, Guam, and Philippines; Spain lost its last American and Pacific colonies.*
4. *Poems should express feelings of Cuban people under what they saw as oppressive Spanish rule.*
5. *Both published newspapers that sensationalized Spanish actions, thus provoking Americans toward war.*

▲ Soldiers of the African American 9th and 10th cavalries are shown here during the Battle of Las Guásimas on June 24, 1898. This victory paved the way for American forces to capture Santiago.

The major American land actions in Cuba began on July 1 as U.S. troops mounted an assault on the Spanish stronghold of Santiago. Their aim was to capture the heights above Santiago—El Caney and San Juan Hill—so that they could aim their guns down on Spanish troops. One U.S. division overcame Spanish forces at El Caney.

In what would become the war's most famous battle, Lieutenant Colonel Teddy Roosevelt (who had resigned his naval post) led a cavalry unit of some 1,000 men toward the garrison on San Juan Hill. Composed largely of athletes from eastern colleges, miners, cowboys, Native Americans, ranchers, and would-be adventurers, the unit was known as the Rough Riders.

Since their horses had not been shipped, the Rough Riders had to charge on foot under intense Spanish fire. The African American 9th and 10th cavalries cleared the way for the final surge. By nightfall U.S. troops controlled the ridge above Santiago. Then on July 3, the U.S. Navy sank the Spanish fleet off the coast of Cuba, resulting in more than 400 Spanish casualties. With their navy crushed, two weeks later, on July 17, Spanish troops in Cuba surrendered. Meanwhile, U.S. troops also defeated Spanish troops in Puerto Rico.

The war was costly for Spain. By the terms of the peace treaty, Spain granted Cuba its independence and ceded Puerto Rico and the Pacific island of Guam (see map on page 220) to the United States. Spain also gave up control of the Philippines in return for a U.S. payment of $20 million.

The United States also paid a price for the war. Some 5,400 soldiers died, nearly 400 in battle and the rest from dysentery, typhoid, malaria, yellow fever, or food poisoning. But the war also brought rewards. By gaining control of overseas territories, the United States secured its position as an imperialist and world power. Expansionists expressed delight, but many Americans were troubled by the quest for empire.

■■ **The United States gained most of Spain's overseas territory through victory in the Spanish-American War.**

SECTION 1 REVIEW

IDENTIFY and explain the significance of the following: imperialism, Te'o Tuvale, José Martí, Valeriano Weyler, William Randolph Hearst, William McKinley, Enrique Dupuy de Lôme, Teller Amendment, Spanish-American War, George Dewey, Emilio Aguinaldo.

LOCATE and explain the importance of the following: American Samoa; Santiago, Cuba; Manila, Philippines; Puerto Rico; Guam.

1. **MAIN IDEA** What led the United States and other industrial powers to turn to imperialism?
2. **MAIN IDEA** What factors caused the United States to become involved in the Spanish-American War?
3. **GEOGRAPHY: PLACE** What territories did the United States gain as a result of the Spanish-American War? How did the war affect Spain?
4. **WRITING TO CREATE** Imagine you are Cuban revolutionary José Martí. Write a poem supporting Cuban independence from Spain.
5. **EVALUATING** How did publishers William Randolph Hearst and Joseph Pulitzer influence the United States to declare war on Spain in 1898?

PREVIEW WORKSHOP

Following is a list of the significant people, places, and terms in this section. You may wish to use this list as a section preview.

People
- William Howard Taft
- Kalakaua
- Liliuokalani

- John Hay
- Matthew Perry

Places
- Hawaii
- Taiwan
- Korea
- Beijing, China
- Yokohama, Japan

Terms
- annex
- Philippine Government Act
- Jones Act of 1916
- spheres of influence
- Open Door policy
- Boxer Rebellion
- Russo-Japanese War

Section 2

EXPANSION IN THE PACIFIC

FOCUS

- **How did the United States deal with Filipino calls for independence?**
- **Why did the U.S. government annex Hawaii?**
- **What role did the United States play in China?**
- **What kind of relationship developed between Japan and the United States in the late 1800s and early 1900s?**

America's war with Spain began over Cuba. But, in addition to establishing a U.S. presence in the Caribbean, the war extended the U.S. presence in Asia and the Pacific. After the war, the United States established political control over the Philippines and added Hawaii to its colonial holdings. The United States also became further involved in affairs in China and took a new interest in Japan.

Hawaiian coin

UPROAR OVER THE PHILIPPINES

When Dewey's fleet steamed into Manila Bay in 1898, few Americans even knew where the Philippines were. President McKinley confessed that before he consulted a globe, he could not locate the islands "within two thousand miles." The Philippines—a group of islands—cover some 100,000 square miles in the Pacific Ocean, southeast of the Chinese coast. Now that the Philippines were "flung into [U.S.] arms by Dewey's guns," Americans faced an urgent question: Should Filipinos be forced to accept U.S. rule?

The debate over annexation. The debate over whether the United States should **annex**, or take control of, the Philippines was rooted in the larger controversy over imperialism raging across the country.

People questioned whether it was proper or wise for the United States to annex any foreign territory and rule its government and its people.

Expansionists argued forcefully in favor of annexation. In addition to making a case for annexation for commercial and naval reasons, some believed that the United States would bring democracy to the Philippines. Others held that the United States had to rule the Philippines to keep out European powers. Charles Denby, a former American

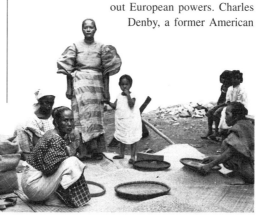
▶ Filipino women are shown winnowing, or separating, rice on Palawan Island.

FOCUS OBJECTIVES

- Describe how the U.S. dealt with Filipino calls for independence.

- Explain why the U.S. government annexed Hawaii.

- Determine the role the U.S. played in China.

- Analyze the relationship that developed between Japan and the U.S. in the late 1800s and early 1900s.

HISTORICAL SIDELIGHTS

The Philippines
When news reached the U.S. of Dewey's victory at Manila Bay, humorist Finley Peter Dunne quipped that Americans weren't sure if the Philippines "were islands or canned goods."

CORE RESOURCES

- **Geography Worksheet 9**
- **Section 2 Daily Quiz**

AV RESOURCES

- **Linking Geography and History Transparency and Worksheet 15**

Teaching the Section

ANNEXATION OR INDEPENDENCE

Organize 12 students into two groups of 6 students each, leaving remaining students to form a large third group. Assign the two small groups the roles of witnesses appearing before a congressional committee considering annexation of the Philippines. Ask one small group to present arguments in favor of annexation and the other to give arguments against it. Have the large group act as the congressional panel: they are to listen to arguments of witnesses, ask questions, and finally vote for or against annexation. Then reorganize groups to allow other class members to act as congressional witnesses for a hearing on the annexation of Hawaii.

MOTIVATING: STUDENT EXPERIENCES

Ask students to locate the Philippines, Japan, and China on a wall map. Ask students to discuss the current relationship between the U.S. and these countries. Then tell students that this section reviews the relationship between the U.S. and these countries in the late 1800s and early 1900s.

PRIMARY SOURCES
Description of Change: excerpted
Rationale: excerpted to focus on main idea

HISTORICAL SIDELIGHTS

McKinley's Decision

President McKinley agonized over whether to recognize Filipino independence or to annex the islands. His ultimate support for annexation reflected widely held attitudes of the time about America's superiority and its duty to spread its culture to other parts of the world. "We could not leave [the Filipinos] to themselves—they were unfit for self-government," McKinley later reported. In addition, he said, America had a responsibility "to educate the Filipinos, and uplift and civilize and Christianize them, and by God's grace to do the best we could by them."

AV TRANSPARENCY

Linking Geography and History Transparency and **Worksheet 15**

---

foreign minister to China, warned opponents of annexation that times had changed:

> 66 I recognize the existence of a national sentiment in accordance with . . . Washington's Farewell Address, which is against the acquisition of foreign territory; but . . . circumstances are changed. . . . We have a great commerce to take care of. We have to compete with the commercial nations of the world in far-distant markets. Commerce, not politics, is king. 99

Opponents of American imperialism responded that, by annexing the Philippines and denying its independence, the United States would violate its own ideals expressed in the Declaration of Independence. In June 1898, opponents of U.S. imperialism formed the Anti-Imperialist League, which proclaimed:

> 66 We regret that it has become necessary in the land of Washington and Lincoln to reaffirm that all men, of whatever race or color, are entitled to life, liberty, and the pursuit of happiness. . . . We insist that the subjugation of any people is "criminal aggression" and open disloyalty to the distinctive principles of our Government. 99

After a fierce debate, the Senate narrowly approved the treaty annexing the Philippines on February 6, 1899. The vote was 57 to 27, barely reaching the two-thirds majority required.

Conquest and early rule. Filipinos, however, did not want to exchange one master for another—gaining independence from Spain only to lose it to the United States. Emilio Aguinaldo had already set up a provisional Filipino government and proclaimed himself president of the Philippine Republic. Now he warned that Filipinos would go to war if "American troops attempt to take forcible possession. Upon their heads will be all the blood which may be shed."

For the next three years, Filipino independence fighters and U.S. soldiers fought for control of the Philippines. U.S. forces captured Aguinaldo in March 1901. When Filipino resistance continued, however, U.S. forces implemented a concentration camp policy as Weyler had done in Cuba. By the time U.S. forces crushed the rebellion in 1902, the cost in Filipino lives was horrendous, estimated in the hundreds of thousands. More than 4,000 U.S. soldiers lost their lives.

In 1902 the U.S. Congress passed the **Philippine Government Act**, also known as the Organic Act. The act decreed that the Philippines would be ruled by a governor and a two-house legislature. The United States would appoint the governor and the legislature's upper house. After peace was

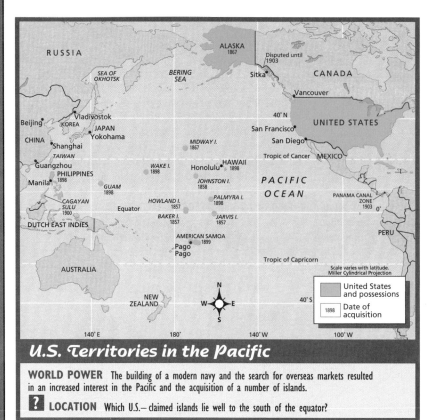

U.S. Territories in the Pacific

WORLD POWER The building of a modern navy and the search for overseas markets resulted in an increased interest in the Pacific and the acquisition of a number of islands.

? **LOCATION** Which U.S.–claimed islands lie well to the south of the equator?

Map Caption Answer
American Samoa

ANNEXING HAWAII

Organize small groups of students to serve as staff members of a U.S. senator. Have the groups prepare memos on the annexation of Hawaii. Memos should outline the issue's history, summarize public opinion in the U.S. and Hawaii, present the arguments for and against annexation, assess the political consequences of each action, and recommend a position for the senator to take. After each staff has reported its recommendation, have the class vote on whether or not to annex Hawaii.

▲ To suppress the Filipino uprising, the United States sent approximately 70,000 troops to the Philippines in 1899. This cartoon shows Emilio Aguinaldo's government crushed by American military might.

restored, Filipino voters would be allowed to elect the legislature's lower house.

Judge William Howard Taft became the first American governor of the Philippines. Taft authorized the construction of public schools, roads, and railroads and improved medical care and sanitation. As the United States reduced and then removed tariffs on Filipino products, U.S. trade with the Philippines flourished.

But Filipinos still lacked the independence for which they had fought so long. The **Jones Act of 1916** gave Filipinos the right to elect both houses of their legislature but stated that independence would have to wait until Congress declared that "a stable government" had been established. The wait would be a long one. The United States finally granted independence to the Philippines on July 4, 1946, nearly half a century after American and Spanish naval guns had shattered the early morning silence of Manila Bay.

■■ Despite Filipino calls for independence, the United States annexed the Philippines and delayed independence until 1946.

*A*CQUIRING HAWAII

Renewed interest in expansion after the Spanish-American War led to demands for U.S. annexation of the Hawaiian Islands, nearly 4,000 miles east of the Philippines. The United States had long been interested in Hawaii for its strategic location along trade routes to China and for its fertile lava-enriched soil. In the 1820s Protestant missionaries from New England traveled to the islands to convert Hawaiians to Christianity. The missionaries' descendants remained, becoming major landholders. By the 1870s Americans living in Hawaii controlled land and trade and exercised growing influence over the Hawaiian government.

When the Hawaiian king, Kalakaua (kah-LAH-KAH-ooh-ah), sought to restrict American influence in 1886, some 400 American businessmen, planters, and traders in Hawaii formed the secret Hawaiian League. Their aim was to overthrow the monarchy and persuade the United States to annex Hawaii.

In 1887 the League forced Kalakaua to sign a new constitution that made the Hawaiian monarch only a figurehead and limited native Hawaiians'

MAKING CONNECTIONS

Economics
The McKinley Tariff Act of 1890 caused huge financial losses for Hawaiian sugar planters. The act placed a bounty on U.S.-grown sugar, in effect subsidizing the U.S. sugar industry and causing sugar prices to plummet. As a result, Hawaiian planters lost some $12 million. This loss caused an even greater desire for Hawaiian annexation among sugar planters, who wanted the benefits that U.S. sugar producers had gained.

BUILDING VOCABULARY

The term *figurehead* originally identified the carved figures attached to the bows of sailing ships. These ornaments, although attractive, had no practical use. Today the term refers to a person who is a boss or chief in name only.

▼ After 1900, pineapples began to rival sugarcane as Hawaii's most important crop. Many of the laborers on Hawaiian plantations were from China, Japan, Korea, and the Philippines.

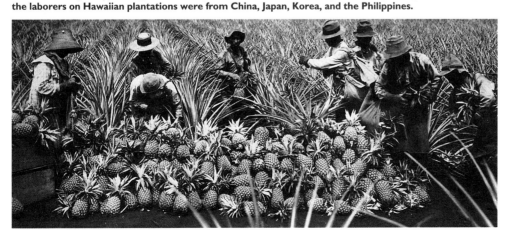

Teaching the Section

THE U.S. AND CHINA

Draw a door on the chalkboard, and call on volunteers to cite the three principles outlined in Hay's Open Door policy as you write them on the door. Then ask students whether or not the American response to the Boxer Rebellion was consistent with the Open Door policy. Ask students to speculate about the motives behind the U.S. response.

U.S.–JAPAN RELATIONSHIP

Work with students to develop a cause-and-effect chart on the chalkboard that illustrates the relationship between the U.S. and Japan from the mid-1800s to 1907. Begin by writing *Perry Arrives in Japan* at the top of the chalkboard and *Russo-Japanese War* at the bottom. Then have students fill in the missing cause-effect relationships and add arrows to link causes and effects. Have students use the chart to explain U.S. views of Japan in the late 1800s and early 1900s.

RECOGNIZING PREJUDICE

Ask students to give examples of American business-people's interventions in Hawaiian affairs. *(Forcing Kalakaua to accept the "Bayonet Constitution," overthrow of Queen Liliuokalani.)* Ask students to speculate whether prejudice toward Hawaiians may have influenced these actions.

🅱 PERSONALITIES IN HISTORY

Liliuokalani was the first and only Hawaiian queen. One of the reasons she agreed to give up her throne was to win pardons for loyal supporters who had been jailed during a revolt to restore her to the throne. In her later life she tried unsuccessfully to obtain federal reimbursement for her property losses. The Hawaiian legislature eventually voted her an annual pension of $4,000. She also received income from a sugar plantation. The Queen wrote "Aloha Oe," meaning "Farewell to Thee," one of Hawaii's most popular songs.

PRIMARY SOURCE

Description of Change: excerpted
Rationale: excerpted to focus on main idea

right to hold office in their own country. Hawaiians criticized what they called the "Bayonet Constitution." That same year, the United States succeeded in getting Kalakaua to grant rights to use Pearl Harbor for a U.S. naval base.

Hawaiian resentment intensified as American interests continued to lobby Washington to annex Hawaii. Then in 1891 Kalakaua died. Succeeding him was his sister, Liliuokalani (li-lee-uh-woh-kuh-LAHN-ee), champion of Hawaiian nationalism, who pledged to regain "Hawaii for Hawaiians."

Liliuokalani was born into a Hawaiian ruling family in 1838. As a young girl she saw the monarchy reclaim Hawaiian independence after a brief British takeover. She would never forget the pride she felt as the Hawaiian flag was again raised over her native land.

Early in her reign, Queen Liliuokalani began working to overturn the Bayonet Constitution and replace it with one that would return power to native Hawaiians. In 1893 she announced her plans to publish a new constitution. The announcement caused the annexationists to swing into action. Forming a Committee of Safety, they forcibly occupied government buildings, declared the end of the monarchy, and set up a provisional government of their own. U.S. Marines stood by as the American foreign minister to Hawaii recognized the provisional government. A deeply saddened Queen Liliuokalani signed a paper giving up her throne:

Queen Liliuokalani

> 66 I, Liliuokalani, . . . protest against any and all acts done against myself and the constitutional government of the Hawaiian kingdom. . . . Now, to avoid any collision of armed forces and perhaps the loss of life, I do, under this protest, and impelled by said forces, yield my authority until such time as the government of the United States shall . . . undo the action of its representatives and reinstate me. 99

▶ Ivory vases and brightly colored fans were some of the many items sold through the lucrative China trade. The fan shows the seaport town of Huang-pu, where American ships took aboard Chinese goods.

The U.S. government never reinstated Liliuokalani. But recognizing that native Hawaiians overwhelmingly opposed annexation, it did not annex Hawaii until 1898. Liliuokalani lived out the rest of her life in Honolulu, a proud reminder of Hawaii's past. She died in 1917 after a severe stroke and was buried in the Royal Mausoleum.

■■ American settlers' response to Queen Liliuokalani's reforms and a renewed interest in overseas colonies led to the U.S. annexation of Hawaii.

*A*MERICAN INVOLVEMENT IN CHINA

The United States had originally become interested in Hawaii because it was the gateway to the China trade. This trade had begun in 1784 when a U.S. trading ship, the *Empress of China,* sailed for the port of Guangzhou (Canton). In 1843 China officially opened five ports to trading ships from the United States and Europe.

For the next 50 years, China's rulers struggled to balance American and European interests to keep them from overrunning the country. In 1895, however, the Chinese government was overrun from another direction. Japan attacked and defeated China, winning from it the large island of Taiwan (Formosa), territory on China's Liaotung Peninsula, and control of Korea.

European powers quickly took advantage of China's weakened position. Great Britain, France, Germany, and Russia pressured the Chinese government to carve the country into separate **spheres of influence**—ports or regions where a particular country would have exclusive rights over trade, mines, and railroads.

Peabody and Essex Museum, Salem, Massachusetts

Practice

GUIDED PRACTICE

Draw a four-column chart on the chalkboard with the headings *Country, Policy Goals, Actions,* and *Effects.* In the first column list *Philippines, Hawaii, China,* and *Japan.* Have students complete the chart by describing the goals of U.S. foreign policy toward each country, the tactics used to achieve those goals, and the impact of U.S. actions on that country.

INDEPENDENT PRACTICE

Ask students to use the information in the Guided Practice to create a political cartoon about American policy toward one of the countries in the chart. Tell students to draw their cartoons from the viewpoint of a citizen from the country they select. Students may wish to include their cartoons in their portfolios.

Review and Assessment

REVIEW Direct students to use the section's four Essential Points as main topics for an outline titled "Expansion in the Pacific." Have students add subtopics to the outline. Then assign the Section 2 Review on p. 224.

ASSESS Assign the **Section 2 Daily Quiz** in *Core Resources.* ▶

The United States feared it would be squeezed out of the China trade. In 1899 Secretary of State John Hay responded by inaugurating an **Open Door policy**, which called for all nations to have equal access to trade and investment in China. Senator Henry Cabot Lodge concluded: "We ask no favors; we only ask that we shall be admitted to that great market upon the same terms with the rest of the world."

In September 1899 Hay began sending a series of Open Door notes to the European powers and Japan. The notes asked them to agree to three principles: (1) to keep all ports in their spheres open to all nations; (2) to allow Chinese officials to collect all tariffs and duties; and (3) to guarantee equal railroad, harbor, and tariff rates in their spheres to all nations trading in China. When the European nations and Japan did not reject the principles outright, Hay announced that the Open Door policy had been accepted.

Chinese resentment of foreigners continued to grow, however. It erupted in the spring of 1900, when a Chinese secret society—the "Fists of Righteous Harmony"—launched a rebellion to drive the "foreign devils" out of the country. They attacked Western missionaries and traders in northern China, killing about 300. Supported by some Chinese government officials, the "Boxers"—the name Westerners gave them because of the "Fists" in their Chinese name—laid siege to the large walled-in foreign settlement in the capital at Beijing (Peking). For eight weeks the siege continued until finally, in August, an international force rescued the foreigners.

The **Boxer Rebellion** ended, but John Hay feared that Japan and other nations would use it as an excuse to seize more Chinese territory. In a second series of Open Door notes, he pressured the foreign powers to observe open trade throughout China and to preserve China's right to rule its own territory. China retained its territory but had to pay foreign powers $333 million in damages for losses sustained during the Boxer Rebellion.

■■ **The United States worked to maintain its trading rights in China through the Open Door policy.**

*A*N EMERGING JAPAN

Japan's 1894 invasion of China marked Japan's emergence as an imperial power. A mere 41 years earlier Japan had ended its almost complete isolation from the rest of the world. From 1639 to the 1850s Japanese rulers had allowed only one Dutch trading ship a year to enter the country. However, Japan's foreign policy had suddenly changed in 1853, when Commodore Matthew Perry of the United States sailed his squadron of black-hulled warships, bristling with guns, into Edo (Tokyo) Bay. President Millard Fillmore had ordered Perry to persuade Japan to open its doors to trade with the rapidly industrializing West. The gifts Perry presented to Japan's rulers symbolized the industrial age: a telegraph transmitter and a model train.

Perry's warships and industrial wonders forced the Japanese to yield to Western demands for trade. But they also convinced Japanese rulers that they must modernize their country—build up its military might and its industry. If they did not, they reasoned, foreigners might gain control of their nation.

Japan rapidly transformed itself into an industrial power and built up its army and navy. Within four decades Japan had become a winner in the struggle for empire rather than a victim of it, as its war with China, and later with Russia, proved.

Japan and Russia were rivals for Chinese territories—especially for Korea and for the fertile soil and mineral riches of Manchuria in northern

▲ **Almost a year after Perry presented gifts to the Japanese, U.S. ships were allowed to trade in the ports of Hakodate and Shimoda.**

MAKING CONNECTIONS

Geography

By 1911 there were more than 50 treaty ports in China in which Westerners were granted the right of extraterritoriality. This meant that they were not subject to the laws of China.

MULTICULTURAL PERSPECTIVES

Some Chinese officials were suspicious of U.S. and European efforts to open relations with China. One Chinese official observed of foreign diplomats that they "think only of profit, and with the meretricious hope of profit they beguile the Chinese people." Have students give their own opinions about whether profit was the main goal of U.S. foreign policy in Asia at that time.

■■ Examine with students some current U.S. attitudes toward Japan. Compare these attitudes with the ways in which Americans viewed Japan in the mid-1850s.

RETEACH Organize students who require reteaching into groups. Ask half the groups to write headlines reflecting the events that took place in the U.S., the Philippines, Hawaii, China, or Japan. Have the remaining groups write two- or three-paragraph news stories explaining each headline.

Closure

Read aloud the quotation by Congressman Henry Cabot Lodge in 1889 on p. 213. Encourage students to explain and cite examples of why this statement was no longer true by 1907.

Extension

COMPARE Have students write a paper that compares manifest destiny with imperialism, explaining the similarities and differences between the two.

INVESTIGATE Have students investigate the terms of the treaty between Japan and Russia that was negotiated by Roosevelt and that won him the Nobel Peace Prize.

Chart Caption Answer
Students should weigh the reasons for U.S. involvement and its consequences.

SECTION REVIEW ANSWERS

IDENTIFY

For significance, see the following pages:
annex (p. 219)
Philippine Government Act (p. 220)
William Howard Taft (p. 221)
Jones Act of 1916 (p. 221)
Kalakaua (p. 221)
Liliuokalani (p. 222)
spheres of influence (p. 222)
John Hay (p. 223)
Boxer Rebellion (p. 223)
Matthew Perry (p. 223)
Russo-Japanese War (p. 224)

LOCATE

For locations, see the map on p. 220.

1. *annexed islands, crushed rebellion, set up government, delayed independence until 1946*
2. *Liliuokalani's plan to replace the Bayonet Constitution, revolt by U.S. settlers*
3. *to protect U.S. trade opportunities*
4. *Reports might suggest that Japan's growing power threatens U.S. influence in China and the Pacific.*
5. *Answers should weigh economic and political benefits against loss of sovereignty.*

U.S. IMPERIALISM

	U.S. Involvement	Interim Status	Current Status
Samoa	Agreement divides islands between U.S. and Germany (1899)	German Samoa achieves independence (1962)	American Samoa under U.S. control
Philippines	Ceded to U.S. (1898)	Philippine Government Act defines government (1902)	Independent republic (1946)
		Declared a commonwealth (1935)	
Cuba	American forces occupy Cuba (1898)	Platt Amendment authorizes U.S. intervention (1902)	Independent republic (1934)
Puerto Rico	Ceded to U.S. (1898)	Foraker Act establishes government (1900)	Declared a commonwealth (1952)
		Application for statehood (1924)	
Hawaii	U.S. annexation (1898)	Application for statehood (1937)	50th state (1959)

Sources: An Encyclopedia of World History, Webster's New Geographical Dictionary

AMERICAN EXPANSIONISM U.S. economic and security interests extended into Asia, the Pacific, the Caribbean, and Latin America at the turn of the century.

? ASSESSING CONSEQUENCES Using one of the countries on the chart as a case study, trace U.S. involvement and its consequences for the country's current status.

China. In February 1904, Japanese troops attacked Russian forces in Manchuria, starting the **Russo-Japanese War**. President Theodore Roosevelt watched the war closely. If Japan won, it might grow dangerously strong. If Russia won, it might cut off U.S. trade with Manchuria.

By May 1905 the Japanese had won a series of crucial battles, and they asked Roosevelt to negotiate peace with Russia. Roosevelt brought representatives of the two countries together at Portsmouth, New Hampshire, where they pounded out a treaty. It granted neither side all it wanted and left both dissatisfied. But it did end the war, and it won the Nobel Peace Prize for Roosevelt.

Aware that Japan might now turn its expansionist eye toward the Pacific, including the U.S.–held Philippines, Roosevelt decided to demonstrate American military might. In late 1907 he sent a fleet of 4 destroyers and 16 battleships, painted a dazzling white, on a 46,000-mile world cruise. The "Great White Fleet" sailed into the Japanese port of Yokohama, where it underscored Roosevelt's later boast that now "the Pacific was as much our home waters as the Atlantic."

■■ The United States came to see Japan, newly emergent as a modern world power, as a rival for influence in China and the Pacific.

SECTION 2 REVIEW

IDENTIFY and explain the significance of the following: annex, Philippine Government Act, Jones Act of 1916, William Howard Taft, Kalakaua, Liliuokalani, spheres of influence, John Hay, Boxer Rebellion, Matthew Perry, Russo-Japanese War.

LOCATE and explain the importance of the following: Hawaii; Taiwan; Korea; Beijing, China; Yokohama, Japan.

1. **MAIN IDEA** How did the United States respond to Filipino demands for independence?
2. **MAIN IDEA** What events led to the U.S. annexation of Hawaii?
3. **MAIN IDEA** What did the Open Door policy attempt to accomplish in China?
4. **WRITING TO EXPLAIN** Imagine you are a U.S. diplomat in Japan in 1905. Write a report to President Roosevelt, explaining why the United States should reevaluate its relationship with Japan.
5. **TAKING A STAND** Do you think the United States is ever justified in annexing a foreign territory? Give reasons for your answer.

PREVIEW WORKSHOP

Following is a list of the significant people, places, and terms in this section. You may wish to use this list as a section preview.

People
■ Leonard Wood
■ Carlos Finlay

Places
■ Guantánamo Bay
■ Panama Canal
■ Colombia
■ Venezuela
■ Dominican Republic
■ Nicaragua
■ Haiti

Terms
■ Platt Amendment

■ protectorate
■ Foraker Act
■ Jones Act of 1917
■ Clayton-Bulwer Treaty
■ Hay-Pauncefote Treaty
■ Hay-Herrán Treaty
■ Hay–Bunau-Varilla Treaty
■ Roosevelt Corollary
■ dollar diplomacy

Section 3

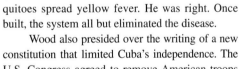

EXPANSION IN LATIN AMERICA

FOCUS OBJECTIVES

■ Determine how the U.S. dealt with Cuba and Puerto Rico after the Spanish-American War.

■ Identify the events that cleared the way for construction of the Panama Canal.

■ Explain how presidents Roosevelt, Taft, and Wilson enforced the Monroe Doctrine.

FOCUS

■ **How did the United States deal with Cuba and Puerto Rico after the Spanish-American War?**

■ **What events cleared the way for construction of the Panama Canal?**

■ **How did presidents Roosevelt, Taft, and Wilson enforce the Monroe Doctrine?**

From 1898 onward, as American power grew in the Pacific, the U.S. role in Latin America expanded as well. Cuba came under strong U.S. control, while Puerto Rico became an out-and-out American possession. The United States built a canal across the Isthmus of Panama in these years, and the U.S. presence was felt throughout Latin America.

President Theodore Roosevelt at Panama Canal site

GOVERNING CUBA AND PUERTO RICO

Both Cuba and Puerto Rico hoped that the peace treaty ending the Spanish-American War would bring independence from Spain followed by the speedy departure of American troops. After all, the Teller Amendment had pledged to Cuba that the United States would allow Cubans to control their government. But Cubans and Puerto Ricans were disappointed. Wanting to restore order quickly in both countries and thus protect U.S. investments, President McKinley set up military governments to rule the islands.

McKinley appointed General Leonard Wood governor of Cuba in 1899. Wood authorized the construction of schools and a sanitation system. U.S. Army doctors Walter Reed and William Gorgas had called for the sanitation system to reduce the mosquito population. Carlos Finlay

▲ Carlos Finlay

(feen-LY), a Cuban doctor, had theorized that mosquitoes spread yellow fever. He was right. Once built, the system all but eliminated the disease.

Wood also presided over the writing of a new constitution that limited Cuba's independence. The U.S. Congress agreed to remove American troops only if Cuba made the **Platt Amendment** part of its constitution. The Platt Amendment (1) limited Cuba's freedom to make treaties with other countries; (2) authorized the United States to intervene in Cuban affairs as it saw necessary; and (3) required Cuba to sell or lease land to the United States for naval and fueling stations. This last clause eventually led to the establishment of the U.S. Navy base at Guantánamo Bay (see map on page 234). In effect, the Platt Amendment made Cuba an American **protectorate**: America promised to protect Cuba from other nations but reserved the right to intervene in Cuba's affairs.

In 1902, after Cuba reluctantly accepted the Platt Amendment, U.S.

CORE RESOURCES

• **Social Studies Skills Worksheet 9**
• **Literature Worksheet 9**
• **Section 3 Daily Quiz**

AV RESOURCES

• *The American Nation* **Videodisc: The Panama Canal**

MOTIVATING:
LINK TO TODAY

Ask students to describe what they know about the relationships that exist between the U.S. and Cuba, Puerto Rico, or Panama today. Then tell students that in this section they will gain some insights into why those relationships are what they are today.

Teaching the Section

CUBA AND PUERTO RICO

List on the chalkboard the three clauses of the Platt Amendment. Ask volunteers to identify the goal of U.S. policy in Cuba and how the clauses of the Platt Amendment furthered this goal. Then have volunteers suggest possible advantages and disadvantages for Cuba of U.S. intervention. Have them speculate about why Cubans were reluctant to agree to the Platt Amendment. Then have students explain how and why the U.S. treated Puerto Rico differently from Cuba.

MULTICULTURAL PERSPECTIVES

The Platt Amendment created long-lasting resentment among Cubans. One Cuban professor denounced the amendment and U.S. imperialism, saying, "We are bound and gagged . . . by your bankers, by your politicians, by your Platt Amendment. . . . We are exiles in our own land." Cuban journalist Carlo Franqui wrote that Cuba was "born deformed because it existed . . . to produce sugar and wealth for U.S. investors." Have students react to these quotes.

HISTORICAL SIDELIGHTS

The Nicaraguan Canal
In the 1880s and 1890s, many U.S. leaders supported building a canal through Nicaragua partly because the French company that controlled the Panama Canal wanted an exorbitant amount—more than $109 million—for its rights. However, U.S. attorney William N. Cromwell persuaded the Republican party to end its support for a Nicaraguan canal. Cromwell worked with Philippe Bunau-Varilla to convince the French company to lower its price to $40 million, and the two took over the French rights. They then worked out a deal with the U.S. for the rights.

troops left. But a U.S. presence remained at the naval base at Guantánamo Bay, which was leased in 1903. Over the next three decades, the United States intervened in Cuba several times. It pressured Cuba into accepting policies favorable to U.S. investors and sent in troops when it decided that the Cuban government could not keep order. The Platt Amendment remained in force until 1934, when America renounced its right to intervene in Cuba. Even then, however, U.S. influence over Cuban affairs remained great.

For Puerto Rico, U.S. policy followed a different course. No Teller Amendment guaranteed independence for Puerto Rico, so the United States ruled the island as a territory like Samoa or the Philippines in the Pacific. But just how these new territories were to be governed raised a thorny legal question for the United States. Were the people of these territories entitled to all the rights of U.S. citizens?

No, ruled the Supreme Court in 1901. The Court argued that the new territories were not fully part of the United States. Therefore, Congress could choose which rights to extend them. The Court affirmed the **Foraker Act** of 1900, which called for Puerto Rico's governor and upper house of the legislature to be appointed by the United States and a lower house to be elected by Puerto Ricans.

The **Jones Act of 1917** made Puerto Ricans American citizens and gave them the right to elect both houses of their legislature. In 1952 Puerto

▲ After Puerto Rico became a U.S. territory, the government built new public schools such as the one shown here.

► The Panama Canal was built by the United States between 1904 and 1914. Shown here are laborers who helped construct the canal.

Rico became a self-governing commonwealth of the United States, which retains ties of citizenship and trade with the mainland.

■■ **After the Spanish-American War, the United States retained a strong influence in Cuba, and Puerto Rico became a U.S. territory.**

THE PANAMA CANAL

With such vital interests in both the Caribbean and the Pacific, the United States looked for a way to cut the travel time between the seas. The long and hazardous voyage around Cape Horn at the southern tip of South America took several weeks. In response the United States proposed digging a canal through a narrow neck of land in Central America to allow the U.S. Navy to police both seas.

Early steps toward a canal. The idea for such a canal was not new. As far back as 1517, Vasco Núñez de Balboa had proposed that a canal be dug across the 50-mile-wide Isthmus of Panama. In 1850 the United States and Great Britain had drawn up the **Clayton-Bulwer Treaty**, proposing an equal partnership to build and run a Central American canal, but they never acted on it. In the 1880s a French company actually worked on a canal across the Isthmus. But after less than 10 years and the loss of some 20,000 lives and more than $280 million, the French abandoned the effort. Deadly tropical diseases, repeated landslides, and bankruptcy killed the project.

Finally, in 1901 President Theodore Roosevelt decided that "after four centuries of conversation" by other countries, it was time for the United States to act. He instructed Secretary of State John Hay to negotiate with Great Britain

226

Changing Ways — A PATH BETWEEN THE SEAS

On August 15, 1914, the SS *Ancon* completed the first passage through the Panama Canal, a 51-mile-long ribbon of waters connecting the Caribbean Sea and the Pacific Ocean. The voyage marked the completion of what Theodore Roosevelt called "the greatest task of its own kind that has ever been performed in the world at all!"

Americans began working on the canal in 1904. Roosevelt was eager "to make the dirt fly" in Panama, but poor working conditions and shortages hampered U.S. efforts from the start. Then in late 1904 a large outbreak of yellow fever hit. By early 1905 the project was at a near standstill.

To put the project back on track, Roosevelt appointed John F. Stevens as chief engineer and architect. Stevens tackled the technical problems, while army colonel Dr. William C. Gorgas worked on improving living conditions. Gorgas, who had helped rid Cuba of tropical diseases, had drinking water purified and buildings screened. Then, to destroy the breeding places of the mosquitoes that transmit yellow fever and malaria, he had swamps drained and standing water coated with oil. By 1906 yellow fever had almost been eliminated. Malaria was under control by 1913.

Panama Canal Zone

Map showing the Panama Canal Zone, with the Caribbean Sea to the north, the Pacific Ocean to the south, and labels including Colón, Cristóbal, Gatun Locks, Gatun Lake, Gaillard Cut, Pedro Miguel Locks, Miraflores Locks, Balboa, Panama, Fort Amador, Río Chagres, Continental Divide, and the Canal Zone. Scale in miles and kilometers, Lambert Conformal Conic Projection.

STRATEGIC INTERESTS Because it took the U.S. naval vessel *Oregon* 66 days to sail from San Francisco around Cape Horn to Key West during the Spanish-American War, pressure increased to build a U.S.–controlled canal through Central America.

? LOCATION If you enter the Panama Canal from the Caribbean Sea on the Atlantic side, which direction will you travel to exit on the Pacific Ocean?

Canal construction soon resumed in force. More than 60 giant steam shovels bit into the land, digging out nearly 160 trainloads of earth each day. Workers numbered more than 43,000, many of whom were recruited from the British West Indies.

Originally, the canal was designed to be built at sea level, but the difficulty of moving millions of tons of dirt and rock prompted a new design—an elevated waterway using locks. One group of workers dredged an approach channel and built a dam and locks on the Atlantic side. Another group dredged a passage from the Pacific through the Bay of Panama and constructed two smaller sets of locks. The hardest job fell to another group, which had to blast an eight-mile-wide path through the mountainous Continental Divide. Geologic faults, heavy rains, and shifting earth caused frequent and often fatal avalanches. But finally, on October 10, 1913, President Wilson signaled crews to dynamite the protective dike at the south end of the canal. In a dramatic finale, water from the two sides rushed together—85 feet above sea level.

The human and economic costs of building the canal were staggering: some 6,000 workers died and about $366 million was spent. But the seemingly impossible had become a reality. The United States—and the rest of the world—now had a "Path Between the Seas."

Changing Ways

A PATH BETWEEN THE SEAS

LINK TO TODAY

The Panama Canal became a vacation destination for wealthy Americans. In 1913, some 20,000 U.S. tourists went to Panama to see the engineering marvel under construction.

■■ Ask students if the Panama Canal is a popular vacation site for U.S. tourists today. Why or why not?

Map Caption Answer
southeast

HISTORICAL SIDELIGHTS

The Big Ditch
In the U.S. the Panama Canal was also known as the "Big Ditch." It lopped some 7,800 miles off the trip between New York City and San Francisco, and it reduced travel time by three weeks. William Gorgas's work in clearing the canal zone of yellow fever proved beneficial in the U.S. as well. Cities such as New Orleans and Mobile implemented the sanitation practices that Gorgas pioneered in order to control infectious diseases.

Teaching the Section

THE PANAMA CANAL

Work with students to create on the chalkboard a time line of the events that cleared the way for the construction of the Panama Canal. Then have students use the time line to write paragraphs explaining how President Roosevelt "took the Canal and let Congress debate." Students may wish to include their paragraphs in their portfolios.

THREE PRESIDENTS AND THE MONROE DOCTRINE

Select three students to role-play presidents Roosevelt, Taft, and Wilson. Organize remaining students into groups to act as journalists from the U.S. and various Latin American countries. Each group should prepare questions for a press conference and interview the three presidents about similarities and differences in their application of the Monroe Doctrine in Latin America and the effects of these actions.

HISTORICAL SIDELIGHTS

Canalimony

Although Roosevelt considered the taking of the canal an achievement equal in magnitude to the Louisiana Purchase or the acquisition of Texas, some American political leaders had second thoughts about how Colombia had been treated. In 1922, the U.S. government paid $25 million to Colombia, an expenditure which many labeled "conscience money" or "canalimony."

COOPERATIVE LEARNING

Organize students into five groups. Within four of the groups assign each student a different Latin American country discussed in the section. Assign the remaining students the role of U.S. diplomats. Have the students of each Latin American group discuss the fairness of the Roosevelt Corollary and dollar diplomacy from their country's perspective and compose a written alternative to these U.S. policies. Then add one or more U.S. diplomats to each group and have the groups negotiate with him or her for acceptance of their policy alternatives.

to end the partnership set up by the Clayton-Bulwer Treaty. In the resulting **Hay-Pauncefote Treaty**, Britain agreed that the United States could build the canal by itself and have "exclusive management and policing of it." In return, the United States promised to keep the canal open to all the world's vessels in wartime as well as in peacetime.

Hay then began negotiations with the Republic of Colombia—of which Panama was then a part. In 1903 the **Hay-Herrán Treaty** was drafted. In return for a 99-year lease on a six-mile strip of land across the Isthmus, the United States agreed to pay Colombia $10 million and a yearly rental of $250,000. But holding out for better terms, Colombia's senate adjourned without ratifying the treaty. A furious President Roosevelt accused the Colombians of blackmail and swore that they must not be allowed "to bar one of the future highways of civilization."

▲ John Hay served as secretary of state from 1898 until his death in 1905.

Revolution in Panama. Events in Panama soon turned in Roosevelt's favor. Key Panamanian leaders who wanted the canal built began plotting revolution against the Colombian government. Helping them was Philippe Bunau-Varilla (boo-noh-vah-ree-yah), the former chief engineer for the French canal-building attempt.

Bunau-Varilla traveled to Washington to get American support for the revolution. On October 9, 1903, he met privately with President Roosevelt. Exactly what was said at the meeting remains unknown, but on November 2 the U.S. gunboat *Nashville* arrived in Panama. The following day, Panamanians began their rebellion. U.S. Marines prevented Colombian forces from reaching the rebels.

On November 4, 1903, the victorious rebels set up a new government and declared Panama an independent nation. Acting with lightning speed, the United States two days later recognized the

▲ This 1903 cartoon shows Roosevelt digging the Panama Canal and throwing dirt in the direction of Colombia, the country that had refused to ratify an earlier canal treaty.

Republic of Panama, and Hay began negotiating a new canal treaty with Panama's special envoy, Bunau-Varilla. The **Hay–Bunau-Varilla Treaty** gave the United States complete and unending sovereignty over a 10-mile-wide Canal Zone.

Did the United States engineer the Panamanian revolution? The facts remain obscure, but President Theodore Roosevelt later boasted, "I took the Canal Zone and let Congress debate." It is clear that U.S. aid to the Panamanian rebels and America's immediate recognition of Panama as an independent nation served American interests and made the Panama Canal possible. American trade and naval power grew stronger because of it, allowing the United States to extend its economic and political interests in Latin America.

■■ The Panamanian revolution and a favorable treaty cleared the way for the United States to build and retain control of the Panama Canal.

*A*PPLYING THE MONROE DOCTRINE

The American interventions in Cuba, Puerto Rico, and Panama were only three instances in a long history of U.S. involvement in Latin America. As far back as 1823, the Monroe Doctrine had cast the United States as protector

Construct on the chalkboard a three-column chart with the headings *Big Stick, Dollar Diplomacy,* and *Democratic Governments.* Have volunteers define each policy, identify the president who followed it, list how it was carried out, and identify countries targeted by each. Write the information on the chart.

INDEPENDENT PRACTICE

Have students write letters to the president as a citizen of one of the countries listed in the Guided Practice. Letters should support or denounce that president's policies toward their country. Students may wish to include their letters in their portfolios.

Review and Assessment

REVIEW Guide students to make an annotated time line for the period from 1898 to 1914, showing key events in the history of U.S–Latin American relations during that time period. Then assign the Section 3 Review on p. 230.

ASSESS Assign the **Section 3 Daily Quiz** in *Core Resources.*

▶

---

of the hemisphere. But for much of the century the doctrine was little more than an idle threat. This changed following the Spanish-American War, as presidents Theodore Roosevelt, William H. Taft, and Woodrow Wilson actively enforced the Monroe Doctrine in an effort to protect U.S. interests in Latin America (see map on page 234).

The Roosevelt Corollary. Latin America, with its wealth of raw materials and potential consumers, attracted a flood of European and American capital during the late 1800s. Much of this capital was in the form of high-interest bank loans. Although many Latin American countries welcomed the loans, difficulty in repaying them often resulted in foreign intervention. In 1902, for example, Great Britain, Germany, and Italy blockaded and attacked Venezuelan ships and ports when the nation failed to repay its loans. President Roosevelt quickly warned the three European powers not to seize any Venezuelan land and convinced them to settle the issue through arbitration.

Roosevelt's actions sent a clear signal that he intended to enforce the Monroe Doctrine. Roosevelt underscored this point in 1904 when the Dominican Republic proved unable to repay its European lenders. Fearing that the Europeans would use force to collect the loans, he issued the **Roosevelt Corollary** to the Monroe Doctrine:

❝ If a nation . . . keeps order and pays its obligations, it need fear no interference from the United States. Chronic wrongdoing . . . in the Western Hemisphere . . . may force the United States, however reluctantly, . . . to the exercise of an international police power. ❞

Without seeking approval from any Latin American nation, Roosevelt assumed the role of "international police officer" in the Western Hemisphere. He had applied in practice the West African proverb he loved to quote: "Speak softly and carry a big stick; you will go far."

Next, Roosevelt convinced the Dominican government to accept U.S. assistance. The United States pledged to use American armed forces to stop any European country from seizing Dominican territory. In exchange, the Dominican government agreed to let the United States collect all Dominican customs duties and turn half over to

YANKEE IMPERIALISM

*A*lthough much of Latin America had at first favored the Monroe Doctrine, support for the policy began to dwindle by the early 1900s. As Peruvian diplomat Francisco García Calderón noted, the Monroe Doctrine took "an aggressive form with Mr. [Theodore] Roosevelt, the politician of the 'big stick.'" Writing in 1913, García Calderón chronicled the list of recent U.S. interventions in Panama, Cuba, the Dominican Republic, and Venezuela. As a result of this "Yankee imperialism," he claimed, "everywhere the Americans of the North are feared" and "hostility against the Anglo-Saxon invaders assumes the character of a . . . crusade." In the view of Mexican scholar Luis Quintanilla, the Roosevelt Corollary had twisted the Monroe Doctrine "from a case of America vs. Europe" to one of "United States vs. America."

foreign creditors. In 1916, when civil disturbances racked the Dominican Republic, the United States government sent in marines. They did not leave until eight years later, in 1924.

■■ **The Roosevelt Corollary established a greater U.S. role in Latin America.**

Some Latin American countries objected to Roosevelt's policy. They argued that every country should maintain control over its own affairs. Some Latin American countries issued a declaration stating that debts owed to other countries could not be collected by force. But despite Latin American protests, intervention continued.

Dollar diplomacy. Roosevelt's successor as president, William H. Taft, further extended U.S. influence in Latin America. Taft favored "substituting dollars for bullets"—economic influence for military force—as a means of protecting U.S.

RETEACH For each subsection in the section, have students write a sentence that summarizes the main idea. Select students to read their statements aloud. Have the group choose the best summary sentence for each section.

Closure

Organize students into groups to decide how the following statement applied to U.S. actions in each of the countries discussed in this section: *The purpose of U.S. foreign policy is to promote and protect U.S. economic or political interests.*

Extension

CREATE Have students create political cartoons that illustrate U.S. policy in Latin America from 1891 to 1914. Students should present and interpret their cartoons for the class.

RESEARCH Direct students to research and report on the steps taken to return the canal to Panama in the year 2000.

Graph Caption Answer
about $1.2 billion

SECTION REVIEW ANSWERS

IDENTIFY

For significance, see the following pages:
Leonard Wood (p. 225)
Carlos Finlay (p. 225)
Platt Amendment (p. 225)
protectorate (p. 225)
Foraker Act (p. 226)
Jones Act of 1917 (p. 226)
Clayton-Bulwer Treaty (p. 226)
Hay-Pauncefote Treaty (p. 228)
Hay-Herrán Treaty (p. 228)
Hay–Bunau-Varilla Treaty (p. 228)
Roosevelt Corollary (p. 229)
dollar diplomacy (p. 230)

LOCATE

For locations, see the map on p. 234.

1. *Cuba became a U.S. protectorate; Puerto Rico became a U.S. territory, then a self-governing commonwealth.*
2. *enabled U.S. to build and control Panama Canal*
3. *All three sent in troops. Taft encouraged U.S. investment and Wilson democratic government as stabilizing forces.*
4. *Speeches might mention the right of each country to maintain control over its own affairs and resources.*
5. *Teller Amendment would have guaranteed Puerto Rico's independence and thus limited the range of U.S. intervention.*

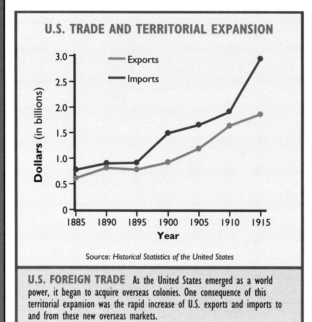

U.S. TRADE AND TERRITORIAL EXPANSION

Source: *Historical Statistics of the United States*

U.S. FOREIGN TRADE As the United States emerged as a world power, it began to acquire overseas colonies. One consequence of this territorial expansion was the rapid increase of U.S. exports and imports to and from these new overseas markets.

? **BUILDING GRAPH SKILLS** What was the difference in the value of U.S. exports and imports by 1915?

the chances of European intervention. By 1914 U.S. capital in Latin America had grown to over $1.6 billion, mainly invested in railroads, mines, and banana and sugar plantations.

Nicaragua was one of the places that Taft put dollar diplomacy to the test. At the invitation of the Nicaraguan president, American bankers made loans totaling $1.5 million to Nicaragua in 1911. The following year, Taft sent more than 2,000 marines to crush a revolt and to protect the U.S. investments that had poured in.

Taft's successor, President Woodrow Wilson, believed that democratic governments, not U.S. dollars, would keep European powers out of Latin America. To keep Germany from taking control of strategic Caribbean territory, Wilson sent marines to several Caribbean countries to put down rebellions and establish constitutional governments. In 1915, when revolution shook Haiti, Wilson sent in marines. Haiti was forced to accept a treaty giving the United States powers in running the Haitian government, and the marines stayed until 1934. Some 1,500 Haitians died resisting U.S. control.

■■ **Taft's dollar diplomacy and Wilson's military interventions increased U.S. political and economic influence in Latin America.**

interests in Latin America (see map on page 234). To implement this policy, which came to be called **dollar diplomacy**, Taft suggested replacing European loans with American ones. Increasing U.S. economic power, Taft argued, would reduce

SECTION 3 REVIEW

IDENTIFY and explain the significance of the following: Leonard Wood, Carlos Finlay, Platt Amendment, protectorate, Foraker Act, Jones Act of 1917, Clayton-Bulwer Treaty, Hay-Pauncefote Treaty, Hay-Herrán Treaty, Hay–Bunau-Varilla Treaty, Roosevelt Corollary, dollar diplomacy.

LOCATE and explain the importance of the following: Guantánamo Bay, Panama Canal, Colombia, Venezuela, Dominican Republic, Nicaragua, Haiti.

1. **MAIN IDEA** How did the U.S. relationship with Cuba and Puerto Rico change after the Spanish-American War?
2. **MAIN IDEA** Why did the United States support the Panamanian rebels and recognize the Republic of Panama?
3. **CONTRASTING** How did presidents Roosevelt, Taft, and Wilson apply the Monroe Doctrine in Latin America?
4. **WRITING TO PERSUADE** Imagine you are a political leader in a Latin American country during this period. Write a speech seeking to persuade the U.S. government not to interfere in the affairs of your country.
5. **HYPOTHESIZING** How might U.S. policy toward Puerto Rico have been different if the Teller Amendment had been extended to apply to that territory?

230

Section 4

CONFLICT WITH MEXICO

FOCUS
- **How did the Mexican Revolution affect relations between the United States and Mexico?**
- **Why did the United States intervene in Mexico?**
- **Why did tensions between the two countries remain strong during Carranza's presidency?**

*D*ollar diplomacy played a significant role in another Latin American country: Mexico. Though many Mexicans uneasily referred to the United States as "the Colossus of the North," economic ties between the two countries increased in the late 19th century. But the Mexican Revolution of 1910 threatened these ties, bringing the two countries to the brink of war.

American artillery along the Mexican border, 1916

THE MEXICAN REVOLUTION

Dollars helped tie Mexico and the United States closer together in the late 19th century, thanks to Mexico's president, Porfirio Díaz. Díaz, who with the political support of wealthy landowners ruled Mexico for more than 30 years, offered special concessions to attract foreign investment. By 1908, U.S. companies controlled three quarters of all Mexican mining operations. Total U.S. investments amounted to almost $1 million by 1913.

Foreign investors helped develop Mexico's economy by building railroads that linked Mexico to U.S. and other foreign markets. But foreign investors and Díaz's friends profited the most from economic growth. Little trickled down to workers and peasants. Indeed, Díaz's policies helped wealthy Mexicans and foreigners take land away from peasants. As a result, most Mexicans—mainly landless peasants and struggling urban workers—lived in poverty.

In 1910 Díaz used force and fraud to defeat opposition candidate Francisco Madero. Peasants, workers, and the middle class, angry at the lack of political democracy, rallied behind Madero in armed revolt against Díaz beginning in November. The rebels defeated Díaz's troops in key cities in northern and central Mexico, forcing Díaz into exile in Paris in 1911. In Mexico's first democratic elections in 30 years, Madero won the presidency.

Madero sought to establish a democratic government, but few agreed on the details. The revolutionary leaders who had supported Madero against

▼ **Women served in military roles during the Mexican Revolution. This 1911 photograph shows a group of female revolutionaries armed with rifles.**

MOTIVATING:
PRIOR KNOWLEDGE

Have students read the section's introductory paragraph. Note that a colossus is a statue or person of gigantic size and power. Ask students to apply what they have learned about U.S. actions in other parts of Latin America to speculate about whether "Colossus of the North" is positive or negative.

Teaching the **Section**

THE MEXICAN REVOLUTION

Assign each of nine volunteers these identities: Porfirio Díaz, Pancho Villa, Francisco Madero, Victoriano Huerta, Venustiano Carranza, Emiliano Zapata, Henry Lane Wilson, Woodrow Wilson, John J. Pershing. Have volunteers line up in any order and without identifying their character explain why and how "he" participated in the revolution and how his actions affected U.S.–Mexican relations. As volunteers present their statements, have students list the speaker's identity on a sheet of paper. When the activity is complete, have students check their lists for accuracy.

HISTORICAL SIDELIGHTS

Wilson *vs.* Wilson

President Wilson was furious at the part played by U.S. ambassador Henry Lane Wilson in the overthrow of the Madero government. In 1913 the president had Wilson recalled. Despite private investments by Americans totaling more than $1 billion, by 1913 President Wilson announced that he was "not the servant of those who wish to enhance the value of their Mexican investments."

 GLOBAL CONNECTIONS

The British regarded President Wilson's opposition to Huerta as impractical and unreasonable. However, the British feared the growing power of Germany and thought that maintaining American goodwill was important in case war broke out in Europe. The British foreign office agreed to advise Huerta to retire from office and recalled its minister from Mexico.

PRIMARY SOURCE

Description of Change: excerpted
Rationale: excerpted to focus on main idea

Díaz thought Madero's plan did not go far enough in such areas as returning land to the peasants. Others, including conservative military officers and wealthy landowners, thought the plan went too far.

Complicating this situation was Henry Lane Wilson, the U.S. ambassador, who did not believe Madero could protect U.S. investments in Mexico. Wilson overstepped his diplomatic role by arranging for factions opposed to Madero to meet and discuss Madero's overthrow. In 1913, backed by wealthy landowners and foreign business interests, General Victoriano Huerta (WER-tah) seized control of the government and had Madero thrown into jail. Huerta's soldiers shot Madero when, they alleged, he attempted to escape.

Madero's murder outraged President Woodrow Wilson. He angrily refused to recognize Huerta, calling his regime a "government of butchers." Civil war raged in Mexico as revolutionary armies battled to drive Huerta out. President Wilson adopted a policy of "watchful waiting," hoping that the revolutionaries would be successful. He also authorized arms sales to the revolutionaries, while refusing to allow arms sales to Huerta's forces.

▲ **Pancho Villa, center, and Emiliano Zapata, right, are shown with their followers in the presidential palace in Mexico City.**

■■ **The Mexican Revolution strained U.S.–Mexican relations as the fighting disrupted Mexico's government and society.**

---

*A*MERICAN INTERVENTION

Four major revolutionary armies continued to fight Huerta. But their leaders—Venustiano Carranza (bay-noos-TYAHN-oh kahr-RAHN-sah), Francisco "Pancho" Villa, Emiliano Zapata, and Álvaro Obregón (oh-bray-GAWN)—were not united. Two of the leaders, Carranza and Villa, actually hated each other. Although the revolutionaries controlled territory throughout Mexico, Wilson worried that they would never be able to defeat Huerta.

In 1914 an incident occurred that gave Wilson an excuse to intervene directly. On April 9, Huerta's soldiers arrested several crew members from the USS *Dolphin*. The U.S. sailors had gone ashore for supplies at the Mexican port of Tampico. The Americans were released unharmed, but Wilson pursued the matter. He backed the American admiral, who demanded an apology and a public ceremony in which Mexico would "hoist the American flag in a prominent position and salute it with twenty-one guns." Huerta made the apology but refused to perform the ceremony.

On April 20 President Wilson went before Congress:

❝ I . . . come to ask your approval that I should use the armed forces of the United States . . . to obtain from General Huerta and his adherents the fullest recognition of the rights and dignity of the United States, even amidst the distressing conditions now unhappily obtaining in Mexico. ❞

Before Congress could act, Wilson learned that a German ship bearing arms for Huerta was heading for the Mexican port of Veracruz. He ordered the U.S. Navy to land marines at Veracruz, take the customs house, and prevent the weapons from being delivered. By the time Congress voted Wilson the authority to use force, the order had been carried out.

THE U.S. AND CARRANZA

Draw on the chalkboard a horizontal line labeled *Justified* on one end and *Unjustified* on the other. Organize students into congressional foreign policy subcommittees. Each group's assignment is to determine whether U.S. intervention in Mexican affairs was justified or unjustified in each of these circumstances: U.S. Marines' landing at Veracruz, Pershing's pursuit of Pancho Villa into Mexico, battle of Carrizal, withdrawal of U.S. troops from Mexico after Carrizal battle, Wilson's request to Carranza to allow the U.S. to intervene in Mexico to protect U.S. investments. Have each group report its findings by placing a mark on the continuum for each action and explaining the placement to the class.

At this critical stage Argentina, Brazil, and Chile—sometimes called the "ABC powers"—organized a conference at Niagara Falls, Ontario, to resolve the crisis. The conference urged Huerta to resign. Since his forces were losing, he complied and fled to Spain. In August 1914 Carranza marched into Mexico City. For the next year the revolutionary generals battled each other for control of the presidency.

■■ **The United States intervened in Mexico to help overthrow the antirevolutionary Huerta government.**

CARRANZA IN POWER

In 1915 Carranza assumed the presidency, and American forces withdrew from Veracruz. The United States recognized Carranza's government in the same year, after he guaranteed that Mexico would respect foreign lives and property.

BIO GRAPHY Venustiano Carranza, with his trim white goatee and his "gentlemanly bearing," hardly fit anyone's picture of a typical revolutionary. Born in 1859 in the state of Coahuila (koh-uh-WEE-luh) in northern Mexico, he was over 50 years old when he took up the rebel cause.

Carranza, who owned a large, profitable ranch, had held many government offices under Díaz. But in 1908 Díaz and Carranza clashed, and three years later, Carranza joined Madero's fight to overthrow Díaz. After Madero was deposed, Carranza helped defeat Huerta's forces. He used his experience as head of a revolutionary army and his considerable political talents to gain the presidency of Mexico.

Venustiano Carranza

Carranza's presidency was marked by conflict. Pancho Villa, who had hoped for U.S. support against Carranza, decided to retaliate against the Americans for recognizing Carranza as president. Villa communicated his plans to rebel leader Emiliano Zapata:

66 We have decided not to fire a bullet more against Mexicans, our brothers, and to prepare and organize ourselves to attack the Americans in their own dens and make them know that Mexico is a land for the free and a tomb for thrones, crowns, and traitors. 99

In March 1916 some 500 of Villa's men crossed the border to raid Columbus, New Mexico. Villa's men burned and looted the surprised town and army post. Seventeen Americans—nine civilians and eight soldiers—were killed, while more than a hundred Mexicans were killed. Villa hoped the raid would provoke American intervention in Mexico that would undermine Carranza's regime. He did not have to wait long for this result.

Without Carranza's approval President Wilson ordered an expedition into Mexico to capture Villa "dead or alive." A week after Villa's raid, General John J. Pershing led a force of some 5,800 men into Chihuahua, Villa's home state. Although Pershing later increased his troop size to more than 10,000 men, Villa eluded capture. The deeper Pershing pushed into Mexican territory, the more the Mexicans resented the Americans.

A battle between Mexican and U.S. troops in June brought the United States and Mexico to the brink of war. Carranza ordered Mexican troops to prevent U.S. soldiers from going any farther south. When one of Pershing's cavalry units attempted to pass through the town of Carrizal, the commander of the Mexican garrison refused passage. Instead of bypassing the town, the U.S. commander entered Carrizal, and a battle ensued.

▲ In 1916 President Wilson sent U.S. soldiers into Mexico to capture Pancho Villa, "dead or alive."

PRIMARY SOURCE
Description of Change: excerpted
Rationale: excerpted to focus on main idea

BIO GRAPHY **PERSONALITIES IN HISTORY**

Carranza was a moderate political reformer who opposed the sweeping social changes that Zapata and Villa favored. After he became president, Carranza did little to institute the far-reaching land reforms that the Constitution of 1917 called for.

MULTICULTURAL PERSPECTIVES

The Mexican Revolution created a great upsurge of immigration to the U.S. Some Mexicans emigrated when their towns were occupied by rebel troops; others, such as Señora Flores de Andrade, went to the U.S. hoping to support the revolution. Flores de Andrade left Chihuahua, Mexico, for El Paso, Texas, in 1906 to raise money and arms to overthrow Díaz. After Madero's execution, however, she grew disenchanted with the struggle, noting with bitterness in the 1920s that "the revolution promised a great deal to the Mexican people but hasn't accomplished anything."

Practice

GUIDED PRACTICE

Write the following statement on the chalkboard: *Concern for U.S. investments justified U.S. intervention in Mexico.* Have volunteers react to this statement as you write key phrases of their responses on the chalkboard. Then change the statement to read: *Concern for Mexican investments justifies Mexican intervention in the U.S.* Compare student reactions to this statement with reactions to the first statement.

INDEPENDENT PRACTICE

Invite students to imagine that they are Mexican citizens. Have them write letters to friends in the U.S., explaining how they feel about U.S. intervention in Mexico during the revolution.

Review and Assessment

REVIEW Ask students to create cause-and-effect charts showing events of the Mexican Revolution and effects of those events on U.S.–Mexican relations. Students may wish to include their charts in their portfolios. Then assign the Section 4 Review on p. 235.

ASSESS Assign the **Section 4 Daily Quiz** in *Core Resources*.

Map Caption Answer
Panama, Nicaragua, Cuba, Haiti, Dominican Republic

HISTORICAL SIDELIGHTS
Constitution of 1917
The 1917 Constitution gave the Mexican government the right to redistribute land from wealthy landowners to peasants, provided factory workers with minimum wages and the right to strike, allowed the president to deport foreigners, limited the powers of the Catholic Church, and provided for free and compulsory public schools.

AV TRANSPARENCY

Linking Geography and History Transparency and **Worksheet 15**

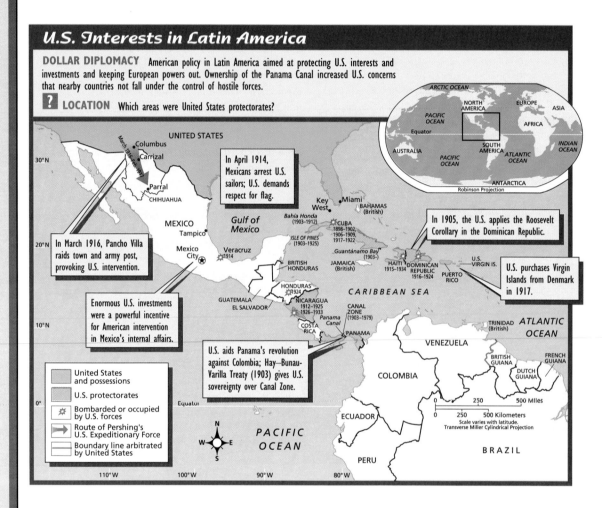

U.S. Interests in Latin America

DOLLAR DIPLOMACY American policy in Latin America aimed at protecting U.S. interests and investments and keeping European powers out. Ownership of the Panama Canal increased U.S. concerns that nearby countries not fall under the control of hostile forces.

? LOCATION Which areas were United States protectorates?

In April 1914, Mexicans arrest U.S. sailors; U.S. demands respect for flag.

In March 1916, Pancho Villa raids town and army post, provoking U.S. intervention.

Enormous U.S. investments were a powerful incentive for American intervention in Mexico's internal affairs.

U.S. aids Panama's revolution against Colombia; Hay–Bunau–Varilla Treaty (1903) gives U.S. sovereignty over Canal Zone.

In 1905, the U.S. applies the Roosevelt Corollary in the Dominican Republic.

U.S. purchases Virgin Islands from Denmark in 1917.

Legend:
- United States and possessions
- U.S. protectorates
- Bombarded or occupied by U.S. forces
- Route of Pershing's U.S. Expeditionary Force
- Boundary line arbitrated by United States

By early September 1916 nearly 150,000 U.S. National Guardsmen were stationed along the Mexican border. But the prospect of armed conflict with Mexico was extremely unpopular in the United States, particularly since events in Europe and on the high seas threatened to pull the United States into World War I (see Chapter 10). Wilson backed down. In exchange for withdrawing U.S. troops, Wilson asked Carranza to adopt a measure that would allow the United States to intervene in Mexico to protect U.S. investments. Carranza refused to limit Mexican sovereignty in this way. Realizing that the threat of war increased with every day U.S. troops remained in Mexico, Wilson ordered U.S. troops withdrawn in January 1917.

In that same year, Carranza approved a sweeping new constitution for Mexico, but he would not have much time to put its provisions in place. In 1920 he was overthrown and killed by forces loyal to another revolutionary leader—Álvaro Obregón.

Obregón and subsequent Mexican presidents gradually implemented the new constitution, which would have important repercussions for U.S. oil companies in Mexico in the 1930s (see Chapter 15).

▪▪ Villa's raid on a U.S. town raised tensions between the United States and Mexico to a dangerous pitch.

COMMENTARY

Expansion in Perspective

In the years from 1890 to 1920, America's global involvement expanded enormously. In some cases this involvement meant actual

RETEACH Ask students, working in pairs, to write sentences that explain how each person in the Preview Workshop is related to the main idea of the subsection in which the person is located.

Closure

Have students reread the warning on p. 215 by Samoan leader Te'o Tuvale to his fellow Samoans and speculate about whether Mexican president Venustiano Carranza would have agreed with it. Have students suggest ways in which Carranza might have reworded Tuvale's statement to reflect Mexico's experience with the U.S.

Extension

CREATE Ask students to investigate the railroads that linked Mexico to U.S. and foreign markets and then to create a map showing these railroads.

RESEARCH Direct students to research the life and legend of Pancho Villa. Have students report to the class on how American movies have characterized Villa and compare these characterizations to what their investigation has revealed about him.

---

military intervention and colonial rule of foreign territories. Although new territory and influence benefited the United States, many Americans believed that overseas expansion helped foreign countries as well. Many supporters of imperialism viewed Samoa, Cuba, Puerto Rico, and other non-European countries as economically backward and uncivilized. Using this doctrine, American imperialists asserted that Americans had a responsibility to bring democracy, prosperity, and order to nonindustrialized nations.

But did U.S. imperialism bring all of these benefits to foreign countries? In Cuba, Puerto Rico, and the Philippines, better sanitation, education, transportation, and public health followed the American flag. And in some cases, such as in Venezuela, U.S. diplomatic actions prevented European countries from colonizing Latin American territory.

U.S. economic and military interventions, however, rarely brought order or democracy to politically troubled countries. U.S. dollar diplomacy in Nicaragua did not prevent a revolt, and the United States brutally suppressed the Filipino independence movement. Although designed to create democracy, the U.S. military governments that were established in many countries often denied citizens a basic democratic principle: political representation.

U.S. attempts to spread American culture sometimes came at the expense of the other country's culture. In Puerto Rico, for example, the U.S. government ordered that English—instead of the native Spanish—be used in classrooms to make Puerto Ricans "good North American citizens." Manuel Maldonado-Denis, a Puerto Rican who grew up under this system, recalled that "Puerto Rican students had to daily swear loyalty to the North American flag in English" and sing "songs in English composed to inspire patriotism in North American students." In this way, Maldonado-Denis concluded, the United States attempted "to rob us of every source of identification with all that is Puerto Rican."

U.S. economic expansion also created resentment against the United States around the world. The millions of dollars that U.S. banks and businesses poured into oil wells, mines, plantations, and railroad projects in poor nations gave the United States control of those nations' natural resources. Poor nations grew angry as they watched their resources and the profits from them flow into the United States. Their struggle to regain control of their own resources would provide a continuing source of tension with the United States.

SECTION 4 REVIEW

IDENTIFY and explain the significance of the following: Porfirio Díaz, Francisco Madero, Victoriano Huerta, Venustiano Carranza, Francisco "Pancho" Villa, Emiliano Zapata, Álvaro Obregón, John J. Pershing.

1. **MAIN IDEA** How were relations between the United States and Mexico affected by the Mexican Revolution?

2. **MAIN IDEA** Why did President Wilson ask Congress for authority to use the armed forces in Mexico?

3. **IDENTIFYING CAUSE AND EFFECT** What event during Carranza's presidency provoked U.S. intervention in Mexico? What effect did this have on relations between the two countries?

4. **WRITING TO EXPLAIN** Imagine you are a landless peasant in Mexico after the overthrow of Porfirio Díaz. Write a letter to a relative in the United States explaining why you took part in the revolution.

5. **SYNTHESIZING** How did U.S. intervention both help and hurt other countries?

DEVELOPING THEMES

Return to the Themes section on p. 212. Have students discuss these again and compare their original responses with those given now. (See p. 211B for suggested answers.)

Chapter Review Answers

WRITING A SUMMARY
See Essential Points in each section for main ideas.

REVIEWING CHRONOLOGY
4, 2, 5, 1, 3
Identifying Cause and Effect
Answers will vary but should make the cause and effect of events clear.

IDENTIFYING PEOPLE AND IDEAS
1. *building an empire by acquiring overseas colonies*
2. *exiled Cuban poet who wrote poems and newspaper articles to promote Cuban independence*
3. *leader of Filipino patriots during Spanish-American War; later Philippine president*
4. *last Hawaiian queen to govern Hawaii; opposed U.S. annexation*
5. *ports or regions in China where another country would have exclusive rights over trade, mines, and railroads*
6. *secretary of state who inaugurated Open Door policy in 1899*
7. *Cuban doctor whose theory that mosquitoes spread yellow fever led to sanitation system that conquered the disease*

8. *Taft's policy of maintaining order in foreign countries through economic influence*
9. *longtime Mexican president whose overthrow by peasants, workers, and middle class launched the Mexican Revolution*
10. *Mexican revolutionary leader who helped defeat Díaz and Huerta, later was president of Mexico*

UNDERSTANDING MAIN IDEAS
1. *for power, prestige, and economic gain; that they needed to control new markets and protect investments, and that the U.S. had a duty to spread Anglo culture and religion*

2. *Positive—built new schools, highways, and railroads; improved medical care and sanitation; increased trade; negative—imposed limits on self-government, delayed independence*
3. *U.S. saw Hawaii as gateway to China trade; Japan's victory in China urged U.S. to protect China trade.*
4. *When the presidents sent marines to these three countries, it showed their willingness to protect American investments from possible European actions in those countries.*
5. *because they wanted Samoa for naval bases and fueling stations; the U.S. retains control of Eastern Samoa, Western is independent*

CHAPTER 9
Review

Spanish-American War begins. U.S. gains control of Puerto Rico, Guam, and Hawaii.	U.S. annexes Philippines. Open Door policy inaugurated.	Boxer Rebellion begins in China.	U.S. recognizes Republic of Panama. Hay–Bunau-Varilla Treaty negotiated. Philippine Government Act passed.	
1898		**1900**		**1902**

WRITING A SUMMARY
Using the essential points of the chapter as a guide, write a summary of the chapter.

REVIEWING CHRONOLOGY
Number your paper 1 to 5. Study the time line above, and list the following events in the order in which they happened by writing the first next to 1, the second next to 2, and so on. Then complete the activity below.
1. Panama Canal completed.
2. U.S. recognizes Republic of Panama.
3. Venustiano Carranza assumes power in Mexico.
4. Open Door policy inaugurated.
5. Russo-Japanese War begins.

Identifying Cause and Effect Select two events from the time line, and in a paragraph, explain the cause-and-effect relationship between them.

IDENTIFYING PEOPLE AND IDEAS
Explain the historical significance of each of the following people or terms.
1. imperialism
2. José Martí
3. Emilio Aguinaldo
4. Liliuokalani
5. spheres of influence
6. John Hay
7. Carlos Finlay
8. dollar diplomacy
9. Porfirio Díaz
10. Venustiano Carranza

UNDERSTANDING MAIN IDEAS
1. What led industrialized nations to seek overseas colonies in the late 19th and early 20th centuries? What arguments did imperialists use to justify the establishment of overseas colonies?
2. What positive and negative effects did U.S. intervention in the Philippines have on that country?
3. How did U.S. relations with Hawaii and Japan eventually lead to American involvement in China?
4. How did U.S. actions in the Dominican Republic, Nicaragua, and Haiti signify Roosevelt's, Taft's, and Wilson's willingness to apply and extend the Monroe Doctrine?

5. Why were the United States, Great Britain, and Germany interested in Samoa? Who finally won control of Samoa?

REVIEWING THEMES
1. **Global Relations** Why was the United States interested in controlling Cuba? Why was Cuba surprised and angered by the position of the American government?
2. **Economic Development** How did the presence of foreign investors in Mexico affect the economy of that country? What problems resulted from these investments?
3. **Democratic Values** Why might some people argue that U.S. actions in the Philippines conflicted with democratic principles?

THINKING CRITICALLY
1. **Evaluating** How did the United States government react to revolutionaries such as Emilio Aguinaldo and Venustiano Carranza?
2. **Analyzing** Why did Japan, unlike China, not come under European spheres of influence?
3. **Hypothesizing** What might have been the effect on U.S. relations with Cuba, Puerto Rico, and the Philippines if the United States had adopted an Open Door policy in each of those countries?

STRATEGY FOR SUCCESS
Review the Skills Handbook entry on Writing a Paper beginning on page 761. Imagine you are a native Hawaiian in 1893 who has witnessed the overthrow of Queen Liliuokalani. What information will you need to collect if you are preparing an article for a local newspaper about this event? Suppose that you are writing a diary entry about the occupation. How will your approach to writing differ in this case?

WRITING ABOUT HISTORY
Writing to Explain Write an essay that traces the negotiations and events that helped the United States build and control the Panama Canal.

REVIEWING THEMES

1. Cuba's location (90 miles from Florida) made it an attractive place for U.S. investments and establishment of naval bases and fueling stations; Cuba expected that U.S. would support its independence.
2. helped develop Mexico's economy through creation of new markets; foreign influence in Mexico's internal affairs and military intervention to protect those investments
3. By annexing the Philippines and denying its independence, the U.S. was violating its own ideals.

THINKING CRITICALLY

1. initially supported their rise to power but turned against them when they did not support U.S. interests
2. Japan transformed itself into a military and industrial power that could compete with European nations.
3. may have promoted broader development or increased instability because of more outside influences and investment

STRATEGY FOR SUCCESS

background information on the event, interviews with participants, chronology of day's events; less formal research, more personal tone

WRITING ABOUT HISTORY

Essays should consider the Clayton-Bulwer Treaty, the Hay-Pauncefote Treaty, the Hay-Herrán Treaty, and the revolution in Panama leading to the Hay–Bunau-Varilla Treaty.

USING PRIMARY SOURCES

because of Villa's nontraditional approach to warfare, the loyalty and bravery of his men, and their dedication to each other and their cause

LINKING HISTORY AND GEOGRAPHY

Paragraphs might mention that because most fighting took place on and around islands, control of the seas was vital to providing troop reinforcements and supplies. The U.S. naval blockade in Cuba and destruction of the Spanish fleets in Cuba and the Philippines led to U.S. victory.

Timeline:

| 1904 | 1910 | 1912 | 1914 | 1916 |

- Russo-Japanese War begins. (1904)
- The Mexican Revolution starts. (1910)
- Panama Canal completed. (1914)
- Venustiano Carranza assumes power in Mexico. Wilson sends marines into Haiti. (1914)
- Pancho Villa's soldiers raid Columbus, New Mexico. (1916)

USING PRIMARY SOURCES

At the height of the Mexican Revolution, American journalist John Reed traveled with the Mexican rebels under the command of Pancho Villa. Read the following excerpt from Reed's book, *Insurgent Mexico,* in which he evaluates Villa's leadership qualities. Why does Reed think that Villa's army will defeat the opposing troops of the Mexican Federal army?

> 66 *Villa had to invent an entirely original method of warfare, because he never had a chance to learn anything of accepted military strategy. . . . Secrecy, quickness of movement, the adaptation of his plans to the character of the country and of his soldiers . . . these are his characteristics. . . . One of the troubles of the Mexican Federal army is that its officers are thoroughly saturated with conventional military theory. [Villa's] soldier is still . . . , above all, a loose, individual, guerrilla fighter. . . . When Villa's army goes into battle he is not hampered by salutes, or rigid respect for officers, . . . or theories of . . . the function of cavalry, infantry and artillery in any particular position. . . . [Villa] does know that guerrilla fighters cannot be driven blindly in platoons around the field in perfect step, that men fighting individually and of their own free will are braver than long volleying rows in the trenches. . . . And where the fighting is fiercest . . . Villa is among them, like any common soldier.* 99

Pancho Villa

LINKING HISTORY AND GEOGRAPHY

Historians have noted that the Spanish-American War was primarily decided at sea. Study the map on page 217 and the text discussion on pages 216–18. Then write a paragraph supporting this view and describing how geography might have influenced U.S. military strategy.

Teddy Roosevelt and the Rough Riders

BUILDING YOUR PORTFOLIO

Complete the following projects independently or cooperatively.

1. **GLOBAL RELATIONS** Imagine you are a member of the State Department in the early 1900s. Write a memorandum to the president that addresses concerns about U.S. relations with Spain, China, Japan, Latin America, or Mexico. Your memorandum should mention specific issues dealing with annexation, colonization, construction of the Panama Canal, or protection of U.S. investments, and propose courses of action.

2. **WAR** Imagine you are a U.S. Army recruiting officer in 1898. Create a series of recruiting posters aimed at attracting a wide range of recruits—such as college students, Native Americans, cowboys, would-be adventurers—to serve in the Spanish-American War.

BUILDING YOUR PORTFOLIO

Have students refer to **Building Your Portfolio Worksheet 2**, assigned at the beginning of Unit 2. Use the worksheet to help students monitor their progress on the portfolio projects.

Assessment

Core Resources
- Reteaching Worksheet 9
- Chapter 9 Tests
- Alternative Assessment Forms

Test Generator

THE U.S. AND THE WORLD

HISTORICAL SIDELIGHTS

Investing "Down Under"

Although Great Britain had held a monopoly over the Australian and New Zealand region since the 18th century, significant economic investment there did not take place until the late 19th century. The discovery of gold and the rise of sheep farming increased British interest in the "land down under." By 1879 Great Britain was importing 300 million pounds of wool annually from Australia alone.

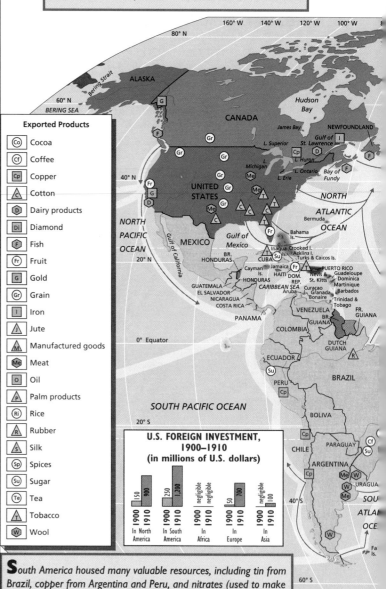

America's GEOGRAPHY

THE UNITED STATES AND THE WORLD

THE Industrial Revolution affected nations throughout the world. By 1914, the eve of World War I, many nations of the world were connected in a complex web of economic trade and investment. The vast majority of this trade and investment was controlled by European nations, particularly Great Britain, which had amassed a huge colonial empire. Japan was the only Asian nation to attempt significant foreign expansion in the early 20th century. Compared to the European empires, the United States had relatively little financial investment in other countries. Yet even the United States expanded its economic and political involvement in foreign nations during this period.

The U.S. and the World, 1900–1914

Foreign landholdings of the United States were very small compared to those of the European empires. The largest American territory, Alaska, appeared to many skeptics to be a useless, frozen wasteland. The discovery of gold, oil, and other useful minerals, however, would prove very valuable to the United States in years to come.

Exported Products

- Co Cocoa
- Cf Coffee
- Cp Copper
- C   Cotton
- D   Dairy products
- Di Diamond
- F   Fish
- Fr Fruit
- G   Gold
- Gr Grain
- I   Iron
- Ju Jute
- M   Manufactured goods
- Me Meat
- O   Oil
- P   Palm products
- Ri Rice
- R   Rubber
- S   Silk
- Sp Spices
- Su Sugar
- Te Tea
- T   Tobacco
- W   Wool

U.S. FOREIGN INVESTMENT, 1900–1910 (in millions of U.S. dollars)

	1900	1910
In North America	150	900
In South America	250	1,200
In Africa	negligible	negligible
In Europe	50	700
In Asia	negligible	100

South America housed many valuable resources, including tin from Brazil, copper from Argentina and Peru, and nitrates (used to make fertilizer and explosives) from Chile. Although the European empires did not attempt to create new colonies in South America, as they did in Africa, they invested heavily in the economic life of self-governing South American countries. The U.S. also increased investment in South America, but most of its investments were concentrated in Central America and the Panama Canal region.

GERMAN FOREIGN INVESTMENT IN 1910*
(in millions of U.S. dollars)

1910	1910	1910	1910	1910
1,150	600	500	2,500	700
In North America	In South America	In Africa	In Europe	In Asia

*All investment data for Germany in 1900 either not available or negligible

Countries and Possessions in 1914

Great Britain	Japan
Denmark	Germany
Netherlands	France
Belgium	Spain
Italy	Portugal
Ottoman	United States
Russia	Independent

Asian empires went through dramatic changes around the turn of the century. China, which had been the largest empire in the world, suffered a series of political crises that led to a loss of many of its territories and eventually to the overthrow of the emperor in 1911. Meanwhile the tiny nation of Japan was becoming the leading Asian power as its empire expanded through military victories over China and Russia.

Europeans had explored and traded in Africa for many years. Except for a few small settlements, there had never been a major effort to colonize the continent. In the late 1800s, however, European countries struggled to claim African lands (and resources) for themselves. This led to a series of wars between European forces and African peoples. By 1914 Liberia, the country founded by American abolitionists in the early 1800s, and Ethiopia were the only self-governing African countries.

BRITISH FOREIGN INVESTMENT, 1900–1910
(in millions of U.S. dollars)

1900	1910	1900	1910	1900	1910	1900	1910	1900	1910
2,250	7,000	1,350	3,700	1,900	2,400	1,250	1,000	1,700	3,500
In North America		In South America		In Africa		In Europe		In Asia	

Chart information from Rand McNally Atlas of World History.

GLOBAL CONNECTIONS

In the late 19th and early 20th centuries, the United States significantly increased its investments in, and trade with, Canada. This economic development was encouraged by the expansion of transcontinental railroads, which opened up previously isolated Canadian regions to new markets. Canada soon became one of the world's leading sources of wheat, nickel, copper, and lumber. Between 1890 and 1914 that country's industrial output increased from some $190 million to more than $500 million.

WORLD WAR I

1914–1920

Chapter Overview

War erupted in 1914 because nationalism and territorial rivalries had turned Europe into a cauldron of hatred. Initially declaring itself neutral, the U.S. slowly was dragged into the conflict. In 1917 the U.S. abandoned its neutrality and entered the war on the Allied side. To aid the nation's war effort, President Wilson called for the complete mobilization of American society.

In November 1918 the warring parties signed an armistice and brought the conflict to an end. President Wilson then moved to forge what he hoped would be a just peace. But the final treaty was a mass of compromises, which the U.S. Senate refused to ratify.

Chapter Planning Guide

CHAPTER 10	CORE RESOURCES	AUDIOVISUAL RESOURCES	PROGRAM RESOURCES
INTRODUCTION pp. 240–241	■ Geography Worksheet 10 ■ Building Your Portfolio Worksheet 2	■ Everyday Life in America Transparency and Worksheet 20	■ *Eyewitnesses and Others*, Volume 2: Reading 35
TEACHING THE CHAPTER pp. 242–267 ■ For expanded coverage of this chapter, see Chapter 23, pp. 628–632; also see Chapter 26.	■ Graphic Organizer 10 ■ Social Studies Skills Worksheet 10 ■ Literature Worksheet 10 ■ Outline Maps 14, 15, 16, 17, 18, 19	■ *The American Nation* Videodisc: Weaponry and Warfare ■ Linking Geography and History Transparency and Worksheet 16	■ Art in American History Transparency and Worksheet 21 ■ *Eyewitnesses and Others*, Volume 2: Readings 32, 33, 34
REVIEW AND ASSESSMENT pp. 268–269	■ Chapter 10 Daily Quizzes ■ Reteaching Worksheet 10 ■ Chapter 10 Tests ■ Alternative Assessment Forms		■ Test Generator

Additional Resources

BOOKS FOR TEACHERS

Bruce, Anthony. *An Illustrated Companion to the First World War.* Viking Penguin, 1990. Documentary of World War I.

Coffman, Edward M. *The War to End All Wars: The American Military Experience in World War I.* University of Wisconsin Press, 1986. Account of American military in World War I.

Schneider, Dorothy and Carl J. *Into the Breach: American Women Overseas in World War I.* Viking Penguin, 1991. Story of the American women who took part in World War I.

BOOKS FOR STUDENTS

* Bosco, Peter. *World War I.* Facts on File, 1991. Overview of WWI.

Freidel, Frank. *Over There: The Story of America's First Great Overseas Crusade.* Temple University Press, 1990. Illustrated account of American involvement in the war.

Hoehling, A. A. *The Last Voyage of the Lusitania.* Outlet Book Co., 1991. Account of the incident that helped to draw the U.S. into the war.

Marshall, S. L. *World War I.* Houghton Mifflin, 1985. Review of military, political, and social aspects of the war.

* for students reading below grade level

MULTIMEDIA MATERIALS

The American Diary—The Price of Peace. Video, 24 min. Aims Media. Reviews U.S. role in the Great War and the struggle for a lasting peace.

The Great War—1918. Video, 60 min. PBS. American involvement in the war told through letters and diaries of soldiers.

Men of Bronze. Video, 58 min. Films Incorporated. Reviews the role of African American soldiers in World War I.

THEMES IN AMERICAN HISTORY

USE WITH PAGES 240-241

*L*isted on the right are the themes emphasized in Chapter 10. The questions in boldface type stimulate critical thinking and provide students with an opportunity to discuss the themes within a broadened context. The questions also appear in the pupil's edition on p. 240.

■ GLOBAL RELATIONS

Why might a country be drawn into an international conflict in spite of efforts to remain neutral? Students might suggest that ties to other nations, such as trade and diplomatic agreements, might make neutrality difficult. The way that the warring nations treat the neutral country might also make it difficult to stay out of the conflict.

■ ECONOMIC DEVELOPMENT

How might fighting a war affect a nation's economy? Students might suggest that war would require increased production of weapons and other military materiel. It might require controls, such as rationing, to make sure that needed materiel are available for the war effort. Rationing and increased war production might result in reduced availability of consumer goods. A war might also bring new workers into the work force to replace workers who enter the armed services.

■ DEMOCRATIC VALUES

How might war affect a government's respect for its citizens' rights? Students might suggest that government efforts to increase wartime national security and to unite the nation behind a war effort could lead to the suppression of dissent. Such actions might result in restrictions of free speech and assembly and other basic rights.

CHAPTER STRATEGIES FOR MEETING INDIVIDUAL NEEDS

LIMITED ENGLISH PROFICIENT LEARNERS

Organize students in pairs to create information cards on the key people, places, and terms introduced in each section. One side of the card should list a name or term; the other side should provide a definition or pertinent biographical, geographical, and historical information.

TACTILE/KINESTHETIC LEARNERS

Have students work in small groups to sketch key events and scenes of American involvement in World War I. Call on volunteers to use their sketches for a "slide show" presentation on the war years.

LEARNERS HAVING DIFFICULTY

Organize students in pairs to construct an annotated outline, section by section, as they read the chapter. Have pairs compare their outlines.

AUDITORY LEARNERS

Suggest that students listen to recordings, or read aloud the lyrics, of American songs that were popular during World War I. Then have students discuss what the songs reveal about life during the war years.

VISUAL LEARNERS

Organize students into four groups and assign each group one of the sections in the chapter. Direct groups to identify a symbol or photograph from the text that best illustrates the main theme of their assigned section. Have each group present and explain its choice.

GIFTED LEARNERS

Ask students to list and describe the major turning points in U.S. foreign affairs from 1914 to 1920. Guide them to evaluate the U.S. response at each point and to identify possible alternative actions that could have been taken.

USING THE CHAPTER FOCUS

■ UNDERSTANDING THE MAIN IDEA

Ask students to read the Understanding the Main Idea paragraph. Then call on volunteers to suggest things that a government might do to mobilize a nation's economy to meet a national emergency, and how government might also mobilize public support. Write responses on a flip chart and retain them. At the close of the chapter, have students review and refine their responses.

THEMES

Have students work individually or in small groups to answer the questions under Themes. Save students' responses so that they can compare them with their responses after studying the chapter. (See p. 239B for suggested answers.)

■ THE TIME LINE

Ask students to copy time-line entries into their notebooks. As students read the chapter, have them write the causes and effects of each event. After they complete the chapter, have students compare their cause-and-effect lists.

CORE RESOURCES

• **Graphic Organizer 10**
• **Geography Worksheet 10**
• **Outline Maps 14, 15, 16, 17, 18, 19**
• **Building Your Portfolio Worksheet 2**

AV RESOURCES

• **Everyday Life in America Transparency and Worksheet 20**

ABOUT THE ILLUSTRATION

Much of Houplines, France, was destroyed before the British finally took the city in a battle on April 9, 1918. Many cities throughout Europe were left decimated by the war. Have students find in magazines or newspapers photographs of cities that have been severely damaged by recent conflicts.

Chapter 10

1914–1920

WORLD WAR I

▼ FOCUS

UNDERSTANDING THE MAIN IDEA

When war enveloped Europe, the United States tried to remain neutral. In 1917, however, the United States joined the Allied cause. The government quickly moved to mobilize the economy and to build public support for the war. Then when the fighting stopped, Wilson worked to shape a just peace. He failed, however, to win congressional support for the treaty he helped write.

THEMES

■ **GLOBAL RELATIONS** Why might a country be drawn into an international conflict in spite of efforts to remain neutral?

■ **ECONOMIC DEVELOPMENT** How might fighting a war affect a nation's economy?

■ **DEMOCRATIC VALUES** How might war affect a government's respect for its citizens' rights?

1914	1915	1917	1918	19
▼	▼	▼	▼	▼
Archduke Franz Ferdinand assassinated.	German U-boat sinks *Lusitania*.	Congress declares war.	Wilson introduces Fourteen Points.	Treaty of Versaille

Have volunteers review the 19th-century record of U.S. neutrality in European conflicts. Then ask students to speculate as to why remaining neutral would be more difficult for the U.S. in the early 20th century. *(U.S. was considered a major power; new technology had made world "smaller" and* *increased ties among nations; U.S. had various diplomatic and economic ties with European nations; new immigrants might put pressure on government to become involved in European affairs.)*

LINK TO THE PAST

In his farewell address President Washington had warned against entangling American "peace and prosperity in the toils of European ambition." The United States had long heeded this advice and tried to remain neutral. But isolation became increasingly difficult as the nation emerged as a world power in the early 1900s.

HISTORICAL SIDELIGHTS

An Unexpected War

The American public was surprised by the outbreak of war in part because, before August 1914, American newspapers devoted relatively less space to foreign affairs than did European newspapers. After the war's outbreak, however, the American press provided readers with fuller coverage of events than could be obtained anywhere else in the world.

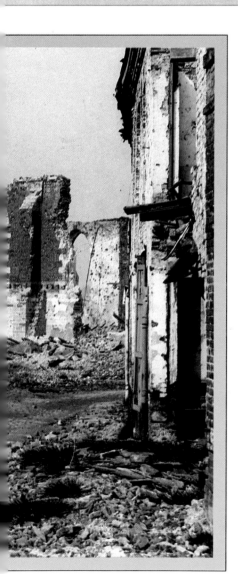

Houplines, France, 1918

On the morning of July 29, 1914, Americans opened their newspapers to screaming headlines announcing the outbreak of war in Europe. The *New York Tribune* proclaimed: "AUSTRIA DECLARES WAR, RUSHES VAST ARMY INTO SERBIA; RUSSIA MASSES 80,000 MEN ON BORDER."

Most Americans reacted with stunned disbelief. Many were grateful that the Atlantic Ocean separated them from Europe. Urging Americans not to take sides, President Wilson attempted to steer a neutral course among the warring nations. With the passing months, however, neutrality became more difficult for the United States. Step by step, events pushed America closer to involvement. Finally, in the spring of 1917, the United States entered the fighting on the side of the Allies—one of some 30 nations on five continents formally to join the war. Before it ended, the war claimed the lives of over 8.5 million people and left some 21 million wounded or maimed.

World War I profoundly affected the American home front. It spurred government regulation of the economy, triggered a great northward migration of African Americans, and unleashed ugly forces of suspicion—even attacks—against dissenters.

President Wilson hoped that a new world order would arise from the ashes of the war. Yet, ironically, when the shooting stopped, the victors imposed a harsh peace on Germany, and the United States refused to join the League of Nations, the organization that embodied Wilson's hopes.

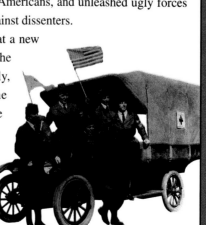

Red Cross unit

FOCUS OBJECTIVES

■ Examine the tensions
that helped bring about
the war in Europe.

■ Describe what life was
like in the trenches.

■ Analyze why most
Americans found it diffi-
cult to remain "impartial
in thought" concerning
the war.

■ Explain how the warring
nations' naval strategies
challenged American
neutrality.

Section 1

WORLD WAR I BREAKS OUT

FOCUS

■ **What tensions helped bring about the war in Europe?**

■ **What was life in the trenches like?**

■ **Why did most Americans find it difficult to remain "impartial in thought" concerning the war?**

■ **How did the warring nations' naval strategies challenge American neutrality?**

Soldier and horse in gas masks

By the early 1900s nationalism, territorial rivalries, and
militarism had turned Europe into a powder keg of hatred and
petty jealousies. An assassination in a small Balkan state provided
the spark that ignited this explosive mix. Within weeks, war gripped
the whole continent. Everyone expected the conflict to end quickly,
but it settled into a deadly stalemate. The United States declared
neutrality, but the personal feelings of many Americans and the
actions of the warring nations tested the country's stand.

THE ORIGINS OF THE WAR

While the Wilson administration grappled with the
problems created by the Mexican Revolution,
another dangerous international situation developed in Europe. On the surface Europe appeared
peaceful—after all, no major conflicts had erupted
since the 1870s. Furthermore, many European
nations had endorsed the recommendations of two
international peace conferences that arbitration be
used to settle disputes among nations. But most
European governments paid no more than lip service to arbitration and international cooperation.
Fear, distrust, and petty jealousies often ruled their
relations with other nations.

Nationalism and territorial rivalries.
At the root of the problem was the intense nationalism that engulfed Europe. Nationalism proved
especially strong in northern, central, and eastern

Europe. There the **Pan-German movement**, led
by Germany, sought to unite all German-speaking
peoples under one flag. In direct opposition,
Russia supported the **Pan-Slavic movement**,
which sought to bring together all the Slavic peoples of central and eastern Europe. These movements seemed destined to come into conflict, for
many Slavs lived in Austria-Hungary, a part of the
German world.

Another source of tension in Europe was
imperialism. European nations, large and small,
coveted land held by their neighbors. In 1908, for
example, Austria-Hungary annexed Bosnia and
Herzegovina. The annexation angered Serbia,
which also had designs on the small Balkan
province. Other countries, too, eyed neighboring
territories. Russia wanted ice-free harbors in the
Baltic Sea and access for Russian warships from
the Black Sea into the Mediterranean. Germany,
the major Baltic power, opposed Russia's ambitions. France wanted to recover Alsace-Lorraine, a

MOTIVATING:
LINK TO TODAY

Ask students what they know about the recent history of the Balkans and tensions that have existed there. As students read the section, have them compare the recent history of the Balkans to the situation there at the outbreak of World War I.

Teaching the Section

CAUSES OF THE WAR

On the chalkboard draw a word web with *World War I* at the center and *Alliances, Assassination of Archduke Franz Ferdinand, Militarism, Nationalism,* and *Imperialism* around it. Then ask volunteers to explain how each satellite word or phrase helped bring about World War I.

French area the Germans had conquered in 1871, and Italy desired nearby territories belonging to Austria-Hungary.

Militarism and alliances. This dizzying tangle of territorial claims helped generate a spirit of **militarism**, or glorification of armed strength, across the continent. Each nation built up its army and navy against the military threat posed by its neighbors. Military buildup quickly turned into an arms race as each nation tried to develop weapons more powerful than those of its neighbors.

European nations also sought to strengthen their military positions through alliances. Germany, Austria-Hungary, and Italy formed the **Triple Alliance**. Great Britain, France, and Russia joined in the **Triple Entente**. In the treaties that cemented these alliances, the members usually promised to aid any other member who came under attack from an outside power.

The spark that led to war. These alliances helped maintain a balance of power, but they also meant that even a minor incident could provoke a war. Many observers feared that if such an incident occurred, it would be in the Balkans—a region so unstable that some called it "the powder keg of Europe." Observers also agreed that the incident

would likely involve nationalist rivalries. As German general Helmuth von Moltke (MAWLT-kuh) remarked in 1912:

> 66 A European war is bound to come sooner or later, and then it will . . . be a struggle between Teuton [German] and Slav. It is the duty of all states who uphold the banner of German spiritual culture to prepare for this conflict. But the attack must come from the Slavs. 99

The attack came in 1914. In June of that year, Archduke Franz Ferdinand, the heir to the Austro-Hungarian throne, paid a goodwill visit to Sarajevo (SAHR-uh-ye-voh), the capital of Bosnia and Herzegovina. As Franz Ferdinand's open motor car proceeded along the city's streets, Serbian nationalist Gavrilo Princip (PREENT-seep) stepped out of the crowd and fired two shots, killing the archduke and his wife, Sofie.

Suspecting—correctly—that the Serbian government knew of Princip's plans, Austria-Hungary declared war on Serbia. The declaration drew each side's allies into the conflict. Russia sided with Serbia; Germany, with Austria-Hungary. Within a week France and Great Britain had declared war on Austria-Hungary and Germany. Despite membership in the Triple Alliance, Italy remained neutral until 1915, when it joined France, Great Britain, Russia, and the other **Allied Powers** against the **Central Powers** of Germany, Austria-Hungary, the Ottoman Empire (Turkey), and Bulgaria. Eventually some 30 nations would take sides in the Great War.

▪▪ **Nationalism, territorial rivalries, militarism, and military alliances created tensions that led to war.**

▼ **Archduke Franz Ferdinand, his wife, and their children pose for a royal family picture.**

▶ **Gavrilo Princip was 19 years old when he assassinated Franz Ferdinand. He was arrested and sentenced to 20 years—the maximum prison penalty for someone under 20 years old.**

Teaching the Section

NAVAL STRATEGIES

Organize students into small groups to study the map on p. 244. Have them use the map to identify and list the countries that comprised the Allied Powers and the Central Powers. Then ask students to use the map to write a paragraph explaining how geography influenced the naval strategies of each side.

GLOBAL CONNECTIONS

The conflict in the Balkans quickly developed into a world war in part because the major belligerents were imperial powers. Soldiers from all over the British Empire, including Canada, India, Australia, and New Zealand, fought under the British flag. French fighting forces were bolstered by troops from French colonies in Africa. And Germany kept thousands of British and African troops busy by waging a hit-and-run campaign in its East African possessions.

Map Caption Answer
on the Eastern Front

MAKING CONNECTIONS

Geography

After the outbreak of war the Russian authorities renamed St. Petersburg *Petrograd* because they felt the original name sounded too Germanic. In 1924 the city was renamed *Leningrad* in memory of the Bolshevik leader V. I. Lenin.

*T*HE EARLY WEEKS OF THE WAR

In 1905, accepting the inevitability of a European war, German military leaders had developed a plan for swift victory. The plan called for German forces to skirt the heavily defended Franco-German border, march through then-neutral Belgium, and invade France across the practically unguarded Belgian border before Great Britain could move its forces across the English Channel. With France and Britain knocked out of the war, Germany could focus on defeating Russia.

On August 3, 1914, the Germans launched their plan, surging into Belgium. German military leaders expected to reach the French border quickly and then sweep across northern France toward Paris. Like their kaiser (ruler), Wilhelm II, they believed that the war would end "before the leaves have fallen from the trees." But thanks to

World War I, 1914–1917

SEVERAL FRONTS The warring powers fought on several battle fronts, with the most intense fighting occurring on the Western Front.

❓ MOVEMENT Where did the Central Powers gain the most territory?

The British blockade succeeds in disrupting German supply lines. As a result, food riots break out in 56 German cities.

The British withdraw from Gallipoli, ending any hope of sending supplies to Russia.

Legend:
- Allied Powers, 1916
- Central Powers, 1916
- Neutral countries
- → Allied forces
- → Central Powers forces
- British naval blockade
- Farthest Russian advance (1914)
- Farthest advance of Central Powers
- Trench line, Western Front
- ☆ Battle
- ▽ Food riots
- German submarine activity

LIFE IN THE TRENCHES

Have students work in small groups to produce a radio newscast titled "A Day in the Trenches." The newscast should include eyewitness accounts or interviews with soldiers about their daily lives and commentary from military experts on how new weapons technology has affected warfare and life in the trenches. If cassette recorders are available, groups may wish to record their newscasts, complete with sound effects. Invite groups to present their newscasts to the class.

▶

the small Belgian army's fierce resistance, the Germans spent nearly three weeks fighting their way across Belgium. As a result, General Joseph Joffre (zhawfruh), the French commander, had time to rush troops to the Belgian border, and the British had time to transport some 90,000 troops to northern France.

These measures managed to slow the German advance but did not stop it. The Germans' superior military might pushed the French and the British back to the Marne River in northeast France. Against heavy odds, the French and the British stopped the Germans early in September 1914 at the **First Battle of the Marne.** From roughly Ypres (eepruh) to Verdun, the German line fell back some 40 miles (see map on page 244). The French and the British launched a counteroffensive but were unable to dislodge the Germans. The Germans had no better luck advancing against the Allies. As 1914 drew to a close, leaders of both sides realized that there would be no quick victory.

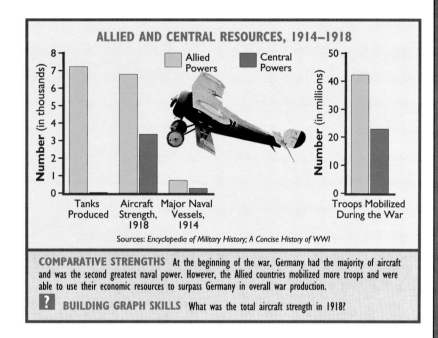

ALLIED AND CENTRAL RESOURCES, 1914–1918

Allied Powers

Central Powers

Number (in thousands): axis 0–8
Number (in millions): axis 0–50

Tanks Produced · Aircraft Strength, 1918 · Major Naval Vessels, 1914 · Troops Mobilized During the War

Sources: *Encyclopedia of Military History; A Concise History of WWI*

COMPARATIVE STRENGTHS At the beginning of the war, Germany had the majority of aircraft and was the second greatest naval power. However, the Allied countries mobilized more troops and were able to use their economic resources to surpass Germany in overall war production.

? **BUILDING GRAPH SKILLS** What was the total aircraft strength in 1918?

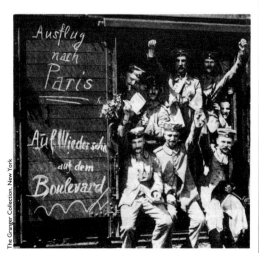

The Granger Collection, New York

▲ This 1914 photograph shows German soldiers traveling to the western front in a train marked with the inscription "A trip to Paris—See you again on the boulevard."

WAR REACHES A STALEMATE

By early 1915 both armies dug in along a front running some 400 miles from the North Sea to the Swiss border. Holed up in trenches and separated by a thin strip of territory called **no-man's land**, both sides struggled to advance.

Trench warfare. Even the most hardened soldier had never encountered anything like **trench warfare**. Britain's field marshal Lord Kitchener lamented, "I don't know what is to be done—this isn't war." In this war most battles began with deafening artillery fire. Then as the smoke and dust from the cannonade cleared, one army would charge the enemy trenches. Most soldiers who succeeded in getting through the barbed wire and land mines strewn across no-man's land were cut down by a hail of bullets from the enemy trenches. In the **Battle of the Somme** in 1916, for example, the British suffered some 60,000 casualties in a single day! All told, this four-month-long battle claimed more than a million dead and wounded.

Maneuvering in the trenches was disheartening. As British soldier Charles Carrington wrote:

66 When moving about in the trenches you turn a corner every few yards, which makes it seem like walking in a maze. It is

Teaching the Section

ATTITUDES ABOUT THE WAR

Ask students to presume that the year is 1915 and that their ancestors immigrated to America from one of the combatant nations of World War I. Direct them to write letters to President Wilson expressing their opinions about America's neutrality policy. Ask representatives of the various ethnic backgrounds to read their letters to the class. Then have the class generalize about why Americans found it difficult to feel impartial about this war. Students may wish to include their letters in their portfolios.

CHALLENGES TO AMERICAN NEUTRALITY

Pair students and ask half the pairs to portray American and German diplomats and the other half, American and British diplomats. Have each "American" draft a note protesting the other country's naval actions and deliver it to the other student. That "diplomat" should return a response that explains and defends that country's naval strategy. Select pairs to read their exchanges to the class.

PRIMARY SOURCES

Description of Change: excerpted
Rationale: excerpted to focus on main idea

BUILDING VOCABULARY

In its developmental stages, the tank was called a *landship*. However, to conceal its identity, the weapon was given the code name *tank* and transported under a tarpaulin marked "portable water tank." By the time the vehicle was used in combat, it was commonly referred to as a *tank*.

MAKING CONNECTIONS

Science

Chlorine gas was the first chemical weapon used in World War I. The far more potent phosgene, produced by the interaction of chlorine and carbon monoxide in sunlight, was introduced later. By the end of the war, however, dichlorodiethyl sulfide was the most common chemical weapon. Better known as "mustard gas" because of its color and smell, it blinded, blistered skin, and seared lungs. Soldiers who survived mustard gas attacks commonly suffered skin, vision, and breathing disorders for years after the war.

impossible to keep your sense of direction and infinitely tiring to proceed at all. When the trenches have been fought over the confusion becomes all the greater. Instead of neat, parallel trench lines, you make the best use of existing trenches which might run in any direction. **99**

Even during lulls in the fighting, life in the trenches proved frightful. Rats and lice plagued the soldiers. Rain flooded the trenches, drenching the soldiers in mud. Artillery fire frequently prevented burial of the dead for days, and exploding shells often unearthed corpses buried earlier. Such unsanitary conditions bred disease, and sickness claimed nearly as many men as bombs and bullets did. The only way out of the trenches, a British soldier observed, was on a stretcher.

New weapons. New weapons added to the horror of trench warfare. The Germans' machine guns fired hundreds of rounds per minute, felling advancing Allied troops like a scythe cutting wheat. The Allies introduced the tank partly to counter the machine gun's deadly impact. First used at the Battle of the Somme in September 1916, the tank produced the intended effect. It

▲ A British tank force is shown here fighting near Amiens, France, in August 1918.

scared the Germans "out of their wits," one British soldier reported, and made them "scuttle like frightened rabbits."

But perhaps the most feared new weapon introduced during World War I was poison gas. No whistling shell announced a gas attack. The green mist silently drifted over the trenches, and the soldiers had only seconds to slip on their gas masks. Any delay meant a slow, suffocating death. After watching a comrade die of poison gas, soldier-poet Wilfred Owen wrote:

66 But someone still was yelling out
and stumbling,
And floundring like a man in fire
or lime . . .
Dim, through the misty panes and
thick green light,
As under a green sea, I saw him
drowning. **99**

■■ Heavy casualties, unsanitary conditions, and fearful new weapons made trench warfare a horrible experience.

▲ Soldiers fought much of World War I from trenches. There they struggled to protect themselves from artillery fire, exposure to all types of weather, and disease and unsanitary conditions.

Continued stalemate. While new military technology produced horrendous casualties on both sides, it did little to break the stalemate on the

Practice

GUIDED PRACTICE

On the chalkboard write phrases identifying the major events covered in this section, leaving space between each phrase. Tell students that these phrases are headlines for news stories. Choose one headline and ask volunteers to give details that might appear in a news story accompanying the headline.

INDEPENDENT PRACTICE

Direct students to choose one of the headlines written on the chalkboard for the Guided Practice activity. Have them first list details about events and then convert these details into a news story that would accompany their selected headlines. Students may wish to include their news stories in their portfolios.

Review and Assessment

REVIEW Have students summarize the major points of the section by writing a paragraph using people, places, and terms listed in the Preview Workshop on p. 242. Ask volunteers to read their summaries to the class. Then assign the Section 1 Review on p. 248.

ASSESS Assign the **Section 1 Daily Quiz** in *Core Resources*.

▶

western front. From 1915 to the spring of 1917, both armies launched offensives that gained them a few miles of territory, which more often than not they quickly lost.

As the months passed, many people wondered whether the fighting would ever stop. They began to suggest that only the intervention of the United States could bring the war to an end.

AMERICAN NEUTRALITY

At the outbreak of the war, most Americans had expressed surprise and horror. After the initial shock, however, Americans tended to look on the war as a faraway conflict that did not involve the United States. As one American diplomat wrote: "Again and ever I thank Heaven for the Atlantic Ocean."

Not surprisingly, then, President Wilson received strong support when he announced a policy of neutrality. All Americans, he urged, ought to be "neutral in fact as well as in name . . . impartial in thought as well as action." Wilson thought that by taking a neutral stance, the United States might help to negotiate a settlement to the conflict. He pursued this goal throughout 1915 and 1916, but without success.

As the war dragged on, most Americans remained neutral in action, but few could claim to be impartial in thought. Some 28 million Americans—almost 30 percent of the population—were immigrants or the children of immigrants. Many men and women of German, Austrian, Hungarian, or Turkish background sympathized with the Central Powers. So did many Irish Americans anxious to free Ireland from Great Britain's rule.

Most Americans, however, backed the Allies. Ties of ancestry, language, and culture bound many Americans to Britain. Strong, long-established links to France also existed. After all, the French had helped Americans win their War of Independence. The British also bolstered American support for the Allies through a skillful propaganda campaign, which painted Germans as brutal warmongers.

■■ **The U.S. government remained neutral, but most Americans— because of ancestral ties or national sympathies—favored one side or the other.**

Challenges to American neutrality.

Despite its policy of neutrality, the United States could not remain untouched by the war. When the war began, the British navy blockaded the German coast and planted explosive mines across the North Sea. The British even stopped American ships bound for ports in neutral countries and examined cargos—including the mail—for goods that might ultimately be destined for Germany. The United States protested, charging that British actions violated American neutrality.

American hostility toward Great Britain faded, however, in the face of German submarine, or U-boat, warfare. Early in 1915 the Germans established a "war zone" around Great Britain. Any ships entering this zone, even those from neutral nations, were liable to U-boat attack. In response, Wilson warned that the United States would, in accordance with international laws of neutrality, hold Germany accountable for any injury to American lives or property on the high seas.

On March 28, 1915, a U-boat sank a British liner in the Irish Sea, killing more than 100 people, including an American. While the United States debated its response, a far more serious incident occurred. On May 7, 1915, a U-boat patrolling off the Irish coast torpedoed the British passenger liner *Lusitania*. The dead included 128 Americans. The *New York Herald* accused the Germans of "piracy on the high seas," and the *New York Times* called the Germans "savages drenched with blood." Outraged Americans agreed. German leaders justified their actions, declaring that they had placed advertisements in U.S. newspapers warning Americans against sailing into the war zone. They also charged that the *Lusitania* was carrying

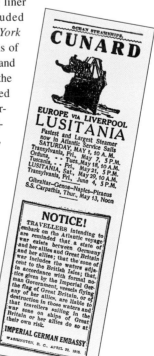

▶ The *Lusitania*'s 1915 voyage announcement carried a warning from the German Embassy against Atlantic sea travel.

RETEACH Organize students into groups and assign each group one of the Focus questions on p. 242. Have group members discuss and write an answer to their question. Ask group representatives to share their answers with the other groups.

Closure

Write this statement on the chalkboard: *Peace in Europe was as difficult to maintain as was American neutrality once war had broken out.* Call on volunteers to cite and evaluate arguments in support of and in opposition to the statement.

Extension

RESEARCH Have students research and report on one of the new weapons of World War I.

CREATE Ask students to assume the role of a World War I European soldier in the trenches and compose a poem that expresses the soldier's feelings about the war.

SECTION REVIEW ANSWERS

IDENTIFY

For significance, see the following pages:
Pan-German movement (p. 242)
Pan-Slavic movement (p. 242)
militarism (p. 243)
Triple Alliance (p. 243)
Triple Entente (p. 243)
Archduke Franz Ferdinand (p. 243)
Gavrilo Princip (p. 243)
Allied Powers (p. 243)
Central Powers (p. 243)
First Battle of the Marne (p. 245)
no-man's land (p. 245)
trench warfare (p. 245)
Battle of the Somme (p. 245)

LOCATE

For locations, see the map on p. 244.

1. *nationalism, territorial rivalries, militarism, alliances*
2. *violated American neutrality, led to U.S. outrage and Wilson's demand that Germany stop unrestricted submarine warfare*
3. *No. Most favored one side or the other because of ancestral ties or national sympathies.*
4. *Diary entries might mention casualties, the effect of weather, unsanitary conditions, and new weapons.*
5. *Responses might suggest that digging in was defensive and that new weapons made attacks horribly costly in human lives.*

▲ The *Lusitania* was photographed shortly before its fateful voyage from New York in 1915.

armaments for England—an accusation that later proved true.

Nevertheless, Wilson fired off an angry protest to the German government, demanding specific pledges against unrestricted submarine warfare. Secretary of State William Jennings Bryan, charging that the president's protest amounted to an ultimatum, resigned. Bryan argued that the United States could not issue ultimatums and remain neutral. The country, he warned, would eventually be drawn into the war.

■■ **British and German naval activities violated the rights of neutral nations and led to American protests.**

THE SINKING OF THE *LUSITANIA*

Germany's Baron von Schwarzenstein offered the following response to the outrage over the sinking of the *Lusitania*:

❝❞t was only after England declared the whole North Sea a war zone . . . that Germany with precisely the same right declared the waters around England a war zone and announced her purpose of sinking all hostile commercial vessels found therein. . . . In the case of the Lusitania the German Ambassador even further warned Americans through the great American newspapers against taking passage thereon. Does a pirate act thus? Does he take pains to save human lives? . . . Nobody regrets more sincerely than we Germans the hard necessity of sending to their deaths hundreds of men. Yet the sinking was a justifiable act of war. . . . The scene of war is no golf links, the ships of belligerent powers no pleasure places. . . . We have sympathy with the victims and their relatives, of course, but did we hear anything about sympathy . . . when England adopted her diabolical plan of starving a great nation? ❞❞

SECTION 1 REVIEW

IDENTIFY and explain the significance of the following: Pan-German movement, Pan-Slavic movement, militarism, Triple Alliance, Triple Entente, Archduke Franz Ferdinand, Gavrilo Princip, Allied Powers, Central Powers, First Battle of the Marne, no-man's land, trench warfare, Battle of the Somme.

LOCATE and explain the importance of the following: Austria-Hungary, Bosnia and Herzegovina, Alsace-Lorraine, Balkans, Belgium.

1. **MAIN IDEA** What factors contributed to the outbreak of World War I?
2. **MAIN IDEA** What effect did Britain and Germany's naval strategies have on American neutrality?
3. **RECOGNIZING POINTS OF VIEW** Did the U.S. government's policy of neutrality reflect the views of most Americans? Why or why not?
4. **WRITING TO DESCRIBE** Imagine you are a British soldier in no-man's land during 1916. Write a diary entry that describes the conditions you experience during trench warfare.
5. **ANALYZING** How might trench warfare and new weapons have contributed to the stalemate on the western front?

PREVIEW WORKSHOP

Following is a list of the significant people, places, and terms in this section. You may wish to use this list as a section preview.

People
■ Robert Lansing
■ Jeannette Rankin
■ John J. Pershing
■ Ferdinand Foch

Places
■ Caporetto
■ Château-Thierry
■ Saint-Mihiel
■ Sedan
■ Meuse River
■ Compiègne

Terms
■ *Sussex* pledge
■ National Defense Act
■ Zimmermann Note
■ Selective Service Act
■ convoy system
■ Bolsheviks
■ Treaty of Brest-Litovsk
■ armistice

Section 2

THE UNITED STATES GOES TO WAR

FOCUS OBJECTIVES

■ Explain why the U.S. finally entered the war.

■ Determine why the U.S. instituted a draft.

■ Describe the part played by the American military in the Allied war effort.

F O C U S

■ **Why did the United States finally enter the war?**
■ **Why did the United States institute a draft?**
■ **What part did the American military play in the Allied war effort?**

*G*ermany's continued violations of American neutrality drew the United States into World War I on the Allied side in 1917. The Americans' entry came none too soon for the Allies, who faced a desperate military situation. As U.S. forces poured into Europe the tide turned. The Germans slowly fell back, and in November 1918 the warring parties signed an armistice. The four-year nightmare had finally ended.

World War I poster

THE ROAD TO WAR

The sinking of the *Lusitania* brought the conflict in Europe closer to home for many Americans. Even so, most still hoped the United States could stay out of the war. Further challenges to American neutrality, however, were not long in coming. In August 1915 two Americans died when a German submarine sank the *Arabic,* another British liner. Then in March 1916 the French passenger vessel *Sussex* was attacked, injuring several Americans. In a sternly worded message to the German government, President Wilson threatened to sever diplomatic ties if Germany did not abandon unrestricted submarine warfare. The German government responded with the *Sussex* **pledge,** a renewal of an earlier promise not to sink liners without warning or without assuring the passengers' safety.

Wilson's actions criticized. Most Americans supported Wilson's approach. However, a number of prominent politicians, including former president Theodore Roosevelt, accused Wilson of not doing enough. Wilson, "that

infernal skunk in the White House," Roosevelt complained, had adopted a course of inaction and was little better than a "coward and weakling."

Others accused Wilson of abandoning neutrality. Former secretary of state William Jennings Bryan argued that Wilson's commercial and trade policies helped the Allies. As secretary of state, Bryan had discouraged American bankers from

▼ **Mrs. Henry Ford and the National Woman's Peace Party organized a telegram campaign in 1915. President Wilson received hundreds of telegrams on Thanksgiving Day from people all over the United States who supported peace.**

CORE RESOURCES

• **Literature Worksheet 10**
• **Section 2 Daily Quiz**

AV **RESOURCES**

• **Linking Geography and History Transparency** and **Worksheet 16**
• **Everyday Life in America Transparency** and **Worksheet 20**

MOTIVATING: PRIOR KNOWLEDGE

Ask students to write a brief response to this question: Basing your answer on what you learned in Section 1, tell what you think might have drawn the U.S. into the war. Ask volunteers to read and explain their responses. Then remind students to check the accuracy of their responses as they read this section.

HISTORICAL SIDELIGHTS

Peace Mission

While Wilson announced his plans for preparedness, some people called for greater efforts toward peace. In late 1915 industrialist Henry Ford hired a ship and invited more than 100 prominent Americans to accompany him on a journey to Europe. Upon their arrival, said Ford, they would establish a permanent peace commission. "We're going to have the boys out of the trenches by Christmas," Ford told journalists. But neither the Allies nor the Central Powers took Ford seriously, and his peace mission failed.

PRIMARY SOURCE

Description of Change: excerpted

Rationale: excerpted to focus on main idea

 GLOBAL CONNECTIONS

The Zimmermann Note also suggested that Mexico should try to persuade Japan to ally with Germany. Such a three-way alliance would have threatened the West Coast and Southwest of the U.S. with invasion.

▲ These Girl Scouts helped the war effort by collecting peach pits. The pits could be ground into a charcoal powder and placed in gas masks to help filter out the poisonous fumes during gas attacks.

making loans to either side, but this policy was soon abandoned. Bryan's successor at the State Department, Robert Lansing, encouraged trade in war materials, especially with the Allies. By 1916 arms sales to the Allies stood at some $500 million, about 80 times the amount sold in 1914.

Preparedness and peace. Bryan's fears increased when Wilson launched a military "preparedness" program. The **National Defense Act**, passed in June 1916, increased the number of soldiers in the regular army from some 90,000 to about 175,000, with an ultimate goal of about 223,000 men. It also set the size of the National Guard at some 450,000 troops and provided for their training. Another bill, passed two months later, appropriated $313 million to build up the navy.

President Wilson assured Americans that he had not abandoned neutrality. Running on the slogan "He Kept Us Out of War," Wilson won reelection in 1916, narrowly defeating the Republicans' Charles Evans Hughes.

Wilson still hoped to negotiate a settlement to the war. In a January 1917 speech, he called for "peace without victory." A lasting peace, he said, had to be one between equals, not between victor and vanquished. Once again, however, Britain and Germany rejected Wilson's effort to mediate.

Diplomatic relations broken. On February 1, 1917, Germany resumed full-scale U-boat warfare. The Germans were gambling that their U-boat fleet could defeat the Allies before the Americans joined the war. Wilson, as he had threatened, broke off diplomatic relations. He also ordered the arming of American merchant ships sailing into the war zone. Nonetheless, German torpedoes sank five American ships.

The publication on March 1, 1917, of an intercepted cable from German foreign secretary Arthur Zimmermann to the German minister in Mexico further heightened tensions. In the event that the United States declared war on Germany, the **Zimmermann Note**, as it was quickly dubbed, instructed the minister to propose to Mexico that it enter an alliance with Germany. With German support, the cable went on, Mexico could "reconquer the lost territory in New Mexico, Texas, and Arizona."

As the weeks passed, Wilson reluctantly concluded that the United States could not stay out of the conflict. On April 2, 1917, the president addressed Congress, asking them to vote on a declaration of war.

CONGRESS DECLARES WAR

A hushed Congress heard Wilson condemn Germany's submarine warfare for its "wanton and wholesale destruction." Wilson, however, did not rest his case solely on the evils of U-boat warfare. He summoned Americans to a crusade for a better world:

> 66 We are glad . . . to fight thus for the ultimate peace of the world and for the liberation of its peoples, . . . for the rights of nations great and small and the privilege of men everywhere to choose their way of life. . . . The world must be made safe for democracy. 99

At these words, cheers and applause rang through the Capitol. A somber Wilson later told an aide: "My message today was a message of death for our young men. How strange it seems to applaud that."

■■ **U-boat activity and the interception of the Zimmermann Note led the United States to declare war on Germany.**

BIO GRAPHY The Senate declared war on April 4; the House, two days later. The vote was not unanimous—6 senators and 50 representatives opposed the declaration. Congresswoman Jeannette Rankin of Montana was among the opposition. "I want to stand by my country," she explained, "but I cannot vote for war."

THE ROAD TO WAR

Organize students into groups, and instruct them to list all the factors that they think contributed to the entry of the U.S. into World War I. Then ask groups to rank their lists from most to least significant factors. Ask groups to present their lists and explain the reasoning for their rankings. As a whole class discuss the differences in groups' rankings.

THE DRAFT

Guide students to hold a "town meeting" on the Selective Service Act. Ask some students to make statements of support for the draft, presenting the reasons for it. Others should state the reasons for their opposition to the draft. When all the speeches have been made, allow the "town" to vote on whether or not it is willing to support the draft.

■■ Ask students if they favor or oppose a draft as an appropriate device for a democratic nation to maintain its military.

Born in Missoula, Montana, in 1880, Rankin was a committed pacifist, social worker, and leader of the women's suffrage movement. In 1916 she became the first woman elected to Congress, and in 1918 she played a key role in the passage of the Nineteenth Amendment. However, with Allied victory only days away, Rankin lost her bid for a Senate seat in the November 1918 elections.

Elected to the House again in 1940, Rankin continued to speak out against the draft and

Jeannette Rankin

military spending, casting the only vote against the United States' entry into World War II. That vote cost her reelection in 1942. She did not give up her pacifism, however. In January 1968, at age 87, Rankin led a march on Washington, D.C., to protest the Vietnam War.

𝑀OBILIZING AMERICAN MILITARY POWER

In his war message on April 2, President Wilson pledged all the nation's "material resources" to the Allied war effort. But what the Allies most urgently needed were fresh troops. Few Americans, however, rushed to volunteer for military service.

On May 18, 1917, Congress responded by passing the **Selective Service Act**, which required men between ages 21 and 30 to register with local draft boards. (The age range was later changed to 18–45) By the end of the war, some 24 million men had registered, and some 2.8 million had been drafted. In fact, more than half of the almost 4.8 million Americans who served in the armed forces were draftees.

Many who supported conscription argued that the draft would help build a more democratic America by bringing together soldiers from different backgrounds. In reality, Native Americans, African Americans, Mexican Americans, and many foreign-born soldiers faced discrimination.

Most foreign-born soldiers, for example, were assigned to segregated units where they were taught civics and English. Congress did, however, offer citizenship to the some 10,000 Native Americans who served during the war.

The more than 370,000 African American recruits experienced particularly harsh discrimination. They were blocked from service in the marines and limited to kitchen duties in the navy. Most African Americans in the army were confined to all-black support units commanded by white officers. And African American draftees sent to army training camps in the South often faced harassment from local whites.

Pressure from the NAACP and other African American organizations convinced the army to open up more opportunities for black soldiers. A school was established to train African American officers, and more blacks were assigned combat duty. The army, however, made no effort to integrate blacks and whites in the same units.

■■ **The United States instituted the draft to bring the armed services up to full force.**

▲ Approximately 1,400 African American officers served during World War I. This officer was stationed in Saint-Dizier, France.

HISTORY *in the Making*

THE DOUGHBOY'S PACK

SETTING THE SCENE

In many ways the experiences of average soldiers in World War I differed from those in previous wars. Point out that some of the supplies provided to U.S. troops, such as steel helmets and gas masks, were responses to what then was called modern warfare.

A MORAL WEAPON?

Tell students that Germans first used poison gas as an offensive weapon in 1915 and that the British soon copied their example. Although used throughout the war by both sides, poison gas was a disappointment to some military commanders because its effectiveness depended heavily on weather conditions. For example, shifting winds might carry the deadly gas back over the very soldiers who launched it. It came to be regarded as an impractical weapon, but not necessarily an unethical one. Point out that the use of chemical weapons today is regarded by many nations as an atrocity.

OVER THERE

With mobilization well under way, American troops sailed to France as part of the American Expeditionary Force (AEF). The first U.S. troops, under the command of General John J. Pershing, reached France in late June 1917. On July 4 thousands of "Yanks," cheered on by huge crowds, marched through Paris to the tomb of the Marquis de Lafayette, the French hero of the American Revolution. "Lafayette, we are here!" proclaimed one of Pershing's aides.

Lieutenant Edward F. Graham wrote home about the sense of purpose that he—and many other soldiers—felt:

❝ The desperate contest between justice and empire . . . is now on. You should be proud to have me . . . participate in the

HISTORY *in the Making*

BY DR. PAUL BOYER

The Doughboy's Pack

History is much more than a study of dates, documents, or facts about influential people. Ordinary objects also leave a historical record about an event or an era. For example, common items provided to soldiers during a war tell a story about how that war was fought.

During World War I the American infantryman—or doughboy, as he was nicknamed—wearily trudged across European battlefields carrying all his necessary equipment inside a canvas "field kit" strapped to his back. Some of the items provided to American soldiers in World War I are shown on these pages. Examine the photographs carefully. What can we learn about the combat experiences of World War I soldiers by studying what they carried?

Begin with the field kit. Examine the cartridge belt attached at waist level. Notice the individual pockets. Each compartment held 10 rounds of ammunition. The around-the-

▶ Soldier equipped with gas mask and steel helmet

waist design with pockets was adopted during World War I because of automatic weapons. Rifles could now fire as many as five bullets per minute, and a soldier needed easy access to large amounts of ammunition during the heat of battle. The cartridge belt served this purpose.

Next notice the shovel strapped to the field kit, with its blade encased inside a protective flap. Until 1918 most of the war on the western front was fought from the trenches. Consequently, digging equipment was a necessity. Each squad shared a variety of tools: shovels, hand axes, pickaxes, and wire cutters. Wire cutters were particularly essential to the needs of World War I infantry. Before a soldier could

reach the enemy's trenches, he had to clear a path through coils of sharp barbed wire. Getting even a small cut from the rusty barbs could prove dangerous—infections in a minor wound often led to the amputation of an arm or a leg.

Now examine the photograph of the American soldier wearing the gas mask and steel helmet. Chlorine gas and mustard gas were highly feared weapons introduced during World War I. The gas mask struggle as a part of the human wall against a second Dark Ages. 🔊

As the weeks went by, American troops arrived in France in ever-swelling numbers. To supply and maintain them, army engineers built docks and railroads and strung up networks of telephone and telegraph lines. They also constructed camps, ammunition dumps, storage sheds, and hospitals.

Some 10,000 American women worked in these hospitals. Emily Vuagniaux, an Army Medical Corps nurse, described life in a battlefield hospital:

🔊 We . . . have worked . . . sometimes 18 hours straight. I have the operating room and they run four tables day and night and have between 200 and 300 patients right off the field, so you may know we are quite close in. 🔊

filtered out poisonous fumes that could suffocate or blind a soldier. The odd-looking rubber contraption was hot and uncomfortable, but crucial to survival. The soldier's steel helmet, as you can see, extended to the top of the ear line. The helmet was designed to help prevent head wounds. A soldier was particularly vulnerable to such injuries when he first peered out from a trench—just before going "over the top."

Next look at a soldier's vital "mess" equipment. The oval "meat can" served as both a skillet and a plate. Sturdy metal containers protected two days' worth of rations from rain, rats, and insects. A doughboy carried two portions of hard biscuits called hardtack. The condiment can had separate compartments for coffee, sugar, and salt. Above the condiment can is a bacon tin. In addition to such supplies, a soldier carried emergency rations such as stringy beef, scornfully called "monkey

meat" by many soldiers. From this mess equipment and the simple nature of the rations, we can assume that a doughboy's supply lines were within a short distance of each squad. More-substantial meals were prepared by a company cook, who followed the combat units.

In addition to the items shown here, an infantryman carried a tent, tent poles, a rain poncho, a bayonet, a blanket, a sewing kit, socks, identification tags, a compass, and a flashlight. On a long march a World War I soldier might have cursed his heavy pack. But he also knew his burden could mean the difference between life and death.

▲ Field kit

◀ Bacon tin

◀ Condiment can

▲ Meat can

PRIMARY SOURCE
Description of Change: excerpted
Rationale: excerpted to focus on main idea

DRUDGERY AND DISCOMFORT

Fully loaded, a doughboy's field kit, including his uniform, weighed between 70 and 90 pounds. U.S. soldiers wore heavy woolen uniforms in every season. Bulky winter overcoats, when drenched by the rain, added even more weight to a soldier's burden.

LINK TO TODAY

Suggest that students make a list of all the items shown on these pages and described in the feature. Ask them to identify items that are probably still necessary for soldiers today. *(shovel, helmet, canteen, gas mask, tent, poncho)*

CRITICAL THINKING

Ask students if they think certain weapons used in warfare can be regarded as humane or moral while others are immoral. Then ask students if they see any contradiction in this idea, pointing out that most offensive weapons are designed to kill one's opponents.

𝒯eaching the 𝒮ection

AMERICAN CONTRIBUTIONS TO VICTORY

Ask students to imagine that they are journalists covering the war for an American newspaper. Direct them to write a commentary on American contributions to the Allied victory. The commentary should be titled "Could the Allies Have Won the War Without Us?" Ask volunteers to read their commentaries to the class. Students may wish to include their commentaries in their portfolios.

▲ Ambulance drivers were responsible for transporting wounded soldiers from the battlefield to hospitals behind the front lines. Many of the ambulance units included women drivers and mechanics.

Thousands more American women went to Europe as volunteers for the Red Cross, the YMCA, or other agencies.

Merchant vessels, escorted by American warships, transported troops, supplies, and volunteers through the submarine-infested North Atlantic. This **convoy system** proved quite effective. Of the more than two million American soldiers who crossed the Atlantic, not one died as the result of an enemy attack on the high seas. Other American warships patrolled the western Atlantic and laid some 70,000 mines in a lethal 240-mile necklace across the North Sea from Norway to the Orkney Islands off Great Britain. This barrier made life hazardous for German U-boats trying to return to their bases.

𝒯HE END OF THE WAR

The Americans' entry into the war came none too soon for the Allies. In an effort to break the deadlock on the western front, the Allies had launched an offensive in the summer of 1917. It failed, shattering the Allied troops' already shaky morale. That fall, mutinies broke out in French units all along the front. In October the Central Powers crashed through Italian lines at Caporetto, on the border between Italy and Austria-Hungary (see map on page 244). Only the arrival of Allied reinforcements saved Italy from collapse.

Worse news arrived from Russia. The Russian people, dissatisfied with working and living conditions, had overthrown the czar in March 1917. Political turmoil continued until November, when the **Bolsheviks**, a branch of the Russian Communist party, seized power. The Bolshevik leader, Vladimir Ilich Lenin, opposed the war. The Bolsheviks signed the **Treaty of Brest-Litovsk** with the Central Powers in March 1918, leaving the Central Powers free to mass their forces on the western front.

Germany's last bid for victory. On March 21, 1918, some one million German troops launched a do-or-die offensive against the Allies. The Germans were backed by some 6,000 heavy guns, including "Big Berthas" capable of firing 250- to 300-pound shells 74 miles. By late May the Germans had pushed the Allies back to the Marne River, only 50 miles from Paris.

General Pershing had originally insisted that American troops fight as a separate army under their own commanders. In light of the situation, however, he agreed to join a unified Allied army under the command of Marshal Ferdinand Foch of France. The introduction of American forces proved decisive. In a last-ditch defense of Paris, American troops helped the French stop the Germans at Château-Thierry on June 3–4. Nearby, a division of American marines counterattacked, recapturing Belleau Wood and two other villages. After fierce fighting, the German advance was halted, and Paris was saved.

On July 15 the Germans threw everything into a final assault around Reims. But the Allied lines held, and Foch ordered a counterattack three days later. The charge, spearheaded by American

Practice

GUIDED PRACTICE

Create a chalkboard chart titled *Aiding the Allies* and list the following items in its left column: *Robert Lansing, National Defense Act, Selective Service Act, American Expeditionary Force, John Pershing,* and *Convoy System.* Ask volunteers to explain how each entry aided the Allies' cause and record their responses in the chart's right column.

INDEPENDENT PRACTICE

Ask students to select the entry from the Guided Practice chart that they think was most important in aiding the Allies. Then direct students to write a paragraph explaining their choice.

Review and Assessment

REVIEW Organize students in small groups to create a four-page pictorial essay titled "The United States and World War I: 1915–1918." Have groups present and explain their essays to the class. Then assign the Section 2 Review on p. 256.

ASSESS Assign the **Section 2 Daily Quiz** in *Core Resources.*

▶

troops, pushed the Germans back. The tide had turned in favor of the Allies.

■■ With the assistance of American troops, the Allies turned the tide against the Germans.

Allied victory. In the late summer Foch seized the initiative, ordering a major offensive along the entire western front. Over the next three months, the Allies pushed deep into German-held territory.

In this offensive the Americans fought as a separate army under Pershing's command and led the attack that pushed the Germans back at Saint-Mihiel, France, in September 1918. The Americans next drove toward Sedan, the French rail center that the Germans had held since 1914. For more than a month the Americans pushed northward along the

Meuse River and through the rugged Argonne Forest, facing artillery and machine-gun fire all the way. The Americans suffered some 120,000 casualties on this drive, but by November they had reached and occupied the hills around Sedan.

Lieutenant Edward Graham was one of the casualties. By the time he died, he no longer saw the war as a noble venture. In his last letter he described it as incomprehensible:

> **66** This is a cowering war—pigmy man huddles in little holes and caves praying to escape the blows of the giant who pounds the earth with blind hammers. **99**

African American troops played a major role in the Argonne offensive. Members of the 369th Infantry, an African American regiment whose men hailed from New York, so distinguished

AV TRANSPARENCY

Everyday Life in America Transparency and **Worksheet 20**

PRIMARY SOURCE

Description of Change: excerpted
Rationale: excerpted to focus on main idea

Map Caption Answer
Belgium and France

HISTORICAL SIDELIGHTS
The Air War
While ground troops grimly struggled for territory yard by yard, the air forces engaged in spectacular aerial "dogfights" high overhead. The U.S. Army Air Service boasted a number of pilots called "aces." The most famous of these was Eddie Rickenbacker. An auto racer who had driven several times in the Indianapolis 500, Rickenbacker began the war as a driver attached to General Pershing's staff. Flying a French-built Spad 13, a wood-and-fabric plane with a top speed of over 200 miles per hour, Rickenbacker shot down 26 German planes.

AV TRANSPARENCY

Linking Geography and History Transparency and **Worksheet 16**

World War I: The Western Front, 1917–1918

GERMAN OFFENSIVE When the Germans signed the Treaty of Brest-Litovsk with Russia in March 1918, some 579,000 German soldiers were able to move to the Western Front.

? **PLACE** Which two countries were largely occupied by the Germans throughout World War I?

Legend:
- Allied Powers
- Central Powers
- Neutral countries
- German forces
- Allied forces
- Front at beginning of German offensive, 1918
- Farthest advance of German forces, 1918
- Armistice line
- Battle
- French army mutinies
- Naval mutinies
- Army mutinies

German Mutinies

RETEACH Ask students, working in pairs, to write sentences that explain how each entry in the Preview Workshop relates to the main idea of the subsection in which it is located. Have pairs share their sentences with the group.

*C*losure

Direct students to create an annotated time line showing the 10 major events of American involvement in World War I. Call on volunteers to present their time lines and justify their choice of events.

*E*xtension

COMPARE Students may wish to examine why it is difficult for a country to remain neutral in time of war. Suggest that they compare the events leading up to the War of 1812 with the process by which the U.S. was drawn into World War I.

RESEARCH Have students research and report on the contributions of African Americans or women to the AEF during World War I.

PRIMARY SOURCE

Description of Change: excerpted
Rationale: excerpted to focus on main idea

SECTION REVIEW ANSWERS

IDENTIFY

For significance, see the following pages:
Sussex pledge (p. 249)
Robert Lansing (p. 250)
National Defense Act (p. 250)
Zimmermann Note (p. 250)
Jeannette Rankin (p. 250)
Selective Service Act (p. 251)
John J. Pershing (p. 252)
convoy system (p. 254)
Bolsheviks (p. 254)
Treaty of Brest-Litovsk (p. 254)
Ferdinand Foch (p. 254)
armistice (p. 256)

LOCATE

For locations, see the maps on pp. 244 and 255.

1. *U-boat activity, interception of Zimmermann Note*
2. *to bring the military to full strength so the Allies would have urgently needed fresh troops*
3. *Students may cite racial discrimination and harassment, segregated units, restricted opportunity in armed forces.*
4. *Memos might mention influx of American warships, troops, and supplies in helping the Allies.*
5. *U.S. might not have been provoked to enter the war, and so Allies might have been defeated.*

256

▲ The armistice ending the war was signed in this railway passenger car on November 11, 1918.

themselves that the French awarded them the *Croix de Guerre* (kwahd i GER), or "Cross of War," a French military honor.

Repeatedly hammered during the Allied offensive, the Central Powers began to disintegrate. Morale in the German military sagged. One soldier, anxious for peace, wrote home:

> ❝ In what way have we sinned, that we should be treated worse than animals? Hunted from place to place, cold, filthy . . . we are destroyed like vermin. Will they *never* make peace? ❞

Mutinies broke out in both the German army and navy. German civilians took to the streets demanding food, not war. Realizing that the war was lost, Wilhelm II fled to the Netherlands in early November. The following day, Germany's new government agreed to an **armistice**, or cease-fire.

On November 8, 1918, German representatives were summoned to Compiègne (kohmp-YAYN), the Allied headquarters, to hear the armistice terms. The Allies demanded that the Germans evacuate France, Belgium, Luxembourg, and Alsace-Lorraine. They also insisted that Germany surrender an enormous amount of war materials, including much of their naval fleet. In addition, the Allies reserved the right to occupy German territory east and west of the Rhine. After brief negotiations the Germans agreed to these harsh terms.

Early on the morning of November 11, the warring parties signed the armistice, and at 11 A.M. the cease-fire went into effect. The constant crashing of guns was replaced, according to one American, by a "silence [that] was nearly unbearable." The Great War, at long last, had ended.

■■
■■ **SECTION 2 REVIEW**

IDENTIFY and explain the significance of the following: Sussex pledge, Robert Lansing, National Defense Act, Zimmermann Note, Jeannette Rankin, Selective Service Act, John J. Pershing, convoy system, Bolsheviks, Treaty of Brest-Litovsk, Ferdinand Foch, armistice.

LOCATE and explain the importance of the following: Caporetto, Château-Thierry, St. Mihiel, Sedan, Meuse River, Compiègne.

1. **MAIN IDEA** What actions provoked the United States to declare war on Germany?
2. **MAIN IDEA** Why did the United States pass the Selective Service Act?
3. **GAINING A MULTICULTURAL PERSPECTIVE** What evidence suggests that conscription did not make America more democratic?
4. **WRITING TO INFORM** Imagine you are Secretary of State Robert Lansing. Write a memorandum to President Wilson that summarizes the effect the American entry into the war had on Allied efforts.
5. **HYPOTHESIZING** How might the war in Europe have been different if Germany had abandoned U-boat warfare?

Chapter 10

SECTION 3

Introducing the Section

PREVIEW WORKSHOP

Following is a list of the significant people and terms in this section. You may wish to use this list as a section preview.

People
- William McAdoo
- Herbert Hoover
- Bernard Baruch
- Carrie Chapman Catt
- Harriot Stanton Blatch
- Victor Berger

Terms
- Food Administration
- Fuel Administration
- Railroad Administration
- War Industries Board
- National War Labor Board
- Great Migration
- Committee on Public Information
- Espionage Act
- Sedition Act

Section 3

THE WAR AT HOME

FOCUS

- **What steps did the federal government take to mobilize the economy for war?**
- **How did the labor force change during the war?**
- **How did the government stifle dissent and rally support for its wartime policies?**

*O*nce the United States entered the war, President Wilson quickly moved to mobilize the nation. The government set up programs to finance the war, to conserve scarce resources, and to redirect industry and labor toward wartime production. Wilson also launched a huge propaganda campaign to mobilize support for the war effort. But as the government whipped up enthusiasm for the war, intolerance of antiwar opinion spread across the land.

Irving Berlin song sheet, 1918

MOBILIZING THE ECONOMY

At the outset of the war, Wilson had noted that "there are no armies in this struggle; there are entire nations armed." To "arm" the nation, Wilson realized, the economy had to be put on a wartime footing.

The first step in this process was raising money to pay for the war, which eventually cost Americans more than $33 billion. The government raised money through four Liberty Bond issues during the war and one Victory Bond issue after the armistice. Posters, parades, and rallies promoted each bond issue. "Every person who refuses to subscribe . . . is a friend of Germany," declared William McAdoo, secretary of treasury and Wilson's son-in-law, and "is not entitled to be an American citizen." These promotions were a huge success, raising some $23 billion for the war.

The government also planned to raise money by increasing taxes. This, however, proved far more difficult than selling bonds. Congress heatedly debated a new tax program for months, finally reaching agreement in October 1917. The new taxes on business incomes and large personal incomes produced about $9 billion for the war—much less than expected.

Mobilizing the economy for war entailed more than raising money, however. It also involved coordinating the actions of government, business,

▲ Movie stars Douglas Fairbanks, Mary Pickford, and Charlie Chaplin lent their support to a Liberty Bond drive in Philadelphia.

FOCUS OBJECTIVES

- List the steps taken by the federal government to mobilize the economy for war.

- Describe how the labor force changed during the war.

- Explain how the government stifled dissent and rallied support for its wartime policies.

MULTICULTURAL PERSPECTIVES

Many African Americans readily subscribed to Liberty Bond drives, even if they had little money to spare. In 1917, for example, bond drives among African American soldiers raised about $800,000. As historians Arthur E. Barbeau and Florette Henri noted, African Americans willingly bought bonds because *"Liberty* was a beautiful word to [people] only a generation removed from slavery."

CORE RESOURCES

- **Social Studies Skills Worksheet 10**
- **Section 3 Daily Quiz**

MOTIVATING: STUDENT EXPERIENCES

Ask students what actions they think would be necessary to prepare the nation to fight a war. Then ask how each action might affect daily life. List their answers on a flip chart. As students read the section, have them compare their responses to the nation's World War I experiences.

Teaching the Section

BOND RALLIES

Have students work in small groups to write a "You Are There" newscast of a war bond rally. Newscasts should include descriptions of the activities as well as interviews with celebrities supporting the rally and with Americans planning to buy bonds. Then invite group members to "broadcast" their newscasts to the class.

MOBILIZING THE ECONOMY

Organize students into groups of four or five. Tell groups that they are President Wilson's economic advisory panel, which has been charged with drawing up a plan to prepare the nation's economy for wartime. Suggest that they divide their plan into three parts—raising money, organizing resources, and organizing industry and labor. Then call on groups to present and explain their plans to the class.

HISTORICAL SIDELIGHTS

Conservation Tactics

To get Hoover's conservation message across to the American people, about 500,000 Food Administration representatives went door to door, handing homemakers cards that requested their cooperation in conserving food.

HISTORICAL SIDELIGHTS

No Idle Threat

Government intimidation to gain wartime cooperation was not limited to the steel industry. During a difficult meeting with automobile executives, Bernard Baruch telephoned the head of the government's Railroad Administration and, within earshot of the executives, asked him to "take down the names of the following factories, and I want you to stop every wheel going in and out." The executives quickly accepted Baruch's suggestions.

and industry. This was done through a multitude of federal war boards. While the federal government never took complete control of the economy, it exercised sweeping economic power through these various agencies. It set the prices and production levels of hundreds of commodities and regulated businesses crucial to the war effort.

CONSERVING FOOD AND FUEL

Among the most successful of the federal war boards were the **Food Administration** and the **Fuel Administration**, which were charged with regulating the production and supply of these essential resources. To direct the Food Administration, Wilson chose Herbert Hoover, a prosperous mining engineer who had managed a food-relief campaign for war-stricken Belgium. Hoover saw his task as twofold: to encourage increased agricultural production and to conserve existing food supplies.

To stimulate wartime production, Hoover guaranteed farmers high prices. Farm production soared. For example, farmers upped wheat production, harvesting some 921 million bushels in 1919—a dramatic increase over the 1917 figure of some 637 million bushels.

▲ **Herbert Hoover, director of the Food Administration**

Announcing that "food will win the war," Hoover called on Americans to reduce their food consumption by observing wheatless and meatless days. To supplement their diets, he suggested they plant "victory gardens" filled with vegetables. The campaign proved very effective—without, as Hoover proudly noted, forced rationing.

The Fuel Administration director, Harry Garfield, the son of the former president, took a similar course of action, encouraging people to observe heatless Mondays. Garfield was not averse to using force, however. When the nation ran short of coal in early 1918, he closed all factories east of the Mississippi for several days.

ORGANIZING INDUSTRY

Hundreds of other boards and agencies regulated industrial production and distribution. For example, the **Railroad Administration**, run by William McAdoo, reorganized the railroads, setting limits on transportation rates and workers' wages.

The work of all these boards was coordinated by the government's central war agency, the **War Industries Board** (WIB). Its director, Wall Street banker Bernard Baruch, had overall responsibility for allocating scarce materials, establishing production priorities, and setting prices. Baruch preferred to persuade business leaders to comply with his wishes. However, when steel owners refused to cut prices, the government threatened to take over their foundries and mills.

At first many business leaders were critical of Wilson's economic mobilization programs. Government intervention, they argued, would permanently damage the American free-enterprise system. As profits soared, however, they ceased to complain.

■■ **The government mobilized for war by setting up programs to raise money, conserve scarce resources, and coordinate government, business, and industry.**

MOBILIZING LABOR

Organized labor moved quickly to gain its share of wartime prosperity. With hundreds of thousands of men drafted into the army and with European immigration slowed to a trickle, industry found itself desperately short of labor as it geared up for the war effort. Taking advantage of this situation, unionized workers across the country went on strike, demanding higher wages and other benefits. Nearly 4,500 strikes involving more than one million workers occurred in 1917 alone. The tactic worked—over the war years, working conditions substantially improved.

To ensure that the voice of labor received a hearing, President Wilson established the **National War Labor Board** (NWLB) in April 1918. Composed of representatives from business and labor, the NWLB arbitrated disputes between workers and employers. In the more than 1,200

THE WARTIME LABOR FORCE

Write the following on the chalkboard, leaving space between each: *Unionization, Women, Immigration,* and *Migration.* Ask volunteers to explain how each of these elements was a factor in creating a wartime labor force. Write a summary of their explanations below the appropriate heading. Then ask students to use the chalkboard information to write a summary paragraph about changes that occurred in the American labor force during World War I. Students may wish to include their paragraphs in their portfolios.

SHAPING PUBLIC OPINION

Conduct class referenda on the creation of the Committee on Public Information and on the passage of the Espionage Act and the Sedition Act. Before each vote, ask volunteers to explain each item and have students discuss whether it is appropriate and necessary in order to rally public support for the war. When the referenda are complete, call on students to explain and defend their votes.

▶

▲ Many American women helped the war effort by working in munitions factories and other industries. Here, a woman loads cartridges for rifles.

cases that it heard, the board ruled in favor of labor more often than not. In this climate of official support, union membership grew rapidly. AFL membership, for instance, rose from some 2 million in 1916 to roughly 3.2 million by 1919. By the end of the decade, some 15 percent of the nonagricultural work force was unionized.

The labor shortage that helped strengthen unions also brought about changes in the work force. The number of women working outside the home grew by about 6 percent during the war. Many of these women took traditionally male jobs. They worked as automobile mechanics, truck drivers, bricklayers, metalworkers, or railroad engineers. In all, some 1.5 million American women worked in industry during the war. Like Norma B. Kastl, an interviewer with a women's service bureau, many women considered employment their patriotic duty:

66 The navy is taking on women as yeomen to do shore duty. . . . Every girl that becomes a yeoman can have the satisfaction of knowing that she is releasing, as from prison, some sailor who had been fuming . . . because he had to spend his days in an office instead of on the deck of a destroyer. 99

Women also helped plan wartime mobilization. Carrie Chapman Catt, a women's suffrage leader, sat on the Women's Committee of the Council of National Defense, a civilian agency organized to support the war effort. Harriot Stanton Blatch, the daughter of Elizabeth Cady Stanton, headed the Food Administration's Speakers' Bureau.

Women's war efforts helped produce one very important political change—the passage of the Nineteenth Amendment. President Wilson, who had wavered on woman suffrage, threw his support behind the amendment in recognition of women's wartime contributions. "The greatest thing that came out of the war," Carrie Chapman Catt later noted, "was the emancipation of women, for which no man fought."

THE GREAT TREK NORTH

The labor shortage that drew women into the work force also spurred immigration from Mexico. Fleeing the Mexican Revolution and lured by southwestern employers who depended on Mexican labor, some 150,000 men and women migrated from Mexico to the United States during the war. Most took agricultural, mining, or railroad jobs in Arizona, California, Colorado, New Mexico, or Texas. But some headed northward for better-paying jobs in such industrial centers as Chicago and Cleveland.

Job opportunities and the prospect of higher wages also brought about one of the most important population shifts in American history—the **Great Migration** of African Americans from the South to northern cities between 1915 and 1930. Persuaded by recruitment agents sent by the Pennsylvania Railroad and other large employers, hundreds of thousands of African Americans moved northward during the war years (estimates range from 200,000 to 550,000). African American newspapers strongly encouraged the migration: "Get out of the South," declared an editorial in the Chicago *Defender.* "Come north . . . The *Defender* says come."

■■ **The wartime labor shortage brought large numbers of women, Mexican immigrants, and African Americans into the work force.**

MULTICULTURAL PERSPECTIVES

African American women who wanted to support the war effort by helping the troops in Europe faced a roadblock of prejudice. Many African American nurses expressed their readiness to serve at the front. The Red Cross, however, ignored their offer. Even so, some evidence suggests that perhaps 300 African American nurses served in battlefield hospitals.

PRIMARY SOURCE

Description of Change: excerpted
Rationale: excerpted to focus on main idea

*P*ractice

GUIDED PRACTICE

Create on the chalkboard a chart titled *Organizing the Home Front.* Ask volunteers to identify actions taken to mobilize the home front to fight World War I. Ask other students to explain the consequences of each action as you record their responses.

INDEPENDENT PRACTICE

Tell students to choose an action from the Guided Practice chart and to write a newspaper editorial about it. Editorials should first explain the action to readers and then either support or challenge it as vital to America's war effort. Students may wish to include their editorials in their portfolios.

*R*eview and *A*ssessment

REVIEW Have students work in small groups to draw up plans for a nonfiction book on the American home front during World War I. Suggest that they include the following: a table of contents and brief descriptions of maps, charts, graphs, and other illustrations. Then assign the Section 3 Review on p. 261.

ASSESS Assign the **Section 3 Daily Quiz** in *Core Resources.*

HISTORICAL SIDELIGHTS

Baseball and the War

Anti-German sentiment spread even to the athletic field. In an exhibition game played two days before the U.S. entered the war, Ty Cobb of the Detroit Tigers slid hard into second base, spiking the New York Giants' Buck Herzog. Cobb then jumped on Herzog, punching him and shouting "German!"

▓▓ Ask students if they are aware of more recent incidents of prejudice in professional sports.

PRIMARY SOURCE

Description of Change: excerpted
Rationale: excerpted to focus on main idea

PRIMARY SOURCE

(for source on p. 261)
Description of Change: excerpted and bracketed
Rationale: excerpted to focus on main idea; bracketed to clarify meaning

260

▲ National guardsmen were called in to preserve the peace during the East St. Louis race riot in July 1917.

African Americans went to the North with great hope. But for many, life in the North proved harsh. Although they enjoyed a better standard of living than they had in the South, racial violence remained a serious problem. The most brutal wartime racial incident occurred in East St. Louis, Illinois, on July 2, 1917. White rioters—egged on by spectators—rampaged through black neighborhoods in an orgy of burning and shooting that left at least 39 dead. Shocked and angered, many African Americans asked themselves why they should fight for freedom in Europe when they enjoyed so little at home.

*M*OBILIZING ATTITUDES

Many Americans—for religious, political, or personal reasons—believed that the United States should have stayed out of the conflict. President Wilson, who wanted all Americans to support the war effort, established the **Committee on Public Information** (CPI) in the spring of 1917. Headed by George Creel, a progressive journalist, the CPI waged a vigorous propaganda campaign to sell the war to Americans.

At first much of the material that the CPI put out was based on fact but censored to present an upbeat picture of the war. Very quickly, however, the CPI began churning out raw propaganda, picturing the Germans as evil monsters. Hollywood joined in, producing movies such as *The Claws of the Hun, The Prussian Cur,* and *The Kaiser, the Beast of Berlin.* These titles vividly

illustrate the message the CPI tried to convey.

CPI pamphlets warned citizens to be on the lookout for German spies. Dozens of "patriotic organizations," with names like the American Protective League and the American Defense Society, sprang up. These groups spied, tapped telephones, and opened mail in an effort to ferret out "spies and traitors."

These groups targeted almost anyone who called for peace, questioned the Allies' progress, or criticized the government's policies. They were particularly hard on German Americans, many of whom lost their jobs. Sometimes this anti-German sentiment took absurd turns. German books vanished from library shelves, schools stopped teaching German language courses, and German music disappeared from concert programs. People even renamed German-sounding items: sauerkraut became liberty cabbage, dachshunds became liberty pups, and hamburger became Salisbury steak.

Vigilantes publicly humiliated people of German heritage by forcing them to kiss the flag, recite the Pledge of Allegiance, or buy war bonds. Sometimes the vigilantes turned violent. In March 1918 John H. Wintherbotham, a midwestern representative for the government's Council of National Defense, reported:

❝ All over this part of the country men are being tarred and feathered and some are being lynched. . . . These cases do not get into the newspapers nor is an effort

◀ Wartime posters inspired people to purchase savings stamps for their country.

RETEACH Write on the chalkboard the names listed in the People section of the Preview Workshop on p. 257. Add to the list: *Harry Garfield, George Creel, Eugene V. Debs*. Then ask volunteers to identify each and to explain how he or she contributed to, or was affected by, American involvement in World War I.

Closure

Suggest that students write a letter to a friend or relative in the U.S. forces in France, explaining how life at home has changed during World War I. Have volunteers share their letters with the class. Students may wish to include their letters in their portfolios.

Extension

EVALUATE Have students prepare for and engage in a debate to evaluate the work of the Committee on Public Information (CPI). The topic for debate is "Resolved: that the CPI's chief task was propaganda, not providing information."

INVESTIGATE Direct students to investigate what life on the home front was like for African Americans and to present their findings in an illustrated report.

ever made to punish the individuals concerned. In fact, as a rule, it has the complete backing of public opinion. **99**

SUPPRESSING DISSENT

Even in this hysterical atmosphere, some Americans continued to oppose the war. Quaker and Mennonite men, committed by faith to nonviolence, refused to take up arms. Considered traitors by many Americans, they faced violence and abuse.

Pacifists like Congresswoman Jeannette Rankin, Senator Robert La Follette, and settlement-house leader Jane Addams never stopped calling for peace. But such declarations held little sway with Wilson, who heaped contempt on the pacifists for their "stupidity."

The Socialist party, too, proclaimed its unalterable opposition to the war. To most party members, the war used the laboring masses as cannon fodder in a capitalist struggle for control of world markets. The Industrial Workers of the World (IWW), the radical labor union, had a similar view of the war and led strikes in a number of war-related industries.

To silence dissenters, Congress passed the **Espionage Act** in June 1917 and the **Sedition Act** a year later. These measures not only outlawed acts of treason but also made it a crime to "utter, print, write, or publish any disloyal . . . or abusive language" criticizing the government, the flag, or the military. Opposition to the draft, to war-bond drives, or to the arms industry also became a crime.

■■ **The Committee on Public Information rallied support for the war, while the Espionage and Sedition acts crushed antiwar dissent.**

More than 1,000 people—including some 200 members of the IWW—were convicted of violating these laws. Victor Berger, a Socialist congressman from Wisconsin, received a 20-year sentence for publishing antiwar articles in his newspaper, the Milwaukee *Leader*. The Socialist party leader Eugene V. Debs went to prison for 10 years for making a speech against the war.

Many Americans, even some who supported the war, believed that the Espionage and Sedition acts violated the First Amendment. The Supreme Court, however, disagreed. In the landmark case *Schenck* v. *United States* (1919), Justice Oliver Wendell Holmes wrote:

66 The question . . . is whether the words used are used in such circumstances and are of such a nature as to create a clear and present danger. . . . When a nation is at war many things that might be said in time of peace . . . will not be endured [and] no Court could regard them as protected by any constitutional right. **99**

This decision was meant to apply to extraordinary circumstances like war. Unfortunately, intolerance of unpopular ideas continued long after the war had ended.

SECTION 3 REVIEW

IDENTIFY and explain the significance of the following: William McAdoo, Herbert Hoover, Food Administration, Fuel Administration, Railroad Administration, War Industries Board, Bernard Baruch, National War Labor Board, Carrie Chapman Catt, Harriot Stanton Blatch, Great Migration, Committee on Public Information, Espionage Act, Sedition Act, Victor Berger.

1. **MAIN IDEA** How did the U.S. government mobilize the economy for war?
2. **MAIN IDEA** What effect did wartime labor shortage have on the work force?
3. **MAIN IDEA** What steps did the government take to shape and control public opinion during the war?
4. **WRITING TO EXPLAIN** Imagine you are an American opposed to the war. Write a newspaper editorial, outlining your reasons for opposing the Committee on Public Information.
5. **EVALUATING** Do you think the U.S. government was justified in taking control of the economy during the war? Why or why not?

SECTION REVIEW ANSWERS

IDENTIFY
For significance, see the following pages:
William McAdoo (p. 257)
Food Administration (p. 258)
Fuel Administration (p. 258)
Herbert Hoover (p. 258)
Railroad Administration (p. 258)
War Industries Board (p. 258)
Bernard Baruch (p. 258)
National War Labor Board (p. 258)
Carrie Chapman Catt (p. 259)
Harriot Stanton Blatch (p. 259)
Great Migration (p. 259)
Committee on Public Information (p. 260)
Espionage Act (p. 261)
Sedition Act (p. 261)
Victor Berger (p. 261)

1. set up programs to raise money; conserved resources; coordinated government, business, and industry
2. strengthened labor unions; brought more women, African Americans, Mexican immigrants into work force, especially in industrial and transportation jobs
3. set up CPI to generate propaganda and rally support for war; passed Espionage Act and Sedition Act to stifle dissent
4. Editorials may mention that search for spies and vigilantism led to violations of people's rights.
5. Students should contrast the benefits of coordination with potential damage to free-enterprise system.

Chapter 10

SECTION
4

Introducing the Section

FOCUS OBJECTIVES

- Identify the two major issues addressed by Wilson's peace plan.

- Explain why Wilson was forced to compromise on his Fourteen Points.

- Determine why the Senate rejected the Treaty of Versailles.

- Evaluate the impact of the war on Europe and on the Middle East.

CORE RESOURCES

• Section 4 Daily Quiz

PREVIEW WORKSHOP

Following is a list of the significant people, places, and terms in this section. You may wish to use this list as a section preview.

People
- Vittorio Orlando
- David Lloyd George
- Georges Clemenceau
- Henry Cabot Lodge

Places
- Czechoslovakia
- Finland
- Estonia
- Latvia
- Lithuania
- Yugoslavia
- Poland
- Saar

Terms
- Fourteen Points
- self-determination
- Big Four
- reparations
- Treaty of Versailles
- mandate system
- irreconcilables
- reservationists
- Balfour Declaration

Section 4

THE LEAGUE OF NATIONS

F O C U S

- **What two major issues did Wilson's peace plan address?**
- **Why was Wilson forced to compromise on his Fourteen Points?**
- **Why did the Senate reject the Treaty of Versailles?**
- **What impact did the war have on Europe and the Middle East?**

President Wilson developed a program for a just peace even before the war ended. This program served as the focus of the Paris Peace Conference in 1919. Wilson had to compromise on many of the points, but the final treaty included the heart of his peace program—the League of Nations. The U.S. Senate, however, rejected the treaty. Without American membership, the League of Nations proved inadequate to solve the world's postwar problems.

Versailles, site of peace-treaty signing

WILSON'S FOURTEEN POINTS

News of the armistice on November 11, 1918, set off a joyful celebration in the United States. Wilson shared the people's great happiness at the Allied victory, but he knew that the task of forging a just peace lay ahead.

This challenge had long been on Wilson's mind. Late in 1917 he had invited a group of scholars to advise him on peace terms. Drawing from their work, Wilson had developed a program for world peace, which he had presented to Congress on January 8, 1918. He called his program the **Fourteen Points** because it contained 14 points, or principles.

Nine of the points dealt with the issue of **self-determination**—the right of people to govern themselves—and with the various territorial disputes created by the war. Other points focused on what Wilson considered the causes of modern war: secret diplomacy, the arms race, violations of freedom of the seas, and trade barriers. But the final point—the establishment of the League of Nations—was the heart of Wilson's program.

◀ **Jubilant Americans celebrate Armistice Day in Washington, D.C., in 1918.**

262

MOTIVATING: PRIOR KNOWLEDGE

Ask students to recall the underlying causes of World War I and to compare them with the reasons that President Wilson gave for entering the conflict. Guide students to use this information to predict what the major controversies surrounding the framing of the peace treaty might have been. Have them review and adjust their predictions as they work through this section.

Teaching the Section

WILSON'S PEACE PLAN

Choose a student to read aloud the excerpt on p. 250 from Wilson's speech of April 1917. Have a volunteer list his principles for a just peace as expressed in the excerpt. Ask other students to explain how Wilson's Fourteen Points addressed each of these principles. Then have the class examine the provisions of the treaty and compare them with his principles. Conclude by asking why Wilson was forced to compromise on his Fourteen Points.

■■ **In his peace plan Wilson aimed to settle territorial disputes and to end the causes of modern war.**

Congress and the American public warmly received the Fourteen Points. The reaction of the Allies, however, proved lukewarm. Moreover, the German government, labeling Wilson an "American busybody," rejected the program.

However, as the war turned against them, the Germans sued for a peace settlement based on the Fourteen Points. Wilson had to push and prod the Allies, but they eventually agreed. After the armistice a peace conference was set for January 1919 in Paris. To make sure that the talks focused on his peace program, Wilson attended the conference.

---

*T*HE PARIS PEACE CONFERENCE

On December 4, 1918, Wilson boarded the *George Washington* for his precedent-setting trip to Europe—he was the first president to cross the Atlantic while in office. As the ship steamed out of New York harbor, a huge crowd gave Wilson a rousing send-off. His reception at the French port of Brest some nine days later proved no less enthusiastic. And on a triumphal tour through France, Britain, and Italy, people welcomed him as a conquering hero. Elated by the cheering throngs, Wilson convinced himself that he had a mandate to shape the peace according to the Fourteen Points.

While Wilson and his fellow leaders gathered to discuss peace, the world was far from peaceful. Across central and eastern Europe, various ethnic groups, now liberated from Austro-Hungarian or Russian rule, clashed over territory. Defeated, Germany teetered on the brink of civil war. In Russia, Bolsheviks fought off the czarists challenge. The Allied powers—including America—had become entangled in the Russian conflict, sending troops to support the czarists effort to overthrow the Bolsheviks.

The other delegates at the conference refused to let Wilson dictate the peace terms. Italy's prime minister, Vittorio Orlando, came to Paris only to make sure his nation got the territories it had been promised on entering the war in 1915. David Lloyd George, Britain's prime minister, had just won an election with such slogans as "Hang the Kaiser." He had no intention of showing generosity

▲ Pictured here are David Lloyd George of England, Naron Sonnino of Italy, Georges Clemenceau of France, and Woodrow Wilson of the United States.

toward the Germans nor of giving up Britain's naval supremacy by accepting Wilson's idea of "freedom of the seas."

The French premier, Georges Clemenceau, wanted to ensure France's security by crushing Germany. Distrustful of Wilson's idealism, Clemenceau growled: "God gave us his Ten Commandments, and we broke them. Wilson gave us his Fourteen Points—we shall see."

As the conference opened on January 18, 1919, Wilson expressed great enthusiasm for the task ahead. But the demands of the other members of the **Big Four**—as Wilson, Orlando, Lloyd George, and Clemenceau became known—soon wore Wilson down. The others insisted that Germany bear the financial cost of the war by making huge payments, called **reparations**, to the Allies. They also wanted several secret spoils-of-war treaties honored. Such demands violated practically every one of the points of President Wilson's peace plan.

Wilson had two options: he could either compromise or walk out. Indeed, at one point he ordered the *George Washington* to stand by to return him to the United States. But he realized that leaving would be an admission of failure. He also feared that without a comprehensive peace agreement, the Bolshevik Revolution might spread from Russia into the already politically unstable regions of central and eastern Europe. More than anything else, however, he wanted to see the creation of the League of Nations. The League, he

---

HISTORICAL SIDELIGHTS
The Tiger

Perhaps the most formidable member of the Big Four was French premier Georges Clemenceau. At age 78, Clemenceau still commanded fear and respect, as his nickname, "the Tiger," indicated. He had begun his political career in the early 1870s, during the Franco-Prussian War. France's humiliating defeat in that conflict was seared into his memory, and he made no secret that he intended to use the Versailles conference to get revenge on Germany.

HISTORICAL SIDELIGHTS
Against Reparations

A British newspaper's demand that Germany "pay [reparations] until the pips squeak" echoed the sentiments of a majority of people in Europe. Yet one voice against this course of action was British economist John Maynard Keynes. In his book *The Economic Consequences of the Peace* (1919), Keynes argued that, first and foremost, the devastated economies of Europe had to be rebuilt. Forcing Germany to pay reparations, he maintained, would only delay that work.

Teaching the Section

THE SENATE REJECTS THE TREATY

Organize students into groups to role-play President Wilson, Senator Lodge, and a news reporter who has brought them together on a radio program. Tell each reporter to interview the president and the senator about their positions on the Treaty of Versailles and to explore possibilities for compromise. Select groups to re-create their interviews for the class. Then discuss the roles that principle and compromise play in resolving conflict, using the treaty issue as an example.

■■ Ask students to describe how the ability to compromise might affect family, school, and peer relationships.

---

believed, would remedy any injustices the treaty might contain. Wilson stayed on.

■■ **Allied demands that Germany pay war damages and that secret treaties be honored forced Wilson to compromise.**

THE TREATY OF VERSAILLES

After six months of debate, the delegates agreed to a peace treaty. The official signing of the **Treaty of Versailles** took place in the magnificent palace of Versailles, just outside Paris, on June 28, 1919. Publicly, the American delegation expressed satisfaction with the document. In private, however, they voiced a different opinion. Secretary of State Robert Lansing confided that he felt "disappointment, . . . regret, and . . . depression." He continued:

> 66 The terms of peace appear immeasurably harsh and humiliating. . . . Resentment and bitterness, if not desperation, are bound to be the consequences of such provisions. . . . We have a treaty of peace, but it will not bring permanent peace because it is founded on the shifting sands of self-interest. 99

According to the treaty, Germany's colonies and the Ottoman Empire (Turkey) were divided among the Allied nations, as specified in the spoils-of-war treaties. At Wilson's insistence, however, the treaty established a **mandate system** that required the new colonial rulers to report on their administration to the League of Nations. To satisfy nationalist longings in central and eastern Europe, the peace treaty also created the new nations of Czechoslovakia and Yugoslavia. (Finland, Estonia, Latvia, Lithuania, and Poland also emerged from the war as independent nations— Poland after nearly 150 years of domination by outside powers.)

The treaty proved a bitter pill for the Germans. Not only did Germany lose its colonies, but France also reclaimed Alsace-Lorraine and won 15-year control of the Saar, an industrial region of Germany rich in coal

Map legend:
- Lost by Germany
- Lost by Bulgaria
- Lost by Austria-Hungary
- Lost by Russia
- Lost by Ottoman empire
- British mandate
- French mandate
- Occupied by Allies

In 1922 the Bolsheviks were firmly in control of Russia, and they organized the Union of Soviet Socialist Republics.

Europe and the Middle East After World War I

END OF EMPIRE Four empires had collapsed by the end of the First World War—the Russian, German, Austro-Hungarian, and Ottoman.

? LOCATION How many countries were created from or received land that had belonged to Russia before the war?

THE IMPACT OF THE WAR

Encourage students to imagine that they are living in Belgium, France, Germany, Russia, or the former Ottoman Empire immediately after World War I. Ask students to write letters to relatives in the U.S., noting the impact that the war has had on the area in which they live. Call on volunteers to read their letters to the class. Students may wish to include their letters in their portfolios.

▶

and iron. In addition, Germany was disarmed, forced to admit full guilt for the war, and assessed billions of dollars in reparations.

Harsh as this treatment was, it would have been much worse but for Wilson's moderating influence. He steadfastly opposed some of the more extreme Allied demands. And, above all, the president made sure that the treaty included a covenant creating the League of Nations.

▲ The first informal meeting of the League of Nations met in Geneva in 1920.

Headquartered in Geneva, the League consisted of a permanent administrative staff; an assembly, where each member nation had one vote; and a council, or executive body. The council was intended to have five permanent members—France, Great Britain, Italy, Japan, and the United States—and four other members that were periodically elected by the assembly.

The League Covenant required member nations to try to resolve disputes peacefully. If negotiations failed, the nations were to observe a waiting period before going to war. If any member nation failed to follow this procedure, the council could apply economic pressure and even recommend the use of force against the offending nation. The heart of the League Covenant—Article 10—required each member nation to "respect and preserve" the independence and territorial integrity of all other member nations.

THE TREATY IN THE SENATE

Returning to America in July 1919, President Wilson worked to win the Senate's consent to the Treaty of Versailles. He believed that he could count on the votes of most Democratic senators, but he would need solid support from Republicans to gain the required two-thirds majority. He faced a difficult task, for most Republican senators had doubts about the treaty. Fourteen of them—called the **irreconcilables**—would have nothing to do with the League of Nations and flatly rejected the treaty. The other 35 Republican senators—the

reservationists—said they could support the treaty if the League Covenant were amended. They particularly objected to Article 10, which seemed to commit the United States to go to war in defense of any League member that came under attack. The Senate's constitutional power to declare war must be protected, they insisted.

Wilson's only hope for consent was to win over close to 20 reservationists. Gaining their support, however, meant compromising on the League, which Wilson refused to do. The more his advisers urged compromise, the more rigid Wilson became.

Henry Cabot Lodge of Massachusetts, head of the Senate Committee on Foreign Relations and Wilson's longtime enemy, led the reservationists. Lodge, too, refused to budge. Playing for time, he bottled up the treaty in the Foreign Relations Committee through the summer of 1919. Angry and frustrated, Wilson took his case to the people. Although he was not feeling well, Wilson began a grueling 9,500-mile speaking tour on September 4. In city after city he ardently defended the treaty. To Wilson's satisfaction, the crowds grew more enthusiastic as the tour went on. Lodge, however, remained unmoved. "The only people who have votes on the treaty," he declared, "are here in the Senate."

On the night of September 25, after an impassioned speech in Pueblo, Colorado, Wilson complained of a splitting headache. His worried doctor ordered him back to Washington, D.C. A few days later, Wilson collapsed from a near-fatal stroke. Wilson lived out the rest of his term in seclusion in the White House, cut off from practically everyone except his wife and his closest aides. Moody, suspicious, and increasingly out of touch with reality, Wilson refused all suggestions of compromise on the treaty.

In November, Lodge presented the treaty, with a list of 14 reservations, to the Senate. Wilson ordered Democratic senators to vote no on the document, thereby rejecting it. The treaty without the list of reservations met the same fate at the hands of the irreconcilables and reservationists. In March

*P*ractice

GUIDED PRACTICE

Work with students to create on the chalkboard a time line of Wilson's efforts to obtain a just peace in Europe. Call on students to offer events to place on the time line.

INDEPENDENT PRACTICE

Ask students to choose an event from the Guided Practice time line and write an editorial that either supports or opposes that event in the process of framing, negotiating, or ratifying terms of peace. Students may wish to include their editorials in their portfolios.

*R*eview and *A*ssessment

REVIEW Direct students to imagine that they are soldiers just returned from Europe. Ask them to write letters to President Wilson, explaining why they are for or against ratification of the Treaty of Versailles. Ask volunteers from both sides to read their letters to the class. Then assign the Section 4 Review on p. 267.

ASSESS Assign the **Section 4 Daily Quiz** in *Core Resources*.

COOPERATIVE LEARNING

Organize students in small work groups to design a "debate page" on the ratification of the Treaty of Versailles. Pages should include statements on the major issues involved in the debate, interviews with ordinary Americans, editorial cartoons, and so on. Allow time for groups to present and discuss their pages.

HISTORICAL SIDELIGHTS

The End of the League
Wilson's supporters periodically brought up the subject of American membership in the League of Nations. In 1923 President Warren G. Harding gave them his final reply. The issue, he said, was "dead. . . . Let it rest in the deep grave to which it has been consigned." Wilson, the architect of the League, died a few months later in February 1924.

PRIMARY SOURCE

Description of Change: excerpted
Rationale: excerpted to focus on main idea

Graph Caption Answer (for graph on p. 267)
Russia, Germany

◀ On his 65th birthday in September 1919, Woodrow Wilson was photographed for the first time since his stroke.

1920 another vote on Lodge's version of the treaty failed, although a number of Democrats broke ranks and sided with the reservationists. A few weeks later, Wilson vetoed a congressional resolution declaring the United States at peace with the Central Powers. There would be no peace treaty, he insisted, without the League of Nations.

■■ **Wilson's refusal to compromise on the League Covenant led to U.S. rejection of the Treaty of Versailles.**

Wilson clutched at the 1920 election as his one remaining hope. He urged the nation to make the election a "great and solemn referendum" on the League Covenant. Americans, however, wanted to put the war and troublesome European problems behind them, and in November they gave the Republican party a landslide victory. By the time Wilson left office, the League of Nations had been established, but without the participation of the United States.

*T*HE GLOBAL IMPACT OF THE WAR

While U.S. leaders debated whether or not to accept the Treaty of Versailles, the Europeans struggled to recover from the war. The destruction and human suffering were almost incomprehensible. In all, over 8.5 million died in battle, and another 21 million were wounded. Germany, with some 6 million dead and wounded, and Russia, with nearly 7 million casualties, suffered the greatest losses. (In contrast, the United States armed forces counted some 112,000 dead.) To add further misery, the influenza epidemic of 1918–1919 killed some 27 million worldwide.

The war had left the industry and agriculture of much of continental Europe in ruins. Northern France was completely destroyed. As British economist John Maynard Keynes observed:

❝ For mile after mile nothing was left. No building was habitable and no field fit for the plow. . . . One devastated area was exactly like another—a heap of rubble, a morass of shell-holes, and tangle of wire. ❞

Those businesses still operating could not produce enough to meet demand, and rampant inflation resulted. In Germany, food shortages were so extreme that it proved almost impossible to keep track of prices.

▼ Verdun was just one of the many cities reduced to rubble by bombing attacks during the war.

▼ American soldiers who fell in France are still remembered and honored in this cemetery.

RETEACH Organize students into small groups. Tell each group to divide the section material, by subsections, among its members. Direct students to write questions about the main ideas presented in their assigned material. Have group members quiz one another with the questions.

Closure

Have students read the comment on p. 267 by historian J. M. Winter. Then ask students to suggest and discuss decisions that world leaders might have made to prevent this outcome.

Extension

INVESTIGATE Students may wish to investigate the role played by First Lady Edith Wilson during President Wilson's illness. Have them report their findings to the class.

CREATE Have students create maps of Europe and the Middle East and Africa before and after World War I, annotating each to point out differences resulting from the war's outcome.

Germany, reeling from the harsh terms of the treaty, seethed with unrest. Throughout the continent, nations vied with one another over territories they thought the treaty ought to have ceded to them. In the Middle East, Arab nations, which had sided with the Allies in hopes of winning their independence from the Ottoman Turks, found themselves living under French and British mandates. Tensions in the region heightened after Britain issued the **Balfour Declaration** in 1917, declaring British support for a Jewish homeland in Palestine.

The new world order, which so many hoped would arise from the ashes of World War I, never materialized. Instead, as historian J. M. Winter noted, "The old order reasserted its will, distributed the spoils of war, and left unresolved the problems which had led to . . . war in 1914."

■■ **The war, which destroyed a generation of young men and left much of Europe in ruins, resolved few prewar issues.**

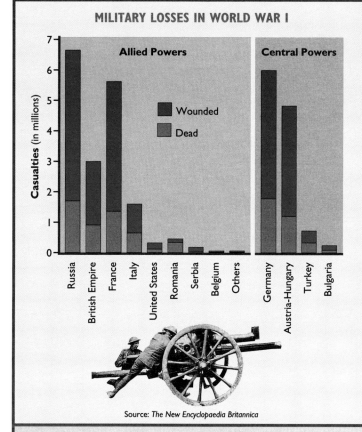

MILITARY LOSSES IN WORLD WAR I

Allied Powers / Central Powers

Casualties (in millions)

■ Wounded
■ Dead

Russia, British Empire, France, Italy, United States, Romania, Serbia, Belgium, Others, Germany, Austria-Hungary, Turkey, Bulgaria

Source: *The New Encyclopaedia Britannica*

A GLOBAL WAR It is estimated that more than 8.5 million soldiers died during World War I; an even higher number suffered from battle-inflicted wounds.

? **BUILDING GRAPH SKILLS** Which Allied power had the highest number of total casualties? Which Central power had the highest casualties?

SECTION REVIEW ANSWERS

IDENTIFY

For significance, see the following pages:
Fourteen Points (p. 262)
self-determination (p. 262)
Vittorio Orlando (p. 263)
David Lloyd George (p. 263)
Georges Clemenceau (p. 263)
Big Four (p. 263)
reparations (p. 263)
Treaty of Versailles (p. 264)
mandate system (p. 264)
irreconcilables (p. 265)
reservationists (p. 265)
Henry Cabot Lodge (p. 265)
Balfour Declaration (p. 267)

LOCATE

For locations, see the map on p. 264.

1. *to settle territorial disputes; to end secret diplomacy, the arms race, and trade barriers; to establish a world body to resolve differences between nations*
2. *that Germany pay war damages and that secret treaties be honored*
3. *terrible destruction and human suffering, massive inflation, created new territorial and nationality issues*
4. *Speeches could mention dislike for League of Nations and fears that Article 10 would limit Senate's power.*
5. *Students might note that by punishing Germany, the Allies sowed the seeds of resentment and revenge.*

SECTION 4 REVIEW

IDENTIFY and explain the significance of the following: Fourteen Points, self-determination, Vittorio Orlando, David Lloyd George, Georges Clemenceau, Big Four, reparations, Treaty of Versailles, mandate system, irreconcilables, reservationists, Henry Cabot Lodge, Balfour Declaration.

LOCATE and explain the importance of the following: Czechoslovakia, Finland, Estonia, Latvia, Lithuania, Yugoslavia, Poland, Saar.

1. **MAIN IDEA** What did Wilson's peace plan hope to accomplish?
2. **MAIN IDEA** What Allied demands forced Wilson to compromise on his Fourteen Points?
3. **ASSESSING CONSEQUENCES** What were some of the effects of the war on Europe and the Middle East?
4. **WRITING TO EXPRESS A VIEWPOINT** Imagine you are a reservationist in the U.S. Senate. Prepare a speech stating your reasons for not supporting ratification of the Treaty of Versailles.
5. **SYNTHESIZING** What aspects of the Treaty of Versailles lend support to Secretary of State Robert Lansing's observation that it was "founded on the shifting sands of self-interest"?

Chapter Review Answers

WRITING A SUMMARY
See Essential Points in each section for main ideas.

REVIEWING CHRONOLOGY
1, 2, 5, 4, 3
Assessing Consequences
Answers will vary but should clearly show how the events selected affected the course of the war.

IDENTIFYING PEOPLE AND IDEAS
1. *glorification of armed strength that contributed to war*
2. *military alliance of Great Britain, France, and Russia in which each member promised to aid any member that came under attack*
3. *Serbian nationalist whose assassination of Archduke Franz Ferdinand provoked World War I*
4. *German government's renewal of promise, following Sussex attack, not to sink ocean liners without warning*
5. *first woman elected to Congress; opposed U.S. entry into wars*
6. *system whereby merchant vessels were escorted by American warships through North Atlantic*
7. *Wall Street banker who served as director of War Industries Board*
8. *shift of African Americans from the South to northern cities between 1915 and 1930*
9. *principle, outlined in Fourteen Points, that people had right to govern themselves*
10. *head of Senate Committee on Foreign Relations who opposed Treaty of Versailles*

UNDERSTANDING MAIN IDEAS
1. *nationalism, territorial rivalries, militarism, and rival alliances*
2. *before—encouraged trade in war materials; after—provided troops and supplies, built transportation and communication networks*
3. *served as nurses and volunteers for the Red Cross, worked in traditionally male jobs in industry, helped plan wartime mobilization through membership in civilian agencies*
4. *program of world peace, self-determination for all nations, solution to territorial disputes, and creation of a League of Nations; Allied demands for German reparations and honoring of secret spoils-of-war treaties*

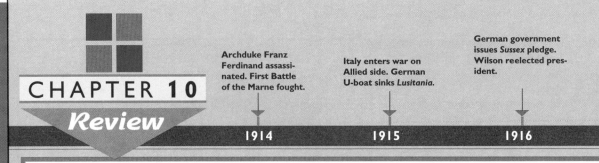

CHAPTER 10
Review

Archduke Franz Ferdinand assassinated. First Battle of the Marne fought.	Italy enters war on Allied side. German U-boat sinks *Lusitania*.	German government issues *Sussex* pledge. Wilson reelected president.
1914	**1915**	**1916**

WRITING A SUMMARY
Using the essential points of the chapter as a guide, write a summary of the chapter.

REVIEWING CHRONOLOGY
Number your paper 1 to 5. Study the time line above, and list the following events in the order in which they happened by writing the first next to 1, the second next to 2, and so on. Then complete the activity below.

1. Archduke Franz Ferdinand assassinated.
2. German U-boat sinks *Lusitania*.
3. National War Labor Board established.
4. Zimmermann Note published.
5. Wilson reelected president.

Assessing Consequences Select two events on the time line, and in a paragraph, explain how they affected the course of the war.

IDENTIFYING PEOPLE AND IDEAS
Explain the historical significance of each of the following people or terms.

1. militarism
2. Triple Entente
3. Gavrilo Princip
4. *Sussex* pledge
5. Jeannette Rankin
6. convoy system
7. Bernard Baruch
8. Great Migration
9. self-determination
10. Henry Cabot Lodge

UNDERSTANDING MAIN IDEAS
1. What tensions contributed to the outbreak of war in Europe?
2. What contributions did the United States make to the Allied war effort both before and after entry into the war?
3. What role did women play in the war effort?
4. What did President Wilson hope to accomplish through his Fourteen Points? Why was he forced to compromise?

REVIEWING THEMES
1. **Global Relations** What factors led the United States to declare war in 1917? Do you think U.S. involvement in the conflict was inevitable? Explain your answer.
2. **Economic Development** How was the American economy mobilized for war?
3. **Democratic Values** How did the U.S. government's attempts to rally support for its wartime policies interfere with First Amendment rights?

THINKING CRITICALLY
1. **Analyzing** What were the positive and the negative effects of the draft in the United States?
2. **Evaluating** What effect did the wartime labor shortage have on unions, women, African Americans, and Mexican Americans?
3. **Hypothesizing** How might the outcome of the war have been different if Wilson had been more willing to compromise on his Fourteen Points?

STRATEGY FOR SUCCESS
Review the Strategies for Success on Interpreting Editorial Cartoons on page 162. Then study the following cartoon, which appeared shortly after the sinking of the *Lusitania*. What clues does the cartoonist give to suggest that Germany humiliated the United States in this incident?

REVIEWING THEMES

1. Students should consider ethnic and cultural ties, German violations of neutral rights, the Zimmermann Note, and business support for Allies as factors in weighing the inevitability of U.S. involvement.
2. money raised through bonds and taxes; actions of government, business, and industry coordinated through war boards; prices and production levels set for commodities; scarce supplies conserved
3. CPI and the Espionage and Sedition acts crushed dissent by targeting anyone who called for peace, questioned the Allies' progress, or criticized government's policies.

THINKING CRITICALLY

1. positive—brought armed services up to full force, created employment opportunities for women and minorities; negative—discrimination against and segregation of minorities and foreign-born in military
2. strengthened unions through strikes and higher average wages, added large numbers of women, African Americans, and Mexican Americans to work force
3. Students might mention that compromise could have led to greater postwar cooperation.

STRATEGY FOR SUCCESS

Wilson's posture as a beggar, the drooping U.S. eagle, and the Kaiser's indifferent coin toss as payment for the sinking of the ship all suggest humiliation.

WRITING ABOUT HISTORY

Letters might consider how discrimination interferes with rights and opportunities, prevents African Americans from becoming better soldiers, and deprives the military of potential talent and leadership.

USING PRIMARY SOURCES

Trench warfare caused men to dehumanize one another and fight not for principle but for survival and revenge.

LINKING HISTORY AND GEOGRAPHY

Trench warfare enabled them to hold their positions and to maintain supply lines.

Zimmermann Note published. Congress declares war. Bolsheviks seize power in Russia.

Wilson introduces Fourteen Points. National War Labor Board established. Congress passes Sedition Act. Armistice signed.

Treaty of Versailles signed.

Republicans win landslide victory.

1917   1918   1919   1920

WRITING ABOUT HISTORY

Writing to Persuade Imagine you are an African American soldier during the war. Write your commanding officer a letter that tries to convince the army to open up more opportunities for black soldiers.

USING PRIMARY SOURCES

In his classic novel about World War I, *All Quiet on the Western Front*, Erich Maria Remarque portrayed the horrible experiences of war through the eyes of German soldiers. Read the following excerpt, which describes an encounter between German and French soldiers. What point is Remarque trying to make about trench warfare?

66 *The moment we are about to retreat three faces rise up from the ground in front of us. Under one of the helmets [I see] a dark pointed beard and two eyes that are fastened on me. I raise my hand, but I cannot throw into those strange eyes; for one mad moment the whole slaughter whirls like a circus round me, . . . then the head rises up, . . . and my hand-grenade flies through the air and into him.*

We make for the rear, pull wire cradles into the trench and leave bombs behind us with the strings pulled, which ensures us a fiery retreat. The machine-guns are already firing from the next position.

Soldiers in trench

We have become wild beasts. We do not fight, we defend ourselves against annihilation. It is not against men that we fling our bombs, what do we know of men in this moment when Death is hunting us down— now, for the first time in three days we can see his face, now for the first time in three days we can oppose him. . . . No longer do we lie helpless, . . . we can destroy and kill, to save ourselves, . . . and to be revenged. 99

LINKING HISTORY AND GEOGRAPHY

Refer to the map on page 244. After the French and the British stopped the German advance at the Marne in 1914, the German army retreated to the Aisne River, halted, and dug themselves into trenches. Why do you think the Germans chose trench warfare rather than retreat into Germany?

BUILDING YOUR PORTFOLIO

Complete the following projects independently or cooperatively.

1. **GLOBAL RELATIONS** In Chapter 9 you portrayed a State Department official concerned with global relations. Building on that experience, imagine you are the U.S. ambassador to Germany in 1915. Write a letter to the Kaiser, protesting German violations of neutral shipping rights.

2. **WAR** In Chapter 9 you portrayed a recruiting officer during the Spanish-American War. Building on that experience, imagine you are a senator committed to U.S. neutrality in World War I. Write a speech that states why the United States should remain neutral.

BUILDING YOUR PORTFOLIO

Have students refer to **Building Your Portfolio Worksheet 2**, assigned at the beginning of Unit 2. Use the worksheet to help students monitor their progress on the portfolio projects.

Assessment

Core Resources
• Reteaching Worksheet 10
• Chapter 10 Tests
• Alternative Assessment Forms
Test Generator

THE SPANISH–AMERICAN WAR

SETTING THE SCENE

José Martí was a leader in the drive for Cuban independence from Spain. Twice exiled from the island for his political activities, he eventually took up residence in New York City. There he continued to work for freedom for his homeland, founding the Cuban Revolutionary party in 1892. Accompanied by a few party members, he staged a revolt on the island three years later. He was killed by Spanish troops two days after writing the diary entry that is excerpted on p. 270.

Like Martí, Lola Rodríguez de Tió was exiled from her homeland because of her political activities. Settling in New York, she became friends with Martí and helped him plan the Cuban revolt of 1895. Her desire for freedom for all peoples of the Caribbean, expressed in her poetry and in her actions, earned her the name "Daughter of the Isles."

UNIT 2

American Letters

The Spanish–American War

As a result of the Spanish-American War, the United States won territories in the Caribbean and the Pacific. In the following selections, Cuban poet and essayist José Martí, Puerto Rican poet Lola Rodríguez de Tió, an anonymous Mexican American poet, and American writers Mark Twain and Edgar Lee Masters explore the meaning of the war for the Caribbean and the United States.

▲ **Lola Rodríguez de Tió**

Diary Entry

by José Martí

[April 25, 1895.] Day of combat. Straight through the woods we are drawing close, already in the claws of Guantanamo. . . . The breast swells with fond reverence and overpowering affection at the sight of the vast landscape of the loved river. We cross it, near a *ceiba* tree, and after greeting a patriot family, overjoyed to see us, we enter the open wood, with sweet sun, rain-washed leaves. As over a carpet go our horses, so thick is the grass. All is garland and leaf, and through the openings, to the right, the green of the cleared fields is visible on the other bank, sheltered and compact. . . . Here as everywhere I am touched by the affection with which we are received, and the unity of soul which will not be allowed to coalesce [grow together], and which will not be recognized, and which will be overridden, harming, at least with the harm of delay, the Revolution in the impulse of its first year. The spirit I sowed, is that which has borne fruit, and that of the Island, and with it, and guiding ourselves by it, we will soon triumph, and with a better victory and for a better peace. ❖

The Song of Borinquen

by Lola Rodríguez de Tió

Awake, Borinqueños,[1]
 for they've given the signal!

Awake from your sleep
 for it's time to fight!

Come! The sound of cannon
 will be dear to us.

At that patriotic clamor
 doesn't your heart burn?

Look! The Cuban will soon be free,
 the machete will give him freedom.

The drum of war announces in its beating
 that the thicket is the place, the meeting place!

Most beautiful Borinquen, we have to follow Cuba;
 you have brave sons who want to fight!

Let us no more seem fearful!
Let us no more, timid, permit our enslavement!

We want to be free already
 and our machete is well sharpened!

Why should we, then, remain so asleep
 and deaf, asleep and deaf to that signal?

▼ *General Toral surrenders the city of Santiago to General Shaftner in 1898.*

270

There's no need to fear, Ricans, the sound of cannon,
for saving the homeland is the duty of the heart!

We want no more despots! Let the tyrant fall!
Women, likewise wild, will know how to fight!

We want freedom and our machete will give it to us!

Let's go, Puerto Ricans, let's go already,
for LIBERTY is waiting, ever so anxious! ❖

---

1 Borinqueños are Puerto Ricans. The word is adapted from
Borinquén, the Native American name for Puerto Rico.

The Voice of the Hispano

Anonymous

Many are the opinions
Against the Hispanic people
And they accuse them of betraying
The American government.

Making an experiment,
They will be disillusioned,
Our brave native men
Do not refuse to be soldiers.

It matters not what is said
Or how our fame is insulted,
As they will fight with pleasure
For the American eagle.

They accuse our native people
Of being rabble,
But they have not proven to be so
On the battlefield.

Like good countrymen
And faithful Americans,
We will free them from that yoke
The humble Cubans. ❖

From To the Person Sitting in Darkness

by Mark Twain

There have been lies; yes, but
they were told in a good cause.
We have been treacherous; but
that was only in order that real
good might come out of apparent
evil. True, we have crushed a
deceived and confiding people; we

have turned against the weak and the friendless who
trusted us; we have stamped out a just and intelligent
and well-ordered republic; we have stabbed an ally in
the back and slapped the face of a guest; we have
bought a Shadow from an enemy that hadn't it to sell;
we have robbed a trusting friend of his land and
liberty; . . . but each detail was for the best. ◆

"Harry Wilmans" From *Spoon River Anthology*

by Edgar Lee Masters

I was just turned twenty-one,
And Henry Phipps, the Sunday-school superintendent,
Made a speech in Bindle's Opera House.
"The honor of the flag must be upheld," he said,
"Whether it be assailed by a barbarous tribe of
    Tagalogs[1]
Or the greatest power in Europe."
And we cheered and cheered the speech and the flag
    he waved
As he spoke.
And I went to the war in spite of my father,
And followed the flag till I saw it raised
By our camp in a rice field near Manila,
And all of us cheered and cheered it.
But there were flies and poisonous things;
And there was the deadly water,
And the cruel heat,
And the sickening, putrid food. . . .
Following the flag,
Till I fell with a scream, shot through the guts.
Now there's a flag over me in Spoon River!
A flag! A flag! ❖

---

1 a people of central Luzon, Philippines

THINKING AND WRITING ABOUT LITERATURE

1. José Martí had just returned to Cuba from his exile in New York when he wrote this diary entry. Which phrases show that he missed Cuba in his absence?
2. Like Martí, Lola Rodríguez de Tió lived in New York and wrote in support of independence from Spain. Whose model does she urge Puerto Ricans to follow?
3. In the anonymous poem, what does the author believe Mexican American soldiers will prove?
4. Mark Twain's controversial essay and Edgar Lee Masters's poem use irony to express the authors' views of the war. Describe both authors' perspectives on the war.

PRIMARY SOURCES

Description of Change: excerpted, bracketed, and footnoted

Rationale: excerpted for space considerations; bracketed and footnoted to clarify meaning

THINKING AND WRITING ABOUT LITERATURE

1. "fond reverence," "overpowering affection," "the loved river," "sweet sun"
2. that of the Cubans, who had already taken up arms against Spain
3. their patriotism and their loyalty to the U.S. government, and that Mexican Americans are not "rabble"
4. Twain believes that the U.S. has deceived its wartime allies (the Philippines, Cuba, Puerto Rico) and robbed them of their liberty. Masters believes that Harry Wilmans's death was in vain and did nothing to promote "the honor of the flag."

RECOGNIZING STEREOTYPES

Guide students through the discussion of how to recognize stereotypes and then have them complete the Practicing the Strategy exercise. Note that stereotypes, though inaccurate, often arise from actual historical events. Have students review the discussion of Francisco "Pancho" Villa's raid on Columbus, New Mexico, on pp. 233–234. Ask students to speculate about what stereotype of Mexicans Villa's raid may have helped create in the U.S. *(the* bandido*)* Discuss how this stereotype might distort an understanding of Villa's motivations for the raid and how it might affect the treatment of Mexican Americans.

PRACTICING THE STRATEGY

1. *African Americans*
2. *The images of blacks in the poster portray either dance or music—African Americans, while being denied opportunities in other areas, often were stereotyped as especially suited to be entertainers.*

Strategies for Success

RECOGNIZING STEREOTYPES

A stereotype is a generalization or oversimplification about a group or culture. Stereotypes deny individual differences by attributing the same characteristics to every member in a group: All poor people are lazy. All Irish drink too much. All African Americans are good athletes. All girls have difficulty with math and science. Most stereotypes are negative and often lead to discrimination and prejudice.

How to Recognize Stereotypes

1. **Examine the message.** Pay close attention to how a person or group is portrayed. Identify generalizations that lack supporting facts. Ask yourself: Are the same qualities being attributed to all individuals in a group?
2. **Note words that signal stereotyping.** Watch for clue words such as *all, always, never,* or *every* that allow no exceptions; their use may signal stereotyping.
3. **Detect bias or prejudice.** Note any bias or tone that indicates prejudice toward the subjects being described.
4. **Use your knowledge.** In evaluating general statements about people, apply what you have learned from your studies or through direct experience with individual classmates, your family members, or others.

Applying the Strategy

In the following passage, Samuel Bryan, an Anglo American sociologist, describes Mexican immigrants in the United States in 1912:

66 Socially and politically the presence of large numbers of Mexicans in this country gives rise to serious problems. . . . They . . . are slow to learn English, . . . move readily from place to place, and do not acquire or lease land to any extent. But their most unfavorable characteristic is their inclination to . . . live in a clannish manner. 99

Bryan's description is an example of the kind of stereotyping that breeds prejudice. First, he lumps together all Mexican immigrants—and, by implication, all Mexican Americans. He ignores the fact that in many areas of the United States stable, prosperous Mexican American communities existed long before Anglo settlement. Second, he blames immigrants for conditions that are a product of their immigrant status. Like members of other immigrant groups, Mexicans often found many jobs closed to them. One area in which

they could find work was farm labor. Because farm labor is seasonal, Mexican farm workers were forced to move often in search of crops to harvest. This migratory existence, coupled with the low wages typical of such farm work, made it difficult for many Mexican immigrants to buy land.

Practicing the Strategy

Study the song poster below. Then, on a separate sheet of paper, answer the following questions.

1. What group is pictured in this song poster?
2. Why can this song poster be considered an example of stereotyping?

BUILDING YOUR PORTFOLIO

Each portfolio project described below is the culmination of the Building Your Portfolio activities in the chapter reviews of Unit 2. First, decide whether you wish students to work individually or in groups on these unit projects. Then permit each student to choose the project on which he or she desires to work. Provide students with copies of **Building Your Portfolio Worksheet 2** from *Core Resources*. This worksheet will guide students step by step to complete their projects.

BUILDING YOUR PORTFOLIO

Outlined below are four projects. Independently or cooperatively, complete one and use the products to demonstrate your mastery of the historical concepts involved.

1 REFORM

In the late 19th century the transformation of the United States from a rural economy to an industrialized, urban society created numerous social problems. In response, the Progressive party sought reforms. Using the portfolio materials you designed in chapters 7 and 8, create a series of Progressive party campaign posters that outline the party's reform goals.

2 DEMOCRATIC RIGHTS

Historians note that progressivism was primarily a white, middle-class movement and thus did not address many of the concerns of working-class women. Using the portfolio materials you designed in chapters 7 and 8, conduct a debate between a white, middle-class progressive and a working-class woman on whether the progressive emphasis on women's suffrage best serves the needs of all women.

3 GLOBAL RELATIONS

The expansionist policies of the United States in the 19th century led to the establishment of U.S. overseas colonies, increased foreign investment, and conflicts with foreign powers. Using the portfolio materials you designed in chapters 9 and 10, create a world map showing areas of U.S. colonization, investment, and conflict through World War I.

4 WAR

The Spanish-American War and World War I brought the United States onto the world stage. Using the portfolio materials you designed in chapters 9 and 10, prepare a speech for delivery to Congress, outlining some of the costs and benefits of America's international role.

PORTFOLIO ASSESSMENT

1. *Campaign posters should show Progressive support of women's suffrage, and reform of political machines, business corruption, poor working conditions, and public health.*
2. *Debates should describe Progressive support of shorter working hours for women, stricter workplace safety standards, and temperance. Debates should also show the importance of higher wages and better working conditions for women workers.*
3. *World maps should show U.S. occupation of Cuba; acquisition of Eastern Samoa, the Philippines, Puerto Rico, and Hawaii; construction of the Panama Canal; intervention in the Dominican Republic, Haiti, and Mexico; investment in Nicaragua and China; Perry's contact with Japan and the voyage of the "Great White Fleet"; and World War I battles in Europe.*
4. *Speeches should address the economic benefits for the U.S. of new colonies, the political benefits for the colonies, and the problems of opposition movements in the colonies.*

Videodisc Review

In assigned groups, develop an outline for a video collage of America in the years between 1897 and 1920. Choose images that best illustrate the major topics of the period. Write a script to accompany the images. Assign narrators to different parts of the script, and present your video collage to the class.

Further Reading

Ettinger, Albert M., and A. Churchill Ettinger. *A Doughboy with the Fighting 69th.* White Mane (1992). Reminiscence of World War I by a soldier of the 69th Rainbow Division.

Hall, Linda B., and Don M. Coerver. *Revolution on the Border: The United States and Mexico, 1910–1920.* University of New Mexico Press (1990). Examines the role that trade and investment played in U.S.–Mexico relations.

Liliuokalani. *Hawaii's Story by Hawaii's Queen.* Charles E. Tuttle (1991). Firsthand account of 19th-century Hawaii.

Schneider, Dorothy, and Carl J. Schneider. *Into the Breach.* Viking (1991). Examines the participation of American women in World War I.

Tuchman, Barbara W. *The Guns of August.* Bantam (1989). Analysis of the events of August 1914 that propelled Europe into World War I.

Prosperity and Crisis ❖ 1920–1945

UNIT OVERVIEW

The prosperity of the 1920s introduced millions of Americans to mass production and mass culture. Rapid change caused social upheaval and led many to question traditional values. By the end of the decade the U.S. had plunged into the worst economic depression in history. Facing unemployment, hunger, and homelessness, Americans looked to President Roosevelt and his New Deal programs for help. Recovery was slow, but the economy fully revived when the U.S. entered World War II. By 1945 the U.S. was the most powerful nation in the free world.

CORE RESOURCES

- **American Almanac Worksheet 3**
- **Building Your Portfolio Worksheet 3**
  You may wish to preview the Unit 3 Review and Building Your Portfolio performance assessment activities on p. 431.

Using the Almanac

Point out that Unit 3 examines the prosperity of the 1920s, the Great Depression and the New Deal years, and American participation in World War II. Call on volunteers to select the almanac entries that best illustrate the lighter side of the 1920s: music, dance, films, and sports.

American ALMANAC

❖ **At Your Leisure**

1924 Americans own 2.5 million radios—up from 2,000 in 1920. By 1937 they spend 4.5 hours a day listening.

1920s Donald Duncan puts his yo-yo on the market.

1930 Lone Ranger's first ride is heard on radio. Hi-yo, Silver!

1935 Americans buy and sell real estate in the board game Monopoly.

1936 Knock-knock jokes are knocked around.

1937 At your local grocery you can find Eskimo Pies, Betty Crocker cake mixes, Wrigley's gum, Rice Krispies, 7-Up, Snickers, Twinkies, Skippy peanut butter, and Spam.

1940 Dick Tracy, Flash Gordon, Superman, and Batman are in the comics.

1943 Teenagers are hot on slumber parties, beach parties, roller rinks, soda shops, and argyle sweaters.

❖ **Fashion Plate**

1920s Gideon Sundback's 1913 invention—the zipper—catches on!

1934 Clark Gable reveals his bare chest in movie; sales of men's undershirts drop.

1942 Pants are popular with women; sales of slacks are five times greater than in 1941.

◀ **Dance marathon**

❖ **America's Music and Dance**

1922 Cornet player Louis "Satchmo" Armstrong helps popularize jazz.

1923 Couple dances over 90 hours, setting dance marathon record.

1927 Duke Ellington's band opens in Harlem's Cotton Club.

1937 About 3,000 teenagers wait in line to see Benny Goodman.

1938 Cuban Desi Arnaz performs in Miami and introduces the conga dance to America.

1942 Glenn Miller's "Chattanooga Choo Choo" is first "gold record," selling over 1 million copies.

▼ **Glenn Miller**

❖ **The Cost of Living**

1920s Eggs cost 68¢ a dozen; milk 17¢ a quart; bread 12¢ a loaf; oranges 63¢ a dozen; coffee 47¢ a pound.

1927 Lawyers make $5,205 per year; teachers make $1,277.

1930 Sneakers cost 39¢; men's suits cost $15.50.

▶ **Desi Arnaz**

America's Music and Dance

Swing, the popular music of the 1930s and 1940s, gave rise to a new language called *jive. Cats* were musicians known for *kicking out,* or improvising, when they played. *Alligators,* or devotees of swing, often could be seen *cuttin' the rug,* or dancing.

🔲 Have students identify and explain some terms associated with today's popular music.

At Your Leisure

Most comic-book heroes were outsiders, often aliens, mutations, or technological creations disguised in some way so that they could pass unnoticed in everyday life. They revealed their true nature only when society was threatened by danger or evil.

🔲 Ask students why comic-book heroes such as Superman and Batman are still popular today.

Fashion Plate

Point out that the lifestyles of young, wealthy people—"glamour girls" and "men about town"—attracted a great deal of publicity and often influenced the fashions of society at large.

🔲 Ask students who, if anybody, influences their fashion decisions.

The Cost of Living

Other 1930s clothes prices: women's—leather shoes, $1.79; raincoat, $2.69; wool sweater, $1.69; men's—shirt, 47¢; silk tie, 55¢; shoes, $3.85.

🔲 Ask students to investigate today's prices of the items listed.

Firsts in America

Earhart's other flying achievements included first nonstop solo flight from Honolulu to California, and a number of altitude and speed records.

🔲 Ask students to identify the flight "firsts" that are being accomplished today.

Sports Extra

Owens's feat stood until Carl Lewis matched it at the 1984 Los Angeles Olympics.

The Silver Screen

Mention that Temple began her movie career at the age of 3 and appeared in some 25 films during the 1930s. She retired from movies at age 21. In later years she served as ambassador to the UN, Ghana, and Czechoslovakia.

🔲 Ask students what child stars are popular today.

► **George Washington Carver**

UNIT 3
Prosperity and Crisis
1920–1945

▼ **Mickey Mouse**

© The Walt Disney Company

❖ The Silver Screen

1921 Heartthrob Rudolph Valentino skyrockets to fame.

1928 Mickey Mouse makes first appearance—Donald Duck follows in 1934 and Bugs Bunny in 1940.

1931 Gangster and horror films rival westerns in popularity.

1936 Shirley Temple is year's biggest star.

▲ **Shirley Temple**

1939 *Stagecoach* makes John Wayne a movie hero.

1946 A record 90 million people go to the movies on average each week!

❖ Sports Extra

1935 Babe Ruth retires with home run record—714!

1936 Jesse Owens wins 4 Olympic gold medals in track and field in Berlin.

1937 Joe Louis is world heavyweight champion.

❖ Firsts in America

1927 Charles Lindbergh makes first solo flight across the Atlantic; in 1932, Amelia Earhart is first woman to do same.

1929 First truly national Hispanic organization—League of United Latin American Citizens, or LULAC—is founded in Texas.

1939 George Washington Carver receives Theodore Roosevelt Medal for extensive research in crop rotation and agricultural chemistry.

1940 Drs. Glenn Seaborg and Edwin McMillan of the University of California, Berkeley, discover plutonium.

XI OLYMPIADE BERLIN 1936

► **Jesse Owens**

𝒜 TURBULENT DECADE

1919–1929

𝒞hapter 𝒪verview

In the years immediately after World War I, the U.S. went through a brief but painful economic recession, labor strikes, and the anti-Communist hysteria known as the "Red Scare." Hoping for a return to the prosperity of the prewar period, voters elected Warren G. Harding, Calvin Coolidge, and then Herbert Hoover as president. Conservative Republicans dominated American politics throughout the decade despite political scandals. Immigrants and racial, ethnic, and religious groups experienced increased hostility during this period.

𝒞hapter 𝒫lanning 𝒢uide

CHAPTER 11	CORE RESOURCES	AUDIOVISUAL RESOURCES	PROGRAM RESOURCES
INTRODUCTION pp. 276–277	■ Building Your Portfolio Worksheet 3	■ Everyday Life in America Transparency and Worksheet 21	
TEACHING THE CHAPTER pp. 278–295 ■ For expanded coverage of pp. 294–295, see Chapter 25, pp. 674–680.	■ Graphic Organizer 11 ■ Social Studies Skills Worksheet 11 ■ Literature Worksheet 11 ■ Geography Worksheet 11 ■ Outline Map 9	■ Linking Geography and History Transparency and Worksheet 17	■ *Eyewitnesses and Others,* Volume 2: Readings 36, 37, 42, 43
REVIEW AND ASSESSMENT pp. 296–297	■ Chapter 11 Daily Quizzes ■ Reteaching Worksheet 11 ■ Chapter 11 Tests ■ Alternative Assessment Forms		■ Test Generator

𝒜dditional 𝑅esources

BOOKS FOR TEACHERS

Cott, Nancy F. *The Grounding of Modern Feminism.* Yale University Press, 1987. Analysis of the campaign for women's suffrage.

Harrison, Alferdteen, ed. *Black Exodus: The Great Migration from the Great American South.* University Press of Mississippi, 1992. Story of the black migration from the South to the urban North.

Leuchtenburg, William E. *The Perils of Prosperity: 1914–32.* University of Chicago, 1958. Distinguished historian's classic study.

BOOKS FOR STUDENTS

Green, Harvey. *The Uncertainty of Everyday Life, 1915–1945.* HarperCollins, 1992. In-depth look at life in the U.S. before, during, and after the "Turbulent Twenties."

* Lawler, Mary. *Marcus Garvey.* Holloway, 1990. Biography of the leader of the Back-to-Africa movement.

* Wade, Linda R. *Warren G. Harding.* Childrens Press, 1989. An easy-to-read biography of the 29th president.

* for students reading below grade level

MULTIMEDIA MATERIALS

The Age of Ballyhoo. Video, 52 min. Republic/SSSS. Cultural history of the 1920s. Includes newsreels of Sacco and Vanzetti.

The Big Red Scare of 1919–1920. Video, 10 min. Multi-Media Productions/SSSS. Traces the origins of anti-Communist and anti-immigrant hysteria in 1919 and 1920.

The Reckless Years. Video, 39 min. Guidance Associates/SSSS. Chronicles the twenties with maps, graphs, cartoons, and historical photographs.

THEMES IN AMERICAN HISTORY

USE WITH PAGES 276–277

Listed on the right are the themes emphasized in Chapter 11. The questions in boldface type stimulate critical thinking and provide students with an opportunity to discuss the themes within a broadened context. The questions also appear in the pupil's edition on p. 276.

■ DEMOCRATIC VALUES

How might a democratic government respond to a perceived threat of revolution? Students might suggest that even a democratic government may try to stifle dissent if many people feel that a revolution threatens their way of life. In such a situation a government might try to intimidate or even to imprison people believed to be responsible for the threat.

■ CULTURAL DIVERSITY

In what ways might ethnic and racial groups respond to acts of discrimination? Students might suggest that members of such groups might try to work together to form their own communities or work to eliminate discrimination by changing attitudes and laws.

■ ECONOMIC DEVELOPMENT

What actions should the federal government take to promote economic prosperity? Students might suggest that the government could pass laws that promote economic development or relax existing regulations that might inhibit development.

CHAPTER STRATEGIES FOR MEETING INDIVIDUAL NEEDS

LIMITED ENGLISH PROFICIENT LEARNERS

Have students work in small groups to role-play interviews with the presidential candidates discussed in Chapter 11. Interviews should show the main differences in candidates and parties.

TACTILE/KINESTHETIC LEARNERS

Have students create campaign buttons, posters, and placards for the Hoover or Smith presidential campaign of 1928. Campaign materials should show differences between candidates and parties.

LEARNERS HAVING DIFFICULTY

Have students work in pairs and pick three events in each section. Then have them write two or three sentences explaining the importance of each event. As a class, create a time line showing all events.

AUDITORY LEARNERS

Have students prepare a radio broadcast of the news of the decade using the events on the chapter time line on pp. 296–297 as ideas for news items.

VISUAL LEARNERS

Have students prepare an advertisement or poster for a movie titled *The 1920s,* which shows key events in those turbulent years and stars key figures in the history of the period.

GIFTED LEARNERS

Have students write an essay comparing the anti-immigrant sentiment of the 1920s with the nativism of the Know-Nothing party of the 1850s.

USING THE CHAPTER FOCUS

■ **UNDERSTANDING THE MAIN IDEA**
Call on a volunteer to read aloud the Understanding the Main Idea paragraph and define the term *probusiness*. Explain that "normalcy" was a term coined by one of the probusiness Republican presidents discussed in this chapter. Have students speculate what this word might mean and why it might be interpreted differently by white war veterans, African Americans, Native Americans, and immigrants.

 THEMES
Have students work individually or in small groups to answer the questions under Themes. Save students' responses so that they can compare them with their responses after studying the chapter. (See p. 275B for suggested answers.)

■ **THE TIME LINE**
Direct students to copy the time-line entries in their notebooks. After they have read about each event on the time line, have them draw an editorial cartoon that focuses on each event.

CORE RESOURCES

- **Graphic Organizer 11**
- **Outline Map 9**
- **Building Your Portfolio Worksheet 3**

AV RESOURCES

- **Everyday Life in America Transparency** and **Worksheet 21**

ABOUT THE ILLUSTRATION

On September 16, 1920, around the noon lunch hour a driver parked a horse and wagon along the curb on Wall Street. Within five minutes the wagon exploded, instantly killing more than 30 people. Hundreds were injured in the blast, and damage to buildings and other property was estimated between a half a million and two million dollars. Although the bomber was never found, police and other officials believed that radicals were to blame for the crime. Ask students to speculate why radicals might have chosen Wall Street for such an act. Then tell students that it was events such as this that characterized the 1920s as a "turbulent decade."

Chapter 11

1919–1929

A TURBULENT DECADE

FOCUS

UNDERSTANDING THE MAIN IDEA

The end of World War I ushered in a period of economic and social instability. Voters, eager to return to "normalcy," elected probusiness Republican presidents, and as the 1920s progressed, prosperity returned. Not all, however, shared the benefits of this economic renewal. Organized labor lost ground, and Native Americans, African Americans, and immigrants faced discrimination.

 THEMES

■ **DEMOCRATIC VALUES**
How might a democratic government respond to a perceived threat of revolution?

■ **CULTURAL DIVERSITY**
In what ways might ethnic and racial groups respond to acts of discrimination?

■ **ECONOMIC DEVELOPMENT** What actions should the federal government take to promote economic prosperity?

1919	1921	1924	1927	1928
Palmer raids begin.	Congress limits immigration.	Congress grants Native Americans citizenship.	Sacco and Vanzetti executed.	Herbert Hoover elected president.

LINK TO THE PAST

Have volunteers recall the changes that took place on the home front during World War I. Focus on changes in the roles of workers—especially women and African Americans. Then tell the class that in this chapter they will look at how the nation made the sometimes turbulent transition from a war machine to a peacetime society.

LINK TO THE PAST

During World War I the government tried to stifle dissent, women took jobs traditionally held by men, and African Americans moved to northern cities. These and other changes in society continued to affect Americans after the war.

MAKING CONNECTIONS

Sociology

Although many Americans yearned for a return to life as they imagined it in prewar America, industrialization had changed forever the way Americans lived. In 1899 electricity powered only about 2 percent of U.S. factories; by 1919 it powered some 31 percent. In 1920 over eight million cars bumped and lurched down U.S. roads, an increase of about 300 percent from 1915. Such developments created opportunities for a radically different life-style for many Americans in the 1920s. Old beliefs and attitudes, however, proved more resistant to change.

*T*he end of World War I brought joyous celebration. As author Malcolm Cowley wrote, "We danced in the streets, embraced old women and pretty girls, swore blood brotherhood with soldiers in little bars, drank with our elbows locked in theirs, reeled through the streets with bottles of champagne." But this joy proved short-lived.

For many Americans life after the war did not appear promising. War veterans returned home to find few jobs available. Those who did find work soon discovered that soaring prices ate up their earnings. Economic and social problems increased. Strikes broke out across the nation, and violent race riots exploded in many American cities. Fueled by wartime fears, anti-immigrant feelings raised social tensions. Looking back on the first years after the war, author and journalist Ray Stannard Baker remarked, "I can recall no period in which life in America looked bleaker."

Aftermath of Wall Street bombing, 1920

World War I veteran with his family, 1919

A TURBULENT DECADE ▪▪ 277

FOCUS OBJECTIVES

- Describe what economic conditions were like after the war.

- Identify how workers reacted to hard times.

- Explain why many Americans feared that a Communist revolution was at hand.

- Analyze what the Sacco and Vanzetti case revealed about America in the early 1920s.

PREVIEW WORKSHOP

Following is a list of the significant people, places, and terms in this section. You may wish to use this list as a section preview.

People
- Ole Hanson
- Edwin Curtis
- A. Mitchell Palmer
- Emma Goldman

- Nicola Sacco
- Bartolomeo Vanzetti

Places
- Seattle, Washington
- Boston, Massachusetts

Terms
- demobilization
- Red Scare
- Palmer raids

Section 1

POSTWAR TROUBLES

FOCUS

- **What were economic conditions like after the war?**
- **How did workers react to hard times?**
- **Why did many Americans fear that a Communist revolution was at hand?**
- **What did the Sacco and Vanzetti case reveal about America in the early 1920s?**

1916 strike sympathizers

The horrors of World War I shocked and disillusioned many Americans. The war, wrote novelist John Dos Passos, had been a "waste of time, waste of money, waste of lives, waste of youth." In response, many Americans tried to return to the way things had been before the war. But there was no going back. Instead of a return to the "old ways," the nation faced economic hardship and social strife.

DEMOBILIZATION

Under the best of conditions, **demobilization**, the shift from a wartime to a peacetime footing, is not an easy task for a nation. The process is made more difficult when the shift is rapid, as was the case after World War I. The war's end caught the

▲ After World War I, millions of veterans scrambled for available jobs. American Legion employment offices, such as this one in Los Angeles, tried to find work for veterans.

American government by surprise—literally. Trains carrying new recruits to boot camp were stopped en route. Within a year some four million soldiers returned to civilian life.

Women were urged to give up their jobs to make room for returning veterans. "The same patriotism which induced women to enter industry during the war should induce them to vacate their positions," declared the New York labor federation. Most of the women who did not respond to patriotic appeals were forced out of jobs traditionally held by men. As a result, the percentage of women in the work force in 1920 fell slightly below what it had been in 1910.

Adding to employment worries was a sky-rocketing cost of living. With peace at hand, consumers went on a spending spree, making purchases they had put off during the war. As the demand for goods outpaced supply, prices soared until the cost of goods and services in 1920 was about twice that of 1914.

Soon, however, this trend reversed as the deep but brief recession of 1920–1921 struck and

---

CORE RESOURCES

• Section 1 Daily Quiz

AV RESOURCES

• Everyday Life in America Transparency and **Worksheet 21**

MOTIVATING:
PRIOR KNOWLEDGE

Ask volunteers to describe what life had been like before the war for many Americans in small-town, rural America. Have students recall the beliefs many had held during the war about what it would accomplish. Tell students this section examines both why the war left many Americans disillusioned and how they reacted to this disillusionment.

Teaching the Section

POSTWAR ECONOMICS

Have students work in groups to prepare skits for a radio show in which a reporter interviews a panel consisting of a female factory worker, housewife/consumer, midwestern grain farmer, and returning war veteran. Each panelist should explain how demobilization has affected his or her life.

prices fell. Demobilization was one of the factors behind the recession. During the war millions of Americans worked in war industries. But at war's end the government canceled more than $2 billion in war contracts. Factories responded by cutting back production and laying off workers. By 1921 some 5 million workers—more than 10 percent of the labor force—were unemployed, and the economy was shrinking.

A farm crisis contributed to the economic problems. Farmers had benefited from wartime markets in Europe. As European farm production revived, however, these markets dried up and farm prices fell. According to the Department of Agriculture, wheat, for example, dropped from $2.16 a bushel in 1919 to less than a dollar a bushel in 1922. Burdened with debt, hundreds of thousands of American farmers lost ownership of their land during the 1920s.

■■ **After the war the cost of living soared, but prices soon fell as a recession took hold and unemployment increased.**

LABOR STRIFE

In 1919, however, Americans were still struggling with rapidly rising prices for food, clothing, and shelter. Workers watched in dismay as runaway inflation ate up their wartime financial gains. Angry and frustrated, they asked for higher wages and shorter hours. But management ignored labor's pleas. In response, many workers walked off the job. In 1919 alone, unions called more than 3,600 strikes—involving more than four million workers.

◀ **Strikes became commonplace in the years after World War I, as workers demanded better wages and conditions. Here, mounted policemen break up a group of Philadelphia strikers in 1919.**

The Seattle general strike. The first strike of 1919 occurred in January, when some 35,000 shipyard workers in Seattle, Washington, walked off the job, demanding higher wages and a shorter workday. Within two weeks 110 local unions voted to join the shipyard workers in a general strike.

The general strike began on February 6 at 10 A.M. An eerie calm fell over the city as 60,000 workers left their jobs. "It was," declared one shipyard worker, "the most beautiful thing I ever seen!"

Alarmed at such a show of unity, Seattle newspapers blamed immigrants, calling the strikers "muddle-headed foreigners" and "riffraff from Europe intent on terrorizing the community." Mayor Ole Hanson denounced the strike as the work of Bolsheviks and called in troops to prevent unrest. But no violent incidents occurred. Instead, the well-disciplined strikers took steps to preserve order and to make sure that food and essential services were available to the community. Nevertheless, the strikers came under increased public pressure to go back to work. After five days they ended the strike without winning any of their demands.

Although the strike had been peaceful, antilabor forces tried to convince the public that Seattle had been on the brink of revolution. Mayor Hanson told the national press:

▲ The *Seattle Union Record* published a special edition on February 6, 1919, announcing the beginning of the general strike.

❝ Revolution . . . doesn't need violence. The general strike . . . is of itself the weapon of revolution, all the more dangerous because quiet. To succeed, it must suspend everything. . . . That is to say, it puts the government out of operation. And that is all there is to revolt—no matter how achieved. ❞

Many people believed these charges. In the end the Seattle strike helped turn public opinion against organized labor.

GLOBAL CONNECTIONS

By early 1915 orders for food to supply the Allies increased demand for U.S. farm products, which meant high prices for crops at home and abroad. Many U.S. farmers borrowed heavily to buy more land and machinery in order to expand production. After the war, overseas demand for U.S. food products dropped sharply, leaving farmers with huge surpluses and lower market prices as they struggled to repay their loans.

MAKING CONNECTIONS
Literature

American author John Dos Passos noted of the spirit of change that threatened many Americans after the war: "Any spring is a time of overturn, but then Lenin was alive, the Seattle general strike had seemed the beginning of the flood. . . . Currents of energy seemed breaking out everywhere as young guys climbed out of their uniforms. . . . In every direction the countries of the world stretched out starving and angry, ready for anything turbulent and new."

PRIMARY SOURCE

Description of Change: excerpted
Rationale: excerpted to focus on main idea

A TURBULENT DECADE ■■ 279

ᴛeaching the ᴛection

LABOR STRIFE

Organize students into three groups. Assign each group one of the following strikes: Seattle shipyard workers, Boston police, steel workers. Have groups imagine they are workers who participated in these strikes. Ask each group to write a letter to their local newspaper explaining their reasons for striking, their opinion of government and public reaction to the strike, the way the strike has been portrayed in the newspapers, and how they feel about the strike's outcome.

■■ Have students give examples of ways they or the American public in general have been affected by media coverage of a controversial issue today. Consider talk shows as well as newspaper and TV news reports.

MULTICULTURAL PERSPECTIVES

African Americans were willing to cross picket lines and work for lower wages than whites because many unions refused to admit them. Despite their exclusion, the official NAACP magazine, *The Crisis,* advised blacks to support the unions: "When colored labor enters into competition with white labor, . . . it must demand the hours and wages of the white worker. . . . To underbid [accept lower wages] . . . is to pull down the standard of living of the working class. . . . The Labor Union is no panacea, but it . . . is proving a force that in the end diminishes race prejudice. A democracy prospers when laborers of all races work together."

PRIMARY SOURCE

Description of Change: excerpted

Rationale: excerpted to focus on main idea

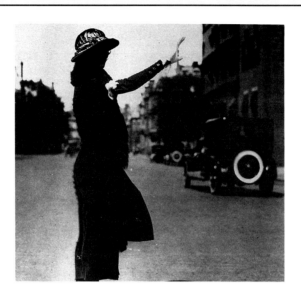

◀ An important issue during the Boston police strike was whether public employees had the right to strike. When policemen refused to report to work, civilians took over traffic control and other public safety jobs.

The Boston police strike. In September 1919 another strike, this time by the Boston police force, further inflamed antilabor sentiments. The Boston police had recently formed a union to seek better pay and working conditions. Although police in other cities had unionized without incident, Boston's police commissioner, Edwin Curtis, refused to recognize the union. Instead, he fired 19 officers for engaging in union activities. In response, some 75 percent of the police force went on strike.

Public order collapsed. Journalist William Allen White described the first night of the strike:

❝ The devil was loose in Boston. . . . Little knots of boys and young men began wandering through the streets. . . . By midnight, the . . . crowds had formed one raging mob, a drunken, noisy, irresponsible mob. . . . Someone threw a loose paving stone through a store window about one o'clock. The tension snapped. . . . By two o'clock, looting had begun. ❞

After two nights of violence, Governor Calvin Coolidge called in the state militia to restore order. The city's newspapers denounced the strikers as "agents of Lenin" and the strike as a "Bolshevist nightmare." The public also came out firmly against the strike. Recognizing that their cause was doomed, the police voted unanimously to

return to work. Curtis, however, refused to reinstate them. Instead, he hired a new force made up of unemployed veterans. Union sympathizers protested. Unmoved, Coolidge backed the commissioner, proclaiming that "there is no right to strike against the public safety by anybody, anywhere, any time." Coolidge's words made him an overnight hero in conservative circles.

The steel strike. Two weeks after the trouble in Boston, the most important strike of 1919 began. In late September some 365,000 steelworkers—many of them immigrants—walked off the job, demanding recognition of their union and protesting low wages and long working hours. This massive walkout threatened to shut down the steel industry.

For years the major steel companies had fought efforts to unionize steelworkers. Now the companies did everything in their power to break the strike. In an effort to divide labor along ethnic lines, they portrayed foreign workers as radicals and called on "loyal" Americans to return to work.

▼ During the steel strike, Pittsburgh policemen arrested dozens of protesters. In a notice printed in several languages, the *Pittsburgh Chronicle Telegraph* declared the strike a failure and urged strikers to go back to work.

RED SCARE AND PALMER RAIDS

Have students identify the reasons for the fear of communism in 1919 and 1920. Then ask students why immigrants and foreigners were particular targets during the Red Scare. Conclude by asking volunteers to take the role of 1920s Americans and to give 15-second statements about why they think a Communist revolution is at hand.

■■ Ask students whether they think a period of hysteria like the Red Scare could happen in the U.S. today and, if so, what groups might be targets. If not, what safeguards would prevent it?

THE TRIAL OF SACCO AND VANZETTI

Divide the class in half to prepare radio news commentaries on the Sacco and Vanzetti trial. Direct each student in the first group to support the conviction of Sacco and Vanzetti. Direct those in the other group to protest the conviction. Call on volunteers to present their commentaries. Then discuss what the case revealed about America in the early 1920s.

▶

The steel bosses also brought in thousands of African Americans and Mexican Americans as replacement workers, and they hired armed thugs to attack the strikers. Strikers were jailed, beaten, or shot. Faced with such tactics, union leaders called off the strike on January 9, 1920. Labor had suffered a crushing defeat. It would be 15 years before unions again tried to organize workers in heavy industry.

■■ **Workers responded to hard times by striking for higher pay and better working conditions, but their efforts largely failed.**

THE RED SCARE

The 1919 strikes were prompted primarily by labor's desire for a fair deal. However, many Americans saw labor unrest as proof that Russia's Bolshevik Revolution of 1917, with its call for a worldwide revolution of workers, was spreading to American shores. This fear of communism reached fever pitch in 1919 and 1920, a period of anti-Communist hysteria known as the **Red Scare**.

Although Communists and Socialists comprised only a tiny fraction of the country's population, some Americans saw "Reds" everywhere. They even implied that Communists controlled many women's organizations. Peace groups, such as the Women's International League for Peace and Freedom, came under particularly strong attack. Antiradical fears reached such heights that several elected members of the New York State Assembly were expelled because they were members of the Socialist party. As journalist Walter Lippmann sarcastically noted:

❝ The people are shivering in their boots over Bolshevism, they are far more afraid of Lenin [the Bolshevik leader] than they ever were of the Kaiser [Wilhelm II, who ruled Germany during World War I]. We seem to be the most frightened lot of victors that the world ever saw. ❞

■■ **The Bolshevik Revolution and the strikes of 1919 led many Americans to fear that a Communist revolution was at hand.**

▲ This cartoon entitled *Put Them Out & Keep Them Out* appeared in the *Philadelphia Inquirer* in 1919 and expressed the fear that Bolshevism was creeping into American society.

The Palmer raids. In 1919 a rash of bomb scares seemed to justify Americans' fears. In April, alert postal clerks discovered 36 bombs in the mail addressed to such prominent citizens as John D. Rockefeller, Supreme Court justice Oliver Wendell Holmes, and Postmaster General Albert Burleson. Then less than a month later, several bombings occurred, one of which damaged the front of Attorney General A. Mitchell Palmer's house. The assailant, an Italian anarchist, died in the blast.

Newspapers began demanding harsh action against radicals. One paper even called for "a few free treatments in the electric chair." Attorney General Palmer, hoping to further his presidential ambitions, responded by launching an anti-Red crusade. He created a special government office to

◀ A. Mitchell Palmer

ⒶⓋ TRANSPARENCY

Everyday Life in America Transparency and **Worksheet 21**

HISTORICAL SIDELIGHTS

A State of Terror
In their zeal to root out the "Reds" in American society, government agents had little respect for their suspects' rights. For example, Justice Department officials beat an alleged Communist while newspaper reporters watched. The reporters were warned that they would be prosecuted if they reported what they had seen. A professor whose "crime" was teaching algebra in Russian was beaten by government agents. Two men accused of being anarchists were detained and tortured at the Justice Department until one killed himself. Reformer Frederic Howe remarked: "Few people would believe the extent to which private hates and prejudices were permitted to usurp government powers."

PRIMARY SOURCE

Description of Change: excerpted and bracketed
Rationale: excerpted to focus on main idea; bracketed to clarify meaning

Practice

GUIDED PRACTICE

Write the following headlines on the chalk-board: *Boston Commissioner Locks Out Police, Federal Officials Arrest 6000 Suspected Radicals, Sacco and Vanzetti Die.* Organize students into two groups. Instruct one group to outline the causes of each event described in the headlines and the other group to outline the effects of the events. Have groups present their outlines to the class.

INDEPENDENT PRACTICE

Have individuals use the headlines and the outlines created in the Guided Practice to write a news story on one of the events. Students may wish to include their news stories in their portfolios.

Review and Assessment

REVIEW Have students work in pairs to create graphic organizers that link the following events in a cause-and-effect relationship: recession of 1920–21, labor unrest, Red Scare, trial of Sacco and Vanzetti. Then assign the Section 1 Review on p. 283.

ASSESS Assign the **Section 1 Daily Quiz** in *Core Resources.*

PRIMARY SOURCE
Description of Change: excerpted
Rationale: excerpted to focus on main idea

BIO GRAPHY PERSONALITIES IN HISTORY

Goldman was deeply troubled by what she saw in Russia. As a strong advocate of free speech, she was outraged when she saw "people raided, imprisoned, and shot for their *ideas!*" She requested and got an interview with Lenin where she confronted him with her concerns. Her decision to speak out in the American press against the Bolsheviks led to isolation and rejection by her former radical friends.

RECOGNIZING PREJUDICE

Webster Thayer, the presiding judge in the Sacco-Vanzetti trial, said of Vanzetti: "This man, although he may not actually have committed the crime . . . is . . . the enemy of our existing institutions. . . . The defendant's ideals are cognate with crime." Have students identify the prejudices toward immigrants and radicals expressed in this quote and explain why it is possible that Sacco and Vanzetti did not get a fair trial.

gather information on radical activities and put J. Edgar Hoover, the future head of the FBI, in charge.

Palmer's most dramatic action was a series of raids to capture alleged radicals. The **Palmer raids** began in November 1919 and peaked on January 2, 1920, when federal officials arrested thousands of suspected radicals in 33 cities nationwide. As journalist Frederick Lewis Allen wrote:

> 66 Over six thousand men were arrested in all, . . . often without any chance to learn what was the explicit charge against them. . . . In Detroit, over a hundred men were herded into a bull-pen measuring twenty-four by thirty feet and kept there for a week. . . . In Hartford, while the suspects were in jail the authorities took the further precaution of arresting . . . all visitors who came to see them. 99

Most of those arrested were poor immigrants newly arrived in the country. In most cases, there was no real evidence against them. In fact, although the government claimed that radicals were "armed to the teeth," only three pistols were seized in the raids.

BIO GRAPHY **Emma Goldman.** During the Red Scare hundreds of foreigners suspected of radical activities were deported to Russia. Among the deportees was Emma Goldman, a noted feminist, writer, and speaker.

Goldman was born in 1869 in Lithuania, a nation that was then part of Russia. Raised in a traditional Jewish family, Goldman was an independent, determined girl who often clashed with her authoritarian father. When she was 15, her father arranged for her to marry a man she did not love. But as she later wrote, "I would not listen to his schemes; I wanted to study, to know life, to travel. Besides, I never would marry for anything but love." So at age 16, Goldman immigrated to the United States.

The young Goldman settled in Rochester, New York, where she took a factory job. Gradually she grew disillusioned with the treatment of foreigners and workers in the United States. In 1889 at age 20, she moved to New York City and entered the world of radical politics. She soon became famous for her fiery speeches. After one such speech in 1893, she was convicted of inciting a riot and sent to prison for a year.

In 1906 Goldman started a radical monthly called *Mother Earth.* In its pages she presented articles on a wide range of topics, from birth control to modern art and literature. Above all, she used the magazine as a forum to defend freedom of speech.

In 1917 Goldman was arrested again, this time for opposing the draft. Two years later, at the height of the Red Scare, she was released from prison and deported to Russia. Like many other radicals, she was eager to see revolutionary Russia up close. "At last . . . ," she wrote, "I would behold . . . the land freed from political and economic masters." Instead of a free land, however, she found a country where freedom of expression was severely limited. Disenchanted, Goldman left Russia in 1921 and spent the rest of her life speaking and writing in Europe.

By mid-1920 public hysteria over radicalism was dying down. The fearful predictions of A. Mitchell Palmer and others that a Communist revolution was close at hand proved to be unfounded. Furthermore, many Americans had never supported the witch-hunting tactics employed by many of the anti-Communist crusaders.

SACCO AND VANZETTI

Although the Red Scare passed, hostility toward foreigners and radicals persisted. This hostility was evident during the 1921 trial of two Italian anarchists, Nicola Sacco and Bartolomeo Vanzetti. Accused of committing murder during a payroll robbery at a factory outside Boston, they were convicted and sentenced to death.

The verdict outraged defenders of civil liberties. They argued that the two men had been

Emma Goldman

RETEACH List these events in order on the chalkboard: *1) WWI ends; 2) skyrocketing prices; 3) strikes of 1919; 4) demobilization; 5) recession of 1920–21; 6) Red Scare; 7) execution of Sacco and Vanzetti.* Have volunteers suggest at least one way each event is related to the one that precedes it.

Closure

Have students speculate how the first few years after the war might have been different if the nation had not experienced first inflation, then a recession.

Extension

RESEARCH Have students research and report to the class on the beliefs and activities of American anarchists in the early 1900s.

INTERPRET Interested students might research the Sacco and Vanzetti case and write an essay explaining whether they think the defendants received a fair trial.

◀ American poet Edna St. Vincent Millay was one of many protesters during the Sacco and Vanzetti trial.

convicted not because of the evidence presented but because they were immigrants and radicals. Even the trial judge had shown bias by declaring that the men's anarchist beliefs were grounds for conviction.

The verdict and subsequent appeals drew worldwide attention. In Paris, New York City, and elsewhere, thousands of people marched in protest. Noted writers and artists rallied to the cause. Calling them "victims of race and national prejudice and class hatred," labor unions contributed to Sacco and Vanzetti's defense fund. The protesters

called for a new trial, but all these pleas failed. On August 23, 1927, Sacco and Vanzetti were executed.

Many Americans believed that radicals like Sacco and Vanzetti deserved to be punished for their views, while others saw them as heroes and martyrs. Historians still debate whether Sacco and Vanzetti were guilty or innocent. All agree, however, that the case reflected the deep divisions tearing at American society in the postwar era.

■■ **The Sacco and Vanzetti case underscored a hostility in the United States toward foreigners and radicals following the war.**

Ben Shahn, *Bartolomeo Vanzetti and Nicola Sacco* (1931–1932)

▶ In the early 1930s immigrant artist Ben Shahn created a series of paintings about the events surrounding the Sacco and Vanzetti trial.

SECTION REVIEW ANSWERS

IDENTIFY

For significance, see the following pages:
demobilization (p. 278)
Ole Hanson (p. 279)
Edwin Curtis (p. 280)
A. Mitchell Palmer (p. 281)
Palmer raids (p. 282)
Emma Goldman (p. 282)
Nicola Sacco (p. 282)
Bartolomeo Vanzetti (p. 282)

LOCATE

For locations, see the map on pp. 776–777.

1. Americans went on a spending spree and the cost of living soared; then unemployment increased, prices fell, and there was a recession.
2. struck for higher pay and better working conditions; efforts largely failed
3. Bolshevik Revolution, strikes of 1919; fear of Communist revolution, Palmer raids and arrests, and deportation of immigrants
4. Articles might mention that both were immigrants and may have been convicted and executed because of their radical beliefs.
5. Answers should note economic impact of postwar demobilization and the effects of the Bolshevik Revolution.

■■ ■ S E C T I O N   **1**   R E V I E W

IDENTIFY and explain the significance of the following: demobilization, Ole Hanson, Edwin Curtis, A. Mitchell Palmer, Palmer raids, Emma Goldman, Nicola Sacco, Bartolomeo Vanzetti.

LOCATE and explain the importance of the following: Seattle, Washington; Boston, Massachusetts.

1. **MAIN IDEA** How did the end of World War I affect the economy?
2. **MAIN IDEA** How did workers respond to deteriorating economic conditions after the war? Were their efforts successful?
3. **IDENTIFYING CAUSE AND EFFECT** What events led to the Red Scare? What were some of the Red Scare's consequences?
4. **WRITING TO INFORM** Imagine you are a reporter covering the Sacco and Vanzetti case. Write an article exploring the public debate surrounding the anarchists' arrest and conviction.
5. **ANALYZING** Why can it be said that international events had a strong impact on American society in the postwar years?

FOCUS OBJECTIVES

- Explain why voters elected Warren G. Harding president in 1920.

- Analyze how the economy fared under Harding.

- Assess the presidency of Calvin Coolidge.

- Describe some effects of the Republicans' probusiness policies.

BUILDING VOCABULARY

The word *nostrum* means a "usually questionable remedy or scheme." It also refers to a medicine with secret ingredients recommended without scientific proof of its effectiveness.

PRIMARY SOURCE

Description of Change: excerpted and bracketed
Rationale: excerpted to focus on main idea; bracketed to clarify meaning

284

Section 2

THE REPUBLICANS IN POWER

FOCUS

- **Why did voters elect Warren G. Harding president in 1920?**
- **How did the economy fare under Harding?**
- **What kind of president was Calvin Coolidge?**
- **What were some effects of the Republicans' probusiness policies?**

Tired of social strife, voters in the 1920 election rejected the party of Woodrow Wilson and elected Republican Warren G. Harding president. Although the Harding years ended in scandal, Harding's Republican successor, Calvin Coolidge, restored a sense of integrity to the White House. As a result, voters elected another Republican president—Herbert Hoover—in 1928.

1924 campaign slogan favoring big business

THE ELECTION OF 1920

With the country in turmoil and Republican voters united once again, Republican leaders felt confident of victory in the 1920 presidential election. As their candidate they nominated Senator Warren G. Harding of Ohio. Harding lacked Woodrow Wilson's razor-sharp intelligence, but he was pleasant and friendly.

Harding ran on a probusiness, antilabor platform that promised tax revision, higher tariffs, limits on immigration, and some aid to farmers. What pleased war-weary voters

◄ With this 1920 campaign ribbon, the Republican party in Pennsylvania urged voters to support the "whole Republican ticket."

the most, however, was Harding's call for a return to "normalcy":

66 America's present need is not heroics but healing, not nostrums [miracle cures] but normalcy, not revolution but restoration, . . . not surgery but serenity, . . . not submergence in internationality but sustainment in triumphant nationality. 99

In contrast, the Democratic candidate, Governor James M. Cox of Ohio, bowed to pressure from President Wilson and stressed support for the League of Nations.

The nation's farmers, suffering from falling farm prices, threw their support behind Harding. Many in the middle class, tired of labor strikes and high taxes, also voted Republican. Americans cast their vote for "normalcy," giving Harding some 60 percent of the popular vote.

▪▪ Anxious for stability after the war and the social strife of the Wilson years, American voters elected a Republican president.

Teaching the Section

THE ELECTION OF 1920

Ask students to explain why a campaign that promised "a return to normalcy" would appeal so strongly to American voters in 1920. Have students speculate how the term "normalcy" could be interpreted by each of these groups: manufacturers, farmers, nativists, isolationists, union workers. Then have students take on the role of a member of one of the groups discussed above and write a paragraph titled "How I Voted in 1920 and Why." Call on volunteers to read their paragraphs to the class. Ask class members to guess the roles of the readers. Students may wish to include their paragraphs in their portfolios.

THE HARDING ADMINISTRATION

From his first day in office, Harding set a very different tone from that of the somber Wilson. Journalist Frederick Lewis Allen commented on the change:

> 66 For four long years the gates of the White House had been locked and guarded with sentries. Harding's first official act was to throw them open, to permit . . . sightseers to roam the grounds and flatten their noses against the executive window-panes. . . . The act seemed to symbolize the return of the government to the people. 99

Focus on the economy. What the Harding administration came to symbolize, however, was—as Harding put it—"less government in business

WARREN G. HARDING
1865–1923

in office
1921–1923

A genial, sociable man, Warren G. Harding was fond of drinking and spending time with his friends. He was the sort "to play poker with all Saturday night," one associate recalled. Under Harding, the White House had more the atmosphere of an Elks or Moose lodge than a stately executive mansion. Liquor flowed freely at Harding's parties, despite Prohibition.

Harding, who did not like being president, compared his position to being in jail. Believing that he was unsuited for the job, he once remarked that he was "a man of limited talents from a small town."

▲ President Harding's cabinet was photographed on the White House lawn at its first meeting in 1921. Secretary of State Charles Evans Hughes is seated to Harding's right, while Vice President Calvin Coolidge is seated to his left.

and more business in government." His probusiness cabinet included such successful businessmen as Secretary of the Treasury Andrew W. Mellon and Secretary of Commerce Herbert Hoover. These men believed that government should not interfere with the economy except to aid business. As a result, the administration had two main economic goals: to reduce the national debt and to promote economic growth.

Wartime spending had driven up the national debt from some $1 billion in 1914 to more than $25 billion in 1919. To eliminate the debt, the head of the newly created Bureau of the Budget, Charles Dawes, set out to slash spending. In 1922, his first year on the job, Dawes succeeded in turning the annual deficit into a surplus.

To achieve the second goal—economic growth—Secretary Mellon proposed eliminating the high wartime taxes imposed on the wealthy. If "government takes away an unreasonable share," he argued, "the incentive to work is no longer there and slackening of effort is the result." Furthermore, he claimed, if taxes were lower, the rich would have more money to invest and the economy would grow. The benefits, Mellon said, would then trickle down to the middle and lower classes in the form of jobs and higher wages. In response to Mellon's program, Congress cut taxes on wealthy Americans during the 1920s.

By 1923 Harding's economic policy appeared to be working. The postwar slump was over, unemployment was low, and most sectors of the economy had entered a period of tremendous growth. Not all sectors were flourishing, however.

PRIMARY SOURCE
Description of Change: excerpted
Rationale: excerpted to focus on main idea

HISTORICAL SIDELIGHTS

Small-town Values
Harding won a landslide victory in 1920 in part because he seemed to stand for many of the values associated with small-town life. Harding's speeches often emphasized that he was a small-town boy who made good. "I grew up in a village of six hundred . . . and I have often referred to it as a fine illustration of the opportunities of American life," Harding said. "There is more happiness in the American village than any other place on the face of the earth." Many voters in 1920 could identify with Harding's roots and dreamed that they too could become self-made successes.

Teaching the Section

THE ECONOMY UNDER HARDING

Select a volunteer to explain Harding's philosophy of "less government in business and more business in government." Have other students cite ways that Harding addressed each goal. Then ask students to state their opinions of Harding's policies. Have the class assess the economy's health under Harding.

The coal industry fell on hard times as oil became a popular fuel source. The producers of cotton and wool textiles suffered because of competition from new synthetic fabrics, such as rayon. These and other "sick industries" signaled that not all was well in the economy.

■■ **The Harding administration's probusiness policies helped fuel an economic boom, but not all sectors of the economy benefited.**

The Harding scandals. Midway through Harding's term, most Americans seemed happy with the nation's course. Yet talk of corruption had begun to haunt the Harding administration. A group of Harding's friends—known as the Ohio Gang—had followed him to Washington and were using their connections with the president to enrich themselves at the public's expense.

The first scandal came to light in the spring of 1923, when it was discovered that Charles Forbes, director of the Veterans' Bureau and Harding's close friend, had received millions of dollars as the result of corrupt schemes. Harding was deeply worried over the Forbes scandal and other signs of wrongdoing in his administration. In June 1923 he confessed to journalist William Allen White, "I have no trouble with my enemies. I can take care of my enemies all right. [It's my] friends . . . that keep me walking the floor nights." Soon after talking to White, Harding set out on an extended tour of the West. In San Francisco on August 2, he died.

After Harding's death other scandals surfaced. In 1924 Attorney General Harry Daugherty,

◀ Teapot Dome and other scandals tarnished the reputation of the Harding administration.

Harding's right-hand man, was forced to resign after it was discovered he had been taking bribes. Worse still was the **Teapot Dome scandal**, which took its name from a government oil reserve in Teapot Dome, Wyoming. According to a Senate investigation, Secretary of the Interior Albert Fall had received loans, cash, and cattle for leasing the oil reserve—along with another reserve in California—to private oil companies. Fall was convicted of accepting bribes and jailed in 1926—the first cabinet member to be imprisoned for crimes committed while in office.

COOLIDGE TAKES CHARGE

After Harding's death Vice President Calvin Coolidge succeeded to the presidency. Immediately he began working to limit the damage from the Harding scandals and to restore the reputation of the presidency.

Coolidge easily won the Republican presidential nomination in 1924. On the 103rd ballot the Democrats, divided between rural and urban wings and split over issues such as prohibition, chose John W. Davis, a corporate lawyer. Both parties faced strong opposition from the Progressive party's nominee, Robert La Follette. Backed by angry farmers and workers, the Progressive platform denounced federal policies favoring business and called for more aid to working people.

Despite these rumblings of discontent, Coolidge won by a landslide, receiving 15.7 million votes to Davis's 8.4 million. La Follette received about 4.8 million votes. Although the Progressive party faded from the scene when La Follette died soon after the election, its strong showing made it clear that not all Americans agreed with the Republicans' emphasis on big business.

In some ways Calvin Coolidge seemed an unlikely man to win the support of so many Americans. Stern

◀ Calvin Coolidge

SILENT CAL

Write on the chalkboard these three text statements about Coolidge: *1) Coolidge seemed an unlikely man to win the support of so many Americans; 2) Coolidge was even more probusiness than Harding; 3) Coolidge took a tightfisted approach to government spending.* Have students work in groups to write a few sentences that explain and support each statement. Then have each group write a generalization evaluating Coolidge, and one or two sentences to support it. Have groups share their evaluations with the class.

EFFECTS OF REPUBLICAN POLICIES

Organize students into groups to review trends and developments during the 1920s in the following areas: business and industry, the environment, farmers, industrial workers. Assign one of these areas to each group and ask it to create a graphic organizer that shows the effects of Republican policies on its assigned topic. Have a spokesperson from each group present and explain its organizer to the class. ▶

PRESIDENTIAL LIVES

CALVIN COOLIDGE
1872–1933

in office 1923–1929

UNITED STATES POSTAGE
$5 ★ CALVIN COOLIDGE 1923–1929 ★ $5

Vermont-born Calvin Coolidge had a stern face and quiet, unemotional manner that made him seem the very picture of cold New England granite. According to his wife Grace, once at a Washington dinner party another guest told Coolidge she had bet that she could make him say at least three words to her. Tight-lipped as usual, Coolidge replied, "You lose."

"Silent Cal" could be as frugal—or even stingy—as he was quiet. Sometimes rather than buying presents, he sent out the boxes of cigars that he himself had received as gifts. Coolidge even refused to share the contents of the stream in front of his vacation home in South Dakota. One day he observed a stranger catching fish from the stream. Coolidge sent a Secret Service agent after the man to retrieve the fish, stating bluntly, "They are my fish."

---

and unemotional, he was known as Silent Cal. His often sour expression inspired one wit's comment that Coolidge looked as if he had been weaned on a pickle. Yet because Coolidge's no-nonsense manner and frugal habits recalled a simpler era, many Americans found him reassuring.

A staunch conservative, Coolidge was even more probusiness than Harding. "The business of America is business," he once declared. "The man who builds a factory builds a temple. The man who works there worships there." Coolidge favored legislation to aid business but generally opposed laws to help farmers or workers, arguing that such legislation stifled private initiative and harmed the economy.

Coolidge also took a tightfisted approach to government spending. In the name of economy, he vetoed a bonus bill designed to aid World War I veterans (Congress passed the bill over his veto). He also vetoed a bill designed to boost farm prices by authorizing the government to buy surplus crops and sell them abroad.

Despite these vetoes the president remained popular and almost certainly could have won reelection in 1928. Instead, to almost everyone's surprise, he announced he would not run.

■■ **Coolidge was a conservative, probusiness president whose no-nonsense style won the support of most Americans.**

THE ELECTION OF 1928

In 1928 the Republicans nominated Secretary of Commerce Herbert Hoover for president. Hoover had a reputation for skill and efficiency. His strongest asset, though, was the nation's apparent prosperity after eight years of Republican rule. In a campaign speech he declared:

66 The poorhouse is vanishing from among us. We have not yet reached the goal, but, given a chance to go forward with the policies of the last eight years, we shall soon . . . be in sight of the day when poverty will be banished from this nation. 99

▲ By the 1928 election Herbert Hoover was known for his integrity and humanitarian ideals.

After a bitter fight the Democrats nominated Governor Alfred E. Smith of New York, a moderate progressive. The party's choice signaled a shift in Democratic strategy—a response, in part, to the Progressive party's strength in the 1924 election. Smith's core support came from urban immigrant voters. By nominating Smith, the Democrats hoped to be seen as "the party of progress and liberal thought," as Franklin Roosevelt put it. Yet Smith had several political liabilities. He was Roman Catholic, he opposed prohibition, and he had ties

---

HISTORICAL SIDELIGHTS

"Sleepy" Cal

Calvin Coolidge was not only silent but sleepy. He slept and napped up to 10 or 11 hours a day. Journalist H. L. Mencken claimed that in Coolidge's years in office, his major feat had been to "sleep more and say less" than any other president.

PRIMARY SOURCE

Description of Change: excerpted

Rationale: excerpted to focus on main idea

MULTICULTURAL PERSPECTIVES

The 1928 presidential campaign symbolized the clash of culture and values in American society. Hoover, a Quaker businessman with roots in rural Iowa, favored Prohibition. Smith, an Irish Catholic who was born in a New York tenement, was a machine politician who openly opposed Prohibition. Many Protestant ministers urged their congregations to vote against Smith. "A Vote for Al Smith Is a Vote for the Pope," warned the Klan. As Smith's campaign train moved across Oklahoma, he could see crosses burning in the fields along his route.

*P*ractice

GUIDED PRACTICE

Draw on the chalkboard a two-column chart with the headings *Harding Administration* and *Coolidge Administration*. Call on students to list the ways that each administration approached the country's economy. Write responses in the appropriate column.

INDEPENDENT PRACTICE

Direct students to use the chart developed in the Guided Practice to write a paragraph that compares Harding's and Coolidge's economic policies and that concludes with a generalization about the effects of Republicans' probusiness policies. Students may wish to include their paragraphs in their portfolios.

*R*eview and *A*ssessment

REVIEW Have students work in pairs to prepare memorials to Harding and Coolidge, highlighting key events in the administration of each and listing their policy successes and failures. Then assign the Section 2 Review on p. 289.

ASSESS Assign the **Section 2 Daily Quiz** in *Core Resources*.

 GLOBAL CONNECTIONS

The Fordney-McCumber Tariff Act had a terrible effect on world trade. The act blocked Europe from selling goods to the U.S., and as a result of retaliatory tariffs imposed by Europe on the U.S., American goods were no longer sold to Europe. In addition, by preventing U.S. war loans from being repaid in goods, the tariff created serious economic problems for European governments—problems that would later help bring down their economies during the global depression of the 1930s.

HISTORICAL SIDELIGHTS

Division over ERA

Women who opposed ERA because they feared it would invalidate protective legislation found allies among conservative groups such as the National Council of Catholic Women, who opposed it because it "seriously menaced . . . the unity of the home and family life" and went against the "essential differences in rights and duties" of the sexes.

---

to New York City's Tammany Hall. All these points stirred strong opposition to Smith's candidacy, especially in the South.

Riding on Smith's handicaps and the economy's strength, Hoover won 58 percent of the popular vote. Smith lost his own state as well as several southern states that went Republican for the first time since Reconstruction. However, Smith did well in the nation's largest cities. His appeal to these voters offered the Democrats hope for the future.

■■ **Herbert Hoover sailed to victory in 1928 on the strength of the economy and his opponent's political liabilities.**

*T*HE EFFECTS OF REPUBLICAN POLICIES

During the 1920s the Republican administrations' probusiness policies helped promote economic growth. Yet these policies also had negative effects on the environment and on many working people.

Business growth and prosperity. One reason for the economic boom that began in 1923 was the availability of surplus capital, in part due to tax cuts. This capital allowed old industries to grow rapidly and new ones to enter the ranks of the corporate giants. The 1920s also saw more than 1,000 **mergers**—the combining of two or more companies. Business favored mergers because they brought greater efficiency and higher profits. By 1930, some 200 corporations owned nearly half the nation's corporate wealth. The government, with its favorable attitude toward business, encouraged this process of consolidation and made little effort to enforce antitrust laws.

▲ **As early as 1917, the corner of 42nd St. and Madison Ave. in New York City was often congested with heavy auto traffic.**

This rapid industrial growth was not without its drawbacks, however. Chemical wastes poured into the nation's rivers and lakes. Cities witnessed increased traffic congestion and air pollution. Yet few Americans saw these consequences of industrial development as problems.

Labor and farming. Workers did not share significantly in business's good fortune during the 1920s. From 1923 to 1929, business profits increased some 60 percent. Over the same period, workers' incomes grew by only about 10 percent. Many workers in "sick industries" even faced pay cuts and unemployment. Farmers were also hit hard, as the postwar slump in farm prices continued into the 1920s.

To help farmers, Congress passed the **Fordney-McCumber Tariff Act** of 1922. The act levied high duties on imported farm products in an effort to boost domestic crop prices. But it brought little relief. Farmers still faced shrinking markets, low prices, high interest rates, and crushing debts.

Organized labor also suffered during the 1920s as the government and courts sought to roll back the gains of the Progressive Era. Federal courts, for example, upheld "yellow-dog contracts," which required employees to promise not to join a union. At the same time, business leaders promoted a policy known as the **American Plan**. The plan called for open shops—factories in which workers could choose not to join unions and management did not have to negotiate with union leaders. As a result, union membership shrank from a high of more than 5 million in 1920 to some 3.6 million in 1923. Without the backing of strong unions, many people continued to work long hours for low wages under often unsafe conditions.

■■ **Republican policies contributed to business growth and general prosperity, but many workers and farmers suffered.**

*T*HE EQUAL RIGHTS AMENDMENT

Regulating hours, working conditions, and wages for women and children had been an important part of the progressive agenda. However, in the 1920s women debated the desirability of such protective legislation. This debate came about because of the National Woman's party's efforts on behalf of the

RETEACH Assign pairs of students a subsection of Section 2. Have each student write a summary of his or her subsection. Combine them into a section summary to be shared with the other pairs.

Closure

Direct students to reread Herbert Hoover's statement on p. 287. Ask students how well they think the quote captures the spirit, philosophy, and policies of the 1920s. Ask students to identify groups that received the greatest benefits from the policies to which Hoover referred. Discuss what groups suffered due to those policies.

Extension

CREATE Invite students to create editorial cartoons that characterize the presidencies of Harding and Coolidge.

COMPARE Have students research the campaign for an Equal Rights Amendment in the 1970s and 1980s and compare its agenda, goals, supporters, and outcome with the Equal Rights Amendment proposed in 1923.

Equal Rights Amendment, introduced into Congress in 1923. Had it passed, the amendment would have given men and women "equal rights throughout the United States." One of the amendment's effects would have been to invalidate protective legislation.

The amendment drew most of its support from middle-class and professional women. They argued that protective legislation discouraged employers from hiring women. Furthermore, they argued, limitations on working hours kept women out of many highly paid jobs.

Opponents of the amendment supported protective legislation as necessary to protect women— few of whom belonged to unions—and their families. Mary Anderson, director of the U.S. Women's Bureau, asserted:

> 66 Women who are wage earners, with one job in the factory and another in the home, have little time and energy left to carry on the fight to better their economic status. They need the help of . . . labor laws. 99

Pauline Newman of the Women's Trade Union League observed that before protective legislation women "were 'free' and 'equal' to work long hours for starvation wages, or free to leave the job and starve!"

Protective legislation did hamper women working in male-dominated occupations. However, few working-class women were employed in such occupations. Thus, they withheld their support for the amendment, which they viewed as benefiting

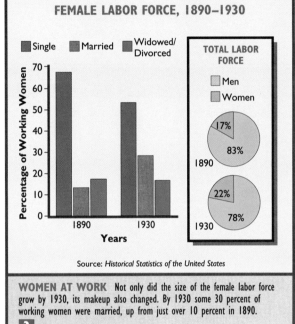

FEMALE LABOR FORCE, 1890–1930

■ Single ■ Married ■ Widowed/Divorced

Percentage of Working Women (y-axis: 0 to 70)

Years: 1890, 1930

TOTAL LABOR FORCE
■ Men ■ Women

1890: 17% / 83%
1930: 22% / 78%

Source: *Historical Statistics of the United States*

WOMEN AT WORK Not only did the size of the female labor force grow by 1930, its makeup also changed. By 1930 some 30 percent of working women were married, up from just over 10 percent in 1890.

? BUILDING GRAPH SKILLS Women made up what percentage of the total labor force in 1890? in 1930?

only middle-class and upper-class women who had the training to enter the professions or skilled trades.

The debate over these issues created deep divisions in the women's movement. It would continue to divide women's organizations until the 1960s.

■■ The debate over the Equal Rights Amendment divided women's groups.

PRIMARY SOURCE

Description of Change: excerpted
Rationale: excerpted to focus on main idea

Graph Caption Answer 17%; 22%

SECTION REVIEW ANSWERS

IDENTIFY

For significance, see the following pages:
Warren G. Harding (p. 284)
Andrew W. Mellon (p. 285)
Herbert Hoover (p. 285)
Charles Dawes (p. 285)
Teapot Dome scandal (p. 286)
Albert Fall (p. 286)
Calvin Coolidge (p. 286)
Alfred E. Smith (p. 287)
mergers (p. 288)
Fordney-McCumber Tariff Act (p. 288)
American Plan (p. 288)

1. *They were anxious for stability after the war.*
2. *conservative and probusiness with a manner that they found reassuring*
3. *lowered unemployment, helped promote industry and business growth and prosperity, but hurt many farmers and workers*
4. *Handbills might mention Hoover's skill and efficiency, nation's prosperity under Republicans, and Smith's liabilities.*
5. *Supporters argued protective legislation discouraged employers from hiring women and kept women out of many highly paid jobs; opponents argued protective legislation helped most women.*

■ ■ ■ SECTION 2 REVIEW

IDENTIFY and explain the significance of the following: Warren G. Harding, Andrew W. Mellon, Herbert Hoover, Charles Dawes, Teapot Dome scandal, Albert Fall, Calvin Coolidge, Alfred E. Smith, mergers, Fordney-McCumber Tariff Act, American Plan.

1. **MAIN IDEA** Why did American voters elect a Republican president in 1920?
2. **MAIN IDEA** What qualities did President Coolidge possess that won the support of most Americans in the 1920s?
3. **ASSESSING CONSEQUENCES** What effect did the probusiness policies of Harding and Coolidge have on the economy?
4. **WRITING TO PERSUADE** Imagine you are a Republican campaigning for Herbert Hoover in 1928. Write a handbill you would distribute to urge other voters to support your candidate.
5. **ANALYZING** Why were women's groups divided over support of the Equal Rights Amendment?

FOCUS OBJECTIVES

■ Describe how Native Americans responded to new efforts to seize tribal land.

■ Summarize factors that gave rise to black nationalism in the 1920s.

■ Analyze what the revival of the Ku Klux Klan and the passage of new immigration laws revealed about the 1920s.

■ Explain why immigration from Mexico increased.

PRIMARY SOURCE

Description of Change: excerpted
Rationale: excerpted to focus on main idea

CORE RESOURCES

• **Literature Worksheet 11**
• **Section 3 Daily Quiz**

[AV] **RESOURCES**

• **Linking Geography and History Transparency and Worksheet 17**

Section 3

A NATION DIVIDED

F O C U S
■ **How did Native Americans respond to new efforts to seize tribal land?**
■ **What gave rise to black nationalism in the 1920s?**
■ **What did the revival of the Ku Klux Klan and the passage of new immigration laws reveal about the 1920s?**
■ **Why did immigration from Mexico increase?**

Although many Americans prospered during the 1920s, deep social and racial divisions still plagued American life. Native Americans, African Americans, and Mexican immigrants all struggled for a place in American society. As African Americans continued to migrate to northern cities, racial tensions increased. The Ku Klux Klan encouraged bigotry not only against African Americans but also against foreigners. Responding to the national mood, Congress passed laws limiting immigration.

Ku Klux Klansman

NATIVE AMERICAN LIFE

For Native Americans the 1920s brought some recognition of the difficulties they faced. The Dawes Act, which attempted to "Americanize"

▲ **Native Americans carry water from a government well in Arizona.**

Indians by dividing tribal land into individual plots (see Chapter 5) had clearly failed. The act's allotment policies—as the Board of Indian Commissioners acknowledged—had often been "a short cut to the separation of . . . Indians from their land and cash."

In the 1920s Native Americans successfully organized to fight new efforts to take tribal land. Native American leaders stopped the Harding administration's attempt to buy back all tribal land. Then in 1922 the different Pueblo tribes of the Southwest organized against the Bursum Bill, which was designed to legalize non–Native American claims to Pueblo land. Furthermore, the bill would limit the power of tribal governments. The Pueblos appealed to all Americans:

66 This bill will destroy our common life and will rob us of everything which we hold dear—our lands, our customs, our traditions. Are the American people willing to see this happen? 99

Call attention to the section title: A Nation Divided. Have students name some of the divisions within American society today and then speculate why some of these divisions also may have existed in the 1920s. Then tell students that in this section they will look more closely at the causes of social tensions in the 1920s.

Teaching the Section

NATIVE AMERICAN RIGHTS

Ask students to analyze the effectiveness of Native Americans' efforts to retain their land. Have them list evidence that the government was beginning to listen to their interests and evidence that improvements in policy still needed to be made.

▶

Many Americans were not. The Pueblos won the support of the General Federation of Women's Clubs and of anthropologists, as well as the support of many other influential men and women. As a result, the *New York Times* could write in January 1923 that the bill was "happily, dead."

In 1924 Congress granted citizenship to all Native Americans, partly in recognition of those who had fought in World War I. But citizenship did not soften the harsh effects of poverty that many Native Americans continued to experience.

■■ **Native Americans organized to fight efforts to take their lands.**

---

*A*FRICAN AMERICANS MOVE NORTH

During the 1920s some 800,000 African Americans joined the hundreds of thousands who had moved to the North during World War I. By 1930 the North's African American population had reached almost 2.5 million, more than double its size in 1910. Large African American communities sprang up in Chicago, Detroit, New York City, and other

▲ A neighborhood strewn with rubble reveals the tragic aftermath of the Chicago race riots in 1919.

northern cities. Harlem, a section of New York City with a large African American population, was called "the capital of Black America."

The North, however, was not free of bigotry. African Americans who had risked their lives in Europe "to make the world safe for democracy" confronted lynch mobs. Others faced discrimination, and as demands for labor eased, African Americans were the first to lose their jobs.

At times, racial tensions erupted violently. One of the worst outbreaks occurred in Chicago in July 1919. The trouble began when a white man

Percentage Change 1920–1930

- More than 100.0% increase
- 50.1–100.0% increase
- 25.1–50.0% increase
- 15.1–25.0% increase
- 10.1–15.0% increase
- 0–10.0% increase
- 0–10.0% decrease
- More than 10.0% decrease

African American Population Changes, 1920–1930

MASS MIGRATION The great increase in African Americans in some northern states meant a decline in their numbers in some other states.

❓ **MOVEMENT** In which states did the African American population more than double?

Teaching the *Section*

RISE OF BLACK NATIONALISM

Invite each student to imagine that he or she is editor of a 1920s African American newspaper. Direct students to write editorials for their newspapers that describe the status of African Americans in the 1920s and that express opinions on the programs and goals of Marcus Garvey. Select students to read their editorials to the class. Students may wish to include their editorials in their portfolios.

THE KKK AND IMMIGRATION QUOTAS

Draw a two-column chart on the chalkboard with the headings *Ku Klux Klan* and *Immigration Act of 1924*. Ask students to list the groups that were discriminated against by the KKK or through passage of the act. List responses on the chart. Then ask students what the chart suggests about the national attitude toward racial and ethnic groups in the 1920s.

HISTORICAL SIDELIGHTS
Pullman Porters
In the 1920s sleeping-car porters had high status in the African American community. Porters were relatively well paid, and such jobs were often the only ones open to black college graduates. However, compared with unionized white railroad workers, porters were grossly underpaid. Beginning in 1925, A. Philip Randolph led the porters in a 12-year fight to get the Pullman Company to recognize their union.

PRIMARY SOURCES
Description of Change: excerpted and bracketed
Rationale: excerpted to focus on main idea; bracketed to clarify meaning

BIO GRAPHY PERSONALITIES IN HISTORY

Garvey was an inspired entrepreneur and promoter who drew by some estimates anywhere from a half a million to two million people to the UNIA. Huge crowds attended Garvey's parades, at which members of his African Legion carried the tricolor UNIA flag. Garvey said the flag was black for the race, red for the blood of the race, and green for the hope of the race.

▲ The NAACP began as an interracial coalition fighting for African Americans' rights. James Weldon Johnson, seated behind the desk, served as executive secretary of the NAACP from 1920 to 1930. Johnson was also a noted author and songwriter.

threw rocks at an African American teenager swimming in Lake Michigan. The boy drowned. The fight that broke out between whites and blacks on shore spread to the rest of the city. The rioting continued for more than a week. White gangs fueled much of the violence as they prowled the slums, attacking African Americans and destroying property. By the time order was restored, 38 people had been killed and 537 injured.

By late 1919, some 25 race riots had erupted around the country. In June 1921, at least 30 people died during a race riot in Tulsa, Oklahoma. One resident described attacks on the black section of town:

> People were seen to flee from their burning homes, some with babes in their arms and leading crying and excited children. . . . [A] machine gun . . . was raining bullets down on our section. 99

Faced with continued violence and discrimination, many African Americans organized to defend their rights. The National Association for the Advancement of Colored People (NAACP) stepped up its legal battle to win equal rights for African Americans and mounted campaigns against lynching and discrimination in housing. The unions' continued failure to help black

workers led labor activist A. Philip Randolph to found the Brotherhood of Sleeping Car Porters in 1925. It became a powerful voice for black workers.

*B*LACK NATIONALISM

Frustrated by the slow pace of change, some African Americans lost hope of ever achieving equality in the United States. What African Americans needed, they said, was a nation of their own. Foremost among these black nationalists was Marcus Garvey.

BIO GRAPHY Garvey, a native of Jamaica, founded the Universal Negro Improvement Association (UNIA) in 1914. UNIA had two main goals: to foster African Americans' economic independence by establishing black-owned businesses and to create an independent

THE BACK–TO–AFRICA MOVEMENT

Marcus Garvey's Back-to-Africa movement drew many followers both in America and in Africa. In 1922 a representative of the king of Abyssinia (Ethiopia) read the following message to a Universal Negro Improvement Association (UNIA) convention:

THROUGH OTHERS' EYES

> **66** *A*ssure them [Garvey's followers] of the cordiality with which I invite them back to the home land, particularly those qualified to help solve our big problems and to develop our vast resources. Teachers, artisans, mechanics, writers, musicians, professional men and women—all who are able to lend a hand in the constructive work which our country so deeply feels, and greatly needs.
>
> Here we have abundant room and great opportunities and here destiny is working to elevate and enthrone a race which has suffered slavery, poverty, persecution and martyrdom, but whose expanding soul and growing genius is now the hope of many millions of mankind. **99**

▶

black homeland in Africa. "We shall now organize," Garvey told the delegates to UNIA's first international convention, "to plant the banner of freedom on the great continent of Africa."

Marcus Garvey

A charismatic speaker, Garvey urged African Americans to draw on their African heritage:

❝ When Europe was inhabited by . . . a race of savages, . . . Africa was peopled with a race of cultured black men, who were masters in art, science and literature. . . . Why, then, should we lose hope? Black men, you were once great; you shall be great again. Lose not courage, lose not faith, go forward. ❞

To foster economic independence, Garvey founded the Black Star Steamship Company in 1919. He urged African Americans to invest in his company so that they "may exert the same influence on the world as the white man does today." Garvey promised investors huge returns, but the company never turned a profit. In 1925 Garvey was jailed for mail fraud in connection with his fund-raising activities. President Coolidge pardoned him in 1927 but ordered him deported. He died in 1940, still clinging to his dream.

Garvey's movement declined after he was jailed. Nevertheless, as one newspaper said in 1927, "He made black people proud. . . . He taught them that black is beautiful." Although other African American leaders, such as W.E.B. Du Bois, shared Garvey's belief in racial pride and solidarity, they opposed his Back-to-Africa movement. They insisted that African Americans should fight for justice and equality in American society.

■■ **Continued discrimination and a growing sense of black pride led to the rise of black nationalism.**

ℭHE RETURN OF THE KU KLUX KLAN

To some degree, racism and discrimination during the 1920s reflected a broader repressive mood in American society. More and more, native-born Protestant Americans distrusted people who seemed different. One sign of this growing intolerance was the resurgence of the Ku Klux Klan.

Like the Klan of post–Civil War days, the new Klan, established in 1915 at Stone Mountain, Georgia, used kidnappings, beatings, and lynchings to terrorize African Americans in the South. However, the Klan also grew rapidly outside the South. In northern and midwestern towns and cities, the Klan targeted not only blacks but also radicals, immigrants, Catholics, and Jews, as well as such threats to traditional moral values as divorce.

The Klan grew slowly at first, but as the Red Scare took hold, membership soared. Reaching its peak in the mid-1920s, the Klan had perhaps as many as five million members. At mass rallies white-robed Klan members burned crosses and spoke out against people and ideas they considered "undesirable." Klan views also influenced politics, helping candidates win elections in such states as Louisiana, Oklahoma, Ohio, Texas—even Oregon. The Klan was particularly powerful in Indiana.

After 1925, however, the Klan declined, and by 1930 its membership had dropped to some 9,000. Rising prosperity and the end of the Red Scare diminished the Klan's appeal, but other factors also contributed. One was the conviction of a Klan leader—Grand Dragon David Stephenson—for second-degree murder. Another was the discovery that Klan promoters were getting rich from membership fees and the sale of regalia. Nevertheless, the Klan did not die out; it continues to spread its message of white supremacy.

▲ **Ku Klux Klan members taught racist attitudes to their children. Here, a baby is being enrolled into the Klan on Independence Day, 1927.**

Practice

GUIDED PRACTICE

Draw a two-column chart on the chalkboard with the headings *Expectations* and *Realities*. In the first column have students list some of the expectations Native Americans, African Americans, and Mexican Americans had about how they should be treated in the U.S. In the second column have students identify ways in which those expectations were or were not met.

INDEPENDENT PRACTICE

Invite students to assume the role of a Native American, African American, or a Mexican American and use the information from the charts created in the Guided Practice to write letters to friends discussing the realities of their lives in the 1920s.

Review and Assessment

REVIEW Ask groups of students to prepare a series of interview questions they could use to gather information from various racial and ethnic groups about life in the 1920s. Have groups exchange their papers and answer the questions they receive. Then assign the Section 3 Review on p. 295.

ASSESS Assign the **Section 3 Daily Quiz** in *Core Resources*.

MULTICULTURAL PERSPECTIVES

The Immigration Act of 1924 angered the Japanese, who saw the quotas as discrimination based on race. In a "Message from Japan to America," the *Japan Times and Mail* complained that the law "stamps Japanese as of an inferior race."

■ Ask students if they think that anti-immigrant sentiment exists in America today. Consider attitudes toward recent non-European immigrant groups.

COOPERATIVE LEARNING

Organize students into groups. Assign each group one of these nationalities: Chinese, Italian, Japanese, Mexican, Russian. Have groups imagine they are immigrants living in the U.S. in 1924. Have each group create an editorial, a letter to the president, and an editorial cartoon reacting to the rise in KKK membership and to the Immigration Act of 1924.

Map Caption Answer
Arizona

IMMIGRATION RESTRICTIONS

During the 1920s the Klan also played on anti-immigrant feelings. Many Americans feared that the country was being overrun by immigrants—in 1920 nearly a quarter of the population was foreign-born or nonwhite. Furthermore, the number of immigrants, which had declined during the war, was once again rising, increasing from some 140,000 in 1919 to some 805,000 in 1921. This dramatic growth, coupled with the widespread belief that immigrants held radical views and took jobs from native-born Americans, led to demands for limits on immigration.

In 1921 Congress passed a law limiting the number of immigrants from each country allowed into the United States. The quota was set at 3 percent of each nationality already in the country in 1910, except for Asians, who were excluded

▲ "Ellis Island Blues" was one of many songs written in the 1920s about the flood of immigrants to the United States after World War I.

altogether. (Immigration from nations in the Western Hemisphere was not limited.) The **Immigration Act of 1924** reduced the quota to 2 percent of the 1890 figures for each national group. This change worked against southern and eastern Europeans because in 1890 most Americans traced their origins to England, Ireland, or northern Europe. While the 1924 law did not exclude Asians, it set the annual quota at only 100 Chinese and 100 Japanese immigrants. In 1925 the restrictions reduced the total number of new immigrants from Europe, Africa, Asia, and Australia to some 153,000.

■ The revival of the Ku Klux Klan and new limits on immigration revealed continued hostility toward racial and ethnic groups.

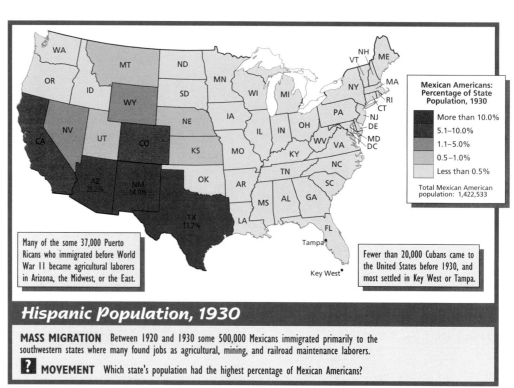

Many of the some 37,000 Puerto Ricans who immigrated before World War II became agricultural laborers in Arizona, the Midwest, or the East.

Fewer than 20,000 Cubans came to the United States before 1930, and most settled in Key West or Tampa.

Mexican Americans: Percentage of State Population, 1930

- More than 10.0%
- 5.1–10.0%
- 1.1–5.0%
- 0.5–1.0%
- Less than 0.5%

Total Mexican American population: 1,422,533

Hispanic Population, 1930

MASS MIGRATION Between 1920 and 1930 some 500,000 Mexicans immigrated primarily to the southwestern states where many found jobs as agricultural, mining, and railroad maintenance laborers.

? **MOVEMENT** Which state's population had the highest percentage of Mexican Americans?

RETEACH Have students work in groups, assigning individuals or pairs the task of outlining subsections of Section 3. Have students exchange outlines and use them to ask questions of other members of their group.

Closure

Have students explain why the phrase "Turbulent Twenties" fits the 1920s and have them suggest other phrases for the decade that might describe the experiences of the racial and ethnic groups living in the U.S. at that time.

Extension

COMPARE Have students compare and report on the KKK of the Reconstruction South, the KKK of the 1920s, and the Klan today.

INVESTIGATE Have students research and report on African American, Mexican American, or other migration to their city or state in the 1920s.

MEXICAN AMERICAN MIGRATION

In the Southwest, employers, particularly in agriculture, railroad construction, and mining, encouraged Mexican immigration, which was not affected by the restrictive legislation of the 1920s. Few people were arriving from Europe and Asia, and southwestern employers were eager to keep a steady flow of workers to fill low-wage jobs. As a result, during the 1920s some 500,000 immigrants arrived from Mexico, where wages were far lower.

Those who took agricultural jobs not only had to accept low pay but many also had to live in ramshackle labor camps. One observer noted:

> 66 Shelters were made of almost every conceivable thing—burlap, canvas, palm branches. . . . We found one woman carrying water in large milk pails from the irrigation ditch. . . . This is evidently all the water which they have in camp. 99

In the 1920s many Mexican immigrants also moved into urban areas. Some were drawn to well-paying factory jobs in cities such as Chicago and Detroit and established new centers of Mexican population in the Midwest. Most, however, migrated to cities in the Southwest—particularly Los Angeles, El Paso, and San Antonio (see map on page 294). Usually the men came alone, and once established, they sent for their wives and children. Many brought other relatives as well, reestablishing extended family networks. These networks helped new arrivals find jobs and housing.

Because of economic hardship, many families allowed their young, unmarried daughters to work outside the home. Many found employment in bakeries, hotels, and laundries, while others worked as maids. Their newfound independence, as one Mexican immigrant woman sadly noted, brought young women "into conflict with their parents. They learn . . . about the outside world, learn how to speak English, and then they become ashamed of their parents who brought them up here." Despite such conflicts, these new immigrants contributed to the mosaic of cultures that helps define American life.

■■ **The promise of jobs drew Mexican immigrants, who were not subject to restrictive quotas, to cities in the Southwest and Midwest.**

▲ Mexican American Victor Villaseñor wrote *Rain of Gold*, a book about his family's experiences as immigrants to California in the 1920s. Shown here is the 1929 wedding of his parents, Juan Salvador and Lupe.

PRIMARY SOURCE
Description of Change: excerpted
Rationale: excerpted to focus on main idea

SECTION REVIEW ANSWERS

IDENTIFY

For significance, see the following pages:
A. Philip Randolph (p. 292)
Marcus Garvey (p. 292)
Immigration Act of 1924 (p. 294)

1. *successfully organized to appeal for public support and to fight measures such as Bursum Bill*
2. *revival of KKK, race riots, passage of Immigration Act of 1924*
3. *slow pace of change, continued violence and discrimination, and growing sense of pride inspired by leaders such as Marcus Garvey*
4. *Diary entries might mention the lure of employment in agriculture, railroad construction, and mining in the Southwest or in factories in the Midwest.*
5. *Students might mention urban population growth, formation of black communities in major cities, eruption of racial tensions, and organization by African Americans to fight lynching and discrimination in housing and employment.*

■■ SECTION 3 REVIEW

IDENTIFY and explain the significance of the following: A. Philip Randolph, Marcus Garvey, Immigration Act of 1924.

1. **MAIN IDEA** In what way did Native Americans fight government attempts to take tribal land?
2. **MAIN IDEA** What events in the 1920s revealed continued hostility toward racial and ethnic groups?
3. **GAINING A MULTICULTURAL PERSPECTIVE** What factors contributed to the rise of black nationalism?
4. **WRITING TO EXPLAIN** Imagine you are a Mexican immigrant in the 1920s. Write a diary entry that explains why you moved to the Southwest or to the Midwest.
5. **EVALUATING** What effect did the migration of African Americans have on the North?

Chapter Review Answers

WRITING A SUMMARY

See Essential Points in each section for main ideas.

REVIEWING CHRONOLOGY

1, 3, 5, 2, 4

Hypothesizing

Scandals might have discredited Harding's probusiness policies and have led to election of a Democrat.

IDENTIFYING PEOPLE AND IDEAS

1. *shift from wartime to peacetime footing*
2. *police commissioner whose refusal to recognize union led to Boston police strike*
3. *period of anti-Communist hysteria, 1919–20*
4. *feminist writer, speaker, and founder of* Mother Earth *who was deported to Russia*
5. *treasury secretary who proposed taxes reduced on wealthy to spur economic growth*
6. *scandal in which government oil reserve in Wyoming was leased to private oil companies*
7. *combining two or more companies to achieve higher profits and greater efficiency*
8. *business leaders' policy favoring open shops, which discouraged union membership*

9. *black nationalist who founded UNIA and supported creation of black homeland in Africa*
10. *act limiting number of immigrants from southern and eastern Europe, Africa, Asia, and Australia into the United States*

UNDERSTANDING MAIN IDEAS

1. *consumers went on spending spree, thus increasing demand; led to cancellation of war contracts, cutbacks in factory production, layoffs of workers, and drop in farm prices*
2. *failed to achieve goals of higher wages and shorter hours; fear of revolution, antilabor propaganda*

helped turn public opinion against organized labor
3. *Both favored reduction in government spending, minimal interference in the economy, lower taxes, limits on immigration, and probusiness laws.*
4. *industries that did not share in 20s prosperity; coal industry suffered as oil became more popular fuel than coal; cotton and wool textiles suffered because of competition from new synthetic fibers.*
5. *events—economic problems, strikes, Red Scare, race riots, rise of KKK; attitudes—anti-immigrant sentiment, racial discrimination, fear of anarchists and Communists*

CHAPTER 11
Review

Palmer raids begin. Marcus Garvey founds Black Star Steamship Company.

Warren G. Harding elected president.

Race riot breaks out in Tulsa, Oklahoma. Congress limits immigration.

Pueblos organize against Bursum Bill.

1919

1921

WRITING A SUMMARY

Using the essential points of the chapter as a guide, write a summary of the chapter.

REVIEWING CHRONOLOGY

Number your paper 1 to 5. Study the time line above, and list the following events in the order in which they happened by writing the first next to 1, the second next to 2, and so on. Then complete the activity below.

1. Palmer raids begin.
2. Calvin Coolidge elected president.
3. Congress limits immigration.
4. Sacco and Vanzetti executed.
5. Equal Rights Amendment introduced into Congress.

Hypothesizing How might political events have been different during the 1920s if President Harding had not died?

IDENTIFYING PEOPLE AND IDEAS

Explain the historical significance of each of the following people or terms.

1. demobilization
2. Edwin Curtis
3. Red Scare
4. Emma Goldman
5. Andrew W. Mellon
6. Teapot Dome scandal
7. mergers
8. American Plan
9. Marcus Garvey
10. Immigration Act of 1924

UNDERSTANDING MAIN IDEAS

1. Why did the cost of living soar after the war? How did demobilization lead to recession and an increase in unemployment?
2. What were the results of the 1919 strikes in Seattle and Boston?
3. How were Warren G. Harding and Calvin Coolidge alike in their approaches to government?
4. What were the "sick industries" during the 1920s? Why did they fail to benefit from the economic boom?
5. What events and attitudes led to increased social tensions during the 1920s?

🏴 REVIEWING THEMES

1. **Democratic Values** What steps did the federal government take during the 1920s to reduce the perceived threat of revolution?
2. **Cultural Diversity** In what ways did Native Americans, African Americans, and Mexican Americans respond to discrimination?
3. **Economic Development** How did Republican probusiness policies attempt to stimulate the economy?

THINKING CRITICALLY

1. **Synthesizing** Why did many Americans vote Republican in the 1920, 1924, and 1928 presidential elections?
2. **Analyzing** Why did many farmers fail to benefit from the economic boom of the 1920s?
3. **Evaluating** Do you think women's groups that opposed the Equal Rights Amendment were justified? Why or why not?

STRATEGY FOR SUCCESS

Review the Strategies for Success on Recognizing Stereotypes on page 272. Then read the following passage from a 1926 article by Hiram Wesley Evans, the Imperial Wizard of the Ku Klux Klan. What group is the subject of this passage? Why can Evans's characterization be considered an example of stereotyping?

> ❝ The alien . . . is unalterably fixed in his instincts, character, thought, and interests by centuries of racial selection and development. . . . He thinks first for his own people, works only with and for them, . . . considers himself always one of them, and never an American. ❞

WRITING ABOUT HISTORY

Writing to Evaluate Write an essay evaluating the impact of the Sacco and Vanzetti case on public opinion.

REVIEWING THEMES

1. Courts acted against unions by supporting "yellow-dog contracts," attorney general launched crusade against and deported suspected radicals, Congress restricted immigration.
2. Native Americans—organized and gained support to keep tribal lands; African Americans—fought for legal rights, supported black nationalism; Mexican Americans—formed communities and family networks in urban areas
3. reduced national debt and lowered taxes to free capital for investment, vetoed bills that increased government spending, encouraged mergers

THINKING CRITICALLY

1. 1920—tired of social strife, war, and higher taxes; 1924—supported probusiness policies that led to economic boom; 1928—favored strong economy that Hoover promised to continue
2. Farmers suffered because of shrinking markets, falling prices, high interest rates on loans, crushing debts, and failure of high tariff laws to bring relief.
3. Answers should weigh the goals of ERA in helping women compete in male-dominated occupations against the benefits of protective legislation in regulating hours, working conditions, and wages for women not protected by unions.

STRATEGY FOR SUCCESS

immigrants; a prejudiced, generalized portrayal of immigrants that is not supported by facts

WRITING ABOUT HISTORY

Essays might mention that the case revealed continued hostility toward foreigners and radicals, that it outraged defenders of civil rights, and that it reflected deep divisions of opinion in 1920s society.

USING PRIMARY SOURCES

Paragraphs should note that the author sympathizes with the strikers' struggle against intolerable conditions and their determined resistance to police attacks.

LINKING HISTORY AND GEOGRAPHY

Students should mention that the greatest concentration of African Americans was in the North and Northeast, while that for Mexican Americans was in the Southwest. Possible factors for population shifts might include more jobs, higher wages, or better working conditions.

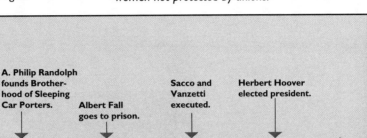

Harding dies. Equal Rights Amendment introduced into Congress.

Congress grants Native Americans citizenship. Immigration Act of 1924 passed. Calvin Coolidge elected president.

A. Philip Randolph founds Brotherhood of Sleeping Car Porters.

Albert Fall goes to prison.

Sacco and Vanzetti executed.

Herbert Hoover elected president.

1923   1925   1927   1929

USING PRIMARY SOURCES

In 1925 more than 11,000 textile workers went on strike in Passaic, New Jersey, to demand better working conditions and higher wages. Read the following excerpt from "The War in Passaic" written by labor activist Mary Heaton Vorse. Then write a paragraph summarizing the author's views of the strike.

❝ Half the picket line is composed of young people. Mothers with children by the hand, older women and high-school boys and girls stream along, their heads thrown back, singing. . . . Passaic sprawling in its winter slush and snow watches its mill-workers make a full-hearted protest against the intolerable conditions in the mills, against the inhuman and unbearable wage cut. . . .

The mayor of Passaic menaced the strikers with a force of three hundred mounted policemen. . . . They charged a crowd of 3,000 strikers, bludgeoned many men, women, and children, and smashed with deliberate intent the persons and cameras of the news photographers. . . . The strikers, armed with gas masks, helmets, and their unbending courage, defied the police successfully—and paraded in peace. . . .

Passaic strikers

The present Passaic strike is only a phase of the long fight of the textile workers for organization and a living wage. . . . When there is such want and suffering, when conditions of toil are so degrading, when the places that human beings live in are so indecent, it becomes the concern of the public at large to make its power felt and to see that this state of things is altered. ❞

LINKING HISTORY AND GEOGRAPHY

Study the African American and Hispanic population maps on pages 291 and 294. Write a brief summary of the population trends shown on each map. Then prepare a list of possible factors that might help explain the population distributions.

BUILDING YOUR PORTFOLIO

Complete the following projects independently or cooperatively.

1. **THE ECONOMY** Imagine you are a World War I veteran in 1919. Write a letter to your senator, explaining why you feel the federal government should help you secure a job. Your letter might mention your concerns about low wages, the high cost of living, and the few employment opportunities available in the postwar economy.

2. **CULTURE AND SOCIETY** Imagine you are an immigrant artist on the staff of Emma Goldman's radical magazine *Mother Earth* in the late 1920s. Create a cover illustration for an upcoming issue that expresses your views about one of the following: the Red Scare, the Sacco and Vanzetti case, labor strikes, or the Equal Rights Amendment.

BUILDING YOUR PORTFOLIO

Have students refer to **Building Your Portfolio Worksheet 3**, assigned at the beginning of Unit 3. Use the worksheet to help students monitor their progress on the portfolio projects.

Assessment

Core Resources
- Reteaching Worksheet 11
- Chapter 11 Tests
- Alternative Assessment Forms

Test Generator

*L*AND USE

HISTORICAL SIDELIGHTS

The Novel Soybean

The nutritious soybean was originally introduced to the United States as a novelty item around 1804. By 1900 some farmers began to produce the crop for livestock grazing, then later for industrial uses and for cattle feed. Soybeans were not used in products for human consumption until after the 1930s, when German chemists developed a method of removing the unpleasant taste and odor from soybean oil.

BUILDING VOCABULARY

In recent years the term *agribusiness* has been used to describe the development of large-scale, commercial farming ventures. The term was first used in 1955 by Assistant Secretary of Agriculture John H. Davis to describe the "vertical integration of agriculture through a company's control of the production, processing, and marketing of farm products."

America's GEOGRAPHY

LAND USE

FOR thousands of years Americans have used the land to grow crops. Many Native American groups cultivated crops on small plots of land long before the arrival of Europeans. In the early days of the republic, most farmers continued to grow food crops on small farms, although many large plantations in the South used the land to grow great quantities of tobacco and cotton. By the late 19th century, improved farm machinery and pesticides allowed farmers to grow larger quantities of food on smaller plots of land. Despite changes in farming techniques, some aspects of American farming have remained the same. For instance, corn is still the primary food crop grown in America—just as it was in the earliest civilizations.

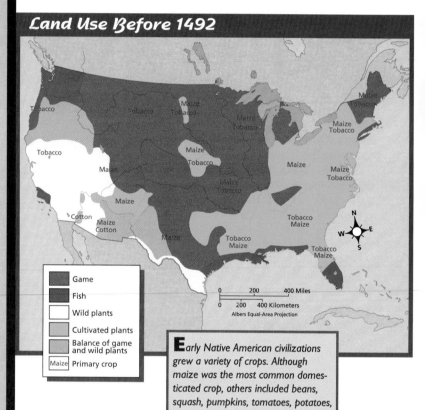

Land Use Before 1492

Legend:
- Game
- Fish
- Wild plants
- Cultivated plants
- Balance of game and wild plants
- Maize — Primary crop

0   200   400 Miles
0   200   400 Kilometers
Albers Equal-Area Projection

Early Native American civilizations grew a variety of crops. Although maize was the most common domesticated crop, others included beans, squash, pumpkins, tomatoes, potatoes, sweet potatoes, peanuts, cashews, pineapples, papayas, avocados, sunflowers, chili peppers, cacao, vanilla, tobacco, indigo, and cotton.

The multipurpose, high-protein soybean has become the agricultural wonder of the 20th century. By 1991 it was the second most-popular crop in the United States. Soybeans are used in the processing of cattle feed, fertilizer, insect sprays, and paint, as well as in food products such as soy sauce, soy milk, baby food, cereals, processed meats, and tofu.

AGRICULTURAL PRODUCTION, 1910–1991

	1910	1991
CORN (in bushels)	2.85 billion	7.75 billion
WHEAT (in bushels)	625 million	1.98 billion
COTTON (in bales)	11.61 million	17.5 million
TOBACCO (in pounds)	1.05 billion	1.66 billion
SOYBEANS (in bushels)	< 50,000	1.99 billion

Sources: *Historical Statistics of the United States, Statistical Abstract of the United States.*

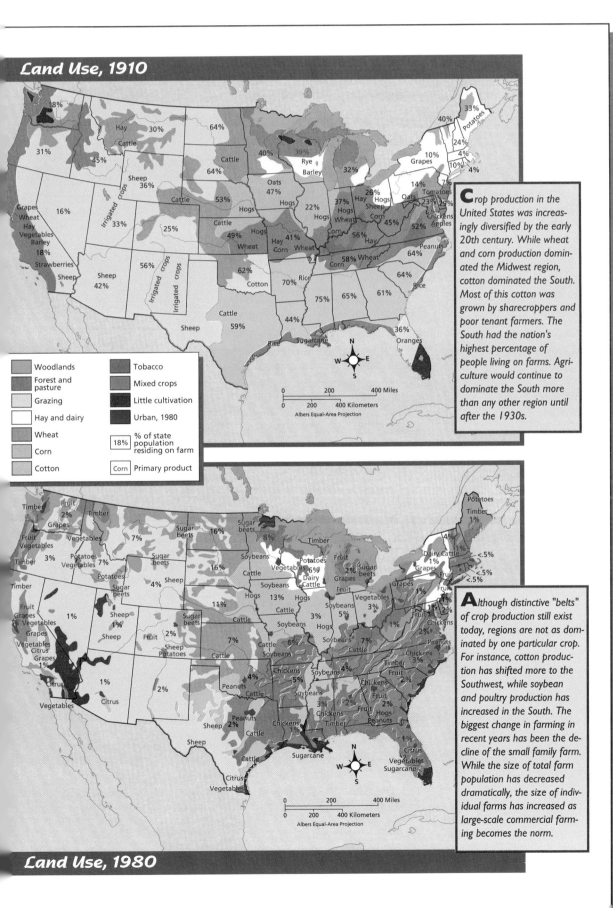

Land Use, 1910

Legend:
- Woodlands
- Forest and pasture
- Grazing
- Hay and dairy
- Wheat
- Corn
- Cotton
- Tobacco
- Mixed crops
- Little cultivation
- Urban, 1980
- 18% = % of state population residing on farm
- Corn = Primary product

Crop production in the United States was increasingly diversified by the early 20th century. While wheat and corn production dominated the Midwest region, cotton dominated the South. Most of this cotton was grown by sharecroppers and poor tenant farmers. The South had the nation's highest percentage of people living on farms. Agriculture would continue to dominate the South more than any other region until after the 1930s.

Although distinctive "belts" of crop production still exist today, regions are not as dominated by one particular crop. For instance, cotton production has shifted more to the Southwest, while soybean and poultry production has increased in the South. The biggest change in farming in recent years has been the decline of the small family farm. While the size of total farm population has decreased dramatically, the size of individual farms has increased as large-scale commercial farming becomes the norm.

Land Use, 1980

HISTORICAL SIDELIGHTS
Farm Monopolies
Small family farms have been disappearing from the American scene at a rapid rate. In 1986 the Congressional Office of Technology Assessment predicted that by the year 2000 about 50,000 large farms would control at least 75 percent of all food production in the United States.

THE JAZZ AGE

1920–1930

Chapter Overview

The 1920s was a decade of rapid technological change, a booming economy, flappers, jazz bands, the Charleston, and the Harlem Renaissance. Fueled by a postwar economy that grew at an unprecedented rate, the prosperity of the 1920s introduced millions of Americans to mass-produced goods as well as to mass culture. This rapid change caused social upheaval, leading many Americans to question traditional values.

THE AMERICAN NATION VIDEODISC PROGRAM
A variety of still images, short videos, and activities are available for you to use as you teach this chapter. See Videodisc Resources in the Core Resources Binder for barcode correlations and suggestions for using the program.

Chapter Planning Guide

CHAPTER 12	CORE RESOURCES	AUDIOVISUAL RESOURCES	PROGRAM RESOURCES
INTRODUCTION pp. 300–301	■ Literature Worksheet 12 ■ Building Your Portfolio Worksheet 3		
TEACHING THE CHAPTER pp. 302–321	■ Graphic Organizer 12 ■ Social Studies Skills Worksheet 12 ■ Geography Worksheet 12	■ *The American Nation Videodisc: The Film Age; Prohibition; Automobile Assembly Line; The 1920s: Americans on the Move; The Wright Brothers* ■ Everyday Life in America Transparency and Worksheet 22	■ Art in American History Transparencies and Worksheets 22, 23, 26, 27, 28 ■ *Eyewitnesses and Others,* Volume 2: Readings 38, 39
REVIEW AND ASSESSMENT pp. 322–323	■ Chapter 12 Daily Quizzes ■ Reteaching Worksheet 12 ■ Chapter 12 Tests ■ Alternative Assessment Forms		■ Test Generator

Additional Resources

BOOKS FOR TEACHERS

Coben, Stanley. *Rebellion Against Victorianism: The Impetus for Cultural Change in 1920s America.* Oxford University Press, 1991. Study of social values in the 1920s.

Smith, Page. *Redeeming the Time, Vol. 8: A People's History of the 1920s and the New Deal.* Viking Penguin, 1991. Early chapters provide a vivid picture of the 1920s.

Vincent, Theodore G. *Voices of a Black Nation: Political Journalism in the Harlem Renaissance.* Africa World Press, 1991. Primary sources from the Harlem Renaissance.

BOOKS FOR STUDENTS

Douglas, George H. *Women of the Twenties.* Saybrook, 1989. Descriptive accounts of the lives of Aimee Semple McPherson, Amelia Earhart, and other notable women.

Lewis, David L. *When Harlem Was in Vogue.* Oxford University Press, 1989. Narrative of major events, trends, and people during the 1920s in Harlem.

*Tames, Richard. *The 1920s (Picture History of the 20th Century Series).* Watts, 1991. Picture history of the major issues and events of the decade.

* for students reading below grade level

MULTIMEDIA MATERIALS

The Story of Henry Ford: Famous Americans of the 20th Century. Video, 55 min. Questar/SSSS. Explores the life and legacy of Ford.

History of the Twentieth Century, 1920–1929. Video, 60 min. ABC Video/SSSS. Expansive overview of Al Capone, Prohibition, and other topics.

A Walk Through the 20th Century With Bill Moyers: The Twenties. Video, 58 min. Corporation for Entertainment and Learning. A study of the personalities and events that shaped the 1920s.

THEMES IN AMERICAN HISTORY

**USE WITH PAGES
299–300**

*Listed on the right are
the themes emphasized in
Chapter 12. The questions in
boldface type stimulate critical
thinking and provide students
with an opportunity to discuss
the themes within a broadened
context. The questions also
appear in the pupil's edition
on p. 300.*

■ ECONOMIC DEVELOPMENT

**How might increased
consumer spending help
improve a nation's econo-
my?** Students might consider
that as more consumers buy
products, factories and other
businesses earn more money.
This might lead to increased
production and thus to more
employment, which would
provide citizens with income
to consume even more products. This consumerism might
spur growth in many industries.

■ TECHNOLOGY AND SOCIETY

**How might new technolo-
gy transform people's
lives?** Students may cite technological advances of which
they are aware and mention
the impact of those advances
on their lives.

■ CULTURAL DIVERSITY

**How might the cultural
traditions of a particular
area or group conflict
with or contribute to a
national culture?** Students
might give examples of how
regional or ethnic customs,
such as fashion or music,
might influence a national culture. Students might also discuss how some customs may
conflict with a nation's traditional mainstream values.

CHAPTER STRATEGIES FOR MEETING INDIVIDUAL NEEDS

LIMITED ENGLISH PROFICIENT LEARNERS

Have students role-play a young person
during the 1920s, such as a flapper, a
singer in a musical, or a writer, and tell
what life was like during this period.

TACTILE/KINESTHETIC LEARNERS

Organize students into small groups to
create scripts for a 1920s drama or comedy radio program that includes creative
sound effects. Call on groups to present
their programs.

LEARNERS HAVING DIFFICULTY

Discuss with students the meaning of key
terms in the chapter, encouraging them
to offer definitions. Then have students
use the key terms to write a brief summary of the chapter.

AUDITORY LEARNERS

Direct students to research and bring to
class a record or tape that illustrates the
music or radio programs of the 1920s.

VISUAL LEARNERS

Have students create a magazine advertisement on a popular product of the
"Roaring Twenties."

GIFTED LEARNERS

Organize students into small groups to
prepare a script for a documentary film
on the changes that took place in U.S.
society during the Jazz Age.

USING THE CHAPTER FOCUS

■ **UNDERSTANDING THE MAIN IDEA**

Ask a volunteer to read aloud the Understanding the Main Idea paragraph. Ask students to suggest what changes may have created social conflict in the 1920s. Ask students if they think that the 1990s are also marked by social conflict and, if so, what changes might have caused it.

THEMES
Have students work individually or in small groups to answer the questions under Themes. Save students' responses so that they can compare them with their responses after studying the chapter. (See p. 299B for suggested answers.)

■ **THE TIME LINE**

Remind students that World War I helped to bring about massive social, political, and technological changes in the U.S. Then encourage students to speculate on the relationships between postwar changes and the events on the time line. Have students review their speculations as they read the chapter.

CORE RESOURCES

• Literature Worksheet 12
• Graphic Organizer 12
• Building Your Portfolio Worksheet 3

ABOUT THE ILLUSTRATION

In the 1920s white northerners first heard jazz music in whites-only nightclubs, such as Chicago's Sunset Club and Harlem's Cotton Club. Although attracted by the music, white audiences also came to see the floor shows, such as the one shown below. In Prohibition-era America, these nightclubs allowed alcohol and offered more-risqué performances than Broadway shows. Draw students' attention to the racial composition of the audience and the performers in the photograph below. Ask students to speculate about the social differences between blacks and whites that this photo reveals.

Chapter 12

1920–1930

THE JAZZ AGE

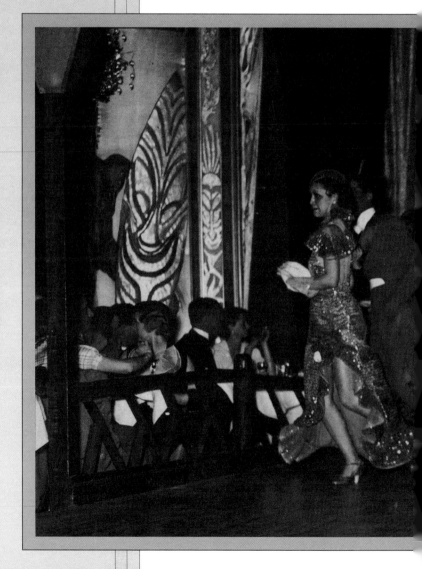

FOCUS

UNDERSTANDING THE MAIN IDEA

Jazz, the upbeat musical form developed by African Americans, helped give the 1920s a unique character. The automobile, advertising, radio programs, and movies also influenced American life. Artists and writers portrayed an American society growing more urban and "modern." Many Americans found the changes of the 1920s unsettling, and the decade was marked by social conflict.

THEMES

■ **ECONOMIC DEVELOPMENT** How might increased consumer spending help improve a nation's economy?

■ **TECHNOLOGY AND SOCIETY** How might new technology transform people's lives?

■ **CULTURAL DIVERSITY** How might the cultural traditions of a particular area or group conflict with or contribute to a national culture?

1920	1925	1926	1927	1928
First radio stations go on the air.	Scopes trial held in Dayton, Tennessee.	Langston Hughes's *Weary Blues* published.	Charles Lindbergh completes first nonstop flight from New York to Paris.	Amelia Earhart crosses Atlantic Ocean by plane.

Ask volunteers to recall the sacrifices made by Americans during World War I. Then have students speculate about how life might have changed for Americans after the Great War and write their responses on a flip chart. Tell students that this chapter focuses on daily life in America after the war. As students read the chapter, have them compare their responses to the information given in the chapter.

LINK TO THE PAST

Americans had cut back on purchasing goods during World War I. With the war over, men and women were eager to buy the new products that postwar American industry offered in abundance.

Jazz floor show in Chicago, 1924

An avalanche of new products transformed the lives of Americans in the 1920s—none more so than the automobile. The automobile changed the way Americans worked, socialized, and ran their households. It also helped change social roles for women. As early as 1907 a poem celebrated the growing independence of women who drove:

> 66 Like the breeze in its flight, or
> the passage of light,
> Or swift as the fall of a star.
> She comes and she goes in a nimbus
> of dust
> A goddess enthroned on a car.
> The maid of the motor, behold her
> erect
> With muscles as steady as steel.
> Her hand on the lever and always
> in front
> The girl in the automobile. 99

New forms of entertainment, including the wildly popular jazz bands, amused Americans in the generally prosperous 1920s. Radio programs, talking pictures, musical performances, and sporting events also entertained millions. But the decade was not all amusement. A small group of writers and artists revitalized American arts with their sober reflections on the war, race relations, and the nature of American society.

Life magazine cover, 1926

The Granger Collection, New York

HISTORICAL SIDELIGHTS

The "New Woman"

The image of the "new woman" belongs very much to the 1920s. Before World War I, in many towns and cities across the country, it was a crime for a woman to drive a car unless accompanied by a man, to smoke in public, or to wear inappropriate clothing—shorts, slacks, or a man's hat, for example. As women's roles in American life expanded during and after the war, such laws began to appear trivial, and local authorities ceased to enforce them.

PRIMARY SOURCE

Description of Change: excerpted
Rationale: excerpted to focus on main idea

FOCUS OBJECTIVES

■ List the factors that led to the economic boom of the 1920s.

■ Identify the processes that changed work habits during the twenties.

■ Describe how the automobile affected American life.

■ Analyze the developments that stimulated consumerism.

Section 1

BOOM TIMES

F O C U S

■ **What factors led to the economic boom of the 1920s?**
■ **Which processes changed work habits during the twenties?**
■ **How did the automobile affect American life?**
■ **What developments stimulated consumerism?**

The Granger Collection, New York

Automobile advertisement, 1920

*The economy prospered in the 1920s. In 1928 wages were a third
higher than they had been in 1914. The gross national product climbed
from $70 billion in 1922 to $100 billion just seven years later. Prosperity
was accompanied by changes in the workplace and a new automobile age.
Salespeople sold cars and a host of other products through aggressive
campaigns that aimed to turn the United States into a nation of consumers.*

PROSPERITY AND PRODUCTIVITY

Many factors led to the boom times of the 1920s. One was the Republicans' probusiness stance. Another was abundant supplies of energy—coal, oil, natural gas, and waterpower, as well as a vast network of electrical power plants. Between 1920 and 1929 fuel oil output doubled, and annual electrical production went from some 56 billion to 114 billion kilowatt-hours. By 1930 over two thirds of all U.S. homes had electricity.

The widespread availability of electricity created a demand for a dizzying array of new electrical appliances—washing machines, sewing machines, cake mixers,

and food grinders. Radio and phonograph sales boomed. Chemical companies also tempted consumers, offering a variety of products made from plastic, rayon, acetate, and other new "wonder" materials. In 1930, textile mills produced more than 118 million pounds of rayon and acetate yarns—more than 13 times the 1920 production level.

A new production technique—the **assembly line**—helped factories churn out goods faster. Around 1913, after adapting techniques used in the slaughterhouses

▶ **The Ford Motor Company introduced assembly-line techniques in its factories as early as 1913. This photograph of a Ford factory was taken in 1924. Henry Ford is shown in the inset.**

MOTIVATING: PRIOR KNOWLEDGE

Call on volunteers to cite events or developments of the early years of the 20th century that might have helped spur an economic boom during the 1920s. *(general probusiness stance, wartime economic expansion, efforts to modernize industry)* List responses on the chalkboard. As students read, have them compare the chalkboard list to the causes of the economic boom that are noted in the section.

Teaching the Section

ECONOMIC BOOM

Organize students into small groups to create a poster or collage that illustrates the major factors that led to the economic boom of the 1920s. Have them write captions for their poster or collage. Then have volunteers explain each group's artwork to the class. Conclude by asking students if any reasons for the boom were not illustrated in the groups' art.

▶

ELECTRICAL PRODUCTION

Kilowatt Hours (in billions) — 1920, 1930: Total U.S. Consumption

Percent — 1920, 1930: Homes with Electricity

Source: *Historical Statistics of the United States*

ABUNDANT ENERGY The use of alternating electric current and powerful transformers allowed electricity to be transmitted over great distances. As a result, electrical use increased dramatically during the 1920s.

? IDENTIFYING CAUSE AND EFFECT By about what percentage did electrical consumption increase from 1920 to 1930?

of Chicago, Henry Ford introduced the assembly line in his Detroit automobile plant. Workers stood in one spot as partially assembled automobiles moved past them on a conveyor belt timed to advance precisely six feet per minute. Bit by bit, workers assembled the 5,000 parts of a Model T, or "Tin Lizzie," until the finished product could be driven out of the factory. Machinery did much of the work of producing individual parts and carrying them to workers. Boasted Ford:

> 66 Every piece of work in the shop moves; it may move on hooks, on overhead chains . . . it may travel on a moving platform, or it may go by gravity, but the point is that there is no lifting or trucking. . . . No workman has anything to do with moving or lifting anything. 99

The assembly line cut the engine assembly time for a Model T in half. Other large car manufacturers quickly followed Ford's lead and installed assembly lines. But few small companies could afford the expense of building or maintaining the new technology. Unable to compete, many were driven out of business. Soon the industry was dominated by three big corporations: Ford, General Motors, and Chrysler.

The assembly line allowed manufacturers to reduce the prices of cars, bringing them within reach of ordinary American families. Automobile registrations during the twenties rose from 8 million to 26 million—an average of one car for every five citizens.

In the 1920s the auto industry was the nation's biggest business. This new industrial giant consumed huge quantities of steel, glass, rubber, and other materials. Gasoline, formerly a troublesome by-product of the petroleum industry, became the industry's most-valued product. By 1929 over one million people labored in the automobile industry or a related business.

■■ Probusiness policies, ample energy, new industries, and the assembly line fueled the economic boom of the 1920s.

*C*HANGES IN WORK

Although assembly lines increased productivity, they had a human cost. Little technical skill was needed to "work the line." Thus, many higher-paid skilled laborers were thrown out of work. But even the people who found jobs on the line suffered. The work was deadening, leading many to quit within a few weeks. To counter the high turnover, Ford limited the workday to eight hours and doubled wages to an unheard-of $5 a day.

Both of these bold steps were welcomed. However, as the wife of one Ford worker noted, the pay increase did not change working conditions:

> 66 The chain system [assembly line] you have is a *slave driver!* My God! Mr. Ford. My husband has come home & thrown himself down & won't eat his supper—so done out! Can't it be remedied? . . . That $5 a day is a blessing—a bigger one than you know but *oh* they earn it. 99

The innovations of "Fordism" were more than matched by those of another movement, "Taylorism." The movement's creator, Frederick W. Taylor, called his approach **scientific management**.

Chart Caption Answer
about 100 percent

HISTORICAL SIDELIGHTS
Engineering
Henry Ford led the way in improving assembly-line techniques. By 1914 the assembly process was refined to the point that a Model T's engine could be built in about 6 hours. Constructing a complete chassis took just 1½ hours. By the time the Model T was discontinued in 1927, approximately 15 million had been sold.

THE AMERICAN NATION VIDEODISC PROGRAM

Automobile Assembly Line

2A   39871   :26

PRIMARY SOURCE
Description of Change: excerpted
Rationale: excerpted to focus on main idea

PRIMARY SOURCE
Description of Change: excerpted and bracketed
Rationale: excerpted to focus on main idea; bracketed to clarify meaning

Teaching the **S**ection

CHANGES IN THE WORKPLACE

Instruct each student to write a letter to an employer from the perspective of a 1920s factory employee, explaining how scientific management and changes in technology have transformed working conditions. Have students read their letters aloud. Ask volunteers to respond to the letters as a 1920s employer would. Students may wish to include their letters in their portfolios.

CAR CULTURE

Organize students into small groups to create charts listing the positive effects and the negative effects of the automobile during the 1920s. Then have representatives from each group create a class chart on the chalkboard. Conclude by asking the class to decide if the automobile was a benefit or a liability for the people of the 1920s.

MULTICULTURAL PERSPECTIVES

Mexican immigrants found jobs at Ford Motor Company plants during World War I. But because of the postwar recession, Ford sent some 3,000 Mexican auto workers back to Mexico in 1920. This forced repatriation slowed Mexican immigration for a time, but by 1923 it had increased. Mexican workers were being drawn to work in factories in Chicago, Detroit, and Pittsburgh. The high rate of Mexican immigration in the 1920s led some labor groups to call for quotas on Mexican immigrants, but such efforts failed.

THE AMERICAN NATION VIDEODISC PROGRAM

The 1920s: Americans on the Move

1B 50587 :34

◀ **Frederick W. Taylor pioneered techniques used to increase workers' output.**

It was based on the idea that every kind of work could be broken down into a series of smaller tasks. Trained observers conducted "time-and-motion" studies to identify these tasks and then set rates of production that people and machines had to meet. Soon "efficiency experts" were applying Taylor's methods to many areas of business.

The assembly line and scientific management changed the types of jobs available to workers. While the number of factory jobs grew only slightly during the 1920s, openings for such white-collar jobs as manager, clerical worker, and salesperson increased from slightly more than 10 million to more than 14 million. Because most of these jobs required that applicants have at least a high-school education, few newly arrived immigrants qualified. Discriminatory hiring practices also closed most of these jobs to African Americans.

Changes in technology affected domestic labor as well. Electrical appliances transformed housework for those who could afford them. Before the introduction of appliances, servants did the laundry and heavy cleaning in most middle- and upper-class homes. With the introduction of electrical appliances, many middle-class housewives took over the jobs they had previously supervised. As a result, many servants were forced to find new employment.

As more families bought cars, housewives also began taking over their families' transportation duties. Before many middle- and upper-class families had cars, their groceries and other supplies had been delivered to their homes. The automobile allowed housewives to assume these responsibilities as well. Thus, like household servants, delivery people often found their jobs in jeopardy.

■■ **Scientific management and new technology transformed working conditions in the 1920s.**

A LAND OF AUTOMOBILES

Just as the automobile assembly line transformed the world of work, so the automobile revolutionized the entire transportation system. By 1930 cars, trucks, and buses had almost completely replaced horse-drawn vehicles. Even railroads and trolley cars lost riders to Ford's "Tin Lizzie" and other automobiles.

To accommodate the increased traffic, more than 400,000 miles of new roads were built during the decade. Alongside the highways sprouted a host of new structures—filling stations, drive-in restaurants, tourist cabins, and billboards.

The automobile enabled rural residents to have greater contact with their neighbors and more access to shopping and leisure activities. Cars linked rural regions to urban areas, making it easier for rural residents to relocate to the booming cities and for city dwellers to visit the country. At the same time, however, the automobile contributed to the depopulation of America's inner

▼ **With some nine million automobiles in use by 1920, more and more families explored the country in their cars. Shown here is an advertisement encouraging motorists to take the Apache Trail Motor Tour through Arizona's National Reserve.**

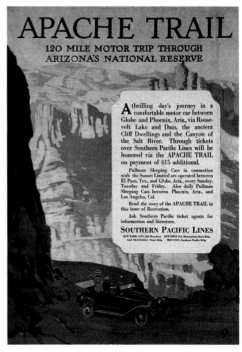

ADVERTISING AND CONSUMERISM

Have students work in pairs to write a slogan or jingle that illustrates the factors that stimulated consumerism in the 1920s. Have pairs present their jingles to the class.

■■ Ask students how and what forms of advertising influence their lives today.

▶

Changing Ways
HITTING THE ROAD

In the 1920s, as millions of Americans purchased automobiles, a new craze swept the nation—the "autotouring" vacation. Guidebooks urged Americans to hit the road:

66 Does father crave to fish for trout and bass and pike and musky? Take him auto-touring. Does sister want to dip in the surf . . . or see the world? Take her automobile vacationing. . . . Does mother sigh for a rest from daily routines? Take her touring. . . . Does baby need fresh mountain air far from flies and heat? Take him auto-camping. 99

Freed from travel restrictions imposed by the schedules and routes of passenger trains, car owners took to the road to see America.

Most motor tourists were city dwellers who vacationed in the country to "get away from it all." But in getting away, they often took a lot of "it" with them. Camping gear for the typical autotourist included a tent, gas stove, heater, cooking utensils, pots and pans, folding table and chairs, spring beds, and blankets.

Autotourists tended to camp together and had a culture all their own. They often dressed in ways that led observers to marvel and to gawk at the same time. One reporter wrote:

▲ Families took advantage of new government autocamps while traveling on the road. This photograph shows a family camping in the 1920s.

66 It was amazing what colorful combinations the knickered rovers [autotourists] managed to attain. They wore veils of all descriptions, flowing Egyptian veils and even gas masks [to keep out road dust]. They wore paper hats that tied under their chins, caps trimmed with the tails of squirrels, skins of rattlesnakes, and quills of porcupines. 99

At first farmers welcomed these visitors from the city. Autotourists broke the isolation of rural life and seemed likely customers for farm produce. But instead of buying fruits and vegetables, vacationers often snitched them from trees and fields. Sometimes campers even milked farmers' cows! They also dumped their garbage on farmers' land. Soon signs banning autotouring appeared in rural areas. One such sign read:

66 Trespassers will B persecuted to the full extent of 2 mongrel dogs which neve was over sochible to strangers and 1 doubl brl shot gun which ain't loaded with sofa pillors. 99

National and state park services, along with town governments, stepped in to keep local people and visitors from clashing. These agencies set up free autocamps to provide tourists with welcome comforts, while keeping them off private land. Electric lighting made it possible for motorists to arrive and set up camp after dark, and gas ranges eliminated the need for firewood.

The heyday of autotourism passed as the prosperity of the 1920s gave way to the depression of the 1930s. But its legacy can be seen today in the continuing appeal of sight-seeing and camping vacations and in the popularity of recreational vehicles.

Changing Ways
HITTING THE ROAD

SETTING THE SCENE
During the early 1900s the practice of autotouring was practically unknown in the U.S. In 1926, however, the American Automobile Association (AAA), founded in 1902, estimated that 12 million campers, using 3 million cars, went autotouring. The AAA attempted to establish a code of responsible behavior for auto-campers. Their booklet, "Courtesy of the Camp," warned campers against dumping trash, destroying trees and bushes, and leaving fires burning.

PRIMARY SOURCES

Description of Change: excerpted

Rationale: excerpted to focus on main idea

PRIMARY SOURCE

Description of Change: excerpted and bracketed

Rationale: excerpted to focus on main idea; bracketed to clarify meaning

Practice

GUIDED PRACTICE
Construct a word web on the chalkboard by first writing the word *automobile* and circling it. Then draw lines radiating from the circle and call on volunteers to cite how the automobile affected America in the 1920s. Add students' responses to the web.

INDEPENDENT PRACTICE
Direct students to create word webs similar to the one constructed in the Guided Practice activity using *work processes* and *advertising* as the circled terms. Students may wish to include their word webs in their portfolios.

Review and Assessment

REVIEW Call on volunteers to give short statements summarizing the main ideas of Section 1. Write responses on the chalkboard. Have students select one statement and write a paragraph that includes supporting details from the section. Then assign the Section 1 Review on p. 307.

ASSESS Assign the **Section 1 Daily Quiz** in *Core Resources.*

MAKING CONNECTIONS
Sociology
Middletown was a pioneering sociological study. The Lynds were the first to apply the methods of cultural anthropology to the study of a Western city. The Lynds returned to Muncie in the 1930s to study the impact of the Great Depression on the city, publishing their findings in their book *Middletown in Transition: A Study in Cultural Conflicts* (1937).

PRIMARY SOURCE
Description of Change: excerpted and bracketed

Rationale: excerpted to focus on main idea; bracketed to clarify meaning

---

cities. Suburbs, now more accessible than ever, attracted thousands of middle-class families.

The automobile also transformed family life. Cars enabled families to enjoy simple drives in the country and elaborate camping trips. The automobile created new social opportunities for teenagers as well. Sociologists Robert Lynd and Helen Lynd, whose book *Middletown* (1929) chronicled life in Muncie, Indiana, wrote:

> 66 The extensive use of this new tool [the automobile] by the young has enormously extended their mobility and the range of alternatives before them; joining a crowd motoring over to a dance . . . twenty miles away may be a matter of a moment's decision, with no one's permission asked. 99

But the automobile had negative effects as well. Critics claimed that cars reduced people's sense of neighborliness. The Lynds observed that "since the advent of the automobile and the movies" Muncie families and neighbors no longer spent "long summer evenings and Sunday afternoons on the porch or in the side yard." Also, by the twenties, cars were already causing pollution, traffic jams, and parking problems. Most serious was the steadily climbing accident rate.

▪▪ **Cars revolutionized the nation's transportation system, eased rural isolation, aided suburban growth, and changed family and community relations.**

---

*C*REATING CONSUMERS

Advertising, which became big business in the 1920s, fueled the demand for cars and other consumer goods. Before World War I, money spent on advertising had totaled some $500 million yearly. By 1929 the total had soared to more than $3 billion. Ads were everywhere. Commercial messages bombarded potential buyers not only in magazines and newspapers but also on billboards and over the new medium of radio.

Advertisements, most of which targeted women, used psychology to play on consumers' hopes and fears. Ads for Borden's milk, for instance, warned mothers that "Hardly a family—well-to-do and poor alike—escapes the menace of malnutrition. Your own child may fall victim to this insidious evil."

Companies used slogans, jingles, and testimonials by celebrities to fix product names in

▶ Advertisements often stressed the ease of operation or low maintenance of the device being offered for sale. This ad for an "unusually quiet" refrigerator appeared in 1927.

▼ Salespeople proudly display a host of new home electrical appliances that proved wildly popular in the 1920s.

RETEACH Ask students to use the section's Essential Points as topics for an outline summarizing the section. Have them add subtopics to the outline.

Closure

Have students imagine they are living in the boom times of the 1920s. Ask them to write paragraphs describing how the new prosperity has affected their lives. Encourage students to share their paragraphs with the class. Students may wish to include their paragraphs in their portfolios.

Extension

ANALYZE Assign small groups of students to review advertisements of the 1920s in period magazines (available in the public library) and analyze the advertising techniques used to sway customers.

INVESTIGATE Have students investigate the life of Henry Ford or the making of the first Model Ts.

customers' minds. Eleanor Roosevelt (whose husband, Franklin D. Roosevelt, was then governor of New York) praised Cream of Wheat, which their son John had eaten since babyhood. The cereal, she was quoted as saying, "has undoubtedly played its part in building his robust physique."

As the number of products expanded to meet the growing demand, new chain stores sprang up around the country. For example, the A & P grocery chain grew from some 3,000 stores in 1922 to about 14,000 by 1925. The chain grocery stores, which slowly replaced the corner markets, stocked a wide variety of new products. The chain stores could do so because cellophane, a transparent wrapping material first produced in the United States in 1924, and quick-freezing techniques preserved fresh foods longer and allowed them to be shipped over longer distances.

Effective merchandising depended above all on clever salespeople. "There are always some people that you can sell anything to if you hammer them hard enough," claimed a car dealer. Door-to-door salespeople hawked everything from cleaning supplies to encyclopedias.

People also bought more because of easy credit. Before the 1920s, consumers bought only a few expensive items, such as pianos and sewing machines, on the installment plan. By mid-decade,

▲ Chain grocery stores did not completely replace the neighborhood grocery. Immigrants continued to shop at family-run groceries such as this one, owned by Antonio and Angeline Tortolano. At such stores customers could buy ethnic foods and talk to shopkeepers in their native language.

buyers purchased about 75 percent of cars on credit. The practice soon spread to many other items. As a car dealer noted:

66 To keep America growing we must keep Americans working, and to keep Americans working we must keep them wanting; wanting more than the bare necessities; wanting the luxuries and frills that make life so much more worthwhile, and installment selling makes it easier to keep Americans wanting. 99

■■ Advertising, merchandising, and installment buying encouraged consumerism.

PRIMARY SOURCE

Description of Change: excerpted
Rationale: excerpted to focus on main idea

SECTION REVIEW ANSWERS

IDENTIFY

*For significance, see the following pages:
assembly line (p. 302)
Henry Ford (p. 303)
Frederick W. Taylor (p. 303)
scientific management (p. 303)
Robert Lynd (p. 306)
Helen Lynd (p. 306)*

1. *probusiness policies, abundant energy supplies, new products and industries, and the assembly line*
2. *assembly line, scientific management, and technological developments*
3. *linked rural and urban areas, aided suburban growth, provided social and recreational opportunities*
4. *Summaries might mention use of slogans and jingles, testimonials from celebrities, and effective packaging of new products as part of its new advertising/merchandising plan.*
5. *positive—fueled economy, transformed housework, promoted consumerism; negative—reduced need for technical skills, made work deadening, encouraged high worker turnover and unemployment*

SECTION 1 REVIEW

IDENTIFY and explain the significance of the following: assembly line, Henry Ford, Frederick W. Taylor, scientific management, Robert Lynd, Helen Lynd.

1. **MAIN IDEA** What factors contributed to the economic prosperity of the 1920s?
2. **MAIN IDEA** What innovations transformed working conditions in the late 1920s?
3. **ASSESSING CONSEQUENCES** How did the invention of the automobile change the way Americans lived?
4. **WRITING TO INFORM** Imagine you are the president of a chain store. Prepare for your board of directors a brief summary of how the company plans to attract new customers.
5. **ANALYZING** Why can it be said that the technological and business innovations of the 1920s had both positive and negative consequences for American society?

FOCUS OBJECTIVES

- List the most popular forms of entertainment during the 1920s.

- Describe the ways young women of the 1920s departed from traditional female behavior.

- Analyze the conflict that Prohibition and Fundamentalism revealed in American society.

Section 2

LIFE IN THE TWENTIES

FOCUS

- **What were the most popular forms of entertainment during the 1920s?**
- **In what ways did young women of the 1920s depart from traditional female behavior?**
- **What did the debate over Prohibition and Fundamentalism reveal about American society in the 1920s?**

The decade of the 1920s has been called the gateway to modern America. For the first time a truly national mass culture emerged in the United States. Commercial radio linked Americans from coast to coast. Instant communications not only entertained people but also informed them about serious developments. The emerging mass culture also brought changes in women's roles and caused conflicts over traditional values.

Matinee idol Rudolph Valentino

POPULAR ENTERTAINMENT

Boom times in the United States meant that many—though not all—Americans had bigger paychecks and more free time than in years past. To help fill their leisure hours, many Americans turned to radio and movies.

Commercial radio arose in the twenties. The first stations, Detroit's WWJ and Pittsburgh's KDKA, went on the air in 1920. By 1929, more than 800 stations reached some 10 million homes—more than a third of the nation's households. "There is radio music in the air, every night, everywhere," gushed a San Francisco newspaper. "Anybody can hear it at home on a receiving set." Along with music, radio stations broadcast sports events, news, and comedy shows.

By the end of the decade, two networks, the National Broadcasting Company (NBC) and the Columbia Broadcasting System (CBS), aired their programs nationwide. Households across the land tuned in to the same programs.

Movies proved equally popular, having grown in both length and complexity since their beginnings in the 1890s. The earliest movie

◄ **Advances in technology made radio more accessible to Americans during the 1920s. This photograph shows a young woman tuning in to a program on her radio set in 1922.**

Call on volunteers to identify radio programs they have listened to or movies they have seen in recent weeks. Then have students discuss what they know about the beginnings of radio and the motion-picture industry. Tell students that this section focuses on the development of radio and the film industry in the U.S., and on other social developments in the 1920s.

▲ Moviegoers during the 1920s stood in line to see romance films starring John Gilbert and Greta Garbo, action films with Douglas Fairbanks, or comedies featuring Charlie Chaplin.

▶ As motion pictures grew in popularity, theater owners built lavish movie palaces with elaborate balconies, box seats, and a pit for live orchestral music.

THE AMERICAN NATION
VIDEODISC PROGRAM
The Film Age

| | | |
| 2A | 07997 | 3:48 |

PRIMARY SOURCE

Description of Change: excerpted and bracketed
Rationale: excerpted to focus on main idea; bracketed to clarify meaning

HISTORICAL SIDELIGHTS

Harlem Globetrotters
Probably the first mass-appeal U.S. basketball team was the all-black Harlem Globetrotters. Orginally called the Savoy Big Five, they first played their games in Chicago's Savoy Ballroom. In 1927, when the ballroom became a skating rink, they took the name Harlem Globetrotters and scheduled all their games on the road. But they became so good that fewer and fewer teams were willing to play them. After winning the World Basketball Tournament in 1940, they adopted the show tactics for which they are best known today.

theaters—called nickelodeons because of the five-cent admission—attracted mainly working-class and immigrant audiences. By the 1920s, lavish movie palaces with names like the Roxy, the Bijou, and the Ritz, were attracting middle-class audiences as well. The more-luxurious theaters had velvet drapes, plush carpets, uniformed ushers, and great theater organs to accompany the silent films. The mass appeal of movie theaters impressed journalist Lloyd Lewis:

66 In the "de luxe" [movie] house every man is a king and every woman a queen. Most of these cinema palaces sell all their seats at the same price,—and get it; the rich man stands in line with the poor. . . . In this suave atmosphere, the differences . . . that determine our lives outside are forgotten. All men enter these portals equal, and thus the movies are perhaps a symbol of democracy. 99

In 1927 Warner Brothers released the first feature-length "talkie," *The Jazz Singer,* starring Al Jolson. Silent-screen stars with high squeaky voices soon found themselves unemployed. In their places emerged new actors with distinctive and appealing voices, among them Gary Cooper and Clara Bow. The advent of sound also led to new film forms, including musicals and newsreels,

short films summing up the news of the day. In 1929 some 80 million Americans flocked to the theaters each week.

■■ **Americans turned to radio and movies for entertainment during the 1920s.**

𝒞ELEBRITIES AND HEROES

When movie star Rudolph Valentino died in 1926 at age 31, mourners lined up for blocks to view his body. In this era of mass culture, actors became instant celebrities. So did other figures in the public eye, especially athletes and pilots.

One sports favorite was Babe Ruth. Ruth dominated baseball from 1920 to 1935, during which time he led the New York Yankees to four World Series championships. In 1927 the spindle-legged, pigeon-toed ball player astounded the sports world with a record 60 home runs. Hard-hitting tennis star Helen Wills wowed audiences

▲ During his long career, Babe Ruth hit 714 home runs—a record not broken until 1974.

Teaching the Section

POPULAR ENTERTAINMENT IN THE 1920s

Organize students into small groups to create a script for a newsreel that describes popular forms of entertainment in the 1920s. Have them use details from the section in their scripts. Ask volunteers from each group to present their scripts to the class.

THROUGH OTHERS' EYES

Ask students to explain why they agree or disagree with Müller-Freienfels's opinion. Then ask if and how his description could apply today.

PRIMARY SOURCE

Description of Change: excerpted and bracketed
Rationale: excerpted to focus on main idea; bracketed to clarify meaning

THE AMERICAN NATION VIDEODISC PROGRAM
The Wright Brothers

1B   51443   :32

BIO
GRAPHY
PERSONALITIES IN HISTORY

Jim Thorpe received long-overdue recognition in 1950, when U.S. sportswriters and broadcasters voted him the country's greatest athlete and football player of the previous 50 years.

THE TWENTIES

Richard Müller-Freienfels, a German professor and writer, studied industrialization and the mass culture that emerged in the early 20th century. Here is his description of American life in the 1920s:

> **❝*A*ll the men seem to be clothed by the same tailor, and all the women seem to have bought their hats at the same shop. . . . The most remarkable thing is that even the people impress one as having been standardized. All these clean-shaven men, all these girls, with their doll-like faces, which are generally painted, seem to have been produced somewhere in a Ford factory, not by the dozen but by the thousand. In no other country are the individuals reduced to such a dead-level as in the United States, and this appears all the more remarkable when we reflect that nowhere [else] is there such a . . . mixture of races and peoples. ❞**

THROUGH OTHERS' EYES

and captured more major tennis championships than any other woman in the world. Wills won the U.S. Open title seven times and Wimbledon eight times. Swimmer Gertrude Ederle broke the world record when she swam the English Channel in 1926 at age 19. She went on to set more than 20 U.S. swimming records and to win several medals in the 1924 summer Olympics.

Few athletes of the 1920s, however, enjoyed greater fame than Jim Thorpe. Born in 1888 in Oklahoma, he was of Sauk, Fox, Irish, and French ancestry. Thorpe attended the Carlisle Indian School in Pennsylvania. There he played every intercollegiate sport the school offered.

Jim Thorpe

After he left Carlisle, Thorpe began training for the Olympics. At the 1912 games, held in Stockholm, Sweden, he became the first contestant to win both the pentathlon and the decathlon. "Sir, you are the greatest athlete in the world," said the Swedish king as he presented Thorpe with his gold medals. "Thanks, King," replied Thorpe with a grin.

A year later Thorpe's triumph turned to ashes. The news became public that he had played semiprofessional baseball for money. (At the time, Olympic athletes had to be amateurs.) Officials erased his name from Olympic record books and confiscated his awards. Many people felt that Thorpe had been treated unfairly; he had not realized that playing baseball for money would disqualify him from track competition.

Thorpe went on to a respectable career in major-league baseball and in the 1920s enjoyed several spectacular years playing professional football. In his later years, which were clouded by illness, he tried to become a movie actor. Not until 1982, 29 years after his death, did an Olympic committee restore his medals.

Probably the greatest celebrity of the 1920s was pilot Charles Lindbergh. In May 1927 he took off in a small single-engine plane, aiming to win a $25,000 prize that had been offered to the first pilot to

▶ **Charles Lindbergh's solo flight across the Atlantic Ocean in 1927 in his plane, *The Spirit of St. Louis*, made him an international celebrity.**

THE NEW WOMAN

Encourage students to imagine they are listening to a 1920s radio talk show on the topic "What's With Today's Young Women?" Ask volunteers to "call" the show with their comments and views to either support or challenge the "new woman's" departure from traditional behavior.

■■ Ask students to compare women's dress and behavior today with the flappers of the 1920s.

PROHIBITION

Have students choose a role (immigrant, religious leader, social reformer, and so on) and write editorials defending or opposing the Volstead Act. Call on volunteers to read their editorials. Use editorials to launch a class discussion on the cultural conflicts revealed by the Prohibition debate.

▶

fly nonstop from New York to Paris. After flying solo for 33 1/2-hours, he landed in France. Americans were delirious with joy. New Yorkers threw a ticker-tape parade for Lindbergh, and President Coolidge received the modest young man at the White House. Lindbergh's flight offered exciting glimpses of a coming era of air travel. The next year, pilot Amelia Earhart became the first woman to cross the Atlantic Ocean by plane.

▲ Flapper styles spread all over the country, even to rural South Texas. Shown here are Idalia Canales and Rosenda García, two cousins who lived in a small town near the Rio Grande and copied the flapper look.

𝒯HE "NEW WOMAN"

Two of the many changes in the 1920s were in women's dress and behavior. Influenced by popular actresses and by the independence of working-class women, some young women exercised new freedom in how they dressed and behaved. These women stopped wearing heavy corsets and started wearing shorter skirts and transparent silk hose. Actress Colleen Moore explained that these changes in dress represented a new independence for women:

❝ Long skirts, corsets, and flowing tresses have gone. . . . The American girl will see to this. She is independent, a thinker [who] will not follow slavishly the ordinances of those who in the past have decreed this or that for her to wear. ❞

People began to call the era's "new women" **flappers**. Flappers enjoyed defying traditional standards of womanly behavior. They wore their dresses daringly short, bobbed their hair, and wore makeup. They also drove cars, participated in sports, and smoked cigarettes.

Flappers gloried not only in their social freedom but also in their economic independence. Young women increasingly worked outside the home, which gave them more freedom to meet people and save money for themselves. If they married, however, they were expected to quit

their paid employment and to fulfill their roles as wives and mothers. As Samuel Gompers, leader of the AFL, made clear in 1921 when he described the winner of the first Miss America beauty pageant, the homemaker was still the ideal of American womanhood:

❝ She represents the type of womanhood America needs— strong, red-blooded, able to shoulder the responsibilities of home-making and motherhood. It is in her type that the hope of the country resides. ❞

■■ The "new woman" of the twenties defied conventions in dress and behavior.

𝒜 CRISIS OF VALUES

For some Americans the flapper symbolized the negative changes overtaking the country in the 1920s. With their unconventional dress and behavior, flappers rejected traditional values. To conservatives, the popularity of romantic movies and cheek-to-cheek dancing seemed signs of increasing immorality. Most critics blamed these "modern" habits on cities, noting with anxiety that radio and movies spread city ways to even the remotest rural areas. Anxiety increased when the census of 1920 revealed that for the first time, more than half of the U.S. population lived in metropolitan areas. In the face of these tremendous changes, arguments raged over such issues as alcohol and religion.

▲ Couples during the 1920s often held each other close in a cheek-to-cheek style while dancing to romantic music such as the tango.

Teaching the Section

FUNDAMENTALISM

Call on volunteers to role-play witnesses before the grand jury deliberating on whether or not John Scopes should be indicted. Some "witnesses" should present the Fundamentalist viewpoint, while others should support Scopes's position. Have the rest of the class act as the grand jury and make a decision on the indictment.

Conclude by asking students to discuss how the Scopes trial symbolized cultural conflict in the 1920s.

■■ Ask students what issues cause cultural conflict in society today.

BUILDING VOCABULARY

The term *bootlegging,* which came into use in the mid-1800s, derives from the smugglers' trick of concealing illegal items in the legs of their boots. During the 1920s the label was applied to smugglers of illegal liquor.

GLOBAL CONNECTIONS

Canada benefited greatly from Prohibition in the U.S. New hotels, bars, and steamboats on the Canadian side of the border, which catered to thirsty American tourists, gave the economy a huge boost. And the more than one million gallons of spirits sold for "export"—in other words, smuggled to the U.S.—produced huge profits for the Canadian liquor monopolies and impressive tax revenues for the Canadian government.

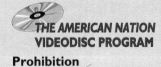

THE AMERICAN NATION **VIDEODISC PROGRAM**

Prohibition

2A   37756   :37

▲ Federal agents such as Izzy Einstein and Moe Smith often went undercover and tried to purchase alcohol in speakeasies. When the alcohol was served, the agents made their arrests.

Prohibition. Progressive reformers had called for a ban on alcohol to combat such urban problems as family violence, crime, and poverty (see Chapter 7). Baptists, Methodists, and other Protestants also opposed drinking. After the Eighteenth Amendment made the manufacture, sale, and transportation of alcoholic beverages illegal in January 1919, Congress passed the **Volstead Act** in October 1919 to enforce the amendment. America entered the era of Prohibition.

In some regions Prohibition was strictly enforced, and drinking declined. But in many parts of the country, especially among immigrants, college students, and some city dwellers, Prohibition was extremely unpopular and widely ignored. Many people treated the reform as an annoyance, if not a joke. They frequented speakeasies, made their own wine or liquor, and bought bootleg (illegal) alcohol that had been smuggled from Canada or the West Indies.

Bootlegging became one of the decade's booming businesses. Criminal gangs in the large cities controlled liquor sales. Gang leaders gained the cooperation of law enforcement officials by bribing or threatening them. Al Capone, the boss of Chicago's underworld,

commanded a small army of heavily armed mobsters. He and other gangsters made millions of dollars.

Gangs branched out to seize control of gambling establishments, houses of prostitution, and dance halls. They also made money through "protection" rackets, collecting money from owners of stores and other businesses by threatening violence if their victims failed to pay.

Prohibition had some positive consequences. Alcoholism declined and so did the number of deaths from alcohol-related causes. Prohibition's negative results, however, drew more attention. Prohibition led to a widespread breakdown of law and order and turned millions of otherwise law-abiding citizens into lawbreakers. Prohibition would later be repealed with the ratification of the **Twenty-first Amendment** in 1933.

Fundamentalism. The increasing popularity of a Protestant movement called **Fundamentalism** also revealed deep cultural conflicts in 1920s America. Fundamentalists believed that every word of the Bible should be regarded as literally true. They attacked Christian "liberals" who had accepted modern scientific learning, such as the theory of evolution. This "modernism," said Fundamentalists, weakened Christianity and contributed to the moral decline of the nation.

Revivalist preachers of the "old-time religion" found an eager audience, both in rural areas and in urban areas where traditional values remained strong. Billy Sunday, who had long preached against alcohol, drew huge crowds to his tent revivals. People were spellbound by Sunday's showmanship and his rousing attacks on dancing, card playing, and drinking. When Prohibition went into effect, he held a funeral service for "John Barleycorn," who personified alcohol, and declared that "the reign of tears is over."

Another popular revivalist of the 1920s was Aimee Semple McPherson, whose practice of faith healing and message of love attracted thousands to her International Church of the Foursquare Gospel, headquartered in Los Angeles. Most of her followers were city dwellers of modest

▼ Aimee Semple McPherson preached for nearly 20 years in a Los Angeles temple built for her by supporters at a cost of $1.5 million.

Practice

GUIDED PRACTICE

Organize students into small groups and direct each group to write dramatic headlines for each of the section's main topics. Have group representatives present their headlines to the class. Then ask the class to select the best headlines and develop brief outlines for newspaper stories to accompany those headlines.

INDEPENDENT PRACTICE

Tell students to use one of the outlines developed in the Guided Practice activity to write a newspaper story on that aspect of life in the U.S. during the 1920s. Students may wish to include their newspaper stories in their portfolios.

Review and Assessment

REVIEW Call on students to take turns answering the Focus questions on p. 308. For each question, record the responses on the chalkboard until no further details can be provided. Then assign the Section 2 Review on p. 314.

ASSESS Assign the **Section 2 Daily Quiz** in *Core Resources.*

▶

Then and Now — CENSORSHIP

The Roaring Twenties was a time of short skirts, bathtub gin, gambling, jazz, and the first talking movies. It was a time when old taboos were falling away one after the other. Alarmed and outraged by what they saw as the breakdown of the nation's moral standards, many community, religious, and government groups took action.

These activists pulled from library and store shelves books and magazines that used foul language, discussed sex frankly, or supported radical political ideas. U.S. Customs officials labeled many foreign books obscene and seized them, including the novel *Ulysses* by Irish author James Joyce.

Groups also targeted the movie industry. Several states and dozens of communities formed censorship boards to ban movies deemed unsuitable for young people. To both stem the tide of censorship and address public concerns over movie content, Hollywood set up in 1924 its own review board, a forerunner of today's movie-rating system, to screen movie content.

The American Civil Liberties Union and other groups opposed these growing

▲ Although James Joyce's *Ulysses* was initially banned, a later federal court ruling declared that it was not obscene and was a true work of literature.

restrictions on the content of movies and literature. They argued that such censorship violated the Constitution's First Amendment, which guarantees freedom of speech and freedom of the press.

Today the battle between censorship and freedom of speech continues. The National Endowment for the Arts (NEA), for example, has come under attack for funding artists whose works some consider obscene. But while some critics judge the art as obscene and unsuitable for public display, the artists defend their right to freedom of expression. The NEA and other agencies are caught in the middle of the battle.

Several rock and rap musicians have also come under fire for recording songs that contain sexually explicit or violent lyrics. In response, the Recording Industry Association of America has begun placing warning labels on any recordings that contain lyrics that might be unsuitable for minors. But many people believe voluntary labeling is not enough. In 1992, for instance, Washington State banned the sale and distribution of certain recordings to minors.

Is such censorship a violation of free speech or a needed form of protection? American society and U.S. courts continue to struggle with this question.

HISTORICAL SIDELIGHTS

Verdict Reversed
Scopes appealed his conviction, and in 1927 the Tennessee supreme court reversed the verdict on a technicality—the judge had set a fine higher than the law prescribed. However, the court upheld the anti-evolution law, which remained on Tennessee's statute books until the 1960s.

---

income, many of them recent migrants from the Midwest. Outfitted in her signature white dress, white shoes, and blue cape, McPherson addressed her followers' concerns about the new doctrines of "communism, socialism, and jazz-ism." McPherson also used radio and magazines to spread her fundamentalist message.

The Scopes trial. Fundamentalism went on trial in a famous court case in July 1925. Earlier that year the Tennessee legislature had outlawed the teaching of Charles Darwin's theory of evolution—a prime target of Fundamentalists—in the state's public schools. To test the law's constitutionality, the American Civil Liberties Union offered to defend any Tennessee schoolteacher who would challenge the statute. John Scopes, a shy high-school biology teacher from Dayton, accepted the offer.

The trial took place in a circus atmosphere. As the trial began in Dayton, the little town was overrun by reporters, farmers in mule-drawn wagons, and big-city lawyers. Scopes's chief defense attorney was salty Clarence Darrow, a famous criminal lawyer from Chicago. The prosecution's

RETEACH Have students work in small groups to chart the major ideas and events presented in the section. Direct each group to indicate on its chart how each item addresses one of the section's Focus questions.

Closure

Ask students to explain why their textbook (on p. 308) characterizes the 1920s as "the gateway to modern America." Require that they give examples to support their explanations.

Extension

COMPARE Ask students to make an oral report comparing the role sports and entertainment played in 1920s American life to the role these pastimes play today.

INVESTIGATE Have students investigate how Canada and Mexico responded to U.S. Prohibition.

PRIMARY SOURCE

Description of Change: excerpted and bracketed **Rationale:** excerpted to focus on main idea; bracketed to clarify meaning

SECTION REVIEW ANSWERS

IDENTIFY

For significance, see the following pages:
Babe Ruth (p. 309)
Helen Wills (p. 309)
Gertrude Ederle (p. 310)
Jim Thorpe (p. 310)
Charles Lindbergh (p. 310)
Amelia Earhart (p. 311)
flappers (p. 311)
Volstead Act (p. 312)
Twenty-first Amendment (p. 312)
Fundamentalism (p. 312)
Aimee Semple McPherson (p. 312)
John Scopes (p. 313)

1. *radio and movies*
2. *broke conventional rules of dress and behavior, had social and economic independence*
3. *Their differences exposed a division between traditional religious values and new values based on science.*
4. *negative—bootlegging, gang control of liquor sales, "protection" rackets; positive—decrease in alcoholism and alcohol-related deaths*
5. *sports figures—instant celebrities because of influence of mass culture; revivalists—popular because changes threatened traditional values*

▶ Clarence Darrow (right) devoted a large part of his legal career to defending the "underdog." This photograph shows him with John Scopes in 1925.

▼ Because the theory of evolution implied that human beings had descended from ape-like creatures, the Scopes trial became known as the "Monkey Trial."

THE CHICAGO DAILY NEWS. BOX SCORE
SCOPES "GUILTY" IN APE CASE

star witness was the elderly William Jennings Bryan, the former Democratic presidential candidate and secretary of state.

The Scopes trial exposed a deep division in American society between traditional religious values and new values based on scientific ways of thought. Bryan represented the many Americans who felt that the theory of evolution contradicted deeply held religious beliefs. Speaking before the trial to an audience of local admirers, Bryan declared:

❝ Our purpose and our only purpose is to vindicate [uphold] the right of parents to guard the religion of their children against efforts made in the name of science to undermine faith in supernatural religion. ❞

Darrow, on the other hand, expressed the views of many other Americans when he attacked the Tennessee law as a threat to free expression. In one of his courtroom speeches, he warned his listeners that "today it is the public school teachers, tomorrow the private, the next day the preachers and the lecturers, the magazines, the books, the newspapers."

Darrow's arguments, however, failed to sway the jury. They found Scopes guilty and fined him $100. The verdict was a victory for Fundamentalists. But press accounts of the trial, which often portrayed Bryan and his cause as narrow-minded, colored many people's views of Fundamentalism.

■■ **The debate over Prohibition and Fundamentalism revealed a crisis of values in 1920s America.**

SECTION 2 REVIEW

IDENTIFY and explain the significance of the following: Babe Ruth, Helen Wills, Gertrude Ederle, Jim Thorpe, Charles Lindbergh, Amelia Earhart, flappers, Volstead Act, Twenty-first Amendment, Fundamentalism, Aimee Semple McPherson, John Scopes.

1. **MAIN IDEA** What two forms of entertainment were most popular among Americans during the 1920s?
2. **MAIN IDEA** How did the flapper represent the "new woman" of the 1920s?
3. **IDENTIFYING VALUES** In what ways did the differing views of Clarence Darrow and William Jennings Bryan in the Scopes trial reflect the clash in values of 1920s America?
4. **WRITING TO INFORM** Write an essay explaining the negative and positive consequences of Prohibition.
5. **HYPOTHESIZING** What social factors might account for the popularity of sports figures and revivalists during the 1920s?

Chapter 12

SECTION 3

Introducing the Section

PREVIEW WORKSHOP

Following is a list of the significant people, places, and terms in this section. You may wish to use this list as a section preview.

People
- Joseph "King" Oliver
- Langston Hughes
- Marian Anderson
- Paul Robeson
- Rose McClendon
- Ernest Hemingway
- Diego Rivera
- Alfred Stieglitz

Places
- Harlem

Terms
- Harlem Renaissance
- Lost Generation
- planned obsolescence

Section 3

A CREATIVE ERA

FOCUS

- **How did African Americans contribute to the arts during the Harlem Renaissance?**
- **Who were the Lost Generation writers, and how did they get their name?**
- **How did the Mexican mural painters approach their art?**
- **How did mass media and advertising affect American culture in the 1920s?**

Louis Armstrong

The decade of the 1920s was a period of great creative energy. African American musicians transformed popular music by introducing the nation to jazz. A new generation of writers explored the problems of postwar American life and the experience of being black. Mexican muralists brought their paintings of social protest to the United States. And new currents in art and architecture swept the nation.

MUSIC AND DANCE

The 1920s has been called the Jazz Age because this was the period when jazz, with its richly complex rhythms, first won a wide following. Jazz originated among African Americans in the South, especially in New Orleans. By the late 1800s, jazz had emerged from a blend of West African and Latin American rhythms, African American spirituals and blues, and European harmonies.

Joseph "King" Oliver, an early jazz great, helped spread jazz northward by moving from New Orleans to Chicago and founding the Creole Jazz Band. In 1922 the great jazz trumpeter Louis Armstrong joined Oliver in Chicago. Pianist and composer Ferdinand "Jelly Roll" Morton also moved north.

▶ **Ferdinand "Jelly Roll" Morton began his career playing ragtime piano in New Orleans. Later, he moved to Chicago where he formed the recording group Red Hot Peppers.**

As it became popular on a national level, jazz was adapted in various ways. White musicians—among them the cornetist and pianist Bix Beiderbecke—incorporated jazz rhythms in their music. George Gershwin's *Rhapsody in Blue,* which

FOCUS OBJECTIVES

- Explain how African Americans contributed to the arts during the Harlem Renaissance.
- Identify the Lost Generation writers and explain how they got their name.
- Describe how the Mexican mural painters approached their art.
- Analyze how mass media and advertising affected American culture in the 1920s.

CORE RESOURCES

- **Literature Worksheet 12**
- **Section 3 Daily Quiz**

AV RESOURCES

- **Everyday Life in America Transparency and Worksheet 22**

THE JAZZ AGE ▪▪ 315

315

MOTIVATING: LINK TO TODAY

Call on volunteers to explain how artists, writers, and musicians influence American society today. Tell students that this section will describe the influences of artists, writers, and musicians on mass culture during the 1920s.

HISTORICAL SIDELIGHTS

The Charleston

The Charleston, a folk dance popular among African Americans throughout the South and in particular, Charleston, South Carolina, took its name from the city with which it was most closely associated. It is remarkably similar to dances found in Trinidad, Nigeria, and Ghana. The Charleston became a national sensation after it was featured in the African American musical *Runnin' Wild* (1923).

AV TRANSPARENCY

Everyday Life in America Transparency and **Worksheet 22**

BIO GRAPHY PERSONALITIES IN HISTORY

Following Rose McClendon's death in 1936, the *Afro-American* hailed her as the "Negro first lady of the dramatic stage." Shortly thereafter the theater she founded, the Negro People's Theatre in Harlem, became part of the Negro Unit of the Federal Theatre Project. Then, in 1937, actor Dick Campbell established the Rose McClendon Players to carry out McClendon's vision of community theater.

▲ During the 1920s jazz music such as "Tin Roof Blues" and "If You Knew Susie Like I Know Susie" became popular hits.

premiered in 1924, "translated" jazz into symphonic form. Jazz also influenced many classical musicians, including such noted composers as Igor Stravinsky and Aaron Copland.

The big bands, both black (Fletcher Henderson's and Duke Ellington's, for instance) and white (such as Paul Whiteman's), popularized jazz for dancing, creating faster and bouncier dances set to jazz rhythms. This new kind of jazz swept the nation via phonograph records, radio, and the movies. Young men and their flapper partners shocked their elders by dancing cheek-to-cheek fox-trots. The Charleston, originally an African dance performed by slaves, became *the* dance of the twenties.

While jazz became universal in the 1920s, it continued to express the particular sadness, pain, and joy of black America. African American poet Langston Hughes noted that through jazz, African Americans were saying "Why should I want to be white? I am a Negro—and beautiful!"

■■ Jazz became widely popular during the 1920s, influencing many other forms of music.

A BLACK RENAISSANCE

African American writers, artists, actors, and musicians in the 1920s expressed a growing black pride. Nowhere was this pride more evident than in the New York City neighborhood of Harlem, the nation's leading African American community. So many important African American writers, musicians, and artists lived in Harlem that this period of artistic development is known as the **Harlem Renaissance**.

The 1920s was a decade of achievement for African American musicians. They popularized not only jazz but also blues and religious songs known

▲ Although known for his work on stage, film, and radio, Paul Robeson also joined movements that fought for better working conditions, racial justice, and world peace.

as spirituals. In 1920 Mamie Smith's recording of "Crazy Blues" made popular the moody melodies of blues for white audiences. Bessie Smith, "the Empress of the Blues," toured widely and made many blues recordings. Marian Anderson, a gifted singer who began her operatic career in the 1920s, and Paul Robeson, singer and actor, incorporated spirituals in their repertoires.

In an era when African Americans were limited in the theatrical roles they were allowed to play, blacks produced and staged several enormously successful Broadway musicals, including Eubie Blake's *Shuffle Along* (1921). African American actors also achieved fame. Charles Gilpin played the title role in Eugene O'Neill's drama *Emperor Jones* in 1920. Paul Robeson made history in 1924 by becoming the first black actor to play a leading role opposite a white actress.

 A leading African American actor of the 1920s was Rose McClendon. Born in 1884 in South Carolina, McClendon moved to New York City as a child. She took part in church

Rose McClendon

HARLEM RENAISSANCE

Ask a volunteer to provide a dramatic reading of Langston Hughes's poem on pp. 317–318 and ask other volunteers to offer interpretations of its meaning. Then have students assume the role of an African American artist, writer, actor, or musician involved in the Harlem Renaissance. Invite them to write an essay or poem explaining how the Harlem Renaissance is an expression of their identity as blacks and as Americans. Have volunteers read their articles to the class. Students may wish to include their writings in their portfolios.

plays but did not become a professional actress until her thirties, after winning a scholarship to the American Academy of Dramatic Art.

McClendon first won fame in *Deep River,* a "native opera with jazz" staged in 1926. Even the simple act of descending a staircase won her praise from critics and fellow actors alike. In later years she played in the Pulitzer Prize–winning tragedy *In Abraham's Bosom,* about a would-be reformer; the first production of *Porgy,* set in Charleston, South Carolina; and *Never No More,* the story of a lynching. Her last role was in Langston Hughes's *Mulatto.*

In addition to directing plays at the Harlem Experimental Theatre, Rose McClendon helped found the Negro People's Theatre in Harlem in 1935. The organization increased opportunities for black actors and playwrights.

As important and impressive as African American contributions to movie and stage were during the Harlem Renaissance, it was above all a literary movement. Black novelists and poets produced work marked by bitterness and defiance but also by joy and hope. In his novel *Home to Harlem* (1928), Jamaica-born Claude McKay explored the excitement and stresses of Harlem life for a returned black soldier. Nella Larsen, born in Chicago of West Indian and Danish ancestry, described the quest for racial identity in her novel *Quicksand* (1928).

Among the most-famous Harlem poets were Langston Hughes and Countee Cullen. Hughes's *Weary Blues* (1926) and Cullen's *Color* (1925) viewed African American life and the African cultural heritage with sensitivity. In the poem "I, Too," Hughes sums up black pride in a few powerful lines:

> 66 I, too, sing America.
>
> I am the darker brother.
> They send me to eat in the kitchen
> When company comes,
> But I laugh,
> And eat well,
> And grow strong.

Harlem Renaissance, 1920s

HARLEM'S EXPANSION Migrants came to New York City from the South and the islands of the West Indies. During the 1920s, some 25 percent of Harlem's black population was foreign born.

? PLACE What was the extent of African American settlement in Harlem in 1920?

Famous club where Duke Ellington and other black entertainers perform for whites-only audiences.

Site of Marcus Garvey's UNIA rallies

This branch library features exhibits by African American artists and poetry readings by Countee Cullen.

Countee Cullen's column, "The Dark Tower," provides the name for this Harlem literary salon.

W.E.B. Du Bois sometimes lectures here, and the Krigwa Players stage plays by African Americans.

Johnson's 1922 anthology, *The Book of Negro Poetry,* helps launch the Harlem Renaissance. His parties draw noted intellectuals, such as Paul Robeson and Clarence Darrow.

- Black settlement in Harlem, 1920
- Black settlement in Harlem, 1930
- Areas predominately African American
- ■ Point of interest

Map Caption Answer
from 130th St. to 145th St., and from 5th Ave. to 8th Ave.

HISTORICAL SIDELIGHTS

Discrimination in Radio

While the radio networks employed black guest performers during the 1920s, they did not hire African Americans as actors or technicians. In addition, some radio programs, such as *Amos 'n' Andy,* in which black characters were portrayed by white actors, contributed to the stereotyping of African Americans.

MULTICULTURAL PERSPECTIVES

African American writer Jessie Fauset served as literary editor of the NAACP's journal, *The Crisis,* in the 1920s. *The Crisis* published many of the Harlem Renaissance writers for the first time. Fauset's encouragement of young writers and her willingness to accept experimental work supported African American exploration of black themes.

PRIMARY SOURCE

Description of Change: excerpted
Rationale: excerpted to focus on main idea

𝒯eaching the 𝒮ection

THE LOST GENERATION

Have students write journal entries from the perspective of young people of the 1920s explaining why they are disillusioned with life in postwar America. Have volunteers share their entries in class. Use these presentations as a starting point for a class discussion on why Gertrude Stein chose the term *lost generation* to characterize young American writers' anger and disappointment in 1920s society.

PRIMARY SOURCE
Description of Change: excerpted
Rationale: excerpted to focus on main idea

HISTORICAL SIDELIGHTS

Americans in Paris

For some members of the Lost Generation, the disillusionment with American society was so complete that they went into exile and lived abroad. Many—Ernest Hemingway among them—gravitated to Paris. Indeed, some scholars have suggested that during the 1920s the French capital was the center of the American literary world. The headquarters for most American writers in Paris was Shakespeare and Company, a bookstore and lending library run by American Sylvia Beach. Hemingway considered Shakespeare and Company "a wonderful place," and he visited it practically every day during his time in Paris.

▲ Langston Hughes

Tomorrow,
I'll be at the table
When company comes.
Nobody'll dare
Say to me,
"Eat in the kitchen,"
Then.

Besides,
They'll see how beautiful I am
And be ashamed—

I, too, am America. 🙰🙰

■■ **African American musicians, actors, and writers in the 1920s flourished, creating a cultural movement known as the Harlem Renaissance.**

𝒯HE LOST GENERATION

The creative spirit of the 1920s expressed itself not only in jazz, but also in the literature of the decade. Many younger writers of the time were haunted by the death and destruction of World War I and scornful of middle-class consumerism and the superficiality of the postwar years. "You are all a lost generation," said poet Gertrude Stein to one such writer, Ernest Hemingway. The label stuck, and scholars refer to writers of the era as the **Lost Generation**.

Ernest Hemingway spent much of his life in France, Spain, and Cuba. An ambulance driver in World War I, he expressed his anger at war's

futility in such novels as *The Sun Also Rises* (1926) and *A Farewell to Arms* (1929). In a famous passage from the latter book, a war veteran explains what the war means to him:

> 🙰🙰 I was always embarrassed by the words sacred, glorious, and sacrifice and the expression in vain. We had heard them . . . and had read them . . . now for a long time, and I had seen nothing sacred, and the things that were glorious had no glory and the sacrifices were like the stockyards at Chicago if nothing was done with the meat except to bury it. 🙰🙰

Disillusionment with World War I echoed in the works of other Lost Generation writers, including John Dos Passos's *Manhattan Transfer* (1925).

Another Lost Generation writer, F. Scott Fitzgerald, was the foremost chronicler of the youthful Jazz Age. In his first novel, *This Side of Paradise* (1920), Fitzgerald described the life of rich college students bored by fast living and hard liquor. In *The Great Gatsby* (1925), Fitzgerald portrayed the emptiness of life devoted to a frenzied struggle to make money and win social status in Prohibition-era America. Sinclair Lewis also criticized American society, satirizing middle-class life in *Main Street* (1920) and *Babbitt* (1922).

■■ **Gertrude Stein called Ernest Hemingway and other postwar writers "a lost generation" because of their anger and disappointment.**

𝒯HE MEXICAN MURALISTS

Another renaissance of the 1920s took place in Mexico and was later brought to the United States by its major artists. This artistic movement stressed Native American traditions and the ideals of the Mexican Revolution of 1910. The artists emphasized the nobility of ordinary people—peasants and other workers—and the tyranny of wealthy capitalists. Their favorite medium was the monumental public mural because, in the words of artist José Clemente Orozco (oh-ROHS-koh), "it cannot be hidden away for the benefit of a certain privileged few. It is for the people. It is for *ALL*."

THE MEXICAN MURALISTS

Have students assume the role of one Mexican muralist discussed in the section. Direct them to write a speech, which they might give to American students, explaining why they chose the mural as their medium as well as why they focused on particular subjects in their work. Ask volunteers to present their speeches to the class. Students may wish to include their speeches in their portfolios.

MASS MEDIA AND CULTURE

Have students work in small groups to draw up plans for a special issue of a current-affairs magazine dealing with the impact of mass media and mass marketing on American culture of the 1920s. Plans should include a table of contents with brief synopses of articles, suggestions for illustrations accompanied by sample captions, and design ideas for a cover. Have groups present and discuss their magazine plans.

▲ Diego Rivera painted many murals that focused on workers and their relationship to industrial production. Shown here is *Entry to the Mine.*

The movement's three major artists—known in Mexico as *los tres grandes,* or "the big three"— were Orozco, David Alfaro Siqueiros (see-KAY-rohs), and Diego Rivera. Each first became known in Mexico in the 1920s and painted murals in the United States in the early 1930s.

Orozco created several murals for American universities, many featuring heroic figures who helped humanity. At New Hampshire's Dartmouth College, Orozco's library murals painted in the early 1930s include the figure of Quetzalcoatl (ket-SAHL-kwaht-uhl), the god who brought the arts of civilization to the Toltecs.

In Los Angeles, Siqueiros painted large-scale murals outdoors, "in the free air," as he put it, "facing the sun, facing the rain, for the masses." His best-known work, *Tropical America* (1932), painted on a wall in a Mexican American section of Los Angeles, featured a crucified Indian. The mural expressed Siqueiros's belief that U.S. imperialism in Latin America was disastrous for Indians. The piece so angered U.S. officials that Siqueiros was deported and the work completely painted over.

Diego Rivera focused on workers' problems and industrial development in his U.S. murals. In his words:

❝ There is more beauty in an electrical plant, with its frank outline and its nervous system of steel transmitting the electric fluid

indispensable to social life, than in the redundant Baroque imitations of European architecture that have contaminated the soil of America. ❞

In a mural at the Detroit Institute of Art, which Rivera painted in 1932, his subject was, fittingly, assembly-line workers in automobile factories.

■■ **The Mexican muralists glorified ordinary people and created art that all could view.**

OTHER CURRENTS IN ART AND DESIGN

Like Rivera, U.S. artists and designers confronted the machine age in their works. They chronicled factories, new technology, workers, and urban landscapes.

Painting and photography. Many American painters of the 1920s depicted urban, industrial settings. Edward Hopper's New York City scenes convey a sense of loneliness. *Early Sunday Morning* (1930) shows a row of darkened stores and a street empty of people. New York City intrigued Georgia O'Keeffe, too. In the 1920s she painted pictures of its factories and tenements. Later she would move to New Mexico and capture the stark beauty of the Southwest.

Photography came into its own as an art form in the early 1900s. Alfred Stieglitz (STEEG-luhts),

Addison Gallery of American Art, Phillips Academy, Andover, MA

▲ This 1928 painting by Edward Hopper is called *Manhattan Bridge Loop.*

*P*ractice

GUIDED PRACTICE

Call on volunteers to identify the major developments in American arts during the 1920s. List responses on the chalkboard, asking students to provide background information on each item.

INDEPENDENT PRACTICE

Have students use the list developed in the Guided Practice to construct an annotated time line on American artistic creativity in the 1920s. Students may wish to include their time lines in their portfolios.

*R*eview and *A*ssessment

REVIEW Have students write 10 questions about Section 3 on individual note cards with the answers on the reverse side. Then divide students into groups of four. Ask them to use their note cards to question the other members of the group. Then assign the Section 3 Review on p. 321.

ASSESS Assign the **Section 3 Daily Quiz** in *Core Resources*.

GLOBAL CONNECTIONS

Industrial design originated at the Bauhaus, a school of design founded by architect Walter Gropius in Germany in 1919. Emphasizing simple, practical designs and attention to craftsmanship, the Bauhaus had a worldwide impact. Its influence was especially marked in the U.S., where some of its members came to teach after the Nazis closed the school in the early 1930s.

PRIMARY SOURCE

Description of Change: excerpted
Rationale: excerpted to focus on main idea

COOPERATIVE LEARNING

Divide the class into groups of four. Assign each group one of these topics on the 1920s to research: music, literature, sports, art. Have groups use their research to create a mural. Students in each group should share assignments among themselves; some might be responsible for research, others for mural design, and still others for writing text to explain the mural.

more than anyone else, gave it new status. Stieglitz's New York gallery influenced many other American artists. His own subjects included airplanes, skyscrapers, and crowded city streets. Charles Sheeler, a photographer and painter, won fame for the "portraits of machinery" he produced for the Ford Motor Company, which commissioned him to photograph its plant near Detroit, Michigan, in 1927.

Industrial design. The machine age that inspired artists also gave rise to a new professional field: industrial design. Spreading from Germany to the United States in the 1920s, industrial design aimed to create objects that were pleasing to look at as well as functional.

Industrial designers, working with such new materials as stainless steel and plastics, developed a wide range of products with a "modern" look. The designers developed streamlining—contours that reduced resistance—for trains, planes, ships, and cars. They also applied streamlining to objects that did not even move, such as radios, clocks, and appliances.

Manufacturers soon learned that a new design for what was essentially the same product boosted sales. They had discovered what came to be called **planned obsolescence**—making products that are designed to go out of style. Auto manufacturers were among the first to take advantage of planned obsolescence. In the early 1920s General Motors introduced the ideas of the yearly model change and the trade-in. Thereafter, many American families routinely traded in their "old" models and bought new cars every year.

Architecture. Industrial design, which combined function and visual appeal, had its counterpart in the world of architecture. Louis Sullivan and Frank Lloyd Wright inspired many other architects to embrace the idea that a building ought to use the materials and follow the forms most suitable to the building's purpose. The structure that most clearly illustrated this principle was the skyscraper, with its clean-cut vertical lines, its use of steel and concrete, its many glass windows, and its relative freedom from ornamentation.

New York City, whose population density and expensive real estate made it more efficient to build upward than outward, witnessed a boom in skyscraper construction during the 1920s. Builders

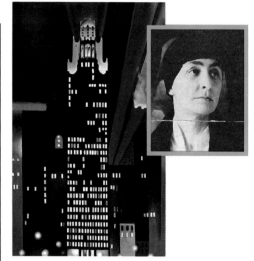

▲ Georgia O'Keeffe (inset) painted this scene, entitled *Radiator Building, Night, New York*, in 1927.

began construction of two landmarks—the Chrysler Building and the Empire State Building.

Civic boosters loved the skyscrapers, but critics had their doubts. A verse of the time protested:

> ❝ THE
> S K Y -
> SCRAPER
> T A L L
> I S A
> WONDER
> TO ALL
> A THING
> TOADMIRE
> BEYOND
> QUESTION
> Butoh!downbelowwherepedestriansgo
> itcertainlyaddstocongestion ❞

COMMENTARY

A Standardized Culture?

What were the social effects of the new mass media and mass marketing of the 1920s? Most historians agree that mass media and mass marketing helped produce a standardized middle-class culture. Movies, radio, advertising, and magazines like The Saturday Evening

RETEACH For each subsection in the section, have students write a sentence that summarizes the main idea. Select students to read their sentences aloud. Have the group choose the best summary sentence for each subsection.

Closure

Encourage students to create poems, songs, or posters that explain why the period from 1920 to 1929 might be called a creative era. Have volunteers present and explain their work. Students may wish to include their poems, songs, or posters in their portfolios.

Extension

ANALYZE Have students investigate and analyze the ways in which jazz influenced classical musicians such as Igor Stravinsky and Aaron Copland.

RESEARCH Encourage students to read further about one of the persons listed in the Preview Workshop and report on that person's contributions during the 1920s.

Post and Time reached every corner of the nation. These new forms of media promoted middle-class ways by presenting an ideal world of hardworking middle-class families. Mass marketing promoted standardization by persuading people to drive the same model cars and buy the same brands of food, soap, and appliances.

Historians recognize, however, that mass media and mass marketing also changed middle-class life. Many Americans—rich and poor, urban and rural—listened and danced to African American–influenced music and dance. Many middle-class women adopted forms of behavior previously associated with working-class women, such as wearing makeup and smoking.

The mass media also helped strengthen working-class, immigrant, and African American cultures. Musical recordings by African Americans, Mexican Americans, and others preserved traditional musical forms. Immigrant and working-class neighborhood movie theaters served as community meeting places. Some local radio stations devoted their programs exclusively to ethnic audiences, offering ethnic music and local news as well as news about the immigrants' homelands. Ethnic newspapers also helped preserve the immigrants' languages and ethnic identities.

While most middle-class families bought the same brands at chain stores, most working-class and immigrant families continued to buy from their local corner groceries. These local grocers, who usually shared the ethnicity of their patrons, extended credit to their customers. The grocers sold traditional ethnic ingredients such as Italian macaroni and Jewish kosher meats, which the chain stores rarely carried. These corner groceries thus allowed ethnic Americans to maintain traditional diets and served as places to swap news and gossip.

The mass media thus helped maintain ethnic cultures while they promoted middle-class values. And when middle-class Americans all over the country copied the style of life presented by the movies, network radio, and mass magazines, they were adopting ways influenced by different cultural perspectives. In short, the mass media and mass marketing supported traditional ways but also spread new ways of thinking and acting throughout the nation.

■■ **Mass media and advertising promoted new and standardized modes of behavior, but also helped sustain traditional cultures.**

SECTION 3 REVIEW

IDENTIFY and explain the significance of the following: Joseph "King" Oliver, Langston Hughes, Harlem Renaissance, Marian Anderson, Paul Robeson, Rose McClendon, Ernest Hemingway, Lost Generation, Diego Rivera, Alfred Stieglitz, planned obsolescence.

LOCATE and explain the importance of the following: Harlem.

1. **MAIN IDEA** In what ways did the artists of the Harlem Renaissance contribute to American culture?

2. **MAIN IDEA** Why were Ernest Hemingway and other young writers of the 1920s called "a lost generation"? Who coined this phrase?

3. **COMPARING** How was the work of José Clemente Orozco similar to that of Diego Rivera?

4. **WRITING TO EVALUATE** How did radio help people maintain long-held customs?

5. **ANALYZING** Why might black artists, writers of the Lost Generation, and Mexican muralists be considered social critics?

SECTION REVIEW ANSWERS

IDENTIFY

For significance, see the following pages:
Joseph "King" Oliver (p. 315)
Langston Hughes (p. 316)
Harlem Renaissance (p. 316)
Marian Anderson (p. 316)
Paul Robeson (p. 316)
Rose McClendon (p. 316)
Ernest Hemingway (p. 318)
Lost Generation (p. 318)
Diego Rivera (p. 319)
Alfred Stieglitz (p. 319)
planned obsolescence (p. 320)

LOCATE

For location, see the map on p. 317.

1. *through music—especially jazz—theater, art, and literature*
2. *because they were discouraged by World War I and disillusioned with middle-class values; Gertrude Stein*
3. *both glorified life of ordinary people and created public mural art that all could view*
4. *Radio reached a broader audience and presented a world of traditional, middle-class values. Some stations also reinforced ethnic customs by directing programs to ethnic audiences.*
5. *They spoke out against oppression, challenged middle-class values, and criticized capitalism.*

THE JAZZ AGE ■■ 321

321

Chapter Review Answers

WRITING A SUMMARY

See Essential Points in each section for main ideas.

REVIEWING CHRONOLOGY

2, 5, 1, 3, 4
Assessing Consequences
popularized sound in movies, resulting in emergence of actors with appealing voices; led to development of new film forms, such as musicals and newsreels

IDENTIFYING PEOPLE AND IDEAS

1. *technique that sped up product assembly*
2. *Frederick W. Taylor's method of breaking down jobs into smaller tasks so as to improve work efficiency*
3. *sociologist who chronicled life in Muncie, Indiana, in the book* Middletown *(1929)*
4. *Native American athlete who won pentathlon and decathlon in 1912 Olympics*
5. *first pilot to fly nonstop from New York to Paris*
6. *Protestant movement believing in literal truth of Bible*
7. *period of African American artistic flowering centered in New York City*
8. *African American theater actor and director*
9. *Mexican muralist whose work focused on workers' problems and on industrial development*
10. *making products that are designed to go out of style*

UNDERSTANDING MAIN IDEAS

1. *Middle-class Americans embraced new musical forms, new products, and new forms of behavior popularized by mass media and advertising.*
2. *disillusionment with World War I, superficiality of middle-class life and emptiness of life devoted merely to making money and winning social status*
3. *popular actresses, independence of working-class women, advertisements, and the automobile*
4. *With more leisure time and more money to spend, Americans sought new ways to entertain themselves, thus encouraging growth of the entertainment industry.*
5. *popularized music such as jazz and blues, and dances such as the Charleston; promoted black cultural pride in literature, theater, and other fields*

CHAPTER 12
Review

First radio stations go on the air.
Eubie Blake's *Shuffle Along* opens.
George Gershwin composes *Rhapsody in Blue.*

1920   1922   1924

WRITING A SUMMARY

Using the essential points of the chapter as a guide, write a summary of the chapter.

REVIEWING CHRONOLOGY

Number your paper 1 to 5. Study the time line above, and list the following events in the order in which they happened by writing the first next to 1, the second next to 2, and so on. Then complete the activity below.

1. Scopes trial held in Dayton, Tennessee.
2. Eubie Blake's *Shuffle Along* opens.
3. *The Jazz Singer* released.
4. Robert Lynd and Helen Lynd's *Middletown* issued.
5. George Gershwin composes *Rhapsody in Blue.*

Assessing Consequences How did *The Jazz Singer* influence the development of American entertainment?

IDENTIFYING PEOPLE AND IDEAS

Explain the historical significance of each of the following people or terms.

1. assembly line
2. scientific management
3. Helen Lynd
4. Jim Thorpe
5. Charles Lindbergh
6. Fundamentalism
7. Harlem Renaissance
8. Rose McClendon
9. Diego Rivera
10. planned obsolescence

UNDERSTANDING MAIN IDEAS

1. How was middle-class life in the 1920s changed by mass media and advertising?
2. What postwar problems did the Lost Generation deal with in their literature?
3. What influences led women to exercise new freedom in dress and behavior?
4. How did the prosperity of the 1920s influence American entertainment?
5. What contributions did African Americans make to the changing American culture of the 1920s?

REVIEWING THEMES

1. **Economic Development** How did advertising, merchandising, and installment buying help the nation's economy in the 1920s?
2. **Technology and Society** How did new technology affect Americans' lives at work and at home?
3. **Cultural Diversity** How did the Mexican muralists celebrate and criticize American culture?

THINKING CRITICALLY

1. **Analyzing** How did increased productivity and consumerism pave the way for future environmental problems?
2. **Synthesizing** Why might the Model T be an appropriate symbol for the 1920s?
3. **Evaluating** How did social changes contribute to the popularity of religious revivals?

STRATEGY FOR SUCCESS

Review the Skills Handbook entry on Taking a Test on page 762. Below is a sample multiple-choice question that might be asked about Chapter 12. Write a paragraph summarizing how you would arrive at the correct answer.

The aspect of industrial design that most increased sales was
   a. scientific management.
   b. advertising.
   c. planned obsolescence.
   d. streamlining.

Ford automobile plant, 1921

REVIEWING THEMES

1. fueled demand for more and new products, which stimulated production and employment
2. Assembly line, scientific management, and new products changed working conditions and types of jobs available to American workers; new appliances and automobiles allowed middle-class women to manage households without servants.
3. Murals glorified aspects of machine age and industry but protested against mistreatment of workers and Native Americans.

THINKING CRITICALLY

1. Increased factory production and automobile traffic began a chain of environmental pollution that has continued to the present.
2. represented changes in production methods and in use of postwar industrial materials; led to transformation of transportation system and of social structure, roles, and values
3. Modern concepts and behavior alarmed many conservatives; revivalists spoke to conservatives' fears and supported traditional values.

STRATEGY FOR SUCCESS

Correct answer is "c." Students should discuss how "a" and "b" can be quickly eliminated because they are not aspects of industrial design; "d" would not necessarily affect sales.

WRITING ABOUT HISTORY

Letters might mention that concerns about teaching evolution have forced the school to eliminate Darwin's theories from curriculum.

USING PRIMARY SOURCES

Paragraphs should consider how Paul Robeson's accomplishments inspired other African Americans to succeed.

LINKING HISTORY AND GEOGRAPHY

Answers might mention that the clustering of African Americans from different backgrounds encouraged the exchange of artistic ideas.

Scopes trial held in Dayton, Tennessee.

Gertrude Ederle breaks world record for swimming English Channel. Langston Hughes's *Weary Blues* published.

The Jazz Singer released. Charles Lindbergh completes first nonstop flight from New York to Paris.

Amelia Earhart crosses Atlantic Ocean by plane.

Ernest Hemingway's *A Farewell to Arms* published. Robert Lynd and Helen Lynd's *Middletown* issued.

1926   **1928**   **1930**

WRITING ABOUT HISTORY

Writing to Explain Imagine you are a high school principal at the time of the Scopes trial. Write a letter to parents, outlining the issues involved in the trial and explaining how the verdict will affect next year's science curriculum.

USING PRIMARY SOURCES

Harlem was the social, cultural, and entertainment capital for many African Americans during the 1920s. In the following excerpt, Howard "Stretch" Johnson talks about the black basketball teams popular in the 1920s and about the influence of Paul Robeson, one of the Harlem Renaissance's major figures. Write a paragraph explaining how Robeson influenced African Americans in the 1920s.

> 66 *The Renaissance Big Five basketball team was a part of [the Harlem Renaissance]....*
>
> *My father was a very fine professional basketball player. He played with a group called the Puritans, which later became the Renaissance Big Five....*
>
> *Paul Robeson played with Alpha fraternity against my father when my father was playing with St. Christopher's, another semipro team that was popular in the '20s. Paul was a great figure. People used to swarm around him when he walked out on the street. He was the inspiration in every walk of life. Those blacks who went in for law had respect for his being a Phi Beta Kappa at Columbia University. Those who aspired to be successful in the athletic field had him as an exemplar [model] with his record at Rutgers, where he got fifteen varsity letters—more varsity A's than any individual who ever went to Rutgers—in football, basketball, track, and baseball.* 99

LINKING HISTORY AND GEOGRAPHY

Refer to the map on page 317. What factors might explain the birth of the Harlem Renaissance during the 1920s?

Young women in Harlem

BUILDING YOUR PORTFOLIO

Complete the following projects independently or cooperatively.

1. **THE ECONOMY** In Chapter 11 you portrayed an unemployed veteran. Building on that experience, imagine you are a prosperous business owner in the 1920s. Create an advertisement for a new household product aimed at the expanding consumer market. Your ad might use psychology, slogans, jingles, or celebrity testimonials to sell your product.

2. **CULTURE AND SOCIETY** In Chapter 11 you portrayed an immigrant artist. Building on that experience, imagine you are an African American artist during the Harlem Renaissance. Create a dance, jazz poem, or painting that expresses cultural pride in your African American heritage.

BUILDING YOUR PORTFOLIO

Have students refer to **Building Your Portfolio Worksheet 3**, assigned at the beginning of Unit 3. Use the worksheet to help students monitor their progress on the portfolio projects.

*A*ssessment

Core Resources
- Reteaching Worksheet 12
- Chapter 12 Tests
- Alternative Assessment Forms

Test Generator

THE GREAT DEPRESSION

1929–1933

Chapter Overview

The excesses of the 1920s, the stock market crash of 1929, and a global economic downturn led to the greatest economic depression in U.S. history. During the Great Depression millions of Americans faced unemployment and hunger. President Herbert Hoover's attempts to deal with the devastation of the Great Depression failed. In 1932 voters elected Franklin Delano Roosevelt to the presidency with hopes that his promised New Deal would solve America's social and economic problems.

Chapter Planning Guide

CHAPTER 13	CORE RESOURCES	AUDIOVISUAL RESOURCES	PROGRAM RESOURCES
INTRODUCTION pp. 324–325	■ Literature Worksheet 13 ■ Building Your Portfolio Worksheet 3		
TEACHING THE CHAPTER pp. 326–345	■ Graphic Organizer 13 ■ Social Studies Skills Worksheet 13 ■ Geography Worksheet 13 ■ Outline Maps 1, 2, 9, 11	■ *The American Nation Videodisc: The Great Depression; Boulder Dam* ■ *Everyday Life in America Transparency and Worksheet 23*	■ *Eyewitnesses and Others*, Volume 2: Readings 41, 44, 47
REVIEW AND ASSESSMENT pp. 346–347	■ Chapter 13 Daily Quizzes ■ Reteaching Worksheet 13 ■ Chapter 13 Tests ■ Alternative Assessment Forms		■ Test Generator

Additional Resources

BOOKS FOR TEACHERS

Galbraith, John Kenneth. *The Great Crash of 1929.* Houghton Mifflin, 1988. Recounts the financial aspects of the crash.

Garraty, John A. *The Great Depression.* Harcourt Brace, 1986. Overview of causes and consequences of the depression.

Klingaman, William K. *Nineteen Twenty-Nine: The Year of the Great Crash.* HarperCollins, 1990. Account of the effects of the crash.

BOOKS FOR STUDENTS

Fausold, Martin L. *The Presidency of Herbert C. Hoover.* University Press of Kansas, 1985. Overview of Hoover's presidency and life.

Meltzer, Milton. *Brother, Can You Spare a Dime?* Facts on File, 1990. Discusses trauma of the depression.

* Schraff, Anne E. *The Great Depression and The New Deal.* Watts, 1990. Explores effects of crash and FDR's programs.

* for students reading below grade level

MULTIMEDIA MATERIALS

Brother Can You Spare a Dime? History in Action. Video, 20 min. Films for the Humanities/SSSS. Depicts causes and effects of the depression.

The Great Depression: Witness to History. Video, 15 min. Guidance Associates/SSSS. Chronicles effects of the depression on everyday life.

Roll of Thunder, Hear My Cry. Video, 115 min. SSSS. Portrays the struggle of southern black landowners during the Great Depression.

THEMES IN AMERICAN HISTORY

**USE WITH PAGES
324–325**

Listed on the right are

the themes emphasized in

Chapter 13. The questions in

boldface type stimulate critical

thinking and provide students

with an opportunity to discuss

the themes within a broadened

context. The questions also

appear in the pupil's edition

on p. 324.

■ ECONOMIC DEVELOPMENT

What factors might cause an economic depression? Students might mention factors such as: overproduction by industries, overuse of credit in place of money, ineffective government economic policies, inequities in the distribution of wealth.

■ GEOGRAPHIC DIVERSITY

How might an economic crisis affect people's choices of where to live? Students might cite that people in regions where there is a scarcity of jobs might move to regions where more jobs are available. For example, impoverished farmers might move into urban areas to find work, or laid-off industrial workers might seek employment in other cities. Job scarcity might also force families to separate.

■ CULTURAL DIVERSITY

How and why might various ethnic groups be affected differently by an economic depression? Students should note that members of some ethnic groups might be laid off before other workers. Because of prejudice and historic disparities in wealth, opportunity, and status, members of these groups might be more drastically affected by such unemployment.

CHAPTER STRATEGIES FOR MEETING INDIVIDUAL NEEDS

LIMITED ENGLISH PROFICIENT LEARNERS

Pair students and have pairs select an illustration from each section in the chapter. Have them write or recite new captions for their selections that explain the significance of the illustrations, tying each one to the section content.

TACTILE/KINESTHETIC LEARNERS

Ask students to choose a specific group of people who were upset with Hoover's policies during the Great Depression. Then have students act out a protest, using banners, signs, and other visuals that they themselves create.

LEARNERS HAVING DIFFICULTY

Have students work in pairs to write answers to the Focus questions in each section. Then have students use their answers to write a brief chapter summary.

AUDITORY LEARNERS

Call on students to assume the roles of persons listed in the chapter's Preview Workshops. Ask them to tell the class the contribution of each person during the depression years.

VISUAL LEARNERS

Have students create posters, charts, and maps that depict the effects of the Great Depression on everyday life in America.

GIFTED LEARNERS

Have students list and describe each of the policies Hoover instituted to deal with the depression. Ask each student to research one of these policies, evaluate its merits and failings, and report his or her findings to the class.

USING THE CHAPTER FOCUS

■ UNDERSTANDING THE MAIN IDEA

Call on a volunteer to read aloud the Understanding the Main Idea paragraph. Ask students to name ways in which a severe economic depression might affect people's lives. List their responses on a flip chart or a sheet of butcher paper. Have students evaluate their answers at the end of the chapter.

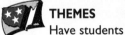 **THEMES**
Have students work individually or in small groups to answer the questions under Themes. Save students' responses so that they can compare them with their responses after studying the chapter. (See p. 323B for suggested answers.)

■ THE TIME LINE

Point out that placing high tariffs on goods coming into the country is one way a government might react to internal economic crises. Ask students what event on the time line signaled that the U.S. was facing economic difficulties in the late 1920s. Have students copy the time line and, as they read the chapter, annotate it with references to the nation's social and economic decline.

ABOUT THE ILLUSTRATION

As the depression hit, Mexican Americans, who were the nucleus of California's farm labor force, formed unions and went on strike against wage reductions. Among the largest was a strike of 18,000 cotton pickers in the San Joaquin Valley in October 1933. The sign in the photograph refers to Pixley, California, where two strikers were killed and several wounded when their union hall was riddled by rifle fire. Despite such violent opposition to their demands, the strikers won a 15-cent increase to 75 cents per 100 pounds of cotton picked. Ask students what "aid" the governor sent to Pixley and how they think the women on the truck might have felt about the governor's "aid."

Chapter 13

1929–1933

THE GREAT DEPRESSION

 FOCUS

UNDERSTANDING THE MAIN IDEA

In 1929 the stock market crashed, causing financial ruin for millions of Americans. The collapse of the stock market was one of several factors that gave rise to the Great Depression. When President Hoover's efforts to revive the economy failed, Americans elected a Democratic president, Franklin D. Roosevelt, to reverse the country's economic decline.

THEMES

■ **ECONOMIC DEVELOPMENT** What factors might cause an economic depression?

■ **GEOGRAPHIC DIVERSITY** How might an economic crisis affect people's choices of where to live?

■ **CULTURAL DIVERSITY** How and why might various ethnic groups be affected differently by an economic depression?

1929	1930	1931	1932
▼	▼	▼	▼
Stock market crashes.	Smoot-Hawley Tariff passed.	Scottsboro Boys case begins.	Franklin Roosevelt elected president.

LINK TO THE PAST

Suggest that a volunteer recall the causes and results of the economic boom of the 1920s. *(Probusiness economic policies of Harding and Coolidge led to a boom in certain industries, which resulted in more products being available and affordable to many Americans.)* Then tell students that in this chapter they will analyze how the attitudes and actions of people in the 1920s led to the Great Depression.

LINK TO THE PAST

The economic boom of the 1920s gave most Americans tremendous faith in the future. For many Americans, prosperity seemed limitless; however, the prosperity was unevenly distributed. The life-style of the Jazz Age also led to enormous debt.

HISTORICAL SIDELIGHTS

Money Pool

In a desperate attempt to save the stock market, six bankers from New York's largest banks met on the fateful Thursday afternoon of October 24, 1929. They formed a pool of $240 million—along with an additional $100 million from other financial firms—to buy stocks, hoping to reverse the panic selling. Although their actions did drive the market up briefly, their efforts failed. Later, they sold most of the stocks they bought, making a profit for themselves.

Mexican American women bound for picket line, 1933

Thursday, October 24, 1929, dawned windy and cool in New York City. Employees of the New York Stock Exchange buttoned their overcoats as they hurried down Wall Street to work. In the first few hours of stock trading, share prices fell sharply. At first, investors remained calm. The market had been shaky in recent weeks but had always resumed its upward trend. Today was different, though. As prices continued to fall, panic struck. Frantic orders to sell stock came pouring in.

All across America, grim-faced investors watched as stock tickers reported the alarming news. The plunge in prices was wiping out the life savings of millions of Americans who had invested in stocks. "One saw men looking defeat in the face," said an eyewitness. "[It was] the smash-up of the hopes of years."

The economic prosperity of the 1920s was over, and the worst economic depression in U.S. history had begun. Over the next several years the American people faced widespread unemployment and poverty. By the time of the 1932 election, they were desperate for a change.

Ticker tape machine

PREVIEW WORKSHOP

Following is a list of the significant terms in this section. You may wish to use this list as a section preview.

Terms
- bull market
- bear market
- margin buying
- Black Thursday

- Black Tuesday
- gross national product
- Great Depression
- Smoot-Hawley Tariff
- business cycle

MOTIVATING:
PRIOR KNOWLEDGE

Call on volunteers to list on the chalkboard warning signs that the U.S. economy was "sick" in the 1920s. Ask students why few people paid attention to these warning signs. Point out that this section explains why the 1929 stock market crash was a direct result of the excesses of the 1920s and analyzes the factors that gave rise to the Great Depression.

FOCUS OBJECTIVES

- Explain why many Americans invested in the stock market in the 1920s.

- Analyze the causes of the stock market crash of 1929.

- List the factors that gave rise to the Great Depression.

Section 1

PROSPERITY SHATTERED

FOCUS

- **Why did many Americans invest in the stock market in the 1920s?**
- **What caused the stock market crash of 1929?**
- **What factors gave rise to the Great Depression?**

Throughout the generally prosperous 1920s, isolated voices warned of problems with the American economy. Some people pointed to the farm crisis and to "sick" industries as problems in need of attention. Yet despite these warnings, most Americans believed that the economy would continue to thrive. Then came the stock market crash of 1929. Stock prices plunged, and investors lost billions of dollars. U.S. industries, already showing signs of weakness, almost ground to a halt.

Newspaper headline,
October 1929

"GET RICH QUICK"

Few Americans other than farmers and the poor worried about the nation's economic health in the late 1920s. Many Americans agreed with Herbert Hoover that the nation was "nearer to the final triumph over poverty than ever before in the history of any land."

This sense of confidence was reflected in the stock market. Stock sales had risen steadily for several years. As demand rose, so did stock prices. Many experts saw no end to the **bull market**—the upward trend in stock prices (as opposed to a **bear market**, or downward trend). Business leaders, such as General Motors executive John J. Raskob, urged Americans to invest, claiming that anyone who put $15 a month in the stock market for 20 years would end up with $80,000—a fortune at the time.

By the late 1920s, stock speculation—"playing" the market by buying and selling to make a quick profit—was widespread. Although speculation fueled economic growth, it also created problems. Rapid buying and selling inflated the prices of stocks to the point that many stocks were selling for more than they were really worth. This speculative buying was fine as long as demand was high, but if investor confidence weakened, prices would tumble.

The situation was made shakier still by **margin buying**—purchasing stocks with borrowed money. Many speculators put up as little as 10 percent of the price of a stock, borrowing the rest. Margin buying worked as long as the bull market continued. If prices fell, though, investors would find themselves deep in debt with no way to pay off their loans. It was a very risky venture.

Although consumer confidence in the market remained high throughout the summer of 1929, a few gloomy voices were heard. In early September, stock analyst Roger Babson wrote: "Sooner or later a crash is coming, and it may be terrific." Some shrewd investors saw the writing on the wall and began to sell their stocks, but most people remained confident in the market. As one eyewitness wrote: "Money is king—but there is something else. It is a high, wild time, a time of riotous spirits and belief in magic rather than cold calculation."

INVESTING IN THE MARKET

Invite students to assume the role of stockbrokers in the late 1920s. Have them work in groups to write brochures aimed at potential investors, explaining why this is a good time to invest. After groups present their brochures, ask class members which brochure would most encourage them to invest in the stock market and why.

CAUSES OF THE CRASH

Discuss with students the concept of scarcity and the relationship between the availability of an item and its value. Ask students to apply this concept to explain the effect that the great speculative demand for stocks had on share prices in the late 1920s. Then ask students to predict what might happen to share prices if a great number of shares were offered for sale over a short period of time. Have a volunteer explain how the practice of margin buying increased the supply of stocks for sale as prices started down, and the further effect this had on prices. Conclude by inviting students to write letters to friends in the role of 1920s stock speculators, explaining why they sold their stock during the crash of 1929. Ask students to read their letters to the class. Students may wish to include their letters in their portfolios.

■■ **Hoping to earn enormous profits from rising stock prices, many Americans invested in the stock market.**

THE STOCK MARKET CRASHES

The magic faltered on October 24, 1929—**Black Thursday**. Large investors, made nervous by various factors, including rising interest rates, suddenly began to sell their shares. The dumping of so much stock on the market jolted investor confidence and caused prices to plunge. Panic gripped Wall Street. A *New York Times* reporter described the crash:

❝ It came with a speed and ferocity that left men dazed. The bottom simply fell out of the market. . . . The streets were crammed with a mixed crowd—agonized little speculators, . . . sold-out traders, . . . inquisitive individuals and tourists seeking . . . a closer view of the national catastrophe. . . . Where was it going to end? ❞

Black Thursday was only the opening stage of a long downward spiral. Prices dropped still lower the following week, as more investors sold their stocks. On October 29—**Black Tuesday**—prices sank to a shocking new low as investors dumped over 16 million shares of stock on the market.

As prices plunged, brokers fired off frantic telegrams to the customers who owed them money. The brokers demanded cash to cover their loans. Unable to raise the funds, thousands of people were forced to sell their stocks at huge losses. Many investors were wiped out. By mid-November the average value of leading stocks had been cut in half, and stockholders had lost some $30 billion. By year's end stock losses exceeded the total cost of U.S. involvement in World War I.

■■ **Speculative buying drove stock prices above their real value. When large-scale selling occurred in October 1929, the market crashed.**

THE DEPRESSION BEGINS

In the first months after the stock market crash, business leaders and public officials insisted that the setback was minor and temporary. President Hoover declared: "We have now passed the worst and . . . shall rapidly recover." But optimistic statements could not conceal the grim truth. By late 1930 it was clear that a major economic depression was under way in the United States and throughout the rest of the world.

From late 1929 to 1933 the U.S. economy sank steadily. In 1929, the last boom year of the period, America's **gross national product**—the total value of all goods and services produced in a given year—reached $103 billion. In 1933, at the depth of the depression, it fell below $56 billion. Over that same period, average income for Americans fell by half. By 1932 the auto and steel industries were producing at just a small fraction of their capacity. Factories and mines stood idle. Railroad cars sat silent and empty. Many companies shut down, and millions of workers lost their jobs.

The banking industry was also hard hit by the

THE CRASH

Company	High Price Sept. 3, 1929	Low Price Nov. 13, 1929
American Telephone and Telegraph	304	197 ¼
General Electric	396 ¼	168 ⅛
General Motors	72 ¾	36
Montgomery Ward	137 ⅞	49 ¼
United States Steel	261 ¾	150
Woolworth	100 ⅜	52 ¼

Source: *Only Yesterday*

FROM RICHES TO RAGS In the days following the stock market crash on October 29, 1929, stock prices continued to fall. Average stock prices reached their lowest point for the year on November 13, 1929, slightly two months after they had reached the high point for the year on September 3.

❓ **BUILDING CHART SKILLS** Which company's stock lost the greatest number of points between September 3 and November 13, 1929?

Teaching the **Section**

THE DEPRESSION BEGINS

Begin a chart on the chalkboard under the heading *Conditions Contributing to the Great Depression.* Call on students to cite the factors that contributed to the Great Depression as you add them to the chart. *(crash of 1929, global economic downturn, debt, easy credit policies, high tariffs, the business cycle, unequal distribution of income)* Then call on volunteers to explain how each factor contributed to the Great Depression.

GLOBAL CONNECTIONS

The global depression left many national governments short of funds. By 1930 the Soviet Union was so short of money that government officials sold 21 paintings from its famous Hermitage Museum to American millionaire Andrew Mellon. The $7 million that the Soviets earned was desperately needed as unemployment grew there.

THE AMERICAN NATION VIDEODISC PROGRAM

The Great Depression

2A   25392   3:24

▲ Panicked by the 1929 stock market crash, many bank depositors stood in long lines to withdraw their money. This photograph was taken in New York City.

depression. After the stock market crash, many debt-ridden investors and businesses could not repay their loans, leaving banks with no incoming funds. Fearing bank failures, many depositors panicked and withdrew their savings. Under the combined weight of these factors, the banking system collapsed.

Between 1930 and 1932 more than 5,000 U.S. banks failed. Customers who went to their banks to withdraw savings often found the doors barred and their money gone. Because bank deposits were not insured, many people lost their life savings. The collapse of one big New York City bank in 1930 wiped out roughly $180 million in savings by some 400,000 depositors, including many poor immigrants.

WHAT CAUSED THE DEPRESSION?

The stock market crash of 1929 jolted the American economy and destroyed individual fortunes, but it alone did not cause the **Great Depression**, the deep economic downturn that gripped the United States between 1929 and the beginning of World War II. At the time, many observers, including President Hoover, blamed the depression on the state of the world economy following World War I. The global economy had suffered enormous setbacks because of the massive war debts incurred by European countries. But this, like the stock market crash, was only a contributing factor. Today economists and historians agree that the root causes of the Great Depression lay in numerous factors, including the American economic system itself.

The troubling twenties. Although the 1920s appeared to be a decade of unlimited

PRESIDENTIAL LIVES

HERBERT HOOVER
1874–1964

in office
1929–1933

As a young man Herbert Hoover was shy and awkward, but very hardworking. Born into a Quaker family in Iowa, he was left an orphan at age nine. He had few friends in college and would wander around with his eyes glued to the ground as if to avoid people. As one of his few friends noted, he had a habit of standing "with one foot thrust forward, jingling the keys in his trouser pocket," chuckling sometimes, but rarely laughing out loud. Even in the White House he remained self-conscious and shy.

After college Hoover rapidly built a career as a successful mining engineer and business consultant. By the age of 40 he was a millionaire. His role as coordinator of food relief during World War I also gave him a reputation as a kind and humanitarian leader. After his presidency he continued to work in public service and wrote many books and articles.

"There is little importance to men's lives," he wrote, "except the accomplishments they leave to posterity."

Practice

GUIDED PRACTICE

Ask students to choose the main events in Section 1. List these events on the chalkboard. Have students develop newspaper headlines, such as the one shown on p. 326, that could be used to describe each event, and write these headlines on the chalkboard. Work with students to develop a list of details that would appear in an article accompanying each headline.

INDEPENDENT PRACTICE

Direct each student to choose one of the headlines and the accompanying details developed in the Guided Practice. Have them write an article that might appear under the headline. Students may wish to include their newspaper articles in their portfolios.

Review and Assessment

REVIEW Have half the students write a letter to the editor in 1929, explaining why they invested in the stock market and how the crash affected them. Have the others write a business article on factors that led to the depression. Select students to read their work aloud. Then assign the Section 1 Review on p. 330.

ASSESS Assign the **Section 1 Daily Quiz** in *Core Resources.* ▶

The Global Depression

UNEMPLOYMENT The worldwide depression created record levels of unemployment.

? PLACE In 1932 which countries had unemployment rates exceeding 30 percent?

United States
America remains determined to collect the war debts despite the European countries' inability to pay them.

Japan
Except from 1930 to 1932, Japan's rate of industrial production continues to climb. Military spending helps fuel this expansion.

France
Unemployment remains low because foreign workers are sent home, and many factory workers return to family farms.

Germany and Italy
Government economic policies and centralized control help bring these countries out of the depression.

South America
Dependent on selling raw materials, Chile, Bolivia, and Peru see exports fall by more than 69 percent from 1928–29 to 1932–33.

USSR
The Communists organize agriculture and build up heavy industry in order to become economically self-sufficient.

23.6% 17.6% 30.8% 31.7% 30.1% 3.2% 2.9% 23.5% 15.4% 15.5% 13.1% 1.9% 22.5% 15.6% 11.0% 4.9% 20.5%* 7.2%

Percentage of Work Force Unemployed
1929   1932
*Figure for Italy is from 1931

Map Caption Answer
Germany, Denmark, Norway

MAKING CONNECTIONS

Sociology

In the late 1920s, installment credit was used to purchase three of every five cars as well as 80 percent of all radios. During the last half of the decade, outstanding installment indebtedness more than doubled—to $3 billion.

🌐 GLOBAL CONNECTIONS

The Smoot-Hawley Tariff raised duties by as much as 50 percent on foreign products entering the U.S. But this action did not alleviate economic conditions in the U.S., and it accelerated the spreading worldwide depression. After the crash Americans stopped investing in Europe, and the tariff severely cut the amount of goods that Europeans could sell in the U.S. Other countries subsequently passed high tariffs of their own, and all countries suffered as a result.

---

economic prosperity, many analysts place primary blame for the Great Depression on economic practices in the 1920s. These practices produced quick profits for some but in the long run contributed to economic chaos. Farm prices, for example, dropped in the 1920s. By the end of the decade, mining, textiles, construction, and other industries were also beginning to suffer.

Another disturbing trend was the widespread dependence on credit. In the late 1920s, the federal government encouraged borrowing by keeping interest rates low. The Republican administrations of the time reasoned that an easy-credit policy would promote business. Easy credit enabled consumers to buy goods when they did

not actually have the money to pay for them. This was not a problem when the economy was booming. Once the economy began to slow and the government raised interest rates, however, many consumers could not pay their debts. After the crash many businesses stopped extending credit altogether.

In 1931 one department store even tried to turn the "credit crunch" to its advantage. While inviting customers to shop and spend as much as they wanted to, it advertised that it would accept only cash. The store claimed to be protecting its patrons from falling into debt. This approach depended on the hope that consumers would keep spending in the face of a depression.

Closure

Have students, in small groups, review the causes of the Great Depression. Then have each group determine which of the causes it thinks was the biggest factor in precipitating the economic crisis. Ask volunteers from each group to explain their group's choice. Discuss each group's choice and reasoning with the rest of the class.

Extension

CREATE Invite students to create a diagram showing the business cycle. Have them write a paragraph explaining the normal business cycle and describing how the cycle differed during the Great Depression.

RESEARCH Suggest that students research and report on worldwide economic conditions in late 1930.

RETEACH Organize students into small groups. Tell each group to divide the section material, by subsections, among its members. Direct students to write questions about the main ideas presented in their assigned material. Have group members quiz one another with the questions.

SECTION REVIEW ANSWERS

IDENTIFY

For significance, see the following pages:
bull market (p. 326)
bear market (p. 326)
margin buying (p. 326)
Black Thursday (p. 327)
Black Tuesday (p. 327)
gross national product (p. 327)
Great Depression (p. 328)
Smoot-Hawley Tariff (p. 330)
business cycle (p. 330)

1. *belief that quick profits could be made by buying and selling stock while prices were rising*
2. *inflated stock prices above their real value*
3. *Nervousness and loss of confidence caused some investors to sell shares, driving down prices and confidence, which led to panic sales; prices plunged and the market crashed.*
4. *Essays might mention the stock market crash of 1929, declining farm prices, weakening of industries, global economic downturn, poor economic practices of the 1920s leading to excess consumer debt, unequal distribution of income, overproduction.*
5. *Answers might note that real wealth was in the hands of very few people. Many other Americans enjoyed "abundance" only because of easy credit that resulted in heavy indebtedness for large segments of the population.*

Unfortunately, by 1931 few debt-ridden consumers had the cash to make any purchases. The illusion of prosperity had prevented many from realizing that the benefits of the economic policies of the 1920s had been unevenly distributed.

A mismanaged economy. Economists cite the unequal distribution of income in America as another central cause of the Great Depression. Between 1923 and 1929 the disposable income of the wealthiest 1 percent of the nation increased by 63 percent while the income of the poorest 93 percent of the nation decreased by 4 percent. As writer Upton Sinclair noted: "The . . . depression is one of abundance, not of scarcity. . . . The cause of the trouble is that a small class has the wealth, while the rest have the debts."

This income gap meant that a large portion of the population did not have the buying power needed to boost the economy. According to many economists, if workers had received better wages for their labor and farmers better prices for their crops, the depression would have been less severe or perhaps could have been avoided.

Even the global factors that Hoover blamed for the depression could have been eased by more-farsighted U.S. policies. Economists point out that the United States contributed to the worldwide economic downturn by placing high tariffs on imported goods. Even after the crash, Congress continued to pass high tariffs, including the highest in U.S. history, the **Smoot-Hawley Tariff** of 1930.

The business cycle. Some economists argue that better fiscal planning in the 1920s could not have prevented the onset of the Great Depression. These economists view depressions as an inevitable part of the **business cycle**—the regular ups and downs of business in a free-enterprise economy. According to business-cycle theory, industries increase production and hire more workers during prosperous times so that eventually surpluses pile up. Industries then cut back on production and lay off workers, causing the start of a recession or a depression.

Events in the Great Depression support business-cycle theory in part. While a wave of new products fueled the economic growth of the 1920s, by the end of the decade fewer Americans were buying expensive goods. Most people who wanted such products, and could afford them, had already bought them. The inability to sell their goods caused many businesses to fail and contributed to the depression.

According to this theory, however, once the surplus goods are sold, industries again gear up for production and the depression comes to an end. But the *length* and *severity* of the Great Depression went far beyond the normal rhythms of the business cycle. Thus it seems impossible to blame the business cycle—or any one factor—for causing the most severe economic depression in U.S. history.

■■ **Many factors contributed to the Great Depression: the global economic downturn, debt, the unequal distribution of wealth, and overproduction.**

■■ **SECTION 1 REVIEW**

IDENTIFY and explain the significance of the following: bull market, bear market, margin buying, Black Thursday, Black Tuesday, gross national product, Great Depression, Smoot-Hawley Tariff, business cycle.

1. **MAIN IDEA** What drove many Americans to participate in the bull market of the 1920s?
2. **MAIN IDEA** How did speculation affect stock prices?
3. **IDENTIFYING CAUSE AND EFFECT** What caused the large-scale selling of stocks in October 1929? What effect did this have on the stock market?
4. **WRITING TO EXPLAIN** Write an essay outlining the factors that contributed to the Great Depression.
5. **ANALYZING** Considering the economic developments of the 1920s, how accurate was Upton Sinclair's statement that the depression was "one of abundance, not of scarcity"?

PREVIEW WORKSHOP

Following is a list of the significant
people and terms in this section.
You may wish to use this list as a
section preview.

People
■ Josefina Fierro de Bright
■ James Hilton
■ James T. Farrell
■ Nathanael West

■ William Faulkner

Terms
■ *mutualistas*
■ breadlines
■ shantytowns

Section 2

HARD TIMES

FOCUS

■ **How did unemployment affect Americans in the 1930s?**
■ **What were urban and rural living conditions like during the Great Depression?**
■ **What did Americans do for entertainment during the period?**

Unemployed worker, 1930

The Great Depression of the 1930s was not the first depression in American history, but it was by far the worst. It lasted for most of the decade, and during that time millions of Americans lost their jobs and sank into poverty. In cities and in rural areas, many people suffered from hunger, homelessness, and despair. Life was not all bleak during the depression, though. Movies, radio, and popular fiction helped lift American spirits.

"WORK IS WHAT I WANT"

Perhaps the clearest sign of the deepening depression was a sharp rise in unemployment. In 1929 some 1.5 million Americans were unemployed; three years later that figure had risen to some 12 million, as ailing and failed businesses laid off their employees. To poet Langston Hughes, it seemed "everybody in America was looking for work."

By 1932, industrial output had fallen to about half that of 1929, resulting in massive layoffs. Even for those who managed to keep their jobs, wages fell dramatically—in some cases to as low as 10 cents an hour. Factory workers' average annual income fell by nearly one third between 1929 and 1933. For the first time in years, immigration to the United States greatly decreased. One despondent Slavic immigrant told a reporter in 1932: "If you had told me, when I come to this country that now I live like this, I shot you dead."

African Americans faced especially difficult times, as economic troubles added to the problem of racial discrimination they already faced. When

factories laid off employees, black workers were often the first to go. In several cities as much as 25 to 40 percent of African Americans were out of work by 1933. One study of Chicago unemployment patterns noted the general view among whites that blacks "should not be hired as long as there are white men without work."

African American women, who made up the vast majority of domestic servants, also suffered

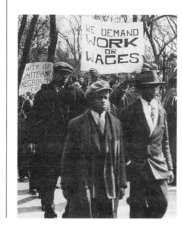

◀ Thousands of unemployed workers gathered before the White House on March 6, 1930, to protest for better unemployment policies.

FOCUS OBJECTIVES

■ Explain how unemployment affected Americans in the 1930s.

■ Describe the urban and rural living conditions during the Great Depression.

■ Identify what Americans did for entertainment during the period.

HISTORICAL SIDELIGHTS

Falling Incomes
Typical of the depression's effects on workers was that a New York subway conductor who earned more than $2,000 per year in 1930 was earning just over $1,200 two years later.

CORE RESOURCES
• **Literature Worksheet 13**
• **Section 2 Daily Quiz**

AV RESOURCES
• **Everyday Life in America Transparency** and **Worksheet 23**

MOTIVATING: STUDENT EXPERIENCES

Ask students how the unemployment rate affects a person's chances of getting a job. Then ask students to describe the psychological impact unemployment might have on a person. Tell them that in this section they will learn how the depression's high unemployment affected Americans.

Teaching the Section

AMERICANS OUT OF WORK

Organize the class into groups of five. Have each group develop a skit demonstrating the effects of unemployment during the Great Depression on a white male factory worker, a black female domestic worker, a white female worker, a black male factory worker, and an immigrant male worker. Have the groups perform their skits before the class.

LIFE IN THE CITY

Ask students to create editorial cartoons illustrating the plight of people living in cities during the Great Depression. Cartoons might focus on ways that people sought relief and on the conditions they faced. Ask volunteers to present and interpret their cartoons for the class. Students may wish to include their cartoons in their portfolios.

Map Caption Answer
South Dakota

PRIMARY SOURCE

Description of Change: excerpted
Rationale: excerpted to focus on main idea

HISTORICAL SIDELIGHTS

Selling Apples

In 1930 the International Apple Shippers Association, searching for a way to get rid of surplus apples, decided to sell the apples on credit to Americans without jobs. The jobless then became street vendors and tried to sell the apples for five cents each, hoping to earn an income. But by the end of 1930 there were about 6,000 apple vendors on the streets of New York.

HISTORICAL SIDELIGHTS

Racial Violence

As the depression worsened so did acts of violence against African Americans. Hilton Butler, a writer for the *New Republic,* reported that black firemen on the railroads in Mississippi were being shot because white workers wanted their jobs. He wrote: "Mississippi, in its own primitive way, had begun to deal with the unemployment problem. . . . Dead men not only tell no tales but create vacancies."

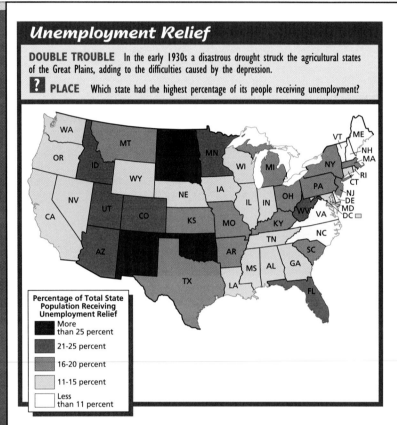

Unemployment Relief

DOUBLE TROUBLE In the early 1930s a disastrous drought struck the agricultural states of the Great Plains, adding to the difficulties caused by the depression.

? PLACE Which state had the highest percentage of its people receiving unemployment?

Percentage of Total State Population Receiving Unemployment Relief
- More than 25 percent
- 21-25 percent
- 16-20 percent
- 11-15 percent
- Less than 11 percent

because of increased competition in domestic and agricultural work.

Some unemployed workers took to selling apples on the street, where on a good day a seller might earn $1.15, causing President Hoover to claim, "Many people have left their jobs for the more profitable one of selling apples." But few people in the depression had any choice over how or where they worked. Some even hitchhiked or hopped freight trains across the country to find jobs.

■■ **During the depression one fourth of the work force lost their jobs. Many had to seek work wherever they could find it.**

massive unemployment. Without regular work, many had to participate in degrading "slave markets," where they would stand on street corners and try to obtain work as maids. One observer of the "Bronx Slave Market" described the typical scene:

❝ Rain or shine, cold or hot, you will find them there—Negro women, old and young—sometimes bedraggled, sometimes neatly dressed . . . waiting expectantly for Bronx housewives to buy their strength and energy for an hour. ❞

Since many employers could hire women more cheaply than men, the percentage of women in the work force actually increased in the 1930s. Most were employed as office workers or domestic servants. But as the percentage of women in the work force rose overall, the percentage of employed African American women actually fell

▲ In the 1930s many couples participated in dance marathons to win money. Some marathons would last for days, until all but one couple dropped from exhaustion.

*L*IFE IN THE CITY

The impact of the depression spread all across America, hitting people in cities and on farms and disrupting family life. Some of the most-lasting images of the period came from urban America, as the depression hit many cities hard. During the early 1930s the federal government did little to aid local communities.

City governments and charitable organizations such as the Red Cross took on the burden of providing direct relief to the needy. Neighbors, especially those in ethnic communities, also helped one another. One elderly African American woman told a visitor: "My neighbors helps me, by bringin' me a little to eat, when they knows I ain't got nothin' in the house to cook."

Mexican American communities formed ***mutualistas,*** or mutual-aid societies, to help local residents. Some Chinese American communities set out open barrels of

LIFE ON THE FARM

Have students work in pairs to write two 1933 newspaper editorials: one discussing the farm crisis, and one calling for help for tenant farmers in the South. Have volunteer pairs read their editorials to the class; then discuss ways in which the farmers were trying to cope with their problems.

▲ Shantytowns appeared outside many towns and cities during the early 1930s. Shown here is a Hooverville in New York City.

rice so that people could draw from them privately, without asking for handouts. Harlem residents organized "rent parties"—large social gatherings that charged a small admission to help pay someone's monthly rent.

Across the country, people struggled daily to feed themselves and their children. Haggard men and women waited in **breadlines** for bowls of watery soup and crusts of dry bread. When one hungry schoolchild was told to go home for lunch, she replied: "It won't do any good. . . . This is my sister's day to eat." By 1932 one out of every five children in New York City suffered from malnutrition. Some Americans suffered long-term health effects in the form of stunted growth, weak bones, and dental problems from these poor diets.

In addition to hunger, homelessness was a serious urban problem during the depression. **Shantytowns**—collections of makeshift shelters built out of packing boxes, scrap lumber, corrugated iron, and other thrown-away items—rose up outside most cities. Blaming an unresponsive president for their plight, the homeless mockingly referred to these shantytowns as Hoovervilles and the newspapers they often slept under as Hoover blankets.

▪▪ With little help from the federal government, urban communities struggled to provide for the hungry and homeless.

LIFE ON THE FARM

The depression also struck hard at rural America, as the farm crisis of the 1920s turned into a disaster in the 1930s. People in the cities needed food but could not pay for it. As demand for farm products shrank, prices plummeted, and farmers found themselves with more goods than they could sell. While people went hungry in the cities, farmers in some areas were forced to let crops rot in the fields and to slaughter excess livestock they could not afford to feed.

As their incomes fell, many farmers were unable to keep up their mortgage payments. While banks foreclosed on farms all across America, some communities banded together to fight back. Often when a bank held a foreclosure auction to sell off a family's possessions, neighbors would

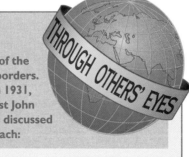

DEPRESSION WORLDWIDE

The depression of the 1930s knew no borders. In a radio talk in 1931, British economist John Maynard Keynes discussed its worldwide reach:

THROUGH OTHERS' EYES

❝*The slump in trade and employment and the business losses . . . are as bad as the worst which have ever occurred in the modern history of the world. No country is exempt. The privation [hardship] and—what is sometimes worse—the anxiety which exist today in millions of homes all over the world is extreme. In the three chief industrial countries of the world, Great Britain, Germany, and the United States, I estimate that probably 12 million industrial workers stand idle. But I am not sure that there is not even more human misery today in the great agricultural countries of the world—Canada, Australia, and South America, where millions of small farmers see themselves ruined by the fall in the prices of their products, so that their receipts after harvest bring them in much less than the crops have cost them to produce.* ❞

MAKING CONNECTIONS
Sociology

The 1920s trend of moving to urban centers reversed itself during the early years of the depression, when more people moved from city to farm than vice versa. Between 1930 and 1935, people left the cities to farm more than one million acres of previously uncultivated land.

HISTORICAL SIDELIGHTS
Riding the Rails
Between September 1931 and April 1932, the Southern Pacific Railroad reported that railroad workers had ejected nearly 417,000 transients—jobless people who had illegally traveled on its railroad cars while trying to find jobs across the country. Eventually Southern Pacific and other railroad companies stopped trying to keep the "hoboes" from hopping their freight trains. Although jumping on trains was very dangerous, sometimes whole families, including children, would illegally ride the trains as they traveled in search of work.

PRIMARY SOURCE
Description of Change: excerpted and bracketed
Rationale: excerpted to focus on main idea; bracketed to clarify meaning

Teaching the Section

MEXICAN AMERICANS AND THE DEPRESSION

Have students stage an organizational meeting of a branch of El Congreso. Call on volunteers to voice examples of discrimination against migrant workers in the Southwest. Then have students suggest actions that the organization might take to fight the discrimination. Have a volunteer list the organization's proposed actions on the chalkboard.

PRIMARY SOURCE

Description of Change: excerpted

Rationale: excerpted to focus on main idea

BIO GRAPHY PERSONALITIES IN HISTORY

El Congreso shifted its goals from militant activism to support of a united national front when the U.S. entered World War II. This change in focus led to the disbanding of the congress, but group leaders found themselves under federal investigation for ties to the Communist party in the years after the war. Anticipating that she would be arrested, Josefina Fierro de Bright left the United States to avoid incriminating friends and associates with her testimony.

arrive and bid absurdly low prices, such as 25 cents for a plow. After the auction they would then give the goods back to the farm family.

Conditions were especially bleak for tenant farmers in the South, where most rural residents already faced crippling poverty. As cotton prices fell from 16 cents per pound in 1929 to below 6 cents in 1931, many tenant farmers, mostly African Americans, were virtually ruined. Some were even forced off the land they had lived on all their lives. While farmers in the Midwest faced an overabundance of food, southern cotton farmers faced scarcity due to poor soil and lack of money to buy food. Gracie Turner, a sharecropper's wife, testified to the hardships of tenant life in the 1930s:

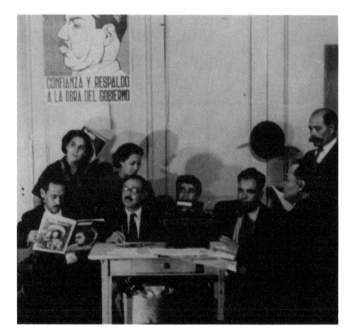

▲ Shown here is a meeting of the Spanish-speaking Congress in Los Angeles, about 1940. This group, known as El Congreso, helped organize Hispanic migrants to fight for their rights.

❝ That's all there is to expect—work hard and go hungry part time. . . . This year's been so hard we had to drop our burial insurance. . . . All it costs is twenty-five cents . . . but they don't come many twenty-five cents in this house. ❞

Migrant farm workers in the Southwest, most of them recent immigrants, also faced great difficulties. As relief costs soared, local authorities chose the cheaper policy of paying Mexican migrants to return to their native land. During the 1930s some 500,000 people of Mexican descent—some of them U.S. citizens—were pressured into leaving the states. Those who remained often faced severe discrimination and poor working conditions.

Some of the Mexican American families who stayed during the depression helped organize resistance to discrimination in the Southwest. One such organizer was Josefina Fierro de Bright, the daughter of migrants who had fled revolution in Mexico to settle in

California. The experience of growing up during the depression in the midst of poverty and ethnic discrimination had a profound effect on the young Fierro. As with many children of the depression, her life was very unstable. Her family had to move often, causing Fierro to change schools eight times. But throughout the hard times her mother always encouraged her to strive for success. "Rely on yourself, be independent," Mrs. Fierro advised. She also emphasized the importance of getting an education.

In 1938, at age 18, Josefina Fierro entered the University of California at Los Angeles. She planned to study medicine, but activism on behalf of the Mexican American community soon took up most of her time. With the aid of her husband, activist Hollywood screenwriter John Bright, she began to lead boycotts of companies that did business in Mexican American communities but did not hire Mexican American workers. Enlisting financial support from a few well-known movie stars, Fierro de Bright also started a radio program for Spanish-speaking audiences.

Josefina Fierro de Bright

FAMILY LIFE AND THE DEPRESSION

Tell students to imagine they are living in the 1930s and their families are suffering great hardship. Ask students to write a journal entry describing how the Great Depression has affected their lives and how they and family members are coping with their difficulties. Ask volunteers to read their journal entries to the class. Students may wish to include their journal entries in their portfolios.

These activities brought her to the attention of a Mexican American group called El Congreso, which was organizing Hispanic migrants to stand up for their rights. In 1939 El Congreso leaders asked Fierro de Bright to help them establish a branch in Los Angeles. Over the next few years, she worked tirelessly, leading marches and hunger strikes, lobbying for expanded relief programs for Hispanic Americans, and encouraging bilingual education for migrant children. "I used to work so hard it used to kill me," she recalled. But throughout her life she never forgot the lessons her mother instilled in her during those early years of the depression. Those memories spurred her efforts to improve the lives of all working people.

■■ **Rural farm workers faced increased hardship during the depression. Some were forced to leave their land.**

FAMILY LIFE IN THE 1930s

On farms and in cities, family members often pulled together and helped one another cope with their difficulties. They shared food and money and provided the support and encouragement their relatives needed to get through hard times. In many cases, relatives doubled up in small houses, and young adults moved back in with their parents.

Economic hardship took its toll on families, however. Some eventually broke apart under the strain. The divorce rate rose during the depression. Many young people put off getting married and starting their own families, which caused marriage

▼ Life was difficult for many families during the depression. Many mothers struggled to make ends meet, such as this wife of an Alabama factory worker who earned one dollar a day.

and birthrates to decline, especially during the early years of the depression. Looking back on those years, a Chicago schoolteacher remarked:

❝ Do you realize how many people in my generation are not married? . . . It wasn't that we didn't have a chance. I was going with someone when the Depression hit. We probably would have gotten married. . . . Suddenly he was laid off. It hit him like a ton of bricks. And he just disappeared. ❞

Life was certainly not easy for women during the depression. In the face of economic hardship, the mothers of hard-hit depression families often played roles of quiet heroism. The daily challenges of putting food on the table, using worn-out appliances, and making clothes and shoes last for one more year brought constant worry. As one woman remarked: "I figured every which way I could to make ends meet . . . but some of [those] ends just wouldn't meet. They just couldn't be stretched far enough to meet." In rural and small-town households, women revived old crafts such as soap making and bread making. Others took jobs outside the home to help support their families.

COMMENTARY

The Psychological Impact of the Depression

The Great Depression affected Americans in countless ways. Some of these effects—such as hunger and homelessness—were temporary for most people. When the depression ended, most Americans got back on their feet. Other effects, though, were longer lasting. In fact, the depression had a major long-term impact on the behavior and the outlook of the millions of Americans who struggled through hard times.

The term depression *could just as easily describe the mood of the country as well as the economy in the 1930s. More than 20,000 Americans committed suicide in 1932, a 28 percent increase over 1929. For middle-class and well-to-do Americans, many of whom had never*

PRIMARY SOURCE
Description of Change: excerpted
Rationale: excerpted to focus on main idea

MULTICULTURAL PERSPECTIVES

Estimates on the number of Mexican Americans repatriated during the 1930s vary from a quarter of a million to half a million. Approximately half of those repatriated were born in America. The treatment of Mexican Americans by U.S. officials in the 1930s increased Mexican American distrust of the U.S. government.

MAKING CONNECTIONS

Health

The effect of the depression on children was illustrated in the following report by the chief of the Children's Bureau, Department of Labor, which appeared in the *New York Times* on June 18, 1932: "A check-up of the [Chicago] city schools revealed today that 11,000 hungry children are being fed by teachers . . . [who themselves] are seriously handicapped by the failure of the Board of Education to pay them."

Teaching the Section

POPULAR CULTURE
IN THE 1930S

Have students work in groups to create an "Entertainment Section" for a newspaper of the 1930s that describes the forms of popular culture during the period. Suggest that they include critics' columns. Post the sections; then call on volunteers to list their choices for a week's entertainment on the chalkboard.

■■ Remind students that in the 1930s there were no televisions, computers, or video games. Ask them which entertainment options of the 1930s they would enjoy the most if they had to choose today. Have students explain their choices.

known poverty, the depression was a cruel blow. Many would never forget the shame they felt at being unemployed, losing their businesses or homes, and being unable to provide for their families. The attitude of an unemployed teacher in New Orleans was typical: "If with all the advantages I've had, I can't make a living, I'm just no good, I guess. I've given up ever amounting to anything. It's no use."

The depression had a devastating effect on the unemployed. Many men whose lives had been dominated by work did not know what to do without a job. They often spent their days just dawdling around the house or roaming the streets. The depression proved equally severe on working women who lost their jobs, especially those whose families depended on two incomes to survive. Many parents who could not support their families were consumed by guilt and self-doubt.

Even after the depression, the memories of those lean years remained vivid. Habits of scrimping and saving, of making every penny count, would stay with members of this generation for the rest of their lives. A strong desire for financial stability and material comforts shaped the outlook of many Americans who came of age during the depression.

▼ Bette Davis

▲ Greta Garbo

Likewise, strong women, such as Bette Davis, Greta Garbo, Mae West, and Marlene Dietrich, lit up the screen, reinforcing the theme of survival in a difficult world.

Meanwhile, upbeat musicals like *Gold Diggers of 1933,* featuring the song "We're in the Money," and comedies portraying the hilarious antics of comedians like the Marx Brothers proved very popular. Movie cartoons also brightened the 1930s, thanks to Walt Disney's Mickey Mouse and Donald Duck characters. Often, Disney cartoons were as popular with movie audiences as the feature films they preceded.

As the movie business flourished, radio also enjoyed its golden age. Radio was immensely popular because it offered free entertainment at home.

*P*OPULAR CULTURE IN THE THIRTIES

Even during hard times, Americans found ways to enjoy themselves. Many people took up inexpensive pastimes, such as reading and playing games at home. Movies and radio also offered a temporary release from economic worries.

The sound explosion. Movies were a big hit during the depression. Talking pictures, which had begun to replace silent films in the late 1920s, enthralled audiences, who flocked to the new movie theaters cropping up in nearly every town. Among the most popular movies of the early 1930s were gangster films, which portrayed tough guys fighting their way to the top against all odds.

▲ Hollywood musicals flourished during the depression. In order to take their minds off their troubles, audiences flocked to see upbeat films such as *Gold Diggers of 1933.*

Practice

GUIDED PRACTICE

Create a two-column chart on the chalkboard with the headings *Urban Life* and *Rural Life*. Call on volunteers to list the impact the depression had on people living in urban and rural communities and add their responses to the chart.

INDEPENDENT PRACTICE

Ask students to assume the role of an urban or rural dweller during the Great Depression. Have them use information from the chart in the Guided Practice activity to write a letter to President Hoover explaining why they need help dealing with the Great Depression. Students may wish to include their letters in their portfolios.

Review and Assessment

REVIEW Have students write a table of contents and an illustration list for a book titled *Hard Times*. Tell them the book should focus on the effects of unemployment, urban and rural living conditions, family life, and recreational activities during the Great Depression. Then assign the Section 2 Review on p. 338.

ASSESS Assign the **Section 2 Daily Quiz** in *Core Resources*. ▶

Then and Now — BASEBALL

By the 1930s baseball was the country's favorite sport and a symbol of American culture, just as it is today. But baseball in the 1930s was in some ways much different from the game we know now.

To be a baseball fan in the 1930s meant taking trips out to the ballpark. Without television to bring the game into people's homes, fans either listened to games on the radio or headed for their local baseball stadium to root for the home team. Games were held only in the daytime until 1930—the year the first night game was held in a major-league park.

Depression-era fans watched such players as home-run king Babe Ruth and pitcher Walter "Boom Boom" Beck. They cheered players who had higher batting averages and hit more home runs than today's players. The ballparks were often smaller than today's stadiums. And the day games favored batters because they could see the ball more clearly during the day than today's players can at night.

However, the biggest difference between baseball then and now was who could play the game. Professional baseball was still racially segregated in the 1930s. White owners maintained a so-called gentleman's agreement not to sign black players. So African Americans formed clubs and leagues of their own.

The Negro National League (NNL) fielded teams in the East such as the Newark Eagles and the New York Black Yankees. The Negro American League (NAL) covered the South and Midwest with clubs like the Kansas City Monarchs and the Chicago American Giants. Players included Hall of Fame pitcher Satchel Paige and William "Judy" Johnson. Turnouts at Paige's games could be as large as any in the majors.

Although they would not sign black players, white club owners rented their ballparks to black teams when white teams were on the road. In fact, it was under just such an arrangement that the Kansas City Monarchs pioneered a portable lighting system and held the first night games in a major-league park. The Monarchs' night games drew such good crowds that within a few years scores of other ballparks also installed lighting.

In the off-season, Satchel Paige and many other baseball players—both black and white—played in Mexico, Cuba, and other countries. Like most Americans in the 1930s, baseball players needed all the money they could earn—their salaries, especially in the black leagues, provided just enough to get by. Today's off-season training camps and million-dollar contracts were unheard of during the depression. Salaries, team rosters, ballparks, and media coverage are all very different today. But the most important element—the enjoyment the game brings—remains the same.

▲ Baseball increased in popularity during the 1930s thanks to the skills of players such as Babe Ruth and Lou Gehrig. This painting by Morris Kantor, *Baseball at Night*, depicts a game from 1934.

RETEACH Organize the class into small groups and assign each group a subsection. Direct each group to develop questions about the main ideas in its subsection. Then have each group exchange its questions with another group and work to answer the questions it receives.

Closure

Refer students to President Hoover's quotation on p. 332: "Many people have left their jobs for the more profitable one of selling apples." Ask students how this statement might reflect the economic conditions of the Great Depression and the attitude of the Hoover administration toward those conditions.

Extension

COMPARE Ask students to research and report on a previous economic depression (1784, 1837, 1893) and compare the similarities and differences between them.

RESEARCH Invite interested students to research the music of Woody Guthrie. Have them give an oral report (with recorded music) or write an essay explaining why Guthrie's songs were popular in the 1930s.

PRIMARY SOURCE
Description of Change: excerpted and bracketed
Rationale: excerpted to focus on main idea; bracketed to clarify meaning

SECTION REVIEW ANSWERS

IDENTIFY

For significance, see the following pages:
mutualistas (p. 332)
breadlines (p. 333)
shantytowns (p. 333)
Josefina Fierro de Bright (p. 334)
James Hilton (p. 338)
James T. Farrell (p. 338)
Nathanael West (p. 338)
William Faulkner (p. 338)

1. *Millions lost their jobs; wages and earnings dropped for others, especially African Americans, but employment of women rose.*
2. *Falling food prices caused surplus in Midwest, scarcity in South, hardship everywhere; drop in farm income led to foreclosures, evictions.*
3. *cities hit hard, received little federal aid; people formed mutual-aid societies, helped hungry with free food; homeless formed shantytowns*
4. *Outlines might mention movies, radio programs, and literature, giving examples in each area.*
5. *Although some pulled together for support, others broke apart as a result of divorce, loss of self-esteem, or suicide. Marriage and birth rates declined.*

During the 1930s the number of radio sets in the United States rose from some 12 million to about 28 million. The most popular programs allowed listeners to forget the hardships of reality. Like the voice of a comforting friend, the opening of a favorite program captured listeners:

> 66 Return with us now to those thrilling days of yesteryear . . . [sound of hoofbeats] . . . From out of the West comes a fiery horse with the speed of light, a cloud of dust, and a hearty 'Hi-yo Silver'—The Lone Ranger rides again! 99

Heroes such as the Lone Ranger, Little Orphan Annie, and the Shadow always triumphed over evil, offering a hopeful message to listeners.

Literature in the early 1930s. The public's desire for entertainment also gave rise to new forms of popular literature. Magazines and comic books offered cheap and accessible forms of entertainment, presenting fantastic heroes such as Superman and Tarzan. One of the best-selling magazines of the time, *Reader's Digest,* presented a selection of condensed articles from various magazines. For families on a limited budget, this "all-purpose" magazine seemed ideal.

Many of the most popular novels of the era also offered escapism. In James Hilton's *Lost Horizon* (1933), a weary traveler stumbles upon a peaceful, prosperous utopia hidden in the mountains of Tibet. The idea of discovering a perfect world appealed to many readers.

Not all fiction of the 1930s was escapist, however. James T. Farrell portrayed the grim

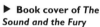
◄ **William Faulkner** used his experiences growing up in Oxford, Mississippi, to create the mythical Yoknapatawpha County—a setting that appeared frequently in his novels.

▶ **Book cover of *The Sound and the Fury***

life of Chicago's Irish immigrants in his *Studs Lonigan* trilogy (1932–1935), while Nathanael West presented the American dream as a nightmare in *Miss Lonelyhearts* (1933). William Faulkner, in novels such as *The Sound and the Fury* (1929) and *As I Lay Dying* (1930), tragically portrayed small-town life in fictional Yoknapatawpha County, Mississippi. Faulkner's novels later earned him the Nobel Prize for literature in 1949 and two Pulitzer prizes—one in 1955 and another in 1963.

■■ **During the 1930s Americans enjoyed many forms of popular culture, including movies, radio programs, and literature.**

SECTION 2 REVIEW

IDENTIFY and explain the significance of the following: *mutualistas*, breadlines, shantytowns, Josefina Fierro de Bright, James Hilton, James T. Farrell, Nathanael West, William Faulkner.

1. **MAIN IDEA** How did the depression affect the work force?
2. **MAIN IDEA** What impact did the Great Depression have on living conditions in rural areas?
3. **MAIN IDEA** How were urban communities affected by the Great Depression? In what ways did individuals and communities try to cope?
4. **WRITING TO DESCRIBE** Imagine you are a magazine editor researching a story on popular culture during the 1930s. Write an outline for an article that describes popular forms of entertainment during this period.
5. **EVALUATING** How did economic hardship alter family life in the 1930s?

Chapter 13

SECTION

3

Introducing the Section

PREVIEW WORKSHOP

Following is a list of the significant people and terms in this section. You may wish to use this list as a section preview.

People
■ Andrew Mellon
■ A. J. Muste
■ Franklin Delano Roosevelt
■ Eleanor Roosevelt

Terms
■ rugged individualism
■ Agricultural Marketing Act
■ Home Loan Bank Act
■ Reconstruction Finance Corporation
■ Bonus Army

Section 3

HOOVER FAILS

FOCUS

■ **What beliefs shaped President Hoover's response to the depression?**
■ **What effect did the Hoover administration's economic policies have on the depression?**
■ **Why did Hoover lose the election of 1932?**

*W**hen the depression began, many Americans had great faith in Herbert Hoover. His skills as a businessman and as an administrator inspired confidence. Under his direction the government undertook some important measures to fight the depression. But they were not enough to end the crisis. As a result, voters in the election of 1932 rejected Hoover in favor of his Democratic opponent, Franklin D. Roosevelt.*

Republican campaign button, 1932

HOOVER'S PHILOSOPHY

The most urgent task confronting President Hoover was to ease the human suffering caused by the depression. Prior to the crash most Americans believed that the government should not interfere in the free-enterprise system. Immediately after the crash, the *New York Times* advised that "the fundamental prescriptions for recovery [are] such homely things as savings . . . and hopeful waiting for the turn." Within a few months, however, the worsening crisis led to calls for the federal government to provide direct relief—food, clothing, shelter, and money—to the needy. Hoover rejected the idea of such government aid, stating:

❝ I do not believe that the power and duty of the [federal] Government ought to be extended to the relief of individual suffering. . . . The lesson should be constantly enforced that though the people support the Government the Government should not support the people. ❞

Direct federal relief, Hoover argued, would create a vast bureaucracy, inflate the federal budget, and undermine the self-respect of people receiving the aid. Instead, Hoover urged Americans to lift themselves up through hard work and strength of character.

Hoover's political beliefs stemmed from the notion of **rugged individualism**—the idea that

▼ **Unemployed workers protested in New York's Times Square in 1933. Demonstrators carried signs indicating they were willing to work for $1 a week.**

FOCUS OBJECTIVES

■ Describe the beliefs that shaped President Hoover's response to the depression.

■ Analyze the effect the Hoover administration's economic policies had on the depression.

■ Explain why Hoover lost the election of 1932.

PRIMARY SOURCE

Description of Change: excerpted and bracketed
Rationale: excerpted to focus on main idea; bracketed to clarify meaning

CORE RESOURCES

• **Social Studies Skills Worksheet 13**
• **Geography Worksheet 13**
• **Section 3 Daily Quiz**

AV RESOURCES

• *The American Nation* **Videodisc: Boulder Dam**

THE GREAT DEPRESSION ■ 339

MOTIVATING:
LINK TO TODAY

Point out that in 1992 President George Bush was faced with many of the same problems that President Herbert Hoover faced 60 years earlier. Point out that, in part, both men lost their reelection bids because of economic problems of their day.

Teaching the Section

HOOVER'S BELIEFS

Organize students into small groups to act as speechwriters for President Herbert Hoover. Have each group write a speech for the president, explaining his philosophy about the role of the federal government in ending the depression. Call on group representatives to present their speeches to the class.

▲ Private charities and organizations such as the Salvation Army helped families in need of assistance by bringing them food and clothing.

▼ Nurses, such as this one in Maryland, often went door-to-door offering people free medical assistance.

success comes through individual effort and private enterprise. He believed that private charities and local communities, not the federal government, could best provide for those in need. "A voluntary deed," said Hoover, "is infinitely more precious to our national ideals and spirit than a thousandfold poured from the Treasury."

Hoover was not alone in his beliefs. Millions of Americans agreed that voluntary efforts were preferable to government intervention. It soon became clear, however, that voluntary efforts alone could not deal with the scale of the depression. Communities and private charities lacked the resources to cope with the ever-rising tide of human misery. Local governments were forced to stretch already inadequate funds to cover growing numbers of needy families. By 1933, for example, families on public welfare in New York City were paid just $23 a month.

In 1930 Hoover appointed the Committee for Unemployment Relief to assist state and local relief efforts. The committee, however, did little beyond urging Americans to contribute more to charity. The human misery of the depression continued practically unchecked.

■■ **Hoover's belief in rugged individualism led him to oppose direct federal relief for those in need.**

*B*OOSTING THE ECONOMY

Although critics would later charge that Hoover's relief plans failed because he did not get the government involved, Hoover was not totally opposed to the government intervening in the economy. In fact, despite his opposition to direct public relief, Hoover's administration played a

▲ President Hoover addressed 250 leaders of finance, industry, and commerce in August 1932. In his speech, Hoover asked business leaders to assume more responsibility for improving the economy.

HOOVER'S POLICIES

Select several volunteers to take turns playing Herbert Hoover at a press conference. Have the rest of the class portray reporters, asking Hoover to explain the economic policies and measures he is taking to end the depression. List the policies and measures on the chalkboard. Then have students choose one policy or measure and write an editorial explaining why that policy or measure is having little effect on the depression. Students may wish to include their editorials in their portfolios.

---

more active role in attempting to shape the economy than any previous administration had.

Stimulating the economy. Within weeks of the stock market crash, Hoover called a White House conference of top business, labor, and political leaders. The *New York Times* hailed the meeting as a step in the right direction, noting:

66 [It is] the largest gathering of noted heads of industrial and other corporations in Washington since the resources of the nation were marshalled for participation in the World War! 99

Hoover urged these leaders to maintain employment and wages voluntarily as a step toward reviving business activity and promoting recovery. At the same time, he issued cheerful public statements designed to boost confidence and get the economy going again.

Unfortunately, most people did not share Hoover's optimism. Many became very cynical toward the administration as trust in government and in business declined. Moaned the chairman of the Republican National Committee: "Every time an administration official gives out an optimistic statement about business conditions, the market immediately drops."

At Hoover's request, Congress funded several public-works programs, among them the giant Hoover Dam on the Colorado River. Hoover expected these projects to achieve two goals: (1) to stimulate business by providing contracts for construction and materials and (2) to provide relief by

◀ Hoover Dam on the Colorado River was completed in 1936. It is the main source of hydroelectric power in the Southwest.

employing jobless workers. Overall, he approved some $800 million in public-works funding. Yet the crisis was so great that even this large amount had little impact on the depression.

Coping with the farm crisis. Hoover also took some steps to ease the plight of farmers. As crop prices fell, Hoover instructed the Federal Farm Board—created through the **Agricultural Marketing Act** of 1929—to buy up surplus wheat, corn, cotton, and other farm products. Officials believed that reducing crop supplies would cause prices to rise. The government could store these commodities and then sell them when prices were higher. The scheme did not work. Farmers at first refused to limit production. Instead, they reacted to low prices by growing more crops. In 1931 the Farm Board stopped buying surplus crops, having already spent some $180 million.

Just as he opposed direct relief for jobless factory workers, Hoover resisted giving direct aid to desperate farmers. He did try to aid farmers indirectly, though, by recommending passage of the **Home Loan Bank Act** in 1932. The act provided money to savings banks, building and loan associations, and insurance companies for low-interest mortgages. Hoover believed that the act would reduce foreclosures on homes and farms and thus allow more farmers to keep their land. He also believed that the act would encourage home construction, boosting employment and increasing the flow of money through the economy.

The Reconstruction Finance Corporation. Hoover also tried to stimulate the economy through the **Reconstruction Finance Corporation** (RFC), created by Congress in February 1932. The RFC lent large sums to railroads, insurance companies, banks, and other financial institutions. By strengthening these key businesses through federal loans, Hoover hoped to reduce bank failures and create more jobs.

By the end of Hoover's term, RFC loans had helped a number of large corporations avoid collapse. Yet the economy continued to decline, in part because the RFC offered too little, too late. It was created while the depression was in full swing, and it provided no direct aid to industries or

PRIMARY SOURCE
Description of Change: excerpted and bracketed
Rationale: excerpted to focus on main idea; bracketed to clarify meaning

HISTORICAL SIDELIGHTS

Building Hoover Dam
The hundreds of people who came to Las Vegas, Nevada, in 1930 to work on the construction of the nearby Hoover Dam often found conditions as bad as in the places from which they came. Just north of Las Vegas, tents and shacks housed hundreds of men, women, and children. When work started in April, the companies that were constructing the dam provided wooden barracks for about 480 single men. People with families, however, were responsible for their own housing until Boulder City, a permanent town, was built. Besides the danger of the actual construction work, workers faced the problem of the unbearable summer heat, which resulted in many heat-related deaths.

THE AMERICAN NATION VIDEODISC PROGRAM
Boulder Dam

1B   52402   :34

Teaching the Section

THE 1932 ELECTION

Have students work in pairs. Have one student assume the role of an interviewer and the other the role of a former Hoover supporter who is voting for FDR in the 1932 election. Ask student pairs to develop interviews in which the voter explains why he or she is voting for FDR. Call on volunteers to present their interviews to the class.

to small businesses, which continued to fail at an alarming rate.

Critics attacked the RFC's trickle-down approach to economic recovery. They argued that money lent to big business would not filter down quickly enough to help the real victims of the depression—ordinary citizens. As one economist put it, this was like putting fertilizer on the branches of a tree—rather than on the roots—to help the tree grow. A more effective approach, said critics, would be to funnel money directly to those in need. This would increase consumers' buying power and thereby stimulate business. Newspaper columnist Walter Lippmann reflected popular sentiments when he wrote:

> 66 It is hard for the country to realize that this era of easy finance is over. . . . In respect to government finance, as in respect to so many other things, Congress and the people of the country have radically to readjust their minds. 99

Government activism. Although President Hoover's policies failed to end the Great Depression, the RFC and other measures—such as the Home Loan Bank Act and funding for public works—represented a major shift in government policy. To a greater degree than ever before, the president and Congress accepted the idea that the federal government can and should do something to boost the economy in times of crisis.

In the early 1930s Treasury Secretary Andrew Mellon had advised the traditional do-nothing approach. He even argued that a short depression would be good for the country because "it will purge the rottenness out of the system." But as the depression became more severe, the government took unprecedented steps to promote recovery. Unfortunately, these measures were not sufficient to halt the downward trend. As Americans continued to suffer, they increasingly blamed their plight on Herbert Hoover.

▲ **Andrew Mellon**

■■ Hoover's limited measures to end the depression did little to ease the crisis.

*R*UMBLINGS OF DISCONTENT

By 1932 Hoover was the most hated man in America. His appearance in movie newsreels provoked boos and catcalls from audiences. And he made little effort to win public support by changing his aloof manner or stiff, boring speeches. "This is not a showman's job," Hoover remarked. "I will not step out of character."

As confidence in Hoover eroded, radical political parties grew more vocal. Both the Communist party and the Socialist party condemned the capitalist system that they believed created the depression. Both parties helped organize several mass protests in the early 1930s. Socialist leader A. J. Muste gathered the jobless into Unemployed Leagues to demand work. The Communist party encouraged labor-union activism and led strikes by migrant farm workers.

A Most Vicious Circle

▲ As the depression worsened, more and more people began to blame President Hoover for their troubles. This cartoon appeared June 1931 in the **Albany** *News*.

Call on students to identify specific groups who were unhappy about Hoover's handling of the depression. List these groups on the chalkboard. Then ask students to imagine themselves as a member of one of these groups and to write a letter to the Republican party, stating his or her frustration with the Hoover administration. Call on volunteers to read their letters to the class. Students may wish to include their letters in their portfolios.

▲ Shown here is lawyer Samuel Leibowitz (left) meeting with Heywood Patterson, one of the principal defendants in the Scottsboro case.

The party also helped expose racial injustice. In 1931 an all-white jury in Scottsboro, Alabama, sentenced eight of nine black youths aged 13 to 21 years to death on a highly questionable rape charge. The Communist party helped supply legal defense for the "Scottsboro Boys" and organized mass demonstrations to overturn the convictions.

Many desperate Americans responded to communist and socialist calls for direct action. Early in 1932, thousands of unemployed men demanding work participated in a hunger march on the Ford auto plant near Detroit. Four were killed when police opened fire. In Seattle, 5,000 unemployed protestors seized a public building. After two days local officials finally forced them out.

Some activism was spontaneous, reflecting the desperation of the times. In rural areas people armed with clubs, pitchforks, and shotguns confronted officials trying to foreclose on homes. Farmers destroyed crops and blocked roads to prevent food from being shipped to market, hoping that limiting food supplies would push prices up. "They say blockading the highway's illegal," an Iowa farmer said. "Seems to me there was a Tea Party in Boston that was illegal too."

The biggest protest was staged by more than 10,000 World War I veterans and their families in May 1932. They came to Washington, D.C., to support a veterans' bonus bill then before Congress. The bill would have granted the veterans—many of whom were unemployed—early payment of pension bonuses due to them for their service during the war. This group was soon dubbed the **Bonus Army**.

At first, officials allowed the Bonus Army demonstrators to live in empty government buildings and to camp in an open area across the Potomac River. When Congress rejected the bonus bill, most of the demonstrators returned home. But about 2,000 veterans stayed, defying orders to leave. In a clash with authorities, two veterans and two policemen were killed. The police requested aid, and President Hoover ordered the army to disperse the squatters.

In late July the army moved in with machine guns, tanks, and tear gas. One woman recalled her husband's experience that day:

66 My husband went to Washington. To march with . . . the bonus boys. He was a machine gunner in the war. He'd say them . . . Germans gassed him in Germany. And [then] his own government . . . gassed him and run him off the country up there with a water hose, half drowned him. 99

▲ More than 10,000 veterans marched to Washington, D.C., in May 1932 to petition Congress for full and immediate payment of pension bonuses earned during World War I.

HISTORICAL SIDELIGHTS
Protests
Encouraged by the Communist party, a group of 500 armed farmers in England, Arkansas, asked a Red Cross administrator for food. When told that there were no more food requisition blanks, the farmers invaded the town's stores. Alarmed, the merchants gave the farmers $900 worth of food.

PRIMARY SOURCE
Description of Change: excerpted and bracketed
Rationale: excerpted to focus on main idea; bracketed to clarify meaning

HISTORICAL SIDELIGHTS
The Scottsboro Boys
The convictions of the "Scottsboro Boys" were overturned twice by the Supreme Court—in 1932 because of inadequate legal representation, and again in 1935 because African Americans were excluded from Alabama juries. The state retried and reconvicted five of the defendants. The case was not finally settled until 1950, when four of the defendants were paroled and the last escaped to Michigan, where officials refused to return him to prison in Alabama.

Practice

GUIDED PRACTICE

Organize the class into the "delegates" at a Democratic platform committee meeting. Call on the "delegates" to list the failures of the Hoover administration and to develop a list of measures the Democratic party will undertake to overcome those failures.

INDEPENDENT PRACTICE

Have students create an editorial cartoon based on the list developed in the Guided Practice. Cartoons should either attack Hoover's failures or support Roosevelt. Students may want to include their cartoons in their portfolios.

Review and Assessment

REVIEW Have students use the section's Essential Points to write a paragraph telling why Hoover was not reelected in 1932. Then assign the Section 3 Review on p. 345.

ASSESS Assign the **Section 3 Daily Quiz** in *Core Resources.*

MULTICULTURAL PERSPECTIVES

In the 1932 election thousands of African Americans supported the Communist party, which had made a special effort to address issues of importance to blacks. One African American, Angelo Herndon, explained why he was attracted to the party, "This much hit me and stuck with me: that the workers could only get things by fighting for them, and that the Negro and the white workers had to stick together to get results. . . . I knew this was what I'd been looking for all my life."

HISTORICAL SIDELIGHTS

Roosevelt's Challenge
Franklin D. Roosevelt nearly died from his bout with polio. After exhaustive physical therapy, he was able to walk with the use of leg braces and a cane. Roosevelt seemed to become a more compassionate person because of his illness. He once said, "If you have spent two years in bed trying to wiggle your big toe, everything else seems easy."

PRIMARY SOURCE

(for source on p. 345)
Description of Change: excerpted
Rationale: excerpted to focus on main idea

Commanded by General Douglas MacArthur (later a hero in World War II), the troops drove the veterans from the buildings, broke up their encampment, and burned their shacks. Hundreds were injured and three killed, including an 11-week-old baby. Many Americans found the government's treatment of the veterans shocking. Across the nation, anger against Hoover grew. As the election of 1932 approached, Americans joked bitterly, "In Hoover we trusted and now we are busted."

▪▪ **Public unrest grew as the depression worsened and Hoover mishandled the Bonus Army protest.**

The ELECTION OF 1932

In the summer of 1932, with elections scheduled for the fall, the Republicans reluctantly renominated Herbert Hoover as their presidential candidate. With public sentiment running strongly against the Republicans, no other member of the party was eager for the nomination. The Democrats, sensing victory, chose Franklin Delano Roosevelt of New York as their candidate.

The Democratic challenger. Roosevelt—who often went by his initials, FDR—was a determined and skillful politician. Born into a wealthy and prestigious family, his background suggested that he would be more likely to identify with the wealthy than with working-class citizens. He could easily have become a Wall Street power broker, but instead he chose a career in public service.

FDR was highly influenced by the progressivism of his distant cousin, former president Theodore Roosevelt, and by that of the former president's niece Eleanor Roosevelt, who married FDR in 1905. Her earnest belief in social reform impressed the young FDR. Mrs. Roosevelt would become one of his most important political assets. A fellow Democrat once said of the relationship between Franklin and Eleanor Roosevelt: "Any good things he may have done during his political career are due to her and any mistakes he may have made are due to his not taking up the matter with his wife."

FDR ran as a vice-presidential candidate in 1920, but his political career appeared to be over when he was paralyzed from the waist down by polio in 1921. Yet with the help of his wife, he overcame his physical challenges and was elected governor of New York in 1928. As governor he gained high marks for his imaginative state relief programs that had instituted unemployment benefits and supported failing industries. In accepting his party's nomination for president, Roosevelt issued a call for a new style of government, declaring:

▼ Franklin D. Roosevelt's support of innovative relief programs while governor of New York made him a strong contender for the 1932 Democratic party presidential nomination (below). The photograph at right shows him campaigning in 1932.

Closure

Draw two columns on the chalkboard. Title one *Pros* and the other *Cons*. Call on students to list the pros and cons of government intervention in economic affairs during the depression. Ask students whether or not they would have supported government intervention and to defend their positions.

Extension

EVALUATE Have students locate and read Hoover's "Rugged Individualism" speech. Ask them to evaluate it from the viewpoint of an industry leader and from the viewpoint of a factory worker.

ANALYZE Suggest that students research the proposals of "Coxey's Army" in 1894. Ask students to analyze whether those proposals might have provided solutions for the Great Depression.

❝ Republican leaders not only have failed in material things, they have failed in national vision, because in disaster they have held out no hope. . . . I pledge you, I pledge myself, to a new deal for the American people. ❞

A change in leadership. The 1932 campaign had one key issue—the depression. While Hoover tried to defend his policies, he realized he had little chance of victory. Roosevelt continually attacked Hoover's record and called for major policy changes, including direct federal relief for the needy, a massive public-works program, and federal regulation of the stock market to prevent fraud. Roosevelt promised to seek a fairer distribution of wealth and to put the political and economic system at "the service of the people."

On election day, Roosevelt and his running mate, John Nance Garner of Texas, carried 42 states, capturing 23 million popular votes and 472 electoral votes to Hoover's 16 million popular votes and 59 electoral votes. The Democrats won decisive majorities in both houses of Congress, solidifying gains they had already made in the congressional election of 1930. As a result, Roosevelt was confident that his programs would have strong support in Congress.

In the 1920s most Americans had credited the Republicans for the era's glowing prosperity. In 1932, voters made it clear that the Republicans would have to take the blame for the depression.

▲ These Roosevelt campaign artifacts were used during the 1932 presidential election.

Many of those who voted for Roosevelt were really voting against Herbert Hoover. But other Americans saw in Roosevelt the kind of dynamic personality they believed could lead the country out of its troubles. Roosevelt had promised a "new deal." During the four months between Election Day and Roosevelt's inauguration on March 4, 1933, Americans waited hopefully to see how the new president would carry out his campaign pledge.

■ **Hoover lost the election of 1932 because voters were upset by the Republicans' handling of the depression and were inspired by Franklin Roosevelt's confidence.**

SECTION REVIEW ANSWERS

IDENTIFY
For significance, see the following pages:
rugged individualism (p. 339)
Agricultural Marketing Act (p. 341)
Home Loan Bank Act (p. 341)
Reconstruction Finance Corporation (p. 341)
Andrew Mellon (p. 342)
A. J. Muste (p. 342)
Bonus Army (p. 343)
Franklin Delano Roosevelt (p. 344)
Eleanor Roosevelt (p. 344)

1. *because he believed that voluntary efforts were preferable to government programs, which he believed would undermine self-respect and inflate the federal budget*
2. *asked Congress to fund some public-works programs, instructed Federal Farm Board to buy surplus farm products, recommended passage of Home Loan Bank Act, created RFC; such limited measures unable to ease huge crisis*
3. *worsening depression, Hoover's mishandling of Bonus Army protest*
4. *Posters might focus on length of depression and confidence in FDR's dynamic leadership.*
5. *The administration might have eased the depression by providing direct federal relief for the needy, and Hoover might have won the 1932 election.*

▪▪ SECTION 3 REVIEW

IDENTIFY and explain the significance of the following: rugged individualism, Agricultural Marketing Act, Home Loan Bank Act, Reconstruction Finance Corporation, Andrew Mellon, A. J. Muste, Bonus Army, Franklin Delano Roosevelt, Eleanor Roosevelt.

1. **MAIN IDEA** Why did President Hoover rely on local and voluntary efforts and oppose direct federal relief for those in need?
2. **MAIN IDEA** What measures did the Hoover administration support to end the depression? Why did they fail?
3. **MAIN IDEA** Why did public unrest grow during the Hoover administration?
4. **WRITING TO EXPRESS A VIEWPOINT** Imagine you are a campaign worker for Franklin Delano Roosevelt. Write a campaign poster explaining why voters should support your candidate in the 1932 election.
5. **HYPOTHESIZING** How might the events of the early 1930s have been different if the Hoover administration had supported direct federal relief?

Chapter Review Answers

WRITING A SUMMARY

See *Essential Points* in each section for main ideas.

REVIEWING CHRONOLOGY

1, 5, 3, 2, 4
Evaluating
The committee urged Americans to give more to charity, reflecting Hoover's belief that private, individual efforts, not the government, should help people in need.

IDENTIFYING PEOPLE AND IDEAS

1. *downward trend in stock prices*
2. *Treasury Secretary who advised the traditional do-nothing approach to depression*
3. *October 29, 1929, day when more than 16 million shares of stock were sold*
4. *mutual-aid societies formed by Mexican American communities to fight the depression*
5. *collections of makeshift shelters used by the homeless*
6. *activist who lobbied for expanded relief programs for Hispanic Americans*
7. *author who portrayed grim life of Chicago's Irish immigrants in* Studs Lonigan *trilogy*

8. *belief that success comes through individual effort and private enterprise*
9. *measure designed to aid farmers by providing money for low-interest mortgages*
10. *veterans who protested in Washington, demanding early payments of pension bonuses*

UNDERSTANDING MAIN IDEAS

1. *speculation for quick profits, ease of margin buying, and confidence in the bull market; speculative buying drove stock prices above their real value, causing large-scale selling, panic, and crash*
2. *Banking system collapsed as debt-ridden investors defaulted on loans, and panic drove depositors to withdraw their savings.*
3. *Economic hardship caused many families to break apart and many young people to put off getting married and starting their own families.*
4. *began limited public-works programs, bought farm surpluses, supported Home Loan Bank Act, created RFC*
5. *Some joined radical political parties, which became more vocal and helped organize mass protests; farmers blocked food shipments in rural areas; Bonus Army marched on Washington, D.C.*

CHAPTER 13
Review

Stock market crashes. William Faulkner's *The Sound and the Fury* published. Agricultural Marketing Act passed.

Smoot-Hawley Tariff passed. William Faulkner's *As I Lay Dying* published.

1929   **1930**

WRITING A SUMMARY

Using the essential points of the chapter as a guide, write a summary of the chapter.

REVIEWING CHRONOLOGY

Number your paper 1 to 5. Study the time line above, and list the following events in the order in which they happened by writing the first next to 1, the second next to 2, and so on. Then complete the activity below.

1. Stock market crashes.
2. Bonus Army marches on Washington, D.C.
3. Scottsboro Boys case begins.
4. James Hilton's *Lost Horizon* and Nathanael West's *Miss Lonelyhearts* published.
5. Smoot-Hawley Tariff passed.

Evaluating How did Hoover's appointment of the Committee for Unemployment Relief show his support for rugged individualism?

IDENTIFYING PEOPLE AND IDEAS

Explain the historical significance of each of the following people or terms.

1. bear market
2. Andrew Mellon
3. Black Tuesday
4. *mutualistas*
5. shantytowns
6. Josefina Fierro de Bright
7. James T. Farrell
8. rugged individualism
9. Home Loan Bank Act
10. Bonus Army

UNDERSTANDING MAIN IDEAS

1. What factors led Americans to invest in the stock market during the 1920s? Why did the stock market crash in 1929?
2. How did the depression affect the banking industry?
3. What effect did the depression have on family life in the 1930s?
4. What measures did President Hoover take to stimulate the economy?
5. What are some of the ways in which people expressed their discontent during the depression?

REVIEWING THEMES

1. **Economic Development** What factors caused the Great Depression?
2. **Geographic Diversity** How did the depression influence where people lived during the 1930s?
3. **Cultural Diversity** How were African Americans and Mexican Americans affected differently by the depression?

THINKING CRITICALLY

1. **Evaluating** How did the depression affect the behavior and outlook of Americans who struggled through those hard times?
2. **Analyzing** Why did Hoover oppose direct federal relief to the needy?
3. **Synthesizing** What major policy changes did Franklin Roosevelt propose during the 1932 presidential campaign?

STRATEGY FOR SUCCESS

Review the Skills Handbook entry on Distinguishing Fact from Opinion on page 750. Then read the following excerpt, in which the editor of the Johnstown *Tribune* warns the city of dangers to be expected from the arrival of the Bonus Army. What opinions does the editor have about the marchers? How might they differ from the opinions of one of the marchers?

> **❝** In any group of the size of the Bonus Army, made up of men gathered from all parts of the country, without discipline, without effective leadership in a crisis, . . . there is certain to be a mixture of undesirables—thieves, plug-uglies [thugs], degenerates. . . . The community must protect itself from the criminal fringe of the invaders. **❞**

WRITING ABOUT HISTORY

Writing to Create Write a poem or lyrics for a song that would reflect the mood of Americans struggling with the depression.

1. *1929 stock market crash, downturn in global economy, poor economic practices of 1920s, decline in farm prices, weakening of major industries, overuse of credit, unequal distribution of income, and overproduction*
2. *Unemployed people moved across country to find jobs; relatives doubled up in small houses; young adults moved back in with their parents.*
3. *African American workers were typically the first to be laid off, black domestic servants lost jobs because of increased competition from white women, many Mexican American agricultural workers in the Southwest were forced to repatriate.*

THINKING CRITICALLY

1. *Many would never forget the shame of unemployment, of losing their businesses or homes, or of being unable to provide for families. A strong desire for financial security and material comforts shaped the outlook of many.*
2. *He thought it would create a vast bureaucracy, inflate federal budget, and undermine self-respect of people receiving aid.*
3. *direct federal relief for the needy, a massive public-works program, federal regulation of stock market to prevent fraud, and a fairer distribution of wealth*

STRATEGY FOR SUCCESS

that the group has no discipline or leadership, that it poses a danger, that it includes criminal elements; marchers might view their group as heroic veterans, marching for a just cause

WRITING ABOUT HISTORY

Poems or songs might recall more prosperous times past, mention despair over present hardships, or express attitudes about the future.

USING PRIMARY SOURCES

a warning that from the ranks of the unemployed a violent revolution could come

LINKING HISTORY AND GEOGRAPHY

Delaware, Maine, New Hampshire, North Carolina, Vermont, Virginia; factors might include differences among the states in their basic industries and economic activities, and the movement of people into or out of the state in search of employment

Herbert Hoover appoints Committee for Unemployment Relief. Scottsboro Boys case begins.	Home Loan Bank Act passed. RFC created. Bonus Army marches on Washington, D.C. Franklin Roosevelt elected president.	James Hilton's *Lost Horizon* and Nathanael West's *Miss Lonelyhearts* published.
1931	**1932**	**1933**

USING PRIMARY SOURCES

As the depression continued into the winter of 1932, the growing numbers of unemployed forced to seek relief in soup kitchens became a familiar sight. In her poem "Bread Line," which was published in January 1932, Florence Converse attempted to make sense of this tragedy. Read the following excerpt from the poem. What point is the poet trying to make?

> *What's the meaning of this queue,*
> *Tailing down the avenue,*
> *Full of eyes that will not meet*
> *The other eyes that throng the street—*
> *The questing eyes, the curious eyes,*
> *Scornful, popping with surprise*
> *To see a living line of men*
> *As long as round the block, and then*
> *As long again? . . .*
>
> .   .   .   .
>
> *What's the meaning in these faces*
> *Modern industry displaces,*
> *Emptying the factory*
> *To set the men so tidily*
> *Along the pavement in a row?*
> *Now and then they take a slow*
> *Shuffling step, straight ahead,*
> *As if a dead march said:*
> *"Beware! I'm not dead."*
>
> .   .   .   .

Breadline

> *A spark can creep, a spark can run;*
> *Suddenly a spark can wink*
> *And send us down destruction's brink.*
>
> .   .   .   .
>
> *What if our slow-match have caught*
> *Fire from a burning thought?*
> *What if we should be destroyed*
> *By our patient unemployed?* **"**

LINKING HISTORY AND GEOGRAPHY

Refer to the map on page 332. Which states had the smallest percentage of people receiving unemployment benefits? What factors might account for variations in the number of people receiving unemployment assistance?

 BUILDING YOUR PORTFOLIO

Complete the following projects independently or cooperatively.

1. **THE ECONOMY** In chapters 11 and 12 you dealt with the postwar economic downswing and the upswing of the 1920s. Building on that experience, imagine you are a cartoonist in 1929. Create an editorial cartoon that criticizes the investment practices that led to the stock market crash.

2. **GLOBAL RELATIONS** Imagine you are a journalist in the 1930s at the height of the Great Depression. Create a series of newspaper headlines that describe the effects of the depression both in the United States and around the world. Headlines might mention stories about individual families, homelessness and food shortages, unemployment, Hoover's political problems, or international trade issues.

 BUILDING YOUR PORTFOLIO

Have students refer to **Building Your Portfolio Worksheet 3**, assigned at the beginning of Unit 3. Use the worksheet to help students monitor their progress on the portfolio projects.

Assessment

Core Resources
- Reteaching Worksheet 13
- Chapter 13 Tests
- Alternative Assessment Forms
Test Generator

THE NEW DEAL

1933–1940

Chapter Overview

When FDR became president in 1933, he attacked the depression with a series of bold new government programs collectively known as the New Deal. Laws were designed to restart the economy through relief, recovery, and reform programs. Projects targeted jobless and needy Americans from urban factory workers to rural farmers. Even the arts benefited from government programs that provided work. Criticism of New Deal programs came from both the left and right. African Americans and other ethnic groups benefited from New Deal programs but faced continued discrimination.

THE AMERICAN NATION VIDEODISC PROGRAM
A variety of still images, short videos, and activities are available for you to use as you teach this chapter. See Videodisc Resources in the Core Resources Binder for barcode correlations and suggestions for using the program.

Chapter Planning Guide

CHAPTER 14	CORE RESOURCES	AUDIOVISUAL RESOURCES	PROGRAM RESOURCES
INTRODUCTION pp. 348–349	■ Building Your Portfolio Worksheet 3	■ Everyday Life in America Transparency and Worksheet 24	■ *Eyewitnesses and Others,* Volume 2: Reading 49
TEACHING THE CHAPTER pp. 350–375 ■ For expanded coverage of pp. 367/370, see Chapter 27, pp. 727–728.	■ Graphic Organizer 14 ■ Social Studies Skills Worksheet 14 ■ Literature Worksheet 14 ■ Geography Worksheet 14 ■ Outline Map 9	■ *The American Nation* Videodisc: Serving the Nation; Marian Anderson	■ Art in American History Transparencies and Worksheets 23, 29, 30, 31, 32, 33 ■ *Eyewitnesses and Others,* Volume 2: Readings 40, 45, 47, 48
REVIEW AND ASSESSMENT pp. 376–377	■ Chapter 14 Daily Quizzes ■ Reteaching Worksheet 14 ■ Chapter 14 Tests ■ Alternative Assessment Forms		■ Test Generator

Additional Resources

BOOKS FOR TEACHERS

Leuchtenburg, William E. *Franklin D. Roosevelt and the New Deal.* Harper-Collins, 1963. A noted historian's scholarly treatment of the years 1932–1940.

Reiman, Richard A. *The New Deal & American Youth: Ideas & Ideals in a Depression Decade.* University of Georgia Press, 1992. Examines role of youth in New Deal.

Rosenbaum, Herbert D., and Elizabeth Bartelme, eds. *Franklin D. Roosevelt: The Man, the Myth, the Era, 1882–1945.* Greenwood, 1987. Biography of FDR.

BOOKS FOR STUDENTS

Allen, Frederick L. *Since Yesterday.* HarperCollins, 1986. Reissue of a classic political and social history of the 1930s.

Daniel, Pete, et al. *Official Images: New Deal Photography.* Smithsonian, 1987. Dramatic images of New Deal photographs accompanied by essays analyzing propaganda techniques used by federal agencies.

*Freedman, Russell. *Franklin Delano Roosevelt.* Houghton Mifflin, 1992. An award-winning biography of FDR by a distinguished writer of nonfiction for young adults.

* for students reading below grade level

MULTIMEDIA MATERIALS

Franklin D. Roosevelt: The Speeches Collection. Video, 40 min. MPI Home Video/SSSS. Includes a speech to CCC workers and a teacher's guide on Roosevelt.

The Great Depression. Video, 31 min. Guidance Associates/SSSS. Traces the depression from 1929 to 1939 and shows how the New Deal changed the power and scope of the federal government.

You May Call Her Madam Secretary. Video, 57 min. Vineyard Video Productions/SSSS. Documents the life of Frances Perkins, the first woman cabinet member.

THEMES IN AMERICAN HISTORY

USE WITH PAGES 348–349

Listed on the right are the themes emphasized in Chapter 14. The questions in boldface type stimulate critical thinking and provide students with an opportunity to discuss the themes within a broadened context. The questions also appear in the pupil's edition on p. 348.

■ ECONOMIC DEVELOPMENT

How can the federal government aid economic recovery? Students might suggest that the federal government could establish programs that encourage businesses to expand and hire workers, provide direct relief to the needy, and sponsor public-works and other projects to employ people.

■ CONSTITUTIONAL HERITAGE

Why might government interference in the economy be considered unconstitutional? Students might recall that the powers enumerated in the Constitution give the federal government little direct control over private businesses unless those businesses are involved in interstate commerce. The federal government might exceed such limits in laws or policies that impact local economic activity.

■ CULTURAL DIVERSITY

What role might the arts play in reflecting ethnic and cultural diversity? Students might mention that novels and plays may reflect the thoughts and experiences of different ethnic groups; paintings might portray scenes of ethnic life; and music may reflect the diversity of traditions within various regions and culture groups.

CHAPTER STRATEGIES FOR MEETING INDIVIDUAL NEEDS

LIMITED ENGLISH PROFICIENT LEARNERS

Organize students into eight groups to create news headlines for the years 1933–1940. Assign each group a different year. Have groups review the chapter to find at least two events that took place during their assigned year. Students should write their headlines on poster paper and create a New Deal collage or bulletin board.

TACTILE/KINESTHETIC LEARNERS

Have students work in groups to prepare skits showing the way the New Deal changed the life of a jobless banker, unemployed factory worker, or artist.

LEARNERS HAVING DIFFICULTY

Organize students into groups to create an "Alphabet Soup" directory of New Deal programs, listing them in alphabetical order with two or three sentences explaining each program's purpose.

AUDITORY LEARNERS

Direct students to interview people who lived during the 1930s to determine their opinions of Roosevelt and New Deal programs. Students might prepare audiotapes of their interviews.

VISUAL LEARNERS

Ask students to imagine they are artists employed by the Federal Arts Project. Have them design a symbol or a poster for a New Deal program.

GIFTED LEARNERS

Have students research and write an essay explaining how FDR's New Deal changed forever the role of government in American life.

USING THE CHAPTER FOCUS

■ **UNDERSTANDING THE MAIN IDEA**

Call on a volunteer to read aloud the Understanding the Main Idea paragraph. Then ask students to draw on what they have learned about the early depression years to speculate on the problems the New Deal would try to solve.

 THEMES Have students work individually or in small groups to answer the questions under Themes. Save students' responses so that they can compare them with their responses after studying the chapter. (See p. 347B for suggested answers.)

■ **THE TIME LINE**

Direct students' attention to the entries for 1939 and 1940. Ask students who have read the books noted, or other books of the 1930s, to discuss major themes and approaches of literature of the time.

CORE RESOURCES

• **Graphic Organizer 14**
• **Social Studies Skills Worksheet 14**
• **Outline Map 9**
• **Building Your Portfolio Worksheet 3**

AV RESOURCES

• **Everyday Life in America Transparency and Worksheet 24**

ABOUT THE ILLUSTRATION

Murals in public buildings, such as this one from a post office, became quite common during the New Deal era. As the government sponsored the construction of new public buildings, it also employed artists to paint murals on them. The program not only provided artists with jobs, but it also helped expose their work to audiences throughout the country. Have students draw sketches for a mural to be painted on a wall in their school. Suggest that their sketches reflect a message about some aspect of their daily lives.

Chapter 14

1933–1940

THE NEW DEAL

 FOCUS

UNDERSTANDING THE MAIN IDEA

To help the nation recover from the Great Depression of the 1930s, President Franklin Roosevelt created a series of programs known as the New Deal. These reforms improved the economy and expanded the role of government in economic life. The government provided jobs to thousands of unemployed workers and provided direct relief to the needy.

THEMES

■ **ECONOMIC DEVELOP-MENT** How can the federal government aid economic recovery?

■ **CONSTITUTIONAL HERITAGE** Why might government interference in the economy be considered unconstitutional?

■ **CULTURAL DIVERSITY** What role might the arts play in reflecting ethnic and cultural diversity?

1933	1935	1936	1937	1939	1940
New Deal launched.	CIO organized.	*Gone with the Wind* published.	GM strike begins.	*The Grapes of Wrath* published.	*Native Son* published.

LINK TO THE PAST

Have students give examples of ways the Hoover administration attempted to deal with the Great Depression and write their responses on the chalkboard. *(called on volunteer organizations, local governments to provide assistance to the needy; urged creation of Reconstruction Finance Corporation and* *passage of Home Loan Bank Act)* Then explain why Hoover's approach was described as "very cautious" and ask students to speculate how government might take a more active role in shaping the economy.

LINK TO THE PAST

The prosperous economic times of the 1920s had come to a devastating end with the stock market crash of 1929 and the Great Depression. President Hoover's administration had been very cautious in dealing with the economic crisis. By electing Franklin Roosevelt in 1932, the nation appeared ready for the federal government to take a more active role in shaping the economy.

HISTORICAL SIDELIGHTS

FDR's Inaugural

Franklin Delano Roosevelt was the last president required to wait four months to take office after being elected. By 1933 the day had long passed when transportation networks and winter travel were obstacles to a new president reaching the capital. So the Constitution's Twentieth Amendment, adopted in 1933, stipulated that the president's term in office should begin and end on January 20 instead of on March 4.

PRIMARY SOURCE

Description of Change: excerpted
Rationale: excerpted to focus on main idea

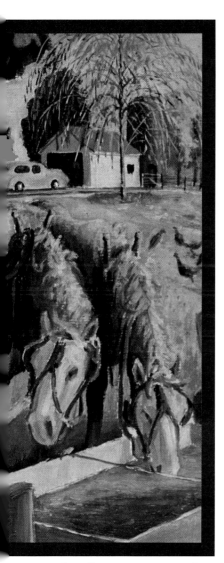

By 1933, Americans had endured three years of economic depression—each year more desperate than the last. On his last day in office, President Hoover was heard to sigh, "We are at the end of our string. There is nothing more we can do." But the new president, Franklin Delano Roosevelt, did not share this despair. In his inaugural address he offered the American people hope:

> 66 First of all let me assert my firm belief that the only thing we have to fear is fear itself—nameless, unreasoning, unjustified terror which paralyzes needed efforts to convert retreat into advance. . . . This Nation asks for action, and action now. 99

Roosevelt's words rang out across the land, lifting Americans from despair and stirring their hopes. Some half a million letters in support of the new president poured into the White House.

Roosevelt's program had three general aims: *relief,* to ease the plight of citizens in economic distress; *recovery,* to restore the economy to health; and *reform,* to correct ills and injustices in American society. Despite much confusion, inefficiency, and political conflict, Roosevelt's measures proved enormously powerful and far-reaching. They restored public hope, aided the unemployed, and gave the government a central role in regulating business and the economy and promoting public welfare.

Post office mural, *Evening on the Farm,* by Orr C. Fisher

National Recovery Administration symbol

FOCUS OBJECTIVES

- Identify the New Deal programs that tackled the banking, farm, and home owners' crises.

- Describe how the New Deal provided relief for the unemployed.

- Explain the effect the New Deal had on the Tennessee Valley region.

PREVIEW WORKSHOP

Following is a list of the significant people, places, and terms in this section. You may wish to use this list as a section preview.

People
- Frances Perkins
- Harry L. Hopkins

Places
- Tennessee River Valley

Terms
- New Deal
- bank holiday
- Emergency Banking Act
- Federal Deposit Insurance Corporation
- Farm Credit Administration
- Home Owners Loan Corporation
- Federal Emergency Relief Administration
- Civil Works Administration
- Civilian Conservation Corps
- National Industrial Recovery Act
- Public Works Administration
- National Recovery Administration
- Agricultural Adjustment Act
- subsidies
- Southern Tenant Farmers' Union
- Tennessee Valley Authority

Section 1

RESTORING HOPE

F O C U S

- **What New Deal programs tackled the banking, farm, and home owners' crises?**
- **How did the New Deal provide relief for the unemployed?**
- **What effect did the New Deal have on the Tennessee Valley region?**

New Yorker magazine cover, 1933

*R*oosevelt wasted no time making good his pledge of "action, and action now." As soon as he arrived in the Oval Office, he confidently proposed programs that would strengthen the nation's teetering banking system and provide relief for the needy. Soon he moved on to attack the deep-seated problems that plagued agriculture and industry. One project would transform an entire region of the country.

*R*OOSEVELT CONFRONTS THE EMERGENCY

Roosevelt's optimism proved contagious. "The whole country is with him," noted humorist Will Rogers, "just so he does something. If he burned down the Capitol, we would cheer and say, 'Well, we at least got a fire started anyhow.'" People were ready for action, even if it meant making mistakes along the way.

Roosevelt did indeed get a fire started. With the help of the Brain Trust, the advisory group that he had formed in 1932 while still governor of New York, the energetic new president drew up 15 relief and recovery measures, his promised "new deal for the American people." Immediately after taking office on March 5, Roosevelt called Congress into special session. Over the next 100 days, Congress approved all

15 measures, which made up the heart of the president's **New Deal** program.

Roosevelt started with the nation's banks, which were in serious trouble. The day after his inauguration, he issued a proclamation closing every bank in the nation for a few days. This so-called **bank holiday** was designed to stop massive withdrawals. On Thursday, March 9, Congress took only a few hours to pass the **Emergency Banking Act**,

▶ Americans listened as Roosevelt discussed important issues in one of his many radio broadcasts.

MOTIVATING: STUDENT EXPERIENCES

Ask students to identify what they know from newspapers, magazines, and television about federal government programs to assist the needy. Have students list responses in their notebooks. Suggest that, as they read the section, students compare items on their lists to the programs instituted by the Roosevelt administration during the First New Deal.

Teaching the Section

BANKING, FARM, AND HOME OWNERS' CRISES

Organize students into three groups. Assign one group banking, another farm problems, and a third the home owners' crisis. Have each group imagine they are members of the Roosevelt brain trust. Direct groups to prepare "fireside chats" for Roosevelt to deliver to the nation, explaining their assigned problem, steps the administration is taking to solve it, and reasons the public should support these policies. Have each group choose a "Roosevelt" to deliver its "chat" to the class.

▪▪ Have students describe some of the ways presidents today use the media to present policies or programs to the public.

▶

THE GREATEST MAN OF THE AGE

THROUGH OTHERS' EYES

J. B. Murray, a young Australian, came to the United States in 1926. He spent the next 11 years working in California orchards, oil fields, and ranches. When Franklin Roosevelt was nominated for the presidency in 1932, Murray became an eager observer of American politics.

"*F*or myself," he later wrote in a book about his travels titled *American Trails*, "I believed in Roosevelt completely, and became engrossed with his campaign. He travelled to distant cities, and into the farming country, and wherever he went left hope behind him. The man's charm of manner and quiet confidence and strength were irresistible." Murray noted that Roosevelt's "personality flooded the countryside like warm sunshine.... The country listened spellbound to [his] clear, confident voice, which assured all that a new era was commencing." Murray concluded, "Listening to his radio talks, I had already marked him down as the greatest man of the age."

---

which authorized the government to examine all banks and allow those that were financially sound to reopen. Roosevelt hoped that the act would restore public confidence in the banking system.

Caught without cash, Americans scrambled to find substitutes for it during the bank holiday. Many used subway and bus tokens, postage stamps, and IOUs. On Sunday evening, March 12, some 60 million anxious Americans tuned in their radios to hear the president explain how the bank holiday would protect their money. In this first of many "fireside chats"—radio broadcasts from the White House—Roosevelt urged people to reinvest in banks. "I can assure you that it is safer to keep your money in a reopened bank than under the mattress," he advised.

The next morning, as banks began reopening, more than $1 billion in deposits flowed into the system. Confidence in banks increased still more when Congress created the **Federal Deposit Insurance**

Corporation (FDIC) in June 1933. This reform insured each bank deposit up to $2,500. (Today, the figure is $100,000 per account.)

Roosevelt then turned his attention to the plight of the farmers. On March 28 he issued an executive order to create the **Farm Credit Administration**, to provide low-interest, long-term loans to farmers. Congress obliged, and with these loans, farmers paid off mortgages and overdue taxes, bought back lost farms, and purchased needed seed, fertilizer, and equipment. In April, Roosevelt asked Congress to create the **Home Owners Loan Corporation** (HOLC) to address the problem of home owners who could not meet their mortgage payments. Again, Congress obliged. By June 1936 the HOLC had saved the homes of some one million American families by granting them low-interest, long-term mortgage loans.

▪▪ The bank holiday and FDIC restored public trust in banks, while the FCA and HOLC provided loans to farmers and home owners.

*R*ELIEF FOR THE NEEDY

Along with these measures the Roosevelt administration also launched a large-scale program of direct relief to the nation's 13 million unemployed. In many ways Roosevelt's direct-relief program completed the agenda that reformers had been trying to get the government to support since the Progressive Era. Through the efforts of Eleanor Roosevelt and Democratic National Committee member Molly Dewson, the president brought in many long-time reformers to direct his programs, including Secretary of Labor Frances Perkins.

In May 1933, at Roosevelt's request, Congress established the **Federal Emergency Relief Administration** (FERA) with half a billion dollars for relief aid to be funneled directly to state and local agencies. One of FDR's most trusted advisers, Harry L. Hopkins, headed the FERA program.

THROUGH OTHERS' EYES

Have students explain what leadership qualities FDR had that Murray admired. Then ask students why such qualities were especially useful in the midst of the depression.

PRIMARY SOURCE

Description of Change: excerpted and bracketed **Rationale:** excerpted to focus on main idea; bracketed to clarify meaning

🌐 GLOBAL CONNECTIONS

Bank failures in the U.S. were followed by bank failures abroad. Europe's flagging economy sank even further in May 1931 with the failure of Austria's largest private bank. Its collapse had a ripple effect throughout eastern Europe.

HISTORICAL SIDELIGHTS

Fireside Chats
During his 12 years as president, FDR gave 30 fireside chats. All began with the greeting "My friends . . ." and were presented in a way that seemed both personal and caring. One historian has said that FDR was like "a father talking about public affairs while sitting with his family in the living room."

Teaching the *Section*

RELIEF FOR THE UNEMPLOYED

Call on volunteers to briefly outline the purposes of the FERA, CWA, and CCC and to explain why each was considered a relief program. Then organize students into three groups and assign to each group one of the programs listed above. Have each group prepare a press release that explains to prospective recipients how they can partici-pate in the program and how they will ben-efit. Have groups present their press releas-es to the class. Encourage other members of the class to act as reporters and ask the pre-senters questions about their programs.

PRIMARY SOURCES

Description of Change: excerpted
Rationale: excerpted to focus on main idea

HISTORICAL SIDELIGHTS

The CCC

CCC workers earned $30 a month in pay, $22 of which was automatically sent home to their families. Although workers took part in forest-fire prevention, mosquito control, and dam and road building, their pri-mary task was tree planting. Of all the trees planted in the first 175 years of the nation's history, more than half were planted by the CCC.

■■ In April 1938, 78 per-cent of the electorate ques-tioned in a Gallup Poll favored making the CCC a permanent part of govern-ment. Ask students how they feel about the value of such a program today.

THE AMERICAN NATION VIDEODISC PROGRAM

Serving the Nation

```
2A     20156     2:54
```

A Washington newspaper reported the eagerness of the FERA director to get relief to the needy:

> ❝ The half-billion dollars for direct relief of States won't last a month if Harry L. Hopkins, the new relief administrator, main-tains the pace he set yesterday in disbursing more than $5,000,000 during his first two hours in office. ❞

By 1935 the total of such direct federal relief aid had risen to some $3 billion. At one point nearly eight million American families were surviving on public assistance.

Americans, however, disliked this kind of aid. They wanted jobs, not handouts. So Hopkins orga-nized the **Civil Works Administration** (CWA) to create jobs. Most of these were "make-work" pro-jects such as raking leaves and picking up park litter. From 1933 to 1934, the CWA paid some $750 mil-lion in wages to some four million men and women.

To aid unemployed young men between ages 18 and 25, Congress established the **Civilian Conservation Corps** (CCC) in 1933. Initially, some 250,000 young men left their homes and went to army camps for CCC training. Once trained, they spread out into the nation's forests, where they planted trees, cleared underbrush, laid out park trails, and developed campgrounds and beaches. For their efforts they earned a dollar a day. Most of their

earnings were sent back home to help their families. Said one CCC veteran of the experience:

> ❝ I really enjoyed it. I had three wonderful square meals a day. . . . They sure made a man out of ya, because you learned that every-body here was equal. There was nobody bet-ter than another in the CCC's. ❞

During its nearly 10-year life, the CCC enrolled more than 2.5 million young men and planted millions of trees, most in the South and the Southwest. The program earned back much of its cost in the value it added to the nation's forests.

■■ **Through the FERA, the CWA, and the CCC, the New Deal granted direct relief to the unemployed and created jobs.**

*H*ELPING THE NATION RECOVER

While New Deal relief programs aided needy Americans, the Roosevelt administration also pur-sued recovery programs to revive the economy. Roosevelt saw relief as a short-term remedy; recovery was his long-term goal.

To stimulate recovery in business and indus-try, the Roosevelt administration poured money into the economy through federal loans and gov-ernment spending—a process sometimes called "priming the pump." Many of the New Deal recovery programs were based on the theories of noted economist John Maynard Keynes, who argued that for a nation to recover fully from a depression, the government had to spend money to create jobs and boost investment.

One of the chief ways in which the Roosevelt administration attempted to prime the economy's pump was through the **National Industrial Recovery Act** (NIRA), which Congress passed in June 1933. The act was designed to stimulate industrial and business activity and reduce unemployment by stabilizing prices, raising wages, limiting workers' hours, and providing jobs. To help achieve these goals,

◀ Some 2.5 million jobless young men were employed by the CCC from 1933 to 1943. During the decade they worked on projects designed to preserve and restore the nation's natural resources.

HELPING THE NATION RECOVER

Call on students to review the major recovery programs of the First New Deal. Suggest that they note the recovery legislation passed by Congress, the agencies that were established as a result, and any criticisms that were leveled against the recovery programs. Then ask students to select a program and design a bumper sticker that supports or opposes that program. Ask volunteers to present and explain their bumper stickers to the class.

THE IMPACT OF THE TVA

Organize students into groups of five and have groups imagine they are the editorial board of a newspaper published in the Tennessee Valley. Have the boards draw up an editorial reply to critics of the Tennessee Valley Authority, pointing out how the program transformed social and economic life throughout the Tennessee River Valley. Have groups present and defend their editorials.

▶

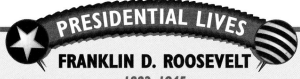

PRESIDENTIAL LIVES

FRANKLIN D. ROOSEVELT
1882–1945

in office
1933–1945

Franklin D. Roosevelt

"Mr. Roosevelt is a unique figure in the modern world: the one statesman . . . who seems able to relax," wrote one journalist about the charismatic leader. Indeed, FDR always appeared to be warm, energetic, and easygoing, despite the enormous pressures that faced his administration. His optimistic outlook may have helped in his recuperation from polio.

The president always hid his private thoughts behind his dazzling smile. One of his speech writers commented that you could never tell what was going on in FDR's "heavily forested interior." Yet, the president relied heavily on instinct and idealism in making decisions. Political philosophy held little value for him. His warm style and compassionate manner, expressed in his weekly "fireside chats," helped win support for many of his programs. Years after the depression many Americans would remember FDR almost as a beloved family member.

---

the NIRA created two new federal agencies—the **Public Works Administration** (PWA) and the **National Recovery Administration** (NRA).

The PWA, under the leadership of Secretary of the Interior Harold Ickes, provided jobs and stimulated business activity by contracting with private firms to construct roads, public buildings, and other public-works projects. Between 1933 and 1939, the PWA spent more than $4 billion on some 34,000 projects.

▲ Roosevelt's approach to government was to recommend a new program, try it, and if it failed, then "admit it frankly and try another." His approach is satirized in this 1934 cartoon.

The NIRA's other arm, the NRA, attempted to promote recovery by encouraging businesses to draw up "codes of fair competition." Under these codes, competing businesses agreed to work together to stabilize prices, wages, hours, and production levels. Businesses were able to do this because the NIRA had suspended antitrust laws. To help protect labor through this period of business self-regulation, Section 7(a) of the NIRA guaranteed workers the "right to organize and bargain collectively through representatives of their own choosing . . . free from the interference, restraint or coercion of employers."

Under the direction of former army general Hugh S. Johnson, the NRA took off on a wave of popular enthusiasm. Parades of workers marched through cities displaying the NRA banner—a blue eagle clutching lightning bolts in its claw, with the slogan "We Do Our Part." Johnson compared the NRA to a fighting army:

> 66 This campaign is a frank dependence on the power and the willingness of the American people to act together as one person in an hour of great danger. . . . The Blue Eagle is a symbol of industrial solidarity and self-government. 99

But enthusiasm soon faded. Businesses did not always obey the codes. Workers complained that the codes held their wages down, while consumers

---

HISTORICAL SIDELIGHTS
The PWA
Major PWA projects included the Triborough Bridge and the Queens-Midtown Tunnel in New York City, the Golden Gate Bridge in San Francisco, and the Grand Coulee Dam in Washington state. Other PWA projects administered the building or restoration of about 5,900 school buildings, 13,000 playgrounds, 2,500 hospitals, and 1,000 airports.

HISTORICAL SIDELIGHTS
Opposition to the NRA
The most outspoken opponents of the NRA were the leaders of the larger industries. Henry Ford, for example, refused to have the "Roosevelt buzzard [the Blue Eagle emblem] on my cars."

PRIMARY SOURCE
Description of Change: excerpted
Rationale: excerpted to focus on main idea

*P*ractice

GUIDED PRACTICE

Draw on the chalkboard a four-column chart with the headings *Measure, Why Needed, Who Benefited, Effects.* In the first column, list major New Deal legislation and agencies discussed in this section. Then help the class to complete the chart.

INDEPENDENT PRACTICE

Have students choose one of the New Deal programs listed in the chart developed in the Guided Practice activity. Ask them to write letters to President Roosevelt from the viewpoint of a person affected by that program, explaining the impact it has had on his or her life. Students may wish to include their letters in their portfolios.

*R*eview and *A*ssessment

REVIEW Have students work in pairs to list and classify each New Deal program in this section as a relief or a recovery program. Have each group identify the relief program and the recovery program that it thinks had the greatest impact on people's lives and explain its choices. Then assign the Section 1 Review on p. 355.

ASSESS Assign the **Section 1 Daily Quiz** in *Core Resources.*

MULTICULTURAL PERSPECTIVES

The STFU was unusual in its ability to bring together people of various backgrounds. In addition to attracting both black and white farmers, the movement was aided by radical farm labor organizers and fundamentalist members who used religious songs and imagery to inspire the group. African Americans A. B. Brookins and John Handcock, for instance, transformed the gospel tune "We Shall Not Be Moved" into an STFU protest song.

MAKING CONNECTIONS

Geography

When it was completed, the TVA operated a system of dams draining an area of some 40,000 square miles. The dams transformed the Tennessee River into a waterway some 300 feet wide, navigable by large ships from Knoxville, Tennessee, about 650 miles to Paducah, Kentucky.

Map Caption Answer

Tennessee, Alabama, Kentucky, Mississippi border

---

complained that the codes pushed prices up. As people lost confidence in the NRA, they joked that it stood for "National Run Around" and "No Recovery Allowed." In 1935 the Supreme Court declared the NIRA (and the NRA) unconstitutional.

*A*GRICULTURAL RECOVERY

To raise farm prices and increase farmers' purchasing power, Roosevelt proposed that farmers cut production. Congress passed the **Agricultural Adjustment Act** (AAA) in May 1933, which established the Agricultural Adjustment Administration (AAA). The AAA paid farmers to reduce their output of cotton, wheat, corn, hogs, rice, tobacco, dairy products, and other commodities. The money for these payments, or **subsidies**, came from taxes levied on food processors, including meat packers, canners, and flour millers.

In one year the plan reduced the cotton crop by more than three million bales, raising cotton prices. Such increased income gave cotton growers and large-scale farmers more cash to spend, thus stimulating overall economic recovery. New Deal

supporters pointed to these favorable results as proof of the value of sound federal planning. But critics of the New Deal farm program pointed out that the taxes on food processors were passed along to consumers in the form of higher prices. Thus, while farmers' incomes rose, the purchasing power of city dwellers declined.

Critics also charged that farmers with large land-holdings benefited far more from the AAA than did small farmers. Often when large landowners cut production, they forced sharecroppers off their land and kept all of the government payments for themselves. Thus, the poorest farmers were forced into deeper poverty. In response, a group of Arkansas sharecroppers, both black and white, formed the **Southern Tenant Farmers' Union** (STFU) in 1934. The union lobbied the government to halt tenant evictions and to force landowners to share payments with the farmers who rented land. Within one year the STFU had grown to more than 10,000 members.

Early in 1936, the Supreme Court struck down the AAA on the grounds that the processing tax was unconstitutional. This decision, like its ruling against the NIRA and NRA, reflected

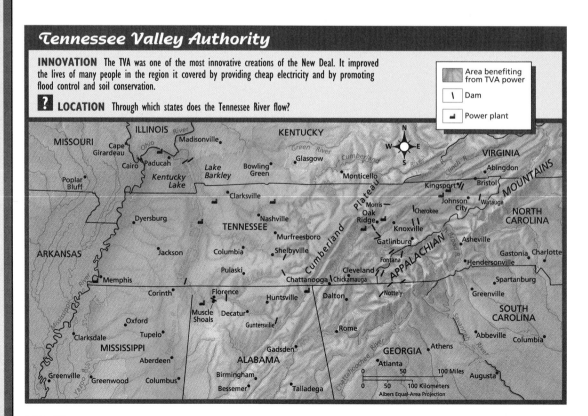

Tennessee Valley Authority

INNOVATION The TVA was one of the most innovative creations of the New Deal. It improved the lives of many people in the region it covered by providing cheap electricity and by promoting flood control and soil conservation.

? LOCATION Through which states does the Tennessee River flow?

RETEACH Organize students into groups and give each group note cards. Have groups write on their note cards six questions about New Deal programs that can be answered with the name of a specific program. For example, "What program insured the savings of bank depositors?" *(FDIC)* Collect questions and hold a quiz bowl.

Closure

On the chalkboard write the following quotation from FDR's first inaugural address: *"The only thing we have to fear is fear itself."* Then call on students to explain how New Deal programs helped to combat this fear.

Extension

CONCLUDE In the late 1980s bank failures occurred in various states. Have students investigate a particular bank failure, determining if the bank was a member of the FDIC and speculating what might have happened if the FDIC had not existed.

INVESTIGATE Have students investigate, and make oral reports on, the PWA or CCC projects that were undertaken in their area.

the Supreme Court's opposition to growing government power.

■■ **To stimulate economic recovery, Congress passed the NIRA to help business and industry and the AAA to aid agriculture.**

*R*EVITALIZING A REGION

The most monumental of all the early New Deal programs was the Tennessee Valley project, which sought to revitalize the seven-state region drained by the Tennessee River and its tributaries (see map on page 354). This rural area was scarred by over-cut forests and frequent flooding. Poverty, malnutrition, disease, and illiteracy plagued its two million residents.

The **Tennessee Valley Authority** (TVA), created in May 1933, transformed the economic and social life of the region. Under the guidance of David E. Lilienthal, the TVA built 38 dams and several power stations that provided electricity, flood control, and recreational facilities for the region. Other TVA projects combated malaria, illiteracy, and soil erosion and tried to improve the region's standard of living, which had barely changed since Reconstruction.

▲ The TVA's system of hydroelectric plants, dams, and navigation channels covers an area of some 41,000 square miles. Shown here is the construction of Norris Dam.

Critics denounced the TVA as overuse of government power. Shareholders in private utility companies, who feared it would cut into their dividends, brought several court cases against the TVA. The Supreme Court, however, refused to strike down the TVA. Probably the best known of the "alphabet soup" of programs created during Roosevelt's First Hundred Days, the TVA remains one of the New Deal's most enduring successes.

■■ **The TVA transformed economic and social conditions throughout the Tennessee River Valley.**

SECTION REVIEW ANSWERS

IDENTIFY
For significance, see the following pages:
New Deal (p. 350)
bank holiday (p. 350)
Emergency Banking Act (p. 350)
FDIC (p. 351)
Farm Credit Administration (p. 351)
HOLC (p. 351)
Frances Perkins (p. 351)
FERA (p. 351)
Harry L. Hopkins (p. 351)
CWA (p. 352)
CCC (p. 352)
NIRA (p. 352)
PWA (p. 353)
NRA (p. 353)
AAA (p. 354)
subsidies (p. 354)
STFU (p. 354)
TVA (p. 355)

LOCATE
For location, see the map on p. 354.

1. *declared "bank holiday," passed Emergency Banking Act, created FDIC; FCA, HOLC*
2. *FERA, CWA, CCC; NIRA, AAA*
3. *area drained by Tennessee River, scarred by overcut forests and flooding*
4. *Letters might mention the construction of power plants and low-cost housing; projects to combat soil erosion, disease, and illiteracy.*
5. *Keynes argued that government must spend money to create jobs and boost investment, just as the New Deal did.*

■■ ■■

S E C T I O N **1** R E V I E W

IDENTIFY and explain the significance of the following: New Deal, bank holiday, Emergency Banking Act, Federal Deposit Insurance Corporation, Farm Credit Administration, Home Owners Loan Corporation, Frances Perkins, Federal Emergency Relief Administration, Harry L. Hopkins, Civil Works Administration, Civilian Conservation Corps, National Industrial Recovery Act, Public Works Administration, National Recovery Administration, Agricultural Adjustment Act, subsidies, Southern Tenant Farmers' Union, Tennessee Valley Authority.

LOCATE and explain the importance of the following: Tennessee River Valley.

1. **MAIN IDEA** How did the Roosevelt administration attempt to restore confidence in the banking system? What New Deal measures provided loans to farmers and home owners?

2. **MAIN IDEA** Which New Deal programs granted direct relief to the unemployed and created jobs? Which programs helped business, industry, and agriculture?

3. **GEOGRAPHY: REGION** Describe the physical characteristics of the Tennessee River Valley.

4. **WRITING TO INFORM** Imagine you are a resident of the Tennessee River Valley in 1935. Write a letter to a critic of the TVA, outlining the positive ways in which the TVA has transformed the region where you live.

5. **ANALYZING** How are the economic theories of John Maynard Keynes evident in the approach that the Roosevelt administration took toward reviving the economy?

PREVIEW WORKSHOP

Following is a list of the significant people and terms in this section. You may wish to use this list as a section preview.

People
- Francis E. Townsend
- Charles E. Coughlin
- Alfred M. Landon

Terms
- Share-Our-Wealth
- Second New Deal
- Works Progress Administration
- National Youth Administration
- Social Security Act
- Rural Electrification Administration
- Wealth Tax Act
- Wagner-Connery Act
- Congress of Industrial Organizations
- sit-down strike
- Farm Security Administration

FOCUS OBJECTIVES

- Identify the criticisms aimed at the New Deal.

- Explain what enabled Roosevelt to win reelection easily in 1936.

- Describe how Roosevelt tried to prevent the Supreme Court from overturning his programs.

- Analyze how the Second New Deal benefited labor and agriculture.

Section 2

NEW CHALLENGES

F O C U S
- **What criticisms were aimed at the New Deal?**
- **What enabled Roosevelt to win reelection easily in 1936?**
- **How did Roosevelt try to prevent the Supreme Court from overturning his programs?**
- **How did the Second New Deal benefit labor and agriculture?**

Once the furious activity of the First Hundred Days ended, the nation anxiously waited to see how well the New Deal would work. Critics were quick to speak out. Rather than slowing the New Deal down, however, these critics made the administration more determined to enact still another series of innovative programs that created jobs, provided security for older Americans, and improved labor and farming conditions.

Townsend Plan sign near Weslaco, Texas

CRITICS OF THE NEW DEAL

Criticism of the New Deal came from both the left and the right of the political spectrum. Liberal and radical critics on the left argued that the New Deal was not going far enough in providing relief, recovery, and reform. Conservatives on the right charged that the New Deal was going too far—pushing government into areas where it had no right to interfere. Conservatives were also concerned about the heavy costs of the New Deal. Although FDR had campaigned for a balanced budget in 1932, the federal deficit rose from roughly $1.3 billion in 1933 to some $3.5 billion in 1936.

Most conservative complaints came from the American Liberty League, made up largely of Republican business interests and disenchanted Democrats led by Al Smith, who accused New Deal supporters of "irresponsible ravings against millionaires and big business." The League complained that the New Deal measures were destroying both the Constitution and free enterprise and would drive the nation into bankruptcy.

Among the liberal opponents of the New Deal was Dr. Francis E. Townsend of California. Townsend wanted the government to grant a pension of $200 a month to every American over 60 years old. All recipients were to spend the pensions within 30 days and thus pump money into the

▲ Huey Long

CORE RESOURCES

• Section 2 Daily Quiz

MOTIVATING:
LINK TO TODAY

Have students name some programs promoted by the current U.S. president and identify ways opponents of these programs make their views known. *(newscasts, talk shows, editorials, voting or lobbying against a program in Congress)* Ask students to describe the ways the president today attempts to counteract such actions.

ᴛeaching the ꜱection

NEW DEAL CRITICS

Organize a portion of the class into four groups. Assign groups the following roles: American Liberty League, Huey Long supporters, conservative business interests and wealthy Americans, and Roosevelt administration officials. Have the first three groups list their criticisms of the New Deal, reasons for these criticisms, and their alternatives. Have groups give their lists to the Roosevelt group to prepare responses. Then choose a moderator from the class and have all groups select a spokesperson to participate in a radio "Crossfire" debate on the merits of the New Deal. After the debate, the class can decide which group most persuasively argued its position.

▶

economy. Father Charles E. Coughlin, the "radio priest," broadcast a similar message from his pulpit in Michigan. He urged the government to nationalize all banks and return to the silver standard.

Huey Long, "the Kingfish," a colorful but corrupt senator from Louisiana, probably had the most radical plan. Like Robin Hood, Long wanted to take from the rich and give to the poor. He claimed that he had done just that as governor of Louisiana, when he had helped the poor by building public housing, roads, and schools and by providing free textbooks to students. Actually, he had financed his state's public-works projects not by taking from the rich, but by imposing higher taxes on everyone—including the poor. In addition, Long and his friends had often profited personally from the projects.

In 1933 Senator Long proposed a radical new kind of relief program, which he called **Share-Our-Wealth**. The program would empower the government to confiscate wealth from the rich through taxes and then provide a guaranteed minimum income and a home to every American family. Long even had his own theme song:

> ❝ Ev'ry man a king, ev'ry man a king,
> For you can be a millionaire,
> There's enough for all people to share.
> When it's sunny June and December too,
> Or in the wintertime or spring:
> There'll be peace without end,
> Ev'ry neighbor a friend,
> With ev'ry man a king. ❞

In spite of Long's reputation for corruption, the Share-Our-Wealth program drew a great deal of popular support. Some critics suspected that Long harbored dreams of becoming a dictator. Such fears led the Communist party and the Socialist party to denounce Long even though his program promised to redistribute wealth. Bolstered by popular support, Long soon threatened to challenge Roosevelt as a third-party candidate in the 1936 election. But both this threat and the Share-Our-Wealth program died when an assassin killed Long in 1935.

∷ Some critics accused the New Deal of pushing government power too far, while others wanted to expand it further.

ᴛHE SECOND NEW DEAL

In the midterm elections of 1934, the Democrats picked up more seats in Congress. The victory, coupled with pressure from the left, encouraged New Deal planners to initiate more public-works programs, a social security plan, and wage and hour improvements for laborers. This series of programs would eventually come to be called the **Second New Deal**. While still providing relief and pursuing recovery, the Second New Deal would increasingly emphasize reform.

The Works Progress Administration.
A works program, the **Works Progress Administration** (WPA), began in April 1935 under the direction of Harry Hopkins. The CWA had ended the previous year, yet unemployment was still high. Millions of American families remained on relief rolls. To create jobs for them, Congress allotted $5 billion for the WPA.

Over the eight years of its life, the WPA employed an estimated 14 million people, with about 2 million working for it at any given time. Workers engaged in a variety of tasks. Male blue-collar workers built or rebuilt a total of some 350 airports, more than 100,000 public buildings, some 78,000 bridges, and about 500,000 miles of roads. White-collar workers took on research projects and teaching jobs. The WPA had a special division for women, but the program often discriminated against women by paying them lower wages than men. On most projects male workers received $5 a day while female workers received only $3 for the same job.

▼ The WPA employed many women, such as this weaver from Kansas, in a variety of jobs.

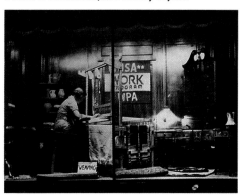

HISTORICAL SIDELIGHTS

Townsend and Coughlin Townsend was an elderly California doctor, whose organization, Old-Age Revolving Pensions, Ltd., had a membership of more than 500,000 by 1935. Radio priest Father Coughlin reached an estimated audience of 10 million weekly. Despite their popularity, neither Townsend nor Coughlin made a significant impact on national public policy. Most observers dismissed the Townsend plan as unfeasible. And Coughlin's following began to dwindle as his sermons became increasingly anti-Semitic in the late 1930s.

PRIMARY SOURCE

Description of Change: excerpted
Rationale: excerpted to focus on main idea

MAKING CONNECTIONS

Literature
Robert Penn Warren's Pulitzer Prize–winning novel *All the King's Men* (1946) was loosely based on the life and career of Huey Long.

Teaching the Section

THE SECOND NEW DEAL

Encourage students to imagine they are New Deal planners. Have them write a report, for presentation to President Roosevelt, indicating why a Second New Deal is necessary and outlining the problems the country still faces and the steps they intend to take to solve these problems. Call on volunteers to read their reports to the class. Students may wish to include their reports in their portfolios.

The WPA tried to help struggling young people between the ages of 16 and 25 by establishing the **National Youth Administration** (NYA), a "junior WPA." The NYA gave young people part-time jobs that provided money to help them stay in school. Within a year the NYA was providing aid to half a million people.

Social Security. Another cornerstone of the Second New Deal was the **Social Security Act**, which Congress passed in August 1935. The act contained three major provisions. First, it provided unemployment insurance for workers who lost their jobs. The funds for this insurance came from a payroll tax on businesses. Second, the act provided pensions for retired workers over age 65. The money for these pensions came from two sources—a payroll tax on employers and a tax on employees' wages. Third, in a shared federal-state program, the act provided payments to the blind, disabled, and elderly and to wives and children of male workers who had died.

At first the Social Security Act covered only a limited segment of the work force. Farmers and the self-employed were excluded, as well as domestic workers, some 60 percent of whom were African American women. Over the years, however, coverage broadened, and the Social Security Act became the model for a wide range of public social welfare programs.

Other programs. Underlying Roosevelt's Second New Deal was the president's belief that the government had not yet "weeded out the overprivileged and . . . effectively lifted up the underprivileged." To help the underprivileged, Roosevelt issued an executive order in May 1935 establishing the **Rural Electrification Administration** (REA). The REA extended power lines into isolated rural areas. Within a few years, only 1 farm in 10 lacked electricity.

To help weed out the overprivileged, Roosevelt went after public utility companies, charging that many were able to set higher prices because they held monopolies over gas and electricity. To reform this system, Congress passed a law giving the government the right to regulate interstate production, transmission, and sale of gas and electricity.

Roosevelt also went after the rich, declaring that tax laws had not done enough "to prevent an unjust concentration of wealth and economic

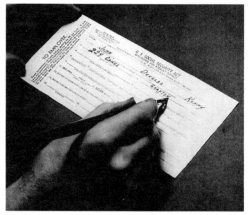

▲ The Social Security Act marked an unprecedented step in providing relief to the unemployed and elderly. In this photograph, a man named John Kenny fills out one of the first applications for a social security number.

power." In response, Congress passed the Revenue Act of 1935. Often referred to as the **Wealth Tax Act**, it sharply increased taxes on the nation's richest people. Corporations had to pay an "excess profits" tax if they made an annual profit greater than 10 percent. A year later, Congress increased corporate taxes again. Business complained bitterly that the tax increase discouraged business expansion.

THE ELECTION OF 1936

By 1936 the depression still lingered. Some 9 million workers lacked regular jobs, and 3.5 million remained on the WPA or the CCC rolls. Many factories remained closed or operated at far less than full capacity. Still, America had made some progress. Since 1932 the national income had jumped from roughly $43 billion to more than $80 billion and unemployment had dropped by nearly three million.

In June 1936 the Democrats enthusiastically nominated Roosevelt for a second term. Labor unions, farmers, those on relief, and even many Republicans also endorsed him. For the first time since Reconstruction, most African Americans living in the North abandoned their traditional ties to the Republican party—"the party of Lincoln"—to support the Democrats. The Republicans nominated the capable but unexciting governor of Kansas, Alfred M. Landon. The Republican platform condemned the New Deal,

ROOSEVELT REELECTED

Have students work in pairs to prepare an interview between a reporter and President Roosevelt in which the president explains what enabled him to win reelection in 1936. Select pairs to conduct their interviews for the class.

▶

NEW DEAL PROGRAMS		
Year	**First New Deal**	**Provisions**
1933	Emergency Banking Act	Gave administration right to regulate banks.
1933	Farm Credit Administration (FCA)	Extended loans to farm owners to refinance loans.
1933	Economy Act	Aimed at balancing the budget.
1933	Civilian Conservation Corps (CCC)	Employed young men on public-works projects.
1933	Federal Emergency Relief Administration (FERA)	Provided relief to the needy.
1933	Agricultural Adjustment Act of 1933 (AAA)	Paid farmers to reduce crops; funded by processing tax later declared unconstitutional.
1933	Tennessee Valley Authority (TVA)	Constructed dam and power projects to improve Tennessee Valley Region.
1933	Home Owners Loan Corporation (HOLC)	Loaned money to home owners to refinance mortgages.
1933	Banking Act of 1933	Created FDIC and prohibited banks from selling stock or financing corporations.
1933	Federal Deposit Insurance Corporation (FDIC)	Insured individual bank deposits.
1933	National Industrial Recovery Act (NIRA)	Established NRA and a series of fair-competition codes for businesses.
1933	National Recovery Administration (NRA)	Regulated industry and raised wages and prices.
1933	Public Works Administration (PWA)	Set up public-works projects to increase employment and business activity.
1933	Civil Works Administration (CWA)	Provided federal jobs to the unemployed.
1934	Securities and Exchange Commission	Regulated securities market.
1934	Federal Housing Administration (FHA)	Insured bank loans for building and repairing homes.

Year	**Second New Deal**	**Provisions**
1935	Works Progress Administration (WPA)	Employed people to do public works, research, and artistic projects.
1935	Soil Conservation Service	Promoted control and prevention of soil erosion.
1935	Rural Electrification Administration (REA)	Provided electricity to rural areas lacking public utilities.
1935	National Youth Administration (NYA)	Provided job training and part-time jobs to students.
1935	National Labor Relations Act (Wagner-Connery Act)	Recognized rights of labor to organize and bargain collectively; regulated labor practices.
1935	Social Security Act	Provided unemployment benefits, pensions for the elderly, and survivor's insurance.
1935	Revenue Act of 1935 (Wealth Tax Act)	Increased taxes on the wealthy.
1937	Farm Security Administration (FSA)	Provided loans to help tenant farmers buy land.
1938	Agricultural Adjustment Act of 1938 (AAA)	Increased government regulation of crop production and payments to farmers.
1938	Revenue Act of 1938	Increased taxes on wealthy businesses.
1938	Fair Labor Standards Act	Established minimum wage of 40 cents per hour and maximum work week of 40 hours for businesses in interstate commerce.

Source: *Encyclopedia of American History*

RELIEF, RECOVERY, AND REFORM Franklin Roosevelt proposed a wide number of programs to aid in the nation's recovery after he assumed office in 1933. These programs became the First New Deal. Two years later he outlined a broader program of social reform in the Second New Deal.

? **BUILDING CHART SKILLS** Which New Deal programs were aimed primarily at helping farmers?

MULTICULTURAL PERSPECTIVES

In the 1932 election campaign, African American Robert Lee Vann, editor of the *Pittsburgh Courier*, advised his black readers to "turn Lincoln's picture to the wall" when they voted for president. In 1936, many did just that, allowing FDR to take a huge share of the black vote in some areas—56 percent in Knoxville, Tennessee, 75 percent in Pittsburgh, Pennsylvania, and 81 percent in New York City, for example.

Have students discuss why African Americans, particularly in the South, voted for the Republican party until the 1930s. Then have students explain why African Americans readily abandoned the Republicans in the 1930s.

Chart Caption Answer
FCA, AAA, REA, FSA, and second AAA

Teaching the Section

ROOSEVELT AND THE SUPREME COURT

Have students work in groups and imagine they are newspaper editors in 1937 shortly after Roosevelt asked Congress to grant him the power to appoint additional Supreme Court justices. Have each group prepare an editorial, accompanied by an editorial cartoon, expressing an opinion on Roosevelt's attempt to "pack" the Court.

■■ Have students speculate how the U.S. legal system might be different today if Roosevelt had won his battle to pack the Court and how the American public would react to such a proposal from the president today.

---

but called for few specific changes in New Deal programs. The Republicans did promise to balance the budget and to reduce federal power by returning more power to the states.

Roosevelt's opponents—mainly business interests upset by new regulations and corporate taxes, conservative newspaper editors, and rich Americans angered by high taxes—renewed their charges that Roosevelt ignored the Constitution. They pointed out that the Supreme Court had overturned the NRA, AAA, and five other key New Deal measures. American individualism, free enterprise, and private property, they insisted, were being abandoned for socialism. Some even charged falsely that the Social Security Act would require everyone to wear metal dog tags!

President Roosevelt entered the fight with great zest. In accepting renomination, he pledged to stay on the course the New Deal had set. He won a smashing victory—with some 28 million popular votes to Landon's 17 million. Roosevelt carried every state but Maine and Vermont—the most lopsided victory in more than a century. The Democrats increased their majorities in both houses of Congress. The coalition that Democrats forged in the election—farmers, southern whites, city dwellers, industrial workers, and northern blacks—would hold together for many elections to come.

■■ **The Democrats, forging a powerful coalition of groups who benefited from the New Deal, easily reelected Roosevelt in 1936.**

ROOSEVELT AND THE SUPREME COURT

Flushed with his triumph and convinced of the power that a solidly Democratic Congress gave him, Roosevelt moved to "reform" the Supreme Court. Angered that the Court had declared several New Deal measures unconstitutional, Roosevelt called attention to the ages of the justices, labeling them "Nine Old Men" (six were 70 or older), and accused them of being stuck in the "horse and buggy" days in their thinking.

In February 1937, two weeks after his second inauguration, Roosevelt asked Congress to grant him the power to appoint one new justice for each of those 70 or older, up to six new justices. The Supreme Court needed "a persistent infusion of new blood," he argued. Roosevelt's proposal triggered a storm of protest across the nation. Critics—Democrats as well as Republicans—charged that this unprecedented "court-packing" would tamper with the delicate balance of legislative, executive, and judicial powers. Dorothy Thompson, a popular political columnist, denounced Roosevelt's scheme as a move toward dictatorship:

66 If the American people accept this last audacity of the President without letting out a yell to high heaven, they have ceased to be jealous of their liberties and are ripe for ruin. This is the beginning of a pure personal government. 99

▶ The negative attitude that many members of the Supreme Court had toward New Deal reforms is satirized in the cartoon *Nine Old Men*.

LABOR'S SECOND NEW DEAL

Invite volunteers to recall the attitudes and actions of government and business toward unions in the late 1800s and early 1900s, and the obstacles to union organization in earlier periods. Ask students what impact the Wagner-Connery Act had on the union movement. Then debate whether the gains in union membership during the 1930s would have been possible if the Great Depression had not occurred.

AGRICULTURE'S SECOND NEW DEAL

Have pairs of students analyze the first and second Agricultural Adjustment Acts. Ask pairs to make lists of aspects of the two acts. Then encourage all pairs to contribute to a chalkboard chart that makes a comparison between the farm policies of the First and Second New Deals and between the results of these policies.

▶

Congress resoundingly denied Roosevelt's request. But this was just one battle in a war that FDR would eventually win. The Supreme Court soon upheld the Social Security Act and the National Labor Relations Act. Many Americans concluded that the justices had decided to become more agreeable to prevent a drastic reform of the Court itself. "A switch in time saves nine," people joked. Over the next four years, seven justices died or retired and were replaced by Roosevelt appointees. By 1945 eight of the nine justices were Roosevelt appointees.

■■ Roosevelt tried to "pack" the Supreme Court with six new members in order to protect his New Deal programs.

▲ As unions became better organized and membership grew, the number of strikes increased. A 1937 sit-down strike is shown above. Workers for a New York City vending company (right) also went on strike later that same year.

THE SECOND NEW DEAL AND LABOR

When the Supreme Court declared the NIRA unconstitutional in May 1935, it struck down Section 7(a), which protected the rights of labor unions. Two months later, however, Congress passed the National Labor Relations Act, also called the **Wagner-Connery Act**, to guarantee labor's right to organize unions and to bargain for better wages and working conditions.

The American Federation of Labor (AFL) continued its efforts to organize workers, including those in such mass-production industries as steel and automobiles. But the AFL did not move fast enough to please gruff, shaggy-browed John L. Lewis, the intimidating leader of the United Mine Workers union. In 1935 Lewis and several other like-minded labor leaders organized the **Congress of Industrial Organizations** (CIO), which tried to unite workers in various industries.

The new CIO unions included all workers, skilled and unskilled, in a given industry. For example, the United Auto Workers (UAW) represented all workers in automotive plants.

Previously, different AFL craft unions had represented different types of autoworkers, such as electricians, welders, or metalworkers. Now all auto workers negotiated as a single powerful union. And in contrast to many AFL branches, the CIO welcomed African American, immigrant, and female members.

The organizing efforts of both the AFL and the CIO resulted in a wave of strikes. One of the most bitter strikes was waged against General Motors (GM) in the winter of 1936–37. The UAW had been trying to unionize GM factories, but the company had been fighting the union's efforts. Meanwhile, GM workers were growing increasingly frustrated with frequent layoffs, abuses of power by management, and work speedups. On December 31, 1936, this frustration led to a **sit-down strike**.

Instead of leaving the automotive plants, workers occupied the factories and pledged to remain until management met their demands. Wives, daughters, and female workers formed the Women's Auxiliary and the Women's Emergency

MULTICULTURAL PERSPECTIVES

Women played important roles in the unions in the 1930s, including African American Pauline Taylor, who organized steelworkers during a 1937 strike in Youngstown, Ohio. Taylor noted: "Anybody who did anything different than what the company wanted was called Communist. . . . I was just a housewife . . . but I would go out on the picket line and work. . . . The contact was made through people that I would know. . . . My work with the foreign born was more than it was even with the black workers until they got used to what I was doing. . . . They accused me of being a Communist. . . . But [the company] couldn't get me like they wanted to because I was not employed. And I could go on any picket line I wanted to go on."

Practice

GUIDED PRACTICE

Make a four-column chart on the Second New Deal. Label the columns *Measures, Goals, Who Benefited, Criticisms.* Have volunteers complete the chart. Then ask students which of these measures they think had the most long-lasting effects.

INDEPENDENT PRACTICE

Have students select one of the Second New Deal programs from the chart developed in the Guided Practice activity. Then ask them to compose lyrics to a song or rap that illustrate the benefits or criticisms of their selected program. Students may wish to include their work in their portfolios.

Review and Assessment

REVIEW Have pairs of students write two or three sentences identifying groups who might have supported each of these New Deal programs and explaining why critics might have opposed them: WPA/NYA, Social Security, Wealth Tax, Wagner-Connery Act, second AAA. Then assign the Section 2 Review on p. 363.

ASSESS Assign the **Section 2 Daily Quiz** in *Core Resources.*

MAKING CONNECTIONS

Economics

The sit-down strike had two advantages over other tactics. It prevented owners from replacing strikers with newly hired workers. Owners also delayed taking violent actions against sit-down strikers for fear the attacks might result in damage to their businesses.

PRIMARY SOURCE

Description of Change: excerpted
Rationale: excerpted to focus on main idea

HISTORICAL SIDELIGHTS

FSA Avoids Discrimination

Because FSA leader Will Alexander insisted that no discrimination exist in the treatment of applicants for the loans made by the agency, thousands of African Americans were able to own farms for the first time.

GLOBAL CONNECTIONS

FDR also had his admirers abroad. British political scientist Harold Laski said of the New Deal: "Success or failure, it bears . . . the hallmarks of great leadership. Improvised in haste, devised under the grim pressure of crisis. . . . It stands out in remarkable . . . contrast to the economic policy of any other capitalist government in the world."

Brigade to picket outside the plants in support of the union. Many women felt their lives were changed by this experience. They soon took up the cause of equal pay for men and women in the auto industry. Said one female activist:

> 66 I'm living for the first time with a definite goal. . . . Just being a woman isn't enough anymore. I want to be a human being with the right to think for myself. 99

Finally, after six weeks, General Motors gave in and granted the UAW the right to organize GM workers. Within eight months the UAW membership grew to some 400,000. Owing in part to the Wagner-Connery Act, total union membership shot up from about 4 million in 1936 to some 9 million in 1939.

■■ **The Wagner-Connery Act guaranteed the rights of labor, increasing union membership and activity.**

THE SECOND NEW DEAL AND FARMERS

The Second New Deal also brought relief for farmers. When the Supreme Court struck down the Agricultural Adjustment Act in January 1936, Congress created another program to replace it. Like the AAA, the new program aimed to keep farm prices high by cutting crop production. To avoid opposition from the Supreme Court, however, Congress combined crop reduction with a soil conservation plan—a legitimate governmental activity.

The Second New Deal also sought to help tenant farmers, sharecroppers, and migrant farm workers. The rise of the Southern Tenant Farmers' Union had brought a backlash of violence against sharecroppers by landowners and authorities in the South, forcing some union members to conduct their activities in secrecy. Then in 1936 the union organized

▶ Migrant workers experienced grinding poverty and set up crude homes near where they worked. Shown here is a migrant Mexican family in Imperial Valley, California.

▲ The depression left many African Americans struggling to find work. This photograph shows people from Memphis, Tennessee, being transported to Arkansas for a day's work in the cotton fields.

a series of strikes by cotton pickers in five states. In 1937 Congress created the **Farm Security Administration** (FSA) to make low-interest, long-term loans to tenant farmers and sharecroppers to buy farms. The FSA also established camps where migrant farm workers could find shelter and medical care.

The Roosevelt administration recognized that the soil conservation program did not do enough to limit farm production. So in 1938 Congress passed a second Agricultural Adjustment Act. The government continued to pay farmers to withdraw land from production and to practice conservation, but it also authorized the Department of Agriculture to limit the amount of specific crops that could be brought to market each year. When harvests exceeded these limits, the government stored the surpluses until prices rose. Farmers cooperating in this program could get government loans based on the value of their stored crops.

RETEACH Organize students so that approximately the same number are assigned to each subsection of the section. Direct each student to write a question about the material in his or her assigned subsection. Then use the questions to quiz the entire group.

Closure

Write the following statement by FDR on the chalkboard: *"Government has a final responsibility for the well-being of its citizenship. If private cooperative endeavor fails to provide work for willing hands and relief for the unfortunate ... government ... must make fitting response."* Have students explain how FDR, in the Second New Deal, carried out the views expressed in this statement.

Extension

CONTRAST Have students contrast the lives and views of Huey Long and Dr. Francis E. Townsend and identify examples of how some of their views were reflected in New Deal programs.

INTERPRET Have students read three historians' views of FDR's plan to reorganize the Supreme Court and write an essay titled "FDR's Court Packing: Major Mistake or Calculated Risk That Paid Off?"

All in all, New Deal agricultural policy compiled a mixed record. Farm income did rise from 1933 to 1937, but critics pointed out that higher farm prices not only hurt consumers but also caused American farm products to lose out in highly competitive foreign markets. Critics also complained about the large cost of farm subsidies. But the farm legislation of the 1930s had some successes. It helped many farmers escape economic disaster, saved homes, and increased the fertility of millions of acres of land through conservation programs.

■■ **The Second New Deal increased farm income; aided tenant farmers, sharecroppers and migrant workers; and encouraged soil conservation.**

BUSINESS SLUMP, POLITICAL SETBACKS

During 1936 and early 1937, the economy seemed to be improving, but in August 1937 it again plunged downward. Stung by criticism of excessive government spending, Roosevelt had begun cutting back on New Deal relief and public-works programs in 1936. Unfortunately, private industry was not yet strong enough to employ those dropped from government rolls because of the cutbacks. In addition, withholding Social Security taxes from workers' paychecks further reduced the flow of money into the economy. By the autumn of 1937, factories were closing and unemployment was rising. Republicans called this period of economic activity "Roosevelt's recession."

President Roosevelt and Congress again primed the economic pump by increasing government lending and spending. The Reconstruction Finance Corporation rescued troubled businesses. The Works Progress Administration quickly doubled the number of workers on its payroll from some 1.5 million to about 3 million. By the fall of 1938, unemployment had declined and industrial production had increased.

As the 1938 midterm elections drew near, Roosevelt decided to reenergize the New Deal (and to punish Democrats who had voted against his Supreme Court reform plan) by opposing conservative Democrats in Congress who did not support the Second New Deal. He actually urged voters to turn these Democrats out of office!

Just as his "court-packing" scheme had backfired, however, so did his attempt to "purge" the Democratic party. All but one member of Congress whom Roosevelt opposed won reelection. Moreover, voters elected still more Democrats who opposed New Deal programs. Adding to Roosevelt's dismay, the Republicans gained 7 seats in the Senate and 80 in the House. Though the Democrats still maintained majorities in both houses of Congress, their margin was much narrower. Faced with increasing criticism from all sides, FDR decided not to propose any new reforms in 1939, marking an end to the New Deal era.

SECTION REVIEW ANSWERS

IDENTIFY

For significance, see the following pages:
Francis E. Townsend (p. 356)
Charles E. Coughlin (p. 357)
Share-Our-Wealth (p. 357)
Second New Deal (p. 357)
WPA (p. 357)
NYA (p. 358)
Social Security Act (p. 358)
REA (p. 358)
Wealth Tax Act (p. 358)
Alfred M. Landon (p. 358)
Wagner-Connery Act (p. 361)
CIO (p. 361)
sit-down strike (p. 361)
FSA (p. 362)

1. *Conservatives claimed that it took government power too far; liberals claimed that it did not go far enough in providing relief, recovery, and reform.*
2. *guaranteed rights of labor; increased farm income, aided farm workers, encouraged soil conservation*
3. *to protect his New Deal programs*
4. *Pamphlets should be aimed at farmers, southern whites, city dwellers, industrial workers, and northern blacks and should outline benefits of the New Deal.*
5. *Those who criticized the New Deal for not providing enough relief revealed liberal values of the left; those who criticized it as ruining the free-enterprise system revealed conservative values of the right.*

SECTION 2 REVIEW

IDENTIFY and explain the significance of the following: Francis E. Townsend, Charles E. Coughlin, Share-Our-Wealth, Second New Deal, Works Progress Administration, National Youth Administration, Social Security Act, Rural Electrification Administration, Wealth Tax Act, Alfred M. Landon, Wagner-Connery Act, Congress of Industrial Organizations, sit-down strike, Farm Security Administration.

1. **MAIN IDEA** What charges did some critics level against the New Deal?
2. **MAIN IDEA** How did the Wagner-Connery Act benefit labor? How did other Second New Deal programs benefit agriculture?
3. **MAIN IDEA** Why did Roosevelt try to "pack" the Supreme Court with six new members?
4. **WRITING TO EXPRESS A VIEWPOINT** Imagine you are a Democratic campaign worker during the 1936 election. Write a campaign pamphlet aimed at the "Roosevelt coalition," explaining why you think FDR should be reelected.
5. **IDENTIFYING VALUES** How did criticisms of the New Deal reveal the values held by the left and the right?

PREVIEW WORKSHOP

*Following is a list of the significant
people, places, and terms in this
section. You may wish to use this
list as a section preview.*

People
■ Marian Anderson
■ Robert C. Weaver
■ Mary McLeod Bethune
■ Antonio Luhan
■ John Collier

■ Pare Lorentz
■ Dorothea Lange

Places
■ Dust Bowl

Terms
■ American Indian Defense
  Association
■ Indian Reorganization Act
■ Okies

FOCUS OBJECTIVES

■ Explain how African
Americans fared during
the New Deal era.

■ Identify the gains Native
Americans made during
the 1930s.

■ Describe the effect the
Dust Bowl had on the
Southwest population.

RECOGNIZING PREJUDICE

Ask students to explain how
the responses of Harold
Ickes and Eleanor Roo-
sevelt to the DAR's treatment of Anderson helped
fight prejudice. Suggest that
students consider how the
responses of these two
prominent people might
have influenced ordinary
Americans or made it easier
for others to stand up
against bigotry.

**THE AMERICAN NATION
VIDEODISC PROGRAM**
Marian Anderson

2A   38876   :32

CORE RESOURCES

• **Literature
  Worksheet 14**
• **Section 3 Daily Quiz**

AV RESOURCES

• *The American Nation
  Videodisc: Marian
  Anderson*

Section 3

LIFE IN THE NEW DEAL ERA

FOCUS

■ **How did African Americans fare during the New Deal era?**
■ **What gains did Native Americans make during the 1930s?**
■ **What effect did the Dust Bowl have on the Southwest population?**

*A*frican Americans, Native Americans, Mexican
Americans, and displaced farmers remained
among the nation's poorest groups during the
depression years. They faced not only economic
hardship but also prejudice and hostility. The New
Deal, however, did make some efforts to help
these groups.

Thomas Hart Benton's *Ploughing It Under*, 1939

A STRUGGLE FOR AFRICAN AMERICANS

New Deal programs succeeded to a large degree in
helping African Americans economically. Some
programs, however, were tainted by discrimination. The FERA and later the WPA became the
greatest sources of relief and work for African
American males. Some 200,000 young black men
flocked to the CCC, where they found work and
training, though they were strictly segregated from
whites. The TVA employed black workers, but they
were not allowed to live in the model towns built by
the TVA. NRA codes often set lower wages for
blacks than for whites, a practice that led some
African American leaders to call the NRA the
"Negro Run Around" or "Negroes Ruined Again."
Social Security also discriminated indirectly against
African Americans since most were agricultural or
domestic workers not eligible for benefits.

The discrimination evident in the programs
was reflective of social attitudes. The depression
increased racial tensions in the country, especially
in the South. Twenty-four black people were

lynched in 1933 alone. Fearing political backlash
from the South, Roosevelt did little to support legislation that might bring civil equality for African
Americans, such as a federal antilynching law
sponsored by the NAACP. Eleanor Roosevelt,
however, became a champion of racial justice.
Black leaders often commented on Mrs.
Roosevelt's unusual ability to understand the struggles of African Americans. "We [whites] are
largely to blame" for poverty among the black
community, she once said. It was her goal to see
educational and economic opportunities open up
for African Americans.

Interior Secretary Harold Ickes, a former
president of the Chicago NAACP, also tried to
respond to the concerns of African Americans.
When the Daughters of the American Revolution
(DAR) refused to let the gifted black concert
singer Marian Anderson perform in their

MOTIVATING:
PRIOR KNOWLEDGE

Ask students to recall the impact of the Great Depression on African Americans, Native Americans, and Mexican Americans. Call on volunteers to explain how prejudice added to the economic difficulties that these groups faced. Then ask students to speculate what steps the government might take to assist such Americans.

Teaching the Section

NEW DEAL FOR AFRICAN AMERICANS?

Have students work in groups to role-play a meeting of FDR's black cabinet. Direct groups to discuss the New Deal's positive and negative impact on African Americans. Have group representatives report the results of the discussions. Then have the class use these reports to write a memo to FDR about the inequalities and benefits

of the New Deal programs for African Americans, and ways in which the programs might be improved.

■■ Ask students why the depression increased racial tensions and whether they think economic conditions affect race relations today.

◄ When Marian Anderson (inset) was denied the use of concert facilities at Constitution Hall, she gave a free concert from the steps of the Lincoln Memorial on Easter Sunday, 1939.

MULTICULTURAL PERSPECTIVES

Arthur Mitchell became the nation's first black Democratic congressman in 1934. In a speech the following year he observed: "Mr. Roosevelt has appointed more Negroes to responsible governmental positions than the last three Republican administrations taken together. . . . I believe that under this administration the Negroes . . . have the best opportunity that has come to them during my lifetime."

PRIMARY SOURCE

Description of Change: excerpted and bracketed
Rationale: excerpted to focus on main idea; bracketed to clarify meaning

BIO GRAPHY PERSONALITIES IN HISTORY

In 1904 when Bethune started her school in a rented house in Daytona Beach, Florida, she had five students and almost no money. Three years later she moved the school to Faith Hall, a building constructed on land that had once been used as a town dump. By 1923 the school had 600 students and joined with the Methodist church's Cookman Institute to eventually become Bethune-Cookman College.

Constitution Hall, both Ickes and Mrs. Roosevelt reacted strongly. Roosevelt resigned her longtime membership in the DAR, stating that "to remain as a member implies approval of that action." She and Ickes then arranged for Anderson to give a free concert at the Lincoln Memorial, which attracted an audience of some 75,000.

Long before this incident, Ickes had brought in several prominent African Americans to advise his department on racial matters, including Robert C. Weaver, the first African American to obtain a Ph.D. in economics from Harvard. Weaver was just one of many African Americans who received high-level government jobs during the New Deal era. FDR named more than 100 blacks to major departments of the federal government, more than any other president since Ulysses S. Grant. These appointees included a wide variety of experts, from legal scholars to educators, social workers, and newspaper editors.

A core group of African American government officials evolved into the Federal Council on Negro Affairs, which became known as the black cabinet or the black brain trust. According to Robert Weaver, their "common cause was to maximize the participation of blacks in all phases of the New Deal." They met weekly at the home of Mary McLeod Bethune, the dynamic director of the Division of Negro Affairs in the National Youth Administration.

BIO GRAPHY Mary McLeod Bethune's journey to prominence in Washington began in 1875 in Mayesville, South Carolina, where she was born the 15th of 17 children to farmers who had once been slaves. The young girl's chances for an

education seemed slim, since the Mayesville school was for whites only. But with the aid of a Presbyterian mission school and a series of scholarships, she eventually attended the Moody Bible Institute in Chicago. Bethune originally intended to become a missionary in Africa but soon found her mission to be educating African American children. She once said of her decision:

❝ The drums of Africa still beat in my heart. They will not let me rest while there is a single Negro boy or girl without a chance to prove his [or her] worth. ❞

In 1904 she founded a primary school for black girls in Florida, which eventually evolved into Bethune-Cookman College, a four-year coeducational institution with a predominantly African American student body.

Bethune became involved with numerous African American groups, including the NAACP and the Urban League. In 1935 she helped unite all national organizations for African American women into the National Council of Negro Women. Through her work with this association, she became close friends with Eleanor Roosevelt, who insisted that Bethune be appointed to work with the NYA. Bethune fought hard, though not always successfully, to rid the NYA of

Mary McLeod Bethune

Teaching the Section

INDIAN REORGANIZATION ACT

Call on volunteers to review and summarize the Dawes General Allotment Act (see Chapter 5). Then ask the class to explain how the Indian Reorganization Act shifted the focus of the federal government's Native American policy. Conclude by asking students to assume the role of Native Americans to write a letter to the editor on the problems they face in revitalizing their culture. Select students to read their letters to the class. Students may wish to include their letters in their portfolios.

■■ Have students report on the ways that Native Americans today are reviving and celebrating their cultural heritage.

PRIMARY SOURCE
Description of Change: excerpted and bracketed
Rationale: excerpted to focus on main idea; bracketed to clarify meaning

MULTICULTURAL PERSPECTIVES

Critics of the Indian Reorganization Act like Rupert Costo, a Cahuilla, felt that it did not offer Native Americans true self-government. He resented the fact that "any plans the Indians might have for . . . self-government would have to be first submitted to the interior secretary or commissioner of Indian affairs for supervision and approval." Sioux critic Ramon Roubideaux argued that "self-government by permission is no self-government at all."

racism. Although Bethune left government service after the NYA ended in 1944, she continued to work on behalf of civil rights and educational opportunities for young African Americans until her death in 1955.

■■ **African Americans gained economic assistance and a voice in government during the New Deal. But little progress was made toward ending discrimination.**

A NEW DEAL FOR NATIVE AMERICANS

As the New Deal era began, life for many Native Americans was very bleak. A late 1920s report on Native American life across the country listed numerous problems that plagued their communities. Inadequate housing, poor health care, and malnutrition left many of the nation's more than 300,000 Native Americans easy prey for epidemics.

Native Americans argued that their culture had been stripped away by measures like the Dawes Act (see Chapter 5), which had ended tribal government and authorized the sale of tribal land to individuals. Antonio Luhan, a member of the Taos Pueblo in New Mexico, described how government policies and the Bureau of Indian Affairs commissioners who enforced them overwhelmed Native American culture:

❝ We had Commissioners against us who tried to stop our ceremony dances and our [religious] dances. They nearly destroy us; call our ways bad or immoral or something, and put in the paper they are going to stop us. ❞

In the 1920s Luhan had shown a white social worker named John Collier the poor living conditions in Native American communities. Deeply moved, Collier founded the **American Indian Defense Association**, which fought to protect religious freedom and tribal property for Native Americans. For the next decade Collier championed Indian reform efforts. In 1933 President Roosevelt appointed Collier as the new commissioner of Indian Affairs. Almost immediately Collier tried to change the government's direction by revitalizing Native American life and culture. "Anything less than to let Indian culture live on would be a crime against the earth itself," Collier declared.

To put these reform ideas into law, Congress passed the **Indian Reorganization Act** of 1934. Reversing the Dawes Act policy, the new law tried to revive tribal rule. The act provided funds to start tribal business ventures and to pay for the college education of young Native Americans. It also ordered Congress "to promote the study of Indian civilization and preserve and develop . . . Indian arts, crafts, skills, and traditions."

▲ The Indian Reorganization Act encouraged Native Americans to preserve their cultural traditions. Shown here is Angelia La Moose, a young girl in the Flathead tribe, wearing a traditional Native American dress.

◄ This 1930 photograph shows a Native American home on the San Xavier Indian Reservation in Arizona.

THE DUST BOWL

Read the following statements to the class: 1) *Thousands of Okies leave Dust Bowl for California;* 2) *Migrant farm workers face falling wages and increasing unemployment;* 3) *Wages of migrant farm workers stabilize.* Direct students to write two or three sentences detailing the causes that might have brought about these effects. Call on volunteers to read and discuss the causes they have identified.

▶

Critics complained that Collier had not obtained enough input from the tribes themselves in formulating policies and that the programs decreased the power of women in some tribes. Still, two thirds of the nation's Native American tribes voted to participate in the new programs.

■■ **New Deal policies encouraged Native Americans to reclaim and revitalize their cultural heritage.**

---

*T*HE STRUGGLE FOR A PLACE IN THE SUN

Toward the end of the 1930s, a billboard appeared on Route 66 just outside Tulsa, Oklahoma, that proclaimed: "NO JOBS in California. If YOU are looking for work—KEEP OUT!" The message was clear. The market for migrant workers on the West Coast was glutted. The sign was directed at the thousands of migrant farmers from the Midwest who traveled to California in the mid-1930s. Driven off their land by the forces of nature, they sought a better life in the Southwest.

The Dust Bowl. In the mid-1930s a severe drought struck the Great Plains—the Texas and Oklahoma panhandles and parts of Colorado, New Mexico, and Kansas. As the topsoil loosened and dried, winds picked it up and turned this 50-million-acre region into a wasteland. Throughout the **Dust Bowl**, as the region came to be called, windswept dust clouds darkened the skies at noon and buried fences and farm machinery. Dust crept into houses through tiny cracks; ships reported great dust clouds hundreds of miles out to sea. One Texas farmer recalled:

> ❝ If the wind blew one way, here came the dark dust from Oklahoma. Another way and it was the gray dust from Kansas. Still another way, the brown dust from Colorado and New Mexico. Little farms were buried. And the towns were blackened. ❞

To prevent future dust bowls, the Department of Agriculture started extensive programs in soil-erosion control. The most dramatic was a shelterbelt of some 217 million trees that CCC workers planted. This windbreak stretched through the Great Plains from Texas to Canada.

By 1939 the amount of dried-out farmland had decreased dramatically. But it was too late to save the many Dust Bowl farmers who had already *(continued on page 370)*

The Dust Bowl, 1930s

Legend:
- ■ Worst-hit area of Dust Bowl
- ■ Dust Bowl area
- ■ Other areas with severe wind erosion
- → Prevailing winds
- → Migration route

John Steinbeck's investigation of the plight of Dust Bowl emigrants in California's Central Valley for a San Francisco newspaper served as the basis for *The Grapes of Wrath*.

ECOLOGICAL DISASTER During World War I farmers planted wheat on dry lands that had been used to pasture cattle. Without the natural grass cover, wind picked up the soil during the drought years and sent "black blizzards" across the country.

❓ MOVEMENT Which directions did the prevailing winds carry the dust?

PRIMARY SOURCE

Description of Change: excerpted
Rationale: excerpted to focus on main idea

HISTORICAL SIDELIGHTS

Dust Storms
A March 1935 dust storm blew away twice the amount of dirt dug up during the construction of the Panama Canal. A month later a dust storm in the Texas panhandle destroyed wheat worth an estimated $20 million.

HISTORICAL SIDELIGHTS

Stopping Erosion
The shelterbelt plan—which was Roosevelt's own—was roundly criticized. Governor "Alfalfa Bill" Murray of Oklahoma, for example, scoffed that the plan was "like trying to grow hair on a bald head." But, much to the surprise of Murray and other critics, the shelterbelt succeeded in slowing erosion.

Map Caption Answer
northeast, east, southeast

HISTORY
in the Making

PHOTOGRAPHING THE DEPRESSION

SETTING THE SCENE

The primary mission of the FSA was to provide mortgages for farm families and labor camps for migrant workers. However, Roosevelt and the FSA wisely saw that documenting the tragedies of farm families could influence public opinion.

HISTORY
in the Making

BY DR. PAUL BOYER

Photographing the Depression

Many Americans at first were suspicious of the New Deal programs. The tradition of self-reliance ran deep in the United States. President Roosevelt believed that opponents of federal relief programs might change their minds if they saw the frightful conditions under which migrant farm workers and city dwellers lived. With Roosevelt's encouragement numerous federal agencies, including the Department of the Interior, the Works Progress Administration (WPA), the Department of Agriculture, and the Farm Security

Administration (FSA), hired photographers in the 1930s to travel across the country and document the lives of ordinary Americans.

No agency used photography more effectively than the FSA, whose staff amassed

more than 250,000 images of American life during the depression. Roy E. Stryker, head of the FSA historical section, assembled an all-star team of photographers that included Walker Evans, Ben Shahn, Arthur Rothstein, and Dorothea Lange.

► Russell Lee photographed these carrot field workers in Santa Maria, Texas, waiting to begin their day.

◄ In Missouri, 1939, Arthur Rothstein captured the mood of this sharecropper's child after the boy's family had been evicted from their land.

To make sure his photographers were prepared, Stryker often tutored them before sending them out on assignment. For example, former print journalist Carl Mydans was set to "go South and 'do cotton'" for the FSA. Learning that Mydans knew virtually nothing about the subject, Stryker postponed the trip. Mydans recalled what happened next:

66 We sat down and we talked almost all day about cotton. We went to lunch and we went to dinner, and we talked well into the night. He [Stryker] talked about cotton as an agricultural product, cotton as a commercial product, the history of cotton in the South, what cotton did to the history of the U.S.A. and how it affected areas outside the U.S.A. By the end of that evening, I was ready to go off and photograph cotton! 99

▶ *Migrant Mother* **is one of Dorothea Lange's most famous photographs of the depression.**

Other photographers, such as Dorothea Lange, were already well grounded in understanding the social and economic forces that shaped rural Americans' lives in the 1930s. Lange often traveled for weeks at a time, working up to 14 hours a day. One of her most famous photographs, *Migrant Mother,* showed an exhausted single mother whose children subsisted chiefly on vegetables they scavenged from California fields. When it appeared in 1936, *Migrant Mother* inspired Californians to defy powerful growers' associations and insist on decent, government-sponsored housing for seasonal harvesters.

Migrant Mother was not the only photograph to fulfill Roosevelt's goal of gaining support for government

programs. From 1936 to 1941, FSA photographs were widely published in government pamphlets and in *Time, Life,* and other magazines. The pictures prompted an outpouring of congressional and public support for federal relief.

Today, the FSA photographs are housed in the Library of Congress and provide an invaluable source of information for historians. They are a detailed visual record of the 1930s that allows researchers today to "see" life in depression America. These photographs have thus enabled historians and citizens alike to step back in time to a crucial period in our history.

◀ **Ben Shahn photographed these rural West Virginia residents heading into Scotts Run to obtain food from relief workers in 1935.**

▶

MORE ABOUT FSA STAFF

Roy Stryker was an economics professor at New York's Columbia University when he was asked to start the FSA's historical section. The first photographer he hired was one of his students, Arthur Rothstein. Rothstein shot dramatic photos of the Dust Bowl storms. After a brief stay at the FSA, Carl Mydans became one of the first staff photographers at *Life*. But Stryker continued to influence Mydans's work. "I often hear Stryker's voice guiding me when I make pictures," Mydans once said. FSA photographer Ben Shahn is perhaps better known today for his paintings on themes of social concern.

PRIMARY SOURCE

Description of Change: excerpted and bracketed **Rationale:** excerpted to focus on main idea; bracketed to clarify meaning

CRITICAL THINKING

Ask students in what ways the photographs taken for the FSA were both art and propaganda. Have students explain who the audience might have been for these photographs and what they hoped to teach.

*P*ractice

GUIDED PRACTICE

Direct students' attention to the photographs featured in History in the Making on pp. 368–369. Guide them in analyzing these photographs by asking them to follow these steps: 1) Determine the subject; 2) Study the details; 3) Determine the photographer's viewpoint; 4) Using information developed in the first three steps, determine the usefulness of the photographs as a historical record of life in the depression.

INDEPENDENT PRACTICE

Direct students to select another photograph from this section. Have them analyze their selection according to the steps outlined in the Guided Practice activity. Call on volunteers to present and discuss their analyses.

*R*eview and *A*ssessment

REVIEW Have students in groups of four role-play a conversation among an African American, a Native American, a Mexican American, and a Filipino in which they contrast their experiences in the 1930s. Select groups to re-create their conversations for the class. Then assign the Section 3 Review on p. 371.

ASSESS Assign the **Section 3 Daily Quiz** in *Core Resources*.

PRIMARY SOURCE
Description of Change: excerpted
Rationale: excerpted to focus on main idea

MULTICULTURAL PERSPECTIVES

Many California landowners hired Filipino workers to do "stoop labor"—strenuous hand work that involved a great deal of bending over. These landowners argued that Filipinos were well suited to stoop work because of their small size. One Japanese farmer noted that in his fields "the Fils do all the stoop labor. They are small and work fast." Yet many Filipino workers suffered from severe back problems because of their work. One Filipino migrant recalled that "at night, I'd feel all kinds of pain in my body—my back, my arm." Another worker complained, "Many people think that we don't suffer from stoop work, but we do."

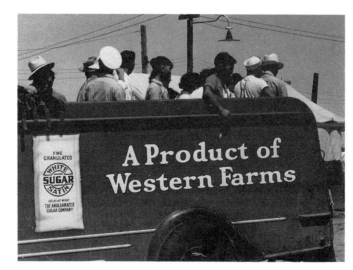

▲ Many Japanese Americans on the West Coast also worked as migrant field laborers. These men labored in sugar fields as far north as Oregon.

66 When we moved to California, we would work after school. Sometimes we wouldn't go. "Following the crops," we missed much school. Trying to get enough money to stay alive the following winter, the whole family picking apricots, walnuts, prunes. . . . We were taken advantage of quite a bit by the labor contractor and the crew pusher. 99

Mexican Americans also faced job competition from Filipino laborers. During the 1920s the Filipino population of California had grown to more than 30,000. Like Mexican American migrants, most Filipinos worked in agriculture. When the depression hit, both groups faced tough economic times, but the Filipino workers attempted to combat decreasing wages by organizing. Throughout the early 1930s the Filipino Labor Union launched a series of strikes to protest wage reductions. In 1936 the American Federation of Labor sponsored the Field Workers Union, a combined organization for Mexican American and Filipino laborers.

The unions were able to keep wages from falling too much. However, as more Okies arrived, competition for migrant work increased. Thus life for all migrants remained difficult.

▪▪ **Dust Bowl refugees moved to the West, where they competed with Mexican Americans and Filipinos for migrant farm work.**

---

lost their land. Packing their meager belongings into battered old cars or trucks, they headed west on Route 66, bound for what they saw as a land of promise—California and other parts of the West Coast. There they hoped to find work picking crops. Thousands of them made the trek, and since many came from Oklahoma, they picked up the nickname **Okies**. Once they reached the West Coast, however, they found themselves in desperate competition with other farm laborers looking for work.

Competition for migrant work. Even before the Dust Bowl refugees started arriving, Mexican Americans had been having a hard time finding work in the West. Like African Americans, Mexican Americans often found themselves the victims of discrimination in many New Deal programs. For example, although the CCC did not segregate Mexican Americans, some complained that they were harassed by camp officials, denied clothing, and assigned to kitchen duty more often than non-Hispanics.

Many families continued to seek what little work they could find as migrant farm laborers. A 1935 California survey found that the average income of Mexican American families had fallen below $300 a year. César Chávez, who later became a noted labor leader, recalled growing up in a depression-era migrant family:

*P*ICTURING THE FACE OF THE DEPRESSION

The grim experiences of migrants and others in rural America provided rich subject matter for documentary filmmakers and photographers. These artists created a memorable visual record of the New Deal era. Better than any words could do, their images of the slumped shoulders of

▲ FSA photographer Carl Mydans captured the devastation of soil erosion in Kentucky in 1936.

unemployed men, the staring faces of children, and the worried expressions of prematurely aged women conveyed the human suffering of the era.

In 1936 and 1937 the filmmaker Pare Lorentz directed two documentary films on the era. *The River* depicts the TVA and its effect on the surrounding regions, while *The Plow That Broke the Plains* portrays the devastation of the Dust Bowl. Using few images of people, the films rely heavily on background music and an unseen narrator to enhance the visual images of the depression's impact on the landscape.

In the late 1930s the Farm Security Administration recruited a group of photographers to record American rural life. These photographers included Walker Evans, who depicted life among sharecroppers in rural Alabama; future African American filmmaker Gordon Parks; international photojournalist Margaret Bourke-White; and Dorothea Lange, probably the best-known of the FSA photographers.

 Lange was one of the most talented photographers of the depression era. Born in Hoboken, New Jersey, she decided in her late teens to become a photographer. After studying the craft for several years, she set out to tour the world and record her impressions. Lange was out of money by the time she reached San Francisco, however, so she stayed and opened a portrait studio.

When the depression struck, Lange began to take pictures of the homeless men wandering the streets of San Francisco. Soon the federal government hired her to photograph migrant farmers in California. Her pictures, which carry captions in the farmers' own words, revealed the migrants' poverty and suffering, as well as their great dignity. Lange's most famous picture, *Migrant Mother* (see page 369), is considered a masterpiece.

During World War II, Lange continued her documentary work by taking pictures of Japanese Americans in California internment camps. Later she produced photo essays for *Life* magazine and traveled the world taking pictures. By the time of her death in 1965, she ranked as one of the world's foremost photographers.

The Granger Collection, New York

Dorothea Lange

SECTION 3 REVIEW

IDENTIFY and explain the significance of the following: Marian Anderson, Robert C. Weaver, Mary McLeod Bethune, Antonio Luhan, John Collier, American Indian Defense Association, Indian Reorganization Act, Okies, Pare Lorentz, Dorothea Lange.

LOCATE and explain the importance of the following: Dust Bowl.

1. **MAIN IDEA** How did the New Deal affect African Americans during the 1930s?
2. **MAIN IDEA** How did the Indian Reorganization Act benefit Native Americans?
3. **LINKING HISTORY AND GEOGRAPHY** What factors caused the Dust Bowl during the 1930s?
4. **WRITING TO DESCRIBE** Imagine you are an Okie migrating west in 1939. Write a diary entry describing your experiences on the West Coast.
5. **ANALYZING** How did filmmakers, such as Pare Lorentz, and photographers, such as Dorothea Lange, serve as social critics during the 1930s?

PREVIEW WORKSHOP

Following is a list of the significant people and terms in this section. You may wish to use this list as a section preview.

People
- Margaret Mitchell
- John Steinbeck
- Zora Neale Hurston
- Richard Wright
- Aaron Copland
- Thomas A. Dorsey
- Benny Goodman
- Robert Sherwood
- Lillian Hellman
- Thornton Wilder
- Jacob Lawrence
- Georgia O'Keeffe
- Anna "Grandma" Moses

Terms
- Federal Project No. 1
- Federal Writers' Project
- regionalists

MOTIVATING: STUDENT EXPERIENCES

Have students give examples of ways that music and the other arts reflect concerns present in American society today. Then have students speculate how the concerns of the depression might have affected the work of people in the arts in the 1930s.

FOCUS OBJECTIVES

- Explain how the Federal Project No. 1 aided writers and artists.

- Describe what many novels were like in the late 1930s.

- Identify common themes that were often heard and seen in music, plays, and paintings of the New Deal era.

CORE RESOURCES

- **Section 4 Daily Quiz**

AV RESOURCES

- **Everyday Life in America Transparency and Worksheet 24**

372

Section 4

THE NEW DEAL AND THE ARTS

F O C U S
- **How did Federal Project No. 1 aid writers and artists?**
- **What were many novels like in the late 1930s?**
- **What common themes were often heard and seen in music, plays, and paintings of the New Deal era?**

In attempting to put Americans back to work, the Roosevelt administration did not forget about those who worked in the arts. The WPA established a series of programs to employ writers, actors, musicians, painters, and other artists. Meanwhile literature in the late 1930s began to turn from escapist fantasies to realistic portrayals of the depression, while musicians, playwrights, and painters searched for uniquely American subject matter.

The Granger Collection, New York

1936 poster for WPA production, *Macbeth*

THE WPA PROGRAMS

All workers struggled with unemployment in depression-era America, including artists. Without an audience that could afford to buy their work, most of the nation's writers, stage actors, musicians, and painters lost their means of earning an income. Like workers in other fields, they sought relief from the government. In February 1935 a few writers picketed federal offices in New York City, carrying signs that read "CHILDREN NEED BOOKS. WRITERS NEED BREAD. WE DEMAND PROJECTS."

Later that year, the WPA set aside some $300 million to create **Federal Project No. 1**. This program tried to encourage pride in American culture by aiding unemployed artists in the fields of writing, theater, music, and visual arts.

The WPA's **Federal Writers' Project** (FWP) hired some 6,600 unemployed writers to produce a variety of works, including state travel guides and histories of various ethnic groups. Others conducted oral-history interviews with hundreds of elderly former slaves. Historians still use these sources to study slave life. Members of the project also studied American folklore and wrote down folktales. These eventually became the basis for the best-selling *Treasury of American Folklore* (1944). The FWP eventually won praise as the "biggest literary project in history," producing more than 1,000 books

◀ Unemployed and striking actors picketed outside the hotel where heads of the regional, state, and national offices of the WPA met in July 1939.

FEDERAL PROJECT NO. 1

Ask volunteers to describe the ways writers, actors, musicians, and artists were employed during the New Deal. Have students speculate how the New Deal's art programs changed the role of the arts in everyday life and affected the public's perception of artists and the arts.

■■ Ask students in what ways the federal government supports the arts today.

THE ARTS OF THE NEW DEAL ERA

Organize the class into four groups and assign one of the following art forms to each group: novels, plays, music, and paintings. Direct each group to create a chart or other graphic organizer to present the artists, works, trends, and themes of the New Deal era in its assigned art form. Encourage groups to illustrate their graphic organizers. After each group has shown and explained its graphic organizer to the class,

ask volunteers to describe the themes and characteristics that these organizers have identified as common to American novels and other literary, performing, and fine arts during the Great Depression.

▶

---

and pamphlets. It also helped launch the careers of numerous writers who went on to great success, such as John Steinbeck and Richard Wright.

The WPA's Federal Theatre Project hired unemployed actors, directors, designers, stagehands, and playwrights to encourage theatrical productions. It entertained millions of Americans, bringing productions to many small towns that had never experienced live theater. The Federal Music Project hired musicians to form orchestras and present some 4,000 musical productions per month to audiences across the country. It also hired music researchers to write down popular American folk songs. The Federal Arts Project hired unemployed artists and designers to produce posters for New Deal programs and to teach art in public schools. Others painted murals on public buildings constructed by the PWA.

■■ **Federal Project No. 1 employed various writers and artists and spread their work throughout the country.**

*L*ITERATURE IN THE LATE 1930s

American interest in romantic fiction continued into the late 1930s. One of the best-selling novels of the decade was Margaret Mitchell's *Gone with the Wind* (1936), a sweeping story of the Old South during the Civil War and Reconstruction. Many depression-era readers could relate to the turmoil faced by the novel's main character, Scarlett O'Hara, who survives war and economic chaos. Her uplifting closing line, "After all, tomorrow is another day," inspired readers of the 1930s.

By the end of the decade, many writers had incorporated the experiences of the depression into their works. John Steinbeck, a writer employed by the FWP, produced a gripping picture of the depression era in *The Grapes of Wrath* (1939). The story follows the fortunes of a desperately poor Dust Bowl family as they travel to California:

66 As the dark caught them, they clustered like bugs near to shelter and to water. And because they were lonely . . . , because they had all come from a place of sadness and . . . were all going to a new mysterious place, they huddled together. 99

▲ Some three years in the planning, MGM's production of *Gone with the Wind* was the most eagerly awaited and top-grossing film of 1939.

As it was for the real Okies, life in California is lonely and harsh for Steinbeck's fictional migrant family. Like *Gone with the Wind,* however, Steinbeck's novel includes a hopeful note, as the head of the family, Ma Joad, optimistically states, "They ain't gonna wipe us out. Why, we're the people—we go on."

Other novels described the experiences of ethnic minorities in the era. African American anthropologist Zora Neale Hurston wrote *Their Eyes Were Watching God* (1937), which explores a black woman's search for fulfillment in rural Florida. Richard Wright offered a grim picture of black urban life in *Native Son* (1940), which

◀ *Native Son* by Richard Wright

▶ *Their Eyes Were Watching God* by Zora Neale Hurston

A number of writers gained fame in the 1930s, including Albert Halper, the son of poor Jewish immigrants from Lithuania. Halper's writing reflected on depression-era society. "I am sorry for many things in life," he wrote in 1934. "I am sorry for the small folk who live thin twisted lives, who have to hold onto their job and look alive when the big chief passes by. I am sorry for the broken men who stand against buildings when the wind howls down the street and the snow whirls past the arc lamps. I am sorry . . . for all my old buddies down at the Post Office—the whites, the Negroes, and the Filipinos, who stand hour on hour tossing mail."

PRIMARY SOURCE

Description of Change: excerpted

Rationale: excerpted to focus on main idea

Practice

GUIDED PRACTICE

Tell students to imagine they are reporters preparing to interview one of the artists in this section. Work with students to develop a series of questions they would like the artist to answer.

INDEPENDENT PRACTICE

Have students select one of the people listed in the Preview Workshop. Then ask students to use the questions developed in the Guided Practice activity as the basis for a magazine "profile" of their chosen subject.

Review and Assessment

REVIEW Have students work in small groups to create a four-page pictorial essay titled "A Reflection of the Times: The Art of the 1930s." Call on volunteers to display and discuss their essays. Then assign the Section 4 Review on p. 375.

ASSESS Assign the **Section 4 Daily Quiz** in *Core Resources*.

MAKING CONNECTIONS

Art

Painter George Biddle once said FDR had "done more for painters in this country than anybody else ever did—not only by feeding them . . . but by establishing the idea that paintings are a good thing to have around, and that artists are important."

COOPERATIVE LEARNING

Organize students into four-person groups consisting of a scriptwriter, caption writer, designer, and artist. Direct them to create plans for a museum exhibit titled "The Arts in the 1930s." Groups can design exhibits on literature, music, plays, paintings, or photography, with each group creating a floor plan, description of works, captions for displays, and tour-guide script for its exhibit.

chronicles the journey of a young African American man lost in a racist world where he can never succeed. *Native Son* explores several themes that haunted the 1930s, including class differences, socialism, racism, and urban despair.

■■ **Many novels of the late 1930s reflected the experiences of the depression.**

PERFORMING ARTS IN THE NEW DEAL ERA

American music of the late 1930s increasingly tried to capture uniquely American sounds. As WPA researchers wrote down American folk songs and folktales, composer Aaron Copland used these themes as the basis for his most popular compositions, including *Billy the Kid* (1938).

Interest in African American music continued throughout the 1930s. Black gospel, a cross between jazz and traditional spirituals, gained popularity through the work of African American composer Thomas A. Dorsey —whose songs included "Precious Lord, Take My Hand"—and singers such as Sister Rosetta Tharpe and Mahalia Jackson. Jackson recalled that some ministers initially objected to this new style of music:

▲ Paper fan depicting singer Mahalia Jackson

66 They didn't like the hand-clapping and the stomping and they said we were bringing jazz into the church and it wasn't dignified. Once at church one of the preachers got up in the pulpit and spoke out against me. I got right up, too. I told him I was born to sing gospel music. 99

Jazz continued its rise in popularity, largely because of the development of swing, a smooth big-band style popular in dance halls. The style derived its name from Duke Ellington's 1932 hit "It Don't Mean a Thing If It Ain't Got That Swing." White conductor Benny Goodman helped popularize swing in the late 1930s. He also broke new ground in popular music by integrating his shows with both black and white performers. Meanwhile, other bands, such as those of Count Basie and Glenn Miller, kept the swing sound alive throughout the 1930's.

On the theatrical stage, plays with social significance—that is, plays that dealt with the nation's labor and class problems—drew large audiences. Robert Sherwood's *The Petrified Forest* (1935) attacked the "petrified forest" of ideas destroying America. Lillian Hellman's *The Little Foxes* (1939) exposed the upper-class greed that many believed was undermining America. By the end of the decade, popular plays, like popular music, focused increasingly on American traditions and values. Two examples are Thornton Wilder's *Our Town* (1938), a heartwarming drama of life and death in a small American town around 1900, and William Saroyan's *The Time of Your Life* (1939), which celebrates the diversity of urban America.

▲ Program from Lillian Hellman's *The Little Foxes*

◄ Lillian Hellman

RETEACH Organize students into groups of three and have them assign one Focus question to each member. Direct students to prepare brief answers to their assigned questions and to share their answers with their group.

*C*losure

Have students identify the ways in which the American public benefited from the New Deal programs for artists.

*E*xtension

INTERPRET Have students make an oral presentation on one of the midwestern regionalists, explaining how the artist's work reflects rural traditions.

INVESTIGATE Point out that many of the travel guides developed by the Federal Writers' Project have recently been reprinted. Have students review a section of the guide for their state and report on it to the class.

■ Music—folk songs, gospel, and jazz—and plays—socially significant and traditional—reflected uniquely American styles and themes.

*P*AINTERS EXAMINE LOCAL CULTURE

Like American writers, painters recorded a variety of memorable American images during the depression. Harlem artist Jacob Lawrence portrayed the daily lives of African American heroes, such as Frederick Douglass and Harriet Tubman, while New Mexico artist Georgia O'Keeffe painted haunting images of the southwestern desert landscape.

Perhaps reflecting the New Deal's focus on farmers' problems, many artists of the era looked to rural America for their subject matter. A group of midwestern artists known as the **regionalists** stressed local folk themes and customs. The regionalists included artists such as Thomas Hart Benton of Missouri, John Steuart Curry of Kansas, and Grant Wood of Iowa.

These artists reminded urban art lovers of America's rural traditions. Wood always insisted that his best ideas "came while milking a cow." The most famous of the regionalist paintings is probably Wood's *American Gothic,* which depicts a stern farmer, pitchfork in hand,

▲ Paintings of rustic scenes, such as *Sugaring Off* by Anna "Grandma" Moses, were typical of regionalists and other folk artists of the depression era.

standing beside a sad-eyed woman in front of a humble farmhouse.

As interest in regional culture grew, people began to rediscover the richness of American folk art, such as handmade quilts and woodcarvings. Many obscure folk artists, including the elderly painter Anna "Grandma" Moses, became well-known during this period.

■ American painters, led by the regionalists, explored a diversity of local folk life.

SECTION REVIEW ANSWERS

IDENTIFY

For significance, see the following pages:
Federal Project No. 1 (p. 372)
Federal Writers' Project (p. 372)
Margaret Mitchell (p. 373)
John Steinbeck (p. 373)
Zora Neale Hurston (p. 373)
Richard Wright (p. 373)
Aaron Copland (p. 374)
Thomas A. Dorsey (p. 374)
Benny Goodman (p. 374)
Robert Sherwood (p. 374)
Lillian Hellman (p. 374)
Thornton Wilder (p. 374)
Jacob Lawrence (p. 375)
Georgia O'Keeffe (p. 375)
regionalists (p. 375)
Anna "Grandma" Moses (p. 375)

1. *to encourage pride in American culture and to employ writers and artists*
2. *stressed rural folk themes, customs, and traditions*
3. *focus on American traditions and values*
4. *Pieces should describe how the depression was portrayed in the novel selected.*
5. *Answers should reflect how books by Hurston and Wright, music by Dorsey and Ellington, and paintings by Jacob Lawrence show class differences, racism, urban life, and African American religion in the 1930s.*

■ ■
■ ■
SECTION 4 REVIEW

IDENTIFY and explain the significance of the following: Federal Project No. 1, Federal Writers' Project, Margaret Mitchell, John Steinbeck, Zora Neale Hurston, Richard Wright, Aaron Copland, Thomas A. Dorsey, Benny Goodman, Robert Sherwood, Lillian Hellman, Thornton Wilder, Jacob Lawrence, Georgia O'Keeffe, regionalists, Anna "Grandma" Moses.

1. **MAIN IDEA** Why was Federal Project No. 1 created?
2. **MAIN IDEA** What contribution did regionalists make to American painting?
3. **COMPARING** What common themes did music and plays of the 1930s share?
4. **WRITING TO CREATE** Write a promotional piece for *The Grapes of Wrath, Their Eyes Were Watching God,* or *Native Son* that shows how the novel reflects the experiences of the depression.
5. **GAINING A MULTICULTURAL PERSPECTIVE** How were the experiences of African Americans expressed artistically during the New Deal era?

Chapter Review Answers

WRITING A SUMMARY
See Essential Points in each section for main ideas.

REVIEWING CHRONOLOGY
4, 5, 2, 1, 3
Assessing Consequences
gained appointment to NYA, which she tried to rid of racism; facilitated work of Federal Council on Negro Affairs, a core group of African American government officials

IDENTIFYING PEOPLE AND IDEAS
1. *Roosevelt's relief, recovery, and reform program*
2. *FDR's labor secretary*
3. *money paid to farmers to reduce output of goods*
4. *African American anthropologist and author of* Their Eyes Were Watching God
5. *1935 revenue act that increased taxes on the wealthy*
6. *protest whereby workers occupy factories until labor demands are met*
7. *black brain-trust member and New Deal adviser on racial matters*
8. *commissioner of Indian Affairs who championed Indian reform efforts*
9. *Great Plains region*

turned into wasteland during 1930s by soil erosion and drought
10. *Louisiana senator who proposed Share-Our-Wealth program*

UNDERSTANDING MAIN IDEAS
1. *to restore public confidence in the banking system*
2. *First New Deal focused on direct relief and recovery programs, Second New Deal on social reform.*
3. *increased purchasing power and farm prices through AAA, revitalized rural areas through TVA*

and REA, provided farm loans through FSA, began soil-erosion control and conservation programs through CCC, extended loans through FCA
4. *African Americans—found relief and work mainly through FERA and WPA, appointed to some government offices, faced discrimination in some New Deal programs; Native Americans—revitalized cultural heritage through the Indian Reorganization Act*
5. *Both created visual records of the depression—Lorentz through documentary films, Lange through photographs.*

CHAPTER 14
Review

FDR declares bank holiday. Congress passes 15 New Deal measures.

Southern Tenant Farmers' Union formed. Indian Reorganization Act passed.

Social Security Act, Wealth Tax Act, and Wagner-Connery Act passed. CIO organized. Mary McLeod Bethune helps form National Council of Negro Women. Federal Project No. 1 created.

1933   1935

WRITING A SUMMARY
Using the essential points of the chapter as a guide, write a summary of the chapter.

REVIEWING CHRONOLOGY
Number your paper 1 to 5. Study the time line above, and list the following events in the order in which they happened by writing the first next to 1, the second next to 2, and so on. Then complete the activity below.
1. Aaron Copland composes *Billy the Kid*.
2. CIO organized.
3. Richard Wright's *Native Son* published.
4. FDR declares bank holiday.
5. Indian Reorganization Act passed.

Assessing Consequences How did Mary McLeod Bethune help maximize the participation of African Americans in the New Deal?

IDENTIFYING PEOPLE AND IDEAS
Explain the historical significance of each of the following people or terms.

1. New Deal
2. Frances Perkins
3. subsidies
4. Zora Neale Hurston
5. Wealth Tax Act
6. sit-down strike
7. Robert C. Weaver
8. John Collier
9. Dust Bowl
10. Huey Long

UNDERSTANDING MAIN IDEAS
1. What was the purpose of the bank holiday and the FDIC?
2. How were the economic and social programs of the Second New Deal different from those of the First New Deal?
3. What steps did the government take in the 1930s to aid farmers?
4. How did the New Deal affect African Americans and Native Americans?
5. What contributions did Pare Lorentz and Dorothea Lange make to the New Deal era?

REVIEWING THEMES
1. **Economic Development** How did the Roosevelt administration attempt to promote economic recovery?
2. **Constitutional Heritage** Why might the Supreme Court have declared some New Deal measures unconstitutional?
3. **Cultural Diversity** How did writers and artists of the 1930s reflect the ethnic and cultural diversity of the nation?

THINKING CRITICALLY
1. **Analyzing** Why did some conservative and liberal critics oppose the New Deal?
2. **Evaluating** Do you think that Roosevelt was justified in trying to "pack" the Supreme Court? Why or why not?
3. **Assessing Consequences** How did WPA programs enrich American culture during the 1930s?

STRATEGY FOR SUCCESS
Review the Skills Handbook entry on Identifying the Main Idea beginning on page 748. Examine the photograph below, taken by Margaret Bourke-White in 1937. These residents of Louisville, Kentucky, are waiting in a relief line to receive aid. What contrasts can you see between the experiences of the people in the line and the message on the billboard behind them?

WORLD'S HIGHEST STANDARD OF LIVING
There's no way like the American Way

REVIEWING THEMES

1. enacted measures to safeguard banking system, provided loans to home owners, granted direct relief and jobs to unemployed, spurred economic growth through "pump priming," passed laws protecting labor and benefiting farmers
2. may have believed that some New Deal measures interfered with American individualism, free enterprise, or private property rights
3. Novelists described ethnic experiences, composers integrated music with ethnic themes, playwrights celebrated urban diversity, and artists focused on ethnic heroes and stressed local folk customs.

THINKING CRITICALLY

1. Some conservatives said measures were destroying free enterprise and driving the nation into bankruptcy. Some liberals argued that the New Deal was not going far enough.
2. Evaluations should weigh the system of checks and balances under the Constitution against FDR's reasons for protecting his programs.
3. WPA financed researchers who wrote down American folktales and folk songs; sponsored interviews with former slaves; spread theater, music, and art to rural areas; launched careers of writers and other artists.

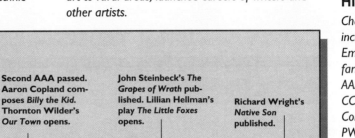

Margaret Mitchell's *Gone with the Wind* published. FDR reelected president.

FDR tries to "pack" Supreme Court. Farm Security Administration created. GM strike begins.

Second AAA passed. Aaron Copland composes *Billy the Kid*. Thornton Wilder's *Our Town* opens.

John Steinbeck's *The Grapes of Wrath* published. Lillian Hellman's play *The Little Foxes* opens.

Richard Wright's *Native Son* published.

1937   **1939**

WRITING ABOUT HISTORY

Writing to Classify Create a chart that classifies the programs of the New Deal according to whether they were designed primarily to help banks, farmers, labor, or business.

USING PRIMARY SOURCES

Jesse Perez worked for the meat-packing industry in Chicago in 1939, during a time when the CIO was attempting to organize workers in the stockyards. Read the following excerpt, which comes from an interview Perez did at that time with a member of the Federal Writers' Project. What does Perez have to say about the treatment of Mexican workers by the company during this time?

> 66 *The bosses in the yards never treat Mexican worker same as rest. I was first to wear CIO button; ever since I start wearing the button they start to pick. I can butcher, but they don't give me job. . . . So when I start telling the boys we have a union for them, almost all join right away. We talk all the time what the union going to do for us, going to raise wages, stop speed-up. The bosses watch and they know it's a union coming.*
>
> *So every day they start saying we behind in the work. They start speeding up the boys more and more every day. . . . We told bosses we working too fast, can't keep up. The whole gang, thirteen men, all stop. Bosses say, we ain't standing for nothing like this. Four days later they fire the whole gang, except two. We took the case in the labor board and . . . now all who was fired got work.*
>
> *Now the bosses try to provoke strike before CIO get ready. . . . We know what they do, we don't talk back, got to watch out they don't play tricks like that.* 99

LINKING HISTORY AND GEOGRAPHY

Describing the effects of the Dust Bowl, John Steinbeck wrote: "The Western States are nervous under the beginning change. . . . A half-million people moving over the country; a million more, restive [restless] to move; ten million more feeling the first nervousness." How did the Dust Bowl influence population shifts in the Southwest?

Scene from the film *The Grapes of Wrath*, 1939

 BUILDING YOUR PORTFOLIO

Complete the following projects independently or cooperatively.

1. **THE ECONOMY** In chapters 11, 12, and 13, you examined the U.S. economy in the 1920s. Building on that experience, imagine you are a New Deal legislator. Write a proposal for a new public works project. Your proposal should describe what the project is, how workers and businesses will benefit, and why your project will be useful to society in terms of relief, recovery, or reform.

2. **CULTURE AND SOCIETY** In chapters 11 and 12 you explored U.S. society in the 1920s. Building on that experience, imagine you are an author in the 1930s. Write a short, realistic passage for your novel that describes the Dust Bowl's effect on your main character.

BETWEEN THE WARS

1921–1941

Chapter Overview

After World War I many nations expected that the U.S. would take a leadership position in world affairs. But the prospects of becoming entangled in another war led the U.S. to limit its leadership role to diplomatic and disarmament conferences. Instead, U.S. attention was focused on affairs at home and in Latin America. However, the worldwide economic depression promoted the rise of dictators in Europe, which made American isolation from European affairs more difficult to maintain and eventually resulted in involvement in another world war.

Chapter Planning Guide

CHAPTER 15	CORE RESOURCES	AUDIOVISUAL RESOURCES	PROGRAM RESOURCES
INTRODUCTION pp. 378–379	■ Building Your Portfolio Worksheet 3	■ Everyday Life in America Transparency and Worksheet 25	
TEACHING THE CHAPTER pp. 380–395 ■ For expanded coverage of p. 383, see Chapter 24, pp. 655–658; for coverage of p. 390, see Chapter 26; for coverage of p. 391, see Chapter 23, pp. 632–633.	■ Graphic Organizer 15 ■ Social Studies Skills Worksheet 15 ■ Literature Worksheet 15 ■ Geography Worksheet 15 ■ Outline Maps 1, 2, 14, 15, 19, 20, 21	■ *The American Nation Videodisc: U.S. Warships in Havana Harbor*	
REVIEW AND ASSESSMENT pp. 396–397	■ Chapter 15 Daily Quizzes ■ Reteaching Worksheet 15 ■ Chapter 15 Tests ■ Alternative Assessment Forms		■ Test Generator

Additional Resources

BOOKS FOR TEACHERS

Alonso, Harriet H. *Peace As a Women's Issue.* Syracuse University Press, 1993. Covers the history of the women's peace movement from the 19th century to modern times.

Black, George. *The Good Neighbor.* Pantheon, 1988. Account of U.S. relations with Central America and the Caribbean.

Scott, William R. *The Sons of Sheba's Race.* Indiana University Press, 1992. In-depth description of the role of African Americans in Italy's war with Ethiopia.

BOOKS FOR STUDENTS

* Allen, Peter. *The Origins of World War II.* Watts, 1992. Part of Witness to History Series; includes illustrations.

Jenkins, Tony. *Nicaragua and the United States: Years of Conflict.* Watts, 1989. Traces the history of U.S. foreign policy in Nicaragua from the 19th century to the present.

Overy, Richard. *The Road to War.* Random House, 1990. Highly readable account of the events leading up to World War II.

* for students reading below grade level

MULTIMEDIA MATERIALS

A New Germany: 1933–1939, Vol. 1. Video, 52 min. Thames Television/ SSSS. Documentary footage of the major political and economic events that led to the spread of Nazism.

Prelude to War: 1935–1939. Video, 25 min. Aims/SSSS. Narrates events leading to Hitler's rise in Germany, the Spanish Civil War, and Japan's aggression toward China.

Seeds of Discord: 1933–1936. Video, 25 min. Aims/SSSS. Covers the rise of Stalin, Hitler, and Mussolini.

U.S. Intervention in Latin America: Witness to History. Video, 15 min. Guidance Associates/SSSS. Analyzes history of U.S. relations with Latin America.

THEMES IN AMERICAN HISTORY

USE WITH PAGES 378–379

Listed on the right are the themes emphasized in Chapter 15. The questions in boldface type stimulate critical thinking and provide students with an opportunity to discuss the themes within a broadened context. The questions also appear in the pupil's edition on p. 378.

■ GLOBAL RELATIONS

How might nations work together to promote world peace? Students may suggest that nations could agree to set limits on weapons, enter into treaties, or form international organizations to monitor world problems.

■ ECONOMIC DEVELOPMENT

What economic problems might wars create? Students may mention that the loss of lives and the destruction of homes, businesses, factories, and transportation networks disrupt a nation's economy. As a result, unemployment might rise, and there may be a shortage of consumer goods.

What political problems might result from these economic difficulties? Economic problems might create dissatisfaction among citizens, which could possibly lead to changes in government policies and leadership.

■ DEMOCRATIC VALUES

What conditions might give rise to a dictatorship? Students may mention that economic downturns might cause citizens to turn to strong leaders to solve a nation's problems. In turn, such a government might use an economic crisis as an excuse to assert more control over its citizens. The presence of a strong military might enable that government to increase its power, while the absence of stable political parties might weaken opposition to the government's restrictions of people's rights.

CHAPTER STRATEGIES FOR MEETING INDIVIDUAL NEEDS

LIMITED ENGLISH PROFICIENT LEARNERS

Have students work in groups to create a visual display for the bulletin board that describes the people involved in and the important events leading to World War II.

TACTILE/KINESTHETIC LEARNERS

Organize the class into groups and have each group create a skit that examines and dramatizes the difficult decisions that different nations' policymakers faced between the wars.

LEARNERS HAVING DIFFICULTY

After students have read the chapter, have them work in pairs, assigning each pair an Essential Point from the chapter. Ask pairs to expand on their topic by writing brief explanations or creating visuals. Have pairs share their explanations or visuals.

AUDITORY LEARNERS

Assign each student to research a person presented in the chapter. Then have students present short biographical sketches to the class, and have other students guess the identity of the person presented.

VISUAL LEARNERS

Have students study the illustrations in this chapter. Ask them to do library research to locate additional images that relate to the chapter content and to share their findings with the class.

GIFTED LEARNERS

Organize students into groups, assigning each of the chapter's sections to two groups. Have each group develop a debate that covers one of the main ideas presented in the section. Ask each pair of groups to present its debate to the class.

USING THE CHAPTER FOCUS

■ UNDERSTANDING THE MAIN IDEA

Have students identify some domestic problems that confront the U.S. today. *(health and welfare issues, homelessness, crime, unemployment)* Write students' responses on the chalkboard. Ask students to speculate how similar problems in some European nations during the 1920s and 1930s could have created conditions that led to war. Have students check the accuracy of their speculations as they read the chapter.

THEMES

Have students work individually or in small groups to answer the questions under Themes. Save students' responses so that they can compare them with their responses after studying the chapter. (See p. 377B for suggested answers.)

■ THE TIME LINE

Have students copy in their notebooks the time line at the bottom of the page. As they read the chapter, have students prepare brief articles about each time-line event that might appear in an encyclopedia. Students should also suggest illustrations that might accompany their articles.

CORE RESOURCES

- Graphic Organizer 15
- Outline Maps 1, 2, 14, 15, 19, 20, 21
- Building Your Port-folio Worksheet 3

AV RESOURCES

- Everyday Life in America Trans-parency and Worksheet 25

378

ABOUT THE ILLUSTRATION

By 1932 the National Socialist, or Nazi, party was the strongest of Germany's seven major political parties. The Nazis attracted almost 14 million of nearly 37 million votes cast in the July election and gained 230 of 608 seats in the Reichstag, the German parliament. This photograph shows supporters of the Nazi party, which in 1933 Hitler declared the only political party legally allowed to operate in Germany. Ask students to speculate what might motivate such enthusiastic support for Hitler's antidemocratic party.

Chapter 15   1921–1941

BETWEEN THE WARS

FOCUS

UNDERSTANDING THE MAIN IDEA

After World War I many Americans hoped to focus on matters at home. Unfortunately, the depression touched off global economic problems. The rise of dictators in Europe set the stage for another war. Dictators also came to power in several Latin American countries. Other countries in Latin America, such as Nicaragua and Mexico, attempted to reduce U.S. influence.

THEMES

- **■ GLOBAL RELATIONS** How might nations work together to promote world peace?

- **■ ECONOMIC DEVELOPMENT** What economic problems might wars create? What political problems might result from these economic difficulties?

- **■ DEMOCRATIC VALUES** What conditions might give rise to a dictatorship?

1921	1926	1931	1933	1939
Washington Conference begins.	Augusto Sandino organizes revolt in Nicaragua.	Japan invades Manchuria.	Adolf Hitler becomes chancellor of Germany.	World War II starts.

■▶ **LINK TO THE PAST**

Call on volunteers to recall the impact the Great Depression had on the U.S. Ask students to speculate why economic hardships might cause Americans to resist military involvement in Europe and Asia and to consider what nonmilitary steps the U.S. might take to reduce international tensions and to promote world peace.

:: LINK TO THE PAST ▶

World War I and the depression created chaos in Europe. Germany was required to pay substantial war reparations, while other European countries owed the United States large war debts. After the war many Americans called for an end to foreign military involvements.

Nazi parade watchers, 1932

"*O*ne word . . . describes the whole feeling in America to-day, and that is *disillusionment* [disappointment]: disillusionment in the leaders, disillusionment in the business men, disillusionment in politics," wrote a friend to British prime minister David Lloyd George in January 1932. This feeling of pessimism arose from the economic strains of the depression and the international chaos caused by World War I. Instead of bringing peace, the end of the war ushered in a period of economic and political instability in Europe.

Many Americans feared that involvement in European affairs might draw the United States into another war. In 1937 the magazine *Christian Century* estimated that "ninety-nine Americans out of a hundred would today regard as an imbecile anyone who might suggest that, in the event of another European war, the United States should again participate in it." In general, the United States backed down from military intervention in foreign countries in the 1920s and 1930s. American efforts on the world stage focused on reducing weapons and improving relations with Latin America.

Nevertheless, conditions brewing in Europe and Asia would soon doom hopes for world peace. In Italy, Germany, and Spain, ruthless dictators came to power by promising to make their countries great through foreign conquest. In Japan, militaristic dreams of empire threatened U.S. interests in China and the Pacific. When the aggressor nations formed an alliance, the stage was set for global war.

Antiwar sheet music, 1940

HISTORICAL SIDELIGHTS
Isolationism

In a 1936 speech at Chautauqua, New York, President Roosevelt echoed the sentiments of the vast majority of U.S. citizens who were against involvement in European conflicts: "I hate war. We can keep out of a war if those who watch and decide possess the courage to say 'no' to those who selfishly or unwisely would let us go to war."

MOTIVATING: LINK TO TODAY

Ask students to give examples of ways that the U.S. promotes world peace today. Then tell students that this section explains how the U.S. attempted to reduce world tensions between 1921 and 1941.

FOCUS OBJECTIVES

- Explain why the U.S. pursued an isolationist foreign policy after World War I.

- Describe how the U.S. tried to promote world peace in the 1920s and 1930s.

- Analyze how war debts and reparations affected European countries after World War I.

Section 1

THE SEARCH FOR PEACE

FOCUS

- **Why did the United States pursue an isolationist foreign policy after World War I?**

- **How did the United States try to promote world peace in the 1920s and 1930s?**

- **How did war debts and reparations affect European countries after World War I?**

Peace activists, 1940

Profoundly disillusioned by the Great War, the United States sought to promote world peace during the 1920s. Fear of becoming involved in another war caused Americans to try to avoid conflict at any cost. As the world slipped into an economic depression and dictators rose to power in Europe in the 1930s, however, the United States found it increasingly difficult to remain isolated from the world's problems.

LEGACIES OF WORLD WAR I

Over 8 million people, including more than 112,000 Americans, had died fighting in the Great War. Yet, because of the postwar chaos in Europe and the founding of a Communist government in the Soviet Union, Americans did not believe that the war had made the world "safe for democracy." The Women's International League for Peace and Freedom summed up the nation's doubts: "War to end war has proved a failure. The war is won, yet nowhere is there peace, security or happiness."

Americans worried about being dragged into another foreign conflict. "We ask only to live our own life in our own way, in friendship and sympathy with all, in alliance with none," declared Senator Hiram W. Johnson in 1922. Such sentiments led the United States to follow a policy of partial **isolationism**, or withdrawal from world affairs, in the 1920s and 1930s.

Isolationists did not want to cut off the United States completely from the affairs of the rest of the world. They merely wanted to avoid what Thomas Jefferson had called "entangling alliances" that could drag the United States into another war. Isolationists also supported U.S. **unilateralism**, that is, one-sided or independent action in foreign affairs.

Isolationism and unilateralism led the United States to shun membership in international organizations set up after the war, such as the League of Nations and the Permanent Court of International Justice (the World Court).

Presidents Coolidge, Hoover, and Roosevelt all proposed that the United States join the World Court, created to solve international disputes. Public opinion, however, ran strongly against membership. The Senate set strict terms for joining in order to guard its right to make treaties. The nations that already belonged to the World Court rejected the Senate's terms, and the matter was dropped.

AN ISOLATIONIST POLICY

Direct students to prepare a short speech to deliver before a class "Senate," explaining why the U.S. should pursue an isolationist policy after World War I. Have volunteers deliver their speeches to the class. Students may wish to include their speeches in their portfolios.

PROMOTING PEACE

Draw on the chalkboard a four-column chart with the headings: *Five Power Agreement, Four Power Treaty, Nine Power Treaty, Kellogg-Briand Pact.* Complete the chart by having students indicate the nations that signed each treaty and provide its terms. Then have volunteers explain how each treaty was intended to contribute to world peace.

WAR DEBTS AND REPARATIONS

Call on three volunteers to represent government officials from the U.S., Germany, and a U.S. ally after World War I. Ask each official to state his or her government's position on war debts and reparations, explaining how the issue is affecting his or her nation. Have remaining class members act as a tribunal to question the officials and challenge their positions. Ask the tribunal to determine an equitable solution to the issue. ▶

■■ **To avoid being drawn into European wars, the United States pursued an isolationist foreign policy after World War I.**

PROMOTING PEACE

Instead of joining international peacekeeping organizations, the United States used diplomacy to promote world peace. American peace groups urged the U.S. government to bring world leaders together to negotiate **disarmament**, or limiting their weapons. Jane Addams, Emily Greene Balch, Jeannette Rankin, and other leaders of the women's movement played important roles in these peace efforts. For their organizing efforts in the United States and abroad, both Addams (in 1931) and Balch (in 1946) received the Nobel Peace Prize.

The Washington Conference. In Washington, D.C., beginning in November 1921, the United States hosted an international conference on naval disarmament and Pacific security. U.S. secretary of state Charles Evans Hughes surprised the other delegates with his bold proposal that the major powers scrap 78 large warships amounting to almost 1.9 million tons. He also called for a 10-year "naval holiday" during which no battleships or battle cruisers would be built.

Hughes proposed that the United States, Great Britain, and Japan scrap enough large warships to bring their naval strength into a ratio of 5:5:3. That is, Great Britain and the United States would be equal in naval strength, with a large-warship tonnage of roughly 525,000 each, while Japan would have some 315,000 tons. Italy and France would both be limited to some 175,000 tons. This plan became known as the **Five Power Agreement**. Marveled one observer: "Secretary

Hughes sank in 35 minutes more ships than all the admirals of the world have sunk in . . . centuries."

The Washington Conference produced other important agreements as well. In the **Four Power Treaty**, Japan, Great Britain, France, and the United States pledged to respect one another's territory in the Pacific. The **Nine Power Treaty**, which included the nations that signed the Five Power agreement as well as the Netherlands, Portugal, Belgium, and China, guaranteed China's territorial integrity and promised to uphold the Open Door policy.

Japan's navy minister, Admiral Kato Tomosaburo, declared that the conference had created "a new order of seapower." He explained Japan's support for disarmament:

> 66 Japan is ready for the new order of thought—the spirit of international friendship and cooperation for the greater good of humanity—which the Conference has brought about. 99

For a time the Washington Conference agreements eased tensions in Asia. Japan withdrew, at least partially, from the Shandong (Shantung) Peninsula it had invaded in 1914 and from parts of Siberia it had occupied during the Russian Revolution. In 1930 Japan's agreement to extend

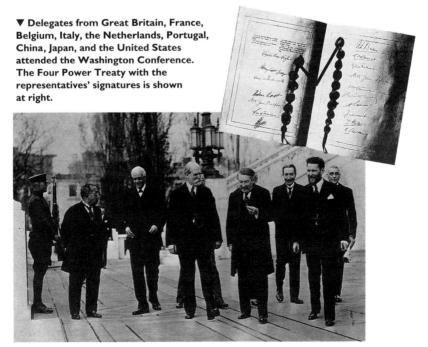

▼ Delegates from Great Britain, France, Belgium, Italy, the Netherlands, Portugal, China, Japan, and the United States attended the Washington Conference. The Four Power Treaty with the representatives' signatures is shown at right.

Practice

GUIDED PRACTICE

Organize students into small groups, and direct each group to write a dramatic headline for a newspaper story on each of the section's main topics. Have each group present its headlines, and then ask the class to devel-

op a brief outline for a newspaper story on each topic.

INDEPENDENT PRACTICE

Tell students to use one of the headlines their group wrote in the Guided Practice activity and the related class outline to write a newspaper story on an aspect of the U.S. effort to promote world peace after World War I. Students may wish to include their stories in their portfolios.

Review and Assessment

REVIEW Have students use the Essential Points of the section as main headings of an outline titled "The Search for Peace." Ask them to use details from the section to add subheads to the outline. Then assign the Section 1 Review on p. 383.

ASSESS Assign the **Section 1 Daily Quiz** in *Core Resources*.

HISTORICAL SIDELIGHTS

Sanctions Against Japan

Although Secretary of State Henry L. Stimson supported economic sanctions against Japan, President Hoover rejected such a penalty. Hoover believed that sanctions would lead to U.S. involvement in a war in a region not vital to U.S. security.

COOPERATIVE LEARNING

Organize students into groups of three to prepare to teach the content that appears under each of the section's three main headings. Each group member should select one of the headings and create a teaching tool, such as an editorial cartoon, newspaper headline, or flowchart, that emphasizes the main idea under their assigned heading. Direct students to create a different teaching tool for each heading. Ask groups to present their plans to the class.

PRIMARY SOURCE

Description of Change: excerpted
Rationale: excerpted to focus on main idea

the holiday on warship construction marked the high point of postwar international cooperation.

Unsuccessful efforts. On April 6, 1927, the 10th anniversary of America's entry into World War I, the French foreign minister, Aristide Briand (ah-ree-steed bree-ahn), proposed that France and the United States enter into an agreement to outlaw war as a means of resolving their differences. The U.S. secretary of state, Frank Kellogg, made a counterproposal that the pact include all nations. Sixty-two countries eventually signed the **Kellogg-Briand Pact**, which outlawed war "as an instrument of national policy" but allowed countries to go to war in self-defense. Unfortunately, the treaty lacked provisions for enforcement. One U.S. senator remarked that the treaty was "as effective to keep down war as a carpet would be to smother an earthquake."

■■ **Through diplomatic conferences and international agreements the United States worked for world peace.**

The pact's weaknesses became clear in September 1931. Japan, whose military leaders were gaining influence, violated all the international agreements and invaded the Chinese territory of Manchuria (see map on page 395). This invasion launched a bloody war between Japan and China. Although many Americans called for

▲ Suffragist and peace activist Carrie Chapman Catt praised the Kellogg-Briand Pact and lobbied Congress for its passage.

▲ These Japanese cavalrymen were photographed in Manchuria in December 1931, some three months after the war between China and Japan had begun.

an economic boycott of Japan, U.S. leaders refused to support sanctions against the Japanese. The failure of diplomacy to prevent Japanese aggression marked the end of attempts at international agreements. Preoccupied by the Japanese invasion and the worldwide economic depression, delegates of the League of Nations' 1932 World Disarmament Conference went home without agreeing to reduce weapons.

WAR DEBTS AND REPARATIONS

The issue of war debts also weakened peace efforts. In the late 1800s European investors had financed U.S. industrial growth, making the United States a **debtor nation** with respect to Europe. After 1914, however, the United States became a **creditor nation**. At the start of World War I, U.S. banks lent money to Great Britain and France so that they could buy armaments in the United States. The U.S. government granted billions more in credit to the Allies. By 1920 the Allies owed more than $10 billion to the United States.

The debtor nations argued that their debts to the United States should be wiped out. David Lloyd George, who had been the British prime minister when the United States entered the war, said:

❝ The United States did not from first to last make any sacrifice or contribution remotely comparable to those of her European Associates, in life, limb, money, material or trade, towards the victory which she shared with them. ❞

RETEACH Organize students into small groups. Tell each group to divide the section material, by subsections, among its members. Direct students to write questions about the main ideas presented in their assigned material. Have group members quiz one another with the questions.

Closure

Read students the following statement made by President Coolidge after World War I: "The world has had enough of the curse of hatred and selfishness, of destruction and war. . . . For the healing of the nations there must be good will and charity, confidence and peace." Have volunteers explain how American foreign policy in the 1920s reflected this attitude.

Extension

RESEARCH Have students research and report on the Japanese conquest of Manchuria.

INVESTIGATE Have students investigate and prepare an oral report on the economic hardships in Germany that were created by reparations.

U.S. officials rejected appeals from Great Britain, France, and Italy to cancel all their war debts. However, the U.S. government reduced the interest rates on the loans and canceled part of the debts. Still, the only way the Allies could pay their war debts to the United States was to collect reparations, or damages, from defeated Germany. In 1921 a reparations commission had set total German reparations at 132 billion gold marks ($32 billion). The Germans bitterly condemned the reparations as too harsh. Chancellor Joseph Wirth paid part of the reparations by borrowing money from Great Britain. The German government also printed paper money, causing massive inflation as the value of the German mark plunged.

In 1931, as the worldwide depression deepened, President Herbert Hoover declared a year's **moratorium**, or halt, on reparation and war-debt payments. The moratorium, however, only prolonged the crisis. Most of the war debts remained

▲ During the 1920s rapid inflation in Germany made most currency worthless. This woman used several million-mark notes to start a breakfast fire.

unpaid. By 1934 none of the debtor nations except Finland could make even a token payment.

America's efforts to collect the war debts sowed resentment in Europe. In Germany the economic hardships created by the reparations made people especially bitter. With his country near financial collapse, Adolf Hitler, a young German politician, hatched a plot to overthrow the German government in 1923. The plot failed, and Hitler was sent to jail. The next year, an international plan temporarily eased Germany's economic crisis by providing loans and extending German debt payments. Continuing German anger over reparations, however, would help bring Hitler to power 10 years later.

■■ Europeans resented America's efforts to collect war debts. German anger over reparations helped Adolf Hitler gain support.

SECTION 1 REVIEW

IDENTIFY and explain the significance of the following: isolationism, unilateralism, disarmament, Emily Greene Balch, Charles Evans Hughes, Five Power Agreement, Four Power Treaty, Nine Power Treaty, Kato Tomosaburo, Kellogg-Briand Pact, debtor nation, creditor nation, moratorium.

LOCATE and explain the importance of the following: Manchuria.

1. **MAIN IDEA** Why did the United States partially withdraw from world affairs after World War I?
2. **MAIN IDEA** What steps did the United States take to work for world peace?
3. **ASSESSING CONSEQUENCES** How did war debts and reparations affect Germany and other European countries?
4. **WRITING TO INFORM** Imagine you are a delegate to the Washington Conference in 1921. Write an essay outlining the goals and accomplishments of the conference.
5. **ANALYZING** Why was the Kellogg-Briand Pact unsuccessful in resolving the conflict in Manchuria?

*Introducing
the Section*

FOCUS OBJECTIVES

- Explain how U.S. relations with Latin America changed in the 1930s.

- Describe how the Great Depression affected Latin American countries.

- Identify the role played by the U.S. in Nicaraguan politics.

- Describe how the U.S. responded when Mexico took over the Mexican oil industry.

PRIMARY SOURCE

Description of Change: excerpted
Rationale: excerpted to focus on main idea

CORE RESOURCES

- **Geography Worksheet 15**
- **Section 2 Daily Quiz**

AV RESOURCES

- **The American Nation Videodisc: U.S. Warships in Havana Harbor**

384

PREVIEW WORKSHOP

Following is a list of the significant people, places, and terms in this section. You may wish to use this list as a section preview.

People
- Maximiliano Hernández Martínez
- Emiliano Chamorro
- Henry Stimson
- Augusto César Sandino
- Adolfo Díaz
- Anastasio Somoza
- Lázaro Cárdenas
- Josephus Daniels

Places
- El Salvador
- Nicaragua

Terms
- Good Neighbor policy
- caudillos
- nationalize

MOTIVATING: PRIOR KNOWLEDGE

Ask students to recall and explain the term *dollar diplomacy*. *(Taft's policy of using loans and investments in Latin America)* Tell students that this section will discuss the use of dollar diplomacy in Latin America in the 1920s and 1930s.

Section 2

RELATIONS WITH LATIN AMERICA

FOCUS

- **How did U.S. relations with Latin America change in the 1930s?**
- **How did the Great Depression affect Latin American countries?**
- **What role did the United States play in Nicaraguan politics?**
- **How did the United States respond when Mexico took over the Mexican oil industry?**

In the 1920s and 1930s the United States preferred to use economic influence—dollar diplomacy—rather than military force to protect its interests in Latin America. For example, conflict between the Mexican government and U.S. oil companies was solved through diplomacy. However, when U.S. interests faced threats in Nicaragua, America sent in the marines.

Woman picking coffee in El Salvador

THE GOOD NEIGHBOR

While the United States tried to avoid war in Europe, presidents Coolidge, Hoover, and Roosevelt all tried to improve relations with Latin American countries. Before his inauguration, Hoover toured Latin America to promote goodwill. Franklin D. Roosevelt spelled out the **Good Neighbor policy** in his inaugural speech of 1933:

❝ In the field of world policy I would dedicate this nation to the policy of the good neighbor—the neighbor who resolutely respects himself and, because he does so, respects the rights of others. ❞

To back up his words, Roosevelt in 1934 canceled the Platt Amendment, by which the United States had claimed the right to intervene in Cuba's affairs. Two years later he gave up the U.S. claim to intervene unilaterally in Panama. Roosevelt also withdrew marines from Haiti, where they had been stationed as an occupying

force since 1915. However, in economic matters the United States often behaved more like an overbearing landlord than a good neighbor.

U.S. investors played a powerful, and sometimes negative, role in Latin America. After World War I, large U.S. companies increased their investments in banana, coffee, and sugar plantations in Central America and the Caribbean.

■■ **In the 1930s the United States pledged to reduce military intervention in Latin America. U.S. business investment continued, however.**

The largest of the American companies was the United Fruit Company, which owned millions of acres in Central America and the Caribbean. In Guatemala it was the largest landowner, exporter, and employer. Besides establishing plantations, United Fruit and other companies built roads and railroads and controlled the ports and shipping lines necessary to export their products. They also tied these regions to the world economy, though

Teaching the Section

RELATIONS WITH LATIN AMERICA

Direct students to assume the role of FDR and prepare a script for a "fireside chat" explaining how his Good Neighbor policy will change U.S. relations with Latin America. Have volunteers deliver their talks. Students may wish to include their scripts in their portfolios.

DEPRESSION AFFECTS LATIN AMERICA

Organize students into small groups to create cause-and-effect charts showing the relationship between the depression, the rise of caudillos, and U.S. foreign policy in Latin America. Then have each group compare its chart with events in Nicaragua.

NICARAGUA AND MEXICO

Have students work in groups to create scripts for a short radio news commentary on U.S. involvement in Nicaraguan and Mexican politics in the 1930s. Commentaries should focus on similarities and differences in U.S. policy toward each country. After each group has "broadcast" its commentary, ask each student to write a paragraph assessing whether Roosevelt's policies toward Mexico showed that the U.S. had become a "good neighbor." ▶

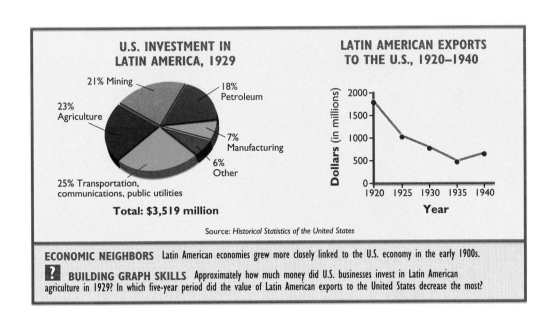

U.S. INVESTMENT IN LATIN AMERICA, 1929

21% Mining
18% Petroleum
23% Agriculture
7% Manufacturing
6% Other
25% Transportation, communications, public utilities

Total: $3,519 million

LATIN AMERICAN EXPORTS TO THE U.S., 1920–1940

Source: *Historical Statistics of the United States*

ECONOMIC NEIGHBORS Latin American economies grew more closely linked to the U.S. economy in the early 1900s.

❓ **BUILDING GRAPH SKILLS** Approximately how much money did U.S. businesses invest in Latin American agriculture in 1929? In which five-year period did the value of Latin American exports to the United States decrease the most?

Graph Caption Answer
about $809 million;
1920–1925

MAKING CONNECTIONS

Sociology
American journalist Carleton Beals traveled through Guatemala in the late 1920s. There he saw railway passengers crammed into second-class coaches and seated on the floor because there were far more cars for carrying bananas than for passengers. When asked about it, Guatemalan President José María Orellana replied, "Yes, bananas are the yellow gold of Guatemala."

PRIMARY SOURCES

Description of Change: excerpted
Rationale: excerpted to focus on main idea

THE AMERICAN NATION VIDEODISC PROGRAM
U.S. Warships in Havana Harbor

2A   41576   :32

profits went mostly to the corporations and wealthy Latin Americans.

In addition to their economic importance in Latin America, the U.S. companies had political power. They made alliances with Latin American landowners and politicians and often played a role in governing the countries in which they operated. The economic and political powers of the large American companies earned them the resentment of many Latin Americans. Chilean poet Pablo Neruda (nay-ROO-thah) wrote:

❝ The Fruit Company, Inc.
reserved for itself the most succulent,
the central coast of my own land,
the delicate waist of America.
It rechristened its territories
as the "Banana Republics." ❞

"Banana republics" were countries run largely to serve the interests of the foreign companies that grew bananas and other crops.

THE RISE OF DICTATORS

The Wall Street crash of 1929 sent shock waves through Latin America. Worldwide depression meant lower prices for coffee, bananas, and other crops on which Latin American economies depended. In El Salvador, coffee prices fell so low

that some plantation owners did not bother to harvest the 1930 coffee crop. Farm wages dropped to eight cents a day.

As workers lost their jobs, the gulf between Latin America's small class of wealthy landowners and the large class of poor landless people widened. The U.S. diplomat Major A. R. Harris commented on the inequality he noted between the classes in El Salvador in 1931:

❝ The first thing one observes . . . is the number of expensive automobiles on the streets. . . . There seems to be nothing between these high-priced cars and the ox-cart with its barefooted attendant. . . . Roughly 90 percent of the wealth of the country is held by about one-half of one percent of the population. ❞

In countries throughout the region, the difficult 1930s brought **caudillos** (kow-THEE-ohs) to power. These caudillos were military leaders who used force to maintain order. In 1932 the caudillo Maximiliano Hernández Martínez brutally crushed a revolt by peasants in El Salvador's hard-hit coffee-growing region. Thousands of peasants were massacred.

During the 1930s caudillos also came to power in Cuba, the Dominican Republic, Guatemala, and Honduras. U.S. diplomats sometimes denounced the caudillos' methods of staying in power: bans on opposition parties and restrictions

Practice

GUIDED PRACTICE

Write *Relations with Latin America* on the chalkboard and circle it. Then draw lines radiating from the circle. Ask students to cite events that affected U.S.–Latin American relations after World War I. As you write each event on a line, ask students to explain how and why it affected those relations.

INDEPENDENT PRACTICE

Have students choose one of the events cited in the Guided Practice activity and, in the role of an American businessperson or a Latin American nationalist, write a newspaper editorial attacking or defending U.S. actions and policy. Students may wish to include their editorials in their portfolios.

Review and Assessment

REVIEW Organize students into four groups and assign each group one of the section's four subsections. Ask each group to create an editorial cartoon that illustrates the Essential Point of their assigned subsection. Have the class interpret each group's cartoon. Then assign the Section 2 Review on p. 387.

ASSESS Assign the **Section 2 Daily Quiz** in *Core Resources*.

HISTORICAL SIDELIGHTS

Dominican Dictator

Rafael Trujillo Molina, dictator in the Dominican Republic, rose to power through the National Guard. He "won" the 1930 presidential election with more votes than registered voters. While in office he promoted his nine-year-old son, Ramfis, to the rank of brigadier general. Trujillo had a hand in Dominican affairs until his assassination in 1961.

MULTICULTURAL PERSPECTIVES

At the Havana Conference in January 1928, Latin American leaders criticized U.S. intervention in Nicaragua. Later, on August 4, 1928, Sandino warned in a letter to 15 Latin American presidents: "Do the Latin American governments think perhaps that the Yankees would be content with the conquest of Nicaragua alone? Have these governments perhaps forgotten that among twenty-one American republics six have already lost their sovereignty? Panama, Puerto Rico, Cuba, Haiti, Santo Domingo, and Nicaragua."

▲ U.S. Army cooks are shown buying produce from Nicaraguan vendors. The baskets contain papayas and alligator pears.

on freedom of speech. However, the United States often supported the caudillos, since they created favorable environments for U.S. businesses.

■■ **The depression wrecked Latin American economies, caused social unrest, and helped bring caudillos to power in many countries.**

INTERVENTION IN NICARAGUA

The United States played a large role in Nicaraguan politics throughout the 1920s and 1930s. In 1925 General Emiliano Chamorro (chah-MAWR-roh) overthrew the government, sparking a bitter civil war.

The United States refused to recognize Chamorro. In May 1926 President Coolidge sent in the marines to protect U.S. commercial interests. He also sent Henry Stimson to negotiate an end to the civil war. Stimson brought the two sides together and they negotiated a peace treaty in May 1927. More important, Stimson called for the abolition of Nicaraguan armed forces. U.S. troops would then train a new Nicaraguan National Guard to maintain order after the withdrawal of U.S. forces.

Augusto César Sandino (sahn-DEE-noh), a general who opposed Chamorro, refused to accept Stimson's proposal. Born in 1893, Sandino was the son of an Indian woman and a well-to-do landowner.

After attending high school, Sandino supervised some of his father's landholdings. He fled his hometown in 1920 to avoid arrest after he shot a man in the leg during a fight. During the next three years, Sandino worked as a mechanic for U.S. companies in Honduras and Guatemala. In 1923 he began working for a U.S.–owned oil company in Tampico, Mexico. There Sandino read about Simon Bolívar, the great hero of Latin American independence struggles.

In 1926, after his return to Nicaragua, Sandino organized a revolt against Chamorro and Chamorro's successor, Adolfo Díaz. He hoped to rid Nicaragua of the Americans, whom he viewed as invaders, and to allow ordinary Nicaraguans to control their country's land and wealth. He planned to help workers and peasants "exploit our own natural resources for the benefit of the Nicaraguan family in general."

Sandino's army, which varied from as few as 30 to as many as 3,000, proved a tough adversary for the U.S. Marines. Although the Americans used aerial bombing for the first time against Sandino's forces, they could not completely destroy the army, which relied on sympathetic farmers to feed and house them.

Augusto César Sandino

The marines never defeated Sandino. The war became increasingly costly for the United States in the midst of the depression. In 1933 President Hoover withdrew the last of the U.S. troops. A year later, the commander of the U.S.–trained National Guard, General Anastasio Somoza, ordered Sandino's assassination. With Sandino dead, organized resistance to Somoza and his military evaporated. Somoza forced out the Nicaraguan president in 1936 and took over the presidency the next year. With U.S. backing, Somoza and other members of his family ruled Nicaragua almost without interruption until the Sandinista revolution (named for Sandino) overthrew the dynasty in 1979.

RETEACH Organize students into small groups and have them assign one Focus question to each member. Direct students to prepare brief answers to the questions and to share their answers with their group.

*C*losure

Ask students to evaluate how "good" a "neighbor" the U.S. was with Latin America in the 1920s and 1930s.

*E*xtension

INVESTIGATE Have students investigate and report on how caudillos came to power in Cuba, the Dominican Republic, Guatemala, or Honduras during the 1930s.

COMPARE Have students research the everyday lives of the poor and the rich in Latin America in the 1930s and write a report that compares and contrasts the two.

■■ The United States opposed Sandino and trained the National Guard, which helped bring Somoza to power.

*R*ELATIONS WITH MEXICO

Perhaps the most severe test of the Good Neighbor policy came when Mexico's president, Lázaro Cárdenas (KAHR-thay-nahs), began to **nationalize**, or assert government control over, that country's oil industry in March 1938. Although the Mexican Constitution of 1917 proclaimed that Mexico controlled all its underground resources (see Chapter 9), U.S. and British firms had continued to own and operate oil companies in Mexico. When the foreign companies refused to meet the demands of Mexican oil workers for higher wages and better working conditions, however, President Cárdenas nationalized the oil fields.

U.S. oil companies hotly criticized the Mexican seizure of their property. They pressed the U.S. State Department to resist the nationalization. Some called for action to oust Cárdenas. Meanwhile, the U.S. ambassador to Mexico, Josephus Daniels, argued for a compromise between the Mexican government and the oil companies. He urged the United States to recognize Mexico's right to control its oil resources but added that U.S. companies should be compensated for the property they had lost.

▲ President Lázaro Cárdenas (center) is shown with Britain's minister to Mexico (left) and Mexico's secretary of foreign relations (right) shortly before diplomatic relations between Mexico and Great Britain were broken in May 1938.

Most Mexicans supported Cárdenas's bold action against the oil companies. Mexicans worried, however, that the United States might invade Mexico to restore U.S. oil companies' property rights. With events in Europe and Asia looking increasingly threatening, however, Roosevelt decided to maintain good relations with Mexico. He acknowledged Mexico's right to control its own resources and urged the oil companies to reach an agreement with the Mexican government for fair compensation. Mexico agreed to the compromise and began payments in 1939.

■■ Roosevelt resisted calls from oil companies for U.S. intervention to protect their interests in Mexico.

■■
■■ SECTION 2 REVIEW

IDENTIFY and explain the significance of the following: Good Neighbor policy, caudillos, Maximiliano Hernández Martínez, Emiliano Chamorro, Henry Stimson, Augusto César Sandino, Adolfo Díaz, Anastasio Somoza, Lázaro Cárdenas, nationalize, Josephus Daniels.

LOCATE and explain the importance of the following: El Salvador, Nicaragua.

1. **MAIN IDEA** How did the United States hope to secure its interests in Latin America after World War I?

2. **MAIN IDEA** What effect did the Great Depression have on Latin America?

3. **IDENTIFYING CAUSE AND EFFECT** How did the United States intervene in Nicaraguan politics throughout the 1920s and 1930s? What was the effect of this intervention?

4. **WRITING TO PERSUADE** Imagine you are Josephus Daniels in 1938. Write a memorandum to President Roosevelt recommending U.S. policy toward Mexico after the oil fields were nationalized.

5. **EVALUATING** Why did Augusto César Sandino organize a revolt against Díaz?

388

PREVIEW WORKSHOP

Following is a list of the significant people, places, and terms in this section. You may wish to use this list as a section preview.

People
- Benito Mussolini
- Adolf Hitler
- Francisco Franco

- Winston Churchill

Places
- Ethiopia
- Rhineland
- Sudetenland
- Munich, Germany
- Yangtze River (Chang Jiang)
- Albania
- Poland

- Finland
- French Indochina

Terms
- Fascist party
- Blackshirts
- Nazi party
- Brownshirts
- anti-Semitism
- *Kristallnacht*
- Spanish Civil War

- Axis Powers
- Munich Conference
- appeasement
- nonaggression pact
- Lend-Lease Act
- blitzkrieg
- Maginot Line
- Atlantic Charter

Section 3

THE ROAD TO WAR

FOCUS

- **What led to the rise of dictatorships after World War I?**
- **How did other countries respond to German aggression?**
- **What caused World War II?**
- **How did the United States move closer to becoming involved in World War II?**

America's isolationist stand faced a severe test when dictators came to power in Italy, Germany, Spain, and Japan in the 1920s and 1930s. Americans tried to stay out of European affairs. Neutrality proved difficult, however, as France and other nations fell before German armies, Great Britain battled for its life, and Japan expanded its territory in Asia.

Japanese women raising money for the war in China

THE RISE OF DICTATORSHIPS

Most European nations after World War I faced inflation and unemployment, which caused political and social unrest. Disagreements over how to solve these problems led to violent clashes between Communists and conservatives. Right-wing military leaders came to power in several countries by promising to end the chaos.

Mussolini in Italy. Although Italy had been on the winning side when World War I ended, many Italians felt they had not benefited from the Treaty of Versailles. Thousands of Italian soldiers returned home after the war only to find themselves jobless. Many joined the Italian Communist party, which urged Italian peasants to take over land and Communist workers to seize factories.

To smash the Communist party and promote his own rise to power, Benito Mussolini founded the **Fascist party** in 1921. The Fascists believed that a military-dominated government should control all aspects of society. Beginning in 1921,

bloody clashes between Communists and Fascists created a situation bordering on civil war. In October 1922 Mussolini led an army of his followers, whose black uniforms gave them the name **Blackshirts**, in a march on Rome. With the support of nationalists, who wanted to strengthen Italy, and of businesspeople who opposed the Socialists and Communists, the Fascists occupied the city.

▲ Benito Mussolini (center), shown here with his followers during their march on Rome, was known as *Il Duce* (eel DOO-chay), or "the leader."

Teaching the Section

RISE OF DICTATORSHIPS

Draw on the chalkboard a four-column chart with the headings *Italy, Germany, Japan, Spain.* Call on volunteers to list the postwar problems of each country and to explain how that country responded to these problems. Then ask students to find parallels between the nations in the chart and to write a general statement summarizing what led to the rise of military dictatorships after World War I. Students may wish to include their summary statements in their portfolios.

The king appointed Mussolini prime minister and granted him dictatorial powers. Mussolini limited freedom of speech, arrested political opponents, and restricted voting rights. Acting on a pledge to make Italy an imperial power, Mussolini sent Italian forces into the African nation of Ethiopia in 1935 (see map on page 392). The small, poorly equipped Ethiopian army proved no match for the Italian dive-bombers and machine guns. The U.S. Congress, fearful of being drawn into the conflict, passed a neutrality act banning arms shipments to both sides. Such an embargo hurt Ethiopia more than Italy, which continued to receive weapons from Germany and oil from U.S. companies.

African Americans raised money to send relief and medical aid to the Ethiopians. Thousands of African Americans volunteered to fight in Ethiopia, but pressure from the U.S. government forced Ethiopia to reject such support. This lack of support convinced other fascist countries, such as Germany, that aggression would go unpunished.

Hitler in Germany. In 1932 Adolf Hitler's National Socialist party, or **Nazi party**, won over 40 percent of the vote, and Hitler became chancellor the next year. While in prison, Hitler had written *Mein Kampf* (*My Struggle*), which laid out his plans to restore German power. Hitler blamed Jews, intellectuals, and Communists for Germany's decline. The book won him many supporters, especially among the middle class and the unemployed ruined by inflation and depression.

Hitler's government, called the Third Reich (the Third Empire), claimed dictatorial powers. Hitler prohibited Jews and non-Nazis from holding government positions, outlawed strikes, and made military service mandatory. Nazi storm troopers, known as **Brownshirts** because of the color of their uniforms, crushed all political opposition.

Hitler's tight control over German industry strengthened the economy and reduced unemployment, allowing him to rearm the country in violation of the Treaty of Versailles. Hitler declared:

❝ The buildup of the armed forces is the most important precondition for . . . political power. . . . How is this political power to be used when it is won? . . . Maybe fighting for new export possibilities, maybe . . . conquest of new *Lebensraum* [space for expansion] in the East. ❞

◀ During the 1930s Nazi posters, such as the one shown here, appealed to those who longed to see Germany restored to its former position as a world power.

The Granger Collection, New York

In March 1936, German troops moved into the Rhineland (see map on page 392). Two years later they overran Austria. Hitler then turned toward the Sudetenland (soo-DAYT-uhn-land), in western Czechoslovakia, where more than three million German-speaking people lived. Hitler demanded that Czechoslovakia turn over the region to Germany. Czechoslovakia refused Hitler's demand.

Meanwhile, Hitler's **anti-Semitism**, or hatred of Jews, became official government policy. He deprived Jews of their German citizenship and authorized the destruction of Jewish property. On November 9, 1938, Nazi thugs burned down synagogues and destroyed Jewish businesses. Known as *Kristallnacht*, "the night of broken glass," the violence provided a chilling preview of the still more-terrible fate that awaited European Jews and others who fell victim to Hitler's murderous rule. Despite outrage at these events, however, Americans were not yet willing to intervene in Germany or to encourage Jewish immigration.

Franco in Spain. Spain did not escape the spread of fascism. In the 1930s Spain faced bitter political conflicts. In 1931 a constitution that limited the power of the military and the Catholic church went into effect. It called for such reforms as universal suffrage, nationalization of public utilities, and land for peasants.

Threatened by the liberal reforms, conservative military men united under the leadership of General Francisco Franco. In July 1936 the Fascist army officers tried to overthrow the government, starting the **Spanish Civil War** between Fascists and Loyalists.

MULTICULTURAL PERSPECTIVES

African American pilot John Robinson was the only American volunteer in the war in Ethiopia. Known as the "Brown Condor," news of his exploits against Mussolini's Blackshirts created excitement in the African American community. When Robinson returned to the U.S. in 1936, he promoted the Ethiopian cause and praised Haile Selassie, the "brave and noble leader" of Ethiopia.

AV TRANSPARENCY

Everyday Life in America Transparency and **Worksheet 25**

PRIMARY SOURCE

Description of Change: excerpted and bracketed **Rationale:** excerpted to focus on main idea; bracketed to clarify meaning

Teaching the Section

RESPONSE TO GERMAN AGGRESSION

Have students write an official statement from the point of view of a policymaker attending the Munich Conference to explain why the European powers settled on the policy of appeasement. Call on volunteers to read their statements. Then ask students to assess the sincerity of European leaders who argued that appeasement would maintain peace. Ask students to cite evidence to support their assessments.

 GLOBAL CONNECTIONS

Between 1900 and 1930 Japan became a major exporter of raw silk, and about half of Japan's peasants depended on its production. During the Great Depression silk prices dropped about 50 percent, dealing a blow to the Japanese economy and impoverishing many peasants. This development became a prime factor in discrediting the policies and leaders of the 1920s and laid the foundation for Japanese militarism.

THROUGH OTHERS' EYES

As Italian and German troops invaded Spain, some Americans recognized the urgency of the Spanish situation. Henry L. Stimson pleaded against Roosevelt's refusal to sell arms to Spain: "If this Loyalist Government is overthrown, it is evident now that its defeat will be solely due to the fact that it has been deprived of its rights to buy . . . the munitions necessary for its defense."

PRIMARY SOURCE

Description of Change: excerpted and bracketed
Rationale: excerpted to focus on main idea; bracketed to clarify meaning

---

After almost three years of fighting, Franco took over the national government with German and Italian military aid. The Soviet Union aided the Loyalists, but Roosevelt's fears of being drawn into a European war kept the United States from sending aid.

Individual Americans, however, did join the fight against fascism. Some 3,000 Americans joined the Abraham Lincoln Brigade, one of several international brigades made up of volunteers who went to Spain. Ernest Hemingway, who covered the Spanish Civil War, expressed his support for the Loyalist cause in the powerful novel *For Whom the Bell Tolls* (1940).

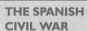

THE SPANISH CIVIL WAR

After the Spanish Civil War, many Loyalists remained bitter over the failure of Western nations to support their cause. In 1940 Julio Alvarez del Vayo, a wartime diplomat for the defeated Spanish Republic, charged that this lack of support had cost the Loyalists the war:

❝*A*part from Russia, from whom she was able, for a time, to buy arms, Republican Spain had no great powers at her side to supply her with men and munitions. . . . Alone, abandoned to their fate, . . . the Spanish people fought for nearly three years against the armed might of the totalitarian states. . . .

My one desire is to show what it would have meant to the Western democracies to have had in Spain a certain ally ready to defend the liberty and dignity of Europe against all attempts at domination and oppression. If . . . Republican Spain had not been defeated, the present war [World War II] would never have begun. . . .

No, it was not Spanish democracy that failed. It was the other democracies who failed to save democratic Spain, as they will one day learn to their cost. ❞

▲ Shown here are Spanish Loyalists leaving Madrid to fight a rebel army advancing on the city.

Militarists in Japan. As German aggression threatened Europe, Japanese expansion loomed in Asia (see map on page 395). Although Japan had moved toward democracy in the 1920s, the leaders of Japan's military forces remained independent of the government. These military men wanted to lessen Japan's reliance on foreign imports, to reduce the influence of Western countries in Asia, and to win for Japan control of new territory throughout Asia.

The creation of a Japanese empire in Asia would give Japan direct control over territories that produced rubber, petroleum, iron, and timber. Worsening economic conditions in Japan strengthened the appeal of the militarists' position.

Japan's 1931 invasion of Manchuria signaled its imperial ambitions. In 1934 and 1935, breaking their Washington Conference pledges, the Japanese began a rapid naval buildup. On July 7, 1937, Japanese and Chinese troops clashed near Beijing (Peking). This incident soon developed into a full-scale war. Japan occupied northern China and launched devastating bombing raids against Chinese cities. Although the League of Nations and the United States condemned Japan's actions, they failed to check Japanese expansion.

■■ In Italy, Germany, Spain, and Japan, postwar problems brought military dictators to power in the 1920s and 1930s.

---

*T*HE RESPONSE TO FASCISM

The spread of fascism in Asia and Europe caused a shake-up in international diplomatic relationships. The most surprising of these realignments was the shift in U.S.–Soviet relations. The Soviets were concerned about curbing the Japanese, who had massed

U.S. RESPONSE TO FASCISM

Direct students to write letters to the editor explaining whether they, as 1930s Americans, support or oppose U.S. neutrality toward expansionist countries. Letters should give reasons for the writers' positions. Call on volunteers with differing viewpoints to read their letters to the class. Students may wish to include their letters in their portfolios.

▶

troops in nearby Manchuria. Hoping "to avert the Japanese danger," Soviet foreign affairs commissar Maksim Litvinov mended diplomatic fences with the United States. In November 1933, after years of hostility between the two countries, the United States formally recognized the Soviet Union.

The fascist powers also formalized their ties. In 1936 the rest of Europe trembled when Germany and Italy formed a military alliance. The two countries became known as the **Axis powers**, which later included Japan.

Roosevelt called for European leaders to meet and resolve their conflicts peacefully. Hitler and Mussolini joined British prime minister Neville Chamberlain and French premier Édouard Daladier (dah-lahd-yay) at Munich in September 1938. The four leaders at the **Munich Conference** signed a pact giving Germany control of the Sudetenland. The European leaders had opted for a policy of **appeasement**, or giving in to demands in an effort to avoid larger conflicts. Many politicians underestimated Hitler's expansionist goals, believing that Hitler sought only to remedy what he considered wrongs created by the Treaty of Versailles. But other politicians, such as Winston Churchill of Great Britain, feared that appeasement would only encourage Hitler to take more territory. Britain and other nations in Europe sped up their rearmament.

▪▪ European leaders tried to appease Hitler to avoid war.

Most Americans denounced the actions of the Axis powers, but isolationism remained strong. American pacifists—religious groups such as the Mennonites and the Society of Friends (Quakers) and groups such as the Committee on the Cause and Cure of War—urged U.S. leaders to reject war as a means of solving conflicts.

A series of neutrality laws passed by Congress from 1935 to 1939 expressed Americans' desire for peace. The neutrality laws (1) prohibited the shipment of U.S. munitions to warring nations, (2) required warring nations that bought goods from America to transport these goods in their own ships, and (3) forbade Americans to travel on the vessels of warring nations.

Not all Americans endorsed neutrality. Many urged the United States to help the nations under attack. If America allowed aggression to go unpunished, they warned, the United States might one day find itself surrounded by powerful enemies.

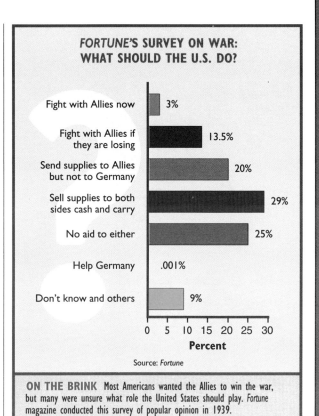

FORTUNE'S SURVEY ON WAR: WHAT SHOULD THE U.S. DO?

- Fight with Allies now — 3%
- Fight with Allies if they are losing — 13.5%
- Send supplies to Allies but not to Germany — 20%
- Sell supplies to both sides cash and carry — 29%
- No aid to either — 25%
- Help Germany — .001%
- Don't know and others — 9%

Percent

Source: *Fortune*

ON THE BRINK Most Americans wanted the Allies to win the war, but many were unsure what role the United States should play. *Fortune* magazine conducted this survey of popular opinion in 1939.

? BUILDING GRAPH SKILLS What percentage of Americans opposed direct military involvement of U.S. forces?

By 1937 President Roosevelt had become convinced that the United States must resist aggression. In October he urged other countries to quarantine, or isolate, expansionist countries. Most Americans, however, were not yet ready to accept U.S. involvement in the quarantine. Proof of this position came in December 1937, when Japanese planes attacked the U.S. gunboat *Panay* and three U.S. oil tankers on China's Yangtze (YANG-SEE) River (Chang Jiang). Several U.S. citizens were killed, and many were wounded. A public opinion poll showed that 54 percent of Americans thought the United States should withdraw from China, rather than risk becoming involved in a war.

War!

U.S. public opinion slowly changed, however, as German aggression continued. In March 1939, Hitler's armies occupied all of Czechoslovakia. Hitler also proposed to annex the Polish port city of

HISTORICAL SIDELIGHTS

Conscientious Objectors

In anticipation of the war, three denominations—Quakers, Mennonites, and Brethren—formed committees to protect the rights of conscientious objectors. One of the most important committees was the Quakers' War Problems Committee. During the war more than 11,000 conscientious objectors worked on soil conservation and reforestation projects in lieu of performing military service.

Teaching the Section

CAUSES OF WORLD WAR II

Write the following on the chalkboard: *World War II Begins.* Ask students to offer events that led to World War II. Using student responses, create a time line of these events on the chalkboard. Then have students suggest policies that world leaders could have employed that might have avoided the German invasion of Poland and the outbreak of war. (*Responses might include calls for arms reduction in Europe, further appeasement, involvement of League of Nations in a settlement, tougher stance toward Germany, preventive war against Germany.*) Discuss each response with the class.

Map Caption Answer
Poland held land between Germany and East Prussia.

HISTORICAL SIDELIGHTS

The Baltic States

The Soviet occupation of Lithuania, Latvia, and Estonia was briefly interrupted in 1941, when Hitler invaded the Soviet Union and occupied the Baltic States. By 1945, however, the three countries were once again under Soviet control. All three states attempted to repel the Soviet takeover, but many members of the opposition were killed or deported to labor camps in Siberia. By 1988 the three republics organized protests favoring sovereignty, and in late 1989 and early 1990, non-Communist governments emerged. In 1990 the new governments declared their intentions to secede from the Soviet Union and became independent the next year after the collapse of the USSR.

German and Italian Expansion, 1935–1941

EXPANSIONIST DICTATORS Hitler's and Mussolini's aggressions brought war to most of Europe for the second time in the 20th century.

? PLACE Why was Poland a likely target for German attack?

Danzig (DAN-sig), but the Poles refused. On April 7, Mussolini's troops invaded Albania.

Awakening at long last to their common peril, Great Britain and France announced that an attack upon Poland would mean war and called on the Soviet Union to join them in resisting further aggression. Instead, on August 23, 1939, the Soviet Union signed a **nonaggression pact** with Nazi Germany. This surprising union came about in part because of a secret clause in the pact in which the two nations agreed to divide Poland between them.

On September 1, 1939, German bombers and armored divisions crashed across the border into Poland. Two days later, Great Britain and France declared war on Germany. World War II had begun. Soviet troops, meanwhile, invaded Poland from the east, occupied the independent nations Estonia, Latvia, and Lithuania, and demanded the right to establish military bases in Finland. When Finland refused, the Soviet Union attacked the small nation and soon annexed part of its territory.

■■ **Allied appeasement failed to halt German aggression. In 1939 the German invasion of Poland sparked World War II.**

U.S. MOVES CLOSER TO WAR

Organize students into groups. Ask them to imagine they are foreign news correspondents assigned to cover World War II. Ask them to identify events that moved the U.S. closer to involvement in the war and to write scripts for a series of radio news stories on those events. Have groups "broadcast" their stories to the class.

THE ATLANTIC CHARTER

Call on volunteers to cite the principles and provisions of the Atlantic Charter and write responses on the chalkboard. Then ask students to explain how each principle was a reaction to a cause of World War II. Encourage students to cite examples in their explanations. Conclude the discussion by asking students to interpret the Atlantic Charter in the context of U.S. "neutrality" in the war. (*showed U.S. was moving closer to involvement*)

▲ This 1939 cartoon satirizes the lack of trust between Germany and the Soviet Union, even after the two nations signed the nonaggression pact.

Roosevelt took steps to aid the European countries under siege. Some three weeks after the German invasion of Poland, he urged Congress to amend the neutrality act that barred the export of munitions. After a six-week debate, Congress agreed on a compromise. The new law allowed any nation to buy munitions from the United States but required that the goods be shipped on foreign vessels.

The European conflict loomed as a major issue in the 1940 election. Both candidates—Roosevelt, who sought a third term, and Republican Wendell Willkie—promised to keep America out of the conflict. In a radio talk on September 3, 1939, Roosevelt pledged: "As long as it remains in my power to prevent, there will be no blackout of peace in the United States."

Roosevelt won his bid for an unprecedented third term. In spite of his public promises to pursue peace, however, he became increasingly alarmed by Japanese and German aggression. He began to view American involvement as unavoidable and started a campaign to prepare U.S. defenses for the likely conflict.

By the end of 1940, U.S. supplies flowed to Great Britain. The British, however, had little cash to pay for needed war materials. Roosevelt proposed that the United States lend or lease arms and other supplies to the British and the other Allies. Congress passed the **Lend-Lease Act** in March 1941. It appropriated $7 billion for ships, planes, tanks, and any other supplies to non-Axis countries.

■ **The United States took its first step toward involvement in the growing European conflict by extending aid to the Allies.**

CONTINUING AGGRESSION

While Hitler carried on his **blitzkrieg** (BLITS-kreeg), or "lightning war," against Poland, the French mobilized. In May 1940, German armored divisions, supported by fighter planes and bombers, crossed the **Maginot Line**, a line of defenses along the French border with Germany. The Germans occupied France; the Netherlands, Belgium, Luxembourg (known as the Low Countries); Denmark; and Norway.

Germany established a puppet government in France headed by Philippe Pétain (pay-tan) and headquartered in the town of Vichy (VISH-ee). A secret French organization known as the Resistance continued to oppose the Germans. In London, French general Charles de Gaulle headed a committee called "Free France," which organized opposition against the Germans.

With the fall of France, Great Britain stood alone. On May 10, 1940, Winston Churchill

▲ Members of the Resistance continued to fight the Germans after the fall of France. This French girl was part of a patrol that hunted down German snipers in Paris late in 1944.

HISTORICAL SIDELIGHTS
Lend-Lease Act

Roosevelt used an intriguing analogy to gain public support for passage of the Lend-Lease Act. He explained that the act was like loaning one's neighbor a garden hose when his or her house is on fire. All one asks is that the hose be returned, or if it is damaged while in use, that it be replaced. Interestingly enough, one of the items in the first shipment of supplies sent to Great Britain under the act was a 9,000-foot fire hose.

HISTORICAL SIDELIGHTS
French Resistance

The French Resistance set up escape routes for Allied aviators, Resistance fighters and Jewish refugees. They also established intelligence gathering groups, underground newspapers, and resistance fighting units to defeat the Nazis. Women played an important part in this effort. In the 1940s, many men viewed women as passive and subordinate, and women in the French Resistance used this stereotype to their advantage, often escaping enemy suspicion because of it. One such woman was Marie Madeleine Fourcade, who assisted the escape to England of hundreds of British and American pilots who were downed in France.

*P*ractice

GUIDED PRACTICE

Organize students into small groups and assign each group one of the following: Italy, Germany, Spain. Ask groups to create cause-and-effect charts that show why and how dictators came to power in each coun-try. Call on volunteers from each group to draw the group's chart on the chalkboard.

INDEPENDENT PRACTICE

Ask students to use the information in the Guided Practice to develop maps that illustrate the rise of dictatorships in Europe in the 1930s. Students should label each country, identify the dictator and/or parties that came to power in the 1920s and 1930s, and annotate their maps with information from the Guided Practice charts.

*R*eview and *A*ssessment

REVIEW Write the following statement on the chalkboard: *Americans found it difficult to avoid foreign entanglements because . . . .* Call on a volunteer to list one reason. Then call on another student to add another reason. Write students' responses on the chalkboard. Then assign the Section 3 Review on p. 395.

ASSESS Assign the **Section 3 Daily Quiz** in *Core Resources.*

 GLOBAL CONNECTIONS

The U.S. embargo caused dissension among Japan's leaders. The embargo effectively ended oil shipments to Japan, which realized that its oil reserves would not see it through a major war. Japan's cabinet settled on a plan of working toward preparedness for war while simultaneously attempting a negotiated settlement. According to the plan, if the diplomatic measures proved unsuccessful, Japan would enter into hostilities against the U.S., Britain, and the Netherlands. Emperor Hirohito opposed the plan and advocated peace over war. Although the U.S. was aware of the plan because it had cracked Japan's diplomatic codes, it was unaware of the dissension among Japanese leaders.

PRIMARY SOURCE

Description of Change: excerpted
Rationale: excerpted to focus on main idea

▲ **RAF combat pilots are shown rushing to their planes to fight German bombers somewhere over French territory.**

became prime minister. With a rare gift for leadership, Churchill rallied the British:

> 66 Hitler knows that he will have to break us in this island or lose the war. . . . Let us therefore brace ourselves to our duties, and so bear ourselves that, if the British Empire and its Commonwealth last for a thousand years, men will still say, "This was their finest hour." 99

On June 10 Italy declared war on France and Great Britain. In August, Hitler unleashed his bombers against Great Britain. The outnumbered British Royal Air Force (RAF) flew day and night to combat the German blitzkrieg.

*T*ENSIONS MOUNT IN THE ATLANTIC

In the face of continuing German attacks, U.S. aid to the Allies gradually increased. By the spring of 1941, German and Italian submarines were turning the North Atlantic into a graveyard of ships. In April, U.S. airplanes and naval vessels began to patrol the Atlantic, notifying British warships of the location of German ships.

A few months later, Roosevelt issued "shoot-on-sight" orders to U.S. warships operating in the North Atlantic "safety zone" America had established in 1939. U.S. warships also began to accompany merchant vessels as far as Iceland. In November, Congress voted to allow U.S. merchant vessels to enter combat areas. Roosevelt armed the merchant vessels and provided them with gun crews.

With the United States moving rapidly toward undeclared war with Germany, Roosevelt and

Churchill met secretly off the coast of Newfoundland in August 1941. The two leaders agreed to a series of principles for international relations. Known as the **Atlantic Charter**, the agreement (1) pledged that the United States and Great Britain would forego territorial expansion, (2) affirmed their respect for the right of every nation to choose its own form of government, and (3) called for freedom of international trade and equal access to raw materials for all countries. Once the war was over, the charter declared, aggressor states should be disarmed, and all nations should work together to rid the world of fear and want.

*T*HE GROWING THREAT FROM JAPAN

As war raged in Europe, Japan added to its conquests in Asia. In July 1941, Japanese troops occupied French Indochina (see map). President Roosevelt immediately froze all Japanese assets in the United States and approved an embargo on shipments of gasoline, machine tools, scrap iron, and steel to Japan. Japan retaliated by freezing all U.S. assets in areas under its control. As a result, trade between the United States and Japan practically ended. To help prevent further Japanese expansion in China, the United States had made China eligible for lend-lease aid earlier in the year.

As U.S. resistance to Japanese aggression grew stronger, Japan's war leaders planned an attack on the United States. Even as the plan went forward, however, a Japanese peace mission visited Washington. On November 20, 1941, this mission demanded that the United States (1) unfreeze Japanese assets, (2) supply Japan's gasoline needs, and (3) cease all aid to China.

The United States had no intention of giving in to the Japanese demands. However, U.S. diplomats kept up the appearance of continuing negotiations with Japan to allow more time to prepare U.S. defenses in the Pacific. By this time the United States had succeeded in breaking the secret code used to send messages between Tokyo and the Japanese mission in Washington, D.C. The Americans knew that the Japanese planned a strike against the United States. The challenge was, as Secretary of War Henry Stimson wrote in his diary, "how we should maneuver them into the position of firing the first shot without allowing too much danger to ourselves."

Closure

Ask students to explain why this section is titled The Road to War. Have them provide evidence from the section that supports such a title.

Extension

INVESTIGATE Instruct students to investigate the immigration of German intellectuals and scientists to the U.S. before World War II.

RESEARCH Invite students to research and report on *Kristallnacht*.

Japanese Expansion, 1931–1941

A PATH OF CONQUEST Japan's military leaders believed that conquering neighboring lands would solve the country's economic problems.

? PLACE What important Chinese cities had Japan captured by 1938?

Map Caption Answer
Shanghai, Beijing, Nanjing, Hangzhou, Tianjin

SECTION REVIEW ANSWERS

IDENTIFY

For significance, see the following pages:
Benito Mussolini (p. 388)
Fascist party (p. 388)
Blackshirts (p. 388)
Adolf Hitler (p. 389)
Nazi party (p. 389)
Brownshirts (p. 389)
anti-Semitism (p. 389)
Kristallnacht (p. 389)
Francisco Franco (p. 389)
Spanish Civil War (p. 389)
Axis Powers (p. 391)
Munich Conference (p. 391)
appeasement (p. 391)
Winston Churchill (p. 391)
nonaggression pact (p. 392)
Lend-Lease Act (p. 393)
blitzkrieg (p. 393)
Maginot Line (p. 393)
Atlantic Charter (p. 394)

LOCATE

For locations, see the maps on pp. 392 and 395.

1. *appeasement; to avoid war*
2. *failure of appeasement policy; German invasion of Poland*
3. *extended aid to the Allies through agreements such as the Lend-Lease Act*
4. *Articles might mention the effects of inflation, unemployment, and political and social unrest.*
5. *A firmer response might have prevented further German aggression.*

SECTION 3 REVIEW

IDENTIFY and explain the significance of the following: Benito Mussolini, Fascist party, Blackshirts, Adolf Hitler, Nazi party, Brownshirts, anti-Semitism, *Kristallnacht*, Francisco Franco, Spanish Civil War, Axis powers, Munich Conference, appeasement, Winston Churchill, nonaggression pact, Lend-Lease Act, blitzkrieg, Maginot Line, Atlantic Charter.

LOCATE and explain the importance of the following: Ethiopia; Rhineland; Sudetenland; Munich, Germany; Yangtze River (Chang Jiang); Albania; Poland; Finland; French Indochina.

1. **MAIN IDEA** What policy did European countries follow in negotiations with Hitler? Why?
2. **MAIN IDEA** What factors led to war in 1939?
3. **MAIN IDEA** What step brought the United States closer toward involvement in the war?
4. **WRITING TO EVALUATE** Imagine you are an American reporter in Europe during the 1920s and 1930s. Write an article that accounts for the rise of dictatorships after World War I.
5. **HYPOTHESIZING** How might events in Europe have been different if European leaders had not decided on an appeasement policy with Hitler?

CHAPTER 15
Review

DEVELOPING THEMES

Return to the Themes section on p. 378. Have students discuss these again and compare their original responses with those given now. (See p. 377B for suggested answers.)

Chapter Review Answers

WRITING A SUMMARY
See Essential Points in each section for main ideas.

REVIEWING CHRONOLOGY
2, 4, 1, 3, 5
Assessing Consequences
Hitler took advantage of appeasement policy and continued the territorial aggression that led to war.

IDENTIFYING PEOPLE AND IDEAS

1. one-sided action in foreign affairs
2. U.S. women's movement leader who received Nobel Peace Prize
3. plan reducing naval strength of U.S., Great Britain, Japan, Italy, and France
4. Latin American military leaders who used force to maintain order
5. Nicaraguan general who led revolt against Díaz
6. assert government control over an industry
7. anti-Semitic author of Mein Kampf, head of Nazi party, and dictator of Germany
8. "the night of broken glass" in 1938 when Nazis destroyed synagogues and Jewish businesses

396

9. 1939 agreement between Germany and the Soviet Union in which both countries agreed not to attack the other
10. British politician who opposed appeasement

UNDERSTANDING MAIN IDEAS
1. fears of entangling alliances and war; growth of dictatorships, failure of appeasement policy to halt Axis aggression
2. economic—increased investments and internal improvements that tied Latin America to world economy; political—made alliances with landowners

and politicians, supported caudillos and military intervention to protect U.S. interests
3. refusal of oil companies to meet workers' demands for better wages and working conditions, right to control Mexican resources
4. hoped to avoid war; feared appeasement would encourage Hitler to seize more land
5. U.S. and Great Britain would forego territorial expansion, respect the right of every nation to self-government, and call for equal access to trade and raw materials; it established principles for building peace in postwar era.

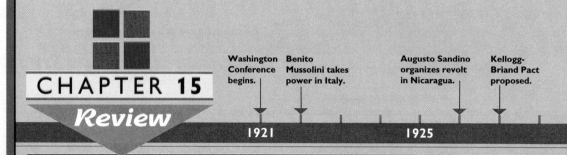

CHAPTER 15
Review

| Washington Conference begins. | Benito Mussolini takes power in Italy. | Augusto Sandino organizes revolt in Nicaragua. | Kellogg-Briand Pact proposed. |

1921   **1925**

WRITING A SUMMARY
Using the essential points of the chapter as a guide, write a summary of the chapter.

REVIEWING CHRONOLOGY
Number your paper 1 to 5. Study the time line above, and list the following events in the order in which they happened by writing the first next to 1, the second next to 2, and so on. Then complete the activity below.

1. Spanish Civil War begins.
2. Washington Conference begins.
3. Lázaro Cárdenas nationalizes Mexican oil fields.
4. Kellogg-Briand Pact proposed.
5. World War II starts.

Assessing Consequences What effect did the Munich Conference have on events in Europe?

IDENTIFYING PEOPLE AND IDEAS
Explain the historical significance of each of the following people or terms.

1. unilateralism
2. Emily Greene Balch
3. Five Power Agreement
4. caudillos
5. Augusto César Sandino
6. nationalize
7. Adolf Hitler
8. *Kristallnacht*
9. nonaggression pact
10. Winston Churchill

UNDERSTANDING MAIN IDEAS
1. What factors encouraged the growth of isolationism in the United States after World War I? What events in the 1930s convinced U.S. leaders to abandon the policy?
2. What economic and political role did the United States play in Latin America?
3. Why did Lázaro Cárdenas nationalize Mexican oil fields in 1938?
4. Why did some European leaders favor a policy of appeasement toward Hitler? Why did others oppose it?
5. What were the provisions of the Atlantic Charter? Why was it adopted?

REVIEWING THEMES
1. **Global Relations** In what ways did countries promote world peace after World War I?
2. **Economic Development** What economic and political problems emerged after World War I?
3. **Democratic Values** How did the fascist dictatorships in Europe limit civil liberties?

THINKING CRITICALLY
1. **Analyzing** How did Benito Mussolini rise to power?
2. **Evaluating** What were the goals of Japan's militarists? Why did they want to create a Japanese empire in Asia?
3. **Synthesizing** How did American approaches to neutrality change between 1935 and 1941?

STRATEGY FOR SUCCESS
Review the Strategies for Success on Interpreting Editorial Cartoons on page 162. Then study the following cartoon, entitled *New Kind of Pump Priming*. What is the cartoonist's message?

Pump Priming—New Style

REVIEWING THEMES

1. formed organizations such as League of Nations and World Court; held diplomatic conferences to negotiate disarmament; reached agreements protecting countries' borders and outlawing war
2. economic—loss of lives and property, war debts and reparations, unemployment and inflation; political—rise of caudillos in Latin America and right-wing dictatorships in Europe and Asia
3. limited freedom of speech, political dissent, and voting rights; persecuted Jews

THINKING CRITICALLY

1. supported by businesspeople and nationalists, who feared the radical politics that emerged from Italy's postwar social unrest
2. to lessen Japan's reliance on foreign imports, to reduce Western influence in Asia, and to create an empire; to give Japan control over territories that produced needed raw materials
3. Early laws limited arms trade with warring nations. After 1939 U.S. increased military and other aid to Allies and increased U.S. military and economic pressure on Germany and Japan.

STRATEGY FOR SUCCESS

The cartoonist is accusing the government of using spending for war preparations and support of Allies to stimulate economic recovery from the depression.

WRITING ABOUT HISTORY

Letters will vary but should describe the struggle between Loyalist and Fascist troops.

USING PRIMARY SOURCES

Wheeler believes act will violate international law, weaken U.S. defenses, and lead the U.S. on the path to war just as it did in World War I, which Wheeler suggests was not worthwhile.

LINKING HISTORY AND GEOGRAPHY

German army did not assault Maginot Line directly, but attacked through Belgium and Ardennes Forest.

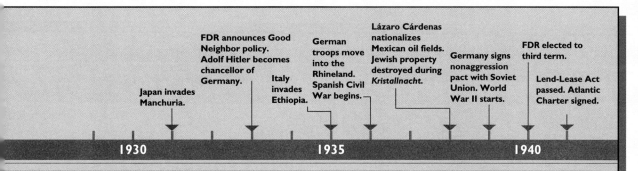

Japan invades Manchuria.

FDR announces Good Neighbor policy. Adolf Hitler becomes chancellor of Germany.

Italy invades Ethiopia.

German troops move into the Rhineland. Spanish Civil War begins.

Lázaro Cárdenas nationalizes Mexican oil fields. Jewish property destroyed during *Kristallnacht*.

Germany signs nonaggression pact with Soviet Union. World War II starts.

FDR elected to third term.

Lend-Lease Act passed. Atlantic Charter signed.

1930   1935   1940

WRITING ABOUT HISTORY

Writing to Describe Imagine you are a Loyalist during the Spanish Civil War. Write a letter to an American friend describing the events during that period.

USING PRIMARY SOURCES

President Roosevelt's proposal of the Lend-Lease Act aroused fierce debate in Congress. Read the following excerpt from isolationist Burton K. Wheeler, a Republican senator from Montana, who argued against passing the measure. What reasons does he give for his stand?

66 *Never before have the American people been asked or compelled to give . . . so completely of their tax dollars to any foreign nation. Never before has the Congress of the United States been asked by any President to violate international law. . . . Never before has the United States given to one man the power to strip this nation of its defenses. . . .*

Approval of this legislation means war, open and complete warfare. I, therefore, ask the American people before they . . . accept it—Was the last World War worthwhile?

If it were, then we should lend and lease war materials. If it were, then we should lend and lease American boys. President Roosevelt has said we would be repaid by England. We will be. . . . Our boys will be returned—returned in caskets, maybe; returned with bodies maimed; returned with minds warped and twisted by sights of horrors and the scream and shriek of high-powered shells. 99

LINKING HISTORY AND GEOGRAPHY

After World War I, France built the Maginot Line, a line of fixed fortifications to protect its border with

Germany. French military commanders felt this series of forts would repel a German attack. Study the map below, which shows the German invasion of France in 1940. How did the German army defeat this French strategy?

BUILDING YOUR PORTFOLIO

Complete the following projects independently or cooperatively.

1. **GLOBAL RELATIONS** In Chapter 13 you portrayed a journalist examining the global effects of the Great Depression. Building on that experience, imagine your assignment is to evaluate the new political trends of the 1930s. Create a chart that compares the similarities and differences among fascist dictators around the world.

2. **WAR** Imagine you are a diplomat at the 1938 Munich Conference. Write a speech aimed at convincing the Allies to abandon their policy of appeasement toward Germany's Adolf Hitler. Your speech might mention *Kristallnacht*, Hitler's repressive domestic policies, German aggression into the Rhineland and Austria, and your opposition toward granting the Sudetenland to Hitler.

BUILDING YOUR PORTFOLIO

Have students refer to **Building Your Portfolio Worksheet 3**, assigned at the beginning of Unit 3. Use the worksheet to help students monitor their progress on the portfolio projects.

Assessment

Core Resources
• Reteaching Worksheet 15
• Chapter 15 Tests
• Alternative Assessment Forms
Test Generator

THE AMERICAN NATION
VIDEODISC PROGRAM
A variety of still images, short videos, and activities are available for you to use as you teach this chapter. See Videodisc Resources in the Core Resources Binder for barcode correlations and suggestions for using the program.

Americans in World War II

1941–1945

Chapter Overview

The Japanese attack on Pearl Harbor drew the U.S. into World War II. In early 1942 the Allies suffered defeats in the Pacific and Europe, but by year's end the tide began to turn. At home, Americans rallied to support the war effort, and the lives of minorities and women were affected. Japanese Americans were interned in relocation camps. African Americans, Mexican Americans, and women entered the wartime work force, but experienced discrimination. Allied invasions of North Africa, Italy, and France and bombardment of German cities led to Germany's surrender. The atomic bomb ended the war with Japan. After the war, the horrors of the Holocaust were revealed, and new power alignments emerged.

Chapter Planning Guide

CHAPTER 16	CORE RESOURCES	AUDIOVISUAL RESOURCES	PROGRAM RESOURCES
INTRODUCTION pp. 398–399	■ Social Studies Skills Worksheet 16 ■ Building Your Portfolio Worksheet 3	■ Everyday Life in America Transparency and Worksheet 26	■ Eyewitnesses and Others, Volume 2: Reading 50
TEACHING THE CHAPTER pp. 400–425 ■ For expanded coverage of this chapter, see Chapter 23, pp. 634–637.	■ Graphic Organizer 16 ■ Literature Worksheet 16 ■ Geography Worksheet 16 ■ Outline Maps 1, 2, 14, 15, 16, 19, 20, 21, 24	■ The American Nation Videodisc: Beyond the Home Front; Japanese Americans in Relocation Camps ■ Linking Geography and History Transparencies and Worksheets 18, 19	■ Eyewitnesses and Others, Volume 2: Readings 51, 52, 53, 54, 55, 56, 57
REVIEW AND ASSESSMENT pp. 426–427	■ Chapter 16 Daily Quizzes ■ Reteaching Worksheet 16 ■ Chapter 16 Tests ■ Alternative Assessment Forms		■ Test Generator

Additional Resources

BOOKS FOR TEACHERS

Bernstein, Alison R. *American Indians and World War II.* University of Oklahoma Press, 1991. Survey of the contributions of Native Americans to the war effort and how the war's aftermath affected Indian affairs.

Hilberg, Raul. *Perpetrators, Victims, Bystanders.* HarperCollins, 1993. A noted historian of the Holocaust looks at Holocaust agents, victims, and collaborators and documents the inaction of the Allies.

Keegan, John. *The Second World War.* Viking Penguin, 1990. A comprehensive history of World War II by a military historian.

BOOKS FOR STUDENTS

Devaney, John. *America Fights the Tide, 1942.* Walker, 1991. Chronicles the year 1942 on the battlefield from the American, German, Japanese, British, and Russian perspectives.

* Meltzer, Milton. *Never to Forget.* HarperCollins, 1991. An introduction to the Holocaust.

Time-Life Books Editors. *WW II: Time–Life Books History of the Second World War.* Prentice-Hall, 1989. Amply illustrated overview of World War II.

* Whitman, Sylvia. *V Is for Victory.* Lerner, 1993. A compendium of facts about the home front.

* for students reading below grade level

MULTIMEDIA MATERIALS

Hiroshima and Nagasaki. Video, 20 min. Zenger/SSSS. Examines the question of whether Truman's decision to drop the bomb on Japan was justified.

The Holocaust: A Teenager's Experience. Video, 30 min. United Learning/SSSS. Holocaust survivor David Bergman tells the story of his years in work camps and death camps, using archival footage and drawings.

The Home Front—1940 to 1945. 3 videos, 180 min. Reader's Digest/SSSS. Documents daily life on the American home front.

USE WITH PAGES 398–399

Listed on the right are the themes emphasized in Chapter 16. The questions in boldface type stimulate critical thinking and provide students with an opportunity to discuss the themes within a broadened context. The questions also appear in the pupil's edition on p. 398.

■ GLOBAL RELATIONS

How might nations coordinate civilian and military resources to win a global war? Students might discuss the difficulties of devising a joint military and supply strategy on which each country can agree. They should, however, recognize the necessity of instituting a multinational command to coordinate the war effort. Students should also point out that each nation would more tightly control production and distribution of goods and information.

■ CULTURAL DIVERSITY

Why might wartime patriotism lead to discrimination against certain groups? Students may suggest that such discrimination could arise because people might question the loyalty of recent emigrants from countries with which a nation is at war. As an example, students might cite the discrimination that German Americans faced in the United States during World War I.

■ TECHNOLOGY AND SOCIETY

What political and moral concerns might a government take into account when developing a potentially destructive technology? Students might note political concerns about the establishment of peace and national security, and the widespread international anxiety that might result when such a technology exists. They might cite moral concerns associated with establishing or maintaining peace through the use or threat of destructive force, and of developing a technology that could have highly destructive effects.

CHAPTER STRATEGIES FOR MEETING INDIVIDUAL NEEDS

LIMITED ENGLISH PROFICIENT LEARNERS

Have pairs of students prepare telephone conversations between World War II soldiers stationed in various parts of the world and family members at home. Conversations should focus on the experiences and feelings of the soldier and family member. Volunteers should dramatize their conversations for the class.

TACTILE/KINESTHETIC LEARNERS

Organize students into small groups and have them select interviews from Studs Terkel's *The Good War: An Oral History of World War II* to dramatize for the class.

LEARNERS HAVING DIFFICULTY

Organize students into groups to create slogans or posters encouraging U.S. civilians to support the war effort by increasing productivity at work, buying war bonds, conserving food, or working against ethnic and racial discrimination.

AUDITORY LEARNERS

Pair students and have them create lists of questions they can use to interview friends, relatives, or others who were teenagers or adults during World War II about their memories of this period. Have students conduct the interviews and compare responses.

VISUAL LEARNERS

Have students create recruitment posters for branches of the armed forces. Posters should encourage Americans to serve their country and explain the importance of an Allied victory.

GIFTED LEARNERS

Direct students to write an essay explaining why they think events such as the Holocaust or the internment of Japanese Americans should be taught in U.S. history classes and what lessons they teach.

USING THE CHAPTER FOCUS

■ UNDERSTANDING THE MAIN IDEA

Call on a volunteer to read aloud the Understanding the Main Idea paragraph. Then ask students to speculate about the challenges the U.S. would face in fighting World War II and the contributions the U.S. could make to the war's outcome.

THEMES

Have students work individually or in small groups to answer the questions under Themes. Save students' responses so that they can compare them with their responses after studying the chapter. (See p. 397B for suggested answers.)

■ THE TIME LINE

Direct students to copy the time line in their notebooks. As they study the chapter, ask them to write details about each time-line event and then to write a summary of each event. At the close of the chapter, call on volunteers to read their summaries to the class.

CORE RESOURCES

- **Graphic Organizer 16**
- **Social Studies Skills Worksheet 16**
- **Outline Maps 1, 2, 14, 15, 16, 19, 20, 21, 24**
- **Building Your Portfolio Worksheet 3**

AV RESOURCES

- **Everyday Life in America Transparency and Worksheet 26**

ABOUT THE ILLUSTRATION

"The attack yesterday on the Hawaiian Islands has caused severe damage to American naval and military forces. Very many American lives have been lost," reported President Roosevelt as he detailed for Congress the devastating outcome of the Japanese attack. The scene below—fuel tanks exploding at the demolished seaplane base at Kaneohe Bay on the east coast of Oahu—depicts one outcome of the surprise attack that stunned Americans. Have students describe how they think they might have felt in December 1941 upon hearing the sudden news on the radio of the bombing of Pearl Harbor.

Chapter 16

1941–1945

AMERICANS IN WORLD WAR II

FOCUS

UNDERSTANDING THE MAIN IDEA

In December 1941 the Japanese bombed Pearl Harbor, bringing the United States into World War II. Americans and their allies battled the Axis powers on land in Europe and North Africa and on sea in the Atlantic, Pacific, and Mediterranean. By August 1945 the Allies defeated the Axis powers, but only after heavy casualties and the atomic bombing of two Japanese cities.

THEMES

- ■ **GLOBAL RELATIONS** How might nations coordinate civilian and military resources to win a global war?

- ■ **CULTURAL DIVERSITY** Why might wartime patriotism lead to increased discrimination against certain groups?

- ■ **TECHNOLOGY AND SOCIETY** What political and moral concerns might a government take into account when developing a potentially destructive technology?

1941	1942	1943	1944	1945
Japanese attack Pearl Harbor.	Bataan Death March occurs.	Zoot-suit riots break out.	D-Day invasion begins.	Japan surrenders.

■■ **LINK TO THE PAST** ▷

The German invasion of Poland in 1939 launched World War II. By 1940, much of Western Europe had fallen to Germany, while Japan expanded its hold on Asia. For a time, the United States maintained its neutrality. Lend-lease aid to the Allies, beginning in 1941, however, marked an important step in U.S. involvement in the conflict.

HISTORICAL SIDELIGHTS
Pearl Harbor

Although Americans were stunned by the attack on Pearl Harbor, the Japanese military had long anticipated such an event. Since 1931 every graduating class of Japan's naval academy had been asked to answer the following exam question: "How would you execute a surprise attack on Pearl Harbor?"

Shortly before 8:00 A.M. on December 7, 1941, the message *"Tora! Tora! Tora!"* was radioed to Japanese carrier ships approaching Hawaii. The signal "Tora," meaning "tiger," launched the long-planned Japanese air-and-sea attack on the U.S. naval base at Pearl Harbor. The heart of America's Pacific Fleet was anchored there, and more than a hundred U.S. planes lined nearby airfields.

In seconds after the attack began, explosions from bombs and torpedoes turned Pearl Harbor into a blazing inferno. When the assault ended less than two hours later, almost 20 American warships and nearly 200 aircraft had been destroyed. Among some 2,400 American dead were 1,103 sailors who were entombed on the *Arizona* when the battleship sank.

The bombing shocked and united Americans. Ann Hoskins, a Connecticut newspaper owner, noticed that before the attack "there was great tension and feelings between people not to intervene. But the minute Pearl Harbor happened, there was utter unity." The next day, a somber President Roosevelt described December 7 as "a date which will live in infamy" and called on Congress for a declaration of war against Japan.

Aftermath of Japanese attack on Hawaii, 1941

Japanese American children during World War II

FOCUS OBJECTIVES

- Explain what obstacles the U.S. faced when it first entered the war.

- Identify the three battles in which the Allies halted Japan's advance in the Pacific.

- Cite two major turning points in the western theater of operations.

- Describe what forms Allied cooperation took.

Section 1

EARLY DIFFICULTIES

FOCUS

- **What obstacles did the United States face when it first entered the war?**
- **In which three battles did the Allies halt Japan's advance in the Pacific?**
- **What were two major turning points in the western theater of operations?**
- **What forms did Allied cooperation take?**

Army nurses evacuated from Bataan

Deeply angered by the bombing of Pearl Harbor, Congress and the American people overwhelmingly supported President Roosevelt's call for war against Japan. Great Britain declared war on Japan as well. On December 11, Japan's allies, Germany and Italy, declared war on the United States, and Congress recognized a state of war with those two nations. World War II had now vastly expanded.

AXIS ADVANTAGES

When the United States entered the war, the Axis powers had two big advantages. First, Germany, Italy, and Japan had already secured firm control of the areas they had invaded. The United States thus faced a long, drawn-out fight on several fronts, including Western Europe, the Pacific, the Mediterranean, and Northern Africa.

Second, Germany was better prepared for war. Since 1933 it had been rearming itself and building airfields, barracks, and military training centers. By the mid-1930s, the Nazis had converted most of the German economy to military production. In contrast, the United States had not begun to prepare for war until 1940, when President Roosevelt called for more money to be devoted to military production. Even then, however, its preparations were limited.

When the United States entered the war, it faced the problems of fighting on many fronts and a lack of preparation.

◀ **Three U.S. sailors in Chicago read about the Japanese attack on Pearl Harbor.**

Ask students if they have seen any movies about World War II and to explain how they reacted to them. Tell students that in this section they will learn about how, after the attack on Pearl Harbor, the U.S. and the Allies cooperated to overcome the powerful offensives mounted by the Axis.

U.S. OBSTACLES

Have volunteers identify Axis strengths and U.S. weaknesses at the time the U.S. entered the war. List responses on the chalkboard. *(Axis strengths: firm control of areas invaded, military preparedness; U.S. weaknesses: necessity to fight on many fronts, lack of preparation for war)* Ask students to speculate about what the U.S. and its allies might do to counter the Axis powers' advantages. Write their responses on the chalkboard.

Hitler, Mussolini, and the Japanese war leaders hoped they could win the conflict before the United States—fighting a two-ocean war—could mobilize its enormous resources. After the Pearl Harbor attack, one Hitler aide warned:

66 We have just one year to cut off Russia from her American supplies. . . . If we don't succeed and the munitions potential of the United States joins up with the manpower potential of the Russians, the war will enter a phase in which we shall only be able to win it with difficulty. 99

WAR IN THE PACIFIC

Japan's assault on Pearl Harbor was only part of a giant offensive throughout the Pacific region. In December the Japanese launched attacks on several other American islands, on the Philippines, and on various British possessions. By the end of the month, Japan controlled Guam, Wake Island, the British colony of Hong Kong, and Thailand.

The year 1942 brought more Japanese victories. In January, Japanese forces took Manila, the capital of the Philippines. The next month, they overran the British naval base at Singapore, and in the **Battle of the Java Sea**, they crushed a fleet of American, British, Dutch, and Australian warships (see map on page 427). By April, Japan had conquered most of the Netherlands East Indies, with its supplies of oil, tin, rubber, and other vital war materials. The Japanese were also driving the British out of Burma.

In the Philippines a small force of Americans and Filipinos under General Douglas MacArthur, commander of U.S. Army troops in the Far East, mounted a heroic but hopeless resistance against the Japanese. After the surrender of Manila, MacArthur's forces withdrew to the Bataan Peninsula across Manila Bay. In March, MacArthur was ordered to Australia but vowed, "I shall return."

Fighting against overwhelming odds, the hungry, sick, exhausted survivors who remained on Bataan surrendered in April. Japanese soldiers forced the some 70,000 survivors to march through the jungle on their way to prison camp. Some 10,000 died on what came to be called the **Bataan Death March** (see map on page 427). U.S. and Filipino soldiers received brutal treat-

JAPAN DECLARES WAR

The day after the Japanese attack on Pearl Harbor, Emperor Hirohito made a speech that was relayed around the world. In it he laid out Japan's reasons for declaring war on the United States and Great Britain:

66 *B*oth America and Britain . . . have aggravated the disturbances in East Asia. . . . These two powers, inducing other countries to follow suit, increased military preparations on all sides of Our Empire. . . . They have obstructed by every means Our peaceful commerce, and finally resorted to a direct severance [cutting off] of economic relations. . . . Patiently have We waited and long have We endured, in hope that Our Government might retrieve the situation in peace. But Our adversaries [enemies], showing not the least spirit of conciliation, have unduly delayed a settlement. . . . Our Empire for its existence and self defense has no other recourse but to appeal to arms and to crush every obstacle in its path. 99

ment at the hands of the Japanese: prisoners were beaten, shot, or prevented from drinking water. The bravery of the Filipino defenders at Bataan inspired thousands of Filipino Americans to enlist in the armed forces. In 1942 alone some 16,000 Filipino Americans in California joined the fight.

By the summer of 1942, the Japanese were poised to strike west at India, south at Australia, and east through Hawaii at the Pacific coast of the United States. At this crucial point, however, the Allies succeeded in halting the Japanese advance in the Pacific. The U.S. Pacific Fleet, commanded by Admiral Chester Nimitz, helped turn the tide with three battles.

The first battle began on May 7, 1942, in the Coral Sea, off the northeastern coast of Australia. A Japanese force on its way to attack Port Moresby, New Guinea, seized Tulagi (too-LAHG-ee) Island,

THROUGH OTHERS' EYES

Ask students to list the reasons Hirohito gives for declaring war. Then have students give reasons why the Allies might reject the validity of Hirohito's explanation.

PRIMARY SOURCE

Description of Change: excerpted
Rationale: excerpted to focus on main idea

PRIMARY SOURCE

Description of Change: excerpted and bracketed
Rationale: excerpted to focus on main idea; bracketed to clarify meaning

MULTICULTURAL PERSPECTIVES

On the Bataan Peninsula, U.S. and Filipino soldiers fought valiantly together. Stories of Filipino bravery at Bataan led to better treatment of Filipinos in the U.S. One California Filipino observed, "No longer on the streetcar do I feel myself in the presence of my enemies. We Filipinos are the same— it is Americans that have changed in their recognition of us."

Teaching the Section

ALLIES HALT JAPANESE IN PACIFIC

Organize students into small groups. Assign each group one of these battles: Coral Sea, Midway, or Guadalcanal. Tell groups their job is to give a military briefing to the press on their assigned battle. The briefing should review the war in the Pacific up to the bat- tle, identify the battle's location, describe the military action, note the battle's out- come, and explain how it furthered the Allied cause. Select groups to present their briefings to the class.

HISTORICAL SIDELIGHTS

Battle of the Coral Sea
The Battle of the Coral Sea initiated a new era in mod- ern naval warfare. For the first time in modern naval battle, the warring fleets, which centered around air- craft carriers, never came close enough to exchange fire. The carriers served as takeoff and landing stations for dive bombers, fighters, and torpedo planes. Japa- nese aircraft destroyed the American carrier *Lexington.* U.S. planes sank the Japa- nese carrier *Shoho.*

AV TRANSPARENCY

Linking Geography and History Transparency and **Worksheet 19**

Map Caption Answer
most of the Netherlands East Indies

▲ Shown here are American and Filipino soldiers at the start of the grueling Bataan Death March in April 1942. Thousands died on the march to a Japanese prison camp.

one of the Solomons. But before the Japanese force could reach its destination, a joint British-American naval force intercepted it. Planes from U.S. carriers damaged a Japanese carrier and destroyed one car- rier and several aircraft. The **Battle of the Coral Sea** was an important victory for the Allies. Although the Allies lost a carrier, the battle stopped the Japanese advance on Australia.

The second naval battle took place early in June 1942. Japan, with the objective of crushing the Pacific Fleet, launched a two-pronged attack. One unit succeeded in occupying two of the Aleutian Islands, near Alaska. This move was

World War II in the Pacific, 1941–1945

TURNING POINT The initiative in the Pacific war passed to the Allies after the Battle of Midway, which cost Japan four aircraft carriers and most of its skilled naval pilots.

? REGION What area did the Allies largely bypass in their island-hopping drive toward Japan?

Have students explain how Germany benefited from the advance into the Soviet Union *(expanded industrial and agricultural base)* and what Germany expected to gain from its North African offensive. *(Suez Canal, Middle East oil fields)* Ask why these goals were important to Germany's war effort. Then ask students to explain how supply problems influenced the outcome of battles at El Alamein and Stalingrad and why these battles are considered turning points in the war. Conclude by having students speculate about how the war might have been different if the Allies had lost either battle.

▲ Although U.S. forces won the Battle of Midway in June 1942, the islands did not escape damage. Japanese bombers hit military installations, including the oil tank shown here.

designed to divert American ships to the north while the Japanese carried out their second offensive, an attack on Midway, two small islands northwest of Hawaii. The United States, however, knew of the Japanese strategy because American experts had broken the Japanese fleet code. Nimitz was therefore able to assemble U.S. aircraft carriers and destroyers north of Midway to fend off the Japanese attack.

Americans and Japanese clashed from June 3 to June 6. U.S. fighters, dive-bombers, and torpedo planes sank four Japanese aircraft carriers and shot down many enemy planes. The American victory at the **Battle of Midway** proved crucial. Japan lost not only ships and planes but also a number of skilled pilots, many of whom had taken part in the Pearl Harbor attack. The battle provided the Americans with valuable experience in naval air warfare and gave people confidence in the carrier-based strike force.

After the Battle of Midway, the United States successfully launched its first offensive. In August 1942, American marines waded ashore at Guadalcanal, another of the Solomon Islands. For six desperate months, with a heavy loss of life, they clung to a toehold around the airport, repelling Japanese attacks from the air, the sea, and the surrounding jungle.

In November the Japanese sent a huge fleet to the Solomons, hoping to regain Guadalcanal. The American fleet defeated the Japanese in a bloody battle. Guadalcanal was secure. The tide of battle in the Pacific had finally turned in the Allies' favor.

■■ **The Allies stopped the Japanese Pacific offensive in the battles of Coral Sea, Midway, and Guadalcanal.**

FIGHTING IN EUROPE AND THE MEDITERRANEAN

By the time of the attack on Pearl Harbor, the Axis powers, which now included Hungary, Romania, and Bulgaria, were in firm control of much of the western theater of operations—Europe and the lands around the Mediterranean. Yugoslavia and Greece had been occupied, and southern Europe was firmly under the Axis boot. Throughout most of 1942, the Axis powers continued to achieve one victory after another.

The Germans and their allies scored victories on many different fronts. German submarines, or U-boats, controlled the Atlantic Ocean, sinking Allied military and merchant ships and nearly cutting off British supply lines. In the first half of 1942, German U-boats sank almost 500 ships off the eastern seaboard of the United States.

In Europe, German troops had penetrated far into the Soviet Union after their initial attack in June 1941. As the Germans advanced, the Soviets lost many industrial centers as well as rich grainfields in the Ukraine (see map on page 404). In the summer of 1942, the Germans pushed toward the oil fields of southern Russia. They also laid siege to Stalingrad (now known as Volgograd). The city mobilized its defenses. For months the men, women, and children defending the city suffered a nightmare of shell fire and starvation.

In North Africa, Italian forces had launched an invasion in 1940. When British troops later began to inflict heavy damage on the Italians, Hitler sent in the German *Afrika Korps* under commander Erwin Rommel.

▼ Erwin Rommel (left) was commander of the German *Afrika Korps* in North Africa.

The term *U-boat* comes from a German word *unterseeboot,* or undersea boat. The term referred to a German submarine. During World War II, the Germans built more than 1,100 U-boats. By war's end, the Allies had sunk over 600 of them.

Teaching the Section

ALLIED COOPERATION

Have students work in pairs to create a graphic organizer that shows the forms Allied cooperation took, including lend-lease programs, joint strategic planning, and agreement on war aims. Have volunteers present their charts. Conclude by having students write paragraphs explaining why joint strategic planning and shared war aims were essential for an Allied victory. Select students to read their paragraphs to the class. Students may wish to include their paragraphs in their portfolios.

Map Caption Answer
in Normandy, France, in 1944

COOPERATIVE LEARNING

Organize students into groups of five. Direct them to use the maps on pp. 402 and 404 and the chapter text to create on butcher paper a wall-size illustrated time line that shows the major World War II battles in Europe, North Africa, and the Pacific. In order to emphasize that some battles in both theaters were taking place simultaneously, ask groups to place the battles in Europe and North Africa above the time line and those in the Pacific below the time line. Students should also note the outcome of each battle on their time lines. Encourage students to divide tasks so that one student locates the battles on the maps, one locates the outcome of each battle in the text, one adds the information to the time line, and the others provide the illustrations.

AV TRANSPARENCY

Linking Geography and History Transparency and **Worksheet 18**

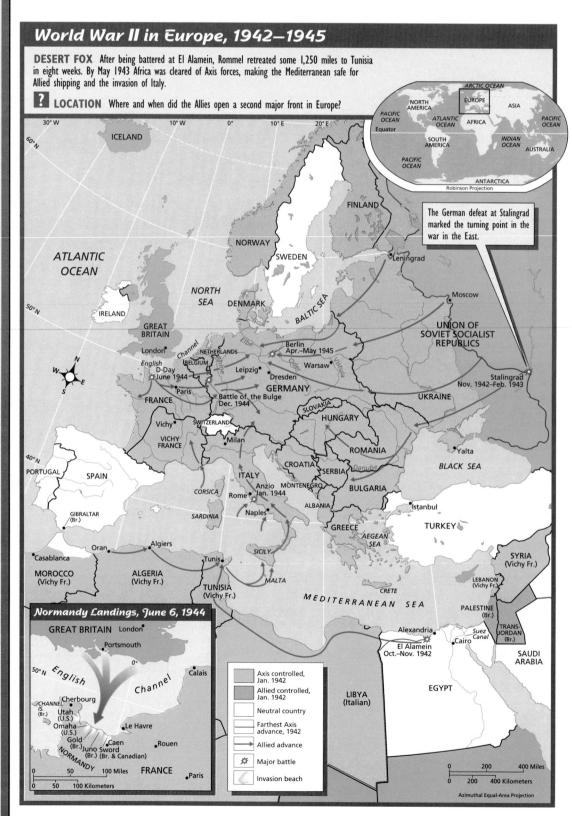

World War II in Europe, 1942–1945

DESERT FOX After being battered at El Alamein, Rommel retreated some 1,250 miles to Tunisia in eight weeks. By May 1943 Africa was cleared of Axis forces, making the Mediterranean safe for Allied shipping and the invasion of Italy.

? LOCATION Where and when did the Allies open a second major front in Europe?

The German defeat at Stalingrad marked the turning point in the war in the East.

Robinson Projection

Normandy Landings, June 6, 1944

GREAT BRITAIN   London
Portsmouth
50°N   English Channel   Calais
CHANNEL IS. (Br.)   Cherbourg
Utah (U.S.)
Omaha (U.S.)   Le Havre
Gold (Br.)   Caen   Rouen
Juno (Br.) Sword (Br. & Canadian)
NORMANDY   FRANCE   Paris
0   50   100 Miles
0   50   100 Kilometers

Axis controlled, Jan. 1942
Allied controlled, Jan. 1942
Neutral country
Farthest Axis advance, 1942
Allied advance
Major battle
Invasion beach

0   200   400 Miles
0   200   400 Kilometers
Azimuthal Equal-Area Projection

Practice

GUIDED PRACTICE

Draw on the chalkboard a three-column chart with the headings *Battle, Outcome, Significance.* In the first column list the key battles on the Pacific front that are discussed in this section, beginning with Pearl Harbor. Have volunteers offer information to complete the chart. Then repeat the process, focusing on Europe and North Africa.

INDEPENDENT PRACTICE

Have students choose one of the battles from the Guided Practice chart and use the information to write a radio news report telling the five W's of the battle: who, what, where, when, why the battle was important. Students may wish to include their news reports in their portfolios.

Review and Assessment

REVIEW Pair students and have pairs create a series of headlines that tracks the course of the war from Pearl Harbor through the Tehran conference. Then assign the Section 1 Review on p. 406.

ASSESS Assign the **Section 1 Daily Quiz** in *Core Resources.*

◀ More than 100,000 Soviet women earned military honors for their participation in the war. Here two snipers, E. Novikova (left) and O. Mokshina (right), wait for hours in the snow to ambush German troops.

▼ Soviet forces laid siege to Stalingrad for 17 months before the German army surrendered in February 1943. Shown here is part of the ruined city shortly after it was liberated.

Rommel, known as the Desert Fox, had advanced as far as El Alamein, Egypt, by July 1942. His troops were ready for a final thrust at the Suez Canal and the oil fields of the Middle East (the European designation for Northeast Africa and Southwest Asia). At the same time, Axis aircraft all but forced British naval craft out of the Mediterranean. In order to reach Egypt, the Middle East, and India, Britain had to send its ships thousands of miles around Africa.

Despite the British forces' transport problems, it was Rommel who suffered most from shortages of men and supplies. The British, led by General Bernard Montgomery, turned this to their advantage. In October, Montgomery attacked, pushing Rommel's *Afrika Korps* steadily westward out of Egypt and into Libya by November. The British victory in the **Battle of El Alamein** helped turn the corner for the Allies in North Africa.

Another turning point came in the fall of 1942, when the Soviets attacked German troops in Stalingrad. Throughout a terrible winter the Germans hung on, forbidden by Hitler to surrender. Trapped in the ruined city with few supplies and little food, the Axis troops finally surrendered in February 1943. After the **Battle of Stalingrad**, less than one third of the original German force of almost 300,000 remained alive. Galina Utkina, a Russian woman, recalled the crucial role Soviet women played in defeating the Germans:

66 Anti-aircraft battalions, air-force regiments and signalling units were made up entirely of women. When the battle reached the city itself, women fought alongside the men. 99

The Allied victories at El Alamein and Stalingrad broke the momentum of the Axis advance. Said British prime minister Winston Churchill: "Before Alamein we never had a victory. After Alamein we never had a defeat."

■■ Setbacks for the Axis powers at El Alamein and Stalingrad were turning points in World War II.

Allied COOPERATION

How had the Allies managed to overcome the powerful offensives mounted by the Axis in both theaters of the war? The ability of the United States to harness its human and industrial resources helped the Allied effort. Through the lend-lease program the United States shipped vast quantities of munitions to its allies. By the end of the war, lend-lease aid totaled more than $50 billion. Of this vast sum, over 60 percent went to Great Britain.

Allied cooperation, which involved joint strategic planning, also helped turn the tide. Just

HISTORICAL SIDELIGHTS

Desert Fox
In his military tactics, Rommel favored speed, surprise, and deception. In March 1941 he bolstered his 5th Panzer Regiment with a "Cardboard Division" made up of dummy tanks mounted on German automobiles. From a distance this impressive array of "tanks" was enough to lead British troops stationed in the nearby Libyan desert to retreat.

PRIMARY SOURCE

Description of Change: excerpted
Rationale: excerpted to focus on main idea

HISTORICAL SIDELIGHTS

Battle of Stalingrad
The five-month Battle of Stalingrad exacted a terrible toll on soldiers and civilians alike—more than one million men, women, and children died. Soldiers fought each other house by house, street by street. The Germans called the battle the War of the Rats. It was the most brutal city fighting of the war.

RETEACH Have students work in groups, assigning individuals or pairs the task of outlining subsections. Have students exchange outlines and use them to ask questions of other members of their group.

Closure

Call on volunteers to explain how the U.S. and the Allies dealt with the challenges of fighting a war on many fronts. In their explanations, students should consider the war strategies agreed upon by FDR and Churchill in Washington.

Extension

COMPARE Have students research and write reports comparing the challenges of weather, climate, and terrain that Allied soldiers faced fighting in North Africa and on Pacific islands.

INTERPRET Through their cartoons and writings, journalists Bill Mauldin and Ernie Pyle kept Americans informed about the war. Have students read and present to the class examples of their work.

SECTION REVIEW ANSWERS

IDENTIFY

For significance, see the following pages:
Battle of the Java Sea (p. 401)
Douglas MacArthur (p. 401)
Bataan Death March (p. 401)
Battle of the Coral Sea (p. 402)
Battle of Midway (p. 403)
Erwin Rommel (p. 403)
Bernard Montgomery (p. 405)
Battle of El Alamein (p. 405)
Battle of Stalingrad (p. 405)
unconditional surrender (p. 406)
Joseph Stalin (p. 406)

LOCATE

For locations, see maps on pp. 402, 404, and 427.

1. *in the battles of the Coral Sea, Midway, Guadalcanal*
2. *German defeats at El Alamein, Stalingrad*
3. *Axis had converted economy to military production and had securely occupied territory. U.S. had to fight on many fronts and had not begun to prepare for war until the summer of 1940.*
4. *Memos might mention lend-lease exchanges, joint strategic planning, and agreement on war aims.*
5. *Japan lost ships, planes, and skilled pilots, while U.S. gained confidence and experience in naval air warfare.*

two weeks after the assault on Pearl Harbor, Churchill and Roosevelt met in Washington, D.C., together with their top military commanders and technical aides. The two leaders and their staffs agreed that defeating the Axis powers in Europe would be the first Allied priority. For the time being, Allied strategy in the Pacific would be defensive rather than offensive.

To formalize their alliance, representatives of 26 Allied countries, calling themselves the United Nations, met in Washington, D.C. On January 1, 1942, they signed the Joint Declaration, which had been drafted by Roosevelt and Churchill. In it the Allies (1) promised full military and economic cooperation in the war effort, (2) agreed that none of them would make a separate peace with the Axis powers, and (3) endorsed the war aims outlined by Roosevelt and Churchill in the Atlantic Charter (see Chapter 15).

Throughout the war Churchill and Roosevelt met frequently. At Casablanca, Morocco, in January 1943, the two leaders agreed to demand the **unconditional surrender** of their enemies. In other words, if the Axis powers gave up, they would have to do so on the Allies' terms. Churchill and Roosevelt also agreed that the Allies should attack Hitler on a second front in order to relieve pressure on the Soviet Union (the first front). The Allies decided to open the second front by invading southern Europe by way of North Africa and the Mediterranean island of Sicily.

▲ Chinese leader Chiang Kai-shek (left), President Roosevelt (center), and British prime minister Winston Churchill (right) are shown at the Cairo Conference in November 1943.

At Cairo in November 1943, Roosevelt and Churchill met with Chiang Kai-shek of China. The leaders outlined Allied strategy against Japan and made plans to restore Japanese-held territories after the war. At Tehran, Iran, shortly afterward, Roosevelt and Churchill met for the first time with Soviet leader Joseph Stalin. Stalin gave his support for Allied war plans.

■■ Cooperation among the Allies took the form of lend-lease exchanges, joint strategic planning, and agreement on war aims.

SECTION 1 REVIEW

IDENTIFY and explain the significance of the following: Battle of the Java Sea, Douglas MacArthur, Bataan Death March, Battle of the Coral Sea, Battle of Midway, Erwin Rommel, Bernard Montgomery, Battle of El Alamein, Battle of Stalingrad, unconditional surrender, Joseph Stalin.

LOCATE and explain the importance of the following: Pearl Harbor, Guam, Wake Island, Hong Kong, Thailand, Bataan, Coral Sea, Midway Islands, Guadalcanal, Ukraine, Stalingrad, El Alamein, Casablanca.

1. **MAIN IDEA** Where did the Allies stop the Japanese Pacific offensive?

2. **MAIN IDEA** What two German setbacks were turning points for the Allies in World War II?

3. **CONTRASTING** What advantages did the Axis powers have over the United States at the beginning of the war?

4. **WRITING TO INFORM** Imagine you are a participant in one of the early wartime conferences. Write a memorandum to the Allies, giving examples of cooperative efforts that could help them win the war.

5. **LINKING HISTORY AND GEOGRAPHY** What was the significance of the American victory at the Battle of Midway for both Japan and the United States?

PREVIEW WORKSHOP

Following is a list of the significant people and terms in this section. You may wish to use this list as a section preview.

People

- James F. Byrnes
- Thomas E. Dewey
- Norman Mineta
- A. Philip Randolph

Terms

- War Production Board
- Selective Training and Service Act
- internment
- Fair Employment Practices Committee
- braceros
- zoot-suit riots

Section 2

THE HOME FRONT

FOCUS

- **How did the United States mobilize for war?**
- **Why were Japanese Americans interned during the war?**
- **What gains did African Americans and Mexican Americans make during the war?**
- **What changes did World War II bring for American women?**

Although World War II was fought on the battlefields of Europe, Asia, and North Africa, American farms and factories also helped win the war. As the United States mobilized its resources for combat, the entertainment industry helped sustain morale. For Japanese Americans the war resulted in confinement in remote camps. For African Americans, Mexican Americans, and women, the conflict brought both new opportunities and reminders that discrimination and inequality still existed in American society.

Seamstresses making flags and banners

MOBILIZING FOR WAR

After the Japanese attack at Pearl Harbor plunged the United States into war, America switched from a peacetime to a wartime economy. Engineer R. W. Danischefsky noted how quickly factory orders came in: "At the time of Pearl Harbor [December 7, 1941] we had five projects in Michigan. By the end of December we had forty-two." To fill these vital orders, union leaders agreed not to organize strikes during the war.

A production boom. The United States soon became the Allies' biggest armaments supplier. Between 1940 and 1945, U.S. war plants produced millions of planes, tanks, jeeps, and guns. Shipbuilders produced thousands of ships, creating a powerful navy and merchant marine.

War production helped create an economic boom. The number of jobless workers, still over 2.5 million in 1942, sank to fewer than 700,000 in 1944. Earnings nearly doubled between 1939 and 1945. People who had stood in breadlines a decade

◀ After the bombing of Pearl Harbor, many existing factories were converted to wartime production. The Firestone Tire & Rubber Company, for example, made antiaircraft guns, tank and submarine parts, and gas masks, as well as tires for all military vehicles.

FOCUS OBJECTIVES

- Describe how the U.S. mobilized for war.
- Explain why Japanese Americans were interned during the war.
- Determine what gains African Americans and Mexican Americans made during the war.
- Examine the changes World War II brought for American women.

MAKING CONNECTIONS

Economics

Due to increased demands of wartime production during the war years, the weekly earnings of a typical factory worker rose from about $25 to about $47.

CORE RESOURCES

- **Social Studies Skills Worksheet 16**
- **Literature Worksheet 16**
- **Section 2 Daily Quiz**

AV RESOURCES

- **The American Nation Videodisc: Beyond the Home Front; Japanese Americans in Relocation Camps**
- **Everyday Life in America Transparency and Worksheet 26**

AMERICANS IN WORLD WAR II ▪ 407

MOTIVATING:
PRIOR KNOWLEDGE

Have volunteers recall the ways the American home front was mobilized to contribute to the war effort during World War I. List student responses on a flip chart. After students complete the section, have them compare the flip-chart list with ways Americans at home contributed to the World War II war effort.

Graph Caption Answer
approximately $250 billion

MULTICULTURAL PERSPECTIVES

Many Native Americans contributed both money and resources to the war effort. For example, Uchee and Creek Indians voted to purchase $400,000 in war bonds, while the Quapaws made a $1 million donation to the war effort and had to be persuaded to accept war bonds in return. A Sioux tribal council voted to postpone receipt of a $5 million government settlement. The Klamath called for building an airfield on their reservation in Oregon to be used for training pilots. The United Pueblos volunteered all of their cars and trucks for the delivery of war-related supplies.

earlier now worked overtime and brought home fat paychecks.

The boom also led to vast population shifts. More than four million workers left their homes to find work in war-industry locations in other states. Sharecroppers, tenant farmers, and others eking out a living on farms flocked to the centers of wartime production—shipyards on the Gulf and Pacific coasts and factories in the Midwest and West. The West especially witnessed phenomenal economic and population growth during the war. The federal government spent billions of dollars to build western factories and military bases. This wartime spending helped the West become a major industrial region after World War II.

American farms also achieved marvels of productivity. Although many agricultural workers went off to fight in the war or to work in wartime factories, productivity remained high. During the war years U.S. farmers produced enough food to supply the American people and the Allies overseas.

Government expansion. Mobilizing for war led to a greatly expanded federal government. The number of federal employees grew from almost one million in 1940 to nearly three million by 1945. The Office of War Mobilization (OWM) coordinated all government agencies involved in producing and distributing civilian goods. Its powerful director, James F. Byrnes, was sometimes called the "assistant president."

The **War Production Board** (WPB) directed the conversion of existing factories to wartime production and supervised the building of new plants. The WPB assigned raw materials to industry, including scrap iron from factories and recyclable tin, aluminum, and fats (used in bullets) from homes.

The WPB (and later the OWM) also coordinated the production and distribution of consumer goods. For instance, it diverted nylon to making parachutes. The WPB even regulated clothing styles in order to save fabric; canceled for the duration of the war were cuffs on men's trousers and pleats in women's skirts.

▶ After the war began, the government conserved valuable resources by establishing rationing programs. Students at Wilson Senior High in Washington, D.C., are shown learning how to use the latest ration book.

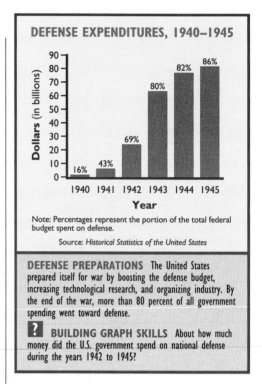

DEFENSE EXPENDITURES, 1940–1945

Note: Percentages represent the portion of the total federal budget spent on defense.

Source: *Historical Statistics of the United States*

DEFENSE PREPARATIONS The United States prepared itself for war by boosting the defense budget, increasing technological research, and organizing industry. By the end of the war, more than 80 percent of all government spending went toward defense.

? BUILDING GRAPH SKILLS About how much money did the U.S. government spend on national defense during the years 1942 to 1945?

Directing the economy. The government also extended its control over the economy. In order to pay for the war, the government increased by more than 10 times the number of Americans who had to pay income tax. The new taxes included most middle- and lower-income groups for the first time. The rest of the money came from borrowing, mainly through war bonds.

The sale of war bonds also helped the government deal with another major concern—keeping inflation down. When incomes remain high but few consumer items are available for people to buy, prices go up and inflation results. Selling war bonds offered one way of siphoning off excess income, thus keeping inflation down.

Teaching the Section

U.S. MOBILIZES FOR WAR

Organize students into seven groups. Assign to each group one of the following roles: factory owner, factory worker, farmer, federal employee, taxpayer, consumer, and draft board member. Have each group discuss—and select a representative to explain to the class—ways that his or her group is contributing to the war effort and how the group has been affected by the expansion of government control that accompanied mobilization.

■■ Examine with students reasons that such agencies as the War Production Board were necessary. Ask students if they think Americans today would accept the same regulation of the economy in the event of war.

▶

The government took other anti-inflationary steps as well. One was rationing, which reduced consumer demand by limiting how much people could buy. The measure also cut civilian purchases of products needed for the war effort. Rationed items included gasoline, heating fuel, tires, coffee, sugar, meat, butter, and canned goods. The government also tried to keep wages and prices down. At first it froze wages, but when the cost of living rose, the government allowed wages to rise by 15 percent.

Raising an army. Gearing up for war meant, along with increased production and expanded government controls, recruiting soldiers. In 1940, before the attack on Pearl Harbor, the United States passed the **Selective Training and Service Act**, which provided for the first peacetime draft in American history. The law required the registration of all men between ages 21 and 35 (age limits later extended from 18 to 37). Local draft boards determined fitness and deferred men for family, religious, or health reasons.

Of the some 15 million members of the armed services during World War II, about two thirds were draftees and the rest volunteers, including more than 300,000 women. Women enrolled in the Women's Auxiliary Army Corps (WAACs), Women's Airforce Service Pilots (WASPs), or auxiliary branches of the navy (WAVES), coast guard (SPARS), and marines. They worked as nurses, did office work, drove vehicles, and ferried planes in order to free men for active duty.

While most women military personnel served on the home front, women in the Army Nurse Corps (ANC) and Navy Nurse Corps (NNC) tended wounded soldiers overseas. Eunice Hatchitt, a nurse who served at Bataan, described the terrible conditions and heavy casualties:

66 Days and nights were an endless nightmare, until it seemed we couldn't stand it any longer. Patients came in by the hundreds, and the doctors and nurses worked continuously under the tents amid the flies and heat and dust. We had from eight to nine hundred victims a day. 99

■■ **The United States mobilized for war by increasing production, expanding government control of the economy, and raising an army.**

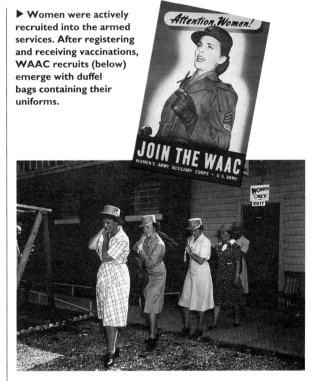

▶ Women were actively recruited into the armed services. After registering and receiving vaccinations, WAAC recruits (below) emerge with duffel bags containing their uniforms.

The urgency of the war effort convinced President Roosevelt, who had led the nation since 1933, to run for an unprecedented fourth term. As the 1944 campaign drew near, Roosevelt told an aide, "God knows I don't want to [run], but I may find it necessary." Roosevelt was nominated with little opposition; his vice-presidential candidate was a Missouri senator, Harry S. Truman.

The Republicans chose Thomas E. Dewey, governor of New York, who had won fame as a district attorney for prosecuting racketeers. However, he lacked Roosevelt's charisma and experience and was defeated by an electoral vote of 99 to Roosevelt's 432.

PROMOTING THE WAR

As it mobilized the nation's resources, the government also worked to keep morale high. This was especially important in the early days of the war, when Allied troops faced many setbacks. The government encouraged the media to do their part. Moviemakers, songwriters, and radio station programmers responded by urging all-out participation in the war effort.

Teaching the Section

PROMOTING THE WAR

Organize students into groups and ask them to outline a script for a radio report on how the media and entertainment industries are promoting the war effort. Groups might also include appropriate interviews in their reports. Select volunteers to "broadcast" their group's reports.

HISTORICAL SIDELIGHTS

Patriotism

Support for the U.S. war effort ran so high that fans began singing "The Star-Spangled Banner" at the beginning of ball games, a tradition that continues today.

HISTORICAL SIDELIGHTS

Japanese Relocation

Support among Californians for Japanese relocation came in part from wartime hysteria and in part from resentment of Japanese Americans' success as merchants, fruit and vegetable farmers, and fishers. Some Japanese Americans fought relocation in the courts. Gordon Hirabayashi in Washington state refused to report to an evacuation center. He argued: "As an American citizen, I wanted to uphold the principles of the Constitution, and the . . . evacuation orders which singled out a group on the basis of ethnicity violated them."

THE AMERICAN NATION
VIDEODISC PROGRAM

Japanese Americans in Relocation Camps

2A   43252   :49

Movie stars advertised war bonds and traveled overseas to entertain the troops. Hundreds of war movies poured out of Hollywood. Some patriotic films, such as *So Proudly We Hail*—about army nurses in the Philippines—built support for the war. Striking a lighter note were comedies like Bob Hope's *Caught in the Draft.* A few films, such as *Wake Island* and *Report from the Aleutians,* offered realistic views of combat. Most, however, romanticized American and other Allied soldiers and stereotypically portrayed the Japanese as treacherous, the Germans as fanatical, and the Italians as cowardly.

Radio stations broadcast both war news and entertainment. Radio correspondents such as Edward R. Murrow and Eric Sevareid gave on-the-scene accounts of war-ravaged Europe. A new federal agency, the Office of War Information (OWI), controlled the flow of war news at home.

Wartime musical hits included "Remember Pearl Harbor" and "Praise the Lord and Pass the Ammunition!" But the biggest hits of the period did not deal directly with the war. African American musicians—including trumpeter Dizzy Gillespie, sax player Charlie Parker, and piano player Thelonious Monk—popularized a new form of jazz, called bebop, or bop. Also popular were such sentimental songs as "White Christmas," which expressed Americans' longing for a return to peace.

The war also affected popular radio serials. Radio stations abandoned spy and sabotage programs for the duration of the war. Some even banned certain sound effects, such as wailing sirens, to avoid alarming listeners.

On the whole, World War II was a popular war. Most Americans put up with shortages, planted "victory gardens" to conserve food, and bought millions of dollars worth of war bonds. Many families proudly displayed window banners with a star—a blue one for a loved one in the service, a gold one to commemorate a death in combat.

JAPANESE AMERICAN RELOCATION

By and large, World War II did not produce the kind of home-front intolerance that occurred during World War I. One tragic exception was the forced relocation and imprisonment, or **internment**, of Japanese Americans living on the Pacific coast. In September 1945, U.S. State Department adviser Eugene Rostow called internment "a tragic and dangerous mistake" and argued that "its motivation and its impact on our system of law deny every value of democracy."

When Pearl Harbor was bombed, about 119,000 people of Japanese ancestry lived in Washington, Oregon, and California. Of these, about a third, the Issei (EE-SAY), had been born in Japan and were regarded by the U.S. government as aliens ineligible for U.S. citizenship. The rest, the Nisei (NEE-SAY), had been born in the United States and were thus American citizens.

People of Japanese ancestry had long suffered racial discrimination in the United States. Laws prevented Japanese immigrants from becoming citizens, and prejudice restricted the kinds of jobs they and their descendants could hold and the neighborhoods where they could live.

▶ This painting of the internment camp at Heart Mountain, Wyoming, was done by Japanese American artist Estelle Ishigo.

◀ Toyo Miyatale photographed this scene in Los Angeles in the early days of World War II. With their belongings piled high on the sidewalk, Japanese Americans wait for the buses that will take them to a relocation assignment center.

JAPANESE RELOCATION

Have students write letters to the editor from the viewpoint of a Japanese American who is about to be interned in a relocation camp. Letters should protest the reasons for internment, explain how internment will disrupt the writer's life, and explain why, as Eugene Rostow noted (p. 410), "its motivation and its impact on our system of law deny every value of democracy." Call on volunteers to read their letters to the class.

Students may wish to include their letters in their portfolios.

■■ Ask students if they think internment of any minority group could happen today. Have students identify legal and other resources that a target group might use to resist such an action.

▶

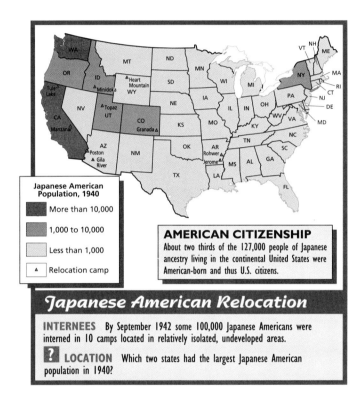

Japanese American Population, 1940

- ■ More than 10,000
- ■ 1,000 to 10,000
- ☐ Less than 1,000
- ▲ Relocation camp

AMERICAN CITIZENSHIP
About two thirds of the 127,000 people of Japanese ancestry living in the continental United States were American-born and thus U.S. citizens.

Japanese American Relocation

INTERNEES By September 1942 some 100,000 Japanese Americans were interned in 10 camps located in relatively isolated, undeveloped areas.

? **LOCATION** Which two states had the largest Japanese American population in 1940?

fearfully watched his neighbors being taken away for questioning by the FBI. He recalled bitterly that "they had done nothing; the only thing that they had done was to be born of Japanese ancestry."

He was 10 years old when his family was uprooted. Mineta wore his Cub Scout uniform on the train, hoping that it would show his loyalty to the United States. After six months in a barracks at the Santa Anita racetrack in southern California, Mineta's family was interned with some 10,000 others at a hastily built camp at Heart Mountain, Wyoming. "These camps were all barbed wire, guard towers, searchlights," recalled Mineta. "They were concentration camps. There's no question about it."

After the war Mineta attended college, became an insurance agent, and went into local politics in San Jose. In 1974 he was elected to the House of Representatives, where he served on several committees and introduced legislation seeking reparations for Japanese American internees.

Like most other internees, Mineta regretted what had happened, but his patriotism never wavered:

❝ Despite the color of our hair and skin, despite the shape of our eyes, the U.S. was our country. I remember how my parents reminded us of that fact. Just before our family was evacuated, my father . . . said, "No matter what happens, *this* is your home." ❞

Patriotism, and the desire to disprove accusations of disloyalty, inspired many young men in the camps to volunteer for military duty (in segregated units).

BIO GRAPHY

When war came, prejudice turned into near hysteria. There was no evidence of disloyalty on the part of any Issei or Nisei. Strong anti-Japanese sentiments among some vocal politicians and residents of western states, however, persuaded the federal government to remove people of Japanese descent from the West Coast. In February 1942 they were ordered to detention camps in Wyoming, Utah, and other states. Here they were imprisoned until 1945—an action upheld by the Supreme Court in 1944.

■■ **Because of prejudice and war hysteria, Japanese Americans living on the West Coast were interned in relocation camps.**

Relocation tragically disrupted the lives of Japanese Americans. They had to leave hurriedly, abandoning or selling their homes and businesses at rock-bottom prices. A government estimate later put Japanese American property losses at $400 million.

One imprisoned Japanese American was Norman Mineta, a Nisei from San Jose, California. On the day of the bombing, the young Mineta

Norman Mineta

Teaching the Section

WARTIME GAINS AND LIMITS

Create a chalkboard chart with columns headed *African Americans* and *Mexican Americans* and rows titled *Opportunities* and *Limitations*. Organize students into groups to discuss the war's consequences for each ethnic group. Then have the groups work together, using information gained from their discussions to complete the chalkboard chart. Conclude by asking students to hypothesize about why the wartime period was marked by racial unrest.

WOMEN IN THE WAR EFFORT

Organize students into groups to create a short segment for a World War II newsreel on women's contributions to the war effort. Segments should include narration, brief scenes of women at work, and comments from women, their supervisors, and their coworkers about women workers and about changes the war has brought to the workplace and to women's lives. Have each group present its newsreel segment to the class.

One Nisei combat team, the 442nd, fought in Europe and became one of the most decorated units in the armed services. Several thousand Japanese Americans also served in the Military Intelligence Service as interpreters and translators in the Pacific.

THE MARCH ON WASHINGTON

For African Americans, World War II brought both continued discrimination and greater opportunities. Many blacks moved into better-paying industrial jobs and played a key role in the military effort. About a million black soldiers served in the armed forces, including several thousand women in the Women's Auxiliary Army Corps. However, despite their protests, African Americans continued to serve in segregated units and until 1943 were kept out of combat. Blacks were usually restricted to menial work.

The millions of black Americans in the labor force in the 1940s also played an important homefront role in the war effort. But they had to struggle to gain acceptance. Many war plants would not hire blacks or would employ them only as janitors. And despite labor leaders' no-strike pledge, some white workers staged strikes, called "hate strikes," to keep black workers out of high-paying factory jobs.

In 1941, before the United States entered the war, African American labor leader A. Philip Randolph planned a march on Washington, D.C., to protest discrimination against black workers.

▲ African Americans served with distinction during the war. These pilots at a training center in Tuskegee, Alabama, study a map before going aloft in 1943.

President Roosevelt wanted to prevent the march, which Randolph predicted would bring 100,000 protesters to the Capitol. Randolph called it off after Roosevelt issued an executive order forbidding racial discrimination in defense plants and government offices.

To enforce the order, the government created the **Fair Employment Practices Committee** (FEPC). The FEPC investigated companies to make sure that all qualified applicants, regardless of race, were considered. The committee, however, lacked enforcement powers and could not prevent the widespread abuses. In addition, African Americans still had to struggle for equality in pay and promotion.

As in World War I, many blacks moved northward to work in war plants. In crowded cities, they faced discrimination in housing. Resulting tensions sometimes led to outbursts of violence against African Americans. In Detroit in 1943, some 25,000 white workers violated the wartime no-strike pledge and staged a hate strike to protest the promotion of African American workers. White residents of one Detroit neighborhood tried to prevent blacks from moving into the newly constructed Sojourner Truth Housing Project. In June of the same year, 25 blacks and 9 whites died in several days of rioting after a fight between blacks and whites at Belle Isle, a popular Detroit park, spread to other parts of the city.

Despite these incidents, most African Americans supported the war. Educator and civil rights activist Mary McLeod Bethune noted that African Americans "feel that the fight against fascism is their fight too," because they realized "that their persecution would be even worse under Hitler."

THE ZOOT-SUIT RIOTS

For Mexican Americans, as for blacks, World War II brought both opportunities and problems. More than 300,000 Mexican Americans served in the military, and 17 earned the Congressional Medal of Honor. The 88th Division, an elite combat unit known as the "Blue Devils," consisted mostly of Mexican Americans.

Mexican Americans also helped meet homefront labor needs. University of Texas history professor Carlos E. Castañeda served as assistant to the chairman of the FEPC and worked to

Practice

GUIDED PRACTICE
Work with the class to develop two lists on the chalkboard—one of the positive changes the war had on the lives of minorities and women on the home front and the other reflecting the negative effects.

INDEPENDENT PRACTICE
Have students pick one of the positive or negative outcomes listed in the Guided Practice activity and create an editorial cartoon that illustrates the experience. Students may wish to include their editorial cartoons in their portfolios.

Review and Assessment

REVIEW Organize a role-play in which volunteers represent a factory owner, farmer, female worker, entertainer, journalist, Japanese American, Mexican American, and African American. Have remaining students interview the role-players about the war years. Then assign the Section 2 Review on p. 414.

ASSESS Assign the **Section 2 Daily Quiz** in *Core Resources*. ▶

▲ These Mexican American infantrymen are being trained to use the rapid-firing Garand rifle at a U.S. Army camp in the South. Because many of these soldiers spoke Spanish, army instructors gave instructions in both English and Spanish.

improve working conditions for Mexican Americans in Texas. In 1945 the FEPC ordered a major Texas oil company to discontinue its hiring and promotion practices that discriminated against Hispanics.

As a result of similar FEPC actions, and the pressing need for workers, many factories opened up jobs to Mexican Americans. Many Mexican Americans moved from the Southwest to industrial centers in the Midwest and on the West Coast. Under a 1942 agreement between the United States and Mexico, thousands of Mexican farm and railroad workers—known as **braceros**—came north to work in the Southwest during World War II.

But prejudice and discrimination against Hispanics in jobs, housing, and recreation facilities caused bitter resentment. Relations grew especially hostile in Los Angeles. Mexican American youths had adopted the fad of wearing zoot suits—outfits with long jackets, pegged trousers, and wide-brimmed hats. In the summer of 1943, sailors roamed the city attacking zoot-suiters in what came to be known as the **zoot-suit riots**. The government eventually clamped down on the sailors, but not before they had viciously beaten many Mexican Americans.

A citizens' committee later determined that the attacks were motivated by racial prejudice. The committee also placed partial responsibility on the police, who had responded to the riots by arresting Mexican Americans, and on biased newspaper reports.

■■ **African Americans and Mexican Americans won better factory jobs during the war but continued to face widespread discrimination.**

ROSIE THE RIVETER

During the depression, the government discouraged women, especially married women, from working. The government now urged them to enter the job market to replace departing servicemen and to help win the war against fascism. One government poster showed a woman worker in bandanna and overalls. The caption read: "I'm Proud . . . my husband <u>wants</u> me to do my part." Advertisements and a popular song promoted "Rosie the Riveter," the symbol of patriotic women defense workers.

From 1940 to 1944 the number of women in the labor force increased by more than four million. Women worked in war plants and replaced men in a host of jobs ranging from newspaper reporting to truck driving. Many of these new workers were married women who were taking jobs outside the home for the first time. Many women already in the paid work force left traditional "women's work" as domestics and other service jobs to work in factories.

■■ **World War II increased women's participation in the paid labor force and allowed them to move into traditionally male jobs.**

Women's participation in the war effort gave many of them a new sense of pride and self-worth. One woman aircraft worker finally felt a sense of achievement after feeling "average" at other jobs:

66 Foremen from other departments come to my machine to ask me to do some work for them if I have time because they say I'm the best countersinker in the vast building! At forty-nine I've at last become not better than average, but the best! 99

HISTORICAL SIDELIGHTS
Women in the Work Force
In the auto industry the number of women production workers went from 1 in 20 in 1940 to 1 in 5 by 1944. However, many women were not offered specialized on-the-job training and were assigned to low-wage jobs. In addition, women workers faced hissing and whistling from their male counterparts. One female machine shop worker noted: "It was very rough for a while, but we were determined to stay, and eventually, the majority of men learned to accept us and respect us as co-workers."

PRIMARY SOURCE
Description of Change: excerpted
Rationale: excerpted to focus on main idea

SECTION 2

RETEACH Ask students, working in pairs, to write sentences that explain how each entry in the Preview Workshop is related to the main idea of the subsection in which it is located. Have pairs share their sentences with the group.

*C*losure

Write these World War II slogans on the chalkboard: *Pay Your Taxes, Beat the Axis; Back the Attack with War Bonds;* and *Don't Let Them Catch Us with Our Plants Down.* Ask students to explain how each slogan reflects the U.S. war effort on the home front.

*E*xtension

ANALYZE Interested students can read the decisions in the two Supreme Court cases *Hirabayashi* v. *United States* (1943) and *Korematsu* v. *United States* (1944), which established the legality of the U.S. internment of Japanese Americans, and write papers commenting on the decisions.

RESEARCH Ask students to research the work of the United Service Organization (USO) during World War II.

SECTION REVIEW ANSWERS

IDENTIFY

For significance, see the following pages:
James F. Byrnes (p. 408)
War Production Board
  (p. 408)
Selective Training and Service
  Act (p. 409)
Thomas E. Dewey (p. 409)
internment (p. 410)
Norman Mineta (p. 411)
A. Philip Randolph (p. 412)
Fair Employment Practices
  Committee (p. 412)
braceros (p. 413)
zoot-suit riots (p. 413)

1. increased industrial production and put production and distribution under government control, financed war and fought inflation by extending income tax to more Americans and by selling war bonds
2. increased women's participation in paid labor force, allowed women to move into traditionally male jobs
3. because prejudice and war hysteria made some Americans question their loyalty
4. Letters might weigh movement into better-paying jobs, service in armed forces against discrimination and struggles for equality in pay and promotion.
5. encouraged media to promote war effort, created OWI; planted "victory gardens" and bought war bonds

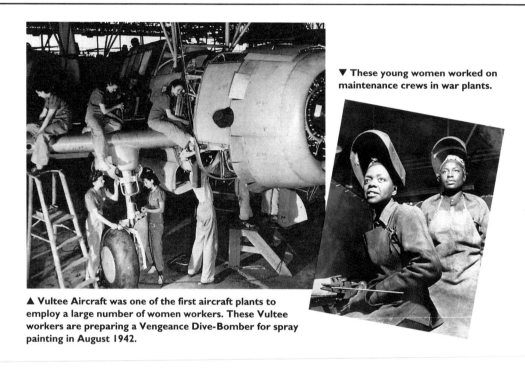

▼ These young women worked on maintenance crews in war plants.

▲ Vultee Aircraft was one of the first aircraft plants to employ a large number of women workers. These Vultee workers are preparing a Vengeance Dive-Bomber for spray painting in August 1942.

A government study in 1942 praised women workers, noting that factories "were practically unanimous in reporting that on the whole the work done by women was considered equal to that of men." Nevertheless, women encountered discrimination. Women workers continued to be paid less than men for the same work. African American women and women over 40 found few employers willing to hire them. Although Frances Perkins, long a supporter of women workers, continued to head the Department of Labor during the war years, wartime federal agencies did little to enforce equal treatment for women workers.

In spite of women's achievements, it was widely assumed—by many women as well as men—that most of the jobs women held during the war were temporary. A manager of a shipyard predicted that "these women who are willing . . . to lend a hand with the war will be the . . . office personnel of . . . the future." The message was clear: in traditionally "masculine" jobs, women were wanted as emergency helpers, not as competition.

SECTION 2 REVIEW

IDENTIFY and explain the significance of the following: James F. Byrnes, War Production Board, Selective Training and Service Act, Thomas E. Dewey, internment, Norman Mineta, A. Philip Randolph, Fair Employment Practices Committee, braceros, zoot-suit riots.

1. **MAIN IDEA** What steps did the United States take to shift from a peacetime to a wartime economy?

2. **MAIN IDEA** How did World War II change life for American women?

3. **RECOGNIZING BIAS** Why did the United States forcibly relocate and imprison Japanese Americans living on the West Coast?

4. **WRITING TO EVALUATE** Imagine you are either an African American or a Mexican American during World War II. Write a letter to your representative in Congress, evaluating the gains you have made during the war.

5. **IDENTIFYING CAUSE AND EFFECT** What did the U.S. government do to keep morale high during World War II? How did most Americans respond to the government's actions?

Section 3

DEFEAT OF THE AXIS POWERS

FOCUS
■ **What did the Allied offensive in North Africa achieve?**
■ **How did the Allies gain final victory in Europe?**
■ **What was the chief objective of Allied assaults in the Pacific?**
■ **Why and when did Japan surrender?**

American supplies and troops began to make a difference in the war by late 1942. But it would take over two more years of hard fighting to defeat the Axis powers. The Allied invasions of North Africa, Italy, and France and the fierce bombardments of German cities forced Germany to surrender in May 1945. In the Pacific, meanwhile, the United States seized Japanese-held islands, including the Philippines. Atomic attacks devastated Japan, and it surrendered in August 1945.

Liberation of Paris, 1944

ALLIED ATTACKS IN THE MEDITERRANEAN

The Allies agreed soon after Pearl Harbor that they would open up a second front against the Axis powers in order to relieve pressure on the Soviet Union. At Churchill's urging, they focused this attack on the Mediterranean region—what Churchill called the "soft underbelly" of the Axis territory.

◀ **"We are out to win the war in the quickest and most economical way," U.S. Army chief of staff George C. Marshall (right) declared in 1943. Marshall was photographed with General Dwight D. Eisenhower in North Africa in June 1943.**

Axis surrender in North Africa. In November 1942, after the British had driven the Germans and Italians into Libya, another Allied force landed in French Northwest Africa in an invasion code-named Operation Torch (see map on page 404). General Dwight D. Eisenhower commanded the invasion force, which consisted of American and British soldiers. As the soldiers established beachheads in Morocco and Algeria, Allied planes and ships cut Axis supply lines from Italy. Then, during the winter of 1942–43, the two Allied land forces—one from the west and the other from the east—began squeezing the Axis troops into a trap between them.

Several fierce battles took place in Tunisia. Finally, in May 1943, the Axis force of some

FOCUS OBJECTIVES
■ Analyze the achievements of the Allied offensive in North Africa.
■ Explain how the Allies gained final victory in Europe.
■ Determine the chief objective of Allied assaults in the Pacific.
■ State why and when Japan surrendered.

 GLOBAL CONNECTIONS
Almost a half-million survivors of the Afrika Corps in North Africa, as well as the first prisoners taken in the Italian campaign, were brought to POW camps in the U.S. and Canada. Many of the POWs were put to work on peanut farms in Florida and in logging camps in West Virginia. The prisoners came to admire the American farmer's way of life. Many POWs returned to the U.S. after the war and obtained U.S. citizenship.

MOTIVATING: PRIOR KNOWLEDGE

Ask students to identify on a map areas held by the Allies and by the Axis powers in late 1942. Have students review the war's turning points and describe how they think Americans at home and on the battlefields might have felt about the war at that time.

MAKING CONNECTIONS

Science

Sonar stands for *"sound navigation and ranging"*—a method of locating and judging the distance of underwater objects by analyzing the sound waves they deflect or give off. Scientists had developed sonar to locate icebergs, but after the outbreak of World War I British and U.S. scientists concentrated their research on using sonar to locate enemy submarines.

HISTORICAL SIDELIGHTS

Dummy Installations

The Allies successfully hid the D-Day landing point through an operation code-named *Fortitude*. While the real invasion force secretly prepared for the Normandy landing, other troops distracted the enemy by mustering in crowded fields in southeastern England accompanied by fake ammunition dumps, hospitals, field kitchens, and artillery made of wood and canvas.

Teaching the Section

THE NORTH AFRICAN OFFENSIVE

Ask for volunteers to role-play a military news briefing in Washington, D.C., to report the successful completion of the Allies' North African campaign. Roles should include: a press officer to coordinate the briefing; staff officers to brief the press on battle locations, tactics, and other geographic aspects; and field officers and soldiers to relate their battlefield experiences. The remainder of the class should portray newspaper reporters at the briefing, asking questions about the information presented and about the potential significance of the victory on the course of the war in Europe.

250,000 men surrendered. The Allies now controlled much of the Mediterranean. This victory also gave American troops valuable combat experience, especially in amphibious assaults.

■■ **The conquest of North Africa gave the Allies increased control over the Mediterranean.**

The invasion of Italy. From North Africa it was not far to the Italian island of Sicily. Allied leaders decided to invade it next in order to clear the Axis forces out of the central Mediterranean and acquire a launching pad for an invasion of the Italian mainland.

Amid high winds and difficult seas, almost half a million troops landed in July 1943 and subdued Sicily in a little over a month. The Italian king named a new prime minister to replace Benito Mussolini and ordered Mussolini's arrest. The Germans, however, were determined not to surrender the peninsula. They took Mussolini to Germany and then set up a base for him in northern Italy.

In September the Italian government signed an armistice with the Allies. Two days later the Allies invaded southern Italy to attack the Germans. Although the Allies took Naples on October 1, they soon bogged down. Hoping to outflank Nazi troops near Rome, they landed to the south at Anzio in January 1944 (see map on page 404); but their attack failed, and they were pinned down for months. Not until June 1944 did the Allies march into Rome, which became the first Axis capital to fall.

American and British forces then began driving slowly north. They were joined by small units of troops from more than 25 countries. After months of bitter mountain warfare, the German occupiers were finally defeated. Mussolini was captured in late April and shot by Italian partisans.

◄ **World War II Victory Medal**

▼ICTORY IN EUROPE

During the months of fighting in the Mediterranean region, the Allies were waging campaigns on several other fronts as well. Although they faced a determined enemy, they eventually overcame all resistance.

Sea and air assaults. In the Atlantic, German U-boats continued to take a staggering toll of Allied ships, lives, and supplies. Not until 1943 did the **Battle of the Atlantic** begin to turn in the Allies' favor. An important factor was the refinement of sonar equipment, which uses sound waves to detect underwater objects. The Allies also developed fast escort ships for convoys and air-bombed German U-boats and submarine yards. By 1944 the Allies had won the Battle of the Atlantic.

In the air, too, 1943 was an important year for the Allies. They intensified their campaign of strategic bombing aimed at destroying German military production and at undermining the morale of the German people. British Royal Air Force (RAF) planes flew chiefly at night, dropping their bombs in the general area of a given target. American aircraft concentrated on precision bombing in daylight raids. By 1944, bombers rained tons of explosives on German factories, supply lines, and military centers. Many German civilians died in these raids.

The invasion of France. Victory in the Battle of the Atlantic and air assaults on Germany paved the way for Operation Overlord—the long-awaited Allied invasion of German-occupied France. Commanded by General Eisenhower, it had involved years of planning. The Allies put in place a system of dummy installations and false clues to convince the Germans that the invasion would take place near Calais.

Instead, the Allies landed to the south, in Normandy. On **D-Day**, June 6, 1944, nearly 5,000 troop transports, landing craft, and warships carried some 150,000 American, British, and Canadian soldiers across the English Channel. Overhead, planes dropped close to 23,000 airborne troops and bombed roads, bridges, and German troop concentrations. Sergeant Ralph G. Martin recalled that "everything was confusion" during the landing made in pounding surf:

Ask students to reread p. 406 on the Allied war aims that FDR and Churchill agreed upon in Washington, D.C., and Casablanca. Then have volunteers recall the situation in the Soviet Union in 1943 and explain why opening a second front was desirable. *(relieve pressure on the Soviets)* Have students analyze how the Italian campaign would further that aim. *(Germany would be forced to move troops from other places in Europe to defend Italy, which could help the Soviets to regain lost territory.)*

Pair students to create a teaching tool to chronicle events in Europe that led to the Allied victory, from the invasion of Italy in July 1943 to Germany's surrender in May 1945. Tell each pair to first decide whether to organize this information on a map, on a flowchart or other graphic organizer, or on a time line. Select pairs to present their work to the class. Then ask volunteers to assess the contribution of naval and air power to the Allies' victory. ▶

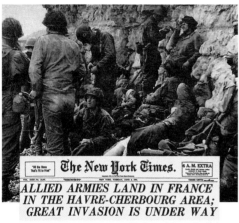

ALLIED ARMIES LAND IN FRANCE IN THE HAVRE-CHERBOURG AREA; GREAT INVASION IS UNDER WAY

The Granger Collection, New York

▲ The *New York Times* announced the Allied invasion of France on June 6, 1944. After landing at Normandy, these American members of the invasion force rest under a cliff before advancing inland.

> 66 Units were mixed up, many of them leaderless, most of them not being where they were supposed to be. Shells were coming in all the time; boats burning; vehicles with nowhere to go bogging down, getting hit; supplies getting wet; boats trying to come in all the time, some hitting mines, exploding. 99

The Germans had fortified the Normandy beaches with concrete bunkers, tank traps, and mines. But the Allied disinformation campaign had done its job. Hitler refused to send reinforcements, believing that the main invasion would occur elsewhere. Although the Allies met determined opposition, they penetrated 15 miles into France in less than a week. Aided by the French Resistance, the Allies drove steadily eastward. They liberated Paris on August 25, 1944. By early September they had landed over two million troops in western Europe. Another Allied force drove northward through France from the Mediterranean. Meanwhile, Soviet troops pressed Germany from the east.

A German counterattack. Although Germany's situation was grave, Hitler would not give up. In September 1944 the Germans launched their first V-2s, long-range rockets aimed at cities in England and Belgium. Once launched, these bombs could not be shot down without causing considerable damage.

By September 1944 the Allies had crossed the German border. As they paused to bring in supplies and to regroup, the Germans launched their last counterattack. In heavy snow, they drove against the Allies in the thickly wooded Ardennes region of Belgium and northern France, pushing them westward to create a dangerous bulge in the Allied lines. In the resulting **Battle of the Bulge**, some 200,000 Germans attacked an initial American force of around 80,000. Because many of the regular troops had been transferred to other areas, much of the fighting was done by "cooks, clerks, mechanics, and radio operators."

Allied reinforcements were rushed to the front, and the Allies pushed the Germans back. Artilleryman Francis Tsuzuki, whose Japanese American battalion pursued the Germans, remembered that "the Germans were retreating so fast. At times we were moving . . . more than 100 miles a day." By January 1945 it was clear that the German offensive had failed. In February Roosevelt, Churchill, and Stalin met at the **Yalta Conference** to plan for the postwar peace. At the conference the leaders agreed to divide and occupy Germany and outlined plans for a new international peace organization.

Last days. During the early months of 1945, Allied bombers continued to blast German industrial and population centers, including Dresden, Leipzig, and Berlin. One of the most devastating—and controversial—attacks hit Dresden in February. This beautiful old city, of little strategic value, was packed with refugees fleeing from the war-torn areas. In one massive two-day attack, Allied bombers caused the worst firestorms of the war. Total civilian deaths have been estimated at between 30,000 and 60,000.

▲ The Allied bombing of Dresden, Germany, left many famous buildings in ruins. Shown here is the damage to the inner court of the Zwinger Museum, which housed a priceless art collection.

HISTORICAL SIDELIGHTS
Bombing of Dresden
While much of Dresden was destroyed by the Allied bombing raids, many of its art treasures were not, since the German government had hidden them outside the city. Although Soviet troops took the art collection in 1945, much of it was returned in the mid-1950s. The damaged Zwinger museum shown in the photograph on this page was one of the few 18th-century structures that survived the bombing raids.

PRIMARY SOURCE
Description of Change: excerpted
Rationale: excerpted to focus on main idea

Teaching the Section

WAR IN THE PACIFIC

Have students work in groups and assume the roles of American military commanders in the Pacific. Ask each group to prepare a briefing explaining the military strategy of island-hopping and its importance. "Commanders" should also create outline maps of the Pacific and locate and label the islands that were involved in the island-hopping strategy. Have volunteers present each group's "briefings" and maps. Then have the class summarize why the recapture of islands was critical to Allied strategy in the Pacific.

 GLOBAL CONNECTIONS

The Coast Watchers
During World War II, Australians living on remote islands in the South Pacific served as the eyes of the Allies. The Australians informed them by radio of Japanese troop movements and rescued shipwrecked sailors and Allied pilots shot down at sea.

BIO GRAPHY PERSONALITIES IN HISTORY
Throughout the early part of 1942, MacArthur disagreed with the U.S. strategy that emphasized Germany's defeat, and he called for a "Japan first" strategy. In mid-1943 MacArthur began his plan for the reconquest of the Philippines. When it was suggested that Admiral Nimitz's forces undertake the campaign, MacArthur bristled and continued to promote himself for the task. Then in 1944, when military leaders questioned the necessity of reconquering the Philippines, he successfully campaigned for his point of view. When MacArthur finally received the go-ahead, he waded onto Leyte beach and made a brief speech. "This is the Voice of Freedom, General MacArthur speaking. People of the Philippines: I have returned!"

In March, Allied troops from the west crossed the Rhine and drove into the heart of Germany. By then, Soviet troops occupied much of Eastern Europe. Churchill wanted the Allies to push east as far and as fast as possible because he was worried that the Russians might later lay claim to territories they seized. But Eisenhower, who did not want military strategy determined by political considerations, halted the Allied advance at the Elbe River in April. The Soviet army agreed to halt momentarily east of Berlin.

On April 30, 1945, Hitler committed suicide in his bunker deep under the ruins of Berlin. As Soviet troops occupied the city, German armies all over Europe stopped fighting. American sergeant Mack Morriss described the grim mood of the fallen city: "There is a feeling that here has ended not only a city but a nation, that here a titanic force has come to catastrophe." Germany surrendered unconditionally on May 7. The next day, known as V-E (Victory in Europe) Day, marked the formal end of the war in Europe. The next month the Allies divided defeated Germany into four occupation zones.

■■ **After winning the Battle of the Atlantic and bombing Germany, the Allies invaded France. Germany surrendered in May 1945.**

*P*ACIFIC OFFENSIVES

In the Pacific, as in the western theater of operations, the Allies went on the offensive by 1943. The planned attack on Japan had two components: (1) air, land, and naval forces would seize Japanese-held islands in the central Pacific and set up air bases there; (2) combined forces would retake New Guinea and then the Philippines. The ultimate objective, of course, was to come within striking distance of Japan itself.

Island-hopping. As early as 1942, the American high command had adopted a policy of **island-hopping**. This meant that troops would attack and seize only certain strategic Japanese-held islands, rather than try to recapture all of them. Japanese garrisons on bypassed islands would be cut off from supplies and troop reinforcements.

In the central Pacific, an island-hopping offensive began in November 1943 in the Gilbert Islands (see map on page 402). Army troops easily took Makin Island. Tarawa Island proved more difficult. Because of a coral reef encircling the island, the marines who landed there, according to Sergeant John Bushemi, had to wade in to the beach "in the face of murderous Japanese fire, with no protection." Almost 1,000 marines lost their lives, and some 2,000 were wounded before the island was secure.

The next important series of landings took place in the Marshall Islands, north of the Gilberts. Here Americans captured several key bases from which they bombed the Truk Islands, the headquarters of the Japanese fleet.

By the summer of 1944, Americans advanced to the Mariana Islands. In June, under cover of intense air and naval bombardment from nearby carriers, landing craft swept in to the beaches of Saipan. The Japanese, determined to take a stand, sent out a big fleet to stop this offensive. In the resulting **Battle of the Philippine Sea**, the United States won a decisive victory, downing hundreds of Japanese planes while only losing some 80 U.S. planes.

Saipan and Guam fell in July and August, respectively. U.S. victories here were especially crucial. The islands provided airstrips from which American bombers could launch missions against the islands of Japan.

Reconquering the Philippines. Despite these setbacks, Japanese resistance proved just as fierce when the Allies began their New Guinea–Philippines campaign in June 1943. Douglas MacArthur, who had earlier evacuated the Philippines, commanded U.S. forces.

BIO GRAPHY MacArthur was born in 1880, the son of distinguished general Arthur MacArthur. After graduating first in his class from West Point, young MacArthur served in the Philippines and was wounded twice in World War I. From

Douglas MacArthur

JAPAN SURRENDERS

As a class, discuss the reasons why Japan surrendered after the bombing of Hiroshima and Nagasaki. Then have students debate this statement: *President Truman's decision to drop the atomic bomb on Japan was a wise one.*

Changing Ways
THE NAVAJO CODE TALKERS

During World War II Native Americans served in several branches of the U.S. armed forces. Their languages allowed them to play a unique role in the Signal Corps, the communication units responsible for coding and sending classified military information. On the basis of the success of a few Native American army groups in code work, the Marine Signal Corps decided in March 1942 to organize a unit composed entirely of Navajos. The marines believed that the Navajo language would be unfamiliar to the Japanese, and thus would provide an unbreakable code. They quickly assembled a group of Navajo soldiers for the job.

The new unit devised and memorized a special Navajo dictionary containing 413 military terms. For example, the Navajo word for "chicken hawk" meant dive-bomber in the code; "humming-bird" meant fighter plane; and "iron fish" meant submarine. Armed with this new code, the Navajo "Code Talkers" first went into action in the fall of 1942 in the Pacific.

Soon after the Code Talkers arrived on the front lines, U.S. field commanders reported that the Navajos' methods reduced the time needed for decoding and encoding messages by half. As radio operators tracking Japanese movements, the Navajos often had to work in especially dangerous conditions behind enemy lines. "The Navajo Code Talkers have proved to be excellent Marines, intelligent, industrious, efficient," one officer wrote. Another remarked, "Were it not for the Navajos, the Marines would never have taken Iwo Jima."

By August 1943 nearly 200 Navajos were participating in the Code Talker program, and by the war's end more than 400 had served in the Marine Signal Corps. Their codes completely baffled the Japanese and were never broken. Though the Navajo Code Talkers made up only a small part of the Allied forces, their contributions to the war effort were invaluable.

▲ Corporal Henry Bake, Jr., (left) and Private George H. Kirk (right) were two members of the Navajo Code Talkers. They are shown operating a portable radio set behind front lines in the Solomon Islands in 1943.

Changing Ways

THE NAVAJO CODE TALKERS

SETTING THE SCENE
Japan had been able to crack every code the United States devised until civil engineer Philip Johnston came up with the idea of using the Navajos as code talkers. He had learned Navajo while his parents were Protestant missionaries among the Navajos. Realizing the need for secret communications from his own experiences in World War I, Johnston believed that the Navajo language would be well suited to sending secret messages. He persuaded the marines to test his idea.

1919 to 1922 he was superintendent of West Point. He took part in the attack on the Bonus Army marchers of 1932 (see Chapter 13), justifying the violence by claiming that Communists were behind this veterans' protest. After serving as a military adviser in the Philippines for several years, MacArthur was recalled to active duty in the summer of 1941. Eventually he was given command of all U.S. Army units in the Pacific.

In many respects, MacArthur was an excellent strategist. No one doubted his courage. But he was also arrogant, and though he demanded absolute loyalty from his subordinates, he did not hesitate to disagree with his superiors.

In the Allied drive to recapture the Philippines, MacArthur led U.S. and Australian troops in a series of landings along the north coast of New Guinea. By late July 1944 they had reached the western end of this large island. Allied forces also took smaller islands nearby, such as the Admiralty Islands.

By the fall of 1944, with New Guinea secure and with its newly won bases in the Marianas, the United States was ready to invade the Philippines.

Practice

GUIDED PRACTICE

Work with students to prepare a time line on the chalkboard to combine the events in the Pacific and Europe that led to the end of World War II. For each event on the time line, have students describe its effect on the Allied war effort.

INDEPENDENT PRACTICE

Have each student pick three events from the Guided Practice time line that he or she considers critical to Allied victory either in Europe or in the Pacific. Instruct students to write a paragraph to justify each choice. Students may wish to include their paragraphs in their portfolios.

Review and Assessment

REVIEW Select students to assume the roles of General Eisenhower, General MacArthur, and President Truman at a "Meet the Press" radio newscast. Have other students serve as members of the press, questioning the panel on the events that led to victory. Then assign the Section 3 Review on p. 421.

ASSESS Assign the **Section 3 Daily Quiz** in *Core Resources*.

MULTICULTURAL PERSPECTIVES

The *kamikaze* pilots went through a ritual-like procedure before takeoff that included a last toast, farewell bids by onlookers, and writing last letters home. The goals of the *kamikazes* were spelled out in the First Order to the *Kamikazes:* "It is absolutely out of the question for you to return alive. Your mission involves certain death. Your bodies will be dead, but not your spirits."

MAKING CONNECTIONS

Science

Scientists from all over the world participated in the Manhattan Project. Among them was German American physicist Maria Mayer, who had come to the U.S. in 1930. Mayer later became the first woman to receive the Nobel Prize in theoretical physics for her contribution to proving the shell-model theory of the nucleus of an atom. This theory posits that the nucleus is made up of concentric shells of protons and neutrons.

PRIMARY SOURCE

Description of Change: excerpted
Rationale: excerpted to focus on main idea

Allied forces poured onto the beaches of the island of Leyte in October. When the Japanese navy counterattacked, the result was the **Battle of Leyte Gulf**, the last, largest, and most decisive naval engagement in the Pacific. The battle was a disaster for the Japanese, who lost four carriers, two battleships, and several cruisers. From this time on, the Japanese fleet no longer presented a serious threat to the Allies.

Allied troops, aided by Filipino guerrillas, fanned out over the islands of the Philippines. Overcoming bitter opposition, they entered Manila in February 1945 and subdued most Japanese defense forces within weeks. "I'm a little late," said MacArthur, "but we finally came."

■■ **Island-hopping and the reconquest of the Philippines brought the Allies within bombing distance of Japan's cities.**

VICTORY IN THE PACIFIC

These Pacific victories gave the United States enough bases to launch B-29 bombers against the Japanese home islands. In a series of devastating night attacks, U.S. planes hit most of the country's major cities. The worst raid, over Tokyo in March 1945, created firestorms that destroyed much of the city.

▼ A few hours after U.S. Marines captured Iwo Jima, naval landing crafts delivered tons of supplies to the island. The slippery volcanic ash made it difficult for marines to keep their footing while carrying the heavy crates.

Japanese civilian morale sagged, but the country's military leaders refused to surrender. In February 1945, when marines attacked Iwo Jima—only 750 miles from Tokyo—they met strong resistance. U.S. marines struggled to take Mount Suribachi, which the Japanese held with a strong system of tunnels and bunkers. The **Battle of Iwo Jima** lasted nearly a month. Some 4,000 marines were killed, while the Japanese lost more than 20,000.

On April 1 the largest landing force in Pacific history invaded Okinawa, located about 350 miles from Japan. Allied soldiers drove the Japanese forces to the southern tip of the island. The **Battle of Okinawa** was perhaps the bloodiest battle of the Pacific war, with American casualties estimated at 49,000 and Japanese losses at over 100,000. Meanwhile, a 700-plane squad of **kamikaze**, or suicide planes, damaged 13 U.S. destroyers. (*Kamikaze* is a Japanese word meaning "divine wind.")

By early April 1945, however, American victory in the Pacific was near. But President Roosevelt did not live to see the end of hostilities with Japan. The world was stunned when he died suddenly on April 12. The new president, Harry S. Truman, wrote candidly about his bewilderment:

▲ The sudden death of President Roosevelt shocked many Americans. Overcome with grief, Sergeant Graham Jackson plays "Going Home" on his accordion while the president's casket passes by.

❝ I did not know what reaction the country would have to the death of a man whom they all practically worshipped. I was worried about the reaction of the Armed Forces. . . . I knew the President had a great many meetings with Churchill and Stalin. I was not familiar with any of these things. ❞

Truman had little time to ponder. In a few weeks he was faced with a tough decision. Although battered by relentless bombing, Japan still had a well-trained army and strong inner defenses. And Germany's surrender in May freed the Allied forces for the war in the Pacific.

By this time, however, the United States had a fearsome new weapon, the atomic bomb. In the top-secret **Manhattan Project**, scientists had been working on a bomb since 1942. They tested it successfully at Alamogordo, New Mexico, on July 16, 1945. The very next day, Truman met with Allied leaders at Potsdam, south of Berlin. On July 26 they demanded Japan's unconditional surrender, which Japan rejected.

Truman proceeded to give the order to use atomic weapons against Japan. On August 6 a U.S. plane called the *Enola Gay* dropped an atomic bomb on Hiroshima. It flattened a huge area of the city and killed more than 75,000. Three days later the United States dropped the second atomic bomb, on Nagasaki. The Japanese estimated that the total number of deaths caused by both bombs—including those who died later from burns and radiation poisoning—was 240,000.

A day before the bombing of Nagasaki, the Soviet Union had declared war on Japan and began

▲ **This aerial photograph shows the devastation in Hiroshima after the atomic bomb was dropped. The watch shown was found in the wreckage, its hands frozen at 8:15—the exact time of the explosion.**

an invasion of Manchuria. The Japanese soon offered to surrender. The formal surrender was signed on September 2, 1945, aboard the battleship *Missouri* in Tokyo Bay.

■■ **After the U.S. atomic bombings of Hiroshima and Nagasaki, Japan surrendered in August 1945.**

SECTION 3 REVIEW

IDENTIFY and explain the significance of the following: Dwight D. Eisenhower, Battle of the Atlantic, D-Day, Battle of the Bulge, Yalta Conference, island-hopping, Battle of the Philippine Sea, Battle of Leyte Gulf, Battle of Iwo Jima, Battle of Okinawa, kamikaze, Harry S. Truman, Manhattan Project.

LOCATE and explain the importance of the following: Sicily, Anzio, Normandy, Dresden, Elbe River, Gilbert Islands, Marshall Islands, Mariana Islands, New Guinea, Leyte, Iwo Jima, Okinawa, Hiroshima, Nagasaki.

1. **MAIN IDEA** What did the Allies accomplish through the military campaign in North Africa?

2. **MAIN IDEA** What events forced Germany to surrender in 1945?

3. **GEOGRAPHY: LOCATION** How did the Allies attempt to regain control of the Pacific? What was the overall aim of this military strategy?

4. **WRITING TO EXPLAIN** Write an essay that explains when and why Japan surrendered.

5. **USING HISTORICAL IMAGINATION** Imagine you are a soldier on either the European or the Pacific front. Write a diary entry that describes conditions you experienced in one of the battles mentioned in the text.

PREVIEW WORKSHOP

Following is a list of the significant people, places, and terms in this section. You may wish to use this list as a section preview.

People
- Elie Wiesel

Places
- Sakhalin Island

- Kuril Islands
- Taiwan
- Hainan

Terms
- Holocaust
- genocide
- superpowers
- revisionists

MOTIVATING:
LINK TO TODAY

Ask students how they think Truman's decision to drop the atomic bomb affected prospects for world peace. Ask volunteers if they think the world today is made more secure or less so by the existence of nuclear weapons. Tell students that in this section they will examine this and other consequences of World War II.

FOCUS OBJECTIVES

- Examine the costs of World War II.

- Explain what the Holocaust was and describe how it affected European Jews.

- Analyze the international consequences of World War II.

Section 4

THE PRICE OF VICTORY

F O C U S
- **What were some of the costs of World War II?**
- **What was the Holocaust? How did it affect European Jews?**
- **What were the international consequences of World War II?**

After years of struggle and sacrifice, World War II ended in victory for the Allies. But the price was high. The toll in lives and property was without precedent. Most alarming was the knowledge—fully revealed only after the defeat of Germany— that Hitler had tried to exterminate all the Jews of Europe. Along with peace came many uncertainties about the future.

Soviet civilians mourn dead soldiers.

COSTS OF THE WAR

The United States and its allies achieved their war aims. Germany's murderous Nazi regime was destroyed. Japanese expansion in Asia was halted and the nation's military warlords overthrown. But the toll in death, suffering, and destruction was appallingly high.

World War II was the most devastating war the world has ever known. When it finally ended, hundreds of cities, from London to Tokyo, lay in ruins. Beautiful churches and palaces were reduced to rubble, and priceless works of art had gone up in smoke. Millions of people lacked heat, electricity, running water, adequate food, or means of traveling from one place to another. In some regions, mile upon mile of field and forest had been reduced to utter desolation.

There is no way of estimating the value of property loss, but two examples indicate its extent. In Düsseldorf, Germany, more than 90 percent of homes could not be lived in. The cities of Kiev and Minsk in the Soviet Union had to be completely rebuilt.

The war took more lives than any other conflict in history and brought untold suffering to civilians. According to one estimate, some 30 million noncombatants lost their lives from bombing, shelling, disease, or starvation. Millions more were injured, were weakened by malnutrition, or lost everything they owned. The Soviet Union and

◀ **Britain's Coventry Cathedral was one of many churches virtually destroyed by bombing attacks during the war. This ceremony was held among the church ruins in February 1941.**

CORE RESOURCES

• **Section 4 Daily Quiz**

COSTS OF WAR

Have students, using the text and chart on p. 423, compare the costs of war for the European and Asian combatants with the costs of war for the U.S. Ask students to explain why the U.S. and France had fewer military deaths than many of the other major combatants and why the U.S. had the fewest civilian deaths.

THE HOLOCAUST

Have students explain why the Holocaust is called genocide. *(not random or sporadic killing, but a deliberate, carefully planned and carried out attempt to destroy Europe's Jews)* Organize students into small groups to identify factors that allowed the Holocaust to take place *(history of anti-Semitism in Europe, Nazi propaganda against Jews, assistance or apathy of non-Jews, inaction of Allied leaders)* and to explain how each contributed to the genocide.

INTERNATIONAL CONSEQUENCES

Write *The Consequences of War* on the chalkboard. Call on volunteers to cite consequences of World War II for both sides and write responses on the chalkboard. Direct students to use the list to write a paragraph explaining the war's short- and long-term effects on the world's people. Have volunteers read their paragraphs to the class. Students may wish to include their paragraphs in their portfolios.

DEATHS IN WORLD WAR II

Country	Military Deaths	Civilian Deaths
ALLIED POWERS		
British Commonwealth	373,372	92,673
France	213,324	350,000
Poland	123,178	5,675,000
Philippines	27,000	91,000
United States	292,131	6,000
Soviet Union	11,000,000	7,000,000
Yugoslavia	305,000	1,200,000
AXIS POWERS		
Bulgaria	10,000	10,000
Germany	3,500,000	780,000
Hungary	200,000	290,000
Italy	242,232	152,941
Japan	1,300,000	672,000
Romania	300,000	200,000

Source: *Encyclopedia Britannica*

THE WAR TO END ALL WARS World War II had an enormous global impact. Tens of thousands of men, women, and children died from causes directly related to the war, and untold numbers lost their homes and livelihoods.

? **BUILDING CHART SKILLS** Which country had the highest overall casualties?

China were especially hard hit. As in World War I, U.S. civilian losses were relatively light. In economic terms, armaments and other military costs probably totaled over $1 trillion.

■■ **World War II resulted in more deaths and destroyed more property than any other war in history.**

𝒯HE HOLOCAUST

No other wartime civilian deaths caused more horror than those of the **Holocaust**, Nazi Germany's systematic slaughter of European Jews. Before the war, Hitler had forced Jews out of most professions and had stripped them of their civil rights (see Chapter 15). The Nazis' goal was a Germany that was *Judenrein*—free of Jews. The Nazi authorities at first encouraged emigration, and about two thirds of all German and Austrian Jews left their countries. Many of those who remained were imprisoned in concentration camps such as Dachau (DAHK-ow) and Buchenwald (BOO-kuhn-wawld).

When Germany occupied France and other countries of Western Europe, and attacked Poland and the Soviet Union, it extended its control over additional thousands of Jews. Now Hitler's war against this people entered a new phase—one of utter savagery. In many regions special squads of German soldiers rounded up Jews and shot them. Elsewhere, Jews were forced into cities and isolated in ghettos. In 1941 the Germans began constructing camps specifically for the purpose of **genocide**—the deliberate annihilation of an entire people. Hitler and senior Nazi officials called this extermination program the "final solution of the Jewish question."

Major death camps were Auschwitz (OWSH-vits), Treblinka, and Majdanek, all in Poland. Here Jewish men, women, and children were transported in sealed railroad cars, marched into rooms disguised as shower facilities, and gassed. Their bodies were then cremated. All told, some six million Jews—two thirds of the Jewish population of Europe—perished.

The Nazis' pitiless slaughter extended to other peoples, too. Other victims, numbering in the

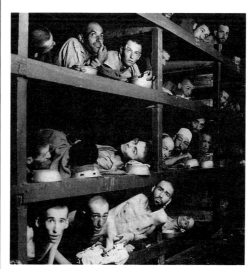

▲ These starving survivors of Buchenwald were photographed in April 1945 after their liberation by Allied soldiers.

Chart Caption Answer
Soviet Union

 GLOBAL CONNECTIONS

As the Nazis implemented their racial policies, Hitler taunted the international community to accept the Jews desperately seeking refuge. "I can only hope," he said, "that the other world which has such deep sympathy . . . will . . . convert this sympathy into practical aid." However, the Évian Conference in July 1938 sent a clear message to Hitler that the Jews had few protectors. Conceived by FDR, the conference brought to Évian, France, delegates from 32 nations. Each explained why it could not accept any Jews. Australia's delegate stated "We don't have a racial problem and we don't want to import one." Venezuela did not want to disturb its "demographic equilibrium." In the end only the Dominican Republic responded positively. It offered to accept 100,000 Jews.

*P*ractice

GUIDED PRACTICE

Work with students to develop a flowchart on the chalkboard that shows the stages and developments of the Nazis' plan for a Germany free of Jews.

INDEPENDENT PRACTICE

Ask students to use the information from the Guided Practice activity to write three journal entries from the viewpoint of a Holocaust survivor. One entry should describe the Nazis' actions toward Jews *before* the war; another, *during* the war; and the last, the psychological effects of the Holocaust on its survivors. Students may wish to include their journal entries in their portfolios.

*R*eview and *A*ssessment

REVIEW Have students write a script for a documentary "The Legacies of World War II." Assign groups the following topics: the costs of war, the Holocaust, the changing balance of power, the beginning of the atomic age. Another group should write an introduction, segment transitions, and conclusion. Then assign the Section 4 Review on p. 425.

ASSESS Assign the **Section 4 Daily Quiz** in *Core Resources*.

HISTORICAL SIDELIGHTS

The *St. Louis*

Although the U.S. could have offered a safe haven to many thousands of Jews fleeing Nazi persecution early in the war, it did not. In 1940 a ship called the *St. Louis* carrying 900 German Jewish refugees tried to land at U.S. ports, but the ship was denied entry. Eventually it returned to Germany, where most of its passengers were sent to Nazi death camps.

PRIMARY SOURCE

Description of Change: excerpted

Rationale: excerpted to focus on main idea

MULTICULTURAL PERSPECTIVES

In April 1993 the U.S. Holocaust Memorial Museum opened in the nation's capital. The federal government donated the museum's site near the Washington Monument to the U.S. Holocaust Memorial Council, an organization set up in 1980 by Congress to create a living memorial to the Holocaust's victims. The museum was built entirely through private donations. Its design incorporates powerful symbols of the death camps—the barbed-wire fences and the guard towers.

---

millions, included Gypsies, Poles, the mentally retarded, religious dissidents, and homosexuals. Communists, Socialists, and other political opponents of the Nazi regime faced imprisonment and death as well.

When the Allies liberated the death camps, they found thousands of starving survivors. One was Elie Wiesel, the Romanian-born American writer. Having been sent first to Auschwitz and then to Buchenwald, he was an emaciated youth of 16 when freed. Hospitalized for two weeks, he recovered. His writings, however, express the deep psychological scars left on concentration camp survivors:

> 66One day I was able to get up, after gathering all my strength. I wanted to see myself in the mirror hanging on the opposite wall. I had not seen myself since the ghetto.
>   From the depths of the mirror, a corpse gazed back at me.
>   The look in his eyes, as they stared into mine, has never left me. 99

The Holocaust took the lives of six million Jews—two thirds of European Jewry.

Why were the Nazis able to carry out the monstrous genocide? They built on a history of anti-Semitism in Europe stretching back to the Middle Ages. A barrage of Nazi propaganda against Jews whipped up this anti-Semitism. Some non-Jews in Nazi-occupied countries assisted or failed to prevent the Nazis from sending their Jewish fellow citizens to the death camps. Others, however, heroically worked to save Jewish lives. Most Germans were afraid to protest; they knew the Nazi secret police imprisoned or killed anyone resisting Hitler's government.

Another factor underlying the Holocaust was the lack of direct action by the Allies. Although reports of mass exterminations surfaced as early as 1941, the Allies believed the reports to be exaggerated. As a result, Allied nations did not open their doors to greater numbers of refugees or attempt to destroy rail lines that led to the death camps.

▶ **British prime minister Winston Churchill (left), President Roosevelt (center), and Soviet leader Joseph Stalin (right) met at Yalta in 1945 to discuss territorial divisions after the war.**

A NEW BALANCE OF POWER

By the time of the Yalta Conference, the political balance of power had clearly shifted. The United States had confirmed its position as the world's strongest nation. Its western European allies, notably Great Britain, had been weakened by the war. The Soviet Union, in spite of the devastation it had undergone, emerged from the war as a mighty force. For the next several decades, the United States and the Soviet Union, as **superpowers**, would dominate the world.

Much of the Soviet Union's new power was based on the territory it had occupied in Eastern Europe during the war. At the Yalta Conference, Roosevelt and Churchill had secretly agreed to accept the Soviet occupation of Polish territory in return for Stalin's vague promise of eventual free elections. When this agreement later became public, some critics blamed Roosevelt and Churchill for giving in to Stalin's demands. But with Soviet troops in control of Poland, they had little choice. Furthermore, Roosevelt wanted to assure Russia's entry into the war against Japan.

By the end of the war, the Soviet Union had absorbed the Baltic nations of Estonia, Latvia, Lithuania, and parts of Czechoslovakia and Romania. After Japan's surrender, the Soviet Union also took control of former Japanese territory, including the Kuril Islands and half of Sakhalin Island, which lie north of Japan. Defeated Japan also lost Inner Mongolia, Manchuria, and the islands of Taiwan (Formosa) and Hainan to China.

Among the many consequences of World War II were the emergence of two superpowers and territorial realignments.

RETEACH For each subsection in Section 4, have students write a sentence that summarizes the main idea. Select students to read their statements aloud. Have the reteaching group choose the best summary sentence for each subsection.

Closure

Ask students what they think was the most enduring legacy of World War II for the U.S. (*Students might mention superpower status, new relationships with former allies and enemies, arms race.*)

Extension

DEBATE Have students research and debate the following statement: *Eisenhower's decision to stop his invasion of Germany at the Elbe River set the stage for Soviet dominance of Eastern Europe.*

EVALUATE Have students consult David Wyman's *The Abandonment of the Jews* and write essays on why American leaders did not act on their knowledge of the Holocaust.

C O M M E N T A R Y

Using the Atomic Bomb

In the field of technology, the war brought several breakthroughs, including synthetic rubber, jet propulsion, and new methods of blood storage and transfusion. One frightening wartime scientific advance was the unleashing of atomic energy for military purposes. In the most controversial decision of World War II, President Truman approved the use of the atomic bomb against Japan. Was the United States justified? Or did it commit a grave error by using nuclear weapons, and against civilians at that?

The decision to fund research on an atomic bomb was made by President Franklin Roosevelt in 1941. He did so in response to fears of scientists in the United States, including Albert Einstein, that German physicists were working on such a weapon. By the time the bomb was successfully tested, Germany was defeated, Roosevelt was dead, and Truman was president.

In announcing the atomic bombing of Japan, Truman defended his decision by noting that Japan had refused to surrender. Truman claimed that dropping the two bombs had prevented an American invasion of Japan, scheduled for early 1946, that might have cost hundreds of thousands of American and Japanese lives. He also portrayed the atomic bomb as the American answer to the Japanese attack on Pearl Harbor. "The Japanese began the war," said Truman. "They have been repaid manyfold."

Some historians have questioned these explanations. (Since these historians have revised the previously accepted version of historical events, they are known as **revisionists**.) They have pointed to evidence that the Japanese were urgently seeking to end the war in the summer of 1945. These historians have suggested that the war could have been won without nuclear weapons and without an invasion of Japan. Some revisionists have argued that Truman and his advisers had another reason for dropping the bomb. They did so not only to end the war but also to demonstrate the power of atomic weapons and thus strengthen the hand of the United States in its postwar dealings with the Soviet Union.

While the debate over the American decision to use atomic weapons continues, all historians agree on the long-range effects of the decision. One result was a dangerous nuclear arms race. In the postwar period the United States, and the rest of the world, would face the challenges of controlling the creation and use of atomic weapons and of harnessing atomic power for peaceful uses.

S E C T I O N   4   R E V I E W

IDENTIFY and explain the significance of the following: Holocaust, genocide, Elie Wiesel, superpowers, revisionists.

LOCATE and explain the importance of the following: Sakhalin Island, Kuril Islands, Taiwan, Hainan.

1. **MAIN IDEA** Why was World War II the most devastating war the world has ever known?
2. **MAIN IDEA** How did the Holocaust affect European Jews?
3. **ASSESSING CONSEQUENCES** Summarize the international consequences of World War II.
4. **WRITING TO DESCRIBE** Imagine you are a soldier who has helped liberate one of the German death camps. Write a letter home that describes what you saw there.
5. **TAKING A STAND** Do you think the United States was justified in using the atomic bomb against Japan? Give reasons for your answer.

SECTION REVIEW ANSWERS

IDENTIFY

For significance, see the following pages:
Holocaust (p. 423)
genocide (p. 423)
Elie Wiesel (p. 424)
superpowers (p. 424)
revisionists (p. 425)

LOCATE

For locations, see the map on p. 402.

1. caused more deaths and destroyed more property than any other war in history
2. The systematic slaughter took the lives of six million Jews—two thirds of European Jewry—and left deep psychological scars on concentration camp survivors.
3. the weakening of Western Europe, emergence of U.S. and Soviet Union as two superpowers, Soviet occupation of Eastern Europe
4. Letters might mention emaciated appearance of survivors, execution chambers within camps, and large number of Jews annihilated.
5. Students should balance the number of lives saved in avoiding an invasion of Japan with the devastation brought about by the bomb's use.

DEVELOPING THEMES

Return to the Themes section on p. 398. Have students discuss these again and compare their original responses with those given now. (See p. 397B for suggested answers.)

Chapter Review Answers

WRITING A SUMMARY
See Essential Points in each section for main ideas.

REVIEWING CHRONOLOGY

5, 1, 3, 2, 4
Assessing Consequences
removed Japanese fleet as threat to Allies in Pacific

IDENTIFYING PEOPLE AND IDEAS

1. *commander of U.S. forces in Pacific*
2. *battle that provided Americans with experience in naval air warfare and created confidence in carrier-based strike force*
3. *Mexican workers who came to the U.S. to work*
4. *agency that directed conversion of existing U.S. factories to wartime production and supervised building of new plants*
5. *Japanese American interned during WW II; as a member of Congress he later worked for reparation payments for other internees*
6. *June 6, 1944, date of Allied invasion of France*
7. *strategy of attacking strategic Pacific islands while bypassing others*
8. *Japanese suicide planes*
9. *deliberate annihilation of an entire people*

10. *Romanian-born American writer who survived Auschwitz and Buchenwald*

UNDERSTANDING MAIN IDEAS

1. *through Japan's bombing of Pearl Harbor, war declarations by Germany and Italy; secure occupied territory and factories already converted to war production*
2. *increased wartime production, expanded federal bureaucracy through WPB and OWM, directed economy, extended taxes and sold war bonds, instituted rationing on specific goods, passed Selective Service Act; urged all-out participation in war effort, publicized war aims, provided pro-war entertainment*
3. *African Americans and Mexican Americans gained factory jobs and fought in the armed services. Women took over jobs traditionally held by male workers, increasing female participation in paid labor force.*
4. *refined sonar equipment, developed fast escort ships for convoys, air-bombed German U-boats and submarine yards*
5. *sent Jews to concentration camps, rounded up Jews and shot them, sent Jews and other victims to camps designed for genocide*

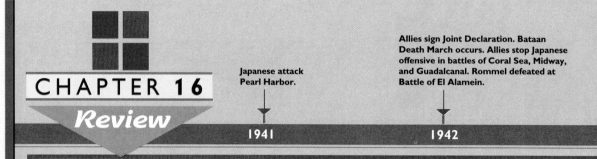

CHAPTER 16
Review

Japanese attack Pearl Harbor.

Allies sign Joint Declaration. Bataan Death March occurs. Allies stop Japanese offensive in battles of Coral Sea, Midway, and Guadalcanal. Rommel defeated at Battle of El Alamein.

1941 | **1942**

WRITING A SUMMARY
Using the essential points of the chapter as a guide, write a summary of the chapter.

REVIEWING CHRONOLOGY
Number your paper 1 to 5. Study the time line above, and list the following events in the order in which they happened by writing the first next to 1, the second next to 2, and so on. Then complete the activity below.

1. Allies sign Joint Declaration.
2. D-Day invasion begins.
3. Zoot-suit riots break out.
4. FDR dies.
5. Japanese attack Pearl Harbor.

Assessing Consequences What was the effect of the Allied victory at the Battle of Leyte Gulf?

IDENTIFYING PEOPLE AND IDEAS
Explain the historical significance of each of the following people or terms.

1. Douglas MacArthur
2. Battle of Midway
3. braceros
4. War Production Board
5. Norman Mineta
6. D-Day
7. island-hopping
8. kamikaze
9. genocide
10. Elie Wiesel

UNDERSTANDING MAIN IDEAS
1. How was the United States drawn into World War II? What advantages did the Axis Powers have over the United States at the beginning of the war?
2. What steps did the U.S. government take to mobilize for war? What did the media do to keep morale high?
3. What gains did African Americans, Mexican Americans, and women make during the war?
4. How did the Allies win the Battle of the Atlantic?
5. How did the Nazis carry out the Holocaust?

REVIEWING THEMES
1. **Global Relations** How did the Allies pool their resources to win World War II?
2. **Cultural Diversity** How did wartime conditions lead to increased discrimination against Japanese Americans?
3. **Technology and Society** What political and moral issues did the development of atomic weapons raise?

THINKING CRITICALLY
1. **Analyzing** What actions did the Allies take to win the war in Europe?
2. **Synthesizing** What were the final costs and consequences of World War II?
3. **Evaluating** Why was the atomic bomb used against Japan? What effect did the use of this weapon have on the war in the Pacific?

WRITING ABOUT HISTORY
Writing to Classify Create a time line listing the important battles and other events leading to the Allied victory in the Pacific.

STRATEGY FOR SUCCESS
Review the Skills Handbook entry on Identifying Cause and Effect beginning on page 749. Then study the poster below, which was issued by the U.S. government during World War II. What cause-and-effect relationship does the poster suggest?

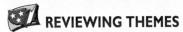
REVIEWING THEMES

1. instituted lend-lease program, engaged in joint strategic plannings, signed the Joint Declaration, agreed on war aims during conferences at Casablanca, Cairo, Tehran, and Yalta
2. Prejudice and war hysteria led many to question the loyalty of people of Japanese descent, resulting in an internment policy.
3. political—concerns over control of atomic weapons and fears of arms race; moral—doubts over use of weapons of such devastating power

THINKING CRITICALLY

1. seized control of Mediterranean, won Battle of the Atlantic, launched offensives on southern, western, and eastern fronts, stepped up bombing of German cities
2. destroyed hundreds of cities, left millions destitute, incurred military costs of probably over $1 trillion, caused nearly 40 million casualties; made U.S. and Soviet Union into superpowers, caused territorial realignments
3. to prevent loss of lives from American invasion of Japan; brought about Japan's surrender, ended war in Pacific

WRITING ABOUT HISTORY

Time lines should include battles of the Coral Sea, Midway, and Guadalcanal in 1942; island-hopping in Gilbert Islands in 1943; battles of Philippine Sea, Saipan, Guam, and Leyte Gulf in 1944; battles of Iwo Jima and Okinawa and use of atomic bomb against Hiroshima and Nagasaki in 1945.

STRATEGY FOR SUCCESS

Careless talk in front of someone who might be a spy could lead to Allied military disaster.

USING PRIMARY SOURCES

Essays might express students' feelings of pity, anger, disgust, and sorrow.

LINKING HISTORY AND GEOGRAPHY

about 60 miles; more than 20 miles; Camp O'Donnell; terrain, weather conditions, and availability of supplies cannot be determined from the map

---

Allied leaders meet at Casablanca, Cairo, and Tehran. Soviets defeat Axis troops at Stalingrad. Allies conquer North Africa. Zoot-suit riots break out.

Allies capture Rome. D-Day invasion begins. Japanese navy defeated at Battle of Leyte Gulf. Germans launch V-2 rockets. FDR reelected president. Allied and German troops clash at Battle of the Bulge.

Allies meet at Yalta. Allies win battles of Iwo Jima and Okinawa. FDR dies. Germany surrenders. U.S. drops atomic bombs on Hiroshima and Nagasaki. Japan surrenders.

1943   **1944**   **1945**

USING PRIMARY SOURCES

After the war, survivors of German concentration camps began to reveal to the world the horrors suffered by Jews and other prisoners. Read the following excerpt from *The Holocaust Kingdom* (1963), written by Alexander Donat, a survivor of Majdanek. Then write an essay expressing your feelings about what you have read.

66 *Usually they were taken there [to the gas chamber] at night, but once I saw the operation in broad daylight. . . . Through a crack in the wall we saw a long procession of living skeletons slowly emerging from Barrack Nineteen on their way to the gate. It was the way we would look in another two, four, or six weeks: it was the way it all ended. Majdanek was an industrial factory for producing corpses: death, the destruction of the greatest number of prisoners in the shortest time at the lowest cost was Majdanek's purpose. Life was treated as something . . . essentially worthless; in fact, contemptible. Death was our constant companion and not a terrible one, for quite often one wished passionately for it. It was life that was terrible, the long, agonizing process of parting from it after it had been shorn of dignity. Life in Majdanek was reduced to its basic elements.* 99

LINKING HISTORY AND GEOGRAPHY

After Allied forces on the Bataan Peninsula surrendered in April 1942, the Japanese ordered them to assemble at Mariveles and then march to San Fernando. From there the prisoners were shipped north by train. Study the map of the Bataan Death March in the next column. About how far did the prisoners have to march to reach San Fernando? About how far did they travel by train? What was their final destination? Why is it not possible to assess the difficulty of the journey from this map?

BUILDING YOUR PORTFOLIO

Complete the following projects independently or cooperatively.

1. **GLOBAL RELATIONS** In chapters 13 and 15 you portrayed a journalist. Building on that experience, imagine you are a member of a peace organization in the United States. Write an essay on ways to resolve international conflicts without war.

2. **WAR** In Chapter 15 you portrayed a diplomat at the beginning of the war. Building on that experience, imagine you are on a government committee examining the effects of the war. Compile statistics that illustrate the effects.

3. **CULTURE AND SOCIETY** In chapters 11, 12, and 14 you explored U.S. society in the 1920s and 1930s. Building on that experience, imagine you are a woman factory worker during World War II. Create a series of journal entries expressing your feelings about life on the home front.

BUILDING YOUR PORTFOLIO

Have students refer to **Building Your Portfolio Worksheet 3**, assigned at the beginning of Unit 3. Use the worksheet to help students monitor their progress on the portfolio projects.

Assessment

Core Resources
• Reteaching Worksheet 16
• Chapter 16 Tests
• Alternative Assessment Forms
Test Generator

SONGS OF THE CITIES

SETTING THE SCENE

Claude McKay and Jean Toomer greatly influenced the development of the Harlem Renaissance. Born in Jamaica, McKay was already a poet of note when he came to the U.S. in 1912. His concentration on the everyday life of African Americans and his angry denunciation of racism set the focus and tone for much Harlem Renaissance literature. Toomer's experimental novel *Cane* (1923) caused a sensation among the young African American artists who became the nucleus of the Harlem Renaissance. It also raised for the first time many of the themes that occupied Harlem Renaissance writers.

Sinclair Lewis employed a mixture of realism and satire to depict his view of life in American small towns. He won the Nobel Prize for Literature in 1930, the first American writer to be awarded the honor.

Toshio Mori's "Lil' Yokohama" was set in the cities of Oakland and San Leandro on San Francisco Bay. The author lived in the Bay area all of his life, with two exceptions. The first was a brief period in which he played professional baseball for the Chicago Cubs; the second was for three years during World War II, when he was confined to an internment camp in Utah.

UNIT 3

American Letters

Songs of the Cities

The Roaring Twenties was an era of cities, when economic prosperity and technological innovations led to a boom in skyscraper construction. Cities continued to expand throughout the Great Depression and World War II. Harlem Renaissance poets Claude McKay and Jean Toomer, novelist Sinclair Lewis, and Japanese American writer Toshio Mori capture the dynamic growth of the cities in the following selections.

▲ Jean Toomer

A Song of the Moon

by Claude McKay

The moonlight breaks upon the city's domes,
And falls along cemented steel and stone,
Upon the grayness of a million homes,
Lugubrious[1] in unchanging monotone.

Upon the clothes behind the tenement,
That hang like ghosts suspended from the lines,
Linking each flat to each indifferent,
Incongruous[2] and strange the moonlight shines.

There is no magic from your presence here,
Ho, moon, sad moon, tuck up your trailing robe,
Whose silver seems antique and so severe
Against the glow of one electric globe.

Go spill your beauty on the laughing faces
Of happy flowers that bloom a thousand hues,
Waiting on tiptoe in the wilding spaces,
To drink your wine mixed with sweet drafts of dews. ❖

1 melancholy
2 not harmonious

From The Blue Meridian

by Jean Toomer

The prairie's sweep in flat infinity,
The city's rise is perpendicular to farthest star,
I stand where the two directions intersect,
At Michigan Avenue and Walton Place,[1]

Level with my countrymen,
Right-angled to the universe.

It is a new America,
To be spiritualized by each new American,
To be taken as a golden grain
And lifted, as the wheat of our bodies,
To matter uniquely man.
I would give my life to see inscribed
Upon the arch of our consciousness
These aims: Growth, Transformation, Love,
That we might become heart-centered towards
   one another,
Love-centered towards God, dedicated to the creation
   of a higher type of man, growing up to Him.
Let new eyes see this statue in the bay,
Let this be quarantine to unbend dreams,
Let old eyes see it in Wall Street and the Loop,[2]
And through this clearing house
Let all pass checks who may. ❖

1 streets in downtown Chicago
2 Chicago's downtown

From Babbitt

by Sinclair Lewis

The towers of Zenith aspired above the morning mist; austere [simple] towers of steel and cement and limestone, sturdy as cliffs and delicate as silver rods. They were neither citadels nor churches, but frankly and beautifully office-buildings.

The mist took pity on the fretted [eroded] structures of earlier generations: the Post Office with its shingle-tortured mansard,[1] the red brick minarets [towers] of hulking old houses, factories with stingy and sooted windows, wooden tenements colored like mud. The city was full of such grotesqueries,[2] but the clean towers were thrusting them from the business center, and on the farther hills were shining new houses, homes—they seemed—for laughter and tranquillity.

Over a concrete bridge fled a limousine of long sleek hood and noiseless engine. These people in evening clothes were returning from an all-night rehearsal of a Little Theater play. . . . Below the bridge curved a railroad, a maze of green and crimson lights. The New York Flyer boomed past, and twenty lines of polished steel leaped into the glare.

In one of the skyscrapers the wires of the Associated Press were closing down. The telegraph operators wearily raised their celluloid eye-shades after a night of talking with Paris and Peking. Through the building crawled the scrubwomen, yawning, their old shoes slapping. The dawn mist spun away. Cues [lines] of men with lunch-boxes clumped toward the immensity of new factories, sheets of glass and hollow tile, glittering shops where five thousand men worked beneath one roof, pouring out the honest wares that would be sold up the Euphrates[3] and across the veldt.[4] The whistles rolled out in greeting a chorus cheerful as the April dawn; the song of labor in a city built—it seemed—for giants. ❖

1 a sloping roof
2 things that are not harmonious
3 river in Southwest Asia
4 grassland of southern Africa

From *Lil' Yokohama*

by Toshio Mori

In Lil' Yokohama, as the youngsters call our community, we have twenty-four hours every day . . . and morning, noon, and night roll on regularly just as in Boston, Cincinnati, Birmingham, Kansas City, Minneapolis, and Emeryville.

When the sun is out, the housewives sit on the porch or walk around the yard, puttering with this and that, and the old men who are in the house when it is cloudy or raining come out

on the porch or sit in the shade and read the newspaper. The day is hot. All right, they like it. The day is cold. All right, all right. The people of Lil' Yokohama are here. *Here, here,* they cry with their presence just as the youngsters when the teachers call the roll. And when the people among people are sometimes missing from Lil' Yokohama's roll, perhaps forever, it is another matter; but the news belongs here just as does the weather.

Today young and old are at the Alameda ball grounds to see the big game: Alameda Taiiku *vs.* San Jose Asahis. The great Northern California game is under way. Will Slugger Hironaka hit that southpaw from San Jose? Will the same southpaw make the Alameda sluggers stand on their heads? It's the great question. . . .

It is Sunday evening in Lil' Yokohama, and the late dinners commence. Someone who did not go to the game asks, "Who won today?" "San Jose," we say. "Oh, gee," he says. "But Slugger knocked another home run," we say. "What again? He sure is good!" he says. "Big league scouts ought to size him up." "Sure," we say.

Tomorrow is a school day, tomorrow is a work day, tomorrow is another twenty-four hours. In Lil' Yokohama night is almost over. On Sunday nights the block is peaceful and quiet. . . .

Something is happening to the Etos of the block. All of a sudden they turn in their old '30 Chevrolet for a new Oldsmobile Eight! They follow this with a new living-room set and a radio and a new coat of paint for the house. On Sundays the whole family goes for an outing. Sometimes it is to Fleishhacker Pool or to Santa Cruz. It may be to Golden Gate Park or to the ocean or to their relatives in the country. . . . They did not strike oil or win the sweepstakes. Nothing of the kind happens in Lil' Yokohama, though it may any day. . . . What then? ❖

THINKING AND WRITING ABOUT LITERATURE

1. What features of the city does Claude McKay describe? Why do you think he wants the moon to shine somewhere else?
2. What are the three things Jean Toomer wishes city dwellers to aspire to?
3. How does Sinclair Lewis describe Zenith's buildings? What do you think he means to show by contrasting the old and new buildings?
4. Why does Toshio Mori describe the daily activities of the Japanese American neighborhood of Lil' Yokohama?

PRIMARY SOURCES

Description of Change: excerpted, bracketed, and footnoted

Rationale: excerpted for space considerations; bracketed and footnoted to clarify meaning

THINKING AND WRITING ABOUT LITERATURE

1. *domes, steel and stone, gray homes, tenement clotheslines; because the poet thinks the moon illuminates only ugliness in the city*
2. *growth, transformation, and love*
3. *The new buildings are simple, sturdy, delicate, and clean, and the old buildings are complicated, "hulking," mud-colored, and grotesque. Lewis is contrasting the city's present and past.*
4. *to show that Japanese Americans live just like other Americans*

RECOGNIZING PROPAGANDA

Guide students through the discussion of how to recognize propaganda and then have them complete the Practicing the Strategy exercise. Point out that in times of national crisis propaganda messages became especially intense in the U.S. Have students work in groups to identify the intended message, the images used, and the techniques employed in the following examples of propaganda: the World War I propaganda posters on pp. 249 and 260; the New Deal poster on p. 349 and sign on p. 356; and the World War II recruiting poster on p. 409. Then have them create posters that could have been used during Operation Desert Storm to build support for the war. Ask students to evaluate how effective one another's posters are.

propaganda posters on pp. 249 and 260; the New Deal poster on p. 349 and sign on p. 356; and the World War II recruiting poster on p. 409.

PRACTICING THE STRATEGY

1. that the German soldiers who died in World War I are martyrs whose deaths will be avenged; Germans who are remembering those who died in the war

2. emotional appeal to sympathy for the war dead; use of the symbolism of altar and blood, in an attempt to liken the deaths to a sacrifice; and sloganlike calls for retaliation and for a renewed Germany

---

Strategies for Success

RECOGNIZING PROPAGANDA

Propaganda is a form of mass communication designed to sway people's attitudes and actions. It appeals primarily to emotion, not reason, using language, symbols, and images. Propaganda is favored by totalitarian regimes, which use it to control the hearts and minds of their people. But propaganda is not always used for sinister purposes. Democracies employ propaganda to discredit their enemies and to gain citizen support for particular policies. Special-interest groups use it in lobbying for or against legislation, and politicians use it in campaigning for election. The following techniques are often used in propaganda:

- **Card-stacking** means presenting just one side of a story. Examples include the selective use of statistics and the parading of opinion as fact.
- **Name-calling** is attaching offensive labels to opponents to cast them in a negative light.
- **Sloganeering** is repetition of catchy, but often empty, statements instead of real arguments.
- **Bandwagon** involves begging support for a cause merely because it is popular. This technique relies on peer pressure to conform.
- **Endorsements** are testimonials by famous people who urge support of a cause. Propagandists hope that people will transfer their liking or respect for the celebrity to the cause.

How to Recognize Propaganda

1. **Look, listen, and read carefully.** Analyze the message being conveyed, noting the use of emotionally charged words. Also examine any imagery: propaganda can be visual.
2. **Recognize the technique used.** Identify the technique being employed (such as card-stacking or name-calling).
3. **Consider the purpose.** Ask yourself: Who is sending the message and why? Decide who is its intended audience and what reaction it is meant to provoke.

Applying the Strategy

During World War II the U.S. government used propaganda techniques to build support for the war. For example, patriotic posters used emotional appeals to encourage people to buy war bonds. The World War II poster in the next column pictures a women with her children. The picture and the words "I gave a man!" are meant to play on workers' emotions and to make them feel guilty if they do not buy war bonds.

The government also used propaganda techniques to recruit women for the nation's defense industry, sounding the theme that "it's a woman's war, too." A government brochure of the time, which used the bandwagon approach and one-sided descriptions of factory labor, read: "Millions of women find war work pleasant and as easy as running a sewing machine, or using a vacuum cleaner."

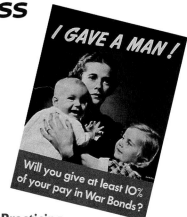

I GAVE A MAN!

Will you give at least 10% of your pay in War Bonds?

Practicing the Strategy

Read the statement below, made in 1927 by Joseph Goebbels (who later became Hitler's propaganda minister) in commemoration of the German soldiers who died in World War I. Then, on a separate sheet of paper, answer the questions that follow.

❝ We think of the two million who grow pale in the graves of Flanders and Poland. . . . We think of . . . all those who gave their lives upon the altar of the future so that Germany might be established again. . . . Retaliation! Retaliation! The day is dawning! . . . We greet you, dead ones. Germany is beginning to glow anew in the dawn of your blood. . . . Let sound the march-beat . . . for freedom! The army of the dead marches with you, you storm troop soldiers, into a better future. ❞

1. What is the message of the excerpt? At whom is it aimed?
2. What clues identify this passage as propaganda?

BUILDING YOUR PORTFOLIO

Each portfolio project described below is the culmination of the Building Your Portfolio activities in the chapter reviews of Unit 3. First, decide whether you wish students to work individually or in groups on these unit projects. Then permit each student to choose the project on which he or she desires to work. Provide students with copies of **Building Your Portfolio Worksheet 3** from *Core Resources*. This worksheet will guide students step by step to complete their projects.

BUILDING YOUR PORTFOLIO

Outlined below are four projects. Independently or cooperatively, complete one and use the products to demonstrate your mastery of the historical concepts involved.

1 THE ECONOMY
The excesses of the 1920s helped trigger the Great Depression. The federal government attempted to get the economy moving through the New Deal. Using the portfolio materials you designed in chapters 11, 12, 13, and 14, create a mural that depicts the economic trends between 1920 and 1940. Your mural might portray the effects of unemployment, consumerism, the depression, or the New Deal.

2 CULTURE AND SOCIETY
American society changed rapidly from the 1920s to the 1940s. Using the portfolio materials you designed in chapters 11, 12, 14, and 16, create a radio program that highlights the issues of the period. Shows might include news of the day, a jazz presentation from the 1920s, a book review from the 1930s, or an interview with women workers from the 1940s.

3 GLOBAL RELATIONS
The world experienced severe economic, political, and social unrest in the years leading up to World War II. Using the portfolio materials you designed in chapters 13, 15, and 16, conduct a debate with representatives from several nations about global relations after World War II. Debates should center around the issue of how the United States should respond in the future to the rise of dictators in other parts of the world.

4 WAR
World War II brought tragedy to millions of people around the world. Using the portfolio materials you designed in chapters 15 and 16, create a design for a war memorial to the victims of World War II. Memorials might commemorate soldiers, prisoners of war, victims of the Holocaust, or civilians killed in the war.

Videodisc Review
In assigned groups, develop an outline for a video collage of American life in the years between 1920 and 1945. Choose images that best illustrate the major topics of the period. Write a script to accompany the images. Assign narrators to different parts of the script, and present your video collage to the class.

Further Reading
Anderson, Jervis. *This Was Harlem: A Cultural Portrait, 1900–1950.* Farrar Straus Giroux (1993). Story of Harlem in the first half of the 20th century.
Berenbaum, Michael. *The World Must Know: The History of the Holocaust as Told in the United States Holocaust Memorial Museum.* Little, Brown (1993). Pictorial and eyewitness history of the Holocaust.

Cohen, Stan. *V for Victory: Pictorial Histories* (1991). Overview of the effect of World War II on Americans on the home front.
Cook, Haruko Taya, and Theodore F. Cook. *Japan at War.* New Press (1992). Accounts of war's effect on the Japanese .
McElvaine, Robert S. *The Great Depression: America, 1929–1941.* Times Books (1984). Overview of the Great Depression.

PORTFOLIO ASSESSMENT

1. *Murals should show the post–World War I bust, the boom period during the 1920s, the stock market crash of 1929, and the Great Depression.*
2. *Radio programs should show students' mastery of one of the following topics: the reasons for the spread of anti-Communist hysteria during the Red Scare; labor problems in the 1920s; the original proposal of the Equal Rights Amendment; the influence of jazz in the 1920s; the impact of the Dust Bowl; or the experiences of women workers during World War II.*
3. *Debates should trace the economic problems leading to the rise of dictators before World War II, U.S. participation in diplomatic conferences between the wars, and the policy of appeasement.*
4. *War memorial designs should show the casualties of Kristallnacht, the Holocaust, the bombing of Hiroshima and Nagasaki, or other military and civilian casualties.*

Introducing the Unit

- **Chapter 17**
  THE POSTWAR YEARS
  1945–1952
- **Chapter 18**
  DECADE OF CONTRASTS
  1950–1960
- **Chapter 19**
  THE SIXTIES
  1960–1970
- **Chapter 20**
  WAR IN VIETNAM
  1954–1975

UNIT OVERVIEW

The U.S. emerged from World War II as the richest and most influential nation in the world. Affluence, abundance, and optimism characterized the postwar period. But the Cold War and the nuclear age contributed to a sense of uncertainty during this time. And in the midst of prosperity, widespread poverty existed. The nation's disfranchised citizens raised other concerns about the reality of the American dream. Similar disillusionment underscored the national debate over the Vietnam War. By the mid-1970s, many Americans were questioning long-standing and cherished perceptions about their country.

CORE RESOURCES

- **American Almanac Worksheet 4**
- **Building Your Portfolio Worksheet 4**
  You may wish to preview the Unit 4 Review and Building Your Portfolio performance assessment activities on p. 551.

Using the Almanac

Use the almanac to begin a class discussion about life in postwar America from 1945 to 1975. Select specific images and statistics and ask students to suggest trends and characteristics of the period that the selections might indicate.

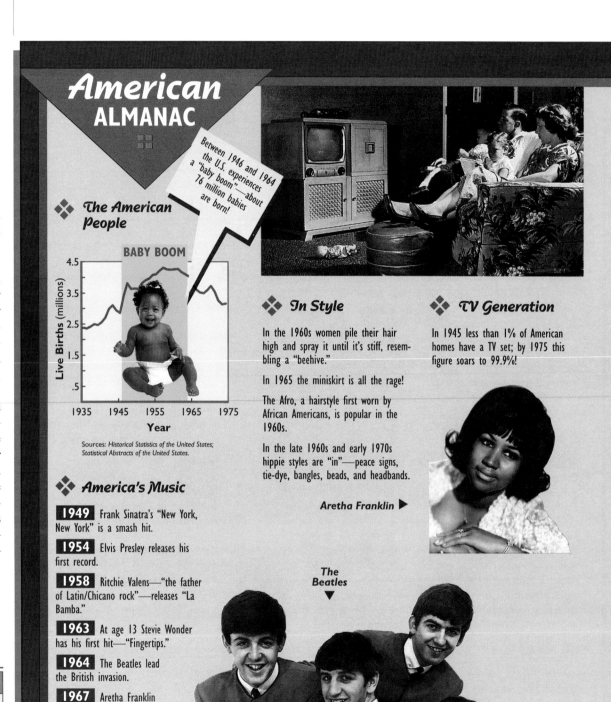

American ALMANAC

Between 1946 and 1964 the U.S. experiences a "baby boom"—about 76 million babies are born!

❖ The American People

BABY BOOM

Live Births (millions)

4.5
3.5
2.5
1.5
.5

1935 1945 1955 1965 1975

Year

Sources: *Historical Statistics of the United States; Statistical Abstracts of the United States.*

❖ America's Music

1949 Frank Sinatra's "New York, New York" is a smash hit.

1954 Elvis Presley releases his first record.

1958 Ritchie Valens—"the father of Latin/Chicano rock"—releases "La Bamba."

1963 At age 13 Stevie Wonder has his first hit—"Fingertips."

1964 The Beatles lead the British invasion.

1967 Aretha Franklin earns "Respect" with her #1 hit.

1970 The Jackson 5 release "ABC"—11-year-old Michael sings lead.

❖ In Style

In the 1960s women pile their hair high and spray it until it's stiff, resembling a "beehive."

In 1965 the miniskirt is all the rage!

The Afro, a hairstyle first worn by African Americans, is popular in the 1960s.

In the late 1960s and early 1970s hippie styles are "in"—peace signs, tie-dye, bangles, beads, and headbands.

❖ TV Generation

In 1945 less than 1% of American homes have a TV set; by 1975 this figure soars to 99.9%!

Aretha Franklin ▶

The Beatles ▼

The American People

The soaring birthrate from 1946 to 1964 became known as the baby boom. The expanding economy meant that couples could afford larger families. But in the 1970s and 1980s, baby boomers found competition for jobs stiffer than it was for their parents.

■■ Have students check a current almanac to determine the birthrate today.

America's Music

Point out that the British invasion greatly influenced American rock music. Yet the Beatles identified African American musicians, such as Chuck Berry, as major influences on their music.

■■ Ask students to identify bands from other countries that they listen to today.

In Style

Point out that many young people in the 1960s, unlike previous generations, were unwilling to adopt the hairstyles and fashions of their parents.

■■ Ask students whether it is important to create their own look or if they dress much like their parents.

TV Generation

Show a video of a popular TV show from the 1950s or 1960s. Ask students about their impressions of the program and how it differs from shows today.

■■ Ask students if they are influenced by the ways that characters behave on TV.

Firsts on Earth and in Space

More than one fifth of the world's population watched the *Apollo 11* moon landing on TV via satellite.

■■ Call on volunteers to suggest what events might attract a large TV audience today.

The Shrinking Dollar

Point out that prices of consumer goods and services rise even during periods of economic stability.

■■ Ask students what a pair of jeans costs today.

The Sporting Life

Mention that Robinson's "first" also signaled the end of the black baseball leagues. As major league clubs rushed to sign black players, African American ball clubs folded.

■■ Call on volunteers to identify the social barriers in sports that are being challenged today.

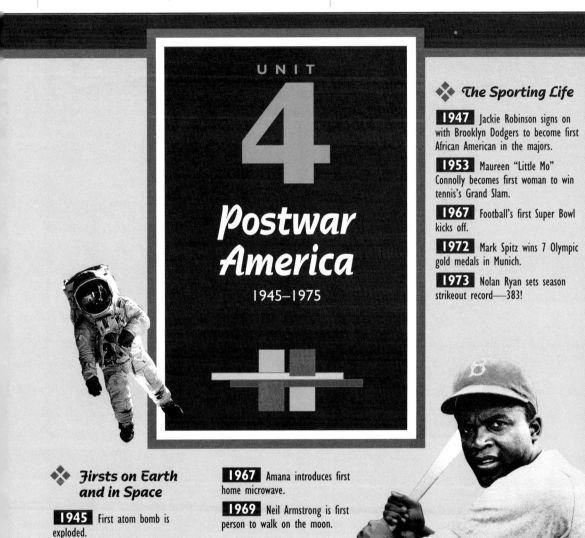

UNIT

4

Postwar America

1945–1975

❖ The Sporting Life

1947 Jackie Robinson signs on with Brooklyn Dodgers to become first African American in the majors.

1953 Maureen "Little Mo" Connolly becomes first woman to win tennis's Grand Slam.

1967 Football's first Super Bowl kicks off.

1972 Mark Spitz wins 7 Olympic gold medals in Munich.

1973 Nolan Ryan sets season strikeout record—383!

❖ Firsts on Earth and in Space

1945 First atom bomb is exploded.

1951 UNIVAC I, first mass-produced computer, is developed.

1953 James Watson and Francis Crick discover DNA.

1955 Dr. Jonas Salk announces successful polio vaccine.

1957 Soviets launch first satellite—*Sputnik I*—U.S. calls for increased math and science education.

1959 Daniel Inouye is first Japanese American and Hiram L. Fong is first Chinese American to serve in Congress; both represent Hawaii.

1962 Rachel Carson's *Silent Spring* helps launch the environmental movement.

1967 Amana introduces first home microwave.

1969 Neil Armstrong is first person to walk on the moon.

❖ The Shrinking Dollar

A pair of jeans costs $3.65 in 1955—by 1975 a pair costs $11.25.

A 16 oz. loaf of white bread in 1960 costs an average of 20.3¢.

◀ **Daniel Inouye**

▲ **Jackie Robinson**

THE POSTWAR YEARS

1945–1952

Chapter Overview

The end of World War II thrust the U.S. into the position of world leadership. While dealing with its own postwar readjustments, the U.S. joined with other allies in occupying Germany and Japan and in organizing the United Nations. A breakdown in U.S.–Soviet relations launched a Cold War and generated a renewed fear of communism at home and abroad. America "fought" the Cold War by providing massive aid to Europe and through economic, political, and military involvement in East Asia and the Middle East.

THE AMERICAN NATION VIDEODISC PROGRAM
A variety of still images, short videos, and activities are available for you to use as you teach this chapter. See Videodisc Resources in the Core Resources Binder for barcode correlations and suggestions for using the program.

Chapter Planning Guide

CHAPTER 17	CORE RESOURCES	AUDIOVISUAL (AV) RESOURCES	PROGRAM RESOURCES
INTRODUCTION pp. 434–435	■ Literature Worksheet 17 ■ Building Your Portfolio Worksheet 4	■ Everyday Life in America Transparency and Worksheet 27	
TEACHING THE CHAPTER pp. 436–457 ■ For expanded coverage of pp. 436–437, see Chapter 24, pp. 659–660; for coverage of pp. 436–439, see Chapter 26; for coverage of pp. 447–448, see Chapter 24, pp. 661–662.	■ Graphic Organizer 17 ■ Social Studies Skills Worksheet 17 ■ Geography Worksheet 17 ■ Outline Maps 1, 2, 9, 14, 15, 17, 18, 20	■ *The American Nation* Videodisc: Jackie Robinson; MacArthur in Korea ■ Linking Geography and History Transparency and Worksheet 20	■ Art in American History Transparencies and Worksheets 34, 35 ■ *Eyewitnesses and Others,* Volume 2: Reading 58
REVIEW AND ASSESSMENT pp. 458–459	■ Chapter 17 Daily Quizzes ■ Reteaching Worksheet 17 ■ Chapter 17 Tests ■ Alternative Assessment Forms		■ Test Generator

Additional Resources

BOOKS FOR TEACHERS

Blair, Clay. *The Forgotten War: America in Korea 1950–1953.* Doubleday, 1989. Chronicles international political history of Korean War.

Brands, H.W. *Inside the Cold War: Loy Henderson & the Rise of the American Empire, 1918–1961.* Oxford University Press, 1991. History of the development of the Cold War.

McCullough, David. *Truman.* Simon & Schuster, 1992. A prize-winning biography of political and private life of Harry S. Truman.

BOOKS FOR STUDENTS

Chafe, William H. *The Unfinished Journey: America since World War II.* Oxford University Press, 1991. American society after 1945.

Halliday, Jon, and Bruce Cumings. *Korea: The Unknown War.* Pantheon, 1988. Examines the war from the perspectives of both North and South Korea.

* Leavell, Perry. *Harry S. Truman.* Chelsea House, 1988. Part of "World Leaders, Past and Present" series.

* for students reading below grade level

MULTIMEDIA MATERIALS

The Cold War: Witness to History. Video, 15 min. Guidance Associates/SSSS. Surveys Cold War conflicts in the aftermath of World War II.

For All the People: The Harry S. Truman Library. Video, 29 min. SSSS. Archival footage and selected speeches survey the Truman era.

Korea: MacArthur's War With Truman. Video, 40 min. Zenger/SSSS. Archival footage, maps, and contemporary images document issues of Korean War.

THEMES IN AMERICAN HISTORY

USE WITH PAGES 434–435

Listed on the right are the themes emphasized in Chapter 17. The questions in boldface type stimulate critical thinking and provide students with an opportunity to discuss the themes within a broadened context. The questions also appear in the pupil's edition on p. 434.

■ GLOBAL RELATIONS

What international and domestic problems might a rivalry between two powerful nations create? Students might mention that the rivalry could lead to military escalation and global competition. The rivalry might create the need for a strong foreign aid program and a robust defense industry at home. Students might disagree about whether this situation would create jobs or drain resources from a nation's economy.

■ TECHNOLOGY AND SOCIETY

How might a society respond to the development of a potentially destructive technology? Students might point out that some people would support such technology, arguing that it would enhance a nation's power and status in the world. Opponents might argue that it could generate fear and distrust among nations and heighten world tensions.

■ DEMOCRATIC VALUES

How might individuals be affected by a government's limitation of civil liberties? Students might provide examples of a government limiting such civil liberties as freedom of speech, the right to due process of law, and the right to privacy. Examples might include government restrictions on the free flow of information during a time when some perceive a nation's security to be threatened, or the effects a government's intelligence-gathering activities might have on citizens' due process rights or privacy rights.

CHAPTER STRATEGIES FOR MEETING INDIVIDUAL NEEDS

LIMITED ENGLISH PROFICIENT LEARNERS

Have students develop clue cards for the people listed in the Preview Workshops. Call on volunteers to present their clues and ask others to identify each person. After each person has been identified, have students select one and write an introduction that might be used by someone honoring that person.

TACTILE/KINESTHETIC LEARNERS

Have students create a series of skits that demonstrate the fears of Americans during the Red Scare period of the late 1940s and the early 1950s.

LEARNERS HAVING DIFFICULTY

Have students recite answers to the Main Idea questions in each Section Review. Then have them write a brief summary of each section.

AUDITORY LEARNERS

Have students research speeches and/or quotations about the Cold War by George Kennan, George C. Marshall, Dean Acheson, Joseph Stalin, and Harry S. Truman. Have students prepare dramatic readings of their selections.

VISUAL LEARNERS

Organize students into small groups to prepare illustrated flowcharts showing the tensions and hostilities that resulted from the Cold War.

GIFTED LEARNERS

Direct students to create a scrapbook of Truman's written and verbal statements. Have students divide the scrapbook into sections that correlate to the chapter's sections. Assign students to write generalizations about the historical significance of each section's quotes.

USING THE CHAPTER FOCUS

■ **UNDERSTANDING THE MAIN IDEA**

Call on a volunteer to read aloud the Understanding the Main Idea paragraph. Ask students to speculate on what problems a country might face in rebuilding from the devastation of war. Write students' responses on the chalkboard and ask them to evaluate their responses as they read the chapter.

 THEMES
Have students work individually or in small groups to answer the questions under Themes. Save students' responses so that they can compare them with their responses after studying the chapter. (See p. 433B for suggested answers.)

■ **THE TIME LINE**

Instruct students to copy the time-line entries into their notebooks. As students read about each event on the time line, have them create cause-and-effect flowcharts for each time-line entry.

CORE RESOURCES

- **Graphic Organizer 17**
- **Literature Worksheet 17**
- **Outline Maps 1, 2, 9, 14, 15, 17, 18, 20**
- **Building Your Portfolio Worksheet 4**

[AV] **RESOURCES**

- **Everyday Life in America Transparency and Worksheet 27**

434

ABOUT THE ILLUSTRATION

Joyful welcomes of returning military personnel, such as the scene shown below, were common after the war. But such happy reunions were often tinged with anxiety because the psychological impact of the war was great for soldiers and civilians alike. Soldiers who had experienced the horrors of war, and who had not seen their families for years, had to readjust to civilian and family life and become reacquainted (or sometimes acquainted) with their children. Women who had worked outside the home for the first time during the war faced potentially new roles within their families. Ask students to write a diary entry from the perspective of a postwar American soldier or civilian, detailing the hopes and fears that person has about the coming years.

Chapter 17   1945–1952

THE POSTWAR YEARS

 FOCUS

UNDERSTANDING THE MAIN IDEA

After World War II many nations struggled to rebuild their war-torn economies. In the United States, wartime production led to a postwar boom. On the international front, however, tensions between the United States and the Soviet Union grew. In 1950, in the midst of the increasing threat of nuclear disaster, the Korean War erupted.

 THEMES

■ **GLOBAL RELATIONS** What international and domestic problems might a rivalry between two powerful nations create?

■ **TECHNOLOGY AND SOCIETY** How might a society respond to the development of a potentially destructive technology?

■ **DEMOCRATIC VALUES** How might individuals be affected by a government's limitation of civil liberties?

1945	1947	1948	1950	1952
▼ Nuremberg trials begin.	▼ Truman Doctrine proposed.	▼ Racial discrimination banned in military and in federal hiring.	▼ North Korea invades South Korea.	▼ U.S. occupation of Japan ends.

Call on volunteers to recall the principles of the Atlantic Charter and write their responses on the chalkboard. *(U.S. and Great Britain would renounce territorial expansion. Every nation has a right to choose its own form of government. There should be freedom of international trade and equal access to raw materials for all countries. Aggressor states should be disarmed, and all nations should work together to rid the world of want and fear.)* As students read the chapter have them compare the charter's provisions for world peace with events and developments in the postwar world.

◧ LINK TO THE PAST

The Churchill-Roosevelt Atlantic Charter of 1941 had called for a free world in which all nations were able to choose their own governments. The agreement, however, did not end imperialism. It took World War II to end Japanese imperialism in Asia and to weaken European colonialism in Asia, Africa, and the Middle East.

Returning U.S. soldiers, 1946

*T*he United States emerged from World War II a world power. Americans realized, however, that with this new role came new challenges. Praising the "brave millions [of soldiers] homeward bound," General Douglas MacArthur in September 1945 urged all Americans "to preserve in peace what we won in war."

In their fight against fascism, American soldiers had helped liberate the surviving victims of Nazi concentration camps. Leon Bass, an African American soldier, believed that the Nazi death camps and the Holocaust had important lessons to teach Americans: "If this could happen [in Germany], it could happen anywhere. It could happen to me. It could happen to black folks in America." Horrified by the Holocaust and inspired by their advances during the war, many African Americans took up the fight for civil rights with increased energy.

The lessons learned from World War II, however, proved difficult to put into practice because of postwar economic chaos and the threat of an all-out nuclear war between the United States and the Soviet Union. Despite the creation of a new international organization to promote peace, Soviet-American tensions escalated and new conflicts broke out. By 1950 the United States was involved in yet another war, this time in Korea.

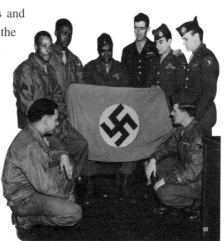

Soldiers with captured Nazi flag

THE POSTWAR YEARS ◧ 435

PREVIEW WORKSHOP

Following is a list of the significant people and terms in this section. You may wish to use this list as a section preview.

People
■ Adolf Eichmann
■ Josef Mengele
■ Klaus Barbie
■ Hideki Tōjō

■ Trygve Lie
■ Eleanor Roosevelt

Terms
■ Potsdam Conference
■ *zaibatsu*
■ Nuremberg trials
■ United Nations

MOTIVATING: PRIOR KNOWLEDGE

Call on a volunteer to describe the U.S. attitude about involvement in world affairs prior to its entrance into World War II. *(generally isolationist)* Ask students to speculate on why U.S. involvement in World War II might have changed that policy. Tell students that this section describes how the U.S. participated in reshaping the world after the war.

FOCUS OBJECTIVES

■ Describe how Germany and Japan were governed after the war.

■ Explain what the war crimes trials accomplished.

■ Analyze why the United Nations was founded.

HISTORICAL SIDELIGHTS

The Potsdam Conference

Although they were shaping the postwar world, the conferees at Potsdam showed their very human natures. At first Truman was drawn to Stalin but was put off by Churchill, whom he considered long-winded. At one party Truman provided violin and piano entertainment, which Churchill hated. He got even by having a Royal Air Force band play loud music all through dinner at a party he hosted.

CORE RESOURCES

• Section 1 Daily Quiz

436

Section 1

HEALING THE WOUNDS OF WAR

FOCUS
■ **How were Germany and Japan governed after the war?**
■ **What did the war crimes trials accomplish?**
■ **Why was the United Nations founded?**

Many Americans gained confidence from the Allied victory. "The war and the victory showed us what we could do in the world," summed up Melville Grosvenor, a magazine editor. Americans now realized that the United States had to take a leading role in the world. One urgent task was dealing with the human suffering and political chaos resulting from the war. The United States worked with the other Allies to restore peace by occupying Germany and Japan and by creating a new international organization, the United Nations.

UN flag

OCCUPATION RULE

After the war Germany and Japan lay in ruins, their wartime governments shattered. A German actress, Hildegard Knef, described a German town "without houses, without windowpanes, without roofs; holes

Allied Occupation Zones, 1945

in the asphalt, rubble, rubbish, rats." An American GI noted that in the area around Tokyo "there was practically nothing left; the rubble did not even look like much." A Japanese American soldier remarked of the devastation: "Tokyo was all flattened, and people were living in holes with corrugated roofs. They were desperate for food." With the fighting over, Germany and Japan now faced the task of rebuilding their governments, economies, and cities under the watchful eyes of the Allies.

The occupation of Germany. The first overseas conference that President Harry S. Truman attended after Roosevelt's death—the **Potsdam Conference** in July 1945—laid the foundation for Germany's postwar status. Truman, Churchill (later replaced by new prime minister Clement Attlee), and Stalin met in Potsdam, Germany, to approve the details of their joint occupation of Germany. The leaders divided Germany into four occupation zones. The British, the French, and the Americans each took control of a zone in the western, industrialized part of Germany. The Soviets agreed to control the poorer,

Teaching the Section

GOVERNMENT IN GERMANY AND JAPAN

Have students create charts comparing the systems of government set up in Germany and Japan after World War II. Have volunteers present their charts. Then discuss possible reasons that Germany and Japan were governed differently.

■■ Ask students how they would react if another nation occupied the U.S.

THE WAR CRIMES TRIALS

Organize students into groups and invite each to imagine that it is a tribunal presiding at war crimes trials after World War II. Ask groups to develop lists of standards, behaviors, and principles against which it will measure defendants who appear before it. Have representatives of each group present and explain its list.

THE UNITED NATIONS

Head five columns on the chalkboard with the five W's: *What, When, Why, Where,* and *Who*. Have students explain the purpose of the United Nations by offering statements for each heading.

▶

▲ This 1946 photograph shows Emperor Hirohito (top) in the Japanese Diet, or legislature, in Tokyo. Hirohito unveiled the new constitution and announced the transfer of his power to the Japanese people and the abolition of the armed forces.

more rural, eastern zone. The four powers also set up occupation zones in Austria and agreed to administer jointly the city of Berlin.

In order to bring stability to the German zones, the occupying powers pledged to crush the Nazi party, reestablish local governments, and rebuild German industry. In addition, the Allies agreed to resettle German refugees.

The conference attendees recognized that the joint occupation of Germany would require cooperation. However, Soviet occupation of much of Eastern Europe created tensions among the Allies. Stalin demanded that the Allies recognize Soviet-backed Poland's claims to German territory it had occupied during the war. The other Allies reluctantly agreed but grew increasingly concerned about Soviet expansion in Eastern Europe. Another source of tension was the Soviet Union's demand for immediate reparations from Germany.

The occupation of Japan. Postwar Japan also faced incredible challenges in its attempts to rebuild. Its economy was in shambles, and Hiroshima and Nagasaki had been devastated by atom bombs. The United States administered

defeated Japan, occupying the island nation from 1945 to 1952.

In addition to helping rebuild the Japanese economy, the United States worked to end Japanese militarism and to create a democratic government. During the occupation Emperor Hirohito remained in the imperial palace, but he became merely a figurehead. Supreme Commander Douglas MacArthur, his staff, and the new Japanese congress ran the country.

Under MacArthur's direction, Japan demobilized more than five million troops and adopted a new constitution in 1947. The constitution set up a democratic system of government, which extended voting rights to women and established separation of church and state. The constitution abolished the Japanese army and navy and prohibited Japan from ever again becoming a military power. Although the constitution bore the clear stamp of American influence, it won support from the Japanese people.

The Japanese also undertook important economic reforms in this period. One program transferred land to Japanese farmers. The government also allowed labor unions to organize and broke up the *zaibatsu*, the huge corporations run by single families that had monopolized the Japanese economy. These political and economic reforms laid the foundation for Japan's tremendous economic recovery after the war.

■■ **After World War II the Allies occupied Germany and Japan and set up new governments in these countries.**

THE WAR CRIMES TRIALS

After the war the Allies also addressed the issue of war crimes. All agreed that convicted German war criminals had to be punished for starting the war and for the Holocaust. By the same token, Japanese war criminals were to be punished for the mistreatment of prisoners of war and for other atrocities committed in Bataan and China.

The German war crimes trials—known as the **Nuremberg trials** because they took place in Nuremberg, the former meeting place of Hitler's Nazi party—began in November 1945. Before an international military tribunal, witnesses gave chilling accounts of Nazi atrocities, including the torture and murder of millions of Jews, Gypsies,

COOPERATIVE LEARNING

Organize students into groups of three. Ask students to assume the roles of policy advisers to General Douglas MacArthur. Tell each group to assign each student a background report on economic, political, or military conditions in Japan after World War II. Have each group use its reports to prepare recommendations for MacArthur on the policies he should implement in governing Japan. Call on students to present their groups' recommendations to the class.

MULTICULTURAL PERSPECTIVES

The U.S. conducted its own war crimes trial against Iva Ikuko Toguri, the Japanese American woman who was known as "Tokyo Rose" during World War II. Toguri had been trapped in Japan during the war and had taken part in anti-Allied propaganda broadcasts. A grand jury convicted Toguri of treason in 1949, and she served more than 6 years of a 10-year sentence.

*P*ractice

GUIDED PRACTICE

Write the main events of the section in headline form on the chalkboard, one at a time. Then choose one of the headlines, and call on volunteers to give details about the event in the headline, as you write responses on the chalkboard.

INDEPENDENT PRACTICE

Instruct students to select one of the headlines from the Guided Practice, list the details of the event, and then use the details to write a news story that might accompany the headline. Students may wish to include their news stories in their portfolios.

*R*eview and *A*ssessment

REVIEW Have students use the section's Essential Points as the main topics of an outline. Direct them to complete the outline by adding subtopics. Then assign the Section 1 Review on p. 439.

ASSESS Assign the **Section 1 Daily Quiz** in *Core Resources*.

GLOBAL CONNECTIONS

After the war many European countries began their own search for Nazi sympathizers. Norway, France, Holland, Belgium, and Denmark all attempted to purge their governments of those suspected of collaborating with the enemy during the war. Thousands were arrested, prison terms and death sentences were handed out, and thousands more were banned from pursuing their professions.

PRIMARY SOURCE

Description of Change: excerpted
Rationale: excerpted to focus on main idea

HISTORICAL SIDELIGHTS

Adolf Eichmann

Adolf Eichmann was tracked down by Israeli agents in 1960 in Argentina. They kidnapped Eichmann and took him to Israel, where a court tried him for war crimes and crimes against humanity. He was found guilty and hanged.

Chart Caption Answer
Security Council

▲ **Allied judges at the Nuremberg trials brought German war criminals to justice. Hermann Göring, commander of the German air force during the war, is shown on the witness stand on May 13, 1946. He later committed suicide in jail.**

and others. Marie Vaillant, a concentration camp survivor, testified:

> ❝ For months, for years we had one wish only: the wish that some of us would escape alive, in order to tell the world what the Nazi convict prisons were like. . . . There was the systematic . . . urge to use human beings as slaves and to kill them when they could work no more. ❞

In September 1946 the tribunal announced its first verdicts. The court had tried 21 Nazi leaders on four charges: planning the war, committing war crimes, committing other crimes against humanity, and conspiring to commit the crimes. Eleven Nazi leaders were sentenced to death; seven received jail sentences; and three were acquitted.

In other trials held in the U.S. occupation zone, thousands of former Nazi officials were tried and jailed, fined, or barred from public office. However, many Nazis—including Adolf Eichmann, the architect of the Jewish extermination program; Josef Mengele (MENG-ge-luh), Auschwitz's "Angel of Death"; and Klaus Barbie, known as the "Butcher of Lyons" for his cruel acts in that French city—escaped immediate prosecution by concealing their identities and fleeing to Latin America.

In the Tokyo war crimes trials, an international tribunal tried more than 20 war leaders. Seven were sentenced to death, including Hideki Tōjō, the wartime premier.

Many Americans, shocked by the evidence of war crimes, argued that more German and Japanese officials should have been punished. Nevertheless, the judges observed legal procedures and tried to avoid acting vengefully. In fact, the trials did set important precedents for international law and the conduct of war. The chief lesson was that nations and individuals can be held accountable for their actions during war. Many countries now accept the principle that war crimes cannot be excused on the grounds that those responsible were "just following orders."

■■ **War crimes trials in Germany and Japan established the principle of individual responsibility for wartime conduct.**

---

*T*HE UNITED NATIONS

During the war, the Allies had met several times to map out strategies to defeat the Axis Powers. In

---

DECISION–MAKING BODIES OF THE UNITED NATIONS

Body	Function
General Assembly	Sets policies.
Security Council	Resolves diplomatic, military, and political disputes.
Economic and Social Council	Deals with human welfare and fundamental rights and freedoms.
International Court of Justice	Handles international legal disputes.
Trusteeship Council	Supervises territories that are not independent.
Secretariat	Performs routine administrative work of the UN.

Sources: Encyclopedia of American History; Funk & Wagnalls New Encyclopedia

MULTICULTURAL COOPERATION The United Nations was established in order to give every member nation a voice in international affairs. The General Assembly includes over 150 countries and uses five official languages—English, Russian, French, Spanish, and Chinese.

❓ **ANALYZING** Which body of the United Nations is responsible for monitoring military aggressions between nations?

RETEACH Ask students, working in pairs, to write sentences that explain how each entry in the Preview Workshop is related to the topic of the subsection in which it is located. Have pairs share their sentences with the reteaching group.

Closure

Ask volunteers to explain what Melville Grosvenor meant by his statement in the section opener on p. 436. Have other students provide details from the section that show his views were an accurate assessment of American foreign policy after the war.

Extension

ANALYZE Have students locate and read the Preamble to the Charter of the United Nations. Have them write an essay comparing the UN preamble to the Preamble of the United States Constitution.

CREATE Ask students to imagine they are teenagers in Germany or Japan after World War II. Have them write a poem or rap that reflects their feelings about another nation occupying their country.

1944, delegates from the United States, Great Britain, the Soviet Union, and China met at Dumbarton Oaks, an estate in Washington, D.C. There they worked out a proposal for a postwar international organization called the **United Nations** (UN). Through the UN, the Allies hoped to continue their alliance by working together to promote world peace.

In April 1945, delegates from 50 nations met in San Francisco to draw up the Charter of the United Nations. The delegates took just eight weeks to write the document. The charter established six bodies: (1) the General Assembly in which all countries shape policy, (2) the Security Council to address military and political problems, (3) the Economic and Social Council, (4) the International Court of Justice, (5) the Trusteeship Council to administer territories, and (6) the Secretariat—headed by the secretary-general—to administer the UN. As permanent members of the Security Council, the United States, the Soviet Union, Great Britain, France, or China could veto any action the UN proposed.

Soon afterward, the Senate overwhelmingly approved American membership in the UN. More than 60 percent of Americans approved of U.S. membership. On October 24, now observed as United Nations Day, the UN officially came into existence when the 29th country approved the UN charter. The UN established its headquarters in New York City. Trygve Lie (TRIG-vuh LEE) of Norway served as the UN's first secretary-general.

From the outset, UN delegates realized that building world peace required both diplomatic and economic cooperation. Eleanor Roosevelt, who, as a U.S. representative to the UN helped shape the Universal Declaration of Human Rights, explained:

> 66 Security requires both control of the use of force and the elimination of want. No people are secure unless they have the things needed not only to preserve existence, but to make life worth living. . . . All peoples throughout the world must know that there is an organization where their interests can be considered and where justice and security will be sought for all. 99

Early critics of the UN insisted that it was doomed to fail because it had no real power to enforce its own decisions. Nevertheless, most Americans were as optimistic as President Truman, who noted in 1945: "This charter points down the only road to enduring peace. There is no other."

▲ **Eleanor Roosevelt chaired the UN Human Rights Commission from 1946 to 1951. She helped draft the Universal Declaration of Human Rights in 1948.**

■■ **The United Nations was founded to promote peaceful cooperation among the nations of the world.**

SECTION REVIEW ANSWERS

IDENTIFY
For significance, see the following pages:
Potsdam Conference (p. 436)
zaibatsu (p. 437)
Nuremberg trials (p. 437)
Adolf Eichmann (p. 438)
Josef Mengele (p. 438)
Klaus Barbie (p. 438)
Hideki Tōjō (p. 438)
United Nations (p. 439)
Trygve Lie (p. 439)
Eleanor Roosevelt (p. 439)

1. *that nations and individuals are accountable for their wartime actions*
2. *to promote international cooperation in the interests of world peace*
3. *Germany—divided into four occupation zones, Nazi party crushed and local governments and industry rebuilt and refugees resettled; Japan—democratic constitution adopted that ended militarism, economy reformed, zaibatsu were broken up*
4. *Letters might mention devastation, economic chaos, and social, economic, and political reforms.*
5. *Students might suggest that such issues affect national security, international relations, and world peace.*

■■
■■
SECTION 1 REVIEW

IDENTIFY and explain the significance of the following: Potsdam Conference, *zaibatsu*, Nuremberg trials, Adolf Eichmann, Josef Mengele, Klaus Barbie, Hideki Tōjō, United Nations, Trygve Lie, Eleanor Roosevelt.

1. **MAIN IDEA** What principle did the war crimes trials in Germany and Japan establish?
2. **MAIN IDEA** What was the purpose of the United Nations?
3. **COMPARING** How did the Allied powers govern Germany and Japan after World War II?
4. **WRITING TO DESCRIBE** Imagine you are a Japanese American soldier in Tokyo in 1946. Write a letter home that describes conditions in Japan after the war.
5. **ANALYZING** Why do you think the United Nations deals with economic and social issues in addition to its peacekeeping efforts?

FOCUS OBJECTIVES

■ Describe how the American economy fared after the war.

■ Explain how the Taft-Hartley Act affected unions.

■ Cite the most important issues in the 1948 election.

HISTORICAL SIDELIGHTS

Mexican American Discrimination

Mexican American veterans faced discrimination upon their return. In one notorious case, a white funeral-home owner in Texas refused to hold services for Felix Longoria, a Mexican American soldier killed in the Pacific. Many Texans were outraged, and U.S. senator Lyndon B. Johnson arranged for Longoria to be buried in Arlington National Cemetery.

AV TRANSPARENCY

Everyday Life in America Transparency and **Worksheet 27**

CORE RESOURCES

• **Section 2 Daily Quiz**

AV RESOURCES

• **The American Nation Videodisc: Jackie Robinson**
• **Everyday Life in America Transparency** and **Worksheet 27**

440

Following is a list of the significant people and terms in this section. You may wish to use this list as a section preview.

People
■ John L. Lewis
■ Sadie Alexander
■ Alben W. Barkley
■ J. Strom Thurmond
■ Henry Wallace

■ Thomas Dewey

Terms
■ GI Bill of Rights
■ Employment Act
■ Council of Economic Advisors
■ Taft-Hartley Act
■ Committee on Civil Rights
■ Dixiecrats
■ Fair Deal

Section 2

THE CHALLENGES OF PEACE

FOCUS

■ **How did the American economy fare after the war?**
■ **How did the Taft-Hartley Act affect unions?**
■ **What were the most important issues in the 1948 election?**

During the difficult transition from war to peace, Americans were apprehensive. Returning veterans were "worried sick about post-war joblessness," according to Fortune *magazine. Many African American, Mexican American, and women workers feared they would lose the economic gains they had made during the war.*

Homecoming, 1945

THE PROBLEMS OF DEMOBILIZATION

At war's end, troop ships headed home. By mid-1946 over nine million servicemen and women had been discharged. The troops received a hero's welcome, but their return also sparked concern. Could the economy absorb all these new workers? The government soon cancelled $23 billion in military contracts, hitting hard the shipyards, munitions factories, aircraft plants, and military bases.

Postwar measures. To prevent a depression and to help war-weary veterans make the difficult transition to civilian life, Congress passed the Servicemen's Readjustment Act of 1944, commonly known as the **GI Bill of Rights**. The act provided pensions and government loans to help veterans start businesses and buy homes or farms. Under the GI Bill, thousands of veterans also received money for tuition, books, and living expenses while they attended college.

▶ Under the GI Bill, many veterans received financial aid to pursue a college education or industrial training. Howard Timian of Milwaukee is shown here studying for an engineering course.

To ensure economic growth, Congress also passed the **Employment Act** of 1946. The act promised that the government would promote full employment and production. It also established the **Council of Economic Advisers** to counsel the president on economic policy.

Despite widespread fears, the postwar depression never materialized. Employment remained high, as plants that had been making tanks and bombers began to produce consumer goods. With world agricultural output shattered by the war, U.S. food exports also remained high. In addition, Americans now began spending the money they had saved from their wartime paychecks.

MOTIVATING:
STUDENT EXPERIENCES

Ask students how they would react if they discovered that they might be replaced at their job by someone else, or that their wages were not keeping up with the cost of living. Tell students that in this section they will analyze the social and economic effects of peace on Americans, and how these effects influenced the 1948 presidential election.

Teaching the Section

THE POSTWAR ECONOMY

Organize students into small groups to create a plan for a two-page magazine spread titled "The American Postwar Economy." Ask groups to write brief summaries of articles that might appear in the spread to explain how veterans, farmers, consumers, and members of ethnic groups fared in the postwar economy.

TAFT-HARTLEY ACT

Ask volunteers to list the provisions of the Taft-Hartley Act. Then have students play the role of business owner or union worker and write a letter to the editor, explaining their support for or their objections to the Taft-Hartley Act. Call on volunteers with opposing viewpoints to read their letters to the class. Students may wish to include their letters in their portfolios.

▶

▲ **A. Philip Randolph and Eleanor Roosevelt are shown here at a 1946 rally at Madison Square Garden to save the Fair Employment Practices Committee. Congress later abolished the committee.**

Not all was rosy on the economic front, however. Government measures encouraged employers to give priority in hiring to veterans. The fears of many women, African Americans, and Mexican Americans were realized as they lost their jobs to returning veterans. During the war these workers had been encouraged to take jobs in vital defense factories. African Americans had been protected from job discrimination by the Fair Employment Practices Committee. Soon after the war, however, Congress abolished the committee.

Many workers were also hit hard by inflation. With the lifting of most wartime price controls in 1946, prices soared. Meat prices went so high that some markets began selling horsemeat. Blaming the Truman administration, angry consumers called the president "Horsemeat Harry."

■■ **Despite fears of a depression, the American economy prospered after the war, though inflation hurt many workers.**

Labor unrest. As inflation worsened, workers took matters into their own hands. Workers who had sacrificed during the depression and the war now craved a better standard of living. Freed of their wartime no-strike pledge, millions of workers walked off the job to win wage increases and to preserve some wartime price controls. In 1946—the most strike-filled year in U.S. history after 1919—almost five million workers walked the picket lines.

President Truman, though a backer of labor unions, opposed these strikes because he feared they would disrupt the economy. In April 1946, when some 400,000 coal miners went on strike, Truman ordered the army to establish government

control of the mines. United Mine Workers' president John L. Lewis responded: "You can't dig coal with bayonets." After the courts slapped heavy fines on the union, though, Lewis ordered the miners back to work. When confronted with striking railway workers, Truman threatened to end the strike by drafting the strikers into the army. Union leaders, however, negotiated an end to the strike without resorting to the draft.

To prevent further strikes, Congress—under Republican control since the 1946 elections—passed an antiunion bill in 1947. This law, known as the **Taft-Hartley Act**, allowed courts to end strikes, outlawed closed-shop agreements (which required union membership for employment), restricted unions' political contributions, and required union officers to swear they were not Communists. President Truman vetoed the bill, but Congress passed it over his veto.

The Taft-Hartley Act stirred angry debate. Conservative supporters argued that the law corrected unfair advantages granted to labor in the Wagner-Connery Act (see Chapter 14). Prolabor opponents denounced it as a "slave labor law."

The act limited the tactics unions could use. Despite these restrictions, however, organized labor continued to make some gains in the postwar years. For example, in 1948 General Motors and the United Automobile Workers (UAW) signed a contract tying wage increases to cost-of-living increases. Union contracts also began to include provisions for such benefits as retirement pensions and health insurance.

■■ **The Taft-Hartley Act placed a variety of restrictions on labor unions.**

◀ **The cartoon *Three Men on a Horse* appeared on February 24, 1953. Union leaders John L. Lewis, Walter Reuther, and George Meany opposed the Taft-Hartley Act's restrictions on labor unions.**

MULTICULTURAL PERSPECTIVES

During World War II and immediately after, Asian American plantation workers in Hawaii organized unions to win better wages and working conditions. Unions lobbied state legislators, who in 1946 passed a law giving the agricultural workers the right to collective bargaining. Saburo Fujisaki, a Nisei union member, explained the union's success: "We had a territory-wide political machine organized. We elected two members of the union to the House of Representatives. We gained respect because we could get votes for people who otherwise couldn't get elected. What we couldn't win across the bargaining table, we decided we'd seek through the Territorial Legislature."

HISTORICAL SIDELIGHTS

Gains for African American Women
By 1953, some 60 percent of the degrees from black colleges were granted to women, as compared to about 35 percent for all women graduating from all colleges in the same time period.

Teaching the **Section**

ISSUES IN THE 1948 ELECTION

Call on volunteers to represent Truman supporters, Dixiecrats, and Progressives during the 1948 election campaign. Have role-players argue the major campaign issues and list their positions on the chalkboard. Then discuss why many Americans expected Truman to lose the election of 1948. Ask students to explain how they would have voted in the election.

MAKING CONNECTIONS

Language Arts
"To err is Truman," was a play on words, taken from Alexander Pope's line in *An Essay on Criticism:* "To err is human, to forgive divine."

HISTORICAL SIDELIGHTS

Shelley v. Kraemer
In the 1948 Supreme Court case *Shelley* v. *Kraemer,* the justices declared that it was unconstitutional for state courts to uphold the restrictive covenant—a written, private agreement between the buyer and seller of a house in which the buyer promised not to sell, rent, or transfer the property to members of specific ethnic groups or religions.

PRIMARY SOURCE

Description of Change: excerpted
Rationale: excerpted to focus on main idea

THE AMERICAN NATION VIDEODISC PROGRAM

Jackie Robinson

2A   42494   :23

THE 1948 ELECTION

By 1948 inflation, high taxes, and labor unrest had eroded public support for Truman. His approval rating stood at 35 percent in March, down from 60 percent the previous year. "To err is Truman," people joked. But Truman was determined to prove his critics wrong. His stand on civil rights for African Americans proved to be an important issue in the 1948 campaign.

The Committee on Civil Rights.
In 1946 African American civil rights groups urged Truman to take action against the racism that stained American society. They pointed out that most African Americans in the South were prevented from voting through the use of poll taxes.

Blacks throughout the nation faced segregation in schools and buses and discrimination in housing and employment. And in many areas African Americans continued to be lynched, a crime that few local courts ever prosecuted. Efforts to battle these conditions met a wall of white resistance.

In December 1946 Truman, distressed by these reports, set up the **Committee on Civil Rights** to examine the issue. The committee's 15 members included African American lawyer Sadie Alexander; Dr. Channing Tobias, director of the Phelps-Stokes Fund, which supported educational opportunities for African Americans; General Electric's president Charles Wilson; and Franklin Roosevelt, Jr.

The committee issued its report, entitled "To Secure These Rights," in October 1947. The report documented widespread civil rights abuses, including discrimination against black veterans and an increase in Ku Klux Klan violence. The committee urged the government to pass an antilynching law and an anti-poll-tax measure and to end discrimination in federal agencies and the military. The report also called for an end to racial segregation in interstate transportation.

▲ Shown here are African American demonstrators outside the convention hall at the 1948 Democratic Convention in Philadelphia.

When Truman did not immediately act on the report's recommendations, African American leader A. Philip Randolph threatened to launch a campaign of civil disobedience if the military remained segregated. The tactic worked. In July 1948 Truman issued executive orders banning racial discrimination in the military and in federal hiring. He also took steps to end employment discrimination by companies working under government contracts.

White southern Democrats were outraged at African American demands for civil rights and at Truman's actions. Senator Olin Johnston of South Carolina angrily explained that the South's electoral votes "won't be for Truman. They'll be for somebody else. He ain't going to be re-elected."

The Democratic convention.
Despite Senator Johnston's bluster, southern opposition did not prevent Truman from being nominated at the Democratic convention in July. Senator Alben W. Barkley of Kentucky was selected to be Truman's running mate. The Democrats hoped to appeal to the former New Deal coalition of farmers, unionized workers, big-city ethnic groups, and African Americans. The Democratic platform called for repeal of the Taft-Hartley Act; an increase in federal aid for housing, education, and agriculture; and broader social security benefits. It also included a strong civil rights plank.

The civil rights issue split the Democratic party. Southern delegates threatened to walk out of the convention. Declaring "LET 'EM WALK," the NAACP argued:

66 There is no room . . . for compromise. . . . Those Democrats who say the

▼ Due to Truman's poor showing in public-opinion polls during the 1948 campaign, the *Chicago Daily Tribune* published an early election-night edition announcing Dewey as the winner.

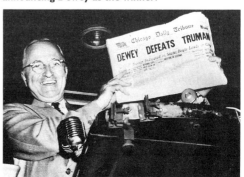

Practice

GUIDED PRACTICE

Ask students to imagine they are advisers to President Truman. Have them name postwar problems that Truman will have to address. List the problems on the chalkboard. Then discuss how each problem might be handled.

INDEPENDENT PRACTICE

Have students choose a problem listed in the Guided Practice and, in their role as advisers to President Truman, have them write a memorandum to the president, explaining the problem and suggesting a solution. Students may wish to include their memorandums in their portfolios.

Review and Assessment

REVIEW Write the following items on the chalkboard: *Demobilization, Taft-Hartley Act,* and *1948 election.* Have students work in groups of three to develop cause-and-effect charts centering on each item. Then assign the Section 2 Review on p. 444.

ASSESS Assign the **Section 2 Daily Quiz** in *Core Resources.* ▶

President's recommendation of such a program is a "stab in the back" of the South are saying they do not choose to abide by the Constitution. They are also saying . . . that the whole section of our nation believes as they do. . . . We *know* it is not true! **99**

After bitter debate the delegates adopted the civil rights plank. Southern delegates stormed out of the convention. They formed the States' Rights party—nicknamed the **Dixiecrats**—which called for continued racial segregation. The Dixiecrats nominated Governor J. Strom Thurmond of South Carolina as their presidential candidate. These explosive divisions were an opening skirmish in a mighty struggle against racism that would soon sweep over the nation.

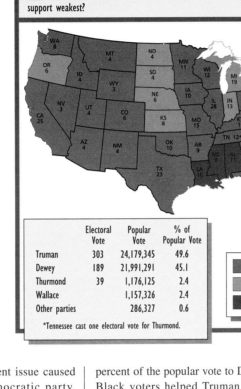

Election of 1948

UNEXPECTED WINNER Truman got slightly less than 50 percent of the popular vote, but had a solid majority in the electoral college.

? REGION In which area of the United States was Truman's support weakest?

	Electoral Vote	Popular Vote	% of Popular Vote
Truman	303	24,179,345	49.6
Dewey	189	21,991,291	45.1
Thurmond	39	1,176,125	2.4
Wallace		1,157,326	2.4
Other parties		286,327	0.6

*Tennessee cast one electoral vote for Thurmond.

Truman (Democratic)
Dewey (Republican)
Thurmond (States' Rights)

HISTORICAL SIDELIGHTS

Whistle-Stop Campaign

President Truman wanted to take his message directly to the people. For 33 days, beginning in September 1948, Truman traveled some 31,000 miles by train, speaking from the rear platform of the train to people in towns across the country. No presidential candidate had ever traveled so far and none would ever again attempt such a campaign by railroad. In a letter to his sister, Truman wrote: "It will be the greatest campaign any President ever made. Win, lose, or draw people will know where I stand."

The race widens. A different issue caused another break within the Democratic party. Troubled by Truman's antilabor actions in 1946, former vice president Henry Wallace and other liberal New Dealers left the Democratic party to found the Progressive party. This group, which was not related to the Progressive party of the early 1900s, called for an extension of the New Deal and for friendly relations with the Soviet Union. The American Communist party supported the Progressive party.

With the Democrats' votes split three ways, the Republicans were confident of victory. They nominated Governor Thomas Dewey of New York as their presidential candidate and Earl Warren, the popular governor of California, as Dewey's running mate. Opinion polls and most newspapers predicted a Dewey victory.

But Truman ran an energetic campaign, attacking the conservatism of the Republicans and the radicalism of the Progressives. As he crisscrossed the country, criticizing the "do-nothing" Republican Congress, crowds began to chant, "Give 'em hell, Harry." In one of the great upsets of U.S. political history, Truman won, gaining 49

percent of the popular vote to Dewey's 45 percent. Black voters helped Truman carry several key states. Workers, farmers, and ethnic voters generally supported Truman, proving that the political coalition that had supported Franklin Roosevelt in the 1930s still held.

■■ **Civil rights and labor issues splintered the Democratic party. Truman, however, ran a tough campaign and won the 1948 election.**

THE FAIR DEAL

Heartened by his victory, Truman urged Congress to continue Roosevelt's New Deal reforms. Proclaiming that "every segment of our population . . . has a right to expect from our government a fair deal," Truman proposed new reforms, which he labeled the **Fair Deal**. Truman's Fair Deal proposed full employment, higher minimum wages, a national health insurance program, affordable

RETEACH Organize students into groups and assign each group a subsection of Section 2. Have each group develop several questions and answers about the main ideas in its assigned material. Then have each group quiz the other groups with its questions.

Closure

Ask students to explain in their own words why they think the author titled this section "The Challenges of Peace." (*Student responses should tie economic, political, and civil rights issues to the transition from war to peace.*)

Extension

COMPARE Have students develop a chart that compares the restrictions imposed on unions by the Taft-Hartley Act of 1947 with the rights they gained under the Wagner Labor Relations Act of 1935.

CREATE Have students create buttons, campaign literature, banners, and other election materials for each of the candidates in the 1948 election.

SECTION REVIEW ANSWERS

IDENTIFY

For significance, see the following pages:
GI Bill of Rights (p. 440)
Employment Act (p. 440)
Council of Economic Advisors (p.440)
John L. Lewis (p. 441)
Taft-Hartley Act (p. 441)
Committee on Civil Rights (p. 442)
Sadie Alexander (p. 442)
Alben W. Barkley (p. 442)
Dixiecrats (p. 443)
J. Strom Thurmond (p. 443)
Henry Wallace (p. 443)
Thomas Dewey (p. 443)
Fair Deal (p. 443)

1. *Economy prospered because of high employment and consumer spending spree, but end of price controls brought inflation that hurt workers.*
2. *reduced the power of labor by allowing courts to end strikes, outlawing closed-shop agreements, and restricting unions' political contributions*
3. *Many lost their jobs to returning veterans.*
4. *Commentaries might mention inflation, high taxes, civil rights, and labor unrest.*
5. *pressure from African American civil rights groups, the findings of the Committee on Civil Rights, Randolph's threat of civil disobedience*

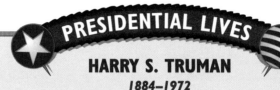

PRESIDENTIAL LIVES

HARRY S. TRUMAN
1884–1972

in office
1945–1953

Harry S. Truman was known to be an honest politician who always spoke his mind. His very direct manner of speaking shocked many people, but impressed others. Once Truman wrote a letter to a music critic who had written a harsh review of a recital by the president's daughter Margaret. In addition to calling the critic "a frustrated old man who never made a success," the president informed him that "I never met you, but if I do

Harry S. Truman
U.S. Postage 8 cents

you'll need a new nose." While some considered this response inappropriate, public opinion strongly supported Truman's defense of his daughter.

While Truman was quick to defend his family and others, he often downplayed his own abilities as president. Many years after he left office he told an interviewer, "I wasn't one of the great Presidents; but I had a good time trying to be one."

housing construction, aid to farmers, and the expansion of welfare benefits.

Most Republicans, and even conservatives in Truman's own party, opposed the president's program. Nevertheless, Truman managed to push through some of his reforms. Between 1949 and 1952 Congress extended social security benefits to some 10 million more people, raised the minimum wage from 40 to 75 cents an hour, and approved programs to clear slums. Congress also expanded federal programs to promote flood control, hydroelectric power, and irrigation.

Overall, though, the Fair Deal had limited success amid an increasingly conservative postwar political climate. Congress failed to repeal the Taft-Hartley Act or to pass a civil rights bill. Most of the New Dealers had resigned from Truman's cabinet in disappointment, leaving business leaders and military men who did not champion the Fair Deal. These domestic issues also unfolded against the backdrop of other pressing concerns that had international implications: conflict with the Soviet Union and almost hysterical fears of communism.

SECTION 2 REVIEW

IDENTIFY and explain the significance of the following: GI Bill of Rights, Employment Act, Council of Economic Advisers, John L. Lewis, Taft-Hartley Act, Committee on Civil Rights, Sadie Alexander, Alben W. Barkley, Dixiecrats, J. Strom Thurmond, Henry Wallace, Thomas Dewey, Fair Deal.

1. **MAIN IDEA** What effect did the end of World War II have on the U.S. economy?
2. **MAIN IDEA** What restrictions did the Taft-Hartley Act place on unions?
3. **GAINING A MULTICULTURAL PERSPECTIVE** How did the end of the war affect women, African American, and Mexican American workers?
4. **WRITING TO INFORM** Imagine you are a political correspondent covering the 1948 election. Write a magazine commentary that outlines the most important issues in the campaign.
5. **ANALYZING** What convinced Truman to desegregate the military and to end discrimination in federal jobs?

Chapter 17

SECTION 3

Introducing the Section

PREVIEW WORKSHOP

Following is a list of the significant people, places, and terms in this section. You may wish to use this list as a section preview.

People
- Nikolai Novikov
- George Kennan
- George C. Marshall

Places
- Greece
- Turkey
- Dardanelles
- Federal Republic of Germany
- German Democratic Republic

Terms
- Cold War
- satellite nations
- containment
- Baruch Plan
- Atomic Energy Act
- Truman Doctrine
- Marshall Plan
- Berlin airlift
- NATO
- Warsaw Pact
- National Security Council
- Central Intelligence Agency
- House Committee on Un-American Activities
- Hollywood Ten
- Internal Security Act

Section 3

THE COLD WAR BEGINS

FOCUS
- **What caused the Cold War?**
- **What did the United States hope to accomplish through the Marshall Plan?**
- **What effects did the Cold War have on American society?**

Soon after World War II, the wartime alliance between the United States and the Soviet Union collapsed. The two countries, at odds because of competing global objectives and different economic and political systems, fought over control of Europe and access to atomic energy.

Berlin airlift, 1948

THE ROOTS OF THE COLD WAR

An intense rivalry between the United States and the Soviet Union began after World War II. With once-mighty Germany, Japan, and Great Britain in ruins, only the United States and the Soviet Union were left to struggle for international dominance. Their competition for global power and influence, which came to be known as the **Cold War**, was waged mostly on political and economic fronts rather than on the battlefield. Nevertheless, the threat of all-out war was always present.

The origins of the Cold War lay in the economic and political differences between the two nations and in each country's perception of the other. Most Americans opposed the foundations of the Soviet state: a state-controlled economy, one-party rule, suppression of religion, and the use of force to crush opposition. The Soviets, on the other hand, criticized American imperialism, racial discrimination, and the treatment of workers. Nikolai Novikov, the Soviet ambassador to the United States, expressed distrust of American international aims:

❝ The foreign policy of the United States . . . is characterized in the postwar period by a striving for world supremacy. . . . Broad plans for expansion have been developed and are being implemented through diplomacy and the establishment of a system of naval and air bases . . . [and] through the arms race. ❞

Americans felt the same way about the Soviets. Soviet expansionism after World War II fueled American mistrust. During World War II the Soviets had taken over the Baltic states of Lithuania, Latvia, and Estonia. Then they captured large areas of Poland and Romania. By war's end the Soviets also controlled Manchuria.

After the war, Stalin made clear his determination to maintain Soviet influence in Eastern Europe, claiming the need for a buffer zone of "friendly nations" on the U.S.S.R.'s western border. He stripped eastern Germany of some 40 percent of its industrial equipment, installed pro-Soviet governments in Poland and Romania, and worked to establish Communist rule throughout Eastern Europe. The countries under Soviet control became known as **satellite nations**.

FOCUS OBJECTIVES

- Identify what caused the Cold War.
- Explain what the United States hoped to accomplish through the Marshall Plan.
- Analyze the effects the Cold War had on Americans.

MAKING CONNECTIONS

Language Arts
The term *Cold War* first appeared in print in 1947, when Walter Lippmann's *The Cold War*, a study of American-Soviet relations, was published.

PRIMARY SOURCE

Description of Change: excerpted and bracketed **Rationale:** excerpted to focus on main idea; bracketed to clarify meaning

CORE RESOURCES

- **Literature Worksheet 17**
- **Geography Worksheet 17**
- **Section 3 Daily Quiz**

■ RESOURCES

- **Linking Geography and History Transparency** and **Worksheet 20**

THE POSTWAR YEARS ■■ 445

445

MOTIVATING: LINK TO TODAY

Ask students if they think that the dissolution of the Soviet Union has eliminated concern about nuclear war and the spread of communism in the world today. Point out that in this section they will learn how such fears sparked the Cold War and how they affected postwar Americans.

Teaching the Section

ROOTS OF THE COLD WAR

Organize the class into two groups. Direct one group to assume the roles of Soviet students and the other the roles of American students after World War II. Have students work in pairs to write letters explaining why they think the other group is responsible for the Cold War. Ask Soviet students to address their letters to Truman and American students to write to Stalin. Call on pairs to read their letters to the class. Then work with the class, using their letters to reach some general conclusions about the roots of the Cold War.

HISTORICAL SIDELIGHTS

Cold War Tensions

Time, in reporting Stalin's speech, described it as "the most warlike pronouncement uttered by any top-rank statesman since V-J Day."

HISTORICAL SIDELIGHTS

Iron Curtain

In February 1945, thirteen months before Churchill spoke of the *Iron Curtain* at Fulton, Missouri, Nazi propaganda minister Joseph Goebbels used the phrase *iron screen* with reference to Russia. The image that inspired their use of similar terms was probably the fireproof iron curtains long used in European theaters.

PRIMARY SOURCE

Description of Change: excerpted

Rationale: excerpted to focus on main idea

Concerned about Stalin's actions, the United States, Great Britain, and France solidified their control of West Germany and revived its industries. The United States also pressured Stalin to withdraw Soviet forces from Iran, the oil-rich Middle Eastern nation that the Soviets had occupied during the war. In April 1946 Stalin finally agreed to withdraw his troops.

In February of the same year, however, Stalin had made a tough speech—dubbed the "Declaration of World War III" by Supreme Court justice William Douglas—proclaiming that capitalism and communism could never coexist. Winston Churchill, Britain's wartime prime minister, answered Stalin in March with an equally tough speech delivered in Fulton, Missouri. Churchill declared that a Soviet "Iron Curtain has descended across the Continent," isolating Western Europe from Soviet-dominated Eastern Europe. Churchill called for closer cooperation between Great Britain and America to check Soviet power.

Churchill's speech was well received in Washington. At the time, George Kennan, a State Department official and Soviet expert, advised similar action. Kennan argued that the Soviet Union's long-term aim was to defeat capitalism and expand the Soviet sphere of influence. He believed that the Soviets would be persistent, yet cautious, expanding only when there were few risks. Kennan explained how American foreign policy could thus stop the spread of communism:

❝ The Soviet pressure against the free institutions of the Western world is something that can be contained by the . . . vigilant application of counterforce at a series of constantly shifting geographical and political points. . . . The Russians look forward to a duel of infinite duration. ❞

Kennan's **containment** doctrine, which aimed to contain, or restrict, Soviet expansion, became the basis for U.S. Cold War strategy. Many Americans, unwilling to return to the appeasement policy of the 1930s, applauded Kennan's stand against communism.

▪▪ The origins of the Cold War lay in U.S.–Soviet global competition, conflicting economic and political systems, and mutual distrust.

*T*HE DEADLOCK OVER ATOMIC WEAPONS

The United States and the Soviet Union soon became locked in a dispute over the control of atomic weapons. This standoff terrified many Americans, who feared a nuclear war. Most people shared lawyer David E. Lilienthal's 1946 assessment that "the awful strength of atomic power . . . directly affects every man, woman, and child in the world." Recognizing this fact, the UN early in 1946 created a commission to draw up a plan for the control of nuclear arms.

At the commission's first meeting, U.S. representative Bernard Baruch called for the creation of a special UN agency with the authority to inspect any nation's atomic-energy installations. This proposal, known as the **Baruch Plan**, would impose penalties on countries violating international controls. Until such a plan was in place, Baruch said, the United States would not reveal any atomic-energy secrets or give up its atomic weapons. At the time, American physicists were developing more-powerful nuclear bombs.

Working feverishly on its own bomb, the Soviet Union rejected all inspection and enforcement provisions. With neither country willing to compromise, hopes for international control of

▼ In July 1946 the United States conducted atomic bomb tests in Bikini Atoll in the western Pacific Ocean. These tests were intended to measure the effects of atomic bombs on warships.

NUCLEAR CONCERNS

Call on a volunteer to explain the purpose of the Atomic Energy Commission. Ask another volunteer to present the Baruch Plan. Then lead a class discussion on how and why each was an outgrowth of the Cold War and why the Cold War made international nuclear cooperation difficult. Conclude by asking students if they think nuclear weapons research should be under military or civilian control.

▶

---

atomic energy died. When the Soviet Union tested its first atomic bomb in 1949, fears of a nuclear-arms race became reality.

Despite the failure of the Baruch Plan, the United States achieved some success in controlling nuclear weapons. Atomic-energy scientists and U.S. peace organizations, such as the Women's International League for Peace and Freedom, urged the U.S. government to establish civilian, rather than military, control of atomic energy. Responding to these appeals, Congress in August 1946 passed the **Atomic Energy Act**. The act set up the Atomic Energy Commission (AEC) under civilian control to oversee nuclear weapons research and to promote peacetime uses of atomic energy. Its main activity, however, became supporting the government's nuclear weapons program.

CONTAINMENT AROUND THE WORLD

As prospects for U.S.–Soviet cooperation dimmed, the Truman administration pursued a more aggressive policy toward the Soviet Union. The U.S. containment policy first took shape in Greece, where a civil war had broken out in 1946. Communist-led rebels battled the Greek monarchy, which relied on military and financial support from Great Britain. In early 1947, however, the British announced that they could no longer continue their aid to Greece. Without aid it seemed likely that Greece's pro-Western government would fall to the Communists and the country would come under Soviet control.

Containment in the Mediterranean. At the same time, the Soviet Union pressured Turkey to give up sole control of the Dardanelles, a narrow strait linking the Black Sea and the Mediterranean. President Truman knew that control of this area would give the Soviets a dominant position in the eastern Mediterranean and would threaten the security of the Suez Canal. In a somber speech before Congress on March 12, 1947, Truman declared: "It must be the policy of the United States to support free peoples who are resisting attempted subjugation [conquest] by armed minorities or by outside pressures."

This statement, which became known as the **Truman Doctrine**, made no mention of the Soviet Union, though clearly Truman had devised it with the Soviets in mind. Agreeing with Truman's

sentiments, Congress soon voted $400 million to aid Greece and Turkey. This action was only a prelude, however, to the more massive foreign-aid program that soon followed.

Containment in Europe. After World War II, European economies were in shambles. In 1948 Germany produced only 45 percent of the goods it had produced before the war. To make matters worse, the winter of 1946–47 brought the worst blizzards in some 50 years. Starvation and chaos loomed. Some Americans believed that the United States should help Europe. They feared that such desperate economic conditions would make Europe more vulnerable to Soviet influence.

Secretary of State George C. Marshall shared this belief. Born in Uniontown, Pennsylvania, in 1880, Marshall graduated from Virginia Military Institute and joined the army. During World War I he served under General Pershing. As army chief of staff during World War II, he attended the Casablanca, Yalta, and Potsdam conferences.

After the war Marshall served briefly as a U.S. envoy to China before Truman appointed him secretary of state in 1947. In a speech at Harvard University on June 5, 1947, Marshall warned that if steps were not taken soon, Europe faced "economic, social, and political" collapse. He then called for a major U.S. effort to promote European recovery "to permit the emergence of political and social conditions in which free institutions can exist." At the same time, Marshall warned that any attempt to block recovery or exploit Europe's difficulties for political ends would face strong American opposition.

George C. Marshall

After Marshall's speech, Truman asked Congress for $17 billion in economic aid for Europe. Truman's request sparked heated debate throughout the United States. Supporters argued that such aid would contain communism by restoring Europe's economic health and would help the U.S. economy as Europeans purchased American goods and military hardware. Opponents said the United States could not afford to "carry Europe on its back."

GLOBAL CONNECTIONS

Although Roosevelt and Churchill had agreed in 1945 to full collaboration in the field of atomic energy between the U.S., the United Kingdom, and Canada, the passage of the Atomic Energy Act terminated virtually all U.S. communications about atomic energy. Truman and Congress felt that the U.S. should keep information about atomic energy to itself since it was valuable and dangerous information. In 1947, feeling betrayed by the Atomic Energy Act, members of Britain's Labour Cabinet called for Britain to begin work on its own atomic bomb.

Teaching the Section

THE MARSHALL PLAN

Call on volunteers to role-play George Marshall and his State Department advisers. Have remaining students work in small groups to develop interview questions to ask Marshall and his advisers about the Marshall Plan. Tell students that the interview should focus on the aims of the Marshall Plan and the part it plays in Truman's overall Cold War strategy. Have each group select a representative for a panel to interview the Marshall group. Conclude by asking all students to write a newspaper article that recaps the interview.

■■ Ask students what types of aid the U.S. provides to other countries today.

GLOBAL CONNECTIONS

Under Soviet pressure, Czechoslovakia, Poland, Romania, and other satellite countries of Eastern Europe refused to participate in the Marshall Plan. Soviet foreign minister V.M. Molotov explained his objections to the Marshall Plan when he said it was "nothing but a vicious American scheme for using dollars to buy its way [into the affairs of Europe]."

HISTORICAL SIDELIGHTS

The Berlin Airlift

When the Soviets blocked off Berlin, it left more than 2 million German citizens, and Allied forces as well, with enough food for only about 36 days, and enough coal for 45. U.S. general Lucius Clay asked for 4,500 tons of supplies a day to be airlifted, knowing that even this amount would not be enough to sustain Berlin during the winter months. By the end of the airlift, British and American aircraft had delivered, in over 277,000 flights, more than 2 million tons of food, fuel, machinery, and other supplies.

PRIMARY SOURCE

Description of Change: excerpted
Rationale: excerpted to focus on main idea

▲ The first cargo of sugar transported under the Marshall Plan is unloaded from the S.S. *Araby* in London in February 1949.

A turning point in the debate came early in 1948, when pro-Soviet Communists overthrew the government of Czechoslovakia. Moved to action by the coup, Congress passed the European Recovery Act, or **Marshall Plan**, in April 1948. The plan, based on Marshall's recommendations, provided some $12 billion in aid to Western Europe over the next four years. For his efforts Marshall won the Nobel Peace Prize in 1953.

■■ **The Marshall Plan aimed to contain the spread of communism by easing economic hardship in Europe.**

CRISIS IN BERLIN

The non-Soviet zone of Germany grew stronger as a result of the Marshall Plan. In early June 1948, Great Britain, France, and the United States announced plans to combine their occupation zones and support the formation of a new West German government.

The Berlin airlift. The Soviets, deeply fearful of renewed German power, opposed this action. On June 24, 1948, the Soviets suddenly blocked all roads, canals, and railways linking Berlin and western Germany, cutting off shipments of food, fuel, and other crucial supplies to the city. The Soviets hoped to drive the Western powers out of Berlin and to delay the formation of a West German government. Berlin had become a pawn in the Cold War chess game.

The British and the Americans responded to the Soviet action with the **Berlin airlift**. Over the next 10 months, U.S. and British planes carried more than two million tons of food and supplies to the people of West Berlin. As one Berliner recalled, the airlift became a lifeline to the rest of the world:

66 Early in the morning, when we woke up, the first thing we did was listen to see whether the noise of aircraft engines could be heard. That gave us the certainty that we were not alone, that the whole civilized world took part in the fight for Berlin's freedom. 99

The success of the Berlin airlift proved a huge embarrassment to the Soviet Union. In May

▲ As tensions mounted, American military police in Berlin warily faced their Soviet counterparts across the dividing line between the Allied and Soviet zones.

THE COLD WAR AT HOME

Direct students to create a web that illustrates the nation's domestic response to the Cold War. Students should write and circle the term *Cold War.* At the end of lines emanating from the circle, students should indicate the ways that the government responded at home to the Cold War. Have volunteers present their webs. Then have class members explain how each government response on the webs illustrates the national climate of concern about communism. Students may wish to include their webs in their portfolios.

Europe After World War II

NEW RUSSIAN EMPIRE The Soviet Union dominated that part of Europe it conquered in the war.

? LOCATION Which nations were members of the Warsaw Pact?

The United States and Canada also were members of NATO.

- NATO member, 1955
- Warsaw Pact member, 1955
- Nonaligned communist nation
- Nonaligned nation
- Territory gained by USSR
- Boundary, 1937

Map Caption Answer
U.S.S.R., Poland, East Germany, Czechoslovakia, Hungary, Romania, Bulgaria, Albania

HISTORICAL SIDELIGHTS
NATO

The signing of NATO marked a radical departure from U.S. tradition. It was the nation's first peacetime military alliance since the signing of the Constitution. President Truman ranked NATO (along with the Marshall Plan) as one of the proudest achievements of his presidency. He was convinced that had NATO been in existence in 1914 and 1939, the world would have been spared two world wars.

AV TRANSPARENCY
Linking Geography and History Transparency and **Worksheet 20**

1949 the Soviets lifted the blockade. On May 9 the Federal Republic of Germany, known as West Germany, was founded. In response, the Soviets set up the German Democratic Republic—East Germany—in the Soviet zone. The division of Germany would last for more than 40 years as a result of Cold War rivalries.

The Western alliance. After the Berlin crisis the United States shifted its attention in Europe from economic recovery to military preparedness. In April 1949 nine Western European nations joined the United States, Canada, and Iceland in a military alliance called the **North Atlantic Treaty Organization**, or NATO.

Under the terms of the NATO treaty, known as the Atlantic Pact, each member nation pledged to defend the others in the event of an outside attack. When Truman submitted the treaty for Senate ratification, debate focused on whether the agreement would allow the United States to go to war without an act of Congress. Concern over this same issue had helped keep the United States out of the League of Nations. This time, however, fear of Soviet expansionism outweighed other concerns. In July 1949 the Senate ratified the treaty.

In 1951 General Dwight D. Eisenhower became the supreme commander of NATO forces. As its contribution to NATO, the United States

Practice

GUIDED PRACTICE

Lead the class in interpreting the cartoon on p. 450. (You may wish to review with students the Strategies for Success on Interpreting Editorial Cartoons on p. 186.) Ask students how caricature, symbols, and labels convey the message in this cartoon.

INDEPENDENT PRACTICE

Direct students to use the techniques discussed in the Guided Practice to create an editorial cartoon about Cold War tensions between the Soviet Union and the U.S. in the 1940s and 1950s. Tell students that their cartoons may be from either the Soviet or the U.S. viewpoint. Students may wish to include their cartoons in their portfolios.

Review and Assessment

REVIEW Direct students to create cause-and-effect charts which show the causes and effects of the Cold War in Europe and at home. Then assign the Section 3 Review on p. 451.

ASSESS Assign the **Section 3 Daily Quiz** in *Core Resources.*

MULTICULTURAL PERSPECTIVES

Although the NAACP accused the Communist party of exploiting race issues, many African Americans were attracted by its message. As one Communist organizer explained, "All my life I'd been sweated and stepped-on and Jim-Crowed. . . . All of a sudden, I had found organizations in which Negroes and whites sat together, and worked together, and knew no difference of race or color."

PRIMARY SOURCE

Description of Change: excerpted
Rationale: excerpted to focus on main idea

HISTORICAL SIDELIGHTS

The Hollywood Ten
During the Hollywood investigation, HUAC interviewed some of the biggest names in the industry, including studio mogul Jack L. Warner, Walt Disney, Gary Cooper, and Ronald Reagan (then an actor involved in the Screen Actors Guild), all of whom testified about Communists in the movie industry.

The Granger Collection, New York

◀ This U.S. cartoon, entitled *Banner of the Non-Soviet Union* (1949), shows that NATO was formed in response to Allied fears of Soviet aggression.

stationed troops in Europe and gave massive military aid to its European allies. The Soviet Union responded in 1955 by forming its own military alliance with other Communist countries in Eastern Europe. This alliance came to be called the **Warsaw Pact**.

THE COLD WAR AT HOME

The Cold War had important consequences within the United States. As a result of Cold War pressures, the United States streamlined its military to allow for peacetime rearmament. In July 1947 Congress replaced the War Department with the Department of Defense, combining the leadership of the army, navy, and air force under the Joint Chiefs of Staff. In addition, Congress set up the **National Security Council** (NSC) to advise the president on strategic matters and established the **Central Intelligence Agency** (CIA) to gather information overseas.

Another Red scare. The Cold War also aroused fears of communism at home. Although Truman opposed communism abroad, some Republicans accused him of allowing Communists in the American government. Responding to such charges, Truman set up the Loyalty Review Board in 1947 to investigate all federal employees. By the end of 1951, more than 20,000 federal workers had been investigated, some 2,000 had resigned, and more than 300 had been fired as "security risks." In most cases the government did not allow dismissed employees to respond to the charges against them.

Meanwhile, Congress cracked down on the Communist party. Leading the anti-Communist crusade in Congress was the

House Committee on Un-American Activities (HUAC), originally established in 1938 to investigate anti-American propaganda. HUAC held a series of hearings to question the political allegiances of members of peace organizations, liberal political groups, and labor unions. In 1947, responding to charges that Hollywood was riddled with Communists, HUAC investigated people in the movie industry. A group of film directors and writers, known as the **Hollywood Ten**, refused to answer HUAC's questions and went to jail. They were blacklisted—denied work in the film industry—and saw their careers destroyed.

The hysteria generated by HUAC spread quickly. One group that bravely spoke out against HUAC, the Women's International League for Peace and Freedom, argued in 1949 that the hearings violated democratic rights:

> ❝ Fully recognizing the danger of fascist and communist totalitarianism, the League believes that such forces can be best opposed by open discussion and by the strengthening of our own democratic procedures, rather than by attempts at direct control. ❞

Because of the league's support for progressive causes, the FBI investigated the national organization and several of its local chapters. The investigation scared many potential members away.

▲ A delegation of Hollywood personalities attended a meeting of HUAC on October 27, 1947. Humphrey Bogart, Lauren Bacall, and Sterling Hayden were among those present.

Closure

Ask a volunteer to explain George Kennan's quote on p. 446. Call on students to provide examples of how the U.S. containment policy was implemented around the world, examples of how the Soviet Union responded to containment, and examples of how Americans at home reacted to the Soviet response.

Extension

ANALYZE Have students research and report on a Soviet satellite nation of their choice, analyzing its political, economic, and/or geographical importance to the Soviet Union.

COMPARE Have students create a chart comparing the U.S. government's response to the Red Scare during the Cold War with its response to the Red Scare following World War I.

HUAC investigations had a similar effect on labor unions and many political groups.

The search for spies. HUAC also investigated individuals accused of spying for the Soviets. In 1948 Whittaker Chambers, who had been a member of the Communist party, accused Alger Hiss of being a Communist spy. Chambers told HUAC that Hiss, a New Deal lawyer who had joined the State Department in 1936, had given him secret State Department documents to pass on to the Soviets.

Hiss denied the charges, but persistent questioning by HUAC member Richard Nixon, a young Republican congressman from California, revealed apparent inconsistencies in Hiss's testimony. In 1950 Hiss was convicted of perjury (lying under oath) and sentenced to five years in prison.

Another notorious spy case also helped fuel domestic fears of communism. In 1951 a U.S. court convicted two Americans, Julius and Ethel Rosenberg, of giving the Soviets atomic-energy secrets during World War II. Defenders of the Rosenbergs claimed that the two were innocent victims of anti-Communist hysteria. Despite worldwide protests on their behalf, however, the Rosenbergs were executed in June 1953. Historians have found evidence for the guilty verdict but agree that the death sentences were extreme reactions in the poisonous Cold War climate.

Other anti-Communist measures included the **Internal Security Act**, passed in 1950. The act

▲ Escorted by a U.S. marshal (left), Julius and Ethel Rosenberg are shown outside of federal court on March 8, 1951, awaiting the result of their trial on charges of conspiracy to commit espionage.

required party members and organizations to register with the federal government. It also imposed strict controls on immigrants suspected of being Communist sympathizers. The anti-Communist hysteria of these years shattered many lives and careers. Today many historians look back on this period as one of the bleakest in American history.

■■ **Cold War anti-communism led to efforts to expose alleged Communists in the United States, creating a climate of fear and suspicion.**

■■ **S E C T I O N   3   R E V I E W**

IDENTIFY and explain the significance of the following: Cold War, Nikolai Novikov, satellite nations, George Kennan, containment, Baruch Plan, Atomic Energy Act, Truman Doctrine, George C. Marshall, Marshall Plan, Berlin airlift, NATO, Warsaw Pact, National Security Council, Central Intelligence Agency, House Committee on Un-American Activities, Hollywood Ten, Internal Security Act.

LOCATE and explain the importance of the following: Greece, Turkey, Dardanelles, Federal Republic of Germany (West Germany), German Democratic Republic (East Germany).

1. **MAIN IDEA** What factors gave rise to the Cold War?

2. **MAIN IDEA** What was the purpose of the Marshall Plan?

3. **ASSESSING CONSEQUENCES** What impact did the Cold War have on U.S. society?

4. **WRITING TO EXPRESS A VIEWPOINT** Imagine you are a court reporter at either the Alger Hiss trial or the trial of Ethel and Julius Rosenberg. Write a letter to a friend abroad explaining the significance of one of the trials.

5. **SYNTHESIZING** How did the U.S. government put George Kennan's containment doctrine into practice?

PREVIEW WORKSHOP

Following is a list of the significant people, places, and terms in this section. You may wish to use this list as a section preview.

- Syngman Rhee
- Dean Acheson
- Douglas MacArthur
- Zhou Enlai

People
- David Ben-Gurion
- Ralph Bunche
- Chiang Kai-shek
- Mao Zedong
- Kim Il Sung

Places
- Palestine
- Israel
- Gaza Strip
- West Bank
- Taiwan

- People's Republic of China
- 38th parallel
- Pusan
- Seoul
- Yalu River

Terms
- Zionism
- Long March

FOCUS OBJECTIVES

- Analyze why Israel and Arab nations went to war.

- Explain how Communists came to power in China.

- Examine what led to the division of Korea.

- Identify who fought in the Korean War.

BUILDING VOCABULARY

The term *Zionism* is derived from the word *Zion,* a hill in Jerusalem on which Solomon's temple stood.

BIO GRAPHY PERSONALITIES IN HISTORY

David Ben-Gurion was born David Gruen. He later adopted the ancient Hebrew name Ben-Gurion.

CORE RESOURCES

- **Social Studies Skills Worksheet 17**
- **Section 4 Daily Quiz**

AV RESOURCES

- *The American Nation Videodisc:*
  MacArthur in Korea

452

Section 4

THE COLD WAR TURNS HOT

FOCUS

- **Why did Israel and Arab nations go to war?**
- **How did Communists come to power in China?**
- **What led to the division of Korea?**
- **Who fought in the Korean War?**

World War II had weakened the grip of European nations on their colonies and spheres of influence in the Middle East and Asia. After the war these former colonies struggled to set up their own governments. The United States became involved in the conflict between Israel and several Arab nations in the Middle East. Concerns over the spread of communism led the United States to support the Nationalists in their struggle against the Communists in China. By 1950 Cold War rivalries drew the United States into outright war in Korea.

U.S. soldiers in Korea, 1952

MIDDLE EAST TENSIONS

Soon after World War II, tensions flared in Palestine, a region at the eastern end of the Mediterranean claimed by both Jews and Arabs. Since World War I, Great Britain had ruled Palestine under a League of Nations mandate. Unable to resolve conflicting claims over the territory, Britain in 1947 turned the problem over to the United Nations. The UN came up with a plan to divide Palestine into two states—one for Jews, the other for Arabs—but Arabs rejected the proposal.

The proposal was a victory for **Zionism**, the movement calling for a Jewish homeland in Palestine. Zionist leader David Ben-Gurion

(ben-goohr-YAWN), born in Plonsk, Russia, in 1886, had fought for just this outcome since the early 1900s. Idealistic and determined, Ben-Gurion sailed to Palestine in 1906. Expelled in 1915 for Zionist activities, he went to the United States to raise money and recruit volunteers among the American Jewish community.

During World War II, Ben-Gurion supported the Allied struggle against Hitler but continued to organize Jewish resistance in Palestine. After the war, Ben-Gurion helped develop land, resettle Jewish refugees, and organize covert activities against British and Arab rule.

With the UN's decision to divide Palestine, Great Britain agreed to give up its control of the region. On May 14, 1948, the last

David Ben-Gurion

MOTIVATING: PRIOR KNOWLEDGE

Call on volunteers to summarize the Cold War aims of the U.S. and the Soviet Union after World War II. Tell students that in this section they will learn how the Cold War between these two superpowers affected other countries that were struggling to set up their own postwar governments.

Teaching the Section

WAR IN THE MIDDLE EAST

Pair students to chronicle events that aroused or increased tensions between Jews and Arabs in the Middle East. Select pairs to list their events on the chalkboard. Then ask volunteers to indicate which events on the chalkboard lists they think were the most important factors in bringing war to the Middle East in 1948. Have the class discuss and evaluate the volunteers' selections.

■■ Ask students to describe the status of this area of the world today.

▶

Legend:
- Israel in June 1948
- Territory Israel gained by January 1949
- Territory Israel held after 1949 armistice
- Boundary of British Mandate of Palestine, 1922–1948
- ⍟ Capital city

LEBANON
SYRIA
SEA OF GALILEE
Haifa
Nazareth
MEDITERRANEAN SEA
Nablus
WEST BANK (to Jordan)
Tel Aviv ⍟
Jaffa
Amman ⍟
Jerusalem
Bethlehem
Gaza
GAZA STRIP (to Egypt)
Hebron
DEAD SEA
EGYPT
ISRAEL
Negev

UN Partition
- Israeli territory
- Arab territory

Jerusalem (International Zone)
PALESTINE
Sinai
EGYPT
1947

JORDAN

0   20   40 Miles
0   20   40 Kilometers
Elat
Lambert Conformal Conic Projection

Israel, 1949

SUCCESS STORY The memory of the Holocaust and the struggle to create a Jewish state unified the Israelis in a common cause.

❓ PLACE Which river divides the West Bank from Jordan?

of the British forces withdrew. Ben-Gurion and other Jewish leaders promptly proclaimed the new state of Israel. Both Truman and Stalin immediately recognized the new nation.

The Arab states, however, did not recognize Israel, since they wanted Palestine to remain an Arab country. Armies from the Arab states of Egypt, Lebanon, Jordan (called Transjordan until 1949), Syria, and Iraq attacked Israel. Although vastly outnumbered in the Arab-Israeli war, Israeli forces under Ben-Gurion's overall command captured and held much of Palestine. Israeli soldiers

counted on an impressive arsenal bought in part with the millions of dollars that poured in from the American Jewish community.

■■ In 1948 war broke out between Israel and Arab nations over the disputed territory of Palestine.

In an effort to end the war, the UN sent a mediator, Count Folke Bernadotte of Sweden, to the Middle East. Bernadotte negotiated a shaky cease-fire, but within months he was assassinated by Israeli extremists. In 1949 a second UN mediator, the American diplomat Ralph Bunche, persuaded both sides to accept an armistice. For his efforts Bunche won the Nobel Peace Prize in 1950—

▲ **Ralph Bunche**

the first African American to receive that honor.

The 1949 agreement gave Israel more territory than the earlier UN partition plan had, but it divided Jerusalem into an Arab east and an Israeli west. The plan gave Egypt control of the Gaza Strip, while Jordan took over the West Bank of the Jordan River. The Arab countries, however, still refused to recognize the state of Israel. Also left unresolved was the fate of the Arabs remaining in Israel and the hundreds of thousands of Arabs who had fled or had been driven out of Israel.

Before the territorial agreements were finalized, Israel held its first parliamentary elections in January 1949. Ben-Gurion became prime minister, a post he held almost continuously until 1963. At his death in 1973, Ben-Gurion was hailed as the chief architect of the state of Israel.

COMMUNIST VICTORY IN CHINA

While the conflict between Arabs and Israelis escalated after World War II, tensions also came to a head in China. The seeds of the conflict were planted in the 1920s. Chiang Kai-shek's Kuomintang (KMT), or Nationalist party, battled the

Teaching the *Section*

COMMUNISM IN CHINA

Organize the class into two groups. Direct students from one group to each write a journal entry from the viewpoint of Chiang Kai-shek explaining why Chinese Communists won control of China. Have students in the remaining group write their journal entries from the viewpoint of Mao Zedong. Call on volunteers from each group to read their entries to the class.

Students may wish to include their journal entries in their portfolios.

MULTICULTURAL PERSPECTIVES

The Chinese American community had a mixed reaction to the Communist victory. The U.S. Chinese Workers' Mutual Aid Association applauded the Communists for "unfetter[ing] the yoke of imperialism, destroy[ing] the reactionary dictatorship of the inept and corrupt Kuomintang and establish[ing] people's rule." On the other hand, the Chinese Six Companies, an important Chinese American organization, aided Chiang in his efforts to overthrow Mao's government.

THE ARAB RESPONSE

THROUGH OTHERS' EYES

Musa Alami, an Arab lawyer and diplomat from Palestine, promoted Palestinian nationalism and unity among the Arab states. After the Arab-Israeli war, Alami published a book, *The Lesson of Palestine* (1949), which examined the causes of the war:

❝*T*he British were the prime causers of the disaster. . . . They were assisted by the Americans and the Russians. . . . We found ourselves face to face with the Jews, and entered into battle with them to decide the future; and in spite of what the British, the Americans, and the Russians had done, it was still within our power to win the fight.

The Arabs failed to defend Palestine. . . . We worked on a local basis, without unity, without totality, without a general command, our defense disjointed and our affairs disordered, every town fighting on its own and only those in areas adjacent to the Jews entering the battle at all. . . . The natural result of all this was disaster and the loss of Palestine. ❞

Chinese Communists. KMT forces held most of northern China, and Communist soldiers controlled parts of southern and central China. But in 1931, when Japan invaded Manchuria, the KMT and the Communists declared a truce and joined forces against the Japanese.

In 1934, however, Chiang broke the truce when he launched what he hoped would be the final battles against the Communist-controlled areas of the south. The KMT forces were successful. From 1934 to 1935 some 100,000 Communists marched nearly 6,000 miles to northern China. Known as the **Long March**, this exodus

▲ Nationalist forces kidnapped Chiang Kai-shek in 1936. This photograph of Chiang with his wife was taken after his release.

helped cement Mao Zedong's leadership of the Chinese Communist party and led to the establishment of a strong base in the north.

Chiang's attacks on the Communists kept him from devoting full attention to stopping further Japanese aggression. By the early 1930s the Japanese controlled Manchuria, Inner Mongolia, and parts of northern China. To prevent the loss of more Chinese territory to the Japanese, a group of KMT soldiers kidnapped Chiang in 1936 and released him only after he agreed to join forces with the Communists against the Japanese. This cooperation continued throughout World War II.

At war's end, however, the conflict resumed. During World War II the Communists had prevented the Japanese from controlling all of northwest China. This effective resistance, plus the reforms that Mao instituted to give land to poor peasants, won more support for the Communists and recruits for their army.

The United States, which had long supported Chiang, did not want to see China become a Communist country. During and after World War II the United States sent economic and military aid, including troops, to China to unite the country under the KMT. Truman sent George Marshall to China in 1946 to arrange a truce, but neither side would compromise.

Although Chiang had helped modernize China by building railroads, roads, and factories, his government was becoming increasingly unpopular. The fight against the Japanese had wrecked the Chinese economy, and the Chinese people faced soaring inflation. Chiang seemed unresponsive to these economic problems. In addition, Chiang made no efforts at land reform to help the desperately poor peasants. Moreover, he presided over an increasingly corrupt and authoritarian government that banned all other political parties. As opposition to Chiang mounted, Mao's forces gained control of most of the country by 1949.

Realizing his defeat, Chiang and his army retreated to the island of Taiwan, off the coast of southeast China. The Chinese Communists established the People's Republic of China. Dismayed by the Communist victory, the United

THE COLD WAR AND KOREA

Organize the class into small groups. Tell each group to create a time line or graphic organizer that illustrates how developments in Korea after World War II were part of the overall Cold War struggle between the Soviet Union and the U.S. over the spread and containment of communism. Have students from each group present and interpret its creation to the class. Then ask volunteers to summarize why Korea was divided.

THE KOREAN WAR

Direct students to create a flowchart that shows the course of the Korean War and that indicates at what points various fighting forces entered the war. Call on volunteers to present their flowcharts. Students may wish to include their flowcharts in their portfolios.

States continued to recognize the Nationalists as China's legal government. The Chinese seat on the UN Security Council, granted to Chiang's Taiwan government after World War II, remained in Nationalist hands until 1971.

■■ **In 1949, after a long struggle with Nationalist forces, Chinese Communists under Mao Zedong won control of China.**

THE KOREAN WAR

Meanwhile, political tensions rose in Korea, a peninsula jutting southward from the northeast corner of China. The Japanese had ruled Korea from 1910 to 1945 but had been driven out by Soviet and American troops at the end of World War II. In 1945 the Allies divided Korea into two parts— North Korea and South Korea—with the border between the two countries set at the **38th parallel.** Soviet forces occupied the North, and American troops held the South.

This division was meant to be temporary, but Cold War tensions cemented it. In 1948 North Korea and South Korea set up separate governments, each claiming to rule the entire country. Communist North Korea, led by Kim Il Sung, became known as the People's Republic of Korea. Kim's government, a Communist dictatorship, redistributed land to poor peasants and nationalized most industries. Although Kim's government limited freedom of speech, it expanded education and established formal equality for women. South Korea, under President Syngman Rhee (SING-muhn REE), called itself the Republic of Korea. The southern republic faced economic and political instability after World War II.

Anxious that South Korea not fall to the Communists as China had, the United States built up the South Korean army as a counterbalance to the Soviet-trained northern forces. By 1949 both the United States and the Soviet Union had pulled their troops out of Korea. The pullout left only the two Korean armies tensely facing each other across the 38th parallel.

■■ **After World War II, Korea was divided into Soviet and American occupation zones. In 1948 North Korea and South Korea established separate governments.**

The Korean War

CHINESE INTERVENTION Fearing UN forces would cross the Yalu River into Manchuria, the Chinese entered the war and invaded Korea.

? **MOVEMENT** How far north of the 38th parallel did the UN forces advance?

HISTORICAL SIDELIGHTS

Korea's Leaders

The two leaders of divided Korea were very different from each other. South Korea was led by 73-year-old, militant anti-Communist Syngman Rhee. Rhee had lived for years as an exile in America, where he earned a doctorate. North Korea was headed by 36-year-old Kim Il Sung. Throughout the 1930s and during World War II, Kim had fought against Japanese troops in Manchuria. After the war he returned to Korea a hero. In their inaugural addresses, Rhee and Kim each vowed to reunite Korea under his own government.

Map Caption Answer
about 200 miles

THE POSTWAR YEARS ■■ 455

455

Practice

GUIDED PRACTICE

Create on the chalkboard a three-column chart with the headings *Middle East, China, Korea*. Call on students to list ways in which the U.S. or the Soviet Union, or both, affected the conflicts that developed in each area.

INDEPENDENT PRACTICE

Have students refer to the Guided Practice chart and write a journal entry from the viewpoint of an Arab, Israeli, Chinese, or Korean explaining how their country has been affected by the Cold War.

Review and Assessment

REVIEW Write each of the main headings in the section in headline form on the chalkboard. Have students write brief details that might appear in a newspaper article under the headline. Then assign the Section 4 Review on p. 457.

ASSESS Assign the **Section 4 Daily Quiz** in *Core Resources*.

The war begins. After repeated clashes between North Korean and South Korean troops, the North Korean army invaded South Korea on June 25, 1950. A perceived shift in American policy may have encouraged the invasion. Earlier that year Secretary of State Dean Acheson had given a speech defining America's "defensive perimeter" against the spread of communism in Asia. This perimeter, an imaginary line stretching from Alaska to the Philippines, did not include Korea. Thus it appeared that the United States would not defend South Korea against invasion.

In an emergency session the UN Security Council called for an immediate cease-fire. (At the time the Soviets were boycotting the Security Council over its refusal to admit Communist China, so their delegate was not on hand to veto the UN resolution.) Two days later, on June 27, President Truman pledged U.S. support for South Korea. That same day, the Security Council adopted a U.S.–sponsored resolution branding North Korea an "aggressor" and calling on UN members to come to South Korea's defense. Truman later explained: "I felt certain that if South Korea was allowed to fall, Communist leaders would be emboldened to override nations closer to our own shores."

Bitter fighting. Acting under the UN resolution, Truman ordered U.S. air and ground forces into action under the command of General Douglas MacArthur. Truman also ordered the U.S. Seventh Fleet to protect Taiwan. Although 15 other UN members contributed assistance, the United States and South Korea played the major role in resisting North Korea's aggression.

At first, however, the onslaught of North Korean forces and their Soviet-made tanks was overwhelming. Outgunned and outmanned, the U.S. and South Korean troops fell back. One soldier, Sergeant Raymond Remp, recalled his first encounter with the North Korean army:

66 Someone fired a green flare, and [the enemy] saw us. . . . They were right on top of us in the hills, firing down on us. . . .
Some colonel—don't know who— said, "Get out the best way you can." . . .
All day and night we ran like antelopes. We didn't know our officers. They didn't know us. We lost everything we had. 99

By August the North Koreans had overrun nearly all of South Korea. The U.S. and South Korean forces were backed into a small area around Pusan, in southeast Korea (see map on page 455).

On September 15, 1950, however, MacArthur launched a powerful counterattack. Coming ashore at Inchon, near the 38th parallel, MacArthur's forces swept inland, recapturing Seoul (SOHL), the capital of South Korea. At the same time, a strong UN army, now well equipped and supported from the air, attacked from the south. Caught in a huge trap, North Koreans surrendered by the thousands. Others fled north across the 38th parallel, with UN forces in hot pursuit. By late October the UN army had reached the Yalu River, the boundary between North Korea and China.

But again the tide turned. Late in November, China entered the war on North Korea's side, sending some 300,000 troops across the Yalu. Chinese foreign minister Zhou Enlai (JOH ENLY) explained why China had intervened:

66 The U.S. imperialists have adopted a hostile attitude towards us . . . while paying

MAJOR EVENTS OF THE COLD WAR	
Year	**Event**
1945	Korea divided into two zones, one occupied by United States and the other by Soviet Union.
1948	U.S. Congress approves Marshall Plan to provide some $12 billion in aid to Western Europe over next four years.
	Soviet Union blocks routes between Berlin and West Germany. Western powers meet blockade with Berlin airlift.
	North Korea and South Korea establish separate governments.
	United States and Soviet Union recognize Israel.
1949	NATO formed.
	Chinese Communists win control of China.
1950	Korean War begins when North Korea invades South Korea.
	China enters Korean War.
1955	Warsaw Pact signed.

Sources: *Encyclopedia of American History; Encyclopedia of World History*

STRUGGLE FOR SUPREMACY The United States and the Soviet Union fought to establish political supremacy across the globe through both diplomatic and military means.

? ANALYZING How did the United States attempt to counteract the influence of the Soviet Union?

RETEACH Write each person's name from Identify in the Section 4 Review on a separate slip of paper. Have each student select one of the slips of paper and explain orally that person's role in the events presented in the section.

Closure

Have volunteers summarize why the U.S. became involved in the conflicts in the late 1940s between the Israelis and Arabs in the Middle East, between the Nationalists and Communists in China, and between North and South Korea in the early 1950s. Then ask students if they think the U.S. should have the responsibility for protecting nations from attack by other nations.

Extension

ANALYZE Have students conduct further research into the conflict between Truman and MacArthur over escalating the war in Korea. Have students analyze each person's position and write an essay in which they defend the actions of each.

RESEARCH Have students research and report on the Long March. Encourage them to use maps or other graphics.

lip service to non-aggression and non-intervention. From the information we got, they wanted to calm China first and after occupying North Korea, they will come to attack China. 99

Outnumbered and with their lines dangerously extended, the UN forces fell back. After desperate fighting and heavy losses in the bitter winter cold, MacArthur's troops finally established a stable defensive line near the 38th parallel.

■■ **During the Korean War, UN forces—mainly U.S. and South Korean soldiers—fought North Korean and Chinese troops.**

The great debate. With China now involved, MacArthur called for a major expansion of the war. He proposed to blockade China's coast, bomb the Chinese mainland, and "unleash" Chiang's Nationalist forces to invade mainland China. This plan stirred fierce public debate. Supporters said it would bring victory in Korea and overthrow the Chinese Communists. Opponents argued that an attack on China could bring the Soviet Union into the conflict and trigger World War III.

President Truman strongly opposed MacArthur's plan because he did not want the war in Korea to lead to another world war. MacArthur, however, refused to accept the Korean War as a limited conflict. Publicly criticizing the president, MacArthur appealed to

▲ In September 1950, U.S. soldiers used hand grenades to remove the remaining North Korean forces from Seoul.

Republican leaders in Congress. He also delivered an ultimatum to the enemy—demanding unconditional surrender—thereby upsetting Truman's plans for peace negotiations. As commander in chief of the military, Truman removed MacArthur from his post in April 1951. General Matthew Ridgway replaced MacArthur as commander of the UN forces.

By the summer of 1951, the war had settled into a stalemate. Bitter fighting continued, but little territory changed hands. Combat in Korea's mountainous terrain became intensely frustrating as the American death toll mounted. Under these circumstances American public opinion gradually turned against the war. The Korean conflict would soon become a major issue in the 1952 presidential election.

PRIMARY SOURCE
Description of Change: excerpted
Rationale: excerpted to focus on main idea

SECTION REVIEW ANSWERS

IDENTIFY
For significance, see the following pages:
Zionism (p. 452)
David Ben-Gurion (p. 452)
Ralph Bunche (p. 453)
Chiang Kai-shek (p. 454)
Long March (p. 454)
Mao Zedong (p. 454)
Kim Il Sung (p. 455)
Syngman Rhee (p. 455)
Dean Acheson (p. 456)
Douglas MacArthur (p. 456)
Zhou Enlai (p. 457)

LOCATE
For locations, see the maps on pp. 453, 455 and 772–773.

1. *because of conflict over Palestine*
2. *Korea divided into Soviet and American zones*
3. *UN forces, made up mainly of U.S. and South Korean soldiers, fought North Koreans and Chinese*
4. *Essays should mention the effects of World War II, U.S. involvement, Chiang's policies, Mao's reforms, and the war between the Communists and Nationalists.*
5. *Students might mention the possibility of overthrowing Communists in Korea and China or the chance that war would have involved more countries.*

SECTION 4 REVIEW

IDENTIFY and explain the significance of the following: Zionism, David Ben-Gurion, Ralph Bunche, Chiang Kai-shek, Long March, Mao Zedong, Kim Il Sung, Syngman Rhee, Dean Acheson, Douglas MacArthur, Zhou Enlai.

LOCATE and explain the importance of the following: Palestine, Israel, Gaza Strip, West Bank, Taiwan, People's Republic of China, 38th parallel, Pusan, Seoul, Yalu River.

1. **MAIN IDEA** Why did war break out between Israel and Arab states in 1948?
2. **MAIN IDEA** How did the end of World War II affect Korea?
3. **MAIN IDEA** What forces fought in the Korean War?
4. **WRITING TO EXPLAIN** Write an essay explaining how the Communists gained control of China in 1949.
5. **HYPOTHESIZING** How do you think the Korean War would have proceeded if MacArthur had been allowed to expand the war into China?

Chapter Review Answers

WRITING A SUMMARY

See Essential Points in each section for main ideas.

REVIEWING CHRONOLOGY

5, 1, 3, 2, 4

Identifying Cause and Effect

Answers will vary but should make the cause and effect of events clear.

IDENTIFYING PEOPLE AND IDEAS

1. postwar organization formed to promote international cooperation
2. first UN secretary-general
3. 1944 measure that helped veterans make transition to civilian life
4. African American lawyer appointed to Committee on Civil Rights in 1946
5. States' Rights party formed by southern Democrats to oppose Truman on civil rights
6. Eastern European countries under Soviet control after WW II
7. State Department official who proposed containment doctrine
8. 1946 act that set up civilian control over atomic energy research
9. ardent Zionist and first prime minister of Israel
10. leader of Communist party in China

458

UNDERSTANDING MAIN IDEAS

1. occupied Germany and Japan and set up new governments; held war crimes trials; helped found UN
2. Employment and food exports remained high as plants produced goods to meet consumer spending spree; soaring prices caused inflation.
3. urged Truman to ban discrimination in military and in federal hiring, served on Committee on Civil Rights, threatened civil disobedience; white southern Democrats formed new party
4. inflation, high taxes, and labor unrest; ran an energetic campaign attacking Republican conservatives, "do-nothing" Congress, and Progressives while keeping support of workers and ethnic voters
5. to protect its borders from feared U.S. invasion

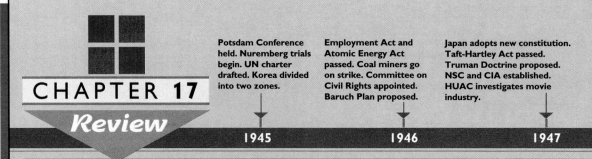

CHAPTER 17
Review

	Potsdam Conference held. Nuremberg trials begin. UN charter drafted. Korea divided into two zones.	Employment Act and Atomic Energy Act passed. Coal miners go on strike. Committee on Civil Rights appointed. Baruch Plan proposed.	Japan adopts new constitution. Taft-Hartley Act passed. Truman Doctrine proposed. NSC and CIA established. HUAC investigates movie industry.
	1945	1946	1947

WRITING A SUMMARY

Using the essential points of the chapter as a guide, write a summary of the chapter.

REVIEWING CHRONOLOGY

Number your paper 1 to 5. Study the time line above, and list the following events in the order in which they happened by writing the first next to 1, the second next to 2, and so on. Then complete the activity below.

1. Committee on Civil Rights appointed.
2. Israel declares its independence.
3. Truman Doctrine proposed.
4. North Korea invades South Korea.
5. UN charter drafted.

Identifying Cause and Effect Select two events on the time line, and in a paragraph, explain the cause-and-effect relationship between them.

IDENTIFYING PEOPLE AND IDEAS

Explain the historical significance of each of the following people or terms.

1. United Nations
2. Trygve Lie
3. GI Bill of Rights
4. Sadie Alexander
5. Dixiecrats
6. satellite nations
7. George Kennan
8. Atomic Energy Act
9. David Ben-Gurion
10. Mao Zedong

UNDERSTANDING MAIN IDEAS

1. How did the United States work with other Allies to restore peace after World War II?
2. Why did postwar fears of a depression never materialize? What effect did the lifting of wartime price controls have on the economy?
3. How did African Americans work for civil rights in the late 1940s? What effect did these actions have on the 1948 election?
4. What factors caused public support for President Truman to plunge by 1948? How did he win the 1948 election?
5. Why did China enter the Korean War on the side of North Korea?

REVIEWING THEMES

1. **Global Relations** What international and domestic tensions resulted from the conflict between the United States and the Soviet Union?
2. **Technology and Society** How did the development of atomic energy affect the United States?
3. **Democratic Values** How did the U.S. government's response to Cold War pressures lead to limitations on civil liberties?

THINKING CRITICALLY

1. **Problem Solving** What steps did the U.S. government take after World War II to make the transition from war to peace?
2. **Analyzing** How did the Taft-Hartley Act attempt to place restrictions on the tactics unions could use to win improvements?
3. **Synthesizing** What were the main causes of the Cold War? How did the Cold War get played out in Korea?

STRATEGY FOR SUCCESS

Review the Strategies for Success on Recognizing Propaganda on page 430. Then read the excerpt below, which comes from an address by J. Edgar Hoover warning of the dangers of communism. What clues identify this passage as propaganda?

> **❝** The Communist Party of the United States . . . is far better organized than were the Nazis. . . . They [the Communists] are seeking to weaken America just as they did . . . when they were aligned with the Nazis. Their goal is the overthrow of our government. **❞**

WRITING ABOUT HISTORY

Writing to Explain Imagine you are an American diplomat in China during 1946. Write a memorandum to President Truman, explaining the reasons for the mounting opposition to Chiang Kai-shek after World War II.

REVIEWING THEMES

1. *international—Cold War, arms race, military confrontations or conflicts in Berlin and Middle East and Asia; domestic—spread of anti-Communist hysteria*
2. *created struggle between those who argued that technology would strengthen U.S. defenses and those who feared that spread of nuclear weapons might lead to war*
3. *Federal employees lost their jobs without being allowed to respond to charges against them. Other government investigations also infringed on free speech and privacy rights in the hunt for suspected Communists.*

THINKING CRITICALLY

1. *acted to help veterans reenter civilian life, promoted full employment and production, controlled labor unrest, and promoted civil rights*
2. *allowed courts to end strikes; outlawed closed-shop agreements; restricted unions' political contributions*
3. *competition between U.S. and U.S.S.R., competing economic and political models, mutual distrust; Communist North Korea, U.S.S.R., and China battled South Korea, U.S., and UN forces*

1948	1949	1950	1951	1952
Racial discrimination banned in military and in federal hiring. Marshall Plan passed. Berlin airlift begins. Israel declares its independence. Dixiecrats formed. Truman elected president.	NATO established. Middle East agreements reached. Communists gain control of China.	Alger Hiss convicted of perjury. Internal Security Act passed. North Korea invades South Korea.	Julius and Ethel Rosenberg convicted.	U.S. occupation of Japan ends.

STRATEGY FOR SUCCESS

use of card-stacking and name-calling by linking Communists and Nazis

WRITING ABOUT HISTORY

Memos should mention Chiang's failure to resolve economic problems, to redistribute land to peasants, and to reform corrupt government.

USING PRIMARY SOURCES

explained his belief in importance of individual rights and argued that the practices being used to ferret out subversives were themselves undemocratic

LINKING HISTORY AND GEOGRAPHY

divided Jerusalem into an Arab east and Jewish west; gave Egypt the Gaza Strip; gave Jordan control of West Bank of Jordan River

USING PRIMARY SOURCES

Attempts to find alleged Communists spread to every level of government. In 1946 President Truman nominated David Lilienthal to head the U.S. Atomic Energy Commission. During Lilienthal's confirmation hearings, Senator Kenneth D. McKellar of Tennessee accused the nominee of being a Communist sympathizer. In Lilienthal's eloquent reply below, how did he defend himself against the charge?

 I believe—and I conceive the Constitution of the United States to rest . . . upon the fundamental proposition of the integrity of the individual. . . .

Any form of government, therefore, and any other institutions which . . . exalt the state or any other institutions above the importance of men, which place arbitrary power over men as a fundamental tenet [belief] of government are contrary to that conception, and, therefore, I am deeply opposed to them.

The communistic . . . form of government falls within this category. . . . The fundamental tenet of communism is that the state is an end in itself, and that therefore the powers which the state exercises over the individual are without any ethical standard to limit them.

That I deeply disbelieve. . . .

I deeply believe in the capacity of democracy to surmount any trials that may lie ahead, provided only that we practice it in our daily lives.

And among the things we must practice is this: that while we seek fervently to ferret out the subversive and anti-democratic forces in the country, we do not at the same time, by hysteria . . . and other unfortunate tactics, besmirch [soil] the very cause that we believe in. 🔊

LINKING HISTORY AND GEOGRAPHY

Refer to the map on page 453. What effect did the 1949 armistice have on both Israeli and Arab territorial boundaries?

BUILDING YOUR PORTFOLIO

Complete the following projects independently or cooperatively.

1. **THE COLD WAR** Imagine that you are a U.S. delegate to the UN conference in San Francisco in 1945. Write a memorandum to the U.S. Senate, detailing world conditions in 1945 that call for the formation of an association of world nations and urging U.S. participation in such an association.

2. **THE GOVERNMENT AND THE ECONOMY** Imagine you are a member of the Department of Labor. Prepare a chart that shows how the U.S. government is assisting returning soldiers through programs designed to help them find civilian jobs, attain college educations, or own their own homes.

3. **CIVIL RIGHTS** Imagine you are a reporter covering the Committee on Civil Rights. Research and prepare a radio piece on why the committee was formed, who its members are, and what it has documented in its official report, "To Secure These Rights."

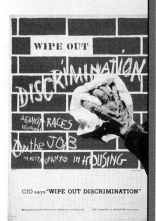

CIO says "WIPE OUT DISCRIMINATION"

BUILDING YOUR PORTFOLIO

Have students refer to **Building Your Portfolio Worksheet 4**, assigned at the beginning of Unit 4. Use the worksheet to help students monitor their progress on the portfolio projects.

Assessment

Core Resources
- Reteaching Worksheet 17
- Chapter 17 Tests
- Alternative Assessment Forms

Test Generator

DECADE OF CONTRASTS

1950–1960

THE AMERICAN NATION VIDEODISC PROGRAM
A variety of still images, short videos, and activities are available for you to use as you teach this chapter. See Videodisc Resources in the Core Resources Binder for barcode correlations and suggestions for using the program.

Chapter Overview

In 1952 Republican Dwight D. Eisenhower was elected president, breaking the Democrats' 20-year hold on the White House. During Eisenhower's presidency Americans continued to focus on the Cold War. As the 1950s drew to a close, however, it seemed possible that U.S.–Soviet relations might improve.

On the domestic front the 1950s were years of great prosperity. Millions of middle-class Americans, living in comfortable suburbs, enjoyed a rising standard of living. But not all shared in this prosperity. Many nonwhites continued to endure prejudice and poverty. By the end of the 1950s, however, many African Americans had begun to push for equality of opportunity.

Chapter Planning Guide

CHAPTER 18	CORE RESOURCES	AUDIOVISUAL RESOURCES	PROGRAM RESOURCES
INTRODUCTION pp. 460–461	■ Literature Worksheet 18 ■ Building Your Portfolio Worksheet 4		■ *Eyewitnesses and Others,* Volume 2: Reading 62
TEACHING THE CHAPTER pp. 462–483 ■ For expanded coverage of pp. 464–466, see Chapter 27, pp. 729–730; for coverage of pp. 471–473, see Chapter 25, pp. 680–681.	■ Graphic Organizer 18 ■ Social Studies Skills Worksheet 18 ■ Geography Worksheet 18 ■ Outline Maps 1, 2, 9, 16, 17, 18, 20	■ *The American Nation* Videodisc: McCarthy and McCarthyism; Bomb Shelters; The Growth of Suburbia; The Interstate Highway System; The Salk Polio Vaccine ■ Linking Geography and History Transparencies and Worksheets 11B, 17A, 20, 21 ■ Everyday Life in America Transparency and Worksheet 28	■ Art in American History Transparencies and Worksheets 36, 37 ■ *Eyewitnesses and Others,* Volume 2: Readings 59, 60, 61
REVIEW AND ASSESSMENT pp. 484–485	■ Chapter 18 Daily Quizzes ■ Reteaching Worksheet 18 ■ Chapter 18 Tests ■ Alternative Assessment Forms		■ Test Generator

Additional Resources

BOOKS FOR TEACHERS

Halberstam, David. *The Fifties.* Random House, 1993. An exhaustive, highly readable review of the decade.

Harvey, Brett. *The Fifties: A Women's Oral History.* HarperCollins, 1993. A study of women's lives in 1950s America.

Inglis, Fred. *The Cruel Peace.* Basic Books, 1993. Study of the myths and realities of the Cold War.

BOOKS FOR STUDENTS

Fried, Richard M. *Nightmare in Red.* Oxford University Press, 1991. Thorough investigation of McCarthyism.

Oakley, J. Ronald. *God's Country: America in the Fifties.* Barricade Books, 1990. Entertaining and informative look at the decade.

*Tames, Richard. *The 1950s: Picture History of the 20th Century.* Watts, 1990. Review of the major issues and events of the decade.

* for students reading below grade level

MULTIMEDIA MATERIALS

The Age of Anxiety. Video, 24 min. AIMS Media. Reviews the Eisenhower years.

The Fragile Balance. Video, 24 min. AIMS Media. Study of the Cold War during the 1950s.

Postwar Hopes, Cold War Fears. Video, 58 min. PBS. Examination of how the Cold War influenced life in the U.S. during the 1950s.

THEMES IN AMERICAN HISTORY

USE WITH PAGES 460–461

Listed on the right are the themes emphasized in Chapter 18. The questions in boldface type stimulate critical thinking and provide students with an opportunity to discuss the themes within a broadened context. The questions also appear in the pupil's edition on p. 460.

■ ECONOMIC DEVELOPMENT

How might an economic boom affect population growth and residential patterns? Students might suggest that economic prosperity could encourage parents to have more children and to seek more affluent neighborhoods, resulting in migration from the cities to the suburbs.

■ CULTURAL DIVERSITY

How can people demonstrate diversity in a society that emphasizes conformity? Students may point out that some people might openly rebel against society. Other people might take a more subtle approach by maintaining ethnic traditions, dressing in nonconformist ways, or challenging mainstream ideas.

■ DEMOCRATIC VALUES

How might a group of people seek to change laws that discriminate against them? Students might suggest that people could challenge those laws in court, stage public protests, and otherwise pressure elected officials to make changes.

CHAPTER STRATEGIES FOR MEETING INDIVIDUAL NEEDS

LIMITED ENGLISH PROFICIENT LEARNERS

Encourage pairs of students to compile a "Then and Now" list about life in the 1950s. Tell them to list key elements of life in the 1950s under the first category. Under the second category, they should indicate whether that element is the same now or explain how it is different.

TACTILE/KINESTHETIC LEARNERS

Have students work in small groups to prepare skits depicting two or three key events of the 1950s. Call on groups to perform their skits.

LEARNERS HAVING DIFFICULTY

Have students work in pairs to create index cards on the key people, places, and terms listed in the chapter's Preview Workshops. One side of the card should list the person, place, or term; the other side should provide pertinent information about the person, place, or term.

AUDITORY LEARNERS

Pair students and assign each pair a person mentioned in the chapter. Have pairs write statements that their assigned person might have said. Call on volunteer pairs to read their statements and have the class identify the person.

VISUAL LEARNERS

Encourage students to use materials in the school and public libraries to locate and photocopy illustrations for a collage that portrays the title of the chapter. Ask volunteers to present and explain their collages to the class.

GIFTED LEARNERS

Direct students to research the impact of the Cold War on everyday life in the U.S. Suggest that they present their findings in an illustrated report.

USING THE CHAPTER FOCUS

■ **UNDERSTANDING THE MAIN IDEA**

Call on a volunteer to read aloud the Understanding the Main Idea paragraph. Then ask students to speculate, based on information in the main idea paragraph, what major developments and trends characterized America during the 1950s. List student responses on a flip chart. Have students evaluate their responses after they have completed the chapter.

 THEMES
Have students work individually or in small groups to answer the questions under Themes. Save students' responses so that they can compare them with their responses after studying the chapter. (See p. 459B for suggested answers.)

■ **THE TIME LINE**

Have students review the time line and point out the entries that concern the Cold War and the entries that concern the civil rights movement. Ask students to construct time lines of the major events of these topics as they read the chapter.

CORE RESOURCES

• Graphic Organizer 18
• Literature Worksheet 18
• Outline Maps 1, 2, 9, 16, 17, 18, 20
• Building Your Portfolio Worksheet 4

ABOUT THE ILLUSTRATION

Point out that the drive for desegregation in the South in part grew out of the experiences of African American military personnel. While serving overseas many African Americans had come into contact with societies different from their own, societies that seemed to pay no heed to their race. African Americans who served in Korea fought in integrated units and returned to the U.S. determined to end racial discrimination and segregation at home. Have students assume the role of the African American airman in the photograph. Ask them to write a journal entry that describes how he might feel about the segregated waiting room.

■ Ask students what methods they might use to combat segregation in public facilities.

Chapter 18

1950–1960

DECADE OF CONTRASTS

FOCUS

UNDERSTANDING THE MAIN IDEA

Though the Korean War came to an end, the Cold War continued in the 1950s, increasing Americans' fears of communism and nuclear war. Meanwhile most Americans experienced economic prosperity, leading white middle-class Americans to move away from cities into suburbs. Popular culture, including television, encouraged conformity, but some groups challenged the practices of American society, especially discrimination against African Americans.

 THEMES

■ **ECONOMIC DEVELOPMENT** How might an economic boom affect population growth and residential patterns?

■ **CULTURAL DIVERSITY** How can people demonstrate diversity in a society that emphasizes conformity?

■ **DEMOCRATIC VALUES** How might a group of people seek to change laws that discriminate against them?

1953	1954	1955	1957	1960
Korean War ends.	Supreme Court issues ruling in *Brown v. Board of Education*.	Montgomery bus boycott begins.	*On the Road* published.	U-2 incident occurs.

■■ LINK TO THE PAST ▶

The end of World War II renewed Americans' optimism about the future. Soon, however, the country was caught up in a Cold War with the Soviet Union. President Truman's commitment to contain the spread of communism led the United States into the Korean War and heightened suspicion that there were Communist spies in America.

HISTORICAL SIDELIGHTS

A Reluctant Candidate

The Democrats and the Republicans both had sought Eisenhower as a presidential candidate in 1948, but he rejected their appeals. Only his announcement that he was a Republican prevented a similar situation from developing in 1952. Republican leaders finally got him to agree to run in 1952 by appealing to his soldier's sense of duty.

United States airman at Atlanta Terminal Station, 1956

*I*n 1952, after 20 years of Democratic rule in the White House, Americans chose Republican Dwight D. Eisenhower for president, echoing the campaign chant "We Like Ike." The Eisenhower era, which occupied much of the 1950s, saw continued conflict in many parts of the world. However, the emergence of new leadership in the Soviet Union raised hopes for a thaw in the Cold War. At home the 1950s brought widespread economic prosperity. The United States had long been the world's richest, most productive nation. Now millions of middle-class Americans enjoyed a rising standard of living, leading many to move away from cities and rural areas into suburbs.

American life was not all rosy, however. Cold War tensions and nuclear-war fears disturbed much of the nation. Moreover, economic prosperity was not shared equally. Rural residents, African Americans, Hispanic Americans, and Native Americans continued to endure poverty and prejudice. By the mid-1950s, however, a new generation of African Americans started to achieve some successes in the long struggle for the equality of opportunity promised in the Fourteenth Amendment.

Watching a 3-D movie, 1953

PREVIEW WORKSHOP

Following is a list of the significant people, places, and terms in this section. You may wish to use this list as a section preview.

People
■ Dwight D. Eisenhower
■ Margaret Chase Smith
■ Nikita Khrushchev

Places
■ Iran
■ Guatemala
■ Suez Canal

Terms
■ hydrogen bomb
■ *Sputnik*
■ National Aeronautics and Space Administration

■ National Defense Education Act
■ brinkmanship
■ Eisenhower Doctrine

Section 1

COLD WAR FEARS

F O C U S

■ **How did the outcome of the Korean War affect Korea?**
■ **What led to Senator Joseph McCarthy's downfall?**
■ **How did President Eisenhower handle threats to U.S. interests in Iran, Guatemala, and Egypt?**
■ **How did the U-2 incident affect the arms race?**

*S*oon after his victory in the 1952 presidential election, Dwight D. Eisenhower kept his campaign promise to end the Korean conflict. But the Cold War continued, generating fears of nuclear weapons and stirring suspicions that Communists had infiltrated every part of American life. On the world stage the Eisenhower administration developed an aggressive policy to fight the spread of communism, while taking steps to improve diplomatic relations with the Soviet Union.

Eisenhower campaign bumper sticker, 1952

*T*HE GENERAL VS. THE EGGHEAD

As 1952 began, President Truman found himself confronted with a host of problems. The Korean War had ground to a bloody stalemate, and peace talks were making little progress. Republicans saw their chance to break the Democrats' 20-year hold on the White House by choosing popular World War II hero General Dwight D. Eisenhower as their presidential candidate. Conservative senator Richard M. Nixon of California served as his running mate.

Truman, recognizing that he had little support even within his own party, decided not to run for reelection. The Democrats selected Governor Adlai E. Stevenson of Illinois as their candidate. Stevenson defended the Fair Deal and Truman's foreign policies. Many voters, however, viewed him as an intellectual out of touch with the common people. Some jokingly referred to Stevenson as an "egghead"—"someone with more brains than hair."

Stevenson also could not match Eisenhower's patriotic appeal. Eisenhower reassured voters that America would remain strong throughout the Cold War. The hero of World War II promised to resist communism and end the Korean War. A triumphant Eisenhower received 55 percent of the popular vote and swept the electoral count 442 to 89.

▼ During the 1952 presidential election, Dwight Eisenhower had promised voters, "I shall go to Korea." Eisenhower fulfilled the promise a month after his presidential victory. Here he is shown eating lunch with his old army outfit.

*T*eaching the *S*ection

THE END OF THE KOREAN WAR

Ask groups of students to imagine they are State Department representatives on a tour of Korea shortly after the signing of the Korean War armistice. Have each group write a report for department officials detailing the impact of the war on Korea, the terms of the armistice, and how the war's outcome might affect future U.S. relations with China and Korea. Call on volunteers to present group reports to the class.

KOREAN WAR ENDS, FEAR CONTINUES

The new president quickly fulfilled his promise to end the war. Eisenhower used military force to get peace negotiations moving. He stepped up bombing raids on North Korea in May 1953 and let it be known that he would use nuclear weapons, if necessary, to end the conflict.

On July 27, 1953, negotiators agreed to an armistice that divided Korea into two nations, Communist North Korea and anti-Communist South Korea, roughly at the 38th parallel—the prewar dividing line. Some Americans questioned whether this outcome in a distant war justified U.S. losses—some 54,000 dead and 103,000 wounded. More than 1.5 million Chinese and Koreans had also died in the conflict. For years after the war, U.S. relations with China and North Korea remained strained.

■■ **The armistice that ended the Korean War created two nations divided at the 38th parallel: North Korea and South Korea.**

The Korean conflict heightened the fears of some that communism was gaining ground in the United States. This anxiety continued even after the war ended. Many Americans became convinced that spies and Communist sympathizers were everywhere. Joseph McCarthy, a U.S. senator from Wisconsin, helped fuel these suspicions.

Senator McCarthy came to public attention in 1950, when he claimed to have a list of known Communists who worked at the State Department. Although he never produced the list, dozens of federal employees lost their jobs after being labeled as "security risks." McCarthy used his position as chairman of the Senate Permanent Subcommittee on Investigations to wage war against all suspected Communist sympathizers in the federal government. With almost no supporting evidence, McCarthy questioned the patriotism—and ruined the reputations—of hundreds of government workers. Many Americans, terrified of communism and the power of the Soviet Union, supported his crusade.

McCarthy's popularity and ruthlessness made many politicians wary of challenging him. One who did, however, was Margaret Chase Smith, a

Republican senator from Maine. Smith was born in the small mill town of Skowhegan, Maine, in 1897. When her husband, Republican congressman Clyde Smith, died in 1940, voters chose her to complete his congressional term.

After four full terms in the house, Smith won a seat in the Senate in 1948, becoming the first woman to be elected to both houses of Congress. Sixteen years later, she became the first woman to seek the Republican nomination for president. When she left the Senate in 1973, her colleagues praised her as a "woman of courage." Smith once said of public service:

Margaret Chase Smith

❝ It must be a complete dedication to the people and to the nation with full recognition that every human being is entitled to courtesy and consideration, that constructive criticism is not only to be expected but sought, that smears are not only to be expected but fought, that honor is to be earned but not bought. ❞

*M*cCARTHY'S DOWNFALL

In 1950 Smith and several other senators issued the "Declaration of Conscience," which condemned those who had turned the Senate into "a forum of hate and character assassination." While she never mentioned McCarthy by name, everyone knew she was referring to him. Few others joined in the condemnation, however. Even President Eisenhower refused to criticize McCarthy.

Most of the critics who did speak out came from the arts or the media. In *The Crucible* (1953), playwright Arthur Miller drew parallels between McCarthyism and the Salem witchcraft trials of 1692. On the television program *See It Now,* newscaster Edward R. Murrow questioned McCarthy's tactics. "We cannot defend freedom abroad," Murrow cautioned, "by deserting it at home." While some viewers praised Murrow, others bombarded him with hate mail.

Teaching the Section

THE ARMY-McCARTHY HEARINGS

Tell students to imagine that they are TV news anchors reporting on the Army-McCarthy hearings. Have them write a 90-second report or commentary on the hearings for the evening news broadcast. Scripts should identify the personalities involved, describe the major incidents, and detail the outcomes. Some students may wish to act as newscasters and "broadcast" their scripts to the class. Use these presentations as a starting point for a class discussion on how the hearings led to McCarthy's downfall. Students may wish to include their scripts in their portfolios.

In 1954 McCarthy's committee investigated charges that Communists had gained a foothold in the U.S. Army. Each day a vast television audience, sometimes as many as 20 million people, tuned in to the Army-McCarthy hearings. McCarthy repeatedly interrupted the circus-like proceedings and frequently ridiculed witnesses. One victim of this treatment said McCarthy "acted like the gangster in a B movie rubbing out someone who had got in his way."

Television exposure of McCarthy's bullying tactics, contrasted with the calm, dignified behavior of army chief counsel Joseph Welch, soon turned public opinion against the senator. At one point when Welch took McCarthy to task for cruelty, the audience in the hearing room broke into applause. A few months later, the Senate—by a vote of 67 to 22—condemned McCarthy for conduct unbecoming a senator.

■■ **McCarthy's behavior during the Army-McCarthy hearings cost him public support.**

NUCLEAR ANXIETY

Americans' fear of nuclear war heightened as the Soviet Union and the United States raced to develop more-powerful nuclear weapons. In 1950 American scientists began work on a **hydrogen bomb**, or H-bomb, which they said would be 1,000 times more powerful than the atomic bomb dropped on Hiroshima and Nagasaki in World War II. The first H-bomb test in 1952 completely vaporized a small island in the Pacific. Some nine months later, the Soviet Union tested their own H-bomb. J. Robert Oppenheimer, one of the creators of the atomic bomb, cautioned:

66 [The United States and the Soviet Union] are like two scorpions in a bottle, each capable of killing the other but only at the risk of his own life.... The atomic clock ticks faster and faster. 99

▲ In the 1950s schools across America frequently took the precaution of holding routine air-raid drills in case of a nuclear attack.

As concerns about nuclear war grew, the government launched a campaign to calm public fears. The federally sponsored book *How to*

THE NUCLEAR ARMS RACE

The testing of increasingly powerful and destructive nuclear weapons by the United States and the Soviet Union in the 1950s alarmed national leaders around the world. In April 1954 Jawaharlal Nehru, Prime Minister of India, voiced his fears:

THROUGH OTHERS' EYES

66 The United States of America and the Union of Soviet Socialist Republics, we are told, possess this [nuclear] weapon and each of these countries has during the last two years effected test explosions, unleashing impacts which in every respect were far beyond those of any weapons of destruction known to man.... We know that its use threatens the existence of man and civilization as we know it.... There can be little doubt about the deep and widespread concern in the world ... about these weapons and their dreadful consequences. But concern is not enough.... We must endeavor with faith and hope to promote all efforts that seek to bring to a halt this drift to what appears to be the menace of total destruction. 99

NUCLEAR ANXIETY

Invite students to imagine that they are a social studies class in the 1950s. Hold a "current events" discussion about proposals for a nuclear test ban. Remind students to keep in mind the Cold War tensions and nuclear anxieties of the time as they role-play the class discussion. Conclude by having students, in their 1950s role, vote on whether they favor or oppose a ban on nuclear testing.

▶

Changing Ways — AMERICANS GO UNDERGROUND

As Cold War tensions and Americans' fear of a Soviet nuclear attack increased in the 1950s, a civil defense craze swept the United States. In 1951 the Federal Civil Defense Administration began a campaign to educate the public on what to do in a nuclear attack. Pamphlets, films, television shows, magazines, and the "Duck and Cover" program for children all encouraged citizens to protect themselves. For example, the *Survival Under Nuclear Attack* booklet urged:

▶ **During the 1950s many children learned about civil defense through the "Duck and Cover" program.**

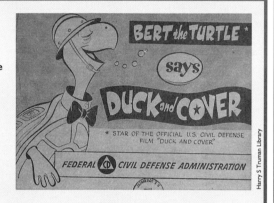

Harry S Truman Library

> 66 You can live through an atom bomb raid and you won't have to have a Geiger counter, protective clothing, or special training in order to do it. The secrets of survival are: KNOW THE BOMB'S TRUE DANGERS. KNOW THE STEPS YOU CAN TAKE TO ESCAPE THEM. 99

Americans' fear increased in 1954 when the U.S. *Bravo* hydrogen-bomb tests in the Pacific Ocean revealed the far-reaching effects of nuclear fallout. The crew of a Japanese

fishing boat 85 miles away from the test site developed radiation sickness. People realized that no one would be safe in a nuclear attack. "The alternatives," one civil defense official said, "are to dig, die, or get out." No one wanted to die, and with little warning of incoming missiles, evacuating would not be possible. So Americans began to dig—constructing an estimated one million backyard fallout shelters by 1960.

Pamphlets like the *Family Fallout Shelter* promoted do-it-yourself home shelters. *Life* magazine even presented building a shelter as a father-and-son project. Shelter manufacturers also sprang up, selling their concrete and steel igloos at county fairs for about $1,500. The typical shelter contained flashlights, a first-aid kit, battery radio,

chemical toilet, and two-week supply of food (mainly canned meats and vegetables) and water. Most shelters were furnished with only metal bunk beds or cots, a table, and chairs, but some had all the comforts of home. One man in Austin, Texas, spent $90,000 on his luxury shelter.

Many people also purchased guns to keep out anyone who tried to enter their shelter during a raid. This survivalist view led many to question the ethics of home bomb shelters. But before this issue could be resolved, the civil defense craze passed. In 1963 the United States, the Soviet Union, and Great Britain signed a treaty ending above-ground nuclear testing. The fear of fallout diminished, and demand for bomb shelters rapidly decreased.

Survive an Atomic Bomb, for example, offered suggestions on how to live through a nuclear attack. Thousands of Americans put these recommendations to use by building backyard bomb shelters. Schoolchildren went through air-raid drills in which they crawled under their desks to protect themselves from radiation.

While a nuclear attack remained only a possibility, radioactive fallout—a by-product of nuclear explosions—already posed a threat. American and Soviet H-bomb tests had spewed tons of radioactive material into the atmosphere. In 1957 Congress held a special hearing on the dangers of radioactive fallout. Defense officials

Changing Ways

AMERICANS GO UNDERGROUND

SETTING THE SCENE

Calls for a civil defense program against nuclear attack came soon after the bombings of Hiroshima and Nagasaki. The scheme taken most seriously during these early days of the atomic age was *urban dispersal*—the resettling of people in small communities in the country's vast open spaces. *Protection in place*—the construction of bomb shelters—replaced dispersal as the most-favored civil defense program during the 1950s.

PRIMARY SOURCE

Description of Change: excerpted
Rationale: excerpted to focus on main idea

THE AMERICAN NATION VIDEODISC PROGRAM

Bomb Shelters

2A   48004   :43

Teaching the Section

FOREIGN-POLICY CONCERNS

Write the following headings on the chalkboard: *Latin America, Middle East, Eastern Europe.* Call on volunteers to identify events that took place in these regions during the 1950s, noting their replies under the appropriate heading. Then ask students to explain how the Eisenhower administration responded to each event. Write answers next to the appropriate event. Have students use information on the chalkboard to discuss how and why U.S. responses to these events differed.

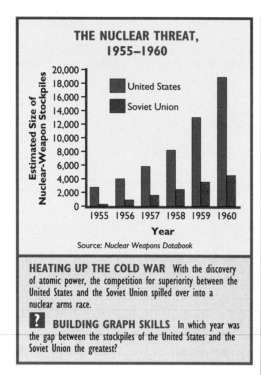

THE NUCLEAR THREAT, 1955–1960

(Bar graph: Estimated Size of Nuclear-Weapon Stockpiles, y-axis 0 to 20,000; x-axis Year 1955, 1956, 1957, 1958, 1959, 1960. Legend: United States, Soviet Union.)

Source: *Nuclear Weapons Databook*

HEATING UP THE COLD WAR With the discovery of atomic power, the competition for superiority between the United States and the Soviet Union spilled over into a nuclear arms race.

? **BUILDING GRAPH SKILLS** In which year was the gap between the stockpiles of the United States and the Soviet Union the greatest?

claimed nuclear testing was perfectly safe, but many scientists argued that radiation released during the tests presented a serious danger to the environment and possibly increased the risk of cancer in human beings. Soon the fear of radiation led to an organized campaign against nuclear testing. In 1957 a group of Americans, including well-known doctor Benjamin Spock, organized the Committee for a Sane Nuclear Policy (SANE). SANE urged the United States to begin negotiations with the Soviet Union to end nuclear tests. Within a year SANE had grown to more than 25,000 members in some 130 chapters across the country.

The arms race surged on, however, especially after the Soviet Union launched the satellite *Sputnik* into orbit around the earth in October 1957. Many Americans feared that this launch proved the United States was falling behind the Soviets in technological development. Eisenhower urged Congress to expand American space technology by establishing the **National Aeronautics and Space Administration** (NASA). In 1958 NASA sent the first American satellite, *Explorer I,* into orbit. That same year Congress approved the **National Defense Education Act**, which appropriated millions of dollars to improve education in science, mathematics, and foreign languages.

✑IGHTING COMMUNISM ABROAD

The Eisenhower administration viewed nuclear arms and technology as central to the government's priority of ending Communist expansion. Secretary of State John Foster Dulles called for the liberation of all nations that had fallen under Soviet control since 1945. To fulfill this aim, the United States would have to confront Communist aggression and not back down—even if that meant going all the way to the brink of war. "The ability to get to the verge without getting into war is the necessary art," Dulles said. This policy of **brinkmanship** rested on the threat of massive retaliation, including the use of nuclear weapons. Eisenhower, however, proved less confrontational than Dulles's policy might have suggested. Instead, he pursued U.S. aims by more covert—secret—means and by diplomacy.

Covert war and the CIA. Eisenhower tested his covert approach to the Cold War in Iran. Shortly after coming to power in 1951, Iranian premier Mohammad Mosaddeq (MAWS-ad-dek) nationalized British-owned oil fields in Iran. After Eisenhower took office he suspended aid to Iran, fearing that nationalization would endanger Western oil purchases. Eisenhower also authorized a covert action by the CIA to organize a military coup against the Iranian leader. The plan, called Operation Ajax, succeeded in having Mosaddeq arrested and replaced with the young pro-American Shah of Iran, Reza Pahlavi (ri-ZAH PAL-uh-vee). While Eisenhower achieved his goal of removing Mosaddeq, this interference in Iranian affairs sowed seeds of anti-American feelings in that country.

In 1954 Eisenhower ordered another covert action, this time in Latin America, where the United States had often intervened in the past. In

"Don't Be Afraid—I Can Always Pull You Back"

◄ The policy of brinkmanship was satirized in this 1956 cartoon. Secretary of State John Foster Dulles is shown pushing Uncle Sam to the brink of war.

from Herblock's Special For Today (Simon & Schuster, 1958)

Organize students into small groups to role-play national security advisers to President Eisenhower. Tell each group to prepare a short report to brief the president about the U-2 incident. Briefings should contain the following elements: 1) background information about the flights and why they were instituted; 2) explanations about what has happened to this flight; 3) suggestions about how to explain this incident to the Soviets. Have groups present their briefings to the class. Then have half the class prepare Eisenhower's message to Khrushchev and the other half prepare Khrushchev's response.

▶

1954 the Guatemalan president, Jacobo Arbenz Guzmán, took possession of uncultivated sections of Guatemala's largest plantations—including those of the American-owned United Fruit Company—to redistribute among the rural poor.

United Fruit Company executives accused the Guatemalan president of being a Communist sympathizer. Eisenhower called on the CIA to gather a small army to oust Arbenz. The CIA-led forces bombed the capital in May 1954 and installed a new pro-U.S. government, which quickly reversed Arbenz's reform program. But American intervention in Guatemala stirred up bitter resentment throughout Latin America.

The Suez crisis. In some cases, Eisenhower used diplomacy rather than covert actions to influence foreign policy. In 1955 the American government offered Egypt financial help to build a large dam at Aswan on the Nile River. However, when Egyptian leader Gamal Abdel Nasser also sought assistance from the Soviet Union, the United States canceled its promised aid. Nasser then seized the Suez Canal, a foreign-owned waterway

MAP LEGEND
- United States and allies
- Soviet Union and allies
- ⊙ Major U.S. base
- ----- North American Defense System (NORAD) Warning line or system
- ✷ Point of conflict

Cold War Defenses

CONTAINMENT The United States ringed the globe with alliances and military bases in an effort to prevent the spread of communism.

❓ **LOCATION** What system did the United States put into place to provide the first warning of a Soviet attack?

that linked the Mediterranean and Red seas (see map on page 561).
Egypt would use canal tolls to build the Aswan Dam, Nasser declared.

Nasser's nationalization of the canal posed many problems, including a threat to the Western oil trade. Egypt also refused to allow ships bound for Israel to pass through the canal. Late in October 1956, Israel launched an attack into Egyptian territory toward the Suez Canal. Great Britain and France, claiming they were protecting

AV TRANSPARENCY
Linking Geography and History Transparency and **Worksheet 20**

MULTICULTURAL PERSPECTIVES

Although the location of Hawaii was a strategic advantage for the U.S., it was not granted statehood until 1959 in part because of the fear of communism. The islands' most powerful union, the International Longshoremen's and Warehousemen's Union, was rumored to be under Communist control. Many members of Congress also were reluctant to create a state with an Asian American majority population that would likely elect Asian Americans to Congress. Indeed, after statehood, Hawaiians elected the first Chinese American senator, Hiram Leong Fong, and a Japanese American congressman, Daniel Ken Inouye.

Map Caption Answer
Ballistic Missile Early Warning System

Practice

GUIDED PRACTICE

Work with the class to create on the chalkboard a time line of events in U.S.–Soviet relations from the Korean War to the U-2 incident. Place each event above or below the line according to class discussion of whether it eased or increased tensions.

INDEPENDENT PRACTICE

Direct students to select an event from the time line developed in the Guided Practice activity. Have them write an "op-ed" column, from the viewpoint of a newspaper columnist living in the 1950s, on how their selected event will affect U.S.–Soviet relations. Call on volunteers to read and discuss their columns. Students may wish to include their columns in their portfolios.

Review and Assessment

REVIEW Provide students with copies of the Preview Workshop list. Direct students to use its people, places, and terms to write a paragraph on Cold War fears in the U.S. Ask volunteers to read their paragraphs to the class. Then assign the Section 1 Review on p. 469.

ASSESS Assign the **Section 1 Daily Quiz** in *Core Resources*.

HISTORICAL SIDELIGHTS

Marines to Lebanon
Nationalist fervor swept across the Middle East in the wake of the Suez crisis. In 1958 a group of army officers killed the king of Iraq and set up a nationalist government. The president of Lebanon, fearing that the new Iraqi government would try to incite unrest in his country, asked the U.S. for assistance. Invoking the Eisenhower Doctrine, the U.S. ordered the marines to Lebanon. As the troops waded ashore, they were greeted by shocked Lebanese sunbathers, who had no idea what was happening.

PRIMARY SOURCE

Description of Change: excerpted
Rationale: excerpted to focus on main idea

MAKING CONNECTIONS

Literature
One outcome of Khrushchev's denunciation of Stalin was a more liberal attitude toward art and artists. For example, the ban on Aleksandr Solzhenitsyn's *One Day in the Life of Ivan Denisovich,* a novel about life in Stalin's prison camps, was lifted. Like Khrushchev's attack, Solzhenitsyn's novel stunned the Soviet people, who were largely unaware of the murderous nature of Stalin's regime.

the canal, seized the Mediterranean end of the waterway a few days later. The Soviet Union threatened war if the three nations did not withdraw from Egypt at once.

The United States faced the difficult task of choosing to support its allies—Britain, France, and Israel—or side with Egypt and the Soviet Union. In the end, Eisenhower supported a UN resolution calling for an immediate cease-fire and the withdrawal of the invading troops. He explained:

> 66 If the United Nations once admits that international disputes can be settled by using force, then we will have destroyed the foundation of the organization and our best hope of establishing a world order. 99

Grudgingly, Britain, France, and Israel withdrew their forces, and the crisis eased.

The Soviet Union's support of Egypt during the Suez crisis bolstered the Soviets' position among the Arab nations. To counter Soviet influence in the Middle East, the president issued the **Eisenhower Doctrine** in January 1957, offering military aid and in some instances American troops to any Middle East nation seeking help in resisting Communist aggression.

■■ **Eisenhower used the CIA to protect U.S. interests in Iran and Guatemala. In the Suez Crisis, he relied on diplomacy.**

Uprising in Eastern Europe. At the same time that the Suez crisis was unfolding, an equally dangerous situation was developing in Eastern Europe. In February 1956 Soviet leader Nikita Khrushchev stunned political observers by denouncing his predecessor, Joseph Stalin, who had died in 1953, for many ruthless crimes. Observers hoped that this move signaled a new era of reform for the Soviet Union and Eastern Europe. Later in 1956, Polish reformers tested Khrushchev by calling for greater political freedom.

Inspired by the example of Poland, thousands of Hungarians took to the streets in late October to demand reform. Moderates seized control of the Hungarian government and called for a Western-style democracy in their nation and for Hungary's secession from the Warsaw Pact. Khrushchev

▲ On November 2, 1956, Hungarian rebels triumphantly waved the tricolored Hungarian flag atop a captured Russian tank. Two days later Soviet troops occupied the main square in front of the Houses of Parliament, where this photograph was taken.

responded with crushing force. On November 4, heavily armed Soviet troops moved into the Hungarian capital, Budapest, and smashed the revolt within days. A new pro-Soviet government imposed martial law and executed or imprisoned the rebel leaders.

Throughout their struggle the Hungarian rebels pleaded for help from the West. Eisenhower worried, however, that intervention in Eastern Europe would lead to all-out nuclear war with the Soviets. He condemned the Soviets' actions but refused to aid the rebels. He did, however, help ease immigration laws to allow more Eastern European refugees into the United States. As a result, some 40,000 Hungarians fled to the United States after the uprising.

To some observers Eisenhower's lack of support for the rebels indicated a retreat from Dulles's talk of liberating Communist-controlled countries. But most of the American public supported Eisenhower, whom they reelected by a landslide against Adlai Stevenson in November 1956.

HOPES RAISED, HOPES DASHED

Near the end of the decade, the United States and the Soviet Union moved to improve their diplomatic relations. In 1959 Vice President Nixon

RETEACH Suggest that students work in small groups, with each student assigned the task of summarizing the information in a subsection by designing a poster. Have groups present their posters.

Closure

Ask a volunteer to define the word *anxiety* for the class. Then point out that the period from the end of World War II to 1960 is sometimes referred to as the "Age of Anxiety." Call on volunteers to discuss whether, based on their study of this section, they would support or challenge this characterization.

Extension

COMPARE Have students compare Truman's and Eisenhower's efforts to stem the spread of communism by answering the following: *Was brinkmanship merely containment under another name? Why or why not?*

RESEARCH Have students consult newspapers and magazines of the period to write a report on how Americans responded to the launching of *Sputnik*.

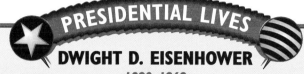

PRESIDENTIAL LIVES

DWIGHT D. EISENHOWER
1890–1969

in office 1953–1961

U.S. 6¢ POSTAGE

DWIGHT D. EISENHOWER

Dwight Eisenhower built his army career slowly. He graduated from West Point in 1915 and worked in an Army camp in Pennsylvania during World War I. Throughout the years between the first and second world wars he moved around the globe, from Panama to the Philippines, becoming a master organizer and coordinator.

In charge of Allied military forces in North Africa in 1943, "he now became," a British colleague explained, "the chairman of a company of great power and resources." As president, Eisenhower continued his military habits of shared leadership. "No man can be a Napoleon in modern war," the president once said. "I don't believe this government was set up to be operated by any one acting alone."

Dwight D. Eisenhower (signature)

---

visited the Soviet Union and Premier Khrushchev came to the United States. Touring Iowa farms, Pittsburgh steel plants, and Hollywood movie studios, the jovial Khrushchev charmed the American media. In Des Moines he jokingly told reporters, "We have beaten you to the moon, but you have beaten us in sausage making." He and Eisenhower agreed to meet at a summit conference in Paris the following year to discuss arms reductions.

In May 1960, however, just before the Paris conference was to open, Khrushchev announced that an American U-2—a high-altitude spy plane—had been shot down over the Soviet Union. At first American officials insisted that it was a

weather-research plane that had strayed off course. But the captured pilot, Francis Gary Powers, admitted he had been on a spying mission.

Khrushchev refused to go ahead with the summit unless the United States halted such spying missions and apologized for past flights. Eisenhower promised that the U-2 flights would stop but did not apologize. Khrushchev refused to meet with Eisenhower again. The brief thaw in the Cold War had come to an abrupt end.

■■ **The U-2 incident halted arms-reduction talks between Khrushchev and Eisenhower.**

SECTION 1 REVIEW

IDENTIFY and explain the significance of the following: Dwight D. Eisenhower, Margaret Chase Smith, hydrogen bomb, *Sputnik*, National Aeronautics and Space Administration, National Defense Education Act, brinkmanship, Eisenhower Doctrine, Nikita Khrushchev.

LOCATE and explain the importance of the following: Iran, Guatemala, Suez Canal.

1. **MAIN IDEA** How did the armistice that ended the Korean War affect Korea?
2. **MAIN IDEA** What effect did the U-2 incident have on relations between the United States and the Soviet Union?
3. **COMPARING** What various tactics did Eisenhower use to protect U.S. interests abroad?
4. **WRITING TO PERSUADE** Imagine you are a reporter covering the Army-McCarthy hearings. Write a commentary explaining why Senator McCarthy should be removed from office.
5. **EVALUATING** What actions by the Soviet Union and the United States heightened Americans' fears of nuclear war?

SECTION REVIEW ANSWERS

IDENTIFY
For significance, see the following pages:
Dwight D. Eisenhower (p. 462)
Margaret Chase Smith (p. 463)
hydrogen bomb (p. 464)
Sputnik (p. 466)
National Aeronautics and Space Administration (p. 466)
National Defense Education Act (p. 466)
brinkmanship (p. 466)
Eisenhower Doctrine (p. 468)
Nikita Khrushchev (p. 468)

LOCATE
For locations, see the maps on pp. 467 and 772–773.

1. *divided Korea, roughly at 38th parallel*
2. *halted arms-reduction talks between Eisenhower and Khrushchev*
3. *used CIA covert actions to overthrow leadership of Iran and Guatemala, used diplomacy during Suez crisis and Hungarian uprising*
4. *Commentaries might mention McCarthy's bullying tactics, "witch-hunt" atmosphere of suspicion.*
5. *H-bomb tests causing radioactive fallout, the start of new arms race after Sputnik launch*

SECTION 2

Introducing the Section

FOCUS OBJECTIVES

- Describe what the economy was like in the 1950s.
- Explain how the population shifted during the decade.
- Describe what early television programming was like.
- Analyze how the work force changed in the 1950s.

Section 2

THE AFFLUENT SOCIETY

FOCUS

- **What was the economy like in the 1950s?**
- **How did the population shift during the decade?**
- **What was early television programming like?**
- **How did the work force change in the 1950s?**

*D*uring *Eisenhower's presidency a rapidly growing economy brought prosperity to many Americans. Newly prosperous whites left the cities for the suburbs, while the rural poor flocked to urban areas in search of jobs. The growth of the suburbs and the spread of television helped create a consumer culture that many of the poorer members of society could not enjoy. Changes in the workplace and the work force also helped transform American society during the 1950s.*

Advertisement for TV dinner

MODERN REPUBLICANISM

President Eisenhower took office in 1953 determined to change the federal government. He pledged to cut the bureaucracy, to curb what he called the "creeping socialism" of the New Deal, to balance the budget, and to reduce government regulation of the economy.

In the first year of his presidency, Eisenhower cut thousands of government jobs and pared billions of dollars from the federal budget. To reduce government influence over the economy, he cut government farm subsidies and turned over federally owned coastal lands for private development.

But despite his pledge to curb "creeping socialism," Eisenhower left the basic social and economic programs of the New Deal–Fair Deal era intact. Under his administration, social security and unemployment benefits expanded, and the minimum wage increased. Eisenhower established the Department of Health, Education, and Welfare, under the supervision of Texan Oveta Culp Hobby. The president also supported the largest increase in educational spending up to that time. This approach to domestic affairs, which Eisenhower described as "conservative when it comes to money and liberal when it comes to human beings," became known as **modern Republicanism**.

Providing funding for social programs, defense, and other government obligations undermined Eisenhower's pledge to balance the federal budget.

◀ As secretary of Health, Education, and Welfare, Oveta Culp Hobby lobbied for legislation providing for a national polio vaccination program.

Teaching the Section

THE 1950s ECONOMY

Organize students into small groups and direct groups to prepare a statement that responds to the following question: *The 1950s—Good Times or Not?* Tell groups to consider such factors as the rate of economic growth, the role of government, who benefited, and who did not. Call on volunteers from each group to present and explain their group's statement to the class.

▶

Only three of the eight budgets he presided over were balanced. Furthermore, during his years in office the federal debt grew by about 9 percent, to $291 billion.

THE "GOOD" YEARS

For many Americans the 1950s was a decade of economic prosperity. The post–World War II spending spree that began in the late 1940s continued into the 1950s. Defense spending, triggered by the Korean War, also boosted growth in the early 1950s. Unemployment and inflation rarely edged above 5 percent. By the mid-1950s more than 60 percent of Americans were earning a "middle-class" income, at that time considered $3,000–$10,000 annually. Never before, the popular media declared, had so many people enjoyed such prosperity. "This is a new kind of capitalism," declared the *Reader's Digest*, "capitalism for the many, not for the few."

Not everyone shared in the good times, however. A 1957 study found nearly 40 million Americans living below or near the poverty line of $3,000 for a family of four. Almost half of the nation's poor lived in rural areas, where they suffered from poor nutrition, inadequate medical care, and lack of education.

■■ The 1950s saw rapid economic expansion and prosperity for many, but the prosperity was not evenly distributed.

PEOPLE ON THE MOVE

The 1950s was a decade of geographic mobility. Millions of newly prosperous whites, especially young couples, moved to the suburbs that sprang up around the nation's cities. At the same time, many poor rural citizens migrated to the cities in search of a better life.

The urban communities. Most of the rural residents who moved to the cities to escape poverty found little improvement in their economic status. By 1960 more than 20 million city dwellers were living in poverty.

While large numbers of poor rural whites flocked to the cities, African Americans constituted

▲ Puerto Rican immigrants developed strong community organizations in their New York neighborhoods. Here, Puerto Rican boys play in the game room of the Good Neighbor Church and Community Center located in Manhattan.

the single largest group in the rural-to-urban movement. In a continuation of the Great Migration, which had begun during World War I (see Chapter 10), African Americans left the South for the industrial cities of the North. This northward movement peaked in the mid-1950s, with the African American population of some northern cities growing by about 2,000 each week.

Wide-scale unemployment caused many Puerto Ricans to leave the island for the mainland. Some 40,000–50,000 migrated annually in the 1950s. About 70 percent of Puerto Rican migrants settled in New York City. Many Mexicans also moved to the States in order to find work. While most immigrants from Mexico had previously settled in rural areas, the new immigrants tended to settle in cities such as Los Angeles, Denver, El Paso, Phoenix, and San Antonio. By 1960 about 80 percent of Hispanic Americans were living in cities.

Relocation under pressure. Thousands of Native Americans also moved to the cities in the 1950s. But unlike other migrants, Native Americans did so under federal pressure. To promote the assimilation of Native Americans into mainstream society, the Eisenhower administration supported passage of the **Relocation Act** of 1956. The act urged Native

▶ In 1958, Native Americans protested when the federal government seized reservation land for a power project in Niagara Falls. This Tuscarora boy was photographed as he walked the picket line.

AV TRANSPARENCY
Linking Geography and History Transparencies and Worksheets 11B, 17A

MAKING CONNECTIONS

Sociology
Poverty in the 1950s was not limited to any particular racial or ethnic group, but certain kinds of people seemed more likely to be poor. For example, nearly one half of all families headed by a woman or someone over the age of 65 were poor. And some 60 percent of poor families were headed by people who had only a grade-school education. Nearly 50 percent of all nonwhite Americans lived in poverty, however.

Teaching the Section

POPULATION SHIFTS

Have students work in small groups to write a script for a five-minute documentary on the population changes that took place in the 1950s. Suggest that students integrate information from the map on p. 472 into their scripts. If video equipment is available, groups may wish to record their documentaries. Call on volunteers to present their documentaries to the class.

MULTICULTURAL PERSPECTIVES

Although thousands of Native Americans relocated to the cities during the 1950s, many eventually returned to the reservations. Native Americans joked that you could send an Indian to the moon without making any arrangements for his return. Just tell him he was being relocated, and he would find his own way home!

Map Caption Answer
the South

AV TRANSPARENCY

Linking Geography and History Transparency and **Worksheet 21**

THE AMERICAN NATION VIDEODISC PROGRAM

The Growth of Suburbia

2B   00599   2:57

Americans to move to urban areas. It even set up relocation offices in major cities to assist newcomers. Many feared that this would deplete the reservations of future leaders and destroy tribal cultures. Oglala Lakota activist Gerald One Feather recalled:

❝ The relocation program had an impact on our . . . government at Pine Ridge [South Dakota]. Many people who could have provided [our] leadership were lost because they had motivation to go off the reservation to find employment or obtain an education. Relocation drained off a lot of our potential leadership. ❞

To hasten relocation, the government adopted a policy of termination in 1953. **Termination** involved ending on a tribe-by-tribe basis the reservation system and most federal funding for Native Americans. Various tribal groups launched protests and lawsuits against the termination policy, considering it an attempt to wipe out Native American communities. By 1958 the Eisenhower administration backed down, saying it would no longer support legislation "to terminate tribes without their consent."

The suburbs. As more poor migrants settled in the cities, many more-prosperous city residents moved to the suburbs. By the end of the decade,

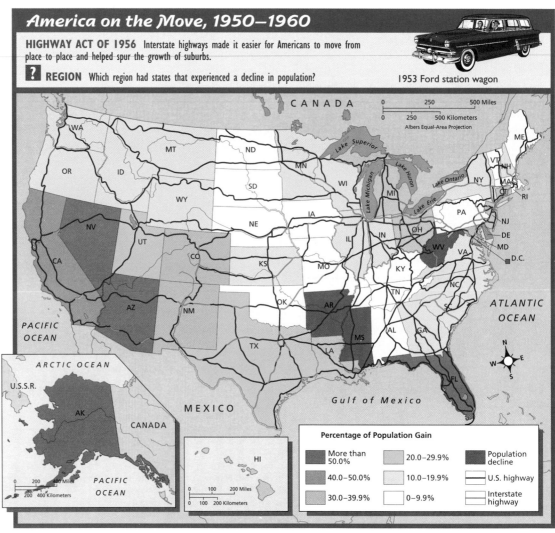

America on the Move, 1950–1960

HIGHWAY ACT OF 1956 Interstate highways made it easier for Americans to move from place to place and helped spur the growth of suburbs.

? REGION Which region had states that experienced a decline in population?

1953 Ford station wagon

Percentage of Population Gain

- More than 50.0%
- 40.0–50.0%
- 30.0–39.9%
- 20.0–29.9%
- 10.0–19.9%
- 0–9.9%
- Population decline
- U.S. highway
- Interstate highway

CONSUMPTION AND CONFORMITY

Call on a student to read aloud the statement by Henry Steele Commager on p. 473 (near top of column 2). Ask students to cite evidence in the section that supports or challenges Commager's statement. Note responses on the chalkboard. Then use the information on the board as the starting point for a class discussion on the validity of Commager's view of American values in the 1950s.

Drawn by Robert Day ©1954, 1982
The New Yorker Magazine, Inc.

"I'm Mrs. Edward M. Barnes. Where do I live?"

▲ **This cartoon satirizing life in the suburbs appeared in *The New Yorker* in 1954.**

close to 60 million Americans—one third of the total population—lived in the suburbs. Many of these suburbs were planned communities.

Suburban growth took off in part because more Americans could afford to purchase homes. Veterans had access to low-interest mortgages from such government agencies as the Veterans Administration (VA) and the Federal Housing Administration (FHA). Private savings and loan associations, too, offered mortgages on relatively easy terms. In addition, the **Highway Act** of 1956 greatly expanded the nation's highway systems, making it easier for suburban residents to commute to jobs in the cities.

The growth of suburbs was also spurred by an expanding population. During the depression and World War II years, many people had postponed getting married or starting a family. After the war, Americans began to get married at earlier ages and in greater numbers than they had for generations. They also had more children. The soaring birth rate accounted for more than 90 percent of the 30-million increase in the population during the 1950s. The decade, many observers said, had experienced nothing less than a **baby boom**.

■■ **Poor whites, African Americans, Hispanic Americans, and Native Americans moved to the cities, while many middle-class Americans moved to the suburbs.**

CONSUMPTION AND CONFORMITY

Suburbanization and prosperity changed the way many Americans lived. Seemingly secure in their jobs and confident of increasing incomes,

Americans went on a buying spree, purchasing between five and seven million new automobiles and an array of household appliances each year.

With an increase in consumerism came a rising emphasis on conformity. Suburban neighbors worked hard to "keep up with the Joneses," or rather, to make sure that they had as many modern conveniences as their neighbors. Scholar Henry Steele Commager noted how conformity affected American values: "What is the new loyalty? It is, above all, conformity. It is the uncritical and unquestioning acceptance of America as it is."

Children became an important focus of suburban life, largely because of the baby boom. Many social activities in the suburbs involved children, such as scouting, music lessons, and athletics. The number of children in schools increased by some 10 million in the 1950s.

The baby boom also led to an emphasis on child rearing, focusing on the role of mothers. Popular magazines, advertisements, and self-help books depicted the perfect wife and mother as a full-time homemaker who devoted all of her energy to making her family happy (and buying all the latest household gadgets). Contrary to these popular images, however, the number of working mothers actually *increased* during the 1950s, from about 3.6 million to some 6.6 million. By the end of the decade, over 39 percent of all women with children ages 6 to 17 worked for wages outside the home.

CHANGES IN MATERIAL STANDARDS OF LIVING, 1940–1955

Households Owning	1940	1955
Automobile	50.0%	71.0%
Television Set	0.0%	76.1%
Refrigerator	44.0%	94.1%
Washing Machine	46.0%	84.1%
Clothes Dryer	0.0%	9.2%
Vacuum Cleaner	38.0%	64.3%

Sources: *The Overworked American; 1956 Statistical Abstract; An Economic History of Women in America; The Proud Decades*

"THE GOOD LIFE" After World War II many American consumers rushed to buy the latest in modern conveniences.

? **BUILDING CHART SKILLS** Which item experienced the greatest increase in ownership?

MAKING CONNECTIONS
Geography

The great surge in suburban housing construction was led by William Levitt. An admirer of Henry Ford, Levitt in the late 1940s adapted mass-production techniques to the building of communities of modestly priced, small, almost identical single-family homes. By the end of the 1950s, other contractors had jumped on the bandwagon, and such developments dotted the outskirts of every major American city.

Chart Caption Answer
television set

*T*eaching the *S*ection

TELEVISION IN THE 1950s

Call on volunteers to role-play a panel of 1950s network television programming executives who are presenting their new programs at a news conference. Have the rest of the class act as reporters and ask the panel questions on the social relevance of the programs, whether or not the programs accurately reflect life in America, and if and how the programs support American values.

■■ Conclude the role-play activity by asking students to identify in what ways the television programs of the 1950s differ from those of today.

HISTORICAL SIDELIGHTS

Working Wives

During the 1950s the wages of the typical working wife boosted the total family income by between 15 and 25 percent.

HISTORICAL SIDELIGHTS

Quiz Show Scandals

Quiz shows were among the most popular television programs. *The $64,000 Question,* for example, regularly drew 85 percent of the audience in its time slot. But the elements of drama and suspense that made these shows so popular proved to be artificial. A 1959 congressional investigation revealed that most of them were rigged. Popular contestants often were given the correct answers beforehand. Some even were coached on ways to answer that would add tension to the show. Such deception led the Federal Communications Commission (FCC) to set strict regulations for television quiz shows.

[AV] TRANSPARENCY

Everday Life in America Transparency and **Worksheet 28**

PRIMARY SOURCE

Description of Change: excerpted

Rationale: excerpted to focus on main idea

▲ The stereotypical "happy housewife" was often used in 1950s advertisements to sell household products to female shoppers.

While it had long been common for mothers of poor families to work for wages, an increasing number of women in the work force were middle-class suburban mothers. Despite the media's image of the typical middle-class family as a stay-at-home wife supported by a well-employed husband, many families needed a second income to share in the middle-class consumer culture. Many of the jobs held by these women were part-time or low-level jobs with little long-term career potential.

Just as the reality of working mothers conflicted with media images of the suburban housewife, so too did the reality of domestic life. Though advertisements portrayed the full-time suburban homemaker as happy and satisfied, many experts argued that isolation at home made women "bored stiff," especially after their children left home. Indeed, many stay-at-home suburban mothers longed to pursue career opportunities once their children were older. Writer Benita Eisler recalled:

❝ For our generation of housewives and mothers, "getting it over with" was our promise to a future deferred. We would "do something" with our college education (or finish it) when we "got out from under" diapers, formulas, car pools. ❞

*T*HE GOLDEN AGE OF TELEVISION

Television helped to reinforce both consumerism and mythical images of American life. By the end of the 1950s, 46 million households owned at least one television set. According to a 1950 survey the average junior high student watched 27 hours of television per week.

Advertising played a major role in television programming. By 1960, advertisers were spending $1.6 billion trying to convince viewers to buy their products. Often one business would sponsor a show, such as *General Electric Theatre* and *Kraft Television Theatre,* so that viewers immediately connected the program with a company. This monopoly on advertising also gave many companies great control over program content. During the height of McCarthyism, many sponsors had actors and writers fired from shows because of their suspected political beliefs.

Sporting events, comedies, variety programs, and quiz shows—such as the World Series, *Your Show of Shows,* and *The $64,000 Question*—shared the airwaves with serious dramas in the early years of television. The most popular program of the decade was the comedy *I Love Lucy,* starring Lucille Ball and Desi Arnaz. Thousands of fans tuned in every week to witness Lucy's slapstick antics. Seventy percent of television viewers tuned in when the character gave birth to a baby boy in one episode.

Though television grew in popularity, it proved a very selective mirror, showing primarily white, middle-class, suburban experiences. Poverty, if shown at all, was a problem all but solved. Working women, ethnic minorities, and inner-city life rarely appeared. When they did, it was usually in a way that reinforced stereotypes.

▼ In 1993, *TV Guide* magazine rated the *I Love Lucy* show as the best sitcom in television history.

CHANGES IN THE WORK FORCE

Encourage students to imagine they are members of an AFL–CIO study group preparing a report on changes in the work force. Suggest that they address the following in their reports: how and why the nature of work changed, which new groups of workers joined the labor force, and how and why organized labor should change its tactics and goals to keep pace with these changes. Call on volunteers to present their reports to the class. Students may wish to include their reports in their portfolios.

Then and Now — PESTICIDES

The 1950s was a decade in which science was king. New discoveries in biology, chemistry, and physics led many to believe that scientific research held the answers to all of the nation's, and even the world's, problems. This was especially the case in agriculture.

The production and use of chemical pesticides and fertilizers soared in the 1950s. One insecticide in particular was hailed as a modern miracle—dichlorodiphenyl-trichloroethane (DDT). DDT and similar pesticides promised farmers increased crop yields and reduced labor expenses. Consumers would benefit as well with higher quality food at a lower cost. These modern chemicals seemed to be a dream come true.

But amid all the praise, Rachel Carson, a former biologist with the U.S. Fish and Wildlife Service, asked, "What has already silenced all the voices of spring in countless towns in America?" In 1962

Carson sent the world a startling message in her book *Silent Spring*. She warned that the indiscriminate use of pesticides, particularly DDT, killed wildlife and polluted the environment. Carson cited a Michigan town that sprayed DDT to kill beetles attacking the town's elm trees. When the elm leaves fell in the fall, they were eaten by worms, which were then eaten by robins. By early spring, almost all the robins in the city were dead.

▲ Workers spray pesticides on fruit trees.

Today, views on the use of DDT and other pesticides have changed dramatically. Public opinion and that of the scientific community now firmly stand behind many of Carson's ideas.

Since the 1960s, possible evidence of cancer and other health problems in field workers and children exposed to DDT has surfaced. And traces of DDT have been found in penguins and seals in Antarctica and in whales off the coast of Greenland—areas far removed from any application of the chemical.

As a result, in 1972 the Environmental Protection Agency (EPA) ordered a ban on domestic uses of DDT, and by the mid-1980s the agency had made addressing pesticide pollution a priority. Now the chemical industry, research scientists, and environmental groups are experimenting with a variety of natural biological controls, such as fungi, bacteria, and "beneficial" insects, to destroy harmful pests.

Carson died in 1964, too soon to see the results of her efforts. Her concerns and warnings inspired a generation of Americans to work toward finding ecologically safe pesticides and fertilizers.

One of the era's most controversial programs was the popular comedy about black urban life, *Amos 'n' Andy*. The show began as a radio program with two white men creating the voices of black characters. When the show moved to television, African American actors took over the roles; but to many viewers, the characters reflected white stereotypes of the black community. The NAACP launched a protest against the program, arguing that it portrayed African Americans as "lazy, dumb and dishonest." Others joined in the protest, and in 1953 *Amos 'n' Andy* left the air. In 1966 the network banned it from being shown in reruns.

■■ **Television provided a variety of programs but often reinforced stereotypes of ethnic groups, women, and American life.**

Practice

GUIDED PRACTICE

On the chalkboard construct a chart with *Moving to the City, Forced Movement,* and *Moving to the Suburbs* as horizontal headings, and *Who, Why,* and *Impact* as vertical headings. Call on volunteers to offer entries for the chart and note their responses.

INDEPENDENT PRACTICE

Have students work individually to create charts, similar to that constructed in the Guided Practice activity, on life in America during the 1950s. Suggest that they use such horizontal headings as *Economic Growth, Poverty and Prosperity, Population Changes, Consumerism, Television,* and *Changes in the Workplace.*

Review and Assessment

REVIEW Suggest that students write the main ideas of the section in the form of newspaper headlines. Ask volunteers to present their headlines to the class. Then assign the Section 2 Review on p. 477.

ASSESS Assign the **Section 2 Daily Quiz** in *Core Resources.*

MAKING CONNECTIONS

Economics

By the end of the 1950s, some 600 corporations—less than one half of 1 percent of all corporations in the U.S.—accounted for more than 50 percent of all corporate income.

PRIMARY SOURCE

Description of Change: excerpted
Rationale: excerpted to focus on main idea

MAKING CONNECTIONS

Sociology

Most women—some 65 percent by 1960—worked in what was called the "pink collar ghetto." This was a work setting in which the majority of employees were women holding low-paying jobs with little opportunity for promotion.

CHANGES IN THE WORKPLACE

Many of the social shifts in America were related to shifts in the work force. Large corporations prospered during the decade. Some 5,000 companies merged together to form larger companies.

Automation. American factories were also changing. Throughout the 1950s companies introduced machines that could perform industrial operations faster and more efficiently than human workers could. This process of **automation** greatly increased productivity. But automation also reduced the number of manufacturing jobs. Many workers began to fear an automated future, as one popular song noted:

> ❝ I walked, walked, walked into the
> foreman's office.
> To find out what was what.
> I looked him in the eye and said,
> "What goes?"
> And this is the answer I got:
> His eyes turned red, then green,
> then blue
> And it suddenly dawned on me—
> There was a robot sitting in the seat
> Where the foreman used to be. ❞

Automation affected America's farms as well, as new machinery boosted production while reducing the labor force. While farm productivity

increased from 1950 to the 1960s, the farm population shrank from 23 million to 15.6 million.

At the same time the number of manufacturing and farming jobs decreased, professional and service jobs increased. Huge new corporations required a multitude of managers, supervisors, and clerical workers. Furthermore, the spending spree of the 1950s created millions of retail jobs. Many of the newly created service jobs were in occupations traditionally filled by women, such as nursing, teaching, retail sales, and clerical work. By 1960, women made up about one third of the total work force. But many women continued to earn much less than men in the same fields, and few received promotions to management jobs.

The new union style. Changes in the work force also influenced organized labor. Boosted in part by the merger of the AFL and CIO in 1955, union membership grew steadily in the mid-1950s, peaking at some 18.5 million in 1956.

To help workers get their fair share of economic prosperity, union leaders abandoned efforts at economic, political, and social reforms in favor of achieving gains in wages and benefits. In order to do so, they sought accommodation, rather than confrontation, with management. George Meany, the AFL–CIO's first president, boasted that he had never led a strike. Further, he said he had no interest in reforming society. His only goal, he stated, was to ensure "an ever rising standard of living" for his members.

Many unions fought for and won guaranteed annual wages and cost-of-living adjustments—automatic pay raises linked to the rate of inflation. In return, unions made concessions, such as accepting automation plans or changes in work rules or production levels.

In the late 1950s newspapers reported corruption and links to organized crime among some union officials. Congress attempted to crack down on union corruption by passing the **Landrum-Griffin Act** of 1959, which banned ex-convicts from holding union offices, required frequent elections of officers, and regulated the investment of union funds. The negative publicity hurt union membership, which steadily declined after 1957.

■■ **The work force changed through automation, an increase in professional and service jobs, and a new approach by union leaders.**

▲ Ford Motor Company closed its Somerville, Massachusetts, plant in 1958. Over 1,000 employees were directly affected by the decision.

RETEACH Organize students so that a roughly equal number are assigned to each subsection of Section 2. Direct each student to write a question about the material in his or her assigned subsection. Then use the questions to quiz the entire group.

Closure

Ask students to use evidence from the section to support or challenge the use of the phrase *the affluent society* as a description of America in the 1950s.

Extension

INVESTIGATE Have pairs of students investigate information about 1950s television programs. Have pairs write a brief synopsis—length, major characters, plot line, and so on—for each program.

CREATE Have students work individually or in small groups to design a poster promoting or criticizing President Eisenhower's modern Republicanism. Call on volunteers to explain their posters.

URBAN RENEWAL

The changing work force also affected those moving to the cities. Automation had eliminated many of the semiskilled jobs traditionally taken by city newcomers. Skilled workers often found that their way to better jobs was blocked by discrimination.

Nowhere was discrimination more obvious than in housing. Prevented by poverty and by discriminatory real-estate practices from moving into newer neighborhoods, African Americans, Hispanics, and Native Americans were generally limited to crowded tenements and old housing in the poorest neighborhoods. Eventually, however, these neighborhoods provided a sense of community for those who lived there. Local stores, churches, and social clubs gave structure to the lives of those struggling to adjust to the cities. As one resident of El Barrio, New York's Puerto Rican neighborhood, observed:

66 This is our neighborhood. . . . We consider this part of the city to be ours. . . . The stores, barbershops, restaurants, butcher shops, churches, funeral parlors, . . . everything is all Latino. 99

Government officials, however, saw only neglected, shabby buildings. To improve inner-city housing, the federal government proposed **urban renewal** programs to replace old, run-down inner-city buildings with new ones. Across the country the government bulldozed older urban neighborhoods to

▲ **A poor family crowds into the kitchen of a small tenement in Harlem, New York City.**

make way for some 417,000 low-income public housing units. Most of these units were cramped apartments, so small, one resident said, "You feel like you can't breathe." The new buildings also had a cold, unfriendly atmosphere. The sense of community that people had felt in the old neighborhoods was gone.

SECTION REVIEW ANSWERS

IDENTIFY
For significance, see the following pages:
Oveta Culp Hobby (p. 470)
modern Republicanism
(p. 470)
Relocation Act (p. 471)
termination (p. 472)
Highway Act (p. 473)
baby boom (p. 473)
automation (p. 476)
George Meany (p. 476)
Landrum-Griffin Act (p. 476)
urban renewal (p. 477)

1. *Poor whites, African Americans, Hispanics, and Native Americans moved to cities; many in middle class moved to suburbs.*
2. *automation, increase in professional and service jobs, new approach by union leaders*
3. *because of economic expansion and spreading prosperity; emphasis on conformity and consumerism*
4. *Articles might argue that TV perpetuates ethnic stereotypes, rarely shows women with careers, portrays families as white, middle-class suburbanites with wage-earning father and homemaker mother.*
5. *crowded minorities into run-down tenements; replaced old neighborhoods with public housing that lost community atmosphere*

SECTION 2 REVIEW

IDENTIFY and explain the significance of the following: Oveta Culp Hobby, modern Republicanism, Relocation Act, termination, Highway Act, baby boom, automation, George Meany, Landrum-Griffin Act, urban renewal.

1. **MAIN IDEA** Describe the shifts in population that occurred during the 1950s. How did these shifts affect city residents?
2. **MAIN IDEA** What changes occurred in the work force during the 1950s?
3. **IDENTIFYING CAUSE AND EFFECT** Why are the 1950s considered boom years? How were American values affected by the economic boom?
4. **WRITING TO EVALUATE** Imagine you are a television critic during the 1950s. Write an article for *TV Guide* that assesses the portrayal of ethnic groups, women, and families on television.
5. **GAINING A MULTICULTURAL PERSPECTIVE** What effect did discrimination in housing have on ethnic groups? Why were some ethnic communities upset with urban renewal programs?

SECTION
3

*Introducing
the Section*

FOCUS OBJECTIVES

■ Explain why the *Brown* v. *Board of Education* decision and the Montgomery bus boycott were major turning points for the civil rights movement.

■ Determine what the Central High School crisis demonstrated about some white southerners' attitudes toward desegregation.

■ Describe how teenagers rebelled against the conformity of the 1950s.

PREVIEW WORKSHOP

Following is a list of the significant people, places, and terms in this section. You may wish to use this list as a section preview.

People
■ Thurgood Marshall
■ Rosa Parks
■ Martin Luther King, Jr.
■ Orval Faubus

■ Ralph Ellison
■ Jack Kerouac

Places
■ Topeka, Kansas
■ Montgomery, Alabama
■ Little Rock, Arkansas

Terms
■ *Brown* v. *The Board of Education of Topeka*

■ Montgomery Improvement Association
■ "Little Rock Nine"
■ Civil Rights Act of 1957
■ Beats
■ silent generation
■ juvenile delinquency
■ rock 'n' roll

Section 3

VOICES OF DISSENT

F O C U S

■ **Why were the *Brown* v. *Board of Education* decision and the Montgomery bus boycott major turning points for the civil rights movement?**

■ **What did the Central High School crisis demonstrate about some white southerners' attitudes toward desegregation?**

■ **How did teenagers rebel against the conformity of the 1950s?**

*A*lthough politics and popular culture in the 1950s emphasized conformity, a few voices spoke out against the system. African Americans, tired of segregation and discrimination, launched the civil rights movement to demand equality. Meanwhile writers, including the Beats, and a new style of music called rock 'n' roll sowed the seeds of rebellion in teenagers.

Rebel Without a Cause
movie poster

*B*ROWN v. BOARD

The NAACP had long waged a campaign against segregation in education, a practice upheld by the Supreme Court's 1896 "separate but equal" doctrine in *Plessy* v. *Ferguson* (see Chapter 4). The NAACP had been able to open some all-white universities and graduate schools to African American students by demonstrating that in most cases separate educational facilities for black students were far inferior to the facilities established for whites only. But the Court continued to maintain that segregation in and of itself was legal.

In 1952 a group of cases that challenged segregation in public schools came before the Supreme Court in the form of *Brown* v. *The Board of Education of Topeka*. The case involved Linda Brown, a young African American student from Topeka, Kansas. Segregation in Topeka's schools prevented her from attending an all-white elementary school a short walk from her home. Instead, she had to travel a long distance over dangerous railroad tracks to get to an all-black school.

Arguing on Brown's behalf, NAACP lawyer Thurgood Marshall introduced data that suggested segregation psychologically damaged African American students by lowering their self-esteem.

▼ **Thurgood Marshall (center) discussed legal strategies for fighting school segregation cases with other NAACP attorneys in 1954.**

MOTIVATING: LINK TO TODAY

Ask students who they think are today's voices of dissent in the U.S. Encourage students to identify the issues protested and the methods used by these persons. Then, as students read the section, have them compare the nature of dissent in the 1990s to dissent in the 1950s.

Teaching the Section

THE CIVIL RIGHTS MOVEMENT

Encourage students to imagine they are involved in the civil rights struggle in the South during the mid-1950s. Have them write a letter to a friend, explaining how they think the Supreme Court decision in *Brown* v. *Board of Education* and the Montgomery bus boycott will affect the civil rights movement and life for African Americans in the future. Call on volunteers to read their letters to the class. Students may wish to include their letters in their portfolios.

▶

Marshall's arguments greatly influenced the Court's ruling, which was issued on May 17, 1954. Written by Chief Justice Earl Warren, the unanimous decision declared that segregation generated

> 66 a feeling of inferiority . . . that may affect [children's] hearts and minds in a way unlikely ever to be undone. . . . In the field of education the doctrine of "separate but equal" has no place. Separate educational facilities are inherently unequal. 99

Many Americans praised the decision as a long overdue step toward ending segregation entirely. Scholar Allison Davis hailed it as the salvation of American industry because it would create more skilled black workers: "The survival of the United States seems to depend upon its developing the ability of millions of our citizens whose capacities have been crippled by segregation."

Some states moved quickly to end school segregation. Many white southern leaders, however, reacted to the decision with alarm. The governor of Virginia, for instance, vowed to use every legal means at his command to maintain segregated schools in his state. Because of the resistance from the South, the Supreme Court issued a ruling in 1955 calling on the federal district courts to end school segregation "with all deliberate speed."

THE MONTGOMERY BUS BOYCOTT

The NAACP next aimed at ending segregation on southern transportation systems, beginning their efforts in Montgomery, Alabama. Local NAACP leaders had been looking for a test case to challenge the practice of forcing African American citizens to ride in the back of buses. On December 1, 1955, Rosa Parks, a black seamstress, provided them with their case when she refused to give up her bus seat to a white passenger.

BIO GRAPHY Born in 1913 in Tuskegee, Alabama, Rosa Parks moved to the Montgomery area at a young age. Her mother was determined that Parks would receive a good education. Montgomery did not have a high school for black students, so her parents sent her to the laboratory school at Alabama State College. Because discrimination prevented her from finding a job that matched her education, she found work as a seamstress. She also became involved in the civil rights movement, holding office in the Montgomery chapter of the NAACP.

In the late 1950s Parks moved to Detroit, where she began working for Congressman John Conyers in 1967. She has continued her commitment to civil rights action and has won numerous awards, including the NAACP's Spingarn Medal, recognizing the "highest or noblest achievement" by an African American.

Rosa Parks

Parks's refusal to give up her seat led to her arrest and conviction for violating the city's segregation laws. In protest, Montgomery's 50,000 African Americans organized a boycott against the bus system. The **Montgomery Improvement Association** (MIA), a group of local civil rights leaders, persuaded the community to continue the boycott while the NAACP and Parks fought her conviction in the courts.

The MIA chose as its spokesperson Martin Luther King, Jr., a 26-year-old Baptist minister who was new to the town. An energetic and charismatic speaker, King could inspire large audiences. His ability to move people helped hold the African American community together as the bus boycott dragged on for months.

White racists tried every method from intimidation to physical violence to break the boycott. White vigilantes attacked and beat boycotters and bombed the houses of King and other MIA leaders. Many boycotters—including Rosa Parks—lost their jobs. But King urged the black community not to respond to violence with more violence. Finally, the peaceful protest worked. In November 1956 the Supreme Court declared both the Montgomery and the Alabama segregation laws unconstitutional. By the end of the year, Montgomery had a desegregated bus system, and the civil rights movement had a new leader—Martin Luther King, Jr.

The successful struggle of thousands of Montgomery blacks to win their basic human rights marked a blow to conformity—and to the general fear of standing up against those in power engendered by Cold War hysteria in America. Not surprisingly, Martin Luther King, Jr., was accused of being a Communist by many who opposed the movement. Some southern whites, however, reluctantly accepted that change had to

---

PRIMARY SOURCE

Description of Change: excerpted and bracketed
Rationale: excerpted to focus on main idea; bracketed to clarify meaning

HISTORICAL SIDELIGHTS

A Southern Manifesto
In 1956 more than 100 southern members of Congress issued a "Southern Manifesto" condemning the Supreme Court's *Brown* ruling as "a clear abuse of judicial power." Only 23 southern members of the House and only 3 southern senators, Lyndon Johnson of Texas among them, refused to sign the document.

HISTORICAL SIDELIGHTS

Spreading the Word
To publicize the boycott, Jo Ann Robinson, a teacher at Alabama State College, stayed up all night printing 35,000 handbills, which she and some of her students distributed throughout the city on the morning of December 2. A local white reporter got one of the handbills and wrote a story on the boycott for his newspaper's December 4 edition. This further helped spread word of the boycott to local African Americans.

Teaching the S*ection*

CENTRAL HIGH SCHOOL CRISIS

Have students work together to produce a *You Are There* program on the events surrounding the desegregation of Central High School in Little Rock. Assign students roles such as reporters, politicians, African American students, white students, school officials, members of the National Guard, African American bystanders, liberal white bystanders, and white segregationists. After students have presented their program, have them discuss the impact of the Central High crisis on the attitudes of whites and African Americans toward segregation.

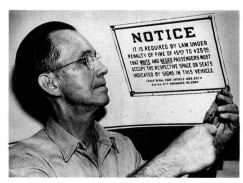

▲ In response to a 1956 court ruling, Dallas buses were ordered to end segregation. Shown here is an employee of the Dallas Transit Company removing a separate seating sign from the rear of a bus.

come. As a South Carolina newspaper declared, "Segregation is going—it's all but gone. . . . The South can't reverse the trend." Even so, other white southerners fought to delay change for as long as possible.

■■ *Brown* v. *Board of Education* and the Montgomery bus boycott marked the first steps toward ending segregation in the South.

S**HOWDOWN IN LITTLE ROCK**

Despite the Supreme Court rulings, school desegregation in the South moved slowly. By the end of the 1956–57 school year, the vast majority of southern school systems remained segregated. In Arkansas, however, school desegregation was progressing with relatively little opposition. Two of the three southern school districts that began desegregation in 1954 were in Arkansas. The Little Rock school board was the first

▶ Elizabeth Eckford bravely walked alone through a crowd of angry, jeering whites before she was turned away from entering Little Rock's Central High School.

in the South to announce it would comply with the *Brown* decision.

Little Rock's desegregation plan was set to begin in September 1957 with the admission of nine black students to the all-white Central High School. However, Governor Orval Faubus, about to embark on a bid for reelection, came out against the desegregation plan. The night before school was to start, he ordered the Arkansas National Guard to surround Central High. He did so, he claimed, to protect the school from attacks by armed protesters. "It will not be possible to restore or to maintain order . . . if forcible integration is carried out tomorrow in the schools of this community," he warned.

No real danger existed, but Faubus's claims panicked the community. When the black students attempted to enter the school, a mob of angry whites and a line of armed National Guardsmen met them. One of the students, Elizabeth Eckford, described the ordeal:

> ❝When I got in front of the school, . . . I didn't know what to do. . . . Just then the guards let some white students through. . . . I walked up to the guard who had let [them] in. . . . When I tried to squeeze past him, he raised his bayonet, and then the other guards moved in. . . . Somebody [in the crowd] started yelling, "Lynch her! Lynch her!"❞

For nearly three weeks the National Guard prevented the students, now known as the "**Little Rock Nine**," from entering the school. Then under

▲ On November 4, 1957, leaders of the Arkansas branch of the NAACP appeared in court to fight an ordinance forcing them to turn over confidential records. State president Daisy Bates (second from the left) played a central role in helping the Little Rock Nine integrate Central High School.

court order, Faubus removed the National Guard. When the nine attempted to enter the school on September 23, the white mob rioted. Deploring the "disgraceful occurrences" at Central High, President Eisenhower ordered some 1,000 federal troops to Little Rock. On September 25, 1957, under the troops' fixed bayonets, the Little Rock Nine finally entered Central High.

In the midst of the Little Rock crisis, President Eisenhower signed the **Civil Rights Act of 1957**. This act, the first civil rights law since Reconstruction, made it a federal crime to prevent qualified persons from voting. It also set up the federal Civil Rights Commission to investigate violations of the law. A follow-up law, passed in 1960, strengthened the courts' powers to protect blacks' voting rights. But prejudice and discrimination continued to be a fact of life for most African Americans. Much remained to be done before they could claim victory in the struggle for civil rights.

■■ The Central High crisis in Little Rock showed that some southern whites were not willing to comply with desegregation.

*R*EBELS AMID CONFORMITY

While the African American community in the South was challenging segregation, other groups were beginning to question the American culture of consumption and conformity. One such group included a handful of writers and scholars who sought to expose what one called the "crack in the picture window" of society.

A number of novelists depicted the experiences of those facing poverty and discrimination. In Ralph Ellison's *Invisible Man* (1952), an African American man searches for his place in a society at once both hostile and indifferent to him. His struggle reflects that of many people left out of mainstream society:

❝I am an invisible man. . . . I am a man of substance, of flesh and bone, fiber and liquids—and I might even be said to possess a mind. I am invisible, understand, simply because people refuse to see me. ❞

Other critics attacked suburban society and the corporate mentality of America. Harvard economist John Kenneth Galbraith warned privileged Americans in *The Affluent Society* (1958) that they were ignoring pressing social issues in their pursuit of material possessions and comfort.

Sociologists William Whyte, C. Wright Mills, and David Riesman criticized the new corporate system. Whyte in *The Organization Man* (1956) and Mills in *White Collar* (1951) argued that the need to conform in a large corporation was wiping out the independent spirit of workers. Riesman argued that the country was facing "a silent revolution against work" because work no longer had meaning for people. Many younger Americans were beginning to agree with him.

The **Beats**, a small but influential group of writers and poets, challenged both the literary

▲ Ralph Ellison received the National Book Award in 1953 for his novel *Invisible Man*.

Practice

GUIDED PRACTICE

List the five major headings of the section on the chalkboard, one at a time. Ask students to make these into headlines for news stories. Invite volunteers to suggest the main points for each story as you note their responses under the appropriate headline.

INDEPENDENT PRACTICE

Direct students to select one headline listed in the Guided Practice activity. Have them use information on the chalkboard to write a news story to accompany the headline. Call on volunteers to read their stories to the class.

Review and Assessment

REVIEW Direct students to read through the section and note all the words that imply dissent. Encourage students to select three of the words and use them to write paragraphs that summarize the section. Then assign the Section 3 Review on p. 483.

ASSESS Assign the **Section 3 Daily Quiz** in *Core Resources*.

COOPERATIVE LEARNING

Organize students into groups of three and assign each group member one of the chapter's sections. Have group members list all the items mentioned in their sections that they might want to include in a time capsule for the 1950s. Then have group members work together to develop a group list of 10 items. Call on group representatives to present and justify their selections.

MULTICULTURAL PERSPECTIVES

Richard Valenzuela, a 17-year-old musician from the Los Angeles area, signed his first recording contract in the late 1950s. At the same time, he changed his surname to Valens so that white disk jockeys would be able to pronounce it. His first two records sold well, especially in the barrios of the big cities, and he appeared to be on the verge of stardom. However, he was killed in a plane crash in 1959. The biographical movie *La Bamba* (1987) secured Valens's position as the pioneer in the fusion of Mexican American music with mainstream rock 'n' roll.

conventions of the day and the life-styles of the middle class. Allen Ginsberg's poem "Howl," for instance, raged against the nuclear threat and the conventions of corporate America. The Beats wrote as they lived—without form, plot, planning, or revision. One of the best-known Beat works, Jack Kerouac's novel *On the Road* (1957), was written in a continuous three-week-long session at the typewriter. Kerouac celebrated the search for individual identity and the rejection of stability. One sentence in the novel caught the essence of the Beat philosophy: "We gotta go and never stop going till we get there."

A "SILENT GENERATION"?

Despite many parents' fears, the Beats never grew into a mass movement among young people. Indeed, many observers dubbed the middle-class youth of the 1950s the **silent generation** because of their seeming willingness to conform to consumer culture without protest. Despite the outward appearance of conformity, however, many young people were beginning to question society and to rebel in subtle ways.

Misunderstood rebels. Many young people discontented with suburban life found meaning in literature and films. Some identified with Holden Caulfield, the main character of J.D. Salinger's *The Catcher in the Rye* (1951). Disgusted by the hypocrisy of the adult world, Holden declared it "crumby" and "phony." Other young people turned

to satirical magazines, such as *MAD,* which dedicated itself to making fun of everything associated with "the American way of life." Many parents worried that reading such magazines would increase **juvenile delinquency**—antisocial behavior by the young.

Several of the most popular films of the decade reflected images of juvenile delinquency and young, angry rebels frustrated with life. Often their anger was directed not at any one particular thing, but at all of society in general. In the 1953 film *The Wild One,* a character asks the young gang leader played by Marlon Brando what he is rebelling against. Brando snarls back, "Whadda ya got?" This image of the rebel with no direction was reinforced in 1955's *Rebel Without a Cause,* starring James Dean, Natalie Wood, and Sal Mineo as teenagers confused about the values of their suburban families. Many teenagers could identify with that confusion.

The rock rebellion. Many teenagers tried to escape the conformity of suburbia through a new type of music called **rock 'n' roll**. This reworking of black rhythm and blues produced a raw sound very different from many tunes of the day, and teenagers claimed it as their own. Cleveland disc jockey Alan Freed coined the term *rock 'n' roll* in 1951, when he started a rhythm-and-blues show aimed at young white audiences. Soon the sound caught on across the country.

Elvis Presley, a truck driver from Memphis, Tennessee, emerged as rock's leading talent. With his sullen good looks, wild body movements, and blues-influenced vocal style, Presley sent shock waves through the white middle class. African American musicians such as Little Richard, Chuck Berry, and Fats Domino, as well as Hispanic performers like Ritchie Valens, profoundly influenced early rock 'n' roll.

Many parents immediately disliked rock 'n' roll. Some critics called it immoral. Others simply dismissed

◀ Teenagers tuned to Dick Clark's *American Bandstand* to listen to the latest rock 'n' roll records and watch the newest groups perform.

RETEACH Have students prepare time lines, with illustrations if they wish, showing the major developments discussed in the section. Invite volunteers to share their time lines. Students may wish to include their time lines in their portfolios.

Closure

Point out that the word *repose* may mean "calm," "tranquility," or "peace." Then write the following on the chalkboard: *The 1950s were years of repose.* Direct students to use information from the section to debate whether or not this characterization of the 1950s in the U.S. is accurate.

Extension

EVALUATE Have students evaluate the social impact of art in the 1950s by writing a review of one of the books or movies mentioned in the section.

COMPARE Ask students to compare the aims and methods of the abolitionists of the mid-1800s to those of civil rights workers of the 1950s.

◀ **Fats Domino**

◀ **Ritchie Valens**

▲ **Elvis Presley**

it as useless noise, pointing out that the lyrics of many popular rock songs did not seem to make any sense, such as in the Silhouettes' 1957 hit "Get a Job":

> 66 Sha da da da
> Sha da da da da
> Bah do
> Bah yip yip yip yip yip yip yip yip
> Mum mum mum mum mum mum
> Get a job. 99

Rock 'n' roll also upset many people by seeming to break down the walls of racial segregation. White rockers such as Presley, Jerry Lee Lewis, and

Buddy Holly shared the airwaves, and often the stage, with noted black artists. While southern officials were worried about sending black and white teenagers to school together, many of those same teens were listening to the same radio stations and sneaking off to attend the same integrated concerts.

■■ **Teenagers rebelled against conformity through literature, films, and rock 'n' roll.**

S E C T I O N 3 R E V I E W

IDENTIFY and explain the significance of the following: *Brown v. The Board of Education of Topeka,* Thurgood Marshall, Rosa Parks, Montgomery Improvement Association, Martin Luther King, Jr., Orval Faubus, "Little Rock Nine," Civil Rights Act of 1957, Ralph Ellison, Beats, Jack Kerouac, silent generation, juvenile delinquency, rock 'n' roll.

LOCATE and explain the importance of the following: Topeka, Kansas; Montgomery, Alabama; Little Rock, Arkansas.

1. **MAIN IDEA** What impact did the decision in *Brown v. Board of Education* and the Montgomery bus boycott have on the civil rights movement?

2. **MAIN IDEA** What did events in Little Rock show about attitudes of some southern whites toward school desegregation?

3. **RECOGNIZING POINTS OF VIEW** What arguments did members of the civil rights movement use to help overturn the "separate but equal" doctrine?

4. **WRITING TO EXPRESS A VIEWPOINT** Write a short story involving a teenage character who expresses his or her view of 1950s society.

5. **USING HISTORICAL IMAGINATION** Imagine you are a member of the Montgomery Improvement Association in 1956. Write a speech you would deliver to the community urging them to continue the boycott against the bus system.

SECTION REVIEW ANSWERS

IDENTIFY
For significance, see the following pages:
Brown v. The Board of Education of Topeka (p. 478)
Thurgood Marshall (p. 478)
Rosa Parks (p. 479)
Montgomery Improvement Association (p. 479)
Martin Luther King, Jr. (p. 479)
Orval Faubus (p. 480)
"Little Rock Nine" (p. 480)
Civil Rights Act of 1957 (p. 481)
Ralph Ellison (p. 481)
Beats (p. 481)
Jack Kerouac (p. 482)
silent generation (p. 482)
juvenile delinquency (p. 482)
rock 'n' roll (p. 482)

LOCATE
For locations, see the map on pp. 776–777.

1. *first steps toward ending segregation in the South*
2. *They were unwilling to comply with desegregation.*
3. *that segregation lowered black students' self-esteem*
4. *Stories might refer to conformity and influence of literature, films, and rock 'n' roll.*
5. *Speeches might mention history of segregation, recent successes, and hope for the future.*

Return to the Themes section on p. 460. Have students discuss these again and compare their original responses with those given now. (See p. 459B for suggested answers.)

Chapter Review Answers

WRITING A SUMMARY

See *Essential Points* in each section for main ideas.

REVIEWING CHRONOLOGY

3, 4, 2, 5, 1
Assessing Consequences
intensified arms race, led to creation of NASA and to launching of Explorer I

IDENTIFYING PEOPLE AND IDEAS

1. *first woman elected to both houses of Congress; McCarthy critic*
2. *policy of confronting Communist aggression by going to brink of war*
3. *Iranian premier overthrown by CIA plot*
4. *policy giving military aid to Middle East nations fighting Communist aggression*
5. *1959 law passed to crack down on union corruption*
6. *name given to soaring birthrate during 1950s*
7. *policy ending reservation system*
8. *NAACP lawyer who argued* Brown v. Board of Education of Topeka
9. *first black students enrolled at Central High School in 1957*
10. *group of writers who challenged literary conventions and middle-class life-styles*

484

UNDERSTANDING MAIN IDEAS

1. *formalized Korea's division into two nations, heightened U.S. fears of communism*
2. *McCarthy's powerful position in Senate, fear of communism; widespread criticism of his tactics, loss of public support after Army-McCarthy hearings*
3. *domestic life—caused suburban growth and baby boom, led to fears of juvenile delinquency, increased consumerism, encouraged conformity; workplace—led to corporate mergers and to automation, created new professional and service jobs, increased number of women in work force*
4. *successes—* Brown v. The Board of Education of Topeka, *which declared segregated schools illegal;* Montgomery bus boycott, *which led to Supreme Court declaration that Montgomery and Alabama segregation laws were unconstitutional; setbacks— Central High School crisis, which showed that many white southerners were not willing to obey the law, though Eisenhower reaffirmed federal authority*
5. *Teenagers used them to rebel against the conformity of the culture.*

CHAPTER 18
Review

I Love Lucy debuts.

Dwight D. Eisenhower elected president. First H-bomb test held. *Invisible Man* published.

Korean War ends.

Army-McCarthy hearings held. Supreme Court issues ruling in *Brown v. Board of Education*.

1950   1952   1954

WRITING A SUMMARY
Using the essential points of the chapter as a guide, write a summary of the chapter.

REVIEWING CHRONOLOGY
Number your paper 1 to 5. Study the time line above, and list the following events in the order in which they happened by writing the first next to 1, the second next to 2, and so on. Then complete the activity below.

1. U-2 incident occurs.
2. Montgomery bus boycott begins.
3. First H-bomb test held.
4. Army-McCarthy hearings held.
5. *On the Road* published.

Assessing Consequences How did the launch of *Sputnik* affect the United States?

IDENTIFYING PEOPLE AND IDEAS
Explain the historical significance of each of the following people or terms.

1. Margaret Chase Smith
2. brinkmanship
3. Mohammad Mosaddeq
4. Eisenhower Doctrine
5. Landrum-Griffin Act
6. baby boom
7. termination
8. Thurgood Marshall
9. "Little Rock Nine"
10. Beats

UNDERSTANDING MAIN IDEAS
1. How did the end of the Korean War affect Korea and the United States?
2. What factors led to the rise of McCarthyism? What events brought about McCarthy's downfall?
3. How did the economic prosperity of the 1950s affect both domestic life and the workplace?
4. What were some of the major successes and setbacks in ending segregated education in the 1950s?
5. How did literature, films, and music affect middle-class teenagers in the 1950s?

REVIEWING THEMES
1. **Economic Development** How were population shifts affected by the economic boom of the 1950s?
2. **Cultural Diversity** How did some people attempt to rebel against the conformity of the 1950s?
3. **Democratic Values** How did Native Americans and African Americans fight discrimination during this decade?

THINKING CRITICALLY
1. **Analyzing** What strategies did President Eisenhower use to fight the spread of communism? Where were these strategies used?
2. **Evaluating** What events contributed to Americans' fears of nuclear war? How were these fears reduced?
3. **Synthesizing** What was the popular image of a mother's role in society during the 1950s? How did this image conflict with reality?

STRATEGY FOR SUCCESS
Review the Skills Handbook entry on Distinguishing Fact from Opinion on page 750. Read the following excerpt, written by a white southerner opposed to the forced integration of schools. Then decide which part of the statement is fact and which is opinion.

> 66 Much of the legislation enacted in the Southern states . . . has been aimed basically at preserving domestic tranquillity as well as racial integrity. This is especially true in the fields of education and recreation, where indiscriminate mingling of the races is bound to bring discord and strife. . . . The closing of such institutions in many cases would be the sensible alternative to the emotional, social, and physical upheaval which would follow on the heels of forced race mixing. 99

WRITING ABOUT HISTORY
Writing to Classify Create a time line that lists the important events of the civil rights movement in this period.

REVIEWING THEMES

1. Poor whites, African Americans, Hispanics, and Native Americans moved from rural areas to industrial cities in North, Northeast, or Southwest; many middle-class whites moved to suburbs.
2. by protesting in the civil rights movement, and by supporting nonconformist literature, films, and rock 'n' roll
3. Native Americans fought termination and relocation programs. African Americans fought TV stereotypes, challenged segregation in courts and through boycotts, and worked for civil rights legislation.

THINKING CRITICALLY

1. brinkmanship and threat of massive retaliation in Korea, covert wars in Iran and Guatemala, diplomacy during Suez crisis and Hungarian uprising
2. building of H-bomb, launch of Sputnik, U-2 incident; through government campaigns, hearings, and activism to decrease nuclear weapons
3. that a woman should be a perfect wife, mother, and full-time homemaker; isolation at home made domestic life boring, need for second income increased number of working mothers

STRATEGY FOR SUCCESS

fact: that legislation has been aimed at tranquility; opinion: that integration will bring discord and that closing the schools is the solution

WRITING ABOUT HISTORY

Time lines should include Brown v. Board of Education, the Montgomery bus boycott, the Central High School crisis, and the Civil Rights acts of 1957 and 1960.

USING PRIMARY SOURCES

Beethoven and Tchaikovsky were classical composers; song reflects desire to break away from musical traditions like theirs and embrace music that is more like rhythm and blues—with energy and a driving beat.

LINKING HISTORY AND GEOGRAPHY

Alaska gave U.S. close contact with Soviet Union and Asia, while Hawaii gave U.S. a better location from which to defend the Pacific Ocean.

AFL merges with CIO. Montgomery bus boycott begins.

Suez crisis occurs. Soviet troops invade Budapest, Hungary.

Sputnik launched. Federal troops ordered to Little Rock. On the Road published.

Explorer I launched.

U-2 incident occurs.

1956   1958   1960

USING PRIMARY SOURCES

Rock 'n' roll music of the 1950s often reflected a desire to break away from old traditions and be more daring. Read the following lyrics from Chuck Berry's "Roll Over Beethoven" (1956). Who are Beethoven and Tchaikovsky? How do the lyrics of the song reflect rebellion and a break from the past?

> 66 Well, I'm gonna write a little letter,
> gonna mail it to my local D.J.
> Yes, it's a jumpin' little record I want
> my jockey to play
> Roll over Beethoven, I gotta hear it
> again today
> You know my temp'rature's risin' and
> the juke box blowin' a fuse
> My heart's beatin' rhythm and my soul
> keeps a singin' the blues
> Roll over Beethoven and tell
> Tchaikovsky the news. 99

Chuck Berry

LINKING HISTORY AND GEOGRAPHY

Alaska and Hawaii became the 49th and 50th states of the union, respectively, in 1959. Study the map in the next column. What strategic advantages of these two areas might have lent support for their statehood during the Cold War?

Alaska and Hawaii

BUILDING YOUR PORTFOLIO

Complete the following projects independently or cooperatively.

1. **THE COLD WAR** In Chapter 17 you served as a UN conference delegate. Building on that experience, prepare a speech outlining UN goals.

2. **CIVIL RIGHTS** In Chapter 17 you were a reporter covering the Committee on Civil Rights. Building on that experience, develop an outline of the civil rights movement from 1945 to 1960.

3. **POPULAR CULTURE** Imagine you are a magazine editor. Create a photo essay that reflects cultural changes in the 1950s.

BUILDING YOUR PORTFOLIO

Have students refer to **Building Your Portfolio Worksheet 4**, assigned at the beginning of Unit 4. Use the worksheet to help students monitor their progress on the portfolio projects.

THE SIXTIES

1960–1970

Chapter Overview

The 1960s were a time of immense change. President John F. Kennedy took office promising to take the country across a "new frontier." His successor, Lyndon Johnson, pushed a profusion of social legislation designed to transform the U.S. into a "Great Society."

The civil rights movement continued the struggle for racial equality, finally gaining ground through the passage of important civil rights and voting rights laws. However, some movement members felt that progress was too slow and called for more militancy.

The 1960s also saw cultural conflict as many young Americans challenged traditional institutions and forms of expression, launching a counterculture of their own.

THE AMERICAN NATION VIDEODISC PROGRAM
A variety of still images, short videos, and activities are available for you to use as you teach this chapter. See Videodisc Resources in the Core Resources Binder for barcode correlations and suggestions for using the program.

Chapter Planning Guide

CHAPTER 19	CORE RESOURCES	AUDIOVISUAL RESOURCES	PROGRAM RESOURCES
INTRODUCTION pp. 486–487	■ Literature Worksheet 19 ■ Building Your Portfolio Worksheet 4	■ Everday Life in America Transparency and Worksheet 29	
TEACHING THE CHAPTER pp. 488–513 ■ For expanded coverage of p. 491, see Chapter 23, pp. 637–642; for coverage of pp. 500–507/510–512, see Chapter 26.	■ Graphic Organizer 19 ■ Social Studies Skills Worksheet 19 ■ Geography Worksheet 19 ■ Outline Maps 1, 2, 9, 12, 13, 14	■ *The American Nation* Videodisc: The Peace Corps: John F. Kennedy's Berlin Speech; The Assassination of John F. Kennedy; VISTA Volunteers; Martin Luther King, Jr.; Malcolm X; César Chávez; The Women's Rights Movement ■ Linking Geography and History Transparency and Worksheet 17B	■ Art in American History Transparency and Worksheet 39 ■ *Eyewitnesses and Others*, Volume 2: Readings 64, 65, 66, 67, 68, 71
REVIEW AND ASSESSMENT pp. 514–515	■ Chapter 19 Daily Quizzes ■ Reteaching Worksheet 19 ■ Chapter 19 Tests ■ Alternative Assessment Forms		■ Test Generator

Additional Resources

BOOKS FOR TEACHERS

Blum, John M. *Years of Discord: American Politics and Society*. Norton, 1992. Highly readable narrative of period.

Friedan, Betty. *It Changed My Life: Writings on the Women's Movement*. Dell, 1991. Essays on a major social movement of the 1960s.

Powledge, Fred. *Free at Last?* HarperCollins, 1992. The civil rights movement through first-person accounts.

BOOKS FOR STUDENTS

*Archer, Jules. *The Incredible Sixties*. Harcourt Brace, 1986. Key events, figures, and movements.

Carson, Clayborne, et al., eds. *Eyes on the Prize Civil Rights Reader*. Viking Penguin, 1991. Accounts of the black struggle for freedom.

Haskins, James, and Kathleen Benson. *The Sixties Reader*. Viking, 1988. Uses primary sources to outline the history of the 1960s.

* for students reading below grade level

MULTIMEDIA MATERIALS

Making Sense of the Sixties: Breaking Boundaries, Testing Limits. Video, 60 min. PBS. A study of the 1960s' youth rebellion and counterculture.

The Second American Revolution, Part II. Video, 58 min. PBS. Details the assault on segregation.

Women in American Life: 1955–1977. Video, 25 min. National Women's History Project. Charts the dramatic changes in women's lives.

USE WITH PAGES 486–487

ℒisted on the right are the themes emphasized in Chapter 19. The questions in boldface type stimulate critical thinking and provide students with an opportunity to discuss the themes within a broadened context. The questions also appear in the pupil's edition on p. 486.

■ GLOBAL RELATIONS

How might foreign policy decisions undermine domestic programs? Students may suggest that foreign policy decisions might require costly measures, such as economic aid to other countries or military spending, that divert resources from domestic programs.

■ DEMOCRATIC VALUES

How might protests help expand democracy? Students might mention that protests could expand democracy by expressing the discontent of groups who feel left out of the political process and/or by calling attention to their problems. In response the government might pass laws or implement policies that expand democracy to empower such groups.

■ CULTURAL DIVERSITY

What are some institutions and traditions that might come under fire by groups questioning conformity? Students might consider institutions such as schools, government agencies, the military, the family, and churches. Traditions might include such things as art, literature, music, styles of dress and hair, language, manners, and life-styles.

ℂHAPTER STRATEGIES FOR MEETING INDIVIDUAL NEEDS

LIMITED ENGLISH PROFICIENT LEARNERS

Pair students and have them create lists of questions they can use to interview friends, teachers, or others who were teenagers or adults during the 1960s about their memories and feelings about this period. Have students conduct the interviews and compare responses.

TACTILE/KINESTHETIC LEARNERS

Have students work in small groups to sketch the key events and scenes of the 1960s. Ask groups to use their sketches to develop a "slide show" or a mural about the decade.

LEARNERS HAVING DIFFICULTY

Organize students into four groups and assign each group one section's Focus questions. Have groups discuss and write answers to their assigned questions. Then have each group share its answer with the other groups.

AUDITORY LEARNERS

Have students listen to a variety of popular music from the 1960s. (Most public libraries should have a wide selection of period recordings.) Ask students to explain to the class what the music discloses about life during the decade.

VISUAL LEARNERS

Organize students in small groups to design a symbol or logo that represents life in the U.S. in the 1960s. Encourage groups to share their symbols or logos.

GIFTED LEARNERS

Encourage students to write an essay analyzing the role that religion played in the 1960s civil rights movement.

USING THE CHAPTER FOCUS

■ UNDERSTANDING THE MAIN IDEA

Call on a volunteer to read aloud the Understanding the Main Idea paragraph. Then point out that many of the changes of the 1960s continue to have an impact on life in the U.S. today. Ask students to note, as they read the chapter, the changes, developments, and innovations of the 1960s that have influenced their lives.

 THEMES

Have students work individually or in small groups to answer the questions under Themes. Save students' responses so that they can compare them with their responses after studying the chapter. (See p. 485B for suggested answers.)

■ THE TIME LINE

Review the time-line entries with students. Point out that some people saw the election of Kennedy as the beginning of a time of hope, and Woodstock as the last act of this period of promise. As students study the chapter, ask them to note the events that marked the rise and decline of hope and promise in the 1960s.

CORE RESOURCES

- **Graphic Organizer 19**
- **Literature Worksheet 19**
- **Outline Maps 1, 2, 9, 12, 13, 14**
- **Building Your Portfolio Worksheet 4**

AV RESOURCES

- **Everday Life in America Transparency and Worksheet 29**

486

ABOUT THE ILLUSTRATION

Some 200,000 people surrounded the Reflecting Pool, between the Washington and Lincoln memorials, at the culmination of the March on Washington on August 28, 1963. The media had predicted that such an event—at the time the largest political gathering in U.S. history—would result in violence. But, buoyed by Martin Luther King, Jr.'s magnificent "I Have a Dream" speech, the crowd remained remarkably peaceful. Point out that President Kennedy and other politicians initially opposed the march because they believed it would result in adverse publicity for the civil rights movement. Then ask students how effective they think such mass demonstrations are in bringing about social change.

Chapter 19

1960–1970

THE SIXTIES

FOCUS

UNDERSTANDING THE MAIN IDEA

The 1960s marked a decade of great change in America. The promise of President John Kennedy's administration was cut short by his assassination. But the new president, Lyndon Johnson, ushered in major social reforms through the Great Society programs, while civil rights leaders finally gained some ground in the struggle for equality. Their success inspired other groups, including some middle-class women and college students, to challenge traditional society.

 THEMES

■ GLOBAL RELATIONS How might foreign policy decisions undermine domestic programs?

■ DEMOCRATIC VALUES How might protests help expand democracy?

■ CULTURAL DIVERSITY What are some institutions and traditions that might come under fire by groups questioning conformity?

1960	1962	1964	1968	1969
▼	▼	▼	▼	▼
John F. Kennedy elected president.	**Cuban missile crisis erupts.**	**Freedom Summer launched.**	**Martin Luther King, Jr., assassinated.**	**Woodstock Music Festival occurs.**

Create a two-column flip chart with the headings *Civil Rights* and *Challenge to Conformity*. Ask students to identify the major events and developments in the struggle for civil rights and the challenge to conformity during the 1950s. Write their responses on the flip chart. *(Civil Rights: 1954—*Brown *v.* Board of Education; *1955–56—Montgomery bus* *boycott; 1957—Central High School crisis in Little Rock, Civil Rights Act. Challenge to Conformity: scholarly and fictional works; movies, such as* The Wild One *and* Rebel Without a Cause; *and rock 'n' roll music.)* As students study the chapter, have them add related entries for the 1960s.

▪▪ LINK TO THE PAST ▶

During the Eisenhower era the Cold War intensified. On the domestic front the civil rights movement gained momentum from the Supreme Court ruling on school desegregation and from the success of the Montgomery bus boycott. By the end of the 1950s, the popular culture's emphasis on conformity and consumerism came under attack from the Beats and rock 'n' roll.

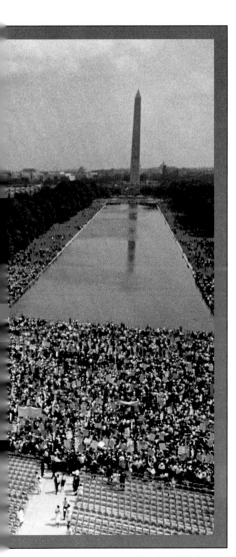

March on Washington
for civil rights, 1963

*I*n 1960, voters chose the youngest man ever elected president, the 43-year-old John F. Kennedy, to succeed one of the oldest presidents up to that time, the 70-year-old Dwight Eisenhower. Kennedy brought a spirit of youth and hope to the nation—a spirit reflected in the dramatic changes of the 1960s. The civil rights movement continued its success, winning expansion of voting rights for African Americans and further breaking down the walls of segregation in the South. Other groups, such as Mexican Americans, Native Americans, and women, also pressed for fairer treatment. Throughout America the generation raised after World War II started to question traditional society through organized protests, music, and the creation of a counterculture.

On the foreign front, the Cold War reached its most dangerous crisis when the United States and the Soviet Union came to the brink of nuclear war in Cuba. Afterward, both nations worked to ease tensions between them. During this period, the United States also increased its involvement in Latin America and Vietnam. As the Vietnam conflict shifted funding from domestic programs, such as President Lyndon Johnson's Great Society reforms, discontent grew within American society. By the end of the 1960s, much of the idealism that began the decade was lost in the wake of violence and division.

African dashiki, worn by American
youths in the 1960s

THE SIXTIES ▪▪ 487

PREVIEW WORKSHOP

Following is a list of the significant people, places, and terms in this section. You may wish to use this list as a section preview.

People
- Richard Nixon
- John F. Kennedy
- Fidel Castro

Places
- Cuba
- Bay of Pigs
- San Cristobal

Terms
- New Frontier
- Equal Pay Act
- flexible response
- Peace Corps

- Alliance for Progress
- Berlin Wall
- Limited Nuclear Test Ban Treaty
- "hot line"

FOCUS OBJECTIVES

- Describe how the Kennedy administration tried to boost the economy.

- Explain the purpose of flexible response.

- Identify the events that sparked the Cuban missile crisis and analyze how it changed Soviet-American relations.

HISTORICAL SIDELIGHTS

A New Beginning

The spirit of change in America was symbolized by the contrast between the outgoing and incoming presidents at Kennedy's inauguration. Eisenhower huddled in a heavy overcoat to combat the chill January air. Kennedy, wearing no topcoat, radiated energy and appeared the very embodiment of youth. The difference between the two provided a vivid illustration of the theme of Kennedy's inaugural address.

CORE RESOURCES

- **Section 1 Daily Quiz**

AV RESOURCES

- *The American Nation* Videodisc: The Peace Corps; John F. Kennedy's Berlin Speech

---

Section 1

THE NEW FRONTIER

F O C U S

- **How did the Kennedy administration try to boost the economy?**
- **What was the purpose of flexible response?**
- **What events sparked the Cuban missile crisis? How did the crisis change Soviet-American relations?**

*P*resident Eisenhower's successor, the 43-year-old John F. Kennedy, brought fresh vigor to the office, promising that his administration would be a "new frontier." On the domestic front, he boosted the economy, mostly by increasing spending on defense and space exploration. Internationally, he first stood firm against the Soviets, then tried to ease Soviet-American tensions. In November 1963, Kennedy's presidency ended suddenly and tragically, its bright promise largely unfulfilled.

President John F. Kennedy and Jacqueline Kennedy in 1961

A NEW BEGINNING

As 1960 began, many voters were looking for someone to inject new life into the White House. Economic recession in the late 1950s, coupled with the Soviet Union's advances in space technology, led many people to fear that the country was falling behind its counterparts.

As expected, the Republicans chose Richard Nixon as their presidential candidate in the upcoming election. His solid performance as Eisenhower's vice president had won him wide support among Republican party members. Trying to appeal to a wide variety of voters, he downplayed his past roles in conservative causes such as the investigations of the House Committee on Un-American Activities.

Senator John F. Kennedy of Massachusetts eventually emerged as the Democratic candidate. The Irish American Kennedy promised to "get America moving again." Voters were impressed with his charm, wit, good looks, and war record. But as a Roman Catholic, he faced falling victim to the same prejudices that had hurt Al Smith's presidential bid in 1928. To neutralize concerns about his religion, Kennedy assured voters that he believed firmly in the separation of church and state.

◄ **The second of four televised debates between Senator John F. Kennedy and Vice President Richard Nixon took place on October 7, 1960.**

Call on volunteers to recall the aims of the domestic agendas of presidents Roosevelt, Truman, and Eisenhower. *(Roosevelt: providing relief, economic recovery, and economic reform during the depression; Truman: extending the New Deal; Eisenhower: balancing liberal social programs with conservative financial policies)*

Then tell students that this section explains President Kennedy's New Frontier agenda, which, on the domestic front, included attempts to boost the economy and to address social problems such as poverty. As students read the section, have them compare the major aims of Kennedy's domestic programs with those of his predecessors.

▶

Nixon led in the polls until the first of four televised debates. Tired and gaunt after an illness, Nixon seemed nervous and uneasy before the cameras. Kennedy, on the other hand, appeared fit, confident, and relaxed. The election was close. Kennedy and his running mate, Lyndon B. Johnson of Texas, defeated Nixon and his running mate, Henry Cabot Lodge, Jr., of Massachusetts, by a margin of fewer than 120,000 popular votes. Their electoral victory was more decisive—303 to 219.

Kennedy was the youngest person ever elected president. His youth helped provide the theme to his inaugural address:

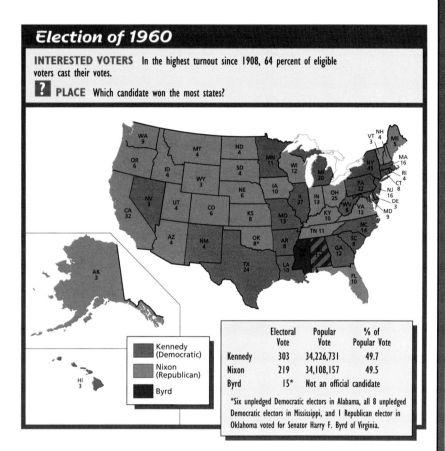

Election of 1960

INTERESTED VOTERS In the highest turnout since 1908, 64 percent of eligible voters cast their votes.

? PLACE Which candidate won the most states?

	Electoral Vote	Popular Vote	% of Popular Vote
Kennedy	303	34,226,731	49.7
Nixon	219	34,108,157	49.5
Byrd	15*	Not an official candidate	

*Six unpledged Democratic electors in Alabama, all 8 unpledged Democratic electors in Mississippi, and 1 Republican elector in Oklahoma voted for Senator Harry F. Byrd of Virginia.

- Kennedy (Democratic)
- Nixon (Republican)
- Byrd

66 Let the word go forth . . . that the torch has been passed to a new generation of Americans. . . . The energy, the faith, the devotion which we bring to this endeavor will light our country and all who serve it. . . . And so, my fellow Americans—ask not what your country can do for you—ask what you can do for your country. 99

THE DOMESTIC FRONTIER

Kennedy stocked his cabinet with young, well-educated men, including his brother Robert as attorney general. These advisers shared the belief that government should offer solutions to national and global problems. Since Kennedy had once compared these problems to a "new frontier," his agenda became known as the **New Frontier**.

One of the first domestic challenges that Kennedy faced was stimulating the economy. To help revive the economy, the president called for an increase in government spending, giving defense and space programs top priority. This emphasis reflected Cold War concerns. In April 1961 Soviet cosmonaut Yuri Gagarin had completed the first orbital space flight, sparking fears that the United States was falling behind in the space race. In late May 1961 Kennedy responded by challenging the nation to "commit itself to achieving the goal, before this decade is out, of landing a man on the moon and returning him safely to earth."

By the end of 1961, inflation was down, but unemployment was still relatively high. Kennedy hoped to keep inflation down and further the recovery by getting labor and business to agree to informal wage and price controls. Businesses had been granting higher wages to workers and then passing the costs on to consumers in the form of higher prices. Kennedy urged businesses to limit prices in return for workers agreeing to fewer pay raises. When U.S. Steel dramatically raised prices in 1962 after workers had agreed to accept small

Teaching the Section

BOOSTING THE ECONOMY

On the chalkboard draw a three-column chart with *Concern, Action,* and *Outcome* as headings. Under *Action* make the following entries: *spending on defense and the space program increased; voluntary price and wage controls suggested; cut in personal and corporate taxes proposed; status of women in America examined by presi-* *dential commission.* Call on volunteers to identify the causes and consequences of these actions, and note their suggestions in the appropriate columns. Then use the chart as the starting point for a class discussion to explore how each action was intended to boost the economy, and to assess the effectiveness of the administration in this area.

HISTORICAL SIDELIGHTS

Workplace Discrimination

The presidential commission on the status of women in America reported that women constituted more than 30 percent of the labor force, most of them employed in low-paid occupations. The commission's report also noted that average wages for women were only about 60 percent of those paid to men doing comparable work.

PRESIDENTIAL LIVES

JOHN F. KENNEDY
1917–1963

in office
1961–1963

Throughout his career in politics, John F. Kennedy presented an image of youth and vigor. Kennedy always looked younger than his years. On several occasions after he entered Congress he was mistaken for a page boy. Once, while he was a senator, a guard tried to stop him from using a special telephone with the warning: "Sorry, mister, these are reserved for the Senators."

Although Kennedy was frequently photographed in sporting activities such as football, sailing, and swimming, his athletic image hid the severe physical pain he suffered through most of his adult life. During World War II he suffered a severe back injury after his naval vessel sank. For the rest of his life, Kennedy would endure extreme pain from this injury and from the effects of Addison's disease. His brother Robert once recalled that "at least one half of the days that he spent on this earth were days of intense physical pain." Publicly, however, he seldom displayed signs of physical strain.

pay raises, Kennedy responded in anger, threatening to cancel government contracts with the company. U.S. Steel soon withdrew the price hike, but the incident further weakened Kennedy's already shaky relationship with the business community.

■■ Kennedy helped boost the economy through increased spending, especially in space and defense programs.

Kennedy also had problems getting cooperation from Congress. A coalition of southern Democrats and conservative Republicans in Congress blocked about two thirds of the president's domestic programs. Early in 1963 Kennedy proposed a $13.5 billion reduction in personal and corporate taxes to boost spending. Congress, however, was not convinced that tax cuts were wise. As 1963 drew to a close, the tax-cut proposal remained tied up in the Senate.

One area of domestic policy that Congress did support involved women's rights. Kennedy appointed a presidential commission to examine the status of women in America. The commission report, completed in 1963, noted that while the number of working women in America had increased in recent years, women still faced discrimination in hiring and received less pay than men for the same jobs.

The president responded by issuing an order requiring the civil service to grant jobs "solely on the basis of ability to meet the requirements of the position, and without regard to sex." The commission report also led to passage of the **Equal Pay Act** in June 1963, which made it illegal for employers to pay female workers less than male workers for the same job.

THE AMERICAN NATION
VIDEODISC PROGRAM

The Peace Corps

2B   35399   1:00

▼ On June 10, 1963, President Kennedy signed into law the Equal Pay Act, which required that women receive pay equal to that of men for performing the same job.

Call on a volunteer to explain the strategy of flexible response and to list the military options it provided for dealing with international crises. Next, have students identify nonmilitary actions Kennedy supported in order to prevent the expansion of communism. Then create on the chalkboard a chart of international events discussed in the section. Ask students to cite how, and to what degree, the Kennedy administration applied military and nonmilitary options to each event and add students' responses to the chart.

KENNEDY AND THE COLD WAR

In foreign affairs Kennedy tended to follow the Cold War policies of his predecessors. As a World War II veteran, he shared Eisenhower's belief in the need for military strength; but unlike his predecessors, Kennedy did not want to rely solely on the threat of nuclear weapons to deter Communist expansion. He preferred to have a range of options open in case of international crises—a strategy called **flexible response**. To expand the nation's options, the Kennedy administration continued the nuclear arms buildup started under Eisenhower and strengthened conventional forces. In addition, the government established special military units like the Green Berets to assist nations struggling to combat communism.

▲ By 1967 some 10,200 Peace Corps volunteers worked in rural communities throughout the world. Shown here is Molly Heit, a schoolteacher in Peru who taught her students how to earn extra money by weaving simple tapestries for tourists.

■■ **Flexible response offered a variety of options for dealing with international conflict.**

Kennedy also supported nonmilitary options to prevent Communist expansion. Offering a helping hand to developing countries, he realized, could serve to strengthen their dependence on the United States and block Soviet intervention. Toward this end, he introduced a number of assistance programs designed to help the developing nations of Africa, Asia, and Latin America. Foremost among these programs was the **Peace Corps**, which sent volunteers to work for two years in developing countries.

The president also introduced a program to expand economic aid to Latin America. The **Alliance for Progress** offered billions of dollars in aid to participating nations. In exchange for money, the countries were expected to develop democratic reforms and encourage capitalism. The alliance was a disappointment, however. By 1963 most of the money that had been given to participating countries was in the hands of corrupt politicians, and few Latin American leaders had enacted reforms. One Latin American writer, Victor Alba, blamed the program's failure on its inability to mobilize the poor majority in Latin American countries:

  ❝ We know who killed the Alliance: the oligarchic governments of Latin America. . . . We know who supplied the poison: the bureaucrats and technicians. And we know who would have defended it if anyone had bothered to let them know that it existed and needed defenders: the people. ❞

THE BAY OF PIGS

Latin America was a special target for aid from the United States because the Soviet Union had recently gained a foothold there. In 1959 an uprising led by Fidel Castro succeeded in overthrowing the Cuban dictator, Fulgencio Batista. Many Americans applauded Castro's success, believing he would bring democracy to Cuba. Castro, however, quickly established a Communist-style dictatorship with strong ties to the Soviet Union.

Fidel Castro

HISTORICAL SIDELIGHTS

The Peace Corps
Kennedy first raised the idea of a Peace Corps in a speech at the University of Michigan during the 1960 presidential campaign. Within days, some 700 Michigan students had volunteered for the nonexistent agency.

PRIMARY SOURCE

Description of Change: excerpted
Rationale: excerpted to focus on main idea

MULTICULTURAL PERSPECTIVES

Latin American reaction to the announcement of the Alliance for Progress was mixed. A Brazilian newspaper called the alliance "an American Marshall Plan . . . destined to transform the 1960s into an historical period of democratic progress." A Venezuelan newspaper praised Kennedy for his "understanding of the reality of Latin America." But a Dominican Republic leader flatly rejected the Alliance, claiming that his country "had already attained and surpassed all the [program's] goals." In Chile right-wing publications declared that the Alliance showed Kennedy to be an "unwitting ally of the communists."

*T*eaching the *S*ection

CUBAN MISSILE CRISIS

Call on volunteers to present a current affairs program on the Cuban missile crisis. One student might act as program moderator/interviewer; others might play the show's guests—such as representatives of the governments involved and policy experts. Still others might act as television reporters offering background stories and reports on developments in the crisis. Remaining class members should "phone in" questions for the show's guests.

INTERNATIONAL CRISES

Pair students and ask each pair to develop a paragraph that explains how the Bay of Pigs, the Berlin Wall, and the Cuban missile crisis were related. Select pairs to read their paragraphs aloud and have the class evaluate each pair's analysis of how these events were connected.

HISTORICAL SIDELIGHTS

Ransom Paid

The Bay of Pigs disaster continued to gnaw at Kennedy, and he sought ways to make amends, especially to the captured invaders languishing in Cuba's jails. Late in 1962 the captives were ransomed for more than $50 million in food and medical supplies and about $3 million in cash. While Kennedy played no role in the negotiations that brought about the exchange, he backed the deal, and his brother Robert, as attorney general, was instrumental in raising the ransom funds.

THE AMERICAN NATION VIDEODISC PROGRAM

John F. Kennedy's Berlin Speech

2B   43456   :42

When Kennedy took office, a plan to overthrow Castro was already in the works. The plan called for an invasion of Cuba by a group of anti-Castro Cuban refugees trained and financed by the Central Intelligence Agency (CIA). Kennedy gave the green light for the plan to proceed.

The invasion was a disaster. When the nearly 1,500 rebels came ashore at Cuba's Bay of Pigs on April 17, 1961, they were quickly pinned down by Cuban forces. The U.S. naval and air support that the rebels expected never materialized—at the last minute Kennedy vetoed

▲ To halt the flow of refugees into West Berlin, East Germans set up blockades along subway and elevated rail lines and cut off key crossing points between both sectors. This photograph shows one view of the Berlin Wall in October 1961.

any direct U.S. involvement. Equally damaging, the invasion failed to spark a popular uprising among the Cuban people. It took Cuban military forces less than 72 hours to crush the invasion and take some 1,200 surviving rebels prisoner.

Kennedy accepted full responsibility for the failed invasion, but his gesture did little to quiet criticism. One American journalist complained that the Bay of Pigs had made the United States look "like fools to our friends, rascals to our enemies, and incompetents to the rest." The invasion also drove Cuban leaders closer to the Soviets.

*T*HE BERLIN CRISIS

The Bay of Pigs convinced Soviet leader Nikita Khrushchev that Kennedy was weak and could be intimidated. During a summit meeting in June 1961, Khrushchev issued an ultimatum: the West must recognize the sovereignty of Communist East Germany and remove all troops from West Berlin.

Kennedy refused, saying that he intended to honor the United States' commitment to defend West Berlin. The situation worsened in mid-August, when the East Germans threw up a barbed-wire barrier across Berlin, cutting off traffic between East and West Berlin. Kennedy responded by sending more American troops to the city. The Soviets also bolstered their military forces there. For a few

days American and Soviet soldiers eyed each other nervously across the barbed wire.

Tensions gradually eased when it became clear that the real goal of Khrushchev's ultimatum had been fulfilled. The barrier had halted the exodus of East Germans, who during the summer of 1961 had fled to the West through Berlin at a rate of some 1,000 per day. In time the East Germans replaced the barbed wire with a wall of gray concrete and watchtowers. The **Berlin Wall** became the most recognizable symbol of the Cold War.

*T*HE MISSILES OF OCTOBER

After Berlin, Khrushchev continued to try to test America's commitment to containment, leading to the Cold War's greatest crisis. To ward off another invasion, Fidel Castro asked the Soviet Union to provide him with defensive weapons. The Soviets complied and also offered *offensive* weapons—nuclear missiles that could reach major cities of the eastern United States.

CIA officials monitored the Soviet arms buildup in Cuba throughout the summer of 1962. But they did not grasp the full extent of the buildup until October 14, when an American U-2 spy plane photographed numerous missile launching pads near the Cuban town of San Cristobal. Additional U-2 flights over the island located

Ask students to suggest what the word *frontier* means to them, noting their responses on the chalkboard. Then lead them in a discussion of why Kennedy chose this word to describe his presidential agenda. List conclusions reached on the chalkboard.

INDEPENDENT PRACTICE

Direct students to use the information developed in the Guided Practice activity to design a poster, logo, or bumper sticker that symbolizes Kennedy's New Frontier. Students may wish to include their designs in their portfolios.

Review and Assessment

REVIEW Encourage students to imagine that they are TV newscasters in 1963. Direct them to write a brief commentary on how well President Kennedy has lived up to the ideals of his New Frontier. Call on volunteers to present their commentaries to the class. Then assign the Section 1 Review on p. 494.

ASSESS Assign the **Section 1 Daily Quiz** in *Core Resources.* ▶

---

more missiles, all of which appeared to be aimed at the United States.

On October 22 Kennedy ordered a naval blockade of Cuba to prevent further deliveries of Soviet weapons. He also demanded that the Soviets remove the missiles. Khrushchev promised to challenge the blockade, calling it "outright banditry." Over the next two days, nuclear war loomed on the horizon. In a frenzy of activity, Soviet military advisers armed the missiles in Cuba. American B-52 bombers armed with nuclear weapons prepared for battle. Meanwhile, Soviet ships sailed toward the blockade line.

Suddenly, on October 24, many of the Soviet ships stopped short of the blockade line, turned, and sailed home. "We're eyeball to eyeball," said Secretary of State Dean Rusk, "and I think the other fellow just blinked." On October 28 Khrushchev agreed to dismantle the missile bases in response to Kennedy's promise not to invade

Cuba. Kennedy also secretly agreed to remove American missiles from some foreign sites.

The event marked a historic turning point in Soviet-American relations. Sobered by their brush with nuclear war, Kennedy and Khrushchev sought to ease tensions between their countries. Kennedy declared that it was time to write a new chapter in the Cold War:

> ❝ If we are to open new doorways to peace, if we are to seize this rare opportunity for progress, if we are to be as bold and farsighted in our control of weapons as we have been in their invention, then let us now show all the world on this side of the wall and the other that a strong America also stands for peace. ❞

In 1963 the United States, the Soviet Union, and Great Britain signed a **Limited Nuclear Test**

PRIMARY SOURCE
Description of Change: excerpted
Rationale: excerpted to focus on main idea

HISTORICAL SIDELIGHTS
At the Brink of War
A number of incidents during the missile crisis brought the superpowers to the very brink of nuclear war. Without orders from Moscow, Soviet troops in Cuba shot down an American U-2. After another U-2 violated Soviet airspace to the north of Alaska, U.S. fighters armed with nuclear weapons took off to protect the plane. In the midst of the crisis, the U.S. Air Force also launched a test missile, which the Soviets thought might be an American first strike. "It was something of a miracle," journalist Tad Szulc commented later, "that we were spared a nuclear war."

1 **Aug. 22:** Kennedy confirms reports of Russian technicians and supplies arriving in Cuba.

2 **Oct. 14:** Aerial surveillance reveals missile on launching pads.

3 **Oct. 22:** Kennedy addresses nation about Soviet threat and announces "quarantine" (blockade) of Cuba.

4 **Oct. 23:** Khrushchev warns that U.S. actions could lead to thermonuclear war.

5 **Oct. 27:** Kennedy accepts Khrushchev's proposal to end the crisis: Soviets will remove missiles and U.S. will end blockade and promise not to invade Cuba.

6 **Oct. 28:** Khrushchev announces that weapons will be returned to the Soviet Union.

⚓ U.S. navy base
✈ U.S. air force base
▼▼ U.S. blockade
| Soviet missile site

Cuban Missile Crisis

NINETY MILES AWAY The United States needed to control the sea lanes to Cuba in order to stop delivery of Soviet missiles, which if launched from Cuba could hit U.S. cities some 2,000 miles away.

❓ **LOCATION** Which bodies of water did the U.S. Navy patrol to enforce the blockade?

Map Caption Answer
Atlantic Ocean, Gulf of Mexico, Caribbean Sea

RETEACH Organize students into small groups and assign each group a subsection of Section 1. Direct each group to develop questions about the main ideas in its subsection. Then have each group exchange its questions with another group and work together to answer the questions it receives.

*C*losure

Lead the class in a discussion of the following statement: *Both in person and in practice, Kennedy was little different from Eisenhower.*

*E*xtension

ANALYZE Have students consult newspapers and magazines of the time to analyze the impact of television on the 1960 presidential election.

INVESTIGATE Ask students to trace the development of the Peace Corps from its creation to the present day. Have them present their findings in an oral report.

PRIMARY SOURCE
Description of Change: excerpted and bracketed
Rationale: excerpted to focus on main idea; bracketed to clarify meaning

---

SECTION REVIEW ANSWERS

IDENTIFY
For significance, see the following pages:
Richard Nixon (p. 488)
John F. Kennedy (p. 488)
New Frontier (p. 489)
Equal Pay Act (p. 490)
flexible response (p. 491)
Peace Corps (p. 491)
Alliance for Progress (p. 491)
Fidel Castro (p. 491)
Berlin Wall (p. 492)
Limited Nuclear Test Ban Treaty (p. 493)
"hot line" (p. 494)

LOCATE
For locations, see the map on p. 493.

1. *through increased spending, suggesting wage and price controls and tax cuts*
2. *a range of options, short of nuclear confrontation, to deal with international conflict*
3. *much of the U.S. exposed to Soviet missiles launched from there*
4. *Reports might mention wage and hiring discrimination and recommend ways to correct inequities.*
5. *believed in military strength but gave greater support to nonmilitary programs to contain communism*

494

CUBAN MISSILE CRISIS

In October 1962 President Kennedy issued an ultimatum to the Soviet Union, demanding that it remove all its missiles from Cuba. For several days the world held its breath as it teetered on the brink of nuclear war. In the end, the Soviets agreed to remove the missiles. Soviet Premier Nikita Khrushchev relates his memory of the crisis:

"*I*t had been, to say the least, an interesting and challenging situation. The two most powerful nations of the world had been squared off against each other, each with its finger on the button. You'd have thought that war was inevitable. But both sides showed that if the desire to avoid war is strong enough, even the most pressing dispute can be solved by compromise. . . . I'll always remember the late President [Kennedy] with deep respect because, in the final analysis, he showed himself to be soberminded and determined to avoid war. He didn't let himself become frightened, nor did he become reckless. He didn't overestimate America's might, and he left himself a way out of the crisis. . . . It was a great victory for us, though, that we had been able to extract from Kennedy a promise that neither America nor any of her allies would invade Cuba. **"**

Ban Treaty to end the testing of nuclear bombs in the atmosphere and under water. A "**hot line**" was also set up between the United States and the Soviet Union. This direct telephone connection enabled leaders of the two countries to communicate directly during a crisis.

■■ The Bay of Pigs and Berlin crises led to the Cuban missile crisis, after which the United States and Soviet Union worked harder for peace.

SECTION 1 REVIEW

IDENTIFY and explain the significance of the following: Richard Nixon, John F. Kennedy, New Frontier, Equal Pay Act, flexible response, Peace Corps, Alliance for Progress, Fidel Castro, Berlin Wall, Limited Nuclear Test Ban Treaty, "hot line."

LOCATE and explain the importance of the following: Cuba, Bay of Pigs, San Cristobal.

1. **MAIN IDEA** How did President Kennedy attempt to stimulate the economy?
2. **MAIN IDEA** What was the advantage of the Kennedy administration's foreign-policy strategy of flexible response?
3. **LINKING HISTORY AND GEOGRAPHY** Why were Americans so concerned with the missile buildup in Cuba?
4. **WRITING TO INFORM** Imagine you are a member of the presidential commission assigned to examine the status of women in America. Write a report that summarizes the findings of the commission and presents recommendations for change.
5. **ANALYZING** How did President Kennedy's approach to foreign affairs differ from that of his predecessors?

PREVIEW WORKSHOP

*Following is a list of the significant
people, places, and terms in this
section. You may wish to use this
list as a section preview.*

People
- Lyndon Johnson
- Lee Harvey Oswald
- Juan Bosch

Places
- Dominican Republic

Terms
- Warren Commission
- War on Poverty
- Office of Economic
  Opportunity
- Great Society
- Medicare

- Medicaid
- Elementary and Secondary
  School Education Act
- Omnibus Housing Act
- Housing and Urban
  Development Act

Section 2

JOHNSON'S GREAT SOCIETY

FOCUS

- **What were the four major concerns of the Great Society programs?**
- **How did the Warren Court decisions affect individual rights?**
- **How did foreign policy concerns affect President Johnson's
  domestic programs?**

*On November 22, 1963, John Kennedy's presidency ended when
he was gunned down in Dallas. The new president, Lyndon
Johnson, pledged himself to the "ideas and ideals" that Kennedy
had "so nobly represented." Johnson sponsored a series of social
programs designed to transform American society. These triumphs
on the domestic scene, however, were soon overshadowed as
foreign policy problems caused Johnson's presidency to unravel.*

LBJ taking the presidential oath
in Dallas, 1963

FOCUS OBJECTIVES

- Identify the four major
  concerns of the Great
  Society programs.

- Explain how the Warren
  Court decisions affected
  individual rights.

- Determine how foreign
  policy concerns affected
  President Johnson's
  domestic programs.

**THE AMERICAN NATION
VIDEODISC PROGRAM**

**The Assassination of
John F. Kennedy**

2B   44810   :32

TRAGEDY IN DALLAS

Kennedy knew he would have to campaign hard to
win reelection in 1964. In November 1963 he traveled to Texas to try to bolster his support there. In
Dallas on November 22, enthusiastic crowds lined
the route of Kennedy's open-car motorcade from
the airport. At about 12:30 P.M., as the motorcade
moved through the downtown area, shots rang out.
Kennedy slumped over, mortally wounded. Within
hours Vice President Lyndon Johnson was sworn
in as president. Over the next four days, the nation
came together to mourn the dead president.
Millions watched the funeral on television. Many
Americans felt that the death of the youthful,
vibrant Kennedy had also killed something in
them. "We'll never be young again," Kennedy
staffer Daniel Patrick Moynihan sadly observed.

    Within hours of the shooting, the Dallas
police had seized Lee Harvey Oswald as a suspect.
Two days after his arrest, while he was being
moved from one jail to another, Oswald was shot
to death by nightclub owner Jack Ruby.

This strange turn of events caused many people to question whether Oswald had acted alone in
killing the president or whether he had been part of
a larger conspiracy. To end speculation, President
Lyndon Johnson named a commission, headed by
Chief Justice Earl Warren, to investigate the assassination. The **Warren Commission**, which spent
10 months reviewing the evidence, concluded that
there was no evidence of conspiracy: both Oswald
and Ruby had acted alone.

JOHNSON TAKES OVER

President Lyndon Johnson appeared very different
from the wealthy, charismatic Kennedy. Born in
the hill country of central Texas, Johnson grew up
in a household that knew, in turn, poverty and relative prosperity. Brash, ambitious, and hardworking,
Johnson rose rapidly through the Democratic party
ranks. By the time he won election to the Senate in
1948, he was a major power in the party.

    A master of compromise, Johnson seemed
to always find the middle course on which most

CORE RESOURCES
- **Social Studies Skills
  Worksheet 19**
- **Section 2 Daily Quiz**

AV RESOURCES
- *The American Nation
  Videodisc: The
  Assassination of
  John F. Kennedy;
  VISTA Volunteers*

THE SIXTIES ▪ 495

𝒯eaching the 𝒮ection

THE GREAT SOCIETY

On the chalkboard draw a two-column chart with *Concerns* and *Actions* as headings. Call on volunteers to list what the Johnson administration believed were the major social problems in the U.S. during the 1960s, noting their suggestions in the first column. *(poverty, civil rights, health care, education, urban renewal)* Ask other students to identify the programs launched by Johnson to address these concerns. Write student responses in the second column. (Note that civil rights legislation is the subject of Section 3.) Then use the chart as a starting point for a class discussion on the impact of Johnson's domestic agenda on the U.S. today.

people could agree. This mastery of the political process, coupled with his years of experience in Washington, enabled Johnson to manage the transition of power with considerable skill and tact. Kennedy's cabinet and advisers stayed on to lend continuity to the Johnson administration.

Announcing in his first cabinet meeting in January 1964 that "the day is over when top jobs are reserved for men," Johnson pledged to add 50 more women to high government offices. Some of his choices included consumer advocate Betty Furness, economists Alice Rivlin and Penelope Thunberg, and Texas legislator Barbara Jordan. Although Johnson was able to appoint only 27 women to high offices, his strong support for women's rights marked a significant break with past administrations.

The new president also promised to appoint more Mexican Americans to high positions. He assigned Vicente T. Ximenes (he-MAY-nays) to chair a presidential committee on Mexican American affairs. Other top appointments went to Héctor P. García, a Texas advocate for Mexican American veterans, and to Raul H. Castro, a noted attorney who later became the first Mexican American governor of Arizona.

As 1964 began, Johnson focused his legislative efforts on three areas: tax cuts, civil rights, and poverty. Within weeks he had persuaded Congress to adopt Kennedy's tax program, which cut personal and corporate income taxes by 4 percent. He then pressured members of Congress to enact the long-stalled civil rights bill (see Section 3) and a comprehensive program to fight poverty.

𝒯HE WAR ON POVERTY

In 1962, social activist Michael Harrington published *The Other America,* a well-documented study of poverty in the United States. The best-selling book shattered the popular notion that all Americans had benefited from the prosperity of the 1950s. Harrington reported that more than 42 million Americans lived on less than $1,000 per year. He issued a direct challenge for leaders to face the reality of poverty:

❝ [The poor exist] within the most powerful and rich society the world has ever known. Their misery has continued while the majority of the nation talked of itself as being "affluent." . . . In this way tens of millions of human beings became invisible. They dropped out of sight and out of mind. . . . How long shall we ignore this underdeveloped nation in our midst? ❞

Harrington also noted that racism still kept many ethnic groups, especially African Americans, in poverty. He warned that the end of legalized segregation would not change the economic condition of most poor blacks. "The laws against color can be removed," he wrote, "but that will leave the poverty that is the historic . . . consequence of color. As long as this is the case, being born a Negro will continue to be the most profound disability that the United States imposes upon a citizen."

President Johnson responded to such concerns by declaring an "unconditional war on poverty in America." To launch his **War on Poverty**, Johnson sent to Congress a bill calling for the establishment of the **Office of Economic Opportunity** (OEO), with a budget of $1 billion, to coordinate a series of new antipoverty programs. These programs included the Job Corps, a work training program for young people between the ages of 16 and 21; Head Start, an education program for preschoolers from low-income families; and VISTA (Volunteers in Service to America), a domestic version of the Peace Corps. The bill passed Congress in late August 1964.

Whereas Kennedy had trouble pushing legislation through Congress, Johnson fulfilled all the major legislative goals of his first term within eight months. Comparing the two administrations, Texas journalist Liz Carpenter concluded: "Kennedy

▲ **VISTA volunteers donated their time and talent to aid poor Americans in the United States and in U.S. territories having limited public services. Shown here is an elementary schoolteacher in the U.S. Virgin Islands.**

THE WARREN COURT AND INDIVIDUAL RIGHTS

List on the chalkboard the Supreme Court cases discussed on p. 498. Then have students work in pairs to write newspaper headlines that state how the decision in each case strengthened individual rights. Call on pairs to read their headlines to the class. Use the headlines as a starting point for a discussion of how the Warren Court during the Johnson years shaped the electoral and criminal justice systems of today.

Ask students whether they think that American society has benefited as a result of these reforms.

FOREIGN POLICY AND THE GREAT SOCIETY

Encourage students to assume the role of Americans who strongly support President Johnson's Great Society programs. Direct them to write a letter to the president, expressing their thoughts about how his increased involvement in foreign affairs will affect the Great Society. Call on volunteers to read their letters aloud. Students may wish to include their letters in their portfolios. ▶

inspired . . . Johnson delivered." Opinion polls showed that Americans were overwhelmingly impressed with Johnson's achievements.

𝒥OHNSON'S VISION FOR AMERICA

Riding this wave of popularity, Johnson easily won the Democratic presidential nomination for the 1964 election. He selected Hubert Humphrey, a liberal senator from Minnesota, as his running mate. Adopting a platform that rejected Eisenhower's modern Republicanism, the Republicans chose Barry Goldwater, a conservative senator from Arizona, as their presidential nominee, with New York congressman William E. Miller as his running mate.

Johnson won by a landslide, taking 61 percent of the popular vote and 486 electoral votes to Goldwater's 52. The Democrats

Goldwater and Johnson campaign dolls, 1964

further increased their majority in both the House and the Senate. The last president to receive such a mandate was Franklin Roosevelt in 1936.

The plan. Long before the election, Johnson had mapped out plans for his presidency. He saw his major task as building a **Great Society**. In this Great Society, he said, poverty and racial injustice would end. All children would have access to an education that enriched their knowledge and enhanced their talents. The cities would serve not only people's physical needs, but also their desire for culture and their "hunger for community." In short, in the Great Society people would be "more concerned with the quality of their goals than the quantity of their goods."

After his election Johnson moved quickly to make the Great Society a reality. While civil rights was a major part of the Great Society legislation, other issues included health care, education, and urban renewal.

The programs. In 1965 Johnson persuaded Congress to establish **Medicare**, a national health insurance program for people over age 65.

PRESIDENTIAL LIVES

LYNDON B. JOHNSON
1908–1973

in office 1963–1969

Many observers saw Lyndon Johnson as the stereotypical Texas politician—loud, brash, and slightly uncouth. Johnson loved to intentionally shock observers with his language, stories, and behavior. Once during an interview he lifted up his shirt for a photographer to display his scar from gall bladder surgery.

Johnson was also a very physical politician. He would shake people's hands until his own bled and slap others on their backs in a friendly gesture. Fellow senators joked that Johnson had two techniques for getting another senator's attention. There was the Half-Johnson—"when he just put a hand on your shoulder"—and the Full-Johnson—"when he put his arm clear around you and thrust his face close to yours." But Johnson's techniques got results.

He was known as a workaholic who drove himself and his staff to exhaustion to complete multiple tasks. "What's the hurry?" one senator asked another about Johnson's busy schedule. "Rome wasn't built in a day." The other senator replied, "No, but Lyndon Johnson wasn't foreman on that job."

Practice

GUIDED PRACTICE

Write the following topic headings on the chalkboard: *Civil Rights, Health Care, Education, Urban Renewal, Individual Rights.* Call on volunteers to identify the major developments in these areas that took place during the Johnson administration and note their responses under the appropriate heading.

INDEPENDENT PRACTICE

Have students select one of the topics listed in the Guided Practice activity and create editorial cartoons or write poems or rap songs to illustrate the developments listed under their selected topic heading. Students may wish to include their work in their portfolios.

Review and Assessment

REVIEW Direct students to use the section's headings as the main topics for an outline of the section. Have students use the text under each heading to add details to their outline. Students may wish to include their outlines in their portfolios. Then assign the Section 2 Review on p. 499.

ASSESS Assign the **Section 2 Daily Quiz** in *Core Resources.*

HISTORICAL SIDELIGHTS

Master of Symbolism
Making use of symbolism as he had with the Medicaid bill signing, Johnson signed the Elementary and Secondary School Education Act in the one-room schoolhouse he had attended as a boy, with his first teacher, Kate Dietrich, looking on.

PRIMARY SOURCE

Description of Change: excerpted
Rationale: excerpted to focus on main idea

MAKING CONNECTIONS

Political Science
The Warren Court also made controversial decisions on freedom of speech and freedom of the press. In a number of cases the Court refined the definition of what could be regarded as obscene—essentially materials that had no redeeming artistic, scholastic, or social qualities. And in *New York Times Co.* v. *Sullivan* (1964), the Court said that published material about a public official, even though it contained falsehoods, could not be considered libelous unless it was written with malice or reckless disregard for the truth.

PRIMARY SOURCE

Description of Change: excerpted and bracketed
Rationale: excerpted to focus on main idea; bracketed to clarify meaning

Congress also authorized funds for states to set up **Medicaid** to provide free health care to the needy. Johnson traveled to Independence, Missouri, to sign the bill in front of 81-year-old Harry Truman, who had first proposed federally funded health insurance in his Fair Deal program.

Johnson also asked Congress to take action on funding for education. In a moving speech, he recalled:

> ❝ My first job after college was as a teacher in Cotulla, Texas, in a small Mexican American school. . . . Somehow you never forget what poverty and hatred can do when you see its scars on the hopeful face of a young child. . . . It never even occurred to me in my fondest dreams that I might have the chance to help the sons and daughters of those students and to help people like them all over this country.
> But now I do have that chance—and I'll let you in on a secret: *I mean to use it.* ❞

Congress responded by passing the **Elementary and Secondary School Education Act** of 1965, which provided $1.3 billion in aid to schools in impoverished areas.

Johnson also persuaded Congress to pass the **Omnibus Housing Act** in 1965, followed by the **Housing and Urban Development Act** of 1968. The acts authorized billions of dollars for urban renewal and housing assistance for low-income families. They also established the Department of Housing and Urban Development (HUD) to oversee all federal housing programs. Robert C. Weaver, a member of the New Deal's "black brain trust" headed this new department, making him the first African American member of a presidential cabinet. Weaver declared that the new programs had made Americans aware that "our cities were filled with poorly housed, badly educated, underemployed, desperate, unhappy Americans."

▲ President Johnson congratulates Robert Weaver after he is sworn in as secretary of HUD.

■■ Civil rights, health care, education, and urban renewal were the major concerns of the Great Society programs.

Great Society laws poured out of Congress at an incredible rate. It was the most hectic period of legislative activity since Franklin Roosevelt's first 100 days.

THE WARREN COURT DECISIONS

Like the Johnson administration, the Supreme Court of the 1960s reflected a spirit of activism. Under the leadership of Chief Justice Earl Warren, the Court tried to continue the trend begun with the 1954 desegregation decision in *Brown* v. *Board of Education* of defining and extending individual rights.

In addition to outlawing segregation across the nation, the Court tried to extend equality in the voting booth with the "one person, one vote" principle. In many congressional districts, sparsely populated rural areas were granted the same number of representatives as densely populated urban areas. In *Baker* v. *Carr* (1962), however, the Court declared that election districts had to be divided by population in order to offer fairly equal representation for everyone.

The Court also issued a series of decisions protecting the rights of those accused of crimes. *Gideon* v. *Wainwright* (1963) declared that the states had to provide lawyers, at public expense, for impoverished defendants charged with serious crimes. *Escobedo* v. *Illinois* (1964) stated that the accused had the right to have a lawyer present during police interrogations. *Miranda* v. *Arizona* (1966) said that accused persons had to be informed of their rights at the time of their arrests.

Many people saw the Supreme Court's actions as an attempt to build a country free of prejudice and inequality, but many others were outraged by such decisions. The Court had overstepped its authority, critics charged, by making law rather than interpreting it. Some went so far as to accuse the chief justice of "high crimes and misdemeanors," erecting billboards that proclaimed "IMPEACH EARL WARREN!" One critic declared:

> ❝ Earl Warren has sinned too grandly for [impeachment]. He has defiled our jurisprudence and made war against the public order. . . . The bench over which he presides has made a mockery of the Supreme Court's appointed function. ❞

RETEACH For each subsection in the section, have students write a sentence that summarizes the main idea. Select students to read their sentences aloud. Have the reteaching group choose the best summary sentence for each subsection.

Closure

Ask students to explain whether they think that Lyndon Johnson upheld the "ideas and ideals" represented by John F. Kennedy. Students should support their position with examples from the text.

Extension

EVALUATE Have students research Head Start, a cornerstone program of the War on Poverty. Ask them to evaluate the program by arguing for or against it on the basis of quality, cost, and results.

INVESTIGATE Encourage students to investigate one of the Warren Court cases discussed on p. 498. Have them present their findings in a report to the class.

■■ The Warren Court's controversial decisions strengthened individual rights.

*F*OREIGN POLICY AND THE GREAT SOCIETY

While the Great Society was taking shape, foreign affairs also drew President Johnson's attention. In addition to dealing with the Vietnam conflict inherited from Kennedy (see Chapter 20), he became involved in the affairs of the Dominican Republic (see map on page 493). The nation's democratically elected president, Juan Bosch, had been ousted by a military coup in 1963. The new leader never really gained control of the country, and in April 1965, factions within the military rebelled, demanding Bosch's return. The American ambassador, believing that Bosch had fallen under Communist influence, insisted that Johnson intervene to "prevent another Cuba."

Johnson responded promptly, sending in a force of some 22,000 marines. With American support, troops loyal to the military government gained the upper hand and the situation stabilized. In 1966, after relatively free and fair elections put a conservative, pro-American government in power, Johnson withdrew the marines.

Many people in Latin America condemned American intervention in the Dominican Republic, labeling it gunboat diplomacy. Even those who

▲ Juan Bosch is shown here on December 18, 1962, two days before being elected president of the Dominican Republic. A military coup removed him from power less than one year later.

supported Johnson's action did so reluctantly. In the United States, however, the majority of the public backed Johnson, praising his aggressive stand against the threat of Communist expansion.

By the spring of 1965 Johnson was also focusing more of his attention on the Vietnam War. As the conflict in Vietnam consumed more of his time, his attention to Great Society programs decreased. In 1966 the government spent about 18 times more on the Vietnam War than it did on the War on Poverty. Citing such statistics, civil rights leader Martin Luther King, Jr., declared that the Great Society had been "shot down on the battlefields of Vietnam."

■■ Foreign policy concerns drew federal funding and President Johnson's attention away from Great Society programs.

SECTION 2 REVIEW

IDENTIFY and explain the significance of the following: Lyndon Johnson, Lee Harvey Oswald, Warren Commission, War on Poverty, Office of Economic Opportunity, Great Society, Medicare, Medicaid, Elementary and Secondary School Education Act, Omnibus Housing Act, Housing and Urban Development Act, Juan Bosch.

LOCATE and explain the importance of the following: Dominican Republic.

1. **MAIN IDEA** What four major concerns did the Great Society programs address?
2. **MAIN IDEA** How did events in Vietnam and Latin America affect President Johnson's domestic programs?
3. **IDENTIFYING VALUES** How did President Johnson's programs reflect values from his early life?
4. **WRITING TO EXPLAIN** Write an essay explaining how the Warren Court decisions strengthened individual rights.
5. **EVALUATING** Why do you think Michael Harrington believed that ending legalized segregation would not change the economic condition of most poor African Americans?

SECTION REVIEW ANSWERS

IDENTIFY
For significance, see the following pages:
Lyndon Johnson (p. 495)
Lee Harvey Oswald (p. 495)
Warren Commission (p. 495)
War on Poverty (p. 496)
Office of Economic Opportunity (p. 496)
Great Society (p. 497)
Medicare (p. 497)
Medicaid (p. 498)
Elementary and Secondary School Education Act (p. 498)
Omnibus Housing Act (p. 498)
Housing and Urban Development Act (p. 498)
Juan Bosch (p. 499)

LOCATE
For location, see the map on p. 493.
1. *civil rights, health care, education, and urban renewal*
2. *directed federal funding and Johnson's attention away from Great Society programs*
3. *Helping the poor, providing equality for all, and improving education reflected his common origins and experience with poverty.*
4. *Essays might focus on influence of Gideon v. Wainwright, Escobedo v. Illinois, and Miranda v. Arizona.*
5. *because ending segregation alone would not change long-term effects of discrimination in housing, education, and employment*

FOCUS OBJECTIVES

- Identify the major tactic of the early civil rights movement and explain how it generated public support for the movement.

- List the events that helped expand legislation on civil rights and voting rights.

- Describe how African American frustration was expressed in the late 1960s.

- Cite other civil rights movements that were inspired by the African American civil rights movement.

CORE RESOURCES

- **Literature Worksheet 19**
- **Geography Worksheet 19**
- **Section 3 Daily Quiz**

AV RESOURCES

- *The American Nation Videodisc: Martin Luther King, Jr.; Malcolm X; César Chávez*
- **Linking Geography and History Transparency and Worksheet 17B**

500

PREVIEW WORKSHOP

Following is a list of the significant people, places, and terms in this section. You may wish to use this list as a section preview.

People
- Malcolm X
- César Chávez

Places
- Greensboro, North Carolina
- Birmingham, Alabama
- Albany, Georgia
- Selma, Alabama
- Memphis, Tennessee

Terms
- Southern Christian Leadership Conference
- nonviolent resistance
- sit-in
- Student Nonviolent Coordinating Committee

- Congress of Racial Equality
- Freedom Riders
- March on Washington
- Civil Rights Act of 1964
- Freedom Summer
- Voting Rights Act
- Black Power
- Kerner Commission
- United Farm Workers
- Chicano movement
- American Indian Movement

Section 3

THE CIVIL RIGHTS MOVEMENT

FOCUS

- **What was the major tactic of the early civil rights movement? How did it generate public support for the movement?**
- **What events helped expand legislation on civil rights and voting rights?**
- **How was African American frustration expressed in the late 1960s?**
- **What other civil rights movements were inspired by the African American civil rights movement?**

As the 1960s began, southern civil rights leaders called for new efforts in the struggle for racial equality. These efforts won passage of important civil rights and voting rights laws in 1964 and 1965. However, some young members of the movement believed that progress was too slow. In the mid-1960s, frustration over the lack of progress exploded into violence in black neighborhoods. Meanwhile, other groups, inspired by African American activism, fought for their rights.

Martin Luther King, Jr., 1963

NONVIOLENCE IN ACTION

After the success of the Montgomery bus boycott (see Chapter 18), southern civil rights leaders met in Atlanta, Georgia, in 1957 to discuss future strategy. They expanded the Montgomery Improvement Association (MIA) into the **Southern Christian Leadership Conference** (SCLC), an alliance of church-based African American organizations dedicated to ending discrimination. The leader of the MIA, the Reverend Martin Luther King, Jr., led the new organization. The SCLC pledged to use **nonviolent resistance** in its protests. Nonviolent resistance required that protesters never resort to violence, even when others attacked them. King called it meeting "the forces of hate with the power of love."

Many non-SCLC members soon took up nonviolent protests on their own. On February 1,

1960, four African American college students sat down at the "whites only" lunch counter of a Greensboro, North Carolina, department store. The management refused to serve them, but they returned the following day, vowing to continue the **sit-in** protest until they received service. News of the Greensboro sit-in quickly spread, and within weeks students began similar demonstrations in cities throughout the South. In April 1960 the leaders of these demonstrations founded the **Student Nonviolent Coordinating Committee** (SNCC, pronounced "snick"), a loose association of student activists from throughout the South.

White response to the sit-ins tested the students' commitment to nonviolence. White racists taunted the demonstrators, dumping food and drinks on them. Sometimes the harassment escalated into physical attacks. But the demonstrators never resorted to violence. By the end of the year, many

MOTIVATING: STUDENT EXPERIENCES

Ask students to identify the actions they would be willing to take to protest laws that they felt were unjust. List their responses on a flip chart. As students read the section, have them compare their list to the actions taken in the 1960s in the struggle for civil rights.

Teaching the Section

NONVIOLENT TACTICS

Organize students into small groups to role-play leaders of a workshop for civil rights workers in the use of nonviolent tactics. Direct them to develop a handout for the workshop on the tactic of nonviolence. Tell them that handouts should include a definition of nonviolence and some examples of nonviolent action that might be used in the civil rights struggle. Call on groups to instruct the class on nonviolent tactics and to explain why learning and using this approach can benefit the civil rights movement.

▶

restaurants and other eating establishments across the South had been integrated.

■■ **Early civil rights activists used nonviolent resistance to fight for equal rights.**

THE FREEDOM RIDES

The success of the sit-ins inspired the **Congress of Racial Equality (CORE)**, a northern-based civil rights group, to launch a protest against segregation in interstate transportation. In May 1961 an integrated group of **Freedom Riders** set off from Washington, D.C., for a trip through the South.

Outside the town of Anniston, Alabama, a white mob fire-bombed one of the two buses carrying the group members and beat the riders as they tried to escape. The riders on the other bus were attacked in Birmingham. When the bus company refused to carry the passengers any farther, CORE called off the ride. Immediately, Nashville SNCC members stepped in to complete the rest of the trip. SNCC leader Diane Nash explained why:

66 If the Freedom Riders had been stopped as a result of violence, I strongly felt that the future of the movement was going to be cut short. The impression would have been that whenever a movement starts, all [you have to do] is attack it with massive violence and the blacks [will] stop. **99**

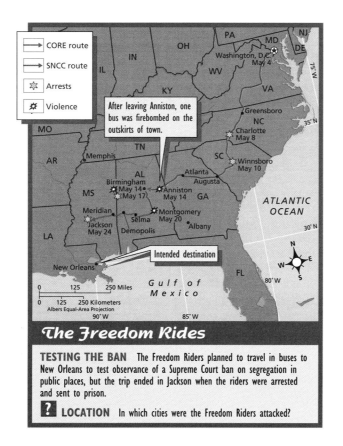

| CORE route |
| SNCC route |
| ☆ Arrests |
| ✷ Violence |

After leaving Anniston, one bus was firebombed on the outskirts of town.

ATLANTIC OCEAN

Washington, D.C. May 4
Greensboro
NC
Charlotte May 8
Winnsboro May 10
Atlanta
Augusta
Birmingham May 14 May 17
Anniston May 14
Montgomery May 20
Meridian
Selma
Jackson May 24
Demopolis
Albany

Intended destination

New Orleans

Gulf of Mexico

0 125 250 Miles
0 125 250 Kilometers
Albers Equal-Area Projection
90° W   85° W

The Freedom Rides

TESTING THE BAN The Freedom Riders planned to travel in buses to New Orleans to test observance of a Supreme Court ban on segregation in public places, but the trip ended in Jackson when the riders were arrested and sent to prison.

❓ LOCATION In which cities were the Freedom Riders attacked?

SNCC sent additional Freedom Riders to Birmingham, where they were quickly arrested by the city commissioner of public safety, T. Eugene "Bull" Connor, and dumped across the state line. The students made their way back to Birmingham and convinced the bus line to take them to Montgomery, where they were once again attacked by a mob. Under pressure from civil rights leaders, Attorney General Robert Kennedy sent federal marshals to protect the riders on the rest of their journey. In Jackson, Mississippi, however, state officials arrested the riders. Outraged by the arrests, hundreds of other protesters tried to carry on the rides. Over the summer more than 300 Freedom Riders traveled the South to protest segregation. In response, Robert Kennedy pressured the Interstate Commerce Commission (ICC) into strengthening its desegregation regulations.

◀ **Stunned Freedom Riders gather outside their bus after it was firebombed by a white mob. In all, 12 people were taken to an Anniston hospital for treatment.**

MAKING CONNECTIONS
Political Science
The Freedom Rides were designed to test the Supreme Court decision of *Boynton v. Virginia* (1960), which held that segregated interstate bus terminals were illegal. "Our intention was to provoke the southern authorities into arresting us and thereby prod the Justice Department into enforcing the law of the land," CORE leader James Farmer said.

Map Caption Answer
Anniston, Birmingham, Montgomery

PRIMARY SOURCE
Description of Change: excerpted and bracketed
Rationale: excerpted to focus on main idea; bracketed to clarify meaning

*T*eaching the *S*ection

INCREASED PUBLIC SUPPORT

Divide the class in half. Then encourage half the students to imagine they are civil rights workers in the South. Have them write letters to a friend, detailing a Freedom Ride, James Meredith's efforts to enroll at the University of Mississippi, or incidents in Birmingham, Alabama, during SCLC protests there. Have the other members of the class read the letters and write a return letter stating how their opinion of the civil rights movement was affected by what they read. Call on volunteers to read their letters to the class.

THE AMERICAN NATION VIDEODISC PROGRAM
Martin Luther King, Jr.

2B   39585   2:09

SUCCESSES AND SETBACKS

The civil rights movement saw many successes; it also saw many setbacks. Despite Supreme Court rulings, many educational institutions remained segregated. In 1962 the NAACP obtained a court order requiring the University of Mississippi to admit African American applicant James Meredith. President Kennedy dispatched federal marshals to ensure that Meredith arrived safely at school. When word got out on the evening of September 30 that Meredith was on campus, a riot broke out that left two people dead. Meredith registered the next day and attended classes the rest of the year under the protection of armed guards.

Events elsewhere tested the effectiveness of nonviolent resistance as a protest tactic. In Albany, Georgia, civil rights organizations staged numerous nonviolent protests against discrimination, but Police Chief Laurie Pritchett was prepared for them. Calling his method of law enforcement meeting "nonviolence with nonviolence," Pritchett quietly arrested all of the protesters without resorting to violence. He arranged to fill all the jails in the surrounding areas with prisoners and continued to fill them for as long as possible, causing the Albany movement to virtually stall out.

Nonviolent resistance proved more effective in Birmingham. In April 1963 the SCLC launched a series of boycotts, sit-ins, and marches to protest the city's segregation laws. Hundreds of demonstrators, including Martin Luther King, Jr., were arrested and jailed. The protests continued to grow until May, when Bull Connor ordered the police to attack the marchers, many of them schoolchildren, with high-pressure fire hoses, dogs, and nightsticks. Scenes of these attacks appeared in newspapers and on television throughout the world, increasing support for the civil rights movement.

■■ **Mob violence against civil rights activists increased public support for the movement.**

*T*HE MARCH ON WASHINGTON

Early in June, President Kennedy urged the passage of a broad new civil rights act designed to end segregation. To show support for Kennedy's civil rights bill, African American leaders called for a huge march on Washington, D.C. On August 28, 1963, more than 200,000 people gathered at the Lincoln Memorial where they heard Martin Luther King, Jr., deliver one of the most moving speeches

MARCH TO FREEDOM

Civil Rights

The Granger Collection, New York

Engraving observing passage of the Civil Rights Act of 1875

1865 Thirteenth Amendment passed.

1866 Fourteenth Amendment passed. ♦ Civil Rights Act passed.

1875 Civil Rights Act passed.

1881 First Jim Crow laws passed.

1860 | 1865 | 1870 | 1875 | 1880 | 1885

1863 Emancipation Proclamation issued.

1873 *Slaughterhouse Cases* limit protection of African American rights under Fourteenth Amendment.

1869 Fifteenth Amendment passed.

Detail from the Emancipation Proclamation

The Granger Collection, New York

1883 Civil Rights Act of 1875 declared unconstitutional.

Freedmen voting in Richmond, Virginia, 1871

THE MARCH ON WASHINGTON

Have students work in groups to present an "on location" newscast at the March on Washington that includes interviews with federal officials, organizers, speakers, and other participants. Newscasts should conclude with a summary of the reasons for the march and an assessment of whether or not it was a success. Have group members "broadcast" their newscasts to the class.

■■ Ask any students who might have taken part in demonstrations, marches, or other activities in support of a cause to describe their feelings and experiences.

▶

in American history. Repeating the phrase "I have a dream," King spoke of a nation in which all Americans would live in harmony (see page 770).

Other speakers, such as A. Philip Randolph, gave eloquent testimony to the long struggle for civil rights in America. SNCC leader John Lewis warned that the younger generation of demonstrators were determined not to give up their struggle until equality was a true reality:

66 By the force of our demands, our determination and our numbers, we shall splinter the segregated South into a thousand pieces, and put them back together in the image of God and democracy. 99

The success of the **March on Washington** raised the spirits of civil rights workers everywhere. But their joy proved short-lived. In mid-September a bomb exploded in a Birmingham church, killing four young African American girls. Then in November an assassin's bullet cut down President Kennedy. The new president, Lyndon Johnson, urged Congress to pass Kennedy's civil rights bill. The **Civil Rights Act of 1964** barred discrimination in employment and in public accommodations and gave the Justice Department the power to bring lawsuits to enforce school desegregation.

■■ **The March on Washington helped bring about passage of the Civil Rights Act of 1964.**

FREEDOM SUMMER AND SELMA

As Congress debated the Civil Rights Act, movement leaders turned their attention to voter registration. In June 1964 they launched **Freedom Summer**, a campaign to register African American voters. It involved nearly 1,000 volunteers, many of them white northerners. Freedom Summer focused on Mississippi, a state with a black population of 45 percent, but where only 5 percent of African Americans were on the voting rolls.

Mississippi had a reputation for racial violence, growing out of the state's many lynchings in the early 20th century and the murder of 14-year-old African American Emmett Till in 1955. Violence quickly struck the Freedom Summer campaign. On June 21 Michael Schwerner and Andrew Goodman, two white New Yorkers, and James Chaney, a black Mississippian, were abducted and killed. Shocked volunteers carried on, but many local blacks feared they would also become the victims of violence if they registered.

Students at Tuskegee Institute

1909 NAACP founded.

1900 New York City race riot occurs.

1908 Ray Stannard Baker's *Following the Color Line* published.

1890   1895   1900   1905   1910

1895 Ida Wells-Barnett publishes lynching study.

The Granger Collection, New York

Ida Wells-Barnett

1896 Plessy supports segregation.

1906 Teddy Roosevelt discharges entire black regiment in Brownsville, Texas.◆Atlanta race riot occurs.

1910 National Urban League founded.

Teaching the Section

EXPANDING VOTER REGISTRATION

Write the following on the chalkboard, leaving space between each entry: *Freedom Summer, Selma's Bloody Sunday, Voting Rights Act.* Call on volunteers to explain how each is related to expanding African American voter registration and write their responses below the corresponding entry. Then direct students to write a summary statement explaining the impact of these events on African American voter registration. Have students compare their statements.

By the end of the summer, only 1,600 African Americans had been added to the voting rolls.

In early 1965, civil rights workers launched a similar registration drive in Selma, Alabama. They invited King, who had won the Nobel Peace Prize the previous year, to lead them. For days African Americans attempted to register at election commission offices in the Selma area, only to face beatings and arrests. Civil rights leaders responded by calling for a protest march from Selma to Montgomery. On Sunday, March 7, some 600 people started on the 50-mile trek.

Just outside Selma, police attacked the marchers. One eight-year-old girl in the march recalled the scene: "I saw those horsemen coming toward me and they had those awful masks on; they rode right through the cloud of tear gas. Some of them had clubs, others had ropes, or whips, which they swung about them like they were driving cattle." Stunned by the fierceness of this attack, thousands of Americans poured into Selma to show support for the marchers. President Johnson was also shocked by Selma's "Bloody Sunday." On March 15, before a joint session of Congress, he asked for speedy passage of a voting rights bill. All Americans, he said, ought to take up the struggle for civil rights, for "it's . . . all of us who must overcome the crippling legacy of bigotry and injustice. And we *shall* overcome."

A week later, under the protection of federal marshals and the National Guard, the marchers completed their journey. Five months later Congress passed the **Voting Rights Act** of 1965, which put the entire registration process under federal control. Within days of the act's passage, federal examiners descended on the South to sign up new African American voters. By 1968 over half of all eligible African Americans in the South were registered.

▪▪ Freedom Summer, Selma's Bloody Sunday, and the Voting Rights Act of 1965 expanded African American voter registration.

*B*LACK POWER

As the civil rights movement grew, many African Americans questioned the effectiveness of nonviolence. Some felt that they should be able to use violence for self-defense. Others began to question the desirability of integration altogether. Using the slogan **Black Power**, many of these leaders argued that African Americans should mobilize to gain

MARCH TO FREEDOM

1915 Guinn v. United States outlaws "grandfather clause."

1919 Marcus Garvey founds Black Star Steamship Company.
◆ "Red Summer"—record number of race riots occur throughout the country.

Race riot in Washington, D.C., 1919

1935 National Council of Negro Women formed.

1915   1920   1925   1930   1935

1917 The U.S. enters World War I. Over 370,000 African Americans serve.

Soldiers of the 369th Infantry Regiment

1925 A. Philip Randolph founds Brotherhood of Sleeping Car Porters.

1934 Southern Tenant Farmers' Union formed.

Members of the STFU

GROWING AFRICAN AMERICAN FRUSTRATION

Draw a line down the center of the chalkboard. To the left of the line, enter the heading *Prior to the Voting Rights Act of 1965;* to the right, enter the heading *After the Voting Rights Act of 1965.* Ask volunteers to identify the distinctive characteristics of the African American struggle for civil rights in these two time periods *(nonviolence before, confrontation after).* Note their responses in the appropriate column.

(Students may wish to consult the "March to Freedom" time line on pp. 502–506.) Then have students write a sentence explaining why the civil rights movement changed after 1965. Encourage students to share and discuss their sentences.

OTHER CIVIL RIGHTS MOVEMENTS

Have students role-play a Mexican American farm worker or a Native American activist and write a journal entry explaining their struggle for equal rights, indicating how that struggle has been influenced by the African American civil rights movement. Call on volunteers to read and discuss their journal entries. Students may wish to include their journal entries in their portfolios. ▶

---

control of economic and political power. Some also argued that since white society caused racism, only separation from white society would help African Americans obtain such power. Although the Black Power slogan was not widely used until the late 1960s, it represented the ideas of many earlier African American leaders, including Marcus Garvey (see Chapter 11) and Malcolm X, a black nationalist who rose to prominence in the early civil rights era.

BIO GRAPHY Malcolm X was born Malcolm Little in 1925. His father was a Baptist minister and organizer for Marcus Garvey. After his father died at the hands of whites, the young Malcolm drifted into a life of crime, eventually ending up in prison. While in prison, he embraced the teachings of Elijah Muhammad's Nation of Islam, or Black Muslims, an offshoot of the orthodox Islamic faith.

Freed in 1952, Malcolm rejected the name Little, handed down to him from some former slaveholder, and used "X" to symbolize his lost African surname. He soon became a leading minister for the Nation of Islam. A powerful orator, Malcolm X championed black separatism and called for freedom to be brought about "by any means necessary." The time for nonviolence had passed, he argued:

❝ You're getting a new generation that has been growing right now, and they're beginning to think with their own minds and see that you can't negotiate up on freedom nowadays. If something is yours by right, then fight for it or shut up. If you can't fight for it, then forget it. ❞

Malcolm X

Malcolm X broke with the Black Muslims in 1964 after a pilgrimage to the Islamic holy city of Mecca. Turning away from separatism, he converted to orthodox Islam and began calling for unity among all people. This break set off a bitter struggle between Malcolm X and the Nation of Islam. In February 1965, Black Muslim assassins gunned down Malcolm X.

Other young activists, however, carried on some of his ideas. In 1966, college students Huey P. Newton and Bobby Seale founded the Black Panther party in Oakland, California, to promote self-determination in the black community. Asserting that blacks could not trust white police officers to protect them, the Black Panthers armed themselves and established citizen patrols to monitor the streets. "War can only be abolished through war," they

BIO GRAPHY **PERSONALITIES IN HISTORY**

While in Mecca, Malcolm X observed pilgrims of all races worshiping and socializing together in complete harmony. This made him realize his beliefs that all whites were "devils" and that integration could never work might be flawed. When he returned to the U.S., he talked not of a separate black state, but of "a society in which people can live like human beings on the basis of equality."

THE AMERICAN NATION VIDEODISC PROGRAM

Malcolm X

2B   28273   4:20

Workers in wartime plant

1941 The U.S. enters World War II. Some one million African Americans serve. ◆ Racial discrimination banned in defense industries and government.

1946 Truman appoints Committee on Civil Rights.

The "Little Rock Nine" and NAACP leaders

1957 Arkansas's "Little Rock Nine" enroll at Central High School. ◆ SCLC founded.

1940   1945   1950   1955   1960

1955 ICC bans segregation on interstate travel. ◆ Montgomery bus boycott begins.

1945 *Smith v. Allright* outlaws "white primaries."

1948 Racial discrimination banned in federal hiring and military.

Civil rights activist Ella Baker

1960 Sit-ins begin in Greensboro, N.C. ◆ SNCC founded. ◆ Civil Rights Act passed. ◆ *United States v. Raines* outlaws literacy tests for voting.

THE SIXTIES ▪▪ 505

Practice

GUIDED PRACTICE

Write on the chalkboard the eight subsection titles of Section 3 and inform students that these are topics for news stories that will appear in a magazine special feature titled "The Civil Rights Movement." Call on volunteers to develop brief story outlines for each topic, noting their suggestions on the chalkboard under the appropriate title.

INDEPENDENT PRACTICE

Direct students to select one of the outlines developed in the Guided Practice activity and to use it to write a news story. Students might also suggest illustrations to accompany their stories. Students may wish to include their stories in their portfolios.

Review and Assessment

REVIEW Ask students to construct an annotated and illustrated map of the 1960s civil rights movement. Suggest that they use the map on p. 501 as a model. Then assign the Section 3 Review on p. 507.

ASSESS Assign the **Section 3 Daily Quiz** in *Core Resources*.

MULTICULTURAL PERSPECTIVES

AIM was founded, in part, because the other Native American organizations in the area were run by boards dominated by whites. The founders, uncertain what to call the new organization, listened to the advice of older, respected tribal members. "Well, you keep saying that you *aim* to do this, you *aim* to do that. Why don't you call it AIM, the American Indian Movement?" the elders suggested.

THE AMERICAN NATION VIDEODISC PROGRAM

César Chávez

```
2B    38963    :21
```

---

declared. Although the Black Panthers were involved in numerous confrontations with police, many African Americans admired their boldness.

FIRE IN THE STREETS

Frustration fueled much of the support for the Black Power movement. Despite the successes of the civil rights movement, discrimination still ruled the lives of most African Americans. In August 1965 frustration became revolt when a routine arrest by Los Angeles police in the black neighborhood of Watts broke into a riot that raged for six days. When the National Guard finally restored order, 34 people were dead, hundreds were injured, and almost 4,000 had been arrested.

Over the next two years, more than 100 riots broke out in cities across the country. The worst came in Detroit, where 43 people lost their lives. A federal report by the **Kerner Commission** charged that white racism was largely responsible for the tensions that led to the riots. "Our nation," the report warned, "is moving toward two societies, one black, one white—separate and unequal."

Seeking to address the frustration of the late 1960s, Martin Luther King, Jr., started to embrace some of the Black Power movement's ideas, such as the need for African Americans to gain economic power. He also became increasingly upset that funding that should have gone for the War on Poverty was being used for the war in Vietnam (see Chapter 20). In March 1968 he called for a Poor People's March on Washington to protest this misuse of government funding.

Before the Poor People's March took place, King went to Memphis, Tennessee, to show his support for a garbage workers' strike. On the evening of April 4, 1968, the man who was the symbol of nonviolence met a violent end when a sniper killed him. Within hours of King's death, black neighborhoods all over the country exploded in outrage. A week of rioting left 46 dead and thousands injured.

■■ **The Black Power movement and the riots of the late 1960s demonstrated growing frustration among African Americans.**

OTHERS INSPIRED BY THE MOVEMENT

King's tragic death and the divisions within the civil rights movement during the 1960s sometimes

MARCH TO FREEDOM

1962 James Meredith enrolls at Ole Miss.

James Meredith attempting to enter Ole Miss

1965 Demonstrators attacked in Selma. ◆ Voting Rights Act passed. ◆ Malcolm X assassinated. ◆ Watts riots occur.

1968 Martin Luther King, Jr., assassinated. ◆ Kerner Report blames white racism for riots.

Coretta Scott King at funeral service, 1968

1965   **1970**

1963 SCLC launches Birmingham protests.

Lunch counter sit-in, 1963

1967 Nearly 100 race riots occur in the U.S. ◆ Kerner Commission appointed.

1964 Freedom Summer project launched in Mississippi. ◆ Civil Rights Act passed. ◆ Mississippi Freedom Democratic party founded. ◆ Twenty-fourth Amendment outlawing poll taxes passed.

1961 CORE sponsors Freedom Rides. ◆ Albany Movement launched.

RETEACH Have students work in groups, assigning individuals or pairs the task of outlining subsections. Direct individuals or pairs to exchange outlines and use them to ask questions of other members of the group.

Closure

Have students discuss whether the civil rights movement accomplished its goals. Have them cite evidence from the section to support their judgments.

Extension

COMPARE Have students write a biographical essay on Martin Luther King, Jr., and Malcolm X comparing their approaches to the civil rights struggle.

INVESTIGATE Have students investigate the work of *La Raza Unida* and present their findings in an oral report.

obscure the gains the movement made, including inspiring other groups, such as Mexican Americans and Native Americans, to fight for their rights. During the 1960s a group that would become the **United Farm Workers** (UFW), led by César Chávez, began to organize migrant workers, most of whom were Mexican Americans, to win better wages and working conditions. Chávez knew that many landowners exploited migrant labor. In 1965 Chávez called a strike of California grape pickers and launched a nationwide boycott of grapes picked by nonunion workers. By 1970 the UFW had won most of its demands. Throughout this struggle Chávez remained committed to using nonviolent resistance.

As in the African American movement for civil rights, many younger members of the Mexican American movement started calling for more-radical action. Young Mexican American college students organized the **Chicano movement**—also known as Brown Power—which emphasized pride in Mexican culture and heritage. Such pride was reflected in the numerous Mexican American political parties that sprang up around the country, most notably *La Raza Unida* ("the united race"), founded in Texas in 1970.

Some Native Americans organized into the Red Power movement, which demanded, among other things, that the U.S. government pay tribes for lands that had been taken from them illegally. In 1968 three Minnesota Chippewas organized the **American Indian Movement** (AIM), which would become the major force in the Red Power movement during the 1970s (see Chapter 21).

In 1969 a group of Red Power advocates occupied the abandoned federal prison on Alcatraz Island near San Francisco. The protesters offered to buy the island from the government with beads and cloth—the same price paid by the Dutch for Manhattan Island. The occupation of Alcatraz lasted for many months, until federal authorities finally removed the protesters by force.

All of these movements shared the African American movement's emphasis on ethnic pride and history. Just a few years earlier, popular culture had emphasized that to be American meant to be white and middle class. Black Power, Brown Power, and Red Power said that all Americans should be proud of their heritages and should fight to correct past injustices against them.

■■ The civil rights movement inspired other groups, such as Mexican Americans and Native Americans, to fight for their rights.

SECTION 3 REVIEW

IDENTIFY and explain the significance of the following: Southern Christian Leadership Conference, nonviolent resistance, sit-in, Student Nonviolent Coordinating Committee, Congress of Racial Equality, Freedom Riders, March on Washington, Civil Rights Act of 1964, Freedom Summer, Voting Rights Act, Black Power, Malcolm X, Kerner Commission, United Farm Workers, César Chávez, Chicano movement, American Indian Movement.

LOCATE and explain the importance of the following: Greensboro, North Carolina; Birmingham, Alabama; Albany, Georgia; Selma, Alabama; Memphis, Tennessee.

1. **MAIN IDEA** What tactic did members of the early civil rights movement use to fight for equal rights? What effect did this tactic have on public opinion?
2. **MAIN IDEA** What event helped bring about passage of the Civil Rights Act of 1964? What incidents helped expand African American voter registration?
3. **MAIN IDEA** How did the African American civil rights movement affect other ethnic movements?
4. **WRITING TO EXPRESS A VIEWPOINT** Imagine you are a Freedom Rider. Write a letter to the editor of a southern newspaper explaining why you feel it is necessary to complete the rides.
5. **TAKING A STAND** Take a stand in support of either Martin Luther King, Jr.'s method of negotiation and nonviolent resistance or Malcolm X's method of separation and self-defense. State the strengths and possible effects of that method on the civil rights movement.

SECTION REVIEW ANSWERS

IDENTIFY

For significance, see the following pages:
SCLC (p. 500)
nonviolent resistance (p. 500)
sit-in (p. 500)
SNCC (p. 500)
CORE (p. 501)
Freedom Riders (p. 501)
March on Washington (p. 503)
Civil Rights Act of 1964 (p. 503)
Freedom Summer (p. 503)
Voting Rights Act (p. 504)
Black Power (p. 504)
Malcolm X (p. 505)
Kerner Commission (p. 506)
United Farm Workers (p. 507)
César Chávez (p. 507)
Chicano movement (p. 507)
AIM (p. 507)

LOCATE

For locations, see the map on p. 501.

1. nonviolent resistance; increased support for movement as violence against activists grew
2. March on Washington; Freedom Summer, Selma's Bloody Sunday, Voting Rights Act
3. inspired Mexican Americans and Native Americans to fight for rights
4. Letters might mention the need to stand up to mob violence and support desegregation laws.
5. Answers will vary but should note differences in goals and methods of each.

Section 4

CULTURE AND COUNTERCULTURE

F O C U S

■ **How did hippies rebel against traditional society?**

■ **What did the revived women's movement do for women?**

■ **How did rock music impact the 1960s?**

"*The times they are a-changin'* " *declared singer Bob Dylan in 1963. He was not referring to the civil rights movement alone. Many young people, rejecting the values of their parents' generation, embraced new styles of music and dress and new ways of life. Others challenged American traditions, including religious practices and the role of women in society. The result was a reinvention of culture that eventually affected the entire nation.*

Hippie, 1967

THE COUNTERCULTURE

The youth rebellion that began in the 1950s with the Beats and rock 'n' roll evolved into a broad movement in the 1960s that challenged the beliefs and traditions of older generations. Growing up during an era of Cold War fears, massive civil rights protests, and the Vietnam War led many children of the baby boom to question the values of American society and to blame their parents for creating the problems that plagued the country. This **generation gap** between the baby boomers and their elders grew ever wider as the decade wore on.

Shaking the ivory tower. The first audible rumblings of the 1960s youth movement occurred on college

campuses among white middle-class students. Many felt frustrated by the conservative curriculum offered at universities. To them, traditional courses seemed out of touch with the real world.

In 1964 discontent exploded into protest at the University of California at Berkeley. Some 70 percent of the students went on strike. Instead of attending classes, they rallied, held sit-ins, and picketed university administration buildings. Their intention, they declared, was to "Shut This Factory Down." By 1965 such chants were echoing from college campuses across the nation. Many students inspired by this experience

◀ **Five hundred policemen were present during the Berkeley student protests in December 1964. Some demonstrators who staged a sit-in were arrested and hauled off to jail.**

Teaching the Section

THE COUNTERCULTURE

Organize students into groups of six to develop skits on the counterculture. Suggest that two students assume the roles of white middle-class college students, two play hippies, and two take the roles of older people. In the skits the students and hippies should defend their values and life-styles and explain why they have chosen to follow them. The older people should question the validity of these values and life-styles. Call on groups to perform their skits.

▶

---

became involved in the political movements of the time. One woman who participated in the student movement at Columbia University recalled the mood of the students:

> 66 There was an incredible exhilaration, that here we were making history, changing the world. . . . Everybody believed that this university would never be the same, that society would be . . . changed, that there'd be a revolution in the United States within five years, and a whole new social order. 99

While some students wanted to change the world, others rebelled by rejecting everything connected with mainstream America, what they called the Establishment. Instead, these **hippies**—as they soon became known—sought to create an alternative life-style, a **counterculture**.

Elements of the counterculture. Like the Beats before them, hippies rejected the materialism and work ethic of past generations in favor of simplicity and doing "your own thing." Many hippies indulged in behavior intended to shock older Americans, such as public displays of nudity and the use of profanity. Most searched for new physical experiences by engaging in permissive sexual behavior or by experimenting with mind-altering drugs, such as LSD (lysergic acid diethylamide), or "acid."

Timothy Leary, a Harvard professor who was fired in 1963 for using LSD on his students, became the drug's leading advocate. Leary invited people to "tune in, turn on, drop out." Many followed his advice. But there was a high price to pay for the experimentation of the era, as reported cases of sexually transmitted diseases and drug addiction increased at an alarming rate.

Some hippies "dropped out" of society by joining rural communes, where they attempted to live collectively in harmony with nature. They rejected most modern conveniences, grew their own food, and shared all property. Some formed their own hippie neighborhoods in run-down urban areas, such as the **Haight-Ashbury** district of San Francisco.

■■ **Hippies rebelled against traditional society by forming their own counterculture.**

▲ The Haight-Ashbury district of San Francisco attracted hippies of all ages. This photograph was taken in May 1968.

QUESTIONING AMERICAN SOCIETY

The counterculture movement reflected a growing sense of skepticism in America. In the 1960s many Americans, even those not active in the counterculture movement, were beginning to question the value of conformity. Many institutions, including traditional churches, came under scrutiny. In the mid-1950s, over 80 percent of Americans said religion could answer all or most of modern society's problems. By 1969, however, 70 percent said that religion was *losing* its influence on American life, leading *Time* magazine to ask, "Is God Dead?"

Americans, especially the young, did not necessarily lack spiritual faith, but many came to lack faith in the ability of the old, established churches to provide spiritual growth in the modern world. The challenges of the nuclear age, some felt, had made conventional religious answers irrelevant. Reflecting the search for alternative answers, the number of college courses in religion—and enrollment in them—grew dramatically, as did interest in Eastern religions such as Zen Buddhism.

The questioning of tradition even extended into the art world. Many new visual artists argued that the art world had become a slave to elite tastes

PRIMARY SOURCE

Description of Change: excerpted

Rationale: excerpted to focus on main idea

BUILDING VOCABULARY

Hippie, which came into popular use in the mid-1960s, is a derivation of the word *hip,* meaning "knowing," or "aware." Some language scholars think that *hip* derives from the West African word *hipi,* which means "to be aware."

MULTICULTURAL PERSPECTIVES

Many hippies became interested in Native American dress and culture. Many Native Americans, however, were not pleased. Peter Nuvamsa, Sr., recalled that when a group of hippies visited his Hopi village, they "offended our way of life. . . . They hugged each other and kissed in public as if they didn't have anything else to do . . . . I went out there and spoke to some of them. I said, 'Why are you here? Why do you behave this way, doing anything that comes into your head? We do not like the way you are behaving. It's not our way.'"

Teaching the Section

THE WOMEN'S MOVEMENT REVIVED

Organize students into small groups to act as leaders of the National Organization for Women (NOW). Direct them to develop a mission statement that explains why the women's movement needs to be revived, describes the role of NOW in that process, and outlines what the organization hopes to achieve—politically, socially, and economically—for women. Ask groups to volunteer to read their statements. Discuss and evaluate each statement after it is presented.

and prejudices. Artists created works only to please a few cultured critics, not to appeal to the majority of non-artists.

As the 1960s began, a number of New York painters and sculptors emerged who wanted to make art more accessible to the general public. They accomplished their goals by using "found objects"—tin cans, furniture, cardboard packaging, cartoon strips, and other everyday articles—as the subjects of their works. The leading proponents of this method, called **pop art**, included Roy Lichtenstein and Claes Oldenberg. Many of Lichtenstein's huge paintings were done in comic-strip style, complete with speech balloons. Oldenberg used a variety of materials to make giant sculptures of such things as hamburgers, toothpaste tubes, and clothespins.

The best-known pop artist, however, was Andy Warhol. His most notable paintings included oversize soup cans, rows of green soda bottles, and a garishly colored rendering of a photograph of Marilyn Monroe reproduced multiple times. Initially, Warhol painted by hand. However, he soon switched to a stencil-printing process called silk screen. Finally, he simply did designs that an army of assistants then reproduced. Warhol's message, that everything—even art—can be mass-produced, both glorified and mocked consumerism. Warhol once predicted that "In the future everyone will be famous for 15 minutes," reflecting consumers' constant desires for new products.

A REVIVED WOMEN'S MOVEMENT

One of the most lasting legacies of the 1960s was its challenge to traditional views of women. After years of inaction, the women's movement experienced a widespread revival.

Sparks of unrest. This revival was sparked in part by the publication of Betty Friedan's *The Feminine Mystique* (1963), which rejected the popular notion that women were content with the roles of wife, mother, and homemaker. Many women, she charged, felt stifled by the "comfortable concentration camp" of domestic life:

> 66 Each suburban wife struggled with it alone. As she made the beds, shopped for groceries, matched slipcover material, ate peanut butter sandwiches with her children, chauffeured Cub Scouts and Brownies, . . . she was afraid to ask even of herself the silent question—"Is this all?" 99

Other women agreed with Friedan. Her book helped motivate women to demand greater opportunities and fairer treatment in the workplace. Although the Civil Rights Act of 1964 outlawed sexual discrimination in employment, the government seemed reluctant to deal with women's grievances. As a result, in 1966 Friedan and other feminists founded the **National Organization for Women** (NOW) to lobby for women's rights. Women began to stand up for themselves in a variety of ways. Some held consciousness-raising sessions to improve their self-esteem. Others took direct action. In 1968, for example, some feminists disrupted the Miss America pageant, charging that beauty contests degraded women.

▶ Pop artists helped make art more accessible to the general public by selecting images that reflected everyday life. Andy Warhol, for example, painted these oversize soup cans in 1965.

Andy Warhol, Campbell's Soup, 1965

Roy Lichtenstein

◀ Many of Roy Lichtenstein's paintings were drawn in a flamboyant, comic-strip style.

A MUSICAL REVOLUTION

Pair students and invite them to imagine that they are American young people during the 1960s. Direct each pair to create a message for a time capsule, to be opened in the 1990s, that describes their music and explains how it was influenced by the developments of their time. Select a number of pairs to read their messages to the class. Then have students compare music as a reflection of social conditions and change in the 1960s to the social role of current musical forms in contemporary society.

HISTORY in the Making

BY DR. ALICE KESSLER-HARRIS

Social History

Until relatively recently, most American history textbooks focused on political history, recounting the deeds of the nation's political, military, and social leaders. Today, however, textbooks have begun to place a greater emphasis on social history.

What is social history? Some 50 years ago the well-known British historian G. M. Trevelyan described social history as "the history of a people with the politics left out." Social historians studied people's private lives rather than political events. They concentrated on the household, giving details about the daily lives of men, women, and children. Though colorful, this history failed to explain larger historical themes.

But social history changed in the 1960s. The civil rights movement, antiwar protests, and the women's movement inspired a new generation of historians. In order to explain how these protest movements arose, historians began studying how African Americans, women, and ethnic groups other than white Protestants contributed to American history. Focusing on ordinary people—workers, women, city dwellers, farmers, immigrants—social historians set out to rewrite the history of the United States.

To do so, these historians sought out new sources and used new methods to reconstruct the daily lives and thoughts of ordinary people. Earlier historians had analyzed only written sources left by political and intellectual leaders. The new social historians uncovered new sources—workers' speeches and letters, oral histories, autobiographies, songs, folklore, reports of chari-

▲ *Roll, Jordan, Roll*, an example of social history by Eugene D. Genovese, explores plantation life in the pre–Civil War South.

table societies, and ethnic and immigrant newspapers. These historians used statistical methods to study how people voted, where they moved, what they ate and drank, how they spent and saved their money, and the size of their families.

The new social historians have created a body of work whose strength lies in its respect for cultural diversity. Their work explores the values and ideas that Americans of different racial, ethnic, and class backgrounds share and do not share. For example, Julia Kirk Blackwelder's *Women of the Depression: Caste and Culture in San Antonio, 1929–39* (1984) shows how people's racial and ethnic backgrounds helped them cope with economic distress.

The new social history also explores the social institutions—families, schools, churches, and so on—that both preserve traditional values and help introduce new ones. This history, however, goes beyond the "old" social history by using social institutions to help explain broader political, economic, or technological changes. For example, Kenneth Jackson's *Crabgrass Frontier* (1985) explains that American families' preference for detached homes of their own helped lead to the growth of suburbs—an important economic and geographic change.

The best social history combines research on political and economic institutions with research on how ordinary people think and act. This combination helps us understand politics and the forces that ultimately create change. In doing so, the new social historians can rightly claim to have updated Trevelyan's definition of social history by creating a history of all Americans with the politics mixed in.

SOCIAL HISTORY

SETTING THE SCENE

The 1960s revival in American social history was fired, in part, by exposure to the works of European social historians. The French *Annales* school of historians emphasized the impact of long-term trends, such as how wheat harvests affected peasant life over a particular time period. In Britain a group of historians focused on the rise of the working class and its role in history. Such research encouraged some young American historians to look at subjects in a different way.

COOPERATIVE LEARNING

Organize students into groups of six and ask each to create a social history time capsule for the 1960s. Group members should divide tasks: some might research suitable items for the capsule, others might "re-create" written or visual items. Call on groups to present and discuss their time capsules.

*P*ractice

GUIDED PRACTICE

Write the four subsection titles on the chalkboard and inform students that these are headings of segments for a magazine article on cultural developments in the 1960s. Ask students what points they would include for each segment and note their ideas under the appropriate heading.

INDEPENDENT PRACTICE

Direct each student to use the information on the chalkboard to write one segment of the article framed in the Guided Practice activity. Encourage students to illustrate, or suggest illustrations for, their segments.

*R*eview and *A*ssessment

REVIEW Have students write 10 questions on Section 4 on individual note cards with the answers on the reverse side. Then divide students into groups of four. Ask them to use their note cards to question the other members of the group. Then assign the Section 4 Review on p. 513.

ASSESS Assign the **Section 4 Daily Quiz** in *Core Resources*.

THE AMERICAN NATION VIDEODISC PROGRAM

The Women's Rights Movement

```
|||||||||||||||||||||||
1B    48258    :32
```

BIOGRAPHY **PERSONALITIES IN HISTORY**

Gloria Steinem was not the first feminist in her family. Her grandmother, Pauline Steinem, served as the president of the Ohio Women's Suffrage Association in the early 1900s and was one of two American delegates to the conference held by the International Council of Women in 1908.

AV **TRANSPARENCY**

Everyday Life in America Transparency and **Worksheet 29**

HISTORICAL SIDELIGHTS

Counterculture Declines

Television images of Haight-Ashbury had drawn to the counterculture hundreds of misfits, drug peddlers, and others who had little interest in peace and happiness. Violence, not love, soon ruled the streets of the hippie mecca. In the fall of 1967, the leaders of the counterculture celebrated "Death of Hippie," a funeral procession through Haight-Ashbury.

512

A new generation. Many young women who had participated in the civil rights movement and counterculture realized that they faced just as much sexual discrimination in those realms as they did in mainstream society. One activist recalled a friend telling her that "you'll never be a radical as long as you don't see how the system affects *you.* You always think it affects other people." By the late 1960s more women inspired by other movements were beginning to stand up for their own rights. One woman who became so inspired was journalist Gloria Steinem.

BIOGRAPHY Gloria Steinem was born on March 25, 1934, in Toledo, Ohio. In 1946 her parents divorced. She spent most of her teenage years taking care of her invalid mother. In 1952 Steinem entered Smith College, where she graduated with honors. "I loved Smith," she recalled. "They gave you three meals a day to eat, and all the books you wanted to read—what more could you want?" Steinem's love of reading and writing led to her desire to become a journalist.

Gloria Steinem

In 1968 she started writing a political column for *New York* magazine, which brought her into contact with activists such as César Chávez and African American Communist Angela Davis. Later that year she wrote her first openly feminist article, "After Black Power, Women's Liberation," which established her as an advocate of the movement. In 1971 she helped found the National Women's Political Caucus to encourage women to run for political office. That same year, she became editor of a new magazine for women entitled *Ms.*

"There is nothing outside of [the movement]," Steinem said. "I once thought I would do this for two or three years and go home to my real life." But she has continued to be a leader in the women's movement, writing several books, lobbying for causes such as the passage of the Equal Rights Amendment (see Chapter 21), and helping found numerous organizations for women, including the Coalition of Labor Union Women and Women Against Pornography.

▪▪ **The 1960s revival of the women's movement challenged traditional views of women.**

---

*M*USICAL REVOLUTION

All of the social and political movements of the 1960s marched to new forms of music. A compelling influence on the youth rebellion of the 1950s, rock 'n' roll continued to reflect social change in the 1960s, while it branched out into a variety of new forms.

The year 1964 marked the musical **British Invasion**—the arrival of such English bands as the Beatles and the Rolling Stones. Looking back to rock 'n' roll and to African American blues for inspiration, these bands created a vibrant, powerful new style of music. Meanwhile, African American artists, many sponsored by Motown Records of Detroit, were experimenting with enhanced blendings of traditional black music. The unique and widely popular style they created became known as the "Motown sound."

The use of electrically amplified instruments, especially the electric guitar, inspired musicians to try innovative—and very loud—sounds on audiences. Seattle native Jimi Hendrix was the master

▼ **Jimi Hendrix, shown here performing at the Isle of Wight in 1970, was one of the most innovative rock 'n' roll guitarists to emerge during the late 1960s.**

▲ **Folk music by artists such as Joan Baez was also popular during the 1960s.**

RETEACH List on the chalkboard the terms from the Preview Workshop at the beginning of this section. Have students respond to the section's Focus questions with sentences containing the terms.

Closure

Refer students to the quote by Bob Dylan that opens the section. Have students discuss the relevance of Dylan's statement by reviewing the changes that took place during the 1960s.

Extension

CREATE Have students create a collage of the counterculture. Suggest that they use 1960s slogans or song titles as captions for their collages. Call on volunteers to present and explain their collages.

CONDUCT Ask students to conduct an interview with an older relative about life in the 1960s. Have students present their findings in an oral report.

of the electric guitar in the 1960s. Folk music also inspired a new type of rock sound as singers such as Joan Baez and Bob Dylan created lyrics that sent a political message to listeners, such as in this 1962 Dylan hit:

> 66 How many years can a mountain exist
> before it's washed to the sea?
> Yes, 'n' How many years can some
> people exist
> before they're allowed to be free?
> Yes, 'n' How many times can a man
> turn his head
> pretending he just doesn't see?
> The answer, my friend, is blowin'
> in the wind,
> The answer is blowin' in the wind. 99

Dylan brought folk music fully into the rock realm in 1965, when he abandoned the acoustic guitar, traditionally used in folk music, in favor of the electric guitar.

Rock music would be the focal point of an event that marked the beginning of the end for the counterculture movement—the Woodstock Music Festival. In August 1969 some 300,000 young people descended on rural upstate New York for the three-day festival, closing the New York State Thruway in the process. Despite driving rain, knee-deep mud, and severe shortages of food and drink, the concert remained a peaceful gathering as listeners reveled in the music of rock's top performers.

▲ In spite of traffic jams, water shortages, lack of public conveniences, and rain, the Woodstock Music Festival in August 1969 was an overwhelming success.

Woodstock was more than just a rock concert. It was a celebration of the era, marking the high point of the counterculture movement. Some four months later, at a free concert held at Altamont Raceway near San Francisco, a security team of Hells' Angels stabbed a fan to death in full view of the stage. The disastrous concert starkly revealed the counterculture's dark side.

▪▪ **Rock music followed the movements of the 1960s and marked the high point of the counterculture at Woodstock.**

PRIMARY SOURCE
Description of Change: excerpted
Rationale: excerpted to focus on main idea

SECTION REVIEW ANSWERS

IDENTIFY
For significance, see the following pages:
generation gap (p. 508)
hippies (p. 509)
counterculture (p. 509)
Timothy Leary (p. 509)
pop art (p. 510)
Roy Lichtenstein (p. 510)
Claes Oldenberg (p. 510)
Andy Warhol (p. 510)
Betty Friedan (p. 510)
National Organization for Women (p. 510)
Gloria Steinem (p. 512)
British Invasion (p. 512)
Jimi Hendrix (p. 512)
Bob Dylan (p. 513)
Woodstock (p. 513)

1. *to create an alternative life-style that rejected traditional values*
2. *caused women to question and challenge traditional roles and views*
3. *brought an examination of traditional values, created a generation gap, increased rates of drug addiction and sexually transmitted diseases*
4. *Articles should note how music reflected social and political changes of the decade.*
5. *commented on consumerism, rejected traditional styles of art elite*

■■ **SECTION 4 REVIEW**

IDENTIFY and explain the significance of the following: generation gap, hippies, counterculture, Timothy Leary, pop art, Roy Lichtenstein, Claes Oldenberg, Andy Warhol, Betty Friedan, National Organization for Women, Gloria Steinem, British Invasion, Jimi Hendrix, Bob Dylan, Woodstock.

1. **MAIN IDEA** Why did hippies form their own counterculture?
2. **MAIN IDEA** What effect did the revival of the women's movement have on traditional views of women?
3. **ASSESSING CONSEQUENCES** What consequences did the youth rebellion of the 1960s have on society?
4. **WRITING TO EVALUATE** Imagine you are a music critic in 1969. Write an article that evaluates the relationship between rock 'n' roll music and the events of the 1960s.
5. **SYNTHESIZING** How did the various works of pop artists reflect American culture in the 1960s?

Chapter Review Answers

WRITING A SUMMARY
See Essential Points in each section for main ideas.

REVIEWING CHRONOLOGY
4, 3, 5, 2, 1
Evaluating
spurred U.S. government to support War on Poverty

IDENTIFYING PEOPLE AND IDEAS
1. *Kennedy's agenda, designed to offer solutions to national and global problems*
2. *program that sent volunteers to work in developing countries*
3. *Communist dictator of Cuba*
4. *commission headed by Chief Justice Earl Warren that concluded there was no evidence of conspiracy in Kennedy assassination*
5. *democratically elected president of Dominican Republic who was ousted by a 1963 military coup*
6. *method of protest that forbids use of violence*
7. *1965 measure that placed voter registration under federal control*
8. *movement organized to emphasize pride in Mexican culture and heritage*
9. *division between baby boomers and older Americans*

10. *journalist and editor of Ms. magazine who helped found the National Women's Political Caucus*

UNDERSTANDING MAIN IDEAS
1. *by applying the principle of flexible response, attempted to overthrow Castro through Bay of Pigs invasion, upheld U.S. commitment to West Berlin, and opposed Soviet missiles in Cuba; by supporting nonmilitary options such as the Peace Corps and Alliance for Progress in developing countries*
2. *to resolve social problems in the U.S.; through legislative efforts and government programs*
3. *belief that members of these groups should be proud of their heritages and should fight to correct injustices against them*
4. *through shocking behavior, use of mind-altering drugs, formation of communes or hippie neighborhoods, rejection of traditional values and behaviors*
5. *won equal pay for equal work through Equal Pay Act, demanded greater opportunities and fairer treatment in work force and other rights; through NOW and similar organizations*

CHAPTER 19
Review

SNCC founded. John F. Kennedy elected president.

Yuri Gagarin makes first manned space flight. Bay of Pigs invaded. Freedom Rides begin. Berlin Wall built.

Michael Harrington's *The Other America* published. Cuban missile crisis erupts.

Equal Pay Act passed. Betty Friedan's *The Feminine Mystique* published. March on Washington occurs. Kennedy assassinated.

1960   1962

WRITING A SUMMARY
Using the essential points of the chapter as a guide, write a summary of the chapter.

REVIEWING CHRONOLOGY
Number your paper 1 to 5. Study the time line above, and list the following events in the order in which they happened by writing the first next to 1, the second next to 2, and so on. Then complete the activity below.

1. Woodstock Music Festival occurs.
2. American Indian Movement organized.
3. Betty Friedan's *The Feminine Mystique* published.
4. Freedom Rides begin.
5. Medicare and Medicaid established.

Evaluating How did Michael Harrington's book *The Other America* influence American domestic policy?

IDENTIFYING PEOPLE AND IDEAS
Explain the historical significance of each of the following people or terms.

1. New Frontier
2. Peace Corps
3. Fidel Castro
4. Warren Commission
5. Juan Bosch
6. nonviolent resistance
7. Voting Rights Act
8. Chicano movement
9. generation gap
10. Gloria Steinem

UNDERSTANDING MAIN IDEAS
1. How did the Kennedy administration propose to deter Communist expansion?
2. What was the purpose of the Great Society? How did President Johnson propose to make the Great Society a reality?
3. What did the Brown Power, Red Power, and Black Power movements have in common?
4. How did young people rebel against conformity during the 1960s?
5. What gains did women make during the 1960s? How did they make these gains?

★☆ REVIEWING THEMES
1. **Global Relations** How did events overseas undermine the Great Society programs?
2. **Democratic Values** How did the Freedom Rides, sit-ins, and other peaceful civil rights protests help expand democracy?
3. **Cultural Diversity** What institutions and traditions were challenged in the late 1960s?

THINKING CRITICALLY
1. **Evaluating** How did the Warren Court's decisions in *Gideon v. Wainwright, Escobedo v. Illinois,* and *Miranda v. Arizona* strengthen individual rights?
2. **Synthesizing** In what ways did African Americans express frustration over their slow progress in achieving civil rights?
3. **Analyzing** What contribution did music and pop art make to society in the 1960s?

STRATEGY FOR SUCCESS
Review the Skills Handbook entry on Reading Charts and Graphs beginning on page 756. Study the graph below, which shows the number of drug arrests reported between 1960 and 1970. In which year did the number of arrests first exceed 100,000? About how many arrests were reported in 1970?

URBAN DRUG ARRESTS, 1960–1970

Number of Cases (in thousands)

Year

Source: *Information Please Almanac*

REVIEWING THEMES

1. Conflicts in Dominican Republic and in Vietnam drew federal funding and Johnson's attention away from domestic programs.
2. drew attention to segregation in South, inspired protests in other areas, attracted public support for civil rights movement, led to laws expanding civil rights and voting rights
3. universities; churches; materialism; work ethic; traditional attitudes and values as expressed in life-styles, art, and music

THINKING CRITICALLY

1. Gideon—states had to provide lawyers for poor defendants charged with serious crimes; Escobedo—accused had the right to have a lawyer present during interrogations; Miranda—accused had to be informed of rights at time of arrest
2. formed Black Power movement to champion black separatism and use of violence, if necessary, to fight for equal rights
3. music—reflected events of 1960s; pop art—commented on consumerism of period, made art more accessible to public

STRATEGY FOR SUCCESS

1967; about 350,000

WRITING ABOUT HISTORY

Essays should contrast Johnson's background and his skill in political compromise with Kennedy's.

USING PRIMARY SOURCES

Students might mention lack of modern conveniences, high levels of disease and infant mortality, and low life-expectancy rates on the reservation.

LINKING HISTORY AND GEOGRAPHY

feared close proximity to U.S. of Soviet allies, refused to compromise on missiles in Cuba, sent troops to Dominican Republic to oppose Bosch

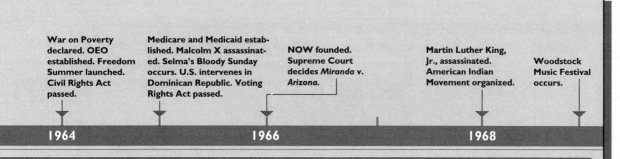

War on Poverty declared. OEO established. Freedom Summer launched. Civil Rights Act passed.	Medicare and Medicaid established. Malcolm X assassinated. Selma's Bloody Sunday occurs. U.S. intervenes in Dominican Republic. Voting Rights Act passed.	NOW founded. Supreme Court decides *Miranda* v. *Arizona*.	Martin Luther King, Jr., assassinated. American Indian Movement organized.	Woodstock Music Festival occurs.

1964   **1966**   **1968**

WRITING ABOUT HISTORY

Writing to Evaluate Write an essay that evaluates the different leadership styles of Lyndon Johnson and John F. Kennedy.

USING PRIMARY SOURCES

Native Americans were one ethnic group in the 1960s whose problems were not addressed by the U.S. government. Read the following excerpt, which comes from an article published in the *New Republic* in 1965, describing conditions on the Pine Ridge Reservation in South Dakota. Then write a paragraph summarizing what you have read.

> **❝** *Practically none of the houses on the reservation has electricity. Half of the houses are without wells nearby; Poverty-Program workers are discovering people hauling water fifteen miles. Indoor plumbing or telephone service is rare. . . .*
>
> *There is a great deal of illness at Pine Ridge. . . . The infant mortality rate is twice that of the nation's, and infectious diseases among small children are a major problem. The incidence of tuberculosis is seventeen times that for the rest of the country. The life expectancy for a person at Pine Ridge is thirty-eight years, compared with sixty-two years nationally. . . .*
>
> *The solution to the Indian problem still is dimly seen to lie in pouring the Indians into the big cities where they will intermingle with everyone else. But the city planners are trying to figure out how to get people out of the cramped city and back into the countryside. If the administration does not pull hard to redevelop these rural areas, it will end up merely fanning the flames in the cities.* **❞**

LINKING HISTORY AND GEOGRAPHY

Refer to the map on page 493. How did geography influence U.S. policy toward Cuba and the Dominican Republic?

BUILDING YOUR PORTFOLIO

Complete the following projects independently or cooperatively.

1. **CIVIL RIGHTS** In chapters 17 and 18 you served as a reporter covering the civil rights movement. Building on that experience, write a memorandum to the manager of your station explaining why the station should provide coverage of the civil rights efforts of African Americans, Hispanic Americans, Native Americans, and women.

2. **THE GOVERNMENT AND THE ECONOMY** In Chapter 17 you prepared a chart of government programs designed to help WWII veterans. Building on that experience, imagine you are a member of Johnson's Great Society. Prepare an illustrated pamphlet that describes government efforts in areas such as health care, urban renewal, or education.

3. **POPULAR CULTURE** In Chapter 18 you prepared a photo essay on American culture during the 1950s. Building on that experience, imagine you are a reporter for *Rolling Stone*, assigned to write an article about the first two decades of rock 'n' roll. Prepare a family tree of rock music, using photos to trace the influence of rhythm and blues, jazz, folk, country, and the British Invasion on American music up to 1970.

BUILDING YOUR PORTFOLIO

Have students refer to **Building Your Portfolio Worksheet 4**, assigned at the beginning of Unit 4. Use the worksheet to help students monitor their progress on the portfolio projects.

Assessment

Core Resources
• Reteaching Worksheet 19
• Chapter 19 Tests
• Alternative Assessment Forms
Test Generator

*U*RBAN AMERICA

The growth of Los Angeles in the 1920s and 1930s was largely because of the expansion of the motion picture industry in Hollywood. The Nestor Company built Hollywood's first film studio in 1911, and numerous other companies followed suit. Most film studios were attracted to the Los Angeles area because of its mild, dry climate and proximity to natural scenery that was ideal for outdoor filming.

America's GEOGRAPHY

URBAN AMERICA

*A*s more people moved into the cities and suburbs after World War II, metropolitan areas —large cities or groups of cities and their surrounding areas—arose. The city of Los Angeles is typical of the 20th-century metropolis. In the 1920s most of the land inside the official city limits was not developed. As the city grew, it engulfed numerous surrounding areas. By the 1980s the Los Angeles metropolitan area encompassed some 80 smaller cities. Like many urban-dwellers, Los Angeles–area residents generally live outside the city and commute to work. This has led to the observation that Los Angeles, like many other metropolitan areas, is in fact "a hundred suburbs in search of a city."

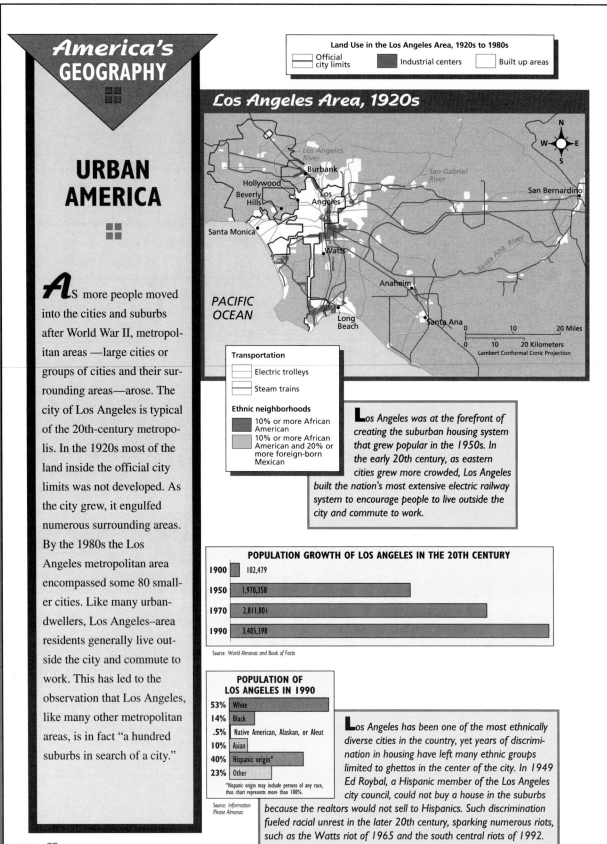

Land Use in the Los Angeles Area, 1920s to 1980s

☐ Official city limits ■ Industrial centers ☐ Built up areas

Los Angeles Area, 1920s

Los Angeles River · Burbank · Hollywood · Beverly Hills · Los Angeles · San Gabriel River · San Bernardino · Santa Monica · Watts · Santa Ana River · Anaheim · PACIFIC OCEAN · Long Beach · Santa Ana

0 10 20 Miles
0 10 20 Kilometers
Lambert Conformal Conic Projection

Transportation
☐ Electric trolleys
☐ Steam trains

Ethnic neighborhoods
■ 10% or more African American
■ 10% or more African American and 20% or more foreign-born Mexican

*L*os Angeles was at the forefront of creating the suburban housing system that grew popular in the 1950s. In the early 20th century, as eastern cities grew more crowded, Los Angeles built the nation's most extensive electric railway system to encourage people to live outside the city and commute to work.

POPULATION GROWTH OF LOS ANGELES IN THE 20TH CENTURY

Year	Population
1900	102,479
1950	1,970,358
1970	2,811,801
1990	3,485,398

Source: World Almanac and Book of Facts

POPULATION OF LOS ANGELES IN 1990

%	Group
53%	White
14%	Black
.5%	Native American, Alaskan, or Aleut
10%	Asian
40%	Hispanic origin*
23%	Other

*Hispanic origin may include persons of any race, thus chart represents more than 100%.

Source: Information Please Almanac

*L*os Angeles has been one of the most ethnically diverse cities in the country, yet years of discrimination in housing have left many ethnic groups limited to ghettos in the center of the city. In 1949 Ed Roybal, a Hispanic member of the Los Angeles city council, could not buy a house in the suburbs because the realtors would not sell to Hispanics. Such discrimination fueled racial unrest in the later 20th century, sparking numerous riots, such as the Watts riot of 1965 and the south central riots of 1992.

Los Angeles Area, 1950s

Transportation
- Freeway completed
- Freeway under construction
- Federal or state highway

Ethnic neighborhoods
- 40% or more African American
- 40% or more Hispanic
- 30% or more Asian

Los Angeles River · Burbank · Hollywood · Beverly Hills · Los Angeles · Santa Monica · San Gabriel River · San Bernardino · Watts · Santa Ana River · Anaheim · PACIFIC OCEAN · Santa Ana · Long Beach

0 10 20 Miles
0 10 20 Kilometers
Lambert Conformal Conic Projection

By the 1940s automobiles had replaced the railway system as the preferred means of transportation in Los Angeles. Construction of a huge freeway network encouraged automobile use, but it also led to a rise in smog pollution—a problem that plagues many cities today. While Los Angeles has grown rapidly, it has also faced numerous problems caused by its geography. The dry climate has contributed to several brush fires in recent years. Lack of an adequate water supply led to the construction of Owens River Aqueduct in 1913, followed by the California Aqueduct in 1973. Los Angeles also lies in an area of heavy earthquake activity. The city has been rocked by numerous earthquakes, including one in January 1994 that killed more than 50 people.

Los Angeles Area, 1980s

Average traffic flow per day
- 200,000 or more vehicles
- 100,000–199,000 vehicles
- 50,000–99,999 vehicles
- 49,999 or fewer vehicles
- Other major road

Ethnic neighborhoods
- 40% or more African American
- 40% or more Hispanic
- 30% or more Asian
- Mixed ethnic population

Los Angeles River · Burbank · Hollywood · Beverly Hills · Los Angeles · Santa Monica · San Gabriel River · San Bernardino · Watts · Santa Ana River · Anaheim · PACIFIC OCEAN · Santa Ana · Long Beach

0 10 20 Miles
0 10 20 Kilometers
Lambert Conformal Conic Projection

By the mid–1980s Los Angeles was the second-largest city in America. Many citizens, worried that the city was growing too rapidly, campaigned for measures to slow growth and improve urban conditions. In 1986 the city passed a measure that cut in half the amount of land available to developers for construction. Also in the mid–1980s the city began working on plans to improve public transportation with a new train and subway system.

HISTORICAL SIDELIGHTS
Freeways
As the traffic flow in large cities increased in the 20th century, so did the expansion of freeways—also called superhighways. These are limited-access, multi-lane highways designed for high-speed traffic. The word *freeway,* which was coined in the 1930s to refer to non-toll roads, now simply refers to the free flow of traffic on these highways. Thus some so-called freeways carry toll charges.

WAR IN VIETNAM

1954–1975

Chapter Overview

In the early 1950s U.S. containment policy focused on Asia. To prevent a Communist victory in Vietnam, the U.S. first supported France's attempts to reestablish rule over its former colony. The U.S. then aided the anti-Communist government of South Vietnam, under attack from the Communist North. Escalating U.S. military involvement failed to produce victory and provoked dissension at home. The Vietnam War ended in 1975, when Communist forces took over South Vietnam.

THE AMERICAN NATION VIDEODISC PROGRAM
A variety of still images, short videos, and activities are available for you to use as you teach this chapter. See Videodisc Resources in the Core Resources Binder for barcode correlations and suggestions for using the program.

Chapter Planning Guide

CHAPTER 20	CORE RESOURCES	**AV** AUDIOVISUAL RESOURCES	PROGRAM RESOURCES
INTRODUCTION pp. 518–519	■ Geography Worksheet 20 ■ Building Your Portfolio Worksheet 4		
TEACHING THE CHAPTER pp. 520–545	■ Graphic Organizer 20 ■ Social Studies Skills Worksheet 20 ■ Literature Worksheet 20 ■ Outline Map 21	■ *The American Nation Videodisc: Vietnam and the Media* ■ *Everyday Life in America Transparency and Worksheet 30*	■ *Eyewitnesses and Others*, Volume 2: Readings 69, 70 ■ Art in American History Transparency and Worksheet 45
REVIEW AND ASSESSMENT pp. 546–547	■ Chapter 20 Daily Quizzes ■ Reteaching Worksheet 20 ■ Chapter 20 Tests ■ Alternative Assessment Forms		■ Test Generator

Additional Resources

BOOKS FOR TEACHERS

Halberstam, David. *The Best and the Brightest.* McKay, 1983. Pulitzer Prize–winning journalist's examination of decision making that led to the war.

Herring, George C. *America's Longest War: The United States and Vietnam, 1950–1975.* McGraw-Hill, 1986. Chronicles the war from earliest U.S. involvement.

Karnow, Stanley. *Vietnam: A History.* Viking Penguin, 1984. Companion to the PBS Series "Vietnam: A Television History."

BOOKS FOR STUDENTS

Edelman, Bernard. *Dear America: Letters Home from Vietnam.* Pocket Books, 1989. Shows war through the eyes of U.S. personnel.

*Hoobler, Dorothy, and Thomas Hoobler. *Vietnam: Why We Fought.* Knopf, 1990. History of Vietnam's foreign relations.

Marshall, Kathryn. *In the Combat Zone: An Oral History of American Women in Vietnam.* Little, Brown, 1987. Examines women's military, medical, and civilian roles.

* for students reading below grade level

MULTIMEDIA MATERIALS

How Far from Home: Veterans after Vietnam. Video, 30 min. Northern Light Productions. Portrays the many problems veterans faced upon returning home.

Vietnam: Chronicle of a War. Video, 88 min. CBS. Walter Cronkite traces history of U.S. involvement.

Why Vietnam? Video, 32 min. U.S. Department of Defense. Shows U.S. government's rationale for fighting in Vietnam.

USE WITH PAGES 518–519

Listed on the right are the themes emphasized in Chapter 20. The questions in boldface type stimulate critical thinking and provide students with an opportunity to discuss the themes within a broadened context. The questions also appear in the pupil's edition on p. 518.

■ GLOBAL RELATIONS

How might global conditions lead one nation to intervene in the affairs of another? Student responses should consider differences in nations' foreign-policy goals, economic interests, and national values. Responses might also reflect students' individual values and beliefs.

■ CONSTITUTIONAL HERITAGE

Why might one branch of government fear another branch becoming too strong? Students should note that the balance of power between branches and the system of checks and balances would be jeopardized.

■ DEMOCRATIC VALUES

What are the limits to the government's responsibility to keep the public informed? Students should consider national security interests versus the need for open government in a democratic system. The development of the atomic bomb during World War II might be a point for debate.

In a democracy, what limits are there to a people's right to protest government actions? Students might suggest that citizens must protest through legal means—peaceful demonstrations, boycotts, elections, recalls, etc.

CHAPTER STRATEGIES FOR MEETING INDIVIDUAL NEEDS

LIMITED ENGLISH PROFICIENT LEARNERS

Have pairs of students write down the boldfaced terms and define them with sketches or short phrases. Ask partners to take turns asking each other questions that use the terms.

TACTILE/KINESTHETIC LEARNERS

Have students work in groups to develop two skits, one illustrating U.S. soldiers' Vietnam experiences, and the other showing confrontation at home between hawks and doves.

LEARNERS HAVING DIFFICULTY

Have pairs of students write brief answers to the questions in each section Focus and two or three sentences summing up each section. Then have them write a short summary of the chapter.

AUDITORY LEARNERS

Have students prepare dramatic readings of important quotations and other critical parts of each section of the chapter.

VISUAL LEARNERS

Have students view a videotape or movie on the Vietnam War. Then have small groups of students make a flowchart showing major events of the war. Students should then list the domestic responses to each event in the chart.

GIFTED LEARNERS

Have students list and describe major turning points in the war. Ask them to evaluate the U.S. response at each point, deciding whether the response should have included withdrawal.

USING THE CHAPTER FOCUS

■ UNDERSTANDING THE MAIN IDEA

Call on a volunteer to read the Understanding the Main Idea paragraph aloud. Ask students what they know about Vietnam from movies, TV programs, and books. List students' comments on a flip chart or butcher paper and have students evaluate their comments after they complete the chapter.

THEMES
Have students work individually or in small groups to answer the questions under Themes. Save students' responses so that they can compare them with their responses after studying the chapter. (See p. 517B for suggested answers.)

■ THE TIME LINE

Point out that events such as the Geneva Conference in 1954 and the unrest that grew in South Vietnam after Diem took power in 1955 heightened Cold War tensions and U.S. fears of the spread of communism. These events helped shape U.S. decisions to increase America's involvement in Vietnam.

Have students note the length of U.S. troop deployment in Vietnam. Ask them to compare it to American involvement in other conflicts (World War I, 1917–1918; World War II, 1941–1945; Korea, 1950–1953).

CORE RESOURCES

- **Graphic Organizer 20**
- **Geography Worksheet 20**
- **Outline Map 21**
- **Building Your Portfolio Worksheet 4**

ABOUT THE ILLUSTRATION

A marine officer takes shelter during the struggle for Hue, one of the most bitter battles of the war. North Vietnamese briefly captured the city in early 1968. U.S. Marines played a decisive role in helping South Vietnamese troops retake the city. In the rubble-strewn streets, U.S. soldiers had a difficult time locating and identifying the enemy. Have students study the marine's expression and stance. Ask them what emotions they think the soldier is feeling.

Chapter 20

1954–1975

WAR IN VIETNAM

FOCUS

UNDERSTANDING THE MAIN IDEA

Most U.S. leaders expected the war in Vietnam to end quickly once U.S. troops and equipment entered the conflict. They did not dream that some 2.6 million Americans would serve in a war that dragged on for more than a decade. Nor did they imagine that antiwar protests would grow to the proportions they did.

THEMES

■ **GLOBAL RELATIONS** How might global conditions lead one nation to intervene in the affairs of another?

■ **CONSTITUTIONAL HERITAGE** Why might one branch of government fear another branch becoming too strong?

■ **DEMOCRATIC VALUES** What are the limits to the government's responsibility to keep the public informed? In a democracy, what limits are there to a people's right to protest government actions?

1954	1955	1965	1973	1975
Geneva Conference held.	Diem comes to power in South Vietnam.	U.S. sends combat troops to Vietnam.	Cease-fire declared.	Saigon falls.

Have students list the reasons that led the U.S. to fight in Korea. Write students' answers on a flip chart or butcher paper and save it. As you move through the chapter, compare the reasons for U.S. involvement in Korea with those for American involvement in Vietnam.

▦ LINK TO THE PAST

The United States had taken the position of opposing the spread of communism anywhere in the world. U.S. troops had recently fought against Communist forces in Korea. Now Americans became involved in a similar war in Vietnam, where the Vietnamese had won their independence from the French a few years earlier.

MAKING CONNECTIONS

Literature
Have students compare Graham Greene's description of the young U.S. adviser with the soldier shown in the photograph. Ask students whether the photograph and Greene's description match.

PRIMARY SOURCE

Description of Change: excerpted
Rationale: excerpted to focus on main idea

A U.S. Marine officer takes cover.

*I*n Graham Greene's novel *The Quiet American* (1955), the narrator sits in a Vietnamese café thinking about a new arrival, the American "adviser" Alden Pyle. According to the narrator, the young American "seemed incapable of harm":

> ❝ Perhaps only ten days ago he had been walking back across the Common in Boston, his arms full of the books he had been reading in advance on the Far East and the problems of China. He didn't even hear what I said; he was absorbed already in the dilemmas of Democracy and the responsibilities of the West; he was determined—I learnt that very soon—to do good, not to any individual person but to a country, a continent, a world. ❞

Greene's Alden Pyle closely resembles the American advisers sent to South Vietnam in the 1950s. This "quiet American," wading into the rough sea of post–World War II Southeast Asia, typifies the early American self-image in Vietnam: confident, serious, and eagerly committed to building a model democracy.

This sense of idealism was grounded in the effort to save Vietnam and the rest of the world from communism, even at great cost to America. The eventual cost—years of war and more than 60,000 Americans dead or missing—was higher than most believed possible. And despite the sacrifices, Vietnam was not "saved." In the war's wake, Americans were left to ponder how early idealism ended in what has been called "a tragedy of epic dimensions."

Vietnam Women's Memorial

Chapter 20

SECTION

1

Introducing the Section

FOCUS OBJECTIVES

- Describe why China and then France sought control of Vietnam.

- Explain why the U.S. refused to back Vietnamese independence in the 1940s and 1950s.

- Identify the reasons why President Kennedy increased U.S. involvement in Vietnam.

PREVIEW WORKSHOP

Following is a list of the significant people, places, and terms in this section. You may wish to use this list as a section preview.

People
- Ho Chi Minh
- Ngo Dinh Diem

Places
- Vietnam
- China
- Red River Delta
- Mekong Delta
- Hanoi
- Saigon/Ho Chi Minh City
- Central Highlands
- Annamite Mountains
- Dien Bien Phu

Terms
- Vietminh
- domino theory
- Vietcong

Section 1

BACKGROUND TO CONFLICT

F O C U S

- **Why did China and then France want to control Vietnam?**
- **Why did the United States refuse to back Vietnamese independence in the 1940s and 1950s?**
- **Why did President Kennedy increase U.S. involvement in Vietnam?**

For centuries invaders coveted the fertile river deltas and coastal lowlands of Vietnam. First China and later France conquered and ruled Vietnam. But the deep desire of the Vietnamese people to be free could not be overcome. During World War II, France began to lose its grip on Vietnam. And as the war came to a close, Vietnamese Communists fought for power, hoping to establish an independent nation. This threat of a Communist takeover soon drew the United States into the conflict.

French colonial occupation in Saigon

THE GEOGRAPHIC SETTING

Fishhook-shaped Vietnam is the easternmost country of Southeast Asia—8,000 miles across the Pacific from the west coast of the United States. It

▲ **Vietnam is one of the world's largest producers of rice, cultivating more than 12 million acres each year.**

is slightly smaller than California, covering 127,207 square miles of mostly hills and dense forests. Lying south of China, Vietnam is bordered on the west by Laos and Cambodia. Its coastline stretches along the Gulf of Tonkin, the South China Sea, and the Gulf of Thailand (see map on page 521).

The population of Vietnam is centered mostly in two areas: the Red River Delta in the far north and the Mekong (MAY-KAWNG) Delta in the south. The Mekong Delta is Vietnam's richest agricultural region, specializing in rice cultivation. Hanoi is the major city of the north and the country's capital, while Ho Chi Minh City (previously South Vietnam's capital, Saigon) is the largest city in the south. Other cities, such as the ports Da Nang and Hue (WAY), are located on the narrow coastal lowlands of central Vietnam.

To the north of the Mekong Delta are the central highlands, sparsely populated and mostly covered by forest. Farther north, the Annamite Mountains form the jagged backbone of Vietnam. Their rugged peaks and dense rain forest separate much of Vietnam from neighboring Laos.

CORE RESOURCES

• **Section 1 Daily Quiz**

520

MOTIVATING:
PRIOR KNOWLEDGE

Call on volunteers to describe U.S. containment policy. Ask students where else in Asia the U.S. had already applied this policy by 1954. *(China, Korea)* Ask them how successful this policy had been.

Teaching the Section

THE GEOGRAPHY OF VIETNAM

Have students work in small groups to draw maps of Vietnam, including major rivers, mountain ranges, highlands, ports, cities, and delta regions. Display the maps on the wall. Call on groups to suggest geographic characteristics of Vietnam that might cause China and France to want to control it. Ask what geographic characteristics might make such control difficult.

▶

CHINESE OCCUPATION

The moist tropical climate of the deltas and coastal lowlands has allowed Vietnamese farmers to grow several crops of rice a year. It was this agricultural abundance that tempted China to invade the Red River Delta around 200 B.C. For more than a thousand years, the Chinese struggled to maintain control over northern and central Vietnam. But the Vietnamese resisted, finally winning limited independence from China in A.D. 939.

In the 1400s China tried to reassert control over Vietnam. A Vietnamese military leader named Le Loi employed guerrilla warfare to defeat the Chinese invaders. Using tactics similar to those later used against the French and Americans, Le Loi's rebels worked as peasants by day; by night they took up arms to attack the Chinese. By 1428 the rebels had driven the Chinese from the country and won independence for Vietnam. Le Loi became the new emperor.

FRENCH OCCUPATION

Vietnam again lost its independence in the surge of European imperialism in the mid-1800s. This time the invaders were French, attracted by the promise of gaining access to Asian trade and of making new Catholic converts.

Despite the stubborn resistance of the Vietnamese, French military power ultimately won out. In 1883 the Vietnamese were forced to grant France complete control of the country. France later combined Vietnam with Laos and Cambodia to form French Indochina, one of France's richest possessions.

■■ **The Chinese and later the French sought control of Vietnam's rich farmlands and trade.**

Ho Chi Minh and Vietnamese independence. Like the Chinese, the French gained control of the land but not the hearts of the Vietnamese. Nationalist feelings remained strong.

Indochina

A TROPICAL PENINSULA The nations of Indochina occupy a peninsula stretching from the mainland of Southeast Asia deep into the tropical waters of the South China Sea.

❓ RELATIVE LOCATION How might Vietnam's location have contributed to its long history of foreign invasion?

Foremost among the nationalists was Nguyen That Thanh (en-gy-EN TAHT TAHN), a world wanderer and man of many names, whose last alias was Ho Chi Minh (HOH CHEE MIN)—"He Who Enlightens."

Ho was born in central Vietnam in 1890, the son of a poor country scholar. In 1911, calling himself Van Ba (Third Son), he got a job as cook on a French merchant ship. After spending a few years at sea, he decided to settle in London. There, while working as a pastry cook in a hotel, Ho learned the English language (he was already fluent in French).

From London, Ho went to Paris, where he soon emerged as a leader of Vietnamese nationalists living in France. Ho joined the French socialists but

BUILDING VOCABULARY

In this instance *Indo* refers to India. Due to the influence of India in the region, some areas in Asia, such as Indochina, came to be labeled in part by their location relative to India.

Map Caption Answer
Its access to trade routes and its climate suited to rice production made it attractive to foreign invaders.

BIO GRAPHY PERSONALITIES IN HISTORY

In 1919 Ho, who was living in France at the time, petitioned the Paris Peace Conference to consider the cause of the Vietnamese people. He asked that the principles of national self-determination enunciated in Wilson's Fourteen Points be applied to Indochina. But Ho was not successful in getting the Big Four to consider his appeal.

 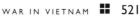

Teaching the **Section**

U.S. POLICY IN VIETNAM

Ask students to explain how Truman's policy of containment in Europe after World War II was related to America's refusal to back Vietnam's independence in Southeast Asia. Poll the class to see how many think that American policy would have been different if Ho Chi Minh had not been a Communist. Call on students to defend their opinions.

THE DOMINO THEORY

Label the spines of six books with the names of Vietnam, Laos, Cambodia, Thailand, Indonesia, and the Philippines. Stand the books in a row with the Vietnam book first. Push "Vietnam" so that it knocks the other books over. Have students explain how this demonstration is related to what Eisenhower feared would happen if Vietnam "fell" to communism.

HISTORICAL SIDELIGHTS

Vietminh Aid U.S.

The Vietminh opposed Japan in World War II. They helped rescue downed U.S. pilots in that war and provided Americans with intelligence information about the Japanese. For this reason, Ho expected at least moral support from the U.S. regarding Vietnam's drive for independence.

GLOBAL CONNECTIONS

The close of World War II saw France's African empire also threatened when in 1945, Algerians began to demand freedom. In 1954, just six months after the French surrender in Vietnam, Algerian nationalists began an all-out struggle for independence. Thus, the French military found itself in another long, bitter guerrilla war—this one lasting nearly eight years until Algeria gained its freedom in 1962.

Ho Chi Minh

soon left them to help organize the French Communist party. Later, Ho claimed that "it was patriotism and not Communism that originally inspired" his quest for Vietnamese independence. By 1923, though, he was convinced that a worldwide Communist revolution was Vietnam's only hope and left Paris to study revolutionary tactics in Moscow.

During the 1920s and 1930s Ho organized and plotted for Vietnamese independence. One French comrade described him as "taut and quivering, with only one thought in his head, his country, Vietnam." Hunted as a Communist, Ho donned disguises as he moved from country to country—sometimes a Chinese journalist, at other times a Buddhist monk with flowing robes.

What Ho awaited was a chance to launch his plan. That chance came during World War II. In 1940 the Japanese army swept down from China to occupy all of French Indochina, the Philippines, Malaya, and Indonesia. In Vietnam the Japanese left the French colonial government in place but controlled it. Early in 1941 Ho slipped secretly into Vietnam to organize a resistance. He called the movement the League for the Independence of Vietnam, or **Vietminh** (vee-ET-MIN). When the Japanese withdrew from Indochina after surrendering to the Allies in August 1945, the Vietminh declared independence.

In Hanoi on September 2, more than half a million people gathered at an independence celebration to hear Ho speak. In an effort to gain American support, the Vietminh leader echoed America's Declaration of Independence: "We hold the truth that all men are created equal, that they are endowed by their Creator with certain unalienable rights, among them life, liberty, and the pursuit of happiness."

At another celebration that day, American army officers joined Vietnamese leaders on the reviewing stand as a Vietnamese band played "The Star-Spangled Banner." U.S. warplanes flew over the gathering in a salute to Vietnam's independence. The French were sure to resist, but the

United States seemed poised to prevent them from reclaiming colonial rule over Vietnam.

France and the Vietminh go to war.

American policy toward Vietnam was soon put to the test. By 1946 the French and the Vietnamese were once again locked in battle. Would America stand with the Vietnamese in this conflict? The answer was no. Not only did President Truman ignore Ho's pleas for assistance, he threw U.S. support behind France.

Why did Truman side with France? First, he viewed France as a vital ally in the struggle against the spread of communism in postwar Europe. Second, he was unwilling to back the Vietminh because of Ho's Communist connections. U.S. advisers feared that communism would engulf Asia (see Chapter 17). This fear was reinforced in 1949 when Mao Zedong's Communists took over China—Asia's most populous country and a former U.S. ally. By 1950 the United States was locked in a bloody ground war to turn back Communist North Korea's invasion of South Korea. Meanwhile, Communist-led nationalist revolts rocked Indonesia, the Philippines, and Malaya.

Because of these developments the focus of America's containment policy broadened to include East Asia. There, U.S. policymakers vowed to hold the line against communism. Truman's successor, Dwight D. Eisenhower, shared this resolve, especially in regard to Southeast Asia. Besides possessing abundant raw materials essential to modern industry, the region was considered of strategic importance in containing the Chinese Communists. Eisenhower warned that if Vietnam fell to communism, the rest of

▶ **At Dien Bien Phu a weary French soldier awaits further shelling by Vietminh guerrillas in early 1954.**

U.S. INVOLVEMENT

Create two columns on the chalkboard. Label one column *Involvement* and the other column *Noninvolvement*. Ask students to imagine that they are advisers to President Kennedy. Call on volunteers to suggest reasons for and against continuing U.S. support for the government of South Vietnam. Then review the two lists that the class has created. Conclude by asking students to name events elsewhere in the world that might have influenced Kennedy to continue to support the Diem government against the Communists. *(Bay of Pigs, Berlin Wall)*

▶

Southeast Asia would soon follow. The president illustrated his point by saying, "You have a row of dominoes set up. You knock over the first one, and what will happen to the last one is a certainty that it will go over very quickly." This idea came to be called the **domino theory**.

■■ **Believing that communism would spread throughout Asia if it took hold in Vietnam, the United States turned down Ho's pleas for help against the French.**

President Eisenhower's commitment to a non-Communist Vietnam was even stronger than Truman's. By 1954 America was paying much of the cost of France's war effort. But even with massive aid, the French suffered defeat after defeat.

Money and military equipment were of limited use against Vietminh guerrilla tactics. The Vietminh chose when and where to attack, struck without warning, and then disappeared into the jungle. In a comment to an American journalist in 1946, Ho Chi Minh had expressed his people's determination to prevail, characterizing the fight as "a war between an elephant"—the French—"and a tiger"—the Vietnamese:

❝ If the tiger ever stands still, the elephant will crush him with his mighty tusks. But the tiger does not stand still. . . . He will leap upon the back of the elephant, tearing huge chunks from his hide, and then the tiger will leap back into the dark jungle. And slowly the elephant will bleed to death. That will be the war of Indochina. ❞

From *America Inside Out* by David Schoenbrun © 1984

Frustrated, the French tried to lure the Vietminh into a conventional battle at Dien Bien Phu (dyen byen FOO), deep within Vietminh-held northern Vietnam. The plan backfired. Some 13,000 French soldiers soon found themselves encircled by more than 50,000 Vietminh troops. The French commander urged his war-weary soldiers to hold out—offering them the hope of a rescue: "The Americans will not let us down; the free world will not let us down."

Help did not come. Although willing to commit money, Eisenhower was reluctant to become directly involved in another Asian war so soon after the Korean War. As a result, the Vietminh defeated the French and on May 7, 1954, forced their surrender.

The Geneva Conference. In the spring of 1954, just one day after the French surrender at Dien Bien Phu, an international conference to settle the Indochina conflict began in Geneva, Switzerland. There, representatives of the French and the Vietminh attempted to map out Indochina's future. The People's Republic of China (Communist China), the United States, Great Britain, the Soviet Union, Laos, and Cambodia joined the discussions.

The Communist Chinese, who had begun aiding the Vietminh in 1950, hoped to limit U.S. influence in the region. They also wished to prevent the establishment of a strong, unified Vietnam on their southern border. The Americans,

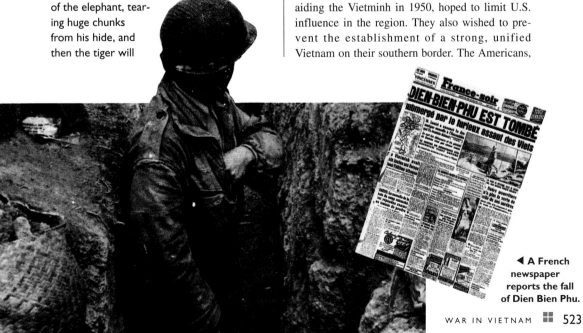

◀ **A French newspaper reports the fall of Dien Bien Phu.**

COOPERATIVE LEARNING

Have students work in small groups to portray U.S. officials formulating policy on Vietnam. Assign members the following roles: an official fearful of Soviet influence and Chinese expansion in Southeast Asia, one convinced Ho Chi Minh is a nationalist who will resist all foreign influence, and one believing that U.S. containment policy in Asia should not be broadened to include Southeast Asia. Groups should write down the policy recommendations that result from their meetings. Call on volunteers to present their groups' recommendations to the class.

PRIMARY SOURCE

Description of Change: excerpted
Rationale: excerpted to focus on main idea

■■ Ask students why Ho compares the French to an elephant and what animal he might have chosen as a comparison for U.S. forces.

Practice

GUIDED PRACTICE

Have volunteers identify periods of external or internal conflict for Vietnam. List the periods on the chalkboard and review them, asking students to provide details about each period.

INDEPENDENT PRACTICE

Using the list developed in the Guided Practice, have students prepare illustrated time lines showing the periods of conflict in Vietnam. Students may wish to include their time lines in their portfolios.

Review and Assessment

REVIEW Have students create an outline of the major points in Section 1. Then assign the Section 1 Review on p. 525.

ASSESS Assign the **Section 1 Daily Quiz** in *Core Resources*.

---

meanwhile, did not want to see Vietnam handed over completely to the Communists.

A cease-fire was agreed to, but no definite political settlement was achieved. Vietnam was temporarily divided at the 17th parallel (17° north latitude). North of the 17th parallel, the Vietminh held undisputed power; south of the line, remnants of the French-controlled government resumed authority. Vietminh forces would withdraw to the north; French forces would withdraw to the south. General elections to reunify the country were scheduled for July 1956. Alarmed that the Communists would likely win a nationwide election, the United States refused to endorse the agreement.

THE REGIME OF NGO DINH DIEM

President Eisenhower estimated that Ho might win a general election by as much as four to one. Still, he hoped that southern Vietnam, at least, might be kept non-Communist. Who could stand against Ho? One possibility was Ngo Dinh Diem (en-GOH DIN de-EM), a former government official under the French. Though lacking Ho's charisma, Diem was enough of a nationalist to be a credible Vietnamese leader.

Diem takes power in the south. Ngo Dinh Diem was strongly anti-Communist. He had spent several years in the United States, where his political views attracted powerful backers. In 1955 Diem became president of the newly established Republic of Vietnam (South Vietnam) following a rigged election—in Saigon, Diem got more than 605,000 votes from the 450,000 registered voters! But Diem knew that he had no chance of winning a nationwide election against Ho. Thus, he refused to call an election in the south when the July 1956 date set by the Geneva Conference rolled around.

Diem, a Roman Catholic, was unpopular from the start. The large Buddhist population resented the favoritism he showed toward Catholics. Peasants disliked his land policies, which favored wealthy landholders. And almost everyone objected that power was solely in the grip of Diem's family. Above all, people feared his ruthless efforts to root out his political enemies. Diem's hated security forces routinely tortured and imprisoned opponents.

By the late 1950s armed revolution had erupted in the south. In 1959, military assistance began

flowing from the north to the Vietminh who had stayed in the south. In 1960 the southern Vietminh formed the National Liberation Front (NLF). The NLF's main goal was the overthrow of the Ngo Dinh Diem regime. Members of this rebel force were called **Vietcong** (Vietnamese Communists) by their opponents, but not all NLF supporters were Communists.

Many peasants joined the ranks of the NLF, some because of government repression. Others joined out of fear: the NLF, like Diem's forces, used terrorist tactics, assassinating hundreds of government officials. Soon much of the countryside was under Vietcong control.

America's involvement deepens. John F. Kennedy, who became president in 1961, fully subscribed to the domino theory. He also was eager to bolster America's image in the world—an image that had been tarnished by the failed Bay of Pigs invasion and the Soviets' raising of the Berlin Wall early in his presidency (see Chapter 19). Coming to the aid of South Vietnam, which Kennedy had once called the "cornerstone of the Free World in Southeast Asia," provided America with a chance to assert its power.

When Kennedy took office, some 700 U.S. military advisers were in South Vietnam training

▼ Ngo Dinh Diem paces the floor of his Saigon palace after crushing an attempt to overthrow his regime in the spring of 1955.

RETEACH Have students work in small groups to answer the questions in the section Focus. Assign each group member a question. Have members share answers with one another.

Closure

Have students reflect on Vietnam's history until 1963. Then ask if they agree with President Kennedy's statement that Vietnam was the "cornerstone of the Free World in Southeast Asia."

Extension

EVALUATE Have interested students evaluate and report on George Kennan's attitude toward U.S. involvement in Vietnam.

RESEARCH Have students research and report on Vietnam's Joan of Arc, Trieu Au, who fought for independence from China in the third century A.D.

Diem's army. Over the course of his administration, Kennedy increased that number to more than 16,000. As Vietcong attacks mounted, Kennedy authorized U.S. forces to engage in direct combat. As a result, the number of Americans killed or wounded climbed from 14 in 1961 to nearly 500 in 1963.

■■ **President Kennedy saw U.S. involvement in Vietnam as a way to halt the spread of communism and strengthen America's image in the world.**

Diem's overthrow. The situation was also escalating politically. South Vietnam's Buddhist leaders now openly opposed Diem's regime. Diem was waging a brutal campaign of repression against Buddhists. Hundreds had been arrested, and many had been killed in the crackdown. In response, several Buddhist monks publicly set themselves on fire. These grisly protests shocked Americans, and U.S. officials in Saigon threatened to withdraw support for Diem unless he ended the repression.

When Diem refused to comply, U.S. leaders gave quiet encouragement to a group of young South Vietnamese army officers plotting Diem's overthrow. The plotters struck in November 1963, murdering both Diem and his brother. Diem's violent assassination upset U.S. advisers, who had been prepared to fly Diem out of the country.

▲ On June 11, 1963, Quang Duc set himself on fire at a busy intersection in Saigon. He was the first of several Buddhist monks who killed themselves to protest Diem's policies.

Kennedy's doubts increase. Diem's overthrow did nothing to ease Kennedy's growing concern over America's involvement in Vietnam. In an interview shortly before Diem's fall, Kennedy had said of the South Vietnamese: "In the final analysis it is their war. They are the ones who have to win or lose it." But we will never know how Kennedy might have handled the situation. Three weeks after Diem's murder, Kennedy himself was assassinated in Dallas.

SECTION REVIEW ANSWERS

IDENTIFY

For significance, see the following pages:
Ho Chi Minh (p. 521)
Vietminh (p. 522)
domino theory (p. 523)
Ngo Dinh Diem (p. 524)
Vietcong (p. 524)

LOCATE

For locations, see the map on p. 521.

1. *France was anti-Communist ally in Europe; feared Ho's Communist connections*
2. *belief in domino theory and desire to bolster America's image in the world*
3. *China—rich farmlands for abundant rice cultivation; France—access to Asian trade, Catholic conversion*
4. *pros—safeguarding Vietnam's abundant raw materials, containing communism; cons—U.S. casualties, financial costs, drain on U.S. resources*
5. *Letters will vary but should argue that Vietnam is seeking to restore its sovereign rights and self-government taken away by China and then France.*

S E C T I O N   **1**   R E V I E W

IDENTIFY and explain the significance of the following: Ho Chi Minh, Vietminh, domino theory, Ngo Dinh Diem, Vietcong.

LOCATE and explain the importance of the following: Vietnam, China, Red River Delta, Mekong Delta, Hanoi, Saigon, central highlands, Annamite Mountains, Dien Bien Phu.

1. **MAIN IDEA** Why did President Truman refuse Ho's requests for help against the French?
2. **MAIN IDEA** What led President Kennedy to increase U.S. involvement in Vietnam?
3. **LINKING HISTORY AND GEOGRAPHY** What attracted the Chinese and the French to Vietnam?
4. **WRITING TO PERSUADE** Imagine you are an adviser to President Eisenhower in 1959. On the basis of what you would know at the time, prepare a statement outlining the pros and cons of U.S. involvement in Vietnam. Then, in a paragraph, make a policy recommendation.
5. **USING HISTORICAL IMAGINATION** In the 1941 Atlantic Charter, President Roosevelt and British Prime Minister Churchill pledged "to see sovereign rights and self-government restored to those who have been forcibly deprived of them." Imagine that you are Ho. Write a letter to President Truman explaining why America should honor this pledge in Vietnam.

PREVIEW WORKSHOP

Following is a list of the significant places and terms in this section. You may wish to use this list as a section preview.

Places
■ Gulf of Tonkin

Terms
■ Tonkin Gulf Resolution
■ escalation
■ Operation Rolling Thunder
■ Ho Chi Minh Trail
■ defoliants
■ search-and-destroy missions
■ pacification

FOCUS OBJECTIVES

■ Discuss why the Tonkin Gulf Resolution raised a constitutional issue.

■ Describe the factors that frustrated U.S. military efforts.

CORE RESOURCES

• **Geography Worksheet 20**
• **Section 2 Daily Quiz**

Section 2

THE WAR ESCALATES

F O C U S

■ **Why did the Tonkin Gulf Resolution raise a constitutional issue?**

■ **What factors frustrated U.S. military efforts in Vietnam?**

"*I am not going to be the President who saw Vietnam go the way China went,*" *vowed Lyndon Baines Johnson, the next American president to inherit the Vietnam War. Throwing U.S. air power and thousands of young American troops into the conflict, Johnson hoped to end the war quickly. But the war in Vietnam would dominate the nation's consciousness for nearly a decade.*

LBJ

THE TONKIN GULF RESOLUTION

The new South Vietnamese government was just as corrupt and ineffective as Diem's, and the NLF continued to gain ground against the South's army (called the ARVN, for Army of the Republic of Vietnam). Secretary of Defense Robert McNamara, a cabinet member held over from the Kennedy administration, returned from a quick trip to Vietnam in December 1963 to give his new boss a sobering report. To prevent a Communist victory, McNamara advised, Johnson would have to increase the American commitment.

A Communist victory in Vietnam was an unthinkable prospect for Johnson. Like previous presidents, he firmly believed it was necessary to stop Communist expansion. Before increasing the U.S. commitment, however, Johnson planned to get congressional backing. Events on the seas off North Vietnam soon gave him the opportunity.

In August 1964 President Johnson announced that U.S. ships had been attacked twice in the Gulf of Tonkin. The president asked Congress to authorize the use of military force "to prevent further aggression." In an overwhelming show of patriotism, Congress passed the **Tonkin Gulf Resolution**, giving the president authority to take "all necessary measures to repel any armed attack against forces of the United States."

Johnson claimed that the attacks in the Gulf of Tonkin were "unprovoked." Later it was revealed that one of the ships, the destroyer *Maddox,* had been engaged in spying in support of South Vietnamese raids against North Vietnam and had fired first. Thus, the first North Vietnamese attack was not without cause. The second, moreover, probably never occurred: it appeared that nervous sailors, caught in stormy weather, had misinterpreted interference on their radar and sonar as enemy ships and torpedoes. Nonetheless, Johnson and his advisers got what they wanted: authority to expand the war as they saw fit. As Johnson admitted later, the resolution was "like Grandma's nightshirt—it covered everything."

Only a few in Congress voiced caution. Wayne Morse of Oregon, one of only two senators to vote against the Tonkin Gulf Resolution,

Remind students that containing communism was one reason for U.S. involvement in Vietnam. Have students write a paragraph supporting or disputing the idea that the end of the Cold War will prevent a situation similar to Vietnam from happening today. Ask volunteers to read their paragraphs to the class.

Teaching the Section

CONSTITUTIONAL ISSUES

Select two students to read aloud the parts of the Constitution that establish the military powers of the president and of Congress (Article II, Section 2, and Article I, Section 8). List these powers on the chalkboard. Have students speculate about which branch the framers of the Constitution intended to have most control over the nation's military power. Then ask what effect the Tonkin Gulf Resolution had on how that power was distributed. Conclude by asking students whether a president should have the power to commit American forces to combat without a declaration of war.

▶

---

warned: "I believe that history will record we have made a great mistake. . . . We are in effect giving the President war-making powers in the absence of a declaration of war." In other words, in passing the resolution, Congress had given up its constitutional power to declare war.

■■ **The Tonkin Gulf Resolution allowed American presidents to fight an undeclared war in Vietnam—contrary to the intent of the U.S. Constitution.**

*A*MERICAN FORCES IN VIETNAM

With the Tonkin Gulf Resolution in his pocket, President Johnson responded to his advisers' call for a buildup, or **escalation**, of American military forces in Vietnam. He ordered the Selective Service, the agency charged with carrying out the military draft, to begin calling up young men to serve in the armed forces. In April 1965 the Selective Service notified 13,700 draftees, and by December some 40,000 had received "greetings" from their local draft boards.

During the war more than 2.6 million Americans served in Vietnam. In the beginning most were professional soldiers, already enlisted in the armed forces. But as the demand for troops grew, more and more draftees were shipped to Vietnam. At the height of the war, American soldiers in Vietnam were, on average, younger (19), poorer, and less educated than those who had served in World War II or in the Korean War.

All young men who registered for the draft did not have an equal chance of serving in Vietnam. One out of four was excused from service for health reasons. Another 30 percent received non-health-related exemptions or deferments (postponements of service), most often for college enrollment. Mainly because of college deferments, young men from higher-income families were the least likely to be drafted. As a result, the poor served in numbers far greater than their proportion in the general population—as they had in most of the previous wars.

African and Hispanic Americans served in combat in especially high numbers, particularly during the early years of the war. Some of these soldiers protested that black and Hispanic soldiers were being asked to do more than their share of the fighting—and dying. In 1965, for example, African Americans accounted for almost 24 percent of all battle deaths, even though they made up only 11 percent of the U.S. population.

BUILDING VOCABULARY

In this instance *resolution* means a formal expression of intent that is voted on by an official body.

HISTORICAL SIDELIGHTS

Tonkin Gulf Resolution
When asked in 1964 whether U.S. ships had been involved in covert raids against the North Vietnamese, Secretary of Defense Robert McNamara said: "Our navy played absolutely no part in, was not associated with, was not aware of, any South Vietnamese actions, if there were any. . . . I say this flatly. This is a fact." However, four years later at Senate Foreign Relations Committee hearings, McNamara admitted the *Maddox* captain knew about the South Vietnamese operations although the captain was unaware of the "details."

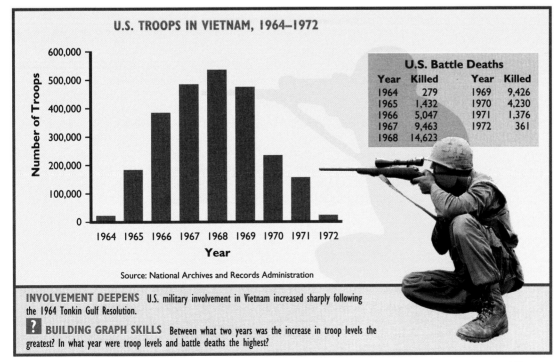

U.S. TROOPS IN VIETNAM, 1964–1972

(Bar graph: Number of Troops, 0 to 600,000, by Year 1964–1972)

	U.S. Battle Deaths			
Year	Killed		Year	Killed
1964	279		1969	9,426
1965	1,432		1970	4,230
1966	5,047		1971	1,376
1967	9,463		1972	361
1968	14,623			

Source: National Archives and Records Administration

INVOLVEMENT DEEPENS U.S. military involvement in Vietnam increased sharply following the 1964 Tonkin Gulf Resolution.

❓ **BUILDING GRAPH SKILLS** Between what two years was the increase in troop levels the greatest? In what year were troop levels and battle deaths the highest?

Graph Caption Answer
1965–1966; 1968

Teaching the Section

VIETNAM AND THE DRAFT

Divide the class into two groups to debate the following: *The draft was a fair way to build up U.S. military forces in Vietnam.* List each group's responses on the chalkboard.

MILITARY EFFORTS

Write the following military strategies on the chalkboard: *bombing, search-and-destroy missions,* and *pacification.* Have students identify the military objective that each strategy was intended to achieve. Then organize the class into three groups and assign a strategy to each group. Direct the groups to evaluate the success of their assigned strategy and to report their findings to the class.

PRIMARY SOURCE

Description of Change: excerpted

Rationale: excerpted to focus on main idea

MULTICULTURAL PERSPECTIVES

Although American air raids were intended to weaken the enemy's will to fight, the bombing actually intensified the nationalism and resistance of the North Vietnamese people. Even those who may have disliked the Communists rallied behind their nation as it came under attack by foreigners. Ton That Tung, a North Vietnamese physician, boasted that "the Americans thought that the more bombs they dropped, the quicker we would fall to our knees and surrender. But the bombs heightened rather than dampened our spirit."

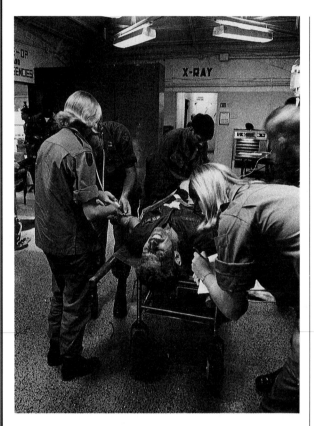

◀ **Most U.S. servicewomen in Vietnam were army nurses assigned to Vietnamese hospitals or to Mobile Army Surgical Hospital (MASH) units.**

Navarra Rhoads, who served in the Army Nurse Corps, later described how complete this detachment could become:

❝ I remember I had completed this amputation and I had the soldier's leg under my arm. I was holding the leg because I had to dress it up and give it to graves registration. . . . This nurse came in and she was scheduled to take the place of another nurse. When she saw me, I went to greet her and I had this leg under my arm. She collapsed on the ground in a dead faint. I thought, "What could possibly be wrong with her?" There I was trying to figure out what's wrong with her, not realizing that here I had this leg with a combat boot still on and half this man's combat fatigue still on, blood dripping over the exposed end. ❞

The AIR WAR

When Johnson sent troops to Vietnam in 1965, he did not anticipate the type of war that Rhoads described. He hoped to use air power to secure a quick victory. Like many of his advisers, the president expected prolonged bombing to pressure the North Vietnamese into negotiating. Toward this end, Johnson launched **Operation Rolling Thunder**, a campaign against military targets in the North, in February 1965. He closely oversaw the operation, boasting that the pilots "can't even bomb an outhouse without my approval."

Though weakening the enemy's will to fight was the air war's eventual goal, Johnson had two more-immediate aims. First, he wanted to assure the South Vietnamese of America's commitment. Second, he wanted to destroy Vietcong supply lines. Weapons and supplies from North Vietnam were coming into South Vietnam by way of the **Ho Chi Minh Trail**. The trail had begun as a network of jungle paths, some of which snaked through nearby Laos and Cambodia. By 1965 North Vietnam had begun converting the trail into a sophisticated communications and transportation system.

Johnson was therefore anxious to bomb the trail. Roads and bridges built to handle heavy trucks were bombed repeatedly, but the resourceful

The most vivid images of the war are of soldiers facing the rigors and terrors of battle. Some confronted the enemy in well-defined battles in the highlands. Others cut their way through the jungle, hearing but seldom seeing the enemy. Still others waded through rice paddies and searched rural villages for guerrilla bands. But most Americans who went to Vietnam were not assigned to combat units. Instead, they served in the thousands of support positions needed to keep the war machine moving: administration, supply and transportation, engineering, medical care, and communications. They were hardly safe, however. Enemy rockets and mortars could—and did—strike anywhere.

Some 10,000 servicewomen were among those who functioned in noncombat positions in Vietnam, most as nurses. Though they did not carry guns into battle, they faced combat horrors daily; eight gave their lives. Another 20,000 to 45,000 women worked in civilian capacities, many as volunteers for humanitarian organizations such as the Red Cross. Like soldiers in the field, these women had to detach themselves from the pain and suffering of war in order to cope. Jacqueline

Practice

GUIDED PRACTICE

Organize students into small groups and direct each group to write a dramatic headline for a newspaper story on each of the section's main topics. Have each group present its headlines and then ask the class to develop a brief outline for a newspaper story on each topic.

INDEPENDENT PRACTICE

Tell students to use one of the headlines their group wrote in the Guided Practice activity and the related class outline to write a newspaper story on an aspect of the U.S. military effort in Vietnam.

Review and Assessment

REVIEW Have students imagine that the year is 1967. Ask them to write a letter to their congressional representative arguing for or against Johnson's Vietnam policy. Students may wish to include their letters in their portfolios. Then assign the Section 2 Review on p. 530.

ASSESS Assign the **Section 2 Daily Quiz** in *Core Resources*.

▶

Vietcong quickly repaired them or made do without them. They constructed many facilities underground as protection against bombing. Some 300,000 people, armed primarily with shovels, worked full time to maintain and expand the Ho Chi Minh Trail.

The U.S. military had estimated that the bombing would bring about North Vietnam's collapse within weeks. When this did not happen, Johnson increased the bombing. By 1967 U.S. fighter bombers were dropping an average of 800 tons of bombs on North Vietnam daily—bombing so heavy that in areas the landscape resembled the cratered surface of the moon. But each escalation failed to bring about the desired results. Frustrated, President Johnson broadened the air war to include strikes against areas of bordering Laos and much of South Vietnam.

In this wider air war, U.S. forces used a variety of deadly weapons, such as napalm—a jellied gasoline mixture used in firebombs—and the "cluster bomb"—which sprayed razor-sharp metal fragments when it exploded. America's arsenal also included **defoliants**, chemicals designed to strip the land of vegetation. The most widely used of these chemicals was Agent Orange. U.S. planes sprayed defoliants over thousands of acres in efforts to expose jungle supply routes and enemy hiding places and to rob the Vietcong of food.

THE GROUND WAR

Although the air war was designed to bring U.S. involvement in Vietnam quickly to an end, it had the opposite effect: North Vietnam—rather than surrendering—sent more troops and supplies south. Because of the widespread bombing, increasing numbers of South Vietnamese joined the ranks of the NLF. Soon the opposition forces included more South Vietnamese than North Vietnamese. The United States countered by launching a ground war. Between March 1965 and the end of 1967, U.S. troop strength grew from some 3,500 to some 486,000.

But sheer numbers were not enough to defeat an enemy who seemed to be everywhere. The NLF, aided by regulars of the North Vietnamese Army (NVA), struck at U.S. patrols or government-held villages and then melted back into the jungle. Vietnamese peasants who appeared peaceful during the day sided with the Vietcong at night.

The Americans conducted thousands of **search-and-destroy missions** in attempts to flush the Vietcong from their hideouts. U.S. ground patrols first located the enemy and then called in air

The Vietnam War

THE HO CHI MINH TRAIL U.S. efforts to destroy the Ho Chi Minh Trail caused the war to spill over into neighboring Laos and Cambodia.

? **PLACE** How did the geography of Vietnam help make the Ho Chi Minh Trail an effective weapon against U.S. and ARVN forces?

HISTORICAL SIDELIGHTS

Agent Orange

The military code name Agent Orange was based on the identifying color stripe on the defoliant's container. From mid-1965 through 1971, the U.S. sprayed more than 11 million gallons of Agent Orange over Vietnam.

🌐 GLOBAL CONNECTIONS

In early 1965 the response by the foreign press to U.S. air strikes against North Vietnam was generally favorable. The South American press and the Southeast Asian press were especially supportive. There was also a general feeling in the foreign press that the U.S. should not widen the war in South Vietnam, although there was general acceptance of the U.S. government's policy of taking action to prevent Communist aggression in South Vietnam.

Map Caption Answer
The trail cut through dense tropical forests and rugged mountains, making it difficult to detect.

RETEACH Organize students into small groups to list the main ideas in the section, using the Essential Points and main heads as a guide. Ask them to use the lists to write questions about the main ideas. Then have groups exchange their questions and discuss answers to the questions they receive.

*C*losure

Draw a stairway on the chalkboard. Fill in steps as students identify U.S. or North Vietnamese actions that escalated the war. Call on students to identify U.S. and North Vietnamese responses to each escalation and insert them in the areas between steps.

*E*xtension

FORMULATE Have students recall previous U.S. military conflicts and find out if presidents usually received widespread support in the conflicts' early stages. Have them formulate hypotheses as to why this pattern might occur.

RESEARCH Have students research and report on the biological and environmental effects of defoliants in Vietnam.

▶ **Trip-wire-activated crossbow traps were one of many kinds of booby traps faced by combat soldiers in the jungles of Vietnam.**

SECTION REVIEW ANSWERS

IDENTIFY

For significance, see the following pages:
Tonkin Gulf Resolution (p. 526)
escalation (p. 527)
Operation Rolling Thunder (p. 528)
Ho Chi Minh Trail (p. 528)
defoliants (p. 529)
search-and-destroy missions (p. 529)
pacification (p. 530)

LOCATE

For location, see the map on p. 529.

1. *gave president war-making powers without a formal declaration of war*
2. *minorities and poor were overrepresented in draft*
3. *Highlands, jungles, and rice paddies favored Vietcong guerrilla tactics and provided cover for movement of enemy troops and supplies.*
4. *Articles might mention the frustration of fighting an unseen enemy in unfamiliar terrain, the danger from enemy rockets and mortars, and the horror of casualties.*
5. *Bombing failed to stop flow of troops and supplies and caused many South Vietnamese to join the NLF.*

support to eliminate them. Once an area was "cleared," the patrols moved on in search of more Vietcong. Snipers and booby traps—from mines to animal snares to pits lined with stakes—made these missions extremely dangerous and frustrating. And villages seldom remained cleared of the NLF.

To deny the enemy any territorial gain, American forces targeted many villages for **pacification**: they moved the residents to refugee camps or cities and then burned the villages. In such warfare, progress could not be shown on a map. Instead, the daily body count of enemy dead became the sole measure of success—and a questionable measure at that. The U.S. military regularly guessed at or inflated the numbers. Said one officer responsible for body-count statistics: "If it's dead and Vietnamese, it's Vietcong."

*A*MERICAN MORALE EBBS

The first U.S. troops had arrived in a hopeful mood. As surely as they carried their packs and rifles, one soldier recalled, they held the "conviction that the Vietcong would be quickly beaten." Most also believed that the cause—defeating communism in South Vietnam—was honorable. This optimistic mood began to fade as the hazards of fighting a nearly invisible foe in an alien landscape sank in.

Equally frustrating was the enemy's will to fight on despite mounting casualties. U.S. war planners believed that superior American technology would win the war. Yet as 1967 ended, success seemed no closer than in 1963. Ho's earlier ominous warning to the French now seemed applicable to Americans: "You can kill ten of my men for every one I kill of yours, but even at those odds, you will lose and I will win."

■■ **U.S. forces were frustrated by their inability to disrupt Vietcong supply lines or make progress against an enemy that melted into the jungle.**

 SECTION 2 REVIEW

IDENTIFY and explain the significance of each of the following: Tonkin Gulf Resolution, escalation, Operation Rolling Thunder, Ho Chi Minh Trail, defoliants, search-and-destroy missions, pacification.

LOCATE and explain the importance of the following: Gulf of Tonkin.

1. **MAIN IDEA** Why did Senator Wayne Morse believe Congress had made a grave mistake in passing the Tonkin Gulf Resolution?

2. **RECOGNIZING POINTS OF VIEW** Why did some people believe the draft was unfair?

3. **GEOGRAPHY: PLACE** How did Vietnam's geography contribute to the U.S. military's inability to defeat the Vietcong?

4. **WRITING TO DESCRIBE** Imagine you are a reporter in Vietnam in 1966. Write a short article describing the conditions faced by U.S. military and civilian personnel in Vietnam.

5. **ANALYZING** Why can it be said that Johnson's attempt to end the war quickly had the opposite effect?

PREVIEW WORKSHOP

*Following is a list of the significant
people and terms in this section.
You may wish to use this list as a
section preview.*

People
- Reverend Martin Luther
  King, Jr.
- J. William Fulbright
- Robert S. McNamara

Terms
- doves
- hawks

Section 3

AMERICANS DIVIDED

FOCUS

- **What were the main reasons some Americans opposed the war?**
- **Why did some Americans label antiwar protesters as disloyal?**

By the end of 1967, over 16,000 Americans had been killed
in Vietnam. Thousands more had been injured or disabled.
And despite the government's optimistic forecasts, a
U.S. victory seemed increasingly distant, if not out of
reach. The fighting dragged on, frustrating soldiers
and citizens alike. Gruesome TV images of terrified
Vietnamese civilians and dead or injured soldiers
brought the fighting home. Some people responded by
demanding that the military be allowed to do whatever it
took to win; others wanted America to pull out of Vietnam.

Peace button

THE MEDIA AND THE WAR

The Vietnam War invaded American homes in
ways no previous conflict had. Free of the tight
press restrictions imposed by the military during
previous wars, war correspondents, photographers,
and TV camera crews accompanied soldiers on
patrol and interviewed people throughout South
Vietnam. Television beamed footage and reports of
the war into people's homes on a nightly basis. As
a result, Americans saw images that seemed to
contradict the government's optimistic reports.

Although such reporters as David
Halberstam of the *New York Times* and Neil
Sheehan of United Press International did not, in
the beginning, question the goal of containing
communism, they did criticize the government's
optimism. As early as 1962 they argued that the
war was not being won and could not be won so
long as America supported the unpopular and corrupt Diem. They also reported on the ineffective-
ness of ARVN troops and accused the U.S. government of inflating enemy body counts to show
progress.

▲ Television images of the war, compellingly reported by correspondents such as Morley Safer, shown here, became a
nightly feature of news programs.

FOCUS OBJECTIVES

- Identify the main rea-
  sons some Americans
  opposed the war.

- Explain why some
  Americans labeled
  antiwar protesters
  as disloyal.

THE AMERICAN NATION
VIDEODISC PROGRAM
Vietnam and the Media

2B   13498   5:43

CORE RESOURCES

- **Social Studies Skills
  Worksheet 20**
- **Literature
  Worksheet 20**
- **Section 3 Daily Quiz**

AV   RESOURCES

- *The American Nation
  Videodisc: Vietnam
  and the Media*
- **Everyday Life in
  America Trans-
  parency** and
  Worksheet 30

MOTIVATING: STUDENT EXPERIENCES

Ask students if they have ever witnessed a protest in person or on television. Discuss what issues were protested and how. Then tell students this section deals with how some Americans protested the Vietnam War.

Teaching the Section

OPPOSING THE WAR

Have students work in pairs to compose short speeches of opposition to the war by each of the following: Reverend Martin Luther King, Jr.; Dr. Benjamin Spock; Students for a Democratic Society; Student Nonviolent Coordinating Committee. Have a volunteer from each pair deliver its speech and ask the class to identify the source.

RIGHT TO PROTEST

Ask students why some Americans opposed the antiwar movement and others supported it. Have a volunteer list the two sets of reasons on the board. Then divide students into groups and conduct a class debate about the loyalty of the antiwar protesters.

COOPERATIVE LEARNING

Have students work in groups of four to prepare short "television broadcasts" in which they assume the following roles: journalist reporting a protest against the war, journalist reporting a demonstration supporting the war, two activists expressing different viewpoints on the Vietnam War. Have groups present their broadcasts to the class.

GLOBAL CONNECTIONS

A large number of Americans became expatriates in Canada to avoid the Vietnam War draft. While Canadian immigration officials estimate that roughly 30,000 American expatriates settled legally in Canada between 1965 and 1972, the American exile organization (AMEX) suggests that the number was closer to 80,000—50,000 illegally and 30,000 legally.

AV TRANSPARENCY

Everyday Life in America Transparency and **Worksheet 30**

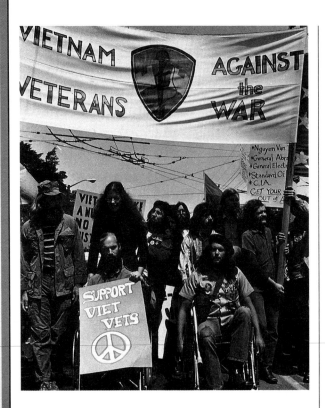

◀ As the war dragged on, the opposition to the war included many Vietnam veterans.

*T*HE ANTIWAR MOVEMENT

A variety of pacifist, religious, civil rights, and student groups shaped the antiwar movement. Among these were peace groups such as Women Strike for Peace and the National Committee for a Sane Nuclear Policy and radical student groups like Students for a Democratic Society (SDS). The movement attracted a broad range of people. Doctors, teachers, ministers, and other professionals joined housewives, retired citizens, and students to protest the war.

SDS and campus protests. By the end of 1965, the SDS had members on 124 college campuses. Though it was only one of many groups opposing the war, in the minds of many Americans, the SDS *was* the antiwar movement. At colleges across the United States, the SDS and other student groups and faculty members held antiwar rallies and debates. These groups particularly criticized the involvement of universities in research and development for the military. They also protested the draft, the presence of the Reserve Officers Training Corps (ROTC) on campus, and the recruitment efforts by the armed services, the CIA, and such defense contractors as Dow Chemical, the manufacturer of napalm.

The antiwar movement builds. The SDS organized the first national antiwar demonstration—held in Washington, D.C., on April 17, 1965. More than 20,000 people participated. After an afternoon of speeches and singing, the crowd marched on the Capitol and delivered to Congress a petition demanding that lawmakers "act immediately to end the war." Because it drew far more people than expected, the march spurred on the antiwar movement. Over the next decade, countless demonstrators, employing tactics largely borrowed from the civil rights movement, protested U.S. involvement in Southeast Asia.

Linking the war to poverty and racism. Civil rights activists were among the most outspoken critics of the war. In 1967 the Reverend Martin Luther King, Jr., spoke of how the war was stealing resources from poverty pro-

*H*AWKS VERSUS DOVES

As the gap between what the government said and what people saw and read widened, doubts at home increased. The administration found itself criticized by both **doves**—people who opposed the war—and **hawks**—people who supported the war's goals. Hawks criticized the way the war was being fought, arguing for more U.S. troops and heavier bombing. Air Force general Curtis LeMay expressed the frustration of many hawks: "Here we are at the height of our power. The most powerful nation in the world. And yet we're afraid to use that power, we lack the will."

Doves opposed the war on many grounds. Pacifists, such as the Reverend Martin Luther King, Jr., believed that all war was wrong. Some doves, such as diplomat George Kennan, were convinced that Vietnam was not crucial to national security. Others objected to the Vietnam War in particular, fearing that the United States might resort to nuclear weapons. Prominent among the war's opponents was the respected pediatrician and author Dr. Benjamin Spock. He and others argued that America was fighting against the wishes of a majority of Vietnamese.

GUIDED PRACTICE

Divide the class into "hawks" and "doves." Take turns asking students from each group reasons for their position on the war. Have a volunteer list responses on the chalkboard under the headings *Hawks* and *Doves*.

■■ Ask students if they consider themselves hawks or doves on the war and to explain their positions.

INDEPENDENT PRACTICE

Have students use the responses from the Guided Practice to design posters, bumper stickers, and buttons that reflect either a hawkish or a dovish attitude toward the Vietnam War. Students may wish to include their designs in their portfolios.

REVIEW Have students use the Essential Points of the section to write a paragraph telling how the Vietnam War divided Americans. Students may wish to include their paragraphs in their portfolios. Then assign the Section 3 Review on p. 534.

ASSESS Assign the **Section 3 Daily Quiz** in *Core Resources*.

▶

---

grams and how that fact heightened his opposition to U.S. involvement in Vietnam:

❝ I watched the program broken and eviscerated [gutted] as if it were some idle political plaything of a society gone mad on war, and I knew that America would never invest the necessary funds or energies in rehabilitation of its poor so long as Vietnam continued to draw men and skills and money like some demonic, destructive suction tube. ❞

Many civil rights activists voiced concern that the U.S. government was sending young African American men off to war in great numbers yet doing little to end racism at home. The Student Nonviolent Coordinating Committee (SNCC), founded in 1960 by African Americans to promote racial equality, expressed the views of growing numbers of blacks:

❝ We take note of the fact that 16 percent of the draftees from this country are

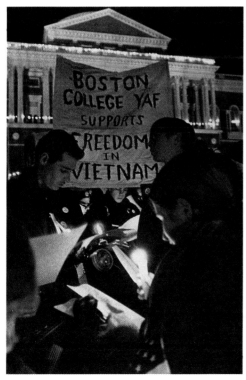

▲ Demonstrations were also organized by those in favor of U.S. politics in Vietnam, such as this rally of the **Young Americans for Freedom**.

Negro, called on to stifle the liberation of Vietnam, to preserve a "democracy" which does not exist for them at home. We ask: Where is the draft for the freedom fight in the United States? ❞

By 1968 blacks were twice as likely as whites to label themselves as doves.

■■ **The antiwar movement focused on two points: Did we have the right to be in Vietnam? Were the sacrifices in lives and domestic programs worth our being there?**

PROTEST VERSUS LOYALTY

Despite their high visibility, antiwar protesters made up a small percentage of the U.S. population. Many Americans opposed the movement, especially its more extreme factions. Some believed that fighting for one's country was a patriotic duty. Others objected to the movement's tactics. People found certain acts of protest, such as burning the American flag, occupying buildings, and burning draft cards, particularly upsetting. Many veterans of past wars were angered by young men who went to prison rather than serve in the military or who fled to Canada to avoid the draft.

Though most Americans who disagreed with the antiwar movement expressed their opposition in private, some organized counterdemonstrations. Demonstrators at these rallies often carried signs proclaiming "America, Love It or Leave It" or "My Country, Right or Wrong."

■■ **Many Americans saw protesters as disloyal. Some believed it was a citizen's patriotic duty to serve in the armed forces. Others objected to antiwar tactics.**

GOVERNMENT CONFLICT

President Johnson and his advisers responded to antiwar protesters by insisting that the United States was helping to defend its ally in Saigon against aggression. If America failed to support

PRIMARY SOURCE

Description of Change: excerpted and bracketed
Rationale: excerpted to focus on main idea; bracketed to clarify meaning

PRIMARY SOURCE

Description of Change: excerpted
Rationale: excerpted to focus on main idea

MULTICULTURAL PERSPECTIVES

Although North Vietnam was not an open society, its leaders clearly understood the concept of democracy. Early in the war the Communists devised a strategy to use the American freedoms to their own advantage. In 1965 they invited a group of American antiwar protesters to Indonesia to meet with North Vietnamese and NLF representatives. At the meeting NLF women described how they had to walk for two weeks just to get out of Vietnam. The North Vietnamese delegates reported that hospitals, schools, and churches in their country were being bombed repeatedly. Upon returning home, the Americans passed this information on to be published in the American free press.

RETEACH Organize students into small groups and assign each group a subsection of Section 3. Tell each group to create a drawing or cartoon that illustrates the main idea of its subsection. Have each group explain its creation.

Closure

Early in the war, North Vietnam's General Giap predicted that as more Americans died in combat, "their mothers will want to know why. The war will not long survive their questions." Ask students whether Giap's prediction seemed to be coming true.

Extension

RESEARCH Have students find and play for the class music associated with the Vietnam War.

ANALYZE Have students research and then write an essay analyzing the media's role in the Vietnam War and stating whether they think the media covered the war's events responsibly.

BIO GRAPHY PERSONALITIES IN HISTORY

Johnson claimed that McNamara was "cracking," that they discussed job options, and that he got McNamara the World Bank presidency. McNamara said he learned of his dismissal via the press.

SECTION REVIEW ANSWERS

IDENTIFY

For significance, see the following pages:
doves (p. 532)
hawks (p. 532)
Reverend Martin Luther
King, Jr. (p. 532)
J. William Fulbright (p. 534)
Robert S. McNamara
(p. 534)

1. *Some believed Vietnam was not crucial to national security; others feared U.S. might use nuclear weapons; still others were pacifists.*
2. *The antiwar movement attracted radical factions and used tactics some thought objectionable or disloyal.*
3. *Letters will vary but should express reasons for the position chosen and outline alternative actions.*
4. *Television presented images of war that conflicted with the government's optimistic reports; troubled economic and social conditions at home caused many Americans to view the war as using resources needed to address domestic problems.*

South Vietnam, asked Secretary of State Dean Rusk, what U.S. ally would ever trust us again?

But the administration also faced criticism in Congress. Doves, such as Senator J. William Fulbright of Arkansas, head of the Foreign Relations Committee, sharply criticized the Johnson administration's policies as too extreme. Fulbright held congressional hearings in 1966 to give the war's critics a forum. These televised hearings gave the antiwar position more credibility with mainstream Americans.

Even within Johnson's circle of advisers, gnawing doubts surfaced. Several senior staffers expressed misgivings about the administration's conduct of the war. Most troubling to the president was the turnabout of his secretary of defense, Robert McNamara.

BIO GRAPHY

By age 44 Robert S. McNamara had already reached the top of the corporate ladder. He was the new president of the Ford Motor Company, the first person to hold that position who was not a descendant of Henry Ford. Then in 1960, after only 34 days in his new job, McNamara received a call inviting him to become secretary of defense for the Kennedy administration.

With his impressive analytical skills, the intense, bespectacled secretary of defense persuaded generals, legislators, national al security advisers—and presidents—to follow his military advice. During the policy debates that led to the escalation of the war, it was McNamara—perhaps more than any other individual—who set America's course. Said Clark Clifford, who

Robert McNamara

later succeeded him as secretary of defense: "McNamara held the key to the President's decision" to grant the military's 1965 request for more troops.

McNamara's many recommendations had failed, however, to achieve their results. As each optimistic forecast proved to be no more than wishful thinking, his confidence slipped; by October 1967 it had eroded altogether. McNamara leveled with President Johnson, telling him that "continuation of our present course of action in Southeast Asia would be dangerous, costly in lives, and unsatisfactory to the American people." But the policy that McNamara had helped shape was firmly entrenched, and Johnson was determined to stay with it. Within days Johnson had eased McNamara out of his cabinet position.

▶ **McNamara sits alone after a presidential press conference announcing further troop shipments to Vietnam.**

Lyndon Baines Johnson Library

 ### SECTION 3 REVIEW

IDENTIFY and explain the significance of each of the following: doves, hawks, Reverend Martin Luther King, Jr., J. William Fulbright, Robert S. McNamara.

1. **MAIN IDEA** Why did some Americans oppose the war?
2. **MAIN IDEA** Why did the antiwar movement trouble some Americans?
3. **WRITING TO PERSUADE** Imagine you are a U.S. senator in 1967 and are either a hawk or a dove. Write the president a letter persuading him to support your view and to change his policies accordingly.
4. **EVALUATING** What roles do you think television coverage and economic and social conditions at home played in shaping American views toward the Vietnam War?

Section 4

WAR AT FULL TIDE

FOCUS
■ **Why did the Tet offensive weaken many Americans' confidence in their government?**
■ **What were the key events of the 1968 presidential campaign?**
■ **How did Nixon set out to end the war? How did Americans react to this plan?**

The year 1968 was a troubled one. It began with a massive military offensive by the NLF and the North Vietnamese that shattered many Americans' confidence in Johnson's handling of the war. Demonstrations and violent riots followed. By year's end some 15,000 more Americans had died in Vietnam, and LBJ's political career lay in ruin. Republican Richard Nixon, who claimed to have a plan to end the war and "win the peace," won the White House. U.S. troops were slowly withdrawing from Vietnam, but the pace of U.S. bombing increased. And when Nixon ordered the invasion of Cambodia in 1970, war protests at home surged to a new high.

Captured NVA weapons

FOCUS OBJECTIVES
■ Understand why the Tet offensive weakened many Americans' confidence in their government.

■ Describe the key events of the 1968 presidential campaign.

■ Explain how Nixon set out to end the war and how Americans reacted to this plan.

THE TET OFFENSIVE

January 30, 1968, was the start of Tet, the Vietnamese New Year. In past years the holiday had been honored by a lull in fighting. However, late that night, as most South Vietnamese and their U.S. allies slept, NLF guerrillas and North Vietnamese troops sprang from their jungle camps and city hideouts to execute a carefully planned strike. Within hours countless villages, more than 100 cities, and 12 U.S. military bases came under attack from nearly 70,000 Communist soldiers (see map, page 529). Heavy fighting raged in such U.S. strongholds as Saigon and Da Nang. At one point the Vietcong even occupied the courtyard of the U.S. Embassy.

North Vietnam expected the **Tet offensive** to bring down the government in the South as the people rallied behind their "liberators." But Hanoi was disappointed. When the assault was over, more than a month later, an estimated 40,000 Communist soldiers lay dead.

General William Westmoreland, commander of U.S. forces in Vietnam, hastened to describe the offensive as a Vietcong defeat. In a military sense, the general had a point. At a cost of 2,000 American and 4,000 ARVN lives, most of the attackers had been repelled. But despite suffering heavy losses, the NLF remained strong in many places. They had faced overwhelming U.S. firepower and were still standing—more determined than ever to fight on.

Even more important was the political effect the offensive had on the United States. Tet jarred American confidence by showing that no part of South Vietnam was secure—not even downtown Saigon. Walter Cronkite, anchor of the *CBS*

MOTIVATING: STUDENT EXPERIENCES

Ask students how they would react if, as they watched the TV news, they regularly saw angry, and sometimes violent, confrontations between groups of Americans. Point out that in the late 1960s this was the case, and many Americans felt that the fabric of society was being ripped apart, perhaps beyond repair.

Teaching the Section

THE TET OFFENSIVE

Have students work in pairs to discuss the following: *The Tet offensive was considered a turning point of the war.* Ask students to write a paragraph explaining this statement from both a military and a political perspective. Call on pairs to read their paragraphs to the class and discuss them.

HISTORICAL SIDELIGHTS

Military Strategy

About a week before the Tet offensive, North Vietnamese troops began a 76-day siege of Khe Sanh. This was intended to distract and draw U.S. forces to an isolated area so the Communists could launch the Tet offensive.

MULTICULTURAL PERSPECTIVES

Vietnamese Communist leaders were surprised and pleased by the political response in the United States to the Tet offensive. To the Communists, the American reaction helped compensate for the attack's failure. "We didn't achieve our main objective," reported General Tran Do, who helped plan the offensive. "Making an impact in the United States . . . had not been our intention—but it turned out to be a fortunate result."

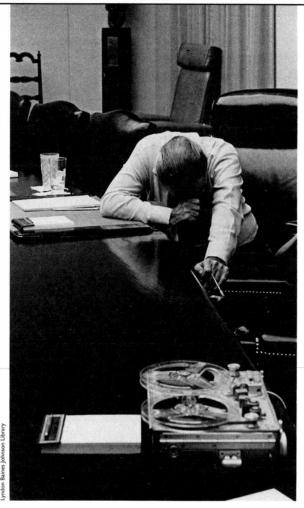

Lyndon Baines Johnson Library

▲ **An emotionally drained Johnson listens to a tape recording made by his son-in-law describing his duty in Vietnam.**

Evening News, expressed America's bewildered mood: "I thought we were winning the war! What the hell is going on?" To one of his aides, President Johnson groaned: "If I've lost Walter, then it's all over. I've lost Mr. Average American."

After Tet, public criticism of the war rose dramatically. Such influential magazines as *Time* and *Newsweek* not only expressed misgivings about the war but also called for its end. Largely because of the shift in public opinion, Johnson denied Westmoreland's urgent request for 206,000 more troops. Though granting a small increase, LBJ made it clear there would be no more.

■■ **The Tet offensive dealt a double blow: it indicated that U.S. leaders had misled the public, and it exposed severe flaws in U.S. military operations in Vietnam.**

*T*HE ELECTION OF 1968

In the wake of the Tet offensive, three out of four Americans disapproved of Johnson's conduct of the war. Early in the 1968 Democratic presidential campaign, antiwar candidate Senator Eugene McCarthy of Minnesota took advantage of this growing dissatisfaction and challenged LBJ. In the March New Hampshire primary, McCarthy won almost as many votes as Johnson.

McCarthy's impressive showing drew another leading critic of the war into the race: Senator Robert F. Kennedy of New York (former U.S. attorney general). RFK's large national following, especially among African Americans, Hispanics, the young, and the poor, made him a strong contender for the Democratic nomination. Shaken by the division within his party, LBJ shocked the nation on March 31. Physically and emotionally exhausted, Johnson announced he would not seek reelection, saying he wished to spend his last months in office trying to end the war.

LBJ's withdrawal from the race left it wide open. Senators McCarthy and Kennedy and Vice President Hubert Humphrey went head-to-head in several state primaries. Kennedy won most of them, particularly the crucial California primary in June. He seemed destined to be the Democratic nominee. But on the night of his California victory, after delivering a speech in a hotel ballroom, RFK was shot. The next day he died—victim of a bullet fired by Sirhan Sirhan, a young Jordanian immigrant. A nation already in shock over the murder of the Reverend Martin Luther King, Jr., two months earlier (see Chapter 19) now had to come to grips with another assassination.

Society seemed to be spinning out of control. Amid the turmoil, the Democrats met in Chicago to settle on a candidate for the November election. The convention was a dispirited affair. President Johnson did not even attend, fearful of the reaction he would cause. And throughout the convention memories of the fallen Robert Kennedy remained hauntingly alive for the demoralized delegates. Vice President Humphrey, despite his close identification with Johnson, received the nomination. He chose Senator Edmund Muskie of Maine as his running mate.

The Democrats' difficulties were underscored by the chaos on the streets outside the convention. Some 10,000 antiwar protesters had massed in the city and camped in Grant Park,

THE 1968 CAMPAIGN

Work with the class to construct on the chalkboard a time line of events during the 1968 presidential campaign. Then have each student assume the role of a candidate and prepare a 15-second "sound bite" reacting to some event on the time line. Select students to present their sound bites to the class. You may wish to have the class guess, from the content of each sound bite, which candidate is being portrayed.

NIXON'S POLICIES

Call on students to identify the policies of President Nixon that led to renewed antiwar protests. Have a volunteer list the policies on the board. Ask students to assume the role of an antiwar protester and to write a letter to Nixon stating reasons for opposition to his policies. Select students to read their letters in class. Students may wish to include their letters in their portfolios.

▶

---

across from the hotel where many delegates were lodged. Of all the college students, longtime activists, and ordinary citizens opposed to the war, perhaps a few hundred came prepared for violent confrontation. In the sweltering August heat, they held rallies, chanting "Hell No! We Won't Go!" and taunting police with shouts of "Pig!"

Outraged to see his city overrun by people he viewed as dangerous revolutionaries, Chicago mayor Richard J. Daley ordered helmeted Chicago police to clear out the protesters. The police attacked on the night of August 28, clubbing protesters and using tear gas to disperse the crowd. Hundreds were injured; hundreds more were hauled to jail. Reporters, passersby, and police were also injured in the fray.

The violent spectacle of protest and police brutality at the Chicago convention raised Republicans' hopes of capturing the White House. At their convention in Miami Beach, the upbeat mood of Republican delegates matched the Florida sunshine. A familiar figure dominated the convention: Richard Nixon. After his defeat by Kennedy in 1960, Nixon also lost a bid for the governorship of California. But since then he had kept in the public eye.

Richard Nixon easily won the nomination. He chose Maryland governor Spiro Agnew as his running mate. Promising a "law-and-order" crackdown on urban crime, Nixon appealed for support to those Americans who neither approved of the disorderly antiwar protests nor wanted a U.S. defeat in Vietnam. Nixon told voters he had a plan to end the Vietnam War, though he revealed no details.

■■ **LBJ's withdrawal and RFK's assassination left Humphrey in an uphill struggle against Nixon in the 1968 presidential campaign.**

As Election Day neared, Humphrey's campaign picked up steam, boosted somewhat by LBJ's announcement in late October of a bombing halt. But time ran out for the Democrats, though the results were close: of 73 million votes cast, Richard Nixon received only some 500,000 more than Hubert Humphrey. Nixon's margin in the electoral college was much wider, however: he carried 32 states to Humphrey's 13. Former Alabama governor George Wallace, who campaigned as the candidate of the newly formed American

▼ Outside the Democratic Convention, Chicago police battled antiwar demonstrators.

Independent party, got some 10 million votes and won 5 states of the Deep South.

NIXON, VIETNAMIZATION, AND CAMBODIA

President Nixon gave foreign affairs his top priority. His key foreign-policy adviser was Henry Kissinger. Together they took important steps to improve relations with Communist China and the Soviet Union (see Chapter 21). But in 1969 Vietnam loomed as the most urgent problem, and Americans watched to see whether Nixon could fulfill his campaign pledge to end the war.

Part of Nixon's end-the-war plan was called **Vietnamization**. It involved turning over the fighting to the South Vietnamese as U.S. troops were gradually pulled out. This strategy, said Nixon, would bring "peace with honor." At best, Nixon hoped, Vietnamization might produce a stable anti-Communist South Vietnam. At worst, it would delay a collapse long enough to spare America the humiliation of outright defeat.

Nixon also hoped that Vietnamization was the key to removing a major obstacle to a peace agreement. The North Vietnamese had warned first Johnson and then Nixon that the United States would have to set a date for troop removals if peace talks were to continue. In February 1970, as U.S. troop withdrawals mounted, Henry Kissinger began meeting secretly in Paris with Le Duc Tho (layd uhk TOH) of North Vietnam.

COOPERATIVE LEARNING

Have students work in small groups to prepare and present documentaries titled "The 1968 Election." Group members should divide tasks so that some students dramatize events, others role-play interviews, and others develop graphics, such as maps and charts. Have groups present their documentaries.

MULTICULTURAL PERSPECTIVES

King's death demoralized many of the African American soldiers in Vietnam. One wrote, "How [could I] be trying to protect foreigners in their country when my hero can't even walk the streets [of America]?"

Practice

GUIDED PRACTICE

Select students to assume the roles of Hubert Humphrey, Eugene McCarthy, Robert Kennedy, and Richard Nixon at a "Meet the Candidates Night." As moderator, ask each candidate to express his views on the issues of the 1968 campaign. Have several other students serve as a panel from the news media to take turns questioning the candidates on their positions. Then turn the meeting over to the rest of the class to question the candidates as members of the audience.

INDEPENDENT PRACTICE

Have students react to issues raised at the "Meet the Candidates Night" by writing newspaper editorials or news reports about the meeting and the views expressed by the candidates.

Review and Assessment

REVIEW Ask students to imagine they voted for Nixon in 1968. Have them write a letter in 1972 to the editor of a newspaper telling why they voted for Nixon and why they would or would not vote for him a second time. Then assign the Section 4 Review on p. 539.

ASSESS Assign the **Section 4 Daily Quiz** in *Core Resources.*

BUILDING VOCABULARY

In this instance *staging* refers to the military term for assembling troops before an action or operation.

AV **TRANSPARENCY**
Everyday Life in America Transparency and **Worksheet 30**

MAKING CONNECTIONS
Sociology

The largest protest of the war took place in Washington, D.C. In late 1969, 45,000 protesters gathered at Arlington National Cemetery. Carrying candles and wearing placards with the names of Americans killed in Vietnam or Vietnamese villages destroyed, the protesters marched to the White House and then to the Capitol. There they deposited the placards in coffins and blew out the candles. The protest continued for 36 hours, culminating in an estimated half million Americans from all over the country pouring into Washington to protest "the war-makers."

PRIMARY SOURCE

(for source on p. 539)
Description of Change: excerpted
Rationale: excerpted to focus on main idea

When Nixon took office, U.S. troop strength in Vietnam stood at about 540,000. He soon ordered a withdrawal of some 25,000 soldiers. Over the next four years, many more came home. But the process was slow. At the end of 1972, about 24,200 Americans still remained in Vietnam.

Publicly, Nixon emphasized Vietnamization; secretly, however, he planned to widen the war—into Cambodia. North Vietnam had been staging troops along the border in neutral Cambodia—safe from U.S. attack—while sending supplies and troops south through Cambodia on the Ho Chi Minh Trail.

Early in 1969 Nixon ordered the widespread bombing of Cambodia. He hoped to destroy North Vietnamese supplies and trails—in line with Johnson's original war aims. He also wanted to send a signal to Hanoi that the United States was willing to respond with force to continued Communist aggression. The air strikes were concealed from Congress, the American people, and key military leaders—even the secretary of the air force.

Because of Cambodia's neutrality, Nixon feared an international uproar. But when a coup ousted Cambodia's ruler in March 1970, Nixon's policy changed. Since the new Cambodian government was pro-American, he made his policy public and justified the air strikes as defense of a friendly nation. Nixon then sent some 80,000 U.S. and ARVN troops into Cambodia.

The invasion destroyed the delicate balance that had kept Cambodia out of the war. NVA troops were forced into the interior of Cambodia, where battles with U.S. and ARVN forces destroyed much of the countryside.

ANTIWAR SENTIMENT INCREASES

News of the bombing and invasion of Cambodia provoked outrage in the United States, particularly on college campuses. When students at Kent State University in Ohio set fire to the campus ROTC building, Ohio's governor vowed to "eradicate" the protesters. On May 4, 1970, National Guard troops sent to control demonstrators shot into a group of students, killing four and injuring nine—some of whom were merely walking across campus.

Ten days later, state police in Jackson, Mississippi, fired at protesters in a dormitory at Jackson State College, killing two students and wounding nine. In outrage at these brutalities, students and faculty on hundreds of college campuses went on strike.

The Cambodian invasion also shocked members of Congress. They too had believed that American involvement in Southeast Asia was ending. Questioning Nixon's constitutional right to extend the war, Congress repealed the Tonkin Gulf Resolution in December 1970. Nixon insisted, however, that this action did not affect his authority to carry on the war. Congressional leaders responded by developing plans to stop the war by ending funding once troop withdrawals were finalized.

In 1971 another incident sparked the antiwar movement. The *New York Times* began publishing a collection of secret government documents relating to the war. Known as the **Pentagon Papers**, they showed that the government had frequently misled the American people about the course of the war. The documents were leaked to the press by Daniel Ellsberg, a former Defense Department official, who had been strongly prowar until

◄ **Four Kent State students were killed during a confrontation between National Guardsmen and some 3,000 rioters.**

Closure

On the chalkboard, write: *By 1972 the U.S. was clearly losing the war from both a military and a political standpoint.* Have students give arguments supporting or contesting the statement.

Extension

ANALYZE Ask students to analyze the reasons why bombing failed to achieve its objectives. Have students compare the Vietnam War with wars in which bombing was effective.

INVESTIGATE Have students investigate the Pentagon Papers and report on their content. Encourage students to discuss whether or not the *New York Times* should have published the documents.

---

spending time in Vietnam studying the effects of the war. While there, he found that few South Vietnamese supported their government. President Nixon tried to block publication of the Pentagon Papers but was unsuccessful.

■■ **Many Americans responded in anger when President Nixon coupled Vietnamization with an invasion of Cambodia.**

THE WAR GOES ON

As commander in chief, President Nixon ordered not only the invasion of Cambodia but also the renewed bombing of North Vietnam, which President Johnson had stopped. Extending the bombings into areas that had been off-limits was part of what the president called the "Madman Theory." As Nixon explained to his chief of staff, H. R. (Bob) Haldeman:

❝ I call it the Madman Theory, Bob. I want the North Vietnamese to believe that I've reached the point where I might do anything to stop the war. We'll just slip the word to them that, "for God's sake, you know Nixon is obsessed about Communists. We can't restrain him when he's angry—and he has his hand on the nuclear button"—and Ho Chi Minh himself will be in Paris in two days begging for peace. ❞

▲ Nixon visits U.S. troops in Vietnam.

Nixon's method was based on his belief that Eisenhower's hints that he might use the atomic bomb had helped end the Korean War. But Nixon miscalculated the opposition's endurance. Rather than ending, the war suddenly grew more fierce.

Hoping to reveal the weaknesses of Nixon's Vietnamization strategy, North Vietnam staged a major invasion of the South in March 1972. NVA troops drove deep into South Vietnam. Nixon responded by ordering heavy bombing of the North, including Hanoi. He also ordered the mining of Haiphong Harbor to prevent Soviet ships from delivering military supplies. Despite these steps, the opposition now held more territory in South Vietnam than ever.

SECTION REVIEW ANSWERS

IDENTIFY

For significance, see the following pages:
Tet offensive (p. 535)
William Westmoreland
  (p. 535)
Eugene McCarthy (p. 536)
Robert F. Kennedy (p. 536)
Richard Nixon (p. 537)
Henry Kissinger (p. 537)
Vietnamization (p. 537)
Le Duc Tho (p. 537)
Kent State University (p. 538)
Jackson State College (p. 538)
Pentagon Papers (p. 538)

LOCATE

For location, see the map on p. 529.

1. *through Vietnamization and air strikes on NVA bases in Cambodia*
2. *success of antiwar candidates in primaries; withdrawal of LBJ from presidential race; violence at Democratic convention in Chicago; election of Nixon*
3. *invasion and bombing of Cambodia*
4. *News releases might mention Nixon's hope that NVA supplies and trails would be destroyed and that North Vietnam would recognize U.S. commitment to stop Communist aggression.*
5. *Answers should contrast desire for information with need for secrecy while planning military strategy.*

■■ **SECTION 4 REVIEW**

IDENTIFY and explain the significance of each of the following: Tet offensive, William Westmoreland, Eugene McCarthy, Robert F. Kennedy, Richard Nixon, Henry Kissinger, Vietnamization, Le Duc Tho, Kent State University, Jackson State College, Pentagon Papers.

LOCATE and explain the importance of the following: Haiphong Harbor.

1. **MAIN IDEA** How did Richard Nixon plan to end the war?
2. **MAIN IDEA** How did the 1968 election signal American dissatisfaction with the war effort?
3. **MAIN IDEA** What Nixon policies led to renewed antiwar protests?
4. **WRITING TO INFORM** Imagine you are Nixon's press agent. Write a news release explaining the reasons for bombing Cambodia.
5. **TAKING A STAND** In wartime, should the U.S. government make all information about the war available to its citizens? Why or why not?

Chapter 20

SECTION 5

Introducing the Section

PREVIEW WORKSHOP

Following is a list of the significant people and terms in this section. You may wish to use this list as a section preview.

People
- George McGovern
- Maya Ying Lin

Terms
- Twenty-sixth Amendment
- War Powers Act

FOCUS OBJECTIVES

- Explain why the U.S. agreed to a cease-fire in January 1973.
- List the factors that contributed to America's inability to win the war.
- Identify the long-term effects the war had on the Vietnamese and American people.

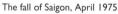

Section 5

THE CEASE–FIRE AND AFTER

FOCUS

- **Why did the United States agree to a cease-fire in January 1973?**
- **What factors contributed to America's inability to win the war?**
- **What long-term effects did the war have on the Vietnamese and American people?**

In 1972 Vietnam again dominated the presidential campaign. Although the war was not yet over, Richard Nixon overwhelmed his antiwar opponent, Democratic senator George McGovern. By early 1973 a cease-fire was signed, finally ending America's most bitterly divisive episode since the Civil War. But the Vietnam War's painful legacy remains.

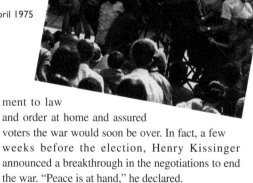

The fall of Saigon, April 1975

NIXON'S REELECTION

Senator George McGovern of South Dakota campaigned in the 1972 Democratic presidential primary as an antiwar candidate. An air force pilot in World War II, McGovern had been a history professor before going into politics. His opposition to the war ran deep. In one emotional Senate speech he declared in a trembling voice: "This chamber reeks of blood." George Wallace opposed McGovern for the Democratic nomination. While at a political rally in Maryland in May, however, Wallace was shot. The injury paralyzed him from the waist down, and he withdrew from the race.

After the disastrous 1968 convention, the Democrats adopted new rules that increased representation of minorities, women, and young people in party organizations. The **Twenty-sixth Amendment**, passed in 1971, had lowered the voting age from 21 to 18. McGovern drew much of his support from these groups, and at the convention he easily captured the nomination.

The Republicans renominated Nixon and Agnew. Nixon again stressed his strong commit-ment to law and order at home and assured voters the war would soon be over. In fact, a few weeks before the election, Henry Kissinger announced a breakthrough in the negotiations to end the war. "Peace is at hand," he declared.

Nixon won the election by a landslide—47 million votes to 29 million for McGovern. In the electoral college, McGovern carried only Massachusetts and the District of Columbia.

A CEASE-FIRE AT LAST

For more than three years Henry Kissinger and North Vietnam's Le Duc Tho had engaged in difficult peace negotiations. Finally, in October 1972 North Vietnam offered a peace plan that Kissinger and President Nixon found generally acceptable. The plan included a cease-fire and pullout of all foreign troops from Vietnam, an end to U.S.

CORE RESOURCES

• **Section 5 Daily Quiz**

540

MOTIVATING:
PRIOR KNOWLEDGE

Ask students what factors contributed to Nixon's victory in the 1968 election and write them on the chalkboard. Ask students if they think Nixon's Vietnam policies were in accord with his 1968 campaign platform. Then tell students this section deals with Nixon's reelection in 1972 and the final steps he took to end the Vietnam War.

𝒯eaching the 𝒮ection

THE 1973 CEASE-FIRE

Begin a flowchart on the chalkboard with the heading "Events Leading to the 1973 Cease-fire." Call on students to cite events that contributed to U.S. agreement to a cease-fire. List students' responses on the flowchart. Ask them to interpret the cause-and-effect relationships in the chart.

military aid, and the creation of a new government in South Vietnam that included Nguyen (en-gy-EN) Van Thieu (the current president), representatives of the NLF, and "neutrals." Thieu, who had not been included in the negotiations, objected to the proposed government, seeing it as a loss of power. Rather than abandon Thieu, the United States rejected the agreement.

When North Vietnam demanded that the agreement be reinstated, Nixon responded by ordering around-the-clock bombing of Hanoi and Haiphong. A furious Nixon declared to the chairman of the Joint Chiefs of Staff: "This is your chance to use military power to win this war, and if you don't, I'll consider you responsible." Some 40,000 tons of bombs rained on the two cities for nearly two weeks, with the barrage only halting for Christmas Day. But the intensive bombing did not sway the North Vietnamese. At the end of December, Nixon called off the bombing and agreed to resume talks.

On January 27, 1973, the negotiators in Paris announced a cease-fire. Although the plan scarcely differed from the one hammered out in October, minor changes allowed each side to claim a diplomatic victory. The United States pledged to withdraw its remaining forces from South Vietnam and to help rebuild Vietnam. The peace settlement also included a prisoner-exchange agreement. It did not, however, address the major issue behind the war—the political future of Vietnam. In urging Thieu to accept the cease-fire, Nixon secretly pledged that if fighting resumed, the United States would come to South Vietnam's aid.

■■ **The United States agreed to a cease-fire in January 1973, after heavy bombing failed to sway the North Vietnamese from their demands.**

Two years after U.S. forces withdrew, Saigon's military regime collapsed. In January 1975, North Vietnamese troops overran the northern part of South Vietnam. South Vietnamese troops retreated in panic, and new waves of refugees poured into Saigon.

In early April the noose around Saigon tightened. The U.S. military hastily evacuated the several thousand Americans still in the city. Some escaped from the U.S. Embassy roof by helicopter

REMEMBERING VIETNAM

Le Ly Hayslip spent the first 20 years of her life in Vietnam. After the war she reflected on what life in a constant state of war had been like:

❝𝓘t was as if life's cycle was no longer birth, growth, and death but only endless dying brought about by endless war. I realized that I, along with so many of my countrymen, had been born into war and that my soul knew nothing else. I tried to imagine people somewhere who knew only peace—what a paradise! How many souls in that world were blessed with the simple privilege of saying good-bye to their loved ones before they died? And how many of those loved ones died with the smile of a life well lived on their lips—knowing that their existence added up to more than a number in a "body count" or another human brick on a towering wall of corpses? Perhaps such a place was America, although American wives and mothers, too, were losing husbands and sons every day in the evil vortex between heaven and hell that my country had become. ❞

as North Vietnamese troops stormed the compound. Some 120,000 Vietnamese who had worked for the Americans were flown to the United States. On April 30, 1975, the Saigon government surrendered unconditionally.

For Americans the Vietnam War was over. The long, costly effort to prevent the creation of a united, independent Vietnam under Communist rule had failed. The war had spread to Cambodia and Laos, which had been ravaged. But the predicted collapse of all Southeast Asia—the falling dominoes—did not happen. Quarrels soon broke out between the Communist leaders of Vietnam and those of China and Cambodia. International communism was not as unified a world force as U.S. policymakers had feared—or had claimed.

THROUGH OTHERS' EYES

Phung Thi Le Ly left her rural village and found work in Saigon, where she married a U.S. civilian contractor. Le Ly's husband died soon after they moved to the U.S. She embarked on a career and owned her own restaurant. A trip back to Vietnam in 1986 inspired her to write a book about her homeland and the aftermath of the war.

Discuss places in the world today where people live in a constant state of war. Have students write a diary entry describing the concerns and feelings they imagine someone would have in such a situation.

HISTORICAL SIDELIGHTS
Nixon on Vietnam
Although publicly optimistic about Vietnamization, Nixon wrote in his diary that the South Vietnamese government was "the weak link in our whole chain. The real problem is that the enemy is willing to sacrifice in order to win, while the South Vietnamese simply aren't willing to pay that much of a price in order to avoid losing."

Teaching the Section

ANALYZING THE WAR

Have students create political cartoons or cartoon strips that illustrate the factors contributing to the U.S. inability to win the war. Call on volunteers to present and explain their cartoons to the class and discuss them. Students may wish to include their political cartoons in their portfolios.

MULTICULTURAL PERSPECTIVES

Vietnamese refugee Phuong Hoang and his family escaped from Vietnam in a 40-foot fishing boat and sailed over 900 miles toward the Philippines before being rescued by the crew of an Italian oil tanker. When asked why he risked the treacherous journey, Hoang replied, "It would have been better to die at sea than to live another day under Communist rule."

HISTORICAL SIDELIGHTS

POW Treatment

U.S. concern about the treatment of its POWs was ongoing. U.S. POWs ate watery soup and a slice of bread or a bowl of rice twice a day. Occasionally they were allowed out of their cells to exercise or to shower. They had no mail privileges and little medical care. In 1969 the U.S. complained to the UN about POW treatment, and families sent representatives to the Paris negotiations to demand information from the Communists. These efforts led to slightly better POW living conditions and some limited mail privileges.

COMMENTARY

Why Did the North Prevail?

Though some people argue that the United States did not lose the Vietnam War, the nation obviously did not achieve its goal—an independent, non-Communist South Vietnam. What contributed to this failure?

People have put forward many reasons to explain why the Communists were able to prevail against ARVN and U.S. forces. Without doubt the Communists' fierce desire for a united Vietnam gave them the will to fight on in the face of overwhelming military opposition. Like the French, American strategists underestimated the strength of this nationalist feeling among the Vietnamese people. For the Vietnamese the war against America was a continuation of their decades-long anticolonial crusade. At the same time, ineffective South Vietnamese leadership undercut the Americans' war effort. A succession of U.S.-sponsored political leaders, most of whom were generals, failed to inspire popular support among the South Vietnamese.

As the war dragged on, a growing number of Americans began doubting that the fall of South Vietnam to communism would seriously threaten America's interests or standing in the world. The climbing death toll and the failure of American leaders to admit the lack of progress resulted in a loss of public trust in the government and a steep decline in support for the war.

Some analysts claim that political and military strategies were at fault—that the United States was not aggressive enough in pursuing its war aims. Others point out that U.S. advisers trained the South Vietnamese forces in conventional warfare rather than in tactics better suited to Vietnam's geography and the enemy's guerrilla tactics. Some even argue that any use of military power to solve an essentially political problem was doomed to failure.

■■ A determined foe, ineffective South Vietnamese leadership, and inappropriate military strategy and tactics all contributed to America's inability to win the war.

VIETNAM AFTER THE WAR

The war ravaged the Vietnamese people. According to Saigon government figures, some 185,000 ARVN soldiers died in combat. Estimates put the number of South Vietnamese civilian dead at nearly a half million. The exact number of Vietcong and North Vietnamese Army war casualties is unknown, but estimates place the total at nearly 1 million dead. In addition, approximately 879,000 Vietnamese were orphaned and 181,000 were disabled. Among the disabled were those exposed to Agent Orange. These people have been plagued by high rates of liver cancer and other illnesses.

Nearly 1.5 million Vietnamese fled Vietnam after the fall of Saigon. Desperate to escape economic and social hardships, many braved the rough South China Sea and Gulf of Thailand in tiny, crowded boats. They were joined by thousands of other Southeast Asian refugees, such as the Hmong

▲ Many Vietnamese were forced to flee their homes following the Vietnam War. This photograph shows a small boat packed with Vietnamese refugees arriving in Hong Kong.

EFFECTS OF THE WAR

Ask students to work in pairs, one student assuming the role of a Vietnamese soldier or civilian and one the role of an American veteran of the war in Vietnam. Have each student in the pair interview the other about the ways the Vietnam War affected them. Call on volunteers to present their interviews to the class. Discuss the effects of the war and list them on the chalkboard.

▶

(MUHNG) of Laos, also fleeing grave postwar conditions. More than 730,000 of these refugees have settled in the United States since the war.

VIETNAM VETERANS AFTER THE WAR

More than 2.6 million Americans were involved in the Vietnam War. More than 58,000 of them died; over 300,000 were wounded, and nearly 2,300 are missing and presumed dead. Improved emergency medical services saved many soldiers with severe wounds that in previous wars would have been fatal. As a result, there are an unprecedented number of paralyzed and otherwise severely disabled Vietnam veterans.

More than 600 Americans were prisoners of war (POWs). Some POWs spent six years or more in North Vietnamese jails, where they endured long periods of solitary confinement and torture.

One of the most visible tragedies of the war has been the fate of its veterans. No ticker-tape parades celebrated the return of soldiers from the Vietnam conflict. On the contrary, veterans often became like lightning rods for the anger, guilt, or shame of fellow citizens frustrated by the war; other Americans met them with stony silence.

The public's negative reaction enraged and demoralized many veterans. They had faced a life-and-death struggle, obeying orders in what they trusted was their country's national interests. In the book *Born on the Fourth of July* (1976), Vietnam veteran Ron Kovic recalled his pain over this lack of support:

> 66 I didn't want to believe it at first—people protesting against us when we were putting our lives on the line for our country. . . . How could they do this to us? Many of us would not be coming back and many others would be wounded or maimed. 99
>
> From *Born on the Fourth of July* by Ron Kovic ©1976

Thousands of Vietnam veterans turned to drugs or failed to kick the drug habits they had developed during the war. Many others had trouble finding jobs or settling down and starting families. Recent estimates indicate that between 250,000 and 350,000 homeless Americans are Vietnam veterans.

Soldiers who were involved in the spraying of defoliants later developed certain forms of can-

▲ One of the legacies of the Vietnam War was the number of paralyzed and severely disabled veterans. Shown here is veteran Earl Robinson as he watches an Armed Forces Day parade in 1976.

cer at an unusually high rate, and children of these veterans had a very high rate of birth defects. Research in the 1970s linked their medical problems to Agent Orange. In 1984 the manufacturers of the chemicals created a relief fund for the veterans and their families, and in 1991 the federal government extended permanent disability benefits to these veterans.

■■ The war left economic, emotional, and physical scars on the people of Vietnam and on many of the Americans who served there.

PUBLIC POLICY LEGACIES

The war shook Americans' confidence in their government. Many were shocked to discover that their leaders had misled them during the war. The actions of Johnson and Nixon raised a crucial constitutional question: under what authority can

Practice

GUIDED PRACTICE

Draw a two-column chart on the chalkboard, with the headings *Military* and *Political*. Have students give reasons for the U.S. failure in Vietnam, identifying each as a military or political factor. Discuss how military and political issues affected each other.

INDEPENDENT PRACTICE

Have students assume the roles of American military personnel in Vietnam. Direct them to use the information from the Guided Practice to write a journal entry about why the United States is not winning the war. Students may wish to include their journal entries in their portfolios.

Review and Assessment

REVIEW Have students write an essay titled "How the Vietnam War Has Affected America." Ask students to read their essays in class. Then assign the Section 5 Review on p. 545.

ASSESS Assign the **Section 5 Daily Quiz** in *Core Resources*.

HISTORICAL SIDELIGHTS

Everlasting Tributes
When the Vietnam Veterans Memorial was built, no one anticipated people would leave flowers, flags, photographs, medals, messages, and other mementos by the "Wall." These items, now numbering in the thousands, are stored in a warehouse.

HISTORICAL SIDELIGHTS

Women in the War
Eight of the Americans whose names appear on the Vietnam Veterans Memorial are women. Only one of these women, First Lieutenant Sharon Lane, Army Nurse Corps, was killed during enemy contact; the majority died in air crashes. In November 1993 a memorial was dedicated in Washington, D.C., to commemorate the contributions of all women who served in Vietnam.

Then and Now   NO MORE VIETNAMS

During the 1991 Persian Gulf War, politicians and commentators often compared it with previous wars—particularly Vietnam. As President George Bush considered using military force to push the Iraqi army out of Kuwait, he assured the nation: "This will not be another Vietnam."

To fulfill this promise, Bush first insured that the Persian Gulf War would not be only America's war. In the United Nations and through direct diplomacy, Bush pushed for international support, including commitments of troops and money from U.S. allies. At home, he asked Congress to authorize the use of force.

With the bulk of world opinion and Congress firmly behind him, Bush then launched a military operation that reflected the lessons learned in Vietnam. Determined to avoid a drawn-out war, he rushed massive numbers of troops, equipment, and supplies to the Gulf. America's military assault would be quick and deadly. And in further contrast to Vietnam, Bush avoided Johnson's tendency to keep tight control on military operations. Instead, he left tactical decisions to his military commanders.

Bush also took a page from the Vietnam War in his approach to media coverage. He did not intend to allow the flow of information from the war zone to erode public support as it had in Vietnam. The U.S. military therefore put tight restrictions on media access to the front lines. It also closely screened what was broadcast so that Americans would not be exposed to the kind of grisly images and grim statistics that fueled the Vietnam antiwar movement.

The president believed that the willingness to use U.S. military power was important to keeping international peace. At the same time, he felt sure that a clear victory over Iraq would rid the nation of the stigma of the Vietnam failure. Most of the news media and general public shared this view. In a special issue about the Persian Gulf victory, *Newsweek* proclaimed that "America's troops exorcised the ghosts of Vietnam."

With the ghosts banished, the men and women returning from the Persian Gulf received a very different welcome than their Vietnam-era counterparts. A surge of gratitude and respect toward all American veterans followed the Gulf War. Even many Americans who opposed the war against Iraq stressed their support for the troops and the sacrifices they made.

OUR TERRIBLE ORDEAL IS OVER.... WE CAN FINALLY PUT THE HORRIBLE WAR *BEHIND* US....

VIETNAM, THAT IS...!

IRAQ VICTORY

presidents wage an undeclared war? To prevent "another Vietnam," Congress passed the **War Powers Act** in 1973. The act reaffirms Congress's constitutional right to declare war by setting a 60-day limit on the presidential commitment of U.S. troops to foreign conflicts.

The Vietnam War also left a dismal economic legacy. The war cost American taxpayers about $150 billion, adding greatly to the national debt and fueling inflation. The war also siphoned off funding that might otherwise have gone to domestic programs, such as those that help the poor.

Above all, Americans learned that there are limits—imposed both by public opinion and by international threats, such as fear of a nuclear war—that can restrict the use of military force. Since Vietnam, leaders have been hesitant to commit U.S. troops in far-off regions without being certain of the consent of the American people and the nation's political allies.

▶ The Vietnam Veterans Memorial— the "Wall"—serves as a tribute to Americans who died in the war.

■■ **The furor surrounding U.S. involvement in Vietnam led Congress to limit the president's war-making powers.**

*H*EALING THE WOUNDS OF THE WAR

Long after the war's end, Americans are still seeking ways to come to terms with the war and its legacies. Perhaps the most moving attempt to heal the rift caused by the war is the Vietnam Veterans Memorial in Washington, D.C., designed by Maya Ying Lin. Lin, a Chinese American, was a young architecture student at Yale when her design was chosen for the national monument. Of the healing aspects of the memorial, she said: "To overcome grief you have to confront it. An honest memorial makes you accept what happened before you overcome it. I think the memorial makes people accept."

Inscribed on a huge wall of black granite are the names of the more than 58,000 Americans who died in Vietnam. Lin insisted that the names be listed in chronological order—not in alphabetical order or by rank—so that "if you were in the war, you could find your time and a few people you knew." Hundreds visit the memorial daily. Some weep or leave flowers or written messages. Others simply ponder what the memorial—by its dark silence—has to tell them.

■■ S E C T I O N 5 R E V I E W

IDENTIFY and explain the significance of each of the following: George McGovern, Twenty-sixth Amendment, War Powers Act, Maya Ying Lin.

1. **MAIN IDEA** What factors led the United States to agree to a cease-fire?
2. **MAIN IDEA** Discuss the effects the war has had both on the Vietnamese people and on many Vietnam veterans.
3. **ASSESSING CONSEQUENCES** What factors helped prevent the United States from achieving its goals in Vietnam? What might the United States have done differently to reach those goals?
4. **WRITING TO PERSUADE** Write a letter to your local chamber of commerce to persuade it to honor local Vietnam veterans in some way.
5. **EVALUATING** What have been some of the long-term effects of the Vietnam War on U.S. foreign and economic policy? Support your answer with specific examples.

★ **DEVELOPING THEMES**

Return to the Themes section on p. 518. Have students discuss these again and compare their original responses with those given now. (See p. 517B for suggested answers.)

Chapter Review Answers

WRITING A SUMMARY
See Essential Points in each section for main ideas.

REVIEWING CHRONOLOGY
3, 5, 4, 1, 2
Identifying Cause and Effect
Answers will vary but should make the cause and effect of events clear.

IDENTIFYING PEOPLE AND IDEAS

1. *leader of Vietnamese independence movement and later of North Vietnam*
2. *idea that if one nation fell to communism, its neighbors might soon follow*
3. *U.S.–backed leader of South Vietnam*
4. *southern Vietnamese rebels who supported NLF*
5. *act passed by Congress giving the president the power to take "all necessary measures" in Vietnam*
6. *chemicals sprayed by U.S. to kill vegetation*
7. *practice of relocating residents and burning their villages to deny Vietcong territorial gains*
8. *people who opposed the war*
9. *massive 1968 military surge by Vietcong and North Vietnamese*
10. *Nixon's plan to turn bulk of fighting over to South Vietnamese*

546

UNDERSTANDING MAIN IDEAS

1. *China "lost" to communism; U.S. hope to strengthen international prestige; belief in the domino theory*
2. *Johnson was determined not to lose in Vietnam; his advisers convinced him the U.S. could win with more troops.*
3. *opposition to all war; Vietnam not crucial to national security; fighting against the wishes of the majority of the Vietnamese people; war was robbing U.S. domestic programs*
4. *The Democratic party was badly split; Nixon promised to end the war.*
5. *shook many people's confidence in government; led to passage of War Powers Act; added to the national debt and fueled inflation; led people to question limits of military force*

CHAPTER 20

Review

War between Vietminh and French begins.

U.S. aids France in Indochina.

French surrender at Dien Bien Phu. Geneva Conference divides Vietnam.

Diem comes to power in South Vietnam.

1945   1950   1955

WRITING A SUMMARY
Using the essential points of the chapter as a guide, write a summary of the chapter.

REVIEWING CHRONOLOGY
Number your paper 1 to 5. Study the time line above, and list the following events in the order in which they happened by writing the first next to 1, the second next to 2, and so on. Then complete the activity below.

1. Students killed at Kent State and Jackson State.
2. Cease-fire declared.
3. Congress passes Tonkin Gulf Resolution.
4. Nixon begins bombing of Cambodia.
5. Tet offensive launched.

Identifying Cause and Effect Select two events on the time line, and in a paragraph, explain the cause-and-effect relationship between them.

IDENTIFYING PEOPLE AND IDEAS
Explain the historical significance of each of the following people or terms.

1. Ho Chi Minh
2. domino theory
3. Ngo Dinh Diem
4. Vietcong
5. Tonkin Gulf Resolution
6. defoliant
7. pacification
8. doves
9. Tet offensive
10. Vietnamization

UNDERSTANDING MAIN IDEAS
1. What were the main reasons the United States became involved in Vietnam?
2. Why did the United States increase its involvement in Vietnam after 1964?
3. What were the main reasons for Americans' opposition to the war?
4. Why did Richard Nixon win the 1968 election?
5. How has the Vietnam War influenced Americans?

★ REVIEWING THEMES
1. **Global Relations** How did the United States' stance on world communism lead to U.S. involvement in Vietnam?
2. **Constitutional Heritage** During the war the executive branch (the president) assumed increasing power. Why did this alarm Congress? What steps did Congress eventually take to safeguard its constitutional powers?
3. **Democratic Values** How did the antiwar protests illustrate American democratic values?

THINKING CRITICALLY
1. **Problem Solving** Imagine you are an adviser to President Kennedy, who is considering sending U.S. combat troops to Vietnam. Write him a memorandum suggesting at least two noncombat ways the United States might contain communism and support South Vietnam.
2. **Evaluating** Do you think LBJ had good reasons to escalate the U.S. war effort? Why or why not?
3. **Hypothesizing** Suppose the United States had won a decisive victory in Vietnam. How might life be different in Vietnam? in America?

STRATEGY FOR SUCCESS
Number your paper 1 to 8. Study the map at the right, noting the numbers on it. Then identify each place on the map by selecting from the names listed below. Write the correct name of each place next to its corresponding number on your paper. There are two extra names on the list.

Mekong River	*Vietnam*	*Laos*
Gulf of Tonkin	*Hanoi*	*Cambodia*
South China Sea	*China*	*Soviet Union*
Ho Chi Minh City		

WRITING ABOUT HISTORY
Writing to Create The Vietnam War is reaching its peak, and you have just been drafted. Write a poem or song that expresses your feelings.

REVIEWING THEMES

1. *U.S. believed communism would spread throughout Asia if it was not contained in Vietnam.*
2. *Congress feared loss of its constitutional powers. It passed the War Powers Act as a safeguard.*
3. *The right to dissent was upheld repeatedly during the war era, illustrating the importance of freedom of speech, assembly, and the press.*

THINKING CRITICALLY

1. *Students might suggest increasing supplies and training of Vietnamese troops or negotiating a settlement.*
2. *Students who say yes might point to the sincere attempt to protect the South Vietnamese. Those who say no might suggest that there had been no formal invitation for U.S. military involvement.*
3. *Students might suggest that Vietnam might not be under Communist control and that the U.S. would be less cautious about becoming involved in foreign entanglements.*

STRATEGY FOR SUCCESS

1. *China*
2. *Hanoi*
3. *Laos*
4. *Mekong River*
5. *Vietnam*
6. *Cambodia*
7. *Ho Chi Minh City (Saigon)*
8. *Gulf of Tonkin*

WRITING ABOUT HISTORY

Poems and songs should express students' feelings about the war era.

USING PRIMARY SOURCES

Essays will vary. Some students might react to the apparent hopelessness expressed.

LINKING HISTORY AND GEOGRAPHY

Paragraphs will vary but should describe why fighting in jungles and mountains is difficult for motorized vehicles.

NLF formed to oppose Diem.

Congress passes Tonkin Gulf Resolution.

First official U.S. combat troops sent to Vietnam. First national antiwar demonstration held.

Tet offensive launched.

Nixon elected president.

U.S. troop withdrawals begin. Nixon begins bombing of Cambodia.

Students killed at Kent State and Jackson State.

Pentagon Papers published.

Cease-fire declared.

Saigon falls.

1960   1965   1970   1975

USING PRIMARY SOURCES

One of the most difficult features of the war for U.S. troops was not knowing who the enemy was. The following poem by a marine who served in Vietnam describes one reaction. Read the poem and in a brief essay state your reaction to it.

Guerrilla War

It's practically impossible
to tell the civilians
from the Vietcong.

Nobody wears uniforms.
They all talk
the same language
(and you couldn't understand them
even if they didn't).

They tape grenades
inside their clothes,
and carry satchel charges
in their market baskets.

Even their women fight;
and young boys,
and girls.

It's practically impossible
to tell civilians
from the Vietcong;

after awhile
you quit trying.

—William Ehrhart

LINKING HISTORY AND GEOGRAPHY

In Vietnam, U.S. forces encountered a physical setting ill suited for motor vehicles and advanced tanks—conventional U.S. war machinery. Review the chapter discussion of Vietnam's physical characteristics and read the following description from Michael Herr's *Dispatches*. Then in a paragraph explain why such terrain made fighting difficult.

 The Highlands of Vietnam are spooky, unbearably spooky, spooky beyond belief. They are a run of erratic mountain ranges, gnarled valleys, jungled ravines and abrupt plains where Montagnard [aborigines living in the Highlands] villages cluster, thin and disappear as the terrain steepens. **99**

BUILDING YOUR PORTFOLIO

Complete the following projects independently or cooperatively.

1. **THE COLD WAR** In chapters 17 and 18 you served as a U.S. delegate to the UN conference. Building on that material, create a chart, photo essay, videotape, or other visual presentation showing the structure of the United Nations. Then write a short statement indicating how the UN might have been used to lessen U.S. military involvement in Vietnam.

2. **CIVIL RIGHTS** In chapters 17, 18, and 19 you served as a reporter covering civil rights movements. Building on that material, write a script for a 15-minute news program that relates the specific concerns of one of the movements to the Vietnam War. Your comments should examine economic and social factors at home, government policies, and conditions in Vietnam.

BUILDING YOUR PORTFOLIO

Have students refer to **Building Your Portfolio Worksheet 4**, assigned at the beginning of Unit 4. Use the worksheet to help students monitor their progress on the portfolio projects.

Assessment

Core Resources
• Reteaching Worksheet 20
• Chapter 20 Tests
• Alternative Assessment Forms
Test Generator

VOICES OF CHANGE

HISTORICAL SIDELIGHTS

Biblical Themes

Some critics have noticed strong Biblical themes in "The Times They Are A-Changin'." "The waters" mentioned in the first verse may refer to the Flood described in Genesis, the first book of the Bible. Images of Old Testament prophets are evoked in the second verse by mention of "writers and critics/Who prophesize." And the battle that will shake windows and rattle walls, mentioned in the third verse, may refer back to Joshua and the Battle of Jericho. The last verse rephrases in a number of ways the lines from the book of Matthew: "But many that are first shall be last; and the last shall be first." This song, one critic concluded, could have been written only by someone well versed in the Bible.

HISTORICAL SIDELIGHTS

Poets' Mecca

Ferlinghetti founded the City Lights Bookstore in San Francisco in 1953. Open until midnight on weekdays and until 2 A.M. on weekends, it quickly became a gathering place for local poets. Through the bookstore, Ferlinghetti published the work of many Beat writers in a paperback series called "Pocket Poets."

UNIT 4

American Letters

Voices of Change

In many ways the postwar years were a troubled time. Americans confronted serious issues, from Cold War fears and war to racial prejudice and social injustice. Singer-songwriter Bob Dylan, San Francisco Beat poet Lawrence Ferlinghetti, African American poet Naomi Long Madgett, and Native American poet-novelist James Welch were among the writers who explored these problems and tensions.

The Times They Are A-Changin'

by Bob Dylan

Come gather 'round people
Wherever you roam
And admit that the waters
Around you have grown
And accept it that soon
You'll be drenched to the bone.
If your time to you
Is worth savin'
Then you better start swimmin'
Or you'll sink like a stone
For the times they are a-changin'.

Come writers and critics
Who prophesize with your pen
And keep your eyes wide
The chance won't come again
And don't speak too soon
For the wheel's still in spin
And there's no tellin' who
That it's namin'.
For the loser now
Will be later to win
For the times they are a-changin'.

Come senators, congressmen
Please heed the call
Don't stand in the doorway
Don't block up the hall

For he that gets hurt
Will be he who has stalled
There's a battle outside
And it is ragin'.
It'll soon shake your windows
And rattle your walls
For the times they are a-changin'.

Come mothers and fathers
Throughout the land
And don't criticize
What you can't understand
Your sons and your daughters
Are beyond your command
Your old road is
Rapidly agin'.

Please get out of the new one
If you can't lend your hand
For the times they are a-changin'.

The line it is drawn
The curse it is cast
The slow one now
Will later be fast
As the present now
Will later be past
The order is
Rapidly fadin'.
And the first one now
Will later be last
For the times they are a-changin'. ❖

▼ Civil rights demonstrators attacked with high-pressure water hoses, 1963

▼ Flower power, 1967

▲ *Voter registration march to Montgomery, Alabama, 1965*

From *I Am Waiting*

by Lawrence Ferlinghetti

I am waiting for my number to be
    called
and I am waiting
for the living end
and I am waiting
for dad to come home
his pockets full
of irradiated silver dollars
and I am waiting
for the atomic tests to end
and I am waiting happily
for things to get much worse
before they improve
and I am waiting
for the Salvation Army to take
    over
and I am waiting
for the human crowd
to wander off a cliff somewhere
clutching its atomic umbrella
and I am waiting
for Ike to act
and I am waiting
for the meek to be blessed
and inherit the earth. . .
and I am waiting for forests and
    animals
to reclaim the earth as theirs
and I am waiting
for a way to be devised
to destroy all nationalisms
without killing anybody
and I am waiting
for linnets[1] and planets to fall like
    rain
and I am waiting for lovers and
    weepers
to lie down together again
in a new rebirth of wonder. . . . ❖

[1] birds of the finch family

Midway

by Naomi Long Madgett

I've come this far to freedom and
    I won't turn back.
I'm climbing to the highway from
    my old dirt track.
    I'm coming and I'm going
    And I'm stretching and
    I'm growing
And I'll reap what I've been
    sowing or my skin's not
    black.

I've prayed and slaved and waited
    and I've sung my song.
You've bled me and you've starved
    me but I've still grown
    strong.
    You've lashed me and you've
    treed me
    And you've everything but
    freed me
But in time you'll know you need
    me and it won't be long.

I've seen the daylight breaking
    high above the bough.
I've found my destination and I've
    made my vow;
    So whether you abhor me
    Or deride me or ignore me,
Mighty mountains loom before me
    and I won't stop now. ❖

Plea to Those Who Matter

by James Welch

You don't know I pretend my
    dumb.
My songs often wise, my bells
    could chase
the snow across these whistle-
    black plains.
Celebrate. The days are grim. Call
    your winds
to blast these bundled streets and
    patronize
my past of poverty and 4-day
    feasts.

Don't ignore me. I'll build my face
    a different way,
a way to make you know that I am
    no longer
proud, my name not strong
    enough to stand alone.
If I lie and say you took me for a
    friend,
patched together in my thin bones,
will you help me be cunning and
    noisy as the wind?

I have plans to burn my drum,
    move out
and civilize this hair. See my nose?
    I smash it
straight for you. These teeth? I
    scrub my teeth
away with stones. I know you help
    me now I matter.
And I—I come to you, head down,
    bleeding from my smile,
happy for the snow clean hands of
    you, my friends. ❖

THINKING AND WRITING ABOUT LITERATURE

1. Why do you think "The Times They Are A-Changin'" became
   an anthem for the youth movement of the 1960s?
2. What image does Lawrence Ferlinghetti paint of life in the 1950s?
3. To whom are the speakers in Naomi Long Madgett's and James
   Welch's poems addressing their message? How are the speakers'
   attitudes similar? How are they different?

THINKING AND WRITING ABOUT LITERATURE

1. because it celebrates the new ideas and beneficial changes that young people can bring about
2. in a state of waiting for an atomic disaster and subsequent rebirth to occur
3. white Americans; both express an awareness of past injustices and a determination to overcome them; Madgett describes the determination of an African American who will not let her spirit be broken; Welch describes a member of an ethnic group who feels that he must transform himself and deny his own ethnic culture in order to become accepted by society

CONDUCTING AN INTERVIEW

Guide students through the discussion of how to conduct an interview and then have them complete the Practicing the Strategy exercise. Point out that oral histories are often invaluable sources of material for historians researching the daily lives of people of a particular era. Have students imagine that they are historians in the year 2030. Have them prepare a short list of questions that would give them information about the daily lives of American students in the 1990s. Then have students use these questions to interview another student. Ask students to write a short report summarizing the results of the interview.

PRACTICING THE STRATEGY

Students' lists will vary but might include such questions as the following: How old were you when the Vietnam War began? When and why did you begin to oppose the war? Can you describe a peace demonstration or march in which you participated? Do you know anyone who served in the armed forces in Vietnam? Since the war, have your views of it changed?

Strategies for Success

CONDUCTING AN INTERVIEW

Historians often conduct interviews with people who witnessed or participated in historical events. Such interviews are called oral histories and are considered primary sources.

One of the largest oral history collections was compiled in the 1930s by the Federal Writers' Project of the WPA. Project members interviewed former slaves to gather their recollections of life in the South under slavery and during Reconstruction. The accounts were first published in 1944 in *Lay My Burden Down.* Historian Charles A. Beard described the accounts as "literature more powerful than anything I have read in fiction."

Effective interviewing involves more than just talking to people. To get the most from an interview, conduct it carefully and accompany it with prior research as well as follow-up analysis.

How to Conduct an Interview

1. **Identify and research the topic.** Gather information on your topic as the basis for questions.
2. **Set up an interview.** Contact the interviewee; identify yourself, state clearly the purpose of the interview, and schedule a convenient time and place to conduct it. Ask whether you may tape-record the interview.
3. **Prepare questions.** Formulate questions to get at the information you need. Plan the interview so that questions logically follow one another.
4. **Conduct the interview.** Be an active listener. Allow responses that go beyond your specific questions, but keep the interview on the topic.
5. **Analyze the interview.** Review and summarize the interview's content, noting what was said with emphasis. Identify statements that are representative of the person's overall views.

Applying the Strategy

Read the following excerpt from Studs Terkel's oral history *Working.* The speaker is Nora Watson, a staff writer for a publisher of health-care literature. Then decide what questions Terkel might have asked to obtain such responses.

> 66 Jobs are not big enough for people. It's not just the assembly line worker whose job is too small for his spirit, you know? . . .
>
> I had expected to put the energy and enthusiasm and the gifts that I may have to work—it isn't happening. They expect less than you can offer. Token labor. . . . I know I'm vegetating and being paid to do exactly that. . . . But then you walk out with no sense of satisfaction. . . . I'm being had. Somebody has bought the right to you for eight hours a day. . . . You know what I mean? 99

Terkel probably began his interview with a question like "How do you spend your workday?" He then may have inquired about how demanding and rewarding the job is. Given Nora Watson's dissatisfaction, his follow-up questions probably encouraged her to reflect further on feeling "underemployed."

Practicing the Strategy

Several oral histories have been written based on interviews with ground and air troops, nurses, support personnel, reporters, and other people who were in Vietnam. But the war can be remembered from many points of view. Prepare a list of questions to use in conducting interviews with people who participated in the antiwar movement. Use chapters 19 and 20 as background for the period.

▼ Studs Terkel

BUILDING YOUR PORTFOLIO

Each portfolio project described below is the culmination of the Building Your Portfolio activities in the chapter reviews of Unit 4. First, decide whether you wish students to work individually or in groups on these unit projects. Then permit each student to choose the project on which he or she desires to work. Provide students with copies of **Building Your Portfolio Worksheet 4** from *Core Resources*. This worksheet will guide students step by step to complete their projects.

BUILDING YOUR PORTFOLIO

Outlined below are four projects. Independently or cooperatively, complete one and use the products to demonstrate your mastery of the historical concepts involved.

 THE COLD WAR
In 1945, representatives of 50 world nations created the United Nations. Using the portfolio materials you designed in chapters 17, 18, and 20, write a report to President Nixon in 1973 recommending or condemning continued U.S. membership in the United Nations. Your report should explain why the United States originally joined the United Nations and evaluate the decision in light of world events between 1945 and 1973.

2 CIVIL RIGHTS
To many Americans, the greatest strides in civil rights came in the 30 years after World War II. African Americans, Hispanic Americans, Americans with disabilities, women, and other groups made progress in securing rights long guaranteed others. Using the portfolio materials you designed in chapters 17, 18, 19, and 20, rehearse and then present your 15-minute news program to the class, making sure the program accomplishes the goals you set and follows your plan of production.

3 THE GOVERNMENT AND THE ECONOMY
In the postwar era, the United States government became increasingly involved in managing and influencing the American economy. Using the portfolio materials you designed in chapters 17 and 19, create a visual display of the different areas of the economy in which the government plays a role. Make sure your display shows how each type of government involvement affects the lives of average citizens.

4 POPULAR CULTURE
In the 1950s and 1960s, advances in science and technology, population growth and shifts, and a rising standard of living helped transform the daily lives of Americans. Using the materials you designed in chapters 18 and 19, present to the class a slide show documenting the changes in everyday life from the 1950s to the 1960s.

Videodisc Review

In assigned groups, develop an outline for a video collage of postwar America. Choose images that best illustrate the major topics of the period. Write a script to accompany the images. Assign narrators to different parts of the script, and present your video collage to the class.

Further Reading
Chafe, William H. *Civilities and Civil Rights.* Oxford (1981). Overview of the formative years of the civil rights movement.

Hampton, Henry, and Steve Fayer. *Voices of Freedom.* Bantam (1990). Oral history of the civil rights movement.

Knox, Donald. *The Korean War: Uncertain Victory.* Harcourt (1988). Oral history of war.

O'Neil, Doris C., ed. *Life—The '60s.* Bullfinch Press (1989). An overview of the 1960s from a social history perspective.

Thompson, Robert Smith. *The Missiles of October.* Simon & Schuster (1992). The story of the Cuban missile crisis.

Young, Marilyn B. *The Vietnam Wars, 1945–1990.* HarperCollins (1991). History of the Vietnam War and its aftermath.

PORTFOLIO ASSESSMENT

1. *Reports should describe the postwar problems that led to the creation of the UN, the UN's role during the 1950s, and the structure of the UN.*

2. *News programs should show, for each of the following, the influence on the struggle for civil rights: the postwar Committee on Civil Rights, the* Brown v. Board of Education *ruling and Montgomery bus boycott of the 1950s, Freedom Rides and other movements of the 1960s, and the Vietnam War.*

3. *Visual displays should show the postwar employment and veteran assistance programs, including the GI Bill; and Johnson's Great Society programs of the 1960s, including Medicare and education and housing programs.*

4. *Slide shows should present the development of rock 'n' roll, the Beat poets and rebelliousness in the 1950s, and the counterculture and British invasion of the 1960s.*

Modern Times ❖ 1970–the Present

Introducing the Unit

- **Chapter 21**
  FROM NIXON TO CARTER
  1970–1980
- **Chapter 22**
  REAGAN, BUSH,
  AND CLINTON
  1980–the Present

UNIT OVERVIEW

President Nixon took action to improve relations with China and the Soviet Union, but the Watergate scandal forced his resignation. His successors, Ford and Carter, grappled with challenges confronting the nation, including a growing sense of discontent. Reagan rode this wave of dissatisfaction into office in 1981 with a conservative agenda. He cut government social programs, lowered taxes, and increased military spending. Bush continued Reagan's policies but failed to pull the U.S. out of its recession. He lost his reelection bid to Clinton in 1992. As Clinton took office, many nations looked to the U.S. for guidance in finding their place in a new world order that followed the collapse of the Soviet Union and the end of the Cold War.

Using the Almanac

Review the almanac entries with students. Then lead a class discussion on what trends for the 21st century the almanac suggests in the areas of U.S. population, the environment, health, space exploration, social change, sports, and leisure.

American ALMANAC

❖ The American People

1990

- White — 75.6%
- African American — 11.8%
- Hispanic American* — 9.0%
- Asian American — 2.8%
- Native American — .7%
- Other — .1%

*Hispanic Americans can be of any race and have not been double counted in the graph.
Source: *Bureau of the Census*

❖ A Healthy Body

WHAT WE EAT*	1975	1990
Red meat	181.1	112.3
Cheese	14.5	24.7
Fresh fruit	85.8	92.2
Sugar	90.2	64.2
Coffee	12.4	10.2

*Pounds per person annually

❖ The Environment

1975 Oregon is first state to ban sale and use of aerosols containing chlorofluorocarbons.

1982 Crowd of about 550,000 gathers in New York for largest antinuclear rally.

1989 Cars are more efficient, averaging 20.5 miles per gallon—up from 13.5 in 1970.

1990 On Earth Day, people leave behind 100 tons of garbage in Central Park.

1971 Cigarette ads are banned from television.

1976 Sales climb 20% for bran cereals.

1989 U.S. surgeon general reports that over 40 million Americans have quit smoking since 1964.

1990 Americans eat 557% more broccoli than in 1971; 7% of the country eats at McDonald's each day.

◀ *Photo of galaxy taken by Hubble telescope*

▼ *Earth Day, 1990*

❖ Up in the Sky

1973 Aboard first piloted SkyLab, 3 men spend 28 days in space.

1983 Guion Bluford is first African American astronaut; Sally Ride is America's first female astronaut.

1990 Hubble telescope is launched, sending back never-before-seen pictures of the galaxy.

1992 Dr. Mae Jemison becomes the first African American woman astronaut.

The American People

Mention that between 1980 and 1990, the Asian American population more than doubled, while the number of Hispanic Americans increased by 53 percent.

■■ Direct students to research the fastest-growing ethnic groups in the U.S. today.

The Environment

Earth Day became a worldwide celebration, with an estimated 200 million people in 140 countries participating in 1990. The major purpose of Earth Day was to heighten awareness of environmental issues.

■■ Ask students who have been involved with environmental issues to share their experiences.

A Healthy Body

A 1990 survey found that only 32 percent of Americans aged 18 to 25 smoked cigarettes—down from 50 percent in 1976.

■■ Ask students if they have changed their eating habits as a result of recent research.

Up in the Sky

In 1986 Richard Rutan and Jeana Yeager became the first people to fly around the world without refueling.

■■ Ask students what personality traits would be useful in undertaking such a flight.

Wide World of Sports

Point out that Aaron ended his career with 755 home runs, a record that many experts believe is unassailable.

■■ Ask students whether individual records have any importance in team sports.

Changing Times

Note that a 1990 Census Bureau survey showed that men and women were marrying at a later age than at any other time in the 20th century—about age 26 for men and nearly 24 for women.

■■ Ask students what they think are the advantages of waiting until they are older to marry.

At Your Leisure

A recent survey showed that 62 percent of U.S. households owned a videocassette recorder and a similar percentage of households subscribed to cable television.

■■ Have students prepare a one-month chart that shows how much time they spend watching movies, videos, and TV.

UNIT

5

Modern Times

1970–the Present

▼ Jenny Fille playing Little League baseball, 1974

❖ At Your Leisure

1971 Disney World opens at a cost of more than $500 million; by 1990 70% of Americans have visited Disney World or Disneyland.

1975 99.9% of American homes have a TV; by 1990 the average American watches almost 7 hours each day.

1990 For every movie ticket bought, 6 videocassettes are rented.

1990 Americans purchase almost $2 billion worth of goods via TV shopping channels.

❖ Changing Times

1972 Andrew Young is first African American congressman from the South since Reconstruction.

1976 Studies show 3 out of 5 marriages end in divorce; 1 out of 5 children lives in single-parent home.

1981 Sandra Day O'Connor is first woman appointed to U.S. Supreme Court.

1984 Geraldine Ferraro is first woman nominated for vice president on a major party ticket.

▲ Sandra Day O'Connor

1988 In Los Angeles 55% of residents speak Spanish.

❖ The Wide World of Sports

1974 Hank Aaron hits his 715th home run, breaking Babe Ruth's record. Girls play Little League baseball for first time.

1984 Olympic games in Los Angeles attract record crowd—5.5 million—despite boycott by Soviets.

1993 Michael Jordan and the Chicago Bulls win their third consecutive NBA championship; playoff series sets NBA record for number of TV viewers.

◀ Michael Jordan

FROM NIXON TO CARTER

1970–1980

Chapter Overview

The 1970s began with great political and social change as President Nixon attempted to deal with pressing domestic problems while improving relations with China and developing a policy of détente with the Soviet Union. But the Watergate scandal forced Nixon to resign. His successor, Gerald Ford, grappled unsuccessfully with many of the domestic issues. In 1976 the nation turned to Jimmy Carter to restore its faith in government. But persistent inflation and Middle East turmoil eroded the public's confidence in him. The 1970s was a decade of gains for women, ethnic groups, and Americans with disabilities.

Chapter Planning Guide

CHAPTER 21	CORE RESOURCES	AUDIOVISUAL (AV) RESOURCES	PROGRAM RESOURCES
INTRODUCTION pp. 554–555	■ Building Your Portfolio Worksheet 5	■ Everyday Life in America Transparency and Worksheet 31	
TEACHING THE CHAPTER pp. 556–579 ■ For expanded coverage of p. 558, see Chapter 24, pp. 663–665; for coverage of p. 559, see Chapter 27, pp. 730–739; for coverage of pp. 570–571/577–578, see Chapter 26; for coverage of pp. 578–579, see Chapter 25, pp. 681–685.	■ Graphic Organizer 21 ■ Social Studies Skills Worksheet 21 ■ Literature Worksheet 21 ■ Geography Worksheet 21 ■ Outline Maps 1, 2, 9, 17, 18, 19, 21	■ *The American Nation Videodisc: The First Landing on the Moon; Nixon in China; The Constitution in Crisis; Richard Nixon Resigns; Ford Pardons Nixon; César Chávez; The Women's Rights Movement* ■ Linking Geography and History Transparencies and Worksheets 12B, 13B	■ Art in American History Transparencies and Worksheets 40, 41, 42, 43 ■ *Eyewitnesses and Others,* Volume 2: Readings 72, 73, 76, 77
REVIEW AND ASSESSMENT pp. 580–581	■ Chapter 21 Daily Quizzes ■ Reteaching Worksheet 21 ■ Chapter 21 Tests ■ Alternative Assessment Forms		■ Test Generator

Additional Resources

BOOKS FOR TEACHERS

Ambrose, Stephen E. *Nixon: Ruin and Recovery, 1973–1990.* Simon & Schuster, 1992. Includes Nixon's private writings and conversations.

Barone, Michael. *Our Country: The Shaping of America from Roosevelt to Reagan.* Free Press, 1990. Chronicles political and social events.

Colodny, Len. *Silent Coup: The Removal of a President.* St. Martin's, 1992. Documents political and personal agendas that combined to destroy Nixon.

BOOKS FOR STUDENTS

* Feinberg, Barbara S. *Watergate: Scandal in the White House.* Watts, 1990. Part of the Twentieth-Century American History series.

Sick, Gary. *October Surprise.* Random, 1992. Account of Iranian hostage situation and 1980 election.

Woodward, Bob, and Carl Bernstein. *All the President's Men.* Simon and Schuster, 1987. Watergate history by Pulitzer Prize–winning journalists who uncovered the scandal.

* for students reading below grade level

MULTIMEDIA MATERIALS

Modern U.S. History, Unit 3: 1969–1981. Video, 46 min. Guidance Associates/SSSS. Focuses on important events of Nixon, Ford, and Carter presidencies.

The Sensational 70s. 10 videos, 60 min. each. SSSS. Focuses on the political, social, and cultural events of the seventies, year by year.

Watergate: The Secret Story. Video, 94 min. CBS/SSSS. Overview of the Watergate break-in and its aftermath.

USE WITH PAGES 554–555

𝓛isted on the right are the themes emphasized in Chapter 21. The questions in boldface type stimulate critical thinking and provide students with an opportunity to discuss the themes within a broadened context. The questions also appear in the pupil's edition on p. 554.

■ ECONOMIC DEVELOPMENT

How might a nation's choice of energy sources affect its economy?
Students might suggest that if a nation relies too heavily on one source of energy, and the supply decreases or cost rises dramatically, the economy could be adversely affected. Students might suggest economic consequences such as higher prices for items manufactured through the use of that energy source or reduced consumption of the source itself, resulting in unemployment in industries related to the source.

■ GLOBAL RELATIONS

How might opening relations with one nation help improve relations with another nation? Students might suggest that if one nation opens relations with another country, that act could also lead to better ties with the other country's allies. In addition, the other country's enemies might seek improved relations with the first nation, so that their enemy will not have better relations with the first nation than they do.

■ CONSTITUTIONAL HERITAGE

Why is it dangerous for one branch of government to withhold information from another branch of government? Students might suggest that by withholding information, one branch could make it more difficult for another branch to carry out its responsibilities under the Constitution. They might note that withholding information therefore could upset the balance of powers as outlined in the Constitution.

𝒞HAPTER STRATEGIES FOR MEETING INDIVIDUAL NEEDS

LIMITED ENGLISH PROFICIENT LEARNERS

Place students into one of three groups and assign each group to represent presidents Nixon, Ford, or Carter. Have students in each group create at least two journal entries that might have been written by their assigned person during his presidency.

TACTILE/KINESTHETIC LEARNERS

Have students create a classroom display or bulletin-board collage that illustrates the diversity in the U.S. population. Then have students give brief talks describing the struggles and achievements of diverse groups during the 1970s.

LEARNERS HAVING DIFFICULTY

Organize students into four groups. Assign each group one section of the chapter. Have each group develop questions and answers about the main ideas in their section. Then have each group quiz the other groups with its questions.

AUDITORY LEARNERS

Have students choose a quote from the chapter text, read the quote aloud, and then paraphrase the quote, explaining its relationship to the chapter content.

VISUAL LEARNERS

Have students study the illustrations and accompanying captions in the chapter. Then have students write a paragraph describing what they believe to be the three most important events that helped shape society in the 1970s.

GIFTED LEARNERS

Have students use magazine and newspaper headlines, stories, and editorial cartoons to create a pictorial museum of the Nixon, Ford, and Carter presidencies. Then have students act as museum tour guides and give oral presentations of the accomplishments and failures of each president.

USING THE CHAPTER FOCUS

■ UNDERSTANDING THE MAIN IDEA

Call on a volunteer to read aloud the Understanding the Main Idea paragraph. Ask students what factors cause people to lose confidence in a president. List students' responses on a flip chart. After students have read the chapter, have them note which factors caused people to lose confidence in the three presidents who held office during the 1970s.

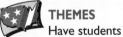 **THEMES**
Have students work individually or in small groups to answer the questions under Themes. Save students' responses so that they can compare them with their responses after studying the chapter. (See p. 553B for suggested answers.)

■ THE TIME LINE

Ask students to write the time-line entries in their notebooks. Have students take notes about each event as they read about it in the chapter. Then have students use the time-line entries as headlines and write articles to accompany their headlines that might appear in a newsmagazine. Students might also suggest illustrations to include with their articles.

CORE RESOURCES

- **Graphic Organizer 21**
- **Outline Maps 1, 2, 9, 17, 18, 19, 21**
- **Building your Port-folio Worksheet 5**

AV RESOURCES

- **Everyday Life in America Transparency and Worksheet 31**

ABOUT THE ILLUSTRATION

In 1976, celebrations of the Bicentennial—the 200th anniversary of the Declaration of Independence on July 4, 1776—were carried on throughout the country. Many events became major historical projects that lasted throughout the year. Ask students if they or any older family members have any mementos from the Bicentennial (these may even include Bicetennial quarters). Have volunteers bring in mementos to share with the class. Ask students how they think the Bicentennial might have affected American morale in the mid-1970s.

Chapter 21

FROM NIXON TO CARTER

 FOCUS

UNDERSTANDING THE MAIN IDEA

Vice President Gerald Ford became president when the Watergate scandal forced Richard Nixon to resign in 1974. Ford lost the 1976 presidential election, however, to Democrat Jimmy Carter. The legacy of the civil rights movement continued through affirmative action programs and busing, which brought about a white backlash, and through activism by numerous groups that had faced discrimination.

THEMES

- **■ ECONOMIC DEVELOP-MENT** How might a nation's choice of energy sources affect its economy?

- **■ GLOBAL RELATIONS** How might opening relations with one nation help improve relations with another nation?

- **■ CONSTITUTIONAL HER-ITAGE** Why is it dangerous for one branch of government to withhold information from another branch of government?

1970	1974	1976	1979
▼	▼	▼	▼
First Earth Day celebration held.	Nixon resigns presidency.	Jimmy Carter elected president.	Iran hostage crisis begins.

LINK TO THE PAST

Throughout the 1960s the United States increased its involvement in the Vietnam War. As the war escalated, so did criticism of it. A weary Lyndon Johnson decided not to run for reelection in 1968. Republican Richard Nixon won the election, promising to end the war in Vietnam and to restore "law and order" to society.

Scene from 1976 bicentennial celebration

"Good evening. This is the thirty-seventh time I have spoken to you from this office." President Richard Nixon's voice cracked with emotion as he addressed the American people on August 8, 1974. Less than two years earlier, he had won reelection in a landslide victory. Now he was announcing his resignation. Facing impeachment for his role in the Watergate affair, the most serious scandal ever to hit the White House, Richard Nixon became the first U.S. president to resign.

Vice President Gerald Ford served out the remainder of Nixon's term. In 1976 the nation elected a Democratic president, Jimmy Carter—a Washington outsider whose promise of honesty in government appealed to many Americans. Carter's popularity soon plummeted, however, and he was voted out of office after just one term.

Amid these political twists and turns, American society changed rapidly as many people moved to the Southwest and new waves of immigrants arrived from Latin America and Asia. In addition, the African American civil rights movement continued to influence other groups seeking equal rights—particularly women, Hispanic Americans, people with disabilities, and Native Americans.

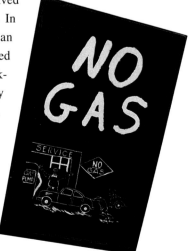

Gas station sign, 1973

PREVIEW WORKSHOP

Following is a list of the significant people, places, and terms in this section. You may wish to use this list as a section preview.

People
- Warren Burger
- Leonid Brezhnev
- Salvador Allende
- Golda Meir

Places
- Israel
- Egypt
- Jordan
- Syria

Terms
- silent majority

- Family Assistance Plan
- southern strategy
- stagflation
- Organization of Petroleum Exporting Countries
- Environmental Protection Agency

- Occupational Safety and Health Administration
- Clean Air Act
- Water Quality Improvement Act
- realpolitik
- Strategic Arms Limitation Talks
- détente

FOCUS OBJECTIVES

- Examine how President Nixon tried to reverse the liberal trends of the Kennedy-Johnson years.

- Describe what caused the energy crisis of the early 1970s.

- List the factors that contributed to the growth of the environmental movement.

- Identify President Nixon's main foreign-policy goal.

THE AMERICAN NATION VIDEODISC PROGRAM

The First Landing on the Moon

2B   51971   :29

Section 1

THE NIXON YEARS

F O C U S

- **How did President Nixon try to reverse the liberal trends of the Kennedy-Johnson years?**
- **What caused the energy crisis of the early 1970s?**
- **What factors contributed to the growth of the environmental movement?**
- **What was President Nixon's main foreign-policy goal?**

*P*resident Nixon tried to steer the nation away from the liberalism of the Kennedy-Johnson years. His conservative agenda, however, was undermined by a Democratic Congress and by serious domestic problems, including a stagnant economy. In foreign affairs, though, the president had greater success. Nixon chalked up his most important achievement by easing tensions with the Communist world.

Chinese leader Mao Zedong and President Richard Nixon

COURTING THE SILENT MAJORITY

On July 20, 1969, Americans cheered as *Apollo 11* astronauts Neil Armstrong and Edwin "Buzz" Aldrin landed their lunar module on the moon. Stepping onto the moon's surface, Armstrong declared, "That's one small step for man, one giant leap for mankind." President Nixon and many other Americans hoped that the leap signaled a shift away from the troubles of the 1960s.

Much of Nixon's support came from middle-class voters weary from the social upheaval of the 1960s. Nixon called these people the **silent majority**—"the forgotten Americans, the non-shouters, the non-demonstrators." He won their votes by pledging to restore law and order and to cut back Democratic programs. Many critics of Johnson's Great Society policies charged that the programs had failed to significantly decrease poverty in America. Instead, critics insisted, these policies had created a complex, inefficient bureaucracy that made people dependent upon the federal government. The welfare system came under particular attack, as the number of welfare recipients climbed from some 3.1 million in 1960 to some 9.7 million in 1970.

◄ **Astronauts Neil Armstrong and Edwin "Buzz" Aldrin made the first lunar landing in 1969. By 1973, five additional Apollo flights had explored the surface of the moon.**

Call on volunteers to name some of the social reforms of the Johnson years. *(Students might cite voting and civil rights legislation; and health, housing, education, and antipoverty programs.)* Tell students that in this section they will learn how Nixon attempted to reverse the social trends of the 1960s while setting precedents in foreign affairs.

NIXON REVERSES TRENDS

Organize students into "White House domestic policy advisory groups" on poverty, civil rights, law and order, and the economy. Assign one group to analyze each of these areas. Tell the groups to summarize developments in their policy area during the 1960s and to suggest actions that the new president might take to reverse the liberal trends of the Kennedy-Johnson years. Ask

representatives from each advisory group to "present" its findings and recommendations to President Nixon. Then call on group members or other students to explain how or why each of Nixon's actions in these areas was intended to achieve his desired result.

▶

Under the existing welfare system, most families received the bulk of aid in the form of services, such as Medicaid. Nixon proposed replacing this system with the **Family Assistance Plan** (FAP), which would guarantee families a minimum income. Supporters of FAP argued that giving money directly to families would cut down on government service programs and the bureaucracy that went with them. Critics, however, charged that such direct aid would only make poor families even more dependent on the federal government. After a heated battle, the Senate voted down the FAP.

In addition to trying to reform the federal bureaucracy, Nixon promised not to ask for any new civil rights legislation. This move was part of the Republicans' **southern strategy**—a plan to woo conservative southern white voters away from the Democratic party. As part of this plan, Nixon also delayed pressuring southern schools to desegregate. When the Supreme Court ruled in 1971 that busing could be used to integrate schools, Nixon denounced the ruling.

The southern strategy also influenced the president's choice of justices for the Supreme Court. Nixon claimed that the liberal rulings of the Warren Court had encouraged lawlessness in America. Such lawlessness, he argued, was demonstrated by a series of prison riots in the late 1960s and the early 1970s. Among the most serious of these was the 1971 rebellion at New York's Attica prison, which resulted in the death of 40 prisoners and guards. When Chief Justice Warren retired in 1969, Nixon appointed a conservative justice, Warren Burger, to head the Court. Two other Nixon nominees to the Court were rejected by the Senate, but the president eventually appointed three more conservative justices: Harry Blackmun, Lewis Powell, and William Rehnquist.

■■ Nixon tried to reverse liberal trends by cutting back on civil rights legislation and appointing conservative justices to the Supreme Court.

TACKLING THE ECONOMY

Reversing the liberal policies of the 1960s was not the only challenge Nixon faced. He also had to tackle a faltering economy. Although the

United States had enjoyed an economic boom during the 1960s, by the time Nixon took office the economy was in trouble. High government spending on social programs and on the Vietnam War had led to a recession and growing unemployment. Normally in times of high unemployment, inflation goes down. Yet in the 1970s,

RICHARD M. NIXON
1913–1994

in office
1969–1974

Richard Milhous Nixon rose to the top ranks of the Republican party through hard work and intense ambition. Growing up in a poor family in California made Nixon determined to be a success and to never give up.

One of the most famous examples of Richard Nixon's ability to bounce back from political challenges came during the 1952 presidential election. Nixon, who was Dwight Eisenhower's vice presidential running mate, had been accused of accepting personal gifts from wealthy businessmen. He went on national television to deny the charges. In what came to be called the "Checkers speech," Nixon admitted to accepting one personal gift. "You know what it was?" the candidate asked. "It was a little cocker spaniel dog . . . black, white, and spotted, and our little girl Tricia, the six-year-old, named it Checkers. . . . And I just want to say this, right now, that regardless of what they say about it, we're going to keep it." The Checkers speech won wide public support and saved Nixon from being dropped from the Republican ticket.

Teaching the Section

THE ENERGY CRISIS

Begin a flowchart on the chalkboard headed *Events Leading to the 1973–74 Energy Crisis*. Call on students to cite events that contributed to the energy crisis and list their responses on the flowchart. Call on volunteers to interpret the cause-and-effect relationships in the chart.

■ Ask students to speculate about how their lives might be affected if the nation suffered a similar energy crisis today.

GLOBAL CONNECTIONS

In response to the Arab oil squeeze, nations around the world undertook energy-saving measures. The Netherlands restricted motorists to two and a half gallons of gas per week. Norway banned Sunday driving. Britain cut street lighting in half, restricted heating and lighting in commercial buildings, and banned small planes from flying on Sunday. France lowered speed limits on highways and imposed an 11 P.M. signoff for weeknight TV. Greece limited Sunday driving to alternate Sundays.

Graph Caption Answer
1979–1981; 2.5 billion

PRIMARY SOURCE

Description of Change: excerpted
Rationale: excerpted to focus on main idea

HISTORICAL SIDELIGHTS

U.S. Gas Hikes
Gasoline shortages led to long lines at gas stations. Accustomed to paying about 30 cents for a gallon of gas, Americans suddenly faced gas prices near a dollar per gallon.

inflation and unemployment both rose. This phenomenon is called **stagflation**.

In August 1971 Nixon took a drastic step to curb inflation by imposing wage and price controls—temporary freezes on wages, prices, and rents. Many people were surprised by the action, since Nixon had long opposed the use of such controls. Labor leaders feared that wage freezes would hurt those earning the lowest wages. AFL–CIO president George Meany called it "Robin Hood in reverse, because it robs from the poor and gives to the rich."

Nixon, however, was bowing to political reality. Only by taking bold action on the economy could he hope to win the upcoming presidential election. The strategy worked. Inflation slowed, and Nixon was reelected in 1972. When he eased controls the following year, though, inflation shot up again. By August 1974 inflation had reached 12 percent. A homemaker from Chicago reflected public sentiments about the economy:

66 You always used to think in this country that there would be bad times followed by good times. Now, maybe it's bad times followed by hard times followed by harder times. 99

THE ENERGY CRISIS

The surging cost of oil was a major cause of inflation during the 1970s. Since World War II the U.S. economy had become increasingly dependent on foreign oil. By the early 1970s the United States was importing one third of its oil needs.

To get higher prices for their oil, several oil-exporting nations, mainly Arab countries, had formed the **Organization of Petroleum Exporting Countries** (OPEC) in 1960. In the fall of 1973, amid a new Arab-Israeli war, OPEC quadrupled oil prices. Many Arab countries cut off oil shipments to the United States as punishment

THE ENERGY CRISIS: OIL PRICES, 1973–1981

U.S. EXPENDITURE ON FOREIGN OIL, 1973–1981

Sources: *World Energy: the Facts and the Future;* inset: *Statistical Abstract of the United States*

OPEC'S OIL Throughout the 1970s the U.S. government struggled to ease the problems caused by skyrocketing oil prices. These efforts were largely unsuccessful because American dependence on foreign oil continually increased.

❓ **BUILDING GRAPH SKILLS** Between which two-year period did the United States experience its biggest increase in oil prices? Approximately how many barrels of foreign oil were purchased in 1975?

for U.S. support of Israel. Although the Arabs lifted their embargo after a few months, the price of oil remained high. Some Americans charged that oil companies were keeping prices artificially high to boost their profits.

The oil embargo and the price hikes caused an energy crisis in the United States during the winter of 1973–74. As the cost of gasoline, heating oil, and electricity soared, some parts of the country experienced severe hardship. One Detroit hospital told its patients to stay in bed to keep warm. "We had so little oil left that we just had to cut back the thermostats," noted one hospital official. "In storage rooms and areas with no patients, it got as low as 40 degrees."

Responding to the crisis, President Nixon announced a program to make the United States less dependent on foreign oil. He called for energy conservation and signed a bill authorizing construction of a pipeline to bring oil south from Alaska. Nevertheless, America's dependence on oil imports grew throughout the 1970s.

■ **The Arab oil embargo and price hikes of 1973 helped provoke an energy crisis in the United States.**

THE ENVIRONMENTAL MOVEMENT

Call on students to identify the major environmental issues of the 1970s. *(air pollution, water pollution, nuclear power)* Direct each student to create an editorial cartoon that might have appeared in a newspaper of the time, expressing concern about one of these issues. Give students an opportunity to review one another's cartoons. Then use the cartoons to spark a class discussion about the relationship between public awareness and the growth of the environmental movement in the 1970s. Conclude by asking students to assess the impact of education and awareness on the environmental movement today. Students may wish to include their editorial cartoons in their portfolios.

NIXON'S FOREIGN POLICY

Write *realpolitik* and *détente* on the chalkboard. Ask volunteers to define them and to describe the role they played in Nixon's foreign policy. Have the class assess the degree to which each approach was a departure from the foreign policies of other Cold War presidents. Then ask students to explain how Nixon's efforts to improve relations with China and the Soviet Union were part of his main foreign-policy goal and how they reflected realpolitik. ▶

CLEANING UP THE ENVIRONMENT

When Nixon took office, few Americans seemed worried about the environment. Two events soon helped increase concern, however. The first was a massive oil spill off the coast of Santa Barbara, California, in 1969. The second was the first Earth Day celebration in April 1970. Across the country huge crowds took part in "teach-ins" and other activities designed to raise awareness of environmental problems. At an Earth Day event in New York City's Central Park, Episcopal priest Paul Moore told a group of schoolchildren: "Unless we stop stealing, exploiting, and ruining nature for our own gain, we will lose everything."

In 1970 Congress responded to growing public concern over the environment by approving the creation of the **Environmental Protection Agency** **(EPA)**, a federal agency with power to enforce environmental laws. Congress also approved the creation of the **Occupational Safety and Health Administration** (OSHA) to make sure that workers were not exposed to unhealthy working conditions. That same year, Congress passed two laws to limit pollution. The **Clean Air Act** set air-quality standards and tough emissions guidelines for car manufacturers. The **Water Quality Improvement Act** made oil companies pay some of the cleanup costs of oil spills and set limits on the discharge of industrial pollutants into water.

■■ **Public concern over air and water quality, coupled with events like Earth Day, fueled the growth of the environmental movement in the 1970s.**

The government also increased support for the use of nuclear energy to replace oil and coal sources. As a relatively clean source of energy that did not rely on limited natural resources, nuclear power seemed to many energy experts to be "the only practicable energy source in sight adequate to sustain our way of life and to promote our economy." By January 1974, 42 nuclear power plants were in operation and over 160 more were under construction or in the planning stages. Yet many critics worried that the risks of a nuclear accident outweighed the advantages of nuclear power.

◀ As concerns over the environment grew, U.S. cities began to stage Earth Day celebrations. Shown here is the 1970 Earth Day event in New York City's Central Park.

FOREIGN AFFAIRS UNDER NIXON

Although domestic issues demanded much of Nixon's attention, his main interest was foreign affairs. Working closely with his national security adviser, Henry Kissinger, Nixon sought to reshape U.S. foreign policy and leave his mark on world affairs.

The Nixon–Kissinger approach. Nixon and Kissinger shared a belief in **realpolitik** ("practical politics")—an approach to foreign policy that emphasized national interests over moral or ethical concerns. Nixon believed that national interests, rather than ideals such as democracy and human rights, should be the guiding force in American foreign policy. Therefore, governments allied with the United States should receive American support, even if they violated human rights.

The chief goal of the Nixon-Kissinger foreign policy was to establish a balance of power among the world's five major powers: the United States, the Soviet Union, Western Europe, Japan, and Communist China. As Nixon explained in 1972:

❝ The only time in the history of the world that we have had any extended period of peace is when there has been a balance of power. It is when one nation becomes infinitely more powerful in relation to its potential competitors that the danger of war arises. ❞

HISTORICAL SIDELIGHTS
Earth Day
The first Earth Day was the creative idea of Wisconsin senator Gaylord Nelson. Credited as the unofficial beginning of today's environmental movement, Earth Day has been held every year since its beginning in 1970 and has evolved into a worldwide event.

■■ Ask students if they have ever participated in an Earth Day event and, if so, ask them to describe their experiences.

PRIMARY SOURCE
Description of Change: excerpted
Rationale: excerpted to focus on main idea

*P*ractice

GUIDED PRACTICE

Ask students to make a headline from each of the section's main headings. List responses on the chalkboard. Have the class select one headline for each heading and use it to create a chalkboard outline for a news story that might appear with that headline.

INDEPENDENT PRACTICE

Direct students to choose one of the outlines developed in the Guided Practice and to use the information to write a news story. Students may wish to include their news stories in their portfolios.

*R*eview and *A*ssessment

REVIEW Have students work in small groups to create graphic organizers for each Essential Point in the section. Ask group members to present and explain their graphic organizers. Then assign the Section 1 Review on p. 561.

ASSESS Assign the **Section 1 Daily Quiz** in *Core Resources.*

**THE AMERICAN NATION
VIDEODISC PROGRAM**
Nixon in China

```
2B     45667    :29
```

PRIMARY SOURCE

Description of Change:
excerpted
Rationale: excerpted to
focus on main idea

HISTORICAL SIDELIGHTS

The CIA and Chile
Following the overthrow of Allende, it was alleged that the CIA had spent $8 million supporting Chilean opposition newspapers, political parties, and right-wing extremist groups. In 1974 Kissinger testified before the Senate Foreign Relations Committee that the money was spent to keep political parties alive, not to overthrow the government. Congressional investigations in 1975 concluded that the CIA's actions were "striking but not unique."

Map Caption Answer

(for map on p. 561)
Iran hostage crisis, Soviet invasion of Afghanistan

▪▪ **Nixon's main foreign-policy goal was to achieve a balance of power that would help reduce international conflict.**

Relations with China and the Soviets.
As part of his plan, President Nixon sought improved relations with the People's Republic of China. By the 1970s China and the Soviet Union—though both still Communist—had become bitter enemies. Nixon believed that improved ties with China would enhance American power in Asia and further divide the Communist world.

Nixon visited China in 1972 in an effort to ease more than 20 years of hostility. The two nations agreed to work together to promote peace in the Pacific region and to develop trade relations and cultural and scientific ties. Furthermore, Nixon promised eventual withdrawal of U.S. forces from Taiwan. This move helped decrease Chinese support for the North Vietnamese. Although many American conservatives were shocked by Nixon's trip, it gave the president leverage to promote a new policy with the Soviet Union.

In May 1972, three months after visiting China, Nixon flew to Moscow for talks with Soviet leader Leonid Brezhnev (BREZSH-nef). The two agreed to promote trade and to cooperate on other issues of mutual concern. At the time, Nixon declared, "There must be room in this world for two great nations with different systems to live together and work together."

Nixon and Brezhnev also signed a treaty limiting nuclear weapons. This treaty, the product of the **Strategic Arms Limitation Talks** (SALT), limited the number of intercontinental nuclear missiles—those capable of traveling long distances to other continents—each nation could have. Although the SALT treaty did not end the arms race, it was a small first step in reducing the nuclear threat. As a result of the peace talks, the United States and the Soviet Union entered into a period of **détente**—the lessening of military and diplomatic tensions between countries.

Trouble spots.
In general, Nixon and Kissinger paid little attention to countries that were not of direct strategic importance to the United States. One exception was the South American nation of Chile. In 1970 Chile elected a Socialist president, Salvador Allende (ah-YAYN-day). Fearing that Allende planned to turn Chile into "another Cuba"—a Communist ally to the Soviet Union—Nixon tried to topple the Allende government. He cut off aid to Chile and provided funds to Allende's opponents in the Chilean military. He also instructed the CIA to disrupt economic and political life in the country. In September 1973 the Chilean army killed Allende and set up a military dictatorship. To many observers, American actions in Chile represented a serious abuse of power.

Shortly after the Chilean coup, conflict erupted in the Middle East. Six years earlier, in 1967, Israel had crushed its Arab neighbors—Egypt, Jordan, and Syria—in the Six-Day War. Embittered by their defeat, the Arab states continued to harass Israel, and Israel continued to strike back. Israeli prime minister Golda Meir recalled the tension between her country and its Arab neighbors:

▲ **Golda Meir**

❝ For years we had been shouting "peace" and hearing the echo "war" come back from the other side. . . . The only time that Arab states were prepared to recognize the existence of . . . Israel was when they attacked it in order to wipe it out. ❞

This simmering conflict was fueled by Cold War competition, with the Soviets providing aid to their Arab allies and with the United States giving most of its support to Israel. Then, in October 1973, Egypt and Syria invaded Israel, seeking to recover land lost in the 1967 war. The attack, which came during the Jewish holiday of Yom Kippur, caught the Israelis by surprise. They soon launched a counterattack, however, that threatened Egypt's capital, Cairo. Facing defeat, Egypt called on the Soviet Union for help.

When the Soviets threatened to send troops into the region, President Nixon put all U.S. forces on alert. A major military confrontation seemed possible. Within days, however, the superpowers persuaded the Arabs and the Israelis to accept a cease-fire. Détente had survived its first critical test, but prospects for a lasting peace in the Middle East remained in doubt.

RETEACH Have students work in groups and assign individuals or pairs the task of outlining subsections of the section. Have students exchange outlines and use them to ask questions of other members of their group.

Closure

On the chalkboard write: *As president, Richard Nixon achieved greater success in foreign affairs than he did with domestic issues.* Call on students to give arguments supporting or contesting the statement.

Extension

RESEARCH Have students research Nixon's trip to China in newsmagazines of the period and analyze the political significance of the trip.

INVESTIGATE Have students investigate the circumstances surrounding the CIA's disruption of Chile's economic and political life and write a paper explaining why many observers considered the disruption to be a serious abuse of power.

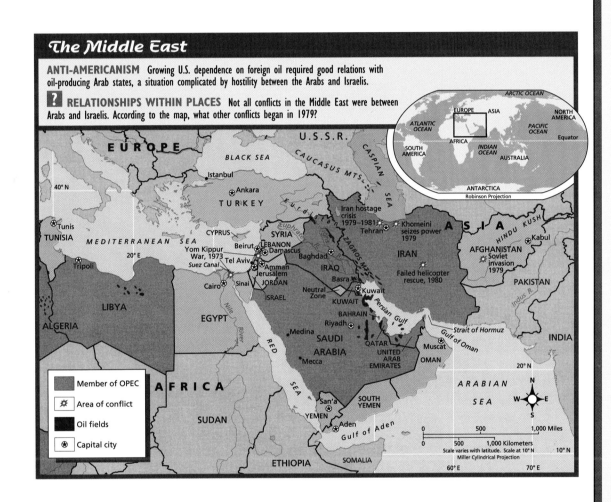

The Middle East

ANTI-AMERICANISM Growing U.S. dependence on foreign oil required good relations with oil-producing Arab states, a situation complicated by hostility between the Arabs and Israelis.

? RELATIONSHIPS WITHIN PLACES Not all conflicts in the Middle East were between Arabs and Israelis. According to the map, what other conflicts began in 1979?

Legend:
- Member of OPEC
- ☼ Area of conflict
- Oil fields
- ⊛ Capital city

▦ SECTION 1 REVIEW

IDENTIFY and explain the significance of the following: silent majority, Family Assistance Plan, southern strategy, Warren Burger, stagflation, Organization of Petroleum Exporting Countries, Environmental Protection Agency, Occupational Safety and Health Administration, Clean Air Act, Water Quality Improvement Act, realpolitik, Leonid Brezhnev, Strategic Arms Limitation Talks, détente, Salvador Allende, Golda Meir.

LOCATE and explain the importance of the following: Israel, Egypt, Jordan, Syria.

1. **MAIN IDEA** What steps did President Nixon take to reverse the liberal policies of the Kennedy and Johnson administrations?

2. **MAIN IDEA** What factors provoked an energy crisis in the United States in 1973?

3. **IDENTIFYING CAUSE AND EFFECT** What events fueled the growth of the environmental movement in the 1970s?

4. **WRITING TO EVALUATE** Imagine you are a member of the National Security Council. Write a memorandum that outlines President Nixon's main foreign-policy goal and evaluates how this goal was threatened by events in the Middle East.

5. **ANALYZING** What was unique about the economy during the early 1970s? How did Nixon propose to deal with this situation?

IDENTIFY

For significance, see the following pages:
silent majority (p. 556)
Family Assistance Plan (p. 557)
southern strategy (p. 557)
Warren Burger (p. 557)
stagflation (p. 558)
OPEC (p. 558)
EPA (p. 559)
OSHA (p. 559)
Clean Air Act (p. 559)
Water Quality Improvement Act (p. 559)
realpolitik (p. 559)
Leonid Brezhnev (p. 560)
SALT (p. 560)
détente (p. 560)
Salvador Allende (p. 560)
Golda Meir (p. 560)

LOCATE

For locations, see the map on p. 561.

1. proposed welfare reform, cut back on civil rights legislation, appointed conservatives to Supreme Court
2. Arab oil embargo, price hikes
3. public concern over air and water quality, events such as Earth Day celebration
4. Memos might mention how the goal of maintaining peace was threatened by possibility of a U.S.–Soviet military confrontation during the 1973 Arab-Israeli war.
5. stagflation—high unemployment and inflation; imposed wage and price controls to curb inflation

PREVIEW WORKSHOP

Following is a list of the significant people and terms in this section. You may wish to use this list as a section preview.

People
- Bob Woodward
- Carl Bernstein
- Sam Ervin
- James McCord

- John Dean
- Archibald Cox
- Gerald Ford
- Jimmy Carter
- Barbara Jordan

Terms
- Watergate
- Saturday Night Massacre

FOCUS OBJECTIVES

- Describe the Watergate scandal.
- Explain why President Nixon resigned.
- Identify the problems President Ford faced during his presidency.

HISTORICAL SIDELIGHTS

Enemies List
The White House "enemies list" contained some 200 names, including politicians, actors, university presidents, and other well-known figures. The White House conducted background investigations on these people in an attempt to find damaging material that could be leaked to newspapers. Senator Edward Kennedy and Speaker of the House Carl Albert were among those on the list.

PRIMARY SOURCE

Description of Change: excerpted
Rationale: excerpted to focus on main idea

CORE RESOURCES

- **Social Studies Skills Worksheet 21**
- **Section 2 Daily Quiz**

AV RESOURCES

- **The American Nation Videodisc: The Constitution in Crisis; Richard Nixon Resigns; Ford Pardons Nixon**

562

Section 2

FROM WATERGATE TO FORD

FOCUS
- **What was the Watergate scandal?**
- **Why did President Nixon resign?**
- **What problems did President Ford face during his presidency?**

Nixon's second term, which began with a sweeping reelection victory, ended less than two years later with his resignation from office. Just as the words Teapot Dome *sum up the scandals of Warren Harding's presidency, the word* Watergate *represents the political abuses of the Nixon years. With Nixon's departure from office, President Gerald Ford tried to restore credibility to the White House.*

Headline announcing Nixon resignation, 1974

CRISIS IN THE PRESIDENCY

Years after Richard Nixon left office, Henry Kissinger reflected on the presidency of his former boss:

> 66 Nixon had three goals: to win by the biggest electoral landslide in history; to be remembered as a peacemaker; and to be accepted by the "Establishment" as an equal. He achieved all these objectives at the end of 1972 and the beginning of 1973. And he lost them all two months later—partly because he turned a dream into an obsession. 99

This obsession began before Nixon won his landslide victory in the 1972 election. Nixon increasingly behaved as though there should be no limitations on his power. He shifted much of the authority of the cabinet, whose appointment required Senate approval, to his personal White House staff. He also hid vital information from Congress and the public. When the news media criticized Nixon's actions, the White House charged them with biased reporting.

Nixon's public actions were nothing compared to what he did in secret to help ensure his reelection. In 1969 he ordered his staff to compile an "enemies list"—made up of critics opposed to his policies—and then tried to smear their reputations. Two years later, in reaction to Daniel Ellsberg's leak of the Pentagon Papers (see Chapter 20), Nixon set up a secret unit called "the plumbers." This group, which included former agents of the CIA and FBI, was ordered to stop leaks and carry out a variety of illegal actions in the name of "national security."

By 1972 these secret activities had mushroomed into a full-scale effort to ensure Nixon's reelection—no matter what it took. This campaign of criminal activity and electoral "dirty tricks," along with subsequent attempts to cover them up, became known as **Watergate**. The scandal took its name from the Watergate building in Washington, D.C. In June 1972 five men carrying wiretap equipment and other spying devices were caught breaking into the Watergate offices of the Democratic National Committee. It was soon

Ask students to name actions or situations that might cause them to question the honesty or integrity of a politician. Then explain that in this section they will learn how the actions of President Nixon led to his resignation and shattered the nation's ideals about integrity in government.

Teaching the *Section*

WATERGATE SCANDAL

Provide the following statement to students: *Compared to the nation's social, economic, and foreign-policy problems in the 1970s, Watergate was an event that did not justify the attention it received.* Organize students into groups to discuss and react to this statement. Ask a representative from each group to report any conclusions it reached.

Then continue with a general class discussion on the statement, calling on individual students to agree or disagree with the groups' conclusions about the importance of the Watergate scandal and to explain their opinions.

▶

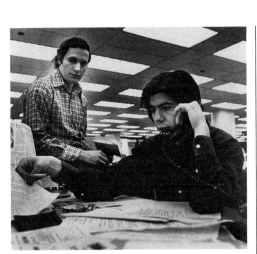

▲ Bob Woodward (left) and Carl Bernstein (right) were two *Washington Post* reporters who investigated the link between the Nixon White House and the Watergate break-in. This photograph was taken in April 1973.

discovered that these men had ties to the White House and were being paid with funds from Nixon's campaign organization, the Committee to Re-elect the President (CREEP).

The administration denied any link to the break-in, calling it a "third-rate burglary." But two *Washington Post* reporters, Bob Woodward and Carl Bernstein, kept digging for the truth. A high-level source, known only as "Deep Throat," revealed that White House officials and CREEP had hired 50 agents to sabotage the Democrats' chances in the 1972 election.

■■ **The Watergate scandal implicated the Nixon administration in illegal activities, which officials later tried to cover up.**

*T*HE WATERGATE INVESTIGATION

As astonishing as Woodward and Bernstein's revelations were, they did not prevent Nixon's reelection. But by the spring of 1973, both the judicial and the legislative branches of government were investigating Watergate. Senator Sam Ervin of North Carolina led the investigations for the Senate. One of the first witnesses to testify was James McCord, an ex-CIA agent who had taken part in the Watergate break-in. McCord admitted that top White House officials had helped plan the

WATERGATE

THROUGH OTHERS' EYES

Foreign journalists were particularly interested in the Watergate case. Many noted that similar scandals exposed by journalists in their countries were often ignored because the popular press had little political influence. For example, although the French followed the Watergate investigation with great interest, an alleged French government attempt to wiretap the offices of a weekly newspaper, *Le Canard Enchaîné*, drew little attention. After Nixon's resignation, French journalist André Fontaine commented in the newspaper *Le Monde*:

❝*W*e no longer knew it, we no longer wanted to believe it. But there's still at least one nation on this earth where the law, decidedly, is stronger than men, where, just named by the President, some judges were capable of making some decisions against him. . . .

The idea that the President of the United States must give up his place to the liberties he took with the truth doesn't leave [Americans] astonished. As for the Watergate scandal, we have heard much that the wiretapping at Le Canard is only a weak replica, the fact is that France has had some others . . . .

Our old . . . countries . . . have become very indulgent toward sins. But the Americans, despite the excesses of competition and counterculture . . . haven't yet loosened the cocoon of moralism, into which the puritans put their political life.❞

break-in and later tried to cover it up. This testimony broke the case wide open.

The biggest bombshells were yet to come. In May, live television coverage of the Senate hearings began. Across the nation millions of Americans sat glued to their sets as senators grilled witnesses and compiled evidence of official misconduct. Eventually several top White House officials were sent to jail. Still, Nixon's role in Watergate remained unclear. Time and again, a key

HISTORICAL SIDELIGHTS
Martha Mitchell
On June 22, 1972, just five days after the Watergate break-in, Martha Mitchell, wife of former attorney general John Mitchell, telephoned UPI reporter Helen Thomas. Mitchell implied that she knew about some improprieties at the White House. According to Thomas, the call ended suddenly, as if "someone took the phone away from [Mitchell's] hand." Three days later Mitchell called Thomas again, claiming that five men had kidnapped her to keep her quiet. The news media ignored the incident, but later many questioned whether the Watergate scandal would have broken sooner if more people had taken Mitchell seriously.

PRIMARY SOURCE
Description of Change: excerpted and bracketed
Rationale: excerpted to focus on main idea; bracketed to clarify meaning

THE AMERICAN NATION VIDEODISC PROGRAM
The Constitution in Crisis

2B   05933   4:13

Teaching the Section

THE ROAD TO RESIGNATION

Work with the class to create on the chalkboard a flowchart listing the events that eventually led to the resignation of President Nixon. Begin the flowchart with the creation of Nixon's "enemies list" in 1969 and carry it through "the plumbers" unit; events of the Watergate break-in, investigation, and cover-up; the Saturday Night Massacre; and the resignation itself in 1974. As the class offers items for the flowchart, call on students to suggest how each event had an impact on the powers and rights established for government and the people under the Constitution.

**THE AMERICAN NATION
VIDEODISC PROGRAM**

Richard Nixon Resigns

2B   47518   1:01

PRIMARY SOURCE

Description of Change:
excerpted
Rationale: excerpted to
focus on main idea

MULTICULTURAL PERSPECTIVES

Worldwide opinions on the results of Watergate varied. One French businessman declared, "The French press is *lamentable,* but the American press is even worse. It's *scandaleux* that your country's press is powerful enough—and irresponsible enough—to politically assassinate one of your greatest presidents." Meanwhile, a British lawyer said, "Watergate didn't really surprise me. After all, corruption is standard practice in American politics. But I still don't understand why it took you two years to get rid of Nixon."

member of the Watergate committee, Senator Howard Baker of Tennessee, asked: "What did the president know and when did he know it?" In June, Nixon's former White House counsel John Dean gave the stunning answer: the president himself had ordered the cover-up.

Nixon denied the charge, and there seemed to be no way to prove it. Then another witness revealed that Nixon had secretly tape-recorded his conversations in the White House. In the tapes, investigators believed, lay the truth behind Watergate. The Justice Department's special prosecutor, Archibald Cox, demanded that Nixon turn over the tapes. Citing "executive privilege," Nixon refused on the grounds that release of the tapes would endanger national security.

In the midst of this controversy, the Justice Department dealt the administration another blow. In October 1973 it charged Vice President Spiro Agnew with income-tax evasion. Agnew pleaded no contest and resigned in exchange for minimal punishment. Nixon then nominated Gerald Ford, the Republican leader in the House of Representatives, as vice president.

NIXON RESIGNS

Shortly before Agnew resigned, a federal judge ordered Nixon to release the tapes. The president refused to comply. On October 20, after Special Prosecutor Cox demanded that he obey the judge, Nixon ordered Attorney General Elliot Richardson to fire Cox. Both the attorney general and Deputy Attorney General William Ruckelshaus resigned rather than obey the order. The task of firing Cox then fell to Robert Bork, the solicitor general, who complied. This series of events, known as the **Saturday Night Massacre,** outraged the public and led to increased calls to impeach Nixon.

Nixon finally agreed to release some of the White House tapes. Vital segments were missing, however, and Nixon again resisted turning over the whole set. It was only months later—after the Supreme Court ordered Nixon to turn over all the tapes—that Americans found out the truth: Nixon had directed the Watergate cover-up and had authorized illegal activities. Still, Nixon refused to step down. Congress responded by recommending impeachment charges against him. Facing almost certain conviction, Nixon finally accepted his fate. On August 8, 1974, he spoke to the nation:

▲ **Gerald Ford is sworn in as the nation's 38th president as his wife, Betty, watches.**

❝ I have never been a quitter. To leave office before my term is completed is opposed to every instinct in my body. But as president I must put the interests of America first. . . . Therefore, I shall resign the presidency effective at noon tomorrow. ❞

■■ **President Nixon resigned rather than face impeachment for his role in covering up the Watergate affair.**

On August 9, 1974, Vice President Gerald Ford was sworn in as the 38th president of the United States. He then nominated Governor Nelson Rockefeller of New York for vice president, and Congress confirmed his choice. For the first time in history, both the president and the vice president held office by appointment.

COMMENTARY

The Larger Meaning of Watergate

Watergate was not the first scandal to taint the presidency. The administration of Ulysses S. Grant, a century before Nixon, was stained by financial scandal. So, too, was the presidency of Warren G. Harding. But Watergate was different. Nixon was the first president to resign from office and the first since Andrew Johnson in 1868 to face a serious threat of impeachment. Unlike Johnson, Nixon's troubles did not result from a power struggle with Congress but from charges of criminal activity.

Furthermore, Watergate did not involve typical political misconduct, such as taking bribes. It challenged the very basis of our constitutional government. Nixon tried to place the presidency above the rule of law and above the constitutional system of balance of powers. Afterward, Congress would try to clean up government corruption by passing several laws, including some limiting the amount of money individuals and corporations could contribute to a political candidate.

Watergate tested our system of constitutional government to the limit, but the system held firm. Vigorous investigative journalism and strong action by the courts and Congress exposed the criminal activities of the Watergate conspirators and forced a president to resign. Watergate underscored the fact that the United States is a government of law, not of individuals.

FORD TRIES TO REUNITE THE NATION

The new president, Gerald Ford, was gifted with the common touch. As leader of the Republicans in the House, he had won the respect of colleagues in both parties for his honesty and unassuming manner. "I'm a Ford, not a Lincoln," he once joked.

But President Ford lost much of this early goodwill when, a month after taking office, he granted Nixon a full pardon. Overnight Ford's popularity rating dropped from 72 percent to 49 percent. His critics charged that now the full truth about Watergate would never emerge. They pointed to the double standard that allowed Nixon to go free while his co-conspirators were punished. Many people suspected that the pardon had been agreed upon in advance in exchange for Nixon's

resignation. President Ford denied this charge. He defended the pardon by saying that a public trial would have prolonged the bitterness and division produced by Watergate. He had acted, he said, to heal "the wounds of the past."

A week later, Ford took another controversial step by offering partial amnesty to Vietnam draft evaders and military deserters who agreed to reaffirm their allegiance to the United States and spend two years performing public service. Supporters of the Vietnam War felt the pardon was unfair to soldiers who had served their country. Meanwhile, only a handful of people accepted the president's offer. Some war resisters, like Dee Knight, contrasted the conditional pardon with the full pardon granted Nixon:

> 66 We knew the clemency was proclaimed just to offset the Nixon pardon, which was an insult. We weren't criminals, and Nixon was, but Ford proposed to pardon Nixon unconditionally while offering "alternative punishment" to us. 99

FORD'S TROUBLES CONTINUE

Ford soon ran into other problems, including conflicts with the Democratic majority in Congress. A moderate conservative, Ford vetoed a number of social-welfare bills sponsored by Democrats. In fact, he vetoed more bills than any other president had in such a short time. As Ford's relations with Congress worsened, he found it increasingly difficult to implement his policies.

One of Ford's main goals was to combat inflation, which was being fueled by the energy

▶ The energy crisis and the rising cost of oil drove the prices of many consumer goods higher in the United States. To win public support for his anti-inflation program, President Ford issued buttons with initials representing "Whip Inflation Now."

THE AMERICAN NATION VIDEODISC PROGRAM

Ford Pardons Nixon

2B   50431   :41

PRIMARY SOURCE

Description of Change: excerpted

Rationale: excerpted to focus on main idea

HISTORICAL SIDELIGHTS

Betty Ford's Activism

While President Ford was embroiled in domestic and foreign affairs, First Lady Betty Ford was drawing attention to important health issues. She was willing to break the silence about health issues that many people were reluctant to discuss. She publicly discussed her bout with breast cancer and urged women to take steps to detect tumors in their early stages. After leaving the White House, Ford became an advocate for the treatment of drug and alcohol abuse after revealing her own addiction to alcohol and pills in 1978.

Practice

GUIDED PRACTICE

Write the following statement by Richard Nixon on the chalkboard: *"When the president does it, that means that it is not illegal."* Ask students to name actions of Nixon that they regard as illegal. List responses on the chalkboard.

INDEPENDENT PRACTICE

Have students choose one of the actions cited in the Guided Practice activity and write an entry for their personal journal on the day that the action became public. Tell students that their journal entries should include their reactions and feelings about the news and a reflection on the action's potential significance for the nation. Students may wish to include their journal entries in their portfolios.

Review and Assessment

REVIEW Have students write a letter to President Ford explaining why they will or will not vote for him in the 1976 election. Students should give details from the section to support their viewpoint. Have volunteers with opposing opinions read and defend their letters before the class. Then assign the Section 2 Review on p. 567.

ASSESS Assign the **Section 2 Daily Quiz** in *Core Resources.*

After retiring from politics, Jordan took a position at the Lyndon Baines Johnson School of Public Affairs, University of Texas at Austin, as a faculty adviser, minority recruiter, and teacher. Explaining her decision to leave politics, Jordan said, "I thought that my role now was to be one of the voices in the country defining where we were, where we were going, what the policies were that were being pursued, and where the holes in those policies were. I felt I was more in an instructive role than a legislative role."

PRIMARY SOURCE

(for source on p. 567)
Description of Change: excerpted
Rationale: excerpted to focus on main idea

PRESIDENTIAL LIVES

GERALD R. FORD
1913–

in office
1974–1977

Gerald Ford faced the difficult task of restoring the nation's confidence in government after the Watergate crisis. Most observers believed that Ford was uniquely qualified to remove the taint of scandal from the White House. Throughout his career he had been known as an honest and likable politician. "The nicest thing about Jerry Ford," said Senator Robert P. Griffin, "is that he doesn't have any enemies." Indeed, when Ford first heard about President Nixon's "enemies list," he responded that "anybody who can't keep his enemies in his head has too many enemies."

EXPERIENCE COUNTS
Elect Gerald R. FORD in '76

Gerald R. Ford

Unlike many politicians, Ford made friends because he always maintained a fair-minded attitude. He was never vengeful when he lost or arrogant when he won. He acquired this attitude from years of playing sports, especially football. He had been a star player for the University of Michigan and received several offers to play for professional teams. Instead he worked his way through law school as a coach and entered politics. Sports remained an influential part of his life, however. He was the most athletic president in the White House since Teddy Roosevelt.

---

crisis and the soaring cost of oil. Like Nixon, Ford tried to curb inflation by cutting federal spending, but this threw the country into a recession and prolonged the nation's economic woes.

In foreign affairs, Ford also continued many of Nixon's policies, including détente. Gradually, however, U.S.–Soviet relations began to unravel. One problem was Soviet emigration policy, which restricted the freedom of Jews and political dissidents to leave the country. When members of Congress criticized this policy, the Soviets canceled a proposed U.S.–Soviet trade pact. Over the next few years, relations continued to sour.

Ford also tried to maintain American influence in Southeast Asia. Toward that end, he requested $722 million in military aid for Cambodia and South Vietnam. But Congress, opposed to further military ventures in Southeast Asia, turned down Ford's request. Then, in May 1975, Cambodian Communists

seized the *Mayaguez,* an unarmed U.S. cargo ship. In response, Ford launched a military action to free the vessel and its crew. Forty-one Americans were killed in the effort to release the 39 crew members. While some applauded the president's actions, others criticized it as hasty and ill-timed. As facts later revealed, the *Mayaguez* crew had already been released when the troops were sent.

▼ **Cambodian Communists seized an unarmed U.S. cargo ship, the *Mayaguez*, in May 1975. President Ford called the action piracy and sent U.S. Marines to free the vessel and its crew.**

RETEACH For each subsection in the section, have students write a sentence that summarizes the main idea. Select students to read their sentences aloud. Have the group choose the best summary sentence for each subsection.

Closure

Return students' attention to Nixon's statement cited in the Guided Practice: "When the president does it, that means that it is not illegal." Ask students whether they agree or disagree with Nixon's point of view. Inform students that Nixon expressed the view in 1977, after he had resigned. Ask students what his actions during Watergate suggest about his views on this subject while he was president.

Extension

COMPARE Have students review the impeachment of President Andrew Johnson and write an essay comparing and contrasting the charges against Johnson with those against President Nixon.

ANALYZE Have students write a paper analyzing the public perceptions of government after Watergate and explaining why most presidents since Ford have campaigned as Washington outsiders.

■■ **Ford clashed with Congress over domestic and foreign policy. During his term U.S.–Soviet relations began to unravel.**

THE ELECTION OF 1976

At the 1976 Republican convention, Ford narrowly won the party's nomination over his more conservative challenger, Ronald Reagan of California. To balance the ticket, the convention nominated conservative senator Robert Dole of Kansas for vice president. At the Democratic convention, Jimmy Carter—a former governor of Georgia—won the nomination, with Senator Walter Mondale of Minnesota as his running mate. Giving the keynote address at the Democratic convention was Congresswoman Barbara Jordan of Texas.

BIO GRAPHY Jordan brought a strong sense of moral authority to the Democratic party. Born in 1936, she grew up in Houston, Texas. She excelled in school and eventually received a law degree from Boston University. In 1966 Jordan became the first African American woman elected to the Texas senate. There her tireless efforts on behalf of social reform won praise from President Lyndon Johnson, who noted, "She proved that black is beautiful before we knew what it meant."

In 1972 Jordan was elected to the U.S. House of Representatives, where she soon gained a reputation as a skilled legislator and brilliant orator. She played a key role in drawing up impeachment charges against President Nixon. At one point

Jordan declared: "I am not going to sit here and be an idle spectator to the . . . destruction of the Constitution." Despite her outstanding record in Congress, in 1978 Jordan announced that she would not run for a fourth term. As a political analyst and adviser, however, she has continued to play a prominent role in national affairs.

Barbara Jordan

In her speech to the 1976 Democratic convention, Jordan declared:

❝ We cannot improve on the system of government handed down to us by the founders of the Republic, but we can find new ways to implement that system and realize our destiny. ❞

The idea of a new approach to government was central to Jimmy Carter's campaign. Little known outside the South, Carter ran as a Washington outsider untainted by Watergate. He promised never to lie to the American people and openly noted that he was a born-again Christian whose religious ethics strongly shaped his political actions. "You can't divorce religious beliefs and public service," he said. In a close election, he captured 297 electoral votes to Ford's 240. After eight years of Republican rule, the Democrats returned to the White House. Many hoped that Carter would be able to reverse the public's mistrust of government.

SECTION REVIEW ANSWERS

IDENTIFY

For significance, see the following pages:
Watergate (p. 562)
Bob Woodward (p. 563)
Carl Bernstein (p. 563)
Sam Ervin (p. 563)
James McCord (p. 563)
John Dean (p. 564)
Archibald Cox (p. 564)
Gerald Ford (p. 564)
Saturday Night Massacre (p. 564)
Jimmy Carter (p. 567)
Barbara Jordan (p. 567)

1. *to avoid being impeached for his role in Watergate cover-up*
2. *loss of public support after he pardoned Nixon, clashes with Congress, continuing inflation, recession, problems in Southeast Asia and with the Soviet Union*
3. *exposed wrongdoing; led to punishment of wrongdoers; reinforced that U.S. is a government of laws, not of individuals; led to laws designed to clean up government corruption*
4. *Articles might mention the link between the break-in and the White House, the testimony given during the Senate hearings, the Nixon tapes, and the court order leading up to the Saturday Night Massacre.*
5. *Ford might have had more public support and cooperation from Congress; he might not have lost 1976 election to Carter.*

■■ SECTION **2** REVIEW

IDENTIFY and explain the significance of the following: Watergate, Bob Woodward, Carl Bernstein, Sam Ervin, James McCord, John Dean, Archibald Cox, Gerald Ford, Saturday Night Massacre, Jimmy Carter, Barbara Jordan.

1. **MAIN IDEA** Why did President Nixon choose to resign from office in 1974?
2. **MAIN IDEA** What difficulties did President Ford face during his time in office?
3. **ASSESSING CONSEQUENCES** What was the significance of the Watergate investigation?
4. **WRITING TO INFORM** Imagine you are an investigative reporter for the *Washington Post,* covering the Watergate scandal. Write an article that outlines the major events in the scandal and the investigation leading up to President Nixon's resignation.
5. **HYPOTHESIZING** How might events have been different if Ford had not pardoned Nixon?

PREVIEW WORKSHOP

Following is a list of the significant people, places, and terms in this section. You may wish to use this list as a section preview.

People
- Rosalynn Carter
- Andrew Young
- Anwar Sadat
- Menachem Begin
- Ayatollah Khomeini
- Ronald Reagan
- John Anderson

Places
- Iran
- South Africa
- Rhodesia (Zimbabwe)
- Afghanistan

Terms
- Department of Energy
- National Energy Act
- human rights
- Panama Canal treaties
- apartheid
- Camp David Accords
- Iran hostage crisis

FOCUS OBJECTIVES

- Identify the critical domestic issues facing the Carter administration.

- Examine how Carter's foreign policy differed from Nixon's.

- Explain why Cold War tensions rose under President Carter.

- Analyze how the Iran hostage crisis affected Carter's presidency.

Section 3

CARTER: THE OUTSIDER AS PRESIDENT

FOCUS

- **What critical domestic issues faced the Carter administration?**
- **How did Carter's foreign policy differ from Nixon's?**
- **Why did Cold War tensions rise under President Carter?**
- **How did the Iran hostage crisis affect Carter's presidency?**

Family member awaiting return of hostages in Iran

On January 20, 1977, Jimmy Carter took the oath as the 39th president of the United States. Initially a popular president, Carter enjoyed some notable successes. But serious problems—including persistent inflation and conflict in the Middle East—eventually helped erode the president's popularity. In 1980 he lost his bid for a second term.

AN "OPEN ADMINISTRATION"

During the presidential campaign, Carter had promised, if elected, to stay in touch with the people. He quickly showed his intentions to keep that promise. Following his inauguration, the president and his family walked down Pennsylvania Avenue to the White House, rather than make the trip in a limousine surrounded by Secret Service.

The Carter style. Carter brought a folksy style to the White House, abandoning much of the pomp and ceremony of previous presidents. Contributing to this informal tone was his colorful family, who became the subject of much public interest. The news media reported on the activities of Carter's young daughter, Amy, and on the views of his outspoken mother, Miss Lillian. Carter's wife, Rosalynn, received even more attention as one of his most trusted advisers. Although critics questioned his wife's influence on policy, the president insisted that she play a prominent role in White House affairs.

Early on, Carter took several steps that indicated a new approach to government. On his first full day in office, he announced an unconditional pardon for most Vietnam-era draft evaders, moving beyond the conditional pardon offered by President Ford. This gesture helped heal lingering divisions over the war. Carter also held several

◀ The Carter family attracted almost as much media attention as the president. Shown here are President Carter with his wife, Rosalynn, and his young daughter, Amy.

Teaching the Section

CARTER'S DOMESTIC ISSUES

Tell each student to choose what he or she believes to be the nation's most pressing domestic problem in the late 1970s and to prepare a message to President Carter, expressing his or her concerns about that issue. Then choose a volunteer to represent Jimmy Carter and conduct a town meeting at which students deliver their messages to the president. Students may wish to include their messages in their portfolios.

PRESIDENTIAL LIVES

JIMMY CARTER
1924–

in office 1977–1981

The common reaction to Georgia governor Jimmy Carter's announcement that he was running for president was "Jimmy who?" Few people outside of his home state were familiar with this peanut farmer from Plains. Soon, however, voters began to discover that there was much more to this southern politician than his large grin. A highly ranked graduate of the United States Naval Academy, Carter had worked as a nuclear engineer before entering politics.

One of the most surprising things about

Carter was his modern relationship with his wife. Rosalynn Carter took an active and public role in political affairs, traveling around the world to represent her husband's views. Meanwhile Jimmy Carter shared in the household chores, such as cooking, caring for their children, and grocery shopping. One interviewer was shocked to see the candidate sewing a button onto his own jacket during the presidential campaign. When asked if he always did his own sewing, Carter simply mumbled with thread in mouth, "Uh-huh."

"town meetings" and radio and television call-in sessions to keep in touch with the people. Unlike Richard Nixon, Jimmy Carter seemed determined to keep his administration open to public view.

Carter's economic policy. One of Carter's first tasks was to stimulate the economy, which was just beginning to emerge from several years of recession. Some eight million Americans—7.8 percent of the work force—were out of work. The unemployment rate among African Americans and Hispanic Americans was a staggering 13 percent.

To revive the economy and create jobs, Carter implemented a series of economic measures, including a corporate tax cut. The Carter administration's policies helped reduce unemployment slightly, but they also fueled inflation, which reached 13.3 percent by 1979. To curb inflation, Carter called for voluntary wage and price controls, along with cuts in funding for social services. But Carter's anti-inflation program produced more unemployment. By the summer of 1980, the economy was once again in recession.

Facing the energy crisis. A major cause of the nation's economic woes was the high cost of imported oil. To reduce the nation's oil dependence, Congress created the **Department of Energy** in 1977. The following year it passed the

National Energy Act to relax controls on the price of natural gas. Despite these efforts, world events continued to affect the nation's energy supply.

In January 1979 a revolution in Iran disrupted world oil shipments. A few months later, OPEC raised the price of oil 50 percent, leading to another U.S. energy crisis (see the chart on page 558). As gasoline supplies dwindled, many gas stations closed or reduced their hours. Tempers flared as frustrated drivers had to wait hours to fill

▼ High energy costs hurt many groups during the late 1970s, especially farmers. On February 6, 1979, protesting farmers drove their tractors down Pennsylvania Avenue to demonstrate in front of the White House.

RECOGNIZING STEREOTYPES

In June 1977 President Carter sent the First Lady on a seven-country diplomatic mission to Latin America. Various members of Congress objected on the basis that she was a woman going into male territory. One congressman told her, "The Latins are macho and they hate gringos and women. What else do you want to know?" But Mrs. Carter proved her critics wrong. After her meetings with leaders in Jamaica and Costa Rica, news that she was discussing pertinent issues preceded her arrival in other Latin American nations, and the leaders of those nations were more prepared to discuss their concerns. According to the First Lady, her mission ended with "a feeling of great willingness, even eagerness, on the part of the leaders . . . to cooperate with us in solving the problems that confronted all our people."

Teaching the Section

FOREIGN-POLICY DIFFERENCES

Pair students to prepare discussions between presidents Carter and Nixon about their foreign policies. Within their dialogues each "president" should explain his approach to foreign policy, state why he thinks it is the better approach, and find fault with the other's approach. Select pairs to re-create their dialogues for the class.

■■ Ask students whether national self-interest or concern for human rights should guide American foreign policy today.

HISTORICAL SIDELIGHTS

The China Syndrome
Public doubts about the safety of nuclear power were exacerbated by the movie *The China Syndrome,* which had been released about two weeks before the Three Mile Island incident. The movie's plot involved a utility company's attempt to cover up a serious accident at a power plant similar to Three Mile Island.

 GLOBAL CONNECTIONS

Brigadier General Omar Torrijos of Panama said that if the U.S. Senate had failed to ratify the treaties, Panama would have resorted to "violent liberation" of the Canal Zone, including the possibility of closing the Panama Canal.

PRIMARY SOURCE

Description of Change: excerpted
Rationale: excerpted to focus on main idea

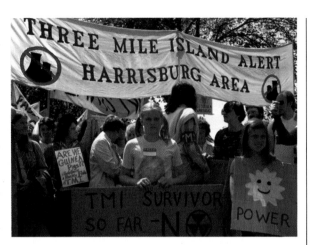

▲ After the disaster at Three Mile Island, residents staged protests that questioned the safety of nuclear power. Protesters urged the government to explore alternative energy research, such as solar power.

their gas tanks. Some people responded by driving less and by embracing other energy-saving measures, such as installing solar heaters in their homes.

In the midst of the oil crisis, another event dramatized America's energy problems. In late March 1979 a nuclear reactor failed at the Three Mile Island power plant in Pennsylvania, nearly causing a catastrophic nuclear meltdown—the melting of the reactor's core. This incident stirred public doubts about nuclear power.

■■ **An economic recession and an energy crisis were among the serious domestic issues facing the Carter administration.**

HUMAN RIGHTS AND FOREIGN POLICY

While Carter was struggling with difficult domestic issues, he was also charting a new course in foreign affairs. Rejecting the realpolitik of the Nixon years, Carter tried to inject moral principles into American foreign policy. Reflecting on past administrations, he declared:

❝ We are deeply concerned . . . by the . . . subtle erosion in the focus and morality of our foreign policy. Under the Nixon-Ford administration, there has evolved a kind of secretive "Lone Ranger" foreign policy—

a one-man policy of international adventure. This is not an appropriate policy for America. ❞

Carter's new approach was most evident in the area of **human rights**—the rights of all people to freedom from unlawful detention or torture. Declaring that "our commitment to human rights must be absolute," Carter called for strong diplomatic and economic pressure on countries that violated human rights.

Not surprisingly, many dictatorships that repressed the rights of their people strongly opposed Carter's policy. Some American diplomats also had doubts. They warned that such meddling in the domestic affairs of other countries might increase world tensions. The United States would resent meddling by other nations in *its* domestic affairs, they pointed out.

■■ **Carter moved away from Nixon's foreign policy of realpolitik to emphasize moral principles and respect for human rights.**

Carter's stand on the Panama Canal caused even greater controversy. He supported Panama's right to control the Canal Zone and pushed for passage of the **Panama Canal treaties**, which granted Panama control over canal operations by the year 2000. Critics charged that Carter was "giving away" the canal. "We built it, we paid for it, it's ours, and . . . we are going to keep it!" declared conservative Republican Ronald Reagan.

Gradually, however, public opinion shifted in Carter's favor, and after a long and bitter debate, the Senate narrowly ratified the treaties in 1978. In

▲ Through the Panama Canal treaties, President Carter proposed that the United States give control of the Canal Zone to Panama by the year 2000.

COLD WAR POLICIES

Assign students one of the following: Panama, Africa, the Soviet Union, or the Middle East. Ask them to prepare a short radio talk that President Carter might give about his policies toward their assigned country or region, and how those actions bring morality to American foreign policy. Select students to "broadcast" their talks to the class. Then ask if Carter's actions in each instance were "meddling" and whether they increased or decreased Cold War tensions.

IRAN HOSTAGE CRISIS

Have students write a letter to President Carter, explaining why the crisis with Iran will affect the way they vote in the 1980 election. Have volunteers read their letters before the class. Students may wish to include their letters in their portfolios.

▶

Latin America, where U.S. control over the canal had long been a sore point, the treaties met with general approval.

CARTER AND THE COLD WAR

Carter's stance on the Panama Canal issue signaled a more flexible approach to relations with developing countries. Carter hoped the approach would improve America's image and diminish the appeal of communism. His policy was evident in Africa, where the United States and the Soviet Union were jockeying for influence among the continent's newly independent states.

Unlike Nixon and Ford, who showed little interest in Africa, Carter tried to win friends among African nations by helping them sort out their problems in their own way. One Carter official noted, "It is not a sign of weakness to recognize that we alone cannot dictate events elsewhere. It is rather a sign of maturity in a complex world."

Carter's ambassador to the United Nations, former civil rights activist Andrew Young, tried to reach out to black African states. He criticized white imperialism in Africa, condemned South Africa's policy of **apartheid** (racial segregation), and supported black majority rule in Rhodesia (now Zimbabwe).

Carter's flexible approach helped smooth relations in Africa and ease Cold War conflict. The easing of tensions was short-lived, however. In December 1979, Soviet troops invaded the country of Afghanistan to install a pro-Soviet leader. The invasion put Soviet troops within striking distance of major oil routes.

Labeling the invasion a threat to peace, President Carter warned the Soviets to withdraw. When they refused, he cut grain sales to the Soviet Union and announced a boycott of the 1980 Summer Olympics in Moscow. Congress also postponed the signing of a key U.S.–Soviet arms-control treaty. Finally, the president warned that any Soviet military action in the Persian Gulf would provoke a military response by the United States.

■■ **Although the U.S. improved relations with developing countries, Cold War tensions increased when the Soviets invaded Afghanistan.**

CARTER AND THE MIDDLE EAST

Not long before the Soviet invasion of Afghanistan, Carter engineered his chief foreign-policy triumph: a Middle East peace accord. Carter had taken office in 1977 amid fears of another Egyptian-Israeli war. Egyptian president Anwar Sadat (sah-DAHT) and Israeli premier Menachem Begin (muh-NAHK-uhm BAY-gin) met for peace talks, but those talks deadlocked.

BIO GRAPHY Anwar Sadat received a great deal of criticism from the leaders of other Arab nations for attempting any peace talks with Israel. Sadat was born in the small village of Mit Abu-Kum on the Nile Delta in 1918. His childhood was heavily influenced by his close-knit family and the local Imam (religious leader), who taught him the principles of the Islamic faith. Soon after graduating from the Egyptian Military Academy in 1938, Sadat joined a group of rebels who wanted to rid Egypt of its constitutional monarchy, which was under British control.

Anwar Sadat

Sadat went to prison in the 1940s for his efforts to liberate Egypt. After being released from prison, he joined the rebel forces who finally overthrew the monarch in 1952. Thereafter Sadat played a central role in shaping Egyptian policy, finally

◀ **As U.S. ambassador to the United Nations, Andrew Young condemned apartheid and sympathized with the concerns of developing nations. His actions made him a controversial figure, and he was forced to resign in 1979.**

Olympic Boycott
More than 50 nations, including West Germany, Japan, and China, chose not to participate in the XXII Olympic Games because of the events in Afghanistan. This action led to 6,000 athletes participating in the games, rather than the projected 10,000. The 300,000 foreign tourists expected in Moscow dropped to about 100,000.

BIO GRAPHY **PERSONALITIES IN HISTORY**

Sadat's public image had been one of his most powerful assets. After he visited Israel in 1977, Egyptians hailed him as the "hero of peace." After Camp David, Egypt's domestic problems—coupled with an explosive press conference during which he accused the foreign press of writing lies about him—helped erode Sadat's image. In September 1981 he ordered the arrest of some 3,000 students, fundamentalists, politicians, and religious leaders and called for the ousting of foreign journalists who had reported his activities. One month later, Sadat was assassinated.

*P*ractice

GUIDED PRACTICE

Create a four-cell chart on the chalkboard with columns labeled *Successes* and *Failures* and rows labeled *Foreign* and *Domestic*. Have the class assess Carter's handling of each event discussed in the section and list that event in the appropriate cell.

INDEPENDENT PRACTICE

Instruct students to choose an event from one of the cells in the Guided Practice chart and create an editorial cartoon that reflects Carter's handling of that situation. Students may wish to include their editorial cartoons in their portfolios.

*R*eview and *A*ssessment

REVIEW Ask students to imagine they voted for Carter in 1976. Have them write a journal entry explaining why they voted for Jimmy Carter. Then instruct them to write a second journal entry citing issues that affected the way they voted in 1980. Then assign the Section 3 Review on p. 573.

ASSESS Assign the **Section 3 Daily Quiz** in *Core Resources*.

PRIMARY SOURCE

Description of Change: excerpted and bracketed
Rationale: excerpted to focus on main idea; bracketed to clarify meaning

PRIMARY SOURCE

Description of Change: excerpted
Rationale: excerpted to focus on main idea

MULTICULTURAL PERSPECTIVES

According to Tass, the Soviet press agency, the reason for Carter's defeat in the 1980 presidential election was his hard-line approach toward the Soviet Union. Tass also claimed that the U.S. boycott of the Summer Olympics in Moscow had severely damaged the Carter administration. After Reagan's victory Soviet Premier Nikolai Tikhonov expressed hope that Reagan would call for a "constructive approach" that would lead to improvement in U.S.–Soviet relations.

Map Caption Answer
(for map on p. 573)
Minnesota and Hawaii

---

becoming president in 1970. As president he played a key role in Middle East events, including trying to pave the road to peace. When Sadat visited Israel in 1977, Premier Begin remarked:

> ❝ The time of the flight between Cairo and Jerusalem is short . . . [but] the distance between them . . . until yesterday, quite large. . . . Sadat passed this distance with heartfelt courage. . . . We, the Jews, know how to appreciate this courage. ❞

But Sadat always downplayed his own role in bringing about peace. He considered his actions a collective effort by the entire country. To him, all Egyptians shared responsibility for the nation's future. He once said:

> ❝ Responsibility cannot be relegated to certain individuals, no matter how good your opinion of them might be; neither can it be confined to groups of people, however good their intentions may be. Responsibility is the entire people's property. ❞

In September 1978 Sadat met with Begin and Carter at Camp David, the presidential retreat in Maryland. There, after 12 days of negotiations, the three agreed on a framework for peace, which became known as the **Camp David Accords**. As a result of their efforts, Sadat and Begin shared the Nobel Peace Prize for 1978. The following year, the two leaders signed a formal peace treaty ending 30 years of war between Egypt and Israel. At the emotion-filled ceremony, each quoted the prophet Isaiah: "And they shall beat their swords into plowshares and their spears into pruning hooks."

The accords did not meet universal approval. Some supporters of Israel accused President Carter of favoring the Arabs in order to appease Arab oil-exporting nations, such as Saudi Arabia. Sadat drew the wrath of other Arab nations, furious at his "betrayal" for making peace with Israel. In 1981, members of an Islamic fundamentalist group within the Egyptian army assassinated Sadat while he was reviewing a military parade.

---

*C*ARTER'S POPULARITY FALLS

Although Carter had chalked up some notable successes as president, by 1980 only 21 percent of

Americans approved of his performance. Nixon's approval rating had not fallen this low even during the depths of Watergate. Carter's drop in popularity was partly due to his lack of political experience. But his troubles also lay in the nature of the problems he faced. The energy crisis, inflation, unemployment, Middle East conflict, and Cold War tensions were highly complicated issues that defied simple solutions. Of all the difficulties he faced, however, none was more damaging than the **Iran hostage crisis**.

Iran had long been regarded as critical to U.S. security in the Middle East. In the 1950s the United States had helped overthrow Iran's leader and restore Shah Reza Pahlavi to power (see Chapter 18). Although the shah's regime was very repressive, the United States always supported him. In 1979, however, followers of a militant Islamic leader, the Ayatollah Khomeini (eye-uh-TOH-luh koh-MAY-nee), forced the shah to flee the country. The new government was outraged when President Carter allowed the shah into the United States for medical treatment. On November 4, 1979, in an effort to force the shah's return to Iran for trial, Iranian militants seized 53 American hostages at the U.S. embassy in Tehran, Iran's capital.

Month after month, the hostage crisis dragged on. In April 1980 a rescue mission failed when U.S. military helicopters crashed in the Iranian desert, killing eight Americans. As frustration over the crisis mounted, public anger at Carter also grew. Many felt that his inability to free the hostages signaled America's decline as a symbol of power. Even one Carter aide admitted that "Khomeini would not have touched the Soviet Embassy."

Echoing these thoughts during the 1980 presidential election campaign, the Republican candidate, Ronald Reagan, attacked Carter as a weak president who had presided over a decline in American power. Reagan's promise to "make America strong

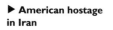

▶ **American hostage in Iran**

Closure

Discuss the advantages and disadvantages of electing a president who is considered an outsider. Ask students to suggest how Carter's outsider status may have influenced his domestic and foreign-policy strategies.

Extension

CONDUCT Ask students to conduct interviews with parents, teachers, or others who experienced the energy crisis of the late 1970s. Have students report their findings to the class in the form of anecdotes.

RESEARCH Have students research additional information about the Camp David Accords and write a summary that identifies the details of the agreement between Egypt and Israel.

again" struck a chord with voters. He and his running mate, George Bush, easily won the election, capturing 489 electoral votes to Carter and Mondale's 49. An independent candidate, John Anderson, failed to capture any electoral votes, but did win almost 7 percent of the popular vote, further reflecting public frustration with the administration. For the first time since 1952, the Republicans won control of the Senate, while the Democrats' hold on the House was reduced somewhat.

After his defeat Carter continued to negotiate for the release of the hostages. On January 20, 1981, after 444 days in captivity, the hostages were finally freed, just moments after Ronald Reagan was sworn in as president.

Election of 1980

REPUBLICAN LANDSLIDE Carter's difficulties at home and abroad doomed his chances for reelection.

? LOCATION Which states did Carter win west of the Mississippi River?

	Electoral Vote	Popular Vote	% of Popular Vote
Reagan	489	43,904,153	50.7
Carter	49	35,483,883	41.0
Anderson		5,720,060	6.6
Other candidates		1,407,793	1.6

Reagan (Republican)
Carter (Democratic)

▪▪ The Iran hostage crisis contributed to Carter's defeat in the 1980 election.

SECTION REVIEW ANSWERS

IDENTIFY

For significance, see the following pages:
Rosalynn Carter (p. 568)
Department of Energy (p. 569)
National Energy Act (p. 569)
human rights (p. 570)
Panama Canal treaties (p. 570)
Andrew Young (p. 571)
apartheid (p. 571)
Anwar Sadat (p. 571)
Menachem Begin (p. 571)
Camp David Accords (p. 572)
Iran hostage crisis (p. 572)
Ayatollah Khomeini (p. 572)
Ronald Reagan (p. 572)
John Anderson (p. 573)

LOCATE

For locations, see the map on pp. 772–773.

1. *recession, energy crisis*
2. *improved U.S. relations with developing nations; Soviet invasion of Afghanistan*
3. *rejected Nixon's realpolitik policy in favor of one emphasizing moral principles and human rights*
4. *Essays might mention Carter's lack of political experience, economic difficulties, and Iran hostage crisis.*
5. *yes—might note that U.S. never owned canal and had no right to it; no— might argue U.S. has always controlled zone and should not give up that control*

SECTION 3 REVIEW

IDENTIFY and explain the significance of the following: Rosalynn Carter, Department of Energy, National Energy Act, human rights, Panama Canal treaties, Andrew Young, apartheid, Anwar Sadat, Menachem Begin, Camp David Accords, Iran hostage crisis, Ayatollah Khomeini, Ronald Reagan, John Anderson.

LOCATE and explain the importance of the following: Iran, South Africa, Rhodesia (Zimbabwe), Afghanistan.

1. **MAIN IDEA** What two serious domestic issues did President Carter face?

2. **MAIN IDEA** How did the Carter administration's approach to the Cold War influence events overseas? What event caused Cold War tensions to increase?

3. **CONTRASTING** Contrast the Carter administration's approach to foreign policy with the Nixon administration's approach.

4. **WRITING TO EXPLAIN** Imagine you are a political analyst covering the 1980 presidential election. Write an essay explaining why Carter has been defeated.

5. **TAKING A STAND** Was Carter right in supporting the Panama Canal treaties? Why or why not?

Chapter 21

SECTION
4

Introducing the Section

FOCUS OBJECTIVES

- Analyze how the civil rights movement continued in the 1970s and describe how some whites responded.

- Explain what Native American leaders fought for during the 1970s.

- Identify the issues that both encouraged and divided the women's movement during the 1970s.

- Describe how the new immigrants in the 1970s helped shape society.

THE AMERICAN NATION VIDEODISC PROGRAM

César Chávez

| 2B | 38963 | :21 |

CORE RESOURCES

- **Literature Worksheet 21**
- **Section 4 Daily Quiz**

AV RESOURCES

- *The American Nation Videodisc: César Chávez; The Women's Rights Movement*
- **Linking Geography and History Transparencies and Worksheets 12B, 13B**

574

PREVIEW WORKSHOP

Following is a list of the significant people and terms in this section. You may wish to use this list as a section preview.

People
- Patricia Harris
- Russell Means
- Wei-Chi Poon

Terms
- League of United Latin American Citizens
- Rehabilitation Act
- Education for All Handicapped Children Act
- affirmative action
- *University of California* v. *Bakke*
- Education Amendments Act
- *Roe* v. *Wade*
- Equal Rights Amendment
- zero population growth
- Sunbelt
- Voting Rights Act of 1975
- Bilingual Education Act

Section 4

A DECADE OF SOCIAL CHANGE

F O C U S

- **How did the civil rights movement continue in the 1970s? How did some whites respond?**
- **What did Native American leaders fight for during the 1970s?**
- **What issues both encouraged and divided the women's movement during the 1970s?**
- **How did the new immigrants in the 1970s help shape society?**

*D*uring the 1970s American society underwent important social changes. African Americans made further gains, despite a growing white backlash. Hispanic Americans, Native Americans, people with disabilities, and women also made legal and economic strides. Amid these changes, society as a whole was evolving as Americans were living longer and moving more often, and new immigrants were swelling the population.

A woman with visual impairment demonstrating for civil rights

*T*HE LEGACY OF THE CIVIL RIGHTS MOVEMENT

The 1970s brought some progress in the area of civil rights. Though a 1975 Civil Rights Commission report found that many African Americans were still being kept from voting by various means, by the end of the 1970s over 4,500 African Americans held elective office—three times the number in 1969. The roster of elected black officials in 1978 included 16 members of the House of Representatives and 170 mayors, including those of Los Angeles, Atlanta, Detroit, and Washington, D.C.

As new African American leaders gained political experience, they formed strong alliances and effective lobbies. They also worked hard to get out the black vote, a key factor in Jimmy Carter's electoral victory in 1976. As president, Carter helped open the doors of the federal government to African Americans, naming more blacks to federal jobs than any previous president. In addition to his

choice of Andrew Young as UN ambassador, Carter appointed the first African American woman to a cabinet post—Patricia Harris as secretary of Housing and Urban Development.

During the 1970s Hispanic Americans also began to reap some rewards for their political struggles of the previous decade. Between 1974 and 1987 the number of elected Hispanic officials in the United States more than doubled. Growing numbers of Hispanic Americans were appointed to federal jobs, while Hispanic groups such as LULAC—**League of United Latin American Citizens**—mounted lobbying efforts and helped raise national awareness of Hispanic concerns. In California the United Farm Workers won a key victory in 1975 with the passage of a state law extending legal protection to migrant farm workers. In addition, the Southwest Voter Registration Education Project helped Hispanic Americans register to vote.

Americans with disabilities also made their voices heard in the 1970s. Why, they asked, should

Ask students to recall important civil rights gains made by African Americans during the 1960s and the methods by which they made these gains. Then explain that in this section students will examine how the civil rights struggle continued in the 1970s as other groups fought for equal treatment and opportunity.

*T*eaching the *S*ection

CIVIL RIGHTS

Have students work in small groups to conceptualize and complete a graphic organizer that summarizes gains made by African Americans, Hispanic Americans, and Americans with disabilities during the 1970s. Ask volunteers from each group to present and explain its graphic organizer to the class. Then discuss with the class why some white Americans might have objected to some of these gains, and how they expressed their objections.

▶

▲ These demonstrators in San Francisco protested lack of access to public transportation by blocking buses during rush hour.

their tax dollars help build public facilities that people in wheelchairs or people with visual disabilities could not easily use? In response to protests, state and local governments passed laws requiring wheelchair ramps and special parking spaces at public facilities. Many public facilities also put up signs in braille to help people who are visually impaired. Congress joined these efforts by passing the **Rehabilitation Act** in 1973, which forbade discrimination in jobs, education, or housing because of physical disabilities. In 1975 it passed the **Education for All Handicapped Children Act**, which required public schools to provide education for children with physical and mental disabilities.

▪▪ The legacy of the civil rights movement continued in the growing political clout of African Americans, Hispanic Americans, and people with disabilities.

A WHITE BACKLASH

The expansion of civil rights during the 1970s was the result of both public and private efforts. In an effort to uphold federal laws against discrimination, the Civil Rights Division of the Department of Justice sued corporations and labor unions to end unfair employment practices. Many schools and businesses also instituted **affirmative action** programs, whereby ethnic minorities and women were given preference in hiring and admission

to make up for previous discrimination.

But the 1970s also brought a white backlash against the civil rights movement. Some white citizens complained that civil rights reform was depriving them of their own rights. One of the first targets of white anger was court-ordered busing to achieve school desegregation. Busing met with strong opposition in a number of cities, most notably Boston. One angry white Bostonian, Jimmy Kelley, warned: "You heard of the Hundred Years War? This will be the eternal war. It will be passed down from father to son."

By the fall of 1974, violent protests against busing had erupted in Boston. Many people were injured in the riots. Yet despite the risks, many

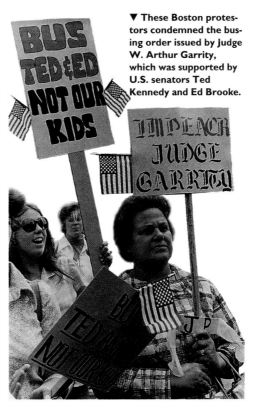

▼ These Boston protestors condemned the busing order issued by Judge W. Arthur Garrity, which was supported by U.S. senators Ted Kennedy and Ed Brooke.

Teaching the Section

NATIVE AMERICANS ORGANIZE

Organize the class into small groups and tell them to assign group members to be either TV journalists or Native Americans in the 1970s. Direct the "journalists" to interview one or more of the "Native Americans" about their opinions of the American Indian Movement (AIM) and its tactics. Journalists also should ask subjects for their opinions about other methods that were used in the 1970s for achieving Native American rights.

🅑🅘🅞 PERSONALITIES IN HISTORY

At age 16, Russell Means transferred from a racially mixed school to a school whose population was comprised almost entirely of whites. There, he grew angry at the taunting and daily insults he received from his classmates. "I guess I was sort of what you'd call a boy named Sioux," he has been quoted as saying. "Every time some wise guy would mouth off I'd figger I had to defend myself for bein' Indian. I got to know what it was like to hate to see it rain."

■■ Ask students what they think Means meant by his last sentence. *(probably that, as a Native American, he was the victim of prejudicial slurs that referred to stereotypical Indian rain dances)*

🅐🅥 TRANSPARENCY

Linking Geography and History Transparency and **Worksheet 12B**

---

black parents believed that busing was necessary. As one African American woman, Rachel Twymon, told her two children who were being bused to a previously all-white school:

❝ I'm afraid this isn't going to be an easy year for either of you. You're going to be called a lot of ugly names. You're going to be spat at, maybe pushed around some. But it's not the first time this has happened and it won't be the last. It's something we have to go through—something *you* have to go through—if this city is ever going to get integrated. ❞

By the late 1970s the busing controversy had quieted down, but anger over affirmative action continued. Many whites argued that affirmative action programs led to reverse discrimination. In 1978 the Supreme Court handed down an important ruling on affirmative action. In *University of California* v. *Bakke*, the Court ruled that a white man, Allan Bakke, had been unfairly denied admission to medical school on the basis of quotas—systems that set aside a fixed number of places for certain groups of people, in this case, African Americans. Although the Court did not rule out all forms of affirmative action, it did strike down quotas as a means of achieving racial equality. In a bitter dissent Justice Thurgood Marshall recalled the history of three centuries of racial discrimination in America and its toll on generations of African Americans: "The dream of America as the great melting pot has not been realized for the Negro; because of his skin color he never even made it into the pot."

■■ **White backlash against civil rights reform erupted in the 1970s, fueled by busing and affirmative action.**

🄽ATIVE AMERICANS ORGANIZE

As part of the broad movement for civil rights, Native Americans also began to organize. Young urban Indians launched the American Indian Movement (AIM) in 1968, calling for a renewal of Native American culture and recognition of Native American rights. In 1972, some 500 AIM members, protesting what they called the "Trail of Broken Treaties," temporarily occupied the Bureau of Indian Affairs (BIA) in Washington, D.C.

🅑🅘🅞 One of the leaders of the BIA occupation was Russell Means, a longtime Indian activist. Born in 1940 on the Pine Ridge Sioux Reservation of South Dakota, Means spent much of his childhood in the San Francisco Bay area. By 1970 he had become a prominent figure in AIM. That year, he gained national attention when he led an AIM occupation of the *Mayflower II*—a replica of the Pilgrim ship—during Thanksgiving Day celebrations in Plymouth, Massachusetts. In a 1971 interview, Means gave his justification for AIM's aggressive tactics:

Russell Means

❝ In all our demonstrations we have yet to hurt anybody or destroy any property. However, . . . we have found that the only way the white man will listen is by us creating a disturbance in his world. ❞

In 1973 Means helped lead AIM's most dramatic action—the seizure of the trading post on the Sioux reservation in Wounded Knee, South Dakota. Here in 1890, U.S. cavalry units had brutally massacred more than 300 Sioux. Now Means declared that the government had two choices: "Either they attack and wipe us out like they did in 1890, or they negotiate our reasonable demands." Means wanted the government to initiate hearings on past broken treaties and investigate alleged misconduct in the Bureau of Indian Affairs.

For 71 days AIM members and U.S. marshals engaged in a grim standoff. Finally, after two people had been killed and one wounded, the government agreed to consider AIM's grievances, and the siege came to an end. The following year, Means and other AIM leaders were put on trial for the Wounded Knee incident. The case was dismissed, however, when defense lawyers presented evidence of government misconduct against AIM.

While AIM's confrontational tactics captured headlines and television attention, other Native American leaders worked to renew tribal life by

---

WOMEN'S MOVEMENT ISSUES

Tell students to imagine they are women in the 1970s. Have students work in pairs to prepare a statement explaining their support or objection to the goals of the women's movement. Advise students that they may prepare their own statements if the pair disagrees. Call on volunteers with opposing viewpoints on each issue to present their statements to the class and to explain the reasons for their views.

IMMIGRANTS SHAPE SOCIETY

Call on students to identify the major sources of immigration in the 1970s, to suggest causes of this immigration, and to compare them with causes of earlier immigration to the U.S. *(economic opportunity and escape from political unrest or oppression, which are historic reasons for U.S. immigration)* Then ask students to cite ways in which the immigrants of the 1970s have affected American society, and again ask for comparisons with the consequences of earlier immigration. *(Students should note similar assimilation and labor force issues and similarities in the political power of some immigrant groups.)*

■■ Ask students whether they believe that programs such as bilingual instruction and non-English voting materials encourage or discourage immigrants' participation in American life and society. ▶

◀ Frustrated over government delays in addressing Native American grievances, AIM leaders resorted to more aggressive tactics. This photograph was taken on March 6, 1973, after members seized the trading post on Wounded Knee reservation.

quieter means, including court action. The Taos Pueblo Indians of New Mexico recovered 48,000 acres of land, including the sacred Blue Lake. Native Americans in Maine, claiming that more than half of the state had been illegally taken from them, won from Congress an $81.5 million award and the right to purchase up to 300,000 acres.

■■ **During the 1970s Indian leaders fought to improve conditions for Native Americans and to take back tribal lands.**

THE WOMEN'S MOVEMENT GAINS MOMENTUM

The women's movement made many advances in the 1970s as leaders worked to shape public policy and elect more women to public office. Many all-male colleges opened their doors to women, while other universities instituted courses in women's studies. In 1972 Congress passed the **Education Amendments Act**, which outlawed sexual discrimination in higher education.

The following year, the Supreme Court handed down a landmark decision affecting women. In the case *Roe v. Wade*, the Court overturned a state law limiting women's access to abortion. The Court ruled that a woman and her doctor, not the state, should make such decisions. While most feminists hailed *Roe v. Wade* as a victory, opponents protested that the ruling violated the right to life of the unborn.

The 1970s also saw a major battle over the **Equal Rights Amendment** (ERA), the proposed

constitutional amendment barring discrimination on the basis of sex (see Chapter 11). The ERA received strong support from the National Organization for Women (NOW) and other women's groups. In testimony before Congress, feminist leader Gloria Steinem asserted:

❝ Women suffer second-class treatment from the moment they are born. They are expected to *be* rather than achieve, to function biologically rather than learn. A brother, whatever his intellect, is more likely to get the family's encouragement and education money, while girls are often pressured to conceal ambition and intelligence. ❞

Congress passed the ERA in 1972, but the amendment still required the approval of at least 38 states. At first, ratification seemed certain, but by

▼ During a news conference, National Women's Political Caucus leaders Bella Abzug, Gloria Steinem, Shirley Chisholm, and Betty Friedan announced their goal to increase the number of women delegates to the 1972 presidential conventions.

Chapter 21
SECTION 4

Practice

GUIDED PRACTICE

Begin a word web by writing *Social Change in the 1970s* in the center of the chalkboard and drawing a circle around it. Draw lines emanating from the circle. Have students add the significant social changes of the 1970s to the end of each line.

INDEPENDENT PRACTICE

Instruct students to select a topic from the word web developed in the Guided Practice activity and to write a paragraph summarizing that change from the perspective of a person who experienced it. Students may wish to include their summaries in their portfolios.

Review and Assessment

REVIEW Have students use the Essential Points of the section to write a paragraph explaining how the civil rights successes of one group may affect other groups. Then assign the Section 4 Review on p. 579.

ASSESS Assign the **Section 4 Daily Quiz** in *Core Resources*.

MULTICULTURAL PERSPECTIVES

Some Native American women were among those who felt that the leaders of NOW did not represent their views. Lorelei DeCora Means, a Winnebago Minneconjou Lakota activist, explained: "We are *American Indian* women, in that order. We are oppressed, first and foremost, as American Indians, as peoples colonized by the United States of America, *not* as women . . . We tend to view those who come to us wanting to form alliances on the basis of . . . 'more important' issues to be a little less than friends, especially since most of them come from the Euroamerican population which benefits most directly from our ongoing colonization."

AV TRANSPARENCY
Linking Geography and History Transparency and **Worksheet 13B**

◄ **Phyllis Schlafly was one of the most vocal critics of the ERA during the 1970s and the 1980s.**

the 1982 deadline set by Congress, the ERA was still three states short of ratification. As a result, it failed to become law.

The women's movement made many political gains; however, it also alienated many women who viewed it as a movement primarily for privileged white women. Many women from working-class and ethnic communities felt that the leaders of NOW simply could not identify with the problems they faced every day.

The movement also alienated many middle-class women who felt that it downgraded the family and condemned women who chose to be full-time homemakers. These women viewed *Roe* v. *Wade* and the ERA as threats to traditional family life. Critics warned that the ERA would "nullify any laws that make any distinction between men and women." Eventually, they argued, men and women would even be forced to share public restrooms! When the ERA failed to win ratification, conservative critic Phyllis Schlafly proclaimed: "The defeat of the Equal Rights Amendment is the greatest victory for women's rights since the woman's suffrage movement of 1920."

▪▪ The women's movement was encouraged by Roe v. Wade and the ERA, but the issues alienated many women from the movement.

A CHANGING POPULATION

As different groups in American society worked for change, the society itself was evolving. Thanks to medical advances, Americans were living longer, a phenomenon referred to as the "graying of America." At the same time, the birthrate was dropping sharply, to an average of two births per woman. For years, experts had been promoting this level of **zero population growth** (ZPG)—a birthrate that replaces the existing population but does not increase it—in hopes of preventing overpopulation.

The divorce rate continued to rise during the 1970s. In 1979, 5.3 divorces were registered per 1,000 Americans, up from 2.2 in 1960. Increasingly, many Americans were abandoning the idea that marriage was necessarily a lifelong commitment.

Americans also moved more often in the 1970s than in the past. During the decade a growing number of Americans migrated from the North and the East to the **Sunbelt** states of the South and the West, seeking a warmer climate and a more suburban life-style. This migration caused the population growth of California, Texas, and Florida to outpace that of the rest of the nation.

Another key factor in America's evolution during this period was continued immigration, mostly from Asia and Latin America. Most Latin American immigrants came from Mexico, but a sizable number also came from the Caribbean. In 1980, for example, nearly 120,000 Cubans fled the

▲ **Many multigenerational Asian families, such as the one pictured here, immigrated to the United States in the 1970s.**

RETEACH Organize students into small groups and assign each a subsection of the section. Tell each group to compose a poem, song, or rap that expresses the theme of its subsection. Have each group perform its composition.

Closure

Ask students to explain why this section is titled "A Decade of Social Change." Ask them to give examples from the text to support their explanations.

Extension

SYNTHESIZE Have students research the controversy surrounding the passage of the Bilingual Education Act of 1974 and write a paper that synthesizes the controversy's issues.

ANALYZE Have students write an essay analyzing why busing was seen as a natural extension of the 1954 Supreme Court ruling in *Brown* v. *Board of Education.*

Communist island for the United States, settling mainly in the Miami area. Economically successful, Cuban Americans became an important interest group in American politics.

China, which opened the way for emigration after President Nixon's visit, supplied some of the new Asian population. Many of these Chinese immigrants were highly skilled and well-educated professionals fleeing political persecution. Despite their backgrounds, however, many found that discrimination and their lack of English skills kept them from obtaining well-paying jobs. The experiences of Wei-Chi Poon, a biology professor from China, and her husband, a skilled architect, were not unique. Neither knew any English when they immigrated to the United States. As a result, she had to toil in a laundry factory for $1.85 an hour, while he took on two low-paying jobs. "We were so busy working and so tired," she recalled, "we had no time and energy to study English."

Congress tried to aid such immigrants by passing two new laws. The **Voting Rights Act of 1975** required states and communities with large numbers of non-English speakers to print voting materials in various foreign languages. The **Bilingual Education Act** of 1974 encouraged public schools to provide instruction to students in their primary languages while they learned

▲ The Bilingual Education Act of 1974 encouraged public schools, such as the one shown here, to provide students with instruction in their primary languages while they learned English.

English. Although some critics opposed bilingual education—claiming that it slowed the assimilation of immigrants into American life—there was little question that the United States was becoming an increasingly multicultural society. Coping with new immigrants, both legal and illegal, would remain an important issue for America.

■■ **Large-scale Asian and Latin American immigration during the 1970s prompted support for bilingual education.**

SECTION REVIEW ANSWERS

IDENTIFY

For significance, see the following pages:
Patricia Harris (p. 574)
League of United Latin American Citizens (p. 574)
Rehabilitation Act (p. 575)
Education for All Handicapped Children Act (p. 575)
affirmative action (p. 575)
University of California v. Bakke (p. 576)
Russell Means (p. 576)
Education Amendments Act (p. 577)
Roe v. Wade (p. 577)
Equal Rights Amendment (p. 577)
zero population growth (p. 578)
Sunbelt (p. 578)
Wei-Chi Poon (p. 579)
Voting Rights Act of 1975 (p. 579)
Bilingual Education Act (p. 579)

1. to fight for improved conditions, to regain lands
2. some became politically influential, prompted support for bilingual education and non-English voting materials
3. increased political power of other groups; resisted education and affirmative action reform
4. Essays should discuss the positive and negative effects on the movement.
5. to seek a warmer climate; increased populations of CA, TX, and FL

SECTION 4 REVIEW

IDENTIFY and explain the significance of the following: Patricia Harris, League of United Latin American Citizens, Rehabilitation Act, Education for All Handicapped Children Act, affirmative action, *University of California* v. *Bakke,* Russell Means, Education Amendments Act, *Roe* v. *Wade,* Equal Rights Amendment, zero population growth, Sunbelt, Wei-Chi Poon, Voting Rights Act of 1975, Bilingual Education Act.

1. **MAIN IDEA** Why did Native Americans begin to organize during this period?

2. **MAIN IDEA** What influence did the Asian and Latin American immigrants in the 1970s have on American society?

3. **IDENTIFYING CAUSE AND EFFECT** How did the impact of the civil rights movement continue into the 1970s? How did some whites respond to this legacy?

4. **WRITING TO EXPRESS A VIEWPOINT** Imagine you are a political observer of the women's movement. Write an essay that summarizes the impact of *Roe* v. *Wade* and the ERA on the movement.

5. **LINKING HISTORY AND GEOGRAPHY** Why did many Americans move to the Sunbelt states during the 1970s? What effect did this migration have on population patterns?

DEVELOPING THEMES

Return to the Themes section on p. 554. Have students discuss these again and compare their original responses with those given now. (See p. 553B for suggested answers.)

Chapter Review Answers

WRITING A SUMMARY

See Essential Points in each section for main ideas.

REVIEWING CHRONOLOGY

2, 3, 1, 4, 5
Evaluating
increased Soviet-American tensions, cut oil supplies to U.S., involved U.S. in the region's search for solutions

IDENTIFYING PEOPLE AND IDEAS

1. *middle-class voters weary from social upheaval of 1960s*
2. *measure setting air quality standards and emissions guidelines for car manufacturers*
3. *Socialist president of Chile overthrown with U.S. help*
4. *series of events on October 20, 1973, that increased calls to impeach Nixon*
5. *congresswoman who gave keynote address at Democratic convention in 1976*
6. *policy of racial segregation in South Africa*
7. *Egyptian president who participated in Camp David Accords*
8. *1973 act that forbade discrimination in jobs, education, or housing because of physical disabilities*

9. *Native American activist and AIM leader*
10. *Supreme Court decision overturning state law limiting access to abortion*

UNDERSTANDING MAIN IDEAS

1. *domestic—followed conservative agenda on law-and-order issues, civil rights, economy; foreign—initiated realpolitik policy, détente with Soviet Union and opening to China*
2. *illegal activities by Nixon administration to smear enemies and win reelection; led to Nixon's resignation and eroded public trust in government*

3. *domestic—conflicts over social welfare programs, inflation; foreign—relations with Soviet Union, Mayaguez incident*
4. *abandoned pomp and ceremony of previous presidents, adopted folksy style, held public forums to keep in touch with people; lack of political experience and failure to resolve economy, energy crisis, and Iran hostage crisis*
5. *increased political participation and legislation concerning special issues, provided new opportunities through affirmative action programs; concerns that civil rights reform deprived whites of their own rights*

CHAPTER 21
Review

First Earth Day celebration held. Salvador Allende elected president of Chile. EPA and OSHA created.	Wage and price controls imposed.	Nixon visits China. SALT treaty signed. Watergate break-in occurs. ERA passed. Nixon reelected president.	Roe v. Wade decided. Egypt and Syria invade Israel. Saturday Night Massacre occurs.

1970   1972

WRITING A SUMMARY

Using the essential points of the chapter as a guide, write a summary of the chapter.

REVIEWING CHRONOLOGY

Number your paper 1 to 5. Study the time line above, and list the following events in the order in which they happened by writing the first next to 1, the second next to 2, and so on. Then complete the activity below.

1. Bilingual Education Act passed.
2. First Earth Day celebration held.
3. Watergate break-in occurs.
4. Panama Canal treaties ratified.
5. Iran hostage crisis begins.

Evaluating How did the Arab-Israeli war affect the United States?

IDENTIFYING PEOPLE AND IDEAS

Explain the historical significance of each of the following people or terms.

1. silent majority
2. Clean Air Act
3. Salvador Allende
4. Saturday Night Massacre
5. Barbara Jordan
6. apartheid
7. Anwar Sadat
8. Rehabilitation Act
9. Russell Means
10. *Roe v. Wade*

UNDERSTANDING MAIN IDEAS

1. How did Nixon's domestic and foreign policies differ from those of his predecessors?
2. What was the origin of the Watergate scandal? What long-term effects did this scandal have on the United States?
3. What domestic and foreign problems did Ford face during his administration?
4. How did Carter attempt to keep his pledge of an "open administration"? Why did he fail to win reelection in 1980?
5. How did the expansion of the civil rights movement during the 1970s affect ethnic groups, women, and people with disabilities? What caused white backlash during this period?

REVIEWING THEMES

1. **Economic Development** How did U.S. dependence on foreign oil affect the economy?
2. **Global Relations** What effect did Nixon's visit to China have on U.S.–Soviet relations?
3. **Constitutional Heritage** Why did Nixon refuse to turn over his White House tapes to the Justice Department? How did his refusal challenge the basis of constitutional government?

THINKING CRITICALLY

1. **Analyzing** What steps did the government take during the 1970s to clean up the environment?
2. **Synthesizing** What domestic and foreign policy actions by Nixon interfered with democratic rights?
3. **Evaluating** Do you think a government is justified in basing a policy of foreign affairs on the principle of human rights? Explain your answer.

WRITING ABOUT HISTORY

Writing to Create Imagine you are a member of the environmental movement. Design a poster for the first Earth Day celebration that illustrates your concerns about the environment.

STRATEGY FOR SUCCESS

Review the Strategies for Success on Conducting an Interview on page 550. Imagine you are a reporter covering the Camp David Accords during 1978. Prepare a list of three questions to use in conducting an interview with either Anwar Sadat or Menachem Begin.

Sadat, Carter, and Begin signing the Camp David Accords, 1978

REVIEWING THEMES

1. Cost of oil fueled inflation and drove up prices of gasoline, heating oil, and electricity; embargo sparked energy crisis, led to concerns over environment, and increased government funding for alternative energy sources.
2. gave Nixon leverage to negotiate SALT treaty, enter into détente
3. because of belief in "executive privilege" and claim that their release would endanger national security; set presidency above law and balance of powers

THINKING CRITICALLY

1. created EPA to enforce environmental laws and OSHA to protect health of workers, passed Clean Air Act and Water Quality Improvement Act, increased support for alternative energy sources
2. domestic—"dirty tricks" campaign, Watergate break-in, refusal to release White House tapes, Saturday Night Massacre; foreign—overthrow of Allende government in Chile
3. Students should balance benefits of basing a foreign policy on moral issues with concerns that such a policy would provoke resentment in other countries and increase world tensions.

WRITING ABOUT HISTORY

Posters will vary but should express concerns over the environmental issue selected.

STRATEGY FOR SUCCESS

Students' lists will vary but might include questions similar to the following: What were your reasons for beginning negotiations? How does this treaty help your country? How do you think this treaty will be accepted by the people in your country?

USING PRIMARY SOURCES

that implementation of court-ordered busing is difficult and can lead to bizarre transportation problems

LINKING HISTORY AND GEOGRAPHY

Nevada and Arizona; South and West

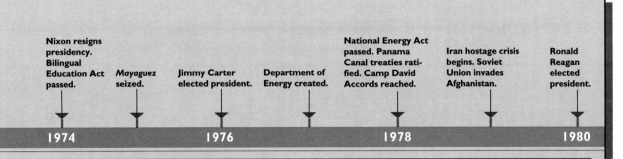

Nixon resigns presidency. Bilingual Education Act passed. | Mayaguez seized. | Jimmy Carter elected president. | Department of Energy created. | National Energy Act passed. Panama Canal treaties ratified. Camp David Accords reached. | Iran hostage crisis begins. Soviet Union invades Afghanistan. | Ronald Reagan elected president.

1974 — 1976 — 1978 — 1980

USING PRIMARY SOURCES

During the 1970s, court-ordered busing was seen as one way of overcoming racial segregation. Read the following excerpt from an account about the effect of busing on West Charlotte High School in Virginia. What is the message of this piece?

> 66 *The district judge . . . made it clear that he wanted socioeconomic integration as well as racial integration. . . .*
>
> *We are presently operating under [a court] order which forbids any change in assignment of a lottery-chosen white student assigned to West Charlotte High even if his family moves away from the area in which he was chosen. This has resulted in some bizarre transportation problems. In one case, we had to assign a driver and bus to pick up one pupil whose family built a new home and moved to the far northerly end of the county, more than 25 miles from West Charlotte High School.* 99

Young antibusing protester

LINKING HISTORY AND GEOGRAPHY

Study the map in the next column, which shows population changes in the United States from 1970 to 1980. Which states had the greatest population growth? Which regions were most affected by population growth?

Percentage Increase in Population
- More than 50.0%
- 25.0%–50.0%
- 15.0%–24.9%
- 5.0%–14.9%
- Less than 5.0%
- Loss

BUILDING YOUR PORTFOLIO

Complete the following projects independently or cooperatively.

1. **POLITICS** Imagine you are a *Washington Post* reporter covering the Senate investigations into the Watergate affair. Write a short article outlining the constitutional issues involved in the Watergate break-in, cover-up, and news coverage.

2. **THE ECONOMY** Imagine you are an economist in the 1970s. Create a flow chart that shows how increases in oil prices overseas ultimately affect the cost of consumer goods in the United States.

3. **GLOBAL RELATIONS** Imagine you are a United Nations delegate from an emerging nation. Conduct an interview with the secretary-general on the role the United Nations should play in establishing a world balance of power amid Cold War conflicts.

BUILDING YOUR PORTFOLIO

Have students refer to **Building Your Portfolio Worksheet 5**, assigned at the beginning of Unit 5. Use the worksheet to help students monitor their progress on the portfolio projects.

A MULTICULTURAL COUNTRY

HISTORICAL SIDELIGHTS

Segregation

In some U.S. cities ethnic and cultural diversity has managed to carry over into individual neighborhoods. But despite advances in civil rights and the diversity of ethnic representation in America, areas in the United States remain racially segregated. A 1992 study of black and white residential patterns found the least segregated cities in the nation to be Jacksonville, NC; Lawton, OK; and Anchorage, AK.

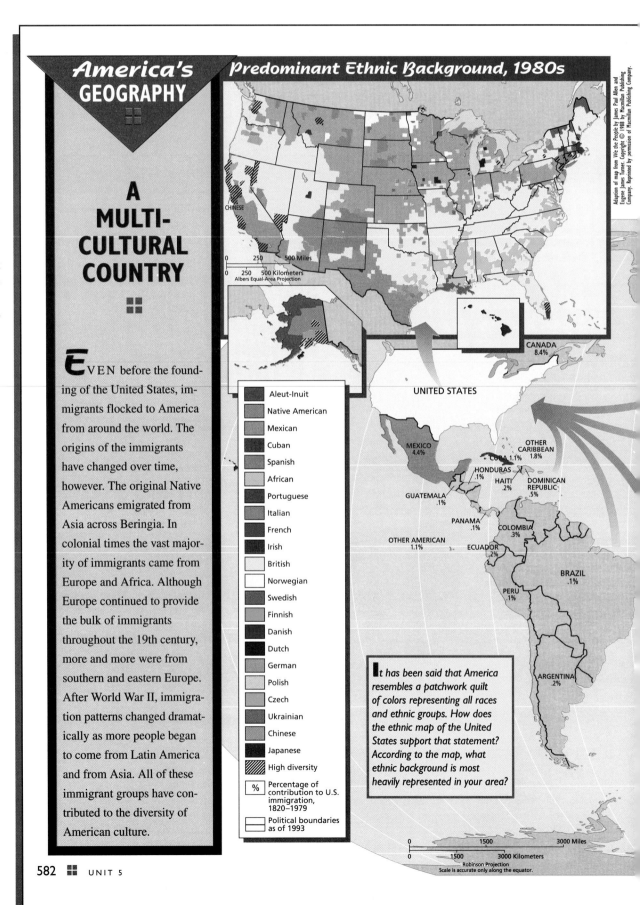

America's GEOGRAPHY

A MULTI-CULTURAL COUNTRY

Predominant Ethnic Background, 1980s

Adaptation of map from *We the People* by James Paul Allen and Eugene James Turner. Copyright © 1988 by Macmillan Publishing Company. Reprinted by permission of Macmillan Publishing Company.

EVEN before the founding of the United States, immigrants flocked to America from around the world. The origins of the immigrants have changed over time, however. The original Native Americans emigrated from Asia across Beringia. In colonial times the vast majority of immigrants came from Europe and Africa. Although Europe continued to provide the bulk of immigrants throughout the 19th century, more and more were from southern and eastern Europe. After World War II, immigration patterns changed dramatically as more people began to come from Latin America and from Asia. All of these immigrant groups have contributed to the diversity of American culture.

Legend:
- Aleut-Inuit
- Native American
- Mexican
- Cuban
- Spanish
- African
- Portuguese
- Italian
- French
- Irish
- British
- Norwegian
- Swedish
- Finnish
- Danish
- Dutch
- German
- Polish
- Czech
- Ukrainian
- Chinese
- Japanese
- High diversity
- % Percentage of contribution to U.S. immigration, 1820–1979
- Political boundaries as of 1993

CHINESE

0   250   500 Miles
0   250   500 Kilometers
Albers Equal-Area Projection

CANADA 8.4%

UNITED STATES

MEXICO 4.4%
CUBA 1.1%
OTHER CARIBBEAN 1.8%
HONDURAS .1%
HAITI .2%
DOMINICAN REPUBLIC .5%
GUATEMALA .1%
PANAMA .1%
COLOMBIA .3%
OTHER AMERICAN 1.1%
ECUADOR .2%
BRAZIL .1%
PERU .1%
ARGENTINA .2%

It has been said that America resembles a patchwork quilt of colors representing all races and ethnic groups. How does the ethnic map of the United States support that statement? According to the map, what ethnic background is most heavily represented in your area?

0   1500   3000 Miles
0   1500   3000 Kilometers
Robinson Projection
Scale is accurate only along the equator.

Contributions to U.S. Immigration

Every day new residents arrive in the United States from throughout the world. In recent years many very small countries, such as Jamaica and El Salvador, have been huge contributors to U.S. immigration. Between 1981 and 1990, some 213,800 Jamaicans immigrated to the U.S.—close to 10 percent of Jamaica's total population in 1982!

TOP TEN CONTRIBUTORS TO U.S. IMMIGRATION, 1981–1990

Country	Percentage of U.S. Immigration
Mexico	23%
Philippines	7%
Vietnam	5%
China	5%
Korea	5%
India	4%
Dominican Republic	3%
El Salvador	3%
Jamaica	3%
Cuba	2%

Chart information from *The World Almanac and Book of Facts 1993* by Mark S. Hoffman. Copyright © 1992 by Pharos Books.

AFRICAN SLAVE ARRIVALS TO THE UNITED STATES, 1701–1810

1701–1720	19,800
1721–1740	50,400
1741–1760	100,400
1761–1780	85,800
1781–1810	91,600

Chart information from *The Atlantic Slave Trade* by Phillip D. Curtin. Copyright © 1969 by The University of Wisconsin Press.

The U.S. Census Bureau did not begin to keep track of immigrant origins until 1820. Since this was after the closing of the African slave trade, census figures on foreign arrivals do not account for the large numbers of Africans who arrived before 1820. The first U.S. census, conducted in 1790, counted African Americans as representing roughly 20 percent of the population.

In recent years immigration to the United States has become much more diverse. Whereas Europe contributed 90 percent of immigrants in the 1880s, it only contributed 10 percent in the 1980s. Three countries—Germany, Scandinavia, and Great Britain alone accounted for 56 percent of immigrants in the 1880s, as much as the top nine countries combined in the 1980s!

CONTRIBUTIONS TO U.S. IMMIGRATION

1821–1830
- Asia <1%
- S. America <1%
- N. America 8%
- Africa <1%
- Other or unknown 23%
- Europe 69%

1881–1890
- Asia 1%
- Other or unknown <1%
- N. America 8%
- Africa <1%
- S. America <1%
- Europe 90%

1931–1940
- Asia 3%
- S. America 3%
- Africa <1%
- Other or unknown <1%
- N. America 28%
- Europe 66%

1981–1990
- Europe 10%
- Other or unknown <1%
- Africa 3%
- S. America 6%
- N. America 42%
- Asia 38%

Due to rounding, percentages do not total 100%.
Chart information from *Statistical Abstract of the United States 1992 and Historical Abstract, 1975.*

Map labels
- OTHER EUROPE .6%
- NORWAY 1.7%
- SWEDEN 2.6%
- FINLAND .1%
- DENMARK .7%
- GREAT BRITAIN .7%
- IRELAND 10.1%
- HOLLAND .7%
- POLAND 1.1%
- BELGIUM .4%
- GERMANY 14.2%
- FRANCE 1.5%
- SWITZERLAND .7%
- FORMER YUGOSLAVIA .2%
- AUSTRIA AND HUNGARY 8.8%
- (UKRAINE)
- RUSSIA AND THE FORMER STATES OF THE SOVIET UNION 6.9%
- SPAIN .5%
- PORTUGAL .9%
- ITALY 10.8%
- GREECE 1.3%
- TURKEY .8%
- LEBANON .1%
- ISRAEL .1%
- JORDAN .1%
- IRAN .1%
- AFRICA .3%
- INDIA .4%
- CHINA 1.1%
- HONG KONG .4%
- VIETNAM .3%
- PHILIPPINES .9%
- KOREA .6%
- JAPAN .8%
- OTHER ASIA .5%
- AUSTRALIA & NEW ZEALAND .2%

Israeli writer Ehud Yonay, commenting on America's continuing appeal to immigrants and tourists, wrote in 1977, "One comes to the United States—always, no matter how often—to see the future. It's what life in one's own country will be like five, ten, twenty years from now."

REAGAN, BUSH, AND CLINTON

1980–the Present

THE AMERICAN NATION VIDEODISC PROGRAM
A variety of still images, short videos, and activities are available for you to use as you teach this chapter. See Videodisc Resources in the Core Resources Binder for barcode correlations and suggestions for using the program.

Chapter Overview

In the 1980s America moved to the right with the election of conservative president Ronald Reagan, who supported cutting taxes and social programs in order to boost the economy. Although Reagan initially took a hard line against the Soviet Union, he welcomed the easing of Cold War tensions after Soviet reformer Mikhail Gorbachev came to power. In 1988 Reagan's vice president, George Bush, was elected president. Bush rose in popularity after the U.S. and its allies defeated Iraq in the Persian Gulf War. But lingering economic problems eroded his popularity and helped Democrat Bill Clinton defeat Bush in the 1992 election.

Chapter Planning Guide

CHAPTER 22	CORE RESOURCES	AUDIOVISUAL RESOURCES	PROGRAM RESOURCES
INTRODUCTION pp. 584–585	▪ Social Studies Skills Worksheet 22 ▪ Literature Worksheet 22 ▪ Building Your Portfolio Worksheet 5		
TEACHING THE CHAPTER pp. 586–611 ▪ For expanded coverage of p. 593, see Chapter 23, pp. 642–643; for coverage of p. 607, see Chapter 24, pp. 665–667; for coverage of pp. 597–599, see Chapter 26, p. 715; for coverage of this chapter, see Chapter 25, pp. 686–693.	▪ Graphic Organizer 22 ▪ Geography Worksheet 22 ▪ Outline Maps 1, 2, 8, 9, 12, 15, 16, 17, 19	▪ *The American Nation* Videodisc: U.S. Troops in the Persian Gulf; Vietnam and the Media; Serving the Nation ▪ Linking Geography and History Transparencies and Worksheets 22, 24 ▪ Everyday Life in America Transparency and Worksheet 32	▪ Art in American History Transparencies and Worksheets 47, 48, 49 ▪ *Eyewitnesses and Others*, Volume 2: Readings 74, 75, 78, 79, 80
REVIEW AND ASSESSMENT pp. 612–613	▪ Chapter 22 Daily Quizzes ▪ Reteaching Worksheet 22 ▪ Chapter 22 Tests ▪ Alternative Assessment Forms		▪ Test Generator

Additional Resources

BOOKS FOR TEACHERS

Allen, Charles F. and Jonathan Portis. *The Comeback Kid: The Life and Career of Bill Clinton.* Carol Publishing Group, 1992. Overview of Clinton's career through 1992 election.

Campbell, Colin, et al., eds. *The Bush Presidency.* Chatham House, 1991. A thoughtful collection of early assessments of Bush administration.

Wills, Garry. *Reagan's America.* Viking Penguin, 1988. Biography focusing on how Reagan's political philosophy took shape and influenced America.

BOOKS FOR STUDENTS

Bowe, Frank. *Equal Rights for Americans with Disabilities.* Watts, 1992. Examines struggle of Americans with disabilities to obtain equal rights.

* Bratman, Fred. *War in the Persian Gulf.* Millbrook Press, 1991. Chronicles the Persian Gulf War.

* Bentley, P. F. *Clinton: Portrait of Victory.* Warner Books, 1993. Pictorial history of 1992 presidential election.

* for students reading below grade level

MULTIMEDIA MATERIALS

A Line in the Sand. Video, 50 min. ABC News/SSSS. Presents the background of the Iraqi invasion of Kuwait and looks at the role of oil in Middle East politics.

History of the 80s. 10 videos, 60 min. each. ABC News/SSSS. Each video documents a different year in the decade, focusing on both foreign and domestic issues.

Reagan's Shield. Video, 60 min. Annenberg/CPB Collection. Looks at Star Wars research and world politics in the Reagan era.

THEMES IN AMERICAN HISTORY

USE WITH PAGES 584–585

*L*isted on the right are the themes emphasized in Chapter 22. The questions in boldface type stimulate critical thinking and provide students with an opportunity to discuss the themes within a broadened context. The questions also appear in the pupil's edition on p. 584.

■ ECONOMIC DEVELOPMENT

What positive and negative effects might measures that cut taxes, social programs, and business regulations have on a nation's economy? Students might suggest that cuts in social programs could reduce government spending and that cuts in taxes and business regulations could stimulate the economy and provide more jobs. They might also note, however, that tax cuts might result in deficit spending. Regulatory cuts could allow business corruption, and social program cuts might lead to increases in crime, poverty, and other social problems.

■ DEMOCRATIC VALUES

How might the use of modern technology increase democratic participation in an election? Students might point out that radio, television, and computer-generated mass mailings could help inform voters about political issues. Communications technology, such as telephones, faxes, and voice mail, could allow voters greater contact with candidates.

CHAPTER STRATEGIES FOR MEETING INDIVIDUAL NEEDS

LIMITED ENGLISH PROFICIENT LEARNERS

Organize students into four groups. Have each group compile a list of the achievements and the failures of the Reagan, Bush, and Clinton presidencies. Have students share their lists.

TACTILE/KINESTHETIC LEARNERS

Organize students into groups to prepare a military briefing for the press—including maps—to show U.S. military operations in Operation Desert Storm.

LEARNERS HAVING DIFFICULTY

Organize students into groups to create posters, campaign slogans, or bumper stickers for the presidential campaigns discussed in this chapter.

AUDITORY LEARNERS

Have students poll classmates, friends, and family members on the 10 most pressing problems of the 1990s. Have students compare answers and identify differences in responses based on age, gender, and race.

VISUAL LEARNERS

Have students create a design for an exhibit for the presidential library of Reagan, Bush, or Clinton. Exhibits should highlight events that took place during the administration chosen.

GIFTED LEARNERS

Have students write an essay comparing economic policies and attitudes toward business in the 1980s with such attitudes and policies in the late 1800s or in the 1920s.

USING THE CHAPTER FOCUS

■ **UNDERSTANDING THE MAIN IDEA**

Call on a volunteer to read aloud the Understanding the Main Idea paragraph. Then ask students why they think the economy is such an important issue for voters.

 THEMES Have students work individually or in small groups to answer the questions under Themes. Save students' responses so that they can compare them with their responses after studying the chapter. (See p. 583B for suggested answers.)

■ **THE TIME LINE**

Have students list in their notebooks the names of the three presidents noted on the time line. Ask them to chart the domestic and foreign policies of each president as they read the chapter. At the close of the chapter, have students write summary statements on each president and how his policies affected Americans.

CORE RESOURCES

• **Graphic Organizer 22**
• **Social Studies Skills Worksheet 22**
• **Literature Worksheet 22**
• **Outline Maps 1, 2, 8, 9, 12, 15, 17**
• **Building Your Portfolio Worksheet 5**

584

ABOUT THE ILLUSTRATION

During the first day of the 100-hour ground campaign in the Persian Gulf War, the 101st Airborne Division launched the largest helicopter assault in history. The 101st was comprised of some 17,000 soldiers, of whom about 900 were women. The photograph shows U.S. soldiers dropped into combat positions from Black Hawk helicopters.

Have students speculate about the challenges of fighting a war on desert terrain. Suggest that they consider such factors as the effects of heat and sand on equipment and armaments, and problems of road building, camouflage, and visibility of supply lines.

Chapter 22

1980–the Present

REAGAN, BUSH, AND CLINTON

FOCUS

UNDERSTANDING THE MAIN IDEA

President Ronald Reagan entered office in 1981 with a series of conservative reforms for the economy and foreign relations. His vice president, George Bush, won the presidency in 1988. Plagued by economic problems that his administration could not address to the satisfaction of voters, Bush lost to Democrat Bill Clinton in the 1992 election. Clinton met with greater success on domestic issues but struggled to define America's place in a new world order.

THEMES

■ **ECONOMIC DEVELOPMENT** What positive and negative effects might measures that cut taxes, social programs, and business regulations have on a nation's economy?

■ **DEMOCRATIC VALUES** How might the use of modern technology increase democratic participation in an election?

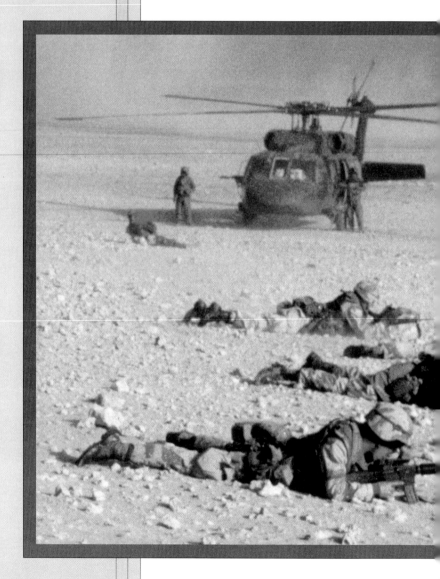

1981	1984	1986	1988	1990	1992
▼	▼	▼	▼	▼	▼
Sandra Day O'Connor appointed to Supreme Court.	Ronald Reagan reelected president.	Tax Reform Law passed.	George Bush elected president.	Iraq invades Kuwait.	Bill Clinton elected president.

Have students recall how the Iran hostage crisis and economic problems affected President Carter's bid for reelection. Tell students this chapter discusses the Reagan, Bush, and Clinton presidencies and the domestic and foreign-policy challenges that each administration faced.

LINK TO THE PAST

Public frustration with government grew in the 1970s as the Watergate scandal broke, the energy crisis emerged, and the economy continued to weaken. As a result, Democrat Jimmy Carter, who promised to reform government, was elected president. The Iran hostage crisis and runaway inflation, however, undermined his presidency, contributing to a Republican victory in the 1980 election.

HISTORICAL SIDELIGHTS
Late Bloomer
Ronald Reagan had not always been a conservative or a Republican. He voted four times for FDR for president and later said that he had been "a near-hopeless hemophilic liberal" during the New Deal era. He began to embrace conservative causes in the 1940s.

Entering the White House on a wave of discontent rising since the Vietnam War, Ronald Reagan promised to set the nation on a new course with his conservative political agenda of lower taxes, fewer federal regulations, cuts in social programs, and increased military spending. Reagan was an ideal president for the television age. Often called "the Great Communicator," he projected a sense of strength and patriotism that reassured Americans troubled by the nation's mounting economic problems and weakened image on the world stage. Television observer John Corry noted of Reagan: "His voice is his greatest weapon. It is not an orator's voice. It is husky, and sometimes it fades to a whisper. Meanwhile, it is extraordinarily intimate. Mr. Reagan does not speak to audiences; he speaks to individuals."

Reagan's vice president, George Bush, was elected president in 1988. Bush's greatest achievements were on the international front. Under his administration, the United States launched a successful invasion of Panama and played a primary role in crushing the Iraqi takeover of Kuwait. Bush's domestic record was less impressive, however. By the time the president ran for reelection in 1992, the country was beset by an ailing economy and other domestic problems. In a campaign that saw the rise of independent candidate H. Ross Perot and an increased role for women, Bush lost to baby-boom Democrat Bill Clinton.

Operation Desert Storm, 1991

Campaign button for presidential candidate H. Ross Perot, 1992

PREVIEW WORKSHOP

Following is a list of the significant people, places, and terms in this section. You may wish to use this list as a section preview.

People
- José Napoleón Duarte
- Geraldine Ferraro
- Sandra Day O'Connor

Places
- Nicaragua
- El Salvador
- Grenada

Terms
- New Right
- Moral Majority
- Reaganomics
- Strategic Defense Initiative
- Solidarity
- Sandinistas
- contras
- Gramm-Rudman-Hollings Act
- Tax Reform Law
- insider trading
- *glasnost*
- *perestroika*
- Intermediate-Range Nuclear Forces Treaty
- Iran-contra affair

FOCUS OBJECTIVES

- Explain Reaganomics and describe how it affected the country.

- Analyze why the Reagan administration considered events in Nicaragua and El Salvador to be important.

- Identify the economic problems that plagued the country during the late 1980s.

- Describe the Iran-contra affair.

Section 1

THE REAGAN MOVEMENT

FOCUS

- **What was Reaganomics? How did it affect the country?**
- **Why did the Reagan administration consider events in Nicaragua and El Salvador important?**
- **What economic problems plagued the country during the late 1980s?**
- **What was the Iran-contra affair?**

*R*onald Reagan's 1980 presidential victory reflected the growing conservative mood of the nation. Adopting Reagan's conservative programs, Congress cut taxes and reduced federal regulation of the economy. As a result, the economy boomed in the mid-1980s. By the end of the decade, however, numerous political scandals and a soaring federal deficit troubled the nation.

President Ronald Reagan and First Lady, Nancy

THE NEW RIGHT

A former liberal Democrat turned conservative Republican, Ronald Reagan appealed to a wide range of voters who were disenchanted with liberal politics. Many moderate and conservative Democrats threw their support behind Reagan, proudly proclaiming themselves Reagan Democrats. Some of Reagan's strongest support, however, came from the political conservatives of the **New Right**. At the forefront of the New Right was Reverend Jerry Falwell's **Moral Majority**—a fundamentalist Christian organization founded in 1978.

Ronald Reagan and the New Right shared the same political goals. Both supported school prayer, a strong defense, and free-market economic policies. Both opposed abortion, the Equal Rights Amendment, gun control, and busing to end racial segregation in schools. To gain support for their causes, the New Right established research centers such as the Heritage Foundation and launched direct mail campaigns.

In addition to helping elect Ronald Reagan president, New Right conservatives were largely responsible for the Republicans gaining control of the Senate in 1980. They also played a significant role in shaping Republican policy throughout the decade. Although Jerry Falwell disbanded the Moral Majority in the late 1980s, New Right conservatives have continued to exert a strong influence in the Republican party.

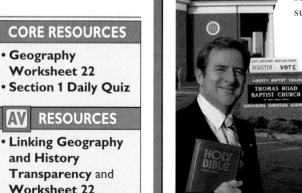

◄ The Reverend Jerry Falwell's Moral Majority encouraged churchgoers to register to vote and support conservative causes.

REAGANOMICS IN ACTION

Ronald Reagan entered office with a comprehensive economic program already mapped out. The program, dubbed **Reaganomics**, was based on the supply-side economics argument that lowering the top income tax rates would spur economic growth. Supporters of Reaganomics claimed that people would use their tax savings to invest in businesses, thereby creating jobs, increasing consumer spending, and generating higher tax revenues. Congress responded by passing a three-year plan to cut federal income taxes by 25 percent.

Congress also supported another part of Reagan's economic plan—drastic cuts in government regulation of industries such as television, trucking, airline, and banking. The Reagan administration's probusiness, antiregulation stance was typified by the Department of the Interior's handling of public lands. Over the angry objections of environmentalists, Secretary of the Interior James Watt leased huge areas of the seafloor to private companies searching for oil and gas. He also leased federal lands to coal companies. In Watt's words, the country should "mine more, drill more, cut more timber."

To Congress's and the public's pleasure, Reaganomics seemed to work. By 1983 the inflation rate had dropped to a manageable 4 percent. With inflation halted, Americans went on a shopping spree similar to those in the 1920s and 1950s. Business revived, the stock market soared, and the future looked bright.

Critics were quick to point out that not all Americans benefited equally from the recovery. Deep cuts in social programs—an important element in Reaganomics—hurt the poor. And although employment rose overall, joblessness remained high among African Americans and Hispanic Americans, especially unskilled workers in the inner cities. Unemployment among factory workers in the Midwest, once America's industrial heartland, also remained high. Homelessness increased dramatically. Critics charged that Reagan's tax cuts favored the wealthy and that spending cuts and deregulation weakened programs that assisted those in need and protected consumers and the environment. They also warned that big tax cuts combined with increased military spending (another important element of Reaganomics) would produce enormous deficits in the federal budget.

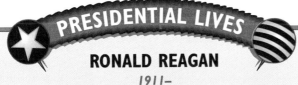

PRESIDENTIAL LIVES

RONALD REAGAN
1911–

in office 1981–1989

Unlike most presidential hopefuls, Ronald Reagan did not begin his political career early in life. Reagan was elected governor of California at age 55, the only office he held until being elected president at age 69. As president, Reagan always projected a young, confident image. One of his particular gifts was a sharp wit. After his first debate with Jimmy Carter in the 1980 election, a reporter asked if he had been nervous appearing on stage with the president. "No, not at all," he replied, then referred to his past career as an actor: "I've been on the same stage with John Wayne."

Reagan's wit helped reassure the nation after a lone gunman shot him on March 30, 1981. As the wounded president was wheeled into the operating room, he looked around at the surgeons and quipped, "Please assure me that you are all Republicans!" While he was recuperating in intensive care, Reagan sent several humorous notes to his staff members, including one that read, "If I had had this much attention in Hollywood, I'd have stayed there!"

*T*eaching the *S*ection

REAGANOMICS

Organize students into six groups. Assign half the groups the role of Reagan supporters and the remaining groups the role of Reagan critics. Have all groups prepare a cost/benefit analysis of Reaganomics. Next to each cost and each benefit have groups indicate who might have been hurt and who might have benefited by these changes.

Then convene a panel of representatives from all the groups to conduct a "Crossfire" roundtable debate on Reaganomics. Have the remainder of the class act as the audience, challenging and asking questions about the positions of panel members.

► Homelessness increased during the 1980s. This homeless shelter is located in Washington, D.C.

▪▪ Reaganomics stimulated the economy by cutting taxes and regulations on industries, but critics claimed the policies hurt the poorest Americans and increased the federal deficit.

*R*EAGAN AND THE COLD WAR

The Reagan administration's emphasis on increased military spending was in part a reflection of Ronald Reagan's strong anti-Communist views. Like British prime minister Margaret Thatcher, he took a hard line against the Soviet Union, even branding it an "evil empire." To counter the Soviet threat, Reagan called for new weapons systems and an increased U.S. presence in such areas as the Indian Ocean and the Persian Gulf.

New weapons. From 1981 to 1985 the Pentagon's budget grew from some $150 billion to about $250 billion. Critics charged that much money was wasted as military contractors padded their bills and officials

► Shown here is an antinuclear protester demonstrating in Copley Square, Boston, 1979.

invested too much in costly weapons that often failed to perform as promised. The MX, a new nuclear missile system, was one program that drew heavy criticism. Reagan's first secretary of state, Alexander Haig, heightened opposition when he suggested that "nuclear warning shots" might be useful in a conventional war.

The talk of nuclear war stirred public fear. In town meetings and state referendums, voters urged a superpower freeze on the testing and deployment of nuclear weapons. Many Americans marched in rallies to show their support for the freeze proposal.

To blunt the nuclear-freeze movement, Reagan proposed the **Strategic Defense Initiative** (SDI), a space-based missile-defense system. SDI stirred controversy. Critics labeled it "Star Wars," after the popular 1977 movie, saying it rested on untested technology and was probably unworkable. They warned that SDI research would intensify the arms race. Reagan countered that SDI would be a weapon for peace—one that killed weapons, not people. He proclaimed in a national address:

❝ I call upon the scientific community in our country, those who gave us nuclear weapons, to turn their great talents now to the cause of mankind and world peace: to give us the means of rendering these nuclear weapons impotent and obsolete. ❞

U.S.–Soviet relations. Even before Reagan took office, U.S.–Soviet relations had cooled because of the Soviet Union's 1979 invasion of Afghanistan (see map on page 561). Relations deteriorated further when, in August 1980, Polish workers in Gdańsk and Szczecin (SHCHET-seen) staged a series of massive strikes to protest high prices and to demand the right to form trade unions free from government or Communist party control. At first, things went well for the strikers. In late August, faced with the threat of a nationwide general strike, the Polish government legalized independent union activity. Labor

REAGAN AND THE COLD WAR

Pair students and ask them to write several sentences explaining how each of these events affected U.S.–Soviet relations: Soviets refuse to withdraw troops from Afghanistan; Reagan calls for SDI; Soviet-backed Polish government closes down Solidarity; Korean airliner is shot down over Soviet air space; U.S. sends nuclear weapons to England and Germany; Soviets boycott 1984 Olympics. Then have each pair choose one event and create two editorial cartoons that show how the event might have been viewed by the Reagan administration and by Soviet leaders. Have volunteer pairs interpret their cartoons for the class.

▲ Many Americans, particularly those of Polish descent, supported the Solidarity movement. These Boston residents marched to show their support.

activists responded by voting on September 17 to form the independent trade union **Solidarity** under the leadership of Lech Walesa (vah-LEN-suh), an electrician at a Gdańsk shipyard who had helped launch the initial series of stikes.

Then in December 1981 the Soviet-backed government changed its stand and instituted martial law. Government troops shut down Solidarity centers and arrested union leaders. Expecting resistance, Soviet troops prepared to "restore order" as they had in Hungary in 1956 and in Czechoslovakia in 1968. Warning the Soviet Union not to invade Poland, Reagan called for new trade restrictions against the Soviets by the United States and its allies. The Soviet Union heeded the warning and stayed out of Poland.

Tensions flared again in 1983. On September 30, the Soviets shot down a Korean airliner over Soviet airspace, killing all 269 passengers, including many Americans. Despite international outcries, the Soviets refused to apologize for the incident, claiming the plane had been spying. Later that year, when the United States sent new

▶ The surrender of the Nicaraguan National Guard to the Sandinistas in July 1979 marked the end of the Somoza regime. Citizens celebrated the rebel victory by dragging a statue of Somoza through the streets of downtown Managua.

nuclear missiles to England and Germany, the Soviets walked out of arms-control talks. When the Soviets boycotted the 1984 Summer Olympics in Los Angeles, relations between the two superpowers sank to their lowest point since the early 1970s.

REAGAN AND LATIN AMERICA

Fearing that the developing nations of Latin America would fall under the influence of the Soviet Union, Reagan pledged to increase U.S. involvement in the region. Of particular interest were the Central American countries of Nicaragua and El Salvador.

In 1979, Nicaraguan rebels known as **Sandinistas** had overthrown the dictatorship of Anastasio Somoza Debayle, whose family had ruled Nicaragua since the 1930s. Soon after Reagan took office, he cut all U.S. aid to Nicaragua on the grounds that the Sandinistas were backed by the Soviet bloc. The Sandinistas, he charged, were exporting revolution by shipping Cuban and Soviet weapons to rebels in El Salvador. When Nicaragua reacted to U.S. pressure by strengthening its ties to the Soviet bloc, Reagan decided that the Sandinista government must go. The assignment of overthrowing the Sandinistas went to the **contras**, a large army recruited, financed, and armed by the CIA. President Reagan called the contras "freedom fighters" and compared them to the founders of the United States.

Many Americans objected to the CIA-sponsored war against the Sandinistas. They foresaw another Vietnam in Central America. Reflecting such fears, Congress began cutting funds for the contras late in 1984. But as the nation would soon learn, the White House continued to finance

Teaching the Section

REAGAN AND LATIN AMERICA

Tell students to imagine that the Senate Foreign Relations Committee will recommend whether to appropriate funds to support the president's policies in Central America. Assign a group to role-play the committee and other groups to represent the Reagan administration, U.S. opposition groups, the governments of Nicaragua and El Salvador, and the insurgents in each nation. Each group should prepare a statement on the situation in one or both countries from its perspective, explaining why events there are or are not important to the U.S. Then have a member of each group testify, the "committee" make a recommendation, and the class vote on funding Reagan's Central American policies. Call on students to explain their votes.

PRIMARY SOURCE
Description of Change: excerpted
Rationale: excerpted to focus on main idea

HISTORICAL SIDELIGHTS
Repression of Rights
A top priority of Reagan's foreign policy, especially in his first term, was to stop expansion of Soviet power outside its Eastern European sphere of influence. This goal led administration officials to overlook human rights abuses committed by anti-Communist dictators, while acting aggressively against equally harsh leftist governments. A *New York Times* reporter who covered Nicaragua suggested that "Nicaraguans today suffer less state repression of fundamental freedoms under their leftist government than do the people of countries . . . like Guatemala and El Salvador whose right-wing governments do not draw the same . . . critical comments from Washington."

Map Caption Answer
Grenada, Panama, Honduras

AV TRANSPARENCY
Linking Geography and History Transparency
and **Worksheet 22**

▲ **José Napoleón Duarte is shown in 1984 speaking to a crowd during his election campaign in El Salvador.**

the contras despite the congressional ban, using funds secretly contributed by wealthy conservatives and foreign governments.

The Reagan administration also involved itself in events in El Salvador. In 1979 a group of young military officers seized power in the country. Though they promised reform, their government proved brutally repressive. The army and special death squads killed and tortured opposition leaders. Soon fighting erupted between government forces and rebels demanding radical reform.

In 1984 José Napoleón Duarte, a moderate, won election by promising to institute reforms and end the civil war. Eager to prevent a rebel victory that might allow El Salvador to fall under Soviet influence, the Reagan administration offered Duarte military and economic aid and sent advisers to train government troops. Duarte met with the rebels as promised, but as he later noted, he never expected success:

66 My government was not out to gain anything, nor would we give anything up. There was little hope for agreement on what each side visualized as the political future of El Salvador. . . . The important thing was to try talking. 99

The civil war raged on until intense international pressure forced both sides to sign a peace treaty in 1992.

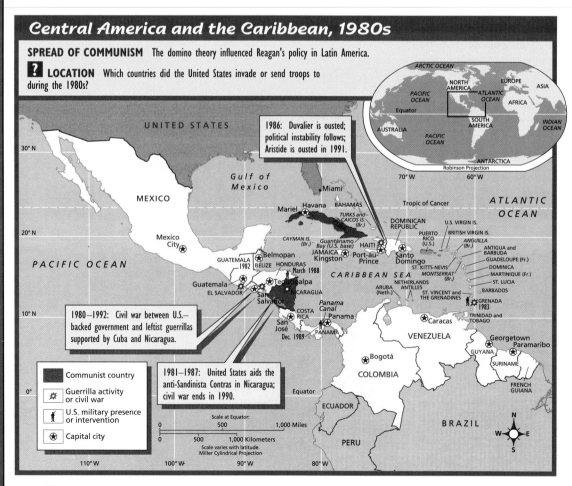

Central America and the Caribbean, 1980s

SPREAD OF COMMUNISM The domino theory influenced Reagan's policy in Latin America.

? LOCATION Which countries did the United States invade or send troops to during the 1980s?

1986: Duvalier is ousted; political instability follows; Aristide is ousted in 1991.

1980–1992: Civil war between U.S.-backed government and leftist guerrillas supported by Cuba and Nicaragua.

1981–1987: United States aids the anti-Sandinista Contras in Nicaragua; civil war ends in 1990.

Communist country
Guerrilla activity or civil war
U.S. military presence or intervention
Capital city

ECONOMIC PROBLEMS

Work with the class to develop a list on the chalkboard of the economic problems facing the U.S. in the late 1980s. *(huge budget deficits, insider trading, stock market crash, failure of S&Ls and banks)* Have volunteers explain why each was a serious economic problem. Then ask students to assess whether or not Reaganomics contributed to these problems and to explain why or why not.

▶

■■ **Latin America, especially Nicaragua and El Salvador, became a crucial interest in the struggle between the United States and the Soviet Union.**

*R*EAGAN TRIUMPHS

Despite criticisms of his policies, Reagan's personal popularity remained high. His emphasis on patriotism and national pride struck a responsive chord with many Americans. While Carter was haunted by his errors, the public seemed quick to forgive and forget any mishaps or scandals in Reagan's administration. Congresswoman Patricia Schroeder once said of the president, "He's just like a Teflon frying pan: Nothing sticks to him."

Among the events that added to Reagan's popularity was a small-scale military action in 1983. On the tiny Caribbean island of Grenada, a military group overthrew the government and killed the prime minister. Several Caribbean nations requested U.S. intervention. On October 25, 1983, some 2,000 U.S. Marines and Army Rangers went ashore on Grenada, overthrew the coup leaders, and set up a government favorable to the United States. The U.S. action in Grenada provided some evidence for Reagan's claim that after the defeat in Vietnam, America was again "standing tall" in the world.

Soon after the Grenada invasion, Reagan announced that he would seek a second term in 1984, with George Bush again as his running mate. Former vice president Walter Mondale won the Democratic nomination. Mondale picked Congresswoman Geraldine Ferraro of New York as his running mate. Ferraro thus became the first woman to run on a major party presidential ticket. Some predicted Ferraro's presence would increase support for the Democratic party among women.

Republicans had been taking steps to increase the presence of women in their own ranks. Reagan appointed several women to high public offices, including Elizabeth Dole as secretary of transportation, Margaret Heckler as secretary of health and human services, and Jeane Kirkpatrick as head of the U.S. delegation to the United Nations—the first woman to hold the post. In 1981 Reagan had also appointed the first woman ever to serve on the Supreme Court—conservative justice Sandra Day O'Connor. Republicans also made a special effort to win the support of women who felt abandoned by the feminist movement. The percentage of female delegates to the Republican convention increased from 24 percent in 1980 to 44 percent in 1984. In the end, Ferraro's presence did not add many votes for the Democrats. On election day Reagan received 54.5 million popular votes to Mondale's 37.6 million. The Republicans swept the electoral vote, 525 to 13.

*T*ROUBLE SIGNS

One issue that arose during the election was the growing conservative emphasis of the Supreme Court. When Chief Justice Warren Burger retired in 1986, Reagan elevated Associate Justice William Rehnquist to chief justice. To fill Rehnquist's position, Reagan nominated conservative Antonin Scalia. When another justice retired in 1987, Reagan nominated Robert Bork, a federal judge and law professor who held a far narrower interpretation of the Bill of Rights than the Court had upheld in recent years.

Bork believed that much of the vast body of civil rights law was unconstitutional. Such views alarmed many people, including many senators. By a 58–42 vote, the Senate rejected Bork, handing Reagan a crushing loss. His next choice, Douglas Ginsberg, withdrew after press reports that he had smoked marijuana as a law professor. At last Reagan found a conservative judge who could also win Senate confirmation, Anthony Kennedy of California.

HISTORICAL SIDELIGHTS
The Kirkpatrick Doctrine
President Reagan's foreign policy was greatly influenced by former political science professor Jeane Kirkpatrick. In a series of books and articles in the late 1970s and early 1980s Kirkpatrick favored U.S. support of authoritarian, right-wing regimes, which she felt could be reformed. She opposed leftist governments because of their anti-American/pro-Soviet stance. As UN ambassador, Kirkpatrick used her post as a platform for her views.

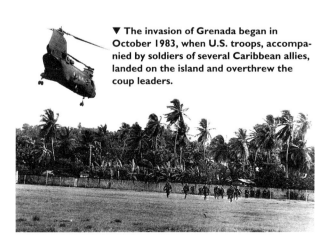

▼ The invasion of Grenada began in October 1983, when U.S. troops, accompanied by soldiers of several Caribbean allies, landed on the island and overthrew the coup leaders.

Teaching the Section

COLD WAR THAW

Call students' attention to the photograph of Reagan and Gorbachev on p. 593. Have them write an imaginary memoir in which one of these men recalls his thoughts as the anti-Communist president embraces the leader of what he once called the "evil empire." Students may wish to include their memoirs in their portfolios.

THE IRAN-CONTRA AFFAIR

Pair students to develop graphic organizers that link the Reagan administration's foreign policies in Iran with its policies in Central America. Select pairs to explain their organizers to the class. Then ask students if they believe these activities were proper. Have students speculate about why the Iran-contra affair of the 1980s did not produce results similar to the Watergate scandal of the 1970s.

Graph Caption Answer
more than 1.5 trillion

HISTORICAL SIDELIGHTS

Tax Reform Law
The 1986 Tax Reform Law removed many low-income Americans from the tax rolls. It eliminated some tax deductions such as those for most interest payments, reduced the amounts taxpayers could deduct for business entertainment, and cut back the benefits that corporations gained from tax credits and depreciation. However, the law also lowered the maximum income tax rate for wealthy Americans from 50 to 28 percent and lowered the tax rate for corporations.

HISTORICAL SIDELIGHTS

S&L Crisis
Deregulation gave the S&L industry greater freedom to invest depositors' funds in high-risk ventures and to make high-risk loans. Without the oversight of government regulators, S&L officials mismanaged or used for their own benefit the savings of thousands of unsuspecting depositors. For example, a group of California S&L officials enjoyed the use of two $17 million jets on which they flew family and friends to condominiums bought with depositors' money.

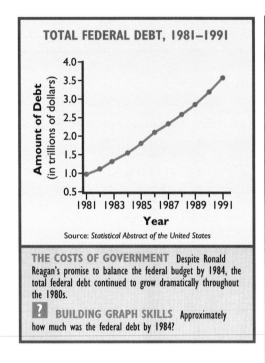

TOTAL FEDERAL DEBT, 1981–1991

Source: *Statistical Abstract of the United States*

THE COSTS OF GOVERNMENT Despite Ronald Reagan's promise to balance the federal budget by 1984, the total federal debt continued to grow dramatically throughout the 1980s.

❓ **BUILDING GRAPH SKILLS** Approximately how much was the federal debt by 1984?

The failure of the Bork nomination was just one of several signs that the "Reagan Revolution" was starting to weaken. Of special concern was the annual federal deficit, which reached over $200 billion in 1985. Seeking to balance the budget with forced spending cuts, Congress passed the Balanced Budget and Emergency Control Act in 1985. Called the **Gramm-Rudman-Hollings Act** after its sponsors, the law required automatic across-the-board cuts in government spending when the deficit exceeded a certain amount. Other legislation took aim at specific problems. The **Tax Reform Law** of 1986, for example, wiped out many rules that gave certain groups special tax breaks.

The stock market also showed signs of trouble. Reagan's tax cuts and business deregulation had stimulated a stock market boom, but with this boom came a wave of illegal **insider trading**—the use of confidential financial information by stockbrokers for personal gain. Several large brokerage firms pleaded guilty to illegal activities and faced severe penalties. These scandals eroded investor trust in stockbrokers.

Then, on October 19, 1987, after several years of growth, the stock market crashed. On paper, stock losses totaled almost $1 trillion. Eastman Kodak saw the value of its stock fall by more than 30 percent. Many other major corporations experienced similar sharp drops in their stocks' values.

Another sign of economic trouble was the crisis that hit the nation's savings and loan (S&L) and banking industries in the late 1980s and early 1990s. Freed of federal regulation, banks and S&Ls, especially in the Southwest, had made risky loans to developers to build office towers, shopping malls, and other projects. In the late 1980s the real-estate market collapsed, and hundreds of S&Ls and banks that had loaned money to developers failed. Since the federal government insures S&L and bank depositors, it had to pay billions of dollars to cover these losses, further straining the federal budget. The federal deficit, the S&L and banking crisis, and other economic problems all remained after Reagan left office.

■■ **By the late 1980s the economy was suffering from a huge federal deficit, the stock market crash, and failures of S&Ls and banks.**

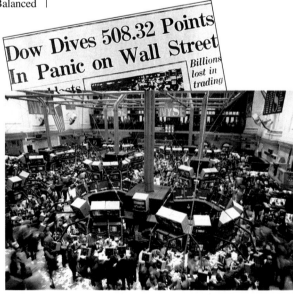

▲ Investors lost billions of dollars during the stock market crash of October 1987. Shown here is the frantic scene on the floor of the New York Stock Exchange on the day of the crash, as traders tried to sell shares and cut losses.

Practice

GUIDED PRACTICE

Assume the role of a radio talk show host. Group students to represent big business owners, Republican and Democratic party workers, homeless people, immigrants from the Soviet Union, African Americans and Hispanic Americans, environmental groups, and industrial workers. Ask these Americans to "call in" to the talk show to give their opinions on the Reagan era.

As students give their opinions, write their responses on the chalkboard.

INDEPENDENT PRACTICE

Have students pick an opinion of a talk show "caller" with whom they agreed or disagreed and write a letter to the radio station, either supporting or challenging the caller's opinion about the Reagan presidency. Students may wish to include their letters in their portfolios.

Review and Assessment

REVIEW Have pairs of students create a "report card" for the Reagan years, giving the president foreign- and domestic-policy grades and including a paragraph about areas that need improvement or that are commendable. Select pairs to summarize their evaluations for the class. Then assign the Section 1 Review on p. 594.

ASSESS Assign the **Section 1 Daily Quiz** in *Core Resources*. ▶

BEFRIENDING "THE EVIL EMPIRE"

President Reagan—and the American people—had much more to cheer about on the international front. The most significant event of Reagan's second term was a dramatic easing of Cold War hostilities. When Mikhail Gorbachev became leader of the Soviet Union in 1985, a new era of Soviet history began. With his nation troubled by a failing economy, a repressive political system, and heavy military costs, Gorbachev introduced a policy of openness, called *glasnost* (GLAZS-nuhst), that promised more freedom for the Soviet people.

Equally dramatic was *perestroika* (per-uh-STROY-kuh)—Gorbachev's plan to restructure the Soviet economy and government. On the economic front he called for increased foreign trade and reduced military spending. The revenues from these changes were to be used to modernize factories. In a startling example of *perestroika*, the Soviet people in 1989 elected representatives to the newly created Congress of People's Deputies, the supreme governing body. It was the first election in Soviet history between competing candidates and the first by secret ballot.

To help achieve his goals at home and focus energy away from Cold War pursuits, Gorbachev pursued détente with the United States. In 1987 after a series of meetings between Gorbachev and President Reagan, the Soviet Union and the United States signed the **Intermediate-range Nuclear Forces** (INF) **Treaty**. This treaty eliminated all medium-range nuclear weapons from Europe and set up inspection procedures to ensure observance of the treaty's terms. Gorbachev also withdrew Soviet troops from Afghanistan. Addressing the United Nations in 1988, Gorbachev said:

> ❝ The use or threat of force no longer can or must be an instrument of foreign policy. . . . All of us, and primarily the stronger of us, must exercise self-restraint and totally rule out any outward-oriented use of force. ❞

In May 1988, as the Senate prepared to ratify the INF Treaty, Reagan boarded a jet for Moscow. In a glare of media attention, the U.S. president and the Soviet leader embraced like old friends.

▲ On June 1, 1988, President Ronald Reagan and Soviet leader Mikhail Gorbachev embraced during a Moscow ceremony celebrating ratification of the INF Treaty.

▪▪ During Reagan's second term U.S.–Soviet relations improved dramatically as Gorbachev instituted *glasnost* and *perestroika*.

THE IRAN-CONTRA AFFAIR

While relations with the Soviet Union were improving, the Reagan administration continued to face frustrating problems in the Middle East and Latin America. These frustrations led to the most serious crisis to hit the Reagan White House—the **Iran-contra affair**.

After Congress cut off funds for the contras' war against Nicaragua's Sandinista government, the Reagan administration sought other sources of funding. At the time, the White House was secretly bargaining with Iran for the release of U.S. hostages held in Lebanon by pro-Iranian groups. As part of the bargain, the administration shipped more than 500 antitank missiles to Iran by way of Israel. Without informing Congress, the administration used the profits from these arms sales to pay for weapons and supplies for the contras.

When the arms sales became public in 1986, Reagan appointed a committee to investigate. The committee cleared Reagan of any direct

GLOBAL CONNECTIONS

After the summit between Reagan and Gorbachev, Gorbachev recalled how he asked Reagan if he still considered the Soviet Union the evil empire: "He [Reagan] said no, and he said that within the walls of the Kremlin . . . in the heart of the evil empire. We take note of that. As the ancient Greeks said, 'Everything flows, everything changes.'"

HISTORICAL SIDELIGHTS

Iran-contra Update
One month before leaving office, President Bush pardoned six former Reagan administration officials who had been charged or convicted in the Iran-contra scandal. The men faced such charges as perjury, obstructing congressional investigations, and withholding information from Congress. In giving the pardons, Bush said that "whether their actions were right or wrong," the six had acted from patriotism.

PRIMARY SOURCE

Description of Change: excerpted
Rationale: excerpted to focus on main idea

PRIMARY SOURCE

(for source on p. 594)

Description of Change: excerpted and bracketed
Rationale: excerpted to focus on main idea; bracketed to clarify meaning

RETEACH Organize students into small groups. Tell each group to divide the section material, by subsections, among its members. Direct students to write questions about the main ideas presented in their assigned material. Have group members quiz one another with the questions.

Closure

Ask students to answer the following questions: *Would you have voted for Ronald Reagan in 1980? Would you have voted for him again in 1984?* Have students give reasons for their opinions.

Extension

COMPARE Have students research and write reports comparing the causes and results of the October 1987 and the 1929 stock market crashes.

INTERPRET Have students read *The Brethren,* which profiles the Supreme Court under Chief Justice Warren Burger, and write a report describing this inside view of the Burger Court's decisions.

SECTION REVIEW ANSWERS

IDENTIFY

For significance, see the following pages:
New Right (p. 586)
Moral Majority (p. 586)
Reaganomics (p. 587)
Strategic Defense Initiative (p. 588)
Solidarity (p. 589)
Sandinistas (p. 589)
contras (p. 589)
José Napoleón Duarte (p. 590)
Geraldine Ferraro (p. 591)
Sandra Day O'Connor (p. 591)
Gramm-Rudman-Hollings Act (p. 592)
Tax Reform Law (p. 592)
insider trading (p. 592)
glasnost (p. 593)
perestroika (p. 593)
INF Treaty (p. 593)
Iran-contra affair (p. 593)

LOCATE

For locations, see the map on p. 590.

1. *reduced inflation and stimulated the economy, but increased federal deficit, hurt the poor, and weakened environmental protection programs*
2. *huge federal deficit, stock market crash, S&L and bank failures*
3. *government repression, civil war; U.S. supporting moderates and democratic reform*
4. *Letters might mention illegal actions by White House aides.*
5. *Dem.—nominated Ferraro; Rep.—more female convention delegates and women appointees*

involvement but heavily criticized other White House officials, some of whom resigned. The secret funding of the contra war soon became known also. It was revealed that Lieutenant Colonel Oliver North, a White House aide, had funneled millions of dollars from the Iranian arms sales to the contras after Congress had forbidden aid.

In 1987, House and Senate committees investigated the affair. North admitted that he and his secretary, Fawn Hall, had destroyed key documents. But North emotionally insisted that he had acted out of loyalty and patriotism. North testified: "I'm not in the habit of questioning my superiors. . . . I don't believe that what we did even under those circumstances is wrong or illegal."

In its report the congressional committee denounced North's activities and criticized the loose White House management style that had allowed North to operate as he did. The chairman of the Senate committee, Senator Daniel Inouye of Hawaii, countered North's claim that he was just following orders. Said Inouye:

❝ [The] colonel was well aware that he was subject to the Uniform Code of Military Justice. . . . And that code makes it abundantly clear that orders of a superior officer must be obeyed by subordinate members—but it is *lawful* orders. . . . In fact, it says members of the military have an obligation to disobey unlawful orders. ❞

In 1988 a court-appointed special prosecutor filed criminal charges against North and President Reagan's national security adviser, Admiral John Poindexter. North was convicted on various charges, including the destruction of government documents and lying to Congress. The conviction was later reversed on a legal technicality.

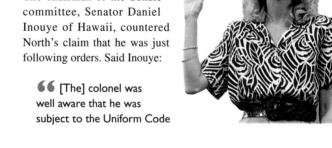

■■ **The Iran-contra affair involved illegal actions by White House aides to provide funding for the Nicaraguan contras through arms sales to Iran.**

◄ **Fawn Hall was called to testify before the congressional committee investigating the Iran-contra affair in 1987.**

SECTION **1** REVIEW

IDENTIFY and explain the significance of the following: New Right, Moral Majority, Reaganomics, Strategic Defense Initiative, Solidarity, Sandinistas, contras, José Napoleón Duarte, Geraldine Ferraro, Sandra Day O'Connor, Gramm-Rudman-Hollings Act, Tax Reform Law, insider trading, *glasnost, perestroika,* Intermediate-range Nuclear Forces Treaty, Iran-contra affair.

LOCATE and explain the importance of the following: Nicaragua, El Salvador, Grenada.

1. **MAIN IDEA** How did Reagan's economic policies both help and hurt the country?
2. **MAIN IDEA** What factors weakened the U.S. economy during the late 1980s?
3. **GAINING A MULTICULTURAL PERSPECTIVE** Imagine you are a citizen of El Salvador in the early 1980s. Describe the political situation in your country and explain why you think the United States is intervening in your country's affairs.
4. **WRITING TO INFORM** Imagine you are a member of the congressional committee appointed to investigate the Iran-contra affair. Write a letter to your constituents that summarizes the results of the investigation.
5. **ASSESSING CONSEQUENCES** How did each political party try to appeal to women voters in the 1984 presidential election?

PREVIEW WORKSHOP

Following is a list of the significant people, places, and terms in this section. You may wish to use this list as a section preview.

People
- Jesse Jackson
- Boris Yeltsin
- Saddam Hussein
- Anita Hill

Places
- Poland
- Azerbaijan
- Kuwait
- Persian Gulf

Terms
- German reunification
- Commonwealth of Independent States

- Operation Desert Storm
- Americans with Disabilities Act
- sexual harassment

Section 2

THE BUSH YEARS

FOCUS OBJECTIVES

- Describe the events that marked the end of the Cold War.

- Contrast Operation Desert Storm with previous American military conflicts.

- Identify the domestic issues that posed problems for President Bush.

FOCUS
- **What events marked the end of the Cold War?**
- **How did Operation Desert Storm differ from previous American military conflicts?**
- **What domestic issues posed problems for President Bush?**

Female soldier during Operation Desert Storm

𝓘n 1988 Vice President George Bush was elected president. While Bush was in office, reform efforts in the Soviet Union led to the end of the Cold War—and eventually to the breakup of the Soviet Union. Bush was determined to prove America's leadership in what he termed the "new world order," and his popularity soared after U.S. troops defeated the Iraqis in the Persian Gulf War. But Bush faced many challenges at home, including a persistent economic recession.

𝓣HE 1988 ELECTION

With the popular Reagan constitutionally prevented from running again, the Democrats hoped to win the White House in 1988. African American leader Jesse Jackson, who had run in 1984, was among those seeking the Democratic nomination. Jackson hoped to attract a "Rainbow Coalition"—a diverse group of voters representing all races and classes. Few political observers had taken

◄ Seeking to unite a "Rainbow Coalition" of voters, Jesse Jackson ran for the Democratic party's presidential nomination in both 1984 and 1988.

Jackson's candidacy seriously in 1984, although he helped generate the largest African American voter turnout ever for a Democratic primary.

By the 1988 election, Jackson's appeal had expanded to encompass a wide range of voters. On "Super Tuesday," the largest single day of primary voting, Jackson won more votes than any other candidate. Governor Michael Dukakis of Massachusetts, however, won the largest number of delegates and eventually gained the nomination. Dukakis, the son of Greek immigrants, selected Senator Lloyd Bentsen of Texas as his running mate. Vice President George Bush won the Republican presidential nomination with young Indiana senator Dan Quayle as his running mate.

The 1988 presidential campaign proved to be one of the dirtiest in recent years. Initially, Bush tried to appeal to voters' sense of optimism by

CORE RESOURCES
- **Section 2 Daily Quiz**

AV RESOURCES
- ***The American Nation Videodisc: U.S. Troops in the Persian Gulf; Vietnam and the Media***
- **Linking Geography and History Transparency** and **Worksheet 24**

MOTIVATING: STUDENT EXPERIENCES

Ask volunteers to recall their experiences watching, hearing, or reading about Operation Desert Storm and the Persian Gulf War. Ask how they felt about their country and their president during the conflict. Have them speculate on why presidential popularity usually increases during a war just as it decreases during economic hard times.

Teaching the Section

THE 1988 ELECTION

Ask students to assume the role of voters in the 1988 election. Have them write a letter to the editor expressing their reactions to the negative ads used in the campaign. Call on volunteers to read their letters to the class. Students may wish to include their letters in their portfolios.

Graph Caption Answer
1984; about 5,000 crimes per 100,000 people

RECOGNIZING PREJUDICE

Skillful use of misleading and negative ads helped Bush to portray Dukakis as soft on crime. The Willie Horton ad, for example, blamed Dukakis for the incident when in fact the Massachusetts prison furlough program that had allowed Horton out of jail on a weekend pass was set up by Dukakis's Republican predecessor. Have students identify the racial stereotype used in the Willie Horton ad and suggest reasons why critics labeled such ads racist.

■■ Have students give examples of negative campaigning in local or state elections. Ask students how they think this type of advertising affects the election process.

Map Caption Answer
Dukakis

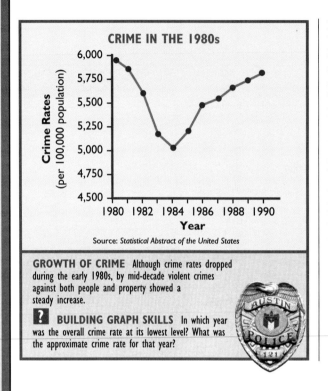

CRIME IN THE 1980s

Crime Rates (per 100,000 population)

Source: *Statistical Abstract of the United States*

GROWTH OF CRIME Although crime rates dropped during the early 1980s, by mid-decade violent crimes against both people and property showed a steady increase.

? **BUILDING GRAPH SKILLS** In which year was the overall crime rate at its lowest level? What was the approximate crime rate for that year?

promising "a kinder and gentler nation." Toward the end of the campaign, however, most of the Republican ads took a negative approach. For instance, despite Bush's weak environmental record, one commercial attacked Dukakis's record by showing scenes of Massachusetts' polluted Boston Harbor.

The most controversial advertising, however, was designed to sway voters troubled by the rising crime rate, which had jumped by over 12.5 percent between 1984 and 1988 (see chart). In a series of commercials and print ads, the Republicans painted Dukakis as weak on crime by associating him with convicted murderer Willie Horton and a Massachusetts prison program that provided prisoners with weekend passes. While out on a pass, Horton had attacked a Maryland couple.

Although some critics charged that the ads were racist (Horton was African American), Dukakis resisted using similarly negative ads in his own campaign. Instead, he tried to win support by promoting his skills as a manager, arguing that the election should be about competence. Most of

Election of 1988

LOW VOTER TURNOUT Only some 50 percent of those eligible voted in 1988, the lowest percentage since the election of 1924.

? **LOCATION** Which candidate carried Washington, D.C.?

▲ 1988 campaign button

	Electoral Vote	Popular Vote	% of Popular Vote
Bush	426	48,886,097	53.4
Dukakis	111	41,809,074	45.6
Other candidates	1	899,638	1.0

*West Virginia cast 1 electoral vote for Senator Lloyd Bentsen of Texas

☐ Bush (Republican)
■ Dukakis (Democratic)

THE END OF THE COLD WAR

Have students work in small groups to write scripts for a five-minute television news story on the fall of communism in Eastern Europe and the Soviet Union. Suggest that groups include in their scripts ideas for visuals to illustrate the story. Ask groups to present and discuss their news stories. Then lead the class in a discussion on how the fall of the Soviet Union has affected American policy.

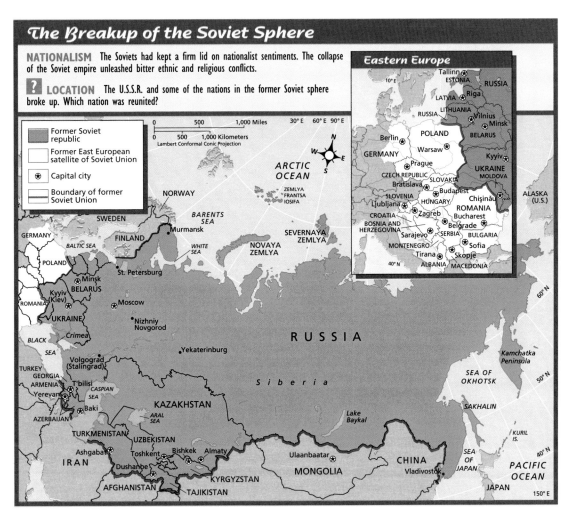

The Breakup of the Soviet Sphere

NATIONALISM The Soviets had kept a firm lid on nationalist sentiments. The collapse of the Soviet empire unleashed bitter ethnic and religious conflicts.

? LOCATION The U.S.S.R. and some of the nations in the former Soviet sphere broke up. Which nation was reunited?

Dukakis's early support evaporated, however, as voters grew skeptical of his abilities. In the November election, Bush won 426 electoral votes to Dukakis's 112. But the Democrats did increase their majorities in both houses of Congress and kept control of most state legislatures.

THE COLD WAR ENDS

Bush, who had served in numerous appointed government positions, including director of the CIA and representative to China, concentrated much of his attention on foreign affairs. He was determined to prove America's world leadership. Bush's first chance came in December 1989 when he sent U.S. troops to arrest Panama's president Manuel Noriega, who was wanted on drug charges in the United States.

Events in the Soviet Union soon pushed Bush's goal of American world leadership even further. Historians are still debating how far Mikhail Gorbachev really intended to go with the economic and political reform of the Soviet system. Undoubtedly, he meant to institute real change. But many argue that it is unlikely he foresaw the end result—the breakup of the Soviet Union and the collapse of Communist rule. Once set in motion, however, Gorbachev's reforms took a course all their own.

Gorbachev's efforts to modernize and expand the Soviet economy led to a dramatic easing of Cold War tensions with the United States. They also indirectly assisted the democratic movements that swept Eastern and Central Europe in 1989 and 1990. No longer willing or able to bear the costs of propping up Communist regimes around the world, the Soviet Union announced in 1989 that it was

Teaching the Section

THE THREAT OF TERRORISM

Organize students into groups to discuss the problem of international terrorism. Tell the groups to consider such topics as the nature of terrorism, recent changes in terrorist tactics, and the impact that terrorism could have on the U.S. Ask groups to share their conclusions with the class.

WORKING FOR PEACE

Organize students into three groups. Have each group imagine it is the United Nations Security Council in the early 1990s. Assign each group the task of formulating a plan to resolve regional conflicts in one of the following areas: Somalia, South Africa, or the former states of Yugoslavia. Suggest to students that their plans may include a variety of possible solutions. Have a representative from each group share its plan with the class.

HISTORY *in the Making*

THE FREEDOM OF INFORMATION ACT

SETTING THE SCENE

Recent statistics show that the FBI is one of the most difficult agencies from which to pry information. In 1990 the agency dealt with nearly 19,000 requests for information. Some 78 percent of these requests—14,897 in all—were closed without releasing any documents. Such requests, the FBI claimed, were not filed correctly, or they sought information that was not available. Further, the average time for handling a request—whether information was released or not—ran about 340 days, and the agency had a backlog of more than 9,000 unanswered applications. With new requests running at more than 15,000 a year, FBI compliance with FOIA is unlikely to improve.

CRITICAL THINKING

Mention that agencies often reject requests for information in the interests of "national security." Ask students to explain in which situations, if any, this might be a valid reason for denying access to government documents.

HISTORY *in the Making*

DR. PAUL BOYER

The Freedom of Information Act

Under the Freedom of Information Act (FOIA), anyone is supposed to be able to examine the records of U.S. federal agencies. Many people expected the FOIA to be particularly useful for scholars of political history. In reality, however, many scholars have found their use of the law severely limited by government red tape.

The congressional call for the Freedom of Information Act originated during the 1950s, when Senator Joseph McCarthy accused numerous government employees of harboring Communist sympathies. Several members of Congress began to push for an act that would allow easy access to government files on people accused of being Communists. By the time Congress passed the law in 1966, all government files were supposed to be open to the public unless national security needs clearly justified their exclusion.

Many government officials, however, claimed that the FOIA interfered with Cold War politics. In some circumstances, they argued, foreign agents might be reluctant to pass information on to American agencies for fear that the information might be made public through the FOIA. As a result of such concerns, numerous amendments were made to the FOIA to grant agencies exemptions from the law. Critics argue that such exemptions, coupled with the complicated way the government handles FOIA requests, have made the law virtually useless. This situation has been particularly troubling to scholars of political history, who cannot fairly evaluate government actions without inside information.

In the post–Cold War era, many observers have begun to press for an overhaul of the FOIA. One strong supporter of FOIA reform has been former Middle East journalist Terry Anderson. Anderson was captured by Islamic terrorists in 1985 and held hostage until December 1991. After his release, Anderson attempted

▲ Terry Anderson tried to use the FOIA to obtain information for his 1993 book *Den of Lions.*

to use the FOIA to research a book about his captivity. Anderson wrote to 10 agencies requesting information on himself, his fiancée, two other hostages held with him, and an Islamic group implicated in the hostage crisis.

Anderson received no useful information from his requests. Some agencies tried to delay answering for as long as possible. Others sent him information that did not relate to his requests or that came from public news reports he could easily have obtained elsewhere. In some cases, when he did receive classified documents, they were so heavily edited that they were useless. For example, one agency sent him 62 pages of documents, of which, Anderson found, "26 were totally blank, 20 showed only addresses with all the text [blacked out], 3 were newspaper reports, and 3 were reports on terrorism outside the Middle East."

As more people push for reform of the law they say is "outmoded by Cold War assumptions," scholars are hopeful that government documents will become more accessible. If reform of the FOIA opens new files to researchers, it may allow historians to examine and evaluate the Cold War period in a new light.

▶

▲ **Pro-democracy demonstrations, such as the one shown here, helped bring on the collapse of Communist party rule in Russia.**

adopting a policy of nonintervention in Eastern Europe. Thus, the Soviets did nothing when Poland and Hungary moved toward free elections and when the Communist governments in Czechoslovakia and Romania fell.

The Soviets also did nothing to assist Communist leaders when pro-democracy demonstrations broke out in East Germany in the fall of 1989. Throughout the fall, tens of thousands of East Germans fled to the West through Hungary. Then in October demonstrators forced Communist leader Erich Honecker to resign. In an attempt to restore calm, the East German government opened the Berlin Wall on November 9 and lifted restrictions on travel to the West. But it was already too late; the pressure for **German reunification**—the reuniting of East and West Germany as one nation—was too great. After free elections, the two nations were united as the Federal Republic of Germany on October 3, 1990, without opposition from Gorbachev.

By 1991 Gorbachev had problems of his own in the Soviet Union. Alarmed by the pace of reforms, Communist hard-liners attempted to oust him. On August 18, 1991, they placed Gorbachev under house arrest at his vacation home on the Crimean Sea. The coup collapsed by August 21, but Gorbachev's days in power were numbered. On December 1 the Ukrainians voted for independence. A week later the presidents of Ukraine, Russia, and Belarus declared that the Soviet Union was "ceasing its existence" and that they were forming the **Commonwealth of Independent States** (CIS). Gorbachev resigned as president of the Soviet Union on December 25 and turned over control of the armed forces to Boris

Yeltsin, the president of Russia. By the end of 1991, the Soviet Union had completely disbanded. Eventually the former Soviet republics of Armenia, Azerbaijan, Kazakhstan, Kyrgyzstan, Moldova, Tajikistan, Turkmenistan, Uzbekistan, and Georgia joined the CIS.

■■ **The collapse of communism in Eastern Europe, the fall of the Berlin Wall, and the breakup of the Soviet Union marked the end of the Cold War.**

THE PERSIAN GULF WAR

As the Soviet Union began breaking up, many people wondered how the role of the United States might change with the end of the Cold War. Bush assumed a leadership role in August 1990 when Iraq, led by ruler Saddam Hussein, invaded neighboring Kuwait, a major oil producer.

Operation Desert Storm. The United Nations condemned the attack, imposed economic sanctions on Iraq, and set a deadline for Iraq's withdrawal from Kuwait. As the January 15, 1991, deadline neared, military forces representing the United States, Britain, France, Egypt, and Saudi Arabia prepared for war. In all, some 690,000 allied troops—including some 540,000 Americans—amassed along the border of Kuwait. On January 16, the allied forces began bombing attacks on Iraqi forces and military and industrial installations.

The ground assault began on February 23. Within days the Iraqis had been driven back, and Kuwait's ruling al-Sabah family returned to power. American casualties included some 150 killed and 450 wounded. An estimated 100,000 Iraqis died. U.S. air attacks also severely damaged the Iraqi capital, Baghdad, and other cities. Many hailed the success of **Operation Desert Storm**. The commander of the U.S. forces, General H. Norman Schwarzkopf, received a hero's welcome in New York City. Bush's approval rating soared to nearly 90 percent following the war. Many people also attributed much of the war's success to the leadership of General Colin Powell.

 Colin Powell was born in New York City in 1937. The son of Jamaican immigrants, Powell earned a bachelor's degree in

Teaching the Section

OPERATION DESERT STORM

Point out that the Persian Gulf War was a popular war with the American public and that it boosted President Bush's popularity. Have students speculate about how both the high-tech nature of the battles and live television coverage might have contributed to public enthusiasm. Have students suggest other factors that added to public support.

(Students may suggest support for Bush's aims, dislike of Saddam Hussein, the limited duration of the conflict and the comparatively low numbers of American casualties.)

Map Caption Answer
by outflanking Iraq's main forces, precipitating their retreat

PERSONALITIES IN HISTORY

After the success of Operation Desert Storm, Colin Powell was considered by members of both major parties to be a potential political candidate. Powell's popularity with the public and silence about his political views led him to be compared to another general who had exhibited these characteristics—Dwight Eisenhower.

THE AMERICAN NATION VIDEODISC PROGRAM

U.S. Troops in the Persian Gulf

2B   49621   :28

Desert Storm, 1991

IRAQI STRATEGY Saddam Hussein peppers Israel with Scud missiles in an effort to draw Israel into the war, and thereby drive Arab countries out of the coalition against him.

? MOVEMENT How did allied strategy defeat Iraq?

1 Jan. 17: Operation Desert Storm begins with massive bombing of strategic targets in Iraq and Kuwait.

3 Iraqis set oil fields and storage tanks ablaze and pump oil into the Persian Gulf in an effort to foul a Saudi desalinization plant.

2 Deployment of U.S. Marines off the coast makes the Iraqis expect an amphibious landing.

4 Feb. 23: The four-day ground war begins.

7 Feb. 27: Allies liberate Kuwait City from retreating Iraqi invaders. Bush announces cease-fire.

6 Feb. 26: Helicopters bring in the 101st Air Assault Division to block the escape of Iraqi forces.

5 Feb. 25: Iraqi Scud missile kills 28 U.S. service personnel in their barracks.

TURKEY — Incirlik
CYPRUS
MEDITERRANEAN SEA
SYRIA
LEBANON — Damascus
Haifa
ISRAEL
Tel Aviv
Jerusalem — Amman
Suez Canal
JORDAN
Sinai
EGYPT — Aqaba
Gulf of Aqaba
RED SEA
Mosul — Erbil
IRAQ
Baghdad — Salman Pak, Tuwaitha
IRAN
Nasiriyah
Basra
KUWAIT — Kuwait City
Khafji
SAUDI ARABIA — Dhahran — BAHRAIN
Riyadh
Persian Gulf
QATAR — Abu Dhabi
OMAN
Strait of Hormuz
UNITED ARAB EMIRATES

ARCTIC OCEAN
EUROPE ASIA NORTH AMERICA
ATLANTIC OCEAN AFRICA PACIFIC OCEAN
SOUTH AMERICA INDIAN OCEAN AUSTRALIA Equator
ANTARCTICA
Robinson Projection

Legend:
- Allied countries
- Neutral countries
- ○ U.S. base
- ✿ Allied bombing
- ✸ Scud missile attack
- ☢ Iraqi nuclear site
- ▷ Allied advance
- Iraqi forces
- U.S. naval vessels
- ▲ Oil field

0   150   300 Miles
0   150   300 Kilometers
Lambert Conformal Conic Projection

geology from the City College of New York and an MBA from George Washington University. Upon finishing his schooling, Powell devoted his professional life to the U.S. Army. He served in Europe, the United States, Vietnam, and Korea. In 1989, Powell became the first African American and the youngest person ever to be appointed Chairman of the

Colin Powell

Joint Chiefs of Staff—the nation's highest-ranking uniformed officer.

When Powell retired from the U.S. Army in September 1993, he reflected on America's role in the new world order. "History and destiny have made America the leader of the world that would be free," he commented. "And the world that would be free is looking to us for inspiration."

A unique war. Operation Desert Storm differed from previous American military engagements. It was won almost entirely by the use of high-tech weaponry. And, although reporters had to rely on military briefings for information, television reporters provided unprecedented live coverage of the air war. Millions sat glued to their

WAR AND TELEVISION

Divide the class in half. Ask one group to discuss the ways live television coverage might increase popular support for a war. Encourage the other group to discuss how television coverage might hurt military efforts. Have each group appoint a spokesperson to present the group's point of view to the rest of the class.

▶

THE GULF WAR

Although the Persian Gulf War was brief, many people were caught in the crossfire, including the residents of Israel. To retaliate against UN forces, Iraq launched an attack on Israel. Sari Nusseibeh, a Palestinian philosopher living in Israel when fighting broke out, recalled his impressions as the war raged around him and his family:

❝*It was January 29, 13 days since the aerial bombardment in the Gulf War had started. For fully two weeks we had been placed under a total 24-hour curfew, interspersed only by three 2-hour intervals in which we were allowed to do our shopping. All of us—my wife, my three children, and myself—had taken to sleeping together on the floor of the sitting-dining area of our apartment. This way we kept each other company through the Scud [missile] scares (yes, even we Palestinians felt tense whenever the sirens blew, as we wondered each* time where the rockets would fall, and what deadly poison they might be . . . carrying).

For almost two weeks we lived in a state of suspension between TV scenes of missiles hitting Iraqi targets and footage of missiles flying over our heads. We were but one family in a population of 1.5 million Palestinians who had been confined to their homes. But Palestinian sufferings and fears were not aired on TV screens during that period—only the children giving vent to their primitive instincts of joy as missiles of destruction missed them and flew toward the enemy.❞

---

television sets as news correspondent Bernard Shaw reported the first allied bombings on Iraq:

❝ This is [pause] something is happening outside. . . . The skies over Baghdad have been illuminated. We're seeing bright flashes going off all over the sky. ❞

Military technology quickly became the star of the show as coverage of the war expanded. The technological nature of the war highlighted another unique aspect of Operation Desert Storm—the significant role played by women. More than 35,000 American women—some 6 percent of U.S. troops—served in the Persian Gulf conflict. Eleven of these women soldiers were killed and two taken prisoner. Though the U.S. military banned women from serving as combat pilots, they served in almost every other capacity—including flying support planes and working on missile crews.

The role of women in Desert Storm and the nature of the war caused many people to question the usefulness of banning women from combat. With technology playing an increasingly significant role in modern warfare, critics argued that

physical strength—and the differences between men and women—would become less important than technological skill. Over the past few years, the number of women in the military had increased to the point that U.S. Air Force colonel Douglas Kennett commented that his branch of the service "couldn't go to war without women and we couldn't win without them." In August 1991 the Senate removed the ban on women serving as combat pilots but continued to limit service in ground battles.

■■ **Operation Desert Storm was unique for its use of high-tech weaponry, live television coverage, and use of women soldiers.**

PROBLEMS AT HOME

Bush's success in foreign affairs won him much popularity and international praise, but some critics charged that he was neglecting problems at home. Bush did win some acclaim when he

---

Chapter 22
SECTION 2

Practice

GUIDED PRACTICE

Work with the class to develop two lists on the chalkboard—one listing the accomplishments of the Bush presidency and another listing the problems that lessened Bush's popularity.

INDEPENDENT PRACTICE

Using the information from the lists developed in the Guided Practice activity, have students imagine they are encyclopedia writers in the year 2010. Have each write an entry on the Bush presidency. Students may wish to include their entries in their portfolios.

Review and Assessment

REVIEW Organize students into groups to prepare a time line of the key events in this section. Ask each group to select for its time line events that represent the successes and challenges of Bush's presidency. Have students explain their choices. Then assign the Section 2 Review on p. 603.

ASSESS Assign the **Section 2 Daily Quiz** in *Core Resources*.

HISTORICAL SIDELIGHTS

Thomas-Hill Hearings
After the bruising Senate confirmation hearings, Thomas became Supreme Court justice by the narrowest margin in this century (52–48).

MAKING CONNECTIONS

Political Science
Shortly after Thomas's confirmation, angry opponents protested with signs that read "WE WILL REMEMBER NEXT NOVEMBER." Many translated their anger over Hill's questioning by Senate investigators into action, putting their support behind such women's political action groups as the National Women's Political Caucus. A single ad showing Thomas before an imaginary panel of female senators raised $61,000 for NWPC political campaigns. Anger over the Thomas-Hill hearings, coupled with fears about changes in abortion law, helped the pro-choice Democratic women's political network known as Emily's List to raise $6 million for the 1992 candidates it supported.

PRESIDENTIAL LIVES

GEORGE BUSH
1924–

in office 1989–1993

Following a popular and charismatic president such as Ronald Reagan was not easy for George Bush. Throughout the 1988 campaign he was constantly fighting "the wimp factor"—the accusation that he was a weak politician and a better follower than leader. This charge seemed particularly ironic for Bush, who had served bravely as a pilot in World War II.

At the age of 18, George Bush became one of the youngest commissioned pilots in the navy. He flew 58 missions in all

and was shot down once. Bush's experiences in war may have contributed to his strong interest in foreign affairs. During his presidency, memories of World War II came back to him when he considered committing troops to battle. "When it came time for me to send our kids . . . to the Middle East," he once said, "I thought back on my own experiences in combat and what it was like to be shot at. . . . Having been in combat rounded out my awareness of the human cost of war."

signed into law the 1990 **Americans with Disabilities Act**, which prohibits discrimination against people with mental or physical disabilities in employment or in access to transportation, telephone services, and public buildings. As the 1992 presidential campaign approached, however, several other domestic issues began to concern the public and undermine the president's support.

The Thomas-Hill hearings. Bush continued Reagan's efforts to move the Supreme Court in a conservative direction. In 1990 he filled a vacancy on the Court with David Souter, a conservative New Hampshire judge. In 1991 when Thurgood Marshall announced his retirement,

Bush nominated Clarence Thomas, a conservative African American judge and former head of the federal Equal Employment Opportunity Commission (EEOC), to take his place.

During the confirmation hearings, law professor Anita Hill, a former associate of Thomas's at the EEOC, accused the nominee of **sexual harassment**—the use of unwelcome sexual language or behavior that creates a hostile working environment. In televised hearings, the Senate Judiciary Committee investigated her charges. The tactics used by some members of the committee,

▶ During confirmation hearings for Supreme Court nominee Clarence Thomas (left), law professor Anita Hill (right) accused Thomas of sexual harassment. The Senate approved Thomas's nomination, in spite of an outcry by female activists.

602 ■ CHAPTER 22

Closure

Have students use the section's main headings to create a graphic organizer that depicts Bush's presidency. Call on volunteers to present their organizers to the class. Students may wish to include their organizers in their portfolios.

Extension

RESEARCH Have students research and report on weapons, military tactics and strategies, media coverage, the role of allies, or key personalities in the Persian Gulf War.

EXPLAIN Have students research the role of women in combat and write papers expressing their feelings on the topic.

which included suggestions that Hill could be "destroyed and belittled" for testifying, outraged many women. After the Senate narrowly approved the Thomas nomination, many women vowed to show their disapproval in the next election.

Across the country the hearings stirred debate about sexual harassment. Many women told of experiencing harassment as they tried to succeed in male-dominated fields. One Senate aide explained why some women, including herself, tolerated harassment:

> 66 You know what the code is, and if you want to be involved, you know what you have to tolerate. It's happened to me, and I never call anyone on it. You have to show you are tough enough to take a certain kind of harassment. 99

The debate became more heated after news broke of wide-scale sexual harassment of female officers at a naval convention in September 1991. An earlier Pentagon study had revealed that two thirds of the women in the military had been sexually harassed by colleagues. Such revelations prompted the military to increase punishment of sexual harassment.

The economy. Many women reported that they tolerated sexual harassment because they could not afford to lose their jobs. Many people could understand such feelings as the nation became more concerned with the economy. The federal deficit, which surged to $282 billion in 1991, was expected to climb to $350 billion in 1992. The costs of the Persian Gulf War and the bailout of the S&L and banking industries added to the deficit.

The trade gap persisted as well. Though the trade deficit had declined from its 1990 high of almost $102 billion, in 1991 it still stood at about $66 billion. Japan's massive annual sales of automobiles and electronic goods to U.S. consumers accounted for a large portion of the gap. On a 1992 trade mission to Japan, President Bush and U.S. business leaders tried—with little success—to persuade the Japanese to increase imports from the United States.

Adding to these economic woes, a recession hit in 1990. As the economy continued to falter, unemployment rose. The number of Americans living below the poverty line grew by more than two million in 1990. However, states facing budget deficits cut their welfare programs. Throughout the nation, economic problems compounded many urban problems. Once home to major companies such as Bethlehem Steel and Goodyear, Los Angeles in the 1980s and early 1990s witnessed the loss of many high-paying factory and defense-industry jobs. Such loss of inner-city jobs was repeated across the country. Despite repeated predictions of recovery, the recession hung on throughout 1992, complicating President Bush's reelection hopes.

■■ **Domestically, Bush faced troubles over the Thomas-Hill hearings and the sagging economy.**

SECTION REVIEW ANSWERS

IDENTIFY

For significance, see the following pages:
Jesse Jackson (p. 595)
German reunification (p. 599)
Commonwealth of
*   Independent States (p. 599)*
Boris Yeltsin (p. 599)
Saddam Hussein (p. 599)
Operation Desert Storm
*   (p. 599)*
Americans with Disabilities
*   Act (p. 602)*
Anita Hill (p. 602)
sexual harassment (p. 602)

LOCATE

For locations, see the maps on pp. 597 and 600.

1. *collapse of communism in Eastern Europe, fall of Berlin Wall, breakup of Soviet Union*
2. *use of high-tech weaponry, live television coverage, role of women*
3. *economy, Thomas-Hill hearings*
4. *Speeches should address the role of technology and the increased number of women in the military.*
5. *Answers will vary but should address the level of African American participation in the 1984 and 1988 elections.*

SECTION 2 REVIEW

IDENTIFY and explain the significance of the following: Jesse Jackson, German reunification, Commonwealth of Independent States, Boris Yeltsin, Saddam Hussein, Operation Desert Storm, Americans with Disabilities Act, Anita Hill, sexual harassment.

LOCATE and explain the importance of the following: Poland, Azerbaijan, Kuwait, Persian Gulf.

1. **MAIN IDEA** What three events signaled the end of the Cold War?
2. **MAIN IDEA** What was unique about Operation Desert Storm?
3. **MAIN IDEA** What domestic problems plagued President Bush?
4. **WRITING TO PERSUADE** Imagine you are in the U.S. Army. Write a speech explaining why women in the military should have the same opportunities as men.
5. **ASSESSING CONSEQUENCES** How did Jesse Jackson's "Rainbow Coalition" campaign affect the 1984 and 1988 elections?

PREVIEW WORKSHOP

Following is a list of the significant people and terms in this section. You may wish to use this list as a section preview.

People
- H. Ross Perot
- Ruth Bader Ginsburg
- Jean-Bertrand Aristide

Terms
- Omnibus Budget Reconciliation Act
- AIDS
- Family and Medical Leave Act
- universal coverage
- employer mandate

MOTIVATING: STUDENT EXPERIENCES

Ask students to think about a recent election in their community. What were the primary issues? How did the candidates address these issues? List student responses on the chalkboard.

FOCUS OBJECTIVES

- Discuss the features that characterized the 1992 election.

- Describe the issues on which President Clinton met with legislative success, and explain why health care reform proved more troublesome.

- Analyze the U.S. reaction to conflicts in various foreign nations.

THE AMERICAN NATION VIDEODISC PROGRAM

Serving the Nation

| 2A | 20156 | 2:54 |

CORE RESOURCES

- **Section 3 Daily Quiz**

AV RESOURCES

- *The American Nation* **Videodisc: Serving the Nation**
- **Everyday Life in America Trans-parency** and **Worksheet 32**

604

Section 3

CLINTON TAKES OVER

F O C U S

- **What features characterized the 1992 election?**
- **On which issues did President Clinton meet with legislative success? Why did health care reform prove more troublesome?**
- **How did the United States react to conflicts in various foreign nations?**

*A*fter his election in 1992, President Bill Clinton focused much of his energy on domestic issues such as the economy, crime, and health care. Foreign-policy issues, however, proved troublesome. Although the Middle East took an important step toward peace, conflict increased in parts of Eastern Europe, Africa, and the Caribbean.

Rally supporting AIDS research

THE 1992 ELECTION

As 1991 ended, most political observers expected Bush to win reelection despite the nation's economic woes. The president was still riding a wave of popularity from the Persian Gulf War. Only a few Democrats were willing to challenge him.

Among these Democrats was Governor Bill Clinton of Arkansas. Born in 1946, Clinton reflected the concerns of many members of his "baby boomer" generation. He opposed the war in Vietnam and for a time tried to avoid being drafted. He was also heavily influenced by the idealism of the Kennedy era. Reflecting the impact of the civil rights movement, he believed strongly in the value of diversity and equality.

The other major presidential candidate was independent H. Ross Perot, a billionaire from

▲ **Bill Clinton**

Texas, who ran as an outsider to the political process. He promised to bring a populist reform movement to Washington, D.C., by decreasing the influence of political lobbyists and by giving the public a greater voice in government. He also promised to use his business skills to reform the economy. Perot's message appealed to many voters who were growing frustrated with President Bush's inability to improve the economy.

The 1992 election proved to be different from any other in recent history. After years of low voter participation, people turned out in droves to make their voices heard. Candidates used forums such as television talk shows and radio call-in programs to answer questions directly from the public.

One group of voters who insisted on being heard were women, especially those outraged by the Thomas-Hill hearings. Shortly after the hearings, activist Eleanor Smeal had declared: "The Senate did more in one week to underscore the critical need for more women in the Senate than feminists have been able to do in 25 years." Women responded by running for office in record numbers.

THE 1992 ELECTION

Ask students to identify issues that arose during the 1992 presidential election. List student responses on the board. Divide the class into groups, and assign each group one of the listed issues. Have each group explain why its assigned issue is important to the U.S.

The increase in women candidates led the press to dub 1992 "the year of the woman." Many of these candidates won. Four prominent women Democrats gained U.S. Senate seats, including Patty Murray of Washington and African American Carol Moseley-Braun of Illinois. California filled both of its Senate seats with women—Barbara Boxer and Dianne Feinstein. Californian Lynn Woolsey, a divorced mother of three, became the first member of the House to have ever received welfare. And in the presidential race, some observers suggested that Clinton's wife, Hillary Rodham Clinton, a talented lawyer, was qualified to run for president herself.

▶ Ben Nighthorse Campbell became the only Native American in the U.S. Senate after his victory in the 1992 senatorial election.

▲ Hillary Rodham Clinton advised her husband on a number of key issues during the 1992 presidential campaign.

Acknowledging this fact, Bill Clinton said during the 1992 campaign that voters would be getting "two for the price of one" if he were elected.

In the end, it was Bill Clinton's message of economic and social reform, rather than his wife, that brought him victory in the 1992 national election. Clinton and his running mate, Senator Al Gore of Tennessee, won 43 percent of the popular vote and 370 electoral votes to the Bush-Quayle ticket's 38 percent of the popular vote and 168 electoral votes. Although Perot and his running mate, Admiral William Stockdale, did not win any electoral votes, they captured 19 percent of the popular vote—the most of any independent presidential campaign since that of Theodore Roosevelt in 1912.

■■ The 1992 election saw increased voter participation, numerous reform candidates, and the election of baby boomer Bill Clinton to the presidency.

HISTORICAL SIDELIGHTS

"Read My Lips"
Bush's 1992 bid for president was also hurt by what some supporters perceived as his broken promise on taxes. While campaigning in 1988, Bush made a famous campaign promise: "Read my lips: No New Taxes." In 1990 he signed into law a bill increasing taxes by $137 billion over 5 years.

HISTORICAL SIDELIGHTS

Year of Women
In 1992, 117 women ran for seats in Congress, 40 more than in 1990. Of that number, 21 were members of ethnic minority groups, up from 14 in 1990.

■■ Ask students if they agree with this statement by Jeannette Rankin, the first woman to be elected to Congress: "We're half the people; we should be half the Congress."

PRESIDENTIAL LIVES

BILL CLINTON
1946–

in office
1993–

Bill Clinton's presidency marked many firsts in the White House. He was the first president born in the post–World War II era and the first president from Arkansas. Clinton was also the first president to play the saxophone at his own inaugural celebration.

Clinton's career goal as a young teenager was to become a jazz musician. He was heavily influenced by African American jazz artists and early rock 'n' roll stars such as Elvis Presley. He excelled at playing the saxophone and was offered numerous music scholarships to college after he graduated from high school. Although Clinton went on to make a career in politics, he frequently used his musical talents in campaigns, such as during the 1992 presidential election when, wearing dark glasses, he played the saxophone on a popular late-night talk show. Despite his love of music, Clinton believes that he made the right career choice. "I would have been a very good musician," he has noted, "but not a great one."

Teaching the *Section*

HELP FOR WORKING PARENTS

Have students imagine they are members of a lobby group favoring government and business support for day care. Have students write speeches they would use to explain to Congress and/or private businesses why the need for such services is growing, who would benefit from such services, and why the federal government and businesses should provide financial support for such services. Call on volunteers to present their speeches. Students may wish to include their speeches in their portfolios.

Changing Ways

NATIVE AMERICAN RENEWAL: A CASE STUDY

SETTING THE SCENE

Water rights are a key issue for many Native American groups. The Shoshones and Arapahos on the Wind River Reservation in Wyoming turned to the courts to help them reclaim their water rights. In a 1989 case, the Supreme Court upheld their right to one third of the water that originates on their reservation. A former Shoshone tribal councilman noted: "We're simply protecting our sacred, sovereign rights. A lot of people in the West aren't accustomed to seeing Indians stand up for themselves."

BIO GRAPHY PERSONALITIES IN HISTORY

Wilma Mankiller's distinctive last name came from an 18th-century warrior ancestor. As chief of the second largest Indian nation in the U.S., Mankiller worked with a $52 million annual budget to run health clinics, businesses, and cultural programs. In 1990 Mankiller signed an agreement with the U.S. government that gave the Cherokee nation direct control of $6.1 million in federal funding.

Changing Ways

NATIVE AMERICAN RENEWAL: A CASE STUDY

The economic problems facing the United States in the 1980s and 1990s presented special problems for the nation's nearly two million American Indians, more than 20 percent of whom lived on or near reservations. As in earlier years, joblessness, lack of education, and poor health care made life hard for many Native Americans. But cultural renewal, economic ventures, and successful claims of treaty rights offered promise.

The Shoshone-Bannock Indians of Fort Hall Reservation in Idaho were among the Native Americans who successfully pressed their treaty claims. In 1990, using the terms of an 1868 treaty with the United States, the Shoshone-Bannock won the right to use water from the Snake River to irrigate their farmlands. The decision was the result of more than 25 years of American Indian efforts to win greater political autonomy and economic self-sufficiency.

BIO GRAPHY
Wilma Mankiller, former chief of the 108,000–strong Cherokee Nation, launched one of the most significant renewal efforts. Mankiller was born in Tahlequah, Oklahoma, in 1945. She spent her early years on a farm, where her family faced economic hardships and lived without indoor plumbing or electricity.

When Mankiller was 12, the farm failed after two drought years. Her family then moved to San Francisco, California, under the Bureau of Indian Affairs' relocation program. The adjustment to city life was difficult for Mankiller, who recalled, "One day I was [in Oklahoma] and the next day I was trying to deal with the mysteries of television, indoor plumbing, neon lights and elevators."

She soon became active in the American Indian Movement, which inspired her to become more involved in her community. In the mid-1970s Mankiller moved back to Oklahoma. She completed college and began working to promote economic growth in the Cherokee Nation. Stressing self-esteem and community self-help, Mankiller helped develop rural water systems, improve housing, and develop new businesses.

In 1985 Mankiller became the first woman principal chief, and in 1987 she won a tough four-way race and a subsequent runoff election. Mankiller compared her job to "running a small country, a medium-size

Wilma Mankiller

▲ The Shoshone-Bannock Indians successfully sued the U.S. government in 1990 to reclaim irrigation rights that had been guaranteed to them in an 1868 treaty.

corporation, and being a social worker." In addition to helping Cherokee communities create new jobs and better health care, the Cherokee Nation sponsored a program to teach students how to read and write the Cherokee language. "I can't help but feel hopeful about our future," Mankiller noted in her 1990 State of the Nation address:

❝ I think the strongest thing I see as I travel around to Cherokee communities and talk with people is their tenacity [persistence]. Despite everything that's happened to our people throughout history we've managed to hang on to our culture, we've managed to hang on to our sense of being Cherokee. ❞

WORKING ON THE ECONOMY

Have the class discuss the issue of tax increases and spending cuts. Encourage students to consider why members of Congress might oppose these measures. Record student responses on the chalkboard.

INTERNATIONAL TRADE

On the chalkboard, make a two-column chart. Label the first column *Pros* and the second *Cons*. Have students discuss the possible effects of lowering trade barriers. Record student responses in the appropriate column.

▶

CLINTON'S APPOINTMENTS

Once in office Clinton quickly set about implementing the reforms he had promised during the campaign. To help him achieve his vision of change, Clinton put together the most racially diverse and gender-balanced cabinet in U.S. history. His appointees included Mexican American Henry Cisneros as secretary of housing and urban affairs and African Americans Ron Brown and Joycelyn Elders as secretary of commerce and surgeon general, respectively. Other women appointees included Press Secretary Dee Dee Myers, Attorney General Janet Reno, and Secretary of Health and Human Services Donna Shalala. After a long search, Clinton also chose distinguished judge Ruth Bader Ginsburg to fill a vacancy on the Supreme Court.

BIO GRAPHY Ruth Bader was born in 1933 in Brooklyn, New York. In 1954 she graduated from Cornell University with high honors in government. That same year she married fellow student Martin D. Ginsburg. She then attended law school, first at Harvard and then at Columbia University. Although she tied for first-place rank in her class at Columbia, a Supreme Court justice refused to give her a clerkship on the grounds that he was unprepared to hire a woman.

Despite this initial setback, Ginsburg was able to secure a clerkship for a U.S. district judge and then went on to teach law at Rutgers and Columbia. She became Columbia's first woman professor to receive tenure. Then, as director of the Women's Rights Project of the American Civil Liberties Union in the 1970s, Ginsburg argued six landmark cases on gender equality before the Supreme Court. She won five of the cases.

Ruth Bader Ginsburg

In 1980 Ginsburg became a federal judge, a position she retained until taking her place on the Supreme Court. Becoming the Court's second female justice, Ginsburg remarked that her nomination would contribute "to the end of the days when women, at least half the talent pool in our society, appear in high place only as one-at-a-time performers."

TACKLING THE ECONOMY

Once President Clinton had appointed his cabinet, his biggest challenge was to improve the economy. He began by proposing a plan for a new budget. Attempting to reduce the deficit, Clinton called for some spending cuts. He also proposed to increase taxes for the wealthy and for corporations.

As a result, many members of Congress—particularly Republicans—were opposed to Clinton's reforms. Ultimately, the **Omnibus Budget Reconciliation Act** did pass, in August 1993. The vote, however, was extremely close in both chambers—218 to 216 in the House, 51 to 50 in the Senate—with the tie-breaking vote cast by Vice President Al Gore. Had any one Congressperson who had voted for the bill decided to vote against it instead, the bill would not have passed. And not a single Republican voted for the bill, the first time in history that a major U.S. legislative act was passed without receiving any votes from the minority party.

Despite the fierce opposition, the passage of the bill was hailed by the Clinton administration and others as a great success. "After a long season of denial and drift and decline, we are seizing control of our economic destiny," proclaimed Clinton. A few months after the budget bill was passed, Clinton made even further progress toward his vision of a healthy economy when Congress voted to ratify a free trade agreement lowering trade barriers between the United States, Canada, and Mexico (see Chapter 24).

TACKLING CRIME

After Clinton had cleared the budget hurdle, he turned his attention to other domestic issues. One of these was crime, which had continued to grow since the 1980s. By the early 1990s, nearly 2 million violent crimes—including some

Teaching the **S***ection*

FAMILY AND MEDICAL LEAVE ACT

Pair students and invite them to imagine that they are single parents, working parents, or chief executives of large businesses. Have students write letters to President Clinton describing their reactions to his decision to sign the Family and Medical Leave Act. Select pairs to read their letters aloud. Then discuss with the class the advantages and disadvantages of this legislation.

HEALTH IN THE 1990S

Have students work in small groups to write an outline for a script for a TV documentary titled "The 1990s—Health Care Crisis." In preparing their scripts, students should consider what factors led to the crisis and how the U.S. government responded. Students might also suggest visuals such as charts and graphs that might be included in their documentary. Call on groups to present their script outlines.

GLOBAL CONNECTIONS

Rising crime rates were a problem throughout Russia during the early 1990s. In 1992 there were 2.76 million registered crimes in Russia, an increase of some 27 percent over 1991. Government officials expected the number of crimes to rise by about 600,000 annually over the next two years. One of the most alarming developments noted by officials was the rise in the number of young criminal offenders. Minors—people under age 16—committed about 200,000 crimes in 1992. And from 1988 to 1992, the number of Russian criminals aged 14 or 15 increased by over 50 percent.

AV TRANSPARENCY

Everyday Life in America Transparency and **Worksheet 32**

COOPERATIVE LEARNING

Divide the class into small groups. Ask each group to discuss the pros and cons of an employer mandate. Each group should develop a plan for health care reform that would provide universal coverage. Have groups present their plans to the class, and have the class vote to determine the best plan.

25,000 murders—were being committed each year. In 1992 the number of violent crimes involving handguns reached some 931,000, up almost 21 percent from 1991. Some of the increase in crime was due to the rising international drug trade, a multibillion-dollar operation.

In a January 1994 poll, 93 percent of the respondents said that it should be an "absolute" national priority to address crime. Clinton agreed. "Every day the national peace is shattered by crime," he said in a State of the Union Message. He went on to propose a measure that would impose tougher penalties on criminals, increase the number of police officers, "keep guns out of the hands of criminals," and increase funding for drug treatment and drug education.

By the summer of 1994, a bill endorsed by Clinton arrived in Congress. Despite an initial setback in which the House of Representatives voted not even to consider the bill, the crime bill was revived and passed both the House and the Senate. The final bill eliminated a racial justice provision aimed at taking into account the disproportionate number of black men on death row and trimmed some of the money for crime prevention. But the bill provided for 100,000 new police officers, added to the range of crimes subject to the death penalty, and prohibited the sale and possession of several kinds of assault weapons. Clinton heralded the bill's passage as a major victory for "all law-abiding Americans."

▲ **Afghan farmer collects opium, which is then refined into heroin and sold in the United States, Europe, and other areas.**

■■ During Clinton's first years in office, Congress passed important legislation concerning the budget and crime.

---

*T*HE HEALTH CARE DEBATE

Clinton met with less success on his plan to revamp the nation's health care system. Between

---

1970 and 1990, U.S. spending on health care had risen from $74 billion to $666 billion. The aging population, soaring physicians' fees, higher insurance costs, and more-expensive medical equipment accounted for much of this increase. Rising medical costs hit the poor and those without health insurance especially hard.

Another group experiencing great difficulties under the current system were people with Acquired Immune Deficiency Syndrome, or AIDS. This is the final deadly stage of an illness believed to be caused by the human immunodeficiency virus, or HIV. By March 1993, AIDS had claimed the lives of more than 180,000 Americans, and some one million people had been infected with HIV. Scientists have not been able to find a cure for AIDS, and the costs of treatment can be very high.

As a result of rising costs, and other problems with the nation's health care system, by the early 1990s many Americans were convinced that the system needed to be changed. In February 1993, two weeks after his inauguration, Clinton signed into law the **Family and Medical Leave Act**, which President Bush had twice vetoed. The legislation requires large companies to provide workers up to 12 weeks of unpaid leave for family and medical emergencies without losing their medical coverage or their jobs. Still, Clinton knew that more was needed. He appointed Hillary Rodham Clinton to head a panel to shape a proposal to reform health care.

One of the criticisms of the current system was the fact that some people could not afford health care. Thus, providing **universal coverage**—health care for every American—became a major goal of health care reformers. As Clinton explained in September 1993, the most "urgent priority" was to give "every American health security, health care that can never be taken away." The following January, Clinton warned Congress:

     66 If you send me legislation that does not guarantee every American private health insurance that can never be taken away, you will force me to take this pen, veto the legislation, and we'll come right back here and start all over again. 99

While most people agreed that universal coverage was a worthwhile goal, they disagreed on how best to accomplish it. Furthermore, some

REGIONAL CONFLICTS

List the following regions on the chalk-board: *Commonwealth of Independent States, Africa, Eastern Europe, Middle East.* Refer students to the regional map on p. 597 and the world map on pp. 772–773, and ask volunteers to identify conflicts that took place within the listed regions in the early 1990s. Note their responses under the appropriate chalkboard headings. Then discuss how the disintegration of the Soviet Union might have contributed to events in each of these regions. Ask students to explain why the collapse of Soviet military power might have contributed to instability within Eastern Europe and the former republics of the Soviet Union.

▶

▲ The rising costs of health insurance, doctors' fees, and improved medical equipment created a health-care crisis during the 1990s.

Americans, including many Republicans, strongly opposed the creation of a government-run health care system and argued that paying for such a system would require huge tax increases.

Probably the greatest controversy, however, arose over how to pay for universal coverage. Clinton favored an **employer mandate**, by which all employers would have to pay most of the costs of insurance for every worker. But opponents argued that this would place too great a burden on small business owners who might not be able to afford the costs of insurance.

In 1993 and 1994 several health care bills were proposed in Congress. But no one bill could please everyone—or win the needed majority.

■■ **Despite a widespread desire to reform health care, Congress could not agree on a program.**

THE 1994 MIDTERM ELECTIONS

The administration's ability to shape legislation was further affected by the 1994 midterm election, in which the Republicans won control of both houses of Congress for the first time in 40 years. One woman echoed the mood of many voters when she explained why she had voted for Republican candidates: "I feel like some of the good old boys have been there too long; they're complacent, owe too many people. They're not listening to what [the average American is] saying."

Reflecting the mood of the voters, the Republican leadership promised to dramatically reduce the size and reach of the federal government. Many of those elected had signed Georgia Congressman Newt Gingrich's Contract with America, promising tax cuts, more military spending, a balanced budget, cuts in welfare programs, and term limits. However, even Gingrich admitted that it would be difficult to bring change to Washington.

DEALING WITH THE WORLD

Health care was not the only difficult issue the United States faced in the 1990s. Figuring out what role the country should play in worldwide conflicts also proved challenging for the U.S. government. Events in Eastern Europe, Africa, the Caribbean, and the Middle East all demanded attention of one type or another.

The former Yugoslavia. The end of Communist rule in Eastern Europe unleashed bitter ethnic and local disputes that had formerly been kept in check by Communist authorities. The region that was once the nation of Yugoslavia experienced some of the greatest turmoil.

With the end of the Cold War and the break-up of the Soviet system, Yugoslavia split into several republics in the early 1990s. Unfortunately the new nations could not agree on borders; in Bosnia, ethnic Serbs sought to slice off part of the country and attach it to Serbia.

In their efforts to do so, the Serbs waged a war of terror—including murder, arson, and other atrocities—against the Bosnian Muslims living in the areas the Serbs wanted. This "ethnic cleansing," as it was called, forced many thousands of Muslims to flee—just as the Serbs intended. By the beginning of 1994, some 300,000 people had been killed or wounded in the conflict.

Most of the rest of the world denounced the Serbs' actions. In 1992 the U.S. ambassador to the UN remarked, "Those responsible for the atrocities and gross violations, including . . . 'ethnic cleansing' and other war crimes in the former Yugoslavia, must be brought to justice." Yet although the United Nations sent peacekeeping forces to the area and launched an investigation into the Serbian leaders' alleged war crimes, UN efforts seemed to do little to stop the fighting. Numerous peace plans were suggested only to be rejected by one faction or the other—usually the Serbs.

Furthermore, U.S. and other nations' leaders were hesitant to become directly involved in a civil war that had no obvious, easy solutions. Such involvement would doubtless take hundreds, even thousands, of soldiers' lives, and promised

*P*ractice

GUIDED PRACTICE

Write on the board the subsection titles and inform students that these are topics for news stories about the different challenges faced by Bill Clinton. Call on volunteers to develop brief story outlines for each topic, noting their suggestions under the appropriate title.

INDEPENDENT PRACTICE

Direct students to use one of the story outlines developed in the Guided Practice activity to write a news story about the Clinton presidency. Students may wish to include their stories in their portfolios.

*R*eview and *A*ssessment

REVIEW Have students write a letter to a friend in another country describing the concerns and challenges facing Americans in the 1990s and describing, where applicable, the steps President Clinton took to address the challenges. Select students to read their letters to the class. Then assign the Section 3 Review on p. 611.

ASSESS Assign the **Section 3 Daily Quiz** in *Core Resources.*

MULTICULTURAL PERSPECTIVES

In 1994 Jordan's King Hussein and Israeli prime minister Yitzhak Rabin signed a treaty that ended a 46-year state of war. But not all of the Arab nations were ready to sign treaties with Israel. Syrian president Hafez Assad insisted that Israel return the Golan Heights, which it had occupied since 1967. Assad said that he was willing to establish "peaceful, normal relations with Israel in return for Israel's full withdrawal from the Golan."

to yield few benefits. "We cannot respond ourselves to every alarm," Clinton's secretary of state Warren Christopher said in 1993. Clinton vowed that any U.S. military intervention would have to be part of a major NATO operation, similar to Desert Storm.

Clinton's reluctance to intervene applied not only to the civil war in the former Yugoslavia but also to conflicts in Africa. Civil wars in the East African countries of Somalia and Rwanda in the early 1990s proved particularly troublesome for U.S. policy makers (see Chapter 25).

Haiti. The U.S. reaction to a conflict in the small Caribbean country of Haiti took a slightly different course, largely because Haiti is so close to the United States. A military coup in September 1991 ousted Haiti's first democratically elected president, Jean-Bertrand Aristide. Again, the United States and the UN condemned the action but avoided becoming directly involved. Instead, they imposed economic sanctions on Haiti.

Sanctions, however, turned out to be somewhat ineffective. Because of Haiti's shared border with the Dominican Republic, smugglers found that it was easy to get goods into Haiti illegally. Furthermore, some critics pointed out that rather than encouraging the military leaders to step down, the sanctions were merely making life harder for the Haitian people. As the number of Haitians fleeing to the United States as refugees increased (see Chapter 25), more and more

▼ The U.S. Coast Guard intercepted Haitian refugees, such as the family shown here, and took them to a temporary "tent-city" at Guantánamo Bay Naval Base. Some 2,500 refugees were housed at this base before being returned to Haiti.

people—including Aristide—urged the United States to take stronger measures.

Clinton feared that other Latin American countries would see U.S. military involvement in Haiti as another instance of "Yankee imperialism." However, U.S. and Caribbean leaders agreed on the need to restore democracy. In a joint statement they declared:

66 Our governments are equally united in their determination to take all necessary means to carry out the [UN] Security Council mandate to restore the democratic process in Haiti. 99

In September 1994, with an American invasion about to take place, Haiti's military rulers met with a U.S. negotiating team headed by former president Carter. When Haiti's rulers realized that an invasion had already been launched, they agreed to resign. The next day American forces landed without opposition to occupy Haiti. President Aristide returned on October 15.

■■ The United States and other nations struggled to define their roles in conflicts in the former Yugoslavia, Africa, and Haiti.

The Middle East. In contrast to the regions experiencing increased conflict in the 1990s, the Middle East—plagued by conflict for decades—made some progress toward peace. Although Arabs, Palestinians, and Israelis had by no means resolved all their differences, hopes for harmony were renewed in September 1993, when Palestinian leader Yasir Arafat and Israeli prime minister Yitzhak Rabin signed a new peace accord. The agreement called for limited self-government for Palestinians in parts of the territories occupied by Israel since the 1967 war.

President Clinton, who oversaw the signing of the accord at the White House, called it a "historic and honorable compromise." Though the Clinton administration hosted the signing, the event capped years of efforts by U.S. officials to bring peace to the Middle East. Cyrus Vance, who was secretary of state when the Camp David Accords were signed in 1978, declared of the 1993 agreement: "It is, at long last, what all of us who worked on the issue hoped and dreamed might one day come about. But we feared we would not see it in our lifetime."

Closure

Have students consider President Clinton's statement in his inaugural address that "We have heard the trumpets, we have changed the guard." Ask them to think about events of the Clinton presidency and explain how those events reflected or ignored this idea.

Extension

RESEARCH Have students reseach and report on the different issues surrounding health care reform.

ANALYZE Have students research a social issue of the 1990s, such as AIDS, crime, or unemployment, and report on its causes and experts' recommendations for addressing the problem selected

▲ President Clinton's smile reflects the relief felt by many throughout the world at this historic handshake between Yitzhak Rabin and Yasir Arafat.

C O M M E N T A R Y

The Private Politician in the Public Eye

President Clinton—like Presidents Nixon and Reagan before him—was hampered by charges of wrongdoing. But there was a difference. The Watergate and Iran-contra scandals involved Nixon's and Reagan's actions as president. In Clinton's case, critics and the media focused on his financial dealings and his private life before he was elected president. Other elected officials or candidates faced similar scrutiny of their private lives. Many people believe that such actions, even in the past, are an important indication of character. Others, however, maintain

that actions that have not affected the public have no bearing on a person's ability to govern wisely and morally.

"Whitewater" is a good example of this new phenomenon. During the first years of Clinton's presidency, investigators looked into possible connections between a failed savings-and-loan institution and an Arkansas real estate deal that had involved Clinton when he was the governor of Arkansas. During much of 1993 and 1994, the press and the public struggled to learn whether Clinton had engaged in any illegal or unethical behavior.

Some argued that such efforts were vital. The New York Times wrote, "Journalists have a constitutionally defined obligation to stick with a story as long as there are unanswered questions of political, legal, or moral consequence." Others, however, believed that the whole Whitewater affair was meaningless. "Whitewater . . . is a parody of a political scandal, full of sound and fury, signifying next to nothing," said one Newsweek editorial. "A few years from now, nothing about Whitewater will be remembered."

Whether Whitewater will be remembered remains to be seen. But it seems clear that for a long time into the future, presidents can expect that all their actions will be the subject of much probing.

SECTION REVIEW ANSWERS

IDENTIFY

For significance, see the following pages:
H. Ross Perot (p. 604)
Ruth Bader Ginsburg (p. 607)
Omnibus Budget
  Reconciliation Act (p. 607)
AIDS (p. 608)
Family and Medical Leave Act (p. 608)
universal coverage (p. 608)
employer mandate (p. 609)
Jean-Bertrand Aristide (p. 610)

1. *increased voter participation, many reform candidates, large numbers of women candidates*
2. *economy—tax increases, spending cuts; crime—tougher penalties for criminals, more police officers, increased funding for drug treatment; legislation passed after fierce congressional battles*
3. *breakup of Soviet Union led to new national conflicts and ethnic turmoil*
4. *Essays should address the issues of universal coverage and employer mandates.*
5. *Answers will vary but should balance the threat of fatalities with the benefits of international peace.*

SECTION 3 REVIEW

IDENTIFY and explain the significance of the following: H. Ross Perot, Ruth Bader Ginsburg, Omnibus Budget Reconciliation Act, AIDS, Family and Medical Leave Act, universal coverage, employer mandate, Jean-Bertrand Aristide.

1. **MAIN IDEA** Why was the 1992 election different from any other in recent history?
2. **MAIN IDEA** How did President Clinton propose to improve the U.S. economy and to reduce crime in America? How successful were his proposals in Congress?
3. **MAIN IDEA** Why did the former Yugoslavia experience increased conflict in the early 1990s?
4. **WRITING TO EXPLAIN** Write an essay explaining why health care reform was controversial despite a widespread belief that such reform was necessary.
5. **TAKING A STAND** What role do you think Americans should play in foreign conflicts that do not directly affect the United States?

DEVELOPING THEMES

Return to the "Themes" section on p. 584. Have students discuss these again and compare their original responses to those given now. (See p. 583B for suggested answers.)

Chapter Review Answers

WRITING A SUMMARY
See Essential Points in each section for main ideas.

REVIEWING CHRONOLOGY
2, 5, 3, 1, 4
Analyzing
to limit spending and balance the budget

IDENTIFYING PEOPLE AND IDEAS

1. *Polish independent trade union*
2. *CIA-sponsored army attempting to overthrow Nicaraguan Sandinistas*
3. *first female candidate on major party presidential ticket*
4. *stockbroker's illegal use of confidential financial information for personal gain*
5. *president of Russia*
6. *Iraqi leader whose invasion of Kuwait led to Persian Gulf War*
7. *popular third-party candidate during 1992 election*
8. *female Supreme Court justice appointed by President Clinton*
9. *fatal disease believed to be caused by HIV virus*
10. *health care for all Americans*

UNDERSTANDING MAIN IDEAS

1. *calls for new weapons systems, increased military spending*
2. *During the Reagan and Bush administrations, domestic issues included difficult Supreme Court nominations, the Iran-contra affair, economic problems, and the issue of sexual harassment.*
3. *President Bush worked to build an international coalition during Operation Desert Storm, and his success in bringing nations together for the military effort showed that America was still a world leader.*
4. *high medical and insurance costs, spread of AIDS; problems of universal coverage, funding sources such as employer mandates*
5. *Clinton was reluctant to intervene in Yugoslavia, but he sent troops to Haiti and facilitated the 1993 peace accord between Israel and the Palestinians.*

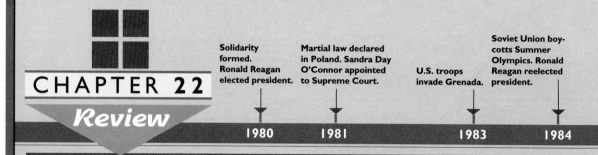

CHAPTER 22
Review

Solidarity formed. Ronald Reagan elected president.	Martial law declared in Poland. Sandra Day O'Connor appointed to Supreme Court.	U.S. troops invade Grenada.	Soviet Union boycotts Summer Olympics. Ronald Reagan reelected president.
1980	**1981**	**1983**	**1984**

WRITING A SUMMARY
Using the essential points of the chapter as a guide, write a summary of the chapter.

REVIEWING CHRONOLOGY
Number your paper 1 to 5. Study the time line above, and list the following events in the order in which they happened by writing the first next to 1, the second next to 2, and so on. Then complete the activity below.

1. U.S. troops invade Grenada.
2. Bill Clinton elected president.
3. Tax Reform Law passed.
4. Solidarity formed.
5. Thomas-Hill hearings occur.

Analyzing What was the purpose of the Gramm-Rudman-Hollings Act?

IDENTIFYING PEOPLE AND IDEAS
Explain the historical significance of each of the following people or terms.

1. Solidarity
2. contras
3. Geraldine Ferraro
4. insider trading
5. Boris Yeltsin
6. Saddam Hussein
7. H. Ross Perot
8. Ruth Bader Ginsburg
9. AIDS
10. universal coverage

UNDERSTANDING MAIN IDEAS
1. How did the Reagan administration fight the Cold War? Why did U.S.-Soviet relations improve in the late 1980s?
2. What domestic challenges did Presidents Bush and Reagan face during their terms?
3. How did President Bush show America's world leadership?
4. Why did Americans want to reform health care in the 1990s? Why did health care reform cause debate?
5. How did events in foreign nations involve the United States in the early 1990s?

REVIEWING THEMES
1. **Economic Development** What effects did Reaganomics have on the country?
2. **Democratic Values** In what ways might technological advances help increase voter participation in the election process?

THINKING CRITICALLY
Comparing and Contrasting How did the scandal surrounding the Iran-contra affair prove both similar to and different from the Watergate scandal?
2. **Synthesizing** Why might 1991, 1992, and 1993 all be called "the year of the woman"?

STRATEGY FOR SUCCESS
Review the Skills Handbook entry on Studying Primary and Secondary Sources beginning on page 758. Then read the following two excerpts from the 1984 presidential campaign. The first is from a speech by Jesse Jackson. The second is from a Republican commercial for Ronald Reagan. How do these two selections reflect different views of America?

“ Our flag is red, white and blue, but our nation is rainbow—red, yellow, brown, black and white. . . . America is not like a blanket—one piece of unbroken cloth, the same color, the same texture, the same size. America is more like a quilt—many patches, many pieces, many colors, many sizes, all woven and held together by a common thread. . . .
  Even in our fractured state, all of us count and fit somewhere. . . . We have not proven that we can win or make progress without each other. We must come together. ”

“ In a town not too far from where you live, a young family has just moved into a new home. Three years ago, even the smallest house seemed completely out of reach. Right down the street, one of the neighbors has just bought himself a new car, with all the options.

REVIEWING THEMES

1. Reaganomics helped to stimulate the economy through tax cuts and fewer regulations on industry, but decreased government support for social programs.
2. Students might mention widespread use of public formats such as TV talk shows and radio call-in programs to involve voters and heighten awareness of the issues.

THINKING CRITICALLY

1. similar—involved secret and illegal actions, led to investigations by Congress, resulted in resignations of key White House officials; different—did not lead to impeachment charges against Reagan or undermine his presidency
2. 1991—publicity for problems of sexual harassment during Thomas-Hill hearings; 1992—increased numbers of women candidates; 1993—presidential appointments of women to top posts

STRATEGY FOR SUCCESS

One emphasizes cultural diversity and the need for more programs and unity. The other emphasizes material comforts and assurance that all is well.

WRITING ABOUT HISTORY

Essays might mention the increased emphasis on social and economic problems represented by passage of these bills.

USING PRIMARY SOURCES

driven out businesses and sources of income

LINKING HISTORY AND GEOGRAPHY

MA, NY, WI, IA, WA, OR

| 1985 | 1986 | 1987 | 1988 | 1989 | 1990 | 1991 | 1992 | 1993 |

Gramm-Rudman-Hollings Act passed. Mikhail Gorbachev becomes leader of Soviet Union.

Tax Reform Law passed. Congress investigates Iran-contra affair. Stock market crashes.

INF Treaty ratified. George Bush elected president.

Berlin Wall falls.

Americans with Disabilities Act passed. Iraq invades Kuwait.

Commonwealth of Independent states formed. Thomas-Hill hearings occur.

Bill Clinton elected president.

Family and Medical Leave Act signed. Ruth Bader Ginsburg appointed to Supreme Court.

The factory down the river is working again. Not long ago, people were saying it probably would be closed forever. . . . Life is better. America is back. **99**

WRITING ABOUT HISTORY
Writing to Explain Write an essay that explains the significance of the passage of the Americans with Disabilities Act, the Omnibus Budget Reconciliation Act, or the Family and Medical Leave Act.

USING PRIMARY SOURCES
The crime problem of the 1980s and 1990s hit African American communities particularly hard. In 1992, for example, African American men between the ages of 16 and 24 were three to four times as likely to be victims of handgun crimes as were their white counterparts. In an interview conducted that same year, Los Angeles's chief of police, Willie L. Williams, expressed his impressions of African American concerns in Los Angeles. According to Williams, how has crime affected African American neighborhoods?

66 Crime . . . has a long-term effect on the [African American] community because it drives out the mom-and-pop businesses, the corner stores, where a lot

Willie L. Williams

of shopping is done. It drives out the source of income for the teenagers and the young adults who don't have a lot of skills or are just going to school to learn skills. It often drives out the source of income for parents who may be living and working at home and working in the area. The cost of crime in the African-American community cannot be underestimated. **99**

LINKING HISTORY AND GEOGRAPHY
Refer to the maps on page 573 and page 596. Which states did the Democratic party win in 1988 that it did not win in 1980?

BUILDING YOUR PORTFOLIO

Complete the following projects independently or cooperatively.

1. **POLITICS** In Chapter 21 you were a reporter covering Watergate. Building on that experience, imagine you are covering the Iran-contra affair. Create a flow chart that traces the Iran-contra transfer of weapons, money, and supplies.

2. **THE ECONOMY** In Chapter 21 you examined oil prices and inflation. Building on that experience, imagine you are one of President Reagan's economic advisers. Prepare a pamphlet describing the principles and goals of Reaganomics.

3. **GLOBAL RELATIONS** In Chapter 21 you portrayed a delegate to the United Nations. Building on that experience, write a speech explaining what effects the end of the Cold War has had on your nation. Your speech should indicate both the positive and the negative ways in which the end of the Cold War has affected your nation.

BUILDING YOUR PORTFOLIO

Have students refer to **Building Your Portfolio Worksheet 5**, assigned at the beginning of Unit 5. Use the worksheet to help students monitor their progress on the portfolio projects.

*A*ssessment

Core Resources
- Reteaching Worksheet 22
- Chapter 22 Tests
- Alternative Assessment Forms

Test Generator

STORIES OF DIVERSITY

UNIT 5

American Letters

Stories of Diversity

More than 10 million immigrants arrived on American shores between 1970 and 1989, most of them from Asia or Latin America. In the following selections, Chinese American author Gish Jen, Mexican American poet Jimmy Santiago Baca, and Philippine-born novelist Jessica Hagedorn explore the struggles of characters who are fully American yet retain ties to their country of origin.

▲ *Jimmy Santiago Baca*

From *Typical American*

by Gish Jen

"We are family," echoed Helen.

"Team," said Ralph. "We should have name. The Chinese Yankees. Call Chang-kees for short."

"Chang-kees!" Everyone laughed.

Ball games became even more fun. Theresa explained how the

▼ **Portrait of a Chinese Family (1985), by Tomie Arai**

Yankees had lost the Series to the Dodgers the year before; they rooted for a comeback. "Let's go Chang-kees!" This was in the privacy of their apartment, in front of their newly bought used Zenith TV; the one time they went to an actual game, people had called them names and told them to go back to their laundry. They in turn had sat impassive as the scoreboard. Rooting in their hearts, they said later. Anyway, they preferred to stay home and watch. "More comfortable." "More convenient." "Can see better," they agreed.

These were the same reasons Ralph advocated buying a car.

"*Seems like someone's becoming[1] one-hundred-percent Americanized,*" Theresa kidded.

"*What's so American? We had a car, growing up. Don't you remember?*" Ralph argued that in fact this way they could avoid getting too Americanized. "*Everywhere we go, we can keep the children inside. Also they won't catch cold.*"

"*I thought we agreed the children are going to be American,*" puzzled Helen.

Ralph furrowed his brow. When Callie turned three they had decided that Mona and Callie would learn English first, and then Chinese. This was what Janis and Old Chao were planning on doing with Alexander; Janis didn't want him to have an accent. For Ralph and Helen, it was a more practical decision. Callie had seemed confused by *outside people* sometimes understanding her and sometimes not. Playing with other children in the park, she had several times started to cry, and once or twice to throw things; she had lost a doll this way, and a dragon. Also, one grabby little boy had, in an ensuing ruckus, lost some teeth. . . .

Now Ralph drummed his fingers. He stopped and smiled.

"*And what better way to Americanize the children than to buy a car!*" ❖

___
1 Italics indicate words spoken in Chinese.

from "Martín IV," Martín and Meditations on the South Valley

by Jimmy Santiago Baca

On visiting days with aunts and
    uncles,
I was shuttled back and forth—
between Chavez bourgeois in the
    city
and rural Lucero sheepherders,
new cars and gleaming furniture
and leather saddles and burlap
    sacks,
noon football games and six packs
    of cokes
and hoes, welfare cards and
    bottles of goat milk.

I was caught in the middle—
between white skinned, English
    speaking altar boy
at the communion railing,
and brown skinned, Spanish
    speaking plains nomadic child
with buffalo heart groaning under-
    world earth powers,
between Sunday brunch at a
    restaurant
and burritos eaten in a tin-roofed
    barn,
between John Wayne on the
    afternoon movie
rifle butting young Braves,
and the Apache whose red
    dripping arrow
was the altar candle in praise of
    the buck
just killed.

Caught between Indio-Mejicano
    rural uncles
who stacked hundred pound sacks
    of pinto beans
on boxcars all day, and worked
    the railroad tracks
behind the Sturgis sheds, who
    sang Apache songs
with accordions, and Chavez
    uncles and aunts

who vacationed and followed the
    Hollywood model
of My Three Sons for their own
    families,
sweeping the kitchen before
    anyone came to visit,
looking at photo albums in the
    parlor. ❖

"Luna Moth" from *Dogeaters*

by Jessica Hagedorn

Without warning, [my mother]
cheerfully announces she is sending me to school in America and
moving there with me for an
indefinite period. I am ecstatic, at
first. Everyone else is stunned. My
father cannot stop her—my
mother has inherited money from
her father and pays for our passage to America. We settle first in
New York, then Boston. I convince myself I am not homesick,
and try not to bring up my father
or brother when I speak. My
mother actually sells a few paintings. The months turn into years.
"Are we going to stay here
forever?" I finally ask her. She
looks surprised. "I don't know
about you, but I love the cold
weather. Go back to Manila if you
want. Tell Raul I miss him more
than he could ever imagine." She
smiles one of her cryptic smiles.
"But he'll have to visit me here if
he wants to see me—" her voice
trails off. . . .

When I finally come home to
Manila to visit, my father warns
me not to bother visiting our old
house. "You'll be disappointed.
Memories are always better."
Smiling apologetically, he tells me
reality will diminish the grandeur
of my childhood image of home.
I take his picture with my new
camera, which later falls in the
swimming pool by accident. The
camera is destroyed, along with
my roll of film. I decide to visit
our old house . . . anyway, borrowing a car from Mikey. Pucha
goes with me; she loves riding
around in cars and doesn't need
any excuse. . . .

My father is right. The house
with its shuttered windows looks
smaller than I remember, and
dingy. The once lush and sprawling garden is now a forlorn landscape of rocks, weeds, and wild
ferns. The bamboo grove has
been cut down. "Let's go," Pucha
whispers, impatient and uninter-
ested. An old man with bright
eyes introduces himself as Manong
Tibo, the caretaker. He unlocks
door after door for us, pulling
aside cobwebs, warning us to be
careful. Rotting floorboards creak
under the weight of our footsteps.
"My bedroom," I say to the old
man, who nods. I am over-
whelmed by melancholy at the
sight of the empty room. A frightened mouse dashes across the
grimy tiled floor. ❖

THINKING AND WRITING ABOUT LITERATURE

1. How do Gish Jen's characters become "Americanized"? What aspects of Chinese culture do they retain?
2. In Baca's poem, what two different ways of life do the two sides of the speaker's family represent? Which do you think he prefers? Why?
3. Why is Jessica Hagedorn's character disappointed when she sees her old home? Do you think she is happy in the United States?

THINKING AND WRITING ABOUT LITERATURE

1. *They buy a television, watch baseball games, teach their children to speak English first, and decide to buy a car. They continue to speak Chinese.*
2. *One side represents mainstream American life and the other represents his ethnic heritage and the lifestyles of many Mexican Americans. He seems to prefer his Lucero relatives, who represent traditional ways of life.*
3. *Her old house is abandoned and is smaller and dirtier than she remembers. She does not seem completely happy in the U.S. because she asks, "Are we going to stay here forever?"*

EVALUATING NEWS STORIES

Guide students through the discussion of how to evaluate news stories and then have them complete the Practicing the Strategy exercise. Ask students to imagine that they are newspaper reporters and have them write a news story on one of the following topics: the Moral Majority, the Strategic Defense Initiative, the health care crisis, Operation Desert Storm, the confirmation hearings of Clarence Thomas, the "Year of the Woman," or the *Challenger* disaster. Each story should include a headline, date, and byline and should answer the questions *who, what, when, where,* and *how.* Students should make use of newspaper and magazine reports when preparing their stories.

PRACTICING THE STRATEGY

Essays will vary according to the topics chosen. Each should include an evaluation of the issue as covered by both print and broadcast media, describing the depth of coverage, presence (if any) of bias in the reporting, and the impact of the story on the student.

Strategies for Success

EVALUATING NEWS STORIES

nformation today comes at us in a flood—from talk shows to tabloids, from the morning headlines to the nightly news. Today's news reporting will become the basis of tomorrow's history, so evaluating news stories contributes to your understanding of current history. News sources, which collectively are called the news media, can be divided into two groups: *broadcast media* and *print media.*

▲ **Bill Clinton jamming on *The Arsenio Hall Show,* 1992**

Broadcast Media

Broadcast media include television and radio. Television is, by far, the dominant medium for news. Surveys show that Americans are much more inclined to watch TV news than to read a daily newspaper. Television, like no other medium, presents the opportunity to witness history in the making. TV and radio can provide on-the-spot, around-the-clock coverage, creating a sense of immediacy. Also, both increasingly offer "instant

analysis" to go with their reporting. Broadcasters like CNN, the 24-hour all-news cable network, and "talk radio" have greatly expanded the amount and kind of news available over the air.

Print Media

Print media include newspapers, weekly newsmagazines like *News-week* and *Time,* and other publications that cover current events. Newspapers, particularly such big-city dailies as the *New York Times* or the *Chicago Tribune,* give detailed accounts of national and world events as they occur. Newsmagazines, which have more time to prepare their stories, specialize in in-depth analyses of issues.

How to Evaluate News Media

To evaluate news reporting, ask questions like the following:

■ **Coverage.** Is the subject treated superficially or in-depth? Does the reporting include information on the background to a story? Does it explore long-range implications of events?
■ **Fairness and accuracy.** Does the reporting stick to the facts? Is it fair and balanced? Is there any recognizable bias in the coverage?
■ **Immediacy and interest.** How close in time is the reporting to the event? Have there been new develop-

ments since the story was written or broadcast? Is the news presented in an interesting way?

Applying the Strategy

Choose a topic that is frequently in the news and that has been covered both in print and on radio and TV. Evaluate recent reporting on the issue in terms of the categories listed above. First, examine how well the reporting covers the *why* and *how* of the event, as well as the *who, what, when,* and *where.* Remember that each story has a wider context, a past and a future; good reporting will bring out these connections. Second, consider whether the story is told objectively. Every reporter has a point of view, so be alert for any expression of bias. Finally, note whether any late-breaking developments have changed the situation as last reported. Evaluate the reporting for the level of interest it creates, keeping in mind that a complex subject such as a financial scandal may be hard to present in exciting images or film footage.

Practicing the Strategy

Choose another current topic and examine reporting about it by each of the following: a TV network news program, a major daily newspaper, a public-radio program, and a national weekly newsmagazine. Write a brief essay evaluating the treatment of the issue or event by the different news media, describing the depth of the coverage offered by each, the presence of bias in any of the reporting, and the way the story affects you.

BUILDING YOUR PORTFOLIO

Each portfolio project described below is the culmination of the Building Your Portfolio activities in the chapter reviews of Unit 5. First, decide whether you wish students to work individually or in groups on these unit projects. Then permit each student to choose the project on which he or she desires to work. Provide students with copies of **Building Your Portfolio Worksheet 5** from *Core Resources*. This worksheet will guide students step by step to complete their projects.

BUILDING YOUR PORTFOLIO

Outlined below are three projects. Independently or cooperatively, complete one and use the products to demonstrate your mastery of the historical concepts involved.

1 POLITICS
The Watergate scandal and the Iran-contra affair challenged the foundation of constitutional government. Using the portfolio materials you designed in chapters 21 and 22, write an editorial that examines the ways in which the Watergate scandal was both similar to and different from the Iran-contra affair.

2 THE ECONOMY
Stagflation and the effects of the energy crisis are only two of the economic problems presidents Nixon, Ford, and Carter struggled with in the 1970s. In the 1980s President Reagan attempted to stimulate the American economy through a series of conservative reforms. Using the portfolio materials you designed in chapters 21 and 22, prepare a presentation on the different ways in which governmental actions and policies regarding the economy of a nation can affect the people of that nation.

3 GLOBAL RELATIONS
During the 1970s and 1980s, the United States opened negotiations with China, improved relations with the Soviet Union, and witnessed the end of the Cold War and the breakup of the Soviet Union. Regional and local conflicts emerged, however, as new nations were torn apart by ethnic and religious struggles. Using the portfolio materials you designed in chapters 21 and 22, conduct a panel discussion about the new world order that highlights the sometimes conflicting interests of the superpowers, industrialized nations, and developing nations.

Videodisc Review

In assigned groups, develop an outline for a video collage of America in the years between 1970 and the present. Choose images that best illustrate the major topics of the period. Write a script to accompany the images. Assign narrators to different parts of the script, and present your video collage to the class.

Further Reading

David, Peter. *Triumph in the Desert: The Challenge, the Fighting, the Legacy.* Random House (1991). Photographic history of the Persian Gulf War.

Edelstein, Andrew J., and Kevin McDonough. *The Seventies: From Hot Pants to Hot Tubs.* Dutton (1990). Social history of the 1970s.

Glynn, Patrick. *Closing Pandora's Box: Arms Races, Arms Control, and the History of the Cold War.* BasicBooks (1992). Analysis of the Cold War from a post–Cold War perspective.

Johnson, Haynes. *Sleepwalking through History: America in the Reagan Years.* Norton (1991). Overview and critical analysis of the Reagan years.

Moore, Jim, with Rick Ihde. *Clinton: Young Man in a Hurry.* The Summit Group (1992). Biography detailing the rise of Bill Clinton to become the 42nd president of the United States.

Virga, Vincent. *The Eighties: Images of America.* Edward Burlingame Books (1992). Photographic essay on life in the United States during the 1980s.

Woodward, Bob, and Carl Bernstein. *The Final Days.* Simon & Schuster (1976). Chronicle of the last days of Richard Nixon's presidency.

PORTFOLIO ASSESSMENT

1. *Editorials should demonstrate an understanding of the roots and consequences of the Watergate scandal and the Iran-contra affair.*

2. *Charts and pamphlets should show the effects of rising oil prices on the U.S. economy in the 1970s and the goals and effects of Reaganomics in the 1980s.*

3. *The panel discussion should show an understanding of the effect on other nations of the Cold War rivalry between the U.S. and the Soviet Union.*

Introducing the Unit

- **Chapter 23**
  IMPERIALISM TO NEW
  WORLD ORDER
- **Chapter 24**
  FROM INDUSTRIALIZATION
  TO GLOBAL ECONOMY
- **Chapter 25**
  THE MOVEMENT OF PEOPLE
  AND IDEAS
- **Chapter 26**
  THE STRUGGLE FOR HUMAN
  RIGHTS
- **Chapter 27**
  A NEW ENVIRONMENTAL
  AWARENESS

UNIT OVERVIEW

The momentous changes
that have taken place in the
United States have not
occured in a vacuum.
People and events in other
nations have influenced the
development of the United
States, and events within
U.S. borders have also
exerted an influence over
other countries. The world
has seen dramatic changes
in political and economic
structures, living patterns,
beliefs about human rights,
and attitudes toward the
environment. In order to
fully comprehend the nature
of American beliefs and
developments, it is necessary to understand the
increasingly global nature
of many different issues.

CORE RESOURCES

- **American Almanac
  Worksheet 6**
- **Building Your Port-
  folio Worksheet 6**
  You may wish to pre-
  view the Unit 6 Review
  and Building Your Port-
  folio performance
  assessment activities on
  p. 745.

Using the Almanac

Review the almanac entries with students. Then ask
students to use information in the almanac to write
a one-paragraph portrait of the American experience during the 20th century. Call on volunteers to
read their portraits to the class.

American ALMANAC

❖ Computers and Technology

Today The world's computer and
computer software industry is worth
$360,000,000,000!

1989 The number of telephones
for every 100 people: in New York
City, 56; in Tokyo, 44; in Seoul, 22;
in Mexico City, 6; in Cairo, 4; in
Beijing, 2

COMPUTERS PER 1000 PERSONS, 1993	
U.S.	265
Canada	162
Singapore	116
Japan	84
Mexico	13
China	2

▼ Rickshaw

▼ Breakdancers

❖ Speaking of Which...

English changes all the time. Here are
some recent additions, with the dates
when they are known to have first
been used: *ditsy* (1978), *aerobics*
(1968), *breakdancing* (1982), *user-
friendly* (1970s), *biodegradable,
biorhythm, biosphere, ecosphere*
(mid-20th century).

Some new words have come from
other languages: *apartheid,* from
Afrikaans, spoken in South Africa
(mid-20th century), *moped,* from
Swedish (mid-20th century), *ciao,*
from Italian (early-20th century),
cowabunga, from
Australia (1950s),
futon, from Japanese
(early 1980s), *glas-
nost,* from Russian
(1985), *karaoke,* from
Japanese (1980s),
lambada, from
Brazilian Portuguese,
(1987), *radicchio,*
from Italian (late
1970s).

❖ Getting Around

1980s Americans and people in
the former Soviet Union spent the
same time commuting—though
Americans traveled farther and drove,
while Soviets walked or took public
transportation.

1990 In 1950 there was one
car for every 46 people in the
world—today there is one car for
every 12! The number of people for
every car: in India, 360; in Nigeria,
150; in the United States, 2

Today Traffic jams! The U.S.
General Accounting Offices says traffic
tie-ups cost the country $100 billion
a year in lost productivity. Officials
in Thailand estimate that the country
loses an average of 44 work days
a year because people are stuck in
traffic!

Today Almost 3 million
Americans ride bicycles to work—
three times as many as ten years ago.

Today In India and Pakistan one
out of five, and in Bangladesh more
than two out of five, trips taken are
by cycle rickshaw—a small rickshaw
pulled by a bicycle.

Today In Manila, the Philippines,
commuters on the light rail spend 15
minutes traveling the distance it
sometimes takes 2 hours to drive!

Computers and Technology

Tell students that computers differ from traditional heavy industries because each unit is small in size and has a high value.

▪▪ Ask students to discuss how these characteristics might increase profits.

Getting Around

Point out to students that in 1950 the United States had about as many cars per person as the United Kingdom had in 1980.

▪▪ Ask students why America has such a marked history of car ownership.

Speaking of Which . . .

Explain to students that the English language, even before colonists came to America, was influenced by a number of different languages, including Latin and French.

▪▪ Ask students to name additional words that have come from other languages.

At Your Leisure

Point out that in 1975 Pelé had come out of retirement to play for the Cosmos.

▪▪ Encourage students to name other athletes who decided to return to professional sports after retiring. Ask why an athlete might come back from retirement.

The Global Economy

Tell students that while the population has grown by 108% since 1950, world grain production has grown by 182%, beef and mutton production has increased by 158%, and the fish catch has grown by 355%.

▪▪ Ask students to consider why agricultural production has grown faster than the population.

Changing World

Point out that experts predict that the world's population will total 8.5 billion in 2025, and that 7.1 billion people will live in cities.

▪▪ Ask students to consider the difficulties of living in crowded urban areas.

Our Environment: Keeping Track

Tell students that in some parts of Nicaragua, small amounts of a crop are planted a few weeks early to attract pests, which can then be destroyed by hand or with small amounts of pesticides.

▪▪ Ask students why farmers might reduce pesticide use.

UNIT

6

The American Experience

IN GLOBAL CONTEXT

▼ Brazilian soccer player Pelé

▲ Tropical bird

❖ At Your Leisure

1977 Legendary Brazilian soccer star, Pelé, played his last professional game as a member of the New York Cosmos against his former team, the Santos of Brazil—Pelé almost single-handedly sparked an interest in soccer in the United States.

Today Video Mania! People in the industrialized nations spend $9 billion a year on video games for children.

❖ The Global Economy

1992 From 1950 to 1992 the value of goods traded worldwide grew from $308 million to $3.58 trillion!

❖ Changing World

Today In 1950 a baby born in the industrialized world could expect to live 66 years, while a baby born in the developing world could expect to live about 40 years; in 1994 life expectancy had increased to 75 in the industrialized world and 62 in the developing world.

Today Most of the population growth in the industrialized world occurs in the United States!

Tomorrow For the next several decades the world population will grow—by an expected 90 million or more each year—and 95 percent of the growth will occur in the developing world!

❖ Our Environment: Keeping Track

1980 From 1700 to 1980 world forests and woodlands shrank 20% while croplands grew 460%.

Today 40%-90% of the world's species live in tropical forests.

Today From roughly 1850 to 1950 the number of blue whales has dropped from 200,000 to 2,000; humpback whales, from 125,000 to 10,000; and the Juan Fernandez fur seal, from 4 million to 600. Among the few species that have made recoveries—Pacific gray whales, from 10,000 to 21,000; walruses, from 50,000 to 280,000; Galapagos fur seals, from near extinction to 30,000.

▼ Baby seal

IMPERIALISM TO NEW WORLD ORDER

THE AMERICAN NATION VIDEODISC PROGRAM
A variety of still images, short videos, and activities are available for you to use as you teach this chapter. See Videodisc Resources in the Core Resources Binder for barcode correlations and suggestions for using the program.

Chapter Overview

The late 19th and early 20th centuries saw the growth of great European empires. Even the U.S., despite its support for republican anti-imperialism, sought to build an empire. After World War I, many colonial powers were weakened. World War II continued this process, and in the postwar years decolonization began.

The Cold War, however, complicated the move toward decolonization. Many newly independent nations attempted to remain neutral in the Cold War. Even so, their need for development aid often drew them into close ties with either the United States or the Soviet Union. At the same time, they continued to face problems related to their colonial past.

Chapter Planning Guide

CHAPTER 23	CORE RESOURCES	AUDIOVISUAL RESOURCES	PROGRAM RESOURCES
INTRODUCTION pp. 620–621	■ Building Your Portfolio Worksheet 6		
TEACHING THE CHAPTER pp. 622–643	■ Graphic Organizer 23 ■ Social Studies Skills Worksheet 23 ■ Geography Worksheet 23 ■ Literature Worksheet 23 ■ Outline Maps 1, 2, 12, 14, 16, 17, 19, 20, 21, 22, 24	■ *The American Nation Videodisc:* The Spanish Mission System; The Panama Canal; John F. Kennedy's Berlin Speech ■ Linking Geography and History Transparencies and Worksheets 15, 24 ■ Everyday Life in America Transparencies and Worksheets 19, 25	■ *Eyewitnesses and Others,* Volume 1: Readings 3, 35; Volume 2: Readings 13, 23
REVIEW AND ASSESSMENT pp. 624–625	■ Chapter 23 Daily Quizzes ■ Reteaching Worksheet 23 ■ Chapter 23 Tests ■ Alternative Assessment Forms		■ Test Generator

Additional Resources

BOOKS FOR TEACHERS

Baumgart, Winfried. *Imperialism: The Idea and Reality of British and French Colonial Expansion, 1880–1914.* Oxford University Press, 1982. Critical examination of the arguments and issues surrounding imperialism.

Hobsbawm, E.J. *The Age of Empire: 1875–1914.* Pantheon Books, 1987. Thorough study of the great age of European imperialism.

Kiernan, V.G. *European Empires from Conquest to Collapse, 1815–1960.* Pantheon Books, 1982. Examines the rise and fall of European imperial power.

BOOKS FOR STUDENTS

*Amey, Peter. *Imperialism.* Greenhaven Press, 1980. Reviews the rise and decline of European colonial empires.

Davidson, Basil. *African Civilization Revisited.* Africa World Press, 1991. Later chapters focus on colonization and the struggle for independence.

The Colonial Overlords: TimeFrame AD 1850–1900. Time-Life Books, 1990. Focuses on colonial developments in the late 1800s.

* for students reading below grade level

MULTIMEDIA MATERIALS

Imperialism. Video, 44 min. EAV/SSSS. Examines imperialism and its effects in Latin America, India, and Africa.

Imperialism—Africa. Video, 30 min. Agency for Instructional Technology. Explains imperialism by looking at three countries in Africa.

India: The Brightest Jewel. 16 mm. film, 20 min. Films Incorporated. Focuses on the independence movement in India.

THEMES IN AMERICAN HISTORY

USE WITH PAGES 620-621

Listed on the right are the themes emphasized in Chapter 23. The questions in boldface type stimulate critical thinking and provide students with an opportunity to discuss the themes within a broadened context. The questions also appear in the pupil's edition on p. 620.

■ DEMOCRATIC VALUES

Can a democratic nation have an empire and still be a democracy? Students will point out that democracy is based on the right of people to rule themselves. Imperialism, which is based on one country ruling another, directly contradicts this principle. Students may note that in spite of this belief, democracies such as France, Great Britain, and the U.S. all practiced imperialism at some time.

■ CULTURAL DIVERSITY

How might empires promote cultural diversity? Students will mention that great empires encompass many countries whose people have diverse cultures. If the imperial power encouraged all the people under its rule to follow their own ways, cultural diversity would be promoted.

How might they discourage it? Students may point out that cultural diversity would be discouraged if the imperial power insisted that all people under its rule assimilate and adopt its way of life.

■ GLOBAL RELATIONS

How might small nations avoid becoming entangled in major world rivalries? Students may suggest that the small nations might band together to avoid entanglements in major world rivalries. Some form of alliance would provide mutual protection. It also would increase economic power for the smaller nations and lessen their dependence on the great powers.

CHAPTER STRATEGIES FOR MEETING INDIVIDUAL NEEDS

LIMITED ENGLISH PROFICIENT LEARNERS

Have students work in pairs to select an illustration from each section in the chapter. Ask pairs to write a new caption for each selection that explains the illustration's significance and relation to the section content.

TACTILE/KINESTHETIC LEARNERS

Have students work in small groups to sketch the key events in the rise and decline of imperialism. Ask groups to use their sketches to create a mural or an illustrated time line on imperialism.

LEARNERS HAVING DIFFICULTY

Organize students into four groups. Assign each group one section of the chapter. Have each group develop questions and answers about the main ideas in their section. Then have each group quiz the other groups with its questions.

AUDITORY LEARNERS

Have students research speeches on imperialism by some of the people mentioned in the chapter. Ask students to prepare dramatic readings of the speeches they select.

VISUAL LEARNERS

Organize students into small groups to design posters on imperialism from the viewpoint of either leaders of a late 19th century colonial power or leaders of independence movements in India or Africa. Have groups display and explain their posters.

GIFTED LEARNERS

Encourage students to write an essay supporting or challenging the following statement: *The vast majority of problems facing the world today are the result of imperialism.*

USING THE CHAPTER FOCUS

■ UNDERSTANDING THE MAIN IDEA

Call on a volunteer to read aloud the Understanding the Main Idea paragraph and to define the term *imperialism*. Ask students to speculate on why the two world wars weakened the great European empires. Then have them suggest what the legacies of imperialism might be. Have students review and adjust their speculations as they read the chapter.

THEMES

Have students work individually or in groups to answer the questions under Themes. Save students' responses so that they can compare them with their responses after studying the chapter. (See p. 619B for suggested answers.)

■ THE TIME LINE

Ask students to imagine that the time line entries are newspaper headlines. As they read the part of the chapter that pertains to each entry, have students write short newspaper articles that explain how the event relates to the development of imperialism.

CORE RESOURCES

• **Graphic Organizer 23**
• **Building Your Portfolio Worksheet 6**

620

ABOUT THE ILLUSTRATION

The Boxer Rebellion attempted to drive foreigners out of China in 1900. Years of foreign involvement in China—and the establishment of spheres of influence—encouraged many Chinese to resent the U.S. and European powers. An international military force was able to suppress the rebellion and ensure the safety of foreigners in China. Ask students to name recent conflicts that have involved the U.S. military as part of an international alliance.

Chapter 23

IMPERIALISM TO NEW WORLD ORDER

FOCUS

UNDERSTANDING THE MAIN IDEA

The 20th century began as the great age of European empires. Even the United States briefly engaged in imperialism. But two world wars weakened the empires, which dissolved after World War II. Only the Soviet Union's empire survived into the 1980s, and it too had collapsed by the early 1990s. Yet many legacies of imperialism remain.

THEMES

■ **DEMOCRATIC VALUES**
Can a democratic nation hold an empire and still be upholding the principles of democracy?

■ **CULTURAL DIVERSITY**
How do empires promote cultural diversity? How do they discourage it?

■ **GLOBAL RELATIONS**
How might small nations avoid becoming entangled in major world rivalries?

1898	1934	1947	1955	1967
Battle of Omdurman leaves thousands of Africans dead.	U.S. Congress passes Tydings-McDuffie Act.	Britain grants India and Pakistan independence.	Bandung Conference held in Indonesia.	Civil war breaks out in Nigeria.

LINK TO THE PAST

Ask students to recall an example of how imperialism and anti-imperialism each shaped American history during the late 19th century. *(imperialism: manifest destiny, expansion in late 19th and early 20th centuries; anti-imperialism: republican ideals, Monroe Doctrine)* Then point out that this chapter reviews the rise and decline of imperialism and analyzes the lasting legacy of colonial rule.

LINK TO THE PAST

The American colonies were established as outposts of the British Empire during the first age of European imperialism. But the success of the American Revolution made the nation a "child" of anti-imperialism. Both imperialism and anti-imperialism continued to shape the history of the United States and the world.

PRIMARY SOURCE
Description of Change: excerpted
Rationale: excerpted to focus on main idea

U.S. soldiers in Shanghai, China, during the Boxer Rebellion, 1900

*D*uring a meeting with a delegation of Methodist missionaries in 1898, President McKinley explained his position regarding annexation of the Philippines. The president said he had prayed long and hard for guidance.

    ❝ And one night late it came to me this way—I don't know how it was, but it came: (1) That we could not give them back to Spain—that would be cowardly and dishonorable; (2) that we could not turn them over to France or Germany—our commercial rivals in the Orient—that would be bad business and discreditable; (3) that we could not leave them to themselves—they were unfit for self-government—and they would soon have anarchy and misrule over there worse than Spain's was; and (4) that there was nothing left for us to do but to take them all, and to educate the Filipinos, and uplift and civilize and Christianize them. ❞

McKinley's attitude was typical of the time. At the height of imperialism, it combined arrogance, ignorance (nearly all the Filipinos were already Christians), and benevolence. But times would change.

Sir Hiram S. Maxim, inventor of the first fully-automatic machine gun (1883)

PREVIEW WORKSHOP

Following is a list of the significant people and terms in this section. You may wish to use this list as a section preview.

■ Battle of Omdurman
■ direct rule
■ indirect rule

People
■ Rudyard Kipling

Terms
■ coaling stations

MOTIVATING: PRIOR KNOWLEDGE

Ask volunteers to suggest reasons for U.S. interest in imperialism during the late 1800s. *(industrialization and increased dependence on world trade, desire for overseas military bases and fueling stations, interest in spreading Christianity and American political system)* As students study the section, have them compare these motives for renewed interest in imperialism on the part of European nations.

FOCUS OBJECTIVES

■ Illustrate how both imperialism and anti-imperialism marked America's early years.

■ Compare American expansion to Russian expansion.

■ Describe the connections that existed between industrialization and imperialism during the late 19th century.

■ Explain why the imperial powers differed in how they governed their colonies.

CORE RESOURCES

• **Geography Worksheet 23**
• **Literature Worksheet 23**
• **Section 1 Daily Quiz**

AV RESOURCES

• *The American Nation* **Videodisc: The Spanish Mission System; The Panama Canal**
• **Linking Geography and History Transparency** and **Worksheet 15**
• **Everyday Life in America Transparency** and **Worksheet 19**

622

Section 1

IMPERIALISM TO WORLD WAR I

FOCUS

■ **How did both imperialism and anti-imperialism mark America's early years?**
■ **How did American expansion compare to Russian expansion?**
■ **What connections existed between industrialization and imperialism during the late 19th century?**
■ **Why did the imperial powers differ in how they governed their colonies?**

Although many Americans believed that imperialism contradicted republicanism, the United States sometimes benefited from imperialism and expansion. By 1900 the United States had joined European powers in a movement to expand overseas.

British soldier, 1778

BORN OF EMPIRE

Americans have never been strangers to imperialism. In many ways, the United States owes its very existence to the first great age of European imperialism, which lasted from the late 1400s to the early 1800s. The founding of Britain's North American colonies during the 17th century was part of a British strategy to gain an advantage in the ongoing struggle against other European nations for trade and territory.

This struggle eventually helped spark the American Revolution. Tired of being treated as pawns in Britain's imperial efforts and of paying taxes to support wars that seemed to have little to do with their own welfare, American colonists declared independence.

▶ **American seamen took to carrying proof-of-citizenship papers to guard against possible impressment by the British navy.**

Even after Americans had won their independence, other nations' imperial ambitions continued to cause trouble. For 30 years after independence, U.S. merchants and sailors repeatedly found themselves caught in European crossfire. When their ships were seized by British and French naval vessels, American merchants lost cargoes. Furthermore, the British forced American sailors into service in the British navy. Twice the disputes that arose over these issues led to hostilities—with France in the 1790s and with Great Britain in the War of 1812.

The troubles with Great Britain and France confirmed Americans' distaste for imperialism. Americans had founded their country on the principle of republicanism—the right of people to rule themselves. Imperialism, which involved one country ruling another, contradicted this principle. And imperialism interfered with the rights of neutral third countries, as the Americans had recently discovered to their regret.

Teaching the Section

THE UNITED STATES AND IMPERIALISM

Work with students to create on the chalkboard a time line showing the role played by imperialism in the development of the U.S. up to the beginning of the 20th century. Then have students use information in the time line to write paragraphs explaining how both imperialism and anti-imperialism marked America's early years. Students may wish to include their paragraphs in their portfolios.

▲ In the early 1830s, under the provisions of the Indian Removal Act, the Choctaws were removed from Mississippi to Indian Territory. This painting of the journey, entitled *Choctaw Removal* (1966), was painted by Choctaw artist Valjean Hessing. Later in the 19th century, many Native Americans were forced onto reservations as settlers pushed even farther west.

Even so, Americans did occasionally benefit from European imperial conflicts. For example, the conflict between the British and the French was one reason the French aided the Patriots in the Revolutionary War. Then when the war ended, Britain granted the United States the eastern half of the Mississippi Valley in an effort to counterbalance French and Spanish territorial ambitions in North America. Americans did not question Britain's motives; they accepted the territory and were happy to have it.

During the 19th century, Americans practiced a kind of imperialism of their own as they expanded across North America. First they streamed into the land they had gained from the British. Soon they pushed even farther west into the Louisiana Territory, Texas, New Mexico, California, and Oregon. Like the Europeans, they gained some of this territory through warfare.

In all of this, Americans continued to voice support for the principles of republican anti-imperialism. They thought of themselves as creating something different from the European empires, and in some respects they were right. While the British, French, and Spanish imperial holdings were far-flung, the new U.S. territories were right next door. Furthermore, while the Europeans kept their holdings as colonies, the U.S. government eventually divided its new territories into states fully equal to the original states.

Yet in another regard American expansion resembled European imperialism. In both cases the wishes of the original inhabitants of the acquired regions were scarcely considered. The Europeans paid little attention to the needs and desires of the native inhabitants living in the colonies they claimed. Similarly, the U.S. government moved Native Americans off their original homelands and onto reservations, often using force.

■■ Although most early Americans disapproved of European imperialism, the United States occasionally benefited from it. Americans even expanded their own territorial holdings.

RUSSIA: ANOTHER LAND EMPIRE

The closest parallel to the American expansion of the 19th century took place halfway around the world, in Russia. Over several centuries, the Russian Empire moved primarily eastward, from its heartland west of the Ural Mountains to the Pacific coast of Asia and even to Alaska (which the United States purchased in 1867). By the 19th century, Russia's expansionist energies were mainly focused on central and far eastern Asia.

▲ During the 1890s Russian colonists expanded into the Far East, occupying villages such as this one near the Pacific coast of Siberia.

MULTICULTURAL PERSPECTIVES

Mexican officials in Texas were well aware of the difficulty of assimilating U.S. settlers. When debating approval of Austin's *empresario* contract, one official urged that the U.S. colonists be settled around San Antonio. He argued that if the colonists settled there, they would in time be assimilated by the city's native inhabitants. The official also stressed the importance of the settlers' being separated from the United States by an expanse of unsettled land.

THE AMERICAN NATION VIDEODISC PROGRAM

The Spanish Mission System

1A   32923   3:02

Teaching the Section

AMERICAN AND RUSSIAN EXPANSION

Draw on the chalkboard a two-column chart with *American Expansion* and *Russian Expansion* as column headings. Ask students to suggest the characteristics of American and Russian expansion, entering their responses in the appropriate column. Then have students use the information in the chart to create pictorial essays titled "American and Russian Expansion—Similarities and Differences." Call on volunteers to present and discuss their essays.

HISTORICAL SIDELIGHTS

Pan-Slavism

Russia's search for a "warm-water port" encouraged Pan-Slavism, or a union of all people who spoke Slavic languages. Nikolai Ia. Danilevskii, a philosopher and writer, suggested that Constantinople, as the center of the Orthodox church, should become Russian territory. He wrote: "What historical significance Constantinople would have if we could wrest her away from the Turks regardless of Europe! What delight would our hearts feel from the radiance of the cross that we would raise atop the dome of St. Sophia! . . .

"But Constantinople should not become Russia's capital. . . . but the capital of a Pan-Slav Union."

Danilevskii's proposed union consisted of much of eastern Europe controlled by the Soviet Union during the Cold War, as well as the former Yugoslavia and portions of present-day Greece and Turkey.

Russian expansion resembled U.S. expansion in a variety of ways. Like the United States, Russia expanded across a large land area by means of agricultural settlement and wars of conquest. In addition, both the Americans and the Russians carried with them their own cultural, economic, and political systems. Both used new industrial technologies, such as great railway systems, to unite their vast territories. And both developed a sense of manifest destiny, as the Americans put it, to justify their expansion.

▲ **The British fought Russian expansion in the Middle East during the mid-1800s. Here a British officer is shown relaxing in camp.**

Some contemporary observers noticed the similarity of the two expansions—the one in Asia, pushing to the Pacific from the west, the other in America, pushing to the Pacific from the east. Alexis de Tocqueville even predicted that Americans and Russians had parallel futures. "Their starting-point is different," Tocqueville wrote, "and their courses are not the same; yet each of them seems marked out by the will of Heaven to sway the destinies of half the globe."

For all the similarities between Russian and American expansion, there were also important differences. For example, in the United States millions of foreign immigrants were among the waves of settlers who moved west. The lands these settlers occupied were inhabited by comparatively small numbers of Native Americans. In Russia, on the other hand, most settlers were ethnic Russians who generally occupied and ruled lands with large non-Russian populations.

Russian expansion was also largely driven by the need to obtain a "warm-water port" that could be used year-round. Many Russian ports were on northern seas and were frozen over during winter months. Russia did have ice-free ports on the Black Sea, but these were of limited use since the Ottoman Empire controlled the outlet from the Black Sea into the Mediterranean. Because overseas trade was essential to a nation's prosperity and security, this limitation worried Russia's rulers. Thus even after reaching the Pacific, Russia continued to look south toward the Mediterranean and the Indian Ocean.

■■ **Like the Americans, Russians expanded across a huge land area. But Russian expansion differed from American expansion in several important ways.**

---

*I*MPERIALISM RENEWED

Russian imperialism was something of an exception in Europe during the first part of the 1800s. Despite their earlier scrambles to acquire colonies, during much of the 1800s most European powers had limited interest in formally annexing new territories. The earlier efforts at maintaining colonies had exhausted them, and domestic concerns—such as political uprisings and industrialization—took up much of their attention.

For most of the century, European powers were content to expand their influence through economic means rather than through direct political control. Britain, for example, established close commercial ties with many Latin American countries. Although these countries remained politically independent, their economic connections to Britain gave the British considerable influence there.

Toward the end of the 19th century, this period of "informal imperialism" gave way to a second great age of European imperialism. By

GREEDY JOHNNIE.
He Has Got a Lot of Good Things.—But How Long Can He Keep Them to Himself?

▲ **This political cartoon satirizes 19th-century British imperialism.**

In the middle of the chalkboard write the word *industrialization* and enclose it in a box. Draw two larger boxes, one above and one below the first, connecting them to the first with lines. Label these boxes *Motivated Imperialism* and *Made Imperialism Possible*. Have students copy this graphic organizer into their notebooks. Ask them to complete the organizer by putting relevant information in the two larger boxes. Call on volunteers to present and discuss their organizers.

COLONIAL ADMINISTRATION

Organize students into small groups to serve as staff members of the U.S. Department of State in the early 1900s. Have groups prepare memos on colonial administration. Memos should describe direct and indirect rule, give examples of countries that use these two kinds of colonial government, and suggest which type the U.S. should adopt and why. Call on groups to present their memos to the rest of the class.

▶

1900 the major industrial powers had divided a substantial portion of the world amongst themselves. The scramble for colonies was most intense in Africa, which the Europeans divided over the span of one generation.

Africa, while the most extreme case, was not the only region in which the imperial powers asserted themselves. In the late 1850s, France began its domination of parts of Southeast Asia, and the British government gained firm control of India. East Asia, while not subject to formal annexation, did not escape the effects of Europe's renewed interest in the rest of the world. Japan and China were forced open to Western trade, and in the 1890s the major expansionist powers divided China into spheres of influence.

The United States joined the ranks of the imperialists when it annexed Hawaii, the Philippines, and various other small territories. The United States also had significant economic interests in China, Japan, and Latin America (see Chapter 9).

A variety of motives lay behind the renewed interest in imperialism. Some people viewed imperialism as a way to spread Christianity. Others claimed that Western culture was superior to the cultures found in other regions of the world and that Westerners thus had a duty to spread their culture as far as possible. British poet Rudyard Kipling called this duty the "white man's burden." British imperialist Cecil Rhodes put it bluntly: "We happen to be the best people in the world, with the highest ideals of decency and justice and liberty and peace, and the more of the world we inhabit, the better it is for humanity." Even U.S. president Theodore Roosevelt echoed the same sentiment:

66 Every expansion of a great civilized power means a victory for law, order, and righteousness. This has been the case in every instance of expansion during the present century, whether the expanding power were France or England, Russia or America. 99

Many historians, however, believe that industrialization was the primary cause for the renewed interest in formal annexation. As countries developed their manufacturing industries, they typically became dependent on foreign countries for raw materials. For example, they looked to India and Egypt for cotton and to Central Africa and

▲ Two female missionaries pose with native guides before heading off into the African interior.

Southeast Asia for rubber. Labor also tended to be cheaper in many Asian and African areas than it was in Europe. In addition, industrialized nations sought foreign markets for their products. The great prize among exporters was China, where millions of Chinese hungered for manufactured goods—or so the industrialized nations hoped.

Industrialization not only provided the motivation for the new imperialism; it also provided the means. Just as railroads had enabled expansion on land, steamships extended the reach of the navies of the industrialized countries.

Ironically, while the development of the steamship made imperialism possible, it also made imperialism appear necessary to the major economic powers. Unlike the sailing vessels of earlier days, the steamships of the late 19th century required periodic refueling. Much as gas stations would become essential to automobiles, **coaling stations**—ports where more coal could be taken on—were essential to steamships. Without coaling stations, the ships could not go where they were wanted and needed. A significant portion of the imperial expansion of the late 1800s and early 1900s was part of an effort to claim the best spots for coaling stations and related maintenance facilities.

Another important product of industrialization—modern weapons—was also vital to imperialist efforts. Modern weapons gave the imperialist countries' soldiers an enormous advantage over the inhabitants of the countries they conquered. The

AV **TRANSPARENCY**
Linking Geography and History Transparency and **Worksheet 15**

PRIMARY SOURCES
Description of Change: excerpted
Rationale: excerpted to clarify meaning

MAKING CONNECTIONS
Geography
Rhodesia was named for Cecil Rhodes, who as head of the British South Africa Company administered a large area of central Africa. In 1980 the country was officially granted independence from the United Kingdom, and its name was changed to Zimbabwe.

AV **TRANSPARENCY**
Everyday Life in America Transparency and **Worksheet 19**

*P*ractice

GUIDED PRACTICE

On the chalkboard create a four-column chart titled "Motivations for Imperialism." Use the following as column heads: *Economic, Strategic, Cultural,* and *Political.* Call on volunteers to give examples of these four types of motives. Enter their responses on the chart.

INDEPENDENT PRACTICE

Organize students into small groups to act as newspaper editorial boards in a western nation. Have groups use information developed in the Guided Practice to write editorials explaining why their country should strive to build a colonial empire. Have groups present and discuss their editorials.

*R*eview and *A*ssessment

REVIEW Direct students to use the section's four Essential Points as main topics for an outline titled "Imperialism to World War I." Have students add subtopics to the outline. Then assign the Section 1 Review on p. 627.

ASSESS Assign the **Section 1 Daily Quiz** in *Core Resources.*

THE AMERICAN NATION VIDEODISC PROGRAM

The Panama Canal

2A   00598   4:07

PRIMARY SOURCE

Description of Change: excerpted
Rationale: excerpted to clarify meaning

Changing Ways

PROTECTING INDIA

SETTING THE SCENE

One of the challenges the British faced in India was the high death rate from malaria. The disease could be treated with quinine, which was derived from a variety of cinchona tree that grew in the South American Andes. Scarcity and shipping costs combined to make the bark enormously expensive, and British scientists set out to transplant the trees in India. Cinchona plantations made quinine widely available, enabling the British to protect themselves and the Indian labor force from the disease.

French-born English writer Hilaire Belloc summarized this advantage in a famous couplet:

> 66 Whatever happens we have got
> The Maxim gun and they have not. 99

Such weapons made it nearly impossible for the inhabitants of the colonized areas to resist the arrival of Western people, goods, and ideas into their midst. For example, when a force of Africans—armed largely with spears and swords—attempted to resist Great Britian's advances into Northeast Africa, British gunfire in the 1898 **Battle of Omdurman** left more than 10,000 Africans dead. Fewer than 50 British soldiers were killed.

In China, which was not actually colonized but was still subjected to many foreign influences, resistance met with greater, but still limited, success. By 1900 many Chinese had become outraged by the effects Western technology and culture were having on China. Such sentiments led to the Boxer Rebellion in 1900 (see Chapter 9).

Changing Ways   PROTECTING INDIA

Sometimes nations expanded into new territories to protect the territories they already had. The British, already in control of India, felt a need to expand into Egypt, East Africa, and the Arabian Peninsula in order to protect the approaches to India. "As long as we rule India," observed one British imperial statesman, Lord Curzon, "we are the greatest power in the world. If we lose it, we shall drop straight away to a third-rate power."

Holding India required two things. First, the British had to maintain the single largest navy in the world to protect the sea routes to India. Second, they had to provide secure ports from which the Royal Navy could carry out this mission. Consequently, by 1860 Britain controlled the strategic routes to India, from Gibraltar in the western Mediterranean to the Cape of Good Hope at the southern tip of Africa.

In 1869 the opening of the Suez Canal sharply reduced the sailing time between Britain and India. The British viewed the Suez Canal as Americans would later see the Panama Canal. With the canal so vital to their national interests, the British did everything in their power to protect it. Between 1869 and 1900, the British took control of Cyprus, Egypt, and parts of East and Central Africa, largely to control and defend access to India through the Suez Canal.

In the late 1890s, control of the canal almost caused Britain to come to blows with France over an outpost in Africa. The place in question, Fashoda, was on the banks of the upper Nile River. The British feared that if the French gained a foothold on the Nile, they might endanger Britain's position downstream in Egypt, which was the key to the Suez Canal.

▲ In November 1869 a procession of ships marked the opening of the Suez Canal.

France was not the only other imperialist power that Britain feared. The British government also saw Russian ambitions to expand southward as a threat not only to British control of India itself but also to British control of the route to India through the Mediterranean Sea, the Suez Canal, and the Indian Ocean. Therefore, Britain worked to extend its influence into central and southwestern Asia. The British policy of containing Russian expansion was called the Great Game. In some ways it was a forerunner of the American containment policy during the Cold War.

RETEACH For each subsection in the section, have students write a sentence that summarizes the main idea. Select students to read their sentences aloud. Have the class choose the best summary sentence for each subsection.

Closure

Have students speculate how the growth of imperialism in the late 1800s might have differed if western countries had not had so many technological advantages over countries in other areas of the world.

Extension

CREATE Have students create cartoons that illustrate the attitudes of leaders of the colonial powers toward the cultures of the regions they colonized. Students should present and interpret their cartoons for the class.

INVESTIGATE Direct students to investigate the great colonial empires that existed in 1914. Ask them to present their findings in an annotated map.

■■ **Industrialization was one of the major motives behind the renewed interest in imperialism. It also helped make imperialism possible.**

COLONIAL ADMINISTRATION

Once they had taken direct control of new territories, the imperialists had to govern them. Different imperialists, however, had different ideas about how best to govern. Two main methods emerged: **direct rule**, in which the colonizing country established a completely new governmental administration, and **indirect rule**, in which the colonizing country ruled through traditional local leaders.

Direct and indirect rule reflected the different objectives of the various imperial powers. France, Belgium, Portugal, and the United States practiced direct rule as part of their plan to westernize their colonial subjects. For the French, Belgians, and Portuguese, this primarily meant cultural assimilation. Once colonial subjects had absorbed enough of the ruling power's culture, they could, at least in theory, become full citizens of the imperial homeland. In French-controlled Senegal, for example, so many Africans qualified for this status that in 1915 four towns along the coast became eligible to vote for representatives to France's Parliament. The United States promoted the English language in its overseas territories, but its primary interests were political and economic rather than cultural. Americans wanted to teach people how to run a constitutional, democratic government and to establish a free-market capitalist economy.

Initially, the British tried both direct and indirect rule. By World War I, however, they had decided against trying to create "Black Englishmen," as some put it. Instead, British colonial administrators maintained that colonial peoples should be helped along their own natural "evolutionary" path from "savagery" to "civilization," just as Europeans had traveled it. Thus the British adopted a policy of indirect rule and tried to leave most aspects of local cultures intact.

Regardless of what type of government the imperialists set up, colonial peoples seldom embraced it. Several decades, however, would pass before conditions made widespread resistance to colonial rule practical.

■■ **Some colonial powers wanted to culturally assimilate their subjects; other powers aimed at cultural "evolution."**

▲ **A U.S. cavalry troop patrols a section of the Great Wall of China during the Boxer Rebellion.**

SECTION REVIEW ANSWERS

IDENTIFY
Rudyard Kipling (p. 625)
coaling stations (p. 625)
Battle of Omdurman (p. 626)
direct rule (p. 627)
indirect rule (p. 627)

1. *Many early Americans objected to imperialism because the country had been founded on the idea that people had the right to rule themselves. Early America benefited from imperialism by gaining territory.*
2. *similarities—both expanded across large land areas through agricultural settlement and war, relying on dominant culture, new technology, and idea of manifest destiny; differences—U.S. relied largely on immigrants while Russia relied on native Russians, while territories conquered by Russians had much higher population than western lands of U.S.*
3. *Industrialization created a need for raw materials and provided new weapons and forms of transportation.*
4. *Letters will vary but should identify the recommended method of colonial rule as well as the reasons that method would be appropriate.*
5. *Answers will vary, but students should note the high numbers of casualties inflicted by modern weapons.*

SECTION 1 REVIEW

IDENTIFY and explain the significance of the following: Rudyard Kipling, coaling stations, Battle of Omdurman, direct rule, indirect rule.

1. **MAIN IDEA** Why did many early Americans oppose imperialism? How did early America occasionally benefit from imperialism?

2. **MAIN IDEA** How was American expansion similar to Russian expansion? How was it different?

3. **IDENTIFYING CAUSE AND EFFECT** How did industrialization contribute to imperialism in the late 1800s and early 1900s?

4. **WRITING TO PERSUADE** Imagine you are a colonial administrator. Write a letter to the government of the colonizing country explaining what type of colonial rule—direct or indirect—you think would best suit the colony. Explain your reasoning.

5. **HYPOTHESIZING** Do you think the Western powers would have been able to establish worldwide empires if they had not had weapons that were more powerful than those of the inhabitants of the colonized territories? Why or why not?

Chapter 23

SECTION

2

Introducing the Section

FOCUS OBJECTIVES

- Analyze the psychological effects World War I had on European imperialism.

- Describe how colonial territories in the Middle East, India, and Indochina moved closer to independence following World War I.

- Identify the factors that led the United States to grant independence to the Philippines.

- Explain how imperialism gained a second wind during the 1930s.

PREVIEW WORKSHOP

Following is a list of the significant people and terms in this section. You may wish to use this list as a section preview.

Terms
- trusteeship
- Tydings-McDuffie Act
- puppet government

People
- Mohandas K. Gandhi
- Manuel Quezon

MOTIVATING: PRIOR KNOWLEDGE

Ask students to recall how imperialism helped to bring about World War I. *(desire to gain land held by neighbors created tensions among European powers)* Then mention that this section discusses the impact of this great conflict on imperialism.

Section 2

IMPERIALISM BETWEEN THE WARS

F O C U S

- **What psychological effects did World War I have on European imperialism?**
- **How did territories in the Middle East, India, and Indochina move closer to independence following World War I?**
- **What factors led the United States to grant independence to the Philippines?**
- **In what respects did imperialism gain a second wind during the 1930s?**

Indian independence leader Mohandas K. Gandhi

World War I halted the latest round of imperial expansion, eroding the self-confidence of the great powers, particularly Britain and France. After the war, nationalists in the colonial regions grew increasingly assertive. The Great Depression further weakened American imperialism, but it strengthened imperialist tendencies in Japan, Italy, and Germany.

WAR AND IMPERIALISM

During the debate over U.S. annexation of the Philippines, anti-imperialist Andrew Carnegie had declared that East Asia was one of the most dangerous regions in the world. "It is in that region the thunderbolt is expected. It is there the storm is to burst," stated Carnegie, referring not literally to the

typhoons that often hit the Philippines but figuratively to the human conflict that might erupt following annexation. Indeed, most American anti-imperialists were not surprised when annexation led to a bloody war in the Philippines (see Chapter 9). In the same way, few anti-imperialists in America or elsewhere were particularly surprised when a much larger war broke out among the major European imperialist powers in 1914.

World War I was only partly caused by imperial rivalries; it had as much to do with the ambitions and fears of the European powers at home. But it had important effects on imperialism. One effect was psychological. Before the war Europeans had considered themselves more enlightened than most other people and therefore specially suited to ruling others. World War I blasted huge holes in this belief. Never had a war

◄ **This church in northeast Poland was transformed into a field hospital during the first German attack on the Russian front in World War I.**

CORE RESOURCES

- **Section 2 Daily Quiz**

AV RESOURCES

- **Everyday Life in America Transparency** and **Worksheet 25**

628

WAR AND EMPIRE

Encourage students to adopt the role of an anti-imperialist politician in a European country. Have them prepare a brief speech, to be given at a political rally, explaining how the events of World War I show that their country should abandon its imperialist policies. Have the class act as the audience at the rally and call on volunteers to deliver their speeches.

▶

killed so many people in so little time, and for so little purpose. If Europe could not even be trusted to manage its own affairs, people asked, how could it hope to manage other countries' affairs?

■■ World War I shook many Europeans' faith in their ability to govern other peoples.

No world leader pressed more publicly for national self-determination—the right of countries to choose their own governments—than President Woodrow Wilson. But to avoid tension with the Allies, Wilson insisted on self-determination only for the countries under the thumb of Germany, Austria-Hungary, and the Ottoman Empire.

Toward this end Article 22 of the covenant of the new League of Nations established the mandate system for the former German and Ottoman colonies. Under this system the victorious powers were to see to the welfare of "peoples not yet able to stand by themselves under the strenuous conditions of the modern world." While the mandate system allowed the victorious imperial powers to expand their territories, it also required them to develop the territories. Under the principle of **trusteeship**, mandate governments were to encourage economic development and provide educational, medical, and other services needed to modernize the new states.

THE MIDDLE EAST

The mandate system took effect most swiftly in the Middle East. The defeated Ottoman Empire was divided into several pieces, which were then parceled out to the victors in the war. (The United States declined to participate in the system.)

France and Britain received the largest Middle Eastern territories. Although they were supposed to be preparing these territories for independence, they concentrated on maintaining some influence in the region. France separated its mandate on the eastern shore of the Mediterranean into two parts: the predominantly Christian Lebanon and the predominantly Muslim Syria. France hoped that Lebanon would continue to maintain its connection to France even after achieving independence.

Great Britain, too, wanted to preserve its connections to the Middle East. Britain's mandates included Iraq, Palestine, and Transjordan—all strategically important areas. With the exception of Palestine, the British had granted independence everywhere in the region by the early 1930s. In exchange for independence, however, the new states had to sign treaties of alliance giving Britain continuing access to the area's strategic waterways, oil resources, and British-established military bases. Consequently, Britain continued to dominate the new states economically, politically, and militarily.

Not everyone approved of the mandate system. Some critics charged that France and Britain were using the system as a disguise for a new form of imperialism. Many inhabitants of the mandated territories had never accepted their former colonial status and thus thought they should have received independence at once. But defenders of the system simply pointed out that without the oversight of the League of Nations the fate of the mandated territories might have been even worse.

HISTORICAL SIDELIGHTS
Independence and Disunity
French troops remained in Syria until complete independence was granted in 1946. Many Syrians hoped to unite with Lebanon, Palestine, and Transjordan in a territory known as Greater Syria. Instead, the establishment of Israel as a Jewish state further divided the region.

▶ Following World War I, the Allies attempted to partition Turkey as well as the rest of the Ottoman Empire. Nationalist leader Mustafa Kemal Atatürk, however, held the nation together with the establishment of the republic of Turkey in 1923. Atatürk attempted to westernize Turkey and is shown here giving instruction in the Roman alphabet.

■■ Under the mandate system, France and Britain were to help the Middle East become fully independent. But they forged permanent ties to the region.

Teaching the Section

THE MIDDLE EAST AND THE MANDATE SYSTEM

Organize students into groups of four to serve as investigating committees for the League of Nations. Direct the committees to write an investigative report on the operation of the mandate system in the Middle East. Reports should include details of how the League of Nations intended the mandate system to work, how it worked in reality, and the impact it had on the peoples living in the mandated areas. Ask groups to present their reports to the class.

INDEPENDENCE MOVEMENTS IN INDIA AND INDOCHINA

Draw an imaginary line to divide the class in half. Have students on one side of the line adopt the role of Mohandas K. Gandhi. Students on the other side should adopt the role of Ho Chi Minh. Then have students write letters explaining how World War I has affected their drive for independence and what approach they should adopt to win their freedom from the imperial powers. Call on volunteers from each group to read their letters to the class.

MULTICULTURAL PERSPECTIVES

After World War I, Ho Chi Minh went to the Versailles conference to encourage greater equality and justice for Vietnam. Ignored by the delegates and unable to find assistance from Western powers, he turned to Communism. In April 1960 he stated, "I gradually came up with the fact that only Socialism and Communism can liberate the oppressed nations and the working people throughout the world from slavery."

THE VICTORIOUS POWERS' TERRITORIES

The same logic and moral reasoning that demanded the breakup of the German and Ottoman empires also applied, presumably, to the overseas empires of the victorious powers, particularly Britain and France. This did not go unnoticed by the inhabitants of the British and French colonies. They too had begun to question Europe's ability to govern other peoples.

British India. In India, for example, some British policies and actions spurred an English-trained Indian lawyer, Mohandas K. Gandhi, to oppose British colonial rule. Over the next few decades, Gandhi used what he called *satyagraha,* insistence on truth, as the basis for a campaign of nonviolent resistance to British rule in India.

India had long had a movement in favor of independence—the Indian National Congress, formed in 1885. But this movement was small and did not include the majority of Indians, most of whom remained untouched by Western culture. As Gandhi became more active in the movement, he realized that he must find a way to make the movement meaningful to most Indians.

To achieve his goal of *swaraj* (self-rule), Gandhi used techniques that many people in India could understand and participate in. For example, he encouraged people to spin and weave their own cloth to protest policies favoring British cotton manufacturers. In 1930 he protested the government monopoly on salt by leading a march to the sea and making his own salt. He was committed to nonviolence. Sometimes Gandhi would fast nearly to death to accomplish his aims; such fasts shamed the British as well as Indians who resorted to violence. He was eventually called Mahatma, or Great Soul, by his followers.

During the 1920s and 1930s Indian nationalism became a powerful force that gradually loosened Britain's hold on India. But Gandhi was not simply trying to return to a precolonial era. He believed that the British had begun a process of nation-building in India by bringing together all of India's various states and peoples. He wanted to continue the process by forging a new sense of national identity among Indians. At the same time, he was convinced that Western civilization was doomed. Many Europeans, Gandhi wrote, "appear to be half mad. . . . One has only to be patient and it [European civilization] will be self-destroyed." Therefore, Gandhi strongly believed, India had to make its own future.

French Indochina. Anti-imperialism grew elsewhere in the colonial world following World War I. At the war's end, Ho Chi Minh, a young Vietnamese nationalist, was living in Paris. While Gandhi was turning toward nonviolence, Ho turned

▲ Mohandas K. "Mahatma" Gandhi is still honored throughout the world for his use of nonviolent resistance to gain India's independence.

RESISTING BRITISH RULE OF INDIA
One of the leaders of the movement for Indian independence was Aurobindo Ghose. Like Gandhi, Ghose was educated in England, and also like Gandhi, Ghose advocated nonviolent resistance to British rule. For Ghose the goal of political independence was similar to the goal of spiritual salvation, and the methods of achieving both were the same:

THROUGH OTHERS' EYES

❝*I*ndia, free, one and indivisible, is the divine realization to which we move, emancipation our aim. . . . Whatever leads only to continued subjection must be spewed out as mere vileness and impurity. Passive resistance may be the final method of salvation in our case or it may be only the preparation for the final sadhana [spiritual self-control]. In either case, the sooner we put it into full and perfect practice, the nearer we shall be to national liberty. ❞

INDEPENDENCE FOR
THE PHILIPPINES

Encourage students to imagine they are editors of a leading American newspaper in the mid-1930s. Direct them to write an editorial titled "It's Time for Philippine Independence." Suggest that in their editorials they mention political and economic reasons for independence. Point out that they also should discuss the role played by Manuel Quezon in the drive for Philippine freedom. Call on volunteers to read their editorials to the class.

FASCIST EXPANSION
IN THE 1930S

Draw on the chalkboard a three-column chart with the headings *Japan, Italy,* and *Germany.* Call on volunteers to explain the reasons these countries gave to justify their expansion and to identify the areas that they seized. Note their responses in the appropriate column. Have students look for parallels among the nations in the chart and to write a general statement summarizing the characteristics of fascist expansion in the 1930s.

Students may wish to include their summary statements in their portfolios.

toward revolutionary communism. Ho listened to French Communists describe the plight of downtrodden workers in France and believed that the relationship between colonies and the mother country was quite similar to the relationship between workers and the ruling class. What would solve the problems of one would solve the problems of the other. "Only Socialism and Communism can liberate the oppressed nations and the working people throughout the world from slavery," he wrote. He became determined to apply this lesson to his Vietnamese homeland. Ho Chi Minh, however, would have to wait a few more decades before his efforts achieved significant results.

■■ Independence movements in India and Indochina grew stronger following World War I.

The Philippines. Ho Chi Minh's views would, in time, place him in conflict with the United States. But during the era after World War I nationalists like Ho and Gandhi could take heart from the words of many Americans. W.E.B. Du Bois spoke of how the imperialist powers exploited the "vast sea of human labor" in China, India, Africa, the West Indies, and elsewhere. According to Du Bois, such workers were

> 66 paid a wage below the level of decent living; driven, beaten, prisoned and enslaved in all but name; spawning the world's raw material and luxury—cotton, wool, coffee, tea, cocoa, palm oil, fibers, spices, rubber, silks, lumber, copper, gold, diamonds, leather. . . . All these are gathered up at prices lowest of the low, manufactured, transformed and transported at fabulous gain; and the resultant wealth is distributed and displayed and made the basis of world power and universal dominion and armed arrogance in London and Paris, Berlin and Rome, New York and Rio de Janeiro. 99

Du Bois was not the only one criticizing imperialism. Although the idea of an American empire had briefly enchanted many Americans, they quickly lost their enthusiasm once they realized the costs of maintaining an empire. For example, many Americans and Filipinos died in the brutal war in the Philippines. And while World War I did not have as strong an impact on the United States as on Europe,

it heightened Americans' suspicions of imperialism. Soon many Americans began to question the U.S. control of the Philippines.

The people of the Philippines sensed American doubts. If Americans could not be coerced into granting independence to the Philippines, they might be shamed into doing so. To further their cause, Filipino leaders adapted to the American way of politics; some became extremely skillful in the art. No Filipino leader was more skillful than Manuel Quezon.

BIO GRAPHY Born in the Tayabas province of the Philippine island of Luzon in 1878, Quezon took to politics early. Quezon had a charismatic personality that many people found nearly irresistible. He especially understood how to appeal to Americans. From 1909 to 1916 he served as the Philippine commissioner in U.S. Congress. In dealings with U.S. leaders, he Americanized his last name to "Casey" and did not hesitate to flatter Americans and praise American principles.

But the flattery and praise had a purpose. He repeatedly reminded the Americans that they could not be true to their principles and

Manuel Quezon

at the same time deny democratic government to Filipinos. In 1923 he joined with other Filipino leaders in sending Washington a complaint against the American governor general of the Philippines. The statement echoed the American colonists' complaints against King George III in the Declaration of Independence:

> 66 He has set to naught all understanding that the Filipino people have had with the American government. . . .
> He has broken asunder the bonds of harmony that had united Americans and Filipinos. . . .
> He has sought to establish a colonial despotism here worse than that which has cursed our country for the last ten generations. 99

Quezon and his comrades hit a sensitive spot in criticizing U.S. rule, especially in doing so in

*P*ractice

GUIDED PRACTICE

Write the subsection headings in headline form on the chalkboard. For each headline, call on volunteers to give information that could be used in a story to accompany the headline. Note responses under the appropriate headline.

INDEPENDENT PRACTICE

Instruct students to select one of the headlines from the Guided Practice. Then have them write news stories that might accompany that headline. Students may wish to include their news stories in their portfolios.

*R*eview and *A*ssessment

REVIEW Have students write 10 questions about Section 2 on individual notecards with the answers on the reverse side. Then divide students into groups of four. Ask them to use their notecards to question the other members of the group. Then assign the Section 2 Review on p. 633.

ASSESS Assign the **Section 2 Daily Quiz** in *Core Resources.*

HISTORICAL SIDELIGHTS

Italian Imperialism
Much of the Italian desire for empire stemmed from dissatisfaction with the 1919 Treaty of Versailles, which did not make significant additons to Italian territories. Although the League of Nations threatened an oil boycott against Italy after the invasion of Ethiopia, the League was soon distracted by European events as Hitler militarized the Rhineland in the spring of 1936.

AV TRANSPARENCY
Everyday Life in America Transparency and **Worksheet 25**

▶This 1929 photograph shows Benito Mussolini, Fascist dictator of Italy, reviewing the Italian bicycle corps on the seventh anniversary of his rise to power.

language reminiscent of Thomas Jefferson. Quezon made Americans uncomfortable when he pointed out the distance between American democratic principles and American colonial practice.

The Great Depression of the 1930s added economic discomfort to the political uneasiness Americans felt regarding their imperial connection to the Philippines. The depression drastically reduced demand for American farm products, and American producers called for protection against competition from Philippine sugar and coconut oil. Similarly, American workers lobbied for protection from competition with Filipino immigrants for jobs. One way to achieve both goals was to grant the Philippines independence. An independent Philippines would be subject to the same tariffs and immigration limits as any other foreign country.

Traditional anti-imperialism combined with this depression-induced self-interest to produce a congressional majority in favor of Philippine independence. In 1934 Congress passed the **Tydings-McDuffie Act**, which promised the Philippines independence at the end of a 12-year transition period.

■■ **Democratic anti-imperialism and economic self-interest eventually led the United States to grant the Philippines independence.**

*J*APANESE, ITALIAN, AND GERMAN EXPANSION

While Americans were turning away from imperialism, other countries were turning toward it.

Japan led the way. Small and resource-poor, Japan looked overseas to support its growing population. As early as 1910 Japan had seized control of Korea, converting it into a colony. During and after World War I, Japan acquired Germany's Pacific possessions. Yet Japanese leaders believed they still needed more space and resources.

They felt the need even more sharply when the Japanese economy took a downturn during the 1930s. In response, Japanese leaders cast an eye toward Manchuria, in northeastern China. Manchuria was full of the kinds of resources Japan wanted, and it was only loosely attached to China.

In 1931 Japan occupied Manchuria and set up a **puppet government**. Although the government was nominally headed by the Chinese, it was really controlled by Japan. "Expansion towards the continent," wrote one leading Japanese banker, Hirozo Mori, "is the destiny of the Japanese people, decreed by Heaven, which neither the world nor we the Japanese ourselves can check or alter."

The significance of the Japanese takeover of Manchuria—and the failure of other nations to prevent it—was not lost on governments elsewhere that sought relief from the depression through foreign expansion. Italy, led by the Fascist dictator Benito Mussolini, invaded and waged a bloody war of conquest against Ethiopia in 1935. As in the case of Japan, the other great powers condemned Italy's action but failed to check its expansion.

The most dangerous of the depression-era imperialists was Adolf Hitler. For years Hitler had dreamed of extending Germany's boundaries; Germany needed *Lebensraum,* or living space, he said. Reviving an old German policy called *Drang*

RETEACH

Have students work in small groups to chart the major ideas and events presented in the section. Direct each group to indicate on its chart how each item addresses one of the section's Focus questions.

*C*losure

Have students use information from the section to explain how World War I helped to bring about the decline of imperialism.

*E*xtension

RESEARCH Have students research and report on *satyagraha,* Mahatma Gandhi's method of challenging British colonial rule in India.

EVALUATE Ask students to evaluate the reasons why Allied leaders did not block fascist expansion in the 1930s. Have students write paragraphs explaining their conclusions.

nach Osten, the drive to the east, Hitler planned to create a new civilization in southern Russia and the Ukraine:

> ❝ The area . . . must be Europeanized! . . . The German agencies and authorities are to have wonderful buildings, the governors' palaces. Around each city, a ring of lovely villages will be placed to within 30 or 40 kilometers. . . . The German cities will be placed, like pearls on a string, and around the cities the German settlements will lie. ❞

German occupation of the region was to be made possible by the extermination or enslavement of the local inhabitants.

Hitler's imperial vision was sweeping. "Germany must either be a world power or there will be no Germany," he said. He never got as far as he planned, but he did rebuild Germany's armed forces, even in defiance of the 1919 Treaty of Versailles. When the great powers did nothing to stop him, he was encouraged to take bolder measures in the late 1930s—the annexation of Austria, the seizure of the Sudetenland, and finally the dismantling of the rest of Czechoslovakia.

Until this last step, other nations—including the United States—had avoided actively interfering with Japanese, Italian, and German expansion. Western leaders were anxious not to repeat the horrors of World War I. Equally important, they feared the expansion of communism and Soviet power. Even though the revolutionaries who had created the Soviet state in 1917 had condemned imperialism along with capitalism, they had gone on to create a new empire of Soviet Socialist Republics. In 1938 Britain's prime minister, Neville Chamberlain, expressed the fears of many when he warned of the dangers of overthrowing Hitler. "Who will guarantee that Germany will not become Bolshevistic [Communist] afterwards?" he asked. Thus no one tried to stop Hitler until it was almost too late and only a large-scale war could prevent further expansion.

■■ **Japan, Italy, and Germany launched new imperialist offensives during the 1930s.**

▲ **Adolf Hitler confers in 1941 with the ambassador of Japan, another nation bent on expansion by military conquest.**

PRIMARY SOURCE
Description of Change: excerpted
Rationale: excerpted to focus on main idea

SECTION REVIEW ANSWERS

IDENTIFY

For significance see the following pages:
trusteeship (p. 629)
Mohandas K. Gandhi (p. 630)
Manuel Quezon (p. 631)
Tydings-McDuffie Act (p. 632)
puppet government (p. 632)

1. *Many Europeans felt that World War I had been brutal and pointless. They were no longer convinced that they were most capable of managing the affairs of other countries.*
2. *After the war the Ottoman Empire was dismantled, and regions were distributed among European powers.*
3. *Many Americans supported independence for the Philippines in order to protect American jobs and exports.*
4. *Essays should reflect the economic troubles of the 1930s that encouraged Germany, Japan, and Italy to expand their empires.*
5. *Responses should reflect the desire for independence as well as the problems posed by imperialism.*

■■ **SECTION 2 REVIEW**

IDENTIFY and explain the significance of the following: trusteeship, Mohandas K. Gandhi, Manuel Quezon, Tydings-McDuffie Act, puppet government.

1. **MAIN IDEA** How did World War I affect European beliefs regarding imperialism?
2. **MAIN IDEA** What effects did World War I have on imperialism in the Middle East?
3. **MAIN IDEA** Why did the U.S. government decide to grant the Philippines independence?
4. **WRITING TO EXPLAIN** Write an essay explaining why Japan, Italy, and Germany wanted to expand their territorial holdings in the 1930s.
5. **USING HISTORICAL IMAGINATION** Imagine you are a leader of the independence movement in India or in Indochina following World War I. How might you persuade people to join the movement?

MOTIVATING: LINK TO TODAY

Ask students to describe what they know about the roles that India and the African nations play on the international scene today. Then tell students that in this section they will gain insight into why and how these nations developed their particular systems of international relations.

FOCUS OBJECTIVES

- Explain how World War II hastened the demise of European imperialism in Asia.

- Identify when most African nations became independent.

- Describe how many former colonies reacted to the Cold War, and note how their goals changed over time.

Section 3

DECOLONIZATION AND THE COLD WAR

F O C U S
- **How did World War II hasten the demise of European colonialism in Asia?**
- **When did most African nations become independent?**
- **How did many former colonies react to the Cold War? How did their goals change over time?**

Even more than World War I, World War II weakened the European powers and strengthened anticolonial nationalist movements. Shortly after the war, decolonization began with a rush. But decolonization was often complicated by the Cold War. Most newly independent countries attempted to remain neutral in the Cold War and formed what came to be called the Third World.

Mohammed Ali Jinnah, head of the Moslem League in British India and first governor general of Pakistan

WAR AND ASIAN NATIONALISM

World War II had a profound effect on imperialism. Where World War I had shattered Europe's sense of moral superiority, World War II shattered its sense of military superiority. Though Japan eventually lost the war, its early victories over American and British forces in the Pacific and in Southeast Asia brought home the point that Asians were fully capable of standing up against the soldiers and technology of the West. Another event from early in the war also had a significant impact on the future of imperialism. Just as President Wilson had thrown America's moral weight behind self-determination in World War I, so too did President Franklin Roosevelt insist that self-determination be a central objective of the anti-Fascist coalition in World War II. Roosevelt's view was embodied in the Atlantic Charter of 1941. Issued in conjunction with British prime minister Winston Churchill, the charter stated:

66 First, [the United States and Britain] seek no aggrandizement [enlargement], territorial or other; Second, they desire to see no territorial changes that do not accord with the freely expressed wishes of the peoples concerned; Third, they respect the right of all peoples to choose the form of government under which they will live; and they wish to see sovereign rights and self-government restored to those who have been forcibly deprived of them. 99

Churchill, however, took few steps toward dissolving the British Empire, and with the war raging on Roosevelt declined to press the point. Nevertheless, the Atlantic Charter became a source of inspiration to colonial peoples around the world.

India. In India, Mahatma Gandhi stepped up the campaign of nonviolent resistance to British rule. Churchill attempted to crush the "Quit India"

THE END OF IMPERIALISM IN INDIA

Organize students into groups of four or five. Provide each group with a piece of butcher paper on which the following headings are written: *How World War II Affected the Indian Independence Movement; How World War II Affected British Attitudes to Colonial Rule in India.* Have groups brainstorm information about these two topics. Direct a group representative to write information under the appropriate heading. Then have members of each group use this information to write a paragraph summarizing the role that World War II played in the demise of European imperialism in Asia. Call on groups to present and discuss their paragraphs.

AN AMERICAN DILEMMA

Encourage students to imagine they are living in the United States in the years immediately after World War II. Have students write letters to the editor of their local newspaper detailing the role that the U.S. should play in the Vietnamese struggle for independence. Students may wish to include their letters in their portfolios.

▶

movement, as the campaign was called, by having tens of thousands of Indian protesters thrown in jail. "I have not become the King's First Minister," he once said, "in order to preside over the liquidation [breakup] of the British Empire."

Yet Churchill's actions served as a stark reminder of the contradiction between the ideals expressed in the Atlantic Charter and the continuing practice of imperialism. A leading newspaper of the Indian nationalist movement wondered in print at the "mysterious silence" that had fallen over Washington, D.C., in the wake of the British crackdown. Many Americans wondered, too, and grew increasingly uncomfortable with their country's failure to denounce British imperialism.

Thus it was with a sigh of relief that Americans viewed the series of events that led to Indian independence. Just as World War II was ending, British voters replaced Churchill with Clement Attlee, the leader of the opposition Labour party. Attlee and the Labour party were not uniformly anti-imperialist. They did believe, however, that after two centuries of British rule, India was ready for independence.

Adding to this belief was the fact that the war left Britain exhausted. Britain and the Allies had won, but the British no longer had the financial resources and were weary of trying to govern other people. The first priority of British voters, as demonstrated by their election of Attlee, was to repair their fortunes at home. India could look out for itself.

Had the Indians made less of an issue of independence, even Attlee might have been inclined to keep the British in India longer. But the war's end only made the Indian nationalists more assertive than ever. They made it plain that a refusal to grant independence would cost Britain dearly—in money, in moral standing, and perhaps in lives of British soldiers.

The British, therefore, agreed to go. In August 1947 the British turned over power to an Indian government. At the same time, they also granted power to the newly established nation of Pakistan, the largely Muslim portion of British India that refused to be associated with predominantly Hindu independent India.

▲ Jawaharlal Nehru, India's first prime minister, reviews troops during 1948 Independence Day ceremonies.

Indonesia. During this same period, and for many of the same reasons, the government of the Netherlands decided to pull out of the Dutch East Indies. The Netherlands had been hit even harder than Britain by the war. Furthermore, the nationalist movement in the Dutch East Indies, led by Achmed Sukarno, was just as determined as the nationalist movement in India.

The Netherlands, however, took a bit longer than Britain to accept decolonization. Several periods of severe fighting broke out between the Dutch and the Indonesians in the years following World War II as the Netherlands resisted giving the region independence. Although the Dutch were able to recapture much territory, the Indonesians would not be defeated. In 1949, after nearly four years of conflict, the Netherlands conceded power to the government of Indonesia.

■■ World War II heartened Asian nationalists and exhausted European imperialists, leading to independence for such countries as India, Pakistan, and Indonesia.

◀ Dr. Achmed Sukarno, an active nationalist for 20 years before Indonesia's independence, became the republic's first president and held that office until 1967.

MULTICULTURAL PERSPECTIVES

In 1929, Gandhi wrote: "What is excellent in British political institutions is there for the whole world to see and copy. The British need not come all the way to India as rulers to teach us political wisdom. Whatever is worth adopting for India must come to her through the process of assimilation, not forcible superimposition."

Teaching the Section

INDEPENDENCE FOR AFRICA

Write the following headings on the chalk-board: *Kenya, Algeria, Belgian Congo.* Then call on a volunteer to read aloud the first Essential Point on page 638. Ask students to explain how the path to independence followed by the three listed countries supports the argument made in the Essential Point. Note the major points of their expla- nations under the appropriate heading. Have students use the information on the chalkboard to write a sentence that makes a generalization about independence movements in Africa.

GLOBAL CONNECTIONS

Pan-Africanism

Between 1919 and 1927 W.E.B. Du Bois organized four Pan-African Congresses calling for African local self-government, improved education, cultural recogni- tion, and the acknowledge- ment of land rights. The fifth Pan-African conference was held in Manchester, England, and although Du Bois was elected president, most of the power was held by continental Africans and West Indians. The U.S. influence was found primar- ily in elements of culture, as writers from the Harlem Renaissance of the 1920s interacted with other black writers from around the world.

▲ Vietnamese nationalists, such as these Annamites captured by French soldiers, opposed the return of French rule to Indochina after World War II.

Vietnam. France, too, was reluctant to let go of its colonies. World War II had been particularly humiliating for the French, who surrendered to the Germans after a mere six weeks of fighting in 1940. Adding insult to injury, Japan took advantage of France's misfortune to strip it of Indochina, its Southeast Asian possession. The final year of the fighting in Europe, during which French soldiers joined the other Allies in liberating France, went part way toward restoring French pride. The gov- ernment in Paris hoped to redeem some of the rest by reclaiming Indochina upon the defeat of Japan.

But the inhabitants of Indochina had other ideas. The leading opposition figure there was Ho Chi Minh, the Vietnamese nationalist who had led the struggle against French imperialism before the war and against Japanese imperialism during the war. The defeat of Japan had led Ho to believe that independence was at hand. Thus when troops returned to reclaim Indochina for France, Ho and many others took up arms in resistance.

Americans were of two minds about the situ- ation in Indochina, just as they had long been of two minds about imperialism. On one hand they sympathized with the Vietnamese desire for inde- pendence. But on the other hand, the U.S. govern- ment was reluctant to anger France. During this period the Cold War was taking shape, and U.S. officials greatly desired French help in fighting the spread of communism worldwide. Further-

more, Ho Chi Minh was not merely a nationalist, but a Communist who proudly proclaimed his desire to bring about a Communist revolution in Vietnam. At a time when the United States was publicly committed to opposing the spread of com- munism, supporting Ho against France seemed out of the question.

The war in Indochina went poorly for France. Ho's guerrilla forces wore the French down. In response, the U.S. government increased its eco- nomic and military assistance to the French in Indochina. But the aid was to no avail, and in 1954 the French government was forced to withdraw from the region (see Chapter 20).

■■ **American choices became com- plicated when nationalists were also Communists, as in Vietnam.**

*I*NDEPENDENT AFRICA

The exhaustion that followed World War II left the European empires in Africa as vulnerable to chal- lenge as the empires in Asia. Africans in all parts of the continent took advantage of their opportu- nity, and most African nations became independent during the late 1950s and early 1960s (see map). In 1960 the British prime minister announced that "the wind of change" was blowing through Africa, driving out colonialism.

The imperial powers, however, did not always let go of their African colonies easily. In Kenya many Africans protested British rule start- ing in the 1940s. Their greatest complaint was that the British owned most of the land in Kenya while many Africans had no land and lived in poverty. When British policy remained unchanged, some Africans— such as Jomo Kenyatta, the leader of the Kenyan inde- pendence movement— became convinced that violence was necessary to achieve their goals.

◄ Kwame Nkrumah, prime minister of Ghana, waves to a crowd cele- brating Ghana's indepen- dence from British rule in 1957.

THE NONALIGNED MOVEMENT

Organize students into small groups to act as delegates to the Bandung Conference in 1955. Have groups prepare a position paper for presentation at the conference. The paper should detail the newly-independent nations' complaints against the former colonial powers, the course they want to follow with respect to the Cold War, and how this course should affect their attempts to get development aid. Select groups to present their papers to the class.

■■ Some politicians have suggested that the giving of aid should be guided by the old adage "He who pays the piper calls the tune." Ask students whether they agree or disagree with this view.

CHANGING GOALS

Suggest that students imagine they are the leaders of a nonaligned country. Ask them to write a 20- to 30-word telegram, to be sent to other members of the nonaligned movement, explaining how and why they are changing their attitudes on nonalignment. Call on volunteers to deliver their telegrams to the rest of the class.

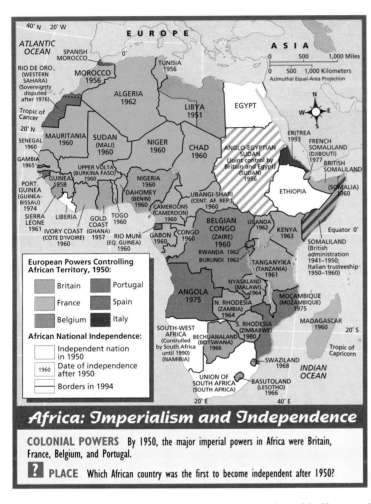

Africa: Imperialism and Independence

COLONIAL POWERS By 1950, the major imperial powers in Africa were Britain, France, Belgium, and Portugal.

? **PLACE** Which African country was the first to become independent after 1950?

Kenyatta expressed his conviction in a 1952 speech in which he discussed the flag of the Kenya African Union (KAU). As African nationalist Karari Njama recalled:

Kenyatta expressed his conviction in a 1952 speech in which he discussed the flag of the Kenya African Union (KAU). As African nationalist Karari Njama recalled:

❝ He [Kenyatta] raised the KAU flag to symbolize African Government. . . . He said, "Black is to show that this is for black people. Red is to show that the blood of an African is the same colour as the blood of a European, and green is to show that when we were given this country by God it was green, fertile and good but now you see the green is below the red and is suppressed." . . . What he said must mean that our fertile lands (green) could only be regained by the blood (red) of the African (black). ❞

Fighting in Kenya broke out in 1952 and continued until 1956. Some 13,000 Africans were killed. Although the independence movement gained even wider support in the late 1950s, Kenya did not officially become independent from Britain until 1963.

In the French African territories, the bloodiest struggle for independence took place in Algeria in North Africa. About one million French colonists lived in Algeria, and in some ways the French considered Algeria a part of France itself. Algerians, however, felt differently, and a nationalist revolt in 1954 sparked a brutal war that raged for several years. Both sides committed many atrocities. Faced with growing opposition to the war, France decided to cut its losses and gave Algeria its independence in 1962.

The Belgian government had no wish to face the bloodshed experienced in Kenya and Algeria. In 1959, when rioting broke out in Belgium's one African colony, the Belgian Congo, the Belgians left even before a successor government was firmly in place. Rival groups engaged in a civil war that wracked the country. Soon the Congo was caught up in the Cold War competition between the United States

▲ This 1964 photograph shows Angolan rebels being instructed in the use of the bazooka.

COOPERATIVE LEARNING

Divide the class into groups of six. Have members develop a chart comparing the challenges posed by independence in each of the following countries: India, Indonesia, Vietnam, Kenya, Algeria, Zaire. Groups should present their charts to the class.

Chapter 23
SECTION 3

*P*ractice

GUIDED PRACTICE

Have students identify the 10 most important events or developments discussed in the section. List the events and developments on the chalkboard and review them, asking students to provide details about each one.

INDEPENDENT PRACTICE

Ask students to use the list developed in the Guided Practice to prepare illustrated time lines showing the history of imperialism from the end of World War II to the height of the Cold War. Students may wish to include their time lines in their portfolios.

*R*eview and *A*ssessment

REVIEW Call on students to take turns answering the Focus questions on p. 634. For each question, record the responses on the chalkboard until no further details can be provided. Then assign the Section 3 Review on p. 639.

ASSESS Assign the **Section 3 Daily Quiz** in *Core Resources*.

HISTORICAL SIDELIGHTS
Balance of Superpowers

Nonalignment was not simply a form of opposition to colonialism, but also was intended to provide greater flexibility in foreign affairs. Nonaligned nations believed that they had the right to side with either superpower in any specific dispute, as long as the superpower's position could be justified. These temporary alliances were designed to allow nonaligned nations to participate in international movements while asserting their independence from the major powers.

and the Soviet Union. Warring parties sought allies where they could, and each superpower hoped to curry favor with the victor in the civil war—whoever that might be. Although the civil war eventually came to an end in the Congo (which changed its name to Zaire in 1971), the country's transition to independence seemed an ominous token of how Cold War rivalries could inflame situations that were explosive enough on their own.

■■ **Although most African nations became independent in the 1950s and 1960s, independence did not always come easily.**

*T*HE NONALIGNED MOVEMENT

The predicament of the Congo was similar to that faced by many small countries in the 1950s and 1960s. Both the United States and the Soviet Union, seeking allies in the Cold War, tried to win the support of the smaller countries by offering them money and supplies. When such devices failed, the superpowers sometimes tried force. For the smaller countries, many of them only recently independent, the international arena of the Cold War could be a dangerous place.

Complicating the situation, many of the newly independent countries remained economically dependent on the old imperial powers. For nationalists anxious to demonstrate their independence, such links could be irritating. It was easier and cheaper, for example, for Nigerians to telephone London than to call nearby Ivory Coast—Nigeria had been a British colony while Ivory Coast had been French.

▲ In 1954, after rebels began a war in Algeria, nomadic families were protected by French troops as they moved from isolated mountain regions.

Neocolonialism. As problems mounted, many new leaders began to blame conditions on the old colonial powers. Some accused the former colonial powers of **neocolonialism**—trying to maintain indirect control over former colonies even after they had achieved independence. As the greatest capitalist power after World War II, the United States, too, was soon accused by many nationalist leaders of practicing this new style of imperialism through economic control. The American role in Cold War events only reinforced this image. When faced with the choice between anti-imperialism and anticommunism, the United States consistently chose anticommunism. The war in Indochina was a case in point.

In reaction to the Cold War rivalries and as a matter of mutual protection, many leaders of the newly independent nations banded together. They formed the **nonaligned movement**, a name that reflected the member nations' policy of neutrality in regard to the two superpowers. One of the founders of the movement was India's new prime minister, Jawaharlal Nehru. Nehru believed that Westerners continued to use the former colonies as pawns in their own quarrels. He hoped to extend Gandhi's doctrine of self-help to other newly independent nations.

■■ **Many former colonies avoided taking sides in the Cold War by forming the nonaligned movement.**

The Third World. To the nonaligned movement the world seemed to be divided into three parts: the First World of the Western capitalist nations, the Second World of the Soviet socialist nations, and the **Third World** made up of all the rest. The Third World first claimed the international spotlight in 1955 when Indonesia hosted a meeting in Bandung, a city on the Indonesian island of Java. The **Bandung Conference** reaffirmed Nehru's suggestion that the former colonies should remain neutral in the Cold War and if necessary should seek help for development from both sides. The conference also inspired the establishment of regional organizations among many Third World nations.

Third World conferences became a regular feature of international politics during the next decade. Moreover, as decolonization spread across Asia and Africa, more and more new countries

638   638 ■■ CHAPTER 23

RETEACH Have students work in groups, assigning individuals or pairs the task of outlining subsections. Direct individuals or pairs to exchange outlines and use them to ask questions of other members of the group.

Closure

Have students use information from the section to explain how the decline of imperialism helped to create a new system of international relations.

Extension

COMPARE Have students write a short essay comparing the ways in which India and Vietnam won independence.

INVESTIGATE Encourage students to investigate the history of the nonaligned movement. Suggest that they present their findings to the class in an oral report.

---

came into being, and most of them joined the nonaligned movement. By the mid-1960s Third World countries made up a majority of members of the United Nations. Though the major industrial powers still controlled the UN Security Council, the General Assembly became an important forum for Third World concerns.

Third World leaders were primarily interested in modernizing and industrializing quickly. Although most complained about being tied to the economies of the former imperial powers, they also depended on foreign aid—including American aid—to pursue their development and modernization programs. Through the nonaligned movement, Third World leaders hoped to keep free of the Cold War struggle and yet obtain the resources they needed for development.

This was not easy. During the Cold War, American foreign aid rarely came without strings attached. The United States saw economic aid as a way to buy allies. To most U.S. leaders, the idea of neutrality in the struggle against worldwide communism was dangerous. John Foster Dulles, secretary of state under President Eisenhower, called it "immoral." Eisenhower himself said, "There can be no neutrals when the question is one of moral values or right and wrong."

American relations with many Third World countries became strained over the issue of neutrality. In the UN many of the Third World leaders denounced American policies as imperialistic. Even so, they continued to apply for aid from both the Western nations and the Soviet Union.

Changing goals. As the nonaligned movement grew larger and more diverse, the policy of neutrality became less important than the goal of development. Soon the movement included some countries that were openly allied with one superpower or the other. Cuba, for example, became a Soviet ally. Pakistan, the Philippines, and several Latin American countries had close ties to the United States.

As a result, the term *Third World* became a synonym for the region of the planet occupied by less developed countries. In addition to the East-West issues of the Cold War, people now spoke of North-South issues—those issues separating the rich, industrialized nations of the northern part of the globe from the poorer countries of the southern part. (These labels were generalizations. New Zealand, for example, was wealthy, though in the Southern Hemisphere, while North Korea, in the Northern Hemisphere, was poor.)

As the colonial empires faded from view, the concerns of those countries that had been part of the empires became increasingly important in international affairs. Though none of these countries possessed the power or wealth of the United States or the Soviet Union, together they held a majority of the world's people. This alone gave them a significance not even the superpowers could ignore.

■■ **Economic development replaced neutrality in the Cold War as the major concern of Third World nations.**

SECTION REVIEW ANSWERS

IDENTIFY

For significance see the following pages:
Clement Attlee (p. 635)
Jomo Kenyatta (p. 636)
neocolonialism (p. 638)
nonaligned movement (p. 638)
Jawaharlal Nehru (p. 638)
Third World (p. 638)
Bandung Conference (p. 638)

LOCATE

For locations, see the map on p. 637.

1. *World War II ended European military superiority and marked the beginning of the dissolution of overseas empires.*
2. *the late 1950s and early 1960s*
3. *by forming the nonaligned movement*
4. *Speeches should indicate the need for foreign aid as well as the necessity of internal improvements.*
5. *Answers will vary but should reflect an analysis of the conditions attached to aid.*

SECTION 3 REVIEW

IDENTIFY and explain the significance of the following: Clement Attlee, Jomo Kenyatta, neocolonialism, nonaligned movement, Jawaharlal Nehru, Third World, Bandung Conference.

LOCATE and explain the importance of the following: Algeria, Kenya, Belgian Congo.

1. **MAIN IDEA** In what ways did World War II lead to independence for several Asian countries?
2. **MAIN IDEA** During what years did most of the nations of Africa become independent?
3. **MAIN IDEA** How did many former colonies try to avoid taking sides in the Cold War?
4. **WRITING TO EXPRESS A VIEWPOINT** Imagine you are a delegate to the Bandung Conference. Prepare a speech discussing how the Third World might obtain the resources necessary for economic development.
5. **EVALUATING** How might the United States have given greater support to independence movements and to newly independent countries?

PREVIEW WORKSHOP

Following is the significant term in this section. You may wish to use this term as part of a section preview.

Term

■ Organization of African Unity

MOTIVATING: STUDENT EXPERIENCES

Ask students to recall information they have read in magazines and newspapers or seen on television news programs about the problems facing many African and Asian countries today. List their responses on a flipchart. As students study the section, have them note which of these problems can be described as legacies of imperialism.

FOCUS OBJECTIVES

■ Describe the problems that newly independent nations faced following decolonization.

■ Explain how Africa continued to feel the effects of imperialism even after most African nations became independent.

■ Illustrate how the nations of Eastern Europe and the Soviet Union resemble former Asian and African colonies.

Section 4

LEGACIES OF IMPERIALISM

FOCUS

■ **What problems did newly independent nations face following decolonization?**

■ **How did Africa continue to feel the effects of imperialism even after most African nations became independent?**

■ **How do the nations of Eastern Europe and the former Soviet Union resemble former Asian and African colonies?**

Once they had gained independence, many former Asian and African colonies continued to face problems related to their colonial histories. And when the Soviet Union collapsed, many Eastern European and former Soviet nations faced similar problems.

Lithuanians holding aloft their country's flag in Vilnius, Lithuania, 1991

PROBLEMS OF INDEPENDENCE

The nonaligned movement helped establish ways in which the newly independent nations might interact with the United States, the Soviet Union, and Europe. But the new nations also had to deal with the realities of setting up political, economic, and social systems—and of addressing domestic conflicts. These were not easy tasks.

◄ N'Garta Tombalbaye, Chad's first president, is shown here at the meeting that established the Organization of African Unity in 1963.

Apart from small groups of Western-educated nationalists, few people in many of the new nations felt any sense of national identity or loyalty to the new states. Some new nations were made up of many diverse groups of people who had never before been politically unified. As the new political leaders struggled with the challenges of governing, many turned to autocratic methods to achieve their goals. Unable to create a sense of national identity among their diverse peoples, many leaders began to practice a kind of ethnic imperialism, relying on their own families and ethnic communities for support. Others used the military to preserve order. Military dictatorships sprang up in many Asian and African nations after independence.

A further problem concerned borders. In many cases, the boundaries established prior to or at independence created terrible conflicts as different cultural groups laid claim to the same territory. India and Pakistan, for instance, fought

PROBLEMS OF INDEPENDENCE

On the chalkboard draw a word web with *End of Imperialism* at the center and *Autocratic Governments, Ethnic Conflicts, Ethnic Imperialism, Illogical Boundaries, Inadequate Training for Government, Military Dictatorships,* and *Underdeveloped Economies* around it. Then ask volunteers to describe the relationship of each satellite term to the process of decolonization. Record their responses in the appropriate place on the word web. Then have students use the information on the chalkboard to write a paragraph explaining how African nations continue to face the effects of imperialism long after independence.

THE COLLAPSE OF THE SOVIET EMPIRE

Organize students into small groups to write scripts for a five-minute television documentary titled "The Soviet Breakup—Decolonization Revisited." Mention that scripts should compare the problems faced by the former Soviet Union and those faced by former Asian and African colonies. Ask groups to present and discuss their scripts.

▶

---

several times over possession of the boundary province of Kashmir and witnessed lasting strife between Muslims and Hindus. In the Middle East the violent conflict between Israelis and Arabs raged for decades.

∎∎ Many newly independent nations faced political instability and ethnic strife.

AFRICA: A CASE STUDY

Africa, in particular, felt the strains created by borders. Back in the 1880s, as the imperialist scramble for African territory was getting underway, the European powers held a conference in Berlin, Germany, to decide how to divide Africa. Looking at a map of the continent, they drew boundaries that were, for the most part, simply based on their own convenience. They failed to consider features that naturally determine borders, such as landforms or cultural groupings. In some cases, borders lumped together hundreds of diverse peoples. Nigeria, for example, became home to over 200 ethnic groups. In other cases, borders split up ethnic groups. The Somali people found themselves divided among Somalia, Ethiopia, and Kenya.

In 1963, after most of the African nations had gained independence, they formed the **Organization of African Unity** (OAU). One of the OAU's main goals was to prevent territorial conflicts among its members. Fearing that redrawing boundaries might spark border disputes, the OAU decided to keep the old colonial boundaries following decolonization. While this decision did limit conflict between African nations, it did not prevent conflict within nations. In Nigeria a separatist movement led to a bloody civil war in 1967. In Sudan, too, ethnic and cultural differences between north and south led to a civil war that dragged on from the mid-1950s to the 1990s. Civil wars and conflicts related to ethnic groupings have affected several other African countries, such as Rwanda (see Chapter 25).

The artificial borders imposed by Europeans were not the only legacies of colonialism left in Africa after independence. Because Europeans made few substantial efforts to develop diversified colonial economies, Africans had little to build on following independence. As a result, they found it difficult to achieve economic self-sufficiency or even to forge new international economic ties. Thus most of the African nations remained economically dependent on their former colonial rulers. Economic dependence on Europe continues today. Only some 5 percent of Africa's total international trade is conducted within Africa.

Economic independence has been hard to achieve in part because many African nations have had difficulty attracting foreign investment due to their size (another result of European-made boundaries), political instability, or poverty. As one investment analyst explained:

> **❝** A lot of African countries, because of their colonial legacy, are so tiny I don't know what they can do. A lot of the products [foreign] companies want to sell, like Coca-Cola [or consumer goods] can't be sold to people without food or running water. **❞**

In some places the Europeans not only failed to develop African economies but also did not adequately prepare Africans themselves for the

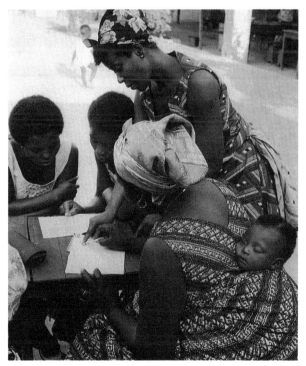

▲ This literacy class in Togo, a small nation in West Africa, helps prepare these women for their role as citizens of a republic.

*P*ractice

GUIDED PRACTICE

Return to the flipchart used in the Motivating activity at the beginning of the section. Review with students the problems that resulted from imperialism. List these problems on the flipchart.

INDEPENDENT PRACTICE

Direct students to select one of the problems from the list developed in the Guided Practice. Encourage them to create an editorial cartoon about their selected problem. Students may wish to include their cartoons in their portfolios.

*R*eview and *A*ssessment

REVIEW Suggest that students write the main ideas of the section in the form of newspaper headlines. Ask for volunteers to present their headlines, and have the class discuss what might be included in articles that accompany the headlines. Then assign the Section 4 Review on p. 643.

ASSESS Assign the **Section 4 Daily Quiz** in *Core Resources.*

PRIMARY SOURCE
Description of Change: excerpted and bracketed
Rationale: excerpted to focus on main idea; bracketed to clarify meaning

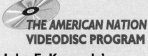

THE AMERICAN NATION VIDEODISC PROGRAM

John F. Kennedy's Berlin Speech

| 2B   43456   :42 |

AV TRANSPARENCY
Linking Geography and History Transparency and **Worksheet 24**

HISTORICAL SIDELIGHTS

Economic Challenges
In 1993 Sergei P. Balan, technical director for a textile factory in Ivanovo, Russia, said, "We've all decided in this factory that we can't rely on the state. If we survive, it will be from our own efforts. And if we go down, we'll go down together." The factory once employed 6,500 people, but by 1993 active employment had dropped to 2,000, and workers received a salary of about $12 per month. The remaining 4,500 employees were on contract and received about $2.49 per month, but had no actual work.

---

challenges they would face following independence. In Zaire (formerly the Belgian Congo), for example, Belgians held most government and business jobs during the colonial period. Africans, meanwhile, received little training—not only in government and business but also in services such as education and health care. Thus when the region became independent in 1960 and the Belgians left, Zaire had few people who had enough experience to manage the country effectively. Zaire was not the only African nation that faced this problem. As Salim Ahmed Salim, the secretary-general of the Organization of African Unity, explained,

> 66 Colonial education, limited to training very low functionaries [government officials], did not prepare the African for the eventual assumption of leadership and management of the affairs of a modern state. 99

In many nations, lack of experience has led to problems of governmental inefficiency, political corruption, and economic planning.

Not all of Africa's problems can be blamed on its colonial heritage. Limited natural resources in some areas, droughts and other natural disasters, and a variety of other obstacles have contributed to many African nations' lack of prosperity. Nevertheless, historians can only guess at what Africa might look like today had it never been colonized.

■■ **Many legacies of imperialism, such as illogical borders and underdeveloped economies, proved problematic for African nations after independence.**

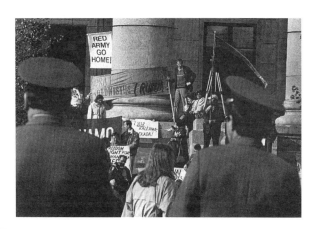

---

*T*HE SOVIET EMPIRE FALLS

As Africa struggled to shake free of colonial influences, the Soviet Union struggled in the mid-1980s to hold together its empire, sometimes referred to as the Soviet sphere. Made up of the Soviet Union's own republics and the satellite nations in Eastern Europe, the Soviet sphere began to collapse in the late 1980s (see Chapter 22). One by one the Eastern European nations broke free of Soviet control. Then the Soviet republics, too, declared independence. The last empire had fallen; the Soviet Union ceased to exist.

The nations created or reshaped by the fall of the Soviet Union found that independence carried its own problems. Like many of the nations that had become independent earlier in the century, the newly independent nations of Eastern Europe and the former Soviet Union have suffered from border disputes, political infighting, and underdeveloped economies. And as in Asia and Africa, ethnic rivalries that a strong central authority had kept in check for years resurfaced.

Yugoslavia has faced the worst of the violence caused by such rivalries (see Chapter 22), but ethnic tensions have affected other countries as well. In the former Soviet Union, the 15 newly independent republics have experienced conflict as different groups struggle for power. Russia and Ukraine have argued over control of the Black Sea fleet, while Christians in the former Soviet republic of Armenia have battled Muslims in neighboring Azerbaijan (az-uhr-by-JAHN). Similarly, some areas of Georgia, a republic just to the east of the Black Sea, have witnessed a rise in ethnic violence between Islamic groups and Georgians, who are traditionally Eastern Orthodox Christian. In some of the new nations of Central Asia, too, fighting has broken out among the region's many ethnic groups.

Economic problems have compounded other problems. Under Soviet control, each satellite nation and Soviet republic produced the goods that it could make or grow best. When the Soviet Union collapsed, however, so too

◄ **Two Soviet soldiers watch proindependence demonstrators in Lithuania in 1990.**

Closure

Encourage students to discuss the role they think the U.S. should play in the post-imperial world. Urge them to justify their arguments with information from the section.

Extension

RESEARCH Have students select a former Asian or African colony and research and write a case study of its imperial legacy.

CREATE Have students create an annotated map showing the new and reshaped nations that emerged from the Soviet collapse. Suggest that they indicate areas that are facing post-imperial problems.

---

did the trade networks that had kept the different regions supplied with necessary goods and resources. Hardships increased as the new nations had to establish new economic links.

Although foreign investment in some Eastern European nations and former Soviet republics is increasing, some investors are hesitant to put money in nations that remain politically and economically unstable. "The political situation in Russia is chaotic," noted one business expert. "It's just a much riskier environment." Even so, many people in Eastern Europe and the former Soviet Union remain cautiously hopeful that free market reforms and increasing democracy will one day bring prosperity.

■■ **The nations of the former Soviet sphere have faced many of the same social and economic problems that have challenged former colonies in Africa and Asia.**

COMMENTARY

America and the Post–Cold War World

As the Cold War was winding down, American commentator Charles Krauthammer wrote, "Nations need enemies. Take away one, and they find another. . . . Countries need mobilizing symbols of 'otherness' to energize the nation and to give it purpose." Krauthammer worried that with the decline of the Soviet Union and the end of the Cold War, America would lose its sense of purpose.

Others took a more optimistic view of what the United States might be able to accomplish in the new world order. Even though the major empires have dissolved and most nations now have the freedom to govern themselves, true democracy remains a dream in many parts of the world. A key question of the 1990s has been whether democratic nations can convince the rest of the world of democracy's ability to help solve social and economic ills. This goal will be accomplished not by military or economic might, but by the power of ideas. In this realm, many people believe, the United States can and must play a central role.

Despite a shifting balance of global power and changing economic realities, the appeal of individual freedom, democratic self-government, and opportunity for all remains as strong as ever. This is especially true for those denied them by repressive rulers or grinding poverty. From South Africa to Eastern Europe to Southeast Asia to Latin America, the vision of democracy and freedom can still become a reality.

SECTION REVIEW ANSWERS

IDENTIFY

For significance see the following page: Organization of African Unity (p. 641)

1. need for new political systems, lack of national identity, ethnic imperialism, arbitrary international boundaries
2. poorly-chosen borders, insufficient economic development, little access to education
3. shared social and economic problems
4. Letters should reflect the difficulties of maintaining a business in a country with an unstable economy.
5. Answers should discuss the effects of arbitrary borders established for colonies and new countries, as well as the lack of political and social systems.

■■ SECTION 4 REVIEW
■■

IDENTIFY and explain the significance of the following: Organization of African Unity.

1. **MAIN IDEA** What were some of the domestic challenges faced by newly independent nations following decolonization?

2. **MAIN IDEA** How did imperialism continue to affect Africa even after most African nations became independent?

3. **COMPARING** In what ways do the nations of the former Soviet sphere resemble former colonies in Africa and Asia?

4. **WRITING TO DESCRIBE** Imagine you are a merchant in a newly independent nation of Africa or of the former Soviet sphere. Write a letter to a friend describing how your business has changed since your country's independence.

5. **ANALYZING** Why did decolonization lead to an increase in ethnic conflict in some nations?

CHAPTER 23
Review

DEVELOPING THEMES

Return to the "Themes" section on p. 620. Have students discuss these again and compare their original responses to those given now. (See p. 619B for suggested answers.)

Chapter Review Answers

WRITING A SUMMARY
See Essential Points in each section for main ideas.

REVIEWING CHRONOLOGY
2, 3, 5, 4, 1
Evaluating
to maintain neutrality during the Cold War

IDENTIFYING PEOPLE AND IDEAS
1. *British author who described "white man's burden"*
2. *ports where ships could take on coal*
3. *new governmental administration established by colonizing country*
4. *encouraging economic and scientific development in colonies*
5. *Philippine leader who criticized U.S. rule*
6. *Manchurian government nominally headed by Chinese but actually controlled by Japan*
7. *Kenyan resistance leader who eventually became president*
8. *maintaining control over former colonies even after independence*
9. *Indian prime minister who founded nonaligned movement*
10. *group of independent African nations seeking to avoid territorial conflict*

644

UNDERSTANDING MAIN IDEAS

1. *Industrialization created a need for raw materials. In addition, new methods of transportation and new weapons were developed.*
2. *The violence of World War I caused many Europeans to question their earlier ideas about moral and cultural superiority. Although a number of colonies, notably those in the Middle East, were able to gain independence, other regions found that they had only exchanged one colonial power for another.*
3. *During the 1930s Japan, Italy, and Germany engaged in imperialism as they sought sources of raw materials and greater prestige.*
4. *World War II marked the beginning of independence movements in Asia. Although independence movements in Africa were slower to succeed, they also developed in the years after World War II.*
5. *The end of imperialism has posed problems related to social structures and political and economic stability.*

	Indian National Congress forms.	Battle of Omdurman leaves thousands of Africans dead.	Boxer Rebellion begins in China.	Japan invades Manchuria.	U.S. Congress passes Tydings-McDuffie Act.
	1885	1898	1900	1931	1934

WRITING A SUMMARY
Using the essential points of the chapter as a guide, write a summary of the chapter.

REVIEWING CHRONOLOGY
Number your paper 1 to 5. Study the time line above, and list the following events in the order in which they happened by writing the first next to 1, the second next to 2, and so on. Then complete the activity below.

1. U.S. Congress passes Tydings-McDuffie Act.
2. Atlantic Charter signed.
3. Kenya becomes independent from Britain.
4. Algerian nationalists revolt against French rule.
5. Indian National Congress forms.

Evaluating What did the leaders of newly independent nations hope to accomplish at the Bandung Conference?

IDENTIFYING PEOPLE AND IDEAS
Explain the historical significance of each of the following people or terms.

1. Rudyard Kipling
2. coaling station
3. direct rule
4. trusteeship
5. Manuel Quezon
6. puppet government
7. Jomo Kenyatta
8. neocolonialism
9. Jawaharlal Nehru
10. Organization of African Unity

UNDERSTANDING MAIN IDEAS
1. How did industrialization contribute to a renewal of imperialism in the late 1800s and early 1900s?
2. Why did World War I change European beliefs about imperialism? How did this change in beliefs affect the Middle East?
3. What major powers engaged in imperialism during the 1930s? What were their primary motives?
4. How did World War II affect European colonialism in Asia? Were the effects the same in Africa?
5. How have legacies of imperialism continued to challenge nations in Asia, Africa, Eastern Europe, and the former Soviet Union?

REVIEWING THEMES
1. **Democratic Values** Why did many early Americans believe that imperialism went against the spirit of democracy?
2. **Cultural Diversity** How did various forms of colonial government reflect differing ideas on the value of cultural diversity within an empire?
3. **Global Relations** What steps did former colonies take to avoid becoming involved in the Cold War? How successful were they?

THINKING CRITICALLY
1. **Synthesizing** In what ways did American expansion in the 1800s and early 1900s resemble European expansion? In what ways did it differ?
2. **Evaluating** What issues should the people of a colony consider in attempts to achieve independence? Support your answer with examples from independence movements in Asia and Africa.
3. **Hypothesizing** Do you think that wide-scale imperialism would still exist today if World Wars I and II had never happened? Why or why not?

STRATEGY FOR SUCCESS
Review the Strategies for Success on Recognizing Stereotypes on page 272. Then read the following excerpt from a book by Frederick Lugard, a British colonial administrator in Africa in the early 1900s. What stereotypes does Lugard use to justify British colonialism in Africa?

❝ As Roman imperialism laid the foundations of modern civilisation, and led the wild barbarians of these islands [Great Britain] along the path of progress, so in Africa to-day we are repaying the debt, and bringing to the dark places of earth, the abode of barbarism and cruelty, the torch of culture

John Bull, which represents Great Britain

REVIEWING THEMES

1. because the U.S. was founded on the belief that people had the right to rule themselves
2. Direct rule provided a completely new administration, and indirect rule allowed the colonizing country to rule through traditional local leaders. Direct rule often worked to change a local culture, while indirect rule focused on political and economic changes.
3. Some formed the nonaligned movement in an attempt to maintain neutrality, while others accepted aid from either the U.S. or the Soviet Union. The quest for neutrality was not always successful, because foreign aid was often necessary for development.

THINKING CRITICALLY

1. similarities—largely ignored wishes of original inhabitants of conquered lands; differences—U.S. territories became states with equal status
2. new political structures, economic systems, educational training, ethnic rivalries; all of these were problems in Asian and African independence movements
3. Answers will vary. Some students may feel that many contemporary nations would still be colonies because European nations would not have been devastated by war. Others may believe that independence movements would have developed even without the effects of the wars.

STRATEGY FOR SUCCESS

Great Britain—"promoted happiness and welfare," "torch of culture and progress," "taught value of liberty"; Africa—"dark places of the earth," "abode of barbarism and cruelty," "primitive"

WRITING ABOUT HISTORY

Speeches should reflect the problems posed by ethnic conflict and the benefits of unity and diversity.

USING PRIMARY SOURCES

Imperialism acts in opposition to the needs of the colony.

LINKING HISTORY AND GEOGRAPHY

National boundaries had changed, particularly in West Africa, and many nations had gained independence.

Timeline:

- **1935** Italy invades Ethiopia.
- **1941** Atlantic Charter signed.
- **1947** Britain grants India and Pakistan independence.
- **1954** France withdraws from Indochina. Algerian nationalists revolt against French rule.
- **1955** Bandung Conference held in Indonesia.
- **1960** Belgium grants the Congo independence.
- **1963** Kenya becomes independent from Britain. Organization of African Unity forms.
- **1967** Civil war breaks out in Nigeria.

and progress. . . . I am profoundly convinced that there can be no question but that British rule has promoted the happiness and welfare of the primitive races. Let those who question it examine the results impartially. If there is unrest, and a desire for independence, . . . it is because we have taught the value of liberty and freedom, which for centuries these peoples had not known. Their very discontent is a measure of their progress. **99**

WRITING ABOUT HISTORY

Writing to Persuade Imagine you are the leader of a newly independent nation that is experiencing conflict among various groups. Write a speech urging the conflicting groups to make peace. Explain why peace would benefit the nation as a whole.

USING PRIMARY SOURCES

Many independence movements gained strength in the period between World War I and World War II. Achmed Sukarno, for example, founded the Partai Nasional Indonesia (PNI) in 1927. In 1930, Indonesia's Dutch rulers attempted to destroy the PNI by arresting Sukarno and other nationalist leaders. Read the following excerpt from a speech Sukarno gave during his defense in the trial. What fundamental contradiction does Sukarno see in imperialism?

66 As long as a nation does not wield political power in its own country, part of its potential, economic, social or political, will be used for interests which are not its interests, but contrary to them. . . .

A colonial nation is a nation that cannot be itself, a nation that in almost all its branches, in all of its life, bears the mark of imperialism. . . . There is no community of interests between the subject and the object of imperialism. Between the two there is only a contrast of interests and a conflict of needs. All interests of imperialism, social,

economic, political, or cultural, are opposed to the interests of the Indonesian people. The imperialists desire the continuation of colonization, the Indonesians desire its abolition. The regulations that came into being under the influence of imperialism are therefore contrary to the interest of the Indonesian people. **99**

LINKING HISTORY AND GEOGRAPHY

Study the map on page 637, which shows how Africa was divided among various European powers in 1950. Then refer to the map on pages 238–239. Focus on the part of the map that shows how Africa was divided among various European powers in 1914. How did imperialism in Africa change between 1914 and 1950?

BUILDING YOUR PORTFOLIO

Complete the following projects independently or cooperatively.

1. **THE ECONOMY** Imagine you are an economist in an independent nation that was under imperial control for the first half of the 20th century. Create a flowchart tracing the relationship between your nation's colonial background and economic factors. Consider the economic motivations that led imperialist powers to take interest in your country originally as well as the economic consequences of imperialism for your nation today.

2. **INDIVIDUAL RIGHTS** Imagine you are a member of an independence movement in a region under imperial control in the mid-1900s. Write a petition to the government of the controlling nation describing how imperialism has interfered with the rights of your region's inhabitants.

BUILDING YOUR PORTFOLIO

Have students refer to **Building Your Portfolio Worksheet 6**, assigned at the beginning of Unit 6. Use the worksheet to help students monitor their progress on the portfolio projects.

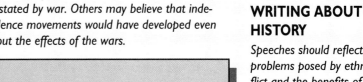

Assessment

Core Resources
- Reteaching Worksheet 23
- Chapter 23 Tests
- Alternative Assessment Forms

Test Generator

ꓞROM INDUSTRIALIZATION TO GLOBAL ECONOMY

Chapter Overview

Industrialization and technological advances in the late 1800s helped make the U.S. a power in the world economy. From this central position, the U.S. played a major role in efforts to increase world trade. After the 1920s these efforts faltered as the world economy underwent major changes and disruptions. To prevent similar disruptions in the future, the U.S. led the way in restructuring the global economy after World War II. Strong economic growth followed, especially in the U.S., Europe, and Japan. Further developments in the late 20th century brought even more changes in the global economy.

Chapter Planning Guide

CHAPTER 24	CORE RESOURCES	AUDIOVISUAL RESOURCES	PROGRAM RESOURCES
INTRODUCTION pp. 646–647	■ Building Your Portfolio Worksheet 6	■ Linking Geography and History Transparencies and Worksheets 11, 11A, 11B, 11C	
TEACHING THE CHAPTER pp. 648–667	■ Graphic Organizer 24 ■ Social Studies Skills Worksheet 24 ■ Literature Worksheet 24 ■ Geography Worksheet 24 ■ Outline Maps 8, 13, 14, 16, 19, 20, 24	■ *The American Nation Videodisc: The Wright Brothers; The Great Depression; The Growth of Suburbia; The Maiden Flight of the Concorde*	■ *Eyewitnesses and Others,* Volume 2: Readings 6, 24, 27, 38, 41, 47
REVIEW AND ASSESSMENT pp. 668–669	■ Chapter 24 Daily Quizzes ■ Reteaching Worksheet 24 ■ Chapter 24 Tests ■ Alternative Assessment Forms		■ Test Generator

Additional Resources

BOOKS FOR TEACHERS

Halberstam, David. *The Next Century.* Updated ed. Avon, 1992. Analyzes global economy on the eve of the 21st century.

Hugill, Peter J. *World Trade Since 1431: Geography, Technology, and Capitalism.* Johns Hopkins University Press, 1993. A review of the history of world trade.

Orme, William A., Jr. *Continental Shift: Free Trade & the New North America.* Washington Post Company, 1993. Examines the effects of NAFTA.

BOOKS FOR STUDENTS

Epping, Randy Charles. *A Beginner's Guide to the World Economy.* Random House, 1992. Offers concise explanations of major world economic issues.

Macmillan, Bill, and Gordon Fell. *Atlas of Economic Issues.* Facts on File, 1992. Presents world economic issues in visual form.

*O'Toole, Thomas. *Global Economics: Economics for Today.* Lerner, 1991. Illustrated explanation of the global economy.

* for students reading below grade level

MULTIMEDIA MATERIALS

The Global Connection. Video, 60 min. HCA/Instructional Video. Points out that economic policy must adapt to accelerating global change.

Pacific Horizons: Economic Change and Challenge. Video, 28 min. Close-Up Foundation/SSSS. Examines the growing importance of the Pacific Rim nations.

The World Bank Story. Video, 20 min. World Bank/SSSS. Explains the history and functions of the World Bank.

THEMES IN AMERICAN HISTORY

USE WITH PAGES 646–647

*L*isted on the right are the themes emphasized in Chapter 24. The questions in boldface type stimulate critical thinking and provide students with an opportunity to discuss the themes within a broadened context. The questions also appear in the pupil's edition on p. 646.

■ TECHNOLOGY AND SOCIETY

How does technology shape economic relations between countries? Students might point out that technological development aids economic growth. An economically developed country might be able to control the flow of goods to developing countries and, therefore, be able to influence those countries economically.

■ GLOBAL RELATIONS

How is conflict harmful to global economic development? Students may mention that in times of war, trade between warring nations is cut off. Further, the belligerents often try to prevent neutral nations from trading with enemies. Wars also harm global economic development because post-war reconstruction is so costly. Some students might also point out that conflict over tariffs or foreign investment might lead to nations adopting protectionist trade policies that harm global economic growth.

■ ECONOMIC DEVELOPMENT

What are the benefits of free trade and protectionism? Students might mention that the major benefit of free trade is that it becomes easier for a country to sell goods in foreign markets, while the greatest benefit of protectionism is that it shields domestic industries from foreign competition.

What are the costs? Students might point out that free trade may hurt domestic industries through unfair foreign competition, which could lead to factory closings and unemployment. Students might mention that protectionist policies could lead other countries to raise their tariffs, and this could result in a drastic decrease in trade.

CHAPTER STRATEGIES FOR MEETING INDIVIDUAL NEEDS

LIMITED ENGLISH PROFICIENT LEARNERS

Have students work in small groups to create illustrated time lines of the major events in the development of the global economy during the 20th century.

TACTILE/KINESTHETIC LEARNERS

Ask students to work in small groups to create scripts for skits about one of the main ideas in the chapter. Have them perform their skits for the class.

LEARNERS HAVING DIFFICULTY

Discuss the meaning and significance of the boldfaced terms in the chapter with students, encouraging them to offer definitions and explanations. Then have students use these terms to write a brief summary of the chapter.

AUDITORY LEARNERS

Direct students to select a quotation from each section and write an introduction to the quote, explaining its subject, its source, and its relevance to the section. Have students read their selections and introductions to the class.

VISUAL LEARNERS

Encourage students to use materials in the school and public libraries to locate and photocopy illustrations for a collage that illustrates the title of the chapter. Ask volunteers to present and explain their collages to the class.

GIFTED LEARNERS

Have students write an essay titled "The World Economy on the Threshold of the 21st Century." Suggest that they focus on the origins of and possible solutions to the major economic challenges faced by the world's nations.

USING THE CHAPTER FOCUS

■ **UNDERSTANDING THE MAIN IDEA**
Call on a volunteer to read aloud the Understanding the Main Idea paragraph. Then ask students to suggest ways in which the global economy has become more unified in the 1990s. Have students evaluate their responses after they have completed the chapter.

 THEMES
Have students work individually or in groups to answer the questions under Themes. Save students' responses so that they can compare them with their responses after studying the chapter. (See p. 645B for suggested answers.)

■ **THE TIME LINE**
Ask students to write the time-line entries in their notebooks. As students study the chapter, have them record the significance of each event to the development of the global economy.

CORE RESOURCES

• **Graphic Organizer 24**
• **Building Your Portfolio Worksheet 6**

646

ABOUT THE ILLUSTRATION

Tell students that currency provides nations with an opportunity to illustrate different elements of their cultures or history. Point out that many coins bear images of national leaders, such as the ruling monarch of the United Kingdom or U.S. presidents. Other coins may include objects or symbols that are commonly associated with that country. For instance, some Norwegian coins include a picture of a reindeer, and the 10-franc coin from Madagascar shows an outline of the island. Ask students what the images on other coins in the illustration may represent.

Chapter 24

FROM INDUSTRIALIZATION TO GLOBAL ECONOMY

FOCUS

UNDERSTANDING THE MAIN IDEA

In the first half of the 20th century the United States became the most powerful country in the world, and this power rested largely on America's economic might. America's economic might rested, in turn, on the nation's ever-closer involvement in the global economy, which grew increasingly unified in the 1900s.

 THEMES

■ **TECHNOLOGY AND SOCIETY** How does technology shape economic relations between countries?

■ **GLOBAL RELATIONS** How is conflict harmful to global economic development?

■ **ECONOMIC DEVELOPMENT** What are the benefits of free trade and of protectionism? What are the costs?

1900	1930	1944	1951	1993
▼ U.S. adopts the gold standard.	▼ Smoot-Hawley Tariff passed.	▼ Bretton Woods conference held.	▼ European Coal and Steel Community formed.	▼ NAFTA ratified.

■■ **LINK TO THE PAST**

International economic affairs played a large role in American history almost from its beginning. For example, if Columbus had not been trying to find a shorter trade route to China, he never would have bumped into the Americas in 1492. American merchants engaged in overseas trade as part of the British Empire, and after independence they ventured out energetically on their own.

Coins from around the world

During the 1830s Frenchman Alexis de Tocqueville visited the United States and forecast a brilliant future for the Americans. Tocqueville said that Americans had both the human and the natural resources to make their country one of the wealthiest and most powerful in the world. No enemy could deprive Americans of "that fertile wilderness which offers resources to all industry"; nor would the Americans be denied "their climate or their inland seas, their great rivers or their exuberant soil."

Tocqueville noted something else. "At the present time . . . ," he wrote, "the nations seem to be advancing to unity. Our means of intellectual intercourse unite the remotest parts of the earth; and men cannot remain strangers to each other, or be ignorant of what is taking place in any corner of the globe."

Events bore out both of Tocqueville's predictions, although not at once. The slavery dispute, the Civil War, and Reconstruction delayed America's rise to world power, and two world wars set back the trend toward global unification. But during the first half of the 20th century, the United States became the most powerful country in the world, largely as a result of its possessing the most powerful economy. And during the second half of the 20th century, the trend toward economic unification resumed.

Bank exchange sign in Madrid, Spain

Chapter 24

SECTION 1

Introducing the Section

FOCUS OBJECTIVES

- Identify some of the effects of industrialization on the American economy during the late 1800s.

- Describe why and where Americans hoped to find new markets for their products in the early 20th century.

- Explain how technological innovations have contributed to the growth of the global economy.

CORE RESOURCES

- **Section 1 Daily Quiz**

AV **RESOURCES**

- **Linking Geography and History Transparency** and **Worksheet 11**
- ***The American Nation Videodisc: The Wright Brothers***

648

PREVIEW WORKSHOP

Following is a list of the significant people and terms in this section. You may wish to use this list as a section preview.

People
- Cyrus Field
- Guglielmo Marconi

Terms
- electronic mail

MOTIVATING: PRIOR KNOWLEDGE

Have students recall the developments that helped to transform the U.S. into a great economic power in the late 1800s. *(technological innovations in industry, communications, energy; rise of big business; new marketing methods)* Ask students to speculate on how an increase in power might lead the U.S. to take a greater role in the world economy. Have them review their responses as they study the section.

Section 1

INDUSTRIALIZATION AND THE REVOLUTION IN TECHNOLOGY

FOCUS

- **What were some of the effects of industrialization on the American economy during the late 1800s?**
- **Why and where did Americans hope to find new markets for their products in the early 20th century?**
- **How have technological innovations contributed to the growth of the global economy?**

Two major developments thrust the United States into a central position in the world economy during the late 19th and early 20th centuries. The first was industrialization, which enabled workers to produce large quantities of goods for export. The second was the introduction of technologies that brought the United States into closer contact with other countries and peoples.

Lithograph of a McCormick Harvesting Machine Company catalog cover

AN INDUSTRIAL GIANT

By 1900 the United States boasted the most powerful industrial economy in the world. Its production of steel—more than 10 million tons in 1900—almost equaled the combined production of Britain and Germany, the world's second and

▼ By 1900 machines such as this steam tractor had greatly increased farm productivity.

third largest steelmakers. Manufactured and processed goods of all kinds, from tractors and trolley cars to cotton cloth and canned hams, poured out of American factories and plants in record quantities.

Industrialization arrived on the farms not long after it hit the cities. Steam-powered combines, gangplows, and other devices allowed farmers to cultivate more land. Production of wheat, corn, cotton, and other crops skyrocketed. Wheat production, for example, increased from 100 million bushels in 1849 to nearly 600 million bushels in 1900. Corn production rose from less than 600 million bushels to over 2.5 billion bushels during the same years.

Industrialization brought the United States unprecedented prosperity, but it also made the American economy more susceptible to the ups and downs of the business cycle. The severe economic downturns of the 1870s and 1890s, which led to numerous bankruptcies and layoffs, reflected the American economy's heightened sensitivity to cycles of boom and bust.

INDUSTRIALIZATION AND THE AMERICAN ECONOMY

On the chalkboard create a cause-effect chain indicating the effects of 19th-century industrialization on the American economy. The first link should be labeled *Rise to Industrial Power,* and the last should read *Need for New Markets.* Ask students to connect the entries by adding links to the chain. Have students use the chain to write a paragraph describing the effects of industrialization.

NEW MARKETS FOR AMERICAN GOODS

Provide students with outline maps of the world, and have them indicate new markets that developed for American goods in the early 20th century. Suggest that students also add pertinent data mentioned in the section, as well as titles and keys. Students may wish to include their maps in their portfolios.

▶

Boom times often led to overproduction. American factories and farms were now generating large quantities of goods, but they were not always able to sell all of these goods—particularly in times of bust. To guarantee future prosperity and the continued growth of the American economy, many observers believed some way had to be found to sell all the products Americans were churning out. President William McKinley bluntly put the matter to a gathering of business and civic leaders:

> 66 There is no use in making a product if you cannot find somebody to take it. The maker must find a taker. You will not . . . make a product unless you can find a buyer for that product after you have made it. 99

■■ **Industrialization brought prosperity but also problems, including recurrent economic downturns and the potential for overproduction.**

LOOKING ABROAD FOR MARKETS

As the 20th century dawned, the most promising place to find the takers and buyers McKinley spoke of appeared to be overseas. If Americans could not or would not buy all the goods U.S. farms and factories were able to produce, then perhaps foreigners would. "The time is not far distant," predicted one New York business editor, "when probably all of the principal industries of the Republic will be either compelled or in a position . . . to seek outlets for their products abroad."

In their search for new markets, American exporters looked to Latin America. Latin America had the advantage of being close at hand. In addition, ever since the announcement of the Monroe Doctrine in 1823, Americans had felt a particular interest in the affairs of the countries to their south. This interest became increasingly economic as time passed. In 1898 the value of U.S. exports to Latin America totaled $90 million; by 1910 that figure had jumped to $263 million.

▲ This Union Pacific timetable suggests the role that railroads played in American expansion westward.

American exporters also sought new markets in East Asia. During the mid-19th century, the United States had followed the lead of Great Britain and other European powers in imposing trade agreements on a reluctant Chinese government. In the 1850s, the United States led the way in opening Japan to foreign commerce. As a result, trade with Asia bloomed. Prior to 1850 the value of U.S. exports to Asia had never totaled more than $4 million annually; in 1900 the value of such exports exceeded $65 million.

▲ As a result of the opening of China and Japan to foreign commerce, trade with East Asia increased. Even Japanese royalty wore western-style clothing.

To many Americans, East Asia represented more than a market for exports—it was a new frontier. From the time of the founding of the British colonies, American history had been a chronicle of westward expansion. Americans had crossed the Appalachians to the Mississippi River, then crossed the Rockies to the Pacific Ocean. Many believed that America's future always lay to the west. But by the 1890s the land frontier in the United States had disappeared as the country's growing population spread. The only way to expand westward was to cross the Pacific to what Europeans had labeled the "Far East."

Although some people called for continued territorial expansion, others argued that commercial expansion—the growth of American overseas trade—would do. And yet others, such as Senator Mark Hanna of Ohio, called for territorial expansion to aid commercial expansion. "If it is commercialism to want the possession of a strategic point giving the American people an opportunity to maintain a foothold in the markets of . . . [China]," remarked Hanna in the debate over U.S. annexation of the Philippines, "for God's sake let us have commercialism."

Commercial expansion would have to do for parts of the world where territorial expansion was out of the question, such as in Europe.

PRIMARY SOURCE
Description of Change: excerpted
Rationale: excerpted to focus on main idea

 GLOBAL CONNECTIONS

U.S. business leaders were not the only people interested in opportunities in Latin America. In 1908 several hundred Japanese immigrants arrived in Brazil. Today, Japanese Brazilian farmers produce about 70 percent of the vegetables and fruit sold in São Paulo, Brazil. Cotia, a Japanese farm cooperative, runs experimental stations and an agricultural school, and exports soybeans, coffee, tea, cotton, and other crops.

Teaching the Section

TECHNOLOGICAL INNOVATION AND WORLD TRADE

List on the chalkboard a number of innovations in communications discussed in the section. Encourage students to suggest how these innovations affected world trade. Note responses under the appropriate innovation. Have students select an innovation and, using information on the chalkboard, design posters or cartoons that illustrate the impact of communications on world trade. Call on volunteers to display and explain their posters or cartoons.

■■ Have students identify recent technological innovations that have encouraged world trade.

HISTORICAL SIDELIGHTS

The Transatlantic Cable
Cyrus Field made four unsuccessful attempts to lay a transatlantic cable. His first two cables broke, and the third failed after four weeks of operation. The fourth broke and sank shortly before completion of the project. Not until his fifth try did Field succeed in linking Europe and North America with telegraph cable.

Throughout its history America's closest economic ties had been with Europe, especially Great Britain and France. Europe had been a source of investment capital for emerging American industries, such as railroads. By the late 19th century, it had gained increasing importance as a market for American exports as well. In 1900 the value of U.S. exports to Europe exceeded $1 billion for the first time.

■■ **At the beginning of the 20th century overproduction caused Americans to look abroad for export markets, especially to Latin America, East Asia, and Europe.**

A SHRINKING PLANET

If the tremendous growth of the American economy during the second half of the 19th century seemed to make deeper involvement in world trade necessary, rapid strides in technology made it possible. The emergence of a global economy depended on innovations in two related areas: transportation and communication.

For most of human history, transportation and communication had been intimately linked. With the exception of communication by carrier pigeon or drum signal, messages traveled no faster than the people who carried them. This remained the case at the beginning of the 19th century, when neither transportation nor communication was much faster than it had ever been.

Technological developments soon changed this. Railroads increased the speed at which people and their messages could travel. A journey across Europe or North America now required days instead of weeks or even months. Although the railroads cost more to build and operate than the animal-drawn vehicles they replaced, they generated more business and thus greater revenues. Between 1860 and 1880, railroad mileage in both Europe and the United States more than tripled.

At sea, steamships gradually replaced sailing vessels after the 1830s. While the steamers were not as fast as

▲ After the 1830s, steamships became a less costly, more reliable means of transporting people and products across the world's oceans.

the swiftest sailing ships, they were more reliable, since they could make headway even on windless days. As a result, a typical voyage across the Atlantic took only 7 or 8 days by 1874, as opposed to the 36 to 48 days a sailing ship might have taken in the 1830s. And by operating on fixed and predictable schedules, the steamships created new business and thereby brought down overall shipping costs. By the mid-1890s, ocean shipping costs were half of what they had been in 1873.

As much as steamships cut travel time across the Atlantic, the invention of the telegraph allowed transatlantic messages to move even faster. In the 1860s an American team headed by Cyrus Field succeeded in laying a permanent telegraph cable

▼ Telegraph cables laid across the floor of the Atlantic Ocean in the 1860s allowed operators to send messages rapidly between North America and Europe.

◄ After the invention of wireless telegraphy, operators were able to send messages long distances without the use of cables.

Practice

GUIDED PRACTICE

Write on the chalkboard the five subsection titles and inform students that these are topics for news stories. Call on volunteers to develop brief story outlines for each topic, noting their suggestions under the appropriate title.

INDEPENDENT PRACTICE

Direct students to use one of the outlines developed in the Guided Practice activity to write a news story on the way industrialization and technological innovation affected development of the world economy during the 19th and 20th centuries. Students may wish to include their stories in their portfolios.

Review and Assessment

REVIEW Have students write 10 questions on Section 1 on individual notecards with the answers on the reverse side. Then divide students into groups of four. Ask them to use their notecards to question the other members of the group. Then assign the Section 1 Review on p. 652.

ASSESS Assign the **Section 1 Daily Quiz** in *Core Resources.* ▶

across the floor of the Atlantic Ocean from North America to Europe. Before long, several cables crossed the ocean floor. While they sped transatlantic communications, the limited number of cables prevented wide-scale use. A 1901 *New York Times* editorial noted:

> 66 At twenty-five cents a word the fourteen Atlantic cables now in operation are fully occupied during the business hours of the day. That means that in this matter demand has outrun supply. 99

Italian scientist Guglielmo Marconi helped solve this problem by inventing a wireless telegraph that could transmit and receive electric signals long distances. On December 12, 1901, Marconi sat at a tower in St. John's, Newfoundland, and received the Morse code signal for the letter *s* from Cornwall, England—nearly 2,000 miles across the Atlantic—with no cables! A writer—the same one who had commented on the inaccessibility of the cables—reported that Marconi's intercontinental wireless telegraphy had the potential to transform "the business and political relations of the peoples of the earth." The writer went on to note:

▲ **Guglielmo Marconi invented the wireless telegraph at age 22.**

> 66 The animating spirit of modern invention is to overcome the obstacles of time and space, "to associate all the races of mankind," by bringing them nearer together. Commerce, of course, has done more than any other agency to make that association intimate and lasting. . . .
>
> It will be the fervent hope of all . . . that wireless telegraphy will very soon prove to be not a mere "scientific toy" but a system for daily and common use. 99

NEW SET OF GOODS

Trade over great distances had existed since prehistoric times, but as long as it was slow and expensive

▲ **As the development of railroad and steamship lines made transatlantic trade faster and cheaper, commodities such as these American cattle bound for British markets became available to millions.**

it was limited to specialty items that only the wealthy could afford. Improved methods of transportation allowed a greater—and cheaper—flow of imports and exports from one country to another. And as prices on certain goods fell, these goods became available to millions of people.

One example directly concerned America's position in the world economy. Prior to the late 19th century, the European market for American wheat had been quite limited. Although American farmers, in general, grew wheat more efficiently—and therefore less expensively—than European farmers, the high cost of transport made the U.S. grain too expensive for most European markets.

The development of railroad and steamship lines trimmed transportation costs dramatically. Now American wheat could undercut European wheat, even with the cost of transportation added in. Moreover, the linking of the continents by telegraph allowed grain dealers to keep in instant touch with their customers. Grain markets are notoriously unstable—prices change wildly with news of droughts, wars, and other disasters. The immediate communications the telegraph afforded allowed the dealers to sell their grain where it would return the greatest profits. As a result, American exports of wheat and flour rose rapidly, from less than $10 million in 1850 to more than $220 million in 1880.

Technological advances made possible not only the trade of greater quantities of goods but also trade in a whole new variety of goods. The introduction in the 1870s and 1880s of refrigeration on ships, for example, expanded trade in perishable goods such as meats, dairy products, and

PRIMARY SOURCES

Description of Change: excerpted
Rationale: excerpted to focus on main idea

MULTICULTURAL PERSPECTIVES

During the late 1800s Hsüeh Fu-ch'eng, a Chinese civil servant, advocated reform through the study of European and American ideas and technology. In 1879, he wrote: "Because of their knowledge of machinery and mathematics, the nations of the West thrive beyond the seas. . . . So that our China can stand up to them, we should make plans for commerce and mining. . . . Skills in crafts and manufacturing should be perfected. . . . Steamships, trains, and the telegraph should be promoted; unless we change, they will be swift and we slow."

THE AMERICAN NATION VIDEODISC PROGRAM

The Wright Brothers

1B   51443   :32

RETEACH Have students work in small groups to chart the major ideas presented in the section. Direct each group to indicate on its chart how each item addresses the section's Focus questions.

Closure

Have students identify the technological innovation that they think had the greatest effect on the development of the world economy during the 19th and 20th centuries. Call on volunteers to reveal and explain their choices.

Extension

CREATE Refer students to the information on p. 649 concerning new markets for the U.S. in the early 1900s. Have them use statistical abstracts and almanacs to create a table that shows the amount of trade the U.S. conducts in these markets today.

INVESTIGATE Ask students to investigate the effect of the "information superhighway" on business. Have them present their findings in a report to the class.

SECTION REVIEW ANSWERS

IDENTIFY

For significance, see the following pages:
Cyrus Field (p. 650)
Guglielmo Marconi (p. 651)
electronic mail (p. 652)

1. *positive—greater variety of manufactured goods, increased farm production; negative—economy tied to business cycle, contributed to overproduction*
2. *to sell surplus goods and products; Latin America, East Asia, Europe*
3. *Advances in communication technology have allowed greater contact between distant regions and markets, and improvements in transportation have made shipping faster and less expensive.*
4. *Advertisements should present the idea that lower transportation costs enable merchants to profit from sales around the world.*
5. *shift away from agriculture to industry; more goods available for purchase*

fruits. Today our grocery stores are filled with all kinds of fresh foods from around the world.

NEW WAYS OF DOING BUSINESS

The types of goods traded are not the only things that have changed as a result of new technology. As the pace of scientific and technological advancements has accelerated over the course of the 20th century, the very ways that people conduct business around the globe have changed. Railroads and steamships have given way to airliners as the preferred means by which people travel long distances. Where a business executive of the early 19th century might have crossed the Atlantic or Pacific once or twice in a lifetime to check on operations overseas, the modern executive does so frequently.

Advances in communications technology have been equally revolutionary for businesses. In 1915 telephone lines linked the U.S. coasts; by the late 1920s telephone service across the Atlantic was available as well. The telephone had two main advantages over the telegraph—it required no special skills to operate and it allowed people to carry on direct conversations. First radio and then television also transformed business. They not only made people aware of events around the world just hours after the events happened but also gave businesses the chance to advertise their products to larger audiences—even to people on distant continents. As a result, American consumer products from McDonald's hamburgers to Levi's blue jeans have been snapped up by people the world over.

▲ **A computer can speed communications with a colleague in the next office or with a Chinese merchant on the other side of the world.**

Today computer networks provide new ways to communicate. **Electronic mail**—commonly called E-mail—allows people to send messages via their computers around the world as easily as they can around the block. Just as important to the global economy are the computer connections among banks, stock exchanges, government offices, and other institutions. Every day, banks electronically whisk millions of dollars from New Delhi to New York, from São Paulo to Seoul, while investors in Toronto purchase stock shares in Tokyo.

■■ **Innovations in communications and transportation have allowed for the freer and more rapid movement of people, merchandise, and information around the globe.**

SECTION 1 REVIEW

IDENTIFY and explain the significance of the following: Cyrus Field, Guglielmo Marconi, electronic mail.

1. **MAIN IDEA** What positive and negative effects did industrialization have on the U.S. economy in the late 19th century?
2. **MAIN IDEA** Why did Americans seek new markets in the early 20th century? Where did they seek those markets?
3. **MAIN IDEA** How have technological innovations influenced world trade?
4. **WRITING TO PERSUADE** Imagine you are an executive of a new U.S. shipping company in 1880. Write an advertisement explaining why farmers and manufacturers should use your company to transport their products to markets.
5. **HYPOTHESIZING** How might the increased involvement of Latin American and Asian countries in the global economy have affected everyday life in these regions?

PREVIEW WORKSHOP

Following is a list of the significant people and terms in this section. You may wish to use this list as a section preview.

People
- Sir Robert Peel
- Charles Gates Dawes

Terms
- gold standard
- Gold Standard Act
- free trade
- Cobden-Chevalier Treaty
- protectionism
- Merchandise Marks Act
- McKinley Tariff
- Dawes Plan

- Young Plan
- devaluation

Section 2

THE GLOBAL ECONOMY TO WORLD WAR II

FOCUS OBJECTIVES

- Explain how the gold standard and free trade encouraged the growth of the world economy.

- Identify the major motive behind protectionism.

- Discuss how World War I changed America's economic position in the world.

- Examine how the Great Depression affected world trade.

FOCUS
- **How did the gold standard and free trade encourage the growth of the world economy?**
- **What was the major motive behind protectionism?**
- **How did World War I change America's economic position in the world?**
- **How did the Great Depression affect world trade?**

𝒯*he gold standard and a movement to reduce tariffs increased world trade in the late 19th century. Between the beginning of the 20th century and World War II, however, the world economy underwent major changes and disruptions—the most important resulting from World War I and the Great Depression of the 1930s.*

£100 British gold coin

𝒯HE GOLD STANDARD

Technological improvements were only partly responsible for the development of the global economy in the late 19th century. Economic policies regarding international trade also played a role. One such policy involved the **gold standard**. Under a gold standard a nation's currency is redeemable in gold at a fixed rate.

Great Britain had long been on the gold standard. But other countries were reluctant to tie their currency to gold because to do so would decrease their control over their currency's value. By the end of the 1800s, however, most industrial nations had adopted the gold standard, persuaded in part by Britain's leading role in the global economy and by the discovery of large gold supplies in California, Australia, Canada, and South Africa.

The United States officially went on the gold standard in 1900 when Congress passed the **Gold Standard Act**. The act declared that the gold dollar "shall be the standard unit of value." The value of every U.S. dollar was set to equal the value of .04837 ounces of pure gold.

The widespread adoption of the gold standard encouraged the development of the world economy. It gave trade greater stability and relieved merchants doing business in foreign countries from worries about exchange rates. For example, an American selling wheat in Germany did not have to gamble on how many dollars the marks paid by the German customer would be worth.

▼ The discovery of gold in parts of the British Empire strengthened Britain's role in the world economy. In 1888 these miners worked for the Republic Gold Company in DeKaap, South Africa.

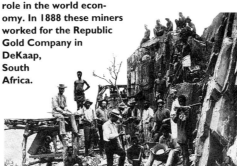

MOTIVATING: LINK TO TODAY

Write the terms *free trade* and *protectionism* on the chalkboard. Then call on volunteers to identify and discuss recent news stories involving these two issues. Have students use these stories to develop class definitions of the two terms. Note the definitions on the chalkboard. Then inform students that Section 2 places the development of the economic policies of free trade and protectionism in a global perspective.

Teaching the **Section**

ENCOURAGING A WORLD ECONOMY

Draw a chart on the chalkboard using *Gold Standard* and *Free Trade* as vertical headings and *Definition, Purpose,* and *Effects* as horizontal headings. Call on volunteers to come to the board and complete the chart. Have students use information in the chart to write a summary of the effects of the gold standard and of free trade on the world economy.

COOPERATIVE LEARNING

Organize students into groups that represent different countries. Each group should decide whether its country supports free trade or protectionism. Groups that support free trade should propose treaties that will eliminate tariff policies. Groups that support protectionist measures should develop tariff policies that will protect domestic industries and increase government revenues. Each group should present its measures to the rest of the class.

With both currencies calculated in terms of gold, the matter was clear from the start.

*F*REE TRADE

Perhaps even more important than the adoption of the gold standard in encouraging international commerce was the move toward **free trade**—international trade free from government regulation. Until the middle of the 19th century, the general rule in international trade had been for governments to levy tariffs against goods from abroad. The tariffs served two main purposes: to supply revenues to the governments and to protect domestic producers from foreign competition.

As with the gold standard, Britain led the way in reducing and even eliminating tariffs. During the 1840s, Great Britain's prime minister, Sir Robert Peel, observed that although a large number of imported goods were subject to British tariffs, most of the British government's tariff revenue came from just a few kinds of goods. Furthermore, Peel reasoned, British industry was the world's most advanced and did not require protection. Thus Peel abolished tariffs on hundreds of items and lowered tariffs on hundreds more.

Peel also believed that an increase in free trade might make it easier to sell British goods in foreign markets—if Britain lowered its tariffs, other countries might do the same. And indeed, following Britain's lead, France and other European countries soon moved toward free trade. In 1860 France and Britain signed the **Cobden-Chevalier Treaty**. The treaty provided that Britain would remove tariffs on most French imports. In return, France would lift a ban on imports of British textiles and would reduce tariffs on many other British goods. Perhaps most importantly, the treaty included a provision that enabled each country to benefit when the other negotiated tariff reductions with a third country.

Soon a network of treaties—each with a similar provision—governed trade among the European nations. Now whenever two countries agreed to a tariff reduction, the reduction applied to almost all of the region's countries. As a result, international trade grew rapidly among the countries lowering their tariff barriers; between 1850 and 1870, trade among the European nations roughly doubled.

■■ **The gold standard and free trade encouraged the development of the world economy by reducing uncertainty and by lowering trade barriers.**

*P*ROTECTIONISM

For all the benefits free trade offered, and for all the growth in international commerce it fostered, free trade still had its opponents. Those who favored **protectionism** wanted protective tariffs, asserting that free trade hurt domestic industries by unfairly exposing them to foreign competition. If foreign-produced goods were available for the same prices as domestically made goods, consumers would have little incentive to buy the domestic goods. This, they argued, would hurt the domestic industries and in some cases might lead to layoffs and unemployment.

When the world economy sank into a depression in the 1870s, many industrialists believed the depression had been caused by the increased international competition brought about by free trade. They clamored for a return to protectionism. At the same time, farmers increased their demands for protection. Prior to 1870 most farmers—particularly in Europe—had not needed economic protection. The expense of overseas shipping prevented competition from imports of farm products such as wheat. But when the drop in transportation costs owing to technological improvements increased competition for the European farmers, they too wanted protection. With protectionism receiving such wide support, numerous countries—beginning with Germany in 1879—approved new tariffs. Before long, tariff wars broke out. Trade between

▶ **This drawing shows an aerial view of Newcastle in the late 19th century. Newcastle was a major industrial city in northern England.**

THE CALL FOR PROTECTIONISM

Organize students into small groups. Have each group assume the role of an editorial board of a late-19th-century newspaper and develop editorials that call for the adoption of a protectionist trade policy. Suggest that they state clearly why protection is necessary. Also, encourage them to use information on the world economy of the late 1800s to support their arguments. Call on boards to present their editorials to the class. Use these presentations as the starting point for a class discussion titled "Free Trade v. Protectionism."

A SHIFT IN ECONOMIC POWER

Have students work in small groups to write scripts for a five-minute television documentary on how World War I changed America's economic position in the world and how the U.S. used its new financial power. Suggest that groups include in their scripts ideas for visuals to illustrate their documentaries. Ask groups to present and discuss their scripts.

▶

France and Italy, for example, declined by half between 1887 and 1898.

Even in Great Britain there was some shift in sentiment—particularly when German imports made inroads in British markets. The **Merchandise Marks Act**, passed by Parliament in 1887, required that foreign goods be labeled to indicate where they were made. Parliament hoped that British consumers would avoid buying goods that were marked "made in Germany."

The United States had never embraced free trade with the enthusiasm of the Europeans. In the years just before the Civil War, however, planters in the South, who generally supported free trade, had managed to keep tariff rates relatively low. But the North's victory in the Civil War enabled the Republican party to dominate national politics, and northern business leaders who favored protectionist policies were well represented in the party. This change, combined with the depressions of the late 1800s, led to a surge of American protectionism.

In 1890, William McKinley, then a U.S. congressman, sponsored a tariff bill which Congress passed that same year. The **McKinley Tariff** increased the number of imported goods subject to tariffs. More importantly, it steeply increased tariff rates. Subsequent measures raised tariff rates even higher. When American voters blamed high tariffs for rising living costs, Congress reduced the rates. However, the United States remained staunchly protectionist.

■■ **Protectionists believed that domestic industries required tariff protection from foreign competition.**

WORLD WAR I AND THE PEACE SETTLEMENT

World War I and the Treaty of Versailles dramatically reshaped the world economy. The war's most important short-term economic effect was the disruption of trade networks that had developed over the previous several decades. The war cut off trade between warring countries and led to attempts to prevent neutral countries from trading with enemies (see Chapter 10).

Debt and payment. A longer-term effect of the war was a shift in the balance of financial power from Great Britain and other European countries to the United States. From the American Revolution until World War I, the United States had been a debtor nation. With abundant resources but relatively little capital, Americans had borrowed money from Europe to finance industrialization and expansion. During World War I, however, the Allied powers turned to the United States for goods and for money to finance the war effort. As a result, the United States became a creditor nation.

After the war, the Allies believed that their debts to the United States should be canceled (see Chapter 15). But the U.S. government argued that the money loaned to the Allies had come from the American people— partly through the sale of Liberty Bonds. Therefore, if the debts were canceled, the American people would be the ones to pay. "All those who would like to see America cancel the European debt," quipped one publication, "are requested to mail in their Liberty Bonds." Even when the U.S. government reduced the interest rates on the loans and arranged a 62-year payment schedule, the Europeans were less than thrilled. "For the next sixty years, the American flag is

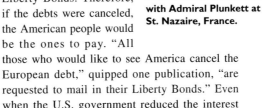

▲ Secretary of the Navy Franklin D. Roosevelt confers with Admiral Plunkett at St. Nazaire, France.

▼ This 1923 cartoon satirizes the debt problem that arose after World War I.

PASSING THE BUCK.

Teaching the **S***ection*

THE GREAT DEPRESSION AND WORLD TRADE

Have students imagine they are economic advisers to the U.S. government or to a European government during the early 1930s. Government ministers have suggested three international economic measures: increased tariffs, departure from the gold standard, and devaluation of the currency.

Students, in the role of advisers, should write a report to the ministers explaining the negative impact these policies will have on the world economy and on international relations. Call on volunteers to read their reports to the class.

BIOGRAPHY PERSONALITIES IN HISTORY

During his years as budget director, Dawes cut government expenses and saved more than one billion dollars. When he left office in 1922, he said, "I am carrying back as souvenirs of this experience the handwritten pasteboard sign in the office door: 'Bureau of the Budget,' and two brooms. I wish I could take back some of the secondhand furniture which we raked up in the Treasury cellars. One cannot successfully preach economy without practicing it."

THE AMERICAN NATION VIDEODISC PROGRAM

The Great Depression

2A	25392	3:24

---

going to look to us like the \$tars and \$tripes," remarked the *London Opinion.*

Repaying the loans, however, was not a simple matter. The Allies—particularly France—could not afford to pay the debt if they themselves did not receive the German reparations required by the Treaty of Versailles. But German inflation left Germany unable to make *any* reparations payments. By November 15, 1923, it took 4.2 trillion marks to buy a single dollar, making the mark worth less than the paper on which it was printed.

The Dawes and Young plans. Economist John Maynard Keynes reflected on the debt situation left by World War I:

❝ The war has ended with everyone owing everyone else immense sums of money. Germany owes a large sum to the Allies. The Allies owe a large sum . . . to the United States. The holders of war loans in every country are owed a large sum by their . . . states. The states, in [their] turn, are owed a large sum by taxpayers. The whole position is in the highest degree . . . vexatious [distressing]. We shall never be able to move again unless we can be free of these paper shackles. ❞

The U.S. government took the first step toward removing the shackles Keynes spoke of by suggesting that a committee be formed to study the issue of the war debts. Chicago banker Charles Dawes was chosen to head the committee.

Charles Gates Dawes was born in Marietta, Ohio, in 1865. After attending law school in Cincinnati, he went on to practice law in Lincoln, Nebraska, from 1887 to 1894. In 1897 he became U.S. comptroller of the currency, but he returned to private business in 1902. Although he remained active in finance throughout his life, Dawes also served as a brigadier general in World War I, the first director of the U.S. Bureau of the Budget, and vice president under Calvin Coolidge. Dawes also wrote several works, including *A Journal of the Great War* (1921) and *Notes as Vice President* (1935).

In 1925 Dawes was awarded—along with Sir Austen

BIOGRAPHY

Charles Dawes

Chamberlain of Britain—the Nobel Peace Prize. He received this award largely for his efforts to deal with the debt-reparations tangle following World War I. In 1924, in what became known as the **Dawes Plan,** Dawes's committee arranged for a \$200 million loan to help Germany meet its reparations payments. Because American bankers were to provide about \$100 million of the loan, the plan set up a payment triangle by which Americans helped finance Germany's reparations payments to the Allies; these payments in turn financed the Allies' war debts to the United States. The Dawes Plan also rewrote the reparations payment schedule.

The plan operated successfully for several years, but it was only a stop-gap measure and was replaced in 1929 by the **Young Plan.** Named for Owen D. Young, chairman of the board of the General Electric Company, this plan spread Germany's reparations payments—totaling about \$26 billion, with interest—over 59 years.

■■ **World War I converted the United States from a debtor nation to a creditor nation. Americans used their new financial power to help stabilize the world economy in the 1920s.**

---

*T*HE GREAT DEPRESSION

The Young Plan might have solved the financial problems caused by World War I, but it never got the chance. After the New York stock market crashed in 1929, similar collapses occurred in other countries. The world soon slipped into the deepest depression it had ever experienced—a depression that thoroughly disrupted world trade and cast the global economy into disarray.

The Young Plan was one of the victims of the depression. As American investment in Germany dried up, Germany was unable to make its reparations payments. As a result, the European Allies could not pay their debts to the United States. Most people, however, felt the effects of the depression more personally. Factory production fell; unemployment increased; basic necessities became unavailable or unaffordable. Author George Orwell observed women "kneeling in the cindery mud and the bitter wind searching for tiny chips of coal" in a British mining town:

GUIDED PRACTICE

Write *World Trade* on the chalkboard and circle it. Then draw five lines radiating from the circle and write one of the following terms at the end of each line: *Gold Standard, Free Trade, Protectionism, Higher Tariffs,* and *Devaluation*. Ask students to explain how each of these terms relates to world trade. Note responses along the appropriate lines.

INDEPENDENT PRACTICE

Have students use information developed in Guided Practice to write a brief essay describing the development of the global economy from the late 1800s to World War II. Students may wish to include their essays in their portfolios.

REVIEW Organize students into groups and assign each group one of the section's subsections. Ask each group to create an editorial cartoon about their assigned subsection. Have the class interpret each cartoon. Then assign the Section 2 Review on p. 658.

ASSESS Assign the **Section 2 Daily Quiz** in *Core Resources*.

▶

> 66 In winter they are almost desperate for fuel; it is more important almost than food. Meanwhile, all round, as far as the eye can see are the slag-heaps . . . of collieries [coal mines], and not one of those collieries can sell all the coal it is capable of producing. 99

In order to stimulate production and employment during the depression, countries adopted two major economic measures. The first was an increase in tariffs, to give domestic industries the advantage in the home market. The U.S. Congress, for example, responded to the onset of the depression by passing the protectionist Smoot-Hawley Tariff of 1930. Many economists warned that the measure, which raised average tariff rates to their highest levels in U.S. history, would trigger retaliatory moves by other countries. The economists were right. In France, where one American said the U.S. tariff was compared to "a declaration of war, an economic blockade,"

the government responded in kind. So did most other countries—even Great Britain, the traditional champion of free trade. By 1931 average tariff rates in 15 European countries were nearly two-thirds higher than in 1927.

The second measure governments used to try to pump life into their economies was to make their currencies cheaper in relation to other currencies. This **devaluation** would make export goods cheaper in foreign markets, thus boosting foreign sales. In order to change the value of their currencies, however, nations had to go off the gold standard. Britain became the first major industrial nation to do so in September 1931. As with tariffs, other nations responded with similar measures. By April 1932, more than 20 countries had left the gold standard.

In 1933 President Roosevelt announced that the United States, too, would no longer tie its currency to gold. Without gold as an internationally agreed-upon standard, currency values wavered uncontrollably.

PRIMARY SOURCE
Description of Change: excerpted and bracketed
Rationale: excerpted to focus on main idea; bracketed to clarify meaning

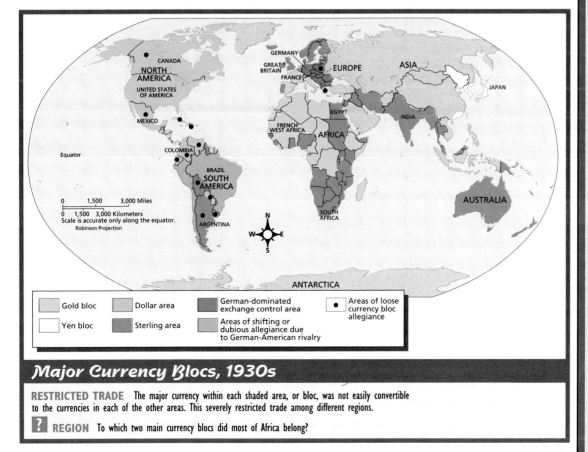

Gold bloc	Dollar area
Yen bloc	Sterling area

German-dominated exchange control area
Areas of shifting or dubious allegiance due to German-American rivalry
● Areas of loose currency bloc allegiance

*M*ajor *C*urrency *B*locs, 1930s

RESTRICTED TRADE The major currency within each shaded area, or bloc, was not easily convertible to the currencies in each of the other areas. This severely restricted trade among different regions.

? **REGION** To which two main currency blocs did most of Africa belong?

Map Caption Answer
gold and sterling

RETEACH For each subsection in the section, have students write a sentence that summarizes the main idea. Select students to read their sentences aloud. Have the class choose the best summary sentence for each subsection.

Closure

Have students speculate on what the world economy would be like if the major industrial nations were still on the gold standard and followed free-trade policies.

Extension

RESEARCH Have students research the effects of America's abandonment of the gold standard on April 19, 1933. Students should report their findings to the class.

ANALYZE Have students analyze why governments adopted protectionist and devaluation policies during the 1930s. Ask them to suggest policies that might have been more successful in bolstering the world economy.

PRIMARY SOURCE

Description of Change: excerpted
Rationale: excerpted to focus on main idea

SECTION REVIEW ANSWERS

IDENTIFY

For significance, see the following pages:
gold standard (p. 653)
Gold Standard Act (p. 653)
free trade (p. 654)
Sir Robert Peel (p. 654)
Cobden-Chevalier Treaty
(p. 654)
protectionism (p. 654)
Merchandise Marks Act
(p. 655)
McKinley Tariff (p. 655)
Charles Dawes (p. 656)
Dawes Plan (p. 656)
Young Plan (p. 656)
devaluation (p. 657)

1. gold standard—stabilized exchange rates; free trade—lowered trade barriers, reduced or even removed tariffs
2. to attempt to counteract the depression of the 1870s
3. European need for wartime goods and capital allowed U.S. to become a creditor nation rather than a debtor nation.
4. Articles should mention the dramatic drop in world trade during the depression. Goals should include ending the tariff wars and reestablishing the gold standard.
5. Answers should discuss the adoption of new European tariffs in response to the Smoot-Hawley Tariff.

THE LONDON ECONOMIC CONFERENCE

THROUGH OTHERS' EYES

As the London conference on the world economic situation opened in the summer of 1933, many people realized that success at the conference would depend on the resolution of a variety of issues. American cooperation, however, was seen as essential to solving the international monetary problem. H. D. Davray, a French journalist, explained his perspective in the British *Saturday Review:*

66 *The economic problems submitted to the Conference cannot be solved at all unless . . . currencies are stabilised and a return to the gold standard established. These are from the French point of view indispensable preliminaries, without which any measures of an economic category that may be recommended will be absolutely futile. . . . The actual world situation is on the verge of catastrophe. . . . If the United States want to save themselves from bankruptcy by devaluation which will lighten their debts and increase the value of their stocks, the idea is reasonable. But such a measure must not result in paralysing and ruining other nations.* 99

While some nations experienced temporary relief as a result of increased tariffs and currency devaluations, the overall effects on world trade were disastrous. In the closest thing the 20th century has seen to a trade war, world trade dropped 40 percent between 1927 and 1933.

In June 1933 the major industrial powers held a conference in London in an attempt to find a way out of the depression. The conference organizers hoped to negotiate an end to the tariff wars, reestablish the gold standard, and promote other forms of international cooperation. Unfortunately, the United States refused to have anything to do with the conference's aim of stabilizing currency.

The United States had recently shown some signs of economic recovery, and many attributed this success to the nation's departure from the gold standard. President Roosevelt was thus hesitant to reinstate the standard. He sent a telegram to the London conference stating that "the sound internal economic system of a nation is a greater factor in its well being than the price of its currency." Without the endorsement of the United States, the London conference accomplished virtually nothing. Thus the depression continued, and the strains it induced intensified the forces propelling nations toward the Second World War.

■■ **The Great Depression provoked trade wars among the major economic powers, creating tensions that contributed to the outbreak of World War II.**

■■ **SECTION 2 REVIEW**

IDENTIFY and explain the significance of the following: gold standard, Gold Standard Act, free trade, Sir Robert Peel, Cobden-Chevalier Treaty, protectionism, Merchandise Marks Act, McKinley Tariff, Charles Dawes, Dawes Plan, Young Plan, devaluation.

1. **MAIN IDEA** What economic policies led to an expansion of the world economy in the late 19th century? How did these policies contribute to expansion?
2. **MAIN IDEA** Why did many nations adopt protectionist policies in the late 19th century?
3. **MAIN IDEA** How and why did America's position in the world economy change after World War I?
4. **WRITING TO EXPLAIN** Imagine you are a delegate to the 1933 London conference seeking to end the Great Depression. Write a newspaper article explaining how the depression has affected world trade and how you propose to address trade problems.
5. **HYPOTHESIZING** Imagine you are the leader of a European nation in 1930. Describe your reaction to the Smoot-Hawley Tariff.

PREVIEW WORKSHOP

Following is a list of the significant people and terms in this section. You may wish to use this list as a section preview.

People
■ Henry Morgenthau

Terms
■ Bretton Woods system

■ fixed exchange rates
■ International Monetary Fund
■ World Bank
■ General Agreement on Tariffs and Trade
■ per capita income
■ European Economic Community

MOTIVATING:
PRIOR KNOWLEDGE

Have students identify the economic policies of the 1930s that disrupted the world economy and international relations. *(higher tariffs, devaluation)* Then ask students to speculate on what measures might have eased the problems caused by these policies. Note responses on the chalkboard or a flip chart.

Section 3

THE ERA OF AMERICAN DOMINANCE

FOCUS OBJECTIVES

■ Explain how the Bretton Woods system aimed to promote peace through commerce.

■ Describe the changes in the international economic landscape following World War II.

■ Identify the trend that the economies of the U.S., Western Europe, and Japan experienced in the 25 years after the war.

PRIMARY SOURCE

Description of Change: excerpted
Rationale: excerpted to focus on main idea

FOCUS

■ **How did the Bretton Woods system aim to promote peace through commerce?**

■ **How did the international economic landscape change following World War II?**

■ **What trend did the economies of the United States, Western Europe, and Japan experience in the 25 years after the war?**

At the end of World War II, the United States took the lead in reordering the world economy. This reordering involved establishing a framework for international trade and investment and reconstructing the war-ruined economies. These efforts were rewarded by more than two decades of strong economic growth, particularly in the United States, Europe, and Japan.

A symbol of the military power that helped make the United States a world leader in the postwar era

A NEW ECONOMIC FRAMEWORK

Even before World War II ended, political leaders and economic experts from around the world had concluded that the monetary and trade policies of the 1930s—the departure from the gold standard,

▼ **Bombing during World War II reduced most French factories to steel skeletons filled with rubble. Lack of production contributed to a devastated postwar economy.**

the competitive currency devaluations, and the high tariffs—had contributed to the onset of the war. As U.S. Secretary of the Treasury Henry Morgenthau explained:

66 All of us have seen the great economic tragedy of our time. We saw the world-wide depression of the 1930's. We saw currency disorders develop and spread from land to land, destroying the basis for international trade and . . . investment and even international faith. In their wake, we saw unemployment and wretchedness. . . . We saw bewilderment and bitterness become the breeders of fascism, and, finally, of war. 99

To avoid the outbreak of another war as a result of similar hostilities, U.S. officials and others resolved to modify international economic policies. "Commerce is the life blood of a free society," wrote President Roosevelt. "We must see to it that the arteries which carry that blood stream

CORE RESOURCES

• **Section 3 Daily Quiz**

AV RESOURCES

• **Linking Geography and History Transparency** and **Worksheet 11B**
• *The American Nation* **Videodisc: The Growth of Suburbia**

Teaching the Section

THE BRETTON WOODS SYSTEM

Ask students to identify problems that were addressed by the Bretton Woods conference. Then ask students to discuss ways conference members worked to solve these problems. List students' answers on the chalkboard.

A NEW ECONOMIC LANDSCAPE

Have students review the information on the Cold War in Chapters 17 and 18. Then divide the class in half. Have one group write a brief presentation explaining why Communist-bloc countries developed their own economic sphere. Have the other group write a similar presentation for capitalist-bloc countries. Call on volunteers from each side to make their presentations to the class.

ECONOMIC GROWTH

Divide the class into three groups. Have one group discuss changes in the U.S. economy after World War II. The second group should discuss U.S. contributions to economic recovery in West Germany, and the third group should discuss the U.S. role in Japan's economic recovery. A representative of each group should summarize the main points of the discussion for the rest of the class.

MAKING CONNECTIONS

Economics

Lord Keynes, an influential British economist, referred to the World Bank and the IMF as "twins" because of the way the two organizations worked together to support the world economy. Two months before the Bretton Woods conference began, he addressed the House of Lords on the need for an international monetary system. "It is extraordinarily difficult to frame any proposals about tariffs if countries are free to alter the value of their currencies without agreement and at short notice. . . . It is very difficult while you have monetary chaos to have order of any kind in other directions."

---

are not clogged again, as they have been in the past, by artificial barriers created through senseless economic rivalries."

At Roosevelt's urging, economic officials from the United States and 43 other countries met at Bretton Woods, New Hampshire, in July 1944 to construct a framework for postwar international economic relations. Their primary goals were to restore the stability of currency and to prevent tariff increases and trade wars like those of the 1930s. The system that emerged from the conference became known as the **Bretton Woods system**.

The first element of the system was an agreement among the major economic powers to maintain **fixed exchange rates** between their currencies. They tied the currencies of Britain, France, and the other countries to the American dollar, which became the system's key currency. To increase stability further, the dollar was tied to gold, at $35 per ounce. In effect, this agreement restored the gold standard to the international economy. To help maintain these fixed exchange rates, the conference created the $8.8 billion **International Monetary Fund**, or IMF.

The conference also established the International Bank for Reconstruction and Development, commonly called the **World Bank**. Credited with $10 billion, the World Bank was to

make loans to boost the economies of the war-damaged countries and to encourage development in the less industrialized countries.

The final part of the Bretton Woods system was the **General Agreement on Tariffs and Trade**, or GATT. Although it did not officially take form until 1947, the agreement represented a commitment by the member governments to the long-term goal of free trade. Over the next few decades, GATT members succeeded in reducing tariffs on a wide variety of goods to their lowest levels in modern history.

■■ **To prevent future economic hostilities, the Bretton Woods system set up fixed exchange rates, the IMF, the World Bank, and an agreement to cut tariffs.**

A NEW ECONOMIC LANDSCAPE

The Bretton Woods system operated in a global economy that differed radically from the pre–World War II economy. The onset of the Cold War divided the world economy into two spheres—the capitalist nations and the communist nations—and economic contact between them virtually ended for about 25 years. Each group believed that its economic and social system was better than that of the other, and neither group wished to do anything that might strengthen the other.

Even among the capitalist countries, economic relationships changed. Many of the European nations—whose economies had dominated the world prior to the war—lay in ruins (see chapters 16 and 17). The U.S. economy, in contrast, emerged from World War II stronger than ever. Government spending on war supplies had boosted the economy, and at the end of the war, Americans produced about two and a half times what they had at the bottom of the depression. For example, steel production in 1944 reached nearly 90 million tons—almost 30 million tons more than annual production had ever been prior to the war and about 60 million tons above yearly totals during much of the depression.

■■ **The Cold War divided the global economy into two spheres. The United States emerged as the capitalist sphere's most economically powerful nation.**

▲ In July 1944, delegates from many countries gathered at Mt. Washington House in Bretton Woods, New Hampshire, to promote international economic harmony.

Practice

GUIDED PRACTICE

Organize students into groups of four or five. Provide each group with a piece of butcher paper on which the following headings are written: *Bretton Woods System, A New Economic Landscape, U.S. Economic Growth, Postwar Economic Recovery in Europe, "Economic Miracle" in West Germany, "Economic Miracle" in Japan.* Have groups brainstorm information about these six topics. Have a group representative note information under the appropriate heading.

INDEPENDENT PRACTICE

Have groups use the information developed in Guided Practice to create a four-page illustrated report titled "The Era of American Dominance." Call on volunteer groups to present and discuss their reports.

Review and Assessment

REVIEW Ask students to work in pairs to write sentences that explain how each entry in the Preview Workshop is related to the main idea of the subsection in which it is located. Have pairs share their sentences with the class. Then assign the Section 3 Review on p. 662.

ASSESS Assign the **Section 3 Daily Quiz** in *Core Resources.* ▶

AMERICAN ECONOMIC GROWTH

Many Americans recognized that government spending on the war effort had helped end the depression. They worried that when the war was over, the economy would nose-dive. According to surveys at the time, some 70 percent of Americans thought that they would be worse off after the war.

Such fears proved groundless. Instead of falling into a depression, the U.S. economy grew dramatically. Between 1945 and 1970, the gross national product (GNP) doubled. One reason for the growth was that at the end of the war, U.S. consumers had plenty of money to spend. Rationing ended shortly after the war, and the pent-up consumer demand kept the economy humming as it shifted from war production to the production of civilian consumer goods.

The economy also boomed because government spending remained high throughout the Cold War. Military spending to rebuild weapons supplies and to fight the Korean War, and later the Vietnam War, kept employment up in defense-related industries. Social programs established during these decades also created jobs and enabled people to maintain their purchasing power.

RECONSTRUCTION AND GROWTH IN EUROPE

Because the United States had the world's most powerful economy following World War II, U.S. officials took the initiative in reconstructing Europe's war-ruined economies. They had two major reasons for doing so. First, if Europe remained weak economically, such weakness could easily spread to the United States. Second, Americans were concerned that a Europe in economic distress might fall prey to communism.

The European Economic Community.

The United States' $12 billion Marshall Plan helped put Europe back on its feet (see Chapter 17). It also had longer-term effects. Although the U.S. aid came mostly in the form of grants and thus did not have to be repaid, it did not come without strings. In order to make the most of assistance and prevent a return to the competition that

▲ German women made up over half of the workforce that cleared away the remains of Berlin's bombed buildings. They were dubbed "rubble women."

had helped bring on World War II, the United States required the European nations to coordinate their economic activities.

The Europeans responded by forming the Organization for European Economic Cooperation to distribute the Marshall Plan aid. Before long, some Europeans were urging economic integration as well as cooperation. To that end, Belgium, France, Italy, Luxembourg, West Germany, and the Netherlands came together in 1951 to form the European Coal and Steel Community (ECSC), which allowed for the free trade of coal, steel, and iron ore among the six member nations.

The success of the ECSC inspired a bolder step in 1957—the formation of the **European Economic Community** (EEC). The treaty that created the EEC explained that the community's purpose was to:

❝ promote the harmonious growth of economic activity in the Community as a

PRIMARY SOURCE

Description of Change: excerpted and bracketed
Rationale: excerpted to focus on main idea; bracketed to clarify meaning

MULTICULTURAL PERSPECTIVES

The Marshall Plan did not offer aid solely to Western Europe. Czechoslovakia agreed to participate in the economic recovery program, and Poland and Hungary indicated some interest. The Soviet Union, however, blocked Eastern European involvement in order to limit the influence of capitalism in Europe.

RETEACH Have students work in groups, assigning individuals or pairs the task of outlining subsections. Direct individuals or pairs to exchange outlines and use them to ask questions of other members of the group.

Closure

Have students write a sentence that summarizes America's role in the global economy during the 25 years after World War II. Call on volunteers to read their sentences to the class.

Extension

COMPARE Encourage students to compare the efforts to rebuild the global economy after World War I with those made after World War II.

INVESTIGATE Have students investigate and report on the activities of the IMF and the World Bank in today's global economy.

SECTION REVIEW ANSWERS

IDENTIFY

For significance, see the following pages:
Henry Morganthau (p. 659)
Bretton Woods system (p. 660)
fixed exchange rates (p. 660)
International Monetary Fund (p. 660)
World Bank (p. 660)
General Agreement on Tariffs and Trade (p. 660)
European Economic Community (p. 661)

1. *established fixed exchange rates, created International Monetary Fund and World Bank, agreed to support free trade*
2. *onset of Cold War divided world between capitalism and communism, devastated European economies looked to U.S. for assistance*
3. *The Marshall Plan provided money to rebuild European nations and required them to work together economically.*
4. *Essays should discuss economic growth in all three areas, indicating that the U.S. provided financial support to Japan and Western Europe.*
5. *Essays should discuss the desire to stabilize currency and avoid tariff wars.*

whole, regular and balanced expansion, augmented [increased] stability, a more rapidly rising standard of living, and closer relations between the participating states. **"**

To achieve these goals, the EEC planned to abolish tariffs and "all barriers to the free movement of persons, services and capital" among members. Indeed, commerce among the EEC countries mushroomed. Trade between France and Germany, for example, grew by about 40 percent from 1958 to 1966. By 1968 tariffs among the six EEC members had been completely abolished.

West Germany. Although all of Western Europe achieved economic recovery in the postwar years, West Germany's recovery was the greatest success story. Immediately after the war, the governments of the victorious powers agreed that Germany should not be allowed to become strong again. As the Cold War developed, however, the United States began looking on West Germany as a barrier to the Soviet Union's westward expansion—and as a key nation in Western Europe's economic revival. Consequently, West Germany was included in the Marshall Plan, and U.S. officials did what they could to foster West Germany's economic growth.

The West German economy soared. In a recovery soon labeled an "economic miracle," unemployment dropped from more than 10 percent in 1950 to less than 1 percent during most of the 1960s. The country's GNP rose from less than 100 million marks in 1950 to more than 500 million marks in 1968. By the 1960s West Germany was the economic envy of the rest of Europe.

JAPAN

Japan's recovery was even more dramatic than Germany's. Before the war Japan had never been as economically powerful as Germany, and Japan received no Marshall Plan aid after the war. Moreover, where much of Germany's revival resulted from trade with its prosperous European neighbors, Japan's neighbors were generally poor.

Yet Japan did have a few advantages. Though not included in the Marshall Plan, Japan received other kinds of American reconstruction assistance. More importantly, its people were industrious and creative in the adoption and development of new technologies. Japan's recovery eventually surpassed Germany's as well as nearly every other country's. Between the late 1940s and the early 1970s, Japan's GNP grew at a rate of more than 10 percent annually. By 1970 Japan had remade itself into an economic powerhouse, the strongest in Asia and one of the strongest in the world.

▪▪ **The years from 1945 to 1970 saw strong economic growth in the United States, Western Europe, and Japan.**

SECTION 3 REVIEW

IDENTIFY and explain the significance of the following: Henry Morgenthau, Bretton Woods system, fixed exchange rates, International Monetary Fund, World Bank, General Agreement on Tariffs and Trade, European Economic Community.

1. **MAIN IDEA** What actions did delegates to the Bretton Woods conference take to promote peace?
2. **MAIN IDEA** How did the end of World War II affect the world economy?
3. **ASSESSING CONSEQUENCES** How did the Marshall Plan affect the European economy?
4. **WRITING TO INFORM** Write an essay detailing the economic developments in the United States, Western Europe, and Japan after World War II.
5. **USING HISTORICAL IMAGINATION** Imagine you represent a country other than the United States at the Bretton Woods Conference. Write an essay that explains why you think international commerce is important to your country.

PREVIEW WORKSHOP

Following is a list of the significant terms in this section. You may wish to use this list as a section preview.

Terms
- oil shocks
- floating exchange rates
- Pacific Rim
- multinational corporations

- European Union
- North American Free Trade Agreement
- Uruguay Round
- World Trade Organization

MOTIVATING: STUDENT EXPERIENCES

Call on volunteers to identify items they use that were made outside the U.S., and have them note the origin of these items. *(clothes made in Central American or Asian countries, athletic shoes made in Taiwan or Korea, audio components made in Asia, autos made in Japan or Europe)* Point out the U.S. participates in a global economy that is becoming more and more unified.

Section 4

A NEW ERA IN TRADE

FOCUS
- **Why has U.S. economic dominance of the world declined since the 1970s?**
- **What part of the world has shown the greatest economic growth in recent decades?**
- **How have multinational corporations and the end of the Cold War affected the global economy?**
- **What agreements reflect a trend toward global free trade?**

The global economy has experienced a dramatic reshaping since the 1970s. The decline of American dominance, the growth of new economic powers and new forms of business investment, and the end of the Cold War are some of the reasons for the changes. Nevertheless, increased free trade has brought the world greater economic unity.

Floating oil production platform in the North Sea, 1984

FOCUS OBJECTIVES
- Explain why U.S. economic dominance of the world has declined since the 1970s.
- Identify the part of the world that has shown the greatest economic growth in recent decades.
- Discuss the effect of multinational corporations and the end of the Cold War on the global economy.
- List the agreements that reflect a trend toward global free trade.

HISTORICAL SIDELIGHTS

Oil Embargo

OPEC members raised oil prices in response to U.S. support for Israel during the 1973 Yom Kippur War. The federal government lowered temperatures in office buildings to 68 degrees, and reduced highway speeds for its vehicles to 50 miles per hour. Officials in one Georgia county prohibited the use of school buses for band and field trips.

OIL SHOCKS

One factor that had encouraged the growth of the industrial economies during the 1950s and 1960s was the availability of oil. Oil was easily transported by pipeline or tanker ship. It was also versatile: oil and the products derived from it could be used to fuel transportation, to heat homes and power factories, to generate electricity, and to manufacture plastics and other products.

Throughout the 1950s and 1960s, oil supplies generally outstripped demand, leaving prices low. In the early 1970s, however, prices rose as demand caught up with supplies. Additional pressure came from OPEC, which repeatedly raised the price of oil during the 1970s (see Chapter 21). By the early 1980s the price of a barrel of oil, which had been less than $3 prior to 1973, stood at more than $30.

The jump in oil prices sent shock waves through the world economy. The **oil shocks**, as the jolts from the price increases were called, tested each country's capacity to adapt. A government official in Japan, which survived the crisis better than most other countries, later recalled: "Both workers and business leaders were very apprehensive after 1973. They feared for the survival of their companies, and so everybody worked together."

▼ **Oil ministers from OPEC's 13 member nations meet to monitor oil production and prices.**

CORE RESOURCES

• **Section 4 Daily Quiz**

 RESOURCES

• **Linking Geography and History Transparency** and **Worksheet 11C**
• *The American Nation* **Videodisc: The Maiden Flight of the Concorde**

Teaching the Section

THE RISE OF NEW ECONOMIC POWERS

Organize students into several groups. Have groups draw up plans for a special issue of a newsmagazine dealing with the decline of American economic dominance and the rise of the Pacific Rim countries. Plans should include a table of contents, suggestions for illustrations and captions, and design ideas for a cover. Have groups present and discuss their magazine plans.

MAKING CONNECTIONS

Economics

Trade among Asian nations has grown dramatically in recent years. By the end of the 1980s, for example, nearly 40 percent of Asian exports went to other Asian countries. Further, about 50 percent of Pacific air cargo moved between Asian countries. And about half the freight handled by the port of Singapore came from its Asian neighbors.

MULTICULTURAL PERSPECTIVES

During the late 1980s, the strength of the Japanese yen encouraged travel to the United States. Many tourists bought luxury items for lower prices than were available in Japan. An American luggage store owner said, "Ninety percent of our clientele is Japanese. If they don't come, we're out of business." Others came for different reasons. One woman said, "We don't want to shop. We come from a small country and want to see a big one." Her husband added, "We also want to see football and baseball games."

THE END OF DOLLAR DOMINANCE

The Bretton Woods financial system did not survive the oil shocks. The supremacy of the dollar enshrined in the Bretton Woods system had come under attack during the 1960s, largely as a result of the economic growth of countries like West Germany and Japan. In 1971 the strain forced the Nixon administration to suspend America's adherence to the gold standard and fixed exchange rates. The oil shocks, by increasing the pressure on the dollar and adding to inflation, killed hopes of a return to the Bretton Woods system.

The system of fixed exchange rates was replaced by a system of **floating exchange rates**. Under the new system the value of a dollar in relation to other currencies could vary, depending on the relative demand for dollars and the other currencies. If Japanese businesses, for example, needed more dollars to pay for imports from the United States, the dollar might rise in value from, say, 250 yen to 300 yen. At least that was the theory.

In reality the dollar fell. During most of the early period following World War II, the dollar's value stood at more than 300 yen. But in the 1980s and early 1990s, the dollar fell continuously against the yen. In June 1994, for example, the dollar was worth less than 100 yen. Although the American economy remained the world's largest, the slippage of the dollar symbolized the end of the era of U.S. dominance of the world economy.

■■ Rising oil prices and the growth of other economic powers brought to a close the era of American dominance of the world economy.

THE PACIFIC RIM

While U.S. economic dominance has declined, the economic power of other countries has quickly risen. In recent decades, the world economy's center of gravity has shifted toward the nations of the **Pacific Rim**, which include Australia, New Zealand, and many East Asian and Southeast Asian nations. In 1991 goods from the Pacific Rim accounted for 39 percent of all imports to the United States. The region's reputation for producing high-quality, low-priced

▲ In recent years high-quality Japanese products such as televisions, radios, and other electronic equipment have captured a large share of the U.S. market.

automobiles, computers, TVs, VCRs, radios, and other goods helped spur demand.

Historically, Japan has been the Pacific Rim's dominant economic power. But in recent years the nations of the Pacific Rim that have experienced the most explosive economic growth are the "Four Tigers"—Taiwan, South Korea, Hong Kong, and Singapore. South Korea, for example, had an average annual growth rate of nearly 10 percent from 1980 to 1990. In contrast, the U.S. growth rate during the same years averaged under 4 percent. Other Asian nations, such as Malaysia, Thailand, and Indonesia, have also shown impressive economic growth in recent years.

China, too, achieved high growth rates during the late 1980s and early 1990s. Although the Chinese government remains Communist, it has allowed economic reform in the direction of free enterprise. Instead of only large state-run factories, there are now some 19 million small companies in rural areas and villages. This reform spurred several years of rapid growth that lifted incomes in much of China and propelled China into the ranks of the major economic powers.

Several factors lie behind the Asian nations' economic success. Asians have worked long hours and saved what they earned, reinvesting the savings to promote economic growth. Furthermore, Asian governments have often taken an active role in encouraging economic development. Critics, however, note that the Asian nations' economic growth has often been based on low wages and thus has not benefited all of the region's peoples.

■■ The nations of the Pacific Rim have experienced rapid economic growth in the 1980s and early 1990s.

MULTINATIONAL CORPORATIONS

Much of the Pacific Rim's economic growth has been fueled by Japanese investors and industries seeking lower labor and land costs. Such efforts have often been led by **multinational corporations**, companies that invest money in or own business ventures around the globe. Japanese corporations such as Honda and Mitsubishi, for instance, have opened factories in the United States. Similarly, many U.S. businesses have set up operations in foreign nations. For example, the New York–based International Telephone and Telegraph (ITT) owns businesses in countries from Bolivia to France. Other companies such as General Motors, Texaco, and International Business Machines (IBM) also operate worldwide.

Sometimes it is difficult to gauge the economic effects of these multinational corporations. In some cases companies can boost employment and development in the countries where they operate. Critics, however, argue that most of the profits go to the country where the corporation is based. Multinational corporations are also sometimes criticized for harming the environment or for changing the cultures in the countries in which they operate.

■ Multinational corporations are playing an increasingly important role in the world economy.

THE END OF THE COLD WAR

Multinational corporations now have a whole new area of the world to invest in. After the breakup of the Soviet Union in the early 1990s, investment money began to flow from the United States and Western Europe to Eastern Europe and the countries of the former Soviet Union. Yet removing the barriers between the two spheres takes time. Most of the countries of what was once the Communist bloc are only beginning to forge close ties with the rest of the world economy.

▲ Multinational corporations have opened several manufacturing plants in the United States. Shown here are workers in the Honda automobile factory in Marysville, Ohio.

Not all nations have benefited from the end of the Cold War. Cuba, for example, which once was supported almost entirely by the Soviet Union, has had to adapt to sharp drop-offs in aid and trade. Similarly, some Africans fear that they will lose investment dollars as Western European nations invest more and more in their Eastern European neighbors.

■ The end of the Cold War has opened new areas for investment in the former Soviet Union and in Eastern Europe.

TOWARD GLOBAL FREE TRADE

In spite of some nations' difficulties, the era since 1945 has been on the whole the most prosperous in modern history. Many economists attribute the era's prosperity to increased free trade. As a result, more and more countries are trying to arrange or expand free-trade agreements.

▲ In 1985 Jacques Delors became president of the European Commission, the body responsible for implementing EC treaties and rules.

Europe. The world's most successful free-trade zone has been in Western Europe. The EEC, after its formation in 1957, grew to include 12 of the leading European economies. In 1967 the group became known as the European Community (EC). Tariffs and other barriers to trade came down further and further until by the late 1980s the goal

Practice

GUIDED PRACTICE

Work with students to develop a list of questions to ask a local business leader his or her opinions on how the role of the U.S. in the global economy has changed. Topics might include the effects of the dollar's decline, the effects of foreign investments in the U.S., and the effects of various trade agreements.

INDEPENDENT PRACTICE

Organize students into small groups and have groups use the list developed in the Guided Practice activity to conduct an interview with a local business leader. Have groups present the results of their interviews to the rest of the class.

Review and Assessment

REVIEW Have students write letters they might send to a friend in another country describing the concerns and challenges the U.S. faces as its role in the global economy changes. Select students to read their letters to the class. Then assign the Section 4 Review or quiz.

ASSESS Assign the **Section 4 Daily Quiz** in *Core Resources*.

HISTORICAL SIDELIGHTS
NAFTA

In 1993, Vice President Al Gore and Ross Perot conducted a televised debate about the effects the North American Free Trade Agreement might have on the U.S. economy. Gore presented Perot with a framed photo of Reed Smoot and Willis Hawley to suggest similarities between opponents of NAFTA and supporters of the restrictive Smoot-Hawley Tariff of 1930.

of a Europe without economic borders was in sight.

To facilitate this goal, the group signed the Maastricht Treaty in 1993. This treaty, aimed at bringing about "an ever-closer union among the peoples of Europe," created the **European Union**. The Union is designed to allow for the free movement of goods, labor, and capital among member nations. Some predict that a full political union—which could include as many as 20 member states by the year 2000—will eventually form in Europe.

NAFTA. Other countries have attempted to copy the European Community's success at eliminating trade barriers. These countries include the United States, Canada, and Mexico. Canada and the United States have long been each other's most important trading partner. During the 1980s leaders in both countries decided to reinforce the relationship by negotiating a free-trade agreement. The pact gained the approval of both governments despite opposition on both sides of the border by some who feared increased competition from the other side.

In the early 1990s Mexico asked to join the group. This represented a significant shift in policy for Mexico. Like many other comparatively poor countries, Mexico had long tended toward protectionism as a way of sheltering domestic industries from the competition of companies in the more advanced economies.

The proposed **North American Free Trade Agreement**, or NAFTA, aroused heated debate in all three countries but especially in the United States. Opponents argued that the low wages paid to Mexican workers would entice U.S. corporations to transfer their operations to Mexico. NAFTA critic H. Ross Perot predicted that if Congress approved NAFTA, Americans would hear a "giant sucking sound" as U.S. jobs were lost to Mexico. Perot was not the only one who feared for the future of domestic employment. In a 1992 poll, 56 percent of

▲ As NAFTA passed narrowly in Congress, opinions continued to differ sharply over whether U.S. workers would lose or gain as a result.

◄ Texas businessman and NAFTA critic H. Ross Perot expressed the concerns of many Americans who feared foreign competition and the loss of domestic jobs to Mexico.

Americans said that protecting U.S. industry and jobs from foreign competition should be the nation's top priority.

Supporters of NAFTA countered that people were not simply producers; they were also consumers. Supporters pointed out that tariffs and other trade barriers raised prices, harming consumers. Free trade would allow each country to specialize in those goods it produced most efficiently and to trade freely for other goods. NAFTA would give the inhabitants of all three countries access to the best possible products at the lowest possible prices. Over 60 percent of U.S. business executives polled in 1992 said that the advantages of free trade in promoting economic activity and efficiency outweighed the costs. In a narrow vote Congress agreed and approved NAFTA in November 1993.

The World Trade Organization. In the background of the debate over NAFTA was another set of trade negotiations involving most of the world's nations. These negotiations, called the **Uruguay Round** of GATT talks, signaled an effort to boost global free trade. Among the important issues covered was the trade of agricultural products and of intellectual property such as movies and computer software.

Although the Uruguay Round was begun in 1986, sharp differences among the major nations over several issues kept them from reaching a final agreement for years. In 1994, however, officials from 125 nations signed an agreement totaling some 22,000 pages. One provision of the agreement reorganized GATT as the **World Trade Organization** (WTO). This new name represents

RETEACH List on the chalkboard the terms from the Preview Workshop at the beginning of this section. Have students respond to the section's Focus questions with sentences containing the terms.

Closure

Have students use information from the section to write a brief paragraph that explains the meaning of the term *economic interdependence.* Call on volunteers to read their paragraphs to the class. Students may wish to include their paragraphs in their portfolios.

Extension

CREATE Have students create an organizational chart that shows the major holdings of an American multinational corporation.

RESEARCH Encourage students to conduct research on the investments American and Western European businesses have made in eastern Europe and the former Soviet Union since the end of the Cold War.

---

its sponsors' hope that the organization will continue to bring cooperation to world trade issues.

■■ **Despite some opposition, the formation of the European Union, NAFTA, and the World Trade Organization reflects a movement toward global free trade.**

▲ **Not everyone prospered as free trade spread throughout the world. This 1992 photograph shows a woman trying to exchange a sweater for fish at a Moscow market.**

COMMENTARY

A Look to the Future

Unfortunately, the prosperity brought about by increased free trade has not spread evenly. Wages remain disturbingly low in many newly industrializing countries. Many African and Latin American nations seem locked in a cycle of poverty from which there is no obvious exit. The formerly Communist countries of Eastern Europe have run into serious problems making the transition to capitalism. And even within the rich countries stubborn pockets of poverty and unemployment remain.

On the whole, however, the world economy as the end of the 20th century approaches is more unified than it has ever been. And economics will play an even greater international role as time passes. As American journalist Bruce W. Nelan observed in 1992,

❝ Just as wars—two World Wars and, equally important, the Cold War—dominated the geopolitical map of the 20th century, economics will rule over the 21st. All the big questions confronting the world in the century ahead are basically economic. ❞

SECTION 4 REVIEW

IDENTIFY and explain the significance of the following: oil shocks, floating exchange rates, Pacific Rim, multinational corporations, European Union, North American Free Trade Agreement, Uruguay Round, World Trade Organization.

1. **MAIN IDEA** What factors led to the decline of U.S. dominance of the world economy since the 1970s?
2. **MAIN IDEA** How have the economies of Pacific Rim countries changed in recent decades?
3. **MAIN IDEA** How has the global economy been changed by the rise of multinational corporations and by the end of the Cold War?
4. **WRITING TO INFORM** Write an essay explaining how global free trade has been supported by recent international agreements.
5. **EVALUATING** Write a paragraph evaluating the arguments made against the idea of global free trade.

PRIMARY SOURCE

Description of Change: excerpted
Rationale: excerpted to focus on main idea

SECTION REVIEW ANSWERS

IDENTIFY

For significance, see the following pages:
oil shocks (p. 663)
floating exchange rates (p. 664)
Pacific Rim (p. 664)
multinational corporations (p. 665)
European Union (p. 666)
North American Free Trade Agreement (p. 666)
Uruguay Round (p. 666)
World Trade Organization (p. 666)

1. oil shocks increased economic pressure on dollar and added to inflation; fixed exchange rates abandoned for system of floating exchange rates
2. have become major producers and consumers, shifting the center of the world economy away from the U.S. and Europe
3. can boost employment and development, but are sometimes accused of harming the environment or changing local cultures
4. Essays should include the effects of the European Union, NAFTA, the Uruguay Round, and the WTO.
5. Paragraphs should discuss concerns about employment issues and foreign competition.

CHAPTER 24
Review

DEVELOPING THEMES

Return to the "Themes" section on p. 646. Have students discuss these again and compare their original responses to those given now. (See p. 645B for suggested answers.)

Chapter Review Answers

WRITING A SUMMARY

See Essential Points in each section for main ideas.

REVIEWING CHRONOLOGY

3, 5, 2, 4, 1
Assessing Consequences
Answers should discuss the widespread adoption of protective tariffs and dramatic fluctuations in currency values.

IDENTIFYING PEOPLE AND IDEAS

1. developed wireless telegraphy
2. allows people around the world to communicate through their computers
3. British prime minister who worked to eliminate tariffs
4. established new schedule for German war debt repayment
5. tied currencies to value of dollar
6. established to provide loans to war-damaged and developing countries
7. responses to rising oil prices in 1970s and 1980s
8. Pacific nations that form new center of world economy
9. companies that invest in or own business ventures around the world
10. organization designed to bring cooperation to world trade issues

UNDERSTANDING MAIN IDEAS

1. Americans looked abroad for markets because overproduction had resulted in a surplus of goods in the U.S. They hoped to find these new markets primarily in Latin America and in Asia.
2. gold standard stabilized currency values, free trade increased trade between nations; wanted to support domestic industries
3. antagonism between capitalist and Communist nations
4. West Germany, Japan
5. oil shocks, system of floating exchange rates, growth of Pacific Rim, spread of multinational corporations, establishment of European Union, development of international trade

France and Great Britain sign the Cobden-Chevalier Treaty. 1860
British Parliament passes the Merchandise Marks Act. 1887
U.S. Congress passes the McKinley Tariff. 1890
U.S. adopts the gold standard. 1900
Marconi sends wireless telegraph across the Atlantic. 1901

WRITING A SUMMARY
Using the essential points of the chapter as a guide, write a summary of the chapter.

REVIEWING CHRONOLOGY
Number your paper 1 to 5. Study the time line above, and list the following events in the order in which they happened by writing the first next to 1, the second next to 2, and so on. Then complete the activity below.

1. Dawes Plan arranged.
2. European Economic Community formed.
3. France and Great Britain sign the Cobden-Chevalier Treaty.
4. Bretton Woods conference held.
5. U.S. adopts the gold standard.

Assessing Consequences How did measures such as the Smoot-Hawley Tariff and the British abandonment of the gold standard affect the world economy in the 1930s?

IDENTIFYING PEOPLE AND IDEAS
Explain the historical significance of each of the following people or terms.

1. Guglielmo Marconi
2. electronic mail
3. Sir Robert Peel
4. Young Plan
5. fixed exchange rates
6. World Bank
7. oil shocks
8. Pacific Rim
9. multinational corporations
10. World Trade Organization

UNDERSTANDING MAIN IDEAS
1. Why did Americans look abroad for markets in the late 19th and early 20th centuries? To what world regions did they turn?
2. How was the global economy affected by a widespread adoption of the gold standard and by an increase in free trade in the late 1800s? Why did some people continue to call for protectionism?
3. Why did two separate economic spheres arise after World War II?
4. What countries experienced rapid economic growth in the 1950s and 1960s?

5. What economic trends and political events have significantly influenced the global economy since the early 1970s?

REVIEWING THEMES
1. **Technology and Society** How did the introduction of steamships and the telegraph contribute to an increase in global trade?
2. **Global Relations** What economic problems did the world experience as a result of World War I?
3. **Economic Development** Why did some people in the United States oppose passage of the North American Free Trade Agreement? What arguments supported the agreement?

THINKING CRITICALLY
1. **Synthesizing** In what ways did the United States benefit economically from both World War I and World War II?
2. **Evaluating** How successful do you think the Bretton Woods system was in preventing the type of economic hostility that had contributed to the outbreak of World War II?
3. **Hypothesizing** What world region do you think will experience the greatest economic growth in the next 25 years? Why?

STRATEGY FOR SUCCESS
Review the Strategies for Success on Interpreting Editorial Cartoons on page 162. Then study the cartoon on the right. What is the cartoonist's message?

The Herblock Gallery, The Washington Post

668

668 ■ CHAPTER 24

REVIEWING THEMES

1. *Faster transportation cut shipping costs, and improved communications gave business leaders more contact with distant areas of the globe.*
2. *massive inflation, worldwide depression, fluctuating currency values*
3. *Opponents of NAFTA felt that the agreement would result in a loss of American jobs. Supporters argued that free trade promoted economic specialization and efficiency.*

THINKING CRITICALLY

1. *Both world wars allowed the United States to become a dominant economic power as a result of wartime destruction in other countries.*
2. *Answers should indicate that the world has not experienced a second economic crisis of the magnitude of the Great Depression.*
3. *Answers will vary but should consider the growth of the Pacific Rim and the development of new trade agreements.*

STRATEGY FOR SUCCESS

The cartoonist seems to be saying that the world economy is unstable and makes Johnson's task of balancing the budget nearly impossible.

WRITING ABOUT HISTORY

Letters should indicate the benefits of stable currencies in other nations and the advantages of maintaining a strong global economy.

USING PRIMARY SOURCES

The document suggests that the U.S. economy is part of a global economy and depends on international stability.

LINKING HISTORY AND GEOGRAPHY

Maps should indicate attempts to find new markets, as well as new sources of labor and production.

1924	1929	1930	1931	1933	1944	1951	1957	1971	1993	1994

- Dawes Plan arranged.
- Young Plan replaces Dawes Plan. New York stock market crashes.
- Smoot-Hawley Tariff passed.
- Great Britain abandons the gold standard.
- U.S. abandons the gold standard. London Conference held.
- Bretton Woods conference held.
- European Coal and Steel Community formed.
- European Economic Community formed.
- U.S. leaves system of fixed exchange rates.
- NAFTA ratified. European Union created out of European Community.
- World Trade Organization formed.

WRITING ABOUT HISTORY

Writing to Persuade Imagine you are a member of Charles Dawes's commission investigating the economic situation left by World War I. Write a letter to American bankers explaining why it would be in their interests to make loans to Germany.

USING PRIMARY SOURCES

While most of the delegates to the Bretton Woods conference believed that greater international cooperation would benefit the economies of individual countries, some people—particularly in the United States—were skeptical. Read the following excerpt from a press release written by U.S. officials as the conference began. How does the document attempt to persuade American citizens that the conference will benefit them?

> 66 *The purpose of the Conference is . . . wholly within the American tradition, and completely outside political considerations. The United States wants, after this war, full utilization of its industries, its factories and its farms; full and steady employment for its citizens, particularly its ex-servicemen; and full prosperity and peace. It can have them only in a world with a vigorous trade. But it can have such trade only if currencies are stable, if money keeps its value, and if people can buy and sell with the certainty that the money they receive on due date will have the value contracted for. . . . With values secured and held stable, it is next desirable to promote world-wide reconstruction, revive normal trade, and make funds available for sound enterprises, all of which will in turn call for American products.* 99

LINKING HISTORY AND GEOGRAPHY

Sketch a map of the world. Using symbols or shading, indicate how economic power has shifted among major world regions over the past 150 years. Then write a paragraph explaining the reasons for the shifts noted on your map.

 BUILDING YOUR PORTFOLIO

Complete the following projects independently or cooperatively.

1. **WAR** Imagine you are an economist at the World Bank assigned to study how wars can affect the economies of different nations. Construct a chart showing how World War I and World War II affected European economies and the U.S. economy.

2. **INTERNATIONAL COOPERATION** Imagine you are an administrator at the World Trade Organization. Prepare a speech explaining how the WTO will benefit the global economy. To support your claims, your speech should include an overview of ways in which international cooperation has helped the global economy in the 20th century.

3. **INDIVIDUAL RIGHTS** In Chapter 23 you portrayed a member of an independence movement who argued that imperialism has interfered with individual rights. Building on that experience, imagine you are a policymaker in a newly independent nation trying to decide how to shape your nation's economy. Write an essay explaining how a nation's economic policies can affect the rights of workers, business owners, consumers, and community members.

Gold coins from the United States, Canada, South Africa, and the Isle of Man

 BUILDING YOUR PORTFOLIO

Have students refer to **Building Your Portfolio Worksheet 6**, assigned at the beginning of Unit 6. Use the worksheet to help students monitor their progress on the portfolio projects.

Assessment

Core Resources
- Reteaching Worksheet 24
- Chapter 24 Tests
- Alternative Assessment Forms
- **Test Generator**

THE GLOBAL ECONOMY

HISTORICAL SIDELIGHTS

Sanctions

Although trade between the U.S. and Asia has increased dramatically during the 20th century, the People's Republic of China is not a member of the World Trade Organization and has had repeated difficulties in gaining a foothold in international commerce. During the early 1990s U.S. officials repeatedly requested that the Chinese government shut down 29 factories making illegal copies of American software, musical recordings, and movies. In February 1995 U.S. President Bill Clinton imposed tariffs on $1 billion of Chinese trade goods. The sanctions were the largest in U.S. history. In return, Chinese officials imposed a tariff on goods imported from the United States.

America's GEOGRAPHY

THE GLOBAL ECONOMY

As the global economy has grown over the past 150 years, a vast array of transportation and communications systems has arisen to support it. Despite this increasing international unity, relationships within the global economy have by no means remained constant. The United States' most important trade partners, for example, used to be the European nations. The percentage of trade with Europe, however, has steadily declined while Asian nations have become increasingly important trading partners. Furthermore, the growth of the global economy has benefited some nations more than others. Many nations, particularly in Africa and Latin America, have found it difficult to develop their economies. Several nations remain poor today.

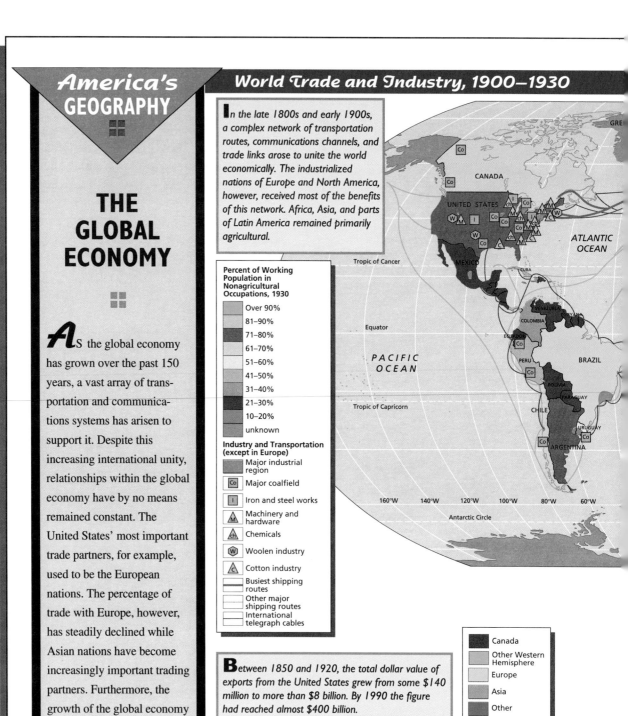

World Trade and Industry, 1900–1930

In the late 1800s and early 1900s, a complex network of transportation routes, communications channels, and trade links arose to unite the world economically. The industrialized nations of Europe and North America, however, received most of the benefits of this network. Africa, Asia, and parts of Latin America remained primarily agricultural.

Percent of Working Population in Nonagricultural Occupations, 1930

- Over 90%
- 81–90%
- 71–80%
- 61–70%
- 51–60%
- 41–50%
- 31–40%
- 21–30%
- 10–20%
- unknown

Industry and Transportation (except in Europe)

- Major industrial region
- Co — Major coalfield
- I — Iron and steel works
- M — Machinery and hardware
- C — Chemicals
- W — Woolen industry
- A — Cotton industry
- Busiest shipping routes
- Other major shipping routes
- International telegraph cables

Between 1850 and 1920, the total dollar value of exports from the United States grew from some $140 million to more than $8 billion. By 1990 the figure had reached almost $400 billion.

- Canada
- Other Western Hemisphere
- Europe
- Asia
- Other

VALUE OF EXPORTS OF U.S. MERCHANDISE: 1850, 1920, 1990

1850
2% 1% 7%
14%
76%

1920
11% 4% 12%
19%
54%

1990
4%
31%
21%
14%
30%

Chart information from *Historical Statistics of the United States, Statistical Abstract of the United States.*

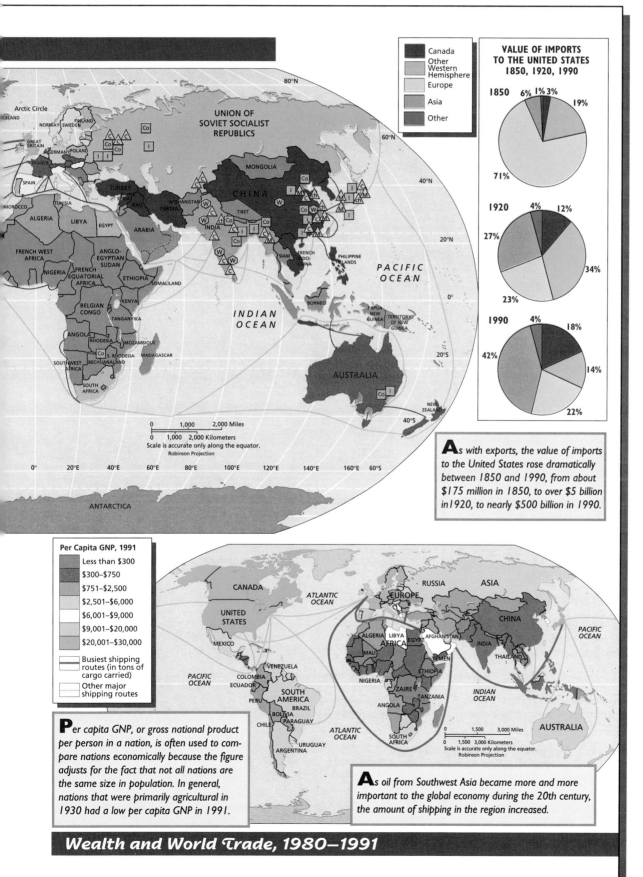

■ Canada		
▨ Other Western Hemisphere		
▨ Europe		
▨ Asia		
■ Other		

VALUE OF IMPORTS TO THE UNITED STATES 1850, 1920, 1990

1850
6% 1% 3%
19%
71%

1920
4% 12%
34%
23%
27%

1990
4% 18%
14%
22%
42%

As with exports, the value of imports to the United States rose dramatically between 1850 and 1990, from about $175 million in 1850, to over $5 billion in 1920, to nearly $500 billion in 1990.

Per Capita GNP, 1991	
▨	Less than $300
▨	$300–$750
▨	$751–$2,500
▨	$2,501–$6,000
□	$6,001–$9,000
▨	$9,001–$20,000
▨	$20,001–$30,000
▭	Busiest shipping routes (in tons of cargo carried)
▭	Other major shipping routes

Per capita GNP, or gross national product per person in a nation, is often used to compare nations economically because the figure adjusts for the fact that not all nations are the same size in population. In general, nations that were primarily agricultural in 1930 had a low per capita GNP in 1991.

As oil from Southwest Asia became more and more important to the global economy during the 20th century, the amount of shipping in the region increased.

MAKING CONNECTIONS

Mathematics

Even though Europe was the source of only 22 percent of imports to the United States in 1990 as compared to 71 percent in 1850, the actual dollar value of the 1990 imports vastly exceeded that of 1850. In fact, the dollar value of imports from Europe in 1990—over $111 billion—was far greater than the dollar value of *all* imports to the United States in both 1850 and 1920.

■■ Ask students to compute the approximate dollar values of each region's imports to the United States in 1990 given a total value of $498 billion.

Wealth and World Trade, 1980–1991

THE MOVEMENT OF PEOPLE AND IDEAS

Chapter Overview

During the 19th and early 20th centuries, millions of people moved from country to country. The U.S. was the single most popular destination for these migrants. As the 20th century progressed, the migrations of people around the globe continued. Growing numbers of migrants were refugees who, because of war and other disasters, left their homes unwillingly.

Ideas, as well as people, moved around the world during this time. Technological developments in the 20th century, however, allowed ideas to spread at a faster and faster rate. This movement of people and ideas has given rise to what might be called a global culture.

Chapter Planning Guide

CHAPTER 25	CORE RESOURCES	AUDIOVISUAL (AV) RESOURCES	PROGRAM RESOURCES
INTRODUCTION pp. 672–673	■ Building Your Portfolio Worksheet 6		
TEACHING THE CHAPTER pp. 674–693	■ Graphic Organizer 25 ■ Social Studies Skills Worksheet 25 ■ Geography Worksheet 25 ■ Literature Worksheet 25 ■ Outline Maps 1, 2, 8, 10, 11, 14, 17, 19, 20, 21, 22	■ *The American Nation Videodisc: A Nation of Immigrants; Early Computer Robot* ■ Linking Geography and History Transparencies and Worksheets 13, 13A, 13B ■ Everyday Life in America Transparency and Worksheet 21	■ *Eyewitnesses and Others,* Volume 1: Readings 10, 35, 43, 51; Volume 2: Readings 2, 5, 16, 22, 31, 76
REVIEW AND ASSESSMENT pp. 694–695	■ Chapter 25 Daily Quizzes ■ Reteaching Worksheet 25 ■ Chapter 25 Tests ■ Alternative Assessment Forms		■ Test Generator

Additional Resources

BOOKS FOR TEACHERS

"The Information Revolution." *BusinessWeek,* special edition, 1994. A number of articles on how communications technology is changing the way people work and live.

Segal, Aaron. *An Atlas of International Migration.* Hans Zell Publishers, 1993. Presents maps and text on migration from the earliest times to the present.

Why Do People Move? SPICE, 1993. Activity package on migration from Latin America.

BOOKS FOR STUDENTS

*Ashabranner, Brent. *Still a Nation of Immigrants.* Cobblehill Books, 1993. Reviews the major issues surrounding immigration to the U.S. today.

Freed, Les, and Frank J. Derfler, Jr. *Building the Information Highway.* Ziff-Davis Press, 1994. Highly entertaining discussion of the latest developments in the Information Revolution.

Hitchcox, Linda. *Refugees.* Franklin Watts, 1990. Looks at the plight of people forced to flee their homes because of war and persecution.

* for students reading below grade level

MULTIMEDIA MATERIALS

Cultural Exchange. Video, 15 min. Agency for Instructional Technology. Shows that world interaction helps bring about cultural exchange.

Immigration in America's History. Video, 11 min. Coronet Instructional Films. Surveys the major waves of immigration to the U.S.

Toward the Global Family. Video, 20 min. Coronet Instructional Films. Addresses the impact of the communications revolution.

THEMES IN AMERICAN HISTORY

USE WITH PAGES 672–673

*L*isted on the right are the themes emphasized in Chapter 25. The questions in boldface type stimulate critical thinking and provide students with an opportunity to discuss the themes within a broadened context. The questions also appear in the pupil's edition on p. 672.

■ CULTURAL DIVERSITY

How might immigration promote cultural diversity in a nation? Students might point out that immigrants arrive with cultural knowledge. An ongoing influx of people with diverse national backgrounds is bound to promote cultural diversity.

■ TECHNOLOGY AND SOCIETY

Why might governments sponsor efforts to develop new communications technologies? Students might point out that adoption of new technologies would enable developing countries to skip intermediate stages of development. In addition, communications developments would enable governments to gain information more quickly.

■ ECONOMIC DEVELOPMENT

How might globalization of sports, movies, and other elements of popular culture influence the development of a global economy? Students may mention that the spread of sports, movies, television shows, and music has exposed people to other cultures all over the world. This often leads to the development of new markets, providing access to the global economy.

CHAPTER STRATEGIES FOR MEETING INDIVIDUAL NEEDS

LIMITED ENGLISH PROFICIENT LEARNERS

After students have read the chapter, have them work in pairs. Assign each pair an Essential Point from the chapter, and ask pairs to expand on their topics by writing brief explanations or by creating visuals. Have pairs share their explanations or visuals.

TACTILE/KINESTHETIC LEARNERS

Have students construct a number of wall maps to illustrate some of the issues discussed in the chapter, such as recent patterns of migration, urbanization, refugee movements and the spread of culture. Encourage students to consult *The New State of the World Atlas* (Simon & Schuster, 1991), by Michael Kidron and Ronald Segal, for ideas.

LEARNERS HAVING DIFFICULTY

Organize students into pairs to construct an annotated outline, section by section, as they read through the chapter. Encourage pairs to compare their outlines and add information to produce an effective chapter overview.

AUDITORY LEARNERS

Have students prepare brief oral presentations on an issue discussed in the chapter. After each presentation, have the other students write summaries of the major points covered. Encourage students to compare their summaries.

VISUAL LEARNERS

Organize students into small groups to design a symbol or logo that represents the theme of the chapter—the movement of people and ideas around the world has helped to create a global culture. Encourage groups to share their symbols or logos.

GIFTED LEARNERS

Encourage students to write an essay on developments in migration and information technology titled "Toward a World Without Borders."

USING THE CHAPTER FOCUS

■ **UNDERSTANDING THE MAIN IDEA**

Call on a volunteer to read aloud the Understanding the Main Idea paragraph. Ask students to suggest how American culture has been influenced by immigrants from other lands. Then ask them how life in other countries has been affected by American culture. Conclude by pointing out that this chapter deals with the global nature of the movements of people and ideas.

 THEMES

Have students work individually or in groups to answer the questions under Themes. Save students' responses so that they can compare them with their responses after studying the chapter. (See p. 671B for suggested answers.)

■ **THE TIME LINE**

Direct students to copy the time-line entries into their notebooks. As students study the chapter, have them note the influence each event had on migration.

CORE RESOURCES

• **Graphic Organizer 25**
• **Building Your Portfolio Worksheet 6**

672

ABOUT THE ILLUSTRATION

Tell students that American sports are popular around the world. Ask them to explain why many Americans enjoy watching sports such as basketball, and why people in other countries might share this interest. List responses on a flipchart or on the chalkboard.

Chapter 25

THE MOVEMENT OF PEOPLE AND IDEAS

FOCUS

UNDERSTANDING THE MAIN IDEA

During the 20th century, migrations have shaped both American and world history. As people moved, they learned new ideas and taught their own traditions to their new neighbors. In the process they helped create a global culture.

 THEMES

■ **CULTURAL DIVERSITY** How might immigration promote cultural diversity in a nation?

■ **TECHNOLOGY AND SOCIETY** Why might governments sponsor efforts to develop new communications technologies?

■ **ECONOMIC DEVELOPMENT** How might globalization of sports, movies, and other elements of popular culture influence the development of a global economy?

1892	1896	1901	1965	1993
Ellis Island opens.	First modern Olympics held in Athens, Greece.	Thomasites arrive in the Philippines.	Immigration Act of 1965 passed.	U.S. Advisory Cour the National Inform Infrastructure crea

LINK TO THE PAST

The first people in America arrived thousands of years ago from Asia. Beginning in the 15th century, a new wave of immigration began—this time from Europe and Africa. The United States was founded in the 18th century by immigrants and their descendants.

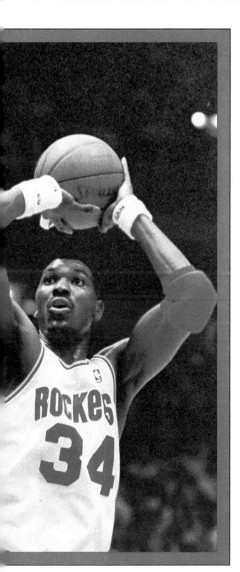

Patrick Ewing and Hakeem Olajuwon during a 1994 NBA championship game

*T*he 1994 championship series of the National Basketball Association (NBA) pitted the Houston Rockets against the New York Knicks. The series turned on the contest of skills between the two teams' centers: Houston's Hakeem Olajuwon and New York's Patrick Ewing.

Millions of Americans tuned their television sets to the series, and the games were broadcast to many other countries as well. By the 1990s basketball, originally developed in Massachusetts, had gained worldwide popularity. NBA games could be seen in more than 75 nations, including Zambia, Finland, and Kuwait. Among the foreign viewers those in Nigeria and Jamaica may have had particular interest in the game. Olajuwon and Ewing both were immigrants to America—Olajuwon from Nigeria, Ewing from Jamaica.

In many ways the 1994 championship series also symbolized trends that extended far beyond the sports world. During the 20th century people migrated between countries in great numbers. Wherever they went they took their ideas, their ways of looking at the world, their music, their games. Shared practices and philosophies led to the development of new traditions. By the end of the 20th century, many people believed that a global culture was emerging.

Indian sitar player Ravi Shankar, a pop idol of the 1960s

GLOBAL CONNECTIONS

Basketball has been played in Italy for more than 60 years, but during the 1980s it grew in popularity to be one of the country's favorite spectator sports, second only to soccer. In 1989 more than 25 percent of Italian television viewers watched Italian league basketball playoffs.

HISTORICAL SIDELIGHTS

Basketball and Philanthropy

A number of NBA players traveled to South Africa in 1994 to put on basketball camps for underprivileged children. Dikembe Mutombo, the Zaire-born center for the Denver Nuggets, recruited Patrick Ewing of the New York Knicks, Alonso Mourning of the Charlotte Hornets, and John Crotty of the Utah Jazz to work at the camps. Mutombo had previously visited basketball camps in Zambia, Kenya, and Somalia. He said, "Although I am from Zaire, I consider all of Africa my home. . . . I just try to give hope to people who have no hope. As my father always reminded me, you should remember where you come from, and you should always give something back."

THE MOVEMENT OF PEOPLE AND IDEAS ■■ 673

PREVIEW WORKSHOP

Following is a list of the significant terms in this section. You may wish to use this list as a section preview.

Terms
- Angel Island
- Thomasites

MOTIVATING: STUDENT EXPERIENCES

Ask volunteers to share what they know about their ancestors and immigration. Then tell students that this section deals with the great wave of migrations that took place in the 19th and early 20th centuries—the period when immigration to the U.S. was at its highest.

FOCUS OBJECTIVES

- Describe how widespread immigration was during the 19th and early 20th centuries.

- Identify the role that the United States played in global migration prior to World War I.

- Explain how pre-World War I migration affected the populations of cities and rural areas.

- List the factors that motivated people to migrate in the 19th and early 20th centuries.

THE AMERICAN NATION VIDEODISC PROGRAM

A Nation of Immigrants

2B	23298	2:45

CORE RESOURCES

- **Section 1 Daily Quiz**

AV **RESOURCES**

- *The American Nation Videodisc: A Nation of Immigrants*
- **Linking Geography and History Transparencies** and **Worksheets 13, 13A**
- **Everyday Life in America Transparency** and **Worksheet 21**

674

Section 1

PATTERNS OF MIGRATION

F O C U S

- **How widespread was migration during the 19th and early 20th centuries?**
- **What role did the United States play in global migration prior to World War I?**
- **How did pre–World War I migration affect the populations of cities and rural areas?**
- **What factors motivated people to migrate in the 19th and early 20th centuries?**

During the 19th and early 20th centuries, millions of people migrated from their birthplaces to other countries and from rural regions to cities. Many of these migrants settled in the United States, attracted by jobs in the booming industries there.

19th-century textile factory

PEOPLE ON THE MOVE

The 19th and early 20th centuries marked one of the world's great ages of migration, affecting all the inhabited continents and most countries. Specific statistics on global migration are difficult to determine because few countries kept good records of those who entered and rarely recorded those who left. Estimates suggest, however, that some 60 million people left Europe during the century before World War I. The stream of European migrants flowed not only to North America but also to South America, to Australia and New Zealand, and to many parts of Africa. From

◀ **Alberto Fujimori, son of Japanese immigrants to Peru, won that country's presidency in 1990.**

China and Japan another wave of people moved into Southeast and South Asia, as well as across the Pacific to the Americas. Several million Japanese emigrants formed communities in Korea, China, the Philippines, Hawaii, and North and South America. From India still other migrants went east to Southeast Asia and west to Africa.

Many people did not plan to relocate permanently but hoped to find economic success and then return to their native countries. Most, however, remained in their new homes. By the 1930s, more than two million Southern Europeans formed an important business class in the North African countries of Egypt, Libya, Tunisia, Algeria, and Morocco. Similarly, Indians and Chinese became successful entrepreneurs in many countries bordering the Indian Ocean. At their height the Indian communities in this region totaled 3 million people, while the Chinese settlers numbered some 12 million.

Although largely ended by the late 19th century, the African slave trade brought about another important movement of peoples. Centuries before the Europeans became involved in the slave trade,

Provide students with outline maps of the world. Then direct students to put the information under the heading *People on the Move* into map form. Suggest that they use annotations where appropriate. When students have completed the map, have them write a caption that makes a generalization about the movement of people in the 19th and early 20th centuries. Students may wish to include their maps in their portfolios.

Encourage students to construct an illustrated time line on the role that migration played in American history up through the early 20th century. Suggest that they record information on immigration on one side of the time line and information about emigration on the other. Call on volunteers to display and discuss their time lines.

▶

Arab slave traders had taken Africans to Southwest Asia and India. Then in the 17th century slaves had become the major factor in the commerce between Africa and the Americas. The size of the slave trade to Asia can only be guessed at because few records exist. However, the Atlantic slave ships landed more than 10 million Africans in North and South America and the Caribbean islands.

■■ **Streams of migration in the 19th and early 20th centuries touched every inhabited continent and nearly every region.**

THE UNITED STATES IN THE WORLD STREAM

The United States sat squarely in the middle of the world stream of migration. Millions entered the United States from abroad; much smaller numbers left the United States for other countries.

Immigration to America. America was the single most popular destination of migrants from other countries. Before the first census of 1790, Great Britain and West Africa provided the largest number of immigrants to the United States. Even after the Revolutionary War, British settlers were drawn to their former colonies, where they could find familiar customs and language. Most Africans, on the other hand, came involuntarily as

▼ This 1883 *Harper's* editorial cartoon illustrates an attitude held by many Americans toward Irish immigrants.

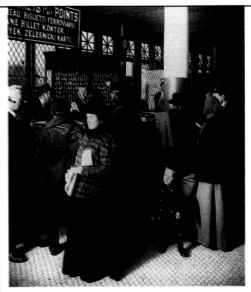

▲ Ellis Island was the first stop for many European immigrants seeking a new life in America.

slaves. After the ban on the importation of slaves went into effect in 1808, however, the number of forced immigrants from Africa dropped.

During the middle part of the 19th century large numbers of Germans and Irish left their homes for the United States. The 1848 discovery of gold in California attracted still more immigrants. Among the gold-seekers were thousands of Chinese, many of whom hoped to make fortunes and return to China. Introducing differences in language and religion, these groups added new cultural elements to the United States.

Immigration to the United States peaked between 1890 and 1914 when some 15 million newcomers landed on American shores. In 1907 alone more than 1.2 million immigrants entered the country. While most of these immigrants came from Europe as before, a growing number arrived from southern and eastern Europe. Of these, Russian Jews, Poles, Ukrainians, Slovaks, Croatians, Slovenes, Hungarians, Romanians, Greeks, and Italians made up the largest groups. Ellis Island in New York Harbor, an immigration station that opened in 1892, was the first sight of America for many of these newcomers.

Many immigrants learned of the opportunities available in the United States from railroad and steamship companies. In fact, convincing foreigners that the United States was the land of opportunity became a major business activity in the late 1800s. The agents of steamship companies and railroads swarmed over Europe, one observer

HISTORICAL SIDELIGHTS

Forming a Nation

Immigrants from many countries played important roles during the Revolutionary War and the early years of the United States. Johann Kalb, who claimed to be a German baron, served as a major general in the Continental Army until his death after the Battle of Camden in 1780. Baron von Steuben, from Prussia, was responsible for training the Continental Army. The Marquis de Lafayette, a 19-year-old French army captain, left France in secret to join the American forces as a major general. He served without pay and provided his own supplies to relieve the financially strapped Second Continental Congress. Alexander Hamilton, who had emigrated from the Leeward Islands to New York in 1772, served in the Continental Army as well as in the first cabinet, as secretary of the treasury.

AV **TRANSPARENCY**

Linking Geography and History Transparency and **Worksheet 13**

Teaching the Section

FROM COUNTRY TO CITY

Organize students into pairs. Encourage pairs to imagine they are working on a history wall chart. Have students complete an entry about migration to the city. Ask pairs to select an appropriate illustration and write a 50-word caption. Have pairs present their entries.

WHY PEOPLE MIGRATE

Select students to play the following roles: a farmer leaving the countryside for a nearby city; an eastern European immigrant heading to the steel mills of Pennsylvania; a Scandinavian immigrant traveling to Minnesota; a European radical on the route to Chicago; a family of Russian Jews trying to get to New York. Have these students, in their roles, make brief statements on why they are migrating. Ask all class members to use the information in the statements to write a paragraph summarizing people's reasons for moving.

■■ Ask students to discuss what might cause them to want to migrate.

PRIMARY SOURCES

Description of Change: excerpted and bracketed
Rationale: Excerpted to focus on main idea; bracketed to clarify meaning

---

MULTICULTURAL PERSPECTIVES

The belief in the need for missions was not limited to Christians during the 19th century. Some members of the German Jewish community in the United States believed that objections to the beliefs and behavior of the new immigrants from eastern Europe could be eliminated if missionaries were "sent to Russia to civilize the Russian Jews rather than have their backwardness ruin the American Jewish community." Rabbi Isaac Mayer Wise asserted that "We are Americans and they are not. We are Israelites of the nineteenth century and a free country, and they gnaw the dead bones of past centuries."

---

noted, "as the locusts covered Egypt!" They painted a tempting—and often false—picture of America. Some railroad companies exaggerated the employment opportunities available in the United States. And the steamship lines charged rock-bottom fares to attract passengers.

Most of the millions who yielded to this hard sell found the journey to the "Promised Land" difficult. The ocean voyage was no pleasure trip for those in the poorest accommodations, called steerage. One Italian immigrant asked:

66 How can a steerage passenger remember that he is a human being when he must first pick the worms from his food . . . and eat in his stuffy, stinking bunk, or in the hot and fetid [bad-smelling] atmosphere of a compartment where 150 men sleep? 99

Nativist response. Although many people in the United States recognized that even native-born Americans were descended from earlier immigrants, others wondered whether these latest arrivals were perhaps too different and too numerous. Some of the opponents of immigration were frankly racist, while others based their opposition on economic factors. One critic claimed that the willingness of many new immigrants to work for very low wages hurt "the native worker and the earlier immigrant . . . , affecting detrimentally the standard of living of hundreds of thousands of workers—workers, too, who are also citizens, fathers, husbands."

Such nativism sometimes prompted or forced immigrants to leave the United States, proving that migration was not a one-way street. Many Chinese who had entered America before passage of the 1882 Chinese Exclusion Act were among those

who left. The Chinese population in the United States plummeted from more than 100,000 in 1890 to less than 65,000 in 1920. Chinese who arrived during this period were detained at **Angel Island**—the West Coast counterpart of Ellis Island—while authorities investigated their claims that they were legal immigrants. One of the detained Chinese wrote this poem on his cell wall:

66 The day I am rid of this prison and attain success,
I must remember that this prison once existed. . . .
All my compatriots [fellow citizens] please be mindful.
Once you have some small gains, return home [to China] early. 99

Emigration from America. Some Americans, searching for new opportunities, also left during this period. Australia's population nearly tripled in the nine years after gold was discovered there in 1851; some of these gold-seekers were Americans lured by the same dreams that had brought so many people to California just a few years earlier. Another gold rush brought Americans to Canada's Yukon Territory in 1897 and 1898. American farmers were also attracted to Canada. Between 1900 and 1920 nearly 300,000 Americans moved north of the border to establish homesteads in Manitoba, Alberta, and Saskatchewan.

One group of emigrants left the United States for what they believed was a loftier goal than land or gold. Christian missionaries—mostly Protestants but some Roman Catholics—sought to convert people in other countries. Many missionaries and church groups focused their attentions on China.

Like China, the Philippines also attracted the attention of missionary societies and teachers. Among the teachers were some 500 young Americans who arrived in Manila in 1901 aboard the steamer *Thomas*. The **Thomasites**, as they were called, saw themselves as representatives of American values. "We are not merely teachers," one of the Thomasites wrote to her parents back in Massachusetts. "We are social assets and emissaries of good will."

Because they also promoted U.S. interests, however, the missionaries were not always welcome. At the time the Thomasites arrived, many Filipinos were resisting the annexation of their country by the United States. Yet in spite of this

▶ Asian immigrants enter the United States at Angel Island in San Francisco Bay (c. 1911).

Practice

GUIDED PRACTICE

On the chalkboard, write the four subsection titles. Inform students that these are topics a newspaper cartoonist has been given to work on. Call on volunteers to offer cartoon ideas—how to represent an idea with a picture, captions, and so on. Note their suggestions under the appropriate title.

INDEPENDENT PRACTICE

Direct students to select one of the topics listed on the chalkboard. Then have them use the ideas developed in the Guided Practice activity to create a cartoon on that topic. Call on volunteers to present and explain their cartoons to the class. Students may wish to include their cartoons in their portfolios.

Review and Assessment

REVIEW Divide the class into groups of four. Assign each group member one of the Focus questions to answer. Then have group members meet with others assigned the same question to come to a consensus on their answer. Have members reconvene in their original groups to share their answers. Then assign the Section 1 Review on p. 678.

ASSESS Assign the **Section 1 Daily Quiz** in *Core Resources.* ▶

▲ These men and boys gather in China to hear an American missionary.

opposition, the Thomasites and their successors—together with the hundreds of thousands of Filipinos who later immigrated to America—forged an important cultural connection between the Philippines and the United States.

∎∎ The United States was the most likely destination of immigrants and the source of a smaller but significant emigration to other countries.

FROM COUNTRY TO CITY

The great migrations of the 19th and early 20th centuries were not only nation-to-nation but also country-to-city movements. Throughout the industrializing world, people were moving from rural regions to cities. This movement to the city was closely tied to the Industrial Revolution. The availability of workers in cities and towns prompted manufacturers to locate their factories there. In turn, the lure of jobs drew even more people to the cities.

In Great Britain, for example, the initial burst of urban growth occurred during the first half of the 19th century in cities such as Birmingham, Manchester, and Liverpool. Birmingham's and Manchester's populations more than tripled between 1800 and 1850, while Liverpool's increased nearly fivefold. As the century progressed, these and other British towns played an increasingly important role in the industrial economy. In 1881 one member of Parliament wrote: "Our towns are the backbone of the nation. They give it strength, cohesion, vitality."

Urban growth followed industrial development throughout Europe. In Italy the change was most notable after 1860, as new industries attracted people to cities and towns. Similarly, in the United States the great population jump in cities occurred in the second half of the 19th century. The population of New York City, for instance, grew from some 2 million to nearly 3.5 million between 1880 and 1900, while Chicago went from some 500,000 to more than 1.5 million. St. Paul, Minneapolis, and Denver also tripled in size. The primary reason for this urban growth was the same as in Britain and other industrializing countries: cities offered the promise of jobs. In the Midwest, for example, many farming areas lost residents to Chicago, Detroit, and other cities, while in New England thousands of farms and scores of rural villages were simply abandoned for the promise of city wages.

Many who witnessed this movement to the cities believed that urban growth was natural and unavoidable. Horace Greeley noted, "We cannot all live in cities, yet nearly all seem determined to do so." The 1920 census seemed to bear out Greeley's observation—for the first time in U.S. history, more than half the people lived in cities.

∎∎ Migration increased city populations, often at the expense of rural populations.

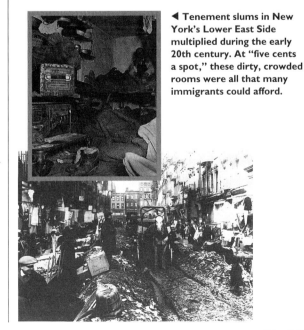

◀ Tenement slums in New York's Lower East Side multiplied during the early 20th century. At "five cents a spot," these dirty, crowded rooms were all that many immigrants could afford.

GLOBAL CONNECTIONS

Not everyone was enthusiastic about the process of urbanization. One Canadian, J.S. Woodsworth, wrote: "The higher the buildings, the less sunshine; the bigger the crowds, the less fresh air. . . . As we penetrate more deeply into its life, we discover evils of which we had hardly dreamed. Pitfalls abound on every side; dark crimes are being committed; dreadful tragedies are being enacted in real life. . . . We look beneath the glittering surface and shrink back from the hidden depths which the yawning darkness suggests. . . . And the horror of it all grows upon us till the city becomes a hateful thing, from which we would flee in despair—a monstrous blot on the face of God's fair earth."

AV **TRANSPARENCY**

Linking Geography and History Transparency and **Worksheet 13A**

AV **TRANSPARENCY**

Everyday Life in America Transparency and **Worksheet 21**

RETEACH Organize students into small groups and assign each group a subsection. Direct each group to develop questions about the main ideas in its subsection. Then have each group exchange its questions with another group and work to answer the questions it receives.

*C*losure

Have students use the section's main headings to create a graphic organizer that depicts patterns of migration in the 19th and early 20th centuries. Call on volunteers to present and explain their organizers to the class.

*E*xtension

INVESTIGATE Invite students to investigate how immigration has affected their city or town. Have them present their findings in a report that explains where the immigrants came from and when they came.

CREATE Encourage students to use information from atlases, almanacs, encyclopedias, and statistical abstracts to create a database on migration patterns in the late 19th and early 20th centuries.

SECTION REVIEW ANSWERS

IDENTIFY

For significance, see the following pages:
Angel Island (p. 676)
Thomasites (p. 676)

1. *Millions of Europeans and Asians settled in other parts of the world; cities grew as people moved from rural areas to find jobs.*
2. *Immigrants contributed to the growth of the United States and added new cultural elements; some left the United States in search of new opportunities.*
3. *Cities grew as people left rural areas in search of jobs.*
4. *Poems should address the problems of leaving home or the excitement and the difficulties experienced by immigrants.*
5. *Paragraphs should note that many migrants moved between regions and between countries in search of better jobs and higher wages, but that many people also moved to other countries to find greater personal freedom.*

678

WHY THEY MOVED

Just as migrants chose to relocate to a variety of areas around the world, they also moved for a variety of reasons. Some people sought improved economic opportunities, while others hoped to find greater personal freedom.

Economic opportunity. The great migrations were caused largely by economic factors, as people looked for better jobs and higher wages. Farmers around the world experienced hard times during the late 19th century, and agriculture seemed a less and less secure source of income. In the cities, however, business and industry appeared to be flourishing. Many people moved to cities in their own countries, while others looked for opportunities abroad. The United States, with the fastest-growing of the large industrial economies, attracted millions of people.

But cities were not the only attraction. Throughout the 19th century and into the 20th century, many of the immigrants to the United States hoped to acquire land, which was cheaper than in Europe. Most had been farmers in their home countries, and many hoped to remain farmers.

▲ A doctor examines Russian Jewish emigrants before they travel as steerage passengers to America.

Some achieved this dream. During the 1800s and 1900s, for example, many German and Scandinavian immigrants established prosperous farms in Minnesota and the upper Middle West. In many cases, though, the hard reality of earning a living upset the immigrants' plans. The dreams of buying a farm were postponed, then postponed again.

Personal freedom. Although economic concerns motivated most immigrants, some sought political freedom. Karl Marx, the German radical and coauthor of the *Communist Manifesto* (1848), fled to England after the failed 1848 revolutions in Europe. Other European radicals settled in the United States.

Other people left their homes for religious reasons. Russian Jews, for instance, had long suffered from discrimination and outright violence. When the chance to leave arose during the 1890s and early 1900s, many did. Some went to South America, others to Canada, but most resettled in the United States. They often met a hostile reception. Edward Ross, a sociologist of the era, railed against "the lower class of Jews of Eastern Europe" who arrived in America as "moral cripples, their souls warped and dwarfed." Yet American anti-Semitism was rarely as violent as in the countries the immigrants had left, and most felt that conditions had changed for the better.

■■ **Most people moved for economic reasons, but the desire for political and religious freedom was also important.**

 S E C T I O N 1 R E V I E W

IDENTIFY and explain the significance of the following: Angel Island, Thomasites.

1. **MAIN IDEA** How did migration affect the various areas of the world during the 19th and early 20th centuries?
2. **MAIN IDEA** How did migration affect the United States during the 19th and early 20th centuries?
3. **MAIN IDEA** How did the population movements that occurred before World War I affect cities and rural areas?
4. **WRITING TO CREATE** Write a poem that expresses how a migrant might feel about leaving home or about starting over in a new land or city.
5. **COMPARING** Write a paragraph comparing the reasons people emigrated to a different country with the reasons people moved from rural areas to cities.

Chapter 25

SECTION 2

Introducing the Section

PREVIEW WORKSHOP

Following is a list of the significant people, places, and terms in this section. You may wish to use this list as a section preview.

People
- Bette Bao Lord

Places
- Bosnia
- Rwanda

Terms
- Displaced Persons Act
- Immigration Act of 1965
- Immigration Act of 1990
- asylum
- Operation Restore Hope

MOTIVATING: LINK TO TODAY

Ask for volunteers to identify the major issues surrounding migration that they have recently read about in magazines and newspapers or seen on television news programs. List these issues on the chalkboard and have students record the list in their notebooks. As students study this section, have them note the origins and historical development of these issues.

Section 2

CHILDREN OF WAR

FOCUS OBJECTIVES
- Describe the effect that World War I and the Great Depression had on migration.
- Explain how World War II and its aftermath influenced the movement of peoples.
- Identify the immigration trends the United States has experienced since the 1960s.
- Determine the migration patterns that marked the 1980s and 1990s.

FOCUS
- **What effect did World War I and the Great Depression have on migration?**
- **How did World War II and its aftermath influence the movement of peoples?**
- **What immigration trends has the United States experienced since the 1960s?**
- **What migration patterns marked the 1980s and 1990s?**

Hutu children in a Rwandan refugee camp, 1994

During the 20th century the migrations of peoples around the globe continued. Economic motivations remained a principal driving force, but growing numbers of migrants were refugees displaced by war and other disasters. By the 1990s tens of millions of people lived outside the countries of their birth.

WORLD WAR I AND ITS AFTERMATH

The outbreak of World War I caused a drop in migration rates. Previously, countries with strained economies had been willing to allow citizens to try their luck elsewhere—and perhaps send money to relatives back at home. When the war began, however, some nations restricted emigration, having decided that the potential emigrants—particularly the young men—would be more useful as soldiers.

Ocean travel also took on new difficulties and risks. Many nations converted passenger ships to troop and cargo carriers, transporting soldiers and equipment to the war zone. Submarines and surface vessels patrolled the sea-lanes, seizing and sometimes sinking enemy ships. Crossing the ocean to start a new life abroad was always a daunting venture; during war it seemed more perilous than ever.

▶ **A passenger ship converted into a troop transport carries grim soldiers to battle during World War I.**

After World War I ended in 1918, the migrations resumed. Immigration to the United States, however, did not reach former levels. Americans who opposed immigration played on people's hostility to wartime enemies to persuade Congress to restrict immigration. The trend continued when Congress passed the Immigration Act of 1924, sharply reducing the number of immigrants allowed into the country.

The economic troubles of the 1930s continued to limit international migration. Now, however,

CORE RESOURCES
- **Section 2 Daily Quiz**

AV RESOURCES
- **Linking Geography and History Transparency** and **Worksheet 13B**

THE MOVEMENT OF PEOPLE AND IDEAS ▦ 679

679

Teaching the Section

MIGRATION SLOWS

Organize students into groups of five. Provide each group with a piece of butcher paper on which is drawn a two-column chart titled "Why Migration Slowed," with *World War I* and *Postwar Years* as column headings. Have group members add information to the chart, round-robin style, until they believe their chart is complete. Select a group to use their chart to explain why migration slowed during World War I and the years after.

the problem was not danger on the high seas or a government's need for soldiers but the collapse of economic opportunity. More than ever, people were willing to look for jobs in other countries. But America's Great Depression was part of an international problem, and few jobs were available anywhere. Moreover, countries that had once welcomed immigrants now closed their borders to keep jobless people from entering. Some nations went even further. During the early 1930s the U.S. government deported some half million Mexican workers out of a belief that they were taking jobs from U.S. citizens (see Chapter 13).

■■ **Both World War I and the Great Depression reduced the movement of peoples across international borders.**

A NEW TYPE OF MIGRATION

Despite the depression the 1930s did mark the beginning of an era of massive displacements of refugees—people forced to flee their homes because of political persecution, war, or natural disasters. For example, after the Nazi party came to power in Germany in 1933, the German government adopted policies designed to drive Jews from positions of influence and even from Germany itself. Many German Jews, especially those with education or skills that might be useful in other countries, left Germany during the 1930s. Albert Einstein, winner of the 1921 Nobel Prize for physics, was one of the most prominent of the refugees from Hitler's Germany to resettle in the United States. A large number of Jews, however, had little choice but to remain in Germany. With

▼ On May 9, 1938, Chinese Americans paraded down the streets of New York City protesting the Japanese invasion of China.

the economic strains of the depression and continuing anti-Semitism, most countries were reluctant to accept large numbers of Jewish refugees.

Europe was not the only region experiencing refugee migration in the 1930s. In the years following Japan's 1931 invasion of Manchuria, Japan extended its control across northern China. Yet despite the continuing Japanese advances and the eventual outbreak of war, many nations refused to accept Chinese immigrants. As a result, refugees were forced to flee to other parts of China. By the time the conflict between China and Japan ended in 1945, 95 million Chinese had become refugees in their own country.

Refugee migration only increased following World War II. Europe had been devastated by the war, and the booming American economy again attracted immigrants. Congress passed the **Displaced Persons Act** of 1948, which enabled some 400,000 European refugees to enter the United States. Many of these immigrants were Jews who had survived the Nazi concentration camps.

Another wave of refugees resulted as European powers pulled out of Asia and Africa and former colonies became independent nations. The difficulties of self-rule often aggravated long-standing tensions. These tensions frequently led to fighting, which, in turn, forced thousands of people to become refugees.

▲ On August 15, 1947, Mohammed Ali Jinnah, governor general of Pakistan, and his sister attended the ceremony marking the beginning of the Dominion of Pakistan.

Great Britain's withdrawal from India in 1947, for instance, brought ethnic and religious conflicts—particularly between Hindus and Muslims—to the forefront. Before they left, the British wanted to reduce the risk of war between these groups. Therefore, the British divided the region into two countries: Pakistan, populated mostly by Muslims, and India, whose residents were mostly Hindus. But people caught on the wrong side of the border often found their lives in danger and fled to safety on the other side.

A NEW KIND OF MIGRATION

Encourage students to study the map titled "The Growing Refugee Problem" on p. 684. Next, provide students with outline maps of the world. Then direct students to create a similar map using the information under the heading *A New Type of Migration*. Suggest that they use arrows to indicate the flow of refugees. They might also use annotations to provide additional information on the map. When students have completed the map, have them write a caption that explains what was "new" about migration in the years after World War II.

IMMIGRATION TO AMERICA SINCE 1965

Organize students into small groups to prepare conversations among immigrants from different countries. They should discuss why they came to the U.S., how they came, and how they were received when they arrived. Call on groups to present their conversations to the class. Have students write paragraphs summarizing the nature of immigration to the U.S. since 1965.

Palestine also experienced turmoil in the 1940s when guerrillas eager to establish a Jewish state fought British rule. The United Nations voted to divide the region in two, providing a homeland for the world's Jews as well as for the region's Arabs (see Chapter 17). Jews from around the world, including the United States, migrated to Palestine. Although much of the world felt sympathy for the plight of displaced Jews, particularly for those who had survived the Nazi Holocaust, many Palestinians bitterly opposed the partition. In 1948 Arab armies attacked Israel.

Israel not only survived the attack but also enlarged its borders. Hundreds of thousands of Palestinians found themselves homeless and destitute, and many ended up in refugee camps in neighboring countries. Nearly one million Palestinians took refuge in Jordan alone, and several hundred thousand others settled in Lebanon. The 1967 Arab-Israeli war created even more refugees as Arabs fled from the territory Israel acquired. The refugee issue has remained a source of conflict between Israel and surrounding countries for decades.

■■ In the years before and after World War II, political, religious, and ethnic conflicts caused many people to become refugees.

IMMIGRATION TO AMERICA SINCE 1965

Rates of immigration to the United States soared after the mid-1960s. This was largely due to the passage of the **Immigration Act of 1965**, which did away with the system admitting fixed percentages of immigrants to the United States based on their countries of origin. The act allowed greater numbers of people into the country. Even though numerical limits on immigration still existed, certain relatives of U.S. citizens were exempt from these limits.

Although a largely unforeseen effect, the act significantly increased the number of immigrants from Asia and Latin America while immigration from Europe slowed. Between 1951 and 1965, for example, Europe supplied over half of all immigrants to the United States; from 1967 through 1978, however, Europeans made up less than one quarter of the total. In contrast, the number of Asians admitted was less than 7 percent in the first period but more than 28 percent in the second.

Motivations. Many of the Asian and Latin American immigrants to the United States since the 1960s have been refugees. The Vietnam War, for example, provoked a flood of refugees from Southeast Asia. After the Communist victory in 1975, many Vietnamese who had supported South Vietnam and the United States feared for their lives. During the next several years, hundreds of thousands of Vietnamese fled their country in crowded boats (see Chapter 20).

Sympathetic to the plight of these "boat people," many Americans worked to provide Vietnamese refugees with shelter and the opportunity for a new life. The U.S. government responded by creating programs that permitted thousands of Vietnamese to immigrate to the United States. Because the war in Vietnam had spilled over into Cambodia and Laos, thousands of people from these countries also fled to the United States.

Many refugees have also fled violence or oppressive governments in Cuba and Central American nations such as Guatemala and El Salvador. And after the military coup in Haiti in 1991, thousands of Haitians fled the growing chaos in their country. The Haitians, however, did not find the United States as open as many other refugees had. Arguing that the Haitians were escaping economic not political conditions, the United States began returning the refugees to Haiti. Many politicians criticized this policy and contrasted it to the special treatment given to Cuban refugees, who were allowed to stay in the United States. U.S. policy toward Cubans changed in 1994, however, when Cuban ruler Fidel Castro threatened to overwhelm Florida with Cuban refugees, eager to flee the island's deepening poverty. Instead of allowing Cubans on homemade rafts to float to Florida, the

▼ An overcrowded sailboat filled with Haitian refugees was intercepted by the U.S. Coast Guard on July 4, 1994.

 GLOBAL CONNECTIONS

Although the United States was the primary destination of refugees from Vietnam and surrounding countries, other nations did receive boat people. More than 48,000 of the 60,103 refugees arriving in Australia between 1975 and 1981 were boat people. Canada, France, West Germany, Japan, and the United Kingdom also accepted these refugees.

AV TRANSPARENCY
Linking Geography and History Transparency and **Worksheet 13B**

HISTORICAL SIDELIGHTS

Immigration Loopholes Not all immigrants are subject to the numerical limitations established by the Immigration Act of 1965. Those who are exempt include spouses and unmarried minor children of U.S. citizens, as well as scientists and artists of exceptional ability. The number of people admitted under these exemptions has grown steadily over time, from some 113,000 in 1976 to 210,761 in 1985.

PERSONALITIES IN HISTORY

During his search for a position in a U.S. hospital, Abraham Verghese discovered a loose network of foreign doctors and students. From these people he was able to gain information about job opportunities and working conditions in hospitals across the country. He wrote, "With a few phone calls, I could establish for any city which hospital to apply to. . . . And the network invariably provided me with the name of someone to stay with."

PRIMARY SOURCE

Description of Change: excerpted and bracketed
Rationale: excerpted to focus on main idea; bracketed to clarify meaning

MAKING CONNECTIONS

Medicine

To Hindus the Ganges River in India is considered holy. Pilgrims come to the river to bathe and to collect the river's water in jars to take home. Unregulated industry and untreated sewage, however, have led to high levels of pollution in the river. In many cases, people who cannot afford to bury their dead choose instead to dump bodies into the river. Doctors and environmentalists say that poor sanitary conditions, as indicated by the pollution of the Ganges, are one cause for the 1994 outbreak of pneumonic plague in Surat.

Then and Now — DISEASE AND MIGRATION

As people moved from one place to another, they carried with them not only their culture and traditions but also viruses and other microbes. For example, shipping and trade routes provided a corridor for outbreaks of bubonic plague. During the 6th, 14th, and 17th centuries rats carried plague-infected fleas to ports throughout Europe and Asia. Similarly, Mongol armies of the 14th century probably carried the disease overland across Asia along with rat-infested supplies.

Other epidemics also accompanied settlers, military forces, and commercial travelers. In the 16th and 17th centuries, European settlers brought smallpox, measles, and other diseases to the Americas, devastating the American Indian populations. In the early 19th century, the British army carried cholera from India into Afghanistan and the Himalayas. And between 1831 and 1833, cholera epidemics struck port cities in Russia, France, England, the United States, and other countries around the world. This epidemic of cholera also appeared in Mecca. Muslim pilgrims who contracted the disease spread cholera across the globe as they returned to their homes.

Epidemics are not confined to the past. Tens of thousands of residents of Surat, India, fled their homes when an outbreak of plague struck in September 1994. More alarming, however, is the spread of new diseases—particularly AIDS—that have no known cure.

AIDS is the final deadly stage of an illness believed to be caused by the human immunodeficiency virus, or HIV. AIDS is believed to have originated in Africa, where it may have spread along long-distance trucking routes. Since the 1980s AIDS has become a global threat. The World Health Organization (WHO) estimated in 1993 that some 2 million persons worldwide had full-blown AIDS and some 13 million others were carrying HIV. In 1992 the United Nations Children's Fund estimated that some 2 million of the world's children had been orphaned by AIDS and predicted that the number would rise to 10 million by the year 2000.

AIDS primarily affects young and middle-aged adults, many of whom are the wage-earners supporting children or aged parents. In developing countries, therefore, AIDS may have a profound effect on the economy as fewer people are able to work. In many ways, AIDS poses social problems that extend far beyond the medical challenges.

 Among those treating AIDS patients is Abraham Verghese. Born in Ethiopia to Indian parents, he studied medicine in India, and then came to the United States to specialize in infectious diseases. In 1985 he became a staff physician at a Veterans Administration hospital in rural Johnson City, Tennessee.

For the next four years, Verghese saw a growing number of patients who were HIV-positive. He wrote:

> 66 Our little town in the heart of the country with 50,000 residents had a hundredfold more cases than the CDC [Center for Disease Control] would have predicted for us. The belief that AIDS would not touch this town had been absurd. 99

In the course of his work, Verghese realized that most of his patients were people who had moved away, acquired the disease, and returned home. To make sense of the suffering he saw, Verghese began to write. In 1994 he published *My Own Country: A Doctor's Story of a Town and Its People in the Age of AIDS,* in which he relates his observations and experiences.

Abraham Verghese

ATTITUDES TOWARD IMMIGRATION

Have students work in small groups to discuss and note the attitudes toward immigration in the 1990s. Have each group use its notes to write a two-minute radio editorial supporting or opposing increased immigration. Have each group choose a representative to air its views. After each presentation, allow time for dissenting opinions.

RECENT PATTERNS IN MIGRATION

List the following regions vertically on the chalkboard: *Former Soviet Union and Eastern Europe, Africa, Asia, Middle East.* For each region, call on volunteers to answer the following questions: Who moved? Why did they move? Where did they move? Enter responses next to the appropriate region. Invite students to work in small groups to develop scripts for a brief television documentary on migration patterns in the late 20th century. Select groups to "broadcast" their documentaries to the class.

▶

Coast Guard picked up the refugees at sea. They were then sent to camps in the U.S. naval base in Guantánamo Bay, Cuba, or in Panama. Many Floridians cheered the new policy. "All of us feel for the rafters," admitted Florida governor Lawton Chiles, "but Florida cannot stand another influx."

As in earlier periods, many of the recent immigrants to the United States have not been refugees, but people seeking economic opportunities that are not available in their home countries. In the past few decades, this has been particularly true of Mexicans. Even though the Mexican immigrants work for wages that are often low by American standards, they are still higher than in Mexico. One immigrant explained:

> 66 There are people who come from Tijuana [a region in northwestern Mexico] who work for six, seven, or eight dollars an hour for work that is worth more than 18 or 20 dollars an hour. They come to work like that because they earn more than they can earn in Tijuana. 99

■■ **In the past few decades, many immigrants have come to the United States from Asia and Latin America.**

The future of U.S. immigration. The 1990 census revealed that immigrants had come to the United States in greater numbers in the 1980s than in any decade since 1910. Many of these immigrants came from Mexico, the Philippines, Vietnam, Korea, China, and India.

The trend toward increased immigration seems likely to continue. President Bush, in signing the **Immigration Act of 1990**, noted that "immigration is not just a link to America's past, it is also a bridge to America's future." The new law increased the number of immigrants and doubled the number of skilled workers allowed into the United States each year.

Immigration, however, remains a controversial topic. Sixty-eight percent of the respondents to a 1992 *Business Week* poll thought that immigration was bad for the country. Many of those polled blamed immigrants for taking jobs away from native-born residents. In some cases the controversy over immigration has stemmed from the fact that many people enter the United States illegally. Many of these illegal immigrants are Latin

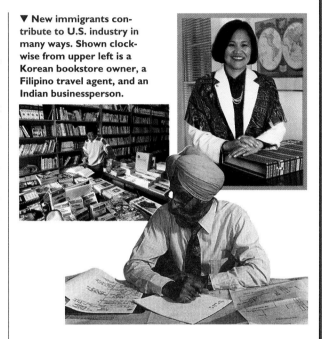

▼ New immigrants contribute to U.S. industry in many ways. Shown clockwise from upper left is a Korean bookstore owner, a Filipino travel agent, and an Indian businessperson.

Americans who cross the long border between Mexico and the United States. But others arrive as well—illegal immigrants from more than 90 countries were apprehended in 1986.

Supporters of immigration argue that immigrants have created new businesses that revitalize urban areas, have helped the U.S. balance of trade by starting their own export companies, and, as employees, have helped U.S. companies become more competitive globally. In addition, supporters of immigration note that many recent immigrants, most notably those from India, the Philippines, China, and Korea, have more years of schooling on average than either native-born Americans or European immigrants. These well-educated immigrants contribute to many U.S. high-tech industries.

As the United States witnesses increased immigration in the coming years, Americans will continue to grapple with the question of whether to welcome immigrants. Bette Bao Lord, a novelist who immigrated as a child to the United States from China, has urged Americans, native-born and immigrant alike, to unite:

> 66 I do not believe that the loss of one's native culture is the price one must pay for becoming an American. On the contrary, I feel doubly blessed. I can choose from two rich cultures those parts that suit my mood or the occasion best. And unbelievable as it

PRIMARY SOURCE
Description of Change: excerpted and bracketed
Rationale: excerpted to focus on main idea; bracketed to clarify meaning

MULTICULTURAL PERSPECTIVES

As Japan grew from a war-damaged country to an economic giant, many Japanese corporations invested in U.S. properties and industry. In 1989 Mitsubishi Estate Company purchased a 51 percent share in the Rockefeller Group, which owns most of New York's Rockefeller Center. Many Americans felt that the sale represented the differences in economic status between Japan and the U.S. To many Japanese citizens, however, American objections seemed to be poorly thought out. Wrote one Yokohama resident, "The U.S. has its own structural problems. . . . Wall Street investment bankers come to us with acquisition proposals every day. Why not regulate their activities first if Americans are really so unhappy about the current situation?"

PRIMARY SOURCE
Description of Change: excerpted
Rationale: excerpted to focus on main idea

*P*ractice

GUIDED PRACTICE

List the section's four main headings on the chalkboard. Call on students to volunteer information they have learned while studying the section. Enter responses under the appropriate heading. Then ask students to suggest how the information might be represented pictorially. Note their ideas next to the appropriate piece of information.

INDEPENDENT PRACTICE

Organize students into groups of four. Ask groups to use information from the Guided Practice to design an exhibit titled "Migration Patterns: From World War I to the Present." Suggest that they organize their exhibit into four sections, one for each of the headings listed in the Guided Practice. Have groups present and discuss their designs.

*R*eview and *A*ssessment

REVIEW Have students use the Essential Points of the section to write a paragraph explaining how migration patterns changed during the 20th century. Then assign the Section 2 Review on p. 685.

ASSESS Assign the **Section 2 Daily Quiz** in *Core Resources.*

HISTORICAL SIDELIGHTS

Soviet Jews

In 1968 Dr. Boris Zuckerman, a Moscow physicist, wrote a letter to the editor of a Soviet newspaper, arguing that neither the constitution nor existing legislation denied people the right to leave the country. When the government did not respond, he wrote a second letter. In addition, Zuckerman called attention to a law requiring that letters written to newspapers about constitutional matters be answered within eight weeks. Within months, exit visas became available for many Jews wishing to leave the Soviet Union.

Map Caption Answer
Rwanda, Afghanistan

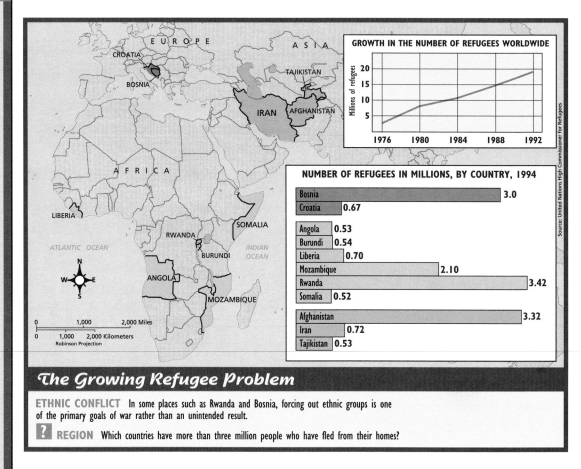

The Growing Refugee Problem

ETHNIC CONFLICT In some places such as Rwanda and Bosnia, forcing out ethnic groups is one of the primary goals of war rather than an unintended result.

? REGION Which countries have more than three million people who have fled from their homes?

---

may seem, shoes tinted red, white and blue go dandy with them all. **99**

*M*IGRATION IN THE NEW WORLD ORDER

Western Europe has also received large numbers of immigrants in recent decades. Since the breakup of the Soviet Union, many Eastern Europeans have pursued new economic opportunities across Europe. Others have sought escape from the conflicts that have sometimes accompanied the end of communism. In the former Yugoslavia, for example, the civil war caused by the fall of communism left thousands homeless. Many people had no choice but to seek refuge in other countries.

Unfortunately, immigrants have occasionally met with violence. In 1991 and 1992 many refugees went to Germany, which had a policy of allowing **asylum**, or a place of protection, to all "persons persecuted on political grounds." In the early 1990s over one million asylum seekers

entered Germany. Germany's citizens, however, were struggling with high unemployment and other economic problems brought about by the unification of East Germany and West Germany. Resentment against immigrants sparked violence, such as in August 1992 when antiforeigner groups rioted, injuring about 150 people.

Many residents of the former Soviet Union have chosen to move south rather than west. The former Soviet republics in Central Asia, for example, have many historic cultural ties to Turkey, Iran, and other Southwest Asian countries. Furthermore, more than a million Jews have emigrated from the former Soviet Union to Israel in recent years, in search of the opportunity to live among other Jews without discrimination.

Some migration in southwest Asia occurred during the Persian Gulf War, when some 5 million people fled areas of violence. These included not only people born in the region, such as Kuwaitis, but also foreign-born workers from Yemen, Egypt, Pakistan, Bangladesh, Sri Lanka, and the Philippines. The Persian Gulf War called attention

RETEACH For each subsection in the section, have students write a sentence that summarizes the main idea. Select students to read their sentences aloud. Have the class choose the best summary sentence for each subsection.

Closure

Pair students and have pairs develop a list of the major issues involving migration, in order of significance, facing the world as we enter the 21st century. Have pairs present and defend their lists.

Extension

EVALUATE

Direct students to read the quotation by Bette Bao Lord on pp. 683–684. Have them write a brief paragraph explaining whether they agree or disagree with Lord's view.

INVESTIGATE

Encourage students to investigate the refugee policy currently followed by the U.S. government. Suggest that they present their findings in an oral report to the class.

to the plight of Kurds, a large ethnic group living in the bordering regions of Iraq, Iran, Syria, Armenia, and Turkey. After Kurds living in Iraq unsuccessfully rebelled against the Iraqi government, some 2 million of them tried to enter Iran and Turkey.

DEVELOPING COUNTRIES

The Kurdish migrations are an example of one of the most important trends in contemporary migration patterns: in recent years, the largest migrations have taken place within and among developing countries. The UN Population Fund reported in 1993 that some 20 to 30 million people in developing countries move from rural to urban areas each year. Although people frequently move to cities looking for jobs and economic opportunities, often they find only poverty. Large shantytowns surround many cities such as São Paulo, Brazil; Jakarta, Indonesia; and Calcutta, India.

In parts of Africa, drought and overgrazing have led to the migration of many people seeking fertile soil. In some countries wars have worsened the effects of already-existing hardships. In Somalia, droughts in the early 1990s caused widespread starvation. When factional fighting broke out amidst the already poor conditions, many Somalis left their homes for refugee camps. In December 1992 UN forces, including many Americans, launched **Operation Restore Hope** to ensure that food and other necessities reached the starving Somali people.

In 1994, ethnic rivalries in Rwanda, a small country in eastern central Africa, turned into a bloody civil war that sent emigration rates skyrocketing. For years strife between the country's two major ethnic groups, the Hutus and the Tutsis, had claimed thousands of lives. But when the nation's president was killed in a plane crash, violence reached epic proportions as the two groups battled for control. Hundreds of thousands of Rwandans were killed in massacres, and a million or more fled the country. On two days in July 1994, nearly 500,000 Hutus flooded west into the nation of Zaire, sometimes at a rate of 30,000 people per hour. One UN official said, "It's a river of people bleeding out of Rwanda!" Refugee camps provided a measure of safety from violence, but disease resulted in many more deaths. By the beginning of August, refugees were dying at a rate of 2,000 per day, and UN and relief agency officials began to encourage those still living to return to Rwanda.

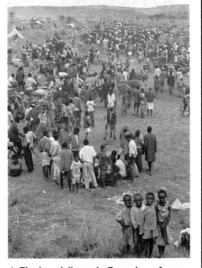

▲ Fleeing civil war in Rwanda, refugees crowd together in a refugee camp in Tanzania, east of Rwanda.

■■ **Ethnic violence and civil wars caused people around the world to migrate during the 1980s and 1990s.**

SECTION REVIEW ANSWERS

IDENTIFY

For significance, see the following pages:
Displaced Persons Act (p. 680)
Immigration Act of 1965 (p. 681)
Immigration Act of 1990 (p. 683)
Bette Bao Lord (p. 683)
asylum (p. 684)
Operation Restore Hope (p. 685)

LOCATE

For locations, refer to the map on p. 684.

1. *Migration slowed as a result of World War I and the Great Depression.*
2. *An increasing number of people became refugees in attempts to escape from conflicts.*
3. *During the 1980s and 1990s people migrated as a result of ethnic violence and civil wars.*
4. *Letters should address the contributions of immigrants as well as the challenges of including immigrants in society.*
5. *Answers will vary but should address fears of increased economic strain as well as the desire to provide opportunities for more people.*

SECTION 2 REVIEW

IDENTIFY and explain the significance of the following: Displaced Persons Act, Immigration Act of 1965, Immigration Act of 1990, Bette Bao Lord, asylum, Operation Restore Hope.

LOCATE and explain the importance of the following: Bosnia, Rwanda.

1. **MAIN IDEA** How did events in the first third of the 20th century affect migration?
2. **MAIN IDEA** How did World War II affect migration?
3. **MAIN IDEA** What factors led people to migrate during the 1980s and 1990s?
4. **WRITING TO EXPRESS A VIEWPOINT** Write the editor of your local newspaper a letter in which you assess the effects of recent immigration on the United States.
5. **ANALYZING** Why might some people oppose and others support increased immigration?

PREVIEW WORKSHOP

Following is a list of the significant terms in this section. You may wish to use this list as a section preview.

- National Information Infrastructure
- teleconferencing
- barcodes

Terms
- Information Revolution
- Internet
- mainframe computers
- minicomputers

MOTIVATING: PRIOR KNOWLEDGE

Have students draw upon information from previous chapters to identify inventions and technological innovations that improved communications. *(telegraph, telephone, television)* As students read the section, have them compare these inventions and innovations with those that brought about the Information Revolution.

FOCUS OBJECTIVES

- Describe the effect that the development of computers had on the spread of information.

- Analyze how developments in information and communications technology have affected businesses.

- Explain how the Information Revolution has increased concerns about privacy.

HISTORICAL SIDELIGHTS

The Space Race
The influence of the German scientists extended beyond the limits of the scientific community. In Huntsville, Alabama, where the space program developed, the civic center is named for Wernher von Braun. And Huntsville itself, once known as the "watercress capital of the world," is now often called "Rocket City, U.S.A."

CORE RESOURCES
- **Section 3 Daily Quiz**

AV RESOURCES
- ***The American Nation** Videodisc:* **Early Computer Robot**

Section 3

THE MOVEMENT OF INFORMATION

F O C U S
- **What effect did the development of computers have on the spread of information?**
- **How have developments in information and communication technology affected businesses?**
- **How has the Information Revolution increased concerns about privacy?**

Throughout most of history, ideas have moved only as quickly as the people who have held them. During the 20th century, however, new technological developments have allowed ideas and information to spread around the world more and more rapidly.

Statue of Albert Einstein in Washington, D.C.

THE SPREAD OF IDEAS

Travelers and migrants have long been responsible for the diffusion of knowledge from one region to another. During the 20th century, for example, Albert Einstein, James Franck, and other Jewish scientists fleeing the Fascists in Europe became key players in America's development of the atomic bomb. After World War II German rocket scientists, such as Wernher von Braun, significantly contributed to both the U.S. and Soviet space programs.

Since the 1940s the spread of knowledge has been enhanced by the development of the computer. The ways in which the computer is transforming society promise to be as profound as the changes that followed the introduction of the printing press. The widespread transfer of information that computers and new information technologies have made possible has become known as the **Information Revolution**.

▶ **Wernher von Braun and his team developed the rocket that launched *Explorer I*, the first U.S. earth satellite, on January 31, 1958.**

Computers provide quick, easy access to information from around the world. For example, the electronic library services of Systems Development Corporation in the United States and Pergamon Infoline in Great Britain contain every patent filed with the U.S. Patent Office since 1971. The National Library of Medicine's service, Medline, indexes some 20,000 journal articles a month. Another service, Lexis, provides access to decisions in U.S. and British courts.

Internet. Because computers can communicate with each other via telephone lines, access to these electronic libraries is fast and easy. Computers can also be linked to allow people to send messages to each other and to gain access to electronic bulletin boards, news, training courses, and various other services. The **Internet**, which links millions of individual computers in more than 80 countries around the world, is the largest of these networks.

The development of the Internet began in the 1960s—in part as a response to the Cold War. The U.S. Department of Defense wanted

COMPUTERS AND THE SPREAD OF COMMUNICATION

List the following on the chalkboard: *Internet, mainframe computers, minicomputers, National Information Infrastructure.* Have students use these terms to create a graphic organizer that shows how computers helped spread information around the world. Students may wish to include their graphic organizers in their portfolios.

A REVOLUTION IN BUSINESS COMMUNICATIONS

Encourage students to imagine they are journalists from a country where the Information Revolution has not yet taken place. Ask them to write an article for their country's readers explaining how developments in communications technology have changed the way businesses operate.

TECHNOLOGY AND PRIVACY

Select five students to act as members of a special congressional committee on computers and privacy. Assign three other students to speak before the committee on this issue. Their presentations should mention why privacy is a problem and what steps might be taken to prevent abuse. After all presentations have been made, have the class come to a consensus on the best way to protect privacy in this computer age.

▶

▲ In 1947 physicists John Bardeen, William Shockley, and Walter H. Brattain invented the transistor, making possible high-speed computers and the Information Revolution.

to find a way for the computer centers at universities and private research laboratories to communicate. The Defense Department was particularly interested in developing a system that could function after a nuclear attack.

The system that was devised in 1969 linked four universities' **mainframe computers**—large, fast computer systems that could process many tasks at once and that could cost millions of dollars. By 1972 the network had expanded to include some 40 members. Because all the computers had equal access to the system and no one computer controlled it, the system could still function even if part of it were destroyed. The design of the system also meant that there was no limit to the network's size.

With the development of **minicomputers**—computers that are smaller, easier to operate, and much cheaper than mainframes—and with the introduction of still smaller and cheaper personal computers in the 1970s, networks expanded to include a wide range of university, business, and individual users. And because these networks ran via public telephone lines rather than the restricted lines that mainframes used, the Internet became even more decentralized. Adding to the trend toward decentralization, the Defense Department opened the network in 1974—without charge—to anyone with access to a computer.

By 1982 Usenet, a network set up to communicate among networks, enabled E-mail to be sent to all computers within a given network and among the various networks. This, in turn, led to the formation of worldwide electronic bulletin boards, or newsgroups. Now people can send short messages, opinion pieces, or articles to all the computers on the network and carry on a discussion with people all over the world who are

interested in the same topics—people they could otherwise never expect to meet.

Although the Internet is widely available, the U.S. government has made significant financial and technological contributions to the system. As part of this investment, the government established the National Science Foundation Network (NSFnet) in the late 1980s. The NSFnet used the latest technology to link a small number of supercomputer centers across the United States. The NSFnet served as the core network or backbone of the Internet by linking the various networks that make up the system. By September 1994, the NSFnet linked some 38,000 other networks around the world. Furthermore, usage has grown to such an extent that some experts estimate that nearly 100 million people will have direct access to the Internet by the end of the century.

National Information Infrastructure.

In 1993 President Clinton created the United States Advisory Council on the **National Information Infrastructure,** headed by Vice President Albert Gore. The government argued for the development of an even more advanced network, the National Information Infrastructure (NII)—or Information Superhighway—that would benefit all Americans by providing:

> ❝ a seamless web of communications networks, computers, databases, and consumer electronics that will put vast amounts of information at users' fingertips. . . [and] help unleash an information revolution. . . .
>
> The NII can transform the lives of the American people—ameliorating [making more tolerable] the constraints of geography, disability, and economic status—giving all Americans a fair opportunity to go as far as their talents and ambitions will take them. ❞

◀ Vice President Albert Gore has worked to make information available to all Americans.

THE AMERICAN NATION VIDEODISC PROGRAM
Early Computer Robot

2A   40641   :27

HISTORICAL SIDELIGHTS

The First Computer
In 1946 scientists developed ENIAC, the first fully electronic computer. ENIAC weighed more than 30 tons and filled over 1,500 square feet—a far cry from the small, lightweight laptop computers available today.

PRIMARY SOURCE

Description of Change: excerpted and bracketed
Rationale: excerpted to focus on main idea; bracketed to clarify meaning

Practice

GUIDED PRACTICE

Call on volunteers to identify the inventions and technological innovations that helped to bring about the Information Revolution. List responses on the chalkboard, asking students to provide background information on each item.

INDEPENDENT PRACTICE

Have students choose one of the inventions or innovations listed in the Guided Practice activity. Encourage them to create a full-page, illustrated magazine or newspaper advertisement to "sell" their selected item. Students may wish to include their advertisements in their portfolios.

Review and Assessment

REVIEW Have students work in small groups to create a four-page pictorial essay titled The *Information Revolution—Moving Information Around the Globe*. Call on volunteers to display and discuss their essays. Then assign the Section 3 Review on p. 689.

ASSESS Assign the **Section 3 Daily Quiz** in *Core Resources*.

 GLOBAL CONNECTIONS

In the early 1990s Roy M. Huffington, the U.S. ambassador to Austria, worked to pair companies in the U.S. with Eastern European partners. Business leaders in the U.S. could indicate their preferences for business opportunities, and computers were used to match each U.S. company with a European counterpart.

MULTICULTURAL PERSPECTIVES

In 1975 the world's first experiment with direct broadcasting by satellite took place in India. The technology was used to provide rural areas with access to educational broadcasts.

PRIMARY SOURCE

Description of Change: excerpted and bracketed **Rationale:** excerpted to focus on main idea; bracketed to clarify meaning

---

How the NII will relate to the Internet is not yet certain. But clearly the government hopes to spur more private-sector investment. In 1994 the National Science Foundation, which has been spending $10 million a year to administer the NSFnet, announced that it was turning the network over to the private sector. "This is an immense change affecting millions of people, and tens of thousands of individual networks," admitted Stephen Wolff, the NSF networking chief. "But the marketplace is there now, and there's no point in having the federal government competing with the private sector."

■■ **New developments in computer technology helped speed the spread of information around the world.**

TRANSFORMING BUSINESS AND INDUSTRY

One of the services that both the Internet and for-profit services provide to companies and individuals is E-mail. The increasing use of E-mail promises to change the way companies are organized. In 1994 Andrew S. Grove, an executive of Intel Corporation, believes that E-mail promotes a more democratic organization:

66 Companies that use E-mail are much faster, much less hierarchical. You can only

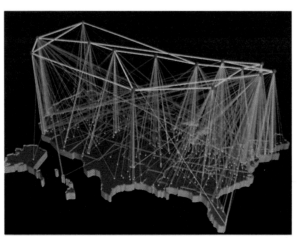

▲ In this view of the **NSFnet,** the purple lines indicate a free flow of information. The white lines show a heavy backup caused by 100 billion bytes of moving data.

use E-mail effectively, though, if you do it yourself [rather than have an assistant screen your mail]. From the moment you do it yourself, you're available to anybody and everybody. The elimination of the screening process in my E-mail . . . tends to lead to a . . . more democratic way of operating—whether it's inside a corporation, inside a country, or across countries. 99

Other developments have also made communication easier. Cellular telephones allow people to make and receive calls no matter how far they may be from their home or office. Satellite links permit **teleconferencing,** which allows people at multiple locations to hold conferences over the telephone or by computer.

Satellites also make two-way interactive television possible. Medical practitioners, for example, have used this technology to improve the treatment of patients in isolated areas. Interactive television enables a doctor to view the treatment of a patient hundreds of miles away and to make recommendations to medical personnel who are administering care.

■■ **Telecommunications advances have begun to change the ways in which business is conducted and services are provided.**

TECHNOLOGY AND THE DEVELOPING WORLD

The introduction of the latest technology to the developing world promises to speed development by skipping intermediate stages of technology. Countries such as China and Hungary that are installing fiber-optic cables and the most up-to-date digital communications technology will gain an edge in global economic competition. For instance, Shanghai, in an effort to become a major financial center, is installing communications equipment as powerful as that used in New York's financial district. Overall, China plans to add some 80 million phone lines and spend some $100 billion over the next decade. While this is a huge sum, it is far less than it would cost to install an older copper-wire, nondigital system.

Closure

Have students use information from the section to write a brief paragraph discussing the costs and benefits of the Information Revolution. Call on volunteers to read their paragraphs to the class. Students may wish to include their paragraphs in their portfolios.

Extension

SYNTHESIZE Have students research the question of whether the Information Superhighway will truly benefit all Americans and write an essay that synthesizes the major arguments on the issue.

INVESTIGATE Encourage students to investigate and report on the most recent technological developments in the Information Revolution.

▲ A portable cellular telephone allows voice communication from virtually anywhere in the world.

Others in the developing world are turning to cellular communications systems, which are carried over radio waves. The advantage of cellular systems is that they are relatively cheap to install. Latin America, where only 7 percent of the population has telephones, has the fastest-growing cellular market in the world. People in Bangkok, Thailand, are also turning to cellular phones because of huge waiting lists for telephones and snarled traffic that traps businesspeople in their cars for hours.

INFORMATION TECHNOLOGY AND PRIVACY

The development of electronic information systems has contributed to new worries about privacy. Many Americans worry that electronic data storage and communication will make private information easily available to others. In some cases, these fears are justified. Today some companies monitor employee use of E-mail, raising new issues of privacy. One E-mail administrator in California supported the privacy of electronic communications with the statement: "You don't read other people's mail, just as you don't listen to their phone conversations."

In some cases, technological innovations provide unexpected opportunities to monitor activities. One 1981-model Cadillac engine included a computer that recorded when systems malfunctioned. The computer also noted when the driver exceeded 80 miles per hour. Electronic **barcodes**, which some libraries use to keep track of their collections, could also be used to provide a record of a borrower's reading habits.

As more and more information is cataloged and made available, a growing number of people are becoming concerned about the possible abuse of knowledge. Credit reports, job applications, and rental agreements result in the collection of personal information that can be entered into a computer and analyzed in any number of ways. Congress has begun to tackle the issue and has proposed legislation to protect the privacy of electronic data such as medical and credit information.

Legislation is not the only means of protecting privacy. A number of corporations, such as IBM, have established detailed privacy protection codes. For those who are concerned about keeping records confidential, the Information Revolution poses new challenges as well as new opportunities.

■■ **Technological developments that make it easier to monitor people's behavior have led to increased concerns about privacy.**

SECTION REVIEW ANSWERS

IDENTIFY

For significance, see the following pages:
Information Revolution (p. 686)
Internet (p. 686)
mainframe computers (p. 687)
minicomputers (p. 687)
National Information Infrastructure (p. 687)
teleconferencing (p. 688)
barcodes (p. 689)

1. Developments in communications, such as advances in computers and satellite technology, have allowed information to spread much more quickly than ever before.
2. Cellular telephones allow people to make telephone calls from nearly any location, and satellites permit teleconferencing and two-way interactive television.
3. Privacy issues generally focus on possible uses of information, such as engine and speed data compiled by automobile computers and records of library use through barcodes.
4. Memos should address the use of communications technology such as satellite transmissions and E-mail to reach large numbers of voters.
5. Essays will vary but should address the speed with which information can travel between distant areas of the world.

■■ SECTION 3 REVIEW

IDENTIFY and explain the significance of the following: Information Revolution, Internet, mainframe computers, minicomputers, National Information Infrastructure, teleconferencing, barcodes.

1. **MAIN IDEA** In the past 25 years, how has new technology affected the spread of information?
2. **MAIN IDEA** How are various businesses likely to be affected by recent technological developments?
3. **MAIN IDEA** What kinds of privacy issues have been raised by the Information Revolution?
4. **WRITING TO EXPLAIN** Write a memo to a political candidate in which you show how new technology could be used to change the way campaigns are conducted.
5. **ASSESSING CONSEQUENCES** Write a short essay discussing the ways in which the Information Revolution could affect the world.

MOTIVATING: STUDENT EXPERIENCES

Quiz students on the sports they watch, their favorite movies and television shows, the music they listen to, and the clothes they wear. Note responses on the chalkboard. Then tell students that in this section they will see that because of the global spread of information and ideas, young people throughout the world share similar tastes.

FOCUS OBJECTIVES

■ Explain how sports has reflected the globalization of culture in the 20th century.

■ Analyze how television and movies have influenced perceptions of other cultures.

■ Discuss how music and fashion have contributed to youth culture around the world.

MULTICULTURAL PERSPECTIVES

In 1994 U.S. baseball fans bemoaned the long-running players' strike that resulted in the cancellation of the baseball season and the World Series. Baseball seasons continued elsewhere, however, as the Yomiuri Giants defeated the Seibu Lions in the Japan Series. Hiromi Makihara, a pitcher for the Giants, said, "It's difficult for Japanese people to understand what is happening in America. It would probably never happen here. If it did, it would last a couple of days, or a month at the most, because people wouldn't allow it to keep going."

Section 4

A GLOBAL CULTURE

FOCUS

■ **How has sports reflected the globalization of culture in the 20th century?**

■ **How have television and movies influenced perceptions of other cultures?**

■ **How have music and fashion contributed to youth culture around the world?**

*W*hen people mingle, they exchange more than technical knowledge and expertise; they also exchange ways of having fun. As people moved from country to country during the 20th century, there emerged something that increasingly could be called a global culture.

An American fast-food restaurant in Bangkok, Thailand

WORLD SPORTS

During the 20th century, technological developments and ease of travel have contributed to the growing popularity of sports. Teams now travel around the world to compete, and individual athletes play for teams outside their own countries. Although the popularity of any individual sport may vary in different countries, the worldwide enthusiasm for athletic competition has enabled many sports to gain a global following.

Historically, sports have often traveled with armies. This is not surprising, since young men—and more recently women—of military age are also of prime age for athletics. Moreover, commanders have supported sports as a way to keep the soldiers fit and hone the competitive edge needed for combat.

The British, who during the 19th century sent soldiers all over the world, carried the game of cricket with them. Today cricket is passionately played in many countries that were once part of Britain's empire, including India, Pakistan, South Africa, Australia, New Zealand, and Jamaica.

Baseball, an American variation of the old English game of rounders, was also carried overseas—this time by U.S. soldiers. Many Italians became devoted baseball fans after American soldiers introduced the game after World War II. The nations of Central America and the Caribbean, which have been periodically occupied by American troops, have produced some notable baseball players. Puerto Rico was the home of Roberto Clemente, the Pittsburgh Pirates slugger of the 1960s and 1970s. Jose Canseco, the 1990s home run hitter, is a native of Cuba.

▶ The Yakult Swallows defeat the Seibu Lions to clinch their first Japan Series title in 15 years.

WORLD SPORTS

Organize students into several groups. Have groups draw up plans for a special insert in a current affairs magazine titled "The Global Nature of Sports." Plans should include a table of contents with brief synopses of articles, suggestions for illustrations accompanied by sample captions, and design ideas for a cover. Have groups present and discuss their magazine plans.

ENTERTAINMENT WITHOUT FRONTIERS

On the chalkboard, write the following: *Television News, Televisions Shows, Movies.* Call on volunteers to provide examples of how these media have helped to create a global culture. Note responses under the appropriate medium. Then have students discuss how these medias present other cultures, and whether these impressions are accurate.

A GLOBAL YOUTH CULTURE

Organize students into several groups to act as T-shirt design teams. Tell the teams their task is to create a design that represents the global youth culture. Suggest that they list the elements of the youth culture first, and then try to incorporate them into the design. Call on groups to display and explain their designs. Encourage interested groups to stencil or paint their designs onto T-shirts.

▶

Baseball is also popular in parts of Asia. Japanese baseball, for example, generates as much enthusiasm in that country as major league baseball does in the United States. Since 1951 hundreds of foreigners, most of them Americans, have gone to Japan to play baseball.

Basketball is another American sport that has gone international during the late 20th century. In the 1990s several European stars made reputations in the United States in the National Basketball Association, and some American players relocated to Europe to play for teams there. In 1990 Boston Celtics general manager Jan Volk said, "The more exposure we get for our teams and players in Europe, the more desirable our players become to the European teams and public." In 1992 Los Angeles Laker Michael Cooper left California to play for Il Messaggero Roma in Italy, where he was offered $1.5 million for his first season, use of a BMW, and a suburban villa.

Europe also offered opportunities for American women basketball players. Though women's basketball was gaining popularity in the United States at the high school and college levels, as of the mid-1990s it had not prospered as a professional sport. Consequently, American women who wished to play professional basketball had to go to Europe. "It's not NBA money," said Vicki Hall, who had played basketball for the University of Texas, referring to her salary for a team in Switzerland. "But I could make more than a decent living there."

While Americans were exporting baseball and basketball, they were importing soccer. Called football in most of the rest of the world, the game is played all over the world. Much of soccer's popularity stems from its simplicity: with a ball and an open patch of ground, anyone can play. The game is within the reach of even the poorest people; where a regulation ball is not available, players have been known to get up games with bundles of rags.

Soccer had long been played in the United States, but its popularity there did not begin to grow until the 1970s and 1980s. Youth soccer leagues were established in cities and towns all across the country and millions of boys and girls signed up to play. Although professional soccer was slow to attract a following in the United States, the selection of the United States as host for the 1994 World Cup championship, which an estimated two billion people watched, appeared likely to give the game a boost.

International sporting events have a long history. The first recorded **Olympic Games** took place in 776 B.C. as part of a religious festival in ancient Greece. The games lost their religious focus after Rome conquered Greece in the 100s B.C. and were officially ended in A.D. 394. In 1894 Baron Pierre de Coubertin, a French educator, proposed reviving the competitions. Two years later the first modern Olympics were held in Athens, Greece. During the next hundred years, the games became a showcase for the global culture of sports. Initially a summer contest for men, the Olympics expanded to include women in 1912 and winter events in 1924. Countries not only competed in the games but also competed to be named host of the Olympics. Over the years the games have been held in Europe, North America, Asia, and Australia.

■■ **Different sports spread around the world, and many became global contests during the 20th century.**

WORLD TELEVISION AND MOVIES

The popularity of competitions such as the World Cup and the Olympics was greatly increased by television. The spread of television helped to create a global culture by permitting people to watch sporting events from almost any part of the world. In 1992 Americans watched the "Dream Team," the U.S. Olympic basketball squad, win the gold medal in Barcelona, Spain. In 1993 and 1994 Chinese viewers saw their country's women distance runners set records all over the world.

▲ This 1993 poster advertising Aladdin in Paris, France, illustrates the worldwide popularity of American films.

News and entertainment are also part of the televised exchange of culture. Cable News Network (CNN) International broadcasts news programs around the world. British productions such as *Mystery!: Prime Suspect* and its sequels won critical acclaim on both sides of the Atlantic. Because their movies and

Practice

GUIDED PRACTICE

Write the three subsection titles on the chalkboard. Call on volunteers to use information from the section to make generalizations about the three listed topics. Note students' generalizations on the chalkboard.

INDEPENDENT PRACTICE

Have students use the generalizations from the Guided Practice activity to write a song or poem titled "A Small World." Encourage students to perform their compositions for the class. Students may wish to include their compositions in their portfolios.

Review and Assessment

REVIEW Have students work in groups to put together a time capsule of a dozen or so items that illustrate the existence of a global culture. Call on groups to describe their items and explain why they chose them. Then assign the Section 4 Review on p. 693.

ASSESS Assign the **Section 4 Daily Quiz** in *Core Resources*.

MULTICULTURAL PERSPECTIVES

Criticism has not kept European visitors away from Euro Disney. In early 1994, visitation was averaging just under one million people per month, making the park the biggest paid tourist destination in Europe.

MAKING CONNECTIONS

Music

Rock 'n' roll had its origins in African American music. In the late 19th and early 20th centuries, elements of traditional spirituals began to be incorporated into mainstream music. New musical forms included jazz, ragtime, and blues. In the early 1950s some artists began to combine blues with other musical forms, as found in songs by Jerry Lee Lewis, Bill Haley, Chuck Berry, and Fats Domino. The new style, rock 'n' roll, sounded distinctly American in its blending of different traditions.

THROUGH OTHERS' EYES

EURO DISNEY

"This is the '90s" declared Disney's head, Michael Eisner, "the decade we reinvent the Disney experience not just in California, but worldwide." However, not everyone welcomed Eisner's vision. When Euro Disney opened outside Paris in April 1992, critics called it a "cultural Chernobyl." "It took a money-hungry little mouse to trigger a debate on issues that we have been evading," noted Jean-Marie Rouart in the Paris newspaper Le Figaro. "Should we allow culture to be ruled by profitability?"

Such concerns on the part of some of the French were not new. In 1982, a decade before Euro Disney opened, France's minister of culture, Jack Lang, warned the world about what he called American cultural imperialism: "Certain great nations who taught us about freedom and called on people to rise up against oppression, yet who today . . . have no other morality than that of profit, . . . seek to impose a uniform culture on the whole world. "

---

television programs do not pose a language barrier, British, Canadian, and Australian productions often have had an edge over other foreign productions in the American market. Some foreign stars, however, have overcome this difficulty; Gérard Depardieu, after a long acting career in France, won American fans with his performance in *Cyrano de Bergerac*—in spite of the need for English subtitles. Others, such as Arnold Schwarzenegger, although foreign born, have become American stars.

Nonetheless, the United States dominates the world market in films and television. American popular culture is the nation's second largest export. In 1993, *Jurassic Park* and 87 other American movies were among the world's 100 most attended films. During the 1980s the television drama *Dallas* seemed to represent American

▶ Technology enables people such as this Kaiapo Indian in Altamira, Brazil, to enjoy a wide variety of entertainment.

---

life to people all over the world. Some worry that it is the worst television programs that receive the widest distribution—because they can be marketed cheaply. For example, American soap operas are wildly popular in Egypt, India, and other developing countries. Others worry about how American movies and television will affect their cultures. In 1994 French minister of culture Jacques Toubon was quoted, calling U.S. domination of the market a "pure monopoly in the worst sense."

Despite such concerns, American performers have also found worldwide popularity, both in and out of movies. Harrison Ford, star of numerous American films such as *Raiders of the Lost Ark* and *Clear and Present Danger*, also acted as spokesperson for a Japanese cable TV channel.

▪▪ **Movies and television moved across international borders, influencing perceptions of different cultures.**

WORLD YOUTH

The international links formed by the entertainment industry have contributed to **cultural diffusion**—the process of spreading cultural practices or beliefs. Teenagers around the world look to television and films for ideas about music and dress.

Music. Although rock 'n' roll was originally an American style, the music quickly gained international popularity. Musical styles continued to evolve and spread around the world, and by the 1980s the growth of cable television allowed music videos to become an important marketing tool for the music industry. This mix of sight and sound is not limited to English-speaking fans or musicians. MTV Asia, broadcast across that

RETEACH Organize the class into small groups. Tell each group to divide the section material, by subsections, among its members. Direct students to write questions about the main ideas presented in their assigned material. Have group members quiz one another with the questions.

Closure

Point out that more than 30 years ago social scientists suggested that the electronic media would reduce distance and isolation so much that the world would become a "global village." Have students discuss whether they feel this prediction has come true.

Extension

INVESTIGATE Have students investigate a recent major sporting event such as the Olympic Games. Have them write a report showing the global nature of their selected event.

CREATE Ask students to create an almanac, similar to those that open the units in this book, titled "Developments in the Global Youth Culture Since 1985." Encourage students to display and discuss their almanacs.

continent, focuses on bands from India and other countries in the region. MTV Europe broadcasts in English, but most of its programming is European and features European musicians. The network reaches some 60 million homes in Europe, and some 88 million viewers in the former Soviet Union receive the network for an hour per week.

Music videos and concert tours provide musicians with worldwide popularity. At any given time U2 of Ireland might be performing in the United States; India's Ravi Shankar in Rio de Janeiro; Cuban-born Gloria Estefan in Rome; and Britain's Rolling Stones in Tokyo. Fans who are unable to get to a concert can find the latest tapes and CDs in stores from Mexico City to Hong Kong.

Clothing. Movies and television also provide teens with inspiration in the world of fashion. In the early 1990s, many copied the "grunge look" of popular musicians. When American director Spike Lee's film *Malcolm X* was released in Japan in 1993, many people became interested in Malcolm's life and beliefs. They also began to wear the same "X"-labeled baseball caps, T-shirts, and jackets that many American youths wore when the film opened in the United States.

Japanese teens have also adopted a range of American casual styles, called *Amekaji*. National Football League (NFL) hats are common among Japanese teens, as are black leather jackets and university warm-up suits. One Japanese advertising executive said, "Sharing in America can release Japanese teenagers from the restraints they live with every day. Through fashion, they can capture a bit of the life-style they can never hope to live."

■■ **Movies, television shows, and music videos have helped to create a kind of global youth culture.**

The export of many kinds of entertainment has provided more links between cultures. Music, sports, movies, and television all allow people in different areas of the world to develop and to share common interests. Furthermore, technology has increased the speed and ease with which entertainment, as well as scientific knowledge, has spread around the world.

▲ **Japanese young people view the latest American styles in Harajuki, a trendy Toyko shopping district.**

SECTION REVIEW ANSWERS

IDENTIFY

*For significance, see the following pages:
Olympic Games (p. 691)
Baron Pierre de Coubertin (p. 691)
Jacques Toubon (p. 692)
cultural diffusion (p. 692)*

1. *Sports have won fans around the world. In addition, athletes often choose to relocate in other countries to play professional sports.*
2. *The media transmits information and speeds the process of cultural diffusion, but many people feel that the images portrayed by the media do not accurately reflect the range of different cultures.*
3. *the spread of movies, television shows, and music videos*
4. *Articles should address concerns about cultural diffusion and describe the economic impact of imported movies and television shows on the domestic entertainment industry.*
5. *Answers will vary but should indicate that sports, music, and fashion have spread around the world in different ways and sometimes appeal to different audiences.*

■■ **S E C T I O N   4   R E V I E W**

IDENTIFY and explain the significance of the following: Olympic Games, Baron Pierre de Coubertin, Jacques Toubon, cultural diffusion.

1. **MAIN IDEA** How has the globalization of culture been affected by athletics?
2. **MAIN IDEA** How do the media contribute to ideas about other cultures?
3. **MAIN IDEA** What factors have contributed to the development of a youth culture around the world?
4. **WRITING TO PERSUADE** Imagine you are the minister of culture in another country. Write an article for a newspaper outlining a policy on imported movies and television programs and explain why you have adopted the policy.
5. **COMPARING** Compare the effects of sports, music, and fashion on the development of a global culture.

Chapter Review Answers

WRITING A SUMMARY
See Essential Points in each section for main ideas.

REVIEWING CHRONOLOGY
1, 2, 5, 3, 4
Synthesizing
Over the course of the century, changes in immigration laws loosened immigration restrictions.

IDENTIFYING PEOPLE AND IDEAS
1. *point of entry for Asian immigrants*
2. *eliminated quota system based on country of origin*
3. *Chinese American novelist who advocates acceptance of immigrants*
4. *place of protection*
5. *UN effort to provide food to starving Somali people*
6. *spreading cultural beliefs and practices*
7. *communications network based on computers*
8. *telephone conferences between people at multiple locations*
9. *French Minister of Culture who opposes spread of U.S. culture*
10. *widespread transfer of information made possible by computers and other new technologies*

UNDERSTANDING MAIN IDEAS
1. During the 19th and early 20th centuries, people moved between all of the inhabited continents. Most people hoped to find better-paying jobs and to improve their lives.
2. The Great Depression and World War II slowed migration, but after World War II many people migrated as refugees.
3. New technologies are providing businesses with the opportunity to communicate more quickly between distant areas. Developing nations are able to use up-to-date information and skip intermediate stages of development. Some people are concerned about privacy issues and the way in which information can be used.
4. Sports, television shows, music videos, and movies enjoy worldwide popularity.

CHAPTER 25 *Review*

Discovery of gold in Australia attracts many immigrants.	Congress passes Chinese Exclusion Act.	First modern Olympics held in Athens, Greece.
	Ellis Island opens.	Thomasites arrive in the Philippines.	Immigration Act of 1924 sharply reduces number of immigrants admitted to the U.S.

1851   1882   1892   1896   1901   1924

WRITING A SUMMARY
Using the essential points of the chapter as a guide, write a summary of the chapter.

REVIEWING CHRONOLOGY
Number your paper 1 to 5. Study the time line above, and list the following events in the order in which they happened by writing the first next to 1, the second next to 2, and so on. Then complete the activity below.

1. Ellis Island opens.
2. Thomasites arrive in the Philippines.
3. U.S. hosts World Cup soccer championship.
4. Congress passes Displaced Persons Act.
5. Internet system links mainframe computers at four universities.

Synthesizing How have the different immigration acts passed by Congress in the 20th century indicated changes in U.S. policy regarding immigration?

IDENTIFYING PEOPLE AND IDEAS
Explain the historical significance of each of the following people or terms.

1. Angel Island
2. Immigration Act of 1965
3. Bette Bao Lord
4. asylum
5. Operation Restore Hope
6. cultural diffusion
7. Internet
8. teleconferencing
9. Jacques Toubon
10. Information Revolution

UNDERSTANDING MAIN IDEAS
1. What patterns of migration marked the 19th and early 20th centuries? What were the main motives behind migration during this period?
2. What economic and political forces affected migration in the 1930s and 1940s?
3. How are new communications technologies transforming businesses and affecting developing nations? What concerns are these new technologies raising?
4. What are some of the forms of recreation and entertainment that have become increasingly popular around the world in recent years?

REVIEWING THEMES
1. **Cultural Diversity** What effect did the Immigration Act of 1965 have on the cultural composition of the U.S. population?
2. **Technology and Society** How did U.S. Defense Department concerns lead to the development of the Internet?
3. **Economic Development** How has an increasingly globalized culture led to increased international trade of various goods such as movies?

THINKING CRITICALLY
1. **Hypothesizing** Do you think the migration patterns that have characterized the 1980s and 1990s will continue to influence international migrations over the next 25 years? Why or why not?
2. **Evaluating** How might the growth of the "Information Superhighway" affect Americans' daily lives?
3. **Synthesizing** In what ways can the movement of people around the world influence the movement of ideas? Support your answer with specific examples.

STRATEGY FOR SUCCESS
Review the Skills Handbook entry on Reading Charts and Graphs beginning on page 756. Study the graph below, which shows the number of jobs in the auto and information processing industries from 1975 to 1993. What effect has the Information Revolution had on the number of jobs in information processing industries? What other conclusions can you draw from the graph? Which of the two types of industries do you think will employ more people in the year 2000? Why?

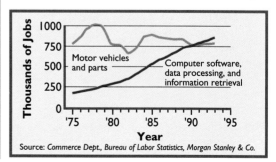

Source: Commerce Dept., Bureau of Labor Statistics, Morgan Stanley & Co.

REVIEWING THEMES

1. loosened restrictions, allowing greater numbers of immigrants from Asia and Latin America
2. The Department of Defense wanted to ease communications between research universities and laboratories and develop a system that would function after a nuclear attack.
3. Movies and clothing styles have spread as people want to adopt elements of other cultures for their own use.

THINKING CRITICALLY

1. Answers will vary but should reflect current immigration trends and attitudes toward immigration.
2. Information will be available even more rapidly, providing people with a wider range of opportunities.
3. Answers should discuss the fact that people bring their cultures with them when they relocate, and may include examples such as the German scientists who worked in the U.S. and the Soviet Union after World War II.

STRATEGY FOR SUCCESS

information processing jobs have increased; auto industries show greater variation in employment levels; information industries appear likely to employ more people by the year 2000 because of growth

WRITING ABOUT HISTORY

Letters should indicate the influence of movies, television shows, music videos, and clothing styles.

USING PRIMARY SOURCES

sees immigration as natural and good for America

LINKING HISTORY AND GEOGRAPHY

natural disasters, wars, lack of employment; deserts, rivers and lakes, oceans, mountains

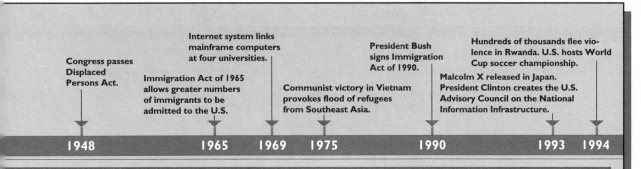

| 1948 | 1965 | 1969 | 1975 | 1990 | 1993 | 1994 |

Congress passes Displaced Persons Act.

Immigration Act of 1965 allows greater numbers of immigrants to be admitted to the U.S.

Internet system links mainframe computers at four universities.

Communist victory in Vietnam provokes flood of refugees from Southeast Asia.

President Bush signs Immigration Act of 1990.

Malcolm X released in Japan. President Clinton creates the U.S. Advisory Council on the National Information Infrastructure.

Hundreds of thousands flee violence in Rwanda. U.S. hosts World Cup soccer championship.

WRITING ABOUT HISTORY

Writing to Create Imagine you are a teenager in a country other than the United States. Write a letter to a friend explaining the extent to which your life is influenced by American culture. Use specific examples to describe what form American cultural influences take.

Crowds outside the Planet Hollywood restaurant in Hong Kong

USING PRIMARY SOURCES

Many writers have reflected on America's diverse cultural heritage. Read the following excerpt taken from a talk by Luis M. Valdez, a Mexican American playwright. How does Valdez view past, present, and future migration to America?

66 *These are painful times, and yet they are very exciting times. Many people in this country are intimidated and frightened by the brown hordes pouring across the border, the nonborder, this border that cannot hold. And so they want to declare English the official language of the United States. But I tell you that you cannot keep something natural from happening. The evolution of America has always involved north and south migration. It was the Europeans who gave it east and west. And we're happy to have it because what that did is to set up the four directions. . . . It's like the bellybutton of the world. Right at that intersection, four roads meet—the white road, the black road, the yellow road, and the*

red road. What they represent to me is the promise of America—that four roads will meet and will bear new fruit in this ancient land. . . . It is important that Europe came to these shores. It is important that Africa came to these shores. It is important that Asia came to these shores. It is important that there was a pre-Columbian America here waiting to blend and to create something greater than the parts. A whole vision of humanity. 99

LINKING HISTORY AND GEOGRAPHY

People sometimes migrate from one area to another in search of a more hospitable environment. What are some of the environmental conditions that might encourage migration? What physical features might make migration difficult?

BUILDING YOUR PORTFOLIO

Complete the following projects independently or cooperatively.

1. **WAR** In Chapter 24 you portrayed an economist studying the economic effects of war. Building on that experience, imagine you are a refugee fleeing from a war in your home country. Write a series of journal entries describing your feelings about the conflict from which you are escaping, the problems you encounter as a refugee, and your plans for the future.

2. **THE ECONOMY** In Chapter 23 you portrayed an economist studying the relationship between imperialism and the economy. Building on that experience, imagine you are the director of a private agency that assists immigrant businesspeople. Prepare a speech on how immigrant businesses are helping to boost your nation's economy.

BUILDING YOUR PORTFOLIO

Have students refer to **Building Your Portfolio Worksheet 6**, assigned at the beginning of Unit 6. Use the worksheet to help students monitor their progress on the portfolio projects.

Assessment

Core Resources
- Reteaching Worksheet 25
- Chapter 25 Tests
- Alternative Assessment Forms

Test Generator

THE STRUGGLE FOR HUMAN RIGHTS

THE AMERICAN NATION
VIDEODISC PROGRAM
A variety of still images, short videos, and activities are available for you to use as you teach this chapter. See Videodisc Resources in the Core Resources Binder for barcode correlations and suggestions for using the program.

Chapter Overview

During the 17th and 18th centuries, some people began to believe that all members of the human race were entitled to certain rights. Events of the 18th and 19th centuries helped to win acceptance of this idea. During the first half of the 20th century, the world experienced horrendous violations of human rights. At the same time, however, a new appreciation of rights developed. After World War II the international community renewed its commitment to fostering a greater respect for human rights. Although great progress has been made, many threats to human rights remain.

Chapter Planning Guide

CHAPTER 26	CORE RESOURCES	AUDIOVISUAL [AV] RESOURCES	PROGRAM RESOURCES
INTRODUCTION pp. 696–697	■ Building Your Portfolio Worksheet 6		
TEACHING THE CHAPTER pp. 698–717	■ Graphic Organizer 26 ■ Social Studies Skills Worksheet 26 ■ Geography Worksheet 26 ■ Literature Worksheet 26 ■ Outline Maps 8, 11, 12, 13, 15, 16, 17, 18, 19, 20, 21, 22	■ *The American Nation Videodisc: Free At Last; The Reform Movement; Weaponry and Warfare; Japanese Americans in Relocation Camps; Martin Luther King, Jr.; The Women's Rights Movement* ■ Linking Geography and History Transparency and Worksheet 5 ■ Everyday Life in America Transparencies and Worksheets 11, 23, 25, 26	■ *Eyewitnesses and Others,* Volume 1: Readings 2, 6, 12, 13, 14, 16, 26, 37, 45, 46, 48, 52, 64, 71, 72, 76; Volume 2: Readings 14, 19, 31, 36, 37, 52, 63, 65, 66, 68, 75
REVIEW AND ASSESSMENT pp. 718–719	■ Chapter 26 Daily Quizzes ■ Reteaching Worksheet 26 ■ Chapter 26 Tests ■ Alternative Assessment Forms		■ Test Generator

Additional Resources

BOOKS FOR TEACHERS

Brownlie, Ian, ed. *Basic Documents on Human Rights,* 3rd ed. Oxford University Press, 1992.

McColm, R. Bruce, et al. *Freedom in the World: Political Rights and Civil Liberties.* Freedom House, 1992. Tracks the progress of human rights worldwide.

Shiman, David. *Teaching Human Rights.* Center for Teaching International Relations, 1993. Activities on issues of justice and rights around the world.

BOOKS FOR STUDENTS

Kronenwetter, Michael. *Taking a Stand Against Human Rights Abuses.* Watts, 1990. Reviews the current status of human rights in the world.

*Rochelle, Belinda. *Witnesses to Freedom: Young People Who Fought for Civil Rights.* Lodestar Books, 1993. Tells the stories of some young human rights advocates.

State of the Peoples: A Global Human Rights Report on Societies in Danger. Beacon Press, 1993. Catalog of worldwide human rights issues.

* for students reading below grade level

MULTIMEDIA MATERIALS

Freedoms. Video, 23 min. Barr Films, Inc. Dramatizes the issue of human rights in the school setting.

International Human Rights. Video, 60 min. Close Up Publishing. Discussion of the worldwide human rights situation led by a representative of Amnesty International.

The Media and Human Rights. Video, 60 min. PBS Video. Discussion on obligation of the media to report human rights abuses.

THEMES IN AMERICAN HISTORY

USE WITH PAGES 696–697

Listed on the right are the themes emphasized in Chapter 26. The questions in boldface type stimulate critical thinking and provide students with an opportunity to discuss the themes within a broadened context. The questions also appear in the pupil's edition on p. 696.

■ DEMOCRATIC VALUES

How is democracy related to human rights? Students should note that one of the characteristics of democracy is the recognition of individual liberty. The basic concept of human rights—that individuals, as human beings, have certain rights—is an extension of the idea of individual liberty.

■ GLOBAL RELATIONS

In what ways can one country encourage others to respect human rights? Students may suggest that a country might use various kinds of pressure to encourage respect for human rights. That country might refuse to sign trade agreements, or it might withhold economic aid. Students may also suggest that a country could set a good example for others by honoring human rights within its own borders.

■ CULTURAL DIVERSITY

Are human rights a universal concept, or do they differ from culture to culture? Students may suggest that the basic human rights—freedom from unlawful imprisonment, freedom from torture, and so on—are universal. Conversely, students may point out that the U.S. emphasizes individual rights. Other cultures, however, place greater emphasis on community rights. Human rights may therefore be defined differently in these cultures.

CHAPTER STRATEGIES FOR MEETING INDIVIDUAL NEEDS

LIMITED ENGLISH PROFICIENT LEARNERS

Organize the class into two groups. Have one group write questions about the people listed in the Preview Workshop for each section. Have the other group write questions about the terms listed in each section's Preview Workshop. Have groups pose their questions to the class.

TACTILE/KINESTHETIC LEARNERS

Have students work in small groups to prepare skits depicting three or four key turning points in the progress of human rights. Call on groups to perform their skits for the rest of the class.

LEARNERS HAVING DIFFICULTY

Have students create a three-column chart for each section using the following headings: *What I Already Know, What I Expect to Learn, What I Have Learned.* Have students complete columns one and two for each Focus question. After students complete each section, have them fill in column three.

AUDITORY LEARNERS

Have students work in small groups to research important speeches on human rights. Have groups make dramatic readings of five or six speeches. Suggest that they introduce each speech with information that answers such questions as: Who made the speech? When? Where? Why?

VISUAL LEARNERS

Refer students to the civil rights time line on pp. 502–506. Suggest that they construct a similar illustrated and annotated time line showing the progress of human rights around the world.

GIFTED LEARNERS

Ask students to create a biographical dictionary of human rights. In their dictionary, they should include the major personalities mentioned in the chapter.

USING THE CHAPTER FOCUS

■ **UNDERSTANDING THE MAIN IDEA**
Call on a volunteer to read aloud the Understanding the Main Idea paragraph. Then ask students to suggest which rights individuals possess by virtue of membership in the human race. Note suggestions on the chalkboard. Discuss with students why they think the listed items should be recognized and protected as human rights. Conclude by pointing out that Chapter 26 is concerned with the worldwide progress toward establishing and protecting such rights.

 THEMES
Have students work individually or in groups to answer the questions under Themes. Save students' responses so that they can compare them with their responses after studying the chapter. (See p. 695B for suggested answers.)

■ **THE TIME LINE**
Review the time-line entries with students. As students read the chapter, have them note why each entry marked an important step in the progress of human rights.

CORE RESOURCES

• **Graphic Organizer 26**
• **Building Your Portfolio Worksheet 6**

696

ABOUT THE ILLUSTRATION

Tell students that the demonstrations in Tiananmen Square stemmed from a desire for increased political and economic reforms in the People's Republic of China. Ask students to study the photograph and write a brief paragraph describing the people and activities in the picture.

Encourage students to consider why people might be willing to protest publicly in spite of the risk of punishment from their government.

Chapter 26

THE STRUGGLE FOR HUMAN RIGHTS

FOCUS

UNDERSTANDING THE MAIN IDEA

The 20th century witnessed a widening of an earlier contest to extend the sphere of human rights. Increasingly, individuals came to be seen as possessing certain rights simply as members of the human race. The United States was a leader in the struggle, improving its own human rights record and often encouraging other countries to do so as well.

THEMES

■ **DEMOCRATIC VALUES**
How is democracy related to human rights?

■ **GLOBAL RELATIONS** In what ways can one country encourage others to respect human rights?

■ **CULTURAL DIVERSITY**
Are human rights a universal concept, or do they differ from culture to culture?

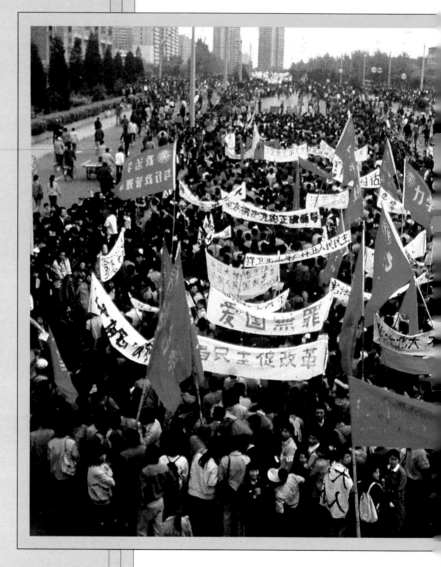

Point out that some scholars suggest that the basis of the human rights concept goes back even further to ancient Greece and Rome and the theory of natural law. According to this theory, all life in the world is ordered by the law of nature. People are obliged to abide by this law, for any violation of it constitutes a moral wrong.

Many of the world's religions have taught the innate worth of all human beings for hundreds, even thousands, of years. The modern concept of human rights, however, grew out of ideas that reached back only to the 17th and 18th centuries.

HISTORICAL SIDELIGHT
Rewriting the Past
In the fall of 1989 Timothy Brook, an American author, traveled to Beijing to investigate the events surrounding the Tiananmen Square massacre. In one video store he found a government-produced videotape describing the protests and the aftermath. The footage on the videotapes had been edited to show that the protesters had started the violence and that the government's suppression of the protest had been justified.

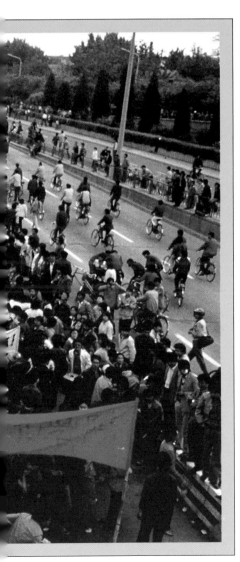

Chinese students in the streets of Beijing, 1989

In the spring of 1989, thousands of students gathered in Beijing, China, to demonstrate in favor of democratic reforms in China. The demonstrators listened to speeches, waved posters, and handed out leaflets demanding that the Chinese government acknowledge the right of the Chinese people to speak their minds and to have a greater say in choosing their leaders.

The centerpiece of the demonstrations was a plaster figure resembling the American Statue of Liberty erected in Tiananmen Square in the heart of the Chinese capital. For more than a century, the American statue had lifted its beacon of democracy and human rights to the world. In 1989 it inspired the Tiananmen Square demonstrators to try to follow the United States' example.

The Chinese government flatly rejected the demonstrators' demands. In a brutal display of force, government troops killed hundreds of demonstrators and wounded hundreds more. Thousands were jailed, many for years. The statue of the "Goddess of Democracy" was smashed to pieces.

The demonstrations in Tiananmen Square showed the global appeal of human rights and the influence of America's example. The massacre showed that the struggle for human rights had far to go.

Tiananmen Square "Goddess of Democracy" statue, May 1989

MOTIVATING: PRIOR KNOWLEDGE

Encourage students to recall documents from the early history of the U.S. that expressed or embraced the concept of human rights. *(Declaration of Independence, U.S. Bill of Rights)* As students read the section, have them note the ideas that inspired the writing of these documents.

FOCUS OBJECTIVES

- Note when the concept of human rights arose, and identify the events that contributed to the development of the concept.

- Discuss how the U.S. antislavery movement was connected to reform movements in other countries.

- Explain what triggered the women's rights movement in the 19th century, and identify the movement's principal demand.

- Describe how progressivism furthered the cause of human rights.

Section 1

HUMAN RIGHTS BEFORE WORLD WAR I

FOCUS

- **When did the modern concept of human rights arise? What events contributed to the development of the concept?**
- **How was the U.S. antislavery movement connected to reform movements in other countries?**
- **What triggered the women's rights movement in the 19th century? What was the movement's principal demand?**
- **How did progressivism further the cause of human rights?**

Various efforts to promote human rights arose during the 18th and 19th centuries. The American and French revolutions focused on the rights of citizens. The antislavery and women's rights movements sought to expand the definition of citizen so as to include more people. The Progressive movement won the vote for American women and protection for American children.

A symbol of the French Revolution, 1789–1799

ORIGINS OF THE HUMAN RIGHTS CONCEPT

The modern concept of human rights is a fairly recent innovation. In ancient and medieval times, certain individuals had rights because of their positions in society: some Athenian Greeks had certain rights as citizens of Athens; feudal nobles had rights as nobles, while peasants had a different set of rights as peasants. But the idea that people had rights simply because they were human beings did not arise in its modern form until the 17th century.

Several 17th- and 18th-century philosophers spoke of natural rights that existed because of the nature of human beings and their relation to society. One such philosopher was John Locke of England. Locke lived during the mid- and late 1600s, when the English Parliament was challenging the absolute power of the king.

Siding with Parliament, Locke believed that individuals had certain rights that governments could

not violate. In fact, the very reason that governments existed, Locke asserted, was to protect individuals' rights. Locke listed the most important of these rights as the rights to life, liberty, and property.

In what became known as the **Glorious Revolution**, Parliament broke the absolute power of the monarchy. As a result, the natural rights Locke identified became part of the political inheritance of the English people—and of those men and women who transplanted themselves from England to North America.

As the natural rights philosophy spread across the Atlantic, it acquired a distinctively American form. This form became apparent in one of history's most important statements on the subject of human rights: the American Declaration of Independence, in which the colonists proclaimed their rights against the government of King George III (see Chapter 2).

The American declaration of rights and the Americans' success in defending these rights inspired people in other countries. Just a few years

ORIGINS OF THE IDEA OF HUMAN RIGHTS

Ask students to imagine they are writers working for a history magazine whose audience consists mostly of 12- to 14-year-olds. They are to write articles on the origins of human rights. Suggest that they develop outlines for the articles detailing the origins of the human rights concept and the various events that contributed to its development.

Encourage them to add ideas for illustrations and special features. Call on volunteers to present and discuss their outlines.

A WORLDWIDE ANTISLAVERY MOVEMENT

Encourage students to imagine they are members of the antislavery movement in the U.S. during the mid-1800s. Ask them to write a brief speech detailing the activities of antislavery movements in other countries, their successes and failures, and the tactics that the American movement might adopt. Have volunteers deliver their speeches to the class.

▶

▲ This painting shows representatives of France's middle class as they met in June 1789 and pledged to write a new constitution.

after the Revolutionary War, residents of Paris, outraged by the French monarchy's excesses, revolted. As the revolution begun by the Parisians spread across France, the newly formed National Assembly issued the **Declaration of the Rights of Man and Citizen**. Like the Declaration of Independence, the French document listed basic rights:

❝ The aim of all political association is the conservation of the natural and inalienable rights of man. These rights are: liberty, property, security and resistance to oppression. ❞

Equality, while not a right in itself, was implied by the declaration's assertion that all men were "equal in rights."

■■ **The modern concept of human rights originated in the 17th century and grew as a result of the American and French revolutions.**

THE ANTISLAVERY MOVEMENT

Thomas Jefferson owned slaves, as did many others who signed the Declaration of Independence. It did not escape the notice of the Declaration's signers that the right of liberty they proclaimed for "all men" was something they themselves denied their slaves. Critics of slavery, of course, also noted this contradiction. But in 1776 the need for unity in the

struggle against Britain seemed to the revolutionary leaders to outweigh the need for consistency regarding human rights. Thus debate over the slavery issue remained relatively quiet.

The slave trade. It did not stay quiet for long, however. In the discussions that produced the Constitution, critics of slavery succeeded in securing a ban on the importation of slaves, albeit after a delay of twenty years. Even the supporters of slavery had difficulty defending the Atlantic slave trade, with its barbarous conditions and appalling death rates. One observer of a ship carrying slaves described how the captives were packed in until "they had not so much room *as a man in his coffin.*"

Criticism of the slave trade was not limited to the United States. At about the time the U.S. Congress was banning the slave trade to the United States, British abolitionists persuaded Parliament to outlaw the slave trade. Subsequently these abolitionists lobbied the British government to pressure other European powers to do the same. At an 1815 meeting among the major European powers, Britain persuaded the other powers to join it in condemning the slave trade.

British abolition. By the time the bans on the slave trade went into effect, the immorality of slavery itself had become an international issue. British abolitionists, led by William Wilberforce, grew

◀ In 1789 William Wilberforce, a prominent British Tory, led the first Parliamentary campaign that attacked slavery.

PRIMARY SOURCE
Description of Change: excerpted
Rationale: excerpted to focus on main idea

AV **TRANSPARENCY**
Linking History and Geography Transparency and **Worksheet 5**

HISTORICAL SIDELIGHTS
Working to End Slavery
In 1776, at the age of 17, William Wilberforce enrolled in Cambridge University. Four years later he won his first election to the House of Commons. In 1787 Wilberforce began a campaign against the British slave trade. Even after his retirement from Parliament in 1825, Wilberforce supported emancipation in British colonies.

ℐeaching the ℐection

RIGHTS FOR WOMEN

Encourage students to imagine they are members of the women's rights movement in the U.S during the 19th century. Have them write letters to a friend in Britain explaining the origins of the movement. Suggest that they end their letters by identi-fying the principal goal of the movement and explaining why this goal is of impor-tance. Call on volunteers to read their letters to the class. Interested students might write a reply from the British friend that details the development and actions of the women's movement in Britain. Students may wish to include their letters in their portfolios.

PROGRESSIVES SUPPORT HUMAN RIGHTS

Organize students into small groups to work as campaign organizers for the Progressive party. Their task is to create a campaign slogan or poster that focuses on the party's support for human rights issues. Call on groups to present and discuss their slogans or posters.

AV TRANSPARENCY

Everyday Life in America Transparency and **Worksheet 11**

THE AMERICAN NATION VIDEODISC PROGRAM

Free At Last

| 1B | 15914 | 2:57 |

increasingly militant in demanding that their government outlaw slavery. Largely as a result of efforts by Wilberforce and others, Parliament voted in 1833 to ban the institution of slavery within the British Empire.

Once the British had put a stop to slavery in their own territories, they tried to end it elsewhere. As British warships patrolled the Atlantic and Indian Oceans during the mid- and late 1800s, they searched for slave ships. When they found such ships, they seized the vessels and released the slaves. Sometimes, however, British efforts back-fired. Some slavers, when they saw British warships approaching, threw slaves overboard in order to prevent their ships from being seized. Nevertheless, the British efforts did reduce the numbers of persons delivered into slavery.

Other movements. The British antislavery movement encouraged abolitionism in other countries. When most of Spain's Latin American colonies claimed and won their independence during the 1810s and 1820s, many abolished slavery at the same time. On the other side of the world, in Russia, reformers called for an end to serfdom. Under this system—similar in some ways to slavery—peasants called serfs were required to work the land they lived on for the benefit of the landowner. Opponents of serfdom in Russia achieved success when Czar Alexander II emancipated the serfs in 1861.

American abolitionists took heart from these foreign efforts to expand human freedom. Leaders

▼ The *Black Man's Lament* shows West Indies slave traders in the mid-1800s separating a man from his family.

▲ Life was often difficult for the peasant class in prerevolutionary Russia.

such as Frederick Douglass and William Lloyd Garrison followed the example of Wilberforce and other reformers overseas in pressing for an end to slavery. Because of the entrenched political position of southern planters, however, American anti-slavery activists found it more difficult than reformers in Britain and Latin America to push abolition to the top of the list of national priorities. But in the 1850s they helped establish the Republican party, which thrust the slavery issue further into politics. Reformers all over applauded Republican Abraham Lincoln's election in 1860. Not all of them cheered the coming of the American Civil War, but without exception they hailed the Emancipation Proclamation and the Thirteenth Amendment abolishing slavery.

▪▪ **The abolitionist movement in the United States was part of an international effort to end slavery and other forms of human bondage.**

ℐHE STRUGGLE FOR WOMEN'S RIGHTS

Many of the most tireless opponents of slavery were women. However, as these women worked for rights for African Americans, they realized that they needed to work for their own rights. As Angelina Grimké stated in 1836: "The investigation of the rights of the slave has led me to a better understand-ing of my own." Elizabeth Cady Stanton and Lucretia Mott came to a similar realization when they were denied the chance to speak at an antislav-ery convention in London (see Chapter 3).

Practice

GUIDED PRACTICE

Call on students to identify the major developments in the progress of human rights up to World War I. Note responses on the chalkboard and ask students to provide details for each entry.

INDEPENDENT PRACTICE

Have students use information developed in the Guided Practice activity to create an annotated flow chart that shows the progress of human rights from the origins of the concept to World War I. Students may wish to include the flow charts in their portfolios.

Review and Assessment

REVIEW Direct students to use the section's headings as the main topics for an outline of the section. Have students use the text under each heading to add details to their outlines. Students may wish to include their outlines in their portfolios. Then assign the Section 1 Review on p. 702.

ASSESS Assign the **Section 1 Daily Quiz** in *Core Resources*.

▶

Moreover, in the abolitionist movement women interested in reform met other women with similar views. Together they learned techniques of organization and education that they could apply on their own behalf. The 1848 Seneca Falls Convention was one of the first efforts at such organization worldwide.

The women's movement in the United States was similar to movements in other countries. Foremost among these was Britain, where women also campaigned in favor of the vote. In 1865 the most active members of the movement established the Women's Suffrage Committee, which was later renamed the London National Society for Women's Suffrage. They believed that the vote would allow them access to Parliament, where they could have even greater influence in establishing women's equality with men.

By the early 1900s, women in Britain had gained the right to vote in local and county elections and to participate in such government bodies as town councils and school boards. In 1907, 10 women were elected mayors of small towns. Nonetheless, women were still barred from voting in national elections.

As opposition in Britain to full women's suffrage persisted, many women became impatient with the long slow struggle. In 1903 feminist Emmeline Pankhurst founded a new women's rights organization, the **Women's Social and Political Union** (WSPU). Disappointed by the British government's continuing refusal to allow women's suffrage, Pankhurst and her followers—who were labeled suffragettes—decided in 1906 to adopt more aggressive tactics.

To get greater publicity and public support, Pankhurst and her followers began to attack public property and tried to get arrested. Once arrested, they often went on hunger strikes. Because the government did not want the women to die while they were in prison, they were often force-fed through tubes stuck into their nostrils. One protester, Mary Leigh, described the experience to her attorney in 1909:

66 The sensation is most painful—the drums of the ears seem to be bursting and there is a horrible pain in the throat and the breast. The tube is pushed down twenty inches. I have to lie on the bed, pinned down by the wardresses [female prison attendants]. 99

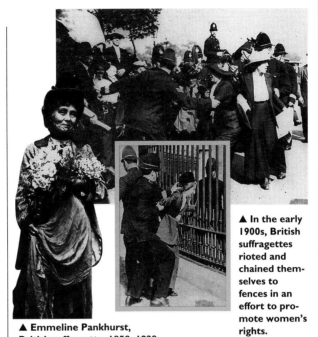

▲ In the early 1900s, British suffragettes rioted and chained themselves to fences in an effort to promote women's rights.

▲ Emmeline Pankhurst, British suffragette, 1858–1928

In response to the suffragettes' tactics, the British government passed an act in 1913 that allowed suffragettes to be released from prison when they became too weak or ill from starvation, and then rearrested as soon as they had recovered enough to serve more of their sentences. This act, which became known as the "Cat and Mouse Act," only made the WSPU more determined. Members increased their attacks on public property. One, Emily Davison, deliberately threw herself under the hooves of the king's horse during a horse race. Although women over the age of 30 gained the right to vote in 1918, it was not until 1928 that all adult women were granted suffrage in Britain.

■■ The movement for women's rights grew out of the antislavery campaign. Its principal early goal was the vote for women.

PROGRESSIVISM AND HUMAN RIGHTS

In the United States the campaign for women's rights became linked during the early years of the 20th century to the Progressive movement. The progressives believed that the answer to the nation's

MULTICULTURAL PERSPECTIVES

In 1913 Emmeline Pankhurst delivered a speech in New York to explain the militancy of many British women suffragists. "Men got the vote because they were and would be violent. The women did not get it because they were constitutional and law-abiding. . . .

". . . Have men ever had to suffer from the laws, more injustice than women suffer?

". . . You are full of sympathy with all struggling people striving for independence. How is it, then, that some of you have nothing but ridicule and contempt and reprobation for women who are fighting for exactly the same thing?"

PRIMARY SOURCE

Description of Change: excerpted and bracketed
Rationale: excerpted to focus on main idea; bracketed to clarify meaning

RETEACH For each subsection in the section, have students write a sentence that summarizes the main idea. Select students to read their sentences aloud. Have the class choose the best summary sentence for each subsection.

Closure

Have students identify what they think is the most important event in the progress of human rights during the time period covered by this section. Encourage them to use information from the section to support their choice.

Extension

ANALYZE Have students analyze the Declaration of Independence (on pp. 32–33) and write an essay showing the influence of John Locke's ideas on this document.

INVESTIGATE Encourage students to investigate and report on the role of the Pankhurst family in the British women's movement. A useful source of information is Midge Mackenzie's *Shoulder to Shoulder* (Alfred A. Knopf, 1975).

SECTION REVIEW ANSWERS

IDENTIFY

For significance, see the following pages:
John Locke (p. 598)
Glorious Revolution (p. 598)
Declaration of the Rights of Man and Citizen (p. 598)
William Wilberforce (p. 598)
Women's Social and Political Union (p. 701)
Emmeline Pankhurst (p. 701)

1. *17th; encouraged people to oppose governments that limited rights*
2. *Britain—antislavery movement; Latin America—independence movements; Russia—movement to end serfdom*
3. *Women were not permitted to participate fully in the abolition movement, prompting many to begin to seek equality for themselves.*
4. *Paragraphs should discuss the Progressive belief that social and political ills could be remedied by expanding democracy.*
5. *Answers will vary, but should include discussion of the kinds of rights mentioned as well as the belief that governments needed to protect the rights of individuals.*

► During the mid-1800s Britain passed labor laws to protect children such as these boys, who worked in a Derbyshire coal mine.

problems—ranging from corrupt city and state governments to corporate monopolies and wasteful exploitation of natural resources—was increased democracy. Women's suffrage fit into the pattern of more democracy, along with such other electoral reforms as the direct primary and the initiative, referendum, and recall. During the first two decades of the new century, women reformers focused on amending the Constitution to guarantee women's right to vote. Success came in 1920 with approval of the Nineteenth Amendment.

The progressive agenda included other items that touched on human rights. Among these were child labor laws. The Industrial Revolution had led to the employment of large numbers of young boys and girls in mills, mines, and other industrial workplaces. The problem first became acute in Britain, where several laws restricting child labor were passed during the 1830s and 1840s. Even so, labor conditions in Britain remained poor, prompting authors such as Charles Dickens to write starkly about the bleak lives of working children.

American progressives were moved by Dickens's stories. They were also moved by American muckraker journalists' accounts and by their own observations of children who toiled long hours in American coal mines and cotton mills. Believing that children deserved protection from exploitation by industrialists, who hired the children because they were cheap, the progressives passed a variety of laws limiting child labor (see Chapter 7).

Critics of the child labor laws argued that such laws did not expand human rights but rather reduced them, by curbing children's right to work as they pleased. Supporters countered that children did not work in coal mines out of free choice but out of economic necessity. They said that child labor laws actually increased the freedom of children by allowing them the right not to work.

■■ **The American progressives' contribution to expanding human rights included winning the vote for women and restricting child labor.**

SECTION 1 REVIEW

IDENTIFY and explain the significance of the following: John Locke, Glorious Revolution, Declaration of the Rights of Man and Citizen, William Wilberforce, Women's Social and Political Union, Emmeline Pankhurst.

1. **MAIN IDEA** During what century did the modern concept of human rights originate? How did the American and French revolutions affect conceptions of rights?

2. **MAIN IDEA** What relationship did the antislavery movement in the United States have with movements in other countries?

3. **MAIN IDEA** What sparked the rise of the women's movement in the 19th century? What was the main goal of people in the movement?

4. **WRITING TO EXPLAIN** Write a paragraph explaining how the Progressive movement contributed to the expansion of human rights.

5. **ANALYZING** How did the American Declaration of Independence reflect the ideas of John Locke about the purpose of government?

Chapter 26

PREVIEW WORKSHOP

Following is a list of the significant terms in this section. You may wish to use this list as a section preview.

Terms
- Geneva Convention
- Red Cross
- Hague Peace Conferences
- American Friends Service Committee
- Universal Declaration of Human Rights

Section 2

THE CRUELTIES OF WAR

FOCUS

- **How did World War I influence thinking about human rights?**
- **What new threats to human rights emerged between the wars?**
- **How did World War II affect human rights?**
- **How did the international community attempt to safeguard human rights following World War II?**

he years from the beginning of World War I to the end of World War II witnessed new challenges to human rights and a new appreciation of those rights. The first war resulted in the slaughter of people by the millions and led to efforts to restrict the use of certain weapons and tactics of war. The interwar years saw the rise of militant fascism, a movement that fostered prejudice. The second war produced suffering on a scale that dwarfed even the first war, but it also produced a new international appreciation for human rights.

American soldiers wearing gas masks, World War I

FOCUS OBJECTIVES

- Explain how World War I influenced thinking about human rights.
- Identify the new threats to human rights that emerged between the wars.
- Describe how World War II affected human rights.
- Evaluate the international community's attempts to safeguard human rights following World War II.

MULTICULTURAL PERSPECTIVES

Although the Red Cross is well known in many countries, the symbol and name are not universal. In almost all Muslim countries the organization is called the Red Crescent, and in Iran it is known as the Red Lion and Sun Society.

THE ULTIMATE VIOLATION

During the early years of the 20th century, the countries of Europe flattered themselves that they had achieved a level of civilization unmatched in human history. Political and other reforms were making the European continent more democratic, more humane, and more enlightened each year. In addition, Europe as a whole had not known a major war for nearly a century. What war there was Europeans tried to humanize, laying down international conventions for its conduct and establishing rules for the treatment of prisoners.

In 1864, for example, 12 nations had agreed to the **Geneva Convention**, which required them to care properly not only for their own sick and wounded soldiers but also for captured enemy soldiers. The Geneva Convention also recognized the efforts of the **Red Cross**, an organization created the previous year by private Swiss citizens to minister

to wounded soldiers of all nations. While the Geneva Convention applied only to warfare on land, the **Hague Peace Conferences** of 1899 and 1907 established provisions to regulate naval warfare.

The horror of war. The world war that broke out in 1914 quickly shattered any sense of self-satisfaction Europeans felt about their approach to warfare. During World War I the European armies killed and maimed each other in unheard-of numbers. In the Battle of the Somme, for example, thousands died in minutes as mass-produced weapons proved how efficiently they could destroy life.

Some weapons seemed more gruesome than others. The damage machine guns and artillery did to human flesh and bone was enough to torment survivors with lifelong nightmares. Poison gas seemed even worse. Unlike guns, gas could not be accurately aimed; it blew and drifted where it would, felling friend and foe alike. And it was

CORE RESOURCES
- **Section 2 Daily Quiz**

AV RESOURCES
- *The American Nation Videodisc:* **Weaponry and Warfare; Japanese Americans in Relocation Camps**
- *Everyday Life in America Transparencies* and **Worksheets 23, 25, 26**

THE STRUGGLE FOR HUMAN RIGHTS ▪▪ 703

MOTIVATING: LINK TO TODAY

Display a large wall map of the world. Call on volunteers to locate on the map regions where wars presently are being fought. Ask other students to identify any human rights issues connected to these wars. Then point out that in this section students will learn that the greatest violations of human rights usually occur during wartime.

*T*eaching the *S*ection

WORLD WAR I AND HUMAN RIGHTS

Organize students into small groups to work as teams of journalists. Ask teams to develop outlines for newspaper articles explaining that even though World War I saw horrendous human rights violations, the peacemaking efforts of governments and individuals created a new appreciation of human rights. Call on team representatives to present their outlines. Have students use these presentations to develop a class outline. Then have students work as individual journalists to write the assigned article.

THE AMERICAN NATION VIDEODISC PROGRAM

Weaponry and Warfare

2A   14847   2:51

PRIMARY SOURCE

Description of Change: excerpted and bracketed **Rationale:** excerpted to focus on main idea; bracketed to clarify meaning

▶ This 1918 photograph shows an American soldier clutching at his throat as he breathes poison gas.

horribly painful, causing those who breathed it to feel that their lungs were on fire. Many gas victims died; others suffered irreparable lung damage and never breathed easily again.

World War I also saw the first significant use of submarines. Prior to World War I, naval blockades had been relatively nonviolent: blockading ships seized vessels but did not destroy them or harm the people aboard. Submarine warfare changed this and added a new form of barbarity to armed conflict. Submarine attacks took their targets by surprise and often sank them without regard for the safety of crew or passengers.

Since the nation using submarines most extensively was Germany, many charges of barbarity were aimed at the German government. The Germans responded to these charges by claiming that the British blockade of Germany was killing more people than were German submarines. The British blockade, by preventing food and other essential supplies from reaching the German people, was contributing to widespread malnutrition and disease. Moreover, children, the elderly, and the sick suffered the most from the shortages caused by the blockade.

War and ethnic conflict.

Other events of the war years also threatened human rights. Ottoman Turkey, for example, took advan-

tage of the war to crush a discontented Armenian minority. The Turks massacred hundreds of thousands of Armenians and forcibly deported hundreds of thousands more. One observer described how Armenians were "brutally dragged out of their native land, torn from their homes and families, . . . penned up in the open like cattle, without shelter, almost no clothing, and irregularly fed with food altogether insufficient." In one Turkish prison camp, the observer continued, "mounds are seen containing 200 or 300 corpses buried in the ground . . . women, children, and old people." Another witness told of other horrors:

> 66 There were 500 Armenians herded together in a stable . . . and locked in. Through an opening in the roof gendarmes [soldiers] threw flaming torches. I saw the flames and heard the screams of the victims, all of whom were burned alive. 99

To the limited extent outsiders knew what was happening—the Ottoman government flatly denied any wrongful activity—there was little anyone could do. Furthermore, the Allies were already at war against Turkey. And at a time when even larger numbers of Allied soldiers were dying in battle elsewhere, atrocities against the Armenians attracted little attention.

■■ **World War I shattered illusions that the world was becoming more humane.**

▼ These Armenian refugees in Adana, Turkey, were among the lucky ones who escaped the Turks during World War I.

NEW THREATS TO HUMAN RIGHTS

Encourage students to work in small groups to develop scripts for a documentary on threats to human rights during the 1930s. Suggest that development teams include the following in their scripts: 1) an explanation of why such political ideologies as communism and fascism posed a threat to individual rights; 2) examples of human rights violations that took place in the 1930s; 3) ideas for illustrations and film clips to be used in the documentary. Call on teams to present and discuss their scripts.

WORLD WAR II AND HUMAN RIGHTS VIOLATIONS

Ask students to imagine they are radio news reporters on location in Europe or Japan at the end of World War II. Have them write brief broadcasts that summarize the human rights violations that took place during the war. Call on reporters to make their broadcasts to the class.

▶

PEACEMAKING AND HUMAN RIGHTS

Yet all the carnage did have an effect. It served as a reminder that the ultimate violation of human rights was war, which in the industrial era left millions dead, often without regard for who was a soldier and who was a civilian.

The war spurred efforts to safeguard human rights by preventing future wars. The most important of these efforts was the establishment of the League of Nations, the international body designed to settle disputes between countries. The World Court, too, attempted to find peaceful resolutions to international disputes. And in the winter of 1921–22, the U.S.-sponsored disarmament conference in Washington resulted in agreements to destroy dozens of warships of the great powers' navies (see Chapter 15).

Private efforts. Not all efforts to promote peace were led by governments. Peace activists in America and elsewhere formed organizations devoted to the study of the causes and prevention of war. For example, the **American Friends Service Committee** (AFSC), which had been founded by Quakers in 1917 to provide "a conscientious service of love for humanity in wartime," created a peace section in 1924. The organization hosted gatherings of pacifist groups in Paris, Berlin, Vienna, Geneva, Warsaw, and Moscow.

The AFSC also provided humanitarian aid to Germany and Poland following World War I. In Germany, the AFSC organized a relief effort that, with the help of many German volunteers, fed over one million children daily during 1921 and 1922. "Feeding the hungry and clothing the naked is spectacular and inspiring work," said the AFSC's 1928 Annual Report. But, the report continued, "it is a much harder task to prevent war, to encourage nations to settle their differences by arbitration, to develop a new type of patriotism."

▲ The American Friends Service Committee's star was first used in 1870 to identify British Quakers providing war relief.

▮▮ Following World War I, the international community and private organizations made efforts to prevent future wars.

The issue of equality. One human rights issue—that of equality—met with less success following World War I. Japan, a member of the winning coalition, asked at the Paris Peace Conference that a statement affirming the principle of racial equality be included in the League of Nations Covenant. The Japanese and other Asians, not to mention Africans, had long labored under the stigma of racial inferiority in dealings with Europeans and Americans. Having helped defeat the German alliance, the Japanese wanted a formal statement of their equality.

The other victors refused. President Wilson knew that he would have enough difficulty getting the Senate to approve the peace treaty. To add a section on racial equality risked increasing opposition among lawmakers from western states, where immigration from Asia had historically been a sensitive issue, and from southern states, where many whites took racial inequality for granted. The British government faced similar political problems and likewise declined to back the Japanese request.

NEW THREATS TO HUMAN RIGHTS

During the 1920s it was possible for human rights advocates to believe they were regaining some of the ground lost during World War I, but during the 1930s they lost this sense of optimism. The Great Depression fostered the rise of Fascist governments in Germany and Spain and strengthened the already-existing Fascist government of Italy.

During the 19th and early 20th centuries, the trend among most countries, especially in Europe and the Americas, had been in the direction of greater individual rights and freedom.

GLOBAL CONNECTIONS

In 1915 Carrie Chapman Catt and Jane Addams organized the Woman's Peace party at a convention in Washington, D.C. The party hoped to limit weapons production, educate children about peace, extend suffrage to women, and improve national economies in an attempt to discourage war. Later that year 47 American women, many of them members of the Woman's Peace party, attended an International Congress of Women held in the Netherlands. Suffragists from 12 different countries attended the conference to advocate peace.

Teaching the Section

PROTECTING HUMAN RIGHTS

On the chalkboard write *Ways to Protect Human Rights*. Below this, write *United Nations* and *Universal Declaration of Human Rights*. Encourage students to write "product descriptions" of these two items. Descriptions should include a brief history of each and the ways in which each provides protection to human rights. Suggest that students add a "warning" sentence to each description, pointing out any limitations to the protection offered. Call on volunteers to share their descriptions with the class.

AV TRANSPARENCY

Everyday Life in America Transparencies and Worksheets 23, 25

HISTORICAL SIDELIGHTS

Anti-Semitism in Sports
The 1936 American Olympic team also included two Jews—Sam Stoller and Marty Glickman, who had won places on the 400-meter relay team. Although both had friends who urged them to boycott the games to protest Nazi policies, Stoller and Glickman hoped to prove publicly that Hitler's views on race were groundless. Instead, the runners were replaced by Jesse Owens and Ralph Metcalfe, who had run in the 100-meter race. Glickman later attributed the decision to anti-Semitism on the part of Dean Cromwell, coach of the relay team, and Avery Brundage, president of the American Olympic Committee. Cromwell and Brundage shared pro-Nazi sentiments and, according to Glickman, hoped "to save Hitler and his entourage the embarrassment of having Jews on that winning podium."

But the rise of fascism and communism reversed the trend. Fascism, like communism in the Soviet Union, was based on the idea that the needs of society were more important than the rights of individuals. In fact, in this view, only the state had rights; individuals had responsibilities. Mussolini explained the concept by comparing individuals within the nation to atoms within the human body. Each was significant only insofar as it worked for the good of the greater being.

Fascism was dangerous to human rights in another way as well. Fascists preached that particular ethnic and racial groups were superior to others. Nazism—the form fascism took in Germany—was the most racist of all. Adolf Hitler and other Nazis gave countless speeches praising the supposed virtues of the "Aryan race" and expressing their distaste for other races and peoples.

Sometimes Hitler's boasting merely made him look foolish. In 1936 Germany hosted the summer Olympic Games. Hitler predicted that Germany's "Aryan" athletes would defeat all others, demonstrating the physical superiority of the German nation. Much to Hitler's disappointment, Jesse Owens of the United States—an African American and therefore, by Hitler's reckoning, a member of one of the inferior races—trounced Germany's athletes, and all others, winning four gold medals. Even as spectators loudly applauded Owens, Hitler remarked to a colleague, "The Americans ought to be ashamed of themselves for

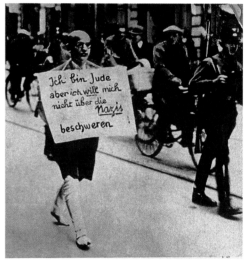

▲ During World War II some German Jews were forced to wear signs reading "I am a Jew, but I will not grumble about the Nazis."

letting their medals be won by Negroes. I myself would never shake hands with one of them."

On other occasions Hitler's racist philosophy had far more vicious consequences. Hitler and the Nazis blamed many of Germany's problems on Jews, carrying anti-Semitism to terrible extremes. The exclusion of "non-Aryans" from the civil service, the stripping of German Jews of their citizenship, and the events of *Kristallnacht* (see Chapter 15) only foreshadowed the horrors of the Holocaust.

The brutality of the 1930s was not limited to Europe. Japan's government was not Fascist, but it was militaristic and violent. Japan invaded China during the 1930s and inflicted mass atrocities on those Chinese not fortunate enough to escape. Japan's 1937 assault on Nanjing (Nanking) was especially horrific. For weeks Japanese soldiers engaged in a campaign of terror against the inhabitants of the city. Millions were left homeless and tens of thousands were killed. One observer said that men, women, and children in the streets "were hunted like rabbits. Everyone seen to move was shot."

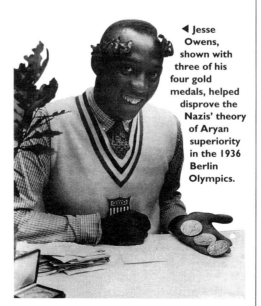

◀ Jesse Owens, shown with three of his four gold medals, helped disprove the Nazis' theory of Aryan superiority in the 1936 Berlin Olympics.

▪▪ **Fascism endangered human rights by preaching the supremacy of the state over the individual and by fostering violent racism. Japanese militarism trampled human rights in China.**

Practice

GUIDED PRACTICE

Write the section's five main headings on the chalkboard. Ask students to suggest ways to visually represent the main idea of the text included under each heading. (Remind students that visuals include charts, tables, and graphs, as well as photographs, cartoons, and drawings.) Note ideas under the appropriate heading.

INDEPENDENT PRACTICE

Organize students into five groups and assign each group one of the headings listed on the chalkboard. Direct groups to use information developed in the Guided Practice activity to create a visual that illustrates the main idea of their assigned heading. Call on groups to combine their visuals into a wall chart titled "Human Rights from World War to World War."

Review and Assessment

REVIEW Provide students with copies of a two-column chart titled "Human Rights Progress to 1950," with *Positive* and *Negative* as headings. Have students use information from the section to complete the chart. Encourage students to compare their charts. Then assign the Section 2 Review on p. 708.

ASSESS Assign the **Section 2 Daily Quiz** in *Core Resources*.   ▶

During the 1930s most Americans did their best to ignore the human rights violations taking place in Europe and Asia. Struggling to cope with the Great Depression, Americans were hesitant to sacrifice their lives and money to safeguard the rights of other people.

MORE WAR, MORE ATROCITIES

Events in Europe, however, soon forced Americans to pay attention. As the troubles of the 1930s erupted into World War II, all the atrocities of World War I were repeated but on an even larger scale. The fighting in the Soviet Union alone left 20 million or more people dead. In China perhaps 15 million died. Germany lost more than 4 million, Japan more than 2 million.

More than any previous war, World War II placed civilians at the center of the fighting. Aerial bombardment of cities played an important role in the strategy of both sides, from the German attacks on London in 1940 to the Allied firebombing of Dresden and Tokyo and the U.S. atomic bombing of Hiroshima and Nagasaki. Unavoidably, and in some cases deliberately, most of the casualties in the bombing attacks against cities were civilians.

Some atrocities took place far from the fighting. Japan, for example, forcibly removed thousands of Korean men from their homeland to work in Japanese war industries and to fight in the war.

And in the most appalling atrocity of the war years—the Nazi Holocaust—some six million Jews and millions of others were killed (see Chapter 16).

▪▪ **World War II witnessed massive violations of human rights, including the attempted genocide of the Jews in the Nazi Holocaust.**

RENEWED HUMAN RIGHTS EFFORTS

With the war raging on and human rights in grave peril, President Roosevelt helped initiate what he termed a "declaration by United Nations." Issued at the start of 1942 by the United States and 25 other nations fighting against Germany and Japan, the declaration reaffirmed the principles of the Atlantic Charter and pledged the signing nations to "defend life, liberty, independence, and religious freedom, and to preserve human rights and justice in their own lands as well as in other lands." The declaration built not only on the Atlantic Charter but also on an earlier speech of Roosevelt's in which he had told Congress that it must be the goal of the United States to guarantee a world founded on "four essential human freedoms—freedom of speech and expression, freedom of worship, freedom from want, freedom from fear."

After the war ended, the international community took further steps to safeguard human rights. In the Nuremberg trials, Nazi leaders were convicted of planning and participating in genocide as well as in a host of other "crimes

◀ On April 30, 1945, prisoners in the concentration camp at Dachau, Germany, cheered as the U.S. Seventh Army set them free.

🔵 **THE AMERICAN NATION VIDEODISC PROGRAM**

Japanese Americans in Relocation Camps

2A	43252 :49

AV TRANSPARENCY
Everyday Life in America Transparency and **Worksheet 26**

MAKING CONNECTIONS

Art

Roosevelt's idea of "four freedoms" appealed to many people. In 1943 artist Norman Rockwell produced a painting called *Four Freedoms* illustrating each concept described by Roosevelt.

RETEACH Organize students into small groups and assign one subsection to each group. Direct each group to develop questions about the main ideas in its subsection. Then have each group exchange its questions with another group and work to answer the questions it receives.

Closure

Refer students to President Roosevelt's list of "four essential human freedoms" on p. 707. Have them discuss if these freedoms describe basic human rights as they see them. Ask them which, if any, rights they would add to the list and why.

Extension

INVESTIGATE Have students investigate the work the American Friends Service Committee does today to support human rights. Suggest that they present their findings in an oral report.

EVALUATE Have students review the Universal Declaration of Human Rights. Ask them to write a brief essay explaining which of the declaration's articles they think is most important.

PRIMARY SOURCE

Description of Change: excerpted
Rationale: excerpted to focus on main idea

SECTION REVIEW ANSWERS

IDENTIFY

For significance, see the following pages:
Geneva Convention (p. 703)
Red Cross (p. 703)
Hague Peace Conferences (p. 703)
American Friends Service Committee (p. 705)
Universal Declaration of Human Rights (p. 708)

1. *World War I caused many people to doubt that respect for human rights was growing. The League of Nations, the disarmament conference of 1921–1922, and a number of private organizations worked to protect human rights.*
2. *fascism—rights belonged only to the state, some racial groups inferior; militarism—used violence to subdue others*
3. *Nuremberg trials, foundation of United Nations, adoption of Universal Declaration of Human Rights*
4. *Brochures should discuss humanitarian aid and pacifism.*
5. *Students should discuss racism, the violence of war, and the development of new weapons, as well as the international nature of efforts to protect human rights.*

▲ **Hideki Tōjō, former Japanese general, testifies on his own behalf during war crimes trials in Tokyo, Japan, on December 26, 1947.**

against humanity." The message was clear: certain human rights must be respected regardless of a person's nationality or ethnic background. This concern with human rights was also enshrined in the United Nations. The new organization committed itself to a new order in the world, as expressed by the preamble to its charter, written in 1945:

> 66 We the peoples of the United Nations determined . . . to reaffirm faith in fundamental human rights, in the dignity and worth of the human person, in the equal rights of men and women and of nations large and small . . . have resolved to combine our efforts to accomplish these aims. 99

The UN charter also declared that the United Nations would promote "universal respect for, and observance of, human rights and fundamental freedoms for all without distinction as to race, sex, language or religion."

Some UN member nations, however, remained unsatisfied with the charter and called for the inclusion of a Bill of Rights. President Truman endorsed this idea, declaring "The Charter is dedicated to the achievement and observance of human rights and fundamental freedoms. Unless we can attain those objectives . . . we cannot have permanent peace and security." On December 10, 1948, the United Nations General Assembly adopted the **Universal Declaration of Human Rights** "as a common standard of achievement for all peoples and all nations." The document went on to list a series of rights held by "all human beings."

As important as the Declaration of Human Rights was, it was not binding on all nations. It was a statement of intent but provided no means of enforcement. Indeed, many countries insisted that any efforts at enforcement would violate another UN principle—the guarantee of national sovereignty. This apparent contradiction would remain an issue for years to come.

■■ **After World War II, the international community tried to protect human rights by forming the UN and by issuing the Universal Declaration of Human Rights.**

■■ SECTION 2 REVIEW

IDENTIFY and explain the significance of the following: Geneva Convention, Red Cross, Hague Peace Conferences, American Friends Service Committee, Universal Declaration of Human Rights.

1. **MAIN IDEA** What effect did World War I have on people's thinking about human rights? What types of efforts to protect human rights arose following the war?
2. **MAIN IDEA** How did fascism in Europe and militarism in Japan affect human rights between World War I and World War II?
3. **MAIN IDEA** What steps did the international community take to safeguard human rights after World War II?
4. **WRITING TO INFORM** Imagine you are a member of a private peace organization during the 1920s. Write a brochure explaining how individuals might promote international peace.
5. **COMPARING** In what ways did World War I and World War II present similar threats to human rights? How were the efforts to protect human rights sparked by both wars similar?

PREVIEW WORKSHOP

Following is a list of the significant people and terms in this section. You may wish to use this list as a section preview.

People
■ Nelson Mandela
■ Simone de Beauvoir
■ Jehan Sadat
■ Benazir Bhutto

Terms
■ Convention on the Elimination of All Forms of Racial Discrimination
■ African National Congress
■ Convention on the Suppression of Apartheid

Section 3

STRIVING FOR EQUALITY

F O C U S

■ **How did the struggle for racial equality progress in the years after World War II?**

■ **What setbacks did the struggle for racial equality experience?**

■ **What features marked the struggle for women's rights in the postwar years?**

Benazir Bhutto, prime minister of Pakistan, 1988

𝓘n the years after World War II, the international community resumed its progress toward greater respect for human rights. Decolonization represented progress toward racial equality, as did the dismantling of the system of racial segregation in the United States. The struggle for equal rights for women, like the struggle for racial equality, increasingly became a worldwide struggle.

THE FIGHT FOR RACIAL EQUALITY

The wave of decolonization that swept across Asia and Africa during the years after World War II (see Chapter 23) represented one of the most important advances for human rights during the 20th century. The essence of the Western imperialism of the late 1800s and early 1900s was the belief that certain groups of people—typically Europeans—were suited to governing themselves and others, and that other groups of people—typically Asians and Africans—were suited to being governed. Thus decolonization was not simply an advance for the principle of political equality; it was also an advance for racial equality.

Worldwide effects of decolonization.

The struggle for decolonization had significant effects on the contest for racial equality in other parts of the world. In the United States, Americans had long prided themselves on being more enlightened, in terms of human rights, than people in most other countries. For the most part this was true, with the glaring exception of the second-class

treatment given African Americans and members of other ethnic minority groups. Yet as long as the countries of Western Europe—those closest to the United States in terms of respect for human rights—held colonies in Africa and Asia, Americans could comfort themselves that their system of racial segregation was, comparatively speaking, not so bad. As the Europeans freed their colonies, however, Americans found themselves in the position of being undeniably backward on the question of race.

This did not escape the notice of civil rights advocates. One of these advocates, Edwin Embree, spoke in 1945 about the changes occurring in the larger world and their importance for African Americans:

> 66 The white man of the Western world is offered his last chance for equal status in world society. If he accepts equality, he can hold a self-respecting place—maybe a leading place—in the new order. . . . But if the Western white man persists in trying to run the show, in exploiting the whole earth, in treating the hundreds of millions of his

FOCUS OBJECTIVES

■ Discuss how the struggle for racial equality progressed in the years after World War II.

■ Identify the setbacks that the struggle for racial equality experienced.

■ Describe the features that marked the struggle for women's rights in the postwar years.

PRIMARY SOURCE

Description of Change: excerpted
Rationale: excerpted to focus on main idea

CORE RESOURCES

• **Section 3 Daily Quiz**

AV RESOURCES

• ***The American Nation Videodisc: Martin Luther King, Jr.; The Women's Rights Movement***

MOTIVATING: PRIOR KNOWLEDGE

Ask students to recall the major events of the struggle for racial and sexual equality in the U.S. during the 1960s. Then point out that this section reviews the American push for civil rights in the context of the worldwide struggle for equality.

Teaching the Section

STRIVING FOR RACIAL EQUALITY

Organize students into small groups. Provide each group with a piece of butcher paper on which you have written the following headings: *Decolonization, Ending Segregation in the U.S.,* and *Actions of the UN.* Have group members add information under each heading, round-robin style, explaining how each helped to further racial equality. Select a group to use their butcher paper to demonstrate to the rest of the class how the struggle for racial equality progressed in the years after World War II.

MULTICULTURAL PERSPECTIVES

Kwame Nkrumah, the first president of the Ghana Republic, was one of the African leaders inspired by civil rights leaders from the Americas. As a student at Lincoln University in Pennsylvania, Nkrumah studied the ideas of Marcus Garvey. Eventually he turned away from Garvey, and later he asserted that the idea of "Africa for the Africans" should not encourage racial discrimination. Nkrumah said, "It only means that Africans shall and must govern themselves in their own countries."

THE AMERICAN NATION VIDEODISC PROGRAM
Martin Luther King, Jr.

2B   39585   2:09

neighbors as inferiors, then the fresh might of the billion and a half nonwhite, non-Western people may in a surging rebellion smash him into nonentity. 🟉🟉

In addition, many of the leaders of the American civil rights movement took inspiration from the methods used by anticolonial leaders. The nonviolent tactics that Mahatma Gandhi used against the British in India served as a particularly important model for U.S. civil rights strategies. Franklin McCain, one of the students who participated in the Greensboro lunch-counter sit-in of 1960, later recalled, "The individual who had probably the most influence on us was Gandhi, more than any single individual." And Martin Luther King, Jr., traveled to India to see the results of Gandhi's efforts and to meet many of his disciples. After King returned he told American civil rights activists that they were taking "honored places in the world-wide struggle for freedom."

Africa and America. The decolonization movement in Africa also had significant repercussions in America. The struggle for civil rights for African Americans and the nationalist movements in Africa already had a historical connection: one of the major influences on African nationalism was the Pan-Africanist movement begun by black American and Caribbean leaders like W.E.B. Du Bois and Marcus Garvey. Then as African nations began to gain independence in the 1950s and 1960s, many

▲ Martin Luther King, Jr., and his wife meet Indian Prime Minister Jawaharlal Nehru on their monthlong visit to India in 1959.

African Americans were inspired by their example to intensify the struggle for equal rights in the United States.

In 1964, for example, African American singer and actor Harry Belafonte sponsored a delegation of members of the Student Nonviolent Coordinating Committee on a tour of Africa. Most of the participants found the experience electrifying. "I saw black men flying the airplanes, driving buses, sitting behind big desks in the bank and just doing everything that I was used to seeing white people do," one SNCC worker, Fannie Lou Hamer, later remembered. Just as African nationalists had been inspired by African American leaders in the struggle for racial equality and civil rights, so now African nationalists were inspiring a new generation of African American leaders. It was not a coincidence that the busiest period of progress toward racial equality in the United States and the busiest period of decolonization in Africa both occurred during the decade between 1955 and 1965.

UN efforts. Legislation promoting racial equality in the United States was mirrored in the United Nations' efforts to end racism throughout the world. In 1965 the UN established the **Convention on the Elimination of All Forms of Racial Discrimination**. Under the terms of this agreement, which took effect in 1969, the signing nations agreed to declare the spread of ideas advocating any form of racial superiority or hatred to be illegal and punishable by law. Even further, the agreement called on the signers to outlaw all organizations engaging in such activities. By 1987, 129 nations had ratified the Convention.

▪▪ **Decolonization, the outlawing of racial segregation in the United States, and UN efforts to end racism worldwide represented steps toward racial equality.**

SOUTH AFRICA

The road toward racial equality was not a one-way street, however. At the same time the United States was beginning to dismantle its system of racial segregation, another country—South Africa—was reinforcing its system. Racial discrimination had been a fact of life in South Africa

SETBACKS IN SOUTH AFRICA

Organize students into several groups to act as the public relations division of a human rights organization. Direct groups to create an advertisement that illustrates the impact of apartheid on the global effort to secure racial equality. Have some groups create full-page newspaper or magazine advertisements. Others might create billboards or radio or television spots. Ask volunteers to present and discuss their advertisements.

THE STRUGGLE FOR WOMEN'S RIGHTS

Have students work in pairs to prepare dialogues in which western and nonwestern women discuss their views of women's rights. Ask volunteer pairs to present their dialogues to the class. Have students take notes as the dialogues are presented. Direct them to use the notes to write a few sentences summarizing points of agreement and disagreement between western and non-western women on the definition of rights.

HISTORY in the Making

BY DR. STERLING STUCKEY

Songs of Freedom

Although African nationalism provided inspiration for civil rights leaders in the United States, the roots of the U.S. civil rights movement lay in America's slave past. The black struggle for equality in the 1950s and 1960s was based on an African American culture of great spiritual depth that had arisen out of the experience of slavery in the South.

As a result of this rich cultural heritage—together with continued and often brutal oppression—the movement for African American rights began not in the North, as many people of the time expected, but in the South. Southern black musical traditions, in particular, helped fuel the civil rights movement in its drive to end racial discrimination and violence against blacks.

Wyatt Tee Walker, an aide to Martin Luther King. Jr., summed up the impact of music on the movement when he stated that "there was no movement in the South that was not a great singing movement." During the Montgomery bus boycott, for example, Georgia Black of the Holt Street Baptist Church—where the boycott officially began—

sang slave songs to inspire blacks to continue to oppose segregated seating on buses:

> We got to hold up the
> Bloodstained banner
> One Day I'm gonna get old
> And Can't fight anymore
> But I'm gonna
> Fight anyhow
> We got to hold it up
> Until we die.

Dorothy Cotton, who worked with the Southern Christian Leadership Conference, recalled that during the 1960s, meetings to encourage blacks to vote "began with the songs of our ancestors. . . . Fannie Lou [Hamer] would stand up and tell tales of intimidation of people on plantations and sing her songs." One of the songs Hamer inspired her listeners with was "This Little Light of Mine":

> The light that shines is the light of Love
> Lights the darkness from above
> It shines on me, and shines on you
> And shows what the power of love can do
>
> I'm gonna shine my light both far and near

> I'm gonna shine my light both bright and clear
> Where there's a dark corner in this land
> I'm gonna let my little light shine.

Singing provided a source of inspiration and strength to the movement especially during periods of hardship. When Freedom Riders were arrested and jailed in Jackson, Mississippi, many of them sang as a way of keeping up their spirits. Prison officials feared the power of the music and threatened to take away the singers' mattresses if they kept singing. But they continued to sing anyway:

> Ain't gonna let nobody turn me 'round
> turn me 'round, turn me 'round
> Ain't gonna let nobody turn me 'round
> I'm gonna keep on a-walking, keep on a-talkin'
> Marchin' up to freedom land.

In 1942, renowned singer and actor Paul Robeson—who himself worked very hard to preserve slave songs—had remarked that he believed southern blacks to be "a race that has come through its trials unbroken, a race of such magnificence of spirit that there exists no power on earth that could crush them." Robeson knew that the freedom struggle to come would be based on the cultural riches of the black past.

▼ Both blacks and whites joined this march for civil rights.

PRIMARY SOURCES
Description of Change: excerpted
Rationale: excerpted to focus on main idea

GLOBAL CONNECTIONS

During Kenya's Mau Mau rebellion of the 1950s, songs were used to educate and politicize the general population and to urge Kenyans to oppose the British. Songs were also used to describe suffering in prison camps and to detail the sacrifices made by rebels.

Practice

GUIDED PRACTICE

Write on the chalkboard the section's main headings and inform students that these are topics for a news story titled "Striving for Equality." Call on volunteers to outline information for each topic, noting their suggestions under the appropriate title.

INDEPENDENT PRACTICE

Direct students to use the outline developed in the Guided Practice activity to write the news story. Students might also suggest illustrations to accompany their stories. Students may wish to include their stories in their portfolios.

Review and Assessment

REVIEW Ask students to work in pairs to write sentences that explain how each entry in the Preview Workshop is related to the main idea of the subsection in which it is located. Have pairs share their sentences with the rest of the class. Then assign the Section 3 Review on p. 713.

ASSESS Assign the **Section 3 Daily Quiz** in *Core Resources.*

MULTICULTURAL PERSPECTIVES

Asma Jahangir, a Pakistani human rights advocate, has supported improvements in the status of religious minorities in Pakistan. She writes: "Minorities should be allowed to preserve their own ethnic and cultural identity, yet encouraged to fight for social reform and change within their own group. They must be encouraged to develop among themselves a consciousness so that minority groups would not be frogs in a well but would have the capacity to unite with national human rights groups to press for change and reform in the society as a whole. . . . The focus should be directed mainly on individual rights while seeking to preserve the humane traditions and practices of minorities."

THE AMERICAN NATION VIDEODISC PROGRAM

The Women's Rights Movement

1B   48258   0:32

712

for many years, but not until the late 1940s did the government put a rigid system of legal separation of the races, called apartheid, into effect.

Ironically, apartheid was to some degree a reaction to the same events that were causing Americans to end their system of segregation. As independence movements gained strength in black Africa, the whites who ruled South Africa, which had gained its independence from Britain in 1910, feared black South Africans' demands for political and social equality. This white minority used apartheid as a way of reinforcing its position against these demands.

Black South Africans protested the policy of apartheid, as did some white South Africans. Many blacks died in the protests, while others were driven into exile. Still others were arrested and sentenced to long prison terms. One such person was Nelson Mandela, a leader of the **African National Congress**, the major black nationalist organization in South Africa.

Many nations around the world also objected to the policy of apartheid. Some imposed economic sanctions on South Africa, and in 1973 the UN General Assembly passed the **Convention on the Suppression of Apartheid**.

■■ **The establishment of apartheid in South Africa represented a step backward in global efforts to secure racial equality.**

▲ This 1990 photograph shows Nelson and Winnie Mandela saluting well-wishers outside South Africa's Victor Vorstor prison. Mandela became the first black president of South Africa in 1994.

WOMEN'S RIGHTS IN THE POSTWAR ERA

As in the struggle to end slavery, women played an important part in the campaign for racial equality. And as in the earlier fight, the struggle on behalf of other people's civil rights made many women aware of the need to fight for their own rights. French feminist Simone de Beauvoir, for example, likened the condition of women in a male-dominated society to that of Asians and Africans under Western imperialism and to that of blacks who suffered under white oppression.

The question of equality for women was not just a Western problem. In parts of Southwest Asia and North Africa, for example, some male authorities sought to restrict women's activities. Though men sometimes cited the Qur'an, the holy book of Islam, as justification for their actions, some prominent Muslim women denied that Islam provided grounds for the subjugation of women. For instance, Jehan Sadat, the wife of Egyptian president Anwar Sadat, declared:

▲ During the mid-1900s Simone de Beauvoir, noted French intellectual and feminist, called for the abolition of the myth of the "eternal feminine."

❝ Nothing in our religion supported the total subservience of women. In no place in the Quran is it written that women must remain at home and do no work in public. No. The Quran treats men and women equally, in life and in death. ❞

Women like Jehan Sadat sometimes traveled to Europe and the United States and observed the comparative freedoms women enjoyed there. For example, by the 1970s nearly all legal barriers to sexual equality in the United States had been eliminated, although the proposed Equal Rights Amendment to the Constitution fell short of the 38-state approval required for ratification (see Chapter 21).

RETEACH Have students work in groups, assigning individuals or pairs the task of outlining subsections. Direct individuals or pairs to exchange outlines and use them to ask questions of other members of the group.

Closure

Have students discuss whether the postwar struggle for equality was successful. Have them cite evidence from the section to support their judgments.

Extension

EVALUATE Have students write an essay evaluating the influence of African independence movements on the civil rights movement in the U.S.

RESEARCH Have students research and write a biographical sketch of one of the women leaders mentioned in the section.

▲ Demonstrators rallied at the Lincoln Memorial on October 12, 1981, in an attempt to obtain ratification of the Equal Rights Amendment.

Although some women of the Middle East called for women's rights comparable to those in the West, others rejected Western notions of women's rights. In the Islamic world particularly, women's rights movements often proclaimed the rights of women not in Western terms but as laid down in the Qur'an. In part, perhaps, this was because, at least in theory, Muslim women had long had some rights which Western women had only recently attained. As Sadat wrote in her autobiography, *A Woman of Egypt*:

66 More than fourteen hundred centuries ago Islam had . . . given women the right to equal education, the right to work and open their own businesses, the right to initiate legal action and the right to buy and sell property. It would take hundreds of years before women from the more "enlightened" countries of Europe were given the same privileges. 99

For example, at a time when few American women held high elective office and none had been seriously considered as a presidential candidate, several foreign countries chose women as their leaders. Indira Gandhi became prime minister of India following an impressive performance as the nation's minister of information and broadcasting. Her actions, contrasted to those of her male colleagues, won her a reputation as "the only man in a Cabinet of old women," according to one bold observer.

Gandhi was not alone. Golda Meir, a Russian-born, American-raised Israeli, assumed the premiership of Israel in 1969. In 1979 Margaret Thatcher became prime minister of Great Britain and held that office longer than any other British prime minister in the 20th century. In the Philippines Corazon Aquino became president in 1986. Benazir Bhutto became the first female leader of an Islamic nation when she was elected prime minister of Pakistan in 1988.

▼ Indira Gandhi, daughter of Jawaharlal Nehru, served as prime minister of India from 1966 to 1977 and from 1980 to 1984.

■■ The struggle for women's rights became increasingly global in the decades after World War II. But not all women defined rights in the same way.

PRIMARY SOURCE
Description of Change: excerpted
Rationale: excerpted to focus on main idea

SECTION REVIEW ANSWERS

IDENTIFY
For significance, see the following pages:
Convention on the Elimination of All Forms of Racial Discrimination (p. 710)
Nelson Mandela (p. 711)
African National Congress (p. 711)
Convention on the Suppression of Apartheid (p. 711)
Simone de Beauvoir (p. 711)
Jehan Sadat (p. 711)
Benazir Bhutto (p. 712)

1. *decolonization, outlawing racial segregation in United States, UN agreements*
2. *reinforced power of white minority over black South Africans and represented a step backward*
3. *Not all women defined rights in the same way, but the number of women political leaders increased.*
4. *Articles should reflect the influence of the Pan-African movement and inspiration of leaders such as Gandhi.*
5. *African nationalists, inspired by the struggle for black suffrage in the U.S., now inspired U.S. civil rights leaders. Women who worked for civil rights for different racial minorities began to question the ways their own rights were limited.*

SECTION 3 REVIEW

IDENTIFY and explain the significance of the following: Convention on the Elimination of All Forms of Racial Discrimination, Nelson Mandela, African National Congress, Convention on the Suppression of Apartheid, Simone de Beauvoir, Jehan Sadat, Benazir Bhutto.

1. **MAIN IDEA** What events advanced the struggle for racial equality following World War II?
2. **MAIN IDEA** How did the establishment of apartheid in South Africa affect the struggle for racial equality?
3. **MAIN IDEA** What were some of the characteristics of efforts to secure women's rights after World War II?
4. **WRITING TO EVALUATE** Imagine you are a U.S. civil rights leader. Write an article that evaluates the relationship between the U.S. civil rights movement and decolonization in Asia and Africa.
5. **SYNTHESIZING** How did the post–World War II movements to secure racial equality and women's rights build on the successes of earlier efforts?

Following is a list of the significant people and terms in this section. You may wish to use this list as a section preview.

People
- Patricia Derian
- Daw Aung San Suu Kyi

Terms
- Covenant on Civil and Political Rights
- Covenant on Economic, Social, and Cultural Rights

MOTIVATING: STUDENT EXPERIENCES

Ask students who have volunteered for an organization dedicated to human rights—Amnesty International, for example—to share their experiences. Then point out that while great progress in human rights has been made in recent years, many challenges remain. Organizations like Amnesty International keep the attention of governments, and individuals, focused on human rights issues.

FOCUS OBJECTIVES

- Discuss how efforts to protect human rights fared in the 1960s and early 1970s.

- Explain how the Carter administration dealt with human rights.

- Identify the human rights improvements that have taken place in recent years and the threats to human rights that remain.

Section 4

THE CONTINUING STRUGGLE

F O C U S

- **How did efforts to protect human rights fare in the 1960s and early 1970s?**
- **How did the Carter administration deal with human rights?**
- **What human rights improvements have taken place in recent years? What threats to human rights remain?**

Beyond the fight for racial and sexual equality, the post–World War II period witnessed a continuing international effort to expand human rights. The United Nations issued important proclamations on human rights, and during the late 1970s the administration of Jimmy Carter made respect for human rights a priority in American diplomacy. A major breakthrough for human rights came with the end of the Cold War, which had led to many rights violations. Yet threats to human rights remained.

Soviet physicist Andrei Sakharov voting in Moscow, 1989

HUMAN RIGHTS AND THE COLD WAR

Human rights continued to be central to UN activities in the decades following decolonization. In 1966 the UN General Assembly approved two covenants on human rights. The first was the **Covenant on Civil and Political Rights**. The nations signing this covenant pledged not to take actions that would interfere with the liberties of individuals.

The second agreement was the **Covenant on Economic, Social, and Cultural Rights**. Its provisions were different from the first set, for many of them required governments not only to refrain from certain actions but also to take positive measures such as providing jobs, increasing educational opportunities, and improving health care.

The absence of any enforcement agency, however, made the covenants little more than promises, and many nations disregarded them. For example, the Soviet Union often subjected political dissidents

such as Andrei Sakharov to "internal exile" in Siberia. Other dissidents were committed to psychiatric hospitals for "antisocial behavior." China, too, was frequently criticized for its treatment of dissidents and for other human rights abuses.

Communist countries were not the only ones where human rights were threatened. Many right-wing regimes—some of which were supported by the U.S. government in its eagerness to fight communism worldwide—also had little tolerance for political dissent. This was particularly true in Central and South America. For example, the Pinochet regime in Chile, which seized power after the 1973 overthrow of Salvador Allende (see Chapter 21), was frequently cited by human rights organizations for its use of torture and for repressing political opposition.

During the postwar years the UN reaffirmed its support for human rights. However, human rights violations continued.

HUMAN RIGHTS DURING THE COLD WAR

Have students work in small groups to prepare the front page of a newspaper that illustrates the major human rights issues of the Cold War years. Suggest that groups include stories that review human rights challenges country by country, examining failures as well as successes. Call on groups to display and discuss their front pages.

A NEW APPROACH TO HUMAN RIGHTS

Select three students to role-play participants in a call-in radio talk show. One student should play the show host, another should play a supporter of President Carter's human rights policy, and the third should play a critic of the Carter policy. Have the host interview the guests on their views. Encourage the rest of the class to participate by "calling-in" questions and comments on the policy.

SUCCESSES AND CHALLENGES

Have students work in small groups to write scripts for a five-minute television news story on human rights improvements in recent years and the threats to human rights that remain. Suggest that groups include in their scripts ideas for visuals to illustrate the story. Ask groups to present and discuss their news stories. Then lead the class in a discussion on what they consider the greatest threat to continuing progress in the area of human rights. ▶

CARTER AND HUMAN RIGHTS

When Jimmy Carter took office as president in 1977, he resolved to make human rights a major concern of U.S. foreign policy. For too long, Carter said, the United States had allowed its fear of communism to govern all actions. For too long the nation had tolerated the human rights abuses of certain regimes simply because they were anticommunist.

To help implement his human rights policy, Carter appointed Patricia Derian as the assistant secretary of state for human rights and humanitarian affairs. Derian, a former civil rights worker from Mississippi, had no patience for those who held that the United States might realistically have to tolerate moderately repressive regimes. She demanded to know what "moderately repressive" meant: "That you only torture half of the people?"

▲ Patricia Derian opposed aid to repressive regimes.

In her work at the State Department, Derian tried to pressure countries to improve their human rights records by linking human rights to U.S. economic aid. For example, when the U.S. government sent offers of aid to Brazil, El Salvador, Guatemala, Uruguay, and Argentina, Derian's staff attached critiques of the human rights records of those countries' governments. Such efforts did not always produce the desired results; many nations refused U.S. aid and criticized Carter for interfering in their internal affairs.

Some human rights advances did, however, occur while Carter was in office. Indonesia, for example, released thousands of political prisoners; Argentina eased up on repression of dissent. Equally important, Carter's policy sent the message that the United States placed human rights at the top of its diplomatic agenda. For the United Nations to issue paper proclamations in favor of human rights was one thing; for the world's most powerful country to employ its political leverage and economic muscle on behalf of human rights was something else.

■■ During the late 1970s President Carter made human rights a centerpiece of U.S. foreign policy.

THE END OF THE COLD WAR

Some of Carter's critics complained that he devoted his main efforts to nations they considered to be minor offenders of human rights, such as Argentina, while leaving major offenders like the Soviet Union alone. This criticism was not entirely justified. For example, Carter engaged in a correspondence with Soviet dissident Andrei Sakharov that outraged the Kremlin and highlighted the need for reform of the Soviet system. Nevertheless, there was something to the claim that human rights would have been advanced more by even small changes in the Soviet Union than by large changes in most smaller countries.

During the late 1980s and early 1990s, changes in the Soviet Union did take place, and they were not small. Just as the breakup of the European empires in Asia and Africa had boosted human rights, so too did the collapse of the Soviet sphere. The region's new governments did not perfectly protect human rights—particularly when ethnic tensions led to violence, as in Yugoslavia. But in general, the new systems were an improvement over what they replaced. Repressive institutions had come crumbling down. Democratic elections gave people a chance to choose their own leaders.

Recent improvements in human rights cannot all be directly linked to the end of the Cold War. In South Africa, for example, apartheid began to crumble in the late 1980s, and in 1990 the South African government released Nelson Mandela and others who had been imprisoned for protesting apartheid. In 1994 the nation held its first election in which blacks were free to vote and elected Nelson Mandela president.

■■ The collapse of the Soviet system and the end of apartheid in South Africa led to improvements in human rights.

▼ In 1988, Armenians rallied in Moscow's Armenian cemetery to protest the treatment of Armenians in Azerbaijan.

MULTICULTURAL PERSPECTIVES

Jimmy Carter was not the only world leader to condemn human rights abuses. In 1989 Pope John Paul II criticized the Hong Kong government for its decision to return Vietnamese refugees to Vietnam, saying, "Our heart cannot remain insensitive and indifferent in the face of such grave decisions that affect so dramatically the lives of many persons, including women and children."

COOPERATIVE LEARNING

Divide the class into small groups. Ask each group to consider how the United States might rely on foreign policy to end human rights abuses in other countries. Groups should develop charts that list pros and cons of each policy element. Have each student present one of the proposed policy measures to the class.

*P*ractice

GUIDED PRACTICE

Ask students to identify countries where human rights violations have occurred recently. List their suggestions on the chalkboard. For each country, ask students to discuss how the U.S. should react. Note their responses on the chalkboard.

INDEPENDENT PRACTICE

Direct students to select one of the countries listed in Guided Practice. Encourage them to write letters to the editor of a local newspaper explaining the steps the U.S. should take to respond to human rights abuses in the country selected. Call on volunteers to read their letters to the class. Students may wish to include their letters in their portfolios.

*R*eview and *A*ssessment

REVIEW Have students write 10 questions on Section 4 on individual notecards with the answers on the reverse side. Then divide students into groups of four. Ask them to use their notecards to question the other members of the group. Then assign the Section 4 Review on p. 717.

ASSESS Assign the **Section 4 Daily Quiz** in *Core Resources.*

HISTORICAL SIDELIGHTS

Chinese Prison Labor
A U.S. government source reported that in 1991, officials from the U.S. consulate in Canton discovered that prison labor was used to make shoes in China. The main destination for the shoes was the United States, even though U.S. policy banned the import of products made in prison.

BIOGRAPHY PERSONALITIES IN HISTORY

In 1994 leaders of Burma's State Law and Order Restoration Council (SLORC) met with Suu Kyi in what many observers felt was an attempt to increase control over opposition to the government. Peter Engardio, a specialist in Asian affairs said, "For SLORC to meet with her is tantamount to recognizing her."

PRIMARY SOURCE

Description of Change: excerpted
Rationale: excerpted to focus on main idea

Chart Caption Answer
because people should have the right to know the charges against them in order to defend themselves

---

*R*EMAINING CHALLENGES

Despite many recent human rights improvements around the world, some nations are still being criticized for violations. For example, although the Communist government of China has permitted economic reform, it has resisted political reform and has stifled dissent, as the Tiananmen Square bloodbath demonstrated. In addition, one human rights group, Human Rights Watch/Asia, reported in 1994 that some 2,000 to 3,000 people executed in China were the main source for organ transplants, and that some prisoners had organs removed while they were still alive.

The rights issue in China stirred considerable interest among Americans when President Clinton announced that the United States would revoke China's trade privileges if the Chinese government did not improve its human rights record. China made few significant changes to its policies, but Clinton backed down and renewed the trade privileges anyway.

Another Asian nation that has come under attack for human rights violations is Burma. After seizing power in 1988, the new military government proceeded to suppress dissenters. One such dissenter was Daw Aung San Suu Kyi (daw awng sahn sue chee).

BIOGRAPHY   Born in 1945, Suu Kyi was the daughter of a hero of the 1940s Burmese independence movement against British rule. Although Suu Kyi lived most of her adult life in the West, she returned to Burma in 1988. With two other opposition leaders, she formed a movement to restore democracy. The military government responded in 1989 by placing her under house arrest. But Suu Kyi's convictions remained firm. Even when the government offered to free her if she ceased her political efforts and left the country, she refused. Her vision of the ideal government was similar to that of many other political reformers throughout the world:

▶ **Daw Aung San Suu Kyi**

❝ To provide the people with . . . peace and security, rulers must observe . . . the concepts of truth, righteousness, and loving kindness. It is government based on these very qualities that the people of Burma are seeking in their struggle for democracy. ❞

HUMAN RIGHTS ABUSES AROUND THE WORLD IN 1993

Amnesty International, a London-based organization that publicizes cases of political repression, torture, and the imprisonment of people for their political beliefs, reported that the following abuses and events took place in 1993:

- **THE WORLD:** More than 100,000 known political prisoners were held without charge or trial in 53 nations. Prisoners were tortured or ill-treated by more than 112 governments.
- **EUROPE:** In the United Kingdom, armed political groups killed 63 civilians. Reports of torture or ill-treatment of detainees were made in 26 nations, including France, Spain, and Turkey.
- **ASIA:** Bombings of homes, hospitals, and mosques left hundreds dead and thousands injured in Afghanistan. Torture and ill-treatment of peaceful protesters, political detainees, and criminal suspects was common in 19 Asian nations, including China and Indonesia.
- **LATIN AMERICA:** Reports of torture and ill-treatment by police were widespread in Venezuela, Mexico, and Peru. Hundreds of people in Colombia were executed without trial.
- **AFRICA:** Hundreds of "disappearances" and executions without trial were reported in 20 African nations, including Angola, Chad, Senegal, and Zaire. In South Africa detainees were tortured by the police and army.
- **THE MIDDLE EAST:** Prisoners of conscience were held in 11 nations, including Morocco, Syria, and Tunisia. Detainees were tortured in 15 countries, including Egypt, Iran, and Israel.

AT GREATEST RISK In many nations the people most likely to suffer from human rights violations in 1993 were human rights supporters. "Human rights defenders often became the first victims of governments trying to build a good human rights image abroad and fearful of the damage human rights activists can do to that image," said Amnesty International.

? **EVALUATING** Why is holding a prisoner without charge considered to be a human rights violation?

Amnesty International Symbol

RETEACH Suggest that students work in small groups, with each student assigned the task of summarizing the information in a subsection by designing a poster. Have groups present their posters.

Closure

Point out that some observers suggested that the collapse of communism led to the creation of a "new world order." Have students discuss whether, in light of recent human rights developments, this is a suitable description of the post-communist world.

Extension

CREATE Encourage students to use information from this text, current affairs magazines, and other sources such as *The New State of the World Atlas* to construct a world map showing areas where human rights are under threat.

EVALUATE Have students read the quote by John Gray on p. 717. Have them write a brief paragraph explaining whether they agree or disagree with Gray's view.

HUMAN RIGHTS OR CULTURAL IMPERIALISM?

Some people, particularly in non-Western nations, object to what they perceive as a Western emphasis on the importance of individual rights. Many claim that their conceptions of rights are governed by a different set of cultural values that place more emphasis on communities of people than on individuals. They claim that when the United States and other Western nations try to impose their sense of human rights on other peoples, these nations are practicing a form of cultural imperialism. "Human rights in Iran are based on Islamic values," said Iran's foreign minister in 1994 in response to complaints from Western human rights groups about some Iranian policies. "We will not accept the values of foreign countries imposed on us under the cover of human rights."

Even some Westerners are critical of Western nations' attempts to influence human rights policies elsewhere. In the British newspaper *The Guardian*, John Gray of Oxford University wrote:

THROUGH OTHERS' EYES

> **❝** *For the most part, Western thought and policy remain based on the premise that Western ideals and practices have universal authority. . . . The American presumption is that any regime that does not conform to Western, and more particularly American, conceptions of human rights is tyrannical and illegitimate. The hubris [arrogant pride] expressed in this American belief is staggering. After all, America ranks foremost among Western societies in its record for homicide and other forms of violent crime. . . . If the U.S. has been unable to protect the ordinary liberties of its citizenry . . . , by what right does it judge the Asian countries?* **❞**

For her efforts, Suu Kyi was awarded the Nobel Peace Prize in 1991. Still under house arrest, however, she was unable to attend the awards ceremony in Oslo, Norway.

▣ **Even in the post–Cold War era, challenges to human rights remained in nations such as China and Burma.**

SECTION 4 REVIEW

IDENTIFY and explain the significance of the following: Covenant on Civil and Political Rights, Covenant on Economic, Social, and Cultural Rights, Patricia Derian, Daw Aung San Suu Kyi.

1. **MAIN IDEA** How did the United Nations show its support for human rights in the 1960s? How successful were the UN efforts at preventing human rights violations over the following years?

2. **MAIN IDEA** What approach did President Carter take toward the issue of human rights in American foreign policy?

3. **IDENTIFYING CAUSE AND EFFECT** What effects did the end of the Cold War have on human rights? How have human rights improved in South Africa?

4. **WRITING TO CREATE** Imagine you are a political prisoner in China or Burma. Write a poem about what events landed you in prison.

5. **TAKING A STAND** To what extent do you think the United States should interfere when other nations take actions that many Americans consider to be human rights violations?

SECTION REVIEW ANSWERS

IDENTIFY

For significance, see the following pages:
Covenant on Civil and Political Rights (p. 714)
Covenant on Economic, Social and Cultural Rights (p. 714)
Patricia Derian (p. 715)
Daw Aung San Suu Kyi (p. 716)

1. *passed covenants supporting human rights, but lacked ability to enforce rulings*
2. *linked economic aid to human rights*
3. *Human rights have improved with the end of the Cold War and the elimination of apartheid.*
4. *Poems should discuss efforts to improve human rights in either nation.*
5. *Answers will vary, but should reflect an understanding of human rights issues and of national sovereignty.*

Chapter Review Answers

WRITING A SUMMARY
See Essential Points in each section for main ideas.

REVIEWING CHRONOLOGY
4, 1, 5, 3, 2
Analyzing
The declaration lacked any means of enforcement.

IDENTIFYING PEOPLE AND IDEAS
1. *English philosopher who argued that governments existed to protect rights*
2. *abolitionist who worked to end slavery in British Empire*
3. *British women's rights organization*
4. *international humanitarian organization*
5. *established provisions to regulate naval warfare*
6. *Egyptian president's wife who described women's rights provided by Muslim law*
7. *French feminist who compared women's status to imperialism*
8. *South African black nationalist organization*
9. *assistant secretary of state for human rights and humanitarian affairs for President Carter*
10. *UN agreement that countries would not take actions limiting individual liberties*

UNDERSTANDING MAIN IDEAS

1. British abolitionists worked to end slavery throughout the British Empire, newly independent Latin American nations outlawed slavery, and Russia ended serfdom.
2. The rise of fascist and militarist governments encouraged racism.
3. Many African leaders were inspired by earlier U.S. civil rights leaders, and they in turn served as models for the American civil rights movement of the 1950s and 1960s.
4. Universal Declaration of Human Rights, Convention on the Elimination of All Forms of Racial Discrimination, Convention on the Suppression of Apartheid, Covenant on Civil and Political Rights, Covenant on Economic, Social, and Cultural Rights
5. spread of democracy and end of repressive institutions; China, Burma, Afghanistan, Indonesia, Venezuela, Mexico, Peru, Angola, Chad, Senegal, Zaire, South Africa, Morocco, Syria, Tunisia, Egypt, Iran, Israel

CHAPTER 26
Review

Parliament bans slavery in the British Empire. — 1833

Seneca Falls Convention held. — 1848

Geneva Convention signed. — 1864

Emmeline Pankhurst forms the Women's Social and Political Union in Britain. — 1903

Quakers found the AFSC. — 1917

WRITING A SUMMARY
Using the essential points of the chapter as a guide, write a summary of the chapter.

REVIEWING CHRONOLOGY
Number your paper 1 to 5. Study the time line above, and list the following events in the order in which they happened by writing the first next to 1, the second next to 2, and so on. Then complete the activity below.

1. UN approves two covenants on human rights.
2. Parliament bans slavery in the British Empire.
3. Tiananmen Square massacre occurs in China.
4. Jesse Owens wins four gold medals at Olympics.
5. Quakers found the AFSC.

Analyzing Why was the Universal Declaration of Human Rights of limited use in stopping human rights violations worldwide?

IDENTIFYING PEOPLE AND IDEAS
Explain the historical significance of each of the following people or terms.

1. John Locke
2. William Wilberforce
3. Women's Social and Political Union
4. Red Cross
5. Hague Peace Conferences
6. Jehan Sadat
7. Simone de Beauvoir
8. African National Congress
9. Patricia Derian
10. Covenant on Civil and Political Rights

UNDERSTANDING MAIN IDEAS
1. How was the struggle to abolish slavery in the 19th century a global effort?
2. What human rights violations occurred during and between World Wars I and II?
3. How was decolonization in Asia and in Africa related to the U.S. civil rights movement?
4. What major UN agreements have tried to promote international respect for human rights?
5. How have human rights improved in the former Soviet sphere? What are some of the nations in which human rights violations continue?

REVIEWING THEMES
1. **Democratic Values** How did the goals of the 19th-century women's movement reflect a link between women's rights and democracy?
2. **Global Relations** How have nations used economic means to encourage other nations to respect human rights? Give examples.
3. **Cultural Diversity** How have conceptions of human rights differed over time and from culture to culture? Give specific examples.

THINKING CRITICALLY
1. **Synthesizing** How did progressivism further the cause of human rights in the United States?
2. **Analyzing** Why did South Africa's white minority institute apartheid following World War II?
3. **Classifying** How might human rights be classified into several different categories?

STRATEGY FOR SUCCESS
Write a rough draft of a news story reporting on a current local, national, or international human rights issue. Then review the Strategies for Success on Evaluating News Stories on page 616. Read the drafts of the news stories prepared by two of your classmates, and take turns evaluating each others' stories. Revise your story after it has been evaluated.

UNITÉ INDIVISIBILITÉ DE LA RÉPUBLIQUE LIBERTÉ ÉGALITÉ FRATERNITÉ OU LA MORT

The motto of the French Revolution, "Unity, indivisibility of the Republic, liberty, equality, fraternity or death" exemplified the growing concern for human rights during the late 18th century.

1. The 19th-century women's movement linked women's rights and democracy by emphasizing voting rights.

2. Nations have used economic measures such as embargoes and tariffs to encourage other nations to respect human rights.

3. Answers will vary, but may reflect the different definitions of rights in the U.S. and in the Muslim world.

THINKING CRITICALLY

1. expanded voting rights, passed child labor laws
2. reinforced white authority over black majority
3. Categories might include gender, suffrage, working conditions, and economic rights.

STRATEGY FOR SUCCESS

News stories should reflect an understanding of contemporary human rights issues. Students should research a particular topic and write a cohesive account of the issue.

WRITING ABOUT HISTORY

Statements should reflect both the style of the documents mentioned and an understanding of human rights issues.

USING PRIMARY SOURCES

Mandela describes economic hardships, poor working conditions, and racism. Answers should reflect an understanding of contemporary conditions in South Africa.

LINKING HISTORY AND GEOGRAPHY

Human rights abuses seem to happen in nearly every country, and frequently involve imprisonment and violence.

Nineteenth Amendment gives U.S. women the vote.

Jesse Owens wins four gold medals at Olympics.

Japan conducts campaign of terror in Nanjing (Nanking).

UN adopts the Universal Declaration of Human Rights.

SNCC members tour Africa.

UN approves two covenants on human rights.

Tiananmen Square massacre occurs in China. Daw Aung San Suu Kyi placed under house arrest in Burma.

Benazir Bhutto elected prime minister of Pakistan.

South Africa holds its first national election open to all South Africans.

| 1920 | 1936 | 1937 | 1948 | 1964 | 1966 | 1988 | 1989 | 1994 |

WRITING ABOUT HISTORY

Writing to Express a Viewpoint In the style of the Declaration of Independence or the Declaration of the Rights of Man and Citizen, write a statement expressing your own conceptions of human rights. Be sure to list the rights that you believe are most important.

USING PRIMARY SOURCES

In 1963 Nelson Mandela was arrested for his role in protesting apartheid in South Africa. Read the following excerpt from his trial, in which Mandela explains some of the grievances held by black South Africans. What human rights violations does Mandela describe in the passage? To what extent do you think conditions in South Africa have improved since the 1960s?

> 66 *We fight against two features which are the hallmarks of African life in South Africa and which are entrenched by legislation which we seek to have repealed. These features are poverty and lack of human dignity. . . .*
>
> *South Africa is the richest country in Africa, and could be one of the richest in the world. But it is a land of extremes and remarkable contrasts. The Whites enjoy what may well be the highest standard of living in the world, whilst Africans live in poverty and misery. Forty per cent of the Africans live in hopelessly overcrowded and, in some cases, drought-stricken Reserves. . . . Thirty per cent are labourers, labour tenants, and squatters on White farms and work and live under conditions similar to those of the serfs of the Middle Ages. . . .*
>
> *The lack of human dignity experienced by Africans is the direct result of the policy of White supremacy. White supremacy implies Black inferiority. . . . Because of this sort of attitude, Whites tend to regard Africans as a separate breed. They do not look upon them*

as people with families of their own; they do not realize that they have emotions—that they fall in love like White people do; that they want to be with their wives and children like White people want to be with theirs; that they want to earn enough money to support their families properly, to feed and clothe them and send them to school. 99

LINKING HISTORY AND GEOGRAPHY

Refer to the chart on page 716. What generalization can you make about where human rights abuses occurred in 1993?

BUILDING YOUR PORTFOLIO

Complete the following projects independently or cooperatively.

1. INTERNATIONAL COOPERATION In Chapter 24 you portrayed a WTO administrator discussing how international cooperation can benefit the global economy. Building on that experience, imagine you are a reporter researching United Nations efforts to protect human rights worldwide over the past few decades. Construct a time line tracing these efforts and write two or three sentences about each entry.

2. INDIVIDUAL RIGHTS In chapters 23 and 24 you explored the effects of imperialism and economic policies on individual rights. Building on that experience, imagine you are a black African in South Africa who has just voted in a national election for the first time. Write a letter to a friend describing the experience and explaining how it fits into the historical struggle for civil rights worldwide.

BUILDING YOUR PORTFOLIO

Have students refer to **Building Your Portfolio Worksheet 6**, assigned at the beginning of Unit 6. Use the worksheet to help students monitor their progress on the portfolio projects.

Assessment

Core Resources
• Reteaching Worksheet 26
• Chapter 26 Tests
• Alternative Assessment Forms
Test Generator

A NEW ENVIRONMENTAL AWARENESS

Chapter Overview

Throughout much of the nation's early history, Americans looked at the natural environment as something to be tamed and exploited. By the beginning of the 20th century, however, many Americans placed greater emphasis on conserving or preserving the country's natural resources. Natural disasters, such as the Dust Bowl, served to increase this focus on conservation and preservation.

In the years after World War II, the proliferation of nuclear weapons and the increased use of pesticides and other chemicals made it clear that environmental issues were a global concern. As the century drew to a close, the United States and other nations continued the search for solutions to the major environmental challenges.

Chapter Planning Guide

CHAPTER 27	CORE RESOURCES	AUDIOVISUAL RESOURCES	PROGRAM RESOURCES
INTRODUCTION pp. 720–721	■ Building Your Portfolio Worksheet 6		
TEACHING THE CHAPTER pp. 722–739	■ Graphic Organizer 27 ■ Social Studies Skills Worksheet 27 ■ Literature Worksheet 27 ■ Geography Worksheet 27 ■ Outline Maps 6, 7, 8	■ Linking Geography and History Transparency and Worksheet 7 ■ Everyday Life in America Transparencies and Worksheets 16, 33 ■ The American Nation Videodisc: Images of America	■ Eyewitnesses and Others, Volume 1: Readings 3, 8, 18; Volume 2: Readings 2, 8, 9, 42, 49
REVIEW AND ASSESSMENT pp. 740–741	■ Chapter 27 Daily Quizzes ■ Reteaching Worksheet 27 ■ Chapter 27 Tests ■ Alternative Assessment Forms		■ Test Generator

Additional Resources

BOOKS FOR TEACHERS

Brown, Lester, et al. *State of the World 1994*, revised ed. Norton, 1994. Draws on wide range of research and statistics to review some of the major global challenges.

Global Resources. Greenhaven Press, 1991. Presents opposing viewpoints on the use of the world's resources.

Pollution. Greenhaven Press, 1994. Presents opposing viewpoints on the environmental effects of pollution.

BOOKS FOR STUDENTS

Herda, D.J., and Madden, Margaret L. *Energy Resources: Toward a Renewable Future*. Franklin Watts, 1991. Chronicles the exploitation of natural resources and the prospects for renewable energy resources.

*Middleton, Nick. *Atlas of Environmental Issues*. Facts on File, 1989. Uses maps to review the world's major environmental problems.

Newton, David E. *Taking a Stand Against Environmental Pollution*. Franklin Watts, 1990. Discusses such issues as energy use, disposal of toxic materials, acid rain, and the greenhouse effect.

* for students reading below grade level

MULTIMEDIA MATERIALS

Energy: The Key to Our Future. 2 videos, 60 min. United Learning/SSSS. Explains what energy is, how it is used, and the pros and cons of various energy sources.

The Environment—New Global Concerns. Video, 20 min. New York Times. Discusses such issues as destruction of the rain forests, ozone depletion, and the greenhouse effect.

Spaceship Earth: Our Global Environment. Video, 25 min. Worldlink. Focuses on three major issues: deforestation, global warming, and ozone depletion.

THEMES IN AMERICAN HISTORY

USE WITH PAGES 720–721

Listed on the right are the themes emphasized in Chapter 27. The questions in boldface type stimulate critical thinking and provide students with an opportunity to discuss the themes within a broadened context. The questions also appear in the pupil's edition on p. 720.

■ TECHNOLOGY AND SCIENCE

How might technological change affect the environment? Students might point out that technological change could have negative and positive effects. For example, some technological advances have created machines that increase pollution of the environment, whereas other advances have brought about safer ways to dispose of garbage and more efficient methods of using scarce natural resources.

■ GLOBAL RELATIONS

In what respects might environmental protection require international cooperation? Students might point out that the major environmental hazards were not created by one nation, nor do they affect one nation. Since environmental hazards have a global impact, the fight to protect the environment should also involve all nations.

■ ECONOMIC DEVELOPMENT

How might a nation balance environmental protection against economic development? Students might note that economic development relies on industrial development. To develop industry, a nation needs to exploit its natural resources. For the sake of economic development, then, a nation might choose to clear forest lands rather than preserve them.

CHAPTER STRATEGIES FOR MEETING INDIVIDUAL NEEDS

LIMITED ENGLISH PROFICIENT LEARNERS

Organize students into small groups. Have groups select an illustration from each section and write an extended caption explaining each illustration's significance and tying it to the section content.

TACTILE/KINESTHETIC LEARNERS

Have students use magazine and newspaper headlines, articles, illustrations, and cartoons to create a bulletin-board collage that shows the global nature of today's environmental challenges. Call on students to explain some of the ways people are meeting these challenges.

LEARNERS HAVING DIFFICULTY

Have pairs of students write brief answers to the questions in each section Focus and two or three sentences summing up each section. Then have pairs write a short summary of the chapter.

AUDITORY LEARNERS

Have students poll classmates, friends, and family members on the most pressing environmental problems facing the world today. Have students compare their poll results and attempt to explain any differences.

VISUAL LEARNERS

Organize students in small groups to design a symbol or logo that represents this chapter's title: "A New Environmental Awareness." Encourage groups to share their symbols or logos.

GIFTED LEARNERS

Have students write a review of today's major environmental issues from the viewpoint of Henry David Thoreau, Victor Shelford, Gifford Pinchot, or John Muir.

USING THE CHAPTER FOCUS

■ UNDERSTANDING THE MAIN IDEA

Call on a volunteer to read aloud the Understanding the Main Idea paragraph. Then ask students to identify the major environmental issues of the late 20th century and explain how these issues are global in nature. Have students evaluate their responses after they have completed the chapter.

■ THEMES

Have students work individually or in groups to answer the questions under Themes. Save students' responses so that they can compare them with their responses after studying the chapter. (See p. 719B for suggested answers.)

■ THE TIME LINE

Review the time-line entries with students, pointing out that some people felt the Chernobyl accident illustrated the global nature of environmental issues. Ask students to speculate on why these people took that view.

CORE RESOURCES

• **Graphic Organizer 27**
• **Building Your Portfolio Worksheet 6**

720

ABOUT THE ILLUSTRATION

Point out that the American whaling industry was well established by the mid-1700s. Colonial Americans hunted whales for meat, oil, and whalebone. The meat provided food, while the oil was a major source of fuel for heating and lighting. Whalebone was used to make such varied items as umbrellas and women's corsets. By the 1850s, the United States had a whaling fleet of some 700 ships. New Bedford and Nantucket in Massachusetts dominated the industry in the Atlantic, while San Francisco was the chief whaling port on the Pacific coast. However, whaling faded in importance with the development of the petroleum industry in the late 1800s.

Have students describe how they might have felt if they were crew members of a whaling ship in the mid-1800s.

Chapter 27

A NEW ENVIRONMENTAL AWARENESS

FOCUS

UNDERSTANDING THE MAIN IDEA

Over the past two centuries, Americans have shifted their thinking on the natural environment away from views emphasizing the need to tame the wilderness to views stressing conservation and preservation. Since World War II, Americans have grown increasingly aware of the global character of environmental issues.

 THEMES

■ **TECHNOLOGY AND SOCIETY** How might technological change affect the environment?

■ **GLOBAL RELATIONS** In what respects might environmental protection require international cooperation?

■ **ECONOMIC DEVELOPMENT** How might a nation balance environmental protection against economic development?

1872	1900	1973	1986	1992
Yellowstone National Park established.	Canadian Forestry Association founded.	Endangered Species Act passed.	Chernobyl accident occurs in Ukraine.	Earth Summit held in Rio de Janeiro.

Mention that the settlers' attitudes toward the environment had a devastating impact on the Native American way of life. To illustrate this point, read the following statement made by Miantonomo, a Narraganset, in 1642:

"Our plains were full of deer, as also our woods, and of turkies, and our coves full of fish and fowl. But these English having gotten our land, they with scythes cut down the grass, and with axes fell the trees; their cows and horses eat the grass, and their hogs spoil our clam banks, and we shall be starved."

PRIMARY SOURCE
Description of Change: excerpted
Rationale: excerpted to focus on main idea

■■ LINK TO THE PAST ▶

American thinking on the environment grew out of a European agricultural tradition that arrived with the first English settlers. This tradition, which taught that nature existed to serve human needs, dominated American attitudes for centuries.

Attacking a right whale (1868), lithograph by Currier & Ives

𝓘n his 1851 novel *Moby-Dick,* Herman Melville painted whaling in vivid detail. Describing the final battle between Captain Ahab and the great white whale, Melville wrote:

❝ The harpoon was darted; the stricken whale flew forward; with igniting velocity the line ran through the groove;—ran foul. Ahab stooped to clear it; he did clear it; but . . . he was shot out of the boat, ere the crew knew he was gone. Next instant, the heavy eye splice in the rope's final end flew out of the stark-empty tub, knocked down an oarsman, and smiting the sea, disappeared in its depths. ❞

Melville's book fared poorly upon publication. The public's reaction had little to do with opposition to whaling, however. The technology of the times kept whaling a relatively equal contest; as in Melville's tale, the whales sometimes killed those trying to kill them. Besides, the oceans were vast. There would always be more whales.

But whaling changed over the years. Hand-hurled harpoons gave way to explosive missiles, oars to high-powered engines, cries of "Thar she blows!" to the ping of sonar. Whaling acquired a grim efficiency that drove the great whales nearly to extinction. By the 1980s the public outcry was so strong that most seafaring nations agreed to ban commercial killing of the great whales.

The shift in public sentiment toward whaling mirrors a larger shift in environmental attitudes that has occurred over the past two centuries. Many people and governments now realize that the world's resources are not limitless.

Pitcher plants drawn by 19th-century German biologist Ernst Haeckel

MOTIVATING: PRIOR KNOWLEDGE

Point out that the attitude of the early settlers was well expressed by William Bradford, a leader of the Pilgrims. He felt that America was "a hideous and desolate wilderness." Have students discuss on what attitudes and beliefs Bradford and others might have based such views.

FOCUS OBJECTIVES

- Describe how most early Americans viewed the wilderness.

- Examine how some 19th-century Americans tried to modify use of the environment.

- Explain how Darwin's work affected views on the environment.

MULTICULTURAL PERSPECTIVES

According to a Crow legend, buffalo jumps, the forced stampeding of buffalo herds over cliffs, began when Old Man Coyote, the creator of the world, challenged a buffalo to a race. "Immediately his challenge was accepted and the race was on. . . . When they approached the cliff, he disappeared quickly. The buffalo herd went over the cliff."

AV TRANSPARENCY

Linking Geography and History Transparency and **Worksheet 7**

CORE RESOURCES

- **Section 1 Daily Quiz**

AV RESOURCES

- **Linking Geography and History Transparency** and **Worksheet 7**
- **Everyday Life in America Transparencies** and **Worksheets 10, 16**

Section 1

OLD ATTITUDES AND NEW

FOCUS

- **How did most colonists and early Americans view the wilderness?**
- **How did some 19th-century Americans try to modify use of the environment?**
- **How did Darwin's work affect views on the environment?**

For much of the nation's early history, Americans placed more emphasis on taming the wilderness than on preserving it. Some people held different views, however, and by the beginning of the 20th century, conservation efforts were growing in number and importance.

American Antiquarian Society

Farm family at work in the fields, 1760s woodcut

SUBDUING THE WILDERNESS

When the first English settlers arrived in Virginia and New England in the early 17th century, the need to preserve the natural heritage of the land was almost the last thing on their minds. On the contrary, most of the new arrivals happily accepted the biblical command to establish control over the earth and "every living thing that moveth upon the earth." For these settlers the wilderness was something to be feared and conquered, not cherished and preserved. From the beginning they set about changing the "remote, rocky, barren, bushy, wild-woody wilderness" into "a second England for fertilness," as Massachusetts colonist Edward Johnson approvingly noted in 1653.

The colonists' approach to nature had grown out of a long tradition of land use. Their ancestors in Europe had been farmers. To them farming meant clearing the land of trees, plowing it, and planting crops. Unlike the Native Americans they encountered, the European colonists had access to metal tools and domesticated animals, which allowed them to bring greater areas of land under cultivation. These farmers transformed the natural environment and deprived many species of the habitat they needed. To the extent the land-clearers thought about it at all, most of them probably believed they had little choice in the matter: they needed the land.

As the U.S. population grew, settlement spread inland from the coast. New technologies increased people's ability to modify the landscape. Better roads made travel faster and cheaper, and the construction of steamboats and canals eventually provided better access to the country's interior. The construction of railroads brought most parts of the country within easy reach of cities and their markets. This spurred further settlement.

The most dramatic effect of the railroad boom on the environment was the destruction of the buffalo herds of the Great Plains. In the prerailroad era, the grasses of the Plains supported millions upon millions of buffalo and a thriving Plains Indian culture. The first railroad line across the Plains was completed in the late 1860s, bringing tourists, farmers, and hunters. At the urging of the

Teaching the Section

Practice

INDEPENDENT PRACTICE

VIEWS OF THE WILDERNESS

Draw on the chalkboard a three-column chart with the headings *Early Americans, 19th-Century Americans,* and *Ecologists.* Have students discuss the historical factors that influenced each group. Then ask how each group viewed the environment. List responses under the appropriate headings.

GUIDED PRACTICE

Write the following names on the chalkboard: Ralph Waldo Emerson, Henry David Thoreau, Samuel Hammond, Charles Darwin, Ernst Haeckel, Henry C. Cowles, Frederic Clements, Victor Shelford. Ask students to describe the roles these individuals played in changing American attitudes on the environment. Note their responses on the chalkboard.

Have students use information developed in Guided Practice to create a "Who's Who" of American environmentalism.

▶ Although the buffalo population once numbered in the millions, its ranks dwindled by the 1870s as hunters were paid from one dollar to three dollars for every hide sold. An 1883 study estimated that some 13 million buffalo had been slaughtered.

farmers, who wanted to fence and plow the grasslands, and the U.S. Army, who wanted to drive Native Americans from the Plains, the hunters slaughtered thousands of buffalo daily. Hardly a generation had passed before the buffalo were on the verge of extinction.

■■ **Most colonists and early Americans believed that nature existed for their benefit and that the wilderness ought to be subdued.**

THE BEGINNINGS OF DISSENT

Even in the early years of the Republic, some citizens did not wish to see America's vast wilderness subdued. In the mid-19th century Ralph Waldo Emerson, Henry David Thoreau, and other **transcendentalists** called for a return to a simple life, one that enabled individuals to regain close touch with the natural world. "In the woods," wrote Emerson, "we return to reason and faith." Voicing a similar sentiment, Thoreau declared: "In Wildness is the preservation of the World."

The transcendentalists and others who shared their views of nature urged that certain lands be set aside in their wild state before the wilderness disappeared entirely. As early as 1859, New York newspaperman Samuel Hammond called for the creation of a nature reserve 100 miles in diameter in New York's Adirondack Mountains. He explained:

❝ I would make it a forest forever. It should be a misdemeanor to chop down a tree, and a felony to clear an acre within its boundaries. The old woods should stand here always as God made them, growing on until the earthworm ate away their roots, and the strong winds hurled them to the ground, and new woods should be permitted to supply the place of the old so long as the earth remained. ❞

Others, such as historian Frederick Jackson Turner, valued the wilderness and the frontier not only for its beauty but also for its effect on the American character. In an 1893 lecture he declared:

❝ The frontier is the line of most rapid and effective Americanization. The wilderness masters the colonist. . . . In short, at the frontier the environment is at first too strong for the man. He must accept the conditions which it furnishes, or perish. . . . Thus the advance of the frontier has meant a steady movement away from the influence of Europe, a steady growth of independence on American lines. ❞

Furthermore, Turner argued, "the most important effect of the frontier has been in the promotion of democracy." This belief in the connection between democracy and the frontier encouraged the efforts of those trying to protect the environment.

■■ **Rejecting the idea of subduing the natural world, some 19th-century Americans favored preserving the wilderness.**

THE BIRTH OF ECOLOGY

During the 19th century, developments in the natural sciences also increased public interest in the environment. Following the 1859 publication of Charles Darwin's *Origin of Species,* the theory of evolution—which argued that those organisms that were best adapted to their environment were most likely to survive and reproduce—took the scientific world by storm.

HISTORICAL SIDELIGHTS

Darwin's Theories

Charles Darwin was careful to distinguish between natural selection and human selection. "Man can act only on external and visible characters; Nature . . . cares nothing for appearances, except in so far as they are useful to any being. She can act on every internal organ. . . . Man selects only for his own good; Nature, only for that of the being which she tends. . . .

It may metaphorically be said that natural selection is daily and hourly scrutinizing, throughout the world, the slightest variations; rejecting those that are bad, preserving and adding up all that are good."

PRIMARY SOURCES

Description of Change: excerpted
Rationale: excerpted to focus on main idea

Review and Assessment

REVIEW Encourage students to outline information in the section that helps to explain the section's title: "Old Attitudes and New." Then assign the Section 1 Review on p. 724.

ASSESS Assign the **Section 1 Daily Quiz** in *Core Resources*.

RETEACH Have groups of students develop questions about ideas in assigned subsections. Have groups exchange questions and answer the questions they receive.

Closure

Have students speculate on how American history might have been different if the early European settlers had been concerned with preserving the natural environment rather than with taming it.

Extension

ANALYZE Encourage students to read selections by Ralph Waldo Emerson or Henry David Thoreau. Have students write a brief analysis of their author's view of nature.

CREATE Have students create a cartoon dealing with environmental issues that illustrates the title of this section: "Old Attitudes and New."

PRIMARY SOURCE

Description of Change: excerpted
Rationale: excerpted to focus on main idea

SECTION REVIEW ANSWERS

IDENTIFY

For significance, see the following pages:
transcendentalists (p. 723)
Samuel Hammond (p. 723)
Charles Darwin (p. 723)
ecology (p. 724)
Ernst Haeckel (p. 724)
Henry C. Cowles (p. 724)
ecosystem (p. 724)
Frederic Clements (p. 724)

1. *During the 17th and 18th centuries, most Americans believed that the environment was designed to meet the needs of humans. During the 19th century, however, more people became concerned about the effects human development had on the wilderness.*
2. *Transcendentalists believed that the environment was a source of reason and faith.*
3. *Ecologists relied on the idea of natural selection in their attempts to determine how species interacted with the environment.*
4. *Essays will vary but should address the issues of conservation and interaction between species.*
5. *Ecologists may be able to provide insight into the workings of the environment and the interdependence of species.*

▲ **Dr. Henry Cowles, seen in this 1924 photograph, proved that the juniper tree he is standing in was nearly 6,000 years old.**

One result of the attention given to the environment was the development of a new science given the name *ecology* in 1866 by German biologist Ernst Haeckel. An enthusiastic supporter of Darwin, Haeckel argued that **ecology**—the study of the interrelationship of plants and animals with each other and with their environment—was a logical outgrowth of the study of evolution. Adopting the Darwinian idea of natural selection, the ecologists tried to identify how changes in the environment might determine which species gained an edge in the struggle for survival.

European botanists were the first to practice ecology, and their studies emphasized the relationship of plants to the environment. For example, Eugenius Warming, a Danish professor, showed how environmental factors such as heat and humidity affected plant growth.

By the 1890s the new science had spread to the United States. One of the first American ecologists, Henry C. Cowles, studied the way in which an **ecosystem**—the interaction of living things with the environment—changes over time. Frederic Clements, who published *Research Methods in Ecology*—the first American book on the subject—argued that climate was the most important factor in determining the survival of competing species.

As the 20th century began, scientists became increasingly interested in the interaction of species with each other as well as with the environment. As one American ecologist, Victor Shelford, wrote:

> ❝ Ecology is the science of communities. A study of the relations of a single species to the environment conceived without reference to communities . . . is not properly included in the field of ecology. ❞

This concern for the whole biological community quite naturally led to a concern for conservation. Furthermore, some members of the new Ecological Society of America—founded in 1915 with Shelford as its first president—saw ecology as a science that would form the basis for natural resource management. In keeping with the progressive spirit of the time, they believed the science of ecology could provide the knowledge necessary to protect the environment.

■■ **Darwin's theory of evolution encouraged people to examine the ways in which humans interacted with the natural environment.**

SECTION 1 REVIEW

IDENTIFY and explain the significance of the following: transcendentalists, Samuel Hammond, Charles Darwin, ecology, Ernst Haeckel, Henry C. Cowles, ecosystem, Frederic Clements.

1. **MAIN IDEA** How did most Americans view the environment during the 17th, 18th, and 19th centuries?
2. **MAIN IDEA** How did the transcendentalists view the environment?
3. **MAIN IDEA** How did Darwin's ideas contribute to the development of the science of ecology?
4. **WRITING TO EXPRESS A VIEWPOINT** Imagine you are an ecologist. Write an essay explaining why you think scientists should study the environment.
5. **EVALUATING** How might ecologists lend support to conservation efforts?

PREVIEW WORKSHOP

Following is a list of the significant people and terms in this section. You may wish to use this list as a section preview.

People
- John Muir
- Aldo Leopold

Terms
- conservation

- Canadian Forestry Association
- preservation

MOTIVATING: PRIOR KNOWLEDGE

Have students review their knowledge of the Progressive movement to suggest one word that sums up the movement's goals. *(reform)* Then ask them to speculate how Progressives might apply reform to environmental issues.

Section 2

EXPANDING HORIZONS

F O C U S
- **How did the progressives view natural resources?**
- **In what ways did the preservationists differ from the conservationists?**
- **How did the Dust Bowl disaster of the 1930s shape environmental thinking in the United States?**

The Progressive Era brought new prominence to environmental issues, but it also sharpened debate between conservationists and preservationists. The ecological disaster of the Dust Bowl made Americans more aware that environmental issues were a national concern.

Lumberjacks in Washington State, 1899

FOCUS OBJECTIVES
- Explain how progressives viewed natural resources.
- Identify the ways in which preservationists differed from conservationists.
- Examine how the Dust Bowl disaster of the 1930s shaped environmental thinking in the United States.

GLOBAL CONNECTIONS
The Canadian lumber industry received a boost from the 1906 San Francisco earthquake and fire. For approximately a year and a half, almost every mill on the Pacific coast operated for 24 hours a day. So much Canadian lumber went to San Francisco that construction in Vancouver was interrupted.

PRIMARY SOURCE
Description of Change: excerpted
Rationale: excerpted to focus on main idea

AV TRANSPARENCY
Everyday Life in America Transparency and **Worksheet 16**

CORE RESOURCES
- **Section 2 Daily Quiz**

AV RESOURCES
- **Everyday Life in America Transparency** and **Worksheet 16**

PROGRESSIVISM AND CONSERVATION

Although few Americans were familiar with the work of ecologists, environmental issues gained a new importance as the Progressive movement became influential around the beginning of the 20th century. Progressives believed government should actively tackle economic and political issues. These issues included control of America's natural resources.

Most progressives believed that the nation's natural resources ought to be used, but used wisely. The term they applied to this policy was **conservation**. For example, most looked with dismay on the large tracts of forests that were being cut with no concern beyond short-term profits. As the progressives sought greater influence in national politics, conservation became one of their priorities.

They got their chance in 1901 when Theodore Roosevelt became president. As a ranchowner in the Dakota Territory, Roosevelt had observed firsthand the way maximum use of ranges and forests, however profitable in the short

run, could cause long-term damage. Believing that people must judge the effects of their actions on the environment, he declared:

> 66 Conservation means development as much as it does protection. I recognize the right and duty of this generation to develop and use the natural resources of our land; but I do not recognize the right to waste them, or to rob, by wasteful use, the generations that come after us. 99

▶ **President Roosevelt appointed forestry expert Gifford Pinchot, shown here, as head of the U.S. Forest Service.**

Teaching the **S**ection

PROGRESSIVES AND NATURAL RESOURCES

Divide the class into small groups. Tell groups they are working on an election campaign for the Progressive party. Their task is to develop a campaign slogan or a 30-second sound bite that explains the Progressive view of natural resources. Have groups display their slogans or "broadcast" their sound bites for the rest of the class.

CONSERVATION VERSUS PRESERVATION

Pair students to role-play conservationists and preservationists. Tell each pair to discuss the similarities and differences in their views of the environment. Choose pairs to re-create the discussion for the class. Then ask each student to write a summary sentence comparing conservation to preservation.

THE DUST BOWL ERA

Organize students into groups of four. Ask groups to role-play advisers to President Franklin D. Roosevelt. Have them discuss the causes and the effects of the Dust Bowl. Then have them develop a brief report proposing steps that the government might take to prevent another Dust Bowl. Select groups to read their reports to the class.

HISTORICAL SIDELIGHTS

The Hetch Hetchy Valley

The most prominent conservation issue of the Progressive Era centered on California's Hetch Hetchy Valley. San Francisco's city government sought to dam the valley, located in Yosemite National Park, to provide a source of drinking water. Although John Muir and the Sierra Club opposed the plan, Congress decided in 1913 to flood the valley.

PRIMARY SOURCE

Description of Change: excerpted

Rationale: excerpted to focus on main idea

▲ The Forest Service tries to prevent trees, such as these California redwoods, from becoming the blackened sticks that remain after a forest fire.

Roosevelt's chief lieutenant in the fight for conservation was Gifford Pinchot. As head of the Forest Service, Pinchot sought to expand the government's control of the nation's forests by enlarging "forest reserves," later called national forests. He also used a system of fees to regulate the use of forest resources.

Roosevelt and other progressives extended their conservation efforts to resources outside the control of the Forest Service. In 1902 Congress passed the Newlands Reclamation Act, which promoted irrigation projects in the West's arid regions. In addition, Roosevelt issued numerous executive orders establishing wildlife refuges across the country. He added Oregon's Crater Lake to the list of national parks and, to discourage the overgrazing that had already laid waste to much of the western range, instituted a system of fees for grazing on public lands.

Conservation issues were not confined to the United States. A number of Canadian officials were strongly influenced by American progressives' view that natural resources should be used wisely. The **Canadian Forestry Association**, founded in 1900, promoted national control of forest areas and called for fire prevention, more forest reserves, and better education for foresters. In 1909 representatives from Canada, Newfoundland, Mexico, and the United States met to identify common environmental problems and to establish national conservation commissions. Only Canada was successful in establishing a permanent commission, however. In Great Britain a private group, the Society for the Promotion of Nature Reserves, was founded in 1912, but it was not until after World War II that the British government established the Nature Conservancy to acquire nature reserves.

■■ **Progressives and other conservationists believed that natural resources should be used, but used wisely.**

PRESERVATION VERSUS CONSERVATION

Roosevelt was not surprised that his efforts on behalf of conservation provoked opposition among people who were making money under the old system. He was more surprised at the objections raised by those who believed that conservation did not go far enough. These people favored **preservation**—that is, they wished to see America's wild areas left essentially untouched.

The preservationists followed in the tradition of Emerson and Thoreau, and their arguments echoed the transcendentalists' belief that the wilderness was a source of spiritual refreshment. Their efforts had led to the founding of the system of American national parks, of which Yellowstone, set aside in 1872, was the first. Yosemite followed in 1890.

The most influential preservationist was John Muir. Muir had led the fight for the creation of Yosemite National Park in California, and he and others of like mind founded the Sierra Club in 1892. Muir joined a deep appreciation for unspoiled nature to a talented pen, and his numerous articles and books placed the issue of preservation squarely before the public.

At a time when industrialization was intensifying the pace of life, Muir called on Americans to catch their breath and enjoy the gifts that nature so freely gave. Many Americans, he declared, had seen the light:

66 Thousands of tired, nerve-shaken, over-civilized people are beginning to find out that going to the mountains is going home; that wildness is a necessity; and that mountain parks and reservations are useful not only as fountains of timber and irrigating rivers, but as fountains of life. 99

Practice

GUIDED PRACTICE

Write the following on the chalkboard: *Approaches to the Environment: From the Progressives to the New Deal Era.* Tell students this is the title of an article to be written for a magazine dealing with environmental issues. Then ask them to suggest an outline for the article. Note suggestions on the chalkboard.

INDEPENDENT PRACTICE

Have students use the outline developed in Guided Practice to write the article. Call on volunteers to read their articles to the class. Students may wish to include their articles in their portfolios.

Review and Assessment

REVIEW Direct students to create an annotated time line of environmental issues in the United States during the first half of the 20th century. Students may wish to include their time lines in their portfolios. Then assign the Section 2 Review on p. 728.

ASSESS Assign the **Section 2 Daily Quiz** in *Core Resources*.

 Another influential preservationist, Aldo Leopold, was one of the first to apply the principles of ecology to wildlife management. After graduating from Yale in 1909, he joined the Forest Service. He

Aldo Leopold

became the nation's leading expert on game, and in 1933 Leopold joined the faculty of the University of Wisconsin. Two years later he joined with others to found the Wilderness Society.

Leopold had begun his career as a firm believer in animal conservation, and he had supported killing wolves to protect deer populations. However, he changed his views on wildlife management after a research trip to Germany, where both forests and deer herds had been carefully managed since the 1400s. German forestry officials had come to recognize the importance of ecological principles to forest management, and in 1914 they started programs to restore mixed forests and wildlife. At the same time, however, German foresters continued to manage the forest for high timber yields and to use supplemental feeding to support large deer herds. The results—an overgrazed forest and stunted deer—dismayed Leopold. He realized that the Germans' techniques left too little room for natural forces and drove out many native species of plants and animals. Returning home convinced of the importance of a balanced environment, Leopold wrote:

66 We Americans, in most states at least, have not yet experienced a bearless, wolfless, eagleless, catless woods. We yearn for more deer and more pines, and we shall probably get them. But do we realize that to get them, as the Germans have, at the expense of their wild environment and their wild enemies, is to get very little indeed? 99

To a certain extent, the difference between the views of the preservationists and the conservationists was a matter of degree. The conservationists

▶ Preservationists fought to save Yosemite's Hetch Hetchy Valley. Shown here before a dam was constructed to supply drinking water to San Francisco, the valley stretched nearly the length and width of Manhattan Island.

believed that some land should be kept off-limits to loggers and ranchers, and the preservationists knew that they could not lock up the entire West.

■■ Conservationists wanted to use wilderness resources wisely, but preservationists contended that wilderness was most valuable when left in its natural state.

*T*HE DUST BOWL ERA

From the 19th century through the first few decades of the 20th century, most environmental debates focused on the West. By the 1930s, however, many Americans were beginning to understand that abuse of natural resources posed problems for the entire nation.

In the early 20th century, American agriculture was centered in the Great Plains. A few people, however, began to ask if the Plains were really suited to farming. They noted that erosion increased and the creeks ran muddier as more and more acres were put to the plow. Terrible dust storms followed weeks of little rain.

Much of the grass that had once covered the Great Plains—and held the topsoil in place—was gone. What had not been plowed under to plant crops had been destroyed by overgrazing. Lamenting the loss, one Texas sheepherder declared that grass "saves us all. . . . Grass is what holds the earth together." Few people, however, listened. As farming and herding increased, the loss of grass and topsoil turned the Plains into an environmental time bomb.

The 1934 *Yearbook of Agriculture* quantified the damage: 100 million acres of cropland had lost

BIO GRAPHY **PERSONALITIES IN HISTORY**

During the 1930s and 1940s Aldo Leopold wrote a series of essays to define and describe his ideas about ecology and ethics. In April 1948 Leopold suffered a heart attack and died while helping his neighbors fight a grass fire near his Wisconsin farm. One year later, many of his essays were published under the title *A Sand County Almanac.*

MULTICULTURAL PERSPECTIVES

A 1936 backpacking trip to Chihuahua, Mexico, provided Leopold with a view of a naturally balanced environment. Settlement and overgrazing by deer were not a problem in that region, because the activities first of the Apaches and later of bandits had discouraged development. This lack of development had allowed wolves and other predators to maintain an ecological equilibrium.

PRIMARY SOURCE

Description of Change: excerpted
Rationale: excerpted to focus on main idea

RETEACH For each subsection in the section, have students write a sentence that summarizes the main idea. Select students to read their sentences aloud. Have the class choose the best summary sentence for each subsection.

Closure

Remind students that the American government played an ever-increasing part in environmental issues during the first half of the 20th century. Have students discuss whether they think this was an appropriate approach for government to take.

Extension

CREATE Have students create a map showing the national park system. Suggest that they accompany their maps with a brief essay describing the development of the National Park Service.

INVESTIGATE Encourage students to investigate the work of the Sierra Club. Have them present their findings in a report to the class.

▲ Windblown topsoil, so desperately needed by Dust Bowl farmers, settles over this abandoned Oklahoma farmstead. Dunelike drifts of soil nearly bury a wagon wheel.

SECTION REVIEW ANSWERS

IDENTIFY

For significance, see the following pages:
conservation (p. 725)
Canadian Forestry Association (p. 726)
preservation (p. 726)
John Muir (p. 726)
Aldo Leopold (p. 727)

1. *Progressives believed in active government intervention to solve problems, including environmental issues.*
2. *preservationists—wanted to prohibit all use of wilderness areas; conservationists —believed the environment should be used wisely rather than exploited*
3. *passed legislation to limit grazing, encourage development of windbreaks, develop flood control projects, plant trees and prevent forest fires*
4. *Essays should discuss the loss of grass on the Great Plains and the spread of acreage under cultivation.*
5. *showed him that predators played an important role in game management and wilderness development*

most or all of the topsoil, and an additional 125 million acres were rapidly losing topsoil. These statistics were driven home by the huge dust storms that raked the Great Plains during the 1930s. Thousands fled the Dust Bowl (see map on page 367). Many left behind houses buried to the windowsills in drifts of grit.

As Congress pondered what to do, a particularly monstrous storm carried dust from the Great Plains to Washington, D.C. The head of the Soil Conservation Service, testifying before a Senate committee, pointed out the window at the windborne soil and commented, "There, gentlemen, goes part of Oklahoma now."

Unable to ignore the environmental catastrophe on the Great Plains, Congress passed legislation to encourage conservation. This legislation, part of Franklin D. Roosevelt's New Deal, included measures to curtail grazing on drought-sensitive grassland and to encourage the planting of trees as windbreaks, and the adoption of other soil-conserving agricultural practices.

Other New Deal programs encouraged the responsible use of natural resources. The Civilian Conservation Corps, for example, sent thousands of young men into the national forests to prevent fires and to plant tree seedlings. The Tennessee Valley Authority combined flood control with electrification projects. The Grand Coulee Dam on the Columbia River provided irrigation as well as hydroelectric power.

■■ **The Dust Bowl disaster demonstrated the need for conservation and made the environment a national concern.**

FDR's conservation programs took much the same approach as those of Theodore Roosevelt. The emphasis these New Deal programs placed on the wise use of resources demonstrated the degree to which environmental problems had acquired national significance.

Although the government supported a policy of conservation, Aldo Leopold and others who supported a policy of preservation continued to influence such government agencies as the Forest Service. After World War II, it was the preservationists who revived the environmental movement in the United States. And as American environmentalists began to deal with a wider range of environmental problems, they adopted a more global perspective.

◄ By using art to promote New Deal programs, painter Ben Shahn (1898–1969) worked to end the despair he depicted in his poster *Years of Dust.*

 SECTION 2 REVIEW

IDENTIFY and explain the significance of the following: conservation, Canadian Forestry Association, preservation, John Muir, Aldo Leopold.

1. **MAIN IDEA** How did the rise of the Progressive movement affect interest in the environment?
2. **MAIN IDEA** How did preservationists and conservationists differ in their views on the environment?
3. **MAIN IDEA** How did the government respond to the problems of the Dust Bowl?
4. **WRITING TO EXPLAIN** Write an essay explaining how agricultural techniques contributed to the problems in the Dust Bowl.
5. **ANALYZING** How did Leopold's trip to Germany influence his views on wildlife conservation?

PREVIEW WORKSHOP

Following is a list of the significant people and terms in this section. You may wish to use this list as a section preview.

People
- Petra Kelly
- Barry Commoner

Terms
- Antarctic Treaty

- Nuclear Nonproliferation Treaty
- nuclear fallout
- food chain
- unilateral disarmament
- Green parties
- smog
- Federal Water Pollution Control Act
- Safe Drinking Water Act
- Endangered Species Act

MOTIVATING: LINK TO TODAY

Call on volunteers to explain the role that environmental concerns played in the last national, state, or local elections. Then point out that this section deals with the development of the environment as a political issue.

FOCUS OBJECTIVES

- Analyze how the development of nuclear weapons encouraged international cooperation.

- Explain how nuclear weapons tests threatened the environment, and describe how people responded.

- Describe how activists used political measures to draw attention to environmental problems.

Section 3

ENVIRONMENTALISM GOES GLOBAL

FOCUS

- **How did the development of nuclear weapons encourage international cooperation on the environment?**

- **How did nuclear weapons tests threaten the environment? How did people respond?**

- **How did activists use political measures to draw attention to environmental problems?**

Antinuclear protester Susan Ginzberg with her son, 1961

During the first three decades after World War II, radioactive fallout from nuclear weapons tests and the effects of large-scale pesticide use made the global nature of threats to the environment unmistakable. The increasing awareness of these threats sparked efforts to change public policy.

THE NUCLEAR AGE

Just as problems of the 1930s and the Great Depression made Americans aware of the importance of ecological problems, later events proved that the environment did not recognize political borders. In the aftermath of World War II, many people were convinced of the need to pay attention to international problems in order to prevent a repeat of the terrible economic, political, and military events of the 1930s and 1940s. Environmental problems were among those cast in global terms.

One of the most pressing environmental problems of the postwar era was the need to prevent nuclear war, which could have disastrous consequences not only for human populations but also for the environment. The worldwide fear of nuclear war led to a number of international agreements designed to limit the development and use of atomic weapons. The **Antarctic Treaty** of 1959 established Antarctica as a nuclear-free zone, and in 1968 the United States, Great Britain, the Soviet Union, and 59 other nations signed the **Nuclear Nonproliferation**

Treaty to keep nuclear weapons technology from spreading to more countries. By 1987 more than 100 nations had ratified the treaty. In spite of these agreements by the 1980s, 24 countries were believed to be capable of building nuclear weapons within a short period of time.

■■ **Fear of the effects of nuclear war encouraged governments to try to stop the proliferation of nuclear weapons.**

NUCLEAR FALLOUT

While the destructive power of a nuclear explosion was obvious, there was another effect, more subtle and difficult to detect—**nuclear fallout**, the radioactive debris that a nuclear explosion produced. For almost two decades after 1945, the countries that had developed nuclear weapons, especially the United States and the Soviet Union, tested their weapons in aboveground explosions. Each test released radioactive particles, which

Teaching the Section

NUCLEAR CONCERNS

Organize students into groups to act as the editorial board of a newspaper. Ask boards to write an editorial supporting international efforts to end the proliferation of nuclear weapons. Call on board representatives to read their editorials to the class.

NUCLEAR TESTING

Call on volunteers to identify and explain the problems created by the testing of nuclear weapons in the atmosphere. Note responses on the chalkboard. Next, divide the class into two groups. Have one group act as members of such groups as SANE and CND and the other act as military and national security officials of the American and British governments. Have the two groups debate how the problems created by nuclear-weapons testing might be overcome.

ENVIRONMENTAL ACTIVISM

Organize students into groups to act as advisers to the Green parties. Their task is to write a party manifesto for an upcoming election campaign. Manifestos should address such questions as: What actions must be taken to protect the environment? Why are these actions necessary? How can these actions be implemented? Select groups to present their manifestos to the class.

GLOBAL CONNECTIONS

A growing number of people and groups supported the idea of a nuclear freeze, which would end nuclear weapons production and reduce existing supplies. By September 1983 the freeze movement involved 156 national and international organizations and brought American professional groups such as the National Conference of Black Lawyers and the American Nurses' Association into contact with peace movements around the world.

▲ Fear of nuclear war and of radioactive fallout led to demonstrations such as this one outside San Francisco's city hall.

prevailing winds blew thousands of miles. Eventually, scientific instruments could detect radioactivity in nearly every area of the planet.

No one knew how nuclear fallout might affect people, but the radiation sickness that developed in the survivors of the Hiroshima and Nagasaki blasts frightened people around the world. Adding to their fears, radioactivity was not just polluting the air, it was showing up in the **food chain**. Rain washed radioactive particles, such as strontium 90, from the atmosphere and deposited them in the soil, where they were absorbed by agricultural crops. When people ate contaminated vegetables and fruits or meat and milk from animals that fed on contaminated plants, they concentrated the radioactive particles in their bodies.

Scientists debated the effects of this radiation. Some pointed out that humans have always been exposed to naturally occurring radiation. Others responded that while this was true, humans had never had this additional exposure. Some of these scientists predicted a rise in the incidence of cancer, particularly in children.

The potential threats nuclear fallout posed sparked an international outcry. Many people also

▶ This Geiger counter, which detects the presence and intensity of radioactivity, helps prospectors locate deposits of uranium—used in producing nuclear energy.

realized that ending nuclear pollution would require international cooperation. In the United States the National Committee for a Sane Nuclear Policy (SANE), formed in 1957, called for an end to testing and to the nuclear arms race. In Great Britain the Campaign for Nuclear Disarmament, or CND, advocated **unilateral disarmament**—the elimination of Britain's nuclear weapons despite the continued presence of nuclear weapons in the United States and the Soviet Union.

Although governments ignored many of the nuclear protests, both the United States and the Soviet Union worked toward eliminating above-ground testing. As President Kennedy pointed out in a speech in 1963, "We all inhabit this planet. We all breathe the same air." Later that year the United States, the Soviet Union, and Great Britain agreed to the Limited Nuclear Test Ban Treaty. However, the successful negotiation of the treaty was primarily due to the discovery of ways to conduct underground nuclear weapons tests. Underground testing satisfied those who contended that continued testing was necessary to protect national security, as well as those who wanted to end radioactive fallout.

▪▪ **The threats posed by radioactive fallout prompted international efforts to pressure governments to limit the production and testing of nuclear weapons.**

POLITICS AND THE ENVIRONMENT

Nuclear destruction and radioactive fallout were not the only new threats to the environment. Pesticide use increased dramatically following the development of new chemicals during World War II. The most popular of the new chemicals was DDT. DDT had first proved its value in 1943 in Naples, Italy, where it was used to prevent an epidemic of typhus by killing the lice that spread the disease.

Despite the benefits, some scientists worried about excessive use of the new pesticides. However, it was Rachel Carson's *Silent Spring,* published in 1962 (see p. 475), that

*P*ractice

GUIDED PRACTICE

Write on the chalkboard the three subsection titles, and inform students that these are topics for news stories. Call on volunteers to develop brief story outlines for each topic, noting their suggestions under the appropriate title.

INDEPENDENT PRACTICE

Direct students to use one of the outlines developed in the Guided Practice activity to write a news story on environmental activism since World War II. Students may wish to include their stories in their portfolios.

*R*eview and *A*ssessment

REVIEW Direct students to create cause-and-effect charts for the development of environmental activism in the United States and in Europe. Then assign the Section 3 Review on p. 732.

ASSESS Assign the **Section 3 Daily Quiz** in *Core Resources*.

▶

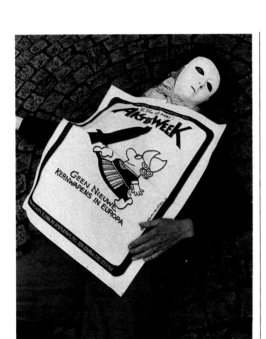

▲ An environmental activist taking part in a 1984 demonstration in Amsterdam's Dam Square dramatically illustrates ecological concerns over the placement of nuclear weapons in Europe.

awakened many people to the dangers that DDT and other pesticides posed to the environment. Carson warned that pesticides threatened more than insects. "These insecticides are not selective poisons. They do not single out the one species of which we desire to be rid," she wrote. "Each of them is used for the simple reason that it is a deadly poison. It therefore poisons all life with which it comes in contact."

As more and more people worried about the threats posed by nuclear fallout and pesticides, they began to pressure governments around the world to take the environment into account when making policy. In the United States, environmental issues developed a political slant only when adopted by a major party. In other nations, however, **Green parties**—so called because their platforms emphasize ecological concerns—forged a more direct link between these issues and politics.

The Greens have drawn most of their support from large urban areas where the effects of pollution and other urban problems tend to be most obvious. Although the parties remain small, the Greens have successfully drawn attention to environmental issues in Great Britain, France, Germany, and other Western European countries.

Germany's *Die Grünen*. The German Green party, *Die Grünen*, has been one of Europe's most successful. *Die Grünen* developed out of a series of protest movements that began in the 1950s with antinuclear protests and then, in the 1960s, centered around student protests against U.S. involvement in Vietnam. During the early 1970s a new wave of protests focused on opposition to nuclear power. Protesters charged that nuclear power presented serious problems—such as pollution from the accidental release of radiation into the atmosphere and contamination of the environment from the disposal of spent radioactive fuel rods. Thousands of people from France, Switzerland, and Germany, for example, protested a planned nuclear power station at Wyhl, in southern Germany.

In the late 1970s when German protest groups began to address various other environmental issues, they came together to form *Die Grünen*. The new party, which won 5.6 percent of the vote and 27 seats in the German parliamentary elections in 1983, based its platform on the "recognition that in a limited world growth cannot be unlimited" and demanded "a policy of active partnership with nature and with the human race." Ecology, explained party activist Manon Maren-Grisebach, would provide the "scientific . . . basis for action." She continued:

❝ But ecology is demanding. At the risk of our own destruction, we cannot ignore its insights; we are not free to act at will because we are forced to obey laws which reach beyond our [selves] and deal with our very existence. ❞

The party also reminded individuals of their responsibility to change environmental policy. In 1982 Petra Kelly, who was then head of *Die Grünen*, asserted "Change . . . has to come from the bottom, not the top."

▶ Environmental activist Petra Kelly addresses the press in Bonn, Germany, on her return from a Moscow peace conference in February 1987.

RETEACH List on the chalkboard the terms from the Preview Workshop at the beginning of this section. Have students respond to the section's Focus questions with sentences containing the terms.

Closure

Draw students' attention to Barry Commoner's four laws of ecology on p. 732. Have students discuss how these laws relate to the environment.

Extension

EVALUATE Ask students to research and evaluate the impact of the Green parties in solving environmental problems. Have them present their conclusions in an oral report.

INVESTIGATE Have students investigate the work of one of the major environmental activist groups in the United States. Encourage students to present their findings in an illustrated written report.

PRIMARY SOURCE

Description of Change: excerpted
Rationale: excerpted to focus on main idea

SECTION REVIEW ANSWERS

IDENTIFY

See the following pages:
Antarctic Treaty (p. 729)
Nuclear Nonproliferation
Treaty (p. 729)
nuclear fallout (p. 729)
food chain (p. 730)
unilateral disarmament (p. 730)
Green parties (p. 731)
Petra Kelly (p. 731)
smog (p. 732)
Federal Water Pollution
Control Act (p. 732)
Safe Drinking Water Act
(p. 732)
Endangered Species Act
(p. 732)
Barry Commoner (p. 732)

1. *Answers should note that although nuclear weapons did spread around the globe, nuclear war did not occur.*
2. *Nuclear weapons tests released radioactive fallout into the atmosphere. People called for unilateral disarmament and supported arms limitations agreements.*
3. *relied on protests, strikes; formed Green parties*
4. *Essays should address the example that would be set by disarmament, as well as the benefits of reducing the global nuclear arsenal.*
5. *Answers will vary, but students may feel that an official party is unnecessary.*

◄ In this 1967 photograph, smog dims the view of the civic center in Los Angeles.

Environmental activism in the United States. Although the idea of an organized Green party failed to win much support in the United States, environmental protests did result in new legislation. In 1970 Congress passed the Clean Air Act, designed to reduce air pollution, including the **smog**—air polluted by chemical fumes, car exhaust, and smoke—that plagued most large cities. The **Federal Water Pollution Control Act** of 1972—better known as the Clean Water Act—and the **Safe Drinking Water Act** of 1974 were aimed at contaminated water. The **Endangered Species Act** of 1973 required the government to take action to safeguard animal species threatened with extinction.

Although the legislation of the early 1970s applied only to the United States, it reflected a growing realization that environmental problems were interrelated. More and more people were coming to appreciate the four laws of ecology that Barry Commoner proposed in his 1971 book *The Closing Circle:*

❝ Everything is connected to everything else.
Everything must go somewhere.
Nature knows best.
There is no such thing as a free lunch. ❞

Although some people disputed the third item, the other items, especially the first, appeared self-evident to many of the world's people.

■■ **Environmental activists became an organized political force in Europe. In the United States environmentalists pressured Congress to pass laws and regulations to protect people and the environment.**

SECTION 3 REVIEW

IDENTIFY and explain the significance of the following: Antarctic Treaty, Nuclear Nonproliferation Treaty, nuclear fallout, food chain, unilateral disarmament, Green parties, Petra Kelly, smog, Federal Water Pollution Control Act, Safe Drinking Water Act, Endangered Species Act, Barry Commoner.

1. **MAIN IDEA** How successful were international efforts to limit the threat of nuclear war? Explain your answer.
2. **MAIN IDEA** What kinds of environmental problems did nuclear weapons tests cause? How did people respond to these threats?
3. **MAIN IDEA** What methods did activists in Europe use to call attention to environmental problems during the 1960s, 1970s, and 1980s?
4. **WRITING TO EXPLAIN** Imagine you are a member of the Campaign for Nuclear Disarmament. Write an essay that explains why Great Britain should adopt a policy of unilateral disarmament.
5. **HYPOTHESIZING** How might voters respond to the development of a Green party in the United States?

PREVIEW WORKSHOP

Following is a list of the significant people, places, and terms in this section. You may wish to use this list as a section preview.

People
■ Chico Mendes

Places
■ Chernobyl
■ Antarctica

Terms
■ biomass
■ biodiversity
■ global warming
■ ozone layer
■ ultraviolet solar radiation
■ chlorofluorocarbons
■ acid rain
■ recycling

■ Third UN Conference on the Law of the Sea
■ Montreal Protocol on Ozone Depletion
■ Convention on Biological Diversity

Section 4

A SMALL PLANET

FOCUS
■ **Why did scientists continue to search for alternative sources of power in the 1990s?**
■ **Why do environmentalists think it is important to protect forest life?**
■ **What are some of the major global environmental problems that have concerned and divided nations? What solutions have been proposed to deal with these concerns?**

*O**f the many problems facing America and the rest of the world in the 1990s, some of the most important related to energy use and the environment. People realized that the earth's reserves of oil, gas, and coal—the fossil-based energy sources that had once seemed unlimited—would someday run out. Many also recognized that industrialization had taken a toll on the natural environment. In future decades the combination of population growth and environmental pollution could make life even more difficult.*

Cleaning waterfowl after the Alaska oil spill, 1989

FOCUS OBJECTIVES
■ Explain why scientists have continued to search for alternative sources of power in the 1990s.

■ Explain why environmentalists think it is important to protect forest life.

■ Identify some of the major global environmental problems that have concerned and divided nations, and examine the solutions that have been proposed to deal with these concerns.

 GLOBAL CONNECTIONS

Accidents like that at Chernobyl, test explosions of nuclear bombs, and the indiscriminate dumping of nuclear waste in landfills and at sea have made radioactive contamination "the number one environmental problem in [Russia]" an adviser to Boris Yeltsin noted. "The way we . . . dealt with the whole issue of nuclear power, . . . was irresponsible and immoral," he concluded.

CORE RESOURCES
• **Section 4 Daily Quiz**

 RESOURCES
• **The American Nation Videodisc: Images of America**
• **Everyday Life in America Transparency** and **Worksheet 33**

LIMITS ON ENERGY RESOURCES

In 1972 the Club of Rome, an international group of scientists, business leaders, and other environmentally concerned individuals, published *The Limits to Growth.* The report projected trends in such critical areas as population growth, food production, and pollution for the next several decades. If current trends continued, the report concluded, the limits to growth on the earth would be reached within a century. Should this occur, the most probable result would be a "sudden and uncontrollable decline in both population and industrial capacity"—in other words, the world's people would face a greatly reduced standard of living, and millions would die from hunger, disease, or war.

Some people criticized the report as far too pessimistic. Human ingenuity, they argued, would

find ways to do things as growing populations pressed against limited resources. They pointed out that the world's energy supply, for example, could be greatly expanded by turning to solar or hydroelectric power. Others claimed nuclear-power plants could supply clean, cheap energy.

Environmentalists, however, argued that some of the proposed solutions to shortages presented new problems. For instance, they continued to warn that nuclear-power plants presented serious hazards. In 1986 the kind of accident protesters had predicted occurred at the Chernobyl nuclear-power plant near Kiev, Ukraine (see map on page 735). The accident sent a cloud of radioactivity drifting across Europe and made the surrounding land unsafe for living things. The Chernobyl disaster pumped 50 times more radioactive material into the environment than the bombs dropped on Hiroshima and Nagasaki in World War II.

Teaching the Section

ALTERNATIVE ENERGY SOURCES

Call on volunteers to identify programs that their community supports to preserve and protect the environment. Note responses on a flip chart. As students read the section, have them compare their local environmental concerns and solutions to those in the global community.

Call on volunteers to identify the various sources of energy mentioned in the section, and note their responses on the chalkboard. Encourage students to discuss the advantages and disadvantages of each energy source, noting the major points of the discussion under the appropriate source. Then ask students to use the information on the chalkboard to write a generalization on why scientists continue to search for alternative sources of energy. Have students compare their generalizations.

MULTICULTURAL PERSPECTIVES

Paiakan, a leader of the Kayapó Indians of the Amazon, provided one description of the interrelated nature of life in the rain forest: "The forest is one big thing; it has people, animals, and plants. There is no point saving the animals if the forest is burned down; there is no point saving the forest if the people and animals who live in it are killed or driven away."

BIOGRAPHY PERSONALITIES IN HISTORY

Chico Mendes received death threats and knew of other environmentalists who had been assassinated in Brazil. He sought protection from any number of authorities, including the Federal Police, the state Tribunal of Justice, and the president of the republic. "Public gestures and a well-attended funeral will not save Amazônia," he said shortly before his death. "I want to live."

PRIMARY SOURCE

Description of Change: excerpted
Rationale: excerpted to focus on main idea

Chernobyl heightened public anxiety over nuclear power. Some called for increased funding for research on alternative energy sources such as solar power, wind power, and **biomass** (materials such as wood or waste products that can be burned or used to make fuel).

■■ **Concerns about limited energy supplies and the safety of nuclear power have sparked interest in alternative energy sources.**

*F*OREST LIFE

As scientists search for new forms of energy, many environmentalists focus on protecting the world's remaining forests and wildlife. Battered by population growth, industrialization, and expanding commercial agriculture and livestock operations, forests are disappearing at an alarming rate. The United Nations Food and Agriculture Organization reports that almost 42 million acres of tropical forests were lost per year between 1981 and 1990.

Experts warn that forests play a vital role in the larger ecosystem. Forests prevent floods and soil erosion. Trees also absorb carbon dioxide; therefore, as forests vanish, more carbon dioxide builds up in the atmosphere, contributing to atmospheric pollution and global warming (see page 736).

▲ **Clearing a piece of Amazon rain forest has become a controversial action now that people understand the importance of trees to the larger ecosystem.**

The debate over the loss of the rain forests is not a simple one. In poor nations, the rain forests are viewed as a source of jobs and income. Business and agricultural interests in developing nations argue that it is unfair for the industrialized world to call on poor nations to make economic sacrifices to preserve the rain forests.

BIOGRAPHY The conflict over the rain forests can be bitter. In the 1980s Chico Mendes, whose family made its living from tapping the sap from rubber trees in the rain forest of Brazil, organized a campaign against the destruction of the Amazonian rain forest by ranchers seeking grazing land for their cattle. Mendes, who was born Francisco Alves Mendes Filho in 1944, grew up with a deep appreciation of nature. "I became an ecologist long before I had ever heard the word," he once recalled.

Chico Mendes

In the 1960s, South American leaders instituted a plan to burn much of the rain forest in order to make way for industrialization and large-scale agriculture. Mendes opposed this destruction by organizing workers who tapped rubber trees and otherwise used the rain forest in environmentally responsible ways. Employing nonviolent methods of resistance such as boycotts and human blockades to stop heavy equipment, the protesters were able to focus worldwide attention on the rain forest.

Still, the burning of the rain forest continued. In 1988 Mendes declared:

❝ In the last half century Amazônia has never seen so many fires as in 1988. They are burning everything. Our airports were closed one week in 1987 because of the smoke. This year they were closed one month for the same reason. When you look down from the airplane, Amazônia is nothing but smoke. How it hurts! ❞

Later that year ranchers killed Mendes. However, the battle to save the Amazon and other tropical forests continues.

PROTECTING FOREST LIFE

Organize students in small groups to act as environmentalists who have been given the task of preparing an oral presentation on why it is necessary to protect endangered species and the rain forests. Have each group suggest methods that can be used to focus attention on these problems. Select groups to make their presentations to the class.

▶

Closely connected to the loss of the rain forests is the danger to **biodiversity**, the wide variety of the earth's plant and animal species. Rain forests are home to about half the earth's species. As the forests vanish, some species may be lost forever. Biologist Edward O. Wilson of Harvard estimates that at the rate rain forest habitat is being destroyed, 25 percent or more of the world's species could become extinct in the next 50 years. Furthermore, the vast majority of these species are undiscovered.

Efforts to save plants and animals are not limited to the rain forests. Activists are campaigning to save from extinction at least some of the species threatened by growing human populations and the spread of cities and industrial areas. For example, Greenpeace, an international environmental organization, has successfully campaigned against whaling. As a result, most countries have joined the International Whaling Commission's moratorium on hunting great whales.

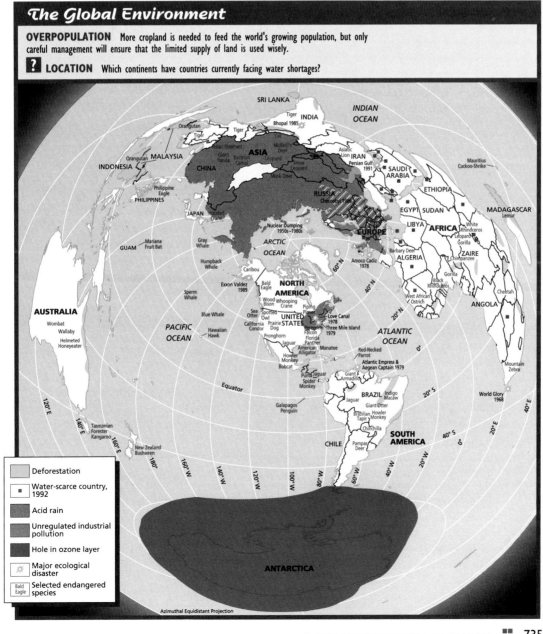

The Global Environment

OVERPOPULATION More cropland is needed to feed the world's growing population, but only careful management will ensure that the limited supply of land is used wisely.

? LOCATION Which continents have countries currently facing water shortages?

Legend:
- Deforestation
- Water-scarce country, 1992
- Acid rain
- Unregulated industrial pollution
- Hole in ozone layer
- Major ecological disaster
- Selected endangered species

Azimuthal Equidistant Projection

MAKING CONNECTIONS
Science

Conservationists in Costa Rica sought to promote biodiversity by cataloging plants, animals, and insects in the Central American rain forest. Costa Rica is smaller than West Virginia, but contains an estimated 500,000 to one million species. The Costa Rican National Biodiversity Institute, called INBIO, focuses on identifying insects and microorganisms, because these species are often ignored in other projects.

Teaching the Section

ENVIRONMENTAL HAZARDS

Write the term *environmental hazards* on the chalkboard and circle it. Draw lines out from the circle. Then ask students to identify the environmental hazards that are threatening human health and survival. (*global warming, ozone depletion, acid rain, water pollution, population explosion*) Write responses at the ends of the lines.

Call on volunteers to explain the causes and effects of each hazard. Close by discussing how such environmental hazards can cause conflict as well as mutual concern among nations.

■■ **Environmentalists are working to prevent deforestation and the extinction of species.**

ENVIRONMENTAL POLLUTION

The rise in global energy consumption and the continued loss of the world's forests have led to growing concern over **global warming**, the gradual increase in the temperature of the earth's atmosphere. Global warming results from the greenhouse effect. The burning of fossil fuels and the cutting and burning of forests have polluted the earth's atmosphere with excess levels of carbon dioxide and with other gases that allow solar radiation to penetrate to the earth's surface while preventing heat from escaping. Scientists warn that over time the greenhouse effect could cause temperate areas to become so hot that crops would wither. The melting of the polar ice caps could flood coastal areas, jeopardizing many cities. Some scientists charge that the greenhouse effect is already harming the environment. Six of the seven hottest years on record since statistics were first kept in the mid-1800s were between 1980 and 1991.

A related danger is the thinning of the **ozone layer**—the thin veil of molecules some 10 to 30 miles above the earth's surface—that protects the earth from **ultraviolet solar radiation** (UV rays). Ultraviolet solar radiation can cause skin cancer, damage marine life, and harm crops. To date, the greatest area of ozone thinning has been in Antarctica (see map on page 735). But environmentalists warn that other areas are thinning at various times of the year. Much of the damage to the ozone layer has been caused by chemicals called **chlorofluorocarbons** (CFCs)—combinations of carbon, chlorine, fluorine, and sometimes hydrogen—which have been pumped into the atmosphere by industrialized nations. CFCs are used in the manufacture of aerosol sprays, refrigerator and air-conditioner coolants, electronics, and plastics.

▲ These aerosol cans appear harmless, but the chlorofluorocarbons they can add to the earth's atmosphere are not.

▶ Acid rain not only injures trees and lakes but also damages buildings and monuments. This statue in St. Peter's Square, Rome, is gradually deteriorating because of exposure to acid rain.

A third hazard of atmospheric pollution is **acid rain**. Factories and automobiles spew sulfur dioxide and nitrogen oxide, which combine with the moisture in the atmosphere and later fall as acid rain, often far from their places of origin. This acid rain gradually kills trees and makes lakes unfit for fish. In the 1980s and the 1990s, regions as distant as southern China, the Appalachian Mountains in eastern North America, the lakes in northern Canada, and the mountains of Central Europe showed the effects of acid rain.

Acid rain has become a major source of conflict between the United States and Canada. Industrial smoke from Michigan factories is believed to have a major effect on rain acidity in Canada. As the United States weakened environmental standards during the 1980s, Canadians strongly protested that this action unfairly affected their environment. As a result, Canada has become one of the leaders in trying to improve global awareness about acid rain, especially in the United States.

The United States has a better record when it comes to dealing with water pollution. Since the Clean Water Act became law in 1972, the United States has made great progress in cleaning up its rivers and lakes. Environmentalists note that water quality has also improved in much of the industrialized world, largely because of better sewage treatment. In many of the cities of the developing world, however, industrial wastes and untreated sewage still pollute water supplies and threaten public health.

Pollution from oil spills also presents serious problems. Spills, such as the 1989 *Exxon*

Valdez accident along the coast of Alaska, kill countless fish and waterfowl and cost millions of dollars to clean up. As a result, environmentalists and many government leaders are calling for stricter controls.

POPULATION EXPLOSION

Many of the world's toughest problems have been made worse by a massive increase in population. In 1994 the world's population was estimated at 5.7 billion, and it was growing by a rate of three people every second. Much of this growth has been concentrated in the developing world. While the population of the industrialized nations grew by only 0.7 percent from 1983 to 1988, in many developing nations it grew by 2 or 3 percent a year. Experts predict that India's population will jump from 866 million in 1991 to 1.3 billion by 2020; Mexico's, from 90 million to 152 million; and Bangladesh's, from 116.6 million to 210 million. By 2020, Africa is expected to account for about 18 percent of the world's population, in contrast to 9 percent in 1950.

Experts suggest that the world's population growth will not begin to slow until women have an average of 2.06 children. The UN estimates that even if this goal is achieved, the world's population will still continue to increase (because so many people will reach child-bearing age in the next 25 years) until it reaches 11.6 billion in 2150.

Many experts on population, however, note that living standards will have to improve for people in the developing world before the world's

▲ These farmers in southern Bangladesh are harvesting rice, the chief crop of this populous nation.

poor think it makes economic sense to have fewer children. Furthermore, some social critics charge that the developed world is unfairly blaming the world's environmental problems on population growth in the developing world, which uses relatively little of the world's resources. Brazilian historian Fatima Vianna Mello argues that unless the developed world is willing to limit its consumption of the world's resources, its call for women in the developing world to have fewer children, "blames the poor people of the world for the tremendous [social

POPULATION SINCE THE YEAR A.D. I

A.D. I	1800	1950	2000	2050	2150
200 Million	I Billion	2 Billion	6.3 Billion*	10.0 Billion*	11.6 Billion*

2025
8.5 Billion*

* Projected by the United Nations Population Fund   Source: *The New York Times*

POPULATION GROWTH Some scientists question how long the earth can support rapid increases in human populations without severely damaging the ecosystem.

❓ BUILDING CHART SKILLS In 1950 the world's population was some 2 billion. About how many times larger will the estimated population be in the year 2000?

*P*ractice

GUIDED PRACTICE

Call on volunteers to identify major energy and environmental challenges that the nation faces today. List responses on the chalkboard, asking students to provide background information on each item.

INDEPENDENT PRACTICE

Have students choose one of the challenges listed in the Guided Practice activity. Then have them create a full-page, illustrated magazine or newspaper advertisement that focuses on their selected challenge. Encourage students to display and discuss their advertisements. Students may wish to include their advertisements in their portfolios.

*R*eview and *A*ssessment

REVIEW Suggest that students write the main ideas of the section in the form of newspaper headlines. Ask volunteers to present their headlines to the class and have class members suggest details for news stories that might accompany the headlines. Then assign the Section 4 Review on p. 739.

ASSESS Assign the **Section 4 Daily Quiz** in *Core Resources.*

 GLOBAL CONNECTIONS

Recycling is a vital activity in Curitiba, Brazil, with its population of more than two million people. Soda bottles are turned into lamps for jogging paths, and old telephone poles are used in construction projects.

HISTORICAL SIDELIGHTS

Products from Garbage
Industries have found creative uses for recycled materials. Sawdust, wood scraps, plastic bags, and industrial shrink-wrap have been combined to make a wood substitute. One brand of hiking shoe contains recycled rubber tires, plastic bottles, and white paper.

COOPERATIVE LEARNING

Organize students into small groups to create a "debate page" on one of the environmental issues discussed in the section. Suggest that pages include pro and con statements, editorial cartoons, and maps. Direct group members to choose tasks involving research, writing, artwork, and design. Allow time for groups to present and discuss their pages.

WOMEN AND POPULATION GROWTH

THROUGH OTHERS' EYES

*S*ome argue that one of the keys to limiting population growth in developing countries is to advance the status of women. As India's former prime minister Indira Gandhi wrote in 1980: "Men and most women are unaware of the potential ability of women. Their lives are entrapped by pre-conceived notions and attitudes from birth onwards. . . . A lower status for women, or lesser opportunity for women, is a handicap for the growth of mankind as a whole." Gandhi believed that if women are granted equality of rights and opportunity, they will no longer be valued primarily for their ability to produce children.

and] environmental imbalances that exist." Other researchers, however, warn that if population growth in the developing world is not reduced, shortages of renewable resources such as land and water, can occur and lead to conflict. In Bangladesh, for example, rapid population growth has contributed to a scarcity of land. As a result, millions of Bangladeshis have migrated to India, sparking ethnic conflict.

▶ Growing populations have overburdened the sanitation resources of many cities. Some cities have loaded their garbage on barges and tried to export it to other areas— often without success. The governor of Florida, for example, refused to allow this New York barge to dock in his state.

▪▪ Environmentalists and government leaders face problems of global warming, ozone depletion, acid rain, water pollution, and growing populations.

*R*ECYCLING AND URBAN GROWTH

As environmental awareness grows, **recycling—** the collection and processing of used items for reuse—has been winning support. Recycling serves two important purposes: it reuses scarce natural resources, and it reduces the mountain of solid waste that must be burned in incinerators, buried in overflowing landfills, dumped into the sea, or shipped to disposal facilities in poorer nations. In 1991 the United States recycled an estimated 14 percent of its solid waste, while Japan recycled 50 percent of its paper and 54 percent of its glass.

Much of the interest in recycling is related to urban growth. Experts predict that by the year 2000 there will be at least 21 cities with populations of 10 million or more. Of these, 18 will be in poor, developing nations. One expert estimates that the enormous amount of garbage created in these cities threatens the health of 40 percent of the urban population in the developing world.

Many cities are making use of innovative systems to recycle garbage. In Cairo, Egypt, some 30,000 Zabaleens (Christians from southern Egypt) collect the city's garbage, sort through it,

---

738

Closure

Ask students to develop a list of world environmental challenges and to compare it to the list they developed in Guided Practice. Then refer students to the statement by the Worldwatch Institute on p. 739. Call on students to indicate whether or not the lists they have developed support the statement.

Extension

INVESTIGATE Encourage students to investigate and report on an alternative energy source under development at the present time.

CREATE Encourage students to use information from atlases, almanacs, encyclopedias, and statistical abstracts to create a database on the major global environmental problems.

---

and sell the reusable parts. Thrown-away food goes to feed pigs. Scrap metal, glass, paper, and plastic are recycled.

One recycling expert notes that Cairo's system has economic as well as environmental benefits:

> 66 Zabaleens make as much as three times the average income in Cairo. In many developing countries, up to 2 percent of the population is supported directly or indirectly by refuse from the upper 20 percent of the population. 99

THE WORLD RESPONDS

Growing environmental dangers stirred the international community to action. For instance, in the 1982 agreements issued by the **Third UN Conference on the Law of the Sea**, participating nations pledged to protect the marine environment of coastal waters and to make the oceans "the common heritage of mankind."

Confronted with the urgent danger of ozone depletion, the international community again took action. The **Montreal Protocol on Ozone Depletion**, signed in Montreal, Canada, in 1987, set standards for reducing the emission of CFCs and other gases that threatened the ozone layer. In 1990, as evidence of ozone depletion grew more alarming, this agreement was made even stricter. Ninety-three nations pledged to halt CFC production entirely within the decade, and more ozone-

damaging chemicals were added to the banned list. In addition, the industrialized nations agreed to contribute $240 million to enable developing countries to purchase alternatives to CFCs.

In 1992, the 20th anniversary of the first United Nations conference on the environment, the UN sponsored the United Nations Conference on Environment and Development—dubbed the Earth Summit—in Rio de Janeiro, Brazil. Attracting delegations from 178 nations and about 1,200 private environmental organizations, the conference yielded some significant compromises. One was a treaty, the **Convention on Biological Diversity**, which went into effect on December 29, 1993. The treaty committed the 167 nations signing it to the protection of biodiversity and mandated that industrialized nations share profits from biotechnology products they bring to market with the developing countries providing the natural resources.

The rise in environmental awareness has also been evident in the growth of private organizations and lobbying groups, such as the international Worldwatch Institute. These groups have tried to work together to promote international cooperation and concern about the environment. As the Worldwatch Institute noted in 1992: "In an environmentally interdependent world, no country can separate its fate from that of the world as a whole."

■■ Recycling and international cooperation are among the solutions promoted to control global environmental hazards.

SECTION REVIEW ANSWERS

IDENTIFY

See the following pages:
biomass (p. 734)
Chico Mendes (p. 734)
biodiversity (p. 735)
global warming (p. 736)
ozone layer (p. 736)
ultraviolet solar radiation (p. 736)
chlorofluorocarbons (p. 736)
acid rain (p. 736)
recycling (p. 738)
Third UN Conference on the Law of the Sea (p. 739)
Montreal Protocol on Ozone Depletion (p. 739)
Convention on Biological Diversity (p. 739)

LOCATE

See the map on p. 735.
1. *called for increased research into alternative energy sources*
2. *prevent floods and soil erosion, absorb carbon dioxide, shelter many species*
3. *destruction of rain forests, loss of species, global warming, thinning of ozone layer, acid rain, population explosion*
4. *Letters should identify local problems and suggest methods of alleviating them.*
5. *Students should mention agreements designed to protect the environment.*

SECTION 4 REVIEW

IDENTIFY and explain the significance of the following: biomass, Chico Mendes, biodiversity, global warming, ozone layer, ultraviolet solar radiation, chlorofluorocarbons, acid rain, recycling, Third UN Conference on the Law of the Sea, Montreal Protocol on Ozone Depletion, Convention on Biological Diversity.

LOCATE and explain the importance of the following: Chernobyl, Antarctica.

1. **MAIN IDEA** How did people respond to the threat of energy shortages?
2. **MAIN IDEA** Why are forests important to the ecosystem?
3. **MAIN IDEA** What are some of the environmental problems facing the world in the 1990s?
4. **WRITING TO PERSUADE** Write a letter to your local newspaper outlining possible solutions to environmental problems in your community.
5. **IDENTIFYING VALUES** Provide support for the view that the international community values a healthy environment.

DEVELOPING THEMES

Return to the "Themes" section on p. 720. Have students discuss these again and compare their original responses to those given now. (See p. 719B for suggested answers.)

Chapter Review Answers

WRITING A SUMMARY
See Essential Points in each section for main ideas.

REVIEWING CHRONOLOGY
5, 1, 3, 2, 4
Analyzing
Answers should address increased concern about pollution and the environment.

IDENTIFYING PEOPLE AND IDEAS

1. *science that focuses on relationships between species and the environment*
2. *idea that environment should be used, but used wisely*
3. *preservationist who applied principles of ecology to wildlife management*
4. *radioactive debris produced by nuclear reaction*
5. *leader of Die Grünen*
6. *elimination of nuclear weapons by one country*
7. *materials such as wood or waste products that can be burned to make fuel*
8. *Brazilian ecologist who worked to save rain forests*
9. *increase in temperature of the earth's surface*
10. *collection and processing of used items for reuse*

UNDERSTANDING MAIN IDEAS

1. People became aware of the ways that they and other species interacted with the environment. The birth of the ecology movement encouraged conservation.
2. preservationists—set aside wilderness areas; conservationists—use environment wisely
3. brought national attention to environmental issues
4. demonstrated that environmental developments could have worldwide effects
5. international agreements, recycling, population control, industrial controls

CHAPTER 27
Review

| Ernst Haeckel names the science of ecology. | Yellowstone National Park established. | Frederick Jackson Turner declares that the frontier promoted democracy. | Canadian Forestry Association founded. | DDT used to prevent a typhus epidemic. | Antarctic Treaty signed. |

1866 — 1872 — 1893 — 1900 — 1943 — 1959

WRITING A SUMMARY
Using the essential points of the chapter as a guide, write a summary of the chapter.

REVIEWING CHRONOLOGY
Number your paper 1 to 5. Study the time line above, and list the following events in the order in which they happened by writing the first next to 1, the second next to 2, and so on. Then complete the activity below.

1. Earth Summit held in Rio de Janeiro.
2. Frederick Jackson Turner declared that the frontier promoted democracy.
3. Antarctic Treaty signed.
4. Canadian Forestry Association founded.
5. Chernobyl accident occurred.

Analyzing How have incidents such as the Chernobyl accident and the *Exxon Valdez* oil spill affected public thinking about the environment?

IDENTIFYING PEOPLE AND IDEAS
Explain the historical significance of each of the following people or terms.

1. ecology
2. conservation
3. Aldo Leopold
4. nuclear fallout
5. Petra Kelly
6. unilateral disarmament
7. biomass
8. Chico Mendes
9. global warming
10. recycling

UNDERSTANDING MAIN IDEAS
1. How did American views of the wilderness change between the colonial period and the 19th century? How did the birth of the ecology movement affect American views of the environment?
2. How did the views of the environment held by preservationists differ from those held by conservationists?
3. What effect did the Dust Bowl disaster have on environmental thinking in the United States?
4. How did the development of nuclear weapons encourage people and governments to look for global solutions to environmental problems?

5. What solutions have been proposed to deal with major environmental problems in the 1990s?

REVIEWING THEMES
1. **Technology and Society** How have technological developments affected the environment?
2. **Global Relations** How have nations tried to work together to solve environmental problems?
3. **Economic Development** How does the need for economic development sometimes influence a country's policy on the environment?

THINKING CRITICALLY
1. **Analyzing** Since the 1960s, how have environmentalists tried to protect forest life?
2. **Evaluating** What effect did progressives have on Americans' views of the environment?
3. **Comparing and Contrasting** How do the links between environmental protest and politics differ in the United States and in Europe?

STRATEGY FOR SUCCESS
Review the Skills Handbook entry on Reading Charts and Graphs beginning on page 756. Study the graph below, which shows changes in the concentration of carbon dioxide in the earth's atmosphere. Carbon dioxide concentrations were fairly stable until the 18th century. During what time period did concentrations increase most dramatically? What historical developments may have contributed to this increase in carbon dioxide concentrations?

CARBON DIOXIDE IN THE ENVIRONMENT

Carbon Dioxide Concentration (ppmv): 360, 340, 320, 300, 280, 260

Year: 1750 1800 1850 1900 1950 2000

Source: *The Cambridge Factfinder*

REVIEWING THEMES

1. increased pollution, greater risk of nuclear radiation
2. international agreements such as Montreal Protocol on Ozone Depletion
3. need for economic development often overrides concern for environment

THINKING CRITICALLY

1. nonviolent protest methods such as boycotts, blockades; campaigns to limit industrial pollution that leads to acid rain; international agreements such as Convention on Biological Diversity
2. encouraged Americans to think about the ways in which they used the environment
3. Europe—organized political parties with environmental platforms; United States—environmental protests, congressional legislation

STRATEGY FOR SUCCESS

after 1950; spread of development and industrialization

WRITING ABOUT HISTORY

Letters should describe party organization and methods used to call attention to environmental issues. Students should explain how official political parties can call constant attention to ecological issues.

USING PRIMARY SOURCES

Radical environmentalists argue that extinction is irreversible, and therefore action must be immediate and dramatic.

LINKING HISTORY AND GEOGRAPHY

Europe, northeastern United States, southeastern Canada; Eastern Europe, Russia, Asia; unregulated pollution is not confined by political boundaries

| 1962 | 1968 | 1972 | 1973 | 1986 | 1987 | 1989 | 1992 | 1993 |

Rachel Carson's *Silent Spring* published.

Treaty on Nonproliferation of Nuclear Weapons signed.

The Limits to Growth published.

Endangered Species Act passed.

Chernobyl accident occurs.

Montreal Protocol on Ozone Depletion signed.

Exxon Valdez spills oil along Alaska coast.

Earth Summit held in Rio de Janeiro.

Convention on Biological Diversity goes into effect.

WRITING ABOUT HISTORY

Writing to Describe Imagine you are an environmental activist in Great Britain, France, or Germany during the 1970s or 1980s. Write a letter to a group of activists in the United States. Describe the role played by the Green party in your chosen country, and explain why you think Green parties are necessary for environmental reform.

USING PRIMARY SOURCES

In the early 1980s a new environmental movement, symbolized by groups such as Earth First!, emerged. The movement abandoned conservative protests against corporations in favor of more-radical actions, such as tree sitting, inserting spikes into trees, and destroying logging equipment. Read the following excerpt from the book *Green Rage*, which profiles this movement. How do radical environmentalists justify the methods they use?

66 *In general, however, radical environmentalism has no pretensions of being a mass movement and does not expect the huge demonstrations the civil rights and antiwar movements produced. It aims to harass more than obstruct, with the hope that the public awareness it generates will do the rest. . . .*

A more important difference in strategy stems from the extreme urgency of the environmental crisis. . . . For the "constancy" of the biocentric civil rights movement, however, there is often no tomorrow. Once an old-growth forest is cut, it will not grow back for hundreds of years, if ever. Once a species becomes extinct the battle is lost. This sense of urgency often motivates the use of ecological civil disobedience, not to make far-reaching changes in society's views of the environment, but merely to buy time for legal redress or for the emergence of public pressure. 99

LINKING HISTORY AND GEOGRAPHY

Refer to the map on page 735. Which areas of the world suffer from acid rain? Which areas include countries that do not regulate industrial pollution? What conclusion can you draw from this information?

BUILDING YOUR PORTFOLIO

Complete the following projects independently or cooperatively.

1. WAR In chapters 24 and 25 you explored the effects of war on nations' economies and on people fleeing from war. Building on that experience, imagine you belong to an environmental organization in the 1950s or 1960s. Create a pamphlet explaining how the Cold War is affecting the environment and urging people to act to prevent further environmental damage from Cold War rivalries.

2. THE ECONOMY In chapters 23 and 25 you explored links between the economy, imperialism, and immigration. Building on that experience, imagine you work for an advertising agency that specializes in environmental topics. Write a script for a commercial urging people to follow ecological practices and explaining why such practices will benefit the economy in the long run.

Button showing 1970s and 1980s antinuclear slogan.

3. INTERNATIONAL COOPERATION In chapters 24 and 26 you examined how nations tried to strengthen the global economy and to protect human rights worldwide. Building on that experience, imagine you are a government official preparing to meet with environmental groups. Make a poster showing how your government has participated in the 1980s and 1990s in international efforts to protect the environment.

BUILDING YOUR PORTFOLIO

Have students refer to **Building Your Portfolio Worksheet 6**, assigned at the beginning of Unit 6. Use the worksheet to help students monitor their progress on the portfolio projects.

Assessment

Core Resources
- Reteaching Worksheet 27
- Chapter 27 Tests
- Alternative Assessment Forms

Test Generator

THE PAINS OF WAR

HISTORICAL SIDELIGHT

Surviving the Holocaust

After his liberation from Buchenwald, Elie Wiesel was taken to France along with other children who had survived the concentration camps. He eventualy studied at the Sorbonne in Paris and became a journalist, traveling to Israel to report on the struggle to establish a Jewish state. In 1958 he moved to New York, and in 1963 he became an American citizen. One year later he retired from journalism to concentrate on his own writing and lecturing, and in 1986 he was awarded the Nobel Peace Prize.

UNIT 6

American Letters

The Pains of War

Numerous wars have marked the 20th century. Some, such as World Wars I and II, have affected Americans as well as many peoples around the world. But all wars are significant to those who experience them personally. Nigerian poet and playwright Wole Soyinka, Romanian-born concentration-camp survivor Elie Wiesel, Vietnamese writer Nguyen Thi Vinh, and Chilean novelist Isabel Allende are among those who have experienced and written about war.

▲ Elie Wiesel

Civilian and Soldier

by Wole Soyinka

My apparition[1] rose from the fall of lead,
Declared, "I'm a civilian." It only served
To aggravate your fright. For how could I
Have risen, a being of this world, in that hour
Of impartial death! And I thought also: nor is
Your quarrel of this world.

            You stood still
For both eternities, and oh I heard the lesson
Of your training sessions, cautioning—
Scorch earth behind you, do not leave
A dubious neutral to the rear. Reiteration
Of my civilian quandary,[2] burrowing earth
From the lead festival of your more eager friends
Worked the worse on your confusion, and when
You brought the gun to bear on me, and death
Twitched me gently in the eye, your plight
And all of you came clear to me.

            I hope some day
Intent upon my trade of living, to be checked
In stride by *your* apparition in a trench,
Signaling, I am a soldier. No hesitation then
But I shall shoot you clean and fair
With meat and bread, a gourd of wine
A bunch of breasts from either arm, and that
Lone question—do you friend, even now, know
What it is all about? ❖

---

1 ghost-like appearance
2 dilemma.

From *Night*

by Elie Wiesel

In front of us flames. In the air that smell of burning flesh. It must have been about midnight. We had arrived—at Birkenau, reception center for Auschwitz.

The cherished objects we had brought with us thus far were left behind in the train, and with them, at last, our illusions.

Every two yards or so an SS man held his Tommy gun[3] trained on us. Hand in hand we followed the crowd.

An SS noncommissioned officer came to meet us, a truncheon in his hand. He gave the order:

"Men to the left! Women to the right!"

Eight words spoken quietly, indifferently, without emotion. Eight short, simple words. Yet that was the moment when I parted from my mother. I had not had time to think, but already I felt the pressure of my father's hand: we were alone. For a part of a second I glimpsed my mother and my sisters moving away to the right. Tzipora held Mother's hand. I saw them disappear into the distance; my mother was stroking my sister's fair hair, as though to protect her, while I walked on with my father and the other men. And I did not know that in that place, at that moment, I was parting from my mother and Tzipora forever. I went on walking. My father held onto my hand.

Behind me, an old man fell to the ground. Near him was an SS man, putting his revolver back in its holster. ❖

---

3 submachine gun

From *Thoughts of Hanoi*

by Nguyen Thi Vinh

The night is deep and chill
as in early autumn. Pitchblack,
it thickens after each lightning
    flash.
I dream of Hanoi:
Co-ngu Road
ten years of separation
the way back sliced by a frontier
    of hatred. . . .

Brother,
how is Hang Dao now?
How is Ngoc Son temple?
Do the trains still run
each day from Hanoi
to the neighboring towns?
To Bac-ninh, Cam-giang, Yen-bai,
the small villages, islands
of brown thatch in a lush green
    sea? . . .

Stainless blue sky,
    jubilant voices of children
stumbling through the alphabet,
    village graybeards strolling to
    the temple,
grandmothers basking in twilight
    sun,
    chewing betel leaves
while the children run—

Brother,
how is all that now?
Or is it obsolete?
Are you like me,
reliving the past,
imagining the future?
Do you count me as a friend
or am I the enemy in your eyes?
Brother, I am afraid
that one day I'll be with the
    March-North Army
meeting you on your way to
    the South.
I might be the one to shoot
    you then

or you me
but please
not with hatred.

For don't you remember how
    it was,
you and I in school together,
plotting our lives together?
Those roots go deep!

Brother, we are men,
conscious of more
than material needs.
How can this happen to us
my friend
my foe? ❖

From *The House of the Spirits*

by Isabel Allende

Then came the roar of the airplanes, and the bombing began. Jaime threw himself to the floor with everyone else, unable to believe what he was seeing; until the day before, he had been convinced that nothing like this would ever happen in his country and that even the military respected the law. Only the President was on his feet. He walked to the window carrying a bazooka and fired it at the tanks below. Jaime inched his way to him and grabbed him by the calves to make him get down, but the President replied with a curse and remained erect.

Fifteen minutes later the whole building was in flames, and it was impossible to breathe because of the bombs and the smoke. Jaime crawled among the broken furniture and bits of plaster that were falling around him like a deadly rain, attempting to help the wounded, but he could only offer words of comfort and close the eyes of the dead. In a sudden pause in the shooting, the President gathered the survivors and told them to leave because he did not want any martyrs or needless sacrifice; everyone had a family, and important tasks lay ahead. "I'm going to call a truce so you can leave," he added. But no one moved. Though a few of them were trembling, all were in apparent possession of their dignity. The bombing was brief, but it left the palace in ruins. By two o'clock in the afternoon the fire had consumed the old drawing rooms that had been used since colonial times, and only a handful of men were left around the President. Soldiers entered the building and took what was left of the first floor. Above the din was heard the hysterical voice of an officer ordering them to surrender and come down single file with their hands on their heads. The President shook each of them by the hand. "I'll go last," he said. They never again saw him alive. ❖

THINKING AND WRITING ABOUT LITERATURE

1. What views regarding the shooting of civilians during warfare does Wole Soyinka present in his poem?
2. Why does Elie Wiesel attribute so much importance to the eight words spoken by the SS officer?
3. How does the speaker in Nguyen Thi Vinh's poem recall Hanoi? How has war changed the speaker's relationship with childhood companions?
4. Why do you think the bombing described by Isabel Allende occurred? Where do the author's sympathies lie?

PRIMARY SOURCES

Description of Change: excerpted and footnoted
Rationale: excerpted for space considerations; footnoted to clarify meaning

THINKING AND WRITING ABOUT LITERATURE

1. *He presents it as meaningless and cruel.*
2. *The words have separated his family and deprived him of the security represented by his mother.*
3. *The speaker recalls Hanoi as a town filled with life. War has made Hanoi a stranger, just as many former friends are strangers and perhaps enemies.*
4. *The bombing seems to have been part of a military coup. The author's sympathies lie with the president and the other people in the palace rather than with the military.*

COMPARING POINTS OF VIEW

Guide students through the explanation of how to identify and compare points of view, and have them complete the Practicing the Strategy exercise. Then have students review the discussion of women's roles in different areas of the world on pp. 712–713. Have students speculate about the significance of women in high political office.

PRACTICING THE STRATEGY

1. *Mello feels that the developed world is also responsible for the problems posed by population growth.*
2. *Her point of view suggests that people in developed nations need to limit their consumption of the world's resources, just as people in developing nations need to limit their patterns of reproduction.*

Strategies for Success

COMPARING POINTS OF VIEW

We all bring to our experiences a point of view, a personal frame of reference from which we see or think about things. Because a variety of factors influence a person's outlook, people often have different—and sometimes conflicting—points of view about a particular topic. Comparing varied views and voices helps us understand the historical debates that have shaped the present, as well as the current debates that will shape the future.

How to Compare Points of View

1. **Note the sources.** Find out about each author or speaker. Check whether each is an authority on the subject under discussion.
2. **Do research.** Find out all you can about the subject.
3. **Compare and contrast the main ideas.** Note similarities and differences in the main ideas being expressed.
4. **Compare supporting details.** Consider whether the ideas are supported by relevant facts, by opinions, or by both. Evaluate the logic of the supporting arguments, and look for any bias.
5. **Evaluate the points of view.** Apply your critical thinking skills to appreciate why people have different points of view and to weigh the accuracy, reliability, and implications of each view.

Applying the Strategy

One of the topics over which people have conflicting points of view concerns the effects that population growth will have on the earth and on future societies. Read and compare the following points of view.

> 66 The effect of higher population density actually seems to be positive. . . . The central benefit of more people in a more developed world is that there are more . . . people to invent new ideas. . . . If population had not increased about 8,000 years ago and made hunting and gathering become less productive, we would be having wild roots, rabbits, and berries for lunch. 99
>
> —Julian Simon, Economist

> 66 There are limits to the rates at which [the] human population . . . can use materials and energy, and there are limits to the rates at which wastes can be emitted without harm. . . . Human society is now using resources and producing wastes at rates that are not sustainable. . . . Even with much more efficient institutions and technologies, the limits of the earth's ability to support population . . . are close at hand. 99
>
> —Meadows, Meadows, and Randers, Population Researchers

Julian Simon, a noted economist, claims that rapid population growth may in fact be a good thing. He points out that the earth's population has grown throughout history and that people have always developed techniques to support the growing population. Based on this historical precedent, Simon is optimistic that people will continue to find ways of supporting larger populations.

Meadows, Meadows, and Randers, researchers who contributed to the 1972 report *The Limits to Growth* and wrote the 1992 sequel *Beyond the Limits,* argue that the earth can support only a finite number of people. In contrast to Simon, they believe that technological advances will not be sufficient to provide for the growing population.

Which point of view comes closest to truth remains to be seen. What is clear, however, is that each point of view has different implications for how political leaders, policymakers, and even ordinary citizens should act. The views we take today regarding the effects of population growth may well shape history for the populations of tomorrow.

Practicing the Strategy

Read the remarks by Brazilian historian Fatima Vianna Mello on pages 737–738. Then, on a separate sheet of paper, answer the following questions.
1. What is Vianna Mello's point of view regarding population growth?
2. What implications does her point of view have for how people—both in developed and developing nations—should act?

BUILDING YOUR PORTFOLIO

Each portfolio project described below is the culmination of the Building Your Portfolio activities in the chapter reviews of Unit 6. First, decide whether you wish students to work individually or in groups on these unit projects. Then permit each student to choose the project on which he or she desires to work. Provide students with copies of **Building Your Portfolio Worksheet 6** from *Core Resources*. This worksheet will guide students step by step to complete their projects.

BUILDING YOUR PORTFOLIO

Outlined below are four projects. Independently or cooperatively, complete one and use the products to demonstrate your mastery of the historical concepts involved.

1 WAR

Wars almost always have profound effects on the economy, the peoples, and the natural environment of a society or even of the entire world. Using the portfolio materials you designed in chapters 24, 25, and 27, develop a series of one-scene plays showing the various effects of wars such as World War I, World War II, and the Cold War. Each play should focus on a different effect or group of people.

2 THE ECONOMY

Nearly every global phenomenon can be linked in some way to economics. Using the portfolio materials you designed in chapters 23, 25, and 27, write a report to be distributed by the World Bank on how nations around the world might improve their economies. Your report should take into account the different economic needs of different nations.

3 INTERNATIONAL COOPERATION

The 20th century has been marked by numerous international efforts to cooperate on such matters as the global economy, human rights, and the environment. Using the portfolio materials you designed in chapters 24, 26, and 27, conduct a panel discussion with representatives from several nations evaluating the effectiveness of various efforts at international cooperation. Discussions might also address how to ensure the success of future efforts.

4 INDIVIDUAL RIGHTS

Even though individual rights have become more inclusive over the past several centuries, even in the 20th century some groups have found their rights limited. Using the portfolio materials you designed in chapters 23, 24, and 26, create a visual display showing how individual rights have been threatened in different parts of the world during the 1900s. Your display should also include examples of improvements in the realm of individual rights.

Videodisc Review

In assigned groups, develop an outline for a video collage of one of the themes discussed in this unit. Choose images that best illustrate the theme throughout the 20th century. Write a script to accompany the images. Assign narrators to different parts of the script, and present your video collage to the class.

Further Reading

Betts, Raymond F. *Uncertain Dimensions: Western Overseas Empires in the Twentieth Century.* University of Minnesota Press (1985). Thematic analysis of imperialism from World War I through decolonization.

Cameron, Rondo. *A Concise Economic History of the World.* Oxford (1993). Overview of international economic history from ancient times to the present.

Drinan, Robert F. *Cry of the Oppressed: The History and Hope of the Human Rights Revolution.* Harper & Row (1987). Overview of efforts to protect human rights since 1945.

Maltby, Richard. *Passing Parade: A History of Popular Culture in the Twentieth Century.* Oxford (1989). Pictorial history of 20th century popular culture in a global context.

Worster, Donald. *Nature's Economy.* Cambridge (1994). A History of Ecological Ideas.

PORTFOLIO ASSESSMENT

1. *Plays should dramatize the effects of war on people, governments, economies, and the environment.*
2. *Reports should suggest improvements in the economies of different nations while recognizing that one solution will not work for all countries.*
3. *Panel discussions should address the need for international cooperation and should develop some agreement to improve conditions in one of the areas listed.*
4. *Displays should illustrate the different threats to individual rights as well as efforts to improve protection of rights.*

Reference
SECTION
▦

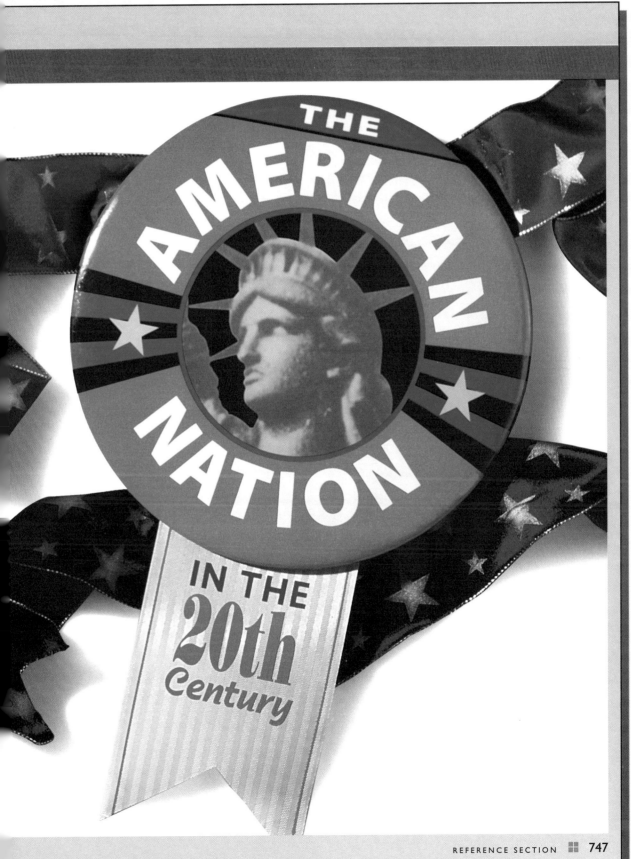

THE AMERICAN NATION

IN THE 20th Century

Your understanding and appreciation of the past will grow as your study skills improve. This Skills Handbook contains instruction on critical thinking strategies and social studies skills that will help you gain a fuller understanding of American history. It explains, for example, how to identify cause and effect and how to distinguish fact from opinion. The lessons in the Handbook equip you to handle historical sources, time lines, maps, and graphs, as well as build your vocabulary and sharpen your research, writing, and test-taking abilities.

1 IDENTIFYING THE MAIN IDEA

In the study of history, the ability to identify what is central is a key to understanding any complex event or issue. *The American Nation in the Twentieth Century* is designed to help you focus on the main ideas in American history. The paragraph titled Understanding the Main Idea that introduces each chapter and the Focus Questions that begin each section are intended to guide your reading. The essential points—the red summary statements placed throughout the text—highlight and reinforce the main ideas presented.

But not everything you read is structured like *The American Nation in the Twentieth Century*. Applying the following guidelines will help you identify the main ideas in what you read.

HOW TO IDENTIFY THE MAIN IDEA

1. **Read introductory material.** Read the title and the introduction, if there is one. They often point to the main ideas to be covered.
2. **Have questions in mind.** Formulate questions that you think might be answered by the material. Having such questions in mind will focus your reading.

NOVA BRITANNIA.
OFFERING MOST
Excellent fruites by Planting in
VIRGINIA.
Exciting all such as be well affected
to further the same.

LONDON
Printed for SAMVEL MACHAM, and are to be sold at
his Shop in Pauls Church-yard, at the
Signe of the Bul-head.
1609.

3. **Note the outline of ideas.** Pay attention to any headings or subheadings. They may provide a basic outline of the major ideas.
4. **Distinguish supporting details.** As you read, distinguish sentences providing supporting details from the general statements they support. A trail of facts may lead to a conclusion that expresses a main idea.

APPLYING YOUR SKILL

Read the following paragraph, from the subsection in Chapter 1 titled "Early English Settlement," to identify its main idea.

66 Attempts at colonization had been made in the 1580s, but they had failed. In 1606, however, King James I issued a charter licensing two merchant groups to organize settlements in Virginia and "to dig, mine, and search for all manner of mines of gold, silver, and copper." The two groups, the Plymouth Company and the London Company, were joint-stock companies, which operate somewhat like corporations do today. Investors shared the cost of starting and maintaining the company; they also shared any profits or losses. Unlike the

Spanish government, which itself organized settlements in the Americas, the English Crown left early colonization to these private companies. 🙶

As the lead sentence indicates, the paragraph focuses on early English colonization efforts. Details are included to explain how colonization efforts were organized under James I. The main idea is best captured in the concluding sentence: Unlike the Spanish government, which itself organized settlements in the Americas, the English Crown left early colonization to these private companies.

PRACTICING YOUR SKILL

Now read the next paragraph of the subsection on early English settlement (page 16), then answer the following questions.

1. What is the paragraph's main idea? How does the author support that idea?
2. What is the relationship of the main ideas of this paragraph and the previous paragraph on joint-stock companies? Combine them into one statement that summarizes the subsection.

2 IDENTIFYING CAUSE AND EFFECT

Identifying and understanding cause-and-effect relationships is crucial to the study of history. To investigate why an event took place, and what else happened as a result of that event, historians ask questions such as: What is the immediate activity that triggered the event? What is the background leading up to the event? Who were the people involved?

HOW TO IDENTIFY CAUSE AND EFFECT

1. **Look for clues.** Certain words and phrases are immediate clues to the existence of a cause-and-effect relationship. Note the examples that follow:

CLUE WORDS AND PHRASES

Cause	Effect
as a result of	aftermath
because	as a consequence
brought about	depended on
inspired	gave rise to
led to	originating from
produced	outcome
provoked	outgrowth
spurred	proceeded from
the reason	resulting in

2. **Identify the relationship.** Read carefully to identify how events are related. Writers do not always state the link between cause and effect. Sometimes a reader of history has to infer the cause or the effect.

3. **Check for complex connections.** Beyond the immediate cause and effect, check for other, more complex connections. Note, for example, whether (1) there were additional causes of a given effect, (2) a cause had multiple effects, and (3) these effects themselves caused further events.

APPLYING YOUR SKILL

The diagrams on page 750 present an important cause-and-effect relationship among the events leading up to the American Revolution. Because of the costs incurred in the French and Indian War, Parliament levied taxes on the colonies to raise revenue—taxation that led colonists

The Granger Collection, New York

1. *search for gold did not provide settlers with necessary food and supplies; details about Smith's orders to the settlers and the assistance provided by Powhatans*
2. *The main idea of the paragraph on joint-stock companies—that unlike the Spanish colonies which were governed directly by the government, the English crown left early colonization in the hands of private companies—provides the cause for the main idea of the paragraph on early English settlement—that private companies focused on the search for gold rather than on maintaining a colony. Student statements should express an understanding of how this emphasis on profit failed to meet the basic needs of the colonists.*

Cause		Effect
Britain incurs huge debt from the French and Indian War.	→	Parliament raises taxes on the colonies.

Cause		Effect/Cause		Effect
Britain incurs huge debt from the French and Indian War.	→	Parliament raises taxes on the colonies.	→	Colonists protest taxation without representation in Parliament.

PRACTICING YOUR SKILL

Students should chart and describe a recent historical development in terms of cause and effect, demonstrating a knowledge of the connections between the actions and the outcomes.

to cry, "No taxation without representation!" A diagram of the first part of this relationship is shown above. The diagram at the top of the next column adds the relationship between the British taxation of colonists and the colonial protests, showing how an effect may in turn become a cause. Such diagrams provide a graphic way of seeing complex relations of events.

PRACTICING YOUR SKILL

From your knowledge of recent American history, choose a sequence of events shaped by cause-and-effect relationships. Draw a chart showing the relationships between the actions and the outcomes. Then write a paragraph that explains the connections.

 # 3 DISTINGUISHING FACT FROM OPINION

Historical sources may contain facts and opinions. Sources such as letters, diaries, and speeches usually express personal views. The ability to distinguish facts from opinions is essential to judge the soundness of an argument or the reliability of a historical account.

HOW TO DISTINGUISH FACT FROM OPINION

1. Identify the facts. Ask yourself: Can it be verified? Determine whether the idea can be checked for accuracy in a source such as an almanac or encyclopedia. If so, it is probably factual; if not, it probably contains an opinion.

2. Identify the opinions. Look for clues that signal a statement of opinion: phrases such as *I think* and *I believe,* comparative words like *greatest* and *more important,* and value-laden words like *extremely* and *ridiculous* imply a judgment, and thus an opinion.

APPLYING YOUR SKILL

Read the following description of George Washington by Thomas Jefferson:

❝ His mind was great and powerful, without being of the very first order; . . . no judgment was ever sounder. It was slow in operation, being little aided by invention or imagination, but sure in conclusion. ❞

Jefferson's assessment—that Washington was neither brilliant nor particularly imaginative as a thinker, but that he possessed sound judgment and decisiveness—is clearly an opinion. Note the comparative words and phrasing: *great . . . without being of the first order, . . . sounder, . . . slow in operation.*

PRACTICING YOUR SKILL

Read the excerpt below, in which Jefferson further evaluates Washington as a commander in battle. Then answer the questions that follow.

❝ . . . Hence the common remark of his officers, of the advantage he derived from councils of war, where hearing all suggestions, he selected whatever was best; certainly no General ever planned his battles more judiciously [carefully]. But if deranged [disrupted] during the course of the action, . . . he was slow in re-adjustment. ❞

1. What fact (or facts) does Jefferson mention in his description of Washington?
2. Which words provide clues to Jefferson's opinion of Washington as a commander?

PRACTICING YOUR SKILL

1. *Fact: Washington listened to his officers' advice.*
2. *word clues: certainly, more judiciously, slow*

4 READING A TIME LINE

Chronology has been called "the skeleton of history." Knowing the chronological order of historical events—that is, the sequence in which they occurred—is essential to understanding them. A time line is a visual framework representing the chronology of a particular historical period. It enables you to see at a glance what happened when. Studying a time line involves seeing relationships between events as well as remembering important dates.

HOW TO READ A TIME LINE

1. **Determine its framework.** Note the years covered and the intervals of time into which the time line is divided.
2. **Study the sequence of events.** Study the order in which the events appear on the time line, noting especially the length of time between events.
3. **Supply missing information.** Think about the people, places, and other events associated with each item on the time line. In this way you can "flesh out" the framework.
4. **Note relationships.** Ask how an event relates to earlier or later events. Look for cause-and-effect relationships and long-term developments.

APPLYING YOUR SKILL

Study the time line below. It lists important events in the history of World War II in the Pacific.

1941	1942	1945
▼	▼	▼
Japan invades Indo-china. U.S. declares embargo against Japan. Japanese attack Pearl Harbor.	Battle of Midway occurs.	U.S. drops bombs on Hiroshima and Nagasaki. Japan surrenders.

When more than one event is listed for the same year, they are stacked with the earliest on top. The entries for 1941 illustrate the background to the surprise attack on Pearl Harbor.

PRACTICING YOUR SKILL

From the time line above, answer the following.

1. What other events might belong on this time line for the years between the attack on Pearl Harbor and the dropping of the atomic bombs?
2. What cause-and-effect relationship is suggested by the sequence of entries for 1945?

5 BUILDING VOCABULARY

In your study of history, you may encounter many new and unfamiliar words. But with regular effort you can master unfamiliar words and turn reading history into an opportunity to enlarge your vocabulary. Following the steps outlined here will assist you in building your vocabulary.

HOW TO BUILD VOCABULARY

1. **Identify unusual words.** As you read, list words that you cannot pronounce or define.
2. **Study context clues.** Study the sentence and paragraph where you find the new term. This setting, or context, may give you clues to the word's meaning through examples or a definition using more familiar words.

3. **Use the dictionary.** Use a dictionary to learn how to say the words on your list and what they mean.
4. **Review new vocabulary.** Look for ways to use the new words—in homework assignments, conversation, or classroom discussions. The best way to master a new word is to use it.

PRACTICING YOUR SKILL

1. What is context? How can it provide clues to a word's meaning?
2. As you read the next chapter, list any unusual words that you find. Write down what you think each word means, then check your definitions against those in a dictionary.

REVIEWING MAP BASICS

Questions about history as well as geography can be answered by consulting maps. Maps convey a wealth of varied information through colors, lines, symbols, and labels. To read and interpret maps, you must be able to understand their language and symbols.

TYPES OF MAPS

A map is an illustration drawn to scale of all or part of the earth's surface. Types of maps include *physical maps, political maps,* and *special-purpose maps.* Physical maps illustrate the natural landscape of an area—the landforms that mark the earth's surface. Physical maps often use shading to show relief—the existence of mountains, hills, and valleys—and colors to show elevation, or the height above or below sea level. The map of the United States on pages 772–73 is a physical map.

Political maps illustrate political units such as states and nations, employing lines to mark boundaries, dots for major cities, and stars or stars within circles for capitals. The map of the United States on pages 774–75 is a political map. Political maps are used also to show information such as territorial changes or military alliances. Special-purpose maps present specific information such as the routes of explorers, the outcome of an election, regional economic activity, or population density. The "Election of 1860" and "The Underground Railroad" maps on these pages are special-purpose maps.

MAP FEATURES

Most maps have a number of features in common. Familiarity with these basic elements makes reading any map easier.

Titles, legends, and labels. A map's title tells you what the map is about. It often includes information on what area is shown and what time period is being represented. The *legend,* or key, explains any special symbols, colors, or shadings used on the map. Labels designate things such as political and geographic place-names as well as physical features like mountain ranges, oceans, and rivers.

Directions and distances. Most maps in this textbook have a *compass rose,* or directional indicator, like the one on "The Underground Railroad" map. The compass rose indicates the four cardinal points: *N* for north, *S* for south, *E* for east, and *W* for west. You can also find intermediate directions—northeast, southeast, southwest, and northwest—using the compass rose. This helps in describing the *relative location* of a place—its location relative to another point of reference. (If a map has no compass rose, assume that north is at the top, east is to the right, and so on.)

Many maps in this textbook include a scale, showing both miles and kilometers, to help you relate distances on the map to actual distances on the earth's surface. You can use a scale to find the distance between any two points.

The global grid. The *absolute location* of any place on the earth is given in terms of *latitude* (number of degrees north or south of the equator) and *longitude*

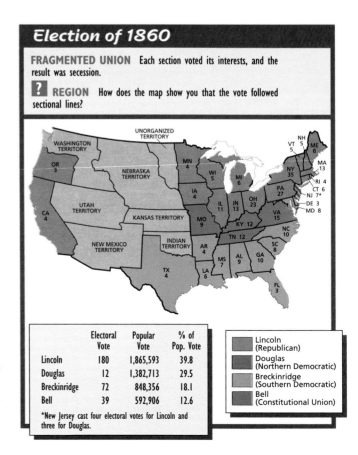

Election of 1860

FRAGMENTED UNION Each section voted its interests, and the result was secession.

? **REGION** How does the map show you that the vote followed sectional lines?

	Electoral Vote	Popular Vote	% of Pop. Vote
Lincoln	180	1,865,593	39.8
Douglas	12	1,382,713	29.5
Breckinridge	72	848,356	18.1
Bell	39	592,906	12.6

*New Jersey cast four electoral votes for Lincoln and three for Douglas.

Lincoln (Republican)
Douglas (Northern Democratic)
Breckinridge (Southern Democratic)
Bell (Constitutional Union)

752 ■■ SKILLS HANDBOOK

(number of degrees east or west of the prime meridian). The *global grid* is created by the intersecting lines of latitude *(parallels)* and lines of longitude *(meridians)*. In *The American Nation in the Twentieth Century,* grid lines sometimes are indicated by tick marks near the edge of the map. Many maps also have *locator maps* (right), which place the area of focus in a larger context, showing it in relation to the entire United States, or the world.

▶ The maps on these two pages are special-purpose maps. On the page opposite is an Albers projection. Above right is a locator map, and below is an example of a tilted perspective.

Robinson Projection

The Underground Railroad

ROAD TO FREEDOM It is estimated that the more than 3,000 members of the Underground Railroad helped from 50,000 to 75,000 enslaved African Americans escape to freedom.

? LOCATION Why do you think Cairo, Illinois, and Cincinnati, Ohio, were important stops on the Underground Railroad?

Map projections. Because the earth is a sphere, it is most accurately represented by a three-dimensional globe. The task of *cartographers,* or mapmakers, is to depict that globe on a flat surface as accurately as they possibly can—to, in the words of 16th-century mapmaker Gerardus Mercator, square the circle. Cartographers do this by transferring the curved coordinates of the globe onto the flat surface in a systematic way. These two-dimensional views of the earth's surface are called *projections.*

To flatten the curved coordinates of a globe, cartographers must squeeze or stretch the global grid of parallels and meridians. Thus every map projection, and therefore every map, distorts to some extent at least one of the following aspects: (1) the shape of land areas, (2) their relative sizes, (3) directions, or (4) distances. Mapmakers choose the projection that least distorts what they wish to show. Most projections in *The American Nation in the Twentieth Century* fall into two broad categories: conformal and equal area.

Conformal projections preserve the shape and scale of small areas around a point or a line. They cannot, however, preserve the shape of large countries or continents because scale varies from point to point. For example, in a world map using a Mercator conformal projection, sizes and shapes are accurate along the equator but distorted toward the poles. As a result, Greenland and South America appear to be the same size even though South America is actually nine times as large as Greenland. The Lambert Conformal Conic projection used on the map of the Bataan Death March on page 327 and for the map of Israel on page 453 are examples of conformal projection.

Equal-area projections show the relative sizes of different countries or continents quite accurately—a square inch or centimeter of paper represents the same number of square miles or kilometers of ground at any point on the map. But the price for this standardization is a distortion of distances and shapes. Most of the maps in *The American Nation in the Twentieth Century* are equal-area projections, with

Albers Equal-Area projections being the most common. The Albers projection is used on most of the U.S. maps—including all of the special-purpose maps like the "Election of 1860"—because it is effective in showing, with a minimum of distortion, large countries with east-west orientations.

Not all of the projections used in this textbook are conformal or equal area. The Robinson projection, used for the locator maps, is an effective compromise between the two categories. It minimizes distortions in size, shape, distance, and direction, although without preserving complete accuracy in any aspect. Other projections are used to give unique perspectives. "The

Indochina

A TROPICAL PENINSULA The nations of Indochina occupy a peninsula stretching from the mainland of Southeast Asia deep into the tropical waters of the South China Sea.

❓ RELATIVE LOCATION How might Vietnam's location have contributed to its long history of foreign invasion?

Underground Railroad" map on page 753 uses a *tilted perspective*. Compare the map to the Albers projection "Election of 1860" map on page 752. Note how the size and shape of the southern states are fairly accurate while the states and territories to the north and west are distorted on the tilted-perspective map. The perspective serves to draw attention to the southern states, the primary focus of the map.

HOW TO READ A MAP

1. **Determine the focus of the map.** Read the map's title and labels to determine the map's focus—its subject and the geographic area it covers.

2. **Study the map legend.** Read the legend and become familiar with any special symbols, lines, colors, and shadings used on the map.

3. **Check directions and distances.** Use the directional indicator and scale as needed to determine direction, location, and distance.

4. **Check the grid lines.** Refer to lines of longitude and latitude, or to a locator map, to fix the area in its larger context.

5. **Determine the projection.** Determine what projection is being used for the map, especially whether it is an equal area or a conformal projection. Ask yourself why this kind of projection has been chosen for the particular map, keeping in mind what its advantages or drawbacks are.

6. **Study the map.** Study the map's basic features and details, keeping its purpose in mind. If it is a special-purpose map, study the specific information being presented.

APPLYING YOUR SKILL

Study the map of Indochina on the opposite page. Use the locator map to determine the region's global location and to help you understand why the region is also called Southeast Asia. The locator map allows you to determine that Indochina is across the Pacific Ocean from the United States. Note that because the map has lines of longitude and latitude and a scale, you can find the absolute locations of each of the national capitals and compare the relative sizes of the countries. The scale even allows you to compare the size of the countries to your state.

This map combines both physical and political features in one map. Note how the use of relief clearly shows the mountains and coastal lowlands. Trace the Red River and Mekong River to their deltas and determine into what bodies of water each flows.

The California Gold Rush

FORTY-NINERS The discovery of gold at Sutter's sawmill on the California Trail drew thousands of people from all over the world.

? PLACE Why did Sacramento and Stockton become important during the gold rush?

Study the borders of the countries that make up Indochina. Note for which countries the Mekong River serves as a border. Also note that Laos is an entirely landlocked country, while Vietnam, on the other hand, has hundreds of miles of coastline on the Gulf of Tonkin, South China Sea, and Gulf of Thailand. Vietnam also has a lengthy mountainous border to its north and west—a geographic fact that has been very important in its history.

PRACTICING YOUR SKILL

For each of the special-purpose maps in this lesson—"Election of 1860" on page 752, "The Underground Railroad" on page 753, and "The California Gold Rush" on this page—answer the following questions.

1. What is the special focus of the map?
2. How is a map helpful in presenting this information?
3. What special symbols, if any, are used on the map?
4. What do the color variations or different lines indicate?

PRACTICING YOUR SKILL

1. **(a)** *state-by-state presidential election results in 1860*
   (b) *the routes escaping slaves took to gain their freedom*
   (c) *the extent of gold mining in California*
2. **(a)** *The clustering of colors for each candidate shows sectional differences.*
   (b) *The scale of the map shows how far slaves had to travel to gain their freedom, and the arrows show that some fled to other countries.*
   (c) *The color and the clustering of the gold mine symbols shows the gold rush area.*
3. **(a)** *none*
   (b) *arrows to show routes*
   (c) *symbol to represent leading gold mines and arrows to show California Trail and supply routes*
4. **(a)** *support for different presidential candidates*
   (b) *percentages of slaves in certain counties and the different routes*
   (c) *trails and supply routes and extent of gold mining*

7 READING CHARTS AND GRAPHS

Charts and graphs are used to organize and present information visually. They categorize and display data in a variety of ways, depending on the type of chart or graph being used and the subject matter of the data. Several different types of charts and graphs are used in this textbook.

CHARTS

You are already familiar with the time line, which is a chart that lists historical events according to their chronological order. For an example of another kind of chronological chart, see the chart "Major Events of the Cold War" on page 456.

Other charts include flowcharts, organizational charts, and tables. A *flowchart* shows a sequence of events or the steps in a process. Cause-and-effect relationships are often shown by flowcharts (see page 750). An *organizational chart* displays the structure of an organization, indicating the ranking or function of its internal parts and the relationships between them. "Decision-Making Bodies of the United Nations" (below left) is an example

of an organizational chart. A *table* is a single, or more often, multicolumn chart that presents data in categories that are easy to understand and compare. Tables, such as "Changes in Material Standards of Living, 1940–1955" (below right), are effective in displaying statistics that vary greatly or would be cumbersome in graph form.

HOW TO READ A CHART

1. **Read the title.** Read the title to identify the focus or purpose of the chart.

2. **Study the chart's parts.** Read the chart's headings, subheadings, and labels to identify the categories used and the specific data given for each category.

3. **Analyze the details.** When reading quantities, note increases or decreases in amounts. When reading dates, note intervals of time. When viewing an organizational chart, follow directional arrows or lines.

4. **Put the data to use.** Form generalizations or draw conclusions based on the data.

DECISION–MAKING BODIES OF THE UNITED NATIONS

Body	Function
General Assembly	Sets policies.
Security Council	Resolves diplomatic, military, and political disputes.
Economic and Social Council	Deals with human welfare and fundamental rights and freedoms.
International Court of Justice	Handles international legal disputes.
Trusteeship Council	Supervises territories that are not independent.
Secretariat	Performs routine administrative work of the UN.

Sources: *Encyclopedia of American History; Funk & Wagnalls New Encyclopedia*

MULTICULTURAL COOPERATION The United Nations was established in order to give every member nation a voice in international affairs. The General Assembly includes over 150 countries and uses five official languages—English, Russian, French, Spanish, and Chinese.

? **ANALYZING** Which body of the United Nations is responsible for monitoring military aggressions between nations?

CHANGES IN MATERIAL STANDARDS OF LIVING, 1940–1955

Households Owning	1940	1955
Automobile	50.0%	71.0%
Television Set	0.0%	76.1%
Refrigerator	44.0%	94.1%
Washing Machine	46.0%	84.1%
Clothes Dryer	0.0%	9.2%
Vacuum Cleaner	38.0%	64.3%

Sources: *The Overworked American; 1956 Statistical Abstract; An Economic History of Women in America; The Proud Decades*

"THE GOOD LIFE" After World War II many American consumers rushed to buy the latest in modern conveniences.

? **BUILDING GRAPH SKILLS** Which item experienced the greatest increase in ownership?

◄ The chart "Decision-Making Bodies of the United Nations" is an organizational chart. "Changes in Material Standards of Living, 1940–1955" is a table.

GRAPHS

There are several types of graphs; each has certain advantages in displaying data for a particular emphasis. A *line graph* plots changes in quantities over time. A line graph has a horizontal axis and a vertical axis. One axis generally lists numbers or percentages, while the other axis is marked off in periods of time. The line is created by plotting data on the grid formed by the intersecting axes and then connecting the dots. "Total Immigration to the U.S., 1860–1900" is an example of a line graph. A *bar graph* can be used to display changes in quantities over time. But most often bar graphs are used to compare quantities within categories. For example, the bar graphs in the "Allied and Central Resources, 1914–1918" chart on this page compare the military resources of the Allied and Central powers during World War I. A *pie graph,* or *circle graph,* displays proportions by showing sections of a whole like slices of a pie, with the whole equaling 100 percent. "Population in the South, 1860" on page 758 features two pie graphs.

HOW TO READ A GRAPH

1. **Read the title.** Read the title to identify the subject and purpose of the graph. Note the kind of graph, remembering what each kind is designed to emphasize.

2. **Study the labels.** To identify the type of information presented in the graph, read the labels that define each axis, bar, or section of the graph.

3. **Analyze the data.** Note increases or decreases in quantities. Look for trends, relationships, and changes in the data.

4. **Put the data to use.** Use the results of your analysis to form generalizations and to draw conclusions.

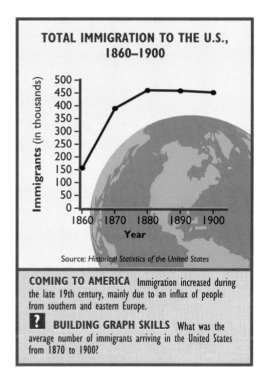

TOTAL IMMIGRATION TO THE U.S., 1860–1900

Source: *Historical Statistics of the United States*

COMING TO AMERICA Immigration increased during the late 19th century, mainly due to an influx of people from southern and eastern Europe.

? BUILDING GRAPH SKILLS What was the average number of immigrants arriving in the United States from 1870 to 1900?

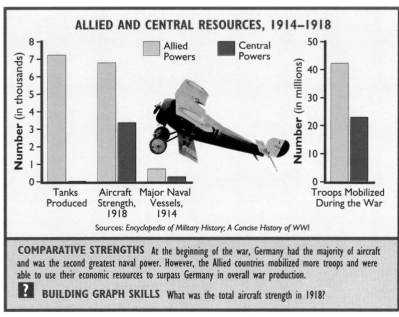

ALLIED AND CENTRAL RESOURCES, 1914–1918

Allied Powers   Central Powers

Tanks Produced | Aircraft Strength, 1918 | Major Naval Vessels, 1914 | Troops Mobilized During the War

Sources: *Encyclopedia of Military History; A Concise History of WWI*

COMPARATIVE STRENGTHS At the beginning of the war, Germany had the majority of aircraft and was the second greatest naval power. However, the Allied countries mobilized more troops and were able to use their economic resources to surpass Germany in overall war production.

? BUILDING GRAPH SKILLS What was the total aircraft strength in 1918?

Study the pie graphs on the South's population on the eve of the Civil War. From the first graph you can see that relatively few whites were slaveholders; for every one who was, about three were not. But it also shows that very few blacks in the South were *not* slaves (only about 1 in 17). The second graph focuses on a small segment of the southern population—slaveholding households. The graph shows that of this segment of the population nearly 75 percent had fewer than 10 slaves, while only 3 percent had 50 or more.

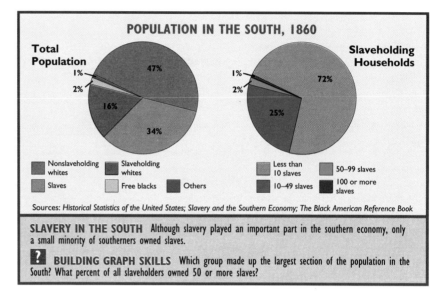

POPULATION IN THE SOUTH, 1860

Total Population

47%
1%
2%
16%
34%

Slaveholding Households

1%
2%
72%
25%

Nonslaveholding whites | Slaveholding whites
Slaves | Free blacks | Others

Less than 10 slaves | 50–99 slaves
10–49 slaves | 100 or more slaves

Sources: *Historical Statistics of the United States; Slavery and the Southern Economy; The Black American Reference Book*

SLAVERY IN THE SOUTH Although slavery played an important part in the southern economy, only a small minority of southerners owned slaves.

? BUILDING GRAPH SKILLS Which group made up the largest section of the population in the South? What percent of all slaveholders owned 50 or more slaves?

PRACTICING YOUR SKILL

Use the line graph on page 757 to answer the following questions.

1. What type of data is illustrated, and what intervals are used for the horizontal axis and the vertical axis?
2. Which decade shows the greatest increase in immigration to the United States? At what number (approximately) does the level of immigration begin to level out? In what year does this occur?
3. What generalizations or conclusions can you draw from the information in this graph?

8 STUDYING PRIMARY AND SECONDARY SOURCES

There are many sources of firsthand historical information, including diaries, letters, editorials, and legal documents such as wills and titles. All of these are *primary sources*. Newspaper reports, too, are considered primary sources, although they are generally written after the fact. The same is true for personal memoirs and autobiographies, which are usually written late in a person's life. The paintings,

photographs, and editorial cartoons that comprise history's visual record also are primary sources. Because they permit a close-up look at the past—a chance to get inside people's minds—primary sources are valuable historical tools.

Secondary sources are descriptions or interpretations of events written after the events have occurred by persons who did not participate in the events. History books, biographies, encyclopedias, and other reference works are examples of secondary sources. Writers of secondary sources have the advantage of knowing the long-range consequences of events. This knowledge helps shape their analyses.

HOW TO STUDY PRIMARY AND SECONDARY SOURCES

1. Study the material carefully. Consider the nature of the material. Is it verbal or visual? Is it based on firsthand

PRACTICING YOUR SKILL

1. *The line graph shows the number of immigrants to the U.S. from 1860 to 1900; the intervals on the horizontal axis are 10 years, and the intervals on the vertical axis are 50,000 people.*
2. *The decade of 1860–69 shows the greatest increase in immigration; immigration begins to level out at roughly 450,000 in 1880.*
3. *Students might conclude from this line graph that immigration to the U.S. tripled from 1860 to 1880 and that almost two million immigrants came to the U.S. in the late 1800s.*

information or on the accounts of others? Note the major ideas and supporting details.

2. **Consider the audience.** Ask yourself: For whom was this message meant originally? Whether a message was intended, for instance, for the general public or for a specific, private audience may have influenced its style or content.

3. **Check for bias.** Watch for words or phrases that signal a one-sided view of a person or event.

4. **When possible, compare sources.** Study more than one source on a topic if available. Comparing sources gives you a more complete, balanced account.

PRACTICING YOUR SKILL

1. What distinguishes secondary sources from primary sources?
2. What advantage do secondary sources have over primary sources?
3. Why should you consider the original audience of a historical source?

Of the following, identify which are primary and which are secondary sources: a newspaper, a private journal, a biography, an editorial cartoon, a deed to property, a snapshot of a family on vacation, a magazine article about the history of the West, an autobiography.

PRACTICING YOUR SKILL

1. *Secondary sources are not firsthand accounts; they are written at a later time by persons not involved in the events they describe.*
2. *Secondary sources can provide a perspective broader than that available in primary sources.*
3. *The style or content of a message may have been shaped by its original, intended audience.*

   primary: newspaper, private journal, editorial cartoon, deed to property, snapshot, autobiography; secondary: biography, magazine article about the history of the West

9 CREATING AN OUTLINE

An outline is a tool for organizing information. It is a logical summary that presents the main points of what you have read or plan to communicate. An outline is an important part of preparing to write a paper. An essay outline, for example, would highlight the main ideas that you intend to express and sketch the details that you want to include for support. An outline is only a skeletal structure. It must be fleshed out in use. But if an outline is thorough and well thought out, it makes writing the final product much easier.

HOW TO CREATE AN OUTLINE

1. **Order your material.** Decide what you want to emphasize or focus on. Order or classify your material with that in mind. Determine what information belongs in an introduction, what should make up the body of your paper, and what to leave for the conclusion.

2. **Identify main ideas.** Identify the main ideas to be highlighted in each section. Make these your outline's main headings.

3. **List supporting details.** Determine the important details or facts that support each main idea. Rank and list them as subheadings, using additional levels of subheadings as necessary. Subheadings must come in pairs, at the least: no *A*'s without *B*'s, no *1*'s without *2*'s.

4. **Put your outline to use.** Structure your essay or report according to your outline. Each main heading, for instance, might form the basis for a topic sentence to begin a paragraph. Subheadings would then

make up the content of the paragraph. In a more lengthy paper, each subheading might be the main idea of a paragraph.

The sample outline below could have been used in preparation for writing about the Louisiana Purchase. Note the several levels of headings that rank the parts of the outline.

I. Republicans favor westward expansion
   A. Settlement of the Trans-Appalachian West
   B. Access to the Mississippi River
      1. Importance of the port of New Orleans
      2. France regains control of Louisiana
         a. Threat to American trade
         b. Obstacle to U.S. westward expansion
II. Jefferson negotiates with France
   A. U.S. diplomats purchase Louisiana
   B. Why France made the sale
      1. Napoléon fails to build empire
         a. Need for naval base in West Indies
         b. Revolt in Saint Domingue (Haiti)
         c. French fail to regain Haiti
      2. Napoléon needs money for war plans

PRACTICING YOUR SKILL

Read the subsection in Chapter 7 titled "Urban Moral Reform" (pages 181–82). Then, using the information you have gained here, create an outline that you could use in writing about this subject.

PRACTICING YOUR SKILL

Student outlines will vary, but main idea should sum up progressive moral reform. Subheadings might include: support of prohibition (ASL and WCTU lead crusade against alcohol; Eighteenth Amendment ratified in 1919) and support of movie censorship (states and cities set up censorship boards; movie industry institutes self-censorship in 1909).

DOING RESEARCH

To complete research papers or special projects, you may need to use resources other than this textbook. Conducting research generally requires you to seek out the resources available in a library.

FINDING INFORMATION

To find a particular book, you need to know how libraries organize their materials. Books of fiction are alphabetized according to the last name of the author. To classify non-fiction books, libraries use the Dewey decimal system and the Library of Congress system. Both systems assign each book a *call number* that tells you its classification.

To find the number, look in the library's *card catalog.* The catalog lists books by author, by title, and by subject. If you know the author or title of the book, finding it is simple. If you do not know this information, or if you just want to find any book about a general subject, look up that subject heading. Some libraries have computerized card catalogs, which can make searching for specific information easier.

Librarians can assist you in using the card catalog and direct you to a book's location. They can also suggest additional resources.

USING RESOURCES

In a library's reference section, you will find encyclopedias, specialized dictionaries, atlases, almanacs, and indexes to recent material in magazines and newspapers. Encyclopedias often will be your best resource. Encyclopedias include biographical sketches of important historical figures; geographic, economic, and political data on individual nations, states, and cities; and discussions of historical events and religious, social, and cultural issues. Entries often include cross-references to related articles.

Specialized dictionaries exist for almost every field. Historical dictionaries such as *The Concise Dictionary of American History* include definitions of historical terms as well as brief descriptions of important laws, court cases, social movements, and more. Geographical

Title

Author

American History in 100 nutshells.

973
TUL

Tuleja, Tad, 1944 -
    American History in 100 nutshells / Tad Tuleja. -- 1st ed. -- New York : Fawcett Columbine, 1992.
        xiii, 241 p. ; 21 cm.

Call number (Library of Congress Catalog number)

Publisher

Includes index.
ISBN 0-449-90346-X (pbk.)

    1. United States --History-- Miscellanea.   I. Title.   II. Title: American History in one hundred nutshells.

E179.T85   1992   973

Other headings under which book is listed

dictionaries—or *gazetteers*—list significant natural physical features and place-names. Pronunciation guides, statistical data, and brief descriptions are also included. *Atlases* contain maps and visual representations of geographic data.

To find up-to-date facts about a subject, you can use almanacs, yearbooks, and periodical indexes. References like *The World Almanac and Book of Facts* include historical information and a variety of statistics about population, the environment, sports, and so on. Encyclopedia yearbooks keep up with recent, significant developments not fully covered in encyclopedia articles.

Periodical indexes, especially *The Readers' Guide to Periodical Literature,* can help you locate articles published in magazines. The *New York Times Index* catalogs the news stories published in the *Times,* the U.S. daily newspaper with perhaps the most in-depth coverage of national and world events.

PRACTICING YOUR SKILL

1. In what two ways are nonfiction books classified?
2. What kinds of references contain information about geography?
3. Where would you look to find recent coverage of a political or social issue?
4. Would you look in an encyclopedia, an atlas, or an American history dictionary to find each of the following items? (a) the latitude of Guatemala (b) a biography of Julius Caesar (c) the purpose of the Taft-Hartley Act (d) the major industries of Cleveland, Ohio

PRACTICING YOUR SKILL

1. *Dewey decimal and Library of Congress systems*
2. *gazetteers, encyclopedias, atlases, and almanacs*
3. The Readers' Guide to Periodical Literature, *the* New York Times Index, *encyclopedia yearbooks, or almanacs*
4. **(a)** *atlas*
   (b) *encyclopedia*
   (c) *American history dictionary*
   (d) *encyclopedia*

WRITING A PAPER

The American Nation in the Twentieth Century provides you with numerous writing opportunities. Section reviews have writing exercises (labeled Writing to Inform, Writing to Persuade, and so on) that give you the chance to write about a historical subject with a particular focus in mind. Chapter reviews contain additional opportunities for writing.

WRITING WITH A PURPOSE

Always keep your purpose for writing in mind. That purpose might be to analyze, to evaluate, to synthesize, to inform, to persuade, to hypothesize, or to take a stand. As you begin, your purpose will determine the most appropriate approach to take; and when you are done, it will help you evaluate how well you have succeeded.

Each different purpose for writing requires its own form, tone, and content. The point of view you are adopting will shape what you write, as will your intended audience. For example, you would take a different tone when writing to a president from the tone you would use with a relative.

HISTORICAL IMAGINATION

Many writing opportunities in *The American Nation in the Twentieth Century* ask you to create a specific type of writing, such as a diary entry, a letter, a newspaper editorial, a poem, or an advertisement. Often such writing about history involves using historical imagination—that is, writing from the perspective of a person living *then* rather than *now*. An assignment may require, for instance, that you address a particular historical figure, such as a former president, or that you write as if living through a specific historical crisis.

HOW TO WRITE A PAPER

Each writing opportunity provided in this textbook will have specific directions about what and how to write. But whether you are writing a diary entry describing your experiences as a western pioneer or an essay about the significance of the frontier, you should follow certain basic steps. The guidelines outlined in the second column (which apply especially to longer papers) can help you plan and improve your writing.

SOME TYPES OF WRITING

- A **diary** is an informal, personal log of your experiences and recollections (or those of someone else in history). Entries are dated and consist of brief accounts of the day's happenings and your reactions.

- A **letter** is a personal communication meant for a specific individual.

- An **advertisement** is an announcement to promote a product or event. Effective ads are direct and to the point, using memorable language, such as jingles and slogans, to highlight important features.

- A newspaper **editorial** is a public statement of an opinion or point of view. It takes a stand on an issue and gives reasons for that stand.

---

1. **Identify your purpose in writing.** Read the directions carefully to identify the purpose for your writing. Keep that purpose in mind as you plan and write your paper.

2. **Consider your audience.** When writing for a specific audience, choose the tone and style that will best communicate your message.

3. **Create an outline.** Think and plan before you begin writing your first draft. Organize themes, main ideas, and supporting details into an outline.

4. **Collect information.** Do research if necessary. Your writing will be more effective if you have many details at hand.

5. **Write a first draft and evaluate it.** In your first draft, remember to use your outline as a guide. Each paragraph should express a single main idea or set of related ideas, with details for support. Be careful to show the relationships between ideas and to use proper transitions—sentences that build connections between paragraphs.

6. **Review and edit.** Revise and reorganize your draft as needed to make your points. Improve sentences by adding appropriate adjectives and adverbs. Make your writing clearer by changing the length or structure of awkward sentences. Replace inexact

1. *the purpose; determines
the most appropriate
approach to take and
helps the writer evaluate
the finished product*

2. *determines format and
tone of one's writing*

3. *reorganize sections, add
appropriate adjectives and
adverbs, change the length
and structure of sentences,
replace inexact words, and
check for proper spelling,
punctuation, and grammar*

wording with more precise word choices. Then check for proper spelling, punctuation, and grammar.

7. Write your final version. Prepare a neat, clean final version. Appearance is important; it may not affect the quality of your writing itself, but it can affect the way your writing is perceived and understood.

PRACTICING YOUR SKILL

1. What factor—more than any other—should affect how and what you write? Why?
2. Why is it important to consider the audience for whom you are writing?
3. What steps should you take to edit a first draft?

12 TAKING A TEST

When it comes to taking a test, for history or any other subject, nothing can take the place of preparation. A good night's sleep added to consistent study habits give you a far better chance for success than hours of late-night, last-minute cramming.

But keeping your mind focused on the test and free from distractions is not all you can do to improve your test scores. Mastering some basic test-taking skills can also help. Keeping up with your daily reading assignments and taking careful notes as you read can turn taking a test into a mere matter of review. Reviewing material that you already know takes less time—and causes less stress—than trying to learn something new under pressure.

You will face several basic types of questions on

▲ *Homework* by Winslow Homer

U.S. history tests: multiple choice, matching, and essay. In answering multiple-choice questions, eliminate any answers that you know are wrong; this will narrow your field of choice. When doing a matching exercise, first go through the entire list, matching those that you are sure of. Then study any that remain.

Read essay questions carefully so that you know exactly what you are being asked to write. If time permits, make an outline of the main ideas and supporting details that you plan to include in your

essay. Keep your answer clear and brief, but cover all necessary points.

HOW TO TAKE A TEST

1. **Prepare beforehand.** This all-important step not only involves studying and reviewing the material prior to the test. It also means being physically rested and mentally focused on the day of the test.

2. **Follow directions.** Read all instructions carefully. Listen closely, particularly if you are being told the directions rather than being given written instructions.

3. **Preview the test.** Skim through the entire test to determine how much time you have for each section. Try to anticipate which areas of the examination will be the most difficult for you. You may wish to allow yourself more time to work on the more difficult sections.

4. **Concentrate on the test.** Do not "watch the clock," but stay aware of the time. If you do not know an answer, move on to the next question. It is best to answer as many questions as you can within the time limit.

5. **Review your answers.** If you have time, return to questions that you skipped or were unsure of and work on them. Review your essays to catch and correct any mistakes in spelling, punctuation, or grammar.

PRACTICING YOUR SKILL

1. How can you improve your chances on multiple-choice questions?
2. Why is it important to skim through the entire test before you begin?
3. Name three things that can help you in taking a test.

**PRACTICING
YOUR SKILL**

1. *by eliminating choices you
know are wrong*

2. *helps in estimating how
much time to take per section or question, anticipating difficult areas, and
pacing through the test*

3. *Answers might include:
consistent study habits,
rest, keeping up with
assignments, taking careful
notes, reviewing material,
concentrating on the test,
ignoring distractions, and
following all directions.*

Thomas Jefferson's First Inaugural Address

March 4, 1801

Friends and Fellow Citizens. . .

All . . . will bear in mind this sacred principle, that though the will of the majority is in all cases to prevail, that will to be rightful must be reasonable; that the minority possess their equal rights, which equal law must protect, and to violate would be oppression. Let us, then, fellow citizens, unite with one heart and one mind. Let us restore to social intercourse [dealings] that harmony and affection without which liberty and even life itself are but dreary things. And let us reflect that, having banished from our land that religious intolerance under which mankind so long bled and suffered, we have yet gained little if we countenance [allow] a political intolerance as despotic, as wicked, and capable of as bitter and bloody persecutions. . . . But every difference of opinion is not a difference of principle. We have called by different names brethren of the same principle. We are all Republicans; we are all Federalists. If there be any among us who would wish to dissolve this Union or to change its republican form, let them stand undisturbed as monuments of the safety with which error of opinion may be tolerated where reason is left free to combat it. I know, indeed, that some honest men fear that a republican government cannot be strong, that this government is not strong enough; but would the honest patriot, in the full tide of successful experiment, abandon a government which has so far kept us free and firm on the theoretic [hypothetical] and visionary fear that this government, the world's best hope, may by possibility want energy to preserve itself? I trust not. I believe this, on the contrary, the strongest government on earth. I believe it the only one where every man, at the call of the law, would fly to the standard of the law, and would meet invasions of the public order as his own personal concern. Sometimes it is said that man cannot be trusted with the government of himself. Can he, then, be trusted with the government of others? Or have we found angels in the forms of kings to govern him? Let history answer this question.

Let us, then, with courage and confidence pursue our own Federal and Republican principles, our attachment to union and representative government. Kindly separated by nature and a wide ocean from the exterminating havoc of one quarter of the globe; too high-minded to endure the degradations of the others; possessing a chosen country, with room enough for our descendants to the thousandth and thousandth generation; entertaining a due sense of our equal right to the use of our own faculties, to the acquisitions of our own industry, to honor and confidence from our fellow citizens, resulting not from birth, but from our actions and their sense of them; enlightened by a benign religion, professed, indeed, and practiced in various forms, yet all of them inculcating [implanting] honesty, truth, temperance, gratitude, and the love of man; acknowledging and adoring an overruling Providence, which by all its dispensations proves that it delights in the happiness of man here and his greater happiness hereafter—with all these blessings, what more is necessary to make us a happy and a prosperous people? Still one thing more, fellow citizens—a wise and frugal government, which shall restrain men from injuring one another, shall leave them otherwise free to regulate their own pursuits of industry and improvement, and shall not take from the mouth of labor the bread it has earned. This is the sum of good government, and this is necessary to close the circle of our felicities [good intentions].

About to enter, fellow citizens, on the exercise of duties which comprehend [include] everything dear and valuable to you, it is proper you should understand what I deem the essential principles of our government and consequently those which ought to shape its administration. I will compress them within the narrowest compass they will bear, stating the general principle, but not all its limitations. Equal and exact justice to all men, of whatever state or persuasion religious or political; peace, commerce, and honest friendship with all nations, entangling alliances with none; the support of the state governments in all their rights, as the most competent administrations for our domestic concerns and the surest bulwarks [defenses] against anti-republican tendencies; the preservation of the general government in its whole constitutional vigor, as the sheet anchor [main support] of our peace at home and safety abroad; a jealous care of the right of election by the people—a mild and safe corrective of abuses which are lopped by the sword of revolution where peaceable remedies are unprovided; absolute acquiescence in [submission to] the decisions of the majority, the vital principle of republics, from which [there] is no appeal but to force, the vital principle and immediate parent of despotism; a well-disciplined militia, our best reliance in peace and for the first moments of war, till regulars may relieve them; the supremacy of the civil over the military authority; economy in the public expense, that labor may be lightly burdened; the honest payment of our debts and sacred preservation of the public faith; encouragement of agriculture, and of commerce as its handmaid; the diffusion of information and arraignment [bringing up] of all abuses at the bar of the public reason; freedom of religion; freedom of the press; and freedom of person under the protection of the *habeas corpus*,* and trial by juries impartially selected. These principles form the bright constellation which has gone before us and guided our steps through an age of revolution and reformation. The wisdom of our sages and blood of our heroes have been devoted to their attainment. They should be the creed of our political faith, the text of civic instruction, the touchstone by which to try the services of those we trust; and should we wander from them in moments of error or of alarm, let us hasten to retrace our steps and to regain the road which alone leads to peace, liberty, and safety.

I repair, then, fellow citizens, to the post you have assigned me. With experience enough in subordinate offices to have seen the difficulties of this the greatest of all, I have learned to expect that it will rarely fall to the lot of imperfect man to retire from this station with the reputation and the favor which bring him into it. Without pretensions to that high confidence you reposed in our first and greatest revolutionary character [Washington] whose pre-eminent services had entitled him to the first place in his country's love and destined for him the fairest page in the volume of faithful history, I ask so much confidence only as may give firmness and effect to the legal administration of your affairs. I shall often go wrong through defect of judgment. When right, I shall often be thought wrong by those whose positions will not command a view of the whole ground. I ask your indulgence for my own errors, which will never be intentional, and your support against the errors of others, who may condemn what they would not if seen in all its parts. The approbation [approval] implied by your suffrage is a great consolation to me for the past, and my future solicitude [concern] will be to retain the good opinion of those who have bestowed it in advance, to conciliate [win over] that of others by doing them all the good in my power, and to be instrumental to the happiness and freedom of all.

Relying, then, on the patronage of your good will, I advance with obedience to the work, ready to retire from it whenever you become sensible how much better choice it is in your power to make. And may that Infinite Power which rules the destinies of the universe lead our councils to what is best, and give them a favorable issue for your peace and prosperity. ❖

Habeas corpus: legal provision guaranteeing a prisoner or detainee the right to be informed of the cause of his or her detention, as a protection against illegal imprisonment.

HISTORICAL DOCUMENT

The Monroe Doctrine

December 2, 1823

At the proposal of the Russian Imperial Government, made through the minister of the Emperor residing here, a full power and instructions have been transmitted to the minister of the United States at St. Petersburg to arrange by amicable negotiations the respective rights and interests of the two nations on the northwest coast of this continent. A similar proposal had been made by His Imperial Majesty to the government of Great Britain, which has likewise been acceded [agreed] to. The government of the United States has been desirous by this friendly proceeding of manifesting the great value which they have invariably attached to the friendship of the Emperor and their solicitude to cultivate the best understanding with his government. In the discussions to which this interest has given rise and in the arrangements by which they may terminate the occasion has been judged proper for asserting, as a principle in which the rights and interests of the United States are involved, that the American continents, by the free and independent condition which they have assumed and maintain, are henceforth not to be considered as subjects for future colonization by any European powers. . . .

The citizens of the United States cherish sentiments the most friendly in favor of the liberty and happiness of their fellow men on that side of the Atlantic [in Europe]. In the wars of the European powers in matters relating to themselves we have never taken any part, nor does it comport with our policy to do so. It is only when our rights are invaded or seriously menaced that we resent injuries or make preparation for our defense. With the movements in this hemisphere we are of necessity more immediately connected, and by causes which must be obvious to all enlightened and impartial observers. The political system of the allied powers [Holy Alliance]* is essentially different in this respect from that of America. This difference proceeds from that which exists in their respective governments; and to the defense of our own, which has been achieved by the loss of much blood and treasure, and matured by the wisdom of their most enlightened citizens, and under which we have enjoyed unexampled felicity, this whole nation is devoted. We owe it, therefore, to candor and to the amicable relations existing between the United States and those powers to declare that we should consider any attempt on their part to extend their system to any portion of this hemisphere as dangerous to our peace and safety. With the existing colonies or dependencies of any European power, we have not interfered and shall not interfere. But with the governments who have declared their independence and maintained it, and whose independence we have, on great consideration and on just principles, acknowledged, we could not view any interposition for the purpose of oppressing them, or controlling in any other manner their destiny, by any European power in any other light than as the manifestation of an unfriendly disposition toward the United States. In the war between those new governments and Spain, we declared our neutrality at the time of their recognition, and to this we have adhered, and shall continue to adhere, provided no change shall occur which,

*Holy Alliance: alliance between France, Austria, Russia, and Prussia.

in the judgment of the competent authorities of this government, shall make a corresponding change on the part of the United States indispensable to their security.

The late events in Spain and Portugal show that Europe is still unsettled. Of this important fact no stronger proof can be adduced [offered] than that the allied powers should have thought it proper, on any principle satisfactory to themselves, to have interposed by force in the internal concerns of Spain. To what extent such interposition may be carried, on the same principle, is a question in which all independent powers whose governments differ from theirs are interested, even those most remote, and surely none more so than the United States. Our policy in regard to Europe, which was adopted at an early stage of the wars which have so long agitated that quarter of the globe, nevertheless remains the same, which is, not to interfere in the internal concerns of any of its powers; to consider the government *de facto* [such as it is] as the legitimate government for us; to cultivate friendly relations with it, and to preserve those relations by a frank, firm, and manly policy, meeting in all instances the just claims of every power, submitting to injuries from none. But in regard to those continents [North and South America] circumstances are eminently and conspicuously different. It is impossible that the allied powers should extend their political system to any portion of either continent without endangering our peace and happiness; nor can anyone believe that our southern brethren [Latin Americans], if left to themselves, would adopt it of their own accord. It is equally impossible, therefore, that we should behold such interposition in any form with indifference. If we look to the comparative strength and resources of Spain and those new governments and their distance from each other, it must be obvious that she can never subdue them. It is still the true policy of the United States to leave the parties to themselves, in the hope that other powers will pursue the same course. . . . ❖

ᵀhe Seneca ᶠalls Declaration of Sentiments

July 19–20, 1848

When, in the course of human events, it becomes necessary for one portion of the family of man to assume among the people of the earth a position different from that which they have hitherto occupied, but one to which the laws of nature and of nature's God entitle them, a decent respect to the opinions of mankind requires that they should declare the causes that impel them to such a course.

We hold these truths to be self-evident: that all men and women are created equal; that they are endowed by their Creator with certain inalienable rights; that among these are life, liberty, and the pursuit of happiness; that to secure these rights governments are instituted, deriving their just powers from the consent of the governed. Whenever any form of government becomes destructive of these ends, it is the right of those who suffer from it to refuse allegiance to it, and to insist upon the institution of a new government, laying its foundation on such principles, and organizing its powers in such form, as to them shall seem most likely to effect their safety and happiness. Prudence, indeed, will dictate that governments long established should not be changed for light and transient causes; and accordingly all experience has shown that mankind are more disposed to suffer while evils are sufferable [bearable], than to right themselves by abolishing the forms to which they were accustomed. But when a long train of abuses and usurpations [seizures] pursuing invariably the same object evinces [reveals] a design to reduce them under absolute despotism, it is their duty to throw off such government, and to provide new guards for their future security. Such has been the patient sufferance [suffering] of the women under this government, and such is now the necessity which constrains them to demand the equal station to which they are entitled.

The history of mankind is a history of repeated injuries and usurpations on the part of man toward woman, having in direct object the establishment of an absolute tyranny over her. To prove this, let facts be submitted to a candid world. . . .

Having deprived her of this first right of a citizen, the elective franchise [right to vote], thereby leaving her without representation in the halls of legislation, he has oppressed her on all sides.

He has made her, if married, in the eye of the law, civilly dead. . . .

Now, in view of this entire disfranchisement [loss of right to vote] of one half of the people of this country, their social and religious degradation—in view of the unjust laws above mentioned, and because women do feel themselves aggrieved, oppressed, and fraudulently deprived of their most sacred rights, we insist that they have immediate admission to all the rights and privileges which belong to them as citizens of the United States.

In entering upon the great work before us, we anticipate no small amount of misconception, misrepresentation, and ridicule; but we shall use every instrumentality [means] within our power to effect our object. We shall employ agents, circulate tracts [pamphlets], petition the state and national legislatures, and endeavor to enlist the pulpit and the press in our behalf. We hope this convention will be followed by a series of conventions embracing every part of the country. . . .

Resolutions

Resolved, That all laws which prevent woman from occupying such a station in society as her conscience shall dictate, or which place her in a position inferior to that of man, are contrary to the great precept of nature, and, therefore, of no force or authority.

Resolved, That woman is man's equal—was intended to be so by the Creator, and the highest good of the race demands that she should be recognized as such. . . .

Resolved, That woman has too long rested satisfied in the circumscribed [narrow] limits which corrupt customs and a perverted [misdirected] application of the Scriptures have marked out for her, and that it is time she should move in the enlarged sphere which her great Creator has assigned her.

Resolved, That it is the duty of the women of this country to secure to themselves their sacred right to the elective franchise.

Resolved, That the equality of human rights results necessarily from the fact of the identity [sameness of essential character] of the race in capabilities and responsibilities. . . .

Resolved, therefore, That, being invested by the Creator with the same capabilities, and the same consciousness of responsibility for their exercise, it is demonstrably the right and duty of woman, equally with man, to promote every righteous cause by every righteous means; and especially in regard to the great subjects of morals and religion, it is self-evidently her right to participate with her brother in teaching them, both in private and in public, by writing and by speaking, by any instrumentalities proper to be used, and in any assemblies proper to be held. . . .

Resolved, That the speedy success of our cause depends upon the zealous and untiring efforts of both men and women, for the overthrow of the monopoly of the pulpit, and for the securing to women an equal participation with men in the various trades, professions, and commerce. ❖

The Emancipation Proclamation

January 1, 1863

**BY THE PRESIDENT OF
THE UNITED STATES OF AMERICA**

A Proclamation

Whereas on the twenty-second day of September, A.D. 1862, a proclamation was issued by the President of the United States, containing, among other things, the following, to wit [namely]:

"That on the first day of January, A.D. 1863, all persons held as slaves within any state or designated part of a state, the people whereof shall then be in rebellion against the United States, shall be then, thenceforward, and forever free; and the executive government of the United States, including the military and naval authority thereof, will recognize and maintain the freedom of such persons and will do no act or acts to repress such persons or any of them, in any efforts they may make for their actual freedom.

"That the Executive will on the first day of January aforesaid, by proclamation, designate the states and parts of states, if any, in which the people thereof, respectively, shall then be in rebellion against the United States; and the fact that any state or the people thereof shall on that day be in good faith represented in the Congress of the United States by members chosen thereto at elections wherein a majority of the qualified voters of such states shall have participated shall, in the absence of strong countervailing [opposing] testimony, be deemed conclusive evidence that such state and the people thereof are not then in rebellion against the United States."

Now, therefore, I, Abraham Lincoln, President of the United States, by virtue of the power in me vested as Commander-in-Chief of the Army and Navy of the United States in time of actual armed rebellion against the authority and government of the United States, and as a fit and necessary war measure for suppressing said rebellion, do, on this first day of January, A.D. 1863, and in accordance with my purpose so to do, publicly proclaimed for the full period of one hundred days from the first day above mentioned, order and designate as the states and parts of states wherein the people thereof, respectively, are this day in rebellion against the United States the following, to wit:

Arkansas, Texas, Louisiana (except the parishes of St. Bernard, Plaquemines, Jefferson, St. John, St. Charles, St. James, Ascension, Assumption, Terrebonne, Lafourche, St. Mary, St. Martin, and Orleans, including the city of New Orleans), Mississippi, Alabama, Florida, Georgia, South Carolina, North Carolina, and Virginia (except the forty-eight counties designated as West Virginia, and also the counties of Berkeley, Accomac, Northampton, Elizabeth City, York, Princess Anne, and Norfolk, including the cities of Norfolk and Portsmouth), and which excepted parts are for the present left precisely as if this proclamation were not issued.

And by virtue of the power and for the purpose aforesaid, I do order and declare that all persons held as slaves within said designated states and parts of states are, and henceforward shall be, free; and that the executive government of the United States, including the military and naval authorities thereof, will recognize and maintain the freedom of said persons.

And I hereby enjoin [order] upon the people so declared to be free to abstain from all violence, unless in necessary self-defense; and I recommend to them that, in all cases when allowed, they labor faithfully for reasonable wages.

And I further declare and make known that such persons of suitable condition will be received into the armed service of the United States to garrison forts, positions, stations, and other places, and to man vessels of all sorts in said service.

And upon this act, sincerely believed to be an act of justice, warranted by the Constitution upon military necessity, I invoke the considerate judgment of mankind and the gracious favor of Almighty God. ❖

Abraham Lincoln's Gettysburg Address

November 19, 1863

Four score and seven years ago our fathers brought forth on this continent a new nation, conceived in liberty, and dedicated to the proposition that all men are created equal.

Now we are engaged in a great civil war, testing whether that nation, or any nation so conceived and so dedicated can long endure. We are met on a great battlefield of that war. We have come to dedicate a portion of that field as a final resting place for those who here gave their lives that that nation might live. It is altogether fitting and proper that we should do this.

But, in a larger sense, we cannot dedicate—we cannot consecrate [make holy]—we cannot hallow—this ground. The brave men, living and dead, who struggled here, have consecrated it far above our poor power to add or detract. The world will little note nor long remember what we say here, but it can never forget what they did here. It is for us, the living, rather, to be dedicated here to the unfinished work which they who fought here have thus far so nobly advanced. It is rather for us to be here dedicated to the great task remaining before us—that from these honored dead we take increased devotion to that cause for which they gave the last full measure of devotion; that we here highly resolve that these dead shall not have died in vain; that this nation, under God, shall have a new birth of freedom; and that government of the people, by the people, for the people, shall not perish from the earth. ❖

The Fourteen Points

January 8, 1918

Gentlemen of the Congress:

It will be our wish and purpose that the processes of peace, when they are begun, shall be absolutely open and that they shall involve and permit henceforth no secret understandings of any kind. The day of conquest and aggrandizement is gone by; so is also the day of secret covenants entered into in the interest of particular governments and likely at some unlooked-for moment to upset the peace of the world. It is this happy fact, now clear to the view of every public man whose thoughts do not still linger in an age that is dead and gone, which makes it possible for every nation whose purposes are consistent with justice and the peace of the world to avow now or at any other time the objects it has in view.

We entered this war because violations of right had occurred which touched us to the quick and made the life of our own people impossible unless they were corrected and the world secured once for all against their recurrence. What we demand in this war, therefore, is nothing peculiar to ourselves. It is that the world be made fit and safe to live in; and particularly that it be made safe for every peace-loving nation which, like our own, wishes to live its own life, determine its own insti-tutions, be assured of justice and fair dealing by the other peoples of the world as against force and selfish aggression. All the peoples of the world are in effect partners in this interest, and for our own part we see very clearly that unless justice be done to others it will not be done to us. The program of the world's peace, therefore, is our program; and that program, the only possible program, as we see it, is this:

I. Open covenants of peace, openly arrived at, after which there shall be no private international understandings of any kind but diplomacy shall proceed always frankly and in the public view.

II. Absolute freedom of navigation upon the seas, outside territorial waters, alike in peace and in war, except as the seas may be closed in whole or in part by international action for the enforcement of international covenants.

III. The removal, so far as possible, of all economic barriers and the establishment of an equality of trade conditions among all the nations consenting to the peace and associating themselves for its maintenance.

IV. Adequate guarantees given and taken that national armaments will be reduced to the lowest point consistent with domestic safety.

V. A free, open-minded, and absolutely impartial adjustment of all colonial claims, based upon a strict observance of the principle that in determining all such questions of sovereignty the interests of the populations concerned must have equal weight with the equitable claims of the government whose title is to be determined.

VI. The evacuation of all Russian territory and such a settlement of all questions affecting Russia as will secure the best and freest cooperation of the other nations of the world in obtaining for her an unhampered and unembarrassed opportunity for the independent determination of her own political development and national policy and assure her of a sincere welcome into the society of free nations under institutions of her own choosing; and, more than a welcome, assistance also of every kind that she may need and may herself desire. The treatment accorded Russia by her sister nations in the months to come will be the acid test of their good will, of their comprehension of her needs as distinguished from their own interests, and of their intelligent and unselfish sympathy.

VII. Belgium, the whole world will agree, must be evacuated and restored, without any attempt to limit the sovereignty which she enjoys in common with all other free nations. No other single act will serve as this will serve to restore confidence among the nations in the laws which they have themselves set and determined for the government of their relation with one another. Without this healing act the whole structure and validity of international law is forever impaired.

VIII. All French territory should be freed and the invaded portions restored, and the wrong done to France by Prussia in 1871 in the matter of Alsace-Lorraine, which has unsettled the peace of the world for nearly fifty years, should be righted, in order that peace may once more be made secure in the interest of all.

IX. A readjustment of the frontiers of Italy shall be effected along clearly recognizable lines of nationality.

X. The peoples of Austria-Hungary, whose place among the nations we wish to see safeguarded and assured, should be accorded the freest opportunity of autonomous development.

XI. Rumania, Serbia, and Montenegro should be evacuated; occupied territories restored; Serbia accorded free and secure access to the sea; and the relations of the several Balkan states to one another determined by friendly counsel along historically established lines of allegiance and nationality; and international guarantees of the political and economic independence and territorial integrity of the several Balkan states should be entered into.

XII. The Turkish portions of the present Ottoman Empire should be assured a secure sovereignty, but the other nationalities which are now under Turkish rule should be assured an undoubted security of life and an absolutely unmolested opportunity of autonomous development, and the Dardanelles should be permanently opened as a free passage to the ships and commerce of all nations under international guarantees.

XIII. An independent Polish state should be erected which should include territories inhabited by indisputably Polish populations, which should be assured a free and secure access to the sea, and whose political and economic independence and territorial integrity should be guaranteed by international covenant.

XIV. A general association of nations must be formed under specific covenants for the purpose of affording mutual guarantees of political independence and territorial integrity to great and small states alike.

In regard to these essential rectifications [righting] of wrong and assertions of right we feel ourselves to be intimate partners of all the governments and peoples associated together against the Imperialists. We cannot be separated in interest or divided in purpose. We stand together until the end.

For such arrangements and covenants we are willing to fight and to continue to fight until they are achieved; but only because we wish the right to prevail and desire a just and stable peace such as can be secured only by removing the chief provocations to war, which this program does not remove. We have no jealousy of German greatness, and there is nothing in this program that impairs it. We grudge her no achievement or distinction of learning or of pacific [peaceful] enterprise such as have made her record very bright and very enviable. We do not wish to injure her or to block in any way her legitimate influence or power. We do not wish to fight her either with arms or with hostile arrangements of trade if she is willing to associate herself with us and the other peace-loving nations of the world in covenants of justice and law and fair dealing. We wish her only to accept a place of equality among the peoples of the world—the new world in which we now live,—instead of a place of mastery.

Neither do we presume to suggest to her any alteration or modification of her institutions. But it is necessary, we must frankly say, and necessary as a preliminary to any intelligent dealings with her on our part, that we should know whom her spokesmen speak for when they speak to us, whether for the Reichstag [German legislature] majority or for the military party and the men whose creed is imperial domination.

We have spoken now, surely, in terms too concrete to admit of any further doubt or question. An evident principle runs through the whole program I have outlined. It is the principle of justice to all peoples and nationalities, and their right to live on equal terms of liberty and safety with one another, whether they be strong or weak. Unless this principle be made its foundation no part of the structure of international justice can stand. The people of the United States could act upon no other principle; and to the vindication of this principle they are ready to devote their lives, their honor, and everything that they possess. The moral climax of this the culminating and final war for human liberty has come, and they are ready to put their own strength, their own highest purpose, their own integrity and devotion to the test. ❖

HISTORICAL DOCUMENT

Martin Luther King, Jr.'s "I Have A Dream" Speech

August 28, 1963

Five score years ago, a great American, in whose symbolic shadow we stand, signed the Emancipation Proclamation. This momentous decree came as a great beacon light of hope to millions of Negro slaves who had been seared in the flames of withering injustice. It came as a joyous daybreak to end the long night of captivity.

But one hundred years later, we must face the tragic fact that the Negro is still not free. One hundred years later, the life of the Negro is still sadly crippled by the manacles of segregation and the chains of discrimination. One hundred years later, the Negro lives on a lonely island of poverty in the midst of a vast ocean of material prosperity. One hundred years later, the Negro is still languished in the corners of American society and finds himself an exile in his own land. So we have come here today to dramatize an appalling condition.

In a sense we have come to our nation's Capital to cash a check. When the architects of our republic wrote the magnificent words of the Constitution and the Declaration of Independence, they were signing a promissory note to which every American was to fall heir. This note was a promise that all men would be guaranteed the unalienable rights of life, liberty, and the pursuit of happiness.

It is obvious today that America has defaulted on this promissory note insofar as her citizens of color are concerned. Instead of honoring this sacred obligation, America has given the Negro people a bad check; a check which has come back marked "insufficient funds." But we refuse to believe that the bank of justice is bankrupt. We refuse to believe that there are insufficient funds in the great vaults of opportunity of this nation. So we have come to cash this check—a check that will give us upon demand the riches of freedom and the security of justice.

We have also come to this hallowed spot to remind America of the fierce urgency of *now.* This is no time to engage in the luxury of cooling off or to take the tranquilizing drug of gradualism. *Now* is the time to make real the promises of democracy. *Now* is the time to rise from the dark and desolate valley of segregation to the sunlit path of racial justice. *Now* is the time to open the doors of opportunity to all of God's children. *Now* is the time to lift our nation from the quicksands of racial injustice to the solid rock of brotherhood.

It would be fatal for the nation to overlook the urgency of the moment and to underestimate the determination of the Negro. This sweltering summer of the Negro's legitimate discontent will not pass until there is an invigorating autumn of freedom and equality. Nineteen sixty-three is not an end, but a beginning. Those who hope that the Negro needed to blow off steam and will now be content will have a rude awakening if the nation returns to business as usual. There will be neither rest nor tranquility in America until the Negro is granted his citizenship rights. The whirlwinds of revolt will continue to shake the foundations of our nation until the bright day of justice emerges.

But there is something that I must say to my people who stand on the warm threshold which leads into the palace of justice. In the process of gaining our rightful place we must not be guilty of wrongful deeds. Let us not seek to satisfy our thirst for freedom by drinking from the cup of bitterness and hatred. We must forever conduct our struggle on the high plane of dignity and discipline. We must not allow our creative protest to degenerate into physical violence. Again and again we must rise to the majestic heights of meeting physical force with soul force.

The marvelous new militancy which has engulfed the Negro community must not lead us to a distrust of all white people, for many of our white brothers, as evidenced by their presence here today, have come to realize that their destiny is tied up with our destiny and their freedom is inextricably bound to our freedom. We cannot walk alone.

And as we walk, we must make the pledge that we shall march ahead. We cannot turn back. There are those who are asking the devotees of civil rights, "When will you be satisfied?"

We can never be satisfied as long as the Negro is the victim of the unspeakable horrors of police brutality.

We can never be satisfied as long as our bodies, heavy with the fatigue of travel, cannot gain lodging in the motels of the highways and the hotels of the cities.

We cannot be satisfied as long as the Negro's basic mobility is from a smaller ghetto to a larger one.

We can never be satisfied as long as a Negro in Mississippi cannot vote and a Negro in New York believes he has nothing for which to vote.

No, no, we are not satisfied, and we will not be satisfied until justice rolls down like waters and righteousness like a mighty stream.

I am not unmindful that some of you have come here out of great trials and tribulations. Some of you have come fresh from narrow jail cells. Some of you have come from areas where your quest for freedom left you battered by the storms of persecution and staggered by the winds of police brutality. You have been the veterans of creative suffering. Continue to work with the faith that unearned suffering is redemptive.

Go back to Mississippi, go back to Alabama, go back to South Carolina, go back to Georgia, go back to Louisiana, go back to the slums and ghettos of our Northern cities, knowing that somehow this situation can and will be changed. Let us not wallow in the valley of despair.

I say to you today, my friends, that in spite of the difficulties and frustrations of the moment I still have a dream. It is a dream deeply rooted in the American dream.

I have a dream that one day this nation will rise up and live out the true meaning of its creed: "We hold these truths to be self-evident; that all men are created equal."

I have a dream that one day on the red hills of Georgia the sons of former slaves and the sons of former slaveowners will be able to sit down together at the table of brotherhood.

I have a dream that one day even the state of Mississippi, a desert state sweltering with the heat of injustice and oppression, will be transformed into an oasis of freedom and justice.

I have a dream that my four little children will one day live in a nation where they will not be judged by the color of their skin but by the content of their character.

I have a dream today.

I have a dream that one day the state of Alabama, whose governor's lips are presently dripping with the words of interposition and nullification, will be transformed into a situation where little black boys and black girls will be able to join hands with little white boys and white girls and walk together as sisters and brothers.

I have a dream today.

I have a dream that one day every valley shall be exhalted, every hill and mountain shall be made low, the rough places will be made plain, and the crooked places will be made straight, and the glory of the Lord shall be revealed, and all flesh shall see it together.

This is our hope. This is the faith with which I return to the South. With this faith we will be able to hew out of the mountain of despair a stone of hope. With this faith we will be able to transform the jangling discords of our nation into a beautiful symphony of brotherhood.

With this faith we will be able to work together, to pray together, to struggle together, to go to jail together, to stand up for freedom together, knowing that we will be free one day.

This will be the day when all of God's children will be able to sing with new meaning, "My country 'tis of thee, sweet land of liberty, of thee I sing. Land where my fathers died, land of the Pilgrims' pride, from every mountainside, let freedom ring."

And if America is to be a great nation, this must become true. So let freedom ring from the prodigious hilltops of New Hampshire. Let freedom ring from the mighty mountains of New York. Let freedom ring from the heightening Alleghenies of Pennsylvania!

Let freedom ring from the snowcapped Rockies of Colorado! Let freedom ring from the curvaceous peaks of California! But not only that; let freedom ring from Stone Mountain of Georgia! Let freedom ring from Lookout Mountain of Tennessee!

Let freedom ring from every hill and molehill of Mississippi. From every mountainside, let freedom ring.

When we let freedom ring, when we let it ring from every village and every hamlet, from every state and every city, we will be able to speed up that day when all of God's children, black men and white men, Jews and Gentiles, Protestants and Catholics, will be able to join hands and sing in the words of the old Negro spiritual, "Free at last! Free at last! Thank God Almighty, we are free at last!" ❖

ATLAS

The World: Political

ARCTIC OCEAN

GREENLAND
(Denmark)

ICELAND

ALASKA
(US)

Godthab

Aleutian Islands

60°N

CANADA

Vancouver

Winnipeg

NORTH
AMERICA

Ottawa

Montreal
Toronto
New York

40°N

Chicago

UNITED
STATES

Washington, D.C.

ATLANTIC

OCEAN

Rabat
Casablanca

MOROCCO

Los Angeles

Houston

BERMUDA
(UK)

WESTERN
SAHARA
(Sovereignty
disputed)

MEXICO

THE
BAHAMAS

Tropic of Cancer

HAWAII (US)

Havana

CUBA

DOMINICAN
REPUBLIC

MAURITANIA

Nouakchott

20°N

Mexico
City

PUERTO RICO (US)

ST. KITTS AND NEVIS

SENEGAL

CAPE VERDE

JAMAICA

HAITI

ANTIGUA AND BARBUDA

Dakar

GUATEMALA

BELIZE

VIRGIN ISLANDS
(US, UK)

DOMINICA

Bamako

Guatemala
City

HONDURAS

ST. LUCIA

BARBADOS

GAMBIA

EL SALVADOR

NICARAGUA

ST. VINCENT AND
THE GRENADINES

GRENADA

GUINEA-BISSAU

GUINEA

Managua

TRINIDAD AND
TOBAGO

PANAMA

Caracas

SIERRA
LEONE

CÔTE
D'IVOIRE

COSTA RICA

VENEZUELA

GUYANA

LIBERIA

Georgetown

Paramaribo

SURINAME

Bogotá

FRENCH GUIANA
(France)

N

COLOMBIA

0° Equator

PACIFIC

Galápagos
Islands
(Ecuador)

Quito

ECUADOR

W   E

KIRIBATI

OCEAN

PERU

S

SOUTH
AMERICA

WESTERN
SAMOA

AMERICAN
SAMOA

Lima

BRAZIL

BOLIVIA

La Paz

Brasília

Sucre

20°S

TONGA

PARAGUAY

Rio de Janeiro

Tropic of Capricorn

CHILE

Asunción

São Paulo

ARGENTINA

ATLANTIC

Santiago

URUGUAY

OCEAN

Buenos
Aires

Montevideo

40°S

FALKLAND
ISLANDS
(UK)

SOUTH GEORGIA
(UK)

SOUTH SANDWICH
ISLANDS (UK)

60°S

160°W

140°W

120°W

100°W

80°W

60°

40°W

20°W

Antarctic Circle

⊛ National capitals

• Other cities

SCALE: at Equator

0   500   1,000 1,500 2,000 Miles

0   1,000   2,000 Kilometers

Projection: Mollweide

United States of America: Physical

PACIFIC OCEAN

Strait of Juan de Fuca

Mount Rainier
14,410 ft
(4392 m)

Columbia River

Cape Mendocino

Klamath Lakes

Goose Lake

Shasta Lake

San Francisco Bay

MONTEREY BAY

COAST RANGES

CASCADE RANGE

COLUMBIA PLATEAU

SIERRA NEVADA

CENTRAL VALLEY

Pyramid Lake

Lake Tahoe

COAST RANGES

Mount Whitney
14,494 ft
(4418 m)

MOJAVE DESERT

Channel Islands

GREAT BASIN

Great Salt Lake

Utah Lake

WASATCH RANGE

UINTA MTS.

Colorado River

GRAND CANYON

Lake Mead

COLORADO PLATEAU

PAINTED DESERT

Gila River

SONORA DESERT

GULF OF CALIFORNIA

SALMON RIVER MTS.

SAWTOOTH MTS.

Snake River

BITTERROOT RANGE

LEWIS RANGE

Milk River

Missouri River

Fort Peck Lake

Yellowstone River

Bighorn River

Powder River

Continental Divide

Granite Peak
12,804 ft
(4200 m)

ROCKY MOUNTAINS

FRONT RANGE

Mount Elbert
14,433 ft
(4400 m)

Pikes Peak
14,110 ft
(4301 m)

SANGRE DE CRISTO MTS.

SAN LUIS VALLEY

Continental Divide

GREAT INTERIOR PLAINS

Lake Sakakawea

Red River

Lake Oahe

BLACK HILLS

Cheyenne River

White River

Niobrara River

North Platte River

South Platte River

Republican River

Smoky Hill River

Kansas River

Minnesota River

Missouri River

Canadian River

Keystone Lake

Eufaula Lake

Lake Texoma

Pecos River

Colorado River

Brazos River

Rio Grande

Amistad Reservoir

Falcon Lake

Padre Island

MEXICO

CANADA

GULF

To understand the relative locations of Alaska and Hawaii as well as the vast distances separating them from the rest of the United States, see the world map.

Kauai

Niihau

Oahu

Molokai

Lanai
Kahoolawe
Maui

PACIFIC OCEAN

Mauna Kea
(13,796 ft
4206 m)

Hawaii

SCALE

| 0 | 75 | 150 Miles |

| 0 | 75 | 150 Kilometers |

ARCTIC OCEAN

Arctic Circle

RUSSIA

BERING STRAIT

St. Lawrence Island

St. Matthew Island

Nunivak Island

BROOKS RANGE

Yukon River

Kuskokwim River

ALASKA RANGE

Mount McKinley
(20,320 ft
6194 m)

CANADA

BERING SEA

Attu Island

Aleutian Islands

PACIFIC OCEAN

Kodiak Island

GULF OF ALASKA

Alexander Archipelago

SCALE

| 0 | 250 | 500 Miles |

| 0 | 250 | 500 Kilometers |

Projection: Albers Equal Area

CANADA

MESABI RANGE

Isle
Royale

Lake Superior

Lake Michigan

Lake Huron

Lake Ontario

Lake Erie

ADIRONDACK MTS.

CATSKILL MTS.

GREEN MTS.

WHITE MTS.

LONGFELLOW MTS.

St. John River

St. Lawrence Seaway

St. Lawrence River

Cape Cod

LONG ISLAND SOUND

Long Island

ALLEGHENY PLATEAU

APPALACHIAN MOUNTAINS

PLAINS

Wisconsin River

Des Moines River

Illinois River

Mississippi River

Lake of the Ozarks

OZARK PLATEAU

OUACHITA MTS.

Lake Barkley

Kentucky Lake

Cumberland River

CUMBERLAND PLATEAU

GREAT SMOKY MTS.

BLUE RIDGE MOUNTAINS

PIEDMONT

DELAWARE BAY

CHESAPEAKE BAY

PAMLICO SOUND

Cape Hatteras

ATLANTIC COASTAL PLAIN

ATLANTIC OCEAN

Toledo Bend Reservoir

COASTAL   PLAIN

Sea Islands

Okefenokee Swamp

Chandeleur Islands

Mississippi Delta

Cape Canaveral

FLORIDA PENINSULA

Lake Okeechobee

The Everglades

GULF OF MEXICO

Cape Sable

Florida Keys

STRAITS OF FLORIDA

THE BAHAMAS

CUBA

ELEVATION

Feet		Meters
13,120		4,000
6,560		2,000
1,640		500
656		200
(Sea level) 0		0 (Sea level)
Below sea level		Below sea level

Ice cap

N
W E
S

SCALE
0   250   500 Miles
0   250   500 Kilometers
Projection: Albers Equal Area

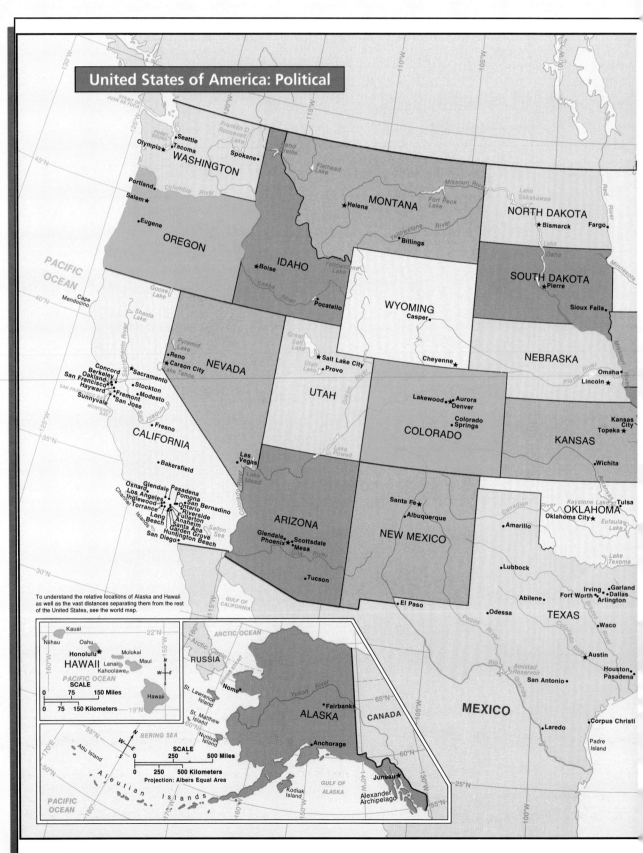

United States of America: Political

Here are the labels visible on the map:

WASHINGTON
- Seattle
- Tacoma
- Olympia ★
- Spokane
- Portland
- Salem ★
- Eugene

OREGON

IDAHO
- Helena ★ (MONTANA)
- Boise ★
- Billings
- Pocatello

MONTANA

NORTH DAKOTA
- Bismarck ★
- Fargo

SOUTH DAKOTA
- Pierre ★
- Sioux Falls

WYOMING
- Casper
- Cheyenne ★

NEBRASKA
- Omaha
- Lincoln ★

NEVADA
- Reno
- Carson City ★

CALIFORNIA
- Concord
- Berkeley
- Oakland
- San Francisco
- Hayward
- Sunnyvale
- Sacramento ★
- Stockton
- Modesto
- Fremont
- San Jose
- Fresno
- Bakersfield
- Glendale
- Oxnard
- Pasadena
- Pomona
- Los Angeles
- Inglewood
- Torrance
- Channel Islands
- San Bernardino
- Ontario
- Riverside
- Fullerton
- Anaheim
- Long Beach
- Santa Ana
- Garden Grove
- Huntington Beach
- San Diego

UTAH
- Salt Lake City ★
- Provo

COLORADO
- Lakewood
- Aurora
- Denver
- Colorado Springs

KANSAS
- Kansas City
- Topeka ★
- Wichita

ARIZONA
- Las Vegas (NEVADA)
- Glendale
- Phoenix ★
- Scottsdale
- Mesa
- Tucson

NEW MEXICO
- Santa Fe ★
- Albuquerque

OKLAHOMA
- Tulsa
- Oklahoma City ★
- Amarillo

TEXAS
- Lubbock
- Abilene
- Odessa
- Irving
- Garland
- Dallas
- Fort Worth
- Arlington
- Waco
- Austin ★
- Houston
- Pasadena
- San Antonio
- Corpus Christi
- Laredo
- Padre Island
- El Paso

PACIFIC OCEAN

Cape Mendocino

GULF OF CALIFORNIA

MEXICO
CANADA

To understand the relative locations of Alaska and Hawaii as well as the vast distances separating them from the rest of the United States, see the world map.

HAWAII
- Kauai
- Niihau
- Oahu
- Honolulu ★
- Molokai
- Lanai
- Maui
- Kahoolawe
- Hawaii

PACIFIC OCEAN

SCALE
0   75   150 Miles
0   75   150 Kilometers

ARCTIC OCEAN
RUSSIA
- Nome
- St. Lawrence Island
- St. Matthew Island
- Nunivak Island
- Fairbanks
- Anchorage
- Juneau ★
- Kodiak Island
- Alexander Archipelago

ALASKA
CANADA

BERING SEA

Aleutian Islands

GULF OF ALASKA

PACIFIC OCEAN

SCALE
0   250   500 Miles
0   250   500 Kilometers
Projection: Albers Equal Area

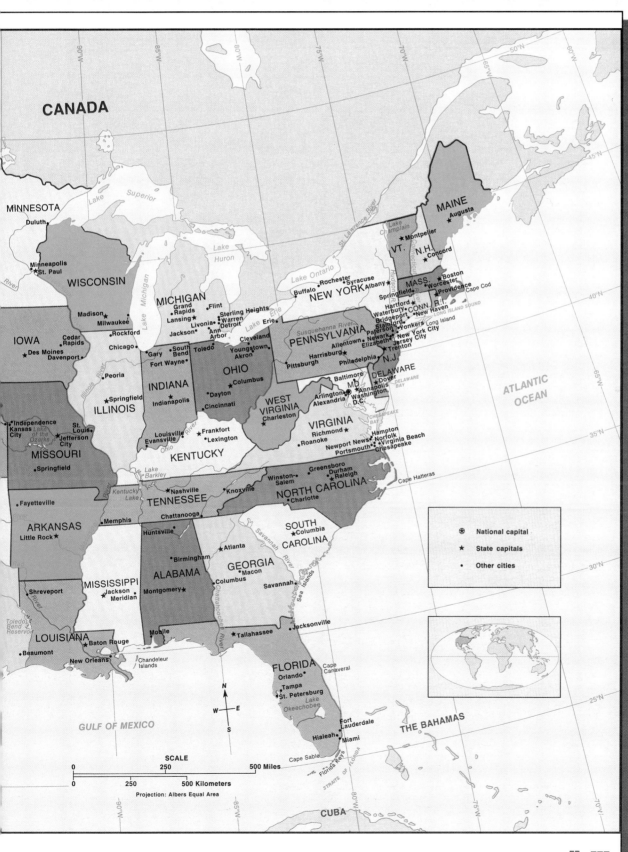

CANADA

MINNESOTA
• Duluth

• Minneapolis
★ St. Paul
WISCONSIN

Lake Superior

Lake Huron

MAINE
Augusta ★

Lake Champlain

VT.
★ Montpelier
N.H.
★ Concord

Lake Ontario

Rochester
Buffalo • • Syracuse
NEW YORK Albany ★

MASS. ★ Boston
Springfield • • Worcester
• Providence
Cape Cod

MICHIGAN
Grand • Flint
Madison ★ Rapids • Sterling Heights
Lansing ★ • Warren
• Milwaukee Livonia • • Detroit
• Rockford Jackson • Ann
Arbor

Hartford ★ CONN. R.I.
Waterbury • ★ New Haven
Bridgeport •
Stamford • Yonkers • Long Island
Paterson • • New York City
Elizabeth • Jersey City
★ Trenton

Lake Erie
Cleveland •
Toledo • Youngstown •
Akron •

PENNSYLVANIA
Susquehanna River
Harrisburg ★
Pittsburgh • • Philadelphia

Allentown •
Newark •
N.J.

IOWA
Cedar • Rapids
★ Des Moines
• Davenport

Chicago •

Gary • South
• Bend
Fort Wayne •

• Peoria

ILLINOIS
★ Springfield

INDIANA
Indianapolis ★

• Dayton

OHIO
• Columbus

• Cincinnati

WEST
VIRGINIA
Charleston ★

Baltimore •
MD. DELAWARE
Annapolis ★ ★ Dover
Arlington ★ Washington, DELAWARE
Alexandria • D.C. BAY

ATLANTIC
OCEAN

MISSOURI
• Independence
Kansas Lake
City of the
Ozarks
★ Jefferson
City
St.
• Louis

Louisville •
Evansville •

Frankfort ★
• Lexington

VIRGINIA
Richmond ★
• Roanoke

Hampton •
Newport News • Norfolk •
Portsmouth • • Virginia Beach
• Chesapeake

CHESAPEAKE
BAY

• Springfield

KENTUCKY

Ohio River

Lake
Barkley

Winston- • Greensboro
Salem • Durham
★ Raleigh

Cape Hatteras

ARKANSAS
Little Rock ★

• Fayetteville

Kentucky
Lake

TENNESSEE
★ Nashville
• Knoxville

Chattanooga •

NORTH CAROLINA
• Charlotte

• Memphis

Huntsville •

SOUTH
CAROLINA
★ Columbia

National capital

State capitals

Other cities

MISSISSIPPI
• Jackson
★ Meridian

ALABAMA
★ Birmingham
Montgomery ★

GEORGIA
★ Atlanta
• Macon
Columbus •

Savannah River

Savannah •

Sea Islands

Shreveport •

Toledo
Bend
Reservoir

LOUISIANA

★ Baton Rouge
• Beaumont

Mobile •

Chattahoochee River

★ Tallahassee

• Jacksonville

New Orleans •
Chandeleur
Islands

FLORIDA
Orlando • Cape
Canaveral
Tampa •
• St. Petersburg
Lake
Okeechobee

N
W E
S

GULF OF MEXICO

• Fort
Lauderdale

THE BAHAMAS

Hialeah • • Miami

Cape Sable

SCALE
0   250   500 Miles

0   250   500 Kilometers
Projection: Albers Equal Area

Florida Keys

STRAITS OF FLORIDA

CUBA

FACTS ABOUT THE STATES

State	Year of Statehood	1990 Population	Reps. in Congress	Area (sq. mi.)	Population Density (sq. mi.)	Capital
Alabama	1819	4,040,587	7	51,705	79.6	Montgomery
Alaska	1959	550,043	1	591,004	1.0	Juneau
Arizona	1912	3,665,228	6	114,000	32.3	Phoenix
Arkansas	1836	2,350,725	4	53,187	45.1	Little Rock
California	1850	29,760,021	52	158,706	190.8	Sacramento
Colorado	1876	3,294,394	6	104,091	31.8	Denver
Connecticut	1788	3,287,116	6	5,018	678.4	Hartford
Delaware	1787	666,168	1	2,045	340.8	Dover
District of Columbia	—	606,900	—	69	9,882.8	—
Florida	1845	12,937,926	23	58,664	239.6	Tallahassee
Georgia	1788	6,478,216	11	58,910	111.9	Atlanta
Hawaii	1959	1,108,229	2	6,471	172.5	Honolulu
Idaho	1890	1,006,749	2	83,564	12.2	Boise
Illinois	1818	11,430,602	20	56,345	205.6	Springfield
Indiana	1816	5,544,159	10	36,185	154.6	Indianapolis
Iowa	1846	2,776,755	5	56,275	49.7	Des Moines
Kansas	1861	2,477,574	4	82,277	30.3	Topeka
Kentucky	1792	3,685,296	6	40,410	92.8	Frankfort
Louisiana	1812	4,219,973	7	47,752	96.9	Baton Rouge
Maine	1820	1,227,928	2	33,265	39.8	Augusta
Maryland	1788	4,781,468	8	10,460	489.2	Annapolis
Massachusetts	1788	6,016,425	10	8,284	767.6	Boston
Michigan	1837	9,295,297	16	58,527	163.6	Lansing
Minnesota	1858	4,375,099	8	84,402	55.0	St. Paul
Mississippi	1817	2,573,216	5	47,689	54.9	Jackson
Missouri	1821	5,117,073	9	69,697	74.3	Jefferson City
Montana	1889	799,065	1	147,046	5.5	Helena
Nebraska	1867	1,578,385	3	77,355	20.5	Lincoln
Nevada	1864	1,201,833	2	110,561	10.9	Carson City
New Hampshire	1788	1,109,252	2	9,279	123.7	Concord
New Jersey	1787	7,730,188	13	7,787	1,042.0	Trenton
New Mexico	1912	1,515,069	3	121,593	12.5	Santa Fe
New York	1788	17,990,455	31	49,108	381.0	Albany
North Carolina	1789	6,628,637	12	52,669	136.1	Raleigh
North Dakota	1889	638,800	1	70,702	9.3	Bismarck
Ohio	1803	10,847,115	19	41,330	264.9	Columbus
Oklahoma	1907	3,145,585	6	69,956	45.8	Oklahoma City
Oregon	1859	2,842,321	5	97,073	29.6	Salem
Pennsylvania	1787	11,881,643	21	45,308	265.1	Harrisburg
Rhode Island	1790	1,003,464	2	1,212	960.3	Providence
South Carolina	1788	3,486,703	6	31,113	115.8	Columbia
South Dakota	1889	696,004	1	77,116	9.2	Pierre
Tennessee	1796	4,877,185	9	42,144	118.3	Nashville
Texas	1845	16,986,510	30	266,807	64.9	Austin
Utah	1896	1,722,850	3	84,899	21.0	Salt Lake City
Vermont	1791	562,758	1	9,614	60.8	Montpelier
Virginia	1788	6,187,358	11	40,767	156.3	Richmond
Washington	1889	4,866,692	9	68,139	73.1	Olympia
West Virginia	1863	1,793,477	3	24,232	74.5	Charleston
Wisconsin	1848	4,891,769	9	56,153	90.1	Madison
Wyoming	1890	453,588	1	97,809	4.7	Cheyenne

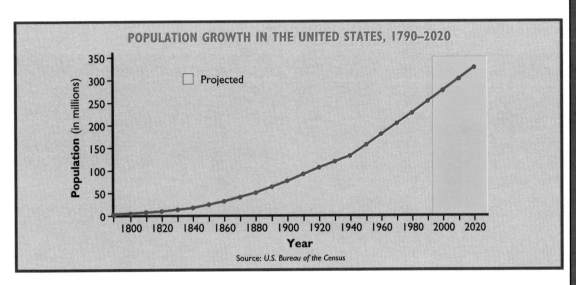

POPULATION GROWTH IN THE UNITED STATES, 1790–2020

Population (in millions) vs. Year

☐ Projected

Source: *U.S. Bureau of the Census*

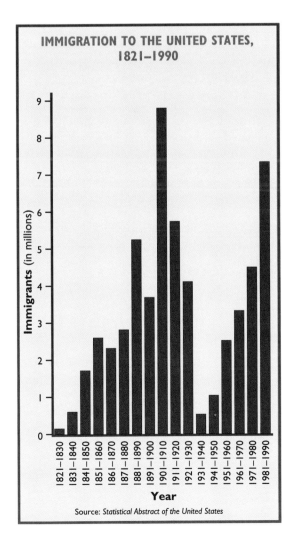

IMMIGRATION TO THE UNITED STATES, 1821–1990

Immigrants (in millions) vs. Year

Source: *Statistical Abstract of the United States*

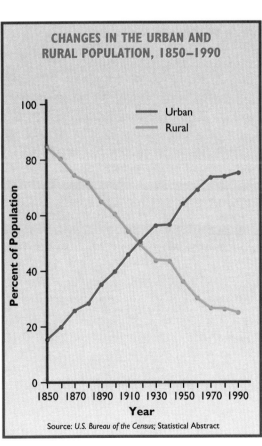

CHANGES IN THE URBAN AND RURAL POPULATION, 1850–1990

Percent of Population vs. Year

— Urban
— Rural

Source: *U.S. Bureau of the Census; Statistical Abstract*

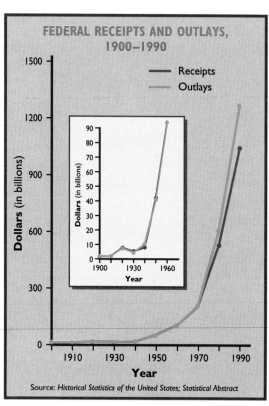

FEDERAL RECEIPTS AND OUTLAYS, 1900–1990

— Receipts
— Outlays

Dollars (in billions)

1500
1200
900
600
300
0

1910 1930 1950 1970 1990

Year

90
80
70
60
50
40
30
20
10

Dollars (in billions)

1900 1930 1960

Year

Source: *Historical Statistics of the United States; Statistical Abstract*

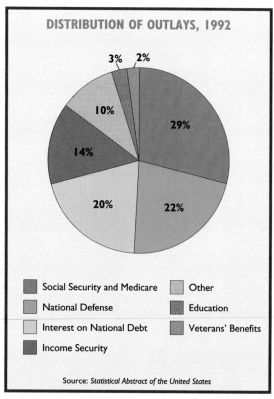

DISTRIBUTION OF OUTLAYS, 1992

3% 2%
10%
14%
29%
20% 22%

Social Security and Medicare   Other

National Defense   Education

Interest on National Debt   Veterans' Benefits

Income Security

Source: *Statistical Abstract of the United States*

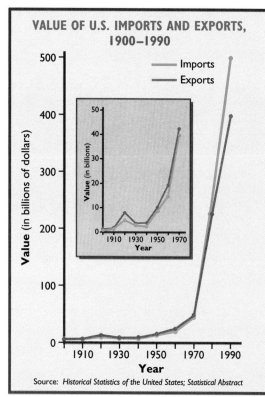

VALUE OF U.S. IMPORTS AND EXPORTS, 1900–1990

— Imports
— Exports

Value (in billions of dollars)

500
400
300
200
100
0

1910 1930 1950 1970 1990

Year

50
40
30
20
10

Value (in billions)

1910 1930 1950 1970

Year

Source: *Historical Statistics of the United States; Statistical Abstract*

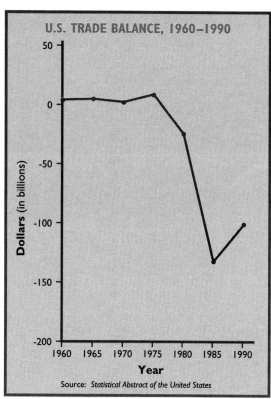

U.S. TRADE BALANCE, 1960–1990

Dollars (in billions)

50
0
-50
-100
-150
-200

1960 1965 1970 1975 1980 1985 1990

Year

Source: *Statistical Abstract of the United States*

PRESIDENTS OF THE UNITED STATES

No.	Name	Born–Died	Years In Office	Political Party	Home State	Vice President
1	George Washington	1732–1799	1789–97	None	VA	John Adams
2	John Adams	1735–1826	1797–1801	Federalist	MA	Thomas Jefferson
3	Thomas Jefferson	1743–1826	1801–09	Republican*	VA	Aaron Burr George Clinton
4	James Madison	1751–1836	1809–17	Republican	VA	George Clinton Elbridge Gerry
5	James Monroe	1758–1831	1817–25	Republican	VA	Daniel D. Tompkins
6	John Quincy Adams	1767–1848	1825–29	Republican	MA	John C. Calhoun
7	Andrew Jackson	1767–1845	1829–37	Democratic	TN	John C. Calhoun Martin Van Buren
8	Martin Van Buren	1782–1862	1837–41	Democratic	NY	Richard M. Johnson
9	William Henry Harrison	1773–1841	1841	Whig	OH	John Tyler
10	John Tyler	1790–1862	1841–45	Whig	VA	
11	James K. Polk	1795–1849	1845–49	Democratic	TN	George M. Dallas
12	Zachary Taylor	1784–1850	1849–50	Whig	LA	Millard Fillmore
13	Millard Fillmore	1800–1874	1850–53	Whig	NY	
14	Franklin Pierce	1804–1869	1853–57	Democratic	NH	William R. King
15	James Buchanan	1791–1868	1857–61	Democratic	PA	John C. Breckenridge
16	Abraham Lincoln	1809–1865	1861–65	Republican	IL	Hannibal Hamlin Andrew Johnson
17	Andrew Johnson	1808–1875	1865–69	Republican	TN	
18	Ulysses S. Grant	1822–1885	1869–77	Republican	IL	Schuyler Colfax Henry Wilson
19	Rutherford B. Hayes	1822–1893	1877–81	Republican	OH	William A. Wheeler
20	James A. Garfield	1831–1881	1881	Republican	OH	Chester A. Arthur
21	Chester A. Arthur	1830–1886	1881–85	Republican	NY	
22	Grover Cleveland	1837–1908	1885–89	Democratic	NY	Thomas A. Hendricks
23	Benjamin Harrison	1833–1901	1889–93	Republican	IN	Levi P. Morton
24	Grover Cleveland		1893–97	Democratic	NY	Adlai E. Stevenson
25	William McKinley	1843–1901	1897–1901	Republican	OH	Garrett A. Hobart Theodore Roosevelt
26	Theodore Roosevelt	1858–1919	1901–09	Republican	NY	Charles W. Fairbanks
27	William Howard Taft	1857–1930	1909–13	Republican	OH	James S. Sherman
28	Woodrow Wilson	1856–1924	1913–21	Democratic	NJ	Thomas R. Marshall
29	Warren G. Harding	1865–1923	1921–23	Republican	OH	Calvin Coolidge
30	Calvin Coolidge	1872–1933	1923–29	Republican	MA	Charles G. Dawes
31	Herbert Hoover	1874–1964	1929–33	Republican	CA	Charles Curtis
32	Franklin D. Roosevelt	1882–1945	1933–45	Democratic	NY	John Nance Garner Henry Wallace Harry S. Truman
33	Harry S. Truman	1884–1972	1945–53	Democratic	MO	Alben W. Barkley
34	Dwight D. Eisenhower	1890–1969	1953–61	Republican	KS	Richard M. Nixon
35	John F. Kennedy	1917–1963	1961–63	Democratic	MA	Lyndon B. Johnson
36	Lyndon B. Johnson	1908–1973	1963–69	Democratic	TX	Hubert H. Humphrey
37	Richard M. Nixon	1913–1994	1969–74	Republican	CA	Spiro T. Agnew Gerald R. Ford
38	Gerald R. Ford	1913–	1974–77	Republican	MI	Nelson A. Rockefeller
39	Jimmy Carter	1924–	1977–81	Democratic	GA	Walter F. Mondale
40	Ronald Reagan	1911–	1981–89	Republican	CA	George Bush
41	George Bush	1924–	1989–1993	Republican	TX	J. Danforth Quayle
42	Bill Clinton	1946–	1993–	Democratic	AR	Albert Gore, Jr.

*The Republican party of the third through sixth presidents is not the party of Abraham Lincoln, which was founded in 1854.

BIOGRAPHIES

A

Abzug, Bella (1920–). Lawyer, politician. U.S. representative, 1971–77; supported legislation to promote federal jobs programs, public transportation, individual right to privacy. Strong advocate of women's rights; helped found the National Women's Political Caucus, 1971. (p. 577)

Adams, John (1735–1826). The 2nd president, 1797–1801. On committee to draft Declaration of Independence; helped negotiate peace after the Revolutionary War. Washington's vice president. Died same day as Jefferson, on 50th anniversary of Declaration of Independence. (p. 63)

Adams, John Quincy (1767–1848). The 6th president, 1825–29. Diplomat; U.S. senator, 1803–08; helped negotiate treaty ending War of 1812; Monroe's secretary of state, 1817–25; negotiated northern U.S. boundary with Britain. U.S. representative, 1831–46. (p. 76)

Anderson, Marian (1902–1993). African American opera singer; toured Europe 1930–35. In 1955 became first African American soloist with NY's Metropolitan Opera. Served as U.S. delegate to United Nations, 1958. Awarded UN Peace Prize, 1977. (pp. 316, 364)

Anthony, Susan B. (1820–1906). Women's suffrage leader; advocate of temperance, abolition of slavery. Helped found National Woman Suffrage Association, 1869; president of National American Woman Suffrage Association, 1892–1900; coauthor *History of Woman Suffrage,* 1881–1902. (p. 208)

Arthur, Chester A. (1829–1886). The 21st president, 1881–85. Collector at port of NY, 1871–79; vice president, 1881. Became president at death of Garfield. (p. 156)

B

Baker, Ella (1903–1986). Civil rights activist; worked with Harlem youth groups and *Negro National News,* 1930s. Worked on recruitment for NAACP, 1940s; president of New York NAACP, 1954; leader in SCLC; helped found SNCC, MS Freedom Democratic party. (p. 505)

Brandeis, Louis D. (1856–1941). Lawyer and jurist; Associate Justice for Supreme Court, 1916–39. Known as "the people's attorney" for taking on cases involving social reform; wrote "Brandeis brief." (p. 175)

Louis D. Brandeis

Buchanan, James (1791–1868). The 15th president, 1857–61. U.S. representative, 1821–31; minister to Russia; U.S. senator, 1834–45; Polk's secretary of state; helped draft Ostend Manifesto, 1854. (p. 90)

Bunche, Ralph (1904–1971). African American diplomat. Chairman political science, Howard University; contributor, Gunnar Myrdal's *An American Dilemma,* 1944. United Nations mediator in Palestine, Africa, Yemen, Cyprus; Nobel Peace Prize, 1950. (p. 453)

Bush, George H.W. (1924–). The 41st president, 1989–93. U.S. representative, 1966–70; appointed UN representative, chairman Republican National Committee by Nixon; appointed director of CIA by Ford. Reagan's vice president, 1981–89. (pp. 585, 602)

C

Carter, James Earl "Jimmy" (1924–). The 39th president, 1977–81. Governor of GA. Known for his campaign for global human rights and Camp David Accords between Egypt and Israel. (p. 569)

Castro, Fidel (1926–). Communist dictator of Cuba. Lawyer, early 1950s. Arrested for leading attempted revolt against dictator Batista, 1953; released from prison, 1955; overthrew Batista, 1959. During Cold War formed close ties with USSR. (p. 491)

Catt, Carrie Chapman (1859–1947). Women's suffragist, peace activist. President, National American Woman Suffrage Association; president International Woman Suffrage Alliance; founded National League of Women Voters, 1920, and National Committee on the Cause and Cure of War, 1925. (pp. 208, 382)

Chávez, César (1927–1993). Mexican American labor leader. Founded Farm Workers United, 1962; led strikes, boycotts against grape growers, lettuce growers; brought about CA Agricultural Labor Relations Act. (pp. 370, 507)

Shirley Chisholm

Chisholm, Shirley (1924–). African American politician; NY teacher, educational adviser. Elected to NY state assembly, 1964. First black female U.S.

representative, 1969–83; first black woman to run for president, 1972 Democratic primary. (p. 577)

Churchill, Winston (1874–1965). British prime minister, 1940–45, 1951–1955. Joined House of Commons, 1901; served in numerous government positions; wrote several books before becoming prime minister, 1940, during WWII. Nobel Peace Prize, 1953. (pp. 393, 446)

Cleveland, Grover (1837–1908). The 22nd and 24th president. President, 1885–89; lost reelection, 1888, to Benjamin Harrison; again president, 1893–97. (p. 156)

Clinton, Hillary Rodham (1947–). First lady. Graduate, Yale Law School; Helped develop 1993 health-care reform package. (p. 605)

Hillary Rodham Clinton

Clinton, William Jefferson "Bill" (1946–). The 42nd president. Nation's youngest governor (of AR). (pp. 604, 605)

Columbus, Christopher (1451–1506). Explorer credited with European discovery of Americas. (p. 10)

Coolidge, Calvin (1872–1933). The 30th president. Vice president, 1921–23; became president at death of Harding, 1923; elected president, 1924, served full term 1925–29. (pp. 280, 287)

Crazy Horse (Ta-sunko-witko) (1842?–1877). Oglala Sioux chief. Led Sioux war of resistance against forced removal to reservation, 1876; victory at Battle of Little Big Horn against Custer, 1876; surrendered, 1877; killed while resisting imprisonment. Called "Strange One" by Sioux. (p. 124)

Custer, George Armstrong (1839–1876). Army officer. Served in Civil War. Joined 7th Calvary Regiment in West; fought many battles against Indians; led Black Hills expedition; killed in Battle of Little Big Horn, "Custer's Last Stand." (p. 124)

Davis, Jefferson (1808–1889). President of Confederacy, 1862–65. Pierce's secretary of war, 1853–57; twice elected U.S. senator. Strong advocate of slavery and secession. Arrested for treason after Civil War; indicted but never tried. (p. 91)

Debs, Eugene V. (1855–1926). Socialist and labor leader. Organizer, American Railway Union, International Workers of the World; imprisoned for role in Pullman strike. Founded Social Democratic party; ran for president five times. (p. 203)

Delany, Martin (1812–1885). African American physician, social reformer, journalist, soldier. Cofounder, coeditor *North Star.* Active abolitionist; worked with Underground Railroad. Attempted to establish African American colony in Nicaragua. (p. 101)

Douglass, Frederick (1817–1895). African American abolitionist, lecturer, author. Born a slave, escaped and settled in MA, 1838. Agent of MA Anti-Slavery Society. Published autobiography, 1845. Lectured in Great Britain and Ireland, 1845–47. Founder, abolitionist newspaper *North Star.* (pp. 82, 101)

Edison, Thomas Alva (1847–1931). "The Wizard of Menlo Park"; founded company that became General Electric. Patented more than 1,000 inventions. (p. 143)

Eisenhower, Dwight David "Ike" (1890–1969). The 34th president, 1953–61. WWII commander in chief of Allied forces, Western Europe, 1943; planned and led defeat of Germany, 1944–45. President,

Columbia University, 1948–53. Supreme commander, NATO forces in Europe, 1951–52. (pp. 415, 469, 522)

Ellison, Ralph (1914–1994). African American writer. Editor, *Negro Quarterly,* 1940s. Novel *Invisible Man* (1952) polled as "the most distinguished single work" published in the United States between 1945 and 1965. (p. 481)

Ralph Ellison

Emerson, Ralph Waldo (1803–1882). Author, Unitarian minister. Became popular writer and lecturer after publication of *Nature,* 1836. Best-known lectures include "The American Scholar," 1837, and "The Divinity School Address," 1838. (p. 723)

Ferraro, Geraldine (1935–). Lawyer, politician. U.S. representative 1978–84. Chosen by Democratic presidential candidate Walter Mondale as running mate, 1984; first woman to run for vice president on a major political party's ticket. (p. 591)

Fillmore, Millard (1800–1874). The 13th president. U.S. representative, 1833–35, 1837–43. U.S. vice president, 1849–50. President, 1850–53, at death of Taylor. Sent Matthew Perry to Japan, 1853. (p. 90)

Fitzgerald, F. Scott (1896–1940). Author. Known for his novels chronicling the Jazz Age (1920s). Worked as scriptwriter in Hollywood, 1937. Work was popular during his lifetime but did not receive critical recognition until long after his death. (p. 318)

Ford, Gerald R. (1913–). The 38th president. U.S. representative, 1948–73; House Republican leader, 1965. Chosen by Nixon as vice

president when Agnew resigned,
1973. Became president when Nixon
resigned, 1974. (p. 566)

Ford, Henry. (1863–1947). Founded
Ford Motor Company. Introduced the
assembly line in his automobile factory,
1913; chartered peace ship in an
unsuccessful effort to end World
War I (1915–1916). (pp. 302, 303)

Franklin, Aretha (1942–). African
American recording artist. Made first
record at age 12. Released around
50 albums since her first in 1961.
Received Grammy Awards for rhythm
and blues, soul-gospel. (p. 432)

Franklin, Benjamin (1706–1790).
Statesman, scientist, author. Publisher
Poor Richard's Almanac. Founded what
became University of PA. Invented
stove, bifocal eyeglasses, lightning
rod; experimented with electricity.
On committee to draft Declaration of
Independence; diplomat to France,
1776–85. (p. xxiv)

Benjamin Franklin

Friedan, Betty (1921–). Author,
feminist. Wrote *The Feminine Mystique,*
1963, saying that many American
women longed for more in life than
being wives and mothers. Founded
National Organization for Women
(NOW), 1966; led campaigns to end
discrimination against women. (p. 510)

Gandhi, Indira (1917–1984). Indian
politician. Official hostess for father,
Prime Minister Jawaharlal Nehru.
President of Congress party; elected
prime minister, 1966; defeated, 1977;
again elected, 1980; assassinated by
Sikh extremists, 1984. (pp. 713, 738)

Garfield, James A. (1831–1881).
The 20th president, 1881. U.S. representative, 1863–80; Republican leader
from 1876; U.S. senator, 1880.
Assassinated, 1881. (p. 156)

Geronimo (1829–1909). Apache chief.
Born AZ. Admitted to warriors' council, Chiricahua Apaches, 1846; nicknamed Geronimo by Mexicans. Led
campaign against whites, 1885–86;
was captured, escaped; surrendered.
Settled at Fort Sill, OK. (p. 126)

Goldwater, Barry M. (1909–).
Public official. U.S. senator from AZ,
1953–65 and 1968–87. Leader of conservative wing of Republicans.
Published *The Conscience of a
Conservative,* 1960. Republican presidential candidate, 1964. (p. 497)

Gorbachev, Mikhail (1931–).
Soviet leader. Became head of USSR's
Communist party, 1985; president of
USSR, 1989. Instituted programs of
economic and political restructuring
(perestroika) and of openness *(glasnost),*
which led to breakup of Soviet Union.
(pp. 593, 597)

Grant, Ulysses S. (1822–1885). The
18th president, 1869–77. As general in
Civil War, broke Confederate control
of MS by capturing Vicksburg. Despite
heavy losses finally wore down
Confederates. Accepted Lee's surrender, 1865. (pp. 102, 109)

Grimké, Angelina (1805–1879) and
Sarah (1792–1873). Sisters, abolitionists, women's rights pioneers.
Became active in abolitionist movement, 1830s. Began fight for women's
rights when criticized for their "shocking" abolitionist behavior. (p. 82)

Hamilton, Alexander (1755–1804).
First secretary of the treasury,
1789–95. Fatally wounded in duel with
Aaron Burr. (p. 61)

Harding, Warren G. (1865–1923).
The 29th president, 1921–23. U.S.
senator, 1915–21. Presidential term
marked by corruption of his
appointees, "the Ohio Gang." Died
on speaking tour. (p. 285)

Harrison, Benjamin (1833–1901).
The 23rd president, 1889–93.
Grandson of W. H. Harrison. U.S.
senator, 1881–87. (pp. 129, 156)

**Harrison, William Henry
(1773–1841).** The 9th president,
1841. Led military campaigns against
Indians; won Battle of Tippecanoe
Creek in War of 1812; defeated
Tecumseh. U.S. representative,
1816–19; U.S. senator, 1825–28. Died
of pneumonia, 1841. (pp. 66, 76)

Hayes, Rutherford B. (1822–1893).
The 19th president, 1877–81. Ran
against Samuel J. Tilden, 1876; contest
decided by electoral commission. To
keep peace with Southern Democrats,
agreed to end military Reconstruction.
(pp. 111, 156)

Hemingway, Ernest (1899–1961).
Writer. Ambulance driver, WWI; cor-
respondent, Spanish Civil War. Created
"Hemingway hero," who displays
unusual courage. Pulitzer Prize for *The
Old Man and the Sea,* 1952. Nobel
Prize for Literature, 1954. (p. 318)

Henry "the Navigator" (1394–1460).
Prince of Portugal; established school
of navigation, directed voyages of
exploration along African coast. (p. 9)

Hobby, Oveta Culp (1905–).
Military leader, statesman. First director of Women's Army Corps, WWI;
first woman promoted to colonel, first
to receive Distinguished Service Medal.
Secretary of health, education, and welfare, 1953–55. Publisher, *The Houston
Post.* (p. 470)

Hoover, Herbert (1874–1964).
The 31st president, 1929–33. U.S. secretary of commerce under Harding

Henry "the Navigator"

and Coolidge, 1921–29. As president secured creation of Federal Farm Board and Reconstruction Finance Corporation. (pp. 287, 328, 339)

Hughes, Langston (1902–1967). African American author. Wrote volumes of poetry, short stories, plays, operas. Awarded NAACP Spingarn Medal, 1960, as "poet laureate of the Negro race." (p. 316)

Hurston, Zora Neale (1889–1968). African American writer, anthropologist. Studied black folklore in the South and the Caribbean. Wrote novels, folklore collections, radio scripts; taught drama at North Carolina College. (p. 373)

Inouye, Daniel (1924–). Asian American statesman. Veteran WWII. U.S. representative, 1950s. First elected to Senate, 1962. Gained national attention during televised Senate investigation of Watergate. (pp. 433, 594)

Jackson, Andrew "Old Hickory" (1767–1845). The 7th president, 1829–37. In War of 1812, defended New Orleans; became national hero. U.S. representative, 1796–97; U.S. senator, 1797–98 and 1823–25. (pp. 67, 75, 76)

Jackson, Jesse (1941–). African American minister, civil rights leader. Worked with Martin Luther King, Jr., 1960s; organized several black self-help projects in Chicago, including Operation Breadbasket and People United to Save Humanity (PUSH). Founder of Rainbow Coalition; presidential candidate. (p. 595)

Jefferson, Thomas (1743–1826). The 3rd president, 1801–09. Drafted Declaration of Independence. Governor of VA, 1779–81; minister to France; first secretary of state, 1790–93; John Adams's vice president,

1797–1801. Founder and designer of University of VA. Died same day as John Adams, on 50th anniversary of the Declaration. (pp. 29, 63)

Johnson, Andrew (1808–1875). The 17th president, 1865–69. Self-educated, tailor. U.S. representative, 1843–53; governor of TN, 1853–57; U.S. senator, 1857–62; Lincoln's vice president, 1865; succeeded to presidency on Lincoln's death. Reconstruction policies led to impeachment, 1868; acquitted. Again U.S. senator, 1875. (pp. 106, 109)

Johnson, Lyndon Baines "LBJ" (1908–1973). The 36th president, 1963–69. U.S. representative, 1937–49; U.S. senator, 1949–61; JFK's vice president, 1961–63, succeeded to presidency on Kennedy's death. As president secured passage of Civil Rights Act of 1964 and Voting Rights Act of 1965. Popularity declined during Vietnam War; did not run for reelection. (pp. 487, 497, 526)

Daniel Inouye

Jones, Mary Harris "Mother" (1830–1930). Labor leader; appeared wherever there was a strike or labor dispute. (pp. 153, 207)

Joseph, Chief (c. 1840–1904). Nez Percé leader. From Wallowa Valley, OR. Fought U.S. troops to retain Nez Percé lands, 1877. Won battles, but when faced with U.S. Army strength, ordered retreat to Canada. Surrendered, resettled in Indian Territory; later returned to Northwest. (p. 125)

Kennedy, John Fitzgerald "JFK" (1917–1963). The 35th president, 1961–63. U.S. representative, 1947–53; U.S. senator, 1953–60. First

Roman Catholic president; assassinated in Dallas, TX, 1963. Won Pulitzer Prize for *Profiles in Courage*, 1956. (pp. 487, 490, 524)

Kennedy, Robert Francis "RFK" (1925–1968). Politician. U.S. attorney general, 1961–64. U.S. senator, 1964–68. Assassinated while campaigning for Democratic presidential nomination, 1968. Wrote *Pursuit of Justice*, 1964. (pp. 489, 536)

Khrushchev, Nikita (1894–1971). Soviet leader. Communist premier, USSR, 1958–64. Promoted space exploration, increase in Soviet standard of living, "peaceful coexistence" with Western nations. Installed Soviet missiles in Cuba, 1962; later withdrew them to end the Cuban missile crisis with President Kennedy. (pp. 468, 492)

King, Martin Luther, Jr. (1929–1968). Minister, civil rights leader. Led Montgomery bus boycott; founded Southern Christian Leadership Conference, 1957. Helped organize March on Washington, 1963. Won Nobel Peace Prize, 1964. Assassinated in Memphis, TN. (pp. 479, 500, 506)

Kirkpatrick, Jeane (1926–). Political scientist, stateswoman. Ambassador to UN, 1981–85. Took tough anti-Communist stance, supported pro-American authoritarian countries; influenced Reagan's foreign policy. (p. 591)

Mary Harris "Mother" Jones

Kissinger, Henry (1923–). Statesman, political scientist. Harvard professor and government consultant, 1950s–60s. Nixon's principal adviser on foreign policy; helped settle end of Vietnam War. Won Nobel Peace Prize, 1973. (pp. 537, 559)

Lee, Robert E. (1807–1870). Civil War general. President of Washington College (now Washington and Lee University), 1865–70. (p. 98)

Lincoln, Abraham (1809–1865). The 16th president. Term spanned Civil War, 1860–65. Wrote Emancipation Proclamation, 1863. Assassinated in 1865. (pp. 90, 91, 106)

Abraham Lincoln

Madison, James (1751–1836). The 4th president, 1809–17. Helped write *The Federalist*. U.S. representative, 1789–97. Sponsored Bill of Rights. Jefferson's secretary of state, 1801–09. (pp. 38, 63)

Mandela, Nelson (1918–). South African anti-apartheid leader. Joined African National Congress, 1944; led protests against South African government, 1950s–60s; sentenced to life in prison. Freed in 1990; elected president of South Africa in 1994. (p. 712)

Marshall, Thurgood (1908–1993). Supreme Court justice, 1967–91. Attorney for NAACP, 1938–61; successfully argued *Brown v. Board of*

Education before Supreme Court. Served on U.S. Court of Appeals, 1961–65; appointed solicitor general, 1965. (p. 478)

McKay, Claude (1890–1948). Harlem Renaissance poet, writer. Moved to U.S. from Jamaica, 1912. First books, *Songs of Jamaica* and *Constab Ballads*, used Jamaican dialect. Also wrote *Harlem Shadows*, 1922; *Banana Bottom*, 1933; *A Long Way from Home*, 1937. (p. 317)

McKinley, William (1843–1901). The 25th president, 1897–1901. U.S. representative, 1877–83 and 1885–91. Elected governor of Ohio, 1892–96. Assassinated in 1901. (pp. 156, 216)

Monroe, James (1758–1831). The 5th president, 1817–25. Fought in Revolution; member Continental Congress. U.S. senator, 1790–94; helped negotiate Louisiana Purchase. Madison's secretary of state, 1811–17, and war, 1814–15. Issued Monroe Doctrine, 1823. (pp. 72, 76)

Mott, Lucretia (1793–1880). Quaker, abolitionist, women's suffrage leader. Helped found Swarthmore College. Active in the Underground Railroad. With Stanton, called Seneca Falls Convention. Founder and first president, American Equal Rights Association, 1866. (p. 82)

Nixon, Richard Milhous (1913–1994). The 37th president, 1969–74. Eisenhower's vice president, 1953–61. In heat of investigation of his role in Watergate scandal, and under threat of impeachment, was first president to resign. (pp. 488, 537, 557)

O'Connor, Sandra Day (1930–). Supreme Court justice. Became first female justice when appointed by Reagan in 1981. In home state of AZ, served as assistant attorney general, state senator, and judge. (p. 591)

O'Keeffe, Georgia (1887–1986). Artist. Developed her painting technique in 1920s when living in NY, with paintings of urban scenes. Won biggest acclaim late in life for her paintings of flowers and Southwest landscapes. (pp. 319, 375)

Georgia O'Keeffe

Paige, Satchel (1906–1982). Baseball player. Pitched in Negro League, 1924–47. Became one of first African American pitchers in American League when he joined Cleveland Indians, 1948. Elected to Baseball Hall of Fame, 1971. (p. 337)

Paul, Alice (1885–1977). Women's suffrage leader. Founded Congressional Union for Woman Suffrage (later the National Woman's party), 1913. Submitted the first Equal Rights Amendment to Congress, 1923. (p. 208)

Perkins, Frances (1882–1965). Stateswoman. Secretary of labor, 1933–45; first female cabinet member. Researched and publicized conditions in sweatshops and factories, 1910s–20s. Helped draft and carry out FDR's labor legislation. Member of Civil Service Commission, 1946–52. (pp. 351, 414)

Pierce, Franklin (1804–1869). The 14th president, 1853–57. Born in NH. U.S. representative, 1833–37; U. S. senator, 1837–42. In Mexican War, 1846–48. As president opened Northwest for settlement. (p. 90)

Polk, James K. (1795–1849). The 11th president, 1845–49. U.S. representative, 1825–39; governor of TN, 1839–41. First "dark horse" candidate. During his presidency the U.S. acquired CA and most of the Southwest. (p. 90)

Randolph, A. Philip (1889–1979). African American labor leader. Organized railroad porters, 1925; convinced FDR to ban discrimination in defense industries and federal bureaus. Vice president AFL–CIO. Led largest civil rights demonstration in U.S. history: March on Washington for Jobs and Freedom, 1963. (pp. 412, 441)

A. Philip Randolph

Reagan, Ronald Wilson (1911–). The 40th president, 1981–89. Contract movie actor, Hollywood; in 52 films, 1937–57. Spokesman and host of weekly TV series for General Electric, 1952–62. Governor of CA, 1966–74. (pp. 586, 587, 591)

Robeson, Paul (1898–1976). African American actor, singer. Stage plays include *Emperor Jones,* 1923; *Show Boat,* 1926; *Othello,* 1943–44. Made first concert appearance singing spirituals in New York City in 1925. Toured U.S., Europe, Russia. Starred in films, 1930s. (p. 316)

Rockefeller, John D. (1839–1937). Oil tycoon and philanthropist. A major benefactor of University of Chicago; established the Rockefeller Institute for Medical Research in 1901; the Rockefeller Foundation in 1913. (pp. 144, 170, 171, 281)

Roosevelt, Eleanor (1884–1962). First lady, author, diplomat, humanitarian. Married Franklin Roosevelt, 1905. Active in Democratic party. Delegate to UN; helped draft Universal Declaration of Human Rights and secure its adoption, 1948. (pp. 344, 364, 439)

Roosevelt, Franklin Delano "FDR" (1882–1945). The 32nd president, 1933–45. Married Eleanor Roosevelt, 1905. Nominee for vice president, 1920; contracted polio, 1921, Governor of NY, 1929–33. Only president elected for third, fourth terms. (pp. 344, 353, 409)

Roosevelt, Theodore (1858–1919). The 26th president, 1901–09. Governor of NY, 1899–1900; McKinley's vice president, 1901; succeeded to presidency on McKinley's death. Served in Cuba with "Rough Riders." Progressive candidate, 1912. (pp. 194, 195, 218)

Ruth, George Herman "Babe" (1898–1948). Baseball player. Nicknamed "Bambino" and "Sultan of Swat." With Boston Red Sox, 1915–19; NY Yankees, 1920–35; Boston Braves, 1935. Hit a record 60 home runs in 1927, a record 714 in career. Elected to Baseball Hall of Fame, 1936. (p. 309)

Schlafly, Phyllis (1924–). Opponent of women's liberation movement; helped defeat ratification of proposed Equal Rights Amendment (ERA). Founded Stop ERA organization, 1972; founded Eagle Forum, group that supports traditional roles of women, 1975. (p. 578)

Smith, Bessie (1898?–1937). African American blues singer. Known for her emotional intensity and earthy realism of style. Recorded almost 200 songs (from 1923), often with major musicians such as Louis Armstrong. Wrote songs such as "Back Water Blues." (p. 316)

Stanton, Elizabeth Cady (1815–1902). Suffragist leader. With Lucretia Mott organized Seneca Falls Convention, 1848. President National

Woman Suffrage Association, 1869–90; from 1851 worked with Susan B. Anthony for the suffrage cause. (pp. 82, 109, 208)

Stein, Gertrude (1874–1946). Author. Moved to Paris, 1903, where leading writers, artists of the day met in her home; wrote experimental prose, poems, operettas. Author of *Tender Buttons,* 1915; *Four Saints in Three Acts,* 1934. (p. 318)

Steinbeck, John (1902–1968). Novelist. Best known for works about agricultural workers: *Of Mice and Men,* 1937; *The Grapes of Wrath,* 1939 (Pulitzer Prize). Other works include *East of Eden,* 1952; *The Winter of Our Discontent,* 1961. Won Nobel Prize, 1962. (p. 373)

Taft, William Howard (1857–1930). The 27th president, 1909–13. Professor of law, Yale, 1913–21; Chief Justice of Supreme Court, 1921–30. (pp. 200, 221, 229)

Taylor, Zachary "Old Rough and Ready" (1784–1850). The 12th president, 1949–50. Entered army, 1808; fought in War of 1812 and Second Seminole War. Defeated Santa Anna at Buena Vista, ending war in northern Mexico. Died in office. (pp. 84, 90)

Phyllis Schlafly

Thatcher, Margaret (1925–). British Prime Minister, 1979–1990. First female leader of a Western political party (Conservative party); first woman in the West to head a national government. (pp. 588, 713)

Thoreau, Henry David (1817–1862).
Writer. Through Ralph Waldo Emerson met transcendentalists. Helped edit *The Dial*, 1842–44. Best known for essay "Civil Disobedience," 1849, and book *Walden*, 1854. (p. 723)

Truman, Harry S. (1884–1972). The 33rd president, 1945–53. U.S. senator, 1935–45. FDR's vice president, 1945; succeeded to presidency on FDR's death. As president established containment policy against USSR, Truman Doctrine, NATO, CIA, and Berlin Airlift; engaged U.S. in Korean War. (pp. 409, 420, 444)

Tubman, Harriet (1820?–1913).
Abolitionist. Escaped from slavery around age 39; became a leading abolitionist; helped more than 300 slaves escape to North by Underground Railroad. During Civil War served as nurse, launderer, and spy for Union in SC; later settled in NY. (p. 100)

George Washington

Tyler, John (1790–1862). The 10th president, 1841–45. U.S. representative, 1817–21; governor of VA, 1825–27; U.S. senator 1827–36. W. H. Harrison's vice president, 1841; succeeded to the presidency on Harrison's death. (p. 76)

Van Buren, Martin (1782–1862). The 8th president, 1837–41. U.S. senator, 1821–28; governor of NY, 1829; Jackson's secretary of state, 1829–31, and vice president, 1833–37. Lost bid for reelection in 1840 and in 1848 as Free-Soil party candidate. (p. 76)

Washington, Booker T. (1856–1915). African American educator. Born enslaved. Chosen to establish and head Tuskegee Institute, AL, for training of blacks in trades and professions. Conservative viewpoint opposed by W.E.B. Du Bois. Author of *Up From Slavery*, 1901. (p. 114)

Washington, George (1732–1799). The 1st president, 1789–97. Commander in chief of Continental Army, Revolutionary War. Set precedents for presidents. (pp. 28, 63).

Wilson, Woodrow (1856–1924). The 28th president, 1913–21. Tried but failed to keep U.S. out of WWI; domestic policies produced three amendments, including women's suffrage, 1920. Author of League of Nations; won Nobel Peace Prize, 1919. Wrote *A History of the American People*, 1902. (pp. 202, 205, 262)

Winnemucca, Sarah (Thoc-me-tony) (1844–1891). Paiute teacher, writer, guide. Lectured on behalf of Paiutes. Opened school in NV for Paiute children. (p. 126)

Sarah Winnemucca

Wright, Frank Lloyd (1867–1959). Architect. Began practice in 1893 in Chicago, producing strikingly original designs. Worked in several styles. Structures include homes and public buildings, such as Guggenheim Museum, NY. (p. 320)

Wright, Richard (1908–1960). African American author. Participated in Federal Writers' Project, 1935–37. Settled in Paris, 1946. Known for fiction dealing with prejudice, alienation, and suffering of urban blacks. Novel *Native Son*, 1940, marked him as a major American writer. (p. 373)

Young, Andrew J., Jr. (1932–   ). African American clergyman. First black U.S. representative from GA since Reconstruction (1972). Worked with National Council of Churches, Southern Christian Leadership Conference. Ambassador to United Nations, 1977–79. (p. 571)

GAZETTEER

Afghanistan
Country of southwest-central Asia. Invaded by the Soviet Union in 1979. Capital: Kabul. (33°N 63°E) *m561, m772–773*

Alabama (AL)   State in the southern U.S. Admitted as a state in 1819. Capital: Montgomery. (33°N 87°W) *m776–777*

Alaska (AK)   U.S. state in northwestern North America. Became a territory in 1912 (first organized in 1884) and a state in 1959. Capital: Juneau. (64°N 150°W) *m776–777*

Albania   Country in southeast Europe on the Adriatic Sea. Invaded by Italy in 1939. Capital: Tiranë. (41°N 20°E) *m392, m597, m772–773*

Algeria   Country in northwestern Africa on the Mediterranean Sea. Capital: Algiers. (29°N 1°E) *m637, m772–773*

Alsace-Lorraine   Region between France, Germany, Belgium, and Switzerland. Part of the German Empire, 1871–1918; returned to France by the Treaty of Versailles, 1919. (48°N 7°E) *m244*

American Samoa   Unincorporated territory of the U.S. in the southern Pacific Ocean. Administered by the U.S. since 1899. (14°S 170°W) *m220*

Antarctica   Continent lying around the South Pole. (80°S 127°E) *m735, m772–773*

Appomattox Courthouse   Virginia town where General Lee surrendered to General Grant, ending the Civil War. (37°N 78°W) *m102*

Arizona (AZ)   State in southwestern U.S. Became a territory in 1863 and a state in 1912. Capital: Phoenix. (34°N 113°W) *m776–777*

Arkansas (AR)   State in south-central U.S. Admitted as a state in 1836. Capital: Little Rock. (35°N 93°W) *m776–777*

Armenia   Republic; member of the Commonwealth of Independent States. Formerly part of the USSR. Independent in 1991. Capital: Yerevan. (41°N 44°E) *m597, m772–773*

Atlanta   Major southern city, capital of Georgia. During the Civil War it was captured and burned by General Sherman, 1864. (33°N 84°W) *m102*

Austria-Hungary   Former monarchy in central Europe. Consisted of Austria, Hungary, Bohemia, and parts of Poland, Romania, Yugoslavia, and Italy. Formed in 1867; lasted until 1918. (47°N 12°E) *m244*

Azerbaijan   Republic; member of the Commonwealth of Independent States. Formerly part of the USSR. Independent in 1991. Capital: Baki. (40°N 47°E) *m597, m772–773*

Bahamas
Country in the Atlantic Ocean consisting of hundreds of islands. Gained independence from Great Britain in 1973. Capital: Nassau. (26°N 76°W) *m22, m772–773*

Balkans   Countries that occupy the Balkan Peninsula, including Albania, Bulgaria, Greece, Romania, the former Yugoslavia, and northwestern Turkey. (43°N 24°E) *m244*

Bangladesh   Country in southern Asia. Formerly part of Bengal, it became part of Pakistan in 1947. In 1971 it became a separate nation. Capital: Dacca. (24°N 90°E) *m772–773*

Beijing   Capital of China. (40°N 116°E) *m220*

Belarus   Republic in Eastern Europe; member of the Commonwealth of Independent States. Formerly part of the USSR. Independent in 1991. Capital: Minsk. (53°N 25°E) *m597, m772–773*

Belgian Congo   *See* Zaire

Belgium   Country in northwest Europe. Invaded by Germany in 1914 and 1940. Capital: Brussels. (51°N 3°E) *m244, m772–773*

Bosnia and Herzegovina   Country annexed to Austria-Hungary in 1908 and Yugoslavia in 1918. Capital: Sarajevo. (44°N 17°E) *m244, m597, m772–773*

Boston   Massachusetts capital on Massachusetts Bay founded in the 17th century. Leading center of anti-British sentiment in the 18th century. (42°N 71°W) *m34*

Brazil   Republic in eastern South America. Largest country on the continent; ruled by Portugal from 1500 to 1822. Empire until 1889. Capital: Brasília. (9°S 53°W) *m772–773*

Cahokia
Settlement founded by the Mississippian culture near present-day St. Louis, Missouri. (38°N 90°W) *m5*

California (CA)   State in western U.S. Admitted as a free state in 1850. Capital: Sacramento. (38°N 121°W) *m776–777*

Cambodia   Republic in southeast Asia. Independent in 1954. Scene of fighting during Vietnam War. Capital: Pnompenh. (12°N 104°E) *m521, m772–773*

Canada   Country in northern North America. Settled by English and French colonists. Ceded to Great Britain in 1763. Declared equal partner of Great Britain, 1931. Capital: Ottawa. (50°N 100°W) *m86, m772–773*

Cape Verde Islands   Group of islands in Atlantic Ocean. Settled by the Portuguese in the mid-1400s; independent in 1975. Capital: Praia. (15°N 26°W) *m239, m772–773*

Caporetto   Town in Slovenia. Scene of World War I defeat of Italian troops in December 1917. *m244*

Château-Thierry   Town in northern France where Allied forces stopped German advance in World War I. (49°N 3°E) *m255*

Chernobyl   City in north-central Ukraine where a nuclear power plant exploded in 1986. (51°N 30°E) *m735*

Chile   Country in southwest South America colonized by Spain in 1541; became independent in 1818. Capital: Santiago. (35°S 72°W) *m238, m772–773*

China (Official name: People's Republic of China)   Country in eastern Asia. After a bitter civil war (1946–49), became a Communist republic; nationalists fled to Taiwan. Capital: Beijing. (36°N 93°E) *m220, m521, m772–773*

Colombia   Country in northwest South America. Capital: Bogotá. (3°N 72°W) *m234, m772–773*

Colorado (CO)   State in southwestern U.S. Became a territory in 1861 and a state in 1876. Capital: Denver. (39°N 107°W) *m776–777*

Compiègne   City in northern France. Armistice ending World War I signed nearby in November 1918. (49°N 2°E) *m255*

Connecticut (CT)   State in northeastern U.S. One of the original Thirteen Colonies. Admitted as a state in 1788. Capital: Hartford. (41°N 73°W) *m776–777*

Cuba   Island country in the Caribbean about 90 miles south of Florida. Capital: Havana. (22°N 79°W) *m493, m772–773*

Czechoslovakia   Former country in central Europe formed in 1918. Communist forces gained control of it in 1948 and kept power until 1989. In 1993 peacefully divided into Czech Republic (Capital: Prague) and Slovakia (Capital: Bratislava). (49°N 16°E) *m264, m392, m597, m772–773*

Delaware (DE)   State in eastern U.S. One of the original Thirteen Colonies. In 1787 became first state to ratify the Constitution. Capital: Dover. (38°N 75°W) *m776–777*

District of Columbia (DC)   Federal district of the U.S. Seat of federal government since 1800. (39°N 77°W) *m776–777*

Dominican Republic   Island country in the Caribbean. Makes up eastern part of island of Hispaniola. Capital: Santo Domingo. (19°N 70°W) *m234, m772–773*

Egypt   Country in northeast Africa on the Mediterranean Sea. Capital: Cairo. (27°N 27°E) *m453, m561, m772–773*

El Salvador   Country in Central America. Capital: San Salvador. (14°N 89°W) *m234, m590, m772–773*

Estonia   Country in northeast Europe. Annexed to the USSR in 1940. Became independent in 1991. Capital: Tallinn. (59°N 25°E) *m264, m597, m772–773*

Ethiopia   Country in eastern Africa; formerly Abyssinia. Capital: Addis Ababa. (7°N 38°E) *m392, m772–773*

Federal Republic of Germany   *See* Germany

Finland   Country in northeast Europe. Capital: Helsinki. (62°N 26°E) *m264, m392, m772–773*

Florida (FL)   State in southeastern U.S. Became a territory in 1822 and a state in 1845. Capital: Tallahassee. (30°N 84°W) *m776–777*

France   Country in western Europe. French Revolution of 1789 overthrew the monarchy. Capital: Paris. (46°N 0°E) *m244, m404*

Gadsden Purchase   Tract of land located in parts of New Mexico and Arizona. Purchased in 1853 by U.S. from Mexico for $10,000,000. *m86*

Georgia (GA)   State in southeastern U.S. One of the original Thirteen Colonies. Admitted as a state in 1788. Capital: Atlanta. (32°N 84°W) *m776–777*

Georgia   Republic; member of the Commonwealth of Independent States. Formerly part of the USSR. Independent in 1991. Capital: T'bilisi. (42°N 43°E) *m597, m772–773*

German Democratic Republic   *See* Germany

Germany   Country in western Europe. Fascist during the 1930s and 1940s. Divided into German Democratic Republic (East Germany) and Federal Republic of Germany (West Germany) after World War II. Reunified in 1990. Capital: Berlin. (51°N 8°E) *m392, m449, m597, m772–773*

Gettysburg   Town in southern Pennsylvania. Scene of major Union victory in the Civil War. Abraham Lincoln delivered Gettysburg Address here in 1863. (40°N 77°W) *m98*

Ghana   Republic in western Africa. Ancient African trading kingdom. Capital: Accra. (8°N 2°W) *m637, m772–773*

Great Britain   Kingdom in western Europe. Consists of England, Scotland, and Wales. Capital: London. (54°N 4°W) *m772–773*

Greece   Balkan country in southern Europe with numerous islands. Capital: Athens. (39°N 21°E) *m449, m772–773*

Grenada   Country in the Caribbean made up of the island of Grenada and the southern Grenadines. Capital: St. George's. (12°N 61°W) *m590*

Guam Pacific island that became U.S. territory after the Spanish-American War. Capital: Agana. (14°N 143°E) *m402*

Guantánamo Bay Bay on southeastern coast of Cuba. U.S. naval station established in 1903. (19°N 75°W) *m234*

Guatemala Republic in Central America. Capital: Guatemala City. (15°N 91°W) *m467, m772–773*

H

Haiti Island country in the Caribbean located on the western part of the island of Hispaniola. Capital: Port-au-Prince. (19°N 72°W) *m234, m590, m772–773*

Hawaii (HI) U.S. state in the central Pacific Ocean comprising the Hawaiian Islands. Admitted as a state in 1959. Capital: Honolulu. (20°N 157°W) *m776–777*

Hiroshima Japanese city; U.S. dropped the first atomic bomb used in warfare on the city in August 1945. (34°N 132°E) *m402*

Hispaniola Columbus and his crew established the colony of La Navidad here in 1492; today comprises the countries of the Dominican Republic and Haiti. (17°N 73°W) *m22*

Homestead Site of a strike at Andrew Carnegie's steel plant in southwestern Pennsylvania. *m154*

I

Idaho (ID) State in northwestern U.S. Admitted as a state in 1890. Capital: Boise. (44°N 115°W) *m776–777*

Illinois (IL) State in north-central U.S. Admitted as a state in 1818. Capital: Springfield. (40°N 90°W) *m776–777*

Indiana (IN) State in north-central U.S. Admitted as a state in 1816. Capital: Indianapolis. (40°N 86°W) *m776–777*

Indian Territory Former territory in south-central U.S. Set aside by the government in 1834 as a homeland for displaced Native Americans. Western section, which became Oklahoma Territory, was opened to white settlement in 1889. In 1907 Indian Territory was merged with Oklahoma Territory to form the state of Oklahoma. (36°N 98°W) *m73*

Indonesia Country in southeast Asia; island chain in the South Pacific. Occasional name for the Malay Archipelago. Capital: Djakarta. (5°S 119°E) *m772–773*

Iowa (IA) State in north-central U.S. Admitted as a state in 1846. Capital: Des Moines. (42°N 94°W) *m776–777*

Iran Country in southwest Asia where 53 Americans were held hostage during the Carter administration. Capital: Tehran. (31°N 53°E) *m561, m772–773*

Iraq Country in southwest Asia. Iraq's invasion of Kuwait led to UN–imposed economic sanctions and to war with the U.S. and the Allies in 1991. Capital: Baghdad. (32°N 43°E) *m561, m600, m772–773*

Ireland Located in the British Isles. Divided between Northern Ireland (Capital: Belfast), which is part of Great Britain, and the independent Republic of Ireland (Capital: Dublin). (54°N 8°W) *m772–773*

Israel Country in southwest Asia on the eastern Mediterranean coast that Jews established after the UN division of Palestine in 1948. Capital: Jerusalem. (32°N 34°E) *m561, m772–773*

Italy Country in southern Europe, which fought on the side of the Allies in World War I. During World War II it was allied with Germany. Capital: Rome. (44°N 11°E) *m772–773*

J

Jamaica Island country in the Caribbean which Columbus visited in 1494. It became a British colony in 1655 and an important sugar producer. Capital: Kingston. (18°N 78°W) *m22, m772–773*

Japan Chain of islands in the western Pacific Ocean. World War II military ally of Germany and Italy. Two of its cities devastated by atomic bombs. Since the war, has played a central role in the global economy. Capital: Tokyo. (37°N 134°E) *m395, m402, m772–773*

Jordan Country of southwest Asia. Capital: Amman. (30°N 38°E) *m453, m561, m772–773*

K

Kansas (KS) Territory in central U.S. Created by Kansas-Nebraska Act in 1854. Admitted to the Union as a free state in 1861. Capital: Topeka. (38°N 99°W) *m776–777*

Kazakhstan Republic; member of the Commonwealth of Independent States. Formerly part of the USSR. Independent in 1991. Capital: Almaty. (49°N 59°E) *m597, m772–773*

Kentucky (KY) State in east-central U.S. Admitted as a state in 1792. Capital: Frankfort. (37°N 87°W) *m776–777*

Kenya Republic in East Africa. Capital: Nairobi. (1°N 37°E) *m637, m772–773*

Korea Peninsula and former country of eastern Asia between the Yellow Sea and the Sea of Japan. Officially divided into two independent nations, North Korea and South Korea, in 1945. (38°N 128°E) *m220, m455*

Kuwait Oil-rich country on the northeast Arabian Peninsula at the head of the Persian Gulf. Invaded by Iraq, it was liberated by the Allies in the Persian Gulf War (1991). Capital: Al Kuwait. (29°N 48°E) *m600, m772–773*

Kyrgyzstan Republic; member of the Commonwealth of Independent States. Formerly part of the USSR. Independent in 1991. Capital: Bishkek. (42°N 28°E) *m597, m772–773*

L

Latvia Country of northern Europe on the Baltic Sea. Capital: Riga. (57°N 24°E) *m772–773*

Liberia   Country on west coast of Africa founded in 1817 by Americans for the resettlement of freed African Americans. Capital: Monrovia. (6°N 10°W) *m772–773*

Lithuania   Country of northern Europe on the Baltic Sea. Declared independence from USSR in March 1990. Capital: Vilnius. (55°N 23°E) *m597, m772–773*

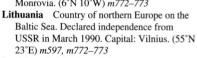

Louisiana (LA)   One of the southeastern states carved out of the Louisiana territory. Admitted as a state in 1812. Capital: Baton Rouge. (31°N 93°W) *m776–777*

M

Maine (ME)   State in the northeastern U.S. Admitted as a state in 1820. Capital: Augusta. (45°N 70°W) *m776–777*

Mali   Country of western Africa. Capital: Bamako. (15°N 0°E) *m637, m776–777*

Manila   Capital and largest city of the Philippines. Located on southwest Luzon Island. (14°N 121°E) *m220*

Maryland (MD)   State in east-central U.S. One of the original Thirteen Colonies. Admitted as a state in 1788. Capital: Annapolis. (39°N 76°W) *m776–777*

Massachusetts (MA)   State in northeastern U.S. One of the original Thirteen Colonies. Admitted as a state in 1788. Capital: Boston. (42°N 72°W) *m776–777*

Meuse River   River in western Europe flowing from northeast France through southern Belgium and the southeast Netherlands to the North Sea. (50°N 5°E) *m255*

Mexican Cession   Area that Mexico ceded to the U.S. at the end of the Mexican War, comprising the present-day states of California, Nevada, and Utah, and parts of Arizona, Colorado, and New Mexico. *m86*

Mexico   Republic in North America, bounded on the north by the U.S. and on the south by Guatemala and British Honduras. Capital: Mexico City. (23°N 104°W) *m772–773*

Michigan (MI)   State in north-central U.S. Admitted as a state in 1837. Capital: Lansing. (46°N 87°W) *m776–777*

Minnesota (MN)   State in north-central U.S. Admitted as a state in 1858. Capital: St. Paul. (46°N 90°W) *m776–777*

Mississippi (MS)   State in southeastern U.S. Admitted as a state in 1817. Capital: Jackson. (32°N 89°W) *m776–777*

Missouri (MO)   State in central U.S. Admitted as a state in 1821. Capital: Jefferson City. (38°N 93°W) *m74, m776–777*

Moldova   Republic; member of the Commonwealth of Independent States. Formerly part of the USSR. Independent in 1991. Capital: Chisinău. *m597, m772–773*

Montana (MT)   State in northwestern U.S. Admitted as a state in 1889. Capital: Helena. (47°N 112°W) *m776–777*

N

Nebraska (NE)   State in central U.S. Admitted as a free state in 1867. Capital: Lincoln. (41°N 101°W) *m776–777*

Nevada (NV)   State in western U.S. Organized as a separate territory in 1861 and admitted as a state in 1864. Capital: Carson City. (39°N 117°W) *m776–777*

New Hampshire (NH)   State in northeastern U.S. One of the original Thirteen Colonies. Admitted as a state in 1788. Capital: Concord. (44°N 71°W) *m776–777*

New Jersey (NJ)   State in eastern U.S. One of the original Thirteen Colonies. Admitted as a state in 1787. Capital: Trenton. (40°N 75°W) *m776–777*

New Mexico (NM)   State in southwestern U.S. Originally Zuni country, ceded to the U.S. by Mexico in 1848. Organized as a territory that included Arizona and part of Colorado in 1850. Admitted as a state in 1912. Capital: Santa Fe. (34°N 107°W) *m776–777*

New York (NY)   State in northeastern U.S. One of the original Thirteen Colonies. Admitted as a state in 1788. Capital: Albany. (42°N 78°W) *m776–777*

Nicaragua   Country of Central America on the Caribbean Sea and the Pacific Ocean. Columbus spotted its Caribbean coastline in 1502. Capital: Managua. (12°N 86°W) *m234, m590, m772–773*

North Carolina (NC)   State in southeastern U.S. One of the original Thirteen Colonies. Admitted as a state in 1789. Capital: Raleigh. (35°N 81°W) *m776–777*

North Dakota (ND)   State in north-central U.S. Admitted as a state in 1889. Capital: Bismarck. (47°N 102°W) *m776–777*

North Korea   (Official name: Democratic People's Republic of Korea) Country on east coast of Asia, bounded on north by China, on east by Sea of Japan, on south by South Korea, and on west by the Yellow Sea and Korea Bay. Capital: P'yongyang. (40°N 127°E) *m455, m772–773*

North Vietnam   *See* Vietnam

O

Ohio (OH)   State in north-central U.S. Originally part of the Northwest Territory. Admitted as a state in 1803. Capital: Columbus. (40°N 83°W) *m776–777*

Oklahoma (OK)   State in south-central U.S. Except for its panhandle, Oklahoma formed part of the Louisiana Purchase. Organized as a territory in 1890 and became a state in 1907. Capital: Oklahoma City. (36°N 98°W) *m776–777*

Oregon (OR)   State in northwestern U.S. Admitted as a state in 1859. Capital: Salem. (43°N 122°W) *m776–777*

Oregon Country   Region encompassing all the land from the California border to Alaska and from the Pacific Ocean to the Rocky Mountains. Held jointly by Great Britain and the U.S., 1818–46, when the international boundary was fixed at the 49th parallel. *m73*

P

Panama   Country in southern Central America occupying the Isthmus of Panama. Capital: Panama City. (8°N 81°W) *m234, m772–773*

Panama Canal   Ship canal, about 51 miles long, crossing the Isthmus of Panama in the Canal Zone and connecting the Caribbean Sea with the Pacific Ocean. *m227*

Pennsylvania (PA)   State in eastern U.S. One of the original Thirteen Colonies. Admitted as a state in 1787. Capital: Harrisburg. (41°N 78°W) *m776–777*

People's Republic of China *See* China

Persian Gulf Arm of the Arabian Sea between the Arabian Peninsula and southwestern Iran in southwest Asia. (27°N 50°E) *m600*

Peru Republic in western South America, bounded on north by Ecuador and Colombia, on east by Brazil and Bolivia, on southern tip by Chile, and on west by the Pacific Ocean. Capital: Lima. (10°S 75°W) *m772–773*

Philippines, Republic of the Archipelago of about 7,100 islands, lying approximately 500 miles off the southeast coast of Asia. Capital: Manila. (14°N 125°E) *m217, m772–773*

Poland Country of central Europe bordering on the Baltic Sea. Capital: Warsaw. (52°N 17°E) *m264, m392, m597, m772–773*

Portugal Country of southwest Europe on the western Iberian Peninsula. Capital: Lisbon. (38°N 9°W) *m239, m772–773*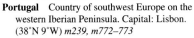

Puerto Rico (PR) Island east of Cuba and southeast of Florida. Ceded to the U.S. after the Spanish-American War. Self-governing commonwealth. Capital: San Juan. (18°N 67°W) *m217, m772–773*

Pullman Former industrial suburb of Chicago, Illinois; since 1889 a southeastern part of Chicago. *m154*

Red River Valley Area along the Red River (also known as Red River of the North) in north-central U.S. and south-central Canada. (48°N 97°W) *m132*

Rhode Island (RI) State in northeastern U.S. One of the original Thirteen Colonies. Admitted as a state in 1790. Capital: Providence. (41°N 71°W) *m776–777*

Richmond State capital, in the east-central part of Virginia on the James River. Capital of the Confederacy in the Civil War; fell in 1865. (37°N 77°W) *m98*

Rio Grande "Great River" that forms the border between Texas and Mexico. (26°N 98°W) *m86*

Russia Country in Eastern Europe and Northwest Asia. Formerly part of USSR. Independent in 1991. Member of the Commonwealth of Independent States. Capital: St. Petersburg, formerly Leningrad. (61°N 60°E) *m772–773*

Rwanda Republic in east-central Africa. Capital: Kigali. (2°S 30°E) *m684, m772–773*

Saar River, about 150 miles long, rising in northeast France and flowing north and northwest to the Moselle River in western Germany. River's valley is also known as the Saar Basin. *m264*

St. Mihiel Village in northeast France on the Meuse River. World War I battle here (1918) was the first major U.S. offensive led by General John J. Pershing. (49°N 5°E) *m255*

San Carlos Reservation Native American reservation located on the Gila River in southeastern Arizona. *m124*

Santiago Cuban seaport captured by American forces during the Spanish-American War. (20°N 76°W) *m217*

Saratoga Former village (now Schuylerville) in eastern New York. Scene of battles that marked the turning point of the Revolutionary War. (43°N 75°W) *m34*

Saudi Arabia Country on the Arabian Peninsula in southwest Asia, bordered on the north by Jordan, Iraq, and Kuwait; the world's second-largest producer of oil. Capital: Riyadh. (22°N 46°E) *m600, m772–773*

Seattle Washington city bounded by Puget Sound and Lake Washington. First settled in the 1850s. Prospered after the coming of the railroad in 1884 and became a boomtown during the Alaskan gold rush of 1897. (47°N 122°W) *m132*

Sedan Town of northeast France on the Meuse River near the Belgian border. Site of important battle in World War I. (50°N 5°E) *m255*

Sierra Leone Country in western Africa on the Atlantic coast. First visited by the Portuguese in the 1460s. Region became a British protectorate in 1896 and achieved independence in 1961. Capital: Freetown. (8°N 12°W) *m239*

Somalia Country of extreme eastern Africa on the Gulf of Aden and the Indian Ocean. Capital: Mogadishu. (3°N 44°E) *m772–773*

South Africa Country of southern Africa on the Atlantic and Indian oceans. Pretoria is the administrative capital, Cape Town the legislative capital, and Bloemfontein the judicial capital. (28°S 25°E) *m772–773*

South Carolina (SC) State in southeastern U.S. One of the original Thirteen Colonies. Admitted as a state in 1788. First state to secede from the Union (1860). Capital: Columbia. (34°N 81°W) *m776–777*

South Dakota (SD) State in north-central U.S. Constituted the southern part of the Dakota Territory. Admitted as a state in 1889. Capital: Pierre. (44°N 102°W) *m776–777*

South Korea (Official name: Republic of Korea) Country on east coast of Asia, bounded on north by North Korea, on east by the Sea of Japan, on south by the Korea Strait, and on west by the Yellow Sea. Capital: Seoul. (36°N 128°E) *m772–773*

South Vietnam *See* Vietnam

Spain Country in southwest Europe, occupying the greater part of the Iberian Peninsula and including the Balearic and Canary islands. Capital: Madrid. (40°N 4°W) *m772–773*

Sudan Country in northeast Africa south of Egypt. Capital: Khartoum. (14°N 28°E) *m772–773*

Syria Country in southwest Asia on the eastern Mediterranean coast. Capital: Damascus. (35°N 37°E) *m561, m772–773*

Taiwan (Official name: Republic of China) Formerly Formosa. Country off the southeast coast of China made up of the island of Taiwan, the Pescadores, and other smaller islands. Capital: Taipei. (37°N 112°E) *m220, m402, m772–773*

Tajikistan   Republic; member of the Commonwealth of Independent States. Formerly part of the USSR. Independent in 1991. Capital: Dushanbe. (39°N 69°E) *m772–773*

Tennessee (TN)   State in south-central U.S. Admitted as a state in 1796. Capital: Nashville. (36°N 88°W) *m776–777*

Texas (TX)   State in south-central U.S. Bounded on south by Gulf of Mexico and Mexico. Known as the Lone Star State because it was an independent republic (1836–45) whose flag featured a single star. Capital: Austin. (31°N 101°W) *m776–777*

Thailand   Formerly Siam. Country in southeast Asia on the Gulf of Thailand. Was a strong supporter of the U.S. in the Vietnam War. Capital: Bangkok. (16°N 101°E) *m402, m772–773*

Trenton   City in west-central New Jersey. Site where American forces under George Washington opened fire on the British in 1776. (40°N 75°W) *m34*

Turkey   Country in southwest Asia and southeast Europe between the Mediterranean and the Black seas. Capital: Ankara. (38°N 32°W) *m449, m772–773*

Turkmenistan   Republic; member of the Commonwealth of Independent States. Formerly part of the USSR. Independent in 1991. Capital: Ashgabat. (40°N 56°E) *m597, m772–773*

Ukraine   Republic; member of the Commonwealth of Independent States. Formerly part of the USSR. Independent in 1991. Central theater of warfare in both world wars. Capital: Kiev. (49°N 30°E) *m404, m597, m772–773*

United Kingdom of Great Britain and Northern Ireland   *See* Great Britain

United States of America   Federal republic, North America. Bounded on north by Canada and (in Alaska) by Arctic Ocean, on east by the Atlantic Ocean, on south by Mexico and the Gulf of Mexico, and on west by the Pacific Ocean. Capital: Washington, D.C. (38°N 110°W) *m772–773, m776–777*

Utah (UT)   State in western U.S. First explored by Coronado expedition, 1540. Admitted as a state in 1896. Capital: Salt Lake City. (39°N 112°W) *m776–777*

Uzbekistan   Republic; member of the Commonwealth of Independent States. Formerly part of the USSR. Independent in 1991. Capital: Toshkent. (42°N 60°E) *m597, m772–773*

Venezuela   Country in northern South America on the Caribbean Sea. Capital: Caracas. (8°N 65°W) *m234, m772–773*

Vermont (VT)   State in northeastern U.S. One of the original Thirteen Colonies. Admitted as a state in 1791. Capital: Montpelier. (44°N 73°W) *m776–777*

Vicksburg   City in western Mississippi on bluffs above the Mississippi River. During the Civil War it was captured by Union troops led by Ulysses S. Grant. (42°N 85°W) *m99*

Vietnam   Southeast Asian country (divided into North Vietnam and South Vietnam between 1954 and 1975) where United States and South Vietnamese forces fought a war against the Communist North Vietnamese. Capital: Hanoi. (18°N 107°E) *m521, m772–773*

Virginia (VA)   State in eastern U.S. One of the original Thirteen Colonies. Admitted as a state in 1788. Capital: Richmond. (37°N 80°W) *m776–777*

Washington (WA)   State in northwestern U.S. Bounded on north by Canadian province of British Columbia and on west by the Pacific Ocean. Admitted as a state in 1889. Capital: Olympia. (47°N 121°W) *m776–777*

Washington, D.C.   Capital of the U.S., on the Potomac River between Virginia and Maryland; also called the District of Columbia. Leading international political center. (39°N 77°W) *m86*

West Virginia (WV)   State in east-central U.S. Admitted as a state in 1863. Part of Virginia until the area refused to endorse the Ordinance of Secession in 1861. Capital: Charleston. (39°N 81°W) *m776–777*

Wisconsin (WI)   State in north-central U.S. First settled by the French, region was ceded to Great Britain in 1763 and became part of the Northwest Territory in 1787. Admitted as a state in 1848. Capital: Madison. (44°N 91°W) *m776–777*

Wyoming (WY)   State in northwestern U.S. Organized as the Wyoming Territory in 1868 and admitted as a state in 1890. Capital: Cheyenne. (43°N 108°W) *m776–777*

Yokohama   Japanese city in southeast Honshu, on the western shore of Tokyo Bay. Almost entirely destroyed by an earthquake and fire in 1923, again largely destroyed by U.S. bombing in World War II. (35°N 139°E) *m220*

Yorktown   Town in southeastern Virginia. Scene of surrender of British forces to the Americans in the Revolutionary War. (37°N 77°W) *m34*

Yugoslavia   Former country in southeast Europe bordering on the Adriatic Sea. It was formed in 1918 and named Yugoslavia in 1929. Today the name is claimed by Serbia and Montenegro. (44°N 17°E) *m264, m597, m772–773*

Zaire   (Official name: Democratic Republic of the Congo; from 1908 to 1960, Belgian Congo) Republic in equatorial Africa. Capital: Kinshasa. (1°S 22°E) *m637, m772–773*

GLOSSARY

This Glossary contains terms you need to understand as you study American history. After each term there is a brief definition or explanation of the meaning of the term as it is used in *The American Nation in the Twentieth Century*. The page number refers to the page on which the term is introduced in the textbook.

Phonetic Respelling and Pronunciation Guide

Many of the key terms in this textbook have been respelled to help you pronounce them. The letter combinations used in the respellings throughout the narrative are explained in the following phonetic respelling and pronunciation guide. The guide is adapted from *Webster's Ninth New Collegiate Dictionary*, *Webster's New Geographical Dictionary*, and *Webster's New Biographical Dictionary*.

MARK	AS IN	RESPELLING	EXAMPLE
a	alphabet	a	*AL-fuh-bet
ā	Asia	ay	AY-zhuh
ä	cart, top	ah	KAHRT, TAHP
e	let, ten	e	LET, TEN
ē	even, leaf	ee	EE-vuhn, LEEF
i	it, tip, British	i	IT, TIP, BRIT-ish
ī	site, buy, Ohio	y	SYT, BY, oh-HY-oh
	iris	eye	EYE-ris
k	card	k	KARD
ō	over, rainbow	oh	oh-vuhr, RAYN-boh
u̇	book, wood	ooh	BOOHK, WOOHD
ȯ	all, orchid	aw	AWL, AWR-kid
ȯi	foil, coin	oy	FOYL, KOYN
au̇	out	ow	OWT
ə	cup, butter	uh	KUHP, BUHT-uhr
ü	rule, food	oo	ROOL, FOOD
yü	few	yoo	FYOO
zh	vision	zh	VIZH-uhn

*A syllable printed in small capital letters receives heavier emphasis than the other syllable(s) in a word.

abolition   Movement to end slavery. **17**

acid rain   Atmospheric pollution that gradually kills trees and makes lakes unfit for marine life. **736**

Adamson Act   Federal law reducing the workday for railroad workers from 10 to 8 hours with no decrease in wages. **207**

affirmative action   Programs giving preference to ethnic minorities and women in jobs or school admission to make up for past discrimination. **575**

African diaspora   Forcible resettlement of millions of African people to the Americas from the 1500s through the 1800s. **9**

African National Congress   The major black nationalist organization in South Africa. **712**

Agricultural Adjustment Act (AAA)   Federal law passed in 1933 to reduce farmers' output, increase crop prices, and establish the Agricultural Adjustment Administration. **354**

Agricultural Marketing Act (1929)   Federal law that created the Federal Farm Board, an agency to help ease the plight of farmers by buying farm surpluses. **341**

AIDS   Acquired Immune Deficiency Syndrome, the final deadly stage of an illness believed to be caused by the human immunodeficiency virus (HIV) **608**

Alien and Sedition Acts (1798)   Series of laws passed by the Federalists to protect the country from foreign influence, limit Republican power, and silence government critics. **64**

Alliance for Progress   President Kennedy's policy of sending economic aid to Latin America; designed to encourage democratic reforms and to promote capitalism. **491**

Allied Powers   World War I alliance that included France, Great Britain, Russia, Italy, and later the United States. **243**

American Anti-Slavery Society   First national antislavery organization devoted to immediate abolition, formed in 1833 by both black and white abolitionists. **82**

American Federation of Labor (AFL)   Organization of independent skilled craft unions founded in 1886 by Samuel Gompers. **155**

American Friends Service Committee Quaker-founded peace organization dedicated to promoting humanity. **705**

American Indian Defense Association Organization that fought to protect religious freedom and tribal property for Native Americans. **366**

American Indian Movement (AIM) Organization, founded in 1968 by Minnesota Chippewas, that became the major force in the Red Power movement during the 1970s. **507**

American Plan Policy, promoted by business leaders during the 1920s, that called for open shops. **288**

Americans with Disabilities Act (1990) Federal law that prohibits discrimination against people with mental or physical disabilities. **602**

American System Henry Clay's federal program for economic development; it included a national bank, a protective tariff, and a national transportation system. **73**

anarchists People who oppose all forms of government. **154**

Angel Island Immigration station in San Francisco Bay opened in 1910 to receive Asian immigrants. **676**

annex Action by which one country takes control of another country or territory. **219**

Antarctic Treaty (1959) International agreement that established Antarctica as a nuclear-free zone. **729**

Antifederalists Individuals who feared a powerful national government and opposed ratification of the U.S. Constitution. **39**

anti-Semitism Hatred of Jews. **389**

apartheid Racial segregation; former racial policy in South Africa. **571**

appeasement Policy of giving in to demands of a country or countries in an effort to avoid major conflicts. **391**

arbitration Hearing in which a third party settles a dispute. **195**

armistice Cease-fire. **256**

Articles of Confederation Agreement, ratified in 1781, in which the 13 colonies established a government of states with each state retaining power over its own affairs. **37**

assembly line Manufacturing technique in which a product is passed along a line of workers and assembled in stages. **302**

assimilation Cultural absorption of a group. **126**

asylum Policy of nations offering a place of protection to anyone being persecuted for political reasons. **684**

Atlantic Charter (1941) Joint declaration of principles for international relations, agreed to by the United States and Great Britain. **394**

Atomic Energy Act (1946) Federal law that placed the Atomic Energy Commission under civilian control to oversee nuclear weapons research and to promote peacetime uses of atomic energy. **447**

automation Manufacturing process that used machines to perform industrial operations faster and more efficiently than human labor. **476**

Axis powers Military alliance of Germany, Italy, and Japan during World War II. **391**

baby boom Soaring birth rate between 1946 and 1964. **473**

Balfour Declaration (1917) Statement issued by Great Britain declaring its support for a Jewish homeland in Palestine. **267**

Bandung Conference (1955) Meeting in Indonesia in which Third World nations reaffirmed the nonaligned movement and established regional organizations among developing countries. **638**

bank holiday (1933) New Deal proclamation that temporarily closed every U.S. bank to stop massive withdrawals. **350**

barcodes Series of vertical bars of varying widths printed on consumer product packages and used for inventory control. **689**

Baruch Plan (1946) Proposal submitted to the UN Atomic Energy Commission for international control of atomic energy. **446**

Bataan Death March (1942) Forced march of Allied prisoners on the Bataan peninsula to a Japanese detention camp, during which thousands died. **401**

Battle of Bunker Hill (1775) Revolutionary War battle in which British troops defeated Patriot forces atop two hills overlooking Boston Harbor. **28**

Battle of El Alamein (1942) British victory in Egypt during World War II that broke the momentum of the Axis advance in North Africa. **405**

Battle of Gettysburg (1863) Union victory during the Civil War that halted General Lee's invasion of the North. **98**

Battle of Iwo Jima (1945) Allied victory in the Pacific during World War II in which Japanese forces lost more than 20,000 troops. **420**

Battle of Leyte Gulf (1944) Decisive naval victory for the Allies during World War II that eliminated the Japanese fleet as a threat in the Pacific. **420**

Battle of Midway (1942) Allied naval victory that helped halt the major Japanese offensive in the Pacific during World War II. **403**

Battle of New Orleans (1815) Battle in which American troops defeated British forces after the War of 1812 had officially ended. **67**

Battle of Okinawa (1945) Allied victory in the Pacific during World War II in which Japanese forces lost more than 100,000 troops. **420**

Battle of Omdurman (1898) British victory in North Africa in which 10,000 African soldiers, armed only with spears and swords, were killed by British gunfire. **626**

Battle of Saratoga (1777) Patriot victory, during Revolutionary War, that convinced France to support the American fight for independence. **35**

Battle of Stalingrad (1942–43) Soviet defeat of German troops during World War II that broke the momentum of the Axis advance in Europe. **405**

Battle of the Atlantic World War II naval war fought between German U-boats and the Allied navy and air force. **416**

Battle of the Bulge (1944) World War II battle in which Allied forces repulsed the final German offensive. **417**

Battle of the Coral Sea (1942) Allied naval victory during World War II in which a joint British-American naval force stopped the Japanese advance on Australia. **402**

Battle of the Java Sea (1942) World War II naval battle in which the Japanese navy defeated a fleet of American, British, Dutch, and Australian warships. **401**

Battle of the Little Bighorn (1876) Native American victory that resulted in the death of U.S. Army general Custer and all the men in his detachment. **124**

Battle of the Philippine Sea (1944) Decisive Allied naval and air victory over the Japanese during World War II. **418**

Battle of the Somme (1916) World War I battle in which the British lost some 60,000 troops in a single day. **245**

Battle of Tippecanoe (1811) Battle in Indiana Territory between U.S. troops and a confederation of Native Americans; ended in defeat for the Indians and made William Henry Harrison a hero. **66**

Battle of Yorktown (1781) Revolutionary War battle in which Patriot troops defeated British forces under General Cornwallis, effectively ending the war. **35**

bear market Downward trend in stock prices. **326**

Beats   Small but influential group of writers and poets who challenged literary conventions and the life-style of the middle class in the 1950s. **481**

benevolent societies   Organizations formed during the turn of the century to support and aid new immigrants. **148**

Beringia   Former land bridge between Siberia and present-day Alaska used by Paleo-Indians to cross from Asia into North America. **4**

Berlin airlift (1948)   Joint effort by U.S. and British air forces to deliver food and supplies into West Berlin after the Soviets blocked all routes into the city. **448**

Berlin Wall   Concrete barrier built in 1961 to cut off traffic between East Berlin and West Berlin. **492**

Big Four   During World War I, term for U.S. president Wilson, French premier Clemenceau, Italian prime minister Orlando, and British prime minister Lloyd George. **263**

Bilingual Education Act (1974)   Federal law encouraging public schools to provide instruction to students in their native languages until they learned English. **579**

Bill of Rights (1791)   First 10 amendments to the Constitution that protect individual liberties. **61**

biodiversity   The wide variety of plant and animal species on the earth. **735**

biomass   Materials, such as wood or waste products, that can be burned or used to make fuel. **734**

black codes   Laws adopted by former Confederates after the Civil War to limit the freedom of former slaves. **107**

blacklists   Lists of union supporters drawn up by employers for the purpose of denying jobs to union workers. **155**

Black Power   African American movement that focused on gaining control of economic and political power to achieve equal rights, by force if necessary. **504**

Blackshirts   Followers of Benito Mussolini. **388**

Black Thursday   October 24, 1929; day investors caused a panic on Wall Street by selling their shares. **327**

Black Tuesday   October 29, 1929; day the stock market crashed. **327**

blitzkrieg   German word for war carried on with great speed and force, used to describe Hitler's "lightning war" against Poland in World War II. **393**

Bolsheviks   Branch of the Russian Communist party that seized power in 1917 following the overthrow of the czar. **254**

bonanza farm   Large-scale farm usually owned by a large company and run like a factory. **131**

Bonus Army   Name given to World War I veterans who marched on Washington, D.C., in 1932 to support a bill granting veterans early payment of pension bonuses. **343**

Boston Massacre (1770)   Clash in Boston between an angry crowd of colonists and British soldiers that resulted in the death of five colonists. **27**

Boston Tea Party (1773)   Protest against British tax on tea in which colonists dumped tea into Boston Harbor. **27**

Boxer Rebellion (1900)   Revolt by a Chinese secret society attempting to drive foreigners out of China. **223**

braceros   Mexican farm workers who came to work in the Southwest during World War II and after. **413**

breadlines   Lines formed by people waiting for free food, such as those that occurred during the Great Depression. **333**

Bretton Woods system   Framework for postwar international economic relations developed by economic officials from the U.S. and 43 other countries. **660**

brinkmanship   Policy promoted by Secretary of State Dulles during the 1950s, which called for threatening all-out war in order to confront Communist aggression. **466**

British Invasion   Revolution in popular music inspired by the 1964 arrival of English rock bands such as the Beatles and the Rolling Stones. **512**

Brownshirts   Nazi storm troopers. **389**

Brown v. The Board of Education of Topeka (1952)   Supreme Court case challenging segregation in public schools; in it the Court ruled that separate educational facilities were unequal. **478**

bull market   Upward trend in stock prices. **326**

Bureau of Indian Affairs   Federal agency established within the War Department in 1824 to administer Native American reservations. **123**

business cycle   Regular ups and downs of business in a free-enterprise economy. **330**

Camp David Accords (1978)   Middle East peace agreement drafted by the U.S., Egypt, and Israel. **572**

Canadian Forestry Association   Conservation group formed in 1900 to promote national control of forest areas, fire prevention, and more forest reserves. **726**

caudillos   Latin American military leaders during the 1930s who used force to maintain order. **385**

Central Intelligence Agency (CIA)   Federal agency created to gather information overseas. **450**

Central Powers   World War I alliance led by Germany, Austria-Hungary, the Ottoman Empire (Turkey), and Bulgaria. **243**

checks and balances   System giving each branch of the federal government the means to restrain the powers of the other two branches. **40**

Chicano movement   Brown Power movement organized by young Mexican American college students to emphasize pride in Mexican culture and heritage. **507**

Chinese Exclusion Act (1882)   Federal law that denied U.S. citizenship to people born in China and prohibited the immigration of Chinese laborers. **148**

chlorofluorocarbons (CFCs)   Compounds, containing carbon, chlorine, fluorine, and sometimes hydrogen; they are suspected of damaging the ozone layer. **736**

circumnavigate   To sail around the world. **12**

Civilian Conservation Corps (CCC)   New Deal agency established in 1933 to employ men on conservation projects. **352**

Civil Rights Act of 1866   Federal law that granted full civil rights, but not voting rights, to everyone born in the U.S. **108**

Civil Rights Act of 1957   Federal law that made it a federal crime to prevent qualified persons from voting. **481**

Civil Rights Act of 1964   Federal law that barred discrimination in employment and public facilities and gave the Justice Department the power to enforce school desegregation. **503**

Civil Rights Bill of 1875   Federal law that prohibited discrimination by businesses serving the public. **111**

Civil Works Administration (CWA)   New Deal agency designed to create jobs during the Great Depression. **352**

Clayton Antitrust Act (1914)   Federal law that clarified and extended the 1890 Sherman Antitrust Act. **205**

Clayton-Bulwer Treaty (1850)   Agreement between the U.S. and Great Britain that proposed an equal partnership in building and running a Central American canal. **226**

Clean Air Act (1970)   Federal law that set air-quality standards and tough emissions guidelines for car manufacturers. **559**

closed shop   Workplace where the employer hires only union members. **176**

coaling stations   Port where steamships take on coal. **625**

Cobden Chevalier Treaty (1860)   Agreement between France and Great Britain that reduced tariffs and removed bans from imports. **654**

Cold War   Competition between the U.S. and the Soviet Union for global power and influence. **445**

Columbian exchange   Transfer of people, ideas, plants, animals, and diseases among the Americas, Europe, Asia, and Africa; initiated by Columbus's voyages. **11**

Committee on Civil Rights   Group established by President Truman in 1946 to document civil rights abuses. **442**

Committee on Public Information (CPI)   Agency established in 1917 that waged a vigorous propaganda campaign to convince Americans to support the war effort. **260**

commonwealth   A democratic nation or state; a federation of states. **17**

Commonwealth of Independent States (CIS)   International organization of sovereign states organized in 1991 by Russia, Ukraine, and Belarus. Other former Soviet republics later became members. **599**

Compromise of 1850   Measures proposed by Henry Clay that temporarily settled differences between the North and the South over slavery issues. **88**

Compromise of 1877   Deal between leading Republicans and southern Democrats that gave the presidency to Rutherford B. Hayes in 1876 in exchange for a promise not to use the military to enforce Reconstruction laws in the South. **111**

Comstock Lode   Rich Nevada silver vein that was the center of frantic prospecting beginning in 1859. **134**

concurrent powers   Powers granted jointly in the United States Constitution to the federal government and the state government. **40**

Congress of Industrial Organizations (CIO)   Labor group organized in 1935 to unite workers in various industries. **361**

Congress of Racial Equality (CORE)   Northern-based civil rights group that launched a protest against segregation in interstate transportation in 1961. **501**

conquistadors   Spanish soldiers who helped conquer the Americas. **13**

conscription   The calling up of people to serve in the military. **100**

conservation   Controlled use and protection of natural resources. **725**

conspicuous consumption   Lavish spending to increase social prestige. **146**

Constitutional Convention   Meeting called in 1787 and held in Philadelphia to strengthen the government, during which delegates wrote and adopted the U.S. Constitution. **38**

containment   Cold War strategy proposed by George Kennan to stop the spread of communism. **446**

Convention on Biological Diversity   Treaty signed in 1993 committing 167 nations to protecting biodiversity and sharing profits from biotechnology. **739**

Convention on the Elimination of All Forms of Racial Discrimination   UN-established agreement enacted in 1969 to declare any advocation of racial hatred illegal and punishable by law. **710**

Convention on the Suppression of Apartheid   Passed by the UN General Assembly in 1973 to discourage apartheid in South Africa. **712**

contras   An army recruited by the CIA to overthrow the Sandinista government of Nicaragua. **589**

convoy system   Use of armed escort vessels to accompany unarmed vessels transporting troops or supplies. **254**

cooperatives   Groups that pool members' resources to sell products directly to urban markets and to buy goods at wholesale prices. **155**

Copperheads   Northern Democrats who sympathized with the South during the Civil War. **101**

corporation   Business organization that is distinct from its owners and that raises the money needed to run the company by selling shares of stock. **143**

cotton gin   Machine invented by Eli Whitney in 1793 to separate seeds from cotton fiber. **79**

Council of Economic Advisers   Federal agency created by the Employment Act of 1946 to counsel the president on economic policy. **440**

counterculture   Culture that holds values and beliefs different from those of established society; for example, the culture of the hippies in the 1960s. **509**

Covenant on Civil and Political Rights   UN General Assembly agreement on human rights that prohibited governments from interfering with individuals' liberties. **714**

Covenant on Economic, Social, and Cultural Rights   UN General Assembly agreement on human rights that required governments to provide jobs, increase opportunity, and improve health care. **714**

creditor nation   Country that loans money to other nations. **382**

crop-lien system   Arrangement in which sharecroppers promised their crops to merchants in exchange for supplies. **113**

Crusades   Series of wars between 1096 and the late 1200s in which Christian crusaders fought Muslims for control of the Holy Land. **7**

cultural diffusion   Process of spreading cultural practices or beliefs from one group to another. **682**

Dawes General Allotment Act (1887)   Federal law that established private ownership of Indian land. **127**

Dawes Plan (1924)   Post–World War I plan that substantially reduced Germany's reparations, loaned Germany $200 million, and set up a new schedule of payments. **656**

D-Day   June 6, 1944; day when Allied soldiers crossed the English Channel to begin their invasion of France. **416**

debtor nation   Country that owes money to other nations. **382**

Declaration of Independence (1776)   Document adopted by the Second Continental Congress that justified and outlined reasons for the American separation from Great Britain. **29**

Declaration of the Rights of Man and Citizen   Document issued by France's National Assembly to outline basic inalienable human rights to liberty, property, security, and resistance to oppression. **699**

defoliants   Chemicals designed to strip land of vegetation. **529**

delegated powers   Powers granted to the federal government in the U.S. Constitution. **40**

demobilization   Shift from wartime preparations to a peacetime economy. **278**

Department of Energy   Federal agency created in 1977 to reduce U.S. dependence on oil. **569**

depression   Sharp drop in business activity accompanied by rising unemployment. **38**

détente   Lessening of military and diplomatic tensions between countries. **560**

devaluation   Reduction in the value of a currency to make it cheaper than other currencies. **657**

direct primary   Nominating election in which voters choose candidates to run in a general election. **191**

direct rule   Imperialistic method of governing in which the colonizing country establishes a completely new governmental administration in hopes of the new colony adopting the imperial culture. **627**

disarmament Reduction or limitation in the amount of a nation's military weapons. **381**

Displaced Persons Act (1948) Federal law that enabled 400,000 European refugees into the U.S. following World War II. **680**

dividends Portions of a company's profits received by its stockholders. **143**

Dixiecrats States' Rights party formed by southern Democrats in 1948; supported continued racial segregation. **443**

doctrine of nullification Theory of the states' right to refuse to obey any act passed by Congress that they consider unconstitutional. **74**

dollar diplomacy President Taft's policy of using economic influence, rather than military force, to protect U.S. interests in Latin America. **230**

domino theory Foreign policy principle of the 1950s and the 1960s stating that if one country fell to communism, neighboring countries would also fall. **523**

doves People who support negotiation and compromise and who oppose war. **532**

Dred Scott **decision** (1857) Supreme Court case in which the Missouri Compromise was declared unconstitutional and in which Scott, a slave, was declared not to be a citizen. **89**

drivers Slave assistants who helped overseers supervise other slaves. **79**

dry farming Techniques to conserve moisture in areas of little rainfall. **131**

Dust Bowl Fifty-million–acre region in the Great Plains that suffered a severe drought in the mid-1930s. **367**

ecology Study of the interrelationships of plants and animals and their environments. **724**

economies of scale Principle of buying supplies in bulk and producing goods in large quantities to lower production costs and increase profits. **144**

ecosystem Interaction of living beings with the environment. **724**

Education Amendments Act (1972) Federal law prohibiting sexual discrimination in higher education. **577**

Education for All Handicapped Children Act (1975) Federal law requiring public schools to provide education for children with physical and mental disabilities. **575**

Eighteenth Amendment (1919) Constitutional amendment that barred the manufacture, sale, or importation of alcoholic beverages; repealed by Twenty-first Amendment. **181**

Eisenhower Doctrine (1957) Policy designed to counter Soviet influence in the Middle East by offering military aid to those nations seeking help in resisting Communist aggression. **468**

elastic clause Constitutional provision that allows Congress to stretch its powers in ways not specifically outlined in the U.S. Constitution. **41**

Electronic mail Messages transmitted electronically via computers; commonly called E-mail. **652**

Elementary and Secondary School Education Act (1965) Federal law that provided $1.3 billion to aid schools in impoverished areas. **498**

Elkins Act (1903) Federal law that prohibited shippers from accepting rebates. **196**

Emancipation Proclamation Decree freeing all slaves living in those areas of the Confederacy that were still in rebellion against the U.S. as of January 1, 1863. **101**

Embargo Act (1807) Measure that stopped shipments of food and other American products to all foreign ports in an effort to maintain U.S. neutrality in European conflicts. **66**

Emergency Banking Act (1933) Federal law authorizing only banks that were financially sound to reopen after the New Deal bank holiday. **350**

employer mandate A call for employers to pay for the majority of the costs of all of their employees' health insurance. **609**

Employment Act (1946) Post–World War II law that established the Council of Economic Advisers and pledged the promotion of full employment and production. **440**

encomienda System that gave Spanish colonists the right to have a certain number of Indians work for them. **11**

Endangered Species Act (1973) Federal law passed to protect species threatened with extinction. **732**

Enforcement Acts Three acts passed by Congress between 1870 and 1871 allowing the government to use military force to stop violence against African Americans. **111**

Environmental Protection Agency (EPA) Federal agency created in 1970 to enforce environmental laws. **559**

Equal Pay Act (1963) Federal law that made it illegal for employers to pay female workers less than male workers for the same job. **490**

Equal Rights Amendment (ERA) Proposed constitutional amendment barring discrimination on the basis of sex. **577**

escalation Increase or buildup of military forces or weapons. **527**

Espionage Act (1917) Federal law designed to outlaw acts of treason and to silence dissenters during World War I. **261**

European Economic Community Economic union formed to promote trade and cooperation among European member nations. **661**

European Union Western European trading bloc formed by the European Community in 1993 with ratification of the Maastricht Treaty. **666**

Fair Deal President Truman's proposed reforms after the 1948 election; for example, a national health insurance program. **443**

Fair Employment Practices Committee (FEPC) Federal commission created in 1941 to prevent job discrimination based on race or ethnic background. **412**

Family and Medical Leave Act (1993) Federal law requiring large companies to provide workers up to 12 weeks of unpaid leave for family and medical emergencies without losing their medical coverage or jobs. **608**

Family Assistance Plan (FAP) President Nixon's proposal to replace the welfare system with a plan that would guarantee families a minimum income. **557**

Farm Credit Administration New Deal agency created in 1933 to give farmers low-interest, long-term loans. **351**

Farmers' Alliance Powerful farm organization formed in 1877 that lobbied to help farmers economically and politically. **156**

Farm Security Administration (FSA) New Deal agency created in 1937 to help tenant farmers and sharecroppers buy farms through low-interest, long-term loans. **362**

Fascist party Political party, founded by Benito Mussolini in 1921, that supported a military-dominated government in control of all aspects of Italian society. **388**

Federal Deposit Insurance Corporation (FDIC) New Deal agency created in 1933 to insure bank savings deposits. **351**

Federal Emergency Relief Administration (FERA)   New Deal agency created in 1933 to funnel relief aid directly to state and local agencies. **351**

Federal Farm Loan Act   Federal law proposed during President Woodrow Wilson's administration that provided low-interest loans to farmers. **207**

federalism   Division and sharing of powers between a strong central government and state governments. **38**

Federalists   Members of a political party who advocated strong national government and favored ratification of the U.S. Constitution. **39**

Federal Project No. 1   New Deal program established in 1935 to aid unemployed artists. **372**

Federal Reserve Act (1913)   Federal law that created a three-level banking system controlled by both private banks and the government. **205**

Federal Trade Commission (FTC)   Government agency established in 1914 to enforce antitrust laws and to investigate corporations engaged in unfair or fraudulent practices. **205**

Federal Water Pollution Control Act (1972)   Federal law passed to regulate contaminated water. **732**

Federal Workmen's Compensation Act   Federal law providing benefits to federal workers injured on the job. **207**

Federal Writers' Project (FWP)   Program that hired unemployed writers to produce a variety of cultural works. **372**

Fifteenth Amendment (1869)   Constitutional amendment that guaranteed that the right to vote could not be denied because of race. **109**

First Battle of Bull Run (1861)   Confederate victory at Manassas Junction, outside of Washington, D.C., that proved the Civil War would last longer than a few months. **97**

First Battle of the Marne (1914)   World War I battle in which French and British forces stopped the German advance in northeast France. **245**

First Continental Congress (1774)   Meeting of delegates from 12 colonies to discuss grievances against Great Britain, including those resulting from the Intolerable Acts. **28**

Five Power Agreement (1921)   Arrangement between the U.S., Great Britain, France, Italy, and Japan to set limits on each nation's naval strength. **381**

fixed exchange rates   Economic system in which the value of a dollar does not vary in relation to other currencies. **660**

flappers   "New women" whose dress and conduct after World War I defied traditional standards of womanly behavior. **311**

flexible response   Strategy adopted by the Kennedy administration of keeping a range of options open for dealing with international crises. **491**

floating exchange rates   Economic system in which the value of a dollar can vary in relation to other currencies, depending on the relative demand for dollars and other currencies. **664**

Food Administration   Government agency responsible for regulating production and supply of food during World War I. **258**

food chain   Order of organisms in ecological communities in which each consumes a lower member and is in turn preyed upon by a higher member. **730**

Foraker Act (1900)   Federal law outlining the organization of Puerto Rico's government. **226**

Fordney-McCumber Tariff Act (1922)   Federal law that placed high duties on imported farm products in an effort to boost domestic crop prices and to help farmers. **288**

forty-niners   Nickname for gold-seekers who went to California, beginning in 1849, to seek their fortune. **86**

Four Power Treaty (1921)   Agreement between the U.S., Great Britain, France, and Japan to respect one another's territory in the Pacific. **381**

Fourteen Points (1918)   President Wilson's program for world peace after World War I that contained 14 principles, including the creation of the League of Nations. **262**

Fourteenth Amendment (1866)   Constitutional amendment that created a national citizenship, thereby extending full citizenship, civil rights, and equal protection under the law to African Americans. **108**

freedom of contract   Right of workers and employers to agree to certain conditions of employment. **175**

Freedom Riders   Integrated group who protested segregation in interstate transportation in 1961. **501**

Freedom Summer   Campaign to register African American voters during the summer of 1964. **503**

freemen   People who enjoy full political and civil liberties. **17**

Free-Soil party   Political party, formed by antislavery Whigs and Democrats in 1848, that opposed the expansion of slavery into the territories. **87**

free trade   International trade free from government regulation. **654**

French and Indian War (1754–63)   Territorial conflict between France and Great Britain over Native American lands in which France lost most of its North American holdings. **19**

Fuel Administration   Government agency responsible for regulating production and supply of fuel during World War I. **258**

Fugitive Slave Act   Law passed as part of the Compromise of 1850 that made it a federal crime to assist runaway slaves. **88**

Fundamentalism   Protestant movement whose followers believe in a literal interpretation of the Bible. **312**

Gadsden Purchase (1853)   Agreement by which the U.S. acquired Mexico's territory south of the Gila River in present-day Arizona and New Mexico for $10 million. **85**

General Agreement on Tariffs and Trade   A commitment to the long-term goal of free trade established by 44 countries at the Bretton Woods conference. **660**

generation gap   Difference in years, attitudes, and cultural beliefs between generations; applied to baby boomers and their elders during the 1960s. **508**

Geneva Convention (1864)   Agreement among 12 nations to care for sick and wounded enemy soldiers as well as their own. **703**

genocide   Deliberate annihilation of an entire people. **423**

German reunification   Reuniting of East Germany and West Germany as one nation in 1990. **599**

Gettysburg Address   Lincoln's speech dedicating a cemetery at the Gettysburg battlefield in which he gave a classic statement of democratic ideals. **98**

GI Bill of Rights (1944)   Servicemen's Readjustment Act, which provided pensions and government loans to help veterans start their own businesses, buy homes or farms, and attend college. **440**

Gilded Age   Name applied to post–Civil War America to describe the corruption and greed that lurked below the surface of industrial society. **152**

glasnost   Policy of openness introduced in the Soviet Union by Mikhail Gorbachev in 1985. **593**

global warming   Gradual increase in the temperature of the earth's atmosphere. **736**

Glorious Revolution (1688)   Bloodless English rebellion that broke the absolute power of the British monarchy, and King James II was replaced by the Protestant rulers Mary and William. **698**

glyph   Picture or symbol used in the Olmec and other picture writing systems. **6**

gold standard   Monetary system in which each dollar is equal to and redeemable for a set amount of gold. **653**

Gold Standard Act (1900)   Federal law declaring the nation's currency to be redeemable in gold at a fixed rate. Adoption of the gold standard encouraged the development of the world economy. **653**

Good Neighbor policy   FDR's policy of promoting goodwill toward Latin America. **384**

graduated income tax   System in which the rate of taxation varies according to income. **156**

Gramm-Rudman-Hollings Act (1985)   Federal law requiring across-the-board cuts in government spending when the deficit exceeds a certain point. **592**

Great Compromise (1787)   Plan approved at the Constitutional Convention in which each state, regardless of size, was given an equal voice in the upper house, while representation in the lower house was determined by population. **38**

Great Depression   Deep economic downturn that gripped the U.S. between 1929 and the beginning of World War II. **328**

Great Migration   Mass movement of Puritans from England to the Americas beginning in 1630. **16**   Mass movement of African Americans from the South to the North between 1915 and 1930. **259**

Great Society   President Lyndon Johnson's economic and social programs during the 1960s. **497**

Great Upheaval (1886)   Year of intense worker strikes and violent labor confrontations in the U.S. **154**

Green parties   Environmentalist political parties in Europe. **731**

gross national product   Total value of all goods and services produced by a country in a given year. **327**

guerrilla warfare   Form of fighting in which forces wear down the enemy with hit-and-run skirmishes. **35**

H

Hague Peace Conferences (1899, 1907)   Meetings that established provisions for the care of enemy soldiers wounded in naval warfare. **703**

Haight-Ashbury   San Francisco district known for its hippie population during the mid-1960s. **509**

hard-rock mining   Technique that involved sinking deep mine shafts to get at ore in quartz veins. **136**

Harlem Renaissance   Period of African American artistic development during the 1920s in New York City's Harlem. **316**

hawks   People who support war or a warlike policy. **532**

Hay-Bunau-Varilla Treaty (1903)   Agreement with Panama giving U.S. control over a 10-mile-wide Canal Zone. **228**

Hay-Herrán Treaty (1903)   Proposed agreement with Colombia that would have given the U.S. a lease to build a canal in Panama. **228**

Haymarket Riot (1886)   Violent confrontation in Chicago between workers, anarchists, and police that helped turn public support against the labor movement. **154**

Hay-Pauncefote Treaty (1901)   Agreement with Great Britain by which the U.S. could build and control a Central American canal. **228**

Hepburn Act (1906)   Federal law that authorized the Interstate Commerce Commission to set railroad rates and to regulate other companies engaged in interstate commerce. **196**

Highway Act (1956)   Federal law that expanded the nation's highway systems. **473**

hippies   Name given to people in the 1960s who rejected everything connected with mainstream America. **509**

Ho Chi Minh Trail   Network of jungle paths used by the North Vietnamese to move weapons and supplies to the Vietcong in South Vietnam. **528**

Hollywood Ten   Group of film directors and writers who went to jail rather than answer questions from the House Committee on Un-American Activities. **450**

Holocaust   Systematic slaughter of European Jews by the Nazis during World War II. **423**

Home Loan Bank Act (1932)   Federal law that provided money to savings banks, building and loan associations, and insurance companies for low-interest mortgages. **341**

Home Owners Loan Corporation (HOLC)   New Deal agency created in 1933 to grant low-interest, long-term mortgage loans to home owners. **351**

Homestead Act (1862)   Federal law that gave public land to any citizen willing to live on the Great Plains and cultivate the land for five years. **128**

horizontal integration   Method of expanding a company by buying other companies involved in the same business. **144**

"hot line"   Telephone connection between the U.S. and the Soviet Union that allowed leaders to communicate directly during a crisis. **494**

House Committee on Un-American Activities (HUAC)   Congressional committee established in 1938 to investigate anti-American propaganda. **450**

Housing and Urban Development Act (1968)   Federal law that, along with the Omnibus Housing Act, provided money for urban renewal and created the Department of Housing and Urban Development. **498**

human rights   Basic rights and freedoms to which all people are entitled, including freedom from unlawful detention or torture. **570**

hunter-gatherers   People who moved from place to place in search of game and edible plants. **4**

hydraulic mining   Technique that uses water pressure to remove mountains of gravel, exposing the minerals underneath. **136**

hydrogen bomb   Weapon approximately 1,000 times more powerful than the atomic bomb. **464**

I

Immigration Act of 1924   Federal law reducing the immigration quota for each nationality to 2 percent of the 1890 figures. **294**

Immigration Act of 1965   Federal law that eliminated the numerical limits and percentages of immigrants to the U.S. **681**

Immigration Act of 1990   Federal law that updated U.S. immigration laws from the 1960s and increased the number of immigrants allowed into the United States each year. **683**

Immigration Restriction League   Group founded in 1894 by well-to-do Bostonians who sought to impose a literacy test on all immigrants. **148**

impeachment   Formal charge of wrongdoing or misconduct brought against a government official. **40**

imperialism   Practice of extending the power of a nation by direct territorial acquisition of colonial empires. **214**

impressment   Practice of kidnapping and forcing people into public service; used by Great Britain in the late 1700s and early 1800s to secure sailors for the British navy. **62**

indentured servants   Persons who agreed to work for a specified time for the person who paid their way to America. **17**

Indian Removal Act (1830)   Federal law that provided for the relocation of Indian nations living east of the Mississippi River to Indian Territory in present-day Oklahoma. **75**

Indian Reorganization Act (1934) Federal law that sought to revive tribal rule by funding tribal business ventures and paying for the college education of Native Americans. **366**

indirect rule Imperialists' method of governing in which the colonizing country rules through traditional leaders, leaving the local culture intact. **627**

Industrial Revolution Shift from hand production to machine production that began in Great Britain in the mid-1700s. **74**

inflation Rise in prices resulting from an increase in the amount of money in circulation relative to the amount of goods available for sale. **37**

Information Revolution Widespread transfer of information made possible by computers and information technologies. **686**

initiative Election reform that gives voters the power to introduce legislation. **191**

insider trading Use of confidential financial information by stockbrokers for personal gain. **592**

Intermediate-range Nuclear Forces (INF) **Treaty** (1987) Agreement that eliminated all medium-range nuclear weapons from Europe and set up inspection procedures to enforce provisions of the treaty. **593**

Internal Security Act (1950) Federal law that required Communist party members and organizations to register with the federal government. **451**

International Monetary Fund $8.8 billion fund established by members of the Bretton Woods conference to maintain the fixed exchange rates for the international economy. **660**

Internet Computer network that allows an estimated 20 million computers in more than 80 countries to communicate and share information. **686**

internment Imprisonment; practice of forced relocation applied to Japanese Americans living on the West Coast after Pearl Harbor. **410**

Interstate Commerce Act (1887) Federal law that regulated railroad freight rates and created an agency to monitor railroad activities. **156**

Intolerable Acts (1774) Series of laws passed by Great Britain to punish Massachusetts for the Boston Tea Party, while strengthening British control over the colonies; also called the Coercive Acts. **28**

Iran-contra affair Name given to the illegal actions taken by White House aides in the 1980s to fund Nicaraguan contras. **593**

Iran hostage crisis (1979–81) Period during which 53 Americans in Iran were seized by followers of militant Islamic leader Ayatollah Khomeini in an attempt to force the return of Shah Reza Pahlavi from exile in the U.S. **572**

Iroquois League Confederation of Indian tribes formed in the 15th or 16th century; also called the Six Nations. **19**

irreconcilables Fourteen Republican senators who opposed the League of Nations and rejected the Treaty of Versailles after World War I. **265**

island-hopping Allied military tactic during World War II in which certain strategic Japanese-held islands in the Pacific were seized, while others were bypassed. **418**

isolationism Policy of avoiding international political or economic alliances; followed by the U.S. during most of the 1920s and 1930s. **380**

Jay's Treaty (1794) Treaty in which Great Britain agreed to abandon its forts in the Northwest Territory in exchange for U.S. payment of debts owed to the British. **63**

Jim Crow laws State laws adopted in the South that were designed to enforce segregation. **114**

joint-stock companies Companies in which investors share the start-up and maintenance costs as well as profits or losses. **15**

Jones Act of 1916 Law that gave Filipinos the right to elect both houses of their legislature, but delayed independence until a stable government was established. **221**

Jones Act of 1917 Law that granted U.S. citizenship to Puerto Ricans and gave them the right to elect both houses of their legislature. **226**

judicial review Supreme Court's right to determine whether laws violate the U.S. Constitution. **64**

Judiciary Act (1789) Law that created the federal court system, including district courts, circuit courts of appeals, and the Supreme Court. **61**

juvenile delinquency Antisocial behavior by the young that is subject to legal action. **482**

kamikaze Japanese planes during World War II assigned to suicide missions against Allied ships. **420**

Kansas-Nebraska Act (1854) Federal law that established popular sovereignty in newly organized territories and overturned the Missouri Compromise. **89**

Keating-Owen Child Labor Act (1916) Proposed federal law that outlawed the interstate sale of products produced by child labor. **207**

Kellogg-Briand Pact (1927) Agreement signed by 62 nations that outlawed war as an instrument of national policy but allowed countries to declare war in self-defense. **382**

Kentucky and Virginia Resolutions State resolutions passed between 1798 and 1799 that declared states should be the final judge of whether a law was unconstitutional. **64**

Kerner Commission Federal Commission that investigated the 1960s riots and reported that white racism was responsible for the violence. **506**

Klondike Gold Rush Flood of prospectors to the Klondike district of Canada's Yukon Territory in the late 1890s in search of gold. **134**

Knights of Labor National union founded in 1869 that consisted of skilled and unskilled workers. **153**

Kristallnacht "Night of broken glass," November 9, 1938, when Nazis burned down synagogues and destroyed Jewish businesses in Germany. **389**

laissez-faire capitalism Theory that opposes government regulation of economic matters. **145**

Land Ordinance of 1785 Federal law that established a system for surveying western lands by townships and selling smaller parcels to the public. **37**

Landrum-Griffin Act (1959) Federal law designed to reduce corruption in labor unions. **476**

League of United Latin American Citizens (LULAC) Hispanic group that lobbied for national awareness of Hispanic concerns and issues. **574**

Lend-Lease Act (1941) Law that appropriated money for the U.S. to lend or lease arms and other supplies to non-Axis countries. **393**

Limited Nuclear Test Ban Treaty (1963) Agreement by the U.S., the Soviet Union, and Great Britain to end the testing of nuclear bombs in the atmosphere or under water. **493**

literacy tests Tests requiring proof of a person's ability to read in order to vote; used in southern states to deny voting rights to African Americans. **114**

"Little Rock Nine" Name given to the African American students who were admitted to an all-white school in Arkansas in 1957. **480**

lockouts Tactic used by employers of barring workers from plants until concessions from workers are obtained. **155**

long drives Overland treks on which cowboys herded cattle from ranches to rail lines. **132**

Long March Exodus of 1934–35 when Communist Chinese marched nearly 6,000 miles to northern China, helping cement Mao Zedong's leadership of the party. **454**

Long Walk Forced march of Navajos to Bosque Redondo, a reservation in eastern New Mexico, following their surrender in early 1864. **125**

loose construction Theory set forth by Alexander Hamilton that the federal government possesses all powers not specifically forbidden by the U.S. Constitution. **62**

Lost Generation Name given by Gertrude Stein to writers of the 1920s whose works expressed disillusionment after World War I. **318**

Louisiana Purchase (1803) U.S. purchase from France of the vast territory of Louisiana for some $15 million. **65**

Loyalists Americans loyal to Great Britain during the Revolutionary War; also called Tories. **35**

M

Maginot Line Line of defenses built by the French after World War I along their border with Germany. **393**

mainframe computers Large, fast computer systems capable of processing many tasks at a time. **687**

mandate system Provision of the Treaty of Versailles that required new colonial rulers to report to the League of Nations on their administration of former Central Power territories. **264**

Manhattan Project Top-secret U.S. project begun in 1942 in which scientists developed the first atomic bomb. **421**

manifest destiny Phrase coined in 1845 to express the belief that the U.S. was destined to extend its boundaries westward to the Pacific Ocean. **84**

Mann-Elkins Act (1910) Federal law that extended the regulatory powers of the Interstate Commerce Commission to telephone and telegraph companies. **199**

Marbury v. *Madison* (1803) Legal case in which the Supreme Court first exercised its right of judicial review. **64**

March on Washington (1963) Demonstration in Washington, D.C., called by African American leaders to show support for President Kennedy's civil rights bill. **503**

margin buying Purchasing stock with borrowed money. **326**

Mariposa War (1850–51) California raids by the Miwoks and the Yokuts to reclaim Native American lands taken over by miners. **87**

market revolution Creation of profitable national markets during the 1800s brought about by new transportation systems and regional specialization. **73**

Marshall Plan (1948) U.S. program that provided some $12 billion in economic aid to Western Europe after World War II; also called the European Recovery Act. **448**

mass transit Public transportation systems, such as commuter trains and subways, that made it possible for workers to live farther away from their jobs. **149**

Mayflower Compact (1620) Document that established Plymouth Colony as a self-governing colony based on the majority rule of male church members. **16**

McKinley Tariff (1890) Federal law increasing the number of imports subject to tariffs and increasing the tariff rate. **655**

Meat Inspection Act (1906) Federal consumer-protection law that required the government inspection of interstate meat shipments. **196**

Medicaid State programs established in 1965 and funded by Congress to provide free health care to the needy. **498**

Medicare Great Society program established in 1965 to provide national health insurance for people over age 65. **497**

Merchandise Marks Act (1887) British law requiring foreign goods be labeled to indicate country of origin. **655**

mergers Combining of two or more companies to achieve greater efficiency and higher profits. **288**

Mexican Cession (1848) Area surrendered by Mexico to the U.S. in the Treaty of Guadalupe Hidalgo; included the present-day states of California, Nevada, and Utah, and parts of Arizona, Colorado, and New Mexico. **85**

Mexican War (1846–48) Conflict between Mexico and the U.S. brought about by the U.S. annexation of Texas and its quest for more territory. **85**

middle class Social class that occupies a position between the wealthy and the poor. **77**

Middle Passage Voyage made by slave ships from Africa across the Atlantic Ocean during which many slaves suffered and died. **17**

militarism Glorification of armed strength and aggressive military preparedness. **243**

minicomputers Computers that are smaller, easier to operate, and less expensive than mainframes. **687**

Missouri Compromise (1820) Act that maintained the balance of slave and free states in Congress by admitting Missouri as a slave state and Maine as a free state, while prohibiting the spread of slavery in the territories to areas north of latitude 36°30´. **74**

modern Republicanism Name given to President Eisenhower's attempt to balance liberal domestic reforms with conservative spending during the 1950s. **470**

monopoly Exclusive control, such as in trade or industry, that eliminates competition. **9, 143**

Monroe Doctrine (1823) U.S. government policy statement in which the Americas were declared off-limits to European expansion. **72**

Montgomery Improvement Association (MIA) Group of civil rights leaders in Montgomery, Alabama, whose members included Martin Luther King, Jr. **479**

Montreal Protocol on Ozone Depletion (1987) International agreement that set standards for reducing the emission of CFCs and other gases. **739**

Moral Majority Fundamentalist Christian political organization founded in 1978 by Reverend Jerry Falwell. **586**

moratorium Authorized period of delay in paying a debt or fulfilling a legal obligation. **383**

Morrill Act (1862) Federal law that gave land to states to establish agricultural colleges. **128**

muckrakers Nickname given by President Theodore Roosevelt to progressive journalists in the early 1900s who exposed political and social evils. **170**

multinational corporations Companies that invest money in or own businesses around the world. **665**

Munich Conference (1938) Meeting attended by government leaders from Great Britain, Italy, France, and Germany in which a pact was signed giving Germany control of the Sudetenland. **391**

mutualistas Mutual-aid societies formed by Mexican American communities to help local residents. **332**

National Aeronautics and Space Administration (NASA) Federal agency established in 1958 to direct American space exploration. **466**

National Association for the Advancement of Colored People (NAACP) Civil rights organization founded in 1909 to work for various social reforms that would benefit African Americans and end racial discrimination. **183**

national bank Central bank with branches in major cities. **62**

National Defense Act (1916) Military "preparedness" program established prior to U.S. entry into World War I that increased the size of the National Guard and the U.S. army. **250**

National Defense Education Act (1958) Federal law that appropriated money to improve education in science, math, and foreign languages. **466**

National Energy Act (1978) Federal law that relaxed controls on the price of natural gas in an effort to ease U.S. dependence on foreign oil. **569**

National Grange Farmers' group founded in 1867 as a social organization that grew into a political force; also called Patrons of Husbandry. **155**

National Industrial Recovery Act (NIRA) Federal law passed in 1933 to stimulate industrial and business activity and to reduce unemployment. **352**

National Information Infrastructure A proposed communications network to make vast amounts of information readily available to the public; known as the Information Superhighway. **687**

nationalism Sense of pride or loyalty to a nation. **72**

nationalize To assert government control or ownership over a business or industry. **387**

National Organization for Women (NOW) Group founded by feminists in 1966 to promote equal rights for women. **510**

National Recovery Administration (NRA) Federal agency that encouraged businesses to draw up "codes of fair competition" as one means of achieving business recovery during the Great Depression. **353**

National Security Council (NSC) Organization created in 1947 by Congress to advise the president on strategic matters. **450**

National War Labor Board (NWLB) Group of representatives from business and labor who arbitrated disputes between workers and employers during World War I. **258**

National Youth Administration (NYA) New Deal agency that provided part-time jobs to people between the ages of 16 and 25. **358**

nativism Policy of favoring native-born Americans over immigrants. **78**

Nazi party Political party, led by Adolf Hitler, that controlled Germany from 1933 to 1945; also called the National Socialist party. **389**

neocolonialism The economic and political policies by which a great power indirectly exerts its influence over former colonies. **638**

New Deal President Franklin Roosevelt's program of providing relief and recovery to the U.S. during the Great Depression. **350**

New Freedom Name given to Woodrow Wilson's progressive program of reform as proposed during the 1912 presidential election. **202**

New Frontier President John Kennedy's political, social, and economic programs of the early 1960s. **489**

new immigrants People, mostly southern and eastern Europeans, who came to the United States in the late 1800s and early 1900s. **147**

Newlands Reclamation Act (1902) Federal law that allowed money from the sale of public land to be used for irrigation and reclamation. **197**

New Nationalism Name given to Theodore Roosevelt's program of social legislation first proposed during the 1910 congressional elections. **201**

New Right Conservatives who showed increased political influence during the 1980s. **586**

Nine Power Treaty (1921) Agreement arising from the Washington Conference that guaranteed China's territorial integrity and promised to uphold the Open Door policy. **381**

Nineteenth Amendment (1920) Constitutional amendment that granted women full voting rights. **208**

no-man's land Thin strip of territory along the Western Front that separated opposing armies during World War I. **245**

nonaggression pact (1939) Temporary alliance in which Germany and the Soviet Union agreed to divide Poland between them. **392**

nonaligned movement Pact formed by the leaders of former colonies to proclaim neutrality toward and establish guidelines for interacting with the superpowers in the Cold War. **638**

nonviolent resistance Strategy of peaceful protest. **500**

North American Free Trade Agreement (NAFTA) International treaty ratified in 1993 to relax trade barriers between the U.S., Canada, and Mexico. **666**

North Atlantic Treaty Organization (NATO) Alliance formed in 1949 whose member nations agreed to protect one another in the event of attack. **449**

Northwest Ordinance (1787) Federal law that established a system for governing the Northwest Territory; also called the Land Ordinance of 1787. **37**

nuclear fallout Radioactive debris produced by a nuclear explosion. **729**

Nuclear Nonproliferation Treaty (1968) Agreement between the U.S., Great Britain, the Soviet Union, and 59 other nations to keep nuclear weapons technology from spreading to more countries. **729**

Nuremberg trials Trials of Nazi war criminals by the Allies that began in 1945. **437**

Occupational Safety and Health Administration (OSHA) Federal agency created in 1970 to protect workers from unhealthful working conditions. **559**

Office of Economic Opportunity (OEO) Government agency formed in 1964 to coordinate antipoverty programs, including the Job Corps, VISTA, and Head Start. **496**

oil shocks Jolts to the world economy caused by a sharp increase in oil prices. **663**

Okies Negative term for farmers, many from Oklahoma, who migrated in 1939 to the West Coast to find work. **370**

Olympic Games Group of modern international athletic contests held every four years in a different city. **691**

Omnibus Budget Reconciliation Act (1993) Budget bill designed to reduce the deficit by spending cuts and taxes on the wealthy. The first major legislative act to pass without any votes from the minority party. **607**

Omnibus Housing Act (1965) Federal law that, together with the Housing and Urban Development Act of 1968, provided money for urban renewal and housing assistance for low-income families. **498**

Open Door policy (1899) U.S. policy, proposed by Secretary of State John Hay, that called for all nations to have equal access to trade and investment in China. **223**

open range Grazing land that the government allowed cattle ranchers to use in the late 1800s. **132**

open shops Nonunion workplaces. **176**

Operation Desert Storm (1991) U.S. military mission that joined allies in driving Iraqi forces from Kuwait. **599**

Operation Restore Hope (1992) United Nations plan to ensure that relief efforts reached famine-stricken Somalia. **685**

Operation Rolling Thunder U.S. bombing campaign against military targets in North Vietnam that began in 1965. **528**

Oregon Country Disputed area of Pacific Northwest occupied jointly by the U.S. and Great Britain after the War of 1812. **72**

Oregon Trail Route to Oregon Country during the 1800s. **85**

Organization of African Unity (1963) Group of African nations formed to maintain peace and prevent territorial conflicts among its members following African independence. **641**

Organization of Petroleum Exporting Countries (OPEC) Group of oil-producing countries, mainly Arab, formed in 1960 to get higher prices for oil exports. **558**

overseers People who supervise workers. **79**

pacification Military tactic used by U.S. troops during the Vietnam War that involved moving residents to refugee camps and burning their villages. **530**

Pacific Railway Act (1862) Federal law that gave land for development of a transcontinental railroad. **128**

Pacific Rim Countries on the western edge of the Pacific Ocean. **664**

Paleo-Indians First people who crossed Beringia into North America. **4**

Palmer raids (1919–20) Raids to capture alleged radicals; launched by Attorney General A. Mitchell Palmer during the Red Scare. **282**

Panama Canal treaties (1978) Agreements granting Panama control over canal operations by the year 2000. **570**

Pan-German movement German efforts prior to World War I to unite all German-speaking peoples under one flag. **242**

Panic of 1819 Economic collapse caused in part by state banks lending money that they could not back with specie. **74**

Pan-Slavic movement Efforts supported by Russia to bring together all Slavic peoples of central and eastern Europe, in direct opposition to the Pan-German movement. **242**

partnerships Business enterprises that are owned by two or more people who are responsible for the businesses' debts. **143**

patio **process** Mining technique developed in Latin America; used mercury to extract silver from ore. **134**

Peace Corps Program established by President John Kennedy in the early 1960s that sends volunteers to developing countries. **491**

Pendleton Civil Service Act (1883) Federal law that created a Civil Service Commission to administer competitive examinations to those seeking government jobs. **153**

Pentagon Papers Secret government documents, published in 1971, that showed how the government had misled Americans about the Vietnam War. **538**

peons Landless laborers, mostly Indians, who worked on Spanish haciendas. **14**

perestroika Mikhail Gorbachev's plan to restructure the Soviet economy and government during the late 1980s. **593**

pet banks State banks that received deposits of federal funds because of their officers' loyalty to the Democratic party and to President Andrew Jackson. **76**

philanthropy Charitable efforts to promote public welfare, such as financing libraries, museums, and art galleries; endowing universities; and establishing theater or music groups. **151**

Philippine Government Act (1902) Federal law decreeing that the Philippines would be ruled by a governor and a two-house legislature. **220**

Pinckney's Treaty (1795) Agreement negotiated with Spain that set the southern boundary of the U.S. near Florida at the 31st parallel. **63**

planned obsolescence Practice of making products that are designed to go out of style. **320**

Platt Amendment Addition to Cuba's constitution, enacted in 1902 and renounced in 1934, that gave the U.S. greater control over Cuban affairs. **225**

Plessy v. Ferguson (1896) Supreme Court case in which the court upheld segregation by ruling that "separate but equal" facilities did not violate the Fourteenth Amendment. **114**

political machines Political organizations, headed by bosses, that used appointments to government jobs to control elections. **152**

poll taxes Fixed taxes imposed on every voter by southern states in an effort to deprive African Americans of the right to vote. **114**

pop art Art form begun in the 1960s that uses everyday objects as subject matter or in the works themselves. **510**

popular sovereignty Right of the people to rule, used as an argument for letting citizens of each new territory decide whether to permit slavery there. **87**

Populist party Political party founded by farmers, labor leaders, and reformers in 1892; also called the People's party. **157**

Potsdam Conference (1945) Overseas meeting attended by the U.S., Britain, and the Soviet Union that laid the foundation for Germany's postwar status. **436**

preservation Keeping wild areas intact and essentially untouched by humans. **726**

Proclamation of 1763 Declaration issued by Great Britain that barred settlement west of the Appalachian Mountains. **26**

progressivism Reform movement concerned with curing the ills caused by industrialization. **168**

prohibition Legal ban on the manufacture, transportation, and sale of alcoholic beverages. **81**

proprietorships Small businesses owned by individuals or families. **143**

protectionism Practice of imposing higher tariffs and stricter barriers against foreign imports in an effort to encourage Americans to purchase domestic goods. **654**

protectorate Country dependent on another for protection. **225**

Protestant Reformation Religious upheaval in Europe begun by Martin Luther in 1517 to protest corruption in the Roman Catholic church. **15**

Public Works Administration (PWA) New Deal agency established in 1933 that contracted with private firms to construct roads, public buildings, and similar projects. **353**

Pueblo Revolt (1680) Attacks by the Pueblo Indians that temporarily drove the Spanish from New Mexico. **13**

puppet government Government established by imperials in a colony in which it seems the colony is in control when in fact the imperial is. **632**

Pure Food and Drug Act (1906)   Federal consumer-protection law that forbade the manufacture or sale of food and patent medicine containing harmful ingredients. **196**

Puritans   English Protestants who sought to "purify" the Anglican church of Catholic rituals and traditions. **16**

Qur'an   Holy book of Islam. **7**

railhead   Town located along a railroad; long cattle drives usually ended there. **132**

Railroad Administration   Federal agency that reorganized railroads and set limits on transportation rates and workers' wages during World War I. **258**

Reaganomics   President Ronald Reagan's economic program built on big tax cuts to encourage business investment. **587**

realpolitik   Approach to foreign policy, adopted by Henry Kissinger and President Richard Nixon, that emphasized national interests over moral or ethical concerns. **559**

recall   Election reform that allows voters to remove an elected official from office by calling for a new election. **191**

reclamation   Process of making damaged land productive. **197**

Reconquista   Ongoing battle to recapture Spanish lands from the Moors that ended in 1492. **10**

Reconstruction   Rebuilding of the former Confederate states to reunite the nation. **106**

Reconstruction Acts (1867)   Federal laws that gave radical Republicans military control of the South. **108**

Reconstruction Finance Corporation (RFC)   Federal agency created in 1932 to stimulate the economy by lending money to railroads, insurance companies, banks, and other financial institutions. **341**

recycling   Collection and processing of used items for reuse. **738**

Red Cross   Organization formed by private Swiss citizens in 1863 to care for wounded soldiers of all nations. Present-day international efforts aid victims of natural disasters. **703**

Red Scare (1919–20)   Period of anti-Communist hysteria after the Bolshevik Revolution in Russia. **281**

referendum   Election reform that allows voters to place a measure on the ballot. **191**

regionalists   Midwestern artists popular in the 1930s who stressed local folk themes and customs in their work. **375**

rehabilitation   Treatment to restore someone to a useful and constructive place in society. **81**

Rehabilitation Act (1973)   Federal law forbidding discrimination in education, in jobs, or in housing because of physical disabilities. **575**

Relocation Act (1956)   Federal law passed to relocate Native Americans to urban areas. **471**

Renaissance   Rebirth of European art and learning spurred by the Crusades. **8**

reparations   Payments of damages. **263**

republic   Form of government in which leaders receive authority from citizens to make and enforce laws. **36**

reservationists   Republican senators who would support the Treaty of Versailles only if the League Covenant were amended. **265**

reserved powers   Powers kept by the states because they are not specifically granted to the federal government or denied to the states by the U.S. Constitution. **40**

revisionists   Historians who revise the previously accepted version of historical events. **425**

rock 'n' roll   Popular music introduced in the 1950s that reworked black rhythm and blues. **482**

Roe v. Wade (1973)   Supreme Court case that overturned a state law limiting a woman's access to an abortion. **577**

Roosevelt Corollary (1904)   Policy that extended the Monroe Doctrine by allowing the U.S. a greater role in maintaining peace and order in the Western Hemisphere. **229**

rugged individualism   Idea that success comes through individual effort and private enterprise. **339**

Rural Electrification Administration (REA)   New Deal agency that brought electricity to isolated rural areas. **358**

Russo-Japanese War (1904–05)   War between Russia and Japan that began with a Japanese attack on Russian forces in Manchuria. **224**

Safe Drinking Water Act (1974)   Federal law enacted to regulate contaminated water. **732**

Sand Creek Massacre (1864)   Slaughter of Cheyenne Indians by U.S. troops at Sand Creek in Colorado Territory. **123**

Sandinistas   Nicaraguan rebels who overthrew the dictatorship of Anastasio Somoza Debayle in 1979. **589**

satellite nations   Countries under the control of the Soviet Union. **445**

Saturday Night Massacre (1973)   Resignation and firing of top government officials who refused to aid President Richard Nixon in the Watergate cover-up. **564**

scientific management   Theory, promoted by Frederick W. Taylor, that every kind of work could be broken into a series of smaller tasks for which rates of production could be set. **303**

search-and-destroy missions   Military attacks that involve looking for and annihilating hidden enemy troops. **529**

Second Continental Congress (1775)   Convention held in Philadelphia in which delegates established the Continental Army and chose George Washington as its commander. **28**

Second Great Awakening   Renewal of religious faith that swept the U.S. beginning in the 1790s. **81**

Second New Deal   Government programs passed after the 1934 elections that provided relief and recovery but emphasized reform. **357**

Second Seminole War (1835–1842)   Resistance by the Seminoles to their removal from Florida; cost more money and lives than any other Indian war in U.S. history. **75**

sectionalism   Loyalty to a particular area of the country. **63**

Sedition Act (1918)   Federal law enacted during World War I that made written criticism of the government a crime. **261**

Selective Service Act (1917)   Federal law that required men to register with local draft boards. **251**

Selective Training and Service Act (1940)   Federal law that provided for America's first peacetime draft. **409**

self-determination   Right of people to govern themselves. **262**

Seneca Falls Convention (1848)   Meeting held in Seneca Falls, New York, that marked the birth of the organized women's rights movement in the U.S. **83**

separation of powers   Allotment of powers between the legislative, executive, and judicial branches of government to prevent any one branch from becoming too powerful. **40**

Separatists Radical English Puritans who broke with the Church of England. **16**

settlement houses Community centers in poor neighborhoods that provided education, recreation, and other services. **150**

Seventeenth Amendment (1913) Constitutional amendment that provided for the direct election of United States senators. **191**

sexual harassment The use of unwelcome sexual language or behavior. **602**

shantytowns Makeshift shelters built by homeless people; for example, the Hoovervilles that were built during the Great Depression. **333**

sharecropping Arrangement under which a sharecropper agreed to work a parcel of land in return for a share of the crop, a cabin, seed, tools, and a mule. **113**

Share-Our-Wealth (1933) Radical relief program proposed by Senator Huey Long to empower the government to confiscate wealth from the rich through taxes and provide a guaranteed minimum income and home to every family. **357**

Shays's Rebellion (1786–87) Farmers' revolt against high taxes and heavy debts, led by Daniel Shays. **38**

Sherman Antitrust Act (1890) Federal law that declared monopolies and trusts illegal. **145**

silent generation Name given to middle-class youth of the 1950s who seemed willing to conform to consumer culture without protest. **482**

silent majority Name given by President Richard Nixon to middle-class voters weary from the social upheaval of the 1960s. **556**

sit-down strike Work stoppage in which workers occupy factories until management meets their demands. **361**

sit-in Strategy of nonviolent protest in which a group enters a public place and refuses to leave. **500**

Sixteenth Amendment (1913) Constitutional amendment that authorized an individual income tax. **199**

smog Air polluted by chemicals, car exhaust, and smoke. **732**

Smoot-Hawley Tariff (1930) High-tariff law that contributed to the global economic downturn of the 1930s. **330**

Social Darwinism Theory, proposed in the late 1800s, that society progressed through competition, with the fittest rising to positions of wealth and power. **150**

Social Gospel Movement by Protestant ministers in the late 1800s that called for people to apply Christian principles to address social problems. **150**

socialism System under which government or worker cooperatives own all means of production and distribution. **176**

Social Security Act (1935) Federal law that provided a system of unemployment compensation and retirement pensions. **358**

Society of American Indians Organization formed by Native Americans to address Indian problems. **184**

Solidarity Polish independent trade union and social movement that was formed in 1980. **589**

Southern Christian Leadership Conference (SCLC) Alliance of church-based African American organizations formed in 1957 and dedicated to ending discrimination. **500**

southern strategy President Richard Nixon's plan to woo conservative southern white voters away from the Democratic party by cutting back on new civil rights legislation. **557**

Southern Tenant Farmers' Union (STFU) Arkansas sharecroppers who lobbied government in 1934 to halt tenant evictions and to force landowners to share payments with tenants. **354**

Spanish-American War (1898) War declared by the U.S. on Spain to protect U.S. investments and to help Cuba overthrow Spanish rule. **216**

Spanish Armada Spanish naval force defeated by England in 1588. **15**

Spanish Civil War War that began in 1936 between Fascists and Loyalists in Spain. **389**

specie Gold or silver coins that a bank held to back up its notes. **74**

spheres of influence Ports or regions in a nation where a foreign country retains exclusive rights over trade, mines, and railroads. **222**

spirituals Songs modeled in part on Christian hymns and in part on African musical forms. **81**

spoils system Political practice, introduced by Andrew Jackson, of giving government jobs to supporters. **75**

Sputnik (1957) Satellite launched by the Soviet Union that led the U.S. to focus more on technological development. **466**

Square Deal Theodore Roosevelt's 1904 presidential campaign slogan pledging fair treatment for business, workers, and the public. **195**

stagflation Economic condition in which inflation is accompanied by unemployment. **558**

Stamp Act (1765) Law enacted by Parliament that placed a tax on all printed matter in the colonies. **27**

stock Certificates of ownership in a company. **143**

stockholders Owners of certificates in a corporation who receive a certain percentage of the corporation's profits through dividends. **143**

Strategic Arms Limitation Talks (SALT) Agreement between the U.S. and the Soviet Union, limiting the number of intercontinental nuclear missiles each nation could have. **560**

Strategic Defense Initiative (SDI) Space-based missile-defense system proposed by President Ronald Reagan in the 1980s to blunt the nuclear-freeze movement; also called "Star Wars." **588**

strict construction Theory set forth by Thomas Jefferson that the federal government possesses only those powers that the U.S. Constitution specifically allows. **62**

strike Tactic used by labor unions in which workers refuse to work until employers meet union demands. **77**

strikebreakers Nonunion workers brought in by a company to replace striking workers. **155**

Student Nonviolent Coordinating Committee (SNCC) Association formed in 1960 by student activists from throughout the South. **500**

subsidies Payments made to farmers to reduce their production of a crop or commodity. **354**

suffrage Right to vote. **83**

Sugar Act (1764) Law enacted by Parliament that set an import tax on foreign sugar, molasses, and other goods to the colonies. **27**

Sunbelt Southern and western states having warm climates and suburban life-styles. **578**

superpowers Nations that possess great power and become dominant in global politics. **424**

supremacy clause Clause in the U.S. Constitution stating that the federal constitution and all federal laws outrank state constitutions and state laws. **40**

Sussex **pledge** (1916) Renewal of promise by Germany not to sink ocean liners without warning or without assuring the passengers' safety. **249**

Taft-Hartley Act (1947) Federal law that extended government regulation of labor unions and included a provision allowing courts to end strikes. **441**

Tariff Act of 1816 Federal law that placed a 25 percent duty on most imported factory goods. **73**

tariffs Taxes on imported or exported goods. **39**

Tax Reform Law (1986) Federal law that eliminated special tax breaks for certain groups. **592**

Teapot Dome scandal (1926) Scandal in which Secretary of the Interior Albert Fall was convicted of accepting bribes for leasing the government oil reserve in Teapot Dome, Wyoming, to private oil companies. **286**

Teleconferencing Satellite links enabling people at different locations to hold conferences over the telephone. **688**

Teller Amendment (1898) Stated that the U.S. claimed no sovereignty, jurisdiction, or control over Cuba. **216**

temperance movement Reform efforts to curb or limit alcohol consumption. **81**

Tennessee Valley Authority (TVA) New Deal agency created in 1933 to develop power stations and dams throughout the Tennessee River Valley. **355**

termination Government policy during the 1950s designed to end the reservation system. **472**

Tet offensive (1968) North Vietnamese attack on South Vietnam during Tet, the Vietnamese New Year. **535**

Texas longhorn Hardy breed of cattle developed by the 1850s that helped make long drives possible. **132**

Texas Revolution (1835) Revolt against Mexico by Tejanos and American settlers in Texas after the loss of state power. **84**

Third UN Conference on the Law of the Sea (1982) International conference in which participating nations agreed to protect the world's oceans. **739**

Third World The developing nations of Africa, Asia, and Latin America. **638**

Thirteenth Amendment (1865) Constitutional amendment that abolished slavery. **107**

38th parallel Border between North Korea and South Korea set by the Allies in 1945. **455**

Thomasites Group of young Americans who arrived in Manila in 1901 to teach American values and forge a cultural connection with the Philippines. **676**

Three-Fifths Compromise (1787) Agreement made at the Constitutional Convention that counted only three fifths of the slave population in determining total state population. **39**

Tonkin Gulf Resolution (1964) Act that gave the president authority to take all necessary measures to repel an armed attack against U.S. forces. **526**

total war Strategy used in the Civil War of striking at the enemy's economic resources in addition to fighting enemy troops. **102**

Townshend Acts (1767) Law enacted by Parliament that placed duties on goods imported by the colonies. **27**

Trail of Tears (1838) Forced relocation of Cherokees from Georgia to Indian Territory, during which many died. **75**

Trans-Appalachian West Area between the Appalachian Mountains and the Mississippi River. **65**

transcendentalists New England intellectuals who believed people could attain perfection and could acquire knowledge about God, self, and the universe. **723**

Treaty of Brest-Litovsk (1918) Agreement signed by the Bolsheviks in which Russia made a separate peace with the Central Powers and withdrew from World War I. **254**

Treaty of Fort Laramie (1851) Agreement that set boundaries for Native American groups and allowed the U.S. government to build roads and forts through Indian Territory. **122**

Treaty of Ghent Agreement signed in 1814 that ended the War of 1812. **67**

Treaty of Guadalupe Hidalgo Agreement ending the Mexican War in 1848 by which Mexico ceded Texas and the rest of its western territory. **85**

Treaty of Medicine Lodge (1867) Agreement that ended a long-standing war between the Sioux and the U.S. **123**

Treaty of Paris (1783) Agreement signed by Great Britain and the U.S. granting the U.S. independence, territory, and fishing rights. **35**

Treaty of Tordesillas (1494) Agreement that divided control over new territories in the Americas between Spain and Portugal. **12**

Treaty of Versailles (1919) Agreement ending World War I that provided for the establishment of the League of Nations. **264**

trench warfare Strategy used during World War I in which opposing armies dug in along the front to defend their positions. **245**

Triple Alliance Military alliance formed by Germany, Austria-Hungary, and Italy prior to World War I. **243**

Triple Entente Military alliance formed by Great Britain, France, and Russia prior to World War I. **243**

Truman Doctrine U.S. policy of giving military and financial aid to those countries resisting Communist rule. **447**

trunk lines Major railroads connected to surrounding areas by feeder or branch lines. **142**

trust Group of companies that give control of their stock to a board of directors, which then runs the companies as a single enterprise. **143**

trusteeship Post–World War I covenant requiring imperial governments to provide economic development and social services to the colonies they governed under League of Nations mandates. **629**

Twelfth Amendment (1804) Constitutional amendment that requires electors to vote for presidential and vice-presidential candidates on separate ballots. **65**

Twenty-first Amendment (1933) Constitutional amendment that repealed Prohibition. **312**

Twenty-sixth Amendment (1971) Constitutional amendment that lowered the voting age from 21 to 18. **540**

Tydings-McDuffie Act (1934) Federal law that granted independence to the Philippines at the end of a 12-year transition period. **632**

u

ultraviolet solar radiation (UV rays) Radiation from the sun that can cause skin cancer, damage marine life, and harm crops. **736**

unconditional surrender Arrangement whereby the loser agrees to the terms of the victor. **406**

Underground Railroad Network that helped slaves escape to the North or Canada before the Civil War. **80**

Underwood Tariff Act (1913) Federal law that reduced tariffs to their lowest levels in 50 years. **205**

unilateral disarmament Voluntary elimination of nuclear weapons despite the presence of nuclear weapons in other nations. **730**

unilateralism One-sided or independent action in foreign affairs. **380**

United Farm Workers (UFW) Organization of migrant workers formed to win better wages and working conditions. **507**

United Nations (UN) International organization formed in 1945 to work for world peace. **439**

universal coverage Health care for every American. **608**

Universal Declaration of Human Rights Series of basic rights held by all human beings that was adopted by the United Nations in 1948. **708**

University of California v. Bakke (1978) Supreme Court decision that struck down quotas as a means of achieving racial equality; in institutions of higher learning, for example. **576**

urban renewal   Programs designed to replace or restore run-down inner-city buildings. **477**

Uruguay Round   Set of negotiations aimed at boosting global free trade among most of the world's nations. **666**

U.S. Department of Agriculture   Government agency created in 1862 to help farmers. **130**

vertical integration   Strategy whereby one company acquires other companies that provide materials and services necessary to the first company. **144**

Vietcong   Vietnamese Communists. **524**

Vietminh   Resistance movement organized by Ho Chi Minh in 1941; also known as the League for the Independence of Vietnam. **522**

Vietnamization   President Richard Nixon's plan to end the Vietnam War by turning over the fighting to the South Vietnamese army and withdrawing U.S. troops. **537**

Virginia Plan   James Madison's proposal during the Constitutional Convention for shifting power away from the states toward a central government. **38**

Volstead Act (1919)   Federal law that enforced the Eighteenth Amendment (Prohibition). **312**

Voting Rights Act (1965)   Federal law that put voter registration under government control. **504**

Voting Rights Act of 1975   Federal law requiring states and communities with large numbers of non-English speakers to print voting materials in various foreign languages. **579**

Wagner-Connery Act (1935)   Federal law that guaranteed labor's right to organize unions and bargain for better wages and working conditions. **361**

War Industries Board (WIB)   U.S. agency during World War I responsible for allocating scarce materials, establishing production priorities, and setting prices. **258**

war of attrition   Forcing an enemy to fight until they run out of supplies, troops, and will. **102**

War on Poverty   President Lyndon Johnson's Great Society programs designed to end poverty in the U.S. **496**

War Powers Act (1973)   Federal law limiting the president's power to send U.S. troops to foreign conflicts. **544**

War Production Board (WPB)   Government agency during World War II that directed the conversion of existing factories to wartime production. **408**

Warren Commission   Group assigned in 1963 to investigate the assassination of President John Kennedy. **495**

Warsaw Pact (1955)   Alliance formed by the Soviet Union and other Communist countries in Eastern Europe. **450**

Water Quality Improvement Act (1970)   Federal law requiring oil companies to pay some oil spill cleanup costs and setting limits on discharge of industrial pollutants into water. **559**

Watergate   Name given to government scandal that began in 1972 and led to President Richard Nixon's resignation in 1974. **562**

Wealth Tax Act (1935)   Federal law that sharply increased taxes on the rich. **358**

Whiskey Rebellion (1794)   Uprising by western Pennsylvania farmers against a tax on whiskey. **62**

Wisconsin Idea   Program of progressive reforms proposed by Wisconsin governor Robert M. "Fighting Bob" La Follette during the early 1900s. **193**

Women's Christian Temperance Union (WCTU)   Reform group in favor of temperance, moral purity, and the rights of women. **181**

Women's Social and Political Union   Faction of women's suffrage movement led by Emmeline Pankhurst whose aggressive tactics helped British women win the right to vote. **701**

Woodstock (1969)   Three-day rock concert in upstate New York that was one of the high points of the counterculture movement. **513**

Works Progress Administration (WPA)   New Deal agency formed in 1935 to create jobs for people on relief. **357**

World Bank   Ten billion dollar institution created to make loans to war-damaged countries and to encourage industrial development in underprivileged countries. **660**

World Trade Organization   Union of 125 nations that signed a final free-trade agreement dedicated to bring cooperation to world trade issues. **666**

Wounded Knee Massacre (1890)   Massacre that occurred between the Sioux on Wounded Knee Creek and the army sent to confiscate the Indians' rifles. **125**

Yalta Conference (1945)   Postwar peace meeting between the U.S., Britain, and the Soviet Union in which plans were made to divide and occupy Germany. **417**

yellow-dog contracts   Agreements many job applicants signed, promising not to join unions. **155**

yeoman farmers   Small farmers who own and cultivate their own land. **78**

Young Plan (1929)   Revision of the Dawes Plan that spread Germany's $26 billion reparations payments over 59 years. **656**

zaibatsu   Huge corporations run by single families that had monopolized the Japanese economy prior to World War II. **437**

zero population growth (ZPG)   Birthrate that replaces existing population but does not increase it. **578**

Zimmermann Note (1917)   Document that showed that Germany was trying to establish a military alliance with Mexico. **250**

Zionism   Movement, originally intended to promote the founding of a Jewish national state, that called for a Jewish homeland in Palestine. **452**

zoot-suit riots (1943)   Racial attacks by U.S. sailors on Mexican American youths in Los Angeles. **413**

American Red Cross, 99
American Revolution: African
    Americans in, 34; battles, *p25,* 28-29,
    34-35, *m34;* causes of, 29; European
    aid in, 35; events leading to, 26-29;
    financing of, 37-38, *p37;* human rights
    in, 698-99; imperialism and, 622, 623;
    Native Americans in, 26; soldiers in,
    p25, p69, p622; victory in, 35; women
    in, 29, 34
American Samoa, 215, *c224*
Americans with Disabilities Act (1990),
    602
American System, 73
amnesty: after Civil War, 106-07; to
    Vietnam draft evaders, 565, 568
Amnesty International, *c716*
Amos 'n' Andy (radio and TV show), 475
Analyzing, xx
anarchists, 154
Anasazi, 6
Anderson, John, 573, *m573*
Anderson, Marian, 80, 316, 364-65,
    p365, 782
Anderson, Mary, 289
Anderson, Robert, 96
Anderson, Terry, 598, *p598*
Andrews, Avery, 189
Angel Island, 676, *p676*
Angola, *p637, c716*
Annamite Mountains, 520, *m521*
annex, 219
Antarctic Treaty (1959), 729
Antarctica, 729, *m735,* 736
Anthony, Susan B., 208, 782
Antietam, Battle of (1862), 98, *m98,* 100
Antifederalists, 39
Anti-Imperialist League, 220
Anti-Saloon League (ASL), 181
anti-Semitism, 389, 678, 680, 706
antislavery movement, 17-18, *p17,* 82,
    p82, 699-700
antitrust legislation, 145, 196, 199, 205
antiwar movement, 532-33, *p532, p548;*
    and election of 1968, 536-37, *p537;*
    growth of, 538-39
Apaches: 122, 126
apartheid, 571; end of, 715; origin of,
    710, 712
*Appeal to the Colored Citizens of the
    World* (Walker), 82
appeasement, 391
Appomattox Courthouse, Confederate
    surrender at, 103
Aquino, Corazon, 713
Arabian peninsula, 626
Arabic (ship), 249
Arab-Israeli War, 453, *m453,* 454, 681
Arab oil embargo (1973), 558, *c558*
Arabs, 610, 640, 681
Arafat, Yasir, 610, *p611*
Aragon, 8
Arai, Tomie, lithograph by, 614
Arapahos, 123
Arbenz Guzmán, Jacobo, 467
arbitration, 195

archaeologists, 4
architecture, 320
Argentina, 715
Aristide, Jean-Bertrand, *m590,* 610
Arizona: mining in, 134; and sheep
    ranching, 133; Spanish exploration
    and settlement of, 13
Arkansas: secession of, 97
Armenia, *m597,* 599, 642, 685
Armenians, 704, *p704, p715*
armistice, and World War I, 256, *p256*
Armory Show, 206, *p206*
Armstrong, Louis "Satchmo," 274
Armstrong, Neil, 433, 556, *p556*
Army-McCarthy hearings, 464
Army Nurse Corps (ANC), 409
Arnaz, Desi, 274, *p274,* 474, *p474*
art: and Armory Show, 206, *p206;* and
    Ash Can School, *p169;* of Mexican
    muralists, 318-19, *p319;* and New
    Deal, *p348-49,* 372-73, 375, *p375;* in
    1920s, 319, *p319;* pop, 510, *p510*
Arthur, Chester A., 153, *p156,* 782
Articles of Confederation, 36-38, *p37*
Ash Can School, *p169*
Asia: baseball in, 691; decolonization in,
    709-10, 634-36; disease in, 682; eco-
    nomic success of, 664; empires of,
    239; foreign investment in, *c239,* 649;
    human rights abuses in, *c716;* after
    independence, 640-41; migration
    within, 674; MTV in, 692-93; post-
    independence refugees in, 680; post-
    1965 immigration from, 681; Russian
    imperialism in, 623-24; as source of
    raw materials, 625; U.S. trade with,
    m670-71
Asian Americans: art of, 614; boat
    people, 542-43, *p542;* and Chinese
    Exclusion Act, 148, 154; immigration
    after Chinese Exclusion Act, 148;
    immigration in late 1800s, *m118-19,*
    147, 148; immigration in 1970s, 555,
    578-79, *p578;* immigration in 1980s,
    683; and labor unions, 148-154; liter-
    ature of, 429, 614, 615; and mining,
    86, *p134,* 135; and railroad construc-
    tion, 129, *p129;* and western settle-
    ment, 130, *p134,* 135; and World
    War II, *p399,* 401, 410-12, *p410,*
    p411, m411
As I Lay Dying (Faulkner), 338
assembly line, 302-03, *p302*
Assignment in Utopia (Lyons), 185
assimilation, 126; literature about, 549
Association of American Painters and
    Sculptors (AAPS), 206
asylum, 684
Atatürk, Kemal, *p629*
Athens, Greece, 691, 698
Atlanta, GA: capture of, in Civil War,
    102; and civil rights, 500
Atlantic, Battle of the (1941-1943), 416
Atlantic Charter (1941), 394, 634, 707
Atlantic Pact, 449
atlases, 760

atomic bomb: deadlock over, 446-47;
    development of, 421, 686; testing of,
    p446; in World War II, 421, *p421,*
    425, 433
Atomic Energy Act (1946), 447
Atomic Energy Commission (AEC), 447
Attlee, Clement, 436, 635
Attucks, Crispus, 27, *p27*
Auschwitz, Poland, 423
Australia, *c239;* cricket in, 690; enter-
    tainment exports to U.S., 692;
    European migration to, 674; gold rush
    in, 676; and global economy, 664
Austria, 389, 633
Austria-Hungary: and mandate system,
    629; and World War I, 242, 243, *m244*
automation, 476
automobiles, 165, *p304, p305;* impact of,
    304, 306; and Japanese, 665; Model T
    Ford, 165, *p165;* production of, 302-
    03, *p302, p322,* 552; statistics on, 618
autotouring, 305
Axis powers, 391
Azerbaijan, *m597,* 599, 642
Aztecs, *m5,* 6, 11, 13

Babbitt (Lewis), 318, 428-29
Babson, Roger, 326
baby boom, 432, *c432,* 473
Baca, Ezequiel de, 164, *p164*
Baca, Jimmy Santiago, 614, *p614,* 615
Bacall, Lauren, *p450*
Back-to-Africa movement, 292, 293
Baez, Joan, *p512,* 513
Baghdad, Iraq: early history, 7; in
    Persian Gulf War, 599
Bahamas, Columbus and, 10-11, *m22*
Bake, Henry, Jr., *p419*
Baker, Ella, 505, 782
Baker, Howard, 564
Baker, Ray Stannard, 171, 227
Baker v. Carr (1962), 498
Bakke, Allan, 576
Balanced Budget and Emergency
    Control Act (1985), 592
Balboa, Vasco Nuñez de, 12-13, 226
Balch, Emily Greene, 381
Balfour Declaration (1917), 267
Ball, Lucille, 474, *p474*
Ballinger, Richard, 200, *p200*
Baltimore, MD, 67
Bandung Conference (1955), 638
Bangkok, Thailand, 689, *p690*
Bangladesh, 737, *p737,* 738
bank holiday, 350-51
banking: in the depression, 327-28; in
    early 1800s, 73, 74; Hamilton's pro-
    posal for, 62; and Jackson, 75-76;
    New Deal programs for, 350-51; in
    1980s and 1990s, 592, 652; and Panic
    of 1819, 74
Banking Act of 1933, *c359*
Bank of the United States: charter of

first, 62; failure to recharter in 1811, 73; Jackson's opposition to second, 75-76; second, 73
Barbie, Klaus, 438
Barcelona, Spain, 691
barcodes, 689
Bardeen, John, *p687*
bar graph, 757
Barkley, Alben W., 442
Barnum & Bailey's Circus, 151
Barrett, Janie Porter, 150
Barton, Clara, 99
Baruch, Bernard, 258, 446
Baruch Plan (1946), 446-47
baseball, 151, *p151,* 164, 275, 309, *p309,* 337, *p337,* 433, *p433,* 553, *p553;* popularity overseas, 690-91
Basie, Count, 374
basketball, in 1990s, 673, 691
Bataan, Philippines: in World War II, *p400,* 401
Bataan Death March (1942), 401, *p402, m427*
Bates, Daisy, *p481*
Batista, Fulgencio, 491
Baumfree, Isabella. *See* Truth, Sojourner
Bay of Pigs, Cuba, 491-92, *m493*
bear market, 326
Beatles, 432, *p432,* 512
Beats, 481-82
Beauregard, P.G.T., 96, 99
Beauvoir, Simone de, 712, *p712*
bebop, 410
Beck, Walter, 337
Begin, Menachem, 571, 572, *p580*
Beiderbecke, Bix, 315
Beijing, China: protests in, *p696-97,* 697
Belafonte, Harry, 710
Belarus, 599
Belgian Congo. *See* Zaire
Belgium: in Africa, 637, *m637;* and European economic integration, 661; imperialism of, 627; at Washington Conference, 381; and World War I, 243, 244, *m244*
Bell, Alexander Graham, xxiv, 143
Belloc, Hilaire, 626
benevolent societies, 148
Ben-Gurion, David, 452-53
Benton, Thomas Hart, 375; painting by, *p364*
Bentsen, Lloyd, 595
Berger, Victor, 261
Beringia, 4
Berlin airlift (1948), *p445,* 448-49
Berlin Wall; construction of, 492, *p492;* fall of, 599
Bernadotte, Folke, 453
Bernstein, Carl, 563, *p563*
Berry, Chuck, 482, 485, *p485*
Bessemer, Henry, 142
Bessemer process, 142
Bethune, Mary McLeod, 365-66, *p365,* 412
Bhutto, Benazir, 713
bicameral legislature, 38

Bicentennial celebration, *p554-55*
bicycling, 1, 618
Big Four, 263
Bilingual Education Act (1974), 579, *p579*
Bill of Rights (1791), 52, 61; text of, 53-54
Bingham, George Caleb, painting by, *p70-71*
biodiversity, 735, 739
biomass, 734
Bird, Ella, 133
Birmingham, England, 677
Black, Georgia, 711
black codes, 107
Blackfeet, 122
Black Kettle, 123
blacklists, 155
Blackmun, Harry, 557
Black Muslims, 505
black nationalism, 292-93
Black Panther party, 505-06
Black Power, 504-06
Blackshirts, 388
Black Star Steamship Company, 293
Black Thursday (October 24, 1929), 327
Black Tuesday (October 29, 1929), 327
Blackwelder, Julia Kirk, 511
Blackwell, Elizabeth, 99, *p99*
Blair, Henry, xxiv
Blake, Eubie, 316
Blatch, Harriot Stanton, 259
"Bleeding Kansas," 89, *p89*
blitzkrieg, 393
"Blue Meridian, The" (Toomer), 428
Bluford, Guion, 552
boat people, 542-43, *p542,* 681
Bogart, Humphrey, *p450*
Bolsheviks, 254
bonanza farm, 131-32, *p131*
Bonnin, Gertrude S., 184, *p184*
Bonus Army (1932), 343-44, *p343*
Booth, John Wilkes, 106, *p107*
bootlegging, 312
Bork, Robert, 564, 591
Bosch, Juan, 499, *p499*
Bosnia: ethnic fighting in, 609-10; and World War I, 242
Bosque Redondo, NM, 125
Boston, MA: in colonial period, 27, *p27;* police strike in, 280, *p280;* in Revolutionary War, 28
Boston Massacre (1770), 27, *p27*
Boston Tea Party (1773), 27
Bourke-White, Margaret, 371, *p376*
Bow, Clara, 309
Bowen, Louise DeKoven, 178
Boxer, Barbara, 605
Boxer Rebellion (1900), 223, *p620-21,* 626, *p627*
Brace, Charles Loring, 180
braceros, 413
Bradford Singers, *p80*
Brain Trust, 350
Brandeis, Louis D., 175, *p175,* 782, *p782*
"Brandeis Brief," 175

Brando, Marlon, 482
Brant, Joseph. *See* Thayendanegea
Brattain, Walter H., *p687*
Braun, Carol Moseley. *See* Moseley-Braun, Carol
Braun, Werhner von, 686, *p686*
Brazil: deforestation in, 734; and Earth Summit, 739; human rights abuses in, 715
"Bread Line" (Converse), 347
breadlines, 333, *p347*
Bretton Woods system, 660, *p660,* 664
Brezhnev, Leonid, 560
Briand, Aristide, 382
brinkmanship, 466
British Invasion, 432, 512
Brooke, Ed, *p575*
Brown, James, 80
Brown, John, 88; raid of, 90
Brown, Linda, 478
Brown, Ron, 607
Brown, William Wells, 1, 79
Brownpower, 507
Brownshirts, 389
Brown v. The Board of Education of Topeka (1952), 478-79, 498
Bruce, Blanche K., 112
Bryan, William Jennings: in election of 1896, 157; in election of 1908, 199; in Scopes trial, 314; as secretary of state, 248, 249-50
Buchanan, James, 89, *p90,* 782
Buchanan v. Warley, 183
Buchenwald, Germany, 423, *p423*
budget, U.S.: deficit under Bush, 603; deficit under Reagan, 592, *c592;* 1900-1990. *c780;* 1992, *c780*
buffalo, *p121,* 126, 722-23, *p723*
Building Vocabulary, 751
Bulgaria, in World War II, 403
Bulge, Battle of the (1944), 417
bull market, 326
Bull Moose party, 201, *p201*
Bull Run: First Battle of (1861), 97, *m98,* 100; Second Battle of (1862), *m98,* 100
Bunau-Varilla, Philippe, 228
Bunche, Ralph, 453, *p453,* 782
Bunker Hill, Battle of (1775), 28
Bureau of Indian Affairs, 123, 137, 184, 576, 606
Burger, Warren: appointment of, to Supreme Court, 557; retirement of, 591
Burleson, Albert, 281
Burma (Myanmar): and military rule, 716; in World War II, 401
Burnham, Daniel, 179, *p179,* 181
Burnside, Ambrose E., 100
Burr, Aaron, 64
Bursum Bill, 290
Bush, George, 602, *p602,* 782; domestic problems of, 601-03; and economy, 603; in election of 1984, 591; in election of 1988, 595-97; in election of 1992, 585, 604, 605; and foreign affairs, 597, 599, 601; and Immigration Act (1990), 683; and legacy of

Vietnam War, 544; and Persian Gulf War, 599; as vice president, 573
business: deregulation of, 587; and health care, 609; impact of technological advances on, 652, 688; regulation of, under Theodore Roosevelt, 195-97; rise of big, 143-45; and Wilson, 205, *p205*, 207
business cycle, 330, 648-49
busing, 557, *p575*, 575-76, 581, 586

cabinet, 61
Cabot, John, 15, *m22*
Cabrillo, Juan Rodríguez, 13, *m22*
Cahokia, 6
Cairo, Egypt: 1943 conference in, 406, *p406;* recycling in, 738-39
Calcutta, India, 685
Calhoun, John C., 74, 87, 88
California: admitted to Union, 88; African Americans in, 86; bonanza farms in, 131, *p131;* Chinese Americans in, *c118,* 148, *p148;* counterculture in, 508-09, *p508, p509;* dance in, 1; election of 1860, 91; election of 1968, 536; and the environment, 559; gold in, 86-87, 675; Great Depression in, 334, 370; Japanese Americans in, 410-11, *m411;* and Mexican Cession, *m86;* Mexican immigration to, 259, *m294,* 295, *p295;* Mexican muralists in, 318-19; in Mexican War, 85; migrant workers in, 367, 369, *p369,* 373, 507; mining in, 86-87, *p120-21;* Native Americans in, 86-87, 122; population migration to, 578; racial unrest in, 576; and sheep ranching, 133; Spanish settlement of, 13-14, 86; U.S. expansion into, 86-87, 623; zoot-suit riots in, 413
California Trail, 86
Californios, 86, 135
call number, 760
Cambodia, 520, *m521;* post–Vietnam War immigrants from, 681; spread of Vietnam War to, 541; U.S. bombing of, 538; U.S. policy toward, 566
Camden, Battle of (1780), *m34,* 35
Campbell, Ben Nighthorse, *p605*
Camp David Accords (1978), 572, 610
Canada: and acid rain, 736; conservation in, 726; entertainment exports to U.S., 692; exploration of, 15, *m22-23;* and French and Indian War, 19; gold rush in, 676; and Montreal Protocol, 739; and NAFTA, 666; in Revolutionary War, 34; Russian Jews in, 678; and Underground Railroad, 80; U.S. immigration to, 676; and War of 1812, 67
Canadian Forestry Association, 726
canals, development of, 73
Cannon, Joseph "Uncle Joe," 201
Canseco, Jose, 690

Cape of Good Hope, 626
capitalism, laissez-faire. *See* laissez-faire capitalism
Capone, Al, 312
card catalog, 760
Cárdenas, Lázaro, 387, *p387*
Cardozo, Francis L., 112
Caribbean: baseball in, 690; Columbus in, *m22;* slave trade to, 675
Carlisle Indian School, 126-27, *p127*
Carnegie, Andrew, 143-44, 150-51, 155, 628
Carnegie Steel Company, 145
Carolinas, settlement of, 18, *p18. See also* North Carolina; South Carolina
Carpenter, Liz, 496-97
Carranza, Venustiano, 176, 232, 233-34, *p233*
Carson, Rachel, 433, 475, 730-31
Carter, Amy, 568, *p568*
Carter, Jimmy, 569, *p569,* 782; criticism of, 572-73; economic policy of, 569; in election of 1976, 567; in election of 1980, 572-73, *m573;* energy policy of, 569-70, *p569, p570;* foreign policy of, 570-72, *p570, p571,* 715; and human rights, 570-71, 715; negotiations in Haiti, 610; presidential style of, 568-69, *p568*
Carter, Lillian, 568
Carter, Rosalynn, 568, *p568,* 569
cartographers, 754
Carver, George Washington, 275, *p275*
Casablanca, Morocco, 406
Cass, Lewis, 87
Castañeda, Carlos E., 412-13
Castile, 8
Castro, Fidel, 491-92, *p491,* 681, 782
Castro, Raul H., 496
Catcher in the Rye, The (Salinger), 482
Catt, Carrie Chapman, 208, 259, *p382,* 782
cattle industry, xxiv, 132-33, *m132,* 651, *p651*
caudillos, 385-86
Cause and Effect, Identifying, xx, 749-50
censorship, 313
Central Intelligence Agency (CIA): and Bay of Pigs, 492; and contras, 589-90; covert activities of, 466-68; creation of, 450
Central Pacific Railroad, 129, *m132*
Central Powers, 243, *c245*
Century of Dishonor (Jackson), 126
CFCs. *See* chlorofluorocarbons
Chad, *c716*
Chamberlain, Austen, 656
Chamberlain, Neville, 391, 633
Chambers, Whittaker, 451
Chamorro, Emiliano, 386
Chancellorsville, Battle of (1863), *m98,* 100
Chaney, James, 503
Charles II (King of England), 18
Charles Town, SC, 18
Charleston (dance), 80, 316
Charleston, SC, 18, 96

Charter of 1606, 15
Charts and Graphs, Reading, 756-58
Château-Thierry, France, 254, *m255*
Chattanooga, Battle of (1863), *p94-95, m99*
Chávez, César, 370, 507, 512, 782
checks and balances, 40-41
Chernobyl nuclear disaster, 733-34
Cherokee Phoenix (newspaper), 1
Cherokees, 75, 606
Chesapeake Bay, settlement of, 17-18
Chestnut, Mary Boykin, 105
Cheyenne, 123
Chiang Kai-shek, 406, *p406,* 454, *p454*
Chicago, IL: African Americans in, 291-92, *p291;* antiwar protest in, 536-37, *p537;* and Haymarket Riots, 154, *c154;* and Hull House, 150; meatpacking industry in, 167, 211, *p211;* Mexican American migration to, 295; planning in, 179, *p179;* population growth of, 677; and Pullman strike, 155; race riot in, 291-92, *p291;* and social reform, 167
Chicano movement, 507
Chickasaws, 75, 93
Chief Joseph. *See* Joseph, Chief
child labor, *p140-41,* 153, *p153,* 173, *p173,* 702; in Great Britain, 702, *p702*
Children's Aid Society, 180
Chile: human rights abuses in, 714; U.S. policy toward, 560
Chiles, Lawton, 683
China: communications advances in, 688; Communist victory in, 454-55; and decline of empire, 239; democracy movement in, *p696-97,* 697; early trade networks, 6; emigrants from, in 1980s, 683; human rights abuses in, 714, 716, *c716;* Japanese emigrants in, 674; Japanese invasion of, 382, 394, *m395,* 632, 680, 706; and Korean War, 456-57; migrants from, 674; missionaries in, 676, *p677;* Nixon visit to, 560; and occupation of Vietnam, 521; in Pacific Rim, 664; refugees in, 680; and resistance to foreign influence, 223, 626; spheres of influence in, 222, 625; television in, 691; U.S. involvement in, 222-23, 625, 649; in Washington Conference, 381; in World War II, 707
Chinese Americans: against Japanese invasion of China, *p680;* and gold mining, 86, *p134,* 135; immigration of, *c118, m118,* 147, 148, *p148;* literature of, 614; nativist attitudes toward, 676, *p676;* population, 1890-1920, 676; and railroad construction, 129, *p129;* and unemployment, 148; and western settlement, *c118,* 130
Chinese Exclusion Act (1882), 148, 154, 676
Chinooks, 86
Chisholm, Shirley, *p577,* 782-83, *p782*
Chivington, John, 123

chlorofluorocarbons (CFCs), 736, 739
Choctaws, 75, *p623*
cholera, 682
Christian Century, 379
Christopher, Warren, 610
Churchill, Winston, 783; and Atlantic
  Charter, 394, 634; and India, 634-35;
  and Iron Curtain speech, 446; in
  World War II, 391, 405, 406, 418; at
  Yalta Conference, 424, *p424*
CIA. *See* Central Intelligence Agency
circle graph, 757
circumnavigate, 12, *m13*
CIS. *See* Commonwealth of Independent
  States
Cisneros, Henry, 607
cities: culture in, 151; in developing
  countries, 685; growth of, in 1800s,
  119, *c164*, 428-29, 677; immigrants
  in, 683; impact of railroads, 142;
  impact of skyscrapers, 148, 320;
  impact of technology, *c119*, 148-49,
  p149; migration to, 677; planning in,
  179, *p179*, 181; poor in, 149, *p149;*
  population of, 516, 677; prosperity of,
  678; recycling in, 738-39; reforms in,
  150-51, *p150*, 178-79, *p179*, 192-93.
  See also specific cities
"Civilian and Soldier" (Soyinka), 742
Civilian Conservation Corps (CCC),
  352, *p352, c359*, 364, 728
Civil Rights Act (1866), 108, *p108*
Civil Rights Act (1957), 481
Civil Rights Act (1964), 503, 510
Civil Rights Bill (1875), 111, p111
civil rights movement: and affirmative
  action, 575; backlash against, 575-76,
  p575; and *Brown* v. *The Board of
  Education*, 478-79, 498; Committee on
  Civil Rights, 442; events in, *c502-06,
  p548, p549;* Freedom Rides in, 501,
  m501, p501; and Freedom Summer,
  503-04; for Hispanic Americans, 507,
  574; impact of decolonization on, 709-
  10; importance of music to, 711; influence of Gandhi on, 710; legacy of,
  574-75; and March on Washington,
  p486-87, 502-03; under Martin Luther
  King, Jr., 479, 500, *p500*, 506;
  Montgomery bus boycott in, 479-80,
  p479; for Native Americans, 507, 576-
  77, *p576, p577;* nonviolence in, 500;
  and people with disabilities, 574-75,
  p575; and segregation fight in Little
  Rock, 480-81, *p480, p481;* successes
  and setbacks in, 502. *See also*
  women's rights movement
Civil War: African Americans in, 101,
  103, *p103;* battles in, *p94-95*, 97-99,
  100, 102-03, *m102, p103;* casualties
  of, *c104;* comparison of sides, 97,
  c97; consequences of, 104; declaration of sides in, 97; European response
  to, 98; fall of Fort Sumter in, 96, *p96;*
  military experience in, 99; northern
  opposition to, 100-01; strategies in,

97-98, *c100*, 101-02; surrender in,
  103-04; war in the East, 98, *m98;* war
  in the West, 98-99, *m99;* women in,
  99-100, *p99*
Civil Works Administration (CWA),
  352, *c359*
Clansman, The (Dixon), 112
Clapton, Eric, 80
Clark, Dick, *p482*
Clark, William, 65
Clay, Henry, 72-73, 74, 88
Clayton Antitrust Act (1914), 205
Clayton-Bulwer Treaty (1850), 226
Clean Air Act (1970), 559, 732
Clean Water Act. *See* Federal Water
  Pollution Control Act
Clear and Present Danger (movie), 692
Clemenceau, Georges, 263, *p263*
Clemens, Samuel Langhorne. *See* Twain,
  Mark
Clemente, Roberto, 690
Clements, Frederic, 724
Cleveland, Grover, 148, 153, *p156*, 157,
  783
Cleveland, OH, 179, 181
Clifford, Clark, 534
climate, 724
Clinton, Bill, 605, *p604, p605*, 783;
  appointments of, 607; and Bosnian
  crisis, 609-10; and China, 716; and
  crime, 607-08; economy under, 607;
  in election of 1992, 585, 604-05; and
  Family and Medical Leave Act, 608;
  and health care reform, 608-09; and
  Information Superhighway, 687; and
  Middle East accord, 610, *p611;* and
  Whitewater affair, 611
Clinton, Hillary Rodham, 605, *p605*,
  608, 783, *p783*
closed shop, 176
Closing Circle, The (Commoner), 732
Clotel (Brown), 1
coaling stations, 625
Coalition of Labor Union Women, 512
Coast Guard, U.S., 683
Cobden-Chevalier Treaty (1860), 654
Cold War, 445, *c456, m467;* and Berlin
  crisis, 448-50, *p448*, 492; and Carter,
  571; commentary on postwar period,
  643; communism in China, 453-55;
  containment in, 447-48; and Cuban
  missile crisis, 492-94, *m493;* deadlock
  over atomic weapons in, 446-47,
  p446; defenses, *m467;* and détente,
  560, 593; and development of
  Internet, 686-87; and domino theory,
  522-23; end of, 597-99, 665; and
  Eastern Europe, 468, *p468;* and
  Eisenhower, 466-68; and Ford, 566;
  and Freedom of Information Act, 598;
  and human rights, 714-15; and impact
  on global economy, 660; and
  Kennedy, 491; and Korean War, 455-
  57, *m455, p457*, 463; Middle East tensions in, 452-53, *m453;* and Nixon,
  559-60; and nuclear bombs, 464-66,

p464, c466; and Reagan, 588-91, 593;
  roots of, 445-46; in the Third World,
  638-39; in U.S., 450-51, *p450, p451;*
  and Vietnam, 636; and Zaire, 637-38
Colfax, Schuyler, 152
Collier, John, 366
Collins, Elizabeth, 135-36
Colombia, *c716*
Colonial America, 16-18, *m23*, 26-28,
  722. *See also* specific colonies
Color (Cullen), 317
Colorado: mining in, 134, 135; Sand
  Creek Massacre in, 123, *m124*
Colored Farmers' Alliance, *p155*
Columbia Broadcasting System (CBS),
  308
Columbian exchange, 11-12
Columbus, Christopher, 3, 10-12, 15,
  783; legacy of, 11-12; voyages of, *m22*
Comanches, 121, 122, 123
Committee for a Sane Nuclear Policy
  (SANE), 466
Committee for Unemployment Relief,
  340
Committee on Civil Rights, 442
Committee on Public Information
  (CPI), 260
Committee on the Cause and Cure of
  War, 391
Committee to Re-elect the President
  (CREEP), 563
Commoner, Barry, 732
Common Sense (Paine), 29
commonwealth, 17
Commonwealth of Independent States
  (CIS), 599
communications: advances in, 142-43;
  and cellular phones, 688, 689, *p689;*
  digital, 688; electronic, 652, 687; and
  global economy, *m670-71;* and
  Information Revolution, 686-88; and
  National Information Infrastructure,
  687-88, *p688;* and newsgroups, 687;
  privacy issues in, 689; and teleconfer-
  encing, 688; transatlantic, 650-52
communism: in Asia, 453-55, 522-23;
  and McCarthyism, 463-64; and Red
  Scare, 281-82, *p281*, 450-51, *p450;*
  rise of, 706
Communist Manifesto (Marx), 678
Communist party (U.S.): and
  Progressive party, 443; and Red Scare,
  281-82, *p281*, 450-51, *p450;* and
  Scottsboro case, 343; and Share-Our-
  Wealth program, 357
Comparing and Contrasting, xx
compass rose, 752
Compromise of 1850, 88
Compromise of 1877, 111
computers: development of, 686; mainframe, 687; minicomputers, 687; net-
  works of, 652. 686-88; numbers of,
  c618; personal, 687; UNIVAC I, 433
Comstock Lode, 134
concentration camps, 423-24, *p423, p707*
Concord, Battle of (1776), 28

Gehrig, Lou, 337
Geiger counter, *p730*
General Agreement on Tariffs and Trade (GATT), 660, 666
General Federation of Women's Clubs, 170, 291
generation gap, 508
Geneva Conference (1954), 523-24
Geneva Convention (1864), 703
Genoa, Italy, 9
genocide, 423
Genthe, Arnold, photograph by, *p185*
geography: of Africa, *m239;* of agriculture, 298-99, *m298-99;* of Asia, *m239;* of Australia, *m239;* of cities, *m516, m517;* of Europe, *m239;* five themes of, 8; and immigration, 118, *m118-19;* and imperialism, 238-39, *m238-39;* of North America, *m238;* of South America, 238, *m238;* of the West, *m189*
George, Henry, 141
George III (king of England), 28, 29, 631, 698
Georgia (CIS), *m597,* 599, 642
Georgia (U.S.): in Civil War, 102; secession of, 91; settlement of, 18
German Americans, 18, 78, *c118, m118, m119,* 130, 247
German reunification (1990), 599
Germany: AFSC aid to, 705; and Berlin airlift, *p445,* 448, *p448;* currency bloc in 1930s, *m657;* and European economic integration, 661-62; expansion of, 632-33; foreign investment in, *c238-39;* Green party in, 731; and Holocaust, 423-24; impact of war debt and reparations on, 382-83, *p383;* inflation in, 383, *p383;* involvement in China, 222-23; and Jewish refugees, 680; and mandate system, 629; Nazis in, *p378-79,* 389, *p389,* 390-91, *m392,* 706; post–World War II occupation of, 436-37, 445; refugees in, 684; and reparations after World War I, 656; reunification of, 599, 684; "rubble women" in, *p661;* signing of nonaggression pact with Soviet Union, 392; and tariff wars, 654-55; wildlife management in, 727; in World War I, 243, 244-45, *m244,* 247-48, 249, *p268,* 704; in World War II, 391-94, 403, *p403, m404,* 405, 417-18, *c423,* 707. *See also* East Germany, West Germany
Geronimo, *m124,* 126, 784
Gershwin, George, 315-16
Gettysburg, Battle of (1863), 98, *m98, c100*
Gettysburg Address, (Lincoln), 98; text of, 768
Ghana, 7, *p636, p640*
Ghose, Aurobindo, 630
Ghost Dance, 125, *p125*
GI Bill of Rights (1944), 440, *p440*
Gibraltar, 626
Gideon v. *Wainright* (1963), 498

Gilded Age, The (Twain and Warner), 152, *p152,* 161
Gillespie, Dizzy, 410
Gilpin, Charles, 316
Gingrich, Newt, 609
Ginsberg, Douglas, 591
Ginsburg, Ruth Bader, 607, *p607*
Ginzberg, Susan, *p729*
glasnost, 593
global grid, 753
global warming, 736
Glorious Revolution, 698
glyph, 6
Goldman, Emma, 282, *p282*
Goldmark, Josephine, 175, *p175*
gold rush: in Australia, 676; in California, 86-87, *p120-21,* 675; in Canada, 676
gold standard, 653-54, 657-58, *m657;* and Bretton Woods system, 660; U.S. abandonment of, 664
Gold Standard Act (1900), 653
Goldwater, Barry M., 497, 784
Gompers, Samuel, 155, 176, 311
Gone with the Wind (Mitchell), 373, *p373*
Goodman, Andrew, 503
Goodman, Benny, 274, 374
Good Neighbor policy, 384-85
Gorbachev, Mikhail, 593, *p593,* 597, 599, 784
Gore, Albert, 605, 607, 687, *p687*
Gorgas, William C., 225, 227
graduated income tax, 156
Gramm-Rudman-Hollings Act (1985), 592
Grange movement, 155-56
Grant, Madison, 184-85
Grant, Ulysses S., 784; in Civil War, 98-99, 101-04, *p109;* and corruption, 152-53; elected president (1868), 109
Grapes of Wrath, The (Steinbeck), 373
Gravier, Charles, 25
Gray, John, 717
Great Britain: and abandonment of gold standard, 657; and abolition of slavery and slave trade, 699-700; African territory, *m637;* and Atlantic Charter, 394; and blitzkrieg, 393-94, *p394;* and border settlement, 85; and Bretton Woods system, 660; child labor in, 702, *p702;* conservation in, 726; and cricket, 690; emigrants from, 675; entertainment exports to U.S., 692; foreign investment and trade of, *c238-39, m238-39;* Glorious Revolution in, 698; and gold standard, 653; during Great Depression, 656-57; Green party in, 731; human rights abuses in, *c716;* imperialism of, 622-23, 624-27, *p624;* and impressment, 62; in India, 630, 634-35; involvement in China, 222, 649; and Jay's Treaty, 63; and Latin America, 624; and Lend-Lease Act, 393; and mandate system, 629; Margaret Thatcher in, 713; in North America, *m22, m23;* and nuclear

weapons, 729; Palestinian independence, 681; and Panama Canal, 226, 228; at Paris Peace Conference, 705; in Persian Gulf War, 599; post–War of 1812 relations with, 67, 72; response to facism, 391; and the South, 98; and South African independence, 712; and tariffs, 654, 655; urban growth in, 677; and War of 1812, 66-67, *p67;* at Washington Conference, 381, *p381;* withdrawal from India, 635, 680; women's suffrage in, 701; and World War I, 243-45, *m244, p246,* 247, *c267,* 704; after World War I, 655; in World War II, *p422. See also* England
Great Compromise (1787), 38
Great Depression, *p324-25;* beginning of, 327-28; causes of, 326, 328-30; and disruption of world trade, 656-58; end of, 661; family life in, 335, *p335;* farm crisis in, 341; global impact of, *m329,* 333, 656-58; Hoover's philosophy on, 339-45, *p340;* and impact on global migration, 680; migrant labor during, 367, 368-69, *p368,* 370, *p370;* and Philippine independence, 632; photographing, 368-69, *p368, p369,* 370-71, *p371;* psychological impact of, 335-36; and rise of fascism, 705; rural life in, 333-35; stock market crash in, 327, *c327;* unemployment in, 331-32, *p331, m332;* urban life in, 332-33, *p333*
Great Gatsby, The (Fitzgerald), 318
Great Migration, 16; of African Americans, 259-60
Great Plains: farming, 130; buffalo on, 722-23; Dust Bowl in, 727-28; Native Americans in, 122; trunk lines crossing, 142
Great Society, 497-98, 499, 556
Great Train Robbery, The (movie), 181-82, *p181*
Great Upheaval (1886), 154
"Great White Fleet," 224
Greece: development of citizens' rights in, 698; Olympics in, 691; in World War II, 403
Greek Americans, 147
Greeley, Horace, 677
Green Berets, 491
Greene, Graham, 519
Greene, Nathanael, 35
greenhouse effect, 736
Green parties, 731
Greenpeace, 735
Green Rage (Manes), 741
Greensboro, NC, 500, 710
Grenada, U.S. invasion of, *m590,* 591, *p591*
Griffith, D. W., 112
Grimké, Angelina, 82, 700, 784
Grimké, Sarah, 784
gross national product, 327, *m671*
Grove, Andrew S., 688
Guadalcanal, in World War II, *m402,* 403

Guam, in World War II, 401, *m402, 418*
Guantánamo Bay, Cuba, 225, 226; Naval Aviation Camp at, *p164, p610;* refugees at, *p610,* 683
Guatemala: human rights abuses in, 715; rise of military dictatorship in, 385; U.S. intervention in, 467
"Guerrilla War" (Ehrhart), 547
guerrilla warfare: in American Revolution, 35; in Vietnam War, 528
Guiteau, Charles, 153
Gulf of Thailand, 520, *m521*
Gulf of Tonkin, 520, *m521,* 526
gun control, 586, 608
Gutenberg, Johannes, 8
Gypsies, 437

hacienda, 14
Haeckel, Ernst, *p721,* 724
Hagedorn, Jessica, 614, 615
Hague Peace Conferences, 703
Haig, Alexander, 588
Haight-Ashbury, 509, *p509*
Hainan, post–World War II, 424
Haiphong Harbor, 539
Haiti: instability in, *m590,* 610; refugees from, 610, *p610,* 681, *p681;* U.S. occupation of, 610; U.S. policy toward, 230; withdrawal of U.S. marines from, 384
Haitians: immigration of, 681, *p681*
Halberstam, David, 531
Haldeman, H. R. (Bob), 539
Hall, Fawn, 594, *p594*
Hall, Vicki, 691
Hamer, Fannie Lou, 710, 711
Hamilton, Alexander, 61-62, 784
Hammond, Samuel, 723
Hanna, Mark, 194-95, 649
Hanoi, Vietnam, 520, *m521,* 522, 535, 539
Hanson, Ole, 279
Harding, Warren G., 284-86, *p285,* 784; death of, 286; domestic policies of, 285-86; election of, in 1920, 284; scandals under, 286, *p286*
hard-rock mining, 136
Harlem Experimental Theatre, 317
Harlem Renaissance, 316-18, *m317;* literature of, 428
Harpers Ferry, 90
Harrington, Michael, 496
Harris, Patricia, 574
Harrison, Benjamin, *p156,* 784
Harrison, William Henry, 66, *p76,* 784
"Harry Wilmans" (Masters), 271
Hawaii: Japanese attack on, *p398-99,* 399, *m402;* Japanese emigrants in, 674; labor in, *p221;* and statehood, *m485;* U.S. acquisition of, 221-22, 625
Hawaiian League, 221-22
hawks, 532
Hay, John, 223, 226, 228, *p228*
Hay-Bunau-Varilla Treaty (1903), 228

Hayden, Sterling, *p450*
Hayes, Rutherford B., 111, *p156,* 784
Hay-Herrán Treaty (1903), 228
Haymarket Riot (1886), 154, *c154*
Hay-Pauncefote Treaty (1901), 228
Hayslip, Le Ly, 541
Haywood, "Big Bill," 176-77
Head Start, 496
health: and cigarettes, 552; and food, 552, *c552*
health care: crisis in, 608; and national health insurance, 443; reform, 608-09; use of interactive television in, 688
Hearst, William Randolph, 215-16
Heckler, Margaret, 591
Heit, Molly, *p491*
Hellman, Lillian, 374, *p374*
Hemingway, Ernest, 318, 390, 784
Henderson, Fletcher, 316
Hendrix, Jimi, 512-13, *p512*
Henry VII (king of England), 8
Henry of Portugal, 9, 784, *p784*
Henry Street Settlement, *p150*
Henson, Matthew, 165
Hepburn Act (1906), 196
Heritage Foundation, 586
Herzegovina: and World War I, 242
Hessing, Valjean, painting by, *p623*
Hicks, Edward, painting by, *p18*
Highway Act (1956), *m472,* 473
Hill, Anita, 602-03, *p602*
Hilton, James, 338
Hindus, in India, 640
hippies, 509
Hirohito, Emperor, 401, 437, *p437*
Hiroshima, *m402,* 421, *p421,* 437, 464, 707
Hispanic Americans: and civil rights movement, 555, 574; in 1930s, *m294;* and poverty, 461; unemployment of, 569, 587; and urban renewal, 477; in Vietnam War, 527; in World War II, 413. *See also* Cuban Americans; Mexican Americans; Puerto Ricans
Hiss, Alger, 451
Historical Documents. *See* individual titles of documents
Historical Imagination, Using, xix
"History of the Standard Oil Company" (Tarbell), 170-71
Hitler, Adolf, 383, 389, 391, *p393,* 394, 418, 632-33, *p633,* 706
HIV. *See* Human Immunodeficiency Virus
Hmong, 542-43
Hobby, Oveta Culp, 470, *p470,* 784
Ho Chi Minh, 521-22, *p522,* 523, 524, 539, 630-31, 636
Ho Chi Minh City, Vietnam, 520, *m521*
Ho Chi Minh Trail, 529, *m529,* 538
Holly, Buddy, 483
Hollywood Ten, 450
Holmes, Oliver Wendell, 261, 281
Holocaust, 423-24, *p423,* 435, 707, *p707*
Holocaust Kingdom, The (Donat), 427
Holt Street Baptist Church, 711

Holy Land, 7
homelessness: in Great Depression, 333, *p333,* 335; in 1980s, 587, *p588;* in former Yugoslavia, 684
Home Loan Bank Act (1932), 341, 342
Home Owners Loan Corporation (HOLC), 351, *c359*
Homer, Winslow, painting by, 762
Homestead Act (1862), 128
Homestead strike, *c154,* 155
Home to Harlem (McKay), 317
Honduras, 385
Honecker, Erich, 599
Hong Kong: and global economy, 664; in World War II, 401, *m402*
Hooker, Joseph "Fighting Joe," 100
Hoover, Herbert, 328, *p328,* 349, 784-85; domestic policies under, 288, *p288;* in election of 1928, 287-88, *p287;* and election of 1932, 344-45; and Great Depression, 327, 328, 332; as head of Food Administration, 258, *p258;* and moratorium on reparations and war debts, 383; philosophy of, 339-44, *p339, p340;* as secretary of commerce, 285; withdraws U.S. troops from Nicaragua, 386
Hoover, J. Edgar, and Palmer raids, 281-82
Hoover Dam, 341, *p341*
Hope, Bob, 410
Hopewells, 6, *p6*
Hopis, 122
Hopkins, Harry, 351-52
Hopper, Edward, 319; painting by, *p319*
horizontal integration, 144
Horton, Willie, 596
"hot line," 494
Houdini, Harry, 164, *p164*
Houplines, France, *p240-41*
House Committee on Un-American Activities (HUAC), 450-51, *p450*
House of Burgesses, 27
House of Mirth (Wharton), 151
House of the Spirits, The (Allende), 743
Housing and Urban Development Act (1968), 498
Houston, Sam, 84
How the Other Half Lives (Riis), 189
Howe, Frederic, 141
Howe, William, 30
Howells, William Dean, 146, 151
Hubble telescope, 552, *p552*
Hue, Vietnam, 520, *m521*
Huerta, Victoriano, 232-33
Hughes, Charles Evans, 250, *p285,* 381
Hughes, Langston, 316, 317-18, *p318,* 785
Hull House, 150, 179
human-environment interaction, 8
Human Immunodeficiency Virus (HIV), 608
human rights, 570, 696-97; abuses, 714-717; *c716;* and Carter, 570-71, 715; and the Cold War, 714-15; and decolonization, 709-10; in former Soviet Union, 714-15; in French Revolution, *p718;* in 1930s, 705-07; in Latin

America, 714, 715; non-Western views of, 717; origins of, 698-99; progessivism and, 702; and racial equality, 705; and slavery, 699-700; UN and, 707-08; and war, 703-05, 707; for women, 701

Humphrey, Hubert: in election of 1964, 497; in election of 1968, 536-37

Hungary: 587; free elections in, 599; Soviet troops in, 589; uprising in (1956), 468, *p468;* in World War II, 403, *m404*

hunger: and AFSC, 705; and Chinese Americans, 332-33; in Great Depression, 332-34, 335, *p337;* and Great Society, 497; and Irish, 78; and Mexican Americans, 332-38; and New Deal, 354; in Somalia, 685

hunter-gatherers, 4

Hurston, Zora Neale, 373, 785

Hussein, Saddam, 599

Hutus, *p679,* 685

hydraulic mining, 136

hydrogen bomb, 464-66

Hypothesizing, xxii

"I Am Waiting" (Ferlinghetti), 549

Ibn Sina, 7

Ickes, Harold, 353, 364-65

Idaho: cattle trails in, *m132;* Indian reservations in, *m124;* mining in, 134

Idrīsī, Abū al-, map drawn by, *p8*

"I Have a Dream" Speech (King), 770-71

Illinois, 73, 90, 173

I Love Lucy (television show), 474, *p474*

IMF. *See* International Monetary Fund

immigrants: *c147;* African, 675; Arab, 147; Armenian, 147; Asian, 86, 118, *c118, m118-19,* 147, 148, 578-79, 681; assimilation of, 184-85, *p185;* British, 675; Cambodian, 681; Central American, 681; Chinese, 129, 147, 148, *p148,* 675, 676, 683; and Civil War draft riots, 100; communities of, 78, 148; Croatian, 675; Cuban, 681, 683; Danish, 18, 130; education levels of, 683; English, 18; European, 675-76, 678, 681; Filipino, 683, *p683;* French Canadian, 147; French Huguenot, 18; German, 18, 78, 130, 675, 678; and gold rush, 675; Greek, 147, 675; Haitian, 681, *p681;* Hungarian, 147, 675; Indian, 683, *p683;* Irish, 78, 129, 130, 675; Italian, 147, 675; Jamaican, 673; Japanese, 147; Jewish, 18, 147; Korean, 683; and labor relations, 279; Laotian, 681; Latin American, 681-82; life of, 78, 148-49; Mennonite, 130; Mexican, 683; new, 147-48; Nigerian, 673; Norwegian, 130; Polish, 147, 675; Puritan, 16-17; Romanian, 675;

Russian Jews, 675, *p678;* Scandinavian, 678; Scotch-Irish, 18; Scots, 18; Slovak, 675; Swedish, 130; Ukrainian, 675; Vietnamese, 681, 683; in West, *p129,* 130; West Indian, 18; working conditions of, 78, 148, 176

immigration, *c147, c779;* Asian, 86, 118, *c118, m118-19,* 147, 148, 578-79, 674; to Australia, 676; boat people, 542-43, *p542,* 681; to Canada, 676; debate over, 683; in 1800s, *cxxiv,* 78, 675; European, *c118, m118-19;* future of, *p683-84;* late 1800s, *c118,* 675; Latin American, 86, 471, 478-79; nativist response to, 78, *p78,* 148, 676; 1920s restrictions on, 294, 680; after 1965, 681; post–World War I, 679; post–World War II, 680-81; of sports figures, 673; to Texas, 84; to U.S., *c779,* 675-76; U.S. attitudes toward, in 1990s, 683

Immigration Act (1924), 294, 679

Immigration Act (1965), 681

Immigration Act (1990), 683

Immigration Restriction League, 148

impeachment, 40; of Andrew Johnson, 108-09, *p109;* and Watergate, 564

imperialism, 214-15, 238-39, 709, 620-43; in Africa, *m637;* and American expansionism, *c224,* 623; and application of Monroe Doctrine, 228-30; British, 624-27, *p624;* and building of Panama Canal, 226-28; and China, 222-23, 625; commentary on, 234-35; European, 622-23, 624-27; and government of Cuba and Puerto Rico, 225-26; and Hawaii, 221-22, 625; and industrialization, 625-27; and Japan, 223-24, 625, 632; and Latin America, *m234,* 625; legacies of, 640-43; and Mexican Revolution, 232-34; motives for, 625-26; and Pacific territories, *m220;* and Philippines, 219-21, 625; Russian, 623-24; and Spanish-American War, 215-18, *m217;* World War I and, 628-31; World War II and, 634-37

impressment, 62, 622, *p622*

Incas, 13

indentured servant, 17

India, 674; Bangladeshis in, 738; British imperialism in, 625, 626; British withdrawal from, 635, 680; cars in, 618; cricket in, 690; disease in, 682; emigrants from, in 1980s, 683; independence of, 634-35; Indira Gandhi in, 713, *p713;* Mohandas Gandhi in, 630, 634-35, 710; MTV and Indian bands, 692-93; popularity of U.S. television in, 692; population of, 737; post-independence conflicts in, 640-41; as source of raw materials, 625

Indiana, 131

Indian Affairs, Bureau of. *See* Bureau of Indian Affairs

Indian National Congress, 630

Indian policy, 126-27

Indian removal, under Jackson, 75, *p623*

Indian Removal Act (1830), 75

Indian Reorganization Act (1934), 366

Indians. *See* Native Americans

indirect rule, 627

Indochina, *m521, m546,* 630-31, 636, *p636*

Indonesia: Bandung Conference in, 638; economic growth in, 664; human rights abuses in, *c716;* human rights advances in, 715; independence of, 635

industrial design, 320

industrialization: early 1800s, 74; after 1850, 141, 142-44, 146-47, 153, 648-49; and impact on migration, 677; and imperialism, 625-27; sources of energy for, 142; world, *m670-71*

Industrial Revolution, 74, 677, 702

Industrial Workers of the World (IWW), 176-77, 261

industry: after World War I, 302-03; automation in, 476; and changes in workstyle, 303-04; in 1800s, 74; in Great Depression, 327-28; growth of, 142-43; in post-Reconstruction South, 114; working conditions in early 1800s, 77; in World War I, 318; in World War II, 407-08

inflation, 37; under Carter, 569; under Ford, 565-66; under Nixon, 558; under Reagan, 587

Information Revolution, 686, *c694*

Information Superhighway. *See* National Information Infrastructure

INF Treaty. *See* Intermediate-range Nuclear Forces Treaty

initiative, 191, 702

Inouye, Daniel, 433, *p433,* 594, 785, *p785*

insider trading, 592

Insurgent Mexico (Reed), 237

interchangeable parts, 74

Interior, Department of, 587

Intermediate-range Nuclear Forces (INF) Treaty (1987), 593

Internal Security Act (1950), 451

International Bank for Reconstruction and Development (World Bank), 660

International Church of the Foursquare Gospel, 312

International Ladies Garment Workers Union (ILGWU), 176

International Monetary Fund (IMF), 660

International Woman Suffrage Conference (1902), 207

Internet, 686-87, 688

internment, 410

Interstate Commerce Act (1887), 156

Interstate Commerce Commission (ICC), 196

Interview, Conducting an, 550

Intolerable Acts (1774), 28

Invisible Man (Ellison), 481, *p481*

IRA. *See* Irish Republican Army

Iran: human rights abuses in, *c716;* Kurds in, 685; Soviet immigrants to, 684; view on human rights, 717

in, 1, 17; settlement of, 16-17, 18; Shays's Rebellion in, 38, *p38*
mass culture, 690-93
mass marketing, 144-45, *p145,* 320-21
mass media, effects of, 320-21. *See also* journalism
mass production, 74
mass transit, 149, *p149*
Masters, Edgar Lee, 271
Maxim, Hiram S., *p621*
Mayaguez (ship), 566, *p566*
Mayas, *m5,* 6
Mayflower Compact, 16
Mayflower II (ship), 576
Mbemba, Nzinga, 12
McAdoo, William, 257-58
McCain, Franklin, 710
McCarthy, Eugene, in election of 1968, 536
McCarthy, Joseph, 463-64, 598
McCarthyism, 463-64, 474
McClellan, George B., 98, 100
McClendon, Rose, 316-17, *p316*
McClure's (magazine) 170, 171
McCord, James, 563
McDowell, Irvin, 97
McGovern, George, in election of 1972, 540
McKay, Claude, 317, 428, 786
McKellar, Kenneth D., 459
McKinley, William, *p156,* 157, *p157,* 786; on annexation of Philippines, 621; assassination of, 194, *p194;* economic policy of, 649; and foreign policy, 216, 219; and tariffs, 655
McKinley Tariff (1890), 655
McMillan, Edwin, 275
McNamara, Robert S., 526, 534, *p534*
McPherson, Aimee Semple, 312-13, *p312*
Meade, George, 98
Meadows, Meadows, and Randers (researchers), 744
Means, Russell, 576, *p576*
Meany, George, 476, 558
measles, 682
Meat Inspection Act (1906), 196
Medicaid, 498
medical care, in Civil War, 99
Medicare, 497
Mediterranean, containment in, 447
Mein Kampf (Hitler), 389
Meir, Golda, 560, *p560,* 713
Mekong Delta, Vietnam, 520, *m521*
Mello, Fatima Vianna, 737-38
Mellon, Andrew W., 285, 342, *p342*
Melville, Herman, 721
Mendes, Chico, 734, *p734*
Menéndez de Avilés, Pedro, 13
Mengele, Josef, 438
Menlo Park, NJ, Edison's workshop in, 143
Mennonites, 130, 391
mentally ill, treatment of, 81
Mercator projections, 754
Merchandise Marks Act (1887), 655

Meredith, James, 502, *p506*
merger, 288
meridians, 753
Mesoamerica, cultures of, 4-6, *m5*
mestizos, 14
Mexican Americans: and cattle industry, 132; in Great Depression, *p324-25,* 332, 334-35, *p334,* 370, 377, 680; literature of, 271, 615; after Mexican War, 85; migration of, in 1920s, 295, *p295;* and mining, 135; muralists, 318-19; in 1950s, 461, 471, 477; in 1970s, 555, 574, 578; as replacement workers, 281; unemployment of, 441; in Vietnam War, 527; in World War I, 251; in World War II, 412-13, *p413;* and zoot-suit riots, 413. *See also* Hispanic Americans
Mexican Cession (1848), 85, *m86*
Mexican Revolution, 231-32, *p231, p232;* American intervention in, 232-33; and Carranza, 233-34
Mexican War (1846–1848), 85
Mexico: human rights abuses in, *c716;* immigration from, 683; and Mexican Cession, 85, *m86;* Mexican War, 85; and NAFTA, 666; population of, 737; revolution in, 231-32, *p231, p232;* Texas relations with, 84-85; U.S. relations with, 387
Mexico City, Mexico, 13, 85, 232
Miami, FL: immigration to, 579; Republican convention of 1968 in, 537; social unrest in, 537
Mickey Mouse, 275, *p275*
middle class: development of, 77; growth of, 146-47
Middle East, *m264, m561;* Arab-Israeli conflict in, 641; human rights abuses in, *c716;* and mandate system, 629; migration within, 684-85; and 1993 peace accord, 610; oil in, 671; policy of Carter, 571-73, *p573;* refugee camps in, 681; Six-Day War in, 560; slave trade to, 674-75; Suez crisis in, 567-68; women in, 712, 713; Yom Kippur War in, 560
Middletown (Lynd and Lynd), 306
Middle West: immigrants in, 678; settlement of, 78
Midway, Battle of (1942), *m402,* 403, *p403*
"Midway" (Madgett), 549
Migrant Mother (photograph), *pxxii,* 369, *p369,* 371
migrant workers, and Great Depression, 334, *p362,* 368-69, 370
migration, global, 674-75; in 1930s, 679-80; of refugees, 680-81; to U.S., 675-76; after World War I, 679
militarism, 243
militarists, rise of, in Japan, 390, 706
Millay, Edna St. Vincent, *p283*
Miller, Arthur, 463
Miller, Glenn, 274, *p274,* 374
Mills, C. Wright, 481

Mineta, Norman, 411, *p411*
minicomputers, 687
mining: as big business, 136-37, *p136;* and California gold rush, 86-87; and western settlement, *p120-21,* 134-37, *p134, p135, p136*
mining communities, life in, 135-36
Minneapolis, MN, 677
Minnesota: bonanza farms in, 131; immigrants in, 678; Indian reservations in, *m124;* railroads in, *m132*
Miranda v. *Arizona* (1966), 498
missionaries, Christian, 621, 625, *p625,* 676-77, *p677*
missions, Spanish, xxiv, *pxxiv,* 13-14, *m23*
Mississippi: in Civil War, 98-99; Freedom Riders in, 501, *m501;* and Freedom Summer, 503-04; race riot in, 502; secession of, 91
Mississippian culture, 6
Miss Lonelyhearts (West), 338
Missouri: settlement of, 74; in Union, 74, 97
Missouri (ship), 421
Missouri Compromise (1820), 74, *m74;* proposed extension of, 87
Mitchell, Margaret, 373
Miwoks, 87, 122
Moby-Dick (Melville), 721
Model T Ford, 165, *p165,* 303
modern Republicanism, 470
Moldova, *m597,* 599
Mondale, Walter: in election of 1976, 567; in election of 1980, 573; in election of 1984, 591
Mongolia, post–World War II, 424
Monk, Thelonious, 410
monopoly, 9, 143
Monroe, James, 72, *p76,* 786
Monroe Doctrine (1823), 72; application of, 228-30; text of, 764-65
Montana: Battle of Little Bighorn in, 124-25, *m124;* Indian reservations in, *m124;* mining in, 134; railroads in, *m132*
Montezuma, Carlos, 184
Montgomery, Bernard, 405
Montgomery bus boycott, 479-80, *p479,* 711
Montgomery Improvement Association (MIA), 479, 500
Montreal, Canada: in French and Indian War, 19; and Protocol on Ozone Depletion, 739
Montreal Protocol on Ozone Depletion (1987), 739
Moral Majority, 586
moratorium, 383
Morgenthau, Henry, 659
Mori, Hirozo, 632
Mori, Toshio, 429
Morocco: Europeans in, 674; human rights abuses in, *c716*
Morrill Act (1862), 128
Morriss, Mack, 418
Morse, Samuel F. B., 142
Morse, Wayne, 526-27

Morton, "Jelly Roll," 315, *p315*
Mosaddeq, Mohammad, 466
Moscow, Russia, 705
Moseley-Braun, Carol, 605
Moses, Anna "Grandma," 375; painting by, *p375*
Mother Earth (magazine), 282
Motown Records, 512
Mott, Lucretia, 82-83, 700, 786
mound builders, 6, *p6*
movement, 8
movies: before 1920, 181-82; in 1920s, 275, 308-09, *p309;* in 1930s, 275, 336, *p336;* in 1940s, 275; in 1950s, 482; as U.S. export, 692; on video-cassettes, 553, *p553;* in World War II, 410
Moynihan, Daniel Patrick, 495
muckrakers, 170-71, 702
Muhammad, 6
Muir, John, 726
Müller-Freienfels, Richard, 310
Muller v. Oregon (1908), 175
Multicultural Perspective, Gaining a, xix
multinational corporations, 665, *p665*
Munich, Germany, 391
Munich Conference (1938), 391
Murphy, Charles, *p190*
Murray, J. B., 351
Murray, Patty, 605
Murrow, Edward R., 410, 463
Mūsā, Mansa, 7, *p7*
music: of African Americans, 80-81, *p80,* 300-01, 315-16, *p315,* 364-65, *p365,* 374, 711; in civil rights movement, 711; and global culture, 692-93; and New Deal, 374; in 1920s, 274, 315-16, *p315, p316;* in 1960s, 434, *p432,* 512-13, *p512, p513;* in 1970s, 432; rock, 80, 482-83, *p482, p483;* videos, 692-93; in World War II, 410
Music Television (MTV), 692-93
Muskie, Edmund, 536
Muslims: in Azerbaijan, 642; in Bosnia, 609; and the Crusades, 7-8; early history, 6-7; in India, 641, 680; and spread of cholera, 682
Mussolini, Benito, 416, *p632;* and individual rights, 706; and invasion of Ethiopia, 632; rise of, 388-89, *p388*
Muste, A. J., 342
mutualistas, 332
MX missile, 588
Mydans, Carl, 369; photograph by, *p371*
Myers, Dee Dee, 607
My Own Country (Verghese), 682

N

NAACP. *See* National Association for the Advancement of Colored People
NAFTA. *See* North American Free Trade Agreement
Nagasaki, Japan, 421, 437, 707, 733
Nanjing (Nanking), China, 706

Narrative of the Life of Frederick Douglass (Douglass), 82
Nash, Diane, 501
Nasser, Gamal Abdel, 467
National Aeronautics and Space Administration (NASA), 466
National American Woman Suffrage Association (NAWSA), 208
National Association for the Advancement of Colored People (NAACP), 164, 183-84, 292, *p292,* 364-65, 475, 478-79, *p478,* 502
National Association of Colored Women, 170
national bank, 62
National Basketball Association (NBA), 673, 691
National Broadcasting Company (NBC), 308
National Child Labor Committee, 173
National Committee for a Sane Nuclear Policy, 532, 730
National Conservation Commission, 197
National Council of Negro Women, 365
National Defense Act (1916), 250
National Defense Education Act (1958), 466
National Endowment for the Arts (NEA), 313
National Energy Act (1978), 569
National Football League (NFL), 693
National Grange, 155-56
National Industrial Recovery Act (1933), 352-53, *c359*
National Information Infrastructure (NII), 687-88
nationalism: in Asia and the Pacific, 630-32; black, 292-93; as cause of World War I, 242-43; post–World War II, 634-37; rise of, 72
nationalize, 387
National Labor Relations Act (1935), *c359,* 361. *See also* Wagner-Connery Act
National Liberation Front (NLF), 524
National Negro Business League, 164
National Organization for Women (NOW), 510, 577-78
National Park Service, 197, *p197, m198*
National Recovery Administration (NRA), 353, *c359*
National Science Foundation Network (NSFnet), 687, 688, *p688*
National Security Council (NSC), 450
National Tuberculosis Association, 179
National Urban League, 183-84
National War Labor Board, 258-59
National Woman's party, 208, 288-89
National Woman's Peace party, *p249*
National Women's Political Caucus, 512
National Youth Administration (NYA), 358, *c359,* 365-66
Native Americans: and American Revolution, 34; assimilation of, 126-27; in Battle of Little Bighorn (1876), 124-25; conflict with settlers, 13, 16,

19, 63, 66, 75, 85-87, 122-26; and cultural renewal, 606; and Dawes General Allotment Act (1887), 127, 290; early cultures of, 4-6, *m5;* education of, 126-27, *p127,* 184, 366; and *encomienda* system, 11; Indian policy, 126-27; in French and Indian War, 19; granting of citizenship to, 291; impact of early colonization on, 10-14; and Indian Removal Act (1830), 75; inventions of, xxiv; and Iroquois League origins, 19; literature of, 549; and Mariposa War (1851), 87; and missions, xxiv; and New Deal, 366-67; in 1920s, 290-91; in 1950s, 461, 471-72, 477; in 1960s, 507, 515; in 1970s, 555, 576-77, *p576, p577;* in 1980s and 1990s, 606; population of, xxiv; progressives, 184; and Relocation Act (1956), 471-72, *p471,* 477; removal of, 75, 93; and reservation policy, 122-23, 137, 623; reservations and battles of, to 1890, *m124;* and Roman Catholic church, 14; and Sand Creek Massacre, 123, in Second Seminole War (1835–1842), 75; and settlement of Pacific Northwest, 85-86; and Society of American Indians, 184; and Trail of Tears (1838), 75; and Treaty of Fort Laramie (1851, 1868), 122, 123, *m124;* and Treaty of Medicine Lodge (1867), 123, *m124;* and treaty rights, 606; and World War I, 251; and World War II, 419; and Wounded Knee Massacre (1890), 125. *See also* names of individual tribes
Native Son (Wright), 373-74
nativism, 78, *p78,* 148, 676
NATO. *See* North Atlantic Treaty Organization
natural rights, 698
natural selection, 724
Navajos, 122, *m124,* 125, 133, 419, *p419*
Navy Nurse Corps (NNC), 409
Nazis: and anti-Semitism, 389, 706; and German aggression, 391-94; and Holocaust, 423-24; rise of Hitler, 383, 389, 706; support for, *p378-79, p389*
NBA. *See* National Basketball Association
NEA. *See* National Endowment for the Arts
Nebraska: and cattle ranching, 132, *m132;* slavery issue in, 89
NFL. *See* National Football League
Negro National League (NNL), 337
Negro People's Theatre, 317
Nehru, Jawaharlal, *p635,* 638, *p710*
Nelan, Bruce W., 667
neocolonialism, 638
Neruda, Pablo, 385
Netherlands: in East Indies, 635; and European economic integration, 661; at Washington Conference, 381
Netherlands East Indies: independence of, 635; in World War II, *m402*
neutrality, of U.S. in World War II, 401

Schroeder, Patricia, 591
Schwarzenegger, Arnold, 692
Schwarzkopf, H. Norman, 599
Schwerner, Michael, 503
scientific management, 303-04
Scopes, John, 303-04; trial of, 303-04, *p304*
Scotch-Irish, 18, 171
Scots, 18
Scott, Dred, 89
Scott, Winfield, 85
"Scottsboro Boys," 343
Seaborg, Glenn, 275
Seale, Bobby, 505-06
search-and-destroy missions, 529
Seattle, WA, general strike in, 279, *p279*
secession, constitutional issues in, 91
Second Amendment (1791), 53
secondary sources, 758
Second Continental Congress (1775), 28, 29, 36
Second Great Awakening, 81
Second Seminole War (1835–1842), 75
sectionalism, 63
Securities and Exchange Commission (1934), *c359*
Sedgwick, Susan, *p29*
segregation, 114, 709; and Black Power, 504-06; in housing, 183-84, 412, 477; and Jim Crow laws, 114; in military, 251, 412; post–World War II, 442; in schools, 478-81, 502, 575-76; southern support of, 484, 557; in transportation, 478-80, 711
Selective Service Act (1917), 251
Selective Training and Service Act (1940), 409
self-determination, 262, 629, 634
Seminoles, 75, *p75*
Seneca Falls Convention (1848), 83, 701
Seneca Falls Declaration of Sentiments, 83, text of, 765-66
Senegal, *c716*
Seoul, South Korea, *m455, 456, p457*
separation of powers, 40
Separatists, 16
Serbia: and ethnic conflicts, 609; and World War I, 242, 243
Serbs, 609
serfdom, 700
Serra, Junípero, 14
Servicemen's Readjustment Act (1944). *See* GI Bill of Rights
settlement houses, 150, *p150*, 172
Sevareid, Eric, 410
Seven Days' Campaign (1862), *m98, 100*
Seven Pines, Battle of (1862), *m98, 100*
Seventeenth Amendment (1913), 191; text of, 56-57
Seventh Amendment (1791), 53-54
Seward, William H.: as secretary of state, 134; and "Seward's Folly," 134; on slavery, 88
sewing machine, 223, *p223*
sexual harassment, 602-03
Seymour, Truman, 103

Shahn, Ben, 368; painting by, *p283;* photograph by, *p369;* poster by, *p728*
Shalala, Donna, 607
Shame of the Cities, The (Steffens), 171, 190
Shanghai, China, *p620-21, 688*
Shankar, Ravi, *p673, 693*
shantytowns, 333, *p333, 685*
sharecropping, 113-114, 334
Share-Our-Wealth (1933), 357
Shaw, Bernard, 601
Shaw, Robert Gould, 103
Shawnees, 66
Shays, Daniel, 38, *p38*
Shays's Rebellion (1786–1787), 38, *p38*
Sheehan, Neil, 531
Sheeler, Charles, 320
Shelford, Victor, 724
Sherman, William Tecumseh, 102-03
Sherman Antitrust Act (1890), 145, 196, 205
Sherwood, Robert, 374
Shiloh, Battle of (1862), 98-99, *m99, 100*
Shockley, William, *p687*
Shoshone-Bannock Indians, 606, *p606*
Siberia, *p623, 714*
Sicily, in World War II, *m404, 416*
Side of Paradise, This (Fitzgerald), 318
Sierra Club, 726
silent generation, 482
silent majority, 556
Silent Spring (Carson), 433, 475, 730-31
Silk Road, 6-7
Simon, Julian, 744
Sinatra, Frank, 432
Sinclair, Upton, 167, 211
Singapore: and global economy, 664; in World War II, 401, *m402*
Sioux, 122, 123
Siqueiros, David Alfaro, 319
Sirhan, Sirhan, 536
Sister Carrie (Dreiser), 171
sit-down strike, 361
sit-in, 500
Sitting Bull, 124-25, *p124*
Six-Day War, 560
Sixteenth Amendment (1913), 199-200; text of, 56
Sixth Amendment (1791), 53
Skills Handbook, 748-62
Skylab, 552
skyscrapers, development of, 148
slash-and-burn agriculture, 4
slave codes, 17
slave culture, 79-81
slavery: in British Empire, 700; critics of, 699-700; cultural heritage of, 711; debate over, 87-89; extension of, 74, *m74;* and Fugitive Slave Act, 88; and Kansas-Nebraska Act, 89; in Latin America, 700; and the Missouri Compromise, 74, *m74;* in South, *p77,* 78-79; in southern colonies, 17-18; and Three-Fifths Compromise, 39
slave(s): living conditions of, 79-80; population, 79, *c79;* rebellion and resis-

tance of, 18, 79-80; and rice production, 18; treatment of, 79-80
slave trade, 9, 11, 12, 17, *p17,* 39, 674-75, 699-700
smallpox, *p11,* 682
Smeal, Eleanor, 604
Smith, Alfred E., 287-88, 356
Smith, Bessie, 316, 787
Smith, John, 16
Smith, Mamie, 316
Smith, Margaret Chase, 463, *p463*
smog, 732, *p732*
Smoot-Hawley Tariff (1930), 330, 657
soccer, 619, 691
Social Darwinism, 150
Social Gospel movement, 150
social history, 511
socialism, 176
Socialist party: and Great Depression, 342; and opposition to World War I, 261; rise of, *c202;* and Share-Our-Wealth program, 357
Social Security Act (1935), 358, *p358, c359,* 361
Society of American Indians, 184
Society of Friends (Quakers), 391
Soil Conservation Service (1935), *c359*
Solidarity, 588-89, *p589*
Solomon Islands, in World War II, 402, *m402,* 403
Somalia, 641, 685
Somalis, 641
Somme, Battle of the (1916), 245, 246, 703
Somoza Debayle, Anastasio, 589
"Song of Borinquen, The" (Rodríguez de Tió), 270-71
"Song of the Moon" (McKay), 428
Sound and the Fury, The (Faulkner), 338, *p338*
Souter, David, 602
South: colonial, *m23;* compared with North, 97, *c97;* cotton in, 79, 299, *m299;* during Reconstruction, 105, 109-11; education in, 81; industrial growth in, 79, 114; population of, 78, *c79,* 97; slavery in, 17-18, 79-80; society in, 78-79; tenant farming and sharecropping in, 113-14, 299, *m299;* treatment of African Americans in, 414
South Africa, 690, 710, 712; end of apartheid in, 715; gold in, 653, *p653;* Nelson Mandela in, 712, *p712,* 715
South America: European migrants to, 674; foreign investment in, 238, *c238, m238;* Japanese emigrants in, 674; Russian Jews in, 678; slave trade to, 675
South Carolina, 18; and nullification, 74; secession of, 91. *See also* Carolinas, settlement of
South China Sea, 520, *m521*
South Dakota, *m124,* 125, *m132*
Southern Christian Leadership Conference (SCLC), 500, 502, 711
southern strategy, 557

Southern Tenant Farmers' Union (STFU), 354, 362
South Korea, 455-57, *m455,* 664
Southwest Voter Registration Education Project, 574
Soviet Union: breakup of, 597, *m597,* 599, 642-43; 715; and Brezhnev, 560; and China, 560; communism in, 706; and Gorbachev, 593, *p593,* 597, 599; human rights abuses in, 714; imperialism of, 633; invasion of Afghanistan, *m561,* 571, 588; under Khrushchev, 468-69, 492-93; 1991 coup in, 599; and Nixon, 559-60; and nonaggression pact with Germany, 392; and nuclear arms race, 464-66, 728; and Poland, 588-89; post-breakup emigrants from, 684; and Reagan, 588-89, 593; response to fascism, 390-91; and *Sputnik,* 433, 466; and Stalin, 424, *p424;* and Suez crisis, 467-68; withdrawal from Afghanistan, 593; in World War II, 403, *m404,* 405, *p405,* 406, 422, *p422,* 424, 707. *See also* Cold War; Russia
Soyinka, Wole, 742
space program: German scientists' contributions to, 686, *p686;* in 1960s, 433, *p433,* 466, 556, *p556;* in 1980s, 552; in 1990s, 552, *p552*
Spain: African territory of, *m637;* aid to American colonies, 35; explorations by, 10-14, *m22;* human rights abuses in, *c716;* imperialism of, 623; negotiation with Portugal, 12; North American colonies of, *m23;* and Pinckney's Treaty, 63; and *Reconquista,* 10; rise of Franco in, 389-90; and search for gold, 11; unification of, 8. *See also* Spanish America
Spanish America, 10-14, *m23;* colonial life in, 14; *encomienda* system in, 11; missions in, xxiv, 13-14, *m23;* social structure of, 14
Spanish-American War, 214-18; causes of, 214-16, *m217;* in Cuba, 215-16, 217-18; in Philippines, *p212-13,* 213, 216; in Puerto Rico, 218. *See also* literature
Spanish Armada, 15
Spanish Civil War, 389-90, *p390*
special purpose map, 752
specie, 74
spheres of influence, 222
Spirit of St. Louis, The (airplane), *p310*
spirituals. *See* music: of African Americans
Spitz, Mark, 433
Spock, Benjamin, 466, 532
spoils system, 75, 153
Spoon River Anthology (Masters), 271
sports, 275, 433, *p433,* 553, *p553;* cricket, 690; global popularity of, 690-91; in late 1800s, 151, *p151;* in 1920s, 309-10, *p309. See also* baseball; basketball; soccer

Sputnik (satellite), 433, 466
Square Deal, 195
Sri Lanka, 684
stagflation, 558
Stalin, Joseph, 424, *p424,* 446, 468
Stalingrad (USSR), 403; Battle of (1942–1943), 405
Stamp Act (1765), *p26,* 27, *p27*
Standard Oil, 144, 145; Tarbell investigation of, 170-71
Standing Rock Reservation, *m124,* 125
Stanford, Leland, 129
Stanton, Edwin M., 108
Stanton, Elizabeth Cady, 82-83, 109, 208, 259, 700, 787
State Department, creation of, 61
steamships, 650, *p650,* 651, 675-76
steel industry: growth of, 142, 143-44, 648; impact of World War II on, 660; 1919 strike in, 280-81, *p280*
Steffens, Lincoln, 170, 171, 189, 190, 192
Stein, Gertrude, 318, 787
Steinbeck, John, 373, 377, 787
Steinem, Gloria, 512, *p512,* 577, *p577*
Stephenson, David, 293
Stereotypes, Recognizing, 272
Stevens, John F., 227
Stevens, Thaddeus, 107
Stevenson, Adlai E., 462, 468
Stieglitz, Alfred, 319-20
Stimson, Henry, 386, 394
stock, 143
Stockdale, William, 605
stockholders, 143
stock market: 1929 crash, 326-27, *c327;* 1987 crash, 592, *p592*
Stowe, Harriet Beecher, 1, 88
Strategic Arms Limitation Talks (SALT), 560
Strategic Defense Initiative (SDI), 588
Strategies for Success. *See* individual strategies
Stravinsky, Igor, 316
strict construction, 62
strikebreakers, 155
strikes: early, 77; 1870-1900, 154-55, *c154;* Homestead, 155, *c154;* police, 280; post–World War I, 279-81, *p279, p280;* Pullman, 155; in steel industry, 280-81, *p280*
Strong, Josiah, 215
Stryker, Roy E., 368, 369
Stuart, Blanche, 165, *p165*
Student Nonviolent Coordinating Committee (SNCC), 500-01, 533, 710
Students for a Democratic Society (SDS), 532
Studs Lonigan (Farrell), 338
submarines, 247, 403, 704
subsidies, 354
subsistence farming. *See* agriculture
suburbs: development of, 149; in 1950s, 472-73, *p473*
Sudan, 641
Sudetenland, 391, *m392,* 633
Suez Canal, 447, 626, *p626*

Suez crisis, 467-68
suffrage, 83. *See also* women's suffrage
suffragettes, 701, *p701*
Sugar Act (1764), 27
Sukarno, Achmed, 635, *p635,* 645
Sullivan, Louis, 320
Sumner, Charles, 107
Sumner, William Graham, 141
Sun Also Rises, The (Hemingway), 318
Sunbelt, 578
Sunday, Billy, 181, 312
Sundback, Gideon, and zipper, 274, *p274*
superpowers, 424
supply-side economics, 587
supremacy clause, 40
Supreme Court, U.S.: and affirmative action, 575, 576; under Burger, 557, 591; Bush appointments to, 602; Clinton appointment to, 607; and education, 478-79, 498; and FDR, 360-61, *p360;* under Marshall, 64; and Nixon appointments to, 557; Reagan appointments to, 591; and reverse discrimination, 576; and *Roe* v. *Wade* (1973), 577; under Taney, 89; under Warren, 479, 498, 557; and Watergate tapes, 564. *See also* specific court cases
Surat, India, 682
Sussex (ship), 249
Sussex **pledge,** 249
Suu Kyi, Daw Aung San, 716-17, *p716*
Swahili, 7
Swedes, 130
Synthesizing, xxii-xxiii
Syria: human rights abuses in, *c716;* Kurds in, 685; and mandate system, 629; and Middle East conflict, 560; relations with Israel, 453

table, 756
Taft, William Howard, 787; as American governor of Philippines, 221; and dollar diplomacy, 229-30; domestic policy of, 199-201; in election of 1908, 199, *p199;* and progressives, 200-01, *p200*
Taft-Hartley Act (1947), 441, 444
Tainos, 11
Taiwan (Formosa): and global economy, 664; after World War II, 424
Tajikistan, *m597,* 599
Taking a Stand, xxiii
Tammany Hall, 152, 288
Taney, Roger B., 89
tanks, in World War I, 246, *p246*
Tanzania, refugee camp in, *p685*
Tarbell, Ida, 170-71, *p170*
Tariff Act (1816), 73
Tariff Act (1828), 74
tariffs, 39; and Bretton Woods System, 660; in European Economic Community, 662, 665-66; General Agreement on Tariffs and Trade, 660, 666; and impact of reductions on

trade, 654-55; McKinley, 655; and NAFTA, 666; Payne-Aldrich, 200; and protectionism, 654-55, 657; and rise of big business, 145; Smoot-Hawley, 330, 657

Ta-sunko-witko. *See* Crazy Horse

taxation: colonial protests over, 26-28; and Shays's Rebellion, 38, *p38*

taxes: and Reaganomics, 587; and Sixteenth Amendment, 199-200

Tax Reform Law (1986), 592

Taylor, Frederick W., 303-04, *p304*

Taylor, Zachary, 787; in election of 1848, 87, *p90;* and Mexican War, 85

Teapot Dome scandal (1926), 286, *p286*

technological innovations: in developing world, 688-89; and imperialism, 625-26; and impact on business, 142-43, 652; and impact on city, 148-49; and impact on global economy, 650-52; in medicine, 688; and right of privacy, 689

Tecumseh, 66, *p66*

Tejanos, 84

teleconferencing, 688

telegraph: development of, 142-43; and impact on global economy, 650-51, *p650;* wireless, *p650,* 651

telephone: cellular, 689, *p689;* development of, xxiv, *p142,* 143; impact on global economy, 652; number of, 618

television: cable, 691-92; and global culture, 691; in households, 432, *p432,* 553; and impact on global economy, 652; influence of, 691-92; interactive, 688; news, 691; in 1950s, 474-75, *p474;* in Persian Gulf War, 600-01; soap operas, 692; as U.S. export, 692

Teller Amendment (1898), 216

temperance movement, 81, 181

tenant farmers: and industrialization, 155; in Great Depression, 334; in New South, 113-14

Ten Bears, 121

tenements, 149, *p149, p477, p677;* and housing reforms, 178

Tennessee: in New Deal, *m354,* 355, *c359,* 364; secession of, 97

Tennessee Valley Authority (TVA), *m354,* 355, *p355, c359,* 364, 728

tennis, 1

Tenochtitlán (Mexico City) 13

Tenth Amendment (1791), 54

Tenure of Office Act (1867), 108

termination policy, 472

Test, Taking a, 762

Tet offensive (1968), 535-36

Texas: annexation of, 85, *m86;* and cattle ranching, xxiv, 132, *m132;* in Civil War, 99; Dust Bowl in, 367, *m367;* Mexican migration to, *m294,* 295, *p295,* 412-13, 471; Mexican settlement of, 84; and Mexican War, 85; mission in, xxiv, *pxxiv;* Republic of, 85; revolution in, 84; secession of, 91; slavery in, 88; Spanish settlement of, 13; Tejanos in, 84; U.S. settlement of, 84, 623

Texas longhorn, 132

Texas Revolution (1835), 84

textiles, 74, 77

Thailand: economic growth of, 664; traffic in, 618; in World War II, 401

Tharpe, Sister Rosetta, 374

Thatcher, Margaret, 588, 713, 787

theater: African American, 316-17; and New Deal, 374-75

Their Eyes Were Watching God (Hurston), 373

Themes in American History, xvi-xvii

Third Amendment (1791), 53

Third UN Conference on the Law of the Sea (1982), 739

Third World, 638-39

Thirteenth Amendment (1865), 107, 700; text of, 55

38th parallel, 455

"This Little Light of Mine," 711

Thoc-me-tony. *See* Winnemucca, Sarah

Thomas, Clarence, 602-03, *p602*

Thomasites, 676-77

Thompson, Dorothy, 360

Thoreau, Henry David, 723, 726, 788

Thorpe, Jim, 184, 310, *p310*

"Thoughts of Hanoi" (Nguyen Thi Vinh), 743

Three-Fifths Compromise (1787), 39

Three Mile Island, PA, disaster at, 570

Thunberg, Penelope, 496

Thurmond, J. Strom, 443

Tiananmen Square, *p696-97,* 697, *p697,* 716

Tiger, Jerome, painting by, *p75*

Tijuana, Mexico, 683

Tilden, Samuel J., 111

Till, Emmett, 503

Tillman, Ben, 111

tilted perspective, 755

Time Line, Reading a, 751

"Times They Are A-Changin', The" (Dylan), 508, 548

Tippecanoe, Battle of (1811), 66

tobacco, in English colonies, 16, 17, *p21*

Tobias, Channing, 442

Tocqueville, Alexis de, 624, 647

Tōjō, Hideki, *p708*

Tokyo, Japan, 707

Tombalbaye, N' Garta, *p640*

Tombouctou, Mali, 7

Tompkins, Sally Louisa, 99-100, *p99*

Tonkin Gulf Resolution (1964), 526-27; repeal of, 538

Toomer, Jean, 428, *p428*

Tories, 35

total war, 102

"To the Person Sitting in Darkness" (Twain), 271

Toubon, Jacques, 692

Townsend, Francis E., 356

Townshend Acts (1767), 27

trade: balance of, *c780;* and Bretton Woods system, 660; with China, 649; colonial, 17, 27; devaluation and, 657-58; in Europe, 654, 661-62, 665-66;

expansion of, 649; foreign investment and, 238, *c238-39, m238-39;* gap in, 603; and General Agreement on Tariffs and Trade, 660, 666; global, 619, *m670-71;* and gold standard, 653-54; during Great Depression, 657-58; impact of technology on global, 650-51; international, 651-52, 653-55; in Middle Ages, 6-8; and NAFTA, 666; with Pacific Rim nations, 664; and territorial expansion, *c230;* U.S. exports (1850-1990), *c670;* U.S. imports (1850-1990), *c671;* U.S.-Japan, 603, 649, *p649;* and World Trade Organization, 666-67. *See also* free trade; tariffs

trading kingdoms, African, 7

Trail of Tears (1838), 75

Trans-Appalachian West, 65

transcendentalists, 723, 726

transcontinental railroad, 128, 129-30, *p129, m132,* 142

transistor, *p687*

Transjordan. *See* Jordan

transportation: and growth of railroads, 142; and impact on global economy, 650, *m670-71;* in Los Angeles, CA, 517, *m517;* in World War I, 679

transportation revolution, 73

Treasury Department, creation of, 61

Treasury of American Folklore, 372

Treaty of Brest-Litovsk (1918), 254

Treaty of Fort Laramie (1851), 122, *m124*

Treaty of Fort Laramie (1868), 123, *m124*

Treaty of Ghent (1814), 67

Treaty of Guadalupe Hidalgo (1848), 85

Treaty of Medicine Lodge (1867), 123, *m124*

Treaty of Paris (1763), 19, 25, 26

Treaty of Paris (1783), 35

Treaty of Tordesillas (1494), 12

Treaty of Versailles (1919), 264-66; and impact on world economy, 655-56

Treaty on European Union. *See* Maastricht Treaty

Treblinka, Poland, 423

trench warfare, 245-46, *p246*

Trenton, Battle of (1776), 34, *m34*

Trevelyan, G. M., 511

Triangle Shirtwaist Company fire, 174-75, 185

Triple Alliance, 243

Triple Entente, 243

Truman, Harry S., 444, *p444,* 459, 788; and atomic bomb, 421, 425; in election of 1944, 409; in election of 1948, 442-43, *p442, m443;* and Fair Deal, 443-44; foreign policy of, 447-50; and Korean War, 455-57; and labor relations, 441; succession to presidency, 420; and UN, 438-39, 708

Truman Doctrine, 447

trunk lines, 142

trust, 143

War Powers Act (1973), 544
War Production Board (WPB), 408
Warren, Earl, 443, 479, 495, 498, 557, 788
Warren Commission, 495
Warsaw Pact (1955), 450, 468
Washington: Indian reservations in, *m124;* railroads in, *m132;* as a territory, *m86*
Washington, Booker T., 114-15, 164, 788
Washington Conference, 381-82, *p381,* 390, 705
Washington, D.C.: antiwar demonstration in, 532; and Bonus Army, 343-44, *p343;* city planning in, 179, 181; in Civil War, 97, 98; corruption in, 190; during first national antiwar demonstration, 532; during Grant administration, 152-53; homeless in, *p588;* Japanese mission to, 394; March on, 502-03; as site of national capital, 62; Vietnam Veterans Memorial in, 545; in War of 1812, 67; and Washington Conference, 381-82, *p381,* 390; and Watergate scandal, 562-64; women's suffrage in, 207
Washington, George, *p63,* 788, *p788;* as commander of Continental Army, 28, *p28,* 34, 35; financial policies of, 61-62; foreign policy of, 62-63; in French and Indian War, *p19,* 28; and frontier problems, 63; inauguration of, 61; at Second Continental Congress, 28
Watergate, 562-64; implications of, 564-65; and resignation of Nixon, 564
Water Quality Improvement Act (1970), 559
Watson, James, 433
Watt, James, 587
Watts riot (1965), 506
WCTU. *See* Women's Christian Temperance Union
Wealth Tax Act (1935), 358
"We Are Soldiers," 711
Weary Blues (Hughes), 317
Weaver, James B., 157
Weaver, Robert C., 365, 498, *p498*
Webster-Ashburton Treaty (1842), *m86*
Welch, James, 549
welfare system, 556-57
Wells-Barnett, Ida, 114-15, *p115*
West, Mae, 336
West, Nathanael, 338
West: and California, 86-87; cattle boom in, xxiv, 132-33; under Confederation, 37; conservation in, 725-27; early interest in, 26; farmers in, 130-31, *p130, p131;* and Gadsden Purchase, 85, *m86;* under Jackson, 75; and Louisiana Purchase, 65-66, *m73;* and manifest destiny, 84; and Mexican Cession, 85, *m86;* Middle, 78; and mining, 86-87, *p120-21,* 134-37, *p134, p135, p136;* myths of, 137; Native American resistance to, 63, 66,

86-87, 122-26, *m124;* and Oregon settlement, 85-86; railroads in, 129-30, *m132, p139,* 142; and Texas, 84-85; and transportation advances, 73; and War of 1812, 66
West African kingdoms, 7
West Berlin, Germany, 492
Western Samoa, 215, *c224*
Western Union, 143
West Germany: post–World War II economic growth, 662
Westmoreland, William, 535
West Virginia: oil industry in, 143; in Union, 97
Wetmore, Claude, 170
Weyler, Valeriano, 215
whaling, *p720-21,* 721, 735
Wharton, Edith, 151
wheat: exports, 651; production of, 648
Wheatley, Phillis, 1, *p1*
Wheeler, Burton K., 397
Whig party, 76, 89
Whiskey Rebellion (1794), 62
White, William Allen, 169, 195, 286
White Collar (Mills), 481
Whitefield, Edwin, painting by, *p26*
Whiteman, Paul, 316
Whitewater affair, 611
Whitman, Narcissa, *p85*
Whitney, Eli, 74, 79
Whyte, William, 481
Wiesel, Elie, 424, 742, *p742*
Wilberforce, William, 699-700, *p699*
Wilder, Thornton, 374
wildlife management, 727
Wilhelm II, 244
Willard, Frances, 181
Williams, T. Harry, 117
Williams, Willie L., 613
Willkie, Wendell, 393
Wills, Helen, 309-10
Wilmot, David, 87
Wilmot Proviso (1846), 87
Wilson, Edward O., 735
Wilson, Henry Lane, 232
Wilson, Woodrow, 205, *p205, p266,* 788; and big business, 205, 207; in election of 1912, 202-03, *m203;* and foreign policy, 230; Fourteen Points of, 262-63, 768-70 (text); inauguration of, 204, *p204;* and labor relations, 207; at Paris Peace Conference, 263-64, *p263,* 705; reforms under, 204-05; and self-determination, 629; stroke of, 265; and U.S. neutrality, 246-48; and Versailles Treaty, 264-66; and women's suffrage, 208; and World War I, 241, 249-51, 257-58, 260
Winnemucca, Sarah, 126, *p126,* 788, *p788*
Winning of the West (T. Roosevelt), 194
Winter, J. M., 267
Wirth, Joseph, 383
Wisconsin: Indian reservations in, *m124;* progressive reforms in, 193
Wisconsin Idea, 193

Wobblies, 177
Wolff, Stephen, 688
Woman of Egypt, A (Sadat), 713
Woman's City Club, 178
women: in American Revolution, 29, 34; in antislavery movement, 82, 700-01; in basketball, 691; in cattle industry, 133; in Civil War, 99-100; in civil rights movement, 712; colonial, 17; education of, *p169,* 170, *c170;* and election of 1984, 591; and election of 1992, 604-05; and harassment, 602-03; and labor movement, 153, 176-77, 297, *p297,* 361-62; in Mexican Revolution, *p231;* in military, 601, 603; Muslim, 712-13; and New Deal programs, 357, *p357,* 358; in 1920s, 311, *p311;* in the Olympics, 691; and opposition to World War I, *p249,* 250-51; in Persian Gulf War, 601; and Plains farming, *p130,* 131; and population, 738; and progressive movement, 169-72, *p172;* in reform movements, 81, 150, 173-74, 181, 183; and sports, 1, 309-10, 433, 553, *p553;* status in non-Western countries, 712-13; at universities, *c170;* in Vietnam War, 528; in West, *p85;* in work force, 77, 146-47, *p146,* 153, *p168, c174,* 259, *p259,* 278, 288-89, *c289;* in World War I, 253-54, *p254,* 259, *p259;* in World War II, 409, 413-14, *p414;* after World War II, 441. *See also* women's rights movement; women's suffrage
Women of the Depression (Blackwelder), 511
Women's Airforce Service Pilots (WASPs), 409
Women's Auxiliary Army Corps (WAACs), 409, *p409*
Women's Christian Temperance Union (WCTU), 181
Women's Committee of the Council of National Defense, 259
Women's International League for Peace and Freedom, 447, 450
women's rights movement: and abolition, 82-83, 700-01; in Great Britain, 701; Kennedy and, 490; in 1960s, 510, 512; in 1970s, 577-78, *p572, p577-78;* origins of, 82-83; postwar, 712-13
Women's Social and Political Union (WSPU), 701
women's suffrage: in Great Britain, 701; U.S. struggle for, 83, 207-08, *p208, m208,* 701-02
Women's Suffrage Committee (Great Britain), 701
Women's Trade Union League, 170, 174, 176, 289
Women Strike for Peace, 532
Wonder, Stevie, 432
Wood, Grant, 375
Wood, Leonard, 225
Wood, Natalie, 482

ACKNOWLEDGMENTS

For permission to reprint copyrighted material, grateful acknowledgment is made to the following sources:

Brandt & Brandt Literary Agents, Inc.: From commencement speech at Harvard by Carlos Fuentes, June 1983. Copyright © 1983 by Carlos Fuentes. Reprinted by permission of Brandt & Brandt Literary Agents, Inc.

Business Week: Excerpt from a letter to the editor by Toshio Fukuhara from "An Eye for an Eye with Japan'?" from *Business Week*, August 28, 1989. Copyright © 1989 by McGraw-Hill, Inc.

The Chicago Tribune: From "The lost pioneers of the West: Riders of the orphan trains finally end their silence" by Hugh Dellios from *The Chicago Tribune*, April 4, 1993. Copyright © 1993 by The Chicago Tribune Company. All rights reserved.

The Christian Science Monitor: Excerpt by Paul Kurdian, manager of a retail business, about sales and Japanese clientele and excerpts by Mari and Mitsuaki Yakoyama about shopping from "Yen's rise against the dollar cuts both ways: America's welcome mat out for

Japanese tourists, now coming in record numbers" by Daniel B. Wood from *The Christian Science Monitor*, vol. 79, no. 86. Copyright © 1987 by The Christian Science Publishing Society.

Clarity Educational Products: Quote by Celia Saparsteen Yanish from *The Life and Times of Rosie the Riveter* by Miriam Frank, Marilyn Ziebarth, and Connie Field. Copyright © 1982 by Clarity Educational Products.

Harold Courlander: From *Hopi Voices: Recollections, Traditions and Narratives of the Hopi Indians*, edited by Harold Courlander. Copyright © 1982 by Harold Courlander. Published by The University of New Mexico Press, Albuquerque.

Democratic National Committee: Television commercial for the 1964 campaign of President Lyndon Johnson.

Elizabeth H. Dos Passos: Quote about the spring of 1919 by John Dos Passos.

Doubleday, a division of Bantam Doubleday Dell Publishing Group, Inc.: From "The Chinese Intervention" from *War in Korea: The Report of a Woman Combat Correspondent* by Marguerite Higgins. Copyright 1951 by Marguerite Higgins.

Lance Fujisaki: From "Saburo Fujisaki: An Oral History," Asian American Studies 129 paper, Spring 1983, University of California, Berkeley.

HarperCollins Publishers, Inc.: From "The Challenge of 1984" from *The Twentieth Century: A People's History* by Howard Zinn. Copyright © 1980, 1984 by Howard Zinn.

Barbara Jordan: Excerpt by Barbara Jordan on her decision to leave politics from *Epic Lives: One Hundred Black Women Who Made a Difference*, edited by Jessie Carney Smith.

Little, Brown and Company: Excerpt by Chico Mendes from *The World Is Burning* by Alex Shoumatoff. Copyright © 1990 by Alex Shoumatoff.

Lorelei DeCora Means: From speech about American Indian women delivered during International Women's Week at the University of Colorado, Boulder, April 1985.

Montgomery Advertiser, AL: Excerpt on desegregation of buses from an interview with Rosa Parks from *Montgomery Advertiser*, February 24, 1982. Copyright © 1982 by Montgomery Advertiser.

National Wildlife Federation: From "Sacred Rights" by Mark Wexler from *National Wildlife*, June/July 1992. Copyright © 1992 by National Wildlife Federation.

Navajivan Trust: Quote by Mohandas Gandhi on British political institutions from *Young India*, March 28, 1929.

New Republic, Inc.: From investigative report on the shooting of black firemen in Mississippi from *The New Republic*, 1930. Copyright 1930 by New Republic, Inc.

The New York Times Company: From a letter by former Secretary of State Henry L. Stimson to *The New York Times*, January 23, 1939. Copyright © 1939 by The New York Times Company.

Ohio Historical Society: From "Women played important roles in union organizing throughout Ohio" and excerpt by German immigrant John Ehmann, a Cincinnati butcher, from *No Strength Without Union: An Illustrated History of Ohio Workers 1803–1980* by Raymond Boryczka and Lorin Lee Cary. Copyright © 1982 by Ohio Historical Society.

Pantheon Books: Quote by Bernadette Devlin from "Movements Challenge the Established Order" from *1968: A Student Generation in Revolt* by Ronald Fraser et al. Copyright © 1988 by Pantheon Books.

Penthouse International, Ltd.: Quote from interview with Vernon Bellecourt by Richard Ballad from *Penthouse*, July 1973. Copyright © 1973 by Penthouse International, Ltd.

St. Martin's Press, Inc.: From *Henry Ford, the Wayward Capitalist* by Carol Gelderman. Copyright © 1981 by St. Martin's Press. Quote by Vo Nguyen Giap from "Into the Abyss, 1965–1966" from *Where the Domino Fell: America and Vietnam, 1945–1990* by James S. Olson and Randy Roberts. Copyright © 1991 by St. Martin's Press, Inc.

Time Inc.: Excerpt by Hiromi Makihara, Yomiuri (Japan) Giants baseball player, from "Away Games" by Tom Verducci from *Sports Illustrated*, October 31, 1994, vol. 81, no. 18. Copyright © 1994 by Time Inc. Excerpt by Dikembe Mutombo, Denver Nuggets basketball star, on his ties to Africa from "World Class" by Rick Telander from *Sports Illustrated*, November 7, 1994, vol. 81, no. 19. Copyright © 1994 by Time Inc.

Mary Tsukamoto and Elizabeth Pinkerton: From "Internment at Jerome, Arkansas" from *We the People: A Story of Internment in America* by Mary Tsukamoto and Elizabeth Pinkerton. Copyright © 1987 by Mary Tsukamoto and Elizabeth Pinkerton.

The University of North Carolina Press: From "Agribusiness" from *Encyclopedia of Southern Culture*, volume 1, *Agriculture–Environment*, edited by Charles Reagan Wilson and William Ferris. Copyright © 1989 by The University of North Carolina Press.

Verso, an imprint of Routledge, Chapman & Hall, Inc.: Quote by Paiakan, Kayapó leader, from "The Ecology of Justice" from *The Fate of the Forest: Developers, Destroyers and Defenders of the Amazon* by Susanna Hecht and Alexander Cockburn. Copyright © 1989 by Susanna Hecht & Alexander Cockburn.

Ling-chi Wang: From unpublished manuscript "Politics of Assimilation and Repression: History of the Chinese in the United States, 1940 to 1970" by Ling-chi Wang, Asian American Studies Library, University of California, Berkeley.

ACKNOWLEDGMENTS

For permission to reprint copyrighted material, grateful acknowledgment is made to the following sources:
Victor Alba: From *Alliance Without Allies: The Mythology of Progress in Latin America* by Victor Alba. Copyright © 1965 by Victor Alba.
American Enterprise Institute for Public Policy Research, Washington, DC: Quote by Julian Simon from *Are World Population Trends a Problem?*, edited, with an introduction, by Ben Wattenberg and Karl Zinsmeister. Copyright © 1985 by American Enterprise Institute for Public Policy Research.
American Heritage Publishing Co., Inc.: From "Before the Colors Fade: Last of the Rough Riders" by V. C. Jones from *American Heritage*, vol. 20, no. 5, August 1969. Copyright © 1969 by American Heritage Publishing Co., Inc.
Terry Anderson: From "My Paper Prison" by Terry Anderson from *The New York Times*, April 4, 1993.
Archives of American Art, Smithsonian Institution: Excerpt by Carl Mydans from interview by Richard K. Doud, April 19, 1964.
The Asia Society: "Thoughts of Hanoi" by Nguyen Thi Vinh, translated by Nguyen Ngoc Bich. Copyright © 1975 by The Asia Society.
Atheneum Publishers, a division of Macmillan Publishers: From "The Black Worker" from *Black Reconstruction in America* by W. E. B. Du Bois. Copyright 1935, © 1962 by W. E. Burghardt Du Bois.
The Atlantic Monthly: From "Bread Line" by Florence Converse from *The Atlantic Monthly*, January 1932. Copyright 1932 by The Atlantic Monthly.
Hugh Austin: Quote by Hugh Austin about the effect of the oil shortage on a Detroit hospital from *Newsweek*, November 19, 1973.
Banco de México, and Dolores Olmedo: From "America Must Discover Her Own Beauty," an unpublished manuscript dated August 3, 1930, by Diego Rivera from The Bertram Wolfe Collection of the Hoover Institution. Copyright © by the Banco de México.
Ann Banks: From "Jesse Perez" by Betty Burke from *First-Person America*, edited and with an introduction by Ann Banks. Copyright © 1980 by Ann Banks.
BBC Enterprises Limited: From "Economy (1931)" from *The Collected Writings of John Maynard Keynes: Volume 9, Essays in Persuasion*. Originally titled "The Problem of Unemployment—II" as published in the *Listener*, January 4, 1931.
Harry J. Benda and John A. Larkin: From speech by Sukarno at his trial, December 1, 1930, from *The World of Southeast Asia* by Harry J. Benda and John A. Larkin. Copyright © 1967 by Harry J. Benda and John A. Larkin.
Chuck Berry: From lyrics from "Roll Over Beethoven" by Chuck Berry.
Bethune-Cookman College Archives: Quote by Mary McLeod Bethune.
John F. Blair, Publisher, Winston-Salem, NC: From "Peter Clifton" from *Before Freedom, When I Just Can Remember*, edited by Belinda Hurmence. Copyright © 1989 by Belinda Hurmence.
Robert Bly: From "The United Fruit Co." by Pablo Neruda from *Neruda and Vallejo: Selected Poems*, chosen and translated by Robert Bly. Copyright © 1971 by Beacon Press.
Brassey's (US), Inc.: From "This Was D-Day" by Sgt. Ralph G. Martin from *YANK: The Story of World War II as Written by the Soldiers* by the Staff of *Yank*, the Army Weekly. Copyright © 1984 by Yank Productions, Inc.
Broadway Video Entertainment, L.P.: From "The Lone Ranger" radio script.
Curtis Brown, Ltd.: Quote by Antonio Luhan from "Commissioner Collier Is on Our Side" from "Winter in Taos" by Mabel Dodge Luhan from *Intimate Memories*. Copyright 1936 by Mabel Dodge Luhan. Published by Harcourt Brace & Co.
Peter N. Carroll: Quote by a Chicago housewife from "The Loss of Connection" and quote by Ralph E. Lapp, energy expert, from "Pinch, Squeeze, Crunch, or Crisis" from *It Seemed Like Nothing Happened: America in the 1970s* by Peter N. Carroll. Copyright © 1982 by Peter Carroll.
Frank Cass & Co. Ltd.: Excerpt by Lord Frederick Lugard from "Conclusion: Value of British Rule" from *The Dual Mandate in British Tropical Africa* by Lord Frederick Lugard. Copyright 1922 by Frank Cass & Co. Ltd.
The Caxton Printers, Ltd.: From "Lil' Yokohama" from *Yokohama, California* by Toshio Mori. Copyright © 1949 by The Caxton Printers, Ltd.
Chelsea Green Publishing Company: From "The Limits: Sources and Sinks" from *Beyond the Limits* by Donella H. Meadows, Dennis L. Meadows, Jørgen Randers. Copyright © 1992 by Donella H. Meadows, Dennis L. Meadows, Jørgen Randers.
Sheyann Webb Christburg: Quote by eight-year-old Sheyann Webb from "The Turbulent Sixties" from *The Enduring Vision: A History of the American People* by Paul S. Boyer et al.
The Christian Science Monitor: "A lot of African countries..." by analyst Bill Moses and "The political situation in Russia..." by professor Debora Spar, from "Developing Nations Win More Investment" by David Rohde from *The Christian Science Monitor*, August 31, 1994. Copyright © 1994 by The Christian Science Publishing Society.
Columbia University Press: Quote by Aurobindo Ghose from "Aurobindo Ghose" from *Sources of Indian Tradition*, compiled by Wm. Theodore de Bary et al. Copyright © 1958 by Columbia University Press.
Confluence Press at Lewis & Clark State College, Lewiston, ID: From "Plea to Those Who Matter" from *Riding the Earthboy 40* by James Welch. Copyright © 1990 by James Welch.
Conservatory of American Letters: From "Guerrilla War" from *The Awkward Silence* by W. D. Ehrhart. Copyright © 1980 by W. D. Ehrhart.
Carl Cowl, Administrator for the Archives of Claude McKay: "A Song of the Moon" from *Selected Poems of Claude McKay*. Published by Harcourt Brace & Company, 1953.
Crisis Publishing Co., Inc.: From "The Bronx Slave Market" by Ella Baker and Marvel Cooke from *The Crisis*, vol. 42, November 1935. Copyright © 1935 by Crisis Publishing Co., Inc.
Daughters of the Utah Pioneers: From "Journal of Priscilla Merriman Evans" from *Heart Throbs of the West* and *Our Pioneer Heritage*, both edited by Kate B. Carter.
Joan Daves Agency as agent for the proprietor for The Heirs of the Estate of Martin Luther King, Jr.: From "War in Vietnam" from *Conscience for Change* by Martin Luther King, Jr. Copyright © 1967 by Martin Luther King, Jr. "I Have a Dream" by Martin Luther King, Jr. Copyright © 1963 by Martin Luther King, Jr.; renewed © 1991 by Coretta Scott King.
Helen Davie: "The Skyscraper" from *Problems of City Life* by Maurice R. Davie. Copyright 1932 by Maurice R. Davie.
Devin-Adair Publishers, Inc., Old Greenwich, CT 06870: From "The Case against Forced Integration" from *The Case for the South* by William D. Workman, Jr. Copyright © 1960 by Devin-Adair Publishers, Inc. All rights reserved.
Dial Press: Excerpt by Edwin Embree from *Marching Blacks*, Second Edition, by Adam Clayton Powell, Jr. Published by Dial Press, 1973.
Mrs. Alexander Donat: From *The Holocaust Kingdom. A Memoir.* by Alexander Donat. Copyright © 1963, 1965 by Alexander Donat.
Doubleday, a division of Bantam Doubleday Dell Publishing Group, Inc.: From "Can Wars Be Just?" by Sari Nusseibeh from *But Was It Just?: Reflections on the Morality of the Persian Gulf War* by Jean Bethke Elshtain et al., translated by Peter Heinegg, edited by David E. Decosse. Copyright © 1992 by Jean Bethke Elshtain, Stanley Hauerwas, Sari Nusseibeh, and George Weigel. From *My Life and Work* by Henry Ford, with Samuel Crowther. Copyright 1922 by Doubleday & Company, Inc. *From When Heaven and Earth Changed Places: A Vietnamese Woman's Journey from War to Peace* by Le Ly Hayslip, with Jay

Wurts. Copyright © 1989 by Le Ly Hayslip and Charles Jay Wurts. From "Wir gedenken der Toten!" from *Aufsätze aus der Kampfzeit* by Joseph Goebbels, translated in *The War That Hitler Won: The Most Infamous Propaganda Campaign in History* by Robert Edwin Herzstein. Copyright © 1978 by Robert Edwin Herzstein. From *The Blue Eagle from Egg to Earth* by Hugh S. Johnson. Copyright 1935 by Hugh S. Johnson. Quote by Walter Cronkite from *Tet!* by Don Oberdorfer. Copyright © 1971 by Don Oberdorfer. From *Woodrow Wilson as I Knew Him* by Joseph P. Tumulty. Copyright 1921 by Joseph P. Tumulty.
Dutton Signet, a division of Penguin Books USA Inc.: From *Movin' on Up* by Mahalia Jackson, with Evan McLeod Wylie. Copyright © 1966 by Mahalia Jackson and Evan McLeod Wylie.
The Economist: Excerpt by Iran's foreign minister from "Iran: Walk in Fear" from *The Economist*, vol. 332, no. 7873, July 23, 1994. Copyright © 1994 by The Economist Newspaper Limited.
Editorial Occidente: Quote by a Puerto Rican resident of El Barrio in New York City from *Trópico en Manhattan* by Guillermo Cotto-Thorner. Published by Editorial Occidente, 1951.
Farrar, Straus & Giroux, Inc.: From "Cabo Haitiano to Dos Rios" from *The America of José Martí*, translated by Juan de Onís. Copyright © 1954 by The Noonday Press, Inc.; renewed copyright © 1982 by Farrar, Straus & Giroux, Inc.
Forbes: Quote by Jan Volk from "Hoops Go Global" by Norm Alster from *Forbes*, October 15, 1990. Copyright © 1990 by Forbes.
The Forum: Quote by a Slav immigrant from "Relief and Revolution" by Charles R. Walker from *The Forum*, August 1932.
Dan Freedman: From "Jacqueline Navarra Rhoads" from *Nurses in Vietnam: The Forgotten Veterans*, edited by Dan Freedman and Jacqueline Rhoads. Copyright © 1987 by Dan Freedman and Jacqueline Rhoads. SEE ALSO: Jacqueline Rhoads.
General Media Publishing Group: From "The World Conference: A French Point of View" by H. D. Davray from *The Saturday Review*, vol. 155, June 24, 1933.
Greenwillow Books, a division of William Morrow and Company, Inc.: Quote about Lyndon Johnson from *With No Apologies: The Personal and Political Memoirs of United States Senator Barry M. Goldwater*. Copyright © 1979 by Barry M. Goldwater.
Greenwood Publishing Group Inc.: Quote by an African American woman from *The American Slave: A Composite Autobiography*, vol. 12, *Georgia Narratives, Part 1*, edited by George P. Rawick. Published by Greenwood Publishing Group Inc., 1978.
Grove Press, Inc.: From "The India of My Dreams" from *My Truth* by Indira Gandhi, presented by Emmanuel Pouchpadass. Copyright © 1980 by Editions Stock. First published in English in 1981 by Vision Books Pvt. Ltd., New Delhi, in collaboration with Editions Stock, Paris.
The Guardian, London: From "The Hubris Is Staggering" by John Gray from *The Guardian*, April 4, 1994. Copyright © 1994 by The Guardian.
Harcourt Brace & Co.: From "Harlem" from *You Must Remember This: An Oral History of Manhattan from the 1890s to World War II* by Jeff Kisseloff. Copyright © 1989 by Jeff Kisseloff. From "The Babbitts of Zenith" from *Babbitt* by Sinclair Lewis. Copyright 1922 by Harcourt Brace & Company; copyright renewed 1950 by Sinclair Lewis.
HarperCollins Publishers, Inc.: From *Only Yesterday: An Informal History of the Nineteen-Twenties* by Frederick Lewis Allen. Copyright 1931 by Frederick Lewis Allen; copyright renewed © 1959 by Agnes Rogers Allen. From "From the Mediterranean" from *Coming to America: A History of Immigration and Ethnicity in American Life* by Roger Daniels. Copyright © 1990 by Visual Education Corporation. From "Greed" from *1929: The Year of the Great Crash* by William K. Klingaman. Copyright © 1989 by William K. Klingaman. "If with all the advantages I've had..." from *The American People: Creating a Nation and a Society*, Second Edition, by Gary B. Nash et al. Copyright © 1990 by HarperCollins Publishers. From "The Quaker as Man of the World" from *Herbert Hoover: Forgotten Progressive* by Joan Hoff Wilson, edited by Oscar Handlin. Copyright © 1975 by HarperCollins Publishers, Inc.
HarperPerennial, a division of HarperCollins Publishers, Inc.: From "Slavery Without Submission" from *A People's History of the United States* by Howard Zinn. Copyright © 1980 by Howard Zinn.
Hikaru Hayashi: Excerpt by Hikaru Hayashi from "American Casual Seizes Japan" by Barry Hillenbrand from *Time*, November 13, 1989.
Heinemann International: From "The Rivonia Trial" from *No Easy Walk to Freedom* by Nelson Mandela. Copyright © 1965 by Nelson Mandela.
James A. Henretta: Quote by Elsa Ponselle, a Chicago schoolteacher, from "Family Values" and quote by a coal miner's daughter about going hungry during the depression from *America's History* by James A. Henretta et al. Published by The Dorsey Press, 1987.
Henry Street Settlement: From "Statements by artists 1963" from *1913 Armory Show 50th Anniversary Exhibition, 1963*, organized by Munson-Williams-Proctor Institute and sponsored by Henry Street Settlement, New York. Copyright © 1963 by Henry Street Settlement, New York, and Munson-Williams-Proctor Institute, Utica, New York. SEE ALSO: Munson-Williams-Proctor Institute.
Hill and Wang, a division of Farrar, Straus and Giroux, Inc.: "Civilian and Soldier" from *Idanre and Other Poems*, by Wole Soyinka. Copyright © 1967 by Wole Soyinka. From *Night* by Elie Wiesel, translated by Stella Rodway. Copyright © 1960 by MacGibbon & Kee; renewed © 1988 by The Collins Publishing Group.
Houghton Mifflin Co.: From *Silent Spring* by Rachel Carson. Copyright © 1962 by Rachel L. Carson; renewed © 1990 by Roger Christie. All rights reserved. From *The Autobiography of Will Rogers*, edited by Donald Day. Copyright 1949 by Rogers Company; copyright renewed 1977 by Donald Day and Beth Day. From *Typical American* by Gish Jen. Copyright © 1991 by Gish Jen. All rights reserved.
Howe Brothers Publishers: Excerpt by Oglala Lakota activist Gerald One Feather from *Indian Self-Rule: First-Hand Accounts of Indian-White Relations from Roosevelt to Reagan*, edited by Kenneth R. Philp. Published by Howe Brothers Publishers, Salt Lake City, UT, 1986.
Independent Woman: Quote by anonymous female aircraft worker from "Comments on 'Womanpower 4F'" from *Independent Woman*, November 1943. Published by the Washington National Federation of Business and Professional Women's Clubs, Inc. Quote by a shipyard manager from "Anchors Aweigh!" by Beatrice Oppenheim from *Independent Woman*, March 1943. Published by the Washington National Federation of Business and Professional Women's Clubs, Inc.
Vera John-Steiner: "The Song of Borinquén" by Lola Rodríguez de Tió from *Borinquén: An Anthology of Puerto Rican Literature*, edited by María Teresa Babín and Stan Steiner.
Estate of Jacob Judson: From unpublished letter of Jacob Judson from *Manuscript Collection*.
Charles H. Kerr & Company, Inc., Chicago: From "The March of the Mill Children" from *The Autobiography of Mother Jones*, edited by Mary Field Parton. Copyright 1925, 1972 by Charles H. Kerr & Company.
Maury Klein, Ph.D.: Quote by Jacob Riis from *Prisoners of Progress: American Industrial Cities, 1850–1920* by Maury Klein and Harvey A. Kantor. Copyright © 1976 by Maury Klein and Estate of Harvey A. Kantor.
Alfred A. Knopf, Inc.: From "The Terror" from *The House of Spirits* by Isabel Allende, translated from the Spanish by Magda Bogin. Copyright © 1985 by Isabel Allende; copyright © 1985 by Alfred A. Knopf, Inc. From "I, Too" by Langston Hughes from *Selected Poems* by Langston Hughes. Copyright 1926 by Alfred A. Knopf, Inc.; renewed © 1954 by Langston Hughes. From "Twymon" from *Common Ground: A Turbulent Decade in the Lives of Three American Families*

Excerpt from *On Politics: A Carnival of Buncombe* by H. L. **Mencken**, edited by Malcolm Moos. Published by Vintage Books, NY, 1960.

Excerpt by Tuscarora chief Clinton Rickard from "A Twentieth-Century Indian Voice" from *Native American Testimony* by Peter **Nabokov**. Copyright © 1978, 1991 by Peter Nabokov.

Quote by Philip **Ortega** from "The Education of Mexican Americans" from the *New Mexico Review*, October 1969. Copyright © 1969 by Philip Ortega.

Quote by George Biddle about President Franklin Roosevelt from *The Roosevelt I Knew* by Frances **Perkins**. Copyright 1946 by Viking Penguin, Inc.

Quote by Rupert Costo, Cahuilla, from *Indian Self-Rule*, edited by Kenneth R. **Philp**. Published by Howe Brothers, Salt Lake City, UT, 1986.

Excerpt from "A Letter to the Rulers of Latin America, August 4, 1928" by Augusto Sandino from *Sandino: The Testimony of a*

Nicaraguan Patriot 1921–1934, compiled and edited by Sergio **Ramírez**, edited and translated by Robert Edgar Conrad. Copyright © 1990 by Princeton University Press. Originally appeared in *El Chipotón*.

Excerpt by Frederic Howe on the domestic terror of the Red Scare and excerpt by Gifford Pinchot after being fired by President Taft from *America Enters the World: A History of the Progressive Era and World War I* by Page **Smith**. Copyright © 1985 by Page Smith. Published by McGraw-Hill Book Company.

Quote by Amanda Burks from *The Long Trail: How Cowboys & Longhorns Opened the West* by Gardner **Soule**. Copyright © 1976 by Gardner Soule. Published by McGraw-Hill Book Company.

Quote by Gordon Hirabayashi from *Strangers from a Different Shore: A History of Asian Americans* by Ronald **Takaki**. Copyright © 1989 by Ronald Takaki. Published by Little, Brown and Company.

Excerpt from *A Colored Woman in a White World* by Mary Church **Terrell**.

Excerpt from a diary entry on being a refugee on board the *St. Louis* by Otto Bergmann from *Voyage of the Damned* by Gordon **Thomas** and Max Morgan Witts.

Quote by a French businessman and quote by a British lawyer from *Watergate: A Crisis for the World, A Survey of British and French Press Reaction Toward an American Political Crisis* by James **Trezise**, James Glen Stovall, and Hamid Mowlana. Copyright © 1980 by James Trezise, James Glen Stovall, and Hamid Mowlana.

Excerpt on job opportunities in hospitals from *My Own Country: A Doctor's Story of a Town and Its People in the Age of AIDS* by Abraham **Verghese**. Copyright © 1994 by Abraham Verghese. Published by Simon & Schuster.

Quote on annexing the Dominican Republic by Theodore Roosevelt from "A Progressive Foreign Policy, 1900–1921" by Lloyd Gardner from *From Colony to Empire: Essays in the History of American Foreign Relations,* edited by William Appleman **Williams**. Published by John Wiley & Sons, Inc., 1972.

840